LAW AND CHILDHOOD STUDIES

Current Legal Issues 2011

VOLUME 14

CURRENT LEGAL PUBLICATIONS

Law and Childhood Studies

Current Legal Issues 2011

VOLUME 14

Edited by
MICHAEL FREEMAN F.B.A.
Professor of English Law
University College London

OXFORD
UNIVERSITY PRESS

OXFORD
UNIVERSITY PRESS

Great Clarendon Street, Oxford OX2 6DP
United Kingdom

Oxford University Press is a department of the University of Oxford. It furthers the University's objective of excellence in research, scholarship, and education by publishing worldwide. Oxford is a registered trade mark of Oxford University Press in the UK and in certain other countries

First published 2012

Impression: 1

British Library Cataloguing in Publication Data
Data available

Library of Congress Cataloguing in Publication Data
Data available

ISBN 978–0–19–965250–1

Printed in Great Britain
on acid-free paper by
CPI Group (UK) Ltd, Croydon, CR0 4YY

Preface

This volume contains papers from the fourteenth annual international interdisciplinary colloquium held in the Law School of UCL. A number of the papers given at the colloquium are not included but the volume is strengthened with the inclusion of some commissioned articles. Childhood studies is a relatively new discipline, and UCL's colloquium in the summer of 2010 is believed to be the first to forge the link between law and this discipline. As such we hope it will be welcomed by all who have an interest in children and childhood. The volume contains papers from across a range of disciplines—children are a relatively new focus for all of us. Barely a generation ago little child law was taught and few had heard of children's rights. There is also a healthy representation of different countries: there are contributors from 12 different countries. The subjects covered range widely: healthcare, restorative justice, child abuse, cyber bullying, son preference, disability, foster care, and corporal chastisement. The range of childhoods surveyed is also wide and includes Africa, Italy, Israel-Palestine, Tanzania, Bangladesh, and Nicaragua. The role of different actors is also explored: obviously children themselves as constructors of their own social world but also judges, parents, foster carers, and not least sociologists and academic and practising lawyers.

We are grateful to Brill, the publishers of the *International Journal of Children's Rights*, for their generous sponsorship. I am grateful, as ever, to Jacqui Bennett and Lisa Penfold, without whom the colloquium would not have come into being.

The 2011 colloquium on 4 and 5 July 2011 was on 'Law and Language'.

The 2012 colloquium, number 16, focuses on 'Law and Global Health'. This will be held on 2 and 3 July 2012. Offers of papers should be addressed to me at michael.freeman@ucl.ac.uk.

Michael Freeman
March, 2011

Contents

List of Abbreviations

AC	Appeal Cases
ACPO	Association of Chief Police Officers
ACRWC	African Charter on the Rights and Welfare of the Child
AIHW	Australian Institute of Health and Welfare
BCSC	Supreme Court of British Columbia
CEDAW	Convention on the Elimination of Discrimination Against Women
CRAGs	Children's Research Advisory Groups
CPS	Crown Prosecution Service
CRC	United Nations Convention on the Rights of the Child
DLR	Dominion Law Reports
ECHR	European Convention on Human Rights
ECtHR	European Court of Human Rights
EHRR	European Human Rights Reports
EWCA	England and Wales Court of Appeal
FLR	Family Law Reports
HRA	Human Rights Act 1998
HRBA	human rights-based approach
ICJ	International Court of Justice
ICCPR	International Covenant on Civil and Political Rights
ICSEC	International Covenant on Social, Economic and Cultural Rights
MDGs	Millennium Development Goals
NGO	non-governmental organization
NIQB	Northern Ireland Queen's Bench Reports
NICCY	Northern Ireland Commissioner for Children and Young People
NZFLR	New Zealand Family Law Reports
NZLR	New Zealand Law Reports
OPT	Occupied Palestinian Territories
OMCT	Organisation Mondiale Contre la Torture
PPP	parental physical punishment
PAR	Participatory Action Research
PDTA	Prenatal Diagnostic Techniques (Regulation and Prevention of Misuse) Act
SCR	Supreme Court Reports (Canada)
CRPD	United Nations Convention on the Rights of Persons with Disabilities
UNDRD	United Nations Declaration on the Right to Development
UNMD	United Nations Millennium Declaration
WLR	Weekly Law Reports

List of Contributors

Anne McGillivray is Professor of Law at the University of Manitoba

Mark Henaghan is Professor and Dean of Law at the University of Otago, Dunedin, New Zealand

John Tobin is Associate Professor at Melbourne Law School

Laura Lundy is a Professor at the School of Education, Queen's University, Belfast

Lesley McEvoy is a Lecturer at the School of Education, Queen's University, Belfast.

Manfred Liebel is Director of the Institute of International Studies on Childhood and Youth (ISCY) and the European Master in Childhood Studies and Children's Rights (EMCR) at the International Academy (INA) at Free University Berlin

Ann Quennerstedt is Associate Professor in Education at Örebro University, Sweden

Julia Sloth-Nielsen is Dean of the Faculty of Law, University of the Western Cape

Hedi Viterbo is a PhD candidate in Law at the London School of Economics. His dissertation examines the legal construction of childhood in the Israeli-Palestinian conflict. He was an adjunct lecturer in the Faculty of Law at Tel Aviv University (Israel), and a visiting researcher at Columbia University (US).

Kay Tisdall is Professor of Childhood Policy and Co-Director of the Centre for Research on Families and Relationships, University of Edinburgh.

Fiona Morrison is a PhD Student at the Centre for Research on Families and Relationships and the School of Political and Social Science, University of Edinburgh.

Priscilla Alderson is Professor Emerita of Childhood Studies at the Institute of Education, University of London

Roberta Bosisio works at the University of Milan, where I cooperates with the Department of Social and Political Studies and with the Department of Law and Politics.

Shannon Moore is Associate Professor of Child and Youth Studies and Director of Women's Studies Department at Brock University, St. Catharines, Ontario, Canada

Richard Mitchell is Associate Professor of Child and Youth Studies at Brock University, St. Catharines, Ontario, Canada

Megan Gollop works at the Centre for Research on Children and Families at the University of Otago

Nicola Taylor works at the Centre for Research on Children and Families at the University of Otago

Jonathan Herring is a Fellow in Law at Exeter College, University of Oxford, where he is a Professor of Law .

Heather Keating is a Senior Lecturer at the University of Sussex.

Anne Cheung works at the Department of Law of The University of Hong Kong.

Ben Matthews is Associate Professor in the Faculty of Law, Queensland University of Technology Brisbane, Australia

Shazia Choudhry is Senior Lecturer in Law at the Queen Mary University of London

Michelle Ratpan is an LLM Graduate in Global Health Law from Georgetown University and The Graduate Institute, Geneva, currently working for the Canadian Department of Justice

Noam Peleg works at the University College London, Faculty of Laws.

Ashleigh Barnes is an Assistant Professor and Assistant Director of the Centre for Women, Law and Social Change at Jindal Global Law School

Bronagh Byrne works at the Queen's University Belfast, Northern Ireland

China Mills is a student at The Education and Social Research Institute (ESRI) and the Discourse Unit at Manchester Metropolitan University.

Kirsty Hughes is Turpin-Lipstein Lecturer in Law at Clare College, University of Cambridge.

Petra Kouvonen works at the Nordic Centre for Welfare and Social Issues

Bronwyn Naylor is Senior Lecturer at the Faculty of Law at Monash University, Victoria, Australia

Bernadette Saunders is Senior Lecturer in Social Work at the Faculty of Medicine, Nursing & Health Sciences, Monash University, Victoria, Australia

Aoife Nolan is Senior Lecturer, Durham Law School

Sofia Johnson Frankenberg works at the Department of Behavioral Sciences and Learning at Linköping University

Jo Bridgeman works at the Centre for Responsibilities, Rights and the Law at Sussex Law School, University of Sussex

1

Introduction

Michael Freeman

The law has always been concerned with children, but prominently so only in the last 30 or so years. And it is not just child law to which one must look to see the way the law thinks about children.[1] There is family law more generally: custody disputes often conceived of children as 'property';[2] children are often marginalized. However, the child is now at the centre of family law, and the image of the child in family law has radically changed.[3] There is little concern today about whether the child is born in or out of marriage—almost as many are born outside marriage as in[4]—and questions of property and succession are marginal. But concerns with new forms of 'property' have emerged: conflicts over name and identity have resulted.[5] All areas of law impact upon children, and have concepts of childhood: contract law engages with capacity and unequal bargaining power;[6] tort law[7] is replete with examples of courts having to grapple with children's sense of responsibility (think of cases about infant trespassers[8]). Criminal law has to confront the child as victim, with all that this entails for process, procedure, and evidence,[9] and the child as perpetrator[10] (the *Bulger* trial shows how ineptly this was done[11]). England and Wales still retains an absurdly low minimum age of criminal responsibility—10[12]—in effect lower than it was with the removal of the *doli incapax* presumption.[13] We can learn a lot about earlier attitudes to disobedient children from Shakespeare.[14] And it is interesting that children should use legal concepts to define their relationships with parents—Cordelia, when asked

[1] See M. King and C. Piper, *How The Court Thinks About Children*, Aldershot: Arena, 1995.

[2] See Butler-Sloss LJ's criticism in *Re B (A Minor) (Residence Order: Ex Parte)* [1992] 2 FLR 1, 5.

[3] See M. Freeman, 'The Child in Family Law' in J. Fionda, *Legal Concepts of Childhood*, Oxford: Hart, 2001, 183–202.

[4] In 2005, 43 per cent of children were born outside marriage, most to couples living together.

[5] Reflected in case law. English examples are *Re P* [2000] Fam 15; *Re J* [1999] 2 FLR 698; *Re H and A* [2002] 1 FLR 1145

[6] See Law Commission, *Law of Contract: Minors' Contracts* (Law Com No 134, 1984).

[7] See R. Bagshaw, 'Children Through Tort' in *op cit*, note 3, 127–50.

[8] See *Adams* v. *Naylor* [1944] 2 All ER 21, 30 ('Children at play are always likely to trespass'). In this case a child trespassed on a mine field to retrieve a tennis ball.

[9] See J. Fortin, *Children's Rights and The Developing Law* (3rd edition), Cambridge: CUP, 2009. See also G. Henderson, 'The European Convention and Child Defendants' (2000) 59 *Cambridge Law Journal* 235.

[10] See A. Levy, '*Children in Court*' in *op cit*, note 3, 99–110.

[11] See M. Freeman, *The Moral Status of Children*, The Hague: Martinus Nijhoff, 1997, 235–53.

[12] There was a brief, and ultimately abortive, extension to 14 in 1969: see Children and Young Persons Act 1969 sections 4 and 70(1). In Scotland it is 8 (but they have a children's hearing system).

[13] Crime and Disorder Act 1998 section 34.

[14] I. Ward, *Law and Literature*, Cambridge: Cambridge University Press, 1995; I. Ward, 'Law, Literature and the Child' in *op cit*, note 3, 111–26.

to define her love for her father, Lear, talks of 'bonds' and 'duties'.[15] 'Law', Ward comments, 'does not admit the emotions of love and family'.[16] And what are we to read into the fact that disobedient children in Shakespeare are all young women? Juliet,[17] Hermia,[18] Kate[19] in *TheTaming Of The Shrew*, Helena in *All's Well*[20](though, of course, there is Prince Hal[21] but was his 'misrule' not an illusion?[22]).

The law developed its concepts of childhood before the discipline of childhood studies emerged. The child was seen as an adult in the making, a future adult, rather than a growing human being. The adult is the finished product, with full competency. We were expected to make sense of childhood *through* adulthood. Lee puts it thus: 'Children's lives and activities in the present are... envisaged... as preparation for the future.'[23] This assumes 'adults' stability and completeness... [that] allows them to act in society, to participate in serious activities like work and politics [while] children's instability and incompleteness mean they are often understood only as dependent and passive recipients of adults' action's'.[24] This view of childhood was nurtured by a number of disciplines, in particular developmental psychology (the work of Piaget being especially prominent),[25] social anthropology (for example, the work of Margaret Mead),[26] and sociology (significantly the work of Talcott Parsons).[27] These disciplines' images of childhood—summarized by Nick Lee[28]—saw children as inadequate, incomplete, and dependent. So, society had to invest in their 'care, training and upbringing since it is children who represent the future of the social world'.[29] Without this conception of the child there was obviously no space for any action of the child as an agent.

A new sociology of childhood emerged in the 1970s and 1980s. It spawned its own journal *Childhood*,[30] and a burgeoning literature.[31] In the UK it led to a major research project.[32] There was (and is) particularly productive work in Scandinavia.[33]

[15] *King Lear*, Act 1, Scene 1, 90–106.

[16] *Op cit*, note 3, 118.

[17] *Romeo and Juliet*, Act 5, Scene 3, 294.

[18] *A Midsummer Night's Dream*. The 'ancient' privilege of Athens allows a father to demand the death of a child who disobeys an injunction to marry (Act 1, Scene 1, 22–45).

[19] A child, but perhaps not a minor. But she will only escape her father's authority when this is transferred to another patriarch (a husband). See, further, J. Schroeder, 'The Taming of the Shrew: The Liberal Attempt To Mainstream Radical Feminist Theory' (1992) 5 *Yale Journal of Law and Feminism* 123–80.

[20] 'The most self-assertive of all Shakespeare's disobedient children' *per* Ward, *op cit*, note 3, 120. There is also Jessica in *The Merchant of Venice*.

[21] *Henry IV*, part 1 and 2.

[22] See his 'I know you all' speech (*Henry IV, Part 1*, Act 1, Scene 2, 190–212).

[23] N. Lee, *Childhood and Society – Growing Up in an Age of Uncertainty*, Maidenhead: Open University Press, 8.

[24] *Ibid*.

[25] *The Child's Conception of The World*, London: RKP, 1929. See also *The Moral Judgement of The Child*, London, RKP, 1932.

[26] *Coming of Age in Samoa*, Harmondsworth: Penguin Books, 1969 (originally published in 1928).

[27] *The Social System*, London: RKP, 1951.

[28] *Op cit*, note 23, 42–3.

[29] Allison James, 'Agency' in (eds.) J. Qvortrup, W.A. Corsaro, and M.S. Hőnig, *The Palgrave Handbook of Children's Studies*, Basingstoke: Palgrave Macmillan, 2009, 37.

[30] This began publication in 1994.

[31] Examples are C. Jenks, *Childhood*, London: Routledge, 1996; A. James and A. Prout, *Constructing and Reconstructing Childhood*, London: Falmer Press, 1997; W. A. Corsaro, *The Sociology of Childhood*, Thousand Oaks, California: Pine Forge Press, 2005. For a different view see J.R. Morss, 'The Several Social Constructions of James, Jessica and Prout' (2002) 10 *International Journal of Children's Rights* 73–88.

[32] The ESRC *Children 5–16: Growing Into the 21st Century*. This attracted 200+ applications. The Programme Director was Alan Prout. I sat on the committee which oversaw the research.

[33] Significant researchers are Jens Qvortrup, Leena Alanen, Ann-Magritt Jensen, Anne Solberg.

The result is a paradigm shift.[34] Instead of talking about children as 'becomings', this new framework emphasized that they were 'beings'.[35] Of course, they are both—which the UN Convention on the Rights of the Child of 1989 recognized.[36]

Why did this shift occur, and occur when it did? There was a child liberation movement in the 1970s,[37] spearheaded by Richard Farson[38] and John Holt,[39] but this seems to have had little influence on the new sociology of childhood. There was no interest then in the ideas of such early thinkers about children's rights as Janusz Korczak[40] or Ellen Key.[41] It barely needs to be said that Piaget, Parsons, Mead, etc were probably totally unaware of what these writers had said. Certainly, they were totally ignored by them. Korczak, in particular, had understood that children could be encouraged to be agents: he pioneered children's parliaments, children's juries, and children's newspapers, and this in Poland in the 1920s.[42] The first serious history of childhood was published (in English) in 1962: although this, Philippe Ariès's *Centuries of Childhood*,[43] is now thought to offer a distorted picture,[44] it was very influential at the time. If, as Ariēs claimed, the 'idea of childhood' had only emerged in the seventeenth century, then perhaps it was a social construction. By the 1970s we had become aware of child abuse[45]—the whistle had been blown on it.[46] Sexual abuse did not rise to the surface for another decade.[47] That children needed to speak out and the need for advocates became all too readily apparent.

There had, of course, been initiatives by the League of Nations in 1924[48]and the United Nations in 1959.[49] Each organization had formulated Declarations of the Rights of the Child. The emphasis in both was on the protection of the child: the

[34] The concept belongs to Thomas Kuhn: see *The Structure of Scientific Revolutions*, Chicago: University of Chicago Press, 1960.

[35] But children have not always been seen as 'becomings'. In the nineteenth century they were 'beings'. See J. Gillis, 'Transitions To Modernity' in *op cit*, note 29, 114–126.

[36] In particular in Articles 3 and 12. The English Children Act of the same year also recognizes both facets.

[37] An early example of which is P. Adams et al,*Children's Rights*, London: Granada, 1972.

[38] *Birthrights*, New York: Macmillan, 1974.

[39] *Escape From Chldhood—The Needs and Rights of Children*, New York: E.P. Dutton, 1974.

[40] He wrote in Polish. His 'The Child's Right To Respect' (1929) is now available in English published by the Council of Europe in 2009. And see G. Eichsteller, 'Janusz Korczak—His Legacy and Its Relevance of Children's Rights Today' (2009) 17 *International Journal of Children's Rights* 377–91.

[41] *The Century of the Child*, New York: Putnams, 1909 (originally published in Swedish in 1900). The twentieth century was to be the 'century of the child'. It was perhaps 'the century of the child professional'.

[42] A good discussion of these is B.J. Lifton, *The King of Children*, London: Chatto and Windus, 1988, an excellent biography of Korczak.

[43] London: Jonathan Cape, 1962.

[44] An early critic is Linda Pollock, *Forgotten Children: Parent-Child Relations From 1500–1900*, Cambridge: CUP, 1983. See further H. Hendrick, 'The Evolution of Childhood in Western Europe c.1400–c.1750' in *op cit*, note 29, 99–213.

[45] The work of Henry Kempe on the 'battered baby' was highly influential. In England, it was the Maria Colwell case in 1973–1974 which brought the subject to the attention of the public.

[46] According to Howard Becker (*Outsiders*, New York: Free Press, 1963) it requires 'moral entrepreneurship'.

[47] With the Cleveland 'affair' in 1987, but it could have been discovered much sooner: see Carol Smart, 'History of Ambivalence and Conflict in the Discursive Construction of the Child Victim of Sexual Abuse' (1999) 8 *Social and Legal Studies* 391.

[48] See D. Marshall, 'Children As An Object of International Relations: An Early History of the Declaration of *Children's Rights*' (1999) 7 *International Journal of Children's Rights* 103.

[49] P. Veerman, *The Rights of the Child and the Changing Image of Childhood*, Dordrecht: Martinus Nijhoff, 1992, 155–80 is a full discussion of both declarations.

clear image of the child within these documents is that of the child as a 'becoming'.[50] The 1959 Declaration had little impact on thinking about children—it passed even writers on children by. Nor should too much significance be attached to the naming of 1979 as the International Year of the Child.[51]

But this was the initiative which ultimately led to the 1989 Convention, which was ratified in haste by most of the world.[52] The Convention recognizes the child as both a 'becoming' (see for example Article 3), and a 'being'. It recognizes the child as an agent, able to participate in decisions (see, in particular, Article 12).[53] It is interesting that as the drafting process was proceeding, the highest court in the UK also recognized that children could take their own decisions. *Gillick*[54] is a landmark case: ahead of its times, it is not surprising that it has not had the impact it deserves.[55] Indeed, there has been a retreat from its implications.[56] The *Tinker* decision seen in the USA was equally significant.[57] But none of these 'events' explains why we began to take a different view of childhood, or why childhood studies emerged.

For whatever reason, the disciplines which had nurtured the 'becoming' model began to question received 'truths'. For example, Piaget's work was shown to be of limited value.[58] It was demonstrated that the thought and reasoning of young children was much more sophisticated than Piaget had claimed. As Woodhead and Faulkner explained: 'What appears to be "faulty" reasoning actually indicates children's ingenious attempts to create sensible meanings for what are, to them, nonsensical situations and contexts'.[59] The structural functionalist agenda of Talcott Parsons was also criticized. It was shown to have placed too much emphasis on the role of social structures and institutions in shaping society, and so left little space for the part individuals (including children) could and did play in society.[60] Dennis Wrong famously accused Parsons of having an over-socialized conception of man.[61] The structure—agency debate began to awaken an interest in children, in particular on the part that children play in the growing-up process and in socialization.

[50] With an emphasis on 'protection', and this primarily for the benefit of future society.

[51] I gave a Public Lecture at UCL to mark the event. See 'The Rights of Children in the International Year of the Child' (1980) 33 *Current Legal Problems* 1–31. Another commemorative publication is Martin Hoyles, *Changing Childhood*, London: Writers and Readers Co-operative, 1979.

[52] Only Somalia and the USA have not ratified the UN Convention on the Rights of the Child. On the USA see D. Cook (2009) 16 *Childhood* 435–39.

[53] There is a large literature putting Article 12 into the context of participation rights more generally. A good example is the 'Special Issue' of an *International Journal of Children's Rights* (2008) 16(3).

[54] *Gillick v. West Norfolk and Wisbech AHA* [1986] AC 112.

[55] It undoubtedly influenced the Children Act 1989. See M. Freeman, *Children, Their Families and the Law*, Basingstoke: Macmillan, 1992, 4. See also M.D.A. Freeman, 'In The Child's Best Interests? Reading the Children Act Critically' (1992) 45(1) *Current Legal Problems* 173–211, and L. Fox Harding, 'The Children Act 1989 in Context: Four Perspectives in Child Care Law and Policy' (1991) *Journal of Social Welfare and Family Law* 179–93; 285–302.

[56] In particular relating to a child's 'refusal' to consent to medical treatment. See *Re R* [1992] Fam 11 and *Re W* [1993] Fam 64. See M. Freeman, 'Rethinking *Gillick*' (2005) 13 *International Journal of Children's Rights* 201.

[57] 393 US 503 (1969).

[58] See M. Donaldson, *Children's Minds*, London: Fontana,

[59] See M. Woodhead and D. Faulkner, 'Subjects, Objects or Participants? Dilemmas of Psychological Research with Children' in P. Christensen and A. James (eds), *Research With Children*, London: Fälmer Press, 2000, 25.

[60] See Chris Jenks, *Childhood*, London: Routledge, 1996, 13–22.

[61] 'The Oversocialized Concept of Man in Modern Sociology' (1961) 26 *American Sociological Review* 183–93.

There were also some significant studies, some now classics. It was shown that working class boys had subtle ways to learn to grasp the social world.[62] Charlotte Hardman suggested children might inhabit a 'self-regulating, autonomic world which does not necessarily reflect early development of adult culture', and that they would be seen as 'social actors'. This article, published in 1973, was not surprisingly reprinted in *Childhood* in 2001.[63] Most interesting of all—at least in my opinion—was Myra Bluebond-Langner's account of the private worlds of dying children.[64] This reveals children as actors in the scripting of death on a cancer ward. It is an ethnographic study based on a Department of Paediatrics in a teaching hospital in the USA. Her aim was to get 'as close as possible . . . to their thought, their interactional strategies, and their structuring of the situation'.[65] And she was able to reveal children's role in the structuring of hospital life, and the relations between parents and children.

By the late 1980s it was recognized that children were 'beings', social actors. This is reflected in the *Gillick* decision, already referred to,[66] where Lord Scarman articulated the view that a child's competence to make her own decision—in this case about contraceptive treatment—depended on her having 'sufficient understanding and intelligence to make the decision',[67] and not on 'any judicially fixed age limit'. Allison James and Alan Prout, writing in 1997, could conclude:

> . . . . children are and must be seen as active in the construction of their own lives, the lives of those around them and of the societies in which they live. Children are not just passive subjects of social structures and processes.[68]

Berry Mayall, writing some 10 years later, confirmed this. She wrote:

> children are social actors . . . . they take part in family relationships from the word go; they express their wishes, demonstrate strong attachments, jealousy and delight, seek justice.[69]

A new paradigm had emerged. Within this paradigm, childhood is understood as a social construction. So, the institution of childhood becomes an interpretive frame for understanding the early years of human life. Sociological (and anthropological) work into childhood began also to conclude that childhood cannot be totally separated from other variables: class, gender, ethnicity, disability, sexual orientation (though this is less discussed). This serves as a corrective to the globalization of a particular concept of childhood, imposed by the 'North' on the 'Third World'. A further feature of the new paradigm is, as James and Prout explain, that:

> childhood and children's social relationships and cultures are worthy of study in their own right, and not just in respect to their social construction by adults.[70]

In addition, it is clear that to talk of a new paradigm is to engage in the process of reconstructing childhood in society. This has particular resonance for children and

[62] P. Willis, *Learning To Labour*, Aldershot: Avebury, 1977: P. Corrigan, *Schooling The Smash Street Kids*, London: Macmillan, 1979.

[63] C. Hardman, 'Can There Be An Anthropology of Children?' (1973) 4 *Journal of the Anthropological Society of Oxford*, 85–99; (2001) 8 *Childhood* 501–17.

[64] *The Private Worlds of Dying Children*, Princeton, NJ: Princeton University, 1979.

[65] *Ibid*, xi. [66] [1986] AC 112, and above note 54. [67] *Ibid*, 186.

[68] *Constructing and Reconstructing Childhood*, London: Falmer Press, 1997, 4.

[69] *Towards A Sociology of Childhood*, Buckingham: Open Univ. Press, 2002, 21.

[70] *Op cit*, note 68, 4.

the way children's rights develop. The clearest statement of the way main features of the new paradigm is set out by Prout and James in the following six points.

1. Childhood is understood as a social construction. As such it provides an interpretive frame for contextualizing the early years of human life. Childhood, as distinct from biological immaturity, is neither a natural nor universal feature of human groups but appears as a specific structural and cultural component of many societies.
2. Childhood is a variable of social analysis. It can never be entirely divorced from other variables such as class, gender, or ethnicity. Comparative and cross-cultural analysis reveals a variety of childhoods rather than a single and universal phenomenon.
3. Children's social relationships and cultures are worthy of study in their own right, independent of the perspective and concerns of adults.
4. Children are and must be seen as active in the construction and determination of their own social lives, the lives of those around them and of the societies in which they live. Children are not just the passive subjects of social structures and processes.
5. Ethnography is a particular useful methodology for the study of childhood. It allows children a more direct voice and participation in the production of sociological data than is usually possible through experimental or survey styles of research.
6. Childhood is a phenomenon in relation to which the double hermeneutic of the social sciences is acutely present. That is to say, to proclaim a new paradigm of childhood sociology is also to engage in and respond to the process of reconstructing childhood in society.[71]

There is now a vast amount of research demonstrating the agency of children. We have greater insight on what punishment means for children[72] (including their understanding of corporal chastisement).[73] We understand better children's understanding of the social organization of time[74] (should children therefore be consulted about the school timetable?). Since parents' involvement is widely regarded as necessary for their children's educational success, it is surprising how little knowledge there was of the part that children can play in the process—but there is now research on this, which indicates that children and young people are constructive and thoughtful commentators on the nature of home-school relations,[75] and the gender and class differences in these processes.[76] We now know more about how children negotiate their parents' divorce,[77] and how they cope with an abusive environment.[78] We have

[71] *Ibid*, 8.

[72] R. Sparks, E. Girling, and M. Smith, 'Children Talking About Justice and Punishment (2000) 8 *International Journal of Children's Rights* 191–209. Another view of 'justice' is R. Bosisio, '"Right" and "Not Right": Representations of Justice in Young People' (2008) 18 *Childhood* 276–94 (see also this volume at 190).

[73] See B.J. Saunders and C. Goddard, *Physical Punishment in Childhood: The Rights of The Child*, Chichester: Wiley-Blackwell, 2010.

[74] See D. Moss, 'Memory, Space and Time: Researching Children's Lives' (2010) 17 *Childhood* 530–844; H. Zeiher, 'Institutionalization As A Secular Trend' in *op cit*, note 29, 137–39, and 131–32.

[75] See S. Etheridge, 'Do You Know You Have Worms on your Pearls? Listening To Children's Voices In The Classroom' in (eds). P. Pufall and R. Unsworth, *Rethinking Childhood*, New Brunswick, NJ: Rutgers University Press, 2004.

[76] *Op cit*, note 29, 31.

[77] C. Smart, B. Neale, and A. Wade, *The Changing Experience of Childhood*, Cambridge: Polity Press, 2001.

[78] See B. Saunders and C. Goddard, 'Some Australian Children's Perception of Physical Punishment in Childhood' (2008) 22 *Children and Society* 405–17.

greater knowledge of what they think of work,[79] of immigrant children's experiences of their neighbourhoods,[80] of children's sense of home, locality, and belonging(s),[81] of their consumption of fashion,[82] of the strategies emphasized by street children to survive.[83] And this is but a snapshot of what is available.

But where do we go from here? Adrian James[84] has recently argued that childhood studies has reached a crossroads in its development because of this very diversity of the interests and agendas being pursued under the interdisciplinary umbrella of childhood studies. The children's rights movement has had a major impact upon childhood studies—this was not anticipated when childhood studies was first emerging.[85] No discussion of the relationship between law and childhood studies can ignore the impact of the United Nations Convention on the Rights of the Child.[86] This offers four general principles (the best interests of the child as a primary consideration;[87] non-discrimination;[88] the right to life, survival, and development;[89] and the child's right to express views freely[90]), and a normative framework of rights. These have been an easy measuring-rod of the status of children in individual societies. They are also a linchpin upon which the UN Committee on the Rights of the Child can build 'General Comments'—there are now 13 of these, the latest building upon Article 19.

To a large extent the Convention emphasizes the universality of childhood. The childhood studies 'movement' by contrast is tending to stress the plurality of childhoods, and so we get talk of 'a right to childhoods'.[91] But Jens Qvortrup has challenged this. To look to plurality is, in his view, to overlook the universality of childhood as a social category. In a paper at an important conference in Oslo in 2005 (as yet not published) he argued that:

> ....the promoters of the plurality thesis typically belong to the social constructionist mood or the post-modernist strands of social research with some reservations against so-called grand narratives... They have a strong sense for perceiving the society as complex and therefore for avoiding simple—or in their view—simplistic—explanations, which at the end of the day typically leads to a preference for uniqueness. Each childhood, therefore, is a unique

[79] See M. Leonard, 'Children's Views on Children's Right To Work: Reflection From Belfast' (2004) 11 *Childhood* 45–62.

[80] M. Bak and K. von Brömssen, 'Interrogating Childhood and Diaspora Through the Voices of Children in Sweden?' (2010) 17 *Childhood* 113–28.

[81] K. Mand, 'I've Got Two Houses: one In Bangladesh and one in London... Everybody Here; Home, Locality and Belonging(s)' (2010) 17 *Childhood* 273–87.

[82] J. Pilcher, 'No Logo? Children's Consumption of Fashion' (2011) 18 *Childhood* 128–41.

[83] P. Mizen and Y. Ofosu-Kusi, 'Asking, Giving, Receiving: Friendship As Survival Strategy Among Accra's Street Children' (2010) 17 *Childhood* 441–54.

[84] 'Competition or Integration? The Next Step in Childhood Studies' (2010) 17 *Childhood* 485–99.

[85] D. Reynaert, M. Bouverne de Bie, and S. Vandevelde, 'A Review of Children's Rights Literature Since the Adoption of the U.N. Convention on the Rights of The Child' (2009) 16 *Childhood* 518–34; D. Hartas, *The Right To Childhoods: Critical Perceptions on Rights, Difference and Knowledge in a Transient World*, London: Continuum, 2008.

[86] See M. Freeman, 'Towards a Sociology of Children's Rights', this volume, 29.

[87] Article 3.

[88] Article 2.

[89] Article 6, and see N. Peleg, this volume, 371 and A. Barnes, this volume, 392.

[90] Article 12. And see M.A. Powell and D. Smith, 'Children's Participation Rights in Research' (2009) 16 *Childhood* 124–42.

[91] See D. Hartas, *The Right To Childhoods*, London: Continuun, 2008

childhood with its particular points of reference which cannot fully be shared by others' childhoods.[92]

There are parallels here with feminism and its debates about whether it should focus on a single gender dichotomy or recognize the diversity of womanhoods. Could 'essentialism' be justified or should race and sexual orientation, for example, be seen as raising different questions?[93] Perhaps the question is whether childhood studies is yet confident enough to abandon the political power of the 'one child' thesis. Does a focus on the plurality of childhoods put at risk the children's rights project? Is this more likely to succeed if we accept its premise that childhood is universal? If it does, children will suffer and I suggest it is those in the developing world who have most to lose.

In another, more recent, paper Qvortrup has made the point that we cannot proliferate into a multiplicity of childhoods until we 'grasp' what childhood is. And 'one good proposition to this effect is that children are as a collectivity set aside from adults'.[94] The law makes a clear dividing line between adulthood and childhood. It is 18 in most legal systems, a fact recognized by Article 1 of the UN Convention.[95] But even in this there are qualifications: for example, recruitment into the armed forces is permitted at 15.[96] And legal systems recognize different ages for different activities: thus English law targets criminal responsibility on children at 10, allows them to consent to medical treatment when *Gillick* competent,[97] and permits marriage at 16.[98] Childhood ends much earlier in practice in much of the world,[99] with children taking on work responsibilities at very young ages. There is concern that they do not become involved in 'the worst forms of labour', which is understandable, but our concern should be with the worst forms of labour whoever is involved in it, whether children or adults. Some argue that, since education is to inculcate skills and discipline to enter the work force, it should be regarded as work.[100] The insight from childhood studies is to ask how children experience schooling, how they exercise their agency in relation to it, and what meaning they attach to it. In relation to these questions there are clearly differences between children in a simple society and not just between cultures: class and gender are significant variables. There are also questions about when childhood begins. Most legal systems, and the Convention, say at birth. But this too is controversial; many regard childhood to start at conception. This is not a subject I will pursue here.[101]

Perhaps surprisingly, given the attention given to the 'being' child, much work in childhood studies remains firmly rooted in the child as a 'becoming'. Where are the

[92] 'The Little "s" and the Prospects for Generational Childhood Studies', *Childhoods Conference*, Oslo, 2005.

[93] See, for example, A. Harris, Race and Essentialism in Feminist Legal Theory' (1990) 42 *Stanford Law Review* 581.

[94] 'Diversity's Temptation—And Hazards', University of Sheffield, 2008.

[95] See M. Freeman, *Article 1*, Leiden: Martinus Nijhoff, forthcoming. See also C. Cassidy, *Thinking Children*, London: Continuum, 2009.

[96] See *Gillick* v. *West Norfolk and Wisbech AHA* [1986] AC 112.

[97] English law's tolerance to younger marriages where personal law allows it is shown in the case of *Mohamed* v. *Knott* [1969] 1 QB 1 (child of at most 13 from northern Nigeria).

[98] See H. Montgomery, *An Introduction To Childhood*, Chichester: Wiley-Blackwell, 2009.

[99] This is condemned in both the UNCRC (see Article 32) and the ILO Convention No 182 (Article 3).

[100] See D. Oldham, 'Childhood As A Mode of Production' in (ed) B. Mayall, *Children's Childhoods Observed and Experienced*, London: Falmer, 1994.

[101] Note the inconsistency between Article 1 of the UNCRC and its Preamble.

successors to Bluebond-Langner?[102] There is little work on how children perceive child abuse or chastisement,[103] and none on their views about the implications of the reproduction revolution: what is it like to be an IVF child? Or a child produced by a surrogate mother?

What is also missing is any real theory of childhood. We are right to reject the Piagets, the Parsons, the Meads, but what is put in their place? There is thus no sociology, as yet, of children's rights.[104] Children's studies surely has something to offer us on the limits of children's rights.[105] On why the Convention of 1989 has not been an unqualified success. On ways to improve the implementation process. On the part children can play in norm-creation when we come to revise the Convention. On whether we need to get 'beyond rights'. On the relationship between rights and social justice.[106] Can the indicators of children's well-being be fitted into a theory about children?[107]

The question is now being asked—and not before time—as to whether childhood studies can improve the lives of children. We certainly have better knowledge of children and their lives as a result of the work done by childhood studies scholars. But has all this work contributed to the empowerment of children? Are children's lives better? Is there more social justice for children? And are childhood studies yet asking what a better life for children looks like? Would this be the same for all children or is it different in the developed world from the developing world?

It is clear that law and childhood studies have much in common, most notably the emphasis on the child as a subject. The children's studies movement takes the implication of this further, for example often seeing the child as a citizen. Each discipline can learn much from the other but I suggest the law has most need of an input. The approaches of the two disciplines are different: one employs a research methodology,[108] the other tests out ideas pragmatically from case to case.

As far as is known, this is the first collection which puts the two disciplines together. Much can be learnt from the papers which follow. They can speak for themselves—no summary can do them justice.

[102] *Op cit*, note 84.

[103] But see Saunders and Goddard, *op cit*, note 73.

[104] See further Freeman, this volume, 29.

[105] And see M. Freeman, 'The Limits of Children's Rights' in (eds.) M. Freeman and P. Veerman, *The Idealogies of Children's Rights*, Dordrecht: Martinus Nijhoff, 1992, 29–46.

[106] But see J. McKendrick, 'Localities: A Holistic Frame of Reference for Appraising Social Justice in Children's Lives' in *op cit*, note 29, 238–55.

[107] See A. Ben-Arieh and I. Frønes, 'Indicators of Children's Well-Being: Theory, Types and Usage' (2007) 83(1) *Social Indicators Research* 1–4.

[108] See H. Beazley, S. Bessell, J. Ennew, and R. Waterson, 'How Are the Human Rights of Children Related To Research Methodology?' in (eds.) A. Invernizzi and J. Williams, *The Human Rights of Children*, Farnham: Ashgate, 2001, 159–78.

2

A State of Imperfect Transformation: Law, Myth, and the Feminine in *Outside Over There*, *Labyrinth*, and *Pan's Labyrinth*

Anne McGillivray[1]

> Blessed is he who has seen these things and undertakes the way beneath the hollow earth: he knows the end of life, he knows the beginning given by Zeus.
>
> Pindar, *Dirges*[2]

> ... down in the underground/you'll find someone true/down in the underground a land serene, a crystal moon/it's only forever/it's not long at all/lost and lonely/that's underground, underground.
>
> David Bowie, 'Underground'[3]

> The state of imperfect transformation, merely hoped for and waited for, does not seem one of torment only, but of positive, if hidden happiness. It is the state of someone who, in his wanderings among the mazes of his psychic transformation comes upon a secret happiness which reconciles him to his apparent loneliness.
>
> C.G. Jung, Mysterium conionctionis[4]

[1] Given at Law and Childhood Studies, Law School, University College London, 2 July 2010, Imagining the Child, The Institute for the Public Life of Arts and Ideas, McGill University, 11 March 2010, and Vision and Voice: Law, Culture and the Humanities, Department of Law, Carleton University, 16 October 2009. I am grateful to Desmond Manderson, McGill University and Suzanne Bouclin, University of Ottawa for their thoughtful critique, to Manitoba law student Charles Murray for his insight, and to Michael Freeman, University College London for his enthusiasm and support. This project received the support of the Legal Research Institute, University of Manitoba.

[2] Fragment 137a, on the Eleusinian Mysteries. 'Happy is he among men upon earth who has seen these mysteries; but he who is uninitiate and who has no part in them, never has his lot of like good things once he is dead, down in the darkness and gloom.' Homer, *Hymn to Demeter* (ca. seventh century BCE), tr. Hugh G. Evelyn-White (London, 1914), lines 434 *et seq.* G. Nagy translates this as 'Olbios among earth-bound mortals is he who has seen these things. But whoever is uninitiated in the rites, whoever takes no part in them, will never get a share [aisa] of those sorts of things [that the initiated get], once they die, down below in the dank realms of mist.' *Homeric Hymn to Demeter* <http://www.uh.edu/~cldue/texts/demeter.html> accessed 4 November 2010.

[3] *Labyrinth* (motion picture) [1986]. Words and music by D. Bowie.

[4] Tr. R.F.C. Hull, *The Collected Works of C.G. Jung* (Princeton, 1969, hereinafter *Works*), vol. 14, para. 623.

2.1 A realm of myth

Childhood is a realm of myth, a submerged geography never outgrown, nor fully known. Stories for children map its landscape.[5] In naming the places of love and fear, progress and transgression, mythic stories fold other worlds within the everyday. For Peter Fitzpatrick, myth 'sets the limits of the world, of what can be meant and done, and transcends these limits in its relation to the sacred'.[6] A messenger between worlds, a trickster or magician (or a child), locates for us 'the profane, mortal world within the sacred', connects us to 'ultimate origins and ultimate identity, with the source and foundational force of all that is', and mediates resolution. If law is derived from and sustained by myth, then, as Desmond Manderson asserts, 'the mythological elements of children's stories ought *themselves* to be regarded as an essential site for the emergence of particular understandings of law'.[7] Children's stories are not 'a series of texts *about* the law' but 'the *fusion* of law and literature' holding 'the key to the constitutive myths and narratives that begin to organize our relationships to law.'[8] That myth may be cloaked in modernity does not diminish its transformative power.[9]

The immutable law of childhood is that children must grow up. Peter Pan is its prime transgressor. In every society, the infant must be made an adult,[10] *infantia* yields to *capax*, and legal innocence becomes legal subjectivity.[11] Knowledge of good and evil means expulsion from the garden of childhood. Myth brings the child safely through the gates. In its telling of origins, transgressions, and reconciliations, myth is both law and the idea of law. Stories for children reflect law in its mythic infancy and original power. Stories featuring child protagonists are powerful reflectors of

[5] 'I don't know whether you have ever seen a map of a person's mind. Doctors sometimes draw maps of other parts of you, and your own map can become intensely interesting, but catch them trying to draw a map of a child's mind, which is not only confused, but keeps going round all the time. There are zigzag lines on it, just like your temperature on a card, and these are probably roads in the island, for the Neverland is always more or less an island... It would be an easy map if that were all, but there is also first day at school, religion, fathers... they are another map showing through'. J.M. Barrie, *Peter and Wendy* (London, 1911), 9.

[6] *The Mythology of Modern Law* (London, 1992), 16. Rejecting Freud's myth of origin, below, Fitzpatrick notes that tales of origin offer powerful images but irresolution is at the centre of law's (premodern) myth. Enlightenment claims to law as a science reject a transcendent figure or a transgressive trickster who mediates resolution. That law supercedes myth is the myth of modern law. The myth of modernity needs the Other—the backward, the myth-ridden, the inscrutable, the savage who may be imagined as a child—to confirm itself as the opposite. It draws on a pseudo-Darwinism to 'explain' how habit- and custom-based societies are overtaken by superior (as more evolved) law-based cultures.

[7] 'From Hunger to Love: Myths of the source, interpretation, and constitution of law in children's literature', Benjamin N. Cardozo School of Law, Jacob Burns Institute for Advanced Legal Studies Research Paper No. 64 (2003) 18. The focus of Manderson's innovative investigation of children's literature as law is Maurice Sendak, *Where the Wild Things Are* (New York, 1963), the first of a trilogy that includes *In the Night Kitchen* (New York, 1970) and *Outside Over There*, discussed herein.

[8] N. 7, above, 15.

[9] Elements of modernity are among the 'new bits, dainty and undainty' that are 'always being added' to the ever-boiling Cauldron of Story. J.R.R. Tolkien, 'On Fairy Stories' in *The Tolkien Reader* (New York, 1966), 52. Fairy tales as myth, as fantasy, are not 'stories about fairies or elves, but stories about Fairy, that is Faërie, the realm or state in which fairies have their being.' The fairy story is a 'sub-creation', a secondary world with its own rules and laws and the 'inner consistency of reality'. Ibid., 88.

[10] 'Child training everywhere seems to be in considerable part concerned with problems which arise from universal characteristics of the human infant and from universal characteristics of adult culture which are incompatible with the continuation of infantile behavior.' J.M. Whiting and I.L. Child, *Child Training and Personality* (Yale, 1953), 63.

[11] Under Roman law, *infantia*, without [legal] speech, ends at seven. From seven to 14, the accuser bore the burden of showing the child is *doli capax*, capable of wrong or malice. At 14, *capax* is presumed.

law's power in everyday life. As Daniel Jutras observes of the mythic realm of Harry Potter and the ordinary one of his Muggle readers, 'the two worlds are not hermetically sealed from one another—their structures mirror one another'.[12] 'The child motif represents the preconscious, childhood aspect of the collective psyche', Jung writes.[13] The child is an image that 'unites the opposites' as 'a mediator, bringer of healing, that is, one who makes whole'.[14] The child at the heart of myth—the child in the story and the child to whom the story is told—symbolizes 'the strongest, the most ineluctable urge in every being, namely the urge to realize itself'.[15] The child of contemporary children's fiction remains linked with the *conception* of childhood emergent in the philosophies of Locke and Rousseau, in which the child is a 'pure point of origin' with access to a lost world or primitive state which she then restores to the adult.[16]

As myth, stories for children do more than shape the incipient subject of law. They *are* law. If childhood is a journey toward law, and if legal subjectivity is to be understood as something more (or other) than enforced obedience to a rule-set, then something more (or other) is needed than the moral foreclosure of the didactic tale and the positivist foreclosure of law. The first is found in the mythic form of the labyrinth and the stories of its travellers. Transcendent in its Heraclitan repetition, it is never the same twice, its meaning never foreclosed. The second is found, among other places, in the critical legal pluralism envisioned by Martha-Marie Kleinhans and Roderick Macdonald.[17] Rejecting both monistic law and the social sciences view of law as social fact, this pluralism presumes that 'knowledge is a process of creating and maintaining myths about realities' and that legal knowledge 'is the project of creating and maintaining self-understandings'.[18] The subject of law is a subject of a plurality of normative orders. As she navigates her way through these orders, or worlds, she becomes a law-inventing, law-subverting genitrix of normativity. 'By highlighting the dynamics of reciprocal construction, a *critical* legal pluralism legitimates interpretations of law apart from those endorsed by officials' because 'the law is within all members of any society that purports to recognize them as legal subjects'.[19]

As tales of the transcendent, as myth, the fantasy or fairy tale offers the uncertainty of meaning that engages Jung's 'state of imperfect transformation'. The labyrinth, an

[12] 'The Legal Dimensions of Everyday Life' (2001) 16 *Canadian Journal of Law & Society* 45. '[T]he appeal of *Harry Potter* lies in the representation of the ordinary complexities of children's lives, of their fears, their joys, aspirations and frustrations in a magical context. The same unresolved tensions and emotions animate the lives of magical heroes and mere mortals in grade school. I would make the same analysis of the legal sphere: in my view, architectural continuity is manifested in the fact that similar tensions or polarities are part of the structure of normative orders at each layer, from the brief encounter to the large-scale human interaction'. Ibid., 64. Comparative law should 'bring the mundane and the very small within its gaze'.

[13] *The Archetypes and the Collective Unconscious,* 2nd ed. *Works*, vol. 9, part 1, 161.

[14] Ibid., 164. [15] Ibid., 170.

[16] J. Rose, *The Case of Peter Pan or The Impossibility of Children's Fiction* (London, 1984, rev. ed. 1992), 10. A new literature emerged to socialize and entertain the 'new child' of the late eighteenth century. The child of children's fiction is 'the one the category itself sets in place, the one which it needs to believe is there for its own purposes.... Suppose, therefore, that Peter Pan is a little boy who does not grow up, not because he doesn't want to, but because someone else prefers that he shouldn't. Suppose, therefore, that what is at stake in *Peter Pan* is the adult's desire for the child'.

[17] 'What is a *Critical* Legal Pluralism?' (1997) 12 *Canadian Journal of Law & Society* 25. Legal pluralism recognizes both a plurality of legal orders in, among others, the colonial encounter, the diversity of sources of law in non- and post-colonial societies, and the production of state law, and a plurality of sites of normativity which may or may not be characterized as law.

[18] Ibid., 39. [19] Ibid., 46.

ancient symbol of transformation, is his metaphor of the psyche. It is ubiquitous in children's fiction. With its convoluted pathways, strange dwellers, and tests of reason and courage, the labyrinth reflects in unsettling ways the normative orders and conflicting rules of the child's everyday world. The nature of the transformation is known only to the child. Its secrets remain locked within. The submerged geography of childhood which holds Jung's maze is Freud's unconscious, where he situates the emergence of sexuality.[20] The child's exit from the labyrinth, then, signals the incipience of the child's sexual maturity and, as I argue, legal maturity as legal subjectivity.

Three contemporary works tell the story of a girl's journey through the labyrinth to retrieve her mother's baby from the goblins. Maurice Sendak's picture book *Outside Over There* (1981)[21] and Jim Henson's film *Labyrinth* (1986)[22] are framed as stories for children. Guillermo del Toro's film *Pan's Labyrinth* (2006) draws on the tropes of children's fiction to tell an adult story of the horrors of war.[23] The hero Theseus strode through the Cretan labyrinth to find a child-eating monster. In these stories, the monster is a baby and the hero is a girl. This Essay asks why. In Part 2.2, I consider the nature of the labyrinth and significations of the mythic labyrinth. In Part 2.3, I summarize the three labyrinth stories and draw connections with Wonderland's Alice. In Part 2.4, I explore the significance of the girl-child and connections between the feminine, the labyrinth, and the law. In Part 2.5, I consider the meanings of goblins. In Part 2.6, I look at the labyrinth and desire.

2.2 The mythic labyrinth

Writing of Borges' labyrinths, Emir Rodriguez-Monegal describes the labyrinth as a 'place of paradox' that fixes movement from form to contemplation, multiplicity to unity, and 'within to without, according to a symbolic progression'.[24] At its centre is a monster or metamorphosed god or a secret that is 'the revelation of one's own being'. It is 'the image of a chaos ordered by human intelligence' and a 'deliberate disorder which contains its own key'. It is an analogy of nature—'an endless river is a labyrinth of water; a forest is a labyrinth of vegetation'; and of human constructs—'a library is a labyrinth of books: any large city is a labyrinth of streets and houses'. In stories for children, the labyrinth is manifested as woods and forests,[25] streams,[26]

[20] N. 16, above, 10. In his Freudian analysis of European fairy tales, Bruno Bettelheim asserts that 'our greatest need and most difficult achievement is to find meaning in our lives' and that 'nothing can be as enriching for child and adult alike as the fairy tale'. Bruno Bettelheim, *The Uses of Enchantment: The Meaning and Importance of Fairy Tales* (New York, 1977), Introduction.

[21] New York: Harper Collins, 1981. In this story, the baby is a girl. Sendak explains: 'I changed the sex of the baby to a sister, thinking, 'God, I don't want anybody to track me on this thing. So it's a baby sister. And Ida hates her baby sister and wishes her gone, wishes her dead.' M. Sendak and H. Schreier, 'They Know Everything: Children and Suffering' at <http://townsendcenter.berkeley.edu/pubs/OP05_Sendak.pdf> accessed 3 November 2010.

[22] Dir. Jim Henson. Perf. David Bowie, Jennifer Connelly. Script Dennis Lee, Jim Henson, Terry Jones. Jim Henson Productions, 1986.

[23] *El Labrinto del Fauno*. Dir. Guillermo del Torro. Perf. Ivan Baquero, Sergi Lopez, Maribel Verdu, Doug Jones, Ariadna Gil, Alex Angulo. Esperanto Films, 2006.

[24] 'Symbols in Borges' Work' (1973) 19 *Modern Fiction Studies* 325.

[25] J. Dashner, *The Maze Runners* (New York, 2009).

[26] C. Kingsley, *The Water-Babies* (London, 1863).

burrows, and caves; as night cities,[27] cities underground,[28] goblin mines and ancient houses[29] and mazes of hedge or stone.[30]

The double-headed axe, insignia of Minos, King of Knossos, is a butterfly, the Bronze Age symbol of transformation. The *labyrinthos* or 'place of the double-headed axe' was built by the artificer Daedalus to house Minotaur, the monstrous son of Minos's wife Pasiphae, Daughter of the Sun, and the bull sent by Poseidon to seduce her.[31] Every ninth year, the king's powers are renewed by a tribute of seven male and seven female children who are left in the labyrinth to starve or be devoured by Minotaur. To end the sacrifice of the innocents, the king's daughter Ariadne aided by Daedalus spins a silken clue to guide her lover Theseus through the labyrinth to slay the monster. The lovers are driven into exile for murdering the prince but the children of Crete are saved.

Demeter the Great Mother, corn-mother and earth-goddess, descends into the Underworld to rescue her daughter Persephone from Hades, Lord of the Dead who, springing from the abyss as she gathers the flowers of spring, violently abducts her to his kingdom underground.[32] Demeter withholds her fruits from the world as she searches for her daughter, until Zeus secures her release. But Persephone has eaten of Hades' fruit and, like the germinating seed, must spend three months of every year underground. Each year Demeter mourns, crops die, and winter comes. Jung links his 'wanderings among the mazes of his psychic transformation' to Demeter's descent into the Underworld and her reunion with Persephone: 'In communing with himself, he finds not deadly boredom and melancholy but an inner partner, more than that, a relationship that seems like a secret love, or like a hidden springtime, when the green seeds sprout from the barren earth, holding out the promise of future harvests.'[33] If Demeter's descent is a descent into the unconscious, then her rescue of Persephone is the rescue of her self, the freeing of suppressed desire.[34]

Orpheus, whose lyre enchants the storms of heaven and seduces all creatures beneath, descends into the underworld to rescue his bride Eurydice, dead of a snake-bite.[35] 'So to the music of his strings he sang, and all the bloodless spirits wept to hear... and the queen and he whose sceptre rules the underworld could not deny the prayer, and called Eurydice. She was among the recent ghosts and, limping from her wound, came slowly forth.'[36] Orpheus took her 'with her this compact that, till he reach the world above and leave Valleys of Hell, he look not back or else the gift would fail' but 'longing to look, he turned his eyes—and straight she slipped away.

[27] M. de Larrabeiti, *The Borribles Trilogy* (London, 2003).

[28] N. Gaimon, *Neverwhere* (London, 1996).

[29] G. MacDonald, *The Princess and the Goblin* (London, 1872), discussed below.

[30] L. Carroll, *Alice's Adventures in Wonderland* (London, 1866) and Ursula K. LeGuinn, *The Tombs of Atuan* (London, 1971). In both works the protagonist is a young girl.

[31] J. Frazier, *The Golden Bough: A Study in Religion and Magic* (London, 1922), 280.

[32] Persephone tells her mother that 'the strong lord, the Host of Many', Hades, 'secretly put in my mouth sweet food, a pomegranate seed, and forced me to taste against my will. Also I will tell how he rapt me away... and carried me off beneath the depths of the earth'. N. 2, above, Homer, lines 405 *et seq*. Also see J. Chevalier and A. Gheerbrant, *A Dictionary of Symbols*, tr. J. Buchanan-Brown (London, 1996), 283, citing Homer. Demeter's search for Persephone parallels that of Aphrodite for Adonis in Syria, Cybele for Attis in Phrygia, and Isis for Osiris in Egypt. N. 31, above, 393.

[33] N. 4, above, continuing the passage cited therein.

[34] Demeter and Persephone are often depicted as identical, denoting the identification of the growing grain with its inert seed, life with afterlife. N. 32, above, Chevalier, 398. The labyrinth, then, is Jung's Dark Mother, the alchemical matrix of transformation.

[35] N. 32, above, 725.

[36] Ca. first century BCE to ca. first century CE, tr. A.D. Melville (Oxford, 1986), 226.

He stretched his arms to hold her and clasped, poor soul, naught but the yielding air. And she, dying again, made no complaint (for what complaint had she save she was loved?) and breathed a faint farewell, and turned again back to the land of spirits whence she came.' Orpheus moves freely between levels of consciousness, overworld and Underworld, and loses Eurydice because he cannot choose.

In their Orphic descent, the celebrants of the Eleusinian Mysteries taught by Demeter experience the cycles of rebirth personified in her reunion with her daughter, and in the horned boy Iacchus, *puer aeternus* and the Child-god of Ovid's *Metamorphoses*.[37] The only child admitted to the mysteries, horned Iacchus is born of Demeter or Persephone and identified with Dionysus, god of trees and the vine.[38] As a vegetation god cycling yearly between life and death, he is a redeemer. As the eternal boy, he is among Jung's archetypes, one of the 'primordial structural elements of the human psyche'.[39] For Jung, the 'higher' and 'complete' (*teleios*) man is begotten by the 'unknown' father and born from Wisdom, and it is he who, in the figure of the *puer aeternus*—'vultu mutabilis albus et ater' ('of changeful countenance, both white and black')—represents our totality, which transcends consciousness'.[40] This 'boy who is born from the maturity of the adult man' is 'not the unconscious child we would like to remain'. The unconscious child and eternal boy of recent myth is Peter Pan who, like Iacchus, connects the everyday with the transcendent Neverland. But Peter Pan is more strongly linked with another horned god, the goat-god Pan, God of All Things, 'chthonic, often lascivious and far from childlike', who drives procreation and preys equally on nymphs and boys.[41] Having escaped the adulthood his parents imagine for him, Peter Pan is also the eternally lost boy.[42] While his many contradictions remain unresolved,[43] he remains the iconic boy of children's fiction.

The labyrinth may be a place of secret happiness but it is a lonely place. Someone or some thing has been lost or stolen. Recovery brings another loss—Ariadne loses her kingdom and Theseus deserts her, every year Demeter is without her daughter, Eurydice is twice dead and Orpheus is torn apart by Maenads. These mythic beings are the fixed and moving points of the journey through the labyrinth, the tied end of Ariadne's clue and the unspooling of its string. Emergence from the labyrinth brings wisdom. For the child traveller, wisdom is tinged with the melancholy of the beginning of the end of childhood.

[37] The Mysteries were celebrated for some 2000 years, over a nine-day period in late September. The culmination of the rites underground may have included a period of blackness in which the initiates contemplate unrelieved death, followed by the reunion of Demeter and Persephone in a blaze of light. E.A. Beach, 'The Eleusinian Mysteries', University of Evansville Ecole Initiative at <http://users.erols.com/nbeach/eleusis.html> accessed 3 November 2010.

[38] N. 31, above, ch. 53.

[39] N. 13, above, 'The Psychology of the Child Archetype' Part 4. On the psychoanalysis of boy-men, see M.-L. von Franz, *The Problem of the Puer Aeternus*, 3rd ed. (Toronto, 2000).

[40] 'Answer to Job' in *Psychology and Religion: West and East*, 2nd ed. *Works*, vol. 11, para. 742, citing Horace, *Epistulae*, II.

[41] A. Yeoman, *Now or Neverland: Peter Pan and the myth of eternal youth, a psychological perspective on a cultural icon* (Toronto, 1998). In early performances of J.M. Barrie's play *Peter Pan* (1902), which predates the book *Peter and Wendy*, Peter carried panpipes and was accompanied by a goat. These props were thought indecent and were abandoned. The death of the goat-god Pan, personification of paganism to the Christian fathers, meant the death of the Greco-Roman order in the face of Christianity. N. 32, above, 734. Pan's likeness was appropriated for that of the devil.

[42] 'I ran away the day I was born... because I heard father and mother... talking about what I was to be when I became a man... I don't want ever to be a man... I want always to be a little boy and to have fun. So I ran away to Kensington Gardens and lived a long long time among the fairies.' N. 5, above, 42.

[43] N. 16, above.

2.3 Three labyrinths and Alice

The Eleusinian underground is a place of darkness punctuated by flashes of brilliance. The celebrant dies in the dark and is reborn. Beyond the mouth of the labyrinth which is also its exit lie elaborate passages twisting back upon themselves. Concealed at its centre is a mystery, an epiphany, a child. Its architecture evokes the architecture of the female body and its processes that body's cycles of menses, gravidity, and parturition. The traveller who completes the journey is bound to secrecy, a secrecy surrounding female rites of blood, begetting, and birth. To return is to be reborn. When the traveller is a pubescent girl—Ida of *Outside Over There* is nine or 10,[44] Sarah of *Labyrinth* is 14, Ofelia of *Pan's Labyrinth* is 11—and what is hidden in the labyrinth is her mother's baby, the labyrinth's convolutes become the involutes of her transforming female body. Her journey is a passage from daughter to mother to self, a growing-in and a growing-up. She shapes the labyrinth by her choices, revealing the labyrinth not as a heterarchy ruled by a monster or a king or a secret priesthood, but as a way she has willed to an end she has chosen. As Alice is the Red King's dream and he is hers, she is the dream of the labyrinth as she dreams it. Its form, myth and meaning exist beyond her, an organic intelligence awakened by her awareness or her presence. She is held within its folds even as its folds mirror that which is hidden within her. Its tests and terrors elicit from her those virtues that the law has historically denied in women—agency, intellect, reason, and courage.

Ida plays her wonder-horn to lull the baby 'but never watched. So the goblins came.' They take the baby and leave behind a changeling made of ice. 'The ice thing only dripped and stared, and Ida mad knew goblins had been there. "They stole my sister away!" she cried, "To be a nasty goblin's bride." ' Wrapped in her mother's cloak, she climbs backward out the window into outside over there, the child's answer to a parent's question, 'Where were you?' She floats above a goblin-haunted labyrinth of hooded pools, caves, doorways, and arches, one revealing the baby as the Lindbergh child.[45] A clue from her father on a label pasted to the sky recalls her to her mission: 'If Ida backwards in the rain would only turn around again and catch those goblins with a tune she'd spoil their kidnap honeymoon.' She lands among the goblins and sees that they are 'just babies like her sister', playing at weddings in their eggshell-littered cave.[46] 'Slyly' Ida plays her horn, the music 'captivating' and then 'frenzied'. The weeping, dancing goblins churn into a stream which she follows home, the baby in her arms. Her imperfect transformation is framed in epithets—poor Ida, Ida mad, foolish Ida, Ida backwards, sly and terrible Ida to the goblins, her father's 'brave, bright little Ida' who must help her mother 'which is just what Ida did'.

[44] N. 21, above.

[45] '*Outside Over There* was the most painful experience of my creative life. It brought on a catastrophe. It was so hard it caused me to have a breakdown. I left the business. I didn't think I could finish it.... I did not anticipate the horror of *Outside Over There*.... Something went amiss in me, a kind of panic, a kind of fear. I had touched on a subject, which is *not* in the book, but which had to be touched on to do the book. I couldn't face painting the pictures. I could not face seeing them all over again and painting Ida. It made me sick to do that.... Ida finds the baby. I refused to let the Lindbergh baby die. I changed history. And that is part of it—but it's a very superficial part'. R. Sutton and M. Sendak, 'An interview with Maurice Sendak', 3 November 2003 at <http://www.mahlerarchives.net/archives/sendak.pdf> accessed 3 November 2010.

[46] The goblins are drawn after the Dionne quintuplets who, with the Lindbergh baby, framed childhood in the Great Depression. N. 21, above.

Labyrinth takes the fairy-tale tropes of *Outside Over There* into the modern.[47] Sarah, resentful of her baby brother, calls up the goblins to take him away. They comply, leaving a goblin changeling briefly writhing in his bed. She must follow the labyrinth to the castle beyond the goblin city to rescue the baby, who will become a goblin if she fails. At the labyrinth's portal, a goblin gardener is flitting fairies. One bites her. She complains, 'I thought fairies did nice things, like granting wishes'. 'Shows what you know', the goblin warns her. It is the first of her many mistakes. Tasting an enchanted peach traps her in a perpetual masked ball from which she escapes to the safety of her doppelganger bedroom in the goblin town dump. She rejects this vestige of her infancy as 'all junk' and returns to her quest. Her labyrinth recapitulates the architectural history of the labyrinth—a stone maze whose walls drip with egg-cluster fruit yields to a cavern maze of speaking stones, a clipped topiary maze, an eighteenth-century hedge maze, backward-twisting forest pathways, the winding streets and crooked houses of the medieval goblin city, and finally the castle's Escher maze of perspective-teasing arches and inside-out staircases.[48] Although Sarah misses, ignores, or rejects many of the labyrinth's clues, she solves logic puzzles, resists the lures of the glam-rock goblin prince, and rallies a force of goblin outliers to fight through to the castle. Its false perspectives require a literal leap of faith to save the baby. When the prince confronts her, she speaks the words of power: 'You have no power over me.' The prince declaims: 'Everything that you wanted I have done. You asked that the child be taken, I took him. You cowered before me, I was frightening. I have reordered time, I have turned the world upside-down, and I have done it all for you. I am exhausted from living up to your expectations.' It is she who made the labyrinth, in the image of her desire.[49]

Pan's Labyrinth is Ofelia's refuge from the fascist colonel who married her mother and sired her foetal brother. A stick insect forms itself into a fairy after a figure in her storybook and leads her into the descending circular stairwell of an ancient labyrinth. Its guardian, a grotesque and mossy faun, tells her that she is the lost daughter of the King of the Underworld. The labyrinth is its portal. To regain her kingdom, she must perform three tasks. The labyrinth is guarded by a fallopian tree, its trunk holding a monstrous toad in whose belly is a golden key. Ofelia tricks the toad into disgorging the key, completing the first task. To retrieve a dagger from the labyrinth, her second task, she enters a chamber painted with gruesome scenes of the murder of children. Near an Auschwitz heap of withered leather baby shoes, a pallid shrivelled naked man sits at a food-laden banquet table, his eyeballs on a plate. Ofelia takes the dagger and, defying instruction, eats three grapes. The pale man, awakened, stumbles after her but is distracted by the fairies. As he catches and devours them, she escapes.[50] Her mother dies in childbirth and her last task is to bring the baby to the

[47] Sarah is a disaffected teen, the prince is an aging rock star, and flitting fairies are pests to be poisoned, but the film holds true to fairytale form. *Outside Over There*, its inspiration, is not found. The credits state:

> 'Jim Henson acknowledges his debt to the works of Maurice Sendak'. *Where the Wild Things* Are, N. 7 above, (the film's Ludo is a Wild Thing) is among Sarah's books.

[48] M.C. Escher, 'Relativity', 1953. Lithograph, and 'Ascending and Descending', 1960. Lithograph.

[49] Sarah's labyrinth-cued bedroom—Escher prints, copies of *Alice in Wonderland* and *Where the Wild Things Are*, a twirling-princess music-box, stuffed toy goblins— would seem to confirms this but a visit from her goblin allies at the end of the film's close suggests otherwise.

[50] The scene follows Francesco Goya, 'Saturn Devouring his Young', painted ca. 1819–1823, Prado, Madrid. Horned Saturn (Cronus, father of Demeter, in Greek myth) is told in prophecy that his son will kill him as he killed his father Uranus. He eats his children as they are born. Only Jupiter survives.

labyrinth. The faun raises the golden dagger over the baby, telling Ofelia that the blood of an innocent is required to open the portal to her Underworld kingdom. She snatches the baby away. Her step-father has tracked her to the labyrinth. He kills her. The innocent is now sacrificed and the last task is complete. She enters her kingdom Underworld. The newly-youthful faun brings her to her father and mother who are arrayed as Hades and Persephone and seated on great thrones.

As in all fairy tales, power is perfected in death—the people are freed of the tyrant, the king or magician or hero sleeps in a cavern under a mountain or a lake until his people call him forth again, the curse is lifted, the world is renewed. The fallopian tree puts out a single flower. But Ofelia is a Persephone powerless to return to the land above. Her labyrinth, like those of Ida and Sarah, mirrors the world of the everyday but Ofelia's worlds are both places of terror. The pale man, with the colonel, is the monstrous father of war, scourge of men, killer of women, devourer of children, the fascistic one-god who steals the powers of good, bad, and trickster gods and obliterates the pantheon. 'It was no accident that in its earliest representations in the decalogue, the icon of law as commandment inscribed in stone was instituted, or founded, upon the destruction of an idol', Peter Goodrich writes. The shattering of the golden calf meant the 'exclusion of difference in its imaginary forms...the Egyptian, the foreigner or stranger...the plurality of sources and of meanings...the feminine'.[51] In his voracious appetite, the monistic father-god must consume all power, however insignificant—a child's above all. Ofelia's tiny magic, like that of Orpheus, lay in the power to mediate between the worlds of the everyday and the transcendent. It is now gone.

Ida, Sarah, and Ofelia follow Alice underground. If Peter Pan is the iconic boy of children's fiction, Alice is its iconic girl. Her rabbit hole leads to a subterranean topiary maze and a baby that she rescues from a Duchess.[52] Behind her looking-glass lies a chessboard labyrinth through which she progresses from pawn to queen.[53] *Alice* is referenced in Ida's Alice band, in the topiary mazes of *Labyrinth* and the Duchess-sized head of its goblin gardener, and in Ofelia's Alice dress and golden key. While Peter Pan forever remains a self-centred crowing infant, Alice rejects the Victorian homiletics parodied in *Alice* and instead draws upon courage, reason, intellect, and logic to cope with her changing state and the mad or childish residents of Wonderland.[54] So Ida uses her music to banish the goblins, Sarah solves logic puzzles and ethical conundrums, and Ofelia relies on trickery and sweet guile.

In choosing which paths to follow and which to reject, the girl is architect of her labyrinth. In making rules for herself and interpreting those of the labyrinth and its creatures, she is no longer a 'passive abider' of law but its transgressive inventor. This is the legal subject imaged in critical legal pluralism.[55] In this view, realities are created and maintained, not by doctrinal law or the external critique of the social

[51] *Oedipus Lex: Psychoanalysis, History, Law* (Berkeley: University of California Press, 1995), 223.

[52] *Alice's Adventures under Ground* (1862, facs. pub. 1886, rep. Ann Arbor: University Microfilms, 1964), handwritten and illustrated by Carroll for Alice Liddell, whose photograph is pasted into the last page. This was re-edited and published as *Alice's Adventures in Wonderland*, n. 30, above, illustrated by John Tenniel. Alice is 'seven and a half' but Liddell, her inspiration, was 11 when Carroll wrote the first *Alice*.

[53] *Through the Looking-Glass and What Alice Found There* (London: Macmillan, 1871).

[54] 'We're all mad here', the Cheshire Cat tells Alice and 'Madness is childhood' for Foucault. The insane 'are regarded as children who had too much strength and make dangerous use of it. They must be given immediate punishments and rewards; whatever is remote has no effect on them'. M. Foucault, *Madness and Civilization: A History of Insanity in the Age of Reason* (New York, 1988), 252.

[55] N. 17, above, 27.

sciences, but by knowledge. Law's subjects 'possess a transformative capacity that enables them to produce legal knowledge and to fashion the very structures of law that contribute to constituting their legal subjectivity'.[56] Wisdom is the secret at the centre of the labyrinth. Knowledge is the labyrinth's fabric. It is elicited from its girl travellers as they resolve its mind-twisting pathways and the twisted homiletics of its creatures, the dicta of Ida's father in the sky, the machinations of the goblin gardener and the goblin prince, and the cruel tricks of the faun.

The labyrinth is a place of 'dangers untold and hardships unnumbered', Sarah's playscript tells her. The child wandering the labyrinth illustrates Jung's 'striking paradox'—'the child is on the one hand delivered helpless into the power of terrible enemies and in continual danger of extinction, while on the other he possesses powers far exceeding those of ordinary humanity'. While he 'may be "insignificant", unknown, "a mere child", he is also divine. Myth . . . emphasizes . . . that the "child" is endowed with superior powers and, despite all dangers, will unexpectedly pull through'.[57] The child traveller's struggle lies not in the journey alone but also in her return to the world of the everyday. How should she reconcile these competing normative orders? Which world is real? Internormative conflict cannot be resolved by external authority, because 'the conflict itself flows only from its recognition and acknowledgment by the legal subject-self'.[58] Resolving internormative conflict requires 'an element of construction or creativity'. If 'subjects control law as much as law controls subjects', then there can be 'no a priori distinction between normative orders because these normative orders cannot exist outside the creative capacity of their subjects'.[59] There is no need, then, to seek 'a separation, nor an eventual hierarchical reconciliation, of multiple legal orders. Normative heterogeneity exists both between various normative regimes which inhabit the same intellectual space, and within the regimes themselves'.[60] Both worlds are real. The normative order of each is reflected or refracted in the other. The mythic labyrinth is and is not in the world of the everyday, as it is and is not within its travellers. Resolving the tensions within and between worlds—'[h]ow legal subjects recognize and react to relations within and between these regimes'—brings 'self-understanding',[61] wisdom.

Although the constitution of the legal subject begins in childhood, a critical vision of law suggests that the legal subject is never fully determined. Still on her journey from *infantia* to *capax*, the girl who has travelled the labyrinth is neither a full legal subject nor fully a woman. Hers is an imperfect transformation.

2.4 The feminine, the labyrinth, and the law

The *puer*, the Divine Child, is androgynous. The protagonist in stories for children is overwhelmingly male. Reading is gendered. Girls read stories about boys but boys seldom read stories about girls. Boys learn to run the world. Girls learn that home is best. Peter Pan's adventures are boys' adventures—fighting pirates, saving exotic maidens, boasting, flying, going to sea—outbound and proto-phallic. Neverland is a place of conquest. Alice's adventures are inbound, proto-uterine, a dream. Her sentences begin with 'I wonder'. Wonderland is a place of speculation. For the Victorians, little girls were 'the purest members of a species of questionable origin, combining as

[56] N. 17, above, 38.
[57] N. 13, above, 170.
[58] N. 17, above, 39.
[59] N. 17, above, 40.
[60] N. 17, above, 44.
[61] N. 17, above, 44.

they did the inherent spirituality of child and woman'.[62] Even so, 'Victorian concepts of the child tended to swing back and forth between extremes of original innocence and original sin; Rousseau and Calvin stood side by side in the nursery' and children are 'quickly . . . transformed into monsters'.[63] Alice is the first strong corrective to the boy hero. Ida, Sarah, and Ofelia are, like Alice, male creations.[64] That the labyrinths and their girl travellers are male visions of female visions lends their stories a frisson of yearning that limns certain images. In bringing these to brightness, others fade away. The girl watching sees the enactment of her own journey in another girl's story, yet male footsteps fall everywhere across these worlds-within-girls.

Uncertain etymology and uneven usage make *girl* one of the most investigated words in English linguistic literature. First recorded at the end of the thirteenth century, it meant a child of either sex.[65] Only from the mid-sixteenth century, when damsel, wench, and maid came into use, did *girl* refer exclusively to a young female. *Girl* became dominant in the seventeenth century, where Ariès locates the birth of the *conception* of childhood.[66] Until the 1990s engagement of popular culture with 'girl power', the usage and connotations of *girl* and *boy* were asymmetrical. This asymmetry permeated the law. Here, 'the place of feminine difference was aligned with the *gynaeceum*, with the private, with the infantile, with impermanence and fantasy'.[67] Boys grow up but girls grow in. 'Uniquely situated as both women and children', girls are marginalized by a combination of gender bias and paternalism in which 'the experience of adulthood defines what it means to be a woman and the experience of being male defines what it is to be a child'.[68]

As the archetypal Child, the girl protagonist is part boy, androgynous. As a male creation, she is trans-gendered, berdache. As a clever girl who outwits the creatures of another world, she is a trickster. As law-inventing and law-subverting genitrix of normativity, both female and child, she paradoxically embodies her own exclusion from the law. 'Woman is compensated by a masculine element and therefore her unconscious has, so to speak, a masculine imprint', Jung writes, which generates 'the

62 N. Auerbach, 'Alice and Wonderland: A Curious Child' (1973) in (ed) H. Bloom, *Lewis Carroll* (New York, 1987), 31 at 32.

63 Ibid., 42. Laurence Stone describes four views of the nature of the child extant in this period, 'the adoption of each of which profoundly affects the way he is treated'—born in original sin, requiring total subordination of the child's will to that of the adult; born *tabula rasa* and malleable; born with a predetermined character and potential, but susceptible to improvement through education; and born pure, to be corrupted by society. *The Family, Sex and Marriage in England 1500–1800* (New York, 1979), 254.

64 *Labyrinth* and *Pan's Labyrinth* are, more than most films, the creations of their directors who exercised unusual control over story development, script, character design, and visual effects. Sendak is illustrator and author of *Outside Over There*.

65 *Boy*, also of uncertain derivation, took on its modern usage after 1400. *Girl* may derive from *gerela, gierela*, referring to unisex clothing, as *brat*, an infant's garment, came to mean *child* in the sixteenth century. A. Bammesberger and J. Grzega, 'ModE Girl and Other Terms for "Young Female Person" in English Language History' (2001) *Onomasiology Online* 2. On the possible derivation of *girl* from *churl*, a low-born person, and related to *kerla*, an old woman or hag, see A. Liberman, *An Analytic Dictionary of English Etymology* (Minneapolis, 2008), 100. For a critical review of the etymology, see A. Curzan, *Gender Shifts in the History of English* (Cambridge, 2003), ch. 5, 'Asymmetrical Word Histories: When Boys could be Girls'.

66 U. Lenker, 'Gerles, Girls, Grrrlz—Girl Power! Cultural Phenomena and the Semantic Changes of *Girl*' in W. Falkner, L. Lipka, and H.-J. Schmit (eds), *Words, Lexemes, Concepts—Approaches to the Lexicon* (Tubingen, 1999), 7. *Teenager* was first recognized in 1947.

67 N. 51, above, 176.

68 N. Taefi, 'The Synthesis of Age and Gender: Intersectionality, International Human Rights Law and the Marginalisation of the Girl-child' (2009) 17 *International Journal of Children's Rights* 345, at 346, 348.

spermatic word'.[69] Jung describes this 'animus' as an elderly father-figure. In law, his compensating 'masculine element' is coverture, a Roman, ecclesiastical and common law doctrine in which the female is in a perpetual state of tutelage to a male. In law, Peter Goodrich asserts, woman is an image and 'the specter of creativity as also of death because femininity is, by tradition, nature: inexorable, material, passionate, and unconscious'.[70] The image of the feminine is 'a desire within wisdom, a fate or seduction within the present, either ignored or denied yet nonetheless inevitable and no less a law for being repeated without being recognized'. It is 'the emblem of another law or law of law, of the contingency and thus fracture of such doctrine, dogma, or jurisprudence that claims the singularity, unity, or closure of legal forms'. As 'a figure of uncertainty, of doubt or desire, foresight or faith, idolatry or immaculate conception, she is many and she is none, both matter and void'.[71] Images of female weakness (*imbecillitas*), vulnerability (*infirmitas*), frailty or fragility (*fragilatas*), frivolity (*levitas*), cunning (*calliditas*), and deception justified the legal disability of girls and women under Roman law.[72] These were taken up with vigour by seventeenth-century churchmen and legalists. Ecclesiastical and secular sanctions placed on women were 'a prohibition of the feminine, of the sensual and of imagination'. Whether the image produced was seductive or repulsive, it 'stood as an obstacle in the path of internal vision' because, 'as contingency, contact, or touch, the feminine would destabilize the universality of law and the abstract character of homosocial community' constructed on the paternal lineage of sons.[73]

Images of the feminine are ambiguous and contradictory. There is 'no common essence... nor indeed is there any common definition of women in law' but a woman whose 'soul and reason is indistinguishable from or even superior to that of men' is worthy of praise.[74] Pubescent but not sexual, displaying the masculine virtues of agency, reason, intellect, and courage, the girl who travels the labyrinth escapes law's dark image of the feminine.[75] With her maturity, it will descend. The labyrinth has prepared her. Homologous to the female body, visionary, fluid, a place of choice, tutelary but not a tutelage, a place of meaning and not of hierarchy, the labyrinth challenges the singularity of monistic law, law as logos, the law of the Father and

[69] 'This results in a considerable psychological difference between men and women, and accordingly I have called the projection-making factor in women the animus, which means mind or spirit.' *The Syzygy: Anima and Animus*, *Works*, vol. 9:2, para. 28f. 'The animus is the deposit, as it were, of all woman's ancestral experiences of man—and not only that, he is also a creative and procreative being, not in the sense of masculine creativity, but in the sense that he brings forth something we might call... the spermatic word.' 'Anima and Animus', *Two Essays on Analytical Psychology*, *Works*, vol. 7, para. 336.

[70] N. 51, above, 37. [71] N. 51, above, 38. [72] N. 51, above, 115.

[73] N. 51, above, 96. To decrease paternity uncertainty, a vast complex of legal and social rules aimed at claustrating women was devised. There is no corresponding uncertainty in maternity.

[74] N. 51, above, 175.

[75] These images persist in the contemporary demonization of women who fail to conform to script. 'When sex murderers are women and their victims are female children, values surrounding womanhood are doubly challenged. Consort with devils may be Hollywood entertainment or a preoccupation of the unreconstructed religious Right but centuries of such beliefs leave the residual metaphor of witch or vampire, the deadly seductive *lamia* and *succubi* fictioned from the dark side of male sexuality. Beginning with Eve in Western tradition, women are imaged as corrupt and corrupting' and (citing *Malleus Malificarm*), 'All wickedness is but little to the wickedness of a woman. Wherefore S. John Chrysostom says on the text, It is not good to marry (*S. Matthew xix*): "What else is woman but a foe to friendship, an unescapable punishment, a necessary evil, a natural temptation, a desirable calamity, a domestic danger, a delectable detriment, an evil of nature, painted with fair colours!"' A. McGillivray, '"A moral vacuity in her which is difficult if not impossible to explain": Law, Psychiatry and the Remaking of Karla Homolka' (1998) 5:2/3 *International Journal of the Legal Profession* 255.

Freud's Oedipal law that brutally subdues the child's desire. 'The child's subjection to the father is by the ordination of God himself', Robert Filmer declares in *Patriarcha*, and the power of the father, of Adam and Abraham, is the locus of the power of the king.[76] This power justifies patriarchal lineage and the suppression of the feminine. Freud locates law's origin in a mythic primal horde ruled by the despotic female-hoarding Father.[77] His sons, the horde, band together to devour him. In their guilt, they enact two primal laws—not to kill the father; not to enjoy women—laws which sublimate and deny the feminine and embody Freud's ubiquitous Oedipus complex.[78] This fundamental element of psychoanalysis represents the moment when the child's (incestuous) desire for the mother is violently severed (a castration) by the jealous father, whom the child then wishes to kill in order to secure the mother for himself. Patriarchal law ruptured the labyrinth's privileging of the feminine and its profound connection with the child long after the labyrinth entered human culture. 'Religion, fathers... they are another map showing through', Barrie writes of the map of Neverland.[79] There are other ways in which to imagine law. The labyrinth is one.

'By imagining law as "a mode of giving particular sense to particular things in particular places", a critical legal pluralism shifts inquiry toward hermeneutic thinking, to thinking of law as "meaning... not machinery".'[80] As a mode that elicits from its traveller an understanding of its rules as meaning, not machinery, the labyrinth may be imagined as law. Labyrinth law is not monist law that seeks, often violently, to bring disparities under a single idea (one god, the Father). It is law as nomos—'the uncountable, incalculable law that distributes emplacements and lines of flight on smooth space', the law that is 'wedded to a very particular type of multiplicity: non-metric, acentered, rhizomatic multiplicities that occupy space without "counting" it and can be "explored only by legwork"'.[81] Transcendence, as wisdom, is immanent in the repetition of the labyrinth's folds. Transcendence, as justice, is immanent in the repetition of law. Drawing on the work of Kierkegaard and the surrealist painter

[76] *Patriarcha or The Natural Power of Kings* (1680), ch. 1, para. 4 at <http://www.constitution.org/eng/patriarcha.htm> accessed 3 November 2010. In his *Second Treatise of Government* (1690) refuting Filmer, John Locke rejects paternal ownership of children and distinguishes parental power from state power. A. McGillivray, 'Children's Rights, Paternal Power and Fiduciary Duty: From Roman law to the Supreme Court of Canada' (2011) 19 *International Journal of Children's Rights* 21–54.

[77] *Totem and Taboo* (1913), tr. J. Strachey (London, 1950). Freud credits his primal horde to Darwin, with scant support. On his replacement of his Seduction Theory in which father-daughter incest is described as fact, with his Oedipus theory in which the daughter desires and therefore imagines the father's seduction, see L. Wolf, *Postcards from the End of the World: Child Abuse in Freud's Vienna* (New York, 1988). On Freud's myth of law, see J.L. Schroeder, 'Totem, Taboo and the Concept of Law: Myth in Hart and Freud' (2009) 1 *Jurisprudence Review* 139.

[78] 'They revoked their deed by forbidding the killing of the totem, the substitute for their father; and they renounced its fruits by resigning their claim to the women who had now been set free. They thus created out of their filial sense of guilt the two fundamental taboos of totemism, which for that very reason inevitably corresponded to the two repressed wishes of the Oedipus complex.' Freud, n. 77, above, 141. Freud speculates that 'the tumultuous mob of brothers were filled with the same contradictory feelings which we can see at work in the ambivalent father complexes of our children and of our neurotic patients. They hated their father, who presented such a formidable obstacle to their craving for power and their sexual desires; but they loved and admired him too.' Ibid., 143.

[79] N. 5, above.

[80] N. 17, above, 42.

[81] A. Philippopoulos-Mihalopoulos, 'Repetition: Deleuze and Kierkegaard on Law, Justice and Art' (University of Westminster School of Law Research Paper No. 10–22, 2010), 7 at <http://ssrn.com/abstract=1581522> accessed 3 November 2010.

de Chirico,[82] Andreas Philippopoulos-Mihalopoulos observes that 'repetition can produce difference by remaining repetition' and that 'repetition characterizes the whole of the legal edifice'.[83] 'When norms (or judgments) repeat themselves, superimposing themselves on a spiral of self-referential production, repetition is "every time once", every time different.'[84] This presents us with 'a law that seems (but is not) coherent, monocular, synthetic. In its repetition, the law fragments in its various perspectives and then, arbitrarily at a given point, regroups and delivers a judgment'. When justice is achieved, judgment is 'the moment of transcendence, where an opening in the architecture, an awning of an arch unexpectedly reveals a piece of the sky. When it takes place, legal transcendence is always within the law, appearing dreamlike behind a normative edifice, in the form of justice'. The labyrinth, like the law, 'repeats itself interminably, every time producing an absolute difference inscribed in its self-referential immanence. Within the folds of its repetition, the law renders itself just, turns itself into justice, and crosses from one point of immanence to another'.[85]

For the labyrinth's traveller, as for the suitor at law, the repetition of 'rhizomatic multiplicities' ends when that which was sought is found—wisdom, justice. In the labyrinth, as in law, the crossing from one to another point of immanence is not effected by the traveller alone, but with and against those dwelling within. These we may call goblins.

2.5 So the goblins came

Earth-bound, secretive, neither for nor against us, the goblins at the margins of human societies are both mentor and nemesis of the labyrinth's girl travellers. If madness is childhood, then goblins embody the metonym. Nietzsche in the voice of Zarathustra declaims: 'The atmosphere rare and pure, danger near and spirit full of a joyful wickedness: these are things well matched. I want to have goblins about me, for I am courageous, the courage which scares away ghosts, creates for itself goblins—it wants to laugh.'[86] For Jung, this is megalomania and 'those goblins are madness already'. He warns: 'You were surrounded by goblins and your solitude was quite a beautiful garden. But don't tell it, because the goblins disappear and instead you have ghosts.'[87]

From the Welsh *coblynau*, the ones who knock, goblins are associated with mountains and caverns.[88] Their rapping brings miners to rich veins of ore. The

[82] Ibid. 'Both Kierkegaard [*Repetition*] and de Chirico [*Piazza d'Italia* series] make use of their material, be this the text or the canvas, while superseding it. But neither of them *departs* from their material. They remain captured, carving out spaces of transcendence among the breaths of recognition, the building and the sky, the demiurge and the public. The enigma of repetition is that its transcendence can only be reached through and then inscribed within immanence.' Ibid., 5. De Chirico draws upon motifs of the labyrinth and the desertion of Ariadne.

[83] Ibid., 2. [84] Ibid., 5. [85] Ibid., 10 (emphasis omitted).

[86] C.G. Jung, *Nietzshe's Zarathustra: Notes of the seminar given in 1934–1939*, (ed) James L. Jarrett (Princeton, 1988), 504. Nietzsche 'would be speaking the truth if he said, "I am afraid. I notice there are goblins about me and no human beings. I have scared human beings away and now ghosts are all over my deserted roads"'. Goblins, then, are the jocular face of fear.

[87] Ibid., 505. 'And where had his normality gone? It had drawn back and left the field to the goblins', ibid., 513.

[88] W. Sykes, *British Goblins: Welsh Folklore, Fairy Mythology, Legends and Traditions* (London, 1890), 24. *Goblin* appears in Middle English in 1320 and *gobelin* in French in the 1500s. A twelfth-century cleric writes of a spirit called Gobelinus haunting Évreux. Associated with underground caverns, the

complex world of *y Tylwyth Teg*, the fair folk, was known to Shakespeare.[89] Puck, a shape-changing *pwca*, calls himself a goblin[90] and Falstaff lampoons the fear of goblins—'God defend me from that Welsh fairy, Lest he transform me to a piece of cheese!'[91]—but goblins are punitive, capricious, and sometimes fatal.[92] Known in Glamorgan by the propitiating euphemism 'mothers' blessing', the fair folk steal babies, leaving a *plentyn-newid* or change-child in its place.[93] The changeling soon grows shrivelled, violent, and idiotic, or unnaturally clever. To compel the child's return, the changeling is held over the fire, beaten, poisoned with foxglove, or tricked into revealing its great age.[94] The mythic labyrinth is an empty place trod by great heroes, with a child-eating monster at its heart. The labyrinth of the girl traveller is populated by child-stealing monsters of other descent.

Goblins represent another sort of fear. The association of goblins with earthy or low sexuality is made in Christina Rossetti's 1862 *Goblin Market*.[95] Laura warns her sister Lizzie, 'We must not look at goblin men, We must not buy their fruits: Who knows upon what soil they fed Their hungry thirsty roots?' But it is Laura who eats the fruit and, 'canker'd, goblin-ridden', awaits the fate of 'Jeanie in her grave who should have been a bride But who for joys brides hope to have Fell sick and died'. Lizzie returns to the goblin men for fruit to ease her sister's pain but they 'Held her hands and squeez'd their fruits Against her mouth to make her eat'. Their bestiality occupies much of the poem—'One had a cat's face, One whisk'd a tail, One tramp'd at a rat's pace, One crawl'd like a snail.' Lizzie's brutal ravishment is accompanied by 'clapping, crowing, Clucking and gobbling... Grunting and snarling... Barking, mewing, hissing, mocking'. Their antecedent is Shakespeare's Puck,

German kobold shares his name with cobalt, a mineral hated by miners for its association with arsenic. *Elementymology & Elements Multidict* at <http://elements.vanderkrogt.net/element.php?sym=Co> accessed 3 November 2010.

[89] '[T]here is ample reason to think that Shakespeare would know of the Welsh fairies themselves: it is plain that in 1595–9 he was interested in matters Welsh.' H.E. Brooks, Introduction, *A Midsummer Night's Dream* (London, 1979), lxxiii. Sykes observes that 'Shakespeare's use of Welsh folk-lore, it should be noted, was extensive and peculiarly faithful'. N. 87, above, 14.

[90] 'I will lead them up and down: I am fear'd in field and town: Goblin, lead them up and down.' N. 88, above, Act III, Sc. 2.

[91] *The Merry Wives of Windsor*, Act V, Sc. 5.

[92] Goblins are not unique to European mythologies. The Sto:Lo of British Columbia, for example, respect the people who live deep in the forest and under the lake, who are 'just the same as us' but different, to be avoided but not feared. Sonny McAlsie, Sto:Lo historian, discussion with the author, 28 June 2005.

[93] N. 88, above, note 1.

[94] N. 87, above, 56. 'That there is nothing especially Welsh in this needs not be pointed out. Apart from the fact that infanticide, like murder, is of no country, similar practices as to changelings have prevailed in most European lands.' Ibid., 57. On Victorian goblins, changelings and murder, see C.G. Silver, *Strange and Secret Peoples: Fairies and Victorian Consciousness* (Oxford, 1999). On changelings as children who fail to thrive or whose mental development is slow or arrested as by autism, see among others S.S. Eberley, 'Fairies and the Folklore of Disability: Changelings, Hybrids and the Solitary Fairy' (1988) 89 *Folklore* 58; for a contrary view, see C.F. Goodey and T. Stainton, 'Intellectual disability and the myth of the changeling myth' (2001) 37 *Journal of the History of the Behavioral Sciences* 223–40. Luther thought disabled children were Satanic changelings, 'only a piece of flesh' which could be killed with impunity. D.L. Ashliman, 'Changelings' (1997) at <http://www.pitt.edu/~dash/changeling.html#10> accessed 3 November 2010. If children of the Tan-Kin of China 'suffer from any lingering malady, and recovery becomes hopeless, they will put it to death with circumstances of great cruelty, believing it not to be their child but a changeling, and fancying that a demon has taken the place of their offspring'. 'Infanticide', *Temple Bar* rep. *New York Times*, 13 August 1882.

[95] *Goblin Market and Other Poems* (Cambridge, 1862).

who boasts: 'Sometime a horse I'll be, sometime a hound, A hog, a headless bear, sometime a fire; And neigh, and bark, and grunt, and roar, and burn, Like horse, hound, hog, bear, fire, at every turn.'[96]

Rossetti's goblins were tamed for children in George MacDonald's 1872 *The Princess and the Goblin*, a story of the labyrinth.[97] In MacDonald's mountain caves, it is not the goblins but their creatures—the 'willed' miscegenation of domestic and wild animals taken 'from the upper regions of light into the lower regions of darkness'—who are a hideous, 'uncouth and varied' mix of bestial forms.[98] The goblins themselves devolved from humans who hid in subterranean caverns and 'grew misshapen in body [as] they had grown in knowledge and cleverness'.[99] The goblin wedding Ida fears for her sister is the foiled wedding of MacDonald's goblin prince Harelip to a human child, a softened version of Jeannie who died 'for joys brides hope to have' and the near-fate of goblin-ridden Laura. The seductive fruit chaining Persephone to Hades for part of every year and sickening Rossetti's girls enchants Sarah into ignoring her mission and brings Ofelia under the pale man's dire gaze. The fruit, with the goblins who offer it, is fed on fell soil. Girls do well to avoid it.

'I have had so many names, old names that only the wind and the trees can pronounce. I am the mountain, the forest and the earth. I am a faun', the faun of *Pan's Labyrinth* tells Ofelia. He is *locus geni*, an ancient being, goat below the waist and man above, goat-horned and goat-eared.[100] The faun is confined to its locus, a mountain or woodland. Goblins creep closer to home. Horace's *puer eternus* 'of changeful countenance, both white and black'[101] fits the faun. Ancient and evil in appearance, its proffered friendship and semblance of goodwill are proven false by the dreadful tasks it sets Ofelia. With her return to her kingdom, its youth is restored and its benign face is shown. A split of man and beast, the faun shares the dual nature of the goblin who is neither man nor beast. 'Of changeful countenance' equally fits the goblins. Helpful and hurtful, childlike and dire, the goblins of the labyrinth, with those of Jung's (and Alice's) beautiful garden, embody childhood's madness. Goblins lie closer to *infantia* than to *capax*. Rule-bound[102] but outside the law, they are *incapax* but not innocent. Chaotic, chthonic, manifesting a rude sexuality and ruder humour, terrifying and delightful in their human mimicry,[103] goblins are *unheimlich*

[96] N. 88, above, Act III, Sc. 3.

[97] N. 29, above. A silken clue spun by a Demeter-like great-grandmother brings the girl safely through the labyrinths of underground caverns and the mountain castle.

[98] N. 29, above, 130. The *Labyrinth* goblins, warty, rubbery, and race-coded brown and black, resemble MacDonald's goblins. Their contrast with the pale elegance of David Bowie's goblin prince and the fuzzy-Muppet goblin allies is unsettling.

[99] N. 29, above, 5.

[100] The Roman faun was later conflated with the goat-footed Greek satyr, follower of Bacchus and another sort of creature.

[101] N. 40, above.

[102] They must, depending on the folklore, obey the rules for identifying a changeling (the changeling must disclose its great age when the mother speaks of brewing ale in an acorn or making a feast in an egg-cup or the changeling is tortured), for releasing a human captive (favour given; indenture served; no food eaten), allowing a human to escape (tests passed; Christian symbols deployed), for taking babies (not a boy dressed as girl; not if protected by iron or a Bible), and giving household help (sweep, bake, brew, or mend if milk is put out for them; sour the household's milk if it is not). They reward and punish at their own caprice. It is tempting to speculate on the nature of goblin law, which by various accounts would be rudimentary, retributive, and old.

[103] 'The coblynau are described as being about half a yard in height and very ugly to look upon, but extremely good-natured, and warm friends of the miner. Their dress is a grotesque imitation of the miner's garb, and they carry tiny hammers, picks and lamps. They work busily, loading ore in buckets,

un-children. The girl must join their games, however silly or inimical, her mission an amusing diversion in their eternal eden of goblin-play. In return, they test her divided loyalties and make manifest the contradictions of her desires.

The stolen baby is more goblin than human. Ida cannot tell the baby from the goblins, Sarah's brother is dressed as a goblin and nearly becomes one, and Ofelia's fetal brother resembles one. Babies suit the goblin world. The girl is too old to turn into a goblin and too young for goblin weddings. However deep she is drawn into their world, she does not belong to it. To rescue the baby is to accept her childhood's incipient end.

2.6 Not the end

The folds of the labyrinth are an imperfect mirror which trues the distortions of desire, distorts that which the traveller had once thought true, or at least inevitable, and disrupts the comforting norms of the everyday. A Persephone of two realms, the girl is now differentiated from her mother: she knows about goblins. The rescue of her infant rival means the end of infantile desire and the beginning of a different relationship. Although she returns to the rule of the father, she does so on her own terms after a hard and secret struggle, his dominion diminished because it is she who chooses to obey. As genitrix of law, her question is no longer the child's question of how the normative order of her parents views her as a subject, but how she should view that order.[104] The goblins manifest the 'multiple narrating selves' within her, to whose scrutiny she is held. If 'knowledge is a process of creating and maintaining myths about realities',[105] then the labyrinth is both knowledge and process. If 'law is within all members of any society that purports to recognize them as legal subjects',[106] then the ordered chaos of the labyrinth inscribed upon its traveller is as much 'law within' as the rules of the everyday. As law's nascent subject, the girl has begun 'to explore the variety of possible worlds and possible selves' and to 'evaluate how [she] wants to live in the worlds open to [her]'.[107] As a pubescent female, as ur-woman, she is at the cusp of innocence and sexual desire. The fell prince, the fallopian tree, the egg-shell littered caves of lost babies, and the dark and bloody passages of the labyrinth presage the coming change. The mother who can tell her what it is all about is, in these stories, silent. The girl must hold secret the mysteries of the labyrinth under a taboo approaching that set on the Eleusinian Mysteries where disclosure is punished by death.[108]

flitting about the shafts, turning tiny windlasses, and pounding away like madmen, but really accomplishing nothing whatever. They have been known to throw stones at the miners, when enraged at being lightly spoken of; but the stones are harmless. Nevertheless, all miners of a proper spirit refrain from provoking them, because their presence brings good luck.' N. 87, above, 24.

[104] 'The self is the irreducible site of normativity and internormativity.' N. 17, above, 36.

[105] N. 17, above, 39. [106] N. 17, above, 46. [107] N. 17, above, 42.

[108] '[T]he true nature of the Mysteries remains shrouded in uncertainty because the participants did, with remarkable consistency, honor their pledge not to reveal what took place in the Telesterion, or inner sanctum of the Temple of Demeter. To violate that oath of secrecy was a capital offense. (Aeschylos, for example, once had to fear for his life on account of coming too close to revealing forbidden truths.)' N 37, above. Homer alludes to the 'awful mysteries which no one may in any way transgress or pry into or utter, for deep awe of the gods checks the voice'. N. 32, above, lines 459 *et seq.*

The labyrinth is a secret that conceals secrets. Its convoluted rules and incalculable geometries determine no outcome. Wisdom is immanent in the repetition of its folds and meaning is within its traveller. In offering a 'perspective of legal meaning' that 'moves through a circle of narrative construction by a dynamic, creative subject',[109] the labyrinth marks the path from childhood toward legal subjectivity. In its mutability, it mimics the changing convolutes and rapidly shifting neural pathways of the adolescent brain.[110] Tales of the labyrinth—of terror and error, test and trial, punctuated by flashing insight and revelations of unimaginable beauty and desire—capture the emotional and cognitive dimensions of adolescence. As the law recognizes in its schema of culpability and punishment, adolescence is itself a state of imperfect transformation.

Goblin fruit poisons the girl who eats it, rendering her desire fixed and immutable. In her state of enchantment, transformation is no longer possible. Persephone is chained to her ravisher while crops die, Rossetti's Laura is sickened with goblin infatuation and Sarah with the glamours of the goblin prince, and fatherless Ofelia, held to the faun's tasks, barely escapes the devouring totemic Father. Like goblin fruit, the 'girl power' embraced by popular culture fixates girls on 'individual subjectivity and desire'.[111] In its 'post-feminist' focus on sexual expression and free choice—the 'capillaries' and not the arteries of feminism—girl power erases the political dimensions of being female and ignores the ramifications of sexual objectification. This 'does not bode well for women, either as authoritative lawyers or as subjects of law', Margaret Thornton observes. Far from celebrating the girl power of popular culture, the labyrinth stories depict their protagonist's clever and courageous escape from the labyrinth's capillaries, those alluring blind alleys and closed caverns of delight that would render her desire insatiable and hold her forever underground.

The girl who braves the labyrinth is neither *infantia* nor *capax* but somewhere in between. Responding to her presence, the labyrinth maps her hidden changing self—her body, brain, and desire. At its centre is a baby, monstrous and unwanted, which is metamorphosed into the revelation of her own being, Wisdom. With the initiates of the Eleusinian Mysteries, she is 'brought face to face with marriage, death and birth' in 'a dark and private space',[112] that 'secret or private world of the female', of Demeter's 'mysteries of death, fertility, magic, and even anger'.[113] The girl's emergence from the labyrinth with a baby boy in her arms is a powerful image of the feminine.[114] It is also a double image of the Divine Child, one at the onset of

[109] N. 17, above, 45.

[110] D. Weinberger, B. Elvevåg, and J. Giedd, 'The Adolescent Brain: A Work in Progress' (June 2005) at <http://www.thenationalcampaign.org/resources/pdf/BRAIN.pdf> accessed 3 November 2010; R.E. Dahl, 'A Framework for Understanding Adolescent Brain Development' [n.d.] at <http://www.wccf.org/pdf/dahl.pdf> accessed 3 November 2010; L. Steinberg, 'Commentary: A behavioral scientist looks at the science of adolescent brain development' in 'Adolescent Brain Development: Current Themes and Future Directions' (2010) 72(1) *Brain and Cognition* 160–4 at <http://www.sciencedirect.com/science/issue/6723-2010-999279998-1578448> accessed 3 November 2010.

[111] M. Thornton, '"Post-Feminism" in the Legal Academy?' (2010) 95 *feminist review* 93 at 97.

[112] H.P. Foley, *The Homeric Hymn to Demeter: Translation, Commentary and Interpretive Essays* (Princeton, 1994), 139.

[113] Ibid., 140.

[114] Her reunion with the baby represents the [re]union with the mother, a joyous return that is at the core of the Eleusinian Mysteries. 'In this way did the two of them spend the whole day, having a like-minded thûmos [realm of consciousness, reason, and emotion], and they gladdened greatly each other's heart and thûmos, hugging each other, and their thûmos ceased having akhos [lamentation]. They

childhood and the other near its close. It signifies the beginning of the end of childhood and the end of the beginning of law. Soon, but not in these stories, the labyrinth that launched her transformation into an inventive, transgressive, and female subject of law will fold itself back into the submerged geography of her childhood. Legal subjectivity will descend.

received joy from each other, and gave it.' Nagy, n. 2, above, line 434 *et seq*. Now of one mind, Demeter and Persephone 'take on maternal responsibility to all mankind'. N. 111, above, 133.

3

Towards a Sociology of Children's Rights

Michael Freeman

The growth of sociological (as well as anthropological and historical) interest in children, of what has come to be called 'children's studies', has coincided broadly with the development of the modern children's rights movement.[1] Although those working within the discipline of sociology are clearly interested in children's rights and their goals are often similar to the motley assemblage of lawyers, philosophers, educationists etc, whose primary goal is to disseminate and propagate children's rights, and are not so interested in understanding the construct we call 'childhood', there has been little dialogue or collaboration between them. The gulf is apparent from an examination of the interests of *Childhood*, the leading journal on the sociology of childhood, and the *International Journal of Children's Rights*. Beginning at roughly the same time,[2] with some overlap of boards, the courses steered by the two have never threatened any collision.[3] It would be nice to think that the same people read both journals, but I think this is wishful thinking.

The two disciplines (though one, the sociology of childhood, is inevitably tighter) have much to offer each other, as, needless to say, they have to anyone concerned with understanding childhood (or rather childhoods) and improving the lives of children.

[1] Leading texts are C. Jenks (ed), *The Sociology of Childhood—Essential Readings* (London, Batsford, 1982); A. James and A. Prout (eds), *Constructing and Reconstructing Childhood* (Basingstoke, Falmer Press, 1990, 2nd ed., 2004); J. Qvortrup et al, *Childhood Matters* (Aldershot, Avebury, 1994); J. Brannen and M. O'Brien, *Children In Families: Research and Policy* (London, Falmer Press, 1996); C. Jenks, *Childhood* (London, Routledge, 1996); A. James, C. Jenks, and A. Prout, *Theorizing Childhood* (Cambridge, Polity Press, 1998); A. Prout, *The Future of Childhood* (London, Routledge, 2004). K. Wells, *Childhood In A Global Perspective* (Cambridge, Polity Press, 2009); H. Montgomery, *An Introduction To Childhood—Anthropological Perspectives on Children's Lives* (Chichester, Wiley-Blackwell, 2009). Two recent significant articles are A.L. James, 'Competition or Integration? The Next Step in Childhood Studies?' (2010) 17 *Childhood* 485–99 and L. Alanen, 'Critical Childhood Studies' (2011) 18 *Childhood* 147–50.

[2] *Childhood* was first published in 1994, a year after the *International Journal of Children's Rights* began publication.

[3] Articles in *Childhood* on children's rights include E. Burman, 'International Child Rights Legislation' (1996) 3 *Childhood* 45–66; M.G. Wyness, 'Policy, Protectivism and the Competent Child' (1996) 3 *Childhood* 431–47; J. Roche, 'Children: Rights, Participation and Citizenship' (1999) 6 *Childhood* 475–93; L. Alanen 'Taking Children's Rights Seriously' (2010) 17 *Childhood* 5–8. Another example of a sociologist engaging with children's rights is B. Mayall, 'The Sociology of Childhood in relation to Children's Rights' (2000) 8 *International Journal of Children's Rights* 243–59. Another is D. Reynaert et al, 'A Review of Children's Rights Literature Since the Adoption of the UNCRC' (2009) 16 *Childhood* 518–34 (there are 28 references to articles in the *International Journal of Children's Rights*). There is an article in *Childhood* also on the ethics of children's rights—a subject rarely addressed by children's rights scholars. See O. Nieuwenhuys, 'The Ethics of Children's Rights' (2008) 15 *Childhood* 4–11. See also the Special Issue of *Childhood* (vol. 13(3), 2006) 'Children's Rights in International Development'. There are also articles offering insights into children's rights in areas not often covered: one example is R. Burr, 'Global and Local Approaches to Children's Rights in Vietnam' (2002) 9 *Childhood* 49–62.

There is an overlap of interests, to some extent a congruence of visions, but aims and perspectives, even world views, diverge.

3.1 The sociology of childhood

Whilst conceding that there are differences of emphasis, even outlook, it is possible to categorize the starting points of the sociologist of childhood as follows.

First, to understand the social order better. This is a goal of the discipline of sociology generally. A study of adult-child relations will inevitably throw light on social organization.

Secondly, to appreciate the ways in which childhood has been used as a strategy to propound versions of social cohesion. I think here of the work of Talcott Parsons[4] and of Jean Piaget,[5] however marginalized their findings are now conceived to be.

Thirdly, to appreciate how (and why) the child has come to represent difference, and, therefore, how, what is constructed as childhood requires explanation, in a way that other forms of deviance do.

Fourthly, to demonstrate, with the support of historical work,[6] that childhood is not a natural phenomenon and cannot be understood as such. Rather it is a social construct, and the meaning of childhood is essentially contested. There are, however, signs that social constructionism is now being questioned.[7]

Fifthly, to grasp how childhood has come to be seen as a stage, rather than as a social practice, with children spoken of as in the process of 'becoming', and therefore in terms of inadequacy, inexperience, and maturity. They are to be 'measured' against an unexplained, unproblematic rational adult world, which is (so it is assumed) both complete and desirable, and, in contrast to childhood, is also static.

3.2 The children's rights movement

The children's rights movement has undergone transformations from child-saving (protecting children), as it was when it first emerged in the second half of the nineteenth century, to propagating the personhood, integrity, and autonomy of children (protecting their rights). The 'kiddie-libbing' movement of the 1970s, associated particularly with Richard Farson[8] and John Holt,[9] has been transcended by, what is now, a dominant model centring on participation in decision-making. Article 12 of

[4] *The Social System* (London, Routledge and Kegan Paul, 1951).

[5] *Psychology and Epistemology*. Tr. P. Wells (Harmondsworth, Penguin, 1972 (originally 1927)).

[6] P. Ariès, *Centuries of Childhood* (London, Jonathan Cape, 1962) (on which see A. Wilson, 'The Infancy of the History of Childhood: An Appraisal of Philippe Ariès' (1980) 19 *History and Theory* 132–54). See also L. Pollock, *Forgotten Children: Parent-Child Relations* 1500–1900 (Cambridge, Cambridge University Press, 1983). A further illustration is K. Hultqvist, 'Changing Rationales for Governing The Child' (1997) 4 *Childhood* 405–24. And see John Modell's argument that we can only understand development as history when we think simultaneously about how changing contexts affect what children appropriate from them, and how children's appropriations modify the contexts that guide development. 'How May Children's Development Be Seen Historically?' (2000) 7 *Childhood* 81–106.

[7] See 'Editorial: The Social Construction of Childhood—And Its Limits' (1998) 5 *Childhood* 131–2.

[8] *Birthrights* (Harmondsworth, Penguin, 1978).

[9] *Escape From Childhood* (Harmondsworth, Penguin, 1975).

the United Nations Convention on the Rights of the Child is a clear formulation of this philosophy in practice.

The primary concerns of the contemporary children's rights movement can be identified thus.

First, to question the relevance of difference, to challenge discrimination.

Secondly, to problematize the relationship between age, regarded at the least as a suspect category, and status.

Thirdly, to flesh out the case—the moral argument—for treating children's rights seriously and, in doing so, to stress the importance of respect for autonomy, dignity, decency, and concern.

Fourthly, to assemble information about the wrongs from which children suffer, whether at home, at school, at work, in the street, and within the context of adult institutions such as courts and penal institutions.

Fifthly, to explore the value and limitations of laws and conventions designed to improve the lives of children, accepting that rights without services are meaningless and that services without resources are impossible, and recognizing the real dangers of symbolic politics, so evident in a world which has signed up to the United Nations Convention whilst watching the lives of children decline.[10]

Sixthly, to advocate the recognition of children's rights as part of a cultural revolution, with an awareness of the role that rights can play in the reconstruction of a society, particularly when there are clear examples of attempts in countries such as South Africa,[11] Mozambique,[12] and in Latin America,[13] where NGOs have used the UN Convention as a moral framework for denouncing child poverty and abuse, and for mobilizing efforts to encode children's rights in legislation after the overthrow of authoritarian regimes.

3.3 Some common ground

From these descriptions, some strands, some links (sometimes clear, sometimes more tenuous) emerge. I would suggest that common ground can be found in the following.

First, both sociologists of childhood and proponents of rights for children accept that, where once children were to be studied as passive beings structured by the social context of the family or the school, now research should focus on children's agency, on the ways that children construct their autonomous social worlds. Hardman wrote in 1973 of the need for children to be studied as people 'in their own right, and not

[10] I emphasize this in my 'Afterword' to *The Moral Status of Children* (The Hague, Kluwer, 1997), 389. For example, 18 million children are in 2011 displaced by conflict and other emergencies. But there has been some progress: thus, today more than 80 per cent of children are immunized (25 years ago it was 10 per cent). In 1990 12.5 million children under five died, mostly from preventable diseases. It is now 8.1 million (12,000 a day less). See further UNICEF, *Child Matters* (Summer 2011). Only two countries have not ratified the UNCRC: Somalia and the USA.

[11] See J. Sloth-Nielsen, 'The Contribution of Children's Rights To The Construction of Society' (1996) 4 *International Journal of Children's Rights* 323–44.

[12] L.F. Sacramento and A.M. Pessoa, 'Implementation of The Rights of the Child in the Mozambique Context' in M. Freeman (ed), *Children's Rights: A Comparative Perspective* (Aldershot, Dartmouth, 1996), 145–64.

[13] See F.J. Pilotti, 'The Historical Development of the Child Welfare System in Latin America' (1999) 6 *Childhood* 408–22.

just as receptacles of adult teaching'.[14] This has been grasped by courts (the *Gillick* decision in England is a paradigmatic case) and by legislators, both national and international.

Secondly, there is recognition of both within the literature that children are persons, not property; subjects, not objects of social concern or control; participants in social processes, not social problems.

Thirdly, both are sensitive to the need to treat children as individuals rather than to categorize them as a collective and undifferentiated class. This means that gender,[15] race, sexual orientation, disability, and all cultural variables become significant.

In addition, both doubt whether—as is all too commonly assumed—adulthood is more important, and both deny that either difference or the well-entrenched belief in a golden age of childhood (what John Holt referred to as 'the walled garden of "Happy, Safe, Protected, Innocent" childhood'[16]) can explain why children were seen as rightless non-persons, or why rights for children were for so long thought of as unnecessary.

Both also accept that childhood has been constructed as, what Chris Jenks calls, a 'protectionist experience',[17] as a period when there is an absence of responsibility and in which there are 'rights to protection and training but not to autonomy'.[18]

There is also a general agreement that these ideas are particularly suspect where such notions are culturally irrelevant, for example, where young children have to work or where criminality by the young is treated no differently from that by adults, as graphically exemplified in England by the James Bulger case and its aftermath.[19]

3.4 What sociology can offer to children's rights

Each of the two disciplines has much to offer the other. In what follows I will emphasize the contribution that sociologists of childhood can make to the development of children's rights. I do not, however, ignore what children's rights thinking can offer towards the understanding of childhood. It is my belief that those who work within, and to propagate, children's rights can find much in sociological literature and research about children to assist them in their goal to improve children's lives, and it is to this I turn first.

First, it is more than a striking coincidence, perhaps even a paradox, that with the growing institutional recognition that children have rights has come the assertion that childhood is a disappearing phenomenon. Indeed, Neil Postman believes that it is because of this that there exists a movement to recast the legal rights of children so that they are, as he sees it, more or less the same as adults. And he cites in evidence Richard Farson's *Birthrights*. For Postman, the evidence for the disappearance of childhood comes from several sources.

[14] 'Can There Be An Anthropology of Children?' (1973) 4 *Journal of the Anthropological Society of Oxford* 85–99 (also in (2001) 8 *Childhood* 501–17).

[15] But see B. Thorne, *Gender Play: Girls and Boys in School* (New Brunswick, NJ, Rutgers University Press, 1993).

[16] *Op cit*, note 9.

[17] *Childhood, op cit*, note 1.

[18] *Per* J. Ennew, *The Sexual Exploitation of Children* (Cambridge, Polity Press, 1986), 21.

[19] Accounts of which are S. Asquith, 'When Children Kill Children' (1996) 3 *Childhood* 99–116; M. Freeman *op cit*, note 10, ch. 12; M. King, *A Better World For Children* (London, Routledge, 1997), ch. 5; and B. Morrison, *As If* (London, Granta Books, 1997).

The evidence displayed by the media themselves, for they not only promote the unseating of childhood through their form and context but reflect its decline in their content. There is evidence to be seen in the merging of the taste and style of children and adults, as well as in the changing perspectives of relevant social institutions, such as the law, schools and sports. And there is evidence of the 'hard' variety—figures about alcoholism, drug use, sexual activity, crime etc, that imply a fading distinction between childhood and adulthood.[20]

It would be wrong to pretend that these trends do not exist, whether in the form of 12-year-old waif-like models exploited by the advertising industry, or in the horrific examples of murders of young children by young children, of which the Bulger case is only the most notorious.

But the Postman thesis nevertheless lacks credence. Childhood was no more created by the printing press than it will be 'disappeared' by the spread and intrusion of electronic media. What we should take from Postman is not his prognosis, but his implication that childhood is a social construction—though this is demonstrated more obviously by others—and the consequences which follow from this. And it certainly does not lead to a denial that children have rights; indeed, quite the contrary.

It does, however, lead to the further recognition that childhood cannot be understood outside the context of other variables, such as class, gender, ethnicity, race, and culture. If childhood is a social construction, then there are 'childhoods' rather than a single, universal, cross-cultural phenomenon. The United Nations Convention on the Rights of the Child adopts, by contrast, a universalist approach to children and to their rights. The sociology of childhood suggests this is wrong. Of course, it does not prescribe an answer—this would exceed its remit. But is the answer to be found in cultural relativism—unquestionably the orthodox view until recently—or in cultural pluralism?[21] The Convention, it is true, says that 'due account' should be taken of the 'importance of the traditions and cultural values of each people for the protection and harmonious development of the child'.[22] These traditions and cultural values are not problematized. There is clear recognition that the child's welfare (which, in the Convention, is a 'primary' consideration[23]) may well be 'trumped' in certain situations (but which?) by 'cultural values and traditions'. And States Parties are required (by Article 24(3)) to 'take effective and appropriate measures with a view to abolishing traditional practices prejudicial to the health of children', but this is in itself qualified by Article 24(4), which provides that states undertake to promote and encourage international co-operation with a view to achieving progressively the full realization of the rights in Article 24.[24]

A second insight which those concerned with children's rights may gain from studies in the sociology of childhood is an understanding of the child as social actor. Sociology enables us to see some of the ways in which the child constructs his/her social world. The world of children's rights has failed to grapple with this perspective. Thus, the United Nations Convention was drawn up by adults—many very committed to a better world for children, but it was a better world as they conceived it. Most commentators on the Convention believe that Article 12 is its linchpin. This, as

[20] *The Disappearance of Childhood* (New York, Vintage Books, 1994, originally published in 1982), 120. And see S. Stephens (ed), *Children And The Politics of Culture* (Princeton, Princeton University Press, 1995) who refers to 'discourses of lost, stolen and disappearing childhoods' and the imaging of 'the domain of childhood as threatened, invaded and "polluted" by adult worlds' (at 9).

[21] See M. Freeman, *op cit*, note 10, ch. 7.

[22] In the Preamble.

[23] See Article 3(1).

[24] See in relation to these issues, G. Douglas and L. Sebba, *Children's Rights and Traditional Values* (Aldershot, Ashgate, 1998).

is well-known, requires States Parties to 'assure to the child who is capable of forming his/her own views the right to express those views freely, on all matters affecting the child, the views of the child being given due consideration in accordance with the age and maturity of the child'. Yet, on the major 'matter' of the contents of the Convention itself, there is no evidence that children or children's groups as such participated or were consulted on drafting, or had any real influence in preliminary discussions. The Convention thus encodes a set of rights and takes an image of childhood from the perspective of the adult world looking in almost as an external observer on the world(s) of children.

The Convention, had it used insights derived from the social world of children, might have made significant additions and amendments. Article 9, for example, gives the child the right not to be separated from parents against their will: the child is given an opportunity to participate in separation proceedings and make views known. But there is no right to representation. A second example is Article 24, which recognizes the right of the child to enjoy the highest attainable standard of health, to have facilities for the treatment of illness and rehabilitation of health, but not as such the right to food,[25] although malnutrition is to be combated. Thirdly, and surprisingly in a Convention on the Rights of the Child, there is no reference to the issue of the consent of the child, relevant in a range of circumstances but particularly with reference to medical treatment. The Convention is thus silent on one of the most controversial issues in relation to children in recent years in England, the question of whether a child—in the reported cases always an adolescent—can refuse consent to medical treatment.[26] It is doubtful whether English judges understood, for example, the inner world of an anorexic and, had they been able to do so, whether they would have come to the conclusion they did in *Re W*[27] in 1992. Fourthly, though a strong case can be made for saying that the Convention makes corporal punishment, even in the context of the home, a practice States Parties should eliminate, Article 19 does not say so directly.[28] With greater understanding of, and greater input from, children, the Convention might well have contained a more explicit prohibition on corporal punishment.

Children should not be 'just passive subjects of social structural determinations', James and Prout, two leading sociologists of childhood, remind us.[29] It has thus become common to parrot the aphorism in the Butler-Sloss report into sexual abuse in Cleveland in North East England that children are social actors, subjects in their own right, not merely objects of social concern or the targets of social intervention.[30] But the implications of this, even after Article 12, have not been properly thought through. The dissonance between children's own experiences of being a child and the institutional form which childhood takes is paralleled by a mismatch between the different understandings of childhood which have been emerging in the writings of sociologists, anthropologists, and historians, and what so often finds its way into laws, institutions, policies, and practices in relation to children.

[25] On which see the Special Issue of the *International Journal of Children's Rights* (vol. 5, no. 4).

[26] See, in particular, the cases of *Re R* [1992] Fam 11 and *Re W* [1993] Fam 64. A more recent case is *Re L* [1998] 2 FLR 810.

[27] See note 26.

[28] And see the important decision of the European Court of Human Rights in *A* v *United Kingdom* [1998] 2 FLR 959. But this has not led to the UK outlawing the smacking of children: Children Act 2004 s. 58.

[29] In *op cit*, note 1, at 4.

[30] See *Report of Inquiry into Child Abuse In Cleveland* (London, HMSO, 1988, Cm. 412).

The sociology of childhood also has much to offer those who fight for children's rights when they grapple, as they must, with such problems as dependency and capacity. The United Nations Convention has done little to reduce the equation that being dependent, as to a greater or lesser extent all children must be, means being deprived of basic rights. Dependency implies a sufficient justification to suspend basic rights to privacy, respect, and individual choice. Being dependent implies being legitimately subject to the often arbitrary and invasive authority of social service providers and other public and private administrators, in the education system for example, who enforce rules with which the dependant must comply, and otherwise exercise power over the conditions of their lives. In meeting the needs of the dependant, often with the aid of social scientific disciplines, welfare agencies also construct those needs themselves. Medical and social service professionals know what is good for those they serve, and those who are dependent do not have the right to claim to know what is good for them. The lessons here go wider than debates about children's rights, but, without question, cast meaningful light on them.

Dependency should not be a reason to be deprived of choice and respect. An important contribution of feminist moral theory has been to question the firmly embedded assumption that moral agency and citizenship rights require as a precondition that a person be independent, totally autonomous. Feminists (Carol Gilligan[31] and Marilyn Friedman[32] being two notable examples) have questioned this deeply-held assumption. It is, they argue, derived from a specifically male experience of social relations, which values competition and voluntary achievement. It is inappropriately individualistic. Dependency is a basic human condition. The United Nations Convention, using largely an autonomous model, would as much as possible give children the opportunity to be independent. But it is also possible, as is argued within feminism,[33] to accord respect and participation rights in decision-making to those who are dependent.

Priscilla Alderson's *Children's Consent To Surgery*[34] is a model of what can be done. She shows how comparatively young, and certainly dependent, children who most children's rights activists would not regard as competent (certainly in the so-called *Gillick* sense which English law has embodied since the mid-1980s) have understanding and abilities well beyond what those who construct a correct childhood believe to be the case. Her work is also significant for bringing out the importance of a child's experiential knowledge—too many who are prepared to link children's rights to knowledge and understanding see this in terms of a bookwork knowledge which is, of course, though they rarely see this, not present in the lives of many adults whose competence is taken for granted.

Questions of competence (or capacity) are also ones upon which sociologists of childhood may have significant contributions to make. When women or people of colour have been denied rights because they have been defined as incompetent, they

[31] *In A Different Voice: Psychological Theory and Women's Development* (Cambridge, Mass., Harvard University Press, 1982). On the ethics of care and children's rights see T. Cockburn, 'Children and the Feminist Ethics of Care' (2005) 12 *Childhood* 71–89.

[32] 'Care and Context in Moral Reasoning' in C. Harding (ed), *Moral Dilemmas: Philosophical Issues In The Development of Moral Reasoning*' (Chicago, 1985).

[33] For example, V. Held, 'A Non Contractual Society' in M. Hanen and K. Nielsen (eds), *Science, Morality and Feminist Theory* (Calgary, University of Calgary Press, 1987).

[34] Buckingham, Open University Press, 1993. And see her *Young Children's Rights* (London, Jessica Kingsley, 2nd ed., 2009) and with Joanna Hawthorne and Margaret Killen, 'The Participation Rights of Premature Babies' (2005) 13 *International Journal of Children's Rights* 31–50.

have been able to redefine themselves as competent beings. This is a hurdle which is much more difficult for children to surmount. Again feminism seemed to offer a way out. This de-emphasizes the significance of competency in rights talk by focusing on individual relationships between children and adults. The writings of Martha Minow are often invoked.[35] But the promise may be more apparent than real: the emphasis on relationships, as Kate Federle has shown, 'presupposes a connection between adults and children that merely underscores children's dependencies rather than rendering them irrelevant'.[36] When our rights talk speaks of children's rights in relationships, it forecloses an honest assessment of the power we have over our children.

Thus, tying rights to relationships is nothing more than a 'sophisticated' version of the argument that children should not have rights because of their incompetencies. The problem may be that we have been seeking to see rights as a quasi-proprietary form. Rather than thinking of rights of 'having', should we rather think of rights of 'being'?[37] Are there rights which children should have simply by virtue of being children? And, can sociologists of childhood advance our understanding of this? Rights of 'being' need not, as most argue rights of 'having' must, be tied to competence or capacity. Rights of 'being' are much more concerned with dignity and decency,[38] two much-neglected concepts, towards understanding of which sociologists (as well as philosophers) can usefully and constructively contribute.

Sociology more generally can offer all sorts of insight to those concerned to improve the status of children using a rights agenda. There are lessons on the limits of participation: gaining access to decision-making bodies does not remove entrenched processes of domination (children do not get power by sitting on school boards or being invited to school conferences at which their future is determined). Sociology in general terms (and the sociology of childhood more particularly) can also throw light on the wrongs from which children suffer and may help us to understand why these wrongs are perpetrated against children. Thus, an understanding of child abuse is enhanced by, what is often called, the 'cultural explanation'.[39] The sociology of childhood may help to explain why children have for so long been seen as property, rather than as persons. Such depersonalization may indeed be a major factor in explaining abuse, including sexual abuse, where children are used as a means to another's sexual ends.

3.5 And in return

The children's rights movement also has important things to say to sociologists of childhood about ways in which we can enhance our understanding of the lives of children. The UN Convention itself offers a touchstone for research: the country reports, which have to be submitted to the Committee on the Rights of the Child, offer invaluable new data and thus opportunities for research.

The language of rights can make visible what has too long been suppressed. It can lead to new stories being heard in public. As Carrie Menkel-Meadow has put it:

[35] 'Rights For The Next Generation: A Feminist Approach To Children's Rights' (1986) 9 *Harvard Women's Journal* 1.

[36] 'Rights Flow Downhill' (1994) 2 *International Journal of Children's Rights* 343–68, at 356.

[37] I draw here on the writings of Luce Irigaray, in particular *Thinking The Difference* (tr. K. Montin) (London, Athlone, 1994).

[38] See A. Margalit, *The Decent Society* (Cambridge, Mass., Harvard University Press, 1996).

[39] See M.D.A. Freeman, *The Rights and Wrongs of Children* (London, Frances Pinter, 1983), ch. 4.

Each time we let in an excluded group, each time we listen to a new way of knowing, we learn more about the limits of our current way of seeing.[40]

The children's rights movement gives children new opportunities to speak, to correct what is partial (in both senses), to throw light on children's lives, the wrongs from which they suffer, on how they perceive the world and the institutions which define and structure their existence.

If we give children the opportunity to challenge, to air their grievances, to articulate the wrongs they perceive themselves as suffering and the losses they feel, they can tell us about the world, as they understand it. Our understanding of children as agents will increase the more we give them a voice. The new third protocol to the UN Convention offers promise here.

It is largely because of children's rights advocacy that there has been legislative change: in England the Children Act 1989 is usually cited, though in Britain the Children (Scotland) Act 1995 is actually a better example which advances the cause of children as active agents in the social process. The 'child' is envisioned in a new light. As James, Jenks, and Prout acknowledge: 'No longer marginal, "the child" is positioned as a social and political actor, a person with opinions, a decision-maker.'[41] Sociologists of childhood are thus offered new material to investigate. If the new legislation empowers, if it redefines the traditional ideological placement of children, what is its effect? And will all the effects be positive? Or will there be negative (if unintended) consequences?

3.6 Conclusion

Those who espouse children's rights have a vision of a better world for children and through this a better world for all. This requires us to gain a better understanding of the lives of children, of what is important to them and how they perceive and construct their social worlds. And nothing can be overlooked. We need to know how they perceive their play,[42] their education,[43] their labour,[44] their friendships;[45] how

[40] 'Excluded Voices: New Voices In The Legal Profession Making New Voices In The Law' (1987) 42 *University of Miami Law Review* 52.

[41] *Op cit*, note 1, 69.

[42] See generally A. James, C. Jenks, and A. Prout, *op cit*, note 1, ch. 5. See also A. Strandell, 'Doing Reality With Play' (1997) 4 *Childhood* 445–64; A.C. Evaldsson and W.A. Corsaro, 'Play and Games In The Peer Cultures of Preschool and Preadolescent Children' (1998) 5 *Childhood* 377–402; and M. Oke et al, 'A Profile of Child's play in Urban India' (1999) 6 *Childhood* 207–20. On citizenship and play see E. Elbés, 'Citizenship in the Making' (1996) 4 *Childhood* 499–514. On the right to play see E.L. Dawson, 'Children And The Right To Play: Lessons From Peru' (1993) 1 *International Journal of Children's Rights* 33–48.

[43] A Pollard and A. Filer, *The Social World of Children's Learning* (London, Cassell, 1996). See also C. Motandon and F. Oslek, 'Children's Perspectives on Their Education' (1998) 5 *Childhood* 247–64. School uniforms raise many issues too: see A. Bodine, 'School Uniforms and Discourses on Childhood' (2003) 10 *Childhood* 43–63; M. Vanderbroek and M. Bouverne-De-Bie, 'Children's Agency and Educational Norms: A Tensed Negotiation' (2006) 13 *Childhood* 127–43.

[44] See A. James, C. Jenks, and A. Prout, *op cit*, note 1, ch. 6 and Special Issue of *Childhood* (vol. 6(1), 1999). On street children see Special Issue of *Childhood* (vol. 3, no. 2, 1996). On sex work see B. Rubenson et al, 'Young sex workers: Ho Chi Minh City Telling Their Life Stories' (2005) 12 *Childhood* 391–411.

[45] See A. James, 'Learning To Be Friends' (1996) 5 *Childhood* 313–30.

they acquire their national consciousness[46] and their concepts of citizenship,[47] their knowledge about medicines[48] and drugs,[49] and their perceptions of risk.[50] What they think of fashion[51] and of justice,[52] of domestic violence[53] and corporal punishment.[54] How they define and create kinship.[55] What they think about religion and ethnic identities.[56] How they experience racism and nationalism[57] and diaspora living.[58] A theme—almost a *leitmotif* of childhood studies—is that childhood is socially constructed. But an important editorial in *Childhood* was entitled 'The Social Construction of Childhood—and Its Limits'.[59] Those who believe in children's rights and in international normative standards such as the United Nations Convention on the Rights of the Child will appreciate this questioning. As the editorial notes: 'Given our proliferating insights into the very different sorts of childhood worlds, how can we conceptualise universal conditions of children's welfare that would constitute legitimate formulations for international children's rights and activism?' This is a challenge to which those concerned to advance children's rights must rise. They cannot ignore the dimensions of class, gender, or disability—subjects which articles in the issue of *Childhood* addressed in the editorial focus upon—but nor can they take refuge in a relativism that will ultimately only fudge moral questions. The challenge can be met and finding ways of meeting it must be a major target. To that end, a dialogue between scholarships—not a confrontation between them—is called for.[60]

[46] See D. Koester, 'Childhood In National Consciousness and National Consciousness in Childhood' (1997) 4 *Childhood* 125–42.

[47] See H. Hengst, 'Negotiating "Us" and "Them": Children's Constructions of Collective Identity' (1997) 4 *Childhood* 43–62. But *cf* T. Cockburn, 'Children and Citizenship in Britain (1998) 5 *Childhood* 99–117.

[48] See A.B. Almarsdóttir and C. Zimmer, 'Children's Knowledge About Medicines' (1998) 5 *Childhood* 265–82.

[49] See S.E. Clausen, 'Parenting Styles and Adolescent Drug Use Behaviour' (1996) 3 *Childhood* 403–14.

[50] P. Kelley, B. Mayall, and S. Hood, 'Children's Accounts of Risk' (1997) 4 *Childhood* 305–24. In relation to divorce see K. Moxnes, 'Risk Factors in Divorce: Perception By The Children Involved' (2003) 10 *Childhood* 131–46. See also K. Backett-Milburn and J. Harden, 'How Children and Their Families Negotiate Risk, Safety and Danger' (2004) 11 *Childhood* 429–48.

[51] See A. König, 'Which Clothes Suit Me? The Presentation of the Juvenile Self' (2008) 15 *Childhood* 225–37; M. Rysst, 'I am only 10 Years Old: Femininities, Clothing-Fashion Codes and the Intergenerational Gap of Interpretation of Young Girls' Clothes' (2010) 17 *Childhood* 76–93; C. Pole, 'Researching Children and Fashion: An Embodied Ethnography' (2007) 14 *Childhood* 67–84; J. Pilcher, 'No Logo? Children's Consumption of Fashion' (2011) 18 *Childhood* 128–41. See also Special Issue of *Childhood* (vol. 12(2), 2005) *Children In and of Commercial Culture*.

[52] R. Bosisio, '"Right" and "Not Right": Representations of Justice In Young People' (2008) 15 *Childhood* 276–94, and also R. Bosisio, this volume, 190.

[53] See C. Överlien and M. Hyden, 'Children's Actions When Experiencing Domestic Violence' (2009) 16 *Childhood* 479–96. And on violence more generally see J. Parkes, 'The Multiple Meanings of Violence: Children's Talk About Life in a South African Neighbourhood' (2009) 14 *Childhood* 401–14.

[54] J-P. Payet and V. Franchi, 'The Rights of the Child and the "Good of the Learners"' (2008) 15 *Childhood* 158–76.

[55] See J. Mason and B. Tipper, 'Being Related: How Children Define and Create Kinship' (2008) 15 *Childhood* 441–60.

[56] F. Moinian, '"I'm just me": Children Talking Beyond Ethnic and Religious Identities' (2009) 16 *Childhood* 31–48.

[57] See J. Habashi, 'Palestine Children Crafting National Identity' (2008) 15 *Childhood* 12–29.

[58] See M. Bak and K. von Brömssen, 'Interrogating Childhood and Diaspora Through The Voices of Children in Sweden' (2010) 17 *Childhood* 113–28; K. Mand, 'I've Got Two Homes: One in Bangladesh and One in London' (2010) 17 *Childhood* 273–87; O. den Besten, 'Local Belonging and "Geographies of Emotions"' (2010) 17 *Childhood* 181–96.

[59] *Op cit*, note 7.

[60] For a rather different article on the sociology of childhood and children's rights see B. Mayall, 'The Sociology of Childhood in Relation To Children's Rights (2000) 8 *International Journal of Children's Rights* 243–59.

4

Why Judges Need to Know and Understand Childhood Studies

Mark Henaghan[1]

4.1 Introduction

Children understand their own world better than anyone else. Each child is unique and sees their own world in their own particular way. Lev Vygotsky, an early contributor to socio-cultural theory, suggested that child development was based on social processes and argued that adults provided the 'scaffolding' for children to build their own worlds.[1A] Vygotsky's theory runs counter to the previously popular Piaget model of how children develop. Jean Piaget's model set out predetermined chronological stages through which each child would pass on their way to becoming an adult.[2] There was little room for the individuality of children; they were all on the conveyor belt of development. This paper is based on the Vygotsky model, where the emphasis is on acting with children to help them understand their world better, and not on them assuming characteristics typical of a particular stage of development.

Leading writers in Childhood Studies, Allison James and Alan Prout make it clear that we should rethink how children are seen in our society.[3] Each child develops according to the particular environment they are in, and according to the influences in that environment. Children are the product of their community and how their individual needs and competencies are met. The more diverse experiences a child has, the richer their development is likely to be. Jim Flynn's work on intelligence supports the theory of Childhood Studies.[4] Flynn has shown categorically through his work

[1] Professor and Dean of the Faculty of Law, University of Otago, Dunedin, New Zealand. The author thanks Antoinette Robinson LLB (Hons) Graduate, Faculty of Law, University of Otago, for her research and in-depth analysis for this chapter and Ruth Ballantyne, Dean's Research Assistant, Faculty of Law, University of Otago, for her invaluable editorial and research assistance.

[1A] For more detailed information about Vygotsky and socio-cultural theory see N. Taylor, 'What Do We Know About Involving Children and Young People in Family Law Decision Making? A Research Update' (2006) 20 *Australian Journal of Family Law* 154 at 154–78; S. Coyle, 'Sociology of Childhood: Implications for Our Practice as Lawyers' (2007) 5 *New Zealand Family Law Journal* 256 at 256–62.

[2] For more detailed information about Piaget see L. Berk, *Child Development* (Boston, 2006).

[3] See generally A. Prout, *Future of Childhood: Towards the Interdisciplinary Study of Children* (London, 2005); A. James, 'Understanding Childhood from an Interdisciplinary Perspective' in P. Pufall and R. Unsworth (eds), *Rethinking Childhood* (New Brunswick, 2004). See also H. Hendrick, 'Constructions and Reconstructions of British Childhood: An Interpretive Study, 1800 to the Present' in A. James and A. Prout (eds), *Constructing and Reconstructing Childhood* (Basingstoke, 1990); C. Jenks, 'Constructing Childhood Sociologically' in M. Kehily (ed), *An Introduction to Childhood Studies* (New York, 2004).

[4] See generally J.R. Flynn, *What is Intelligence?* (Cambridge, 2007).

that our IQ is not something preset or predetermined, but that it develops according to the environmental experiences that we have.[5] For example, as Flynn states:

> A gene-caused performance advantage causes a more-homework-done environment, the latter magnifies the academic performance advantage, which upgrades the environment further by entry into a top stream, which magnifies the performance advantage once again, which gets access to a good university environment.[6]

Childhood Studies requires us to see children from their point of view, based on what is happening in their world, rather than from an external standpoint that assumes how they are likely to see the world at particular ages and stages of development. Most crucially, it treats each child as a unique individual who deserves to be respected and can only be understood by seeing the world through their eyes. The prime justification for giving children rights is respect for their individual dignity and person.[7] The dignity of the child is respected by listening to their views when making decisions about them. Parkinson and Cashmore have shown that most children want to express their views about the important matters in their lives.[8] Decisions that take account of what is happening from the child's point of view are more likely to lead to better arrangements about the child's care. As Baroness Hale says, when a child is given the opportunity to be heard, 'the court will then see the child as a real person, rather than as the object of other people's disputes or concerns'.[9]

4.2 Incorporating Childhood Studies theory into law

Up until 2004, New Zealand used a developmental approach to children's perspectives when making decisions about them. Section 23(2) of the Guardianship Act 1968 required the court to obtain the child's wishes if the child was able to express them and weight was to be given to those wishes, 'having regard to the age and maturity of the child'. What this meant in practice was that young children, particularly those under the age of ten, could have their wishes ignored purely on the basis that they were not of sufficient age and maturity to be able to express 'rational choices' about their lives. On 1 July 2005 the Care of Children Act 2004 came into force. Section 6 of the Care of Children Act 2004 states that a child must be given reasonable opportunities to express *views* on matters affecting the child. *Any views* the child expresses either directly or through a representative *must be taken into account.*[10] Section 7 of the Care of Children Act 2004 provides for the appointment of a lawyer to act for the child. The lawyer must meet with the child, except in exceptional circumstances.[11] The effect of any parenting order must be explained to the child in a way that the child understands,[12] and the child has a right of appeal.[13]

The Care of Children Act 2004 provisions recognize that each child, no matter what their age or so-called maturity, must be given reasonable opportunities to

[5] Ibid. [6] Ibid at 39.

[7] M. Freeman, *The Rights and Wrongs of Children* (London, 1983); J. Fortin, *Children's Rights and the Developing Law* (Cambridge, 2002).

[8] P. Parkinson and J. Cashmore, *The Voice of a Child in Family Law Disputes* (Oxford, 2008).

[9] Baroness Hale, 'Children's Participation in Family Law Decisions Making: Lessons from Abroad' (2006) 20 *Australian Journal of Family Law* 119 at 124.

[10] Care of Children Act 2004, s 6(2)(b). [11] Care of Children Act 2004, s 7(3).

[12] Care of Children Act 2004, s 55(4). [13] Care of Children Act 2004, s 143(3).

express their views. Views are a much wider concept than wishes.[14] Wishes imply that the child has to give a statement about the particular outcome of the case, whereas views may be about anything that is important to the particular child. The court is required to take any expressed views into account. That does not mean the court must make the child's views determinative, but it does require the court to take them into account, no matter how old the child is. The Care of Children Act 2004 is a clear example of Childhood Studies in action. It assumes that each child will have views, no matter what their age, and that those views are important to the child. Thus the court must take the child's views seriously, even if they are not determinative in the particular case.

4.2.1 A judge appears to understand

The first case to come before New Zealand's higher courts after the Care of Children Act 2004 came into force was *C v S*.[15] This case involved a young girl who was four years and three months old at the time of the Family Court hearing. There had been violence and substance abuse in the parents' relationship,[16] thus the young girl had been in the care of the father's niece since birth.[17] The father, who had been convicted for a series of excess breath alcohol offences,[18] wanted the child back in his care.[19] In the Family Court, the child was not given an opportunity to express her views because the Family Court and the lawyer for the child believed she was too young to do so.[20] The lawyer for the father appealed the case to the High Court. The primary focus of the appeal was that the Family Court had not ascertained the child's views, nor taken account of them.[21] Randerson J in the High Court analyses section 6 of the Care of Children Act 2004, which states that it is mandatory to provide a child with reasonable opportunities to 'express views on matters affecting him or her'.[22] Randerson J accepts that views can be expressed in non-verbal ways, and that views are wider than wishes.[23] He explains that:

> [V]iews may cover a wider range of matters such as an assessment of the advantages and disadvantages of being in the care of one party or another; what the child enjoys or does not enjoy about his or her relationship with the adults in question; what matters are important to the child and what are not.[24]

Randerson J accepts that the court's requirement to 'take into account' the views of the child is stronger than the previous legislation that used the words 'have regard to'.[25] So far, so good; however, old habits die hard.

4.2.2 Old habits die hard

Randerson J did not believe that the omission of the words 'age' and 'maturity' in section 6 of the Care of Children Act 2004 meant that a court should not have regard to these factors. Sadly, most judges lack education about Childhood Studies theory and therefore totally miss the significance of the words' omission from the legislation.

[14] See M. Henaghan, 'The Impact of the Care of Children Act 2004 on Family Law Practice', Paper presented at the New Zealand Law Society Family Law Conference (Wellington, 2005); *C v S* [2006] 3 NZLR 420 at [31].
[15] *C v S* [2006] 3 NZLR 420. [16] Ibid at [8]. [17] Ibid at [1]. [18] Ibid at [11].
[19] Ibid at [2]. [20] Ibid at [21]. [21] Ibid at [5]. [22] Ibid at [31]. [23] Ibid.
[24] Ibid. [25] Ibid.

Even on a simple statutory interpretation analysis, removing words from a statute is a clear indication of intent by Parliament that the words are no longer relevant. Ultimately, the court concluded that the failure to hear the child's views was not material because 'it would not have affected the outcome'. Randerson J held that shared day-to-day care with the father had not worked because of his alcohol consumption and, therefore, whatever the child had to say would have made no difference to the overall result. However, this undermines the point made earlier by Randerson J that views are much wider than wishes and this little girl may well have had views about her relationship with her father that should have been taken into account in making sure the arrangements worked in the best possible way for the child.

The father in *C v S*[26] applied to the New Zealand Court of Appeal for leave to appeal the High Court's decision.[27] The Court of Appeal refused leave and held that the purpose of section 6 of the Care of Children Act 2004 was about 'outcomes not just processes'.[28] The court said that section 6 'must be applied in a sensible way'[29] and stated that there is not much point ascertaining the views of a child who is not 'expected to have and express views which would be material to the issue'.[30] The Court of Appeal has also missed the point. The purpose of section 6 is to give a child the right to have input into the decision-making process by raising matters that are important to them. The court cannot expect a child to second-guess what may or may not be material to the decision. Such expectations do not provide scaffolding for a child from which to build their own world. Rather, it requires the child to understand the adult decision-making process and make their submissions accordingly. Such an attitude results in the court missing out on a rich understanding of what is going on in a particular child's life. Once the court hears the child's views, then it may well see materiality in a totally different way. However, for the court to close its mind to the child's views in advance is to silence the child and to turn the law back as though section 6 of the Care of Children Act 2004 was never enacted.

The trend set by the Court of Appeal has been picked up by other High Court judges and was reinforced in *DLB v DLS*.[31] In this case, a young girl aged four years and five months old, who had been interviewed by psychologists in the past, was not given the opportunity to express her views for the Family Court hearing. On appeal, the High Court judge held that it was unrealistic to expect relevant information from a 'little girl of her age'.[32]

4.3 Analysis of 120 Family Court cases 2005–2010

4.3.1 Methods of obtaining children's views in different types of cases

The only way to understand fully the implications of section 6 of the Care of Children Act 2004, and how it is being used in the courts, is to carry out an extensive analysis of cases decided in the Family Court. The Family Court is a specialist court created by statute, where judges are chosen based on their experience, knowledge, personality, and ability to make decisions about families in an appropriate manner.[33]

[26] *C v S* [2006] 3 NZLR 420. [27] *C v S* CA115/06. [28] Ibid at [6]. [29] Ibid at [9].
[30] Ibid. [31] *DLB v DLS* [2007] NZFLR 263. [32] Ibid at [51].
[33] Family Courts Act 1960, s 5.

Four specific case categories were selected in order to see if there are differences in how children are treated based on the primary context in which the case comes to court. Fifteen of the cases involved what is called alienation: where one parent is working strongly to cut the other parent out of the child's life. Forty-seven of the cases involved relocation as the primary issue: where one parent wants to move away to another part of New Zealand or overseas. Thirty of the cases involved issues of violence, and 28 were general issues relating to how much time a child should spend with each particular parent (day-to-day care and contact).

In 119 of the total 120 case sample (99 per cent), a lawyer for the child was appointed.[34] It has become common practice in the New Zealand Family Courts for the lawyer for the child to give a written report to the court about the child's views.[35] In 64 of the total 120 case sample (53 per cent), a specialist psychologist was appointed by the court to interview the children involved.[36] In 39 of the total 120 case sample (33 per cent), a judicial interview took place; and in one case of the total 120 case sample (0.83 per cent), a child was permitted to give evidence directly to the judge in the courtroom.[37] The latter case was unusual and involved a 14-year-old child who strongly wanted to tell the judge their views.

The type of case does have an influence on which methods are used. Alienation cases, where there is a great degree of animosity between the parents, led to psychologists being appointed to ascertain children's views in 13 of the 15 alienation cases (87 per cent). By comparison, psychologists are used in only 26 of the 47 relocation cases (55 per cent), 13 of the 30 violence cases (43 per cent), and 12 of the 28 care and contact cases (43 per cent).

Children's views in alienation cases create difficulties for judges. The child has normally internalized negative views of the so-called alienated parent. A choice has to be made as to whether these views should be given weight, or whether they should be put to one side and the child placed with the alienated parent. For example in *SAM v DLR*[38] the judge said, 'It is clear that R has been coached and his views reflect a home environment that is openly hostile to his paternal family'.[39] A change in primary care was ordered.

Where views are expressed strongly, they can influence the court's decision as to whether or not to change a child's primary care. This was the case in *JR v RCT*[40] where the judge held that:

> [The option of being moved into the care of their alienated mother] is quite contrary to the boys' wishes, and, because of the degree of their polarisation and the depth of their emotions, would almost certainly provoke an extreme reaction in them [. . .] It is quite obvious from the discussion that, harmful as it may be, retaining the status quo is less dangerous to the boys' welfare than any alternative.[41]

[34] Care of Children Act 2004, s 7(2) states that the court must appoint a lawyer to act for a child if the proceedings involve day-to-day care or contact and the case appears likely to proceed to a hearing, unless the court is satisfied that the appointment would serve no useful purpose.

[35] This raises issues of natural justice because it is not possible for the parties to cross-examine the lawyer for the child in court, although the lawyer for the child does present submissions in the case and cross-examine witnesses. For an explanation of how a child's welfare can trump natural justice in some situations see generally J. Caldwell, 'Family Proceedings Concerning Children: The Nature of Natural Justice' (2010) 12 *Otago Law Review* 345.

[36] Care of Children Act 2004, s 33.

[37] *JTP v BTT* FC Invercargill FAM-2008-082-000004, 28 January 2010.

[38] *SAM v DLR* FC Rotorua FAM-2004-073-000025, 17 March 2009.

[39] Ibid at [36].

[40] *JR v RCT* FC Christchurch FAM-2002-009-001773, 22 December 2006.

[41] Ibid at [37] and [41].

In one case[42] the views of the child (a 14-year-old girl) were expressed so strongly that the judge would not interfere with them. The child wanted to have no contact with her mother. The judge concluded:

It is not realistic for Elaine to live with her mother. She wishes, in the strongest terms, to live with her father and have no contact with her mother. This is one of those exceptional cases where I have decided not to interfere with Elaine's wishes even though I am utterly convinced that what Elaine wants is not in her best interests.[43]

It is evident that in difficult cases, such as those involving alienation, courts will tend to give more weight to the evidence of experts. New Zealand's Principal Family Court Judge Peter Boshier has written extra-judicially about the benefits of receiving reports from child psychologists.[44] One benefit is that child psychologists are trained to communicate with children and are therefore better able to listen to them and elicit views that are important to the child. This of course depends totally on whether or not the psychologist involved places a strong emphasis on listening to children. It would be dangerous to assume that the sheer status of the profession is enough to ensure the child is truly being listened to. Another important benefit in having a psychologist obtain the child's views is that psychologists can be cross-examined on the child's views while giving evidence. Where views are obtained by a lawyer for the child or by a judicial interview they are not able to be tested by cross-examination. This denies the parties their natural justice rights in any court hearing where important interests are at stake. The cross-examination process ensures that the psychologist's methods are carefully scrutinized to ensure that their evaluation of the child's views is based on robust research, rather than the particular opinion of the psychologist giving evidence.

In the area of parental alienation there are different schools of thought as to how to evaluate a child's views when they are strongly expressed against a particular parent. Janet Johnston and Vivienne Roseby, in their work *In the Name of the Child*, state that when a child refuses to have contact with a parent who appears appropriate and reasonable, it is quite natural to feel frustrated by what appears to be an aligned position fostered by the parent who has influenced the child against the other parent.[45] Johnston and Roseby argue that there is a tendency in these situations for courts to become 'arbitrary, punitive and coercive with the child'.[46] This loses sight of the child's attempts to cope with what is happening in a difficult, entangled web of parental conflict. Johnston and Roseby suggest that changing care of the child in such situations:

compounds their sense of powerlessness as persons in their own right. In so doing, we collude in the process of rendering children unseen and unheard in custody disputes that are fought fraudulently 'in the name of a child'.[47]

By way of comparison Richard Gardner took the view that the only way to break the deadlock of alienation is to remove the child from the alienating parent and place them with the alienated parent. Gardner proposed this was the only way a child

[42] *JTP v BTT* FC Invercargill FAM-2008-082-000004, 28 January 2010. [43] Ibid at [40].

[44] P. Boshier, 'Involving Children in Decision Making: Lessons From New Zealand' (2006) 20 *Australian Journal of Family Law* 145 at 149.

[45] J.R. Johnston and V. Roseby, *In the Name of the Child: A Developmental Approach to Understanding and Helping Children of Conflicted and Violent Divorce* (New York, 1997).

[46] Ibid at 218.

[47] Ibid.

could see for themselves that the alienated parent was not the person that had been portrayed by the alienating parent.[48]

New Zealand courts have not been totally convinced by one or other of these psychological positions. For example in *ADK v KMR*[49] a 14-year-old boy expressed strong views against his father. The court's first approach was to leave the boy in the care of his mother with gradual supervised contact as a way of establishing contact between the boy and his father. Unfortunately, the mother did not comply with the arrangements and over a period of a year there had only been one attempt to have contact with the father. When the matter returned to court, the judge took the risk of changing the boy's day-to-day care against his wishes. What appeared to reassure the judge was that there was incongruence between what the boy was saying about his father and his outwardly happy demeanour.[50] It was observed that when the boy was returning from a visit with his father he appeared to be 'happy; chatting away to the chaperone and generally appeared to be his normal self'.[51] This was a positive outcome for the child and after being placed with his father he appears to be doing well.[52]

The key is to understand why the child feels the way they do toward the other parent. It may be because of the way the other parent has treated them, or it may be out of loyalty to the parent they are living with. An emphasis on Childhood Studies moves away from the debate of parental alienation as a syndrome and requires the court to listen to the particular child in their particular circumstances. This ensures the court fully understands what is happening in the child's life, rather than drawing on general conclusions from research.

The risk of courts putting too much weight on psychologists' recommendations is that, while psychologists are very well trained in child development, they tend to work with standardized tests. This creates a risk, whereby a child that does not fit into the standardized model, may not have their voice heard. Because of the difficulties in high conflict cases, courts tend to put significant weight on what the psychologists have to say. For example in *Wheelan v Last*[53] the court said 'the advice given to the court by [the psychologist . . . is] to be given more weight that the opinions expressed by others'.[54]

4.3.2 Judicial interviews

Judicial interviews of children, as a way of obtaining their views, have become more common since the enactment of section 6 of the Care of Children Act 2004. The Principal Family Court Judge Peter Boshier has provided guidelines for judges when interviewing children.[55] The guidelines do not fully engage with the wording of section 6 of the Care of Children Act 2004 because they state that judges are to be guided 'by the age and maturity of the child when deciding whether or not to adopt

[48] R. Gardner, *The Parental Alienation Syndrome* (New Jersey, 1992). For a detailed critique of Gardner's work see C. Bruch, 'Parental Alienation Syndrome and Parental Alienation: Getting It Wrong in Child Custody Cases' (2001) 35 *Family Law Quarterly* 527.

[49] *ADK v KMR* FC Hastings FAM-2002-090-001392, 2 October 2009.

[50] Ibid at [10].

[51] Ibid.

[52] Author's conversation with Principal Family Court Judge Peter Boshier (May, 2010).

[53] *Wheelan v Last* FC Lower Hutt FAM-2003-032-000366, 11 July 2005.

[54] Ibid at [111].

[55] P. Boshier, 'Judges' Guidelines—Discussions with Children' in S. Williams, 'Judges Listening to Children Directly in Separation and Divorce Proceedings: Individual, Institutional and International Guidelines', National Judicial Institute of Canada Family Law Program (Toronto, 2010).

[the guidelines]'.[56] Judges who undertake judicial interviews have been uniformly positive about their experiences. One judge said, 'I benefitted from seeing [the child] not so much [because of] what he said, but rather being able to make this decision with his personality in mind'.[57]

Judges appear to be more comfortable with interviewing children where the dispute is over day-to-day care and contact. These are normally disputes over what amount of time a child should spend with each parent. The issue is not whether either of the parents is fit to parent the child; rather, the issue is more one of what care arrangements would work best for the child on, for example, a weekly or fortnightly basis. Judicial interviews in these cases can help judges understand the arrangement from a child's point of view and therefore are more likely to lead to better outcomes.

The area where judicial interviews are used least is in protection cases. In only four of the 30 violence cases (13 per cent) did judges conduct a judicial interview. Section 5(e) of the Care of Children Act 2004 says that when deciding such cases 'the child's safety must be protected'. In the recent Supreme Court case *Kacem v Bashir*[58] the court said that, 'if the safety principle is engaged it is likely to have decisive weight... because of the crucial factual importance of protecting the safety of children'.[59] Assessing risks of safety is predominately assigned to the lawyer for the child, with psychologists being appointed in under half the cases where safety is at issue. Even when the child's safety is at issue, and it is established that a child is at risk, it is still important to the child that the court understands what the child's views are.

4.3.3 Taking account of children's views

Section 6 of the Care of Children Act 2004 requires the court to take a child's views into account, even if it does not necessarily give weight to the child's views. The analysis of the 120 case sample for this paper shows that the 'take account' step is often overlooked. If judges do not think that a child's view is to be given any weight, they do not take it into account. The following examples show how judges prefer to focus on the weight to be given to the child's views, rather than how they have taken account of them. In *HJT v EGT*[60] the judge states:

> [The eight-year-old child] does not have a sufficient level of maturity to understand the implications of relocation, so little weight can be placed on any impression she gives that she would like to go to South Africa with her mother.[61]

In another case the judge made the following statement: 'I place little weight on [the child's] views. The child is 6½ years old and does not have the maturity or cognitive ability to understand what relocation would entail.'[62] In *PSC v BLB*[63] the judge states:

> I am required to take the children's views into account; s6 says that. The youngest child [at four years old] is really too young to express a mature view. The older two children say they

[56] Ibid.

[57] Judge Neal in *Knight v Finn* (2003) NZFLR 38 in S. Jefferson, 'Point and Purpose: The Judicial Interview as a Tool for Ascertaining the Child's Views', Paper presented at the New Zealand Law Society—Advanced Lawyer for the Child—The Winds of Change—Continuing Legal Education Conference (Wellington, 2008).

[58] *Kacem v Bashir* [2010] NZSC 112.

[59] Ibid at [19].

[60] *HJT v EGT* FC Hamilton FAM-2003-019-00896, 3 October 2008.

[61] Ibid at [28].

[62] *FLT v WT* FC Hamilton FAM-2008-019-001111, 28 January 2010 at [108].

[63] *PSC v BLB* FC Waipukarau FAM-020-286-05, 7 May 2008.

do not want to see their father. But there is obvious caution about that, as pointed out by [the psychologist].[64]

In these examples, the judges have gone straight to considering weight and used the criteria of age and maturity that has been specifically removed from the legislation. There is no evidence of these judges taking account of the children's views at all. Therefore, the intended effect of section 6 of the Care of Children Act 2004 is entirely lost.

What these judges should have done is discussed the particular views of the children involved, and then shown how they had taken account of them, before making any decisions about what weight should be given to them. For example a four-year-old girl says she 'really likes' spending weekends with a particular parent but she finds the travelling time 'a little boring and tiring'. The judge would need to incorporate the girl's views into the judgment, saying how they have taken account of them, in the sense of what relevance the child's views have to the overall decision to be made. The judge would then determine the weight to be given to them, not based on age and maturity, but in relation to all the other factors that may be relevant for the particular decision. This is a big switch for judges to make, because they tend to look at the status of children in terms of their age and maturity first, rather than what children say and how it might be relevant to the outcome of the decision. If judges listened more and took greater account of children's views, they may find that decisions as to the weight to be given to the children's views may be quite different. Even if children's views were outweighed by other relevant factors in the case, at least the decisions would show that the particular child has been heard and illustrate where the child's views lie in the matrix of facts the judge has taken into account.

Some judges appear to misunderstand totally what taking a child's view into account entails. One judge said 'Section 6 requires that the child's views must be taken into account [the lawyer for the child] has fulfilled that role'.[65] Judges also need to show how they have taken account of a child's view because the lawyer for the child has a duty to explain the decision to the child,[66] and this would be difficult if the child's views have not been taken account of. Taking a child's views into account also allows the child to see that they have been listened to.

There were some examples in the 120 case sample of judges taking account of children's views. For example in *BU v AC*,[67] which involved allegations of sexual abuse and parental alienation, the judge ascertained the views of each of the three children via a judicial interview and set out the children's views individually.[68] The judge held that the best interests of the children were to remain in the day-to-day care of their mother (despite parental alienation), but set out for each individual child specific contact with their father.[69] This allowed the judge to make a compromise between each of the children's different views and each of their best interests. The judge describes balancing children's views with their best interests thus:

The process for deciding what is in a child's best interests is like to [sic] putting the pieces of a jigsaw puzzle together. Views expressed by a child are an important piece. Children can be

64 Ibid at [16]. There was no further discussion about how the judge gave weight to each child's views in the case.

65 *Sullivan v Nash* FC Manukau FAM-2007-055-000321, 30 April 2008 at [8].

66 Care of Children Act, s 55.

67 *BU v AC* FC Manukau FAM 2001-092-1875, 26 February 2007.

68 Ibid at [43].

69 Ibid at [60].

reassured that when a Judge looks at the jigsaw their piece stands out. Equally though the other pieces cannot be ignored.[70]

In *Rewi-Wetini v Wasser*[71] the primary issue was the safety of the children while they were in their father's care. The children said they wanted to spend more time with their father. The court took these views seriously and ultimately held that 'the girls' wishes can be accommodated to an extent, providing that they do not stay overnight at their father's home and that contact is supervised by [their paternal grandmother]'.[72]

The requirement of section 6 of the Care of Children Act 2004 is that each child's views 'must be ascertained and taken into account'. Of the 62 cases in the 120 case sample in which there were multiple children subject to the proceedings, only 38 (61 per cent) discussed the views of each individual child. Thus, in 23 of the 62 multiple children cases (39 per cent), the court did not consider each individual child in their particular circumstances, despite this being required by section 4 of the Care of Children Act 2004. The court ascertained each individual child's views in 18 of the 23 multiple children relocation cases (78 per cent). However, the court only ascertained each individual child's views in seven of the 11 multiple children alienation cases (64 per cent), seven of the 13 multiple children care and contact cases (54 per cent), and just six of the 15 multiple children violence cases (40 per cent).

In violence cases the overriding concern for the child's safety means that the child's views are more readily disregarded. Relocation cases, on the other hand, require judges to make difficult decisions about whether the status quo should prevail, or whether the relocating parent can move the child to another location. In these cases, the child's views take a more predominate focus, allowing judges to determine how the possible options will impact on each child, given their relationships with each parent and other factors in their lives.

4.3.4 Weight given to children's views

Weight was only given to children's views in five of the 15 alienation cases (33 per cent). Age and maturity factors were seen as relevant in seven of the 15 alienation cases (47 per cent). In 11 of the 47 relocation cases (23 per cent), the children's views were not discussed at all and in 14 of the 47 relocation cases (30 per cent), the weight to be given to the children's views was also not discussed, despite this being required by section 6 of the Care of Children Act 2004. In 22 of the 47 relocation cases (47 per cent), age and maturity factors were discussed. In 14 of the 47 relocation cases (30 per cent), either children's views were discounted because the children were not old enough to understand the consequences of relocation, or the children were deemed too young to express a view. In 15 of the 47 relocation cases (32 per cent), children's views were given weight, and in just 12 of the 47 relocation cases (26 per cent), were children's views followed.

Cases in which children's views were given the least analysis were cases involving violence. In 14 of the 30 violence cases (47 per cent), children's views were not discussed at all. In three of the 30 violence cases (10 per cent), the judge said that the children were too young to express a view. In four of the 30 violence cases (13 per cent), children's views were discounted because they were found to be contrary to

[70] Ibid at [7].
[71] *Rewi-Wetini v Wasser* FC Hamilton FAM-2002-019-1515, 21 September 2005.
[72] Ibid at [80].

the children's best interests. In seven of the 30 violence cases (23 per cent), children's views were discussed, but the weight to be given to them was not analysed at all. In just seven of the 30 violence cases (23 per cent), children's views were considered and followed or partially followed.

In eight of the 28 care and contact cases (29 per cent), the children's views were not discussed. Children's views were given weight in ten of the 28 care and contact cases (36 per cent), but these views were discounted in six of the 28 care and contact cases (21 per cent) because the views were contrary to the children's best interests.

Generally, children's views were most likely to be followed when the children were aged 11 or older and their views were strongly and consistently held. Usually these views revolved around wanting to spend more time with the other parent. Young children under seven years old tended to have their views ignored. Views that were seen as influenced, coached, or aligned were also ignored.

In 21 of the 86 cases in which the children's views were discussed (24 per cent), there was no further discussion of the weight to be given to those views. In 55 cases of the total 120 case sample (46 per cent), the children's views were either not ascertained in the written judgment or, if they were, there was no further consideration of the weight to be given to them. Despite age and maturity being removed as a criteria for assessing weight, in 47 cases of the total 120 case sample (39 per cent), age and maturity of the children were used to determine whether the children were capable of expressing views and whether weight should be attached to the children's views. In 13 cases of the total 120 case sample (11 per cent), the court said that the children were too young to express a view. The children in these cases ranged from one year old to five years old. The following quotations from three of the sample cases illustrate how the court dismisses young children's views:

> This is a case where Hugo [two years old] is too young to express an opinion or indicate his wishes.[73]
>
> Section 6 of the Act makes it clear that a child must be given reasonable opportunity to express any views on the matter affecting the child and that those views must be taken into account. In this case [the child] has only just turned five. He is described as a bright and articulate young boy, but he is too young to express a view.[74]
>
> The children's ages [six and four and a half] preclude the Court receiving their full and independent views and wishes.[75]

In eight cases of the total 120 case sample (seven per cent), ascertained children's views were discounted because of the children's age and maturity. The children in these cases ranged from four-and-a-half years old to 13 years old. Once the age and maturity of children is raised, judges stop listening to children and use the concept of weight to dismiss their views. This is illustrated by the wording used by the judge in the following example:

> Given [seven-year-old child's] age, and the contents of the reports from [the psychologist] in relation to this, I was not prepared to explore reasons for her views.[76]

Age counts for children. Once they are perceived to be at a suitable age, their views can be given weight. In six cases of the total 120 case sample (five per cent), weight was given to children's views because of their age. The children in these cases ranged

[73] *Carey v Walker* FC Dunedin FAM-2003-002-000252, 5 July 2005 at [6].
[74] *WAB v NTTT* FC Wellington FAM-2003-085-2119, 10 August 2005 at [14].
[75] *R v M* FC Hamilton FAM-2007-019-001242, 27 February 2009 at [26].
[76] *BU v AC* FC Manukau FAM-2001-092-1875, 26 February 2007 at [43].

from eight-and-a-half years old to 16 years old. For example as one judge says, 'Having regard to their ages, I find that the children's wishes must be given significant weight'.[77] In another case a judge similarly states, 'Given the ages of the boys, I find that their views must be given considerable weight'.[78]

A further indication that judges have not fully adapted to section 6 of the Care of Children Act 2004 when considering children's views is that, in 39 cases of the total 120 case sample (33 per cent), the court refers to the 'wishes' of the child, instead of the more accurate and wider concept of 'views'. Of the 203 children who were involved in the total 120 case sample, the court followed, or partly followed, the views of 80 (39 per cent) of the children. Thirty-five (44 per cent) of these children were males, and 40 (50 per cent) of these children were girls. Five children (six per cent) were not identified by gender in the judgments. The court uses only initials to indentify the children and in many of the judgments careful reading had to be carried out in order to identify whether the children were male or female.

A significant trend was that of the 80 children whose views were at least partially followed, 41 (51 per cent) had had a judicial interview with the judge and 40 (50 per cent) had a court-appointed psychologist.[79] Psychologists were appointed by the court in 64 cases of the total 120 case sample (53 per cent). This shows there is no significant difference between the rate of cases where children's views are given weight, and the rate of psychologists appointed. However, there is a significant difference when it comes to judicial interviews. Judicial interviews only took place in 39 cases of the total 120 case sample (33 per cent), yet this approach had the highest overall following of children's views.

There are a range of reasons why a judicial interview appears to influence the weight to be attached to a child's views. Firstly, the type of case in which judicial interviews are employed is one explanation for why judicial interviews influence whether or not a child's views are followed. For example, judicial interviews are rare in cases involving protection. It therefore seems that where a judge chooses to pursue a judicial interview and hear the child's views, the views become more meaningful to the judge because they are ascertained with the intention that they would be of assistance to the overall decision. A further factor behind judicial interviews leading to children's views being more likely to be followed is that they enable the children to convey their views directly to the judge, which is likely to give the judge a more specific understanding of what the child's views actually are under section 6 of the Care of Children Act 2004. Finally, judges who interview children may just simply be more in tune with section 6 and the significance of children's development, which means that they are more likely to take children's views into account when they make their final decision.

Aside from considerations of age, the other common reason for not giving weight to children's views was the external influence of others. For example one judge held:

> I find that the children's wishes have been so influenced by Ms Bennett that they cannot be regarded as the children's own. I am unable to place any reliance on those wishes.[80]

[77] *Rewi-Wetini v Wasser* FC Hamilton FAM-2002-019-1515, 21 September 2005 at [63].

[78] *Pehi-Neho v Davis* FC Manukau FAM-2002-055-377, 9 June 2006 at [81].

[79] Some children had both a judicial interview and an appointed psychologist, hence the overlapping figures.

[80] *Bennett v Reeves* FC Hamilton FAM-1999-019-1558, 19 July 2005 at [32].

There were cases where judges did attempt to give effect to children's views in circumstances where the judges could reach a compromise that would still protect the children, but also show that their views were taken seriously. For example in *Rewi-Wetini v Wasser*[81] more contact time was awarded to the father as the girl had requested, but the judge did not go so far as to allow overnight stays due to safety issues.[82]

Some judges went out of their way to show that children's views were not determinative of the outcome, even where the outcome was consistent with what the children had said. For example in *SFW v RAL*[83] the judge reported that the children wanted to spend more than five hours a week with their father. The judge commented:

> That is their view, but while the view must be taken account of, it cannot decide this case. I am the one that has to make that decision and I have to do that as best as I can with what is in front of me [...] I do not think I can place a great deal of weight on what the children said because without the input of the psychologist, it is difficult for me to know just what reliance I can place on their comments.[84]

In the end, the judge made an order that accorded with the children's views and doubled the amount of time they would spend with their father each week. A similar pattern of reasoning was adopted in *GRT v RT*[85] where the judge remained with the status quo (which was what the five- and seven-year-old boys wanted), but the judge said because of their ages, significant weight could not be given to their views. So whilst the judges in these cases found outcomes that accorded with the children's views, they made it very clear their decisions were not based on the children's views, but rather based on what the judges believed was best for the children.

The most consistent pattern of giving weight to children's views is when those views coincide with what the court believes is best for the children, along with the age and maturity of the children. For example one judge held:

> Overall, I consider the advantages to P of extending contact outweigh the disadvantages. Extending contact would accord with her views and would accord with the [best interests] principles in s 5 of the Act to which I have referred.[86]

There was no evidence in the 120 case sample of any gender bias in the application of section 6 of the Care of Children Act 2004. Forty-three cases (36 per cent) were decided by a female judge and 77 (64 per cent) were decided by a male judge. Of the 56 cases where the views of at least one child were not ascertained, or were ascertained and discounted due to age, 18 (32 per cent) were decided by female judges and 38 (68 per cent) by male judges. Of the 50 cases, in which the views of at least one child were followed or partially followed, 18 (36 per cent) were decided by female judges and 32 (60 per cent) were decided by male judges.

There were small changes over time in the case sample, which was made up of Family Court decisions from 2005 to 2010. In day-to-day care and contact cases, there was an increase over time in the appointment of psychologists and the number of cases where children's views were discussed in the judgment. There was a slight increase where the weight to be given to children's views was discussed more in the relocation and alienation categories. There was an increase over time in the relocation

[81] *Rewi-Wetini v Wasser* FC Hamilton FAM-2002-019-1515, 21 September 2005.
[82] Ibid at [76].
[83] *SFW v RAL* FC Lower Hutt FAM-2005-032-000695, 15 November 2006.
[84] Ibid at [16] and [5].
[85] *GRT v RT* FC North Shore FAM-2008-044-002629, 29 March 2010.
[86] *CAH v LJD* FC Porirua FAM-2007-091-000716, 17 July 2009 at [22].

and protection cases of judgments discussing age and maturity in relation to section 6. These are difficult cases, but they do not justify judges introducing irrelevant criteria to dismiss children's views.

4.4 The difference that understanding Childhood Studies will make

When the Care of Children Act 2004 first came into force Judge Jan Doogue wrote an article about the importance of correctly receiving children's views.[87] Judge Doogue said:

> If a child is truly to be given a reasonable opportunity to express their views then it is essential that the person to whom they communicate them has the capability and training to understand that children and adults see the world differently, and use different language to articulate their experiences. The recipient of the views needs to know how to create an environment within which to facilitate the expression of views, both in the very questions that are asked and how they are asked.[88]

An understanding of Childhood Studies will enable judges to understand that children play an active role in the development of their own childhood, that every childhood is unique, and that no one is able to understand a child's world better than the particular child. Childhood Studies requires an effort to understand how the child sees their own unique world. A current member of the Family Court Bench in New Zealand, Judge Stephen Coyle, wrote an article encouraging Family Court professionals to:

> [L]ook to disciplines outside of our comfort zone in our efforts to ensure that the Court is best able to meet the needs of those who appear before it, but in particular, those of children.[89]

Pauline Tapp warns that judges do not always have the appropriate expertise for interviewing children.[90] The fundamental starting point has to be for a judge to understand why it is important to listen to children and ascertain what is happening in their world. The judge must then take account of the children's views in their judgment. The dispute is about the child, yet it is very easy for judges to see the dispute as one between the parents, and the judge's obligation as being merely to make a decision for parents when the parents cannot agree amongst themselves. If children are listened to, children's views become part of the evidence that assists the court in making its decision. This is better than judges looking merely to see if the children's views are deemed relevant to the particular decision they have to make.

A judgment written from a Childhood Studies perspective is built around looking at what is happening, not from the parents' point of view, or the judge's point of view, but primarily from a child's point of view. The ultimate decision is still for the judge, but it is more likely to be a decision about the particular child if the judge fully understands, takes account of, and carefully considers the weight to be given to the

[87] J. Doogue, 'A Seismic Shift or a Minor Realignment? A View from the Bench Ascertaining Children's Views' (2006) 5 *New Zealand Family Law Reports* 198.

[88] Ibid at 201.

[89] S. Coyle, 'Sociology of Childhood: Implications for Our Practice as Lawyers' (2006) 5 *New Zealand Family Law Journal* 256 at 256.

[90] P. Tapp, 'Judges Are Human Too: Conversations Between the Judge and a Child as a Means of Giving Effect to s 6 of the Care of Children Act 2004' (2006) *New Zealand Law Reports* 35.

particular views of the particular child. The weight to be given to the child's views should not be based on the child's age and maturity, but based on all of the circumstances of the particular case.

4.5 Conclusion

The best way to illustrate why judges should be aware of Childhood Studies is to conclude with a practical example. The case of *L v B*[91] concerns a five-year-old boy whose parents had separated when he was three. Both parents lived in Auckland, a large city in the North Island of New Zealand. The mother sought the Family Court's permission to relocate with the child to live a 90-minute drive away in Hamilton. The father opposed the relocation. The child's views were given to the court via the child's representative, the lawyer for the child. The child expressed the following views. Firstly, the child wanted the judge to decide who he should live with because the decision was 'too hard' for the child to make.[92] It was clear the child did not want to disappoint either of his parents. Then the child told the lawyer for the child 'he wants to spend the same time with Mum and Dad'.[93] The child also said that he 'wants to be collected by [his paternal grandmother] from school'.[94]

The Family Court judge was of the view that because of the young boy's 'age and level of maturity' his views were not to be given any significant weight.[95] Ultimately, the Family Court gave permission to the mother to take the child to live with her in Hamilton.

The case was appealed to the High Court in which Potter J held that the Family Court judge was wrong not to accord significant weight to the views of this child in this particular case.[96] Potter J said:

> A five year old cannot be expected to have any appreciation of the range of complex factors involved in a relocation decision, and his views must necessarily reflect his past experience. But in this case, the experience [the child] expressed was positive and confirmed a view consistent with the principle in s 5(b) that he should have continuing relationships with both his parents.[97]

The child had made it very clear that he wanted to spend 'the same time' with his mother and father, and that he wanted to have a closer level of involvement with his paternal grandmother after school.[98] There was no evidence before the court that the child had been subjected to any inappropriate parental influences.[99] Potter J was convinced that the child having continuing contact with both parents would best serve the child's welfare, and that the geographical separation between Auckland and Hamilton would erode the child's opportunities for such ongoing contact.[100]

The child's young age in this case was not used as a reason to minimize the weight to be given to the child's views. Instead, the child's views were seen in the context of the child's world and the child's previous experiences.

Whilst judges are more likely to listen to children's views when they accord with the principles enshrined in section 5 of the Care of Children Act 2004, the child's views in this case illustrate that children are often very sensitive to what is happening

[91] *L v B* HC Auckland CIV-2009-404-005482, 22 January 2010. [92] Ibid at [36].
[93] Ibid. [94] Ibid. [95] Ibid at [34]. [96] Ibid at [111]. [97] Ibid at [109].
[98] Ibid. [99] Ibid at [110]. [100] Ibid at [113].

around them and that they do have views about things that affect them. It is clear that a child's perspective can be of great assistance to the court in coming to a decision that is in the best interests of the particular child in that particular child's circumstances. Listening to a child's views also accords the child with the respect and dignity that they deserve.

5

Courts and the Construction of Childhood: A New Way of Thinking

John Tobin[1]

In an interview with the *Guardian*, Albie Sachs, the celebrated and now retired Justice of the South African Constitutional Court, explained the history of a case in which he held that the imposition of a custodial sentence on a mother was not justified because of the impact on her children. His initial response to the application had been dismissive:

> I said: 'This doesn't raise a constitutional question. She simply wants to avoid going to jail. She doesn't make out a case, and her prospects of success are zero.'
>
> But a female colleague insisted that the case be heard. She said: 'There is something you are missing. What about the children?' Sachs went on:
>
> 'The minute my colleague spoke to me about the importance of the three teenage children of Mrs M, I started to see them not as three small citizens who had the right to grow up into big citizens but as three threatened, worrying, precarious, conflicted young boys who had a claim on the court, a claim on our society as individuals, as children, and a claim not to be treated solely as extensions of the rights of the mother, but in their own terms.'[1A]

As the interview continued, Sachs explained that he had learnt of a similar approach being advocated in Scotland where two thirds of women in prison had children under 18 but there was no provision to take the rights of the children into account during the sentencing of their mother:

> 'This was astonishing,' Sachs told the audience. 'In a totally different legal system, in a totally different society, a conclusion was being reached that is almost identical. It showed that the time has come for new ways of thinking.'

This interview is at once both a cause for concern and hope. Concern because it demonstrates the fragile way in which justice is conceived and delivered. But for the intervention of one judge, there is the real prospect that the mother of three children may have been imprisoned irrespective of the impact on her children. Hope because of the willingness of Sachs and the other members of the South African Court to

[1] BComm, LLB (Hons) (Melb), LLM (Lond), PhD (Melb); Associate Professor, Melbourne Law School. The chapter is based on an earlier and more extensive article on the treatment of children's rights by courts titled, 'Judging the Judges: Are they Adopting the Rights Approach in Matters Involving Children?' (2009) 33 *Melbourne University Law Review* 579. The author would like to thank the editors of the *Melbourne University Law Review* for allowing the reproduction of parts of this article in this chapter. Thanks are also due to the Law Research Service in the Melbourne Law School law library for its excellent research assistance.

[1A] Jackie Kemp, 'Life Sentences', *Guardian* (London) 1 July 2009, 5.

embrace a new way of thinking about children that sought to mitigate the impact of their decision concerning an adult on the lives of children.

The aim of this chapter is to explore what is meant by this new way of judicial thinking in which children are conceived of as independent subjects with rights and entitlements as opposed to mere objects in need of protection and charity. It consists of four parts. Part 5.1 will provide an overview of the ways in which courts have constructed childhood over time. It will be suggested that three broad models have emerged—a proprietary approach, a welfare approach, and more recently a rights based approach. Part 5.2 will detail the features of this newest way of thinking about children and Part 5.3 will provide an overview of the ways in which courts engage with this model. It will be argued that courts' engagement with a rights based approach can be classified along a spectrum that ranges from the non-existent (or invisible) to the substantive with a range of approaches between these extremes. Finally Part 5.4 will identify the legal, institutional, and social factors that influence the extent to which courts engage with this new way of thinking whereby children are conceived of as rights holders. It will be argued that we are on the verge of a new epoch in which the construction of childhood by courts will increasingly be viewed through the prism of rights.

5.1 The ways in which courts construct childhood

5.1.1 The proprietary model

Historically, judges had no reason to conceptualize disputes involving children in terms of their rights. This was a legacy of the Roman doctrine of *patria potestas*—paternal power—which entitled a father not only 'to all the service and all the acquisitions of his child, as much as those of his slave, but he had the same absolute control over his person'.[2] Despite the emergence of rights discourse in the mid-1800s within political and social commentary, children were still excluded from this development.[3] Not surprisingly judges adopted a position that was consistent with this position. The archetypal case for the illustration of this approach is the English decision in the late nineteenth century of *In re Agar-Ellis*[4] in which Bowen LJ warned that any move by a court to override 'the natural jurisdiction' of a father over his child 'would be really to set aside the whole course and order of nature, and it seems to me it would disturb the very foundation of family life'.[5]

There was a significant social, political, and legal movement away from the notion of parental possession over the course of the late nineteenth and early twentieth century, first with the adoption of the welfare model and more latterly with the emergence of children's rights.[6] This paradigm shift, however, has not been universally

[2] James Hadley, *Introduction to Roman Law in Twelve Academical Lectures* (1873) 119, quoted in Bryan A. Garner (ed), *Black's Law Dictionary* (9th ed, 2009), 1287.

[3] For example John Stuart Mill argued in 1859 in *On Liberty* that the liberty principle applied 'only to human beings in the maturity of their faculties' and disqualified from its exercise 'children and young persons below that age which the law may fix as that of manhood and womanhood': John Stuart Mill, *On Liberty* (1859), 8.

[4] (1883) 24 Ch D 317.

[5] Ibid 336.

[6] See John Eekelaar, 'The Emergence of Children's Rights' (1986) 6 *Oxford Journal of Legal Studies* 161.

embraced by courts and the legacy of the parental possession doctrine remains. For example, as recently as 2004 Justice Gummow of the High Court of Australia, in a case concerning the detention of refugee children, remarked that:

> The starting point is the proposition that, at common law, a right of a parent or parents to custody of children who had not reached the age of discretion (14 for boys and 16 for girls) incorporates a '*right of possession*' of the child which includes the right to exercise physical control over that child.[7]

In defence of Gummow J, the context in which this comment was made indicates an intention to construe parental authority as a means by which to protect the interests of the child.[8] However, the construction of this relationship by reference to a parent's right of possession is problematic. The UN Convention on the Rights of the Child (CRC) explicitly rejects this proprietary model in favour of an approach where parents actually have an *obligation* to assist children in the realization of their rights.[9]

The legacy of the proprietary model can also be found in the response of some courts in cases which involve a challenge to the legality of corporal punishment administered by parents. Although there is a trend within national courts to condemn such a practice as a violation of children's rights, this trend is far from universal as the Canadian case of *Canadian Foundation for Children, Youth and the Law v Canada (Attorney General)*[10] illustrates. This case involved a claim that a provision in the Canadian criminal law, which allowed for the reasonable use of force by parents and teachers to discipline children, was a violation of children's rights under the Canadian Charter of Rights and Freedoms. The rationale underlying the majority's rejection of this claim was based on two broad considerations: first, a belief that the relevant law provided 'parents and teachers with the ability to carry out the reasonable education of the child without the threat of sanction by the criminal law';[11] and second, a belief that:

> The decision not to criminalize such conduct is not grounded in devaluation of the child, but in a concern that to do so risks ruining lives and breaking up families—a burden that in large part would be borne by children and outweigh any benefit derived from applying the criminal process.[12]

But the court's ostensible concern for children is misleading. Its real concern is to maintain a family structure in which parents enjoy the right to use physical force against their children—a right that has its genesis in the proprietary model of childhood.

The Canadian Supreme Court has built a reputation for using a robust test of proportionality in which the reasonableness of an interference with a right must be established by the availability of cogent and persuasive evidence and the need to minimally impair the right.[13] But in this case, the majority overlooked these considerations and retreated to assumptions about the need to ensure parents can use corporal

[7] *Re Woolley; Ex parte Applicants M276/2003* (2004) 225 CLR 1, 57–8 ('*Re Woolley*') (emphasis added) (citations omitted).

[8] *Re Woolley* (2004) 225 CLR 1, 55–61, [152]–[167].

[9] Opened for signature 20 November 1989, 1577 UNTS 3, arts 43–4 (entered into force 2 September 1990). See CRC arts 5, 18(1), 27(2).

[10] [2004] 1 SCR 76.

[11] Ibid [59] (McLachlin CJ, and Gonthier, Iacobucci, Major, Bastarache, and LeBel JJ).

[12] Ibid [62] (McLachlin CJ, and Gonthier, Iacobucci, Major, Bastarache, and LeBel JJ).

[13] *R v Oakes* [1986] 1 SCR 103.

punishment against their children and a spurious belief that the family structure will collapse if parents are no longer able to smack their children and are subject to prosecution if they do. This is despite the growing body of evidence that demonstrates the harm of corporal punishment, the reasonable availability of alternative non-physical disciplinary techniques, and the fact that in those jurisdictions where the practice has been banned, there is no evidence to suggest that this has led to the disintegration of the family structure.[14] The majority of the court may not have intended to affirm the proprietary model. But they failed to interrogate the foundations of the assumptions on which they based their decision. This meant they were unable to disenthrall themselves from the lingering impact of the proprietary model on the construction of childhood within society which includes the tolerance of corporal punishment for children.[15]

5.1.2 The welfare model

The welfare model for the treatment of children emerged in the late nineteenth, early twentieth century and has tended to dominate judicial thinking about children ever since. Much has already been written about this model and need not be repeated here. Suffice to say that the development of this model was motivated by the failings of the proprietary model to ensure the protection and welfare of children when in the care of their parents or other adults. Its underlying principle is that children are vulnerable and immature. As such, they lack the capacity and agency to protect themselves against harm or make decisions in their own best interests. Adults, and the institutions created by the State, including courts, must therefore act in a way that secures the best interests of a child.

From a judicial perspective, illustrations of the welfare model and its legacy can be seen in contexts ranging from decisions to prohibit the publication of the names of children in judicial proceedings, decisions to force children to undergo medical treatment against their wishes, and decisions to authorize the sterilization of girls with an intellectual disability. In each of these contexts the need to protect children against harm is achieved by the judicial application of the principle that the best interests of a child are the primary or paramount consideration. But the impact of the welfare model extends beyond an application of the best interests principle. For example, the construction of childhood as a period of immaturity and relative irresponsibility was also a significant factor in the decision of the majority of the US Supreme Court in *Roper v Simmons* to prohibit the death penalty for children under the age of 18.[16] The court held that the death penalty was reserved for the most serious offenders and that children did not fall within this category because '[a] lack of maturity and an underdeveloped sense of responsibility are found in youth more often than in adults and are more understandable among the young. These qualities often result in impetuous and ill-considered actions and decisions'.[17] Although the perception of children as

[14] There is a growing body of literature with respect to these issues much of which is available at <http://www.endcorporalpunishment.org/pages/frame.html> (accessed 28 February 2011).

[15] See *Canadian Foundation for Children, Youth and the Law v A-G (Canada)* [2004] 1 SCR 76, 183 [231] (Deschamps J) ('*Canadian Foundation for Children*'): Deschamps J, dissenting, held that a law allowing for corporal punishment of children by their parents perpetuated notions of children as property.

[16] *Roper v Simmons* 543 US 551, 567 (Kennedy J for Stevens, Kennedy, Souter, Ginsburg, and Breyer JJ) (2005).

[17] Ibid 15.

immature was not the only factor that influenced the majority's reasoning, it played a significant role. Thus it is important to acknowledge that the welfare model carried significant benefits for children relative to the previous model which was based on the proprietary interests of a father in his children. However, as Eekelaar notes, the welfare model 'had its dark side. The duty to advance the interests of the vulnerable carried with it the power to decide what those interests were'.[18] Indeed, it was this concern that contributed to the emergence of the rights based model.

5.1.3 The rights based model

The children's rights movement emerged in the wake of the civil rights and feminist movements in the 1960s. It was against this social and political backdrop, that the Supreme Court of the United States delivered its judgment *In Re Gault*[19] in 1967—a decision that has been described 'as the most important children's rights case in history'.[20] This comment may reflect a very American vision of history but the decision did represent a watershed in relation to the way in which courts conceptualized legal issues in matters involving children. Prior to *In Re Gault* the American juvenile justice system had operated along a welfare model in which their best interests were the concern of the State. This meant that children who engaged in criminal offending were denied due process rights. The US Supreme Court rejected this position and declared that 'neither the Fourteenth Amendment nor the Bill of Rights is for adults alone'.[21] Children, like adults, were entitled to rights.

Importantly *In Re Gault* precipitated a paradigm shift in the 1960s and 1970s in the way in which the US Supreme Court dealt with matters concerning children. For example, in *Tinker v Des Moines Independent Community School District* ('*Tinker*'), a case which dealt with children's right to expression in public schools, it was held that 'students in school as well as out of school are "persons" under our Constitution. They are possessed of fundamental rights which the State must respect...'.[22] In *Planned Parenthood of Central Missouri v Danforth*, Justice Blackmun, in writing the majority opinion concerning an adolescent's right to an abortion, proclaimed that 'constitutional rights do not mature and come into being magically only when one attains the state-defined age of majority. Minors, as well as adults, are protected by the Constitution and possess constitutional rights'.[23] In each of these cases the US Supreme Court was prepared to resist historical perceptions as to the status of children and affirm their independent legal status and entitlement to rights.[24]

A similar trend emerged in other jurisdictions, most notably in the decision of the UK House of Lords in 1986, *Gillick v West Norfolk and Wisbech Area Authority and Anor*,[25] in which it was held that a child who had attained sufficient understanding

[18] John Eekelaar, *Family Law and Personal Life* (Oxford University Press USA, 2008), 13.

[19] 387 US 1 (1967).

[20] Martin Guggenheim, *What's Wrong with Children's Rights* (Harvard University Press, 2005), 7.

[21] *Re Gault* 387 US 1, 13 (Fortas J for Warren CJ, Black, Douglas, Clark, Harlan, Brennan, Stewart, White and Fortas JJ) (1967).

[22] 393 US 503, 511 (Fortas J for Warren CJ, Black, Douglas, Harlan, Brennan, Stewart, White, Fortas, and Marshall JJ) (1969).

[23] 428 US 52, 74 (Blackmun J for Brennan, Marshall, and Blackmun JJ) (1976).

[24] Commentators have lamented that this trend which commenced in the late 1960s has not been continued in the US: Barbara Bennett Woodhouse, 'The Constitutionalization of Children's Rights: Incorpor-ating Emerging Human Rights into Constitutional Doctrine' (1999) 2 *University of Pennsylvania Journal of Constitutional Law* 1, 8.

[25] [1986] 1 AC 112.

and intelligence had the capacity to consent to contraceptive treatment and advice without the consent of her parents. Significantly this decision was widely adopted throughout common law jurisdictions where it challenged the underlying principles of both the proprietary model and the welfare model.[26] Children were no longer to be subject to the exclusive control of their parents. Nor were they to be constructed simply as incompetent and vulnerable beings incapable of expressing their views as to what was in their best interests.

This judicial development in domestic jurisdictions also coincided with the period in which the CRC was being drafted and ultimately adopted in 1989—an instrument which has catapulted the concept of children's rights into all areas of decision making involving children, including the courts. Indeed in 2003 the Committee on the Rights of the Child, the body of independent experts tasked with the responsibility for monitoring States parties' compliance with the CRC, called on all judicial bodies systematically to consider 'how children's rights and interests are or will be affected by their decisions and actions'.[27] A question remains, however, as to what that approach might look like in practice, and it is to this issue that I now turn.

5.2 The features of a substantive rights based approach to the judicial construction of childhood

The rise of the discourse of children's rights has not caused concerns about its content and relevance to disappear. For example, Martin Guggenheim, one of America's leading advocates and academics in the area of children and the law, has argued that the concept of children's rights 'has less substantive content . . . than many would suppose . . . [and] . . . has provided very little by way of a useful analytic tool for resolving knotty social problems'.[28] In contrast the UK scholar Jane Fortin has argued that:

> By articulating children's interests as rights, and incorporating evidence traditionally associated with ideas about their best interests, within such rights, the courts can develop a more structured and analytical approach to decision making.[29]

Such a polarization of views presents a challenge for those courts that may be urged to embrace a rights based approach. What is important to remember, however, is that although Guggenheim and Fortin refer to the same slogan, their understanding of the concept of children's rights is very different. Guggenheim's vision is wedded to the experience of children's rights in the USA whereas Fortin locates her analysis within the context of the Human Rights Act and the European Convention for the Protection of Human Rights and Fundamental Freedoms. The analysis in this

[26] See John Eekelaar, 'The Emergence of Children's Rights' (1986) 6 *Oxford Journal of Legal Studies* 161. Faced with the prospect of a doctor providing contraceptive advice to a young girl without her mother's consent, the lower courts in England were content to maintain a parent's right to physical possession over a child thereby, in the words of Eekelaar, 'annihilating' the prospect for any recognition of the autonomy interests of children: ibid 180. In contrast the majority of the House of Lords were prepared to hold that a child who had attained sufficient understanding and maturity had the full capacity to enter into legal relationships without the consent of his or her parents.

[27] CRC Committee, *General Comment No 5: General Measures of Implementation of the Convention on the Rights of the Child (Articles 4, 42 and 44(6))*, 34th sess, [12], UN Doc CRC/GC/2003/5 (2003) ('*General Comment No 5*').

[28] Guggenheim, above n 20, xii.

[29] Jane Fortin, 'Accommodating Children's Rights in a Post *Human Rights Act* Era' (2006) 69 *Modern Law Review* 299, 326.

chapter proceeds from yet another basis, namely the vision of children's rights under the CRC.

Although this vision is contested there are four core principles that inform a rights based construction of childhood by courts. First, a recognition that children have rights.[30] Second, a recognition that parents have primary responsibility for the care and upbringing of a child. Importantly this relationship is not defined by a parental right of possession or control but an obligation to provide guidance and assistance to a child to ensure the realization of his or her rights, subject to the evolving capacities of the child.[31] Third, a requirement to ensure the best interests of children are, as a minimum, a primary consideration in all matters concerning them.[32] Subject to a few exceptions, such as adoption and child protection, a child's best interests are not to be the paramount consideration for a court in matters concerning children. Thus, whereas the paramountcy principle demands that a child's best interests must be the overriding and dominant (although not exclusive) consideration in any judicial proceedings, the primary principle does not require such a level of judicial deference. At the same time, a child's best interests cannot be readily dismissed and a heavy burden is cast on the party seeking to displace the best interests of the child to establish a legitimate and compelling reason to justify such an approach.[33]

The fourth core principle for courts to consider relates to the process for the determination of a child's best interests. This principle has been repeatedly criticized for its apparent indeterminacy and its potential to be interpreted by reference to the subjective preferences of a decision maker. Under the CRC, however, this principle must be interpreted by reference to the other rights under the CRC.[34] Of particular significance is article 12(1) which provides that a State must assure to a child who is capable of expressing a view, the right to have those views heard in any matters affecting the child. Moreover, article 12(2) specifically provides that a child must be given an opportunity to be heard in any judicial proceedings affecting him or her. This emphasis on the participation of children serves to distinguish a rights based approach from traditional welfare based approaches where children's voices remained, if not completely silenced, then seriously marginalized relative to the views of adults. Importantly, children's views are not necessarily determinative of their best interests under a rights based model and a court must give such views due weight according to the age and maturity of a child.

A further factor for a court to consider when determining the best interests of a child is the availability of any empirical evidence in relation to the child specifically or of children more generally, which is of relevance to the issues before the court. The requirement to adopt an evidence based approach operates to reduce the indeterminacy of the best interests principle and mitigate the potential for judges to substitute their own subjective or speculative preferences as to what amounts to a child's best interests. It therefore serves to allay the concerns expressed by the Chief Justice of the Canadian Supreme Court that the best interests principle is incapable of 'being

[30] See CRC art 2 (the principle of non discrimination).

[31] See CRC arts 5, 18, 27.

[32] See CRC art 3.

[33] Philip Alston, 'The Best Interests Principle: Towards a Reconciliation of Culture and Human Rights' in Philip Alston (ed), *The Best Interests of the Child: Reconciling Culture and Human Rights* (1994) 1.

[34] This argument is based on the principle of internal system coherence. See John Tobin, 'Seeking to Persuade: A Constructive Approach to Human Rights Treaty Interpretation' (2010) 23 *Harvard Human Rights Journal* 1. See also Alston, n 33 above.

identified with some precision'.[35] It may not be amenable to a mathematical formula but a process does exist by which to generate the meaning of a child's best interests in the circumstances of each case. Importantly, this process requires more than an assessment of a child's 'well being'—an approach which was recently adopted by the UK Supreme Court[36] and simply substitutes one ambiguous phrase with another. The process for the determination of a child's best interests requires a consideration of: (a) the wishes of a child; (b) the relevance of any other rights under the CRC; (c) the particular circumstances of the child as informed by the views of any persons caring for, or working with, the child; and (d) any available empirical evidence that may be of relevance.

Having mapped out, albeit in a cursory fashion, the features of a rights based approach that are most salient for courts, it is now appropriate to consider the means by which courts can apply these principles in a substantive way, what I have termed a 'substantive rights' approach. Importantly, this approach is not homogenous. However, in terms of illustrating when a court will satisfy the features of such an approach, it is convenient to examine the different areas in which a consideration of children's rights may be relevant for a court. These are identified as being: (a) the conceptualization of the issues before the court; (b) the procedures to be adopted for the determination of the issues; (c) the meaning to be given to the content of the rights in question; and (d) the substantive reasoning by which to resolve the issues and balance any competing interests.

5.2.1 Conceptualization of the issues

The archetypal example of how to conceptualize the issues in a case concerning children from a substantive rights perspective, is the approach taken by Baroness Hale of Richmond in *R (Williamson) v Secretary of State for Education and Employment* ('*Williamson*').[37] This matter concerned the legality of a ban on corporal punishment in English schools. When the matter finally reached the House of Lords, as it then was, Baroness Hale of Richmond declared:

> My Lords this is and has always been a case about children, their rights and the rights of their parents and teachers. Yet there has been no one here or in the courts below to speak on behalf of children. No litigation friend has been appointed to consider the rights of the pupils.... No non-governmental organisation... has intervened to argue a case on behalf of children as a whole. The battle has been fought on ground selected by the adults.[38]

Prior to the case arriving before Baroness Hale, the matter had managed to traverse its way through the English judicial system without any discussion as to the relevance of children's rights. Instead the case had been confined to an analysis as to the nature of the religious beliefs on which the parents sought to assert their right to have their children subject to physical discipline in schools.[39] Under a substantive

[35] *Canadian Foundation for Children* [2004] 1 SCR 76, 591.

[36] *ZH (Tanzania) v Secretary of State for the Home Department* [2011] 2 WLR 148, 159 [26], 160 [29], 162 [33] ('*Tanzania*').

[37] [2005] 2 AC 246.

[38] Ibid 271 [71].

[39] It is important to note, as Jane Fortin brought to my attention, that the UK Secretary of State had not raised the issue of children's own rights because English law maintains that parents have a right to physically punish their children. Thus procedurally the case was presented to the English courts as if the issue for resolution was confined to the legitimacy of the state's attack on the religious rights of parents. This narrow position however did not prevent Baroness Hale of Richmond from identifying the central

rights approach, in any case concerning children, the issues must be conceptualized through a prism in which the rights of children are identified as being central to the issues to be determined by the court.

5.2.2 The procedures adopted for the resolution of the issues

Not surprisingly the decision of Baroness Hale of Richmond in *Williamson* also provides an illustration of the impact on the procedures of a court when a rights based approach is adopted. After identifying the centrality of children's rights to the issue of corporal punishment, she lamented that:

> ... there has been no one here or in the courts below to speak on behalf of the children. No litigation friend has been appointed to consider the rights of the pupils ... no non-governmental organisation ... has intervened to argue a case on behalf of children as a whole. The battle has been fought on ground selected by the adults.

This concern about an absence of a procedure to assure that children's views were made known to a court, is consistent with the obligation on States parties to the CRC under article 12 to ensure that children must be provided with the opportunity to be heard in any proceedings affecting them either directly or indirectly or through a representative or an appropriate body.[40]

Importantly, a rights based model has an impact on the procedures adopted by a court beyond ensuring adequate representation of a child in a proceeding. They must extend to every aspect of the proceedings including the way in which a child gives evidence, the length of the sitting day, where and with whom a child sits, the physical arrangement of the court itself, the extent to which the public have access to the court, and the publication of any proceedings by the media. A detailed discussion of these issues is beyond the scope of this chapter. By way of illustration, however, the decision of the European Court of Human Rights in *V v United Kingdom*[41] is worth noting. This case related to the conviction of two young boys for the murder of a toddler. The Court held that the failure to adopt procedures tailored to the age of the boys in terms of sitting hours and the court's layout, meant that the boys were unable to participate effectively in the proceedings. This in turn constituted a violation of their right to a fair hearing.[42]

5.2.3 The meaning given to the content of the rights in question

A substantive rights approach to matters concerning children demands an approach that is similar to the way in which feminism has demanded an interpretation of rights that is grounded in and reflects the experiences of women. In other words, courts must inform the content of a right by reference to the experiences of children. Thus, for example, when the European Court of Human Rights had to determine the nature and scope of the right to a fair hearing in *V v United Kingdom*, it considered

importance of children's rights to the issue. Had there been a procedural entitlement for children to receive separate representation it is likely, assuming the involvement of competent counsel, that the relevance of children's rights would have been raised at a much earlier stage in the proceedings.

[40] See Judy Cashmore and Patrick Parkinson, *The Voice of a Child in Family Law Disputes* (Oxford University Press USA, 2008); David Archard and Marit Skivens, 'Balancing a Child's Best Interests and a Child's Views' (2009) 17 *International Journal of Children's Rights* 1.

[41] (1999) 30 EHRR 121.

[42] Ibid 181.

the specific measures required to ensure the effective enjoyment of this right from the perspective of 10-year-old boys as opposed to adults. Similarly, when determining the content of the prohibition against inhuman and degrading treatment, as Baroness Hale of Richmond has noted, 'The European Court of Human Rights has taken particular note of the vulnerability of children in its judgments on the obligations of the state to protect people from inhuman and degrading treatment'.[43] Thus, for example, the European Court of Human Rights has held that the defence of reasonable chastisement did not provide a child with sufficient protection against inhuman and degrading treatment,[44] while a failure by authorities to respond to situations of prolonged neglect and abuse was also a violation of this right.[45]

5.2.4 The substantive reasoning adopted by courts to resolve legal issues that arise in cases concerning children

The final feature of a substantive rights approach concerns the reasoning adopted by a court in the resolution of the relevant legal issues. With respect to those matters where the paramountcy principle applies, such as adoption, as the England and Wales Court of Appeal held in *F and H (Children)*[46] this tends to mean that a child's best interests are 'more important than anything else' and the 'rights of adults are . . . subservient to those of the children'.[47] A substantive rights approach does not mean, however, that the rights and best interests of a child are the only consideration and it remains incumbent upon a court to adopt an inclusive approach whereby due consideration is given to the rights and interests of any other persons that may arise in the context of an issue in which a child's rights and best interests are paramount.[48]

This is exactly what the South African Constitutional Court did in *Du Toit & Anor v The Minister for Welfare and Population Development & Ors* (2003)[49] when it recognized that it was not only the best interests of children that were violated by a prohibition against persons in a same sex relationship from making a joint application for adoption. It also held that this prohibition was a violation of the constitutional right of the adults to equality before the law and protection against unfair discrimination on the basis of their sexual orientation.[50] But in relation to those matters in which a child's interests and rights are merely a primary consideration, a more sophisticated and nuanced balancing of the competing rights must be adopted. This balancing will be required in several different and potentially overlapping contexts. They include when there is a judicial dispute concerning: (i) a child and other children; (ii) a child

[43] *E v Chief Constable of the Royal Ulster Constabulary* [2009] 1 AC 536, 543.

[44] *A v United Kingdom* [1998] VI Eur Court HR 2692, 2699.

[45] *Z v United Kingdom* [2001] V Eur Court HR 1, 24–5; *E v United Kingdom* (2002) 36 EHRR 519, 523–8.

[46] [2007] EWCA Civ 880 (24 August 2008).

[47] Ibid [32] (Wall LJ).

[48] See comments of Sachs J in *S v M (Centre for Child Law as Amicus Curiae)* [2008] 3 SA 232, 249 [26] (Constitutional Court) ('*S v M*') with respect to the provision under the South African constitution, section 28(2) that the best interests of the child have paramount importance in every matter concerning a child ('the fact that the best interests of the child are paramount does not mean that they are absolute. Like all rights in the Bill of Rights their operation has to take account of their relationship with other rights, which might require that their ambit be limited').

[49] [2003] 2 SA 198, 207–8 (Skweyiya AJ for Chaskalson CJ, Langa DCJ, Ackermann, Goldstone, Kriegler, Madala, Ngcobo, O'Regan, Sachs JJ, Du Plessis, and Skweyiya AJJ).

[50] Ibid paras 208–9.

and his or her parents; (iii) a child, his or her parents, and the State; and (iv) a child and the State.

5.2.4.1 A dispute between children

In relation to the resolution of a dispute in which a child's claim to a right must be tempered against the rights of other children, the decision of the House of Lords in *R (on the application of Begum (by her litigation friend)) v Headteacher and Governors of Denbigh High School*[51] provides an example of how to resolve such a case consistently with a substantive rights approach. This matter involved a claim by a young girl that a ban on wearing the Islamic jilbab to her school was a violation of her right to freedom of religion. Although a majority of the Law Lords held there had been no interference with the girl's right, they still proceeded to assess whether the ban would have been reasonable in the circumstances. In concluding that this was the case, some members of the House of Lords placed significant emphasis on the fact that the school had adopted a consultative process in designing its school policy.[52] Importantly, this process enabled several students to express their concerns that if other students were allowed to wear the jilbab, this would place undue social pressure on them to do the same.[53] Thus, the reasonableness of the restriction was informed in part by the need to ensure that the students attending the school were also able to enjoy their effective right to freedom of religion—a decision that was also enabled by the fact that the student claiming the violation of her rights was able to attend other public schools that did not impose a restriction on the wearing of the jilbab.

The significance of this case to this analysis is that it demonstrates the need for courts to give careful consideration to rights of all those children in a dispute which may be of concern to them even in circumstances where they may not be directly involved in the proceedings. As to where the balance must ultimately be drawn by a court, this will depend on the facts of each case. The critical consideration however is the need for a court to give explicit and sensitive consideration to the competing interests of any children in a case.

5.2.4.2 A dispute concerning a child and his or her parents

The classic judicial dispute between a child and his or her parents concerns access to information relevant to family planning or medical procedures to terminate a pregnancy. In such matters, as the above discussion of cases such as *Gillick* demonstrates, courts must not treat children as merely an appendage of their parents to whom the interests of children would become entirely subservient. A substantive rights approach concedes that a child of insufficient maturity and understanding will remain dependent on his or her parents. Indeed, article 5 of the CRC effectively requires that a court, as a representative of the State, must respect the responsibilities, rights, and duties of parents to provide appropriate direction and guidance in the exercise of a child's rights. This responsibility, however, remains subject to the caveat that it must be exercised 'in a manner consistent with the evolving capacities of the child'. Thus, as the House of Lords determined in *Gillick*, a child of sufficient understanding and maturity has the capacity to enter into legal relationships without

[51] [2007] 1 AC 100.

[52] See ibid 117 [33] (Lord Bingham), 119, 125 (Lord Hoffmann), 135 [98] (Baroness Hale of Richmond).

[53] See ibid 125 [65] (Lord Hoffmann); 135 [98] (Baroness Hale of Richmond).

the consent of his or her parents—a position that has been endorsed in numerous jurisdictions by domestic courts.[54]

A grey zone exists, however, in those circumstances in which a child clearly expresses a view which is contrary to the wishes of his or her parents but lacks sufficient understanding and maturity for his or her views to be determinative of the issue. In such cases, a substantive rights approach demands that judges must apply the best interests principle in forming a decision. Importantly, the assessment of the child's best interests is not to be reduced to the views of the parents or indeed those of the presiding judicial officer. Instead the assessment of the child's best interests must involve a process that takes into account any available empirical evidence, the individual circumstance of a child, and the impact of a court's decision on the other rights to which a child is entitled under the CRC.

5.2.4.3 A dispute concerning a child, his or her parents, and the State

Judicial disputes which concern children, their parents, and the State tend to fall into two categories—those in which a child is the dominant subject of concern in the proceedings and those in which he or she is the secondary subject of concern. In relation to the first category this would include cases arising out of circumstances in which the State seeks to take measures to protect and secure the rights of children which are contested by certain parents. Measures to prohibit corporal punishment are an example of such a case. Although the lower courts in England in the case of *Williamson* did not conceptualize this issue in such terms, when the matter went before the House of Lords, Baroness Hale of Richmond was able to identify the interests of all three parties. Importantly, she did not fall into the trap of a superficial rights approach and simply declare that the ban on corporal punishment was lawful because it sought to advance the rights of children. Instead she carefully examined the rights of children and their parents which were relevant in the context of a prohibition of corporal punishment in schools and the role of the State in ensuring that an appropriate balance was struck between these rights. She therefore concluded that the ban on corporal punishment was a limitation on the right of the parents to manifest a belief that their children must be subject to such a practice.[55] But this interference was found to be justified because it pursued a legitimate aim, namely the protection of children's rights including their rights under the CRC.[56]

Importantly, a substantive rights approach does not demand that the balance must always favour the rights and interests of children in disputes which concern children, their parents, and the State. Indeed, in matters where children are the secondary as opposed to the primary subject of concern, there is always the prospect that the balance may favour the rights and interests of the other parties. The approach adopted by Justice Sachs of the South African Constitutional Court in *M v State* (2007) when dealing with the question of whether to imprison a primary caregiver of young children for criminal offences provides a good example of a matter where this may be the case.

The issue before the Constitutional Court was whether the requirement under the South African constitution that a child's best interests must be the paramount

[54] See, eg, *Secretary, Department of Health and Community Services v JWB* (1992) 175 CLR 218 ('*Marion's Case*'); *Re A* (1993) 16 Fam LR 715; *JSC v Wren* (1986) 35 DLR (4th) 419.

[55] *Williamson* [2005] 2 AC 246, 273 [78].

[56] Ibid 274 [80].

consideration in every matter affecting them, required greater consideration of children's rights in the sentencing process than had previously been the case. Justice Sachs, with whom the majority concurred, rejected the submission by the State that it was sufficient to consider the children of an offender as merely a 'personal circumstance' of a defendant to be taken into account in sentencing.[57] Instead he accepted that a child of a primary caregiver is an individual whose interests need to be considered independently and balanced against all the varied interests involved.[58] Importantly, Justice Sachs did not suggest that this balancing exercise would always favour the imposition of a non-custodial sentence on a primary caregiver. Indeed, he explained that '[a] balancing exercise has to be undertaken on a case-by-case basis' in which the State's legitimate interest in punishing offenders, not only the interests of a child, must be given appropriate consideration.[59] On the facts of the case Justice Sachs ultimately decided to suspend the term of imprisonment originally imposed by the lower courts on a mother of three children and place her on a correctional order with various conditions. But it was the 'new way of thinking' that Justice Sachs advocated rather than the outcome that has led to this case being cited in jurisdictions around the world.

5.2.4.4 A dispute concerning a child and the State

The final category of judicial dispute in which children typically tend to be involved concerns those matters where there is a dispute between a child and the State. The most common example of such a dispute is when children are subject to criminal law proceedings. But it may also arise in other circumstances such as an attempt by a student to resist the imposition of, for example, a curfew or restrictions on a child's freedom of expression in schools, deportation proceedings, exclusion from school, or the wearing and/or carrying of religious symbols in schools.

The adoption of a substantive rights approach in the reasoning adopted by judges to resolve such disputes demands that they must proceed on the basis that children have rights and conceptualize the issue in terms of these rights. Once it is established that an interference with these rights has occurred, judges must perform a proportionality analysis to assess carefully whether the interference or limitation with the relevant rights are justified.[60] Under the model of children's rights which is based on the CRC, justification will be established when the limitation is undertaken in pursuit of a legitimate aim and the measures to achieve this aim are reasonable and proportionate in all the circumstances.[61] Importantly, the assessment as to the necessity of a limitation must be made on the basis of objective considerations and the burden of justification will lie with the State which must use no more restrictive means than are required for the achievement of the purpose of the limitation.[62]

[57] The existing approach to sentencing in South Africa was based on what is referred to as the '*Zinn* triad'—a model which considers the nature of the crime, the circumstances of the criminal, and the broader interests of the community.

[58] *S v M* [2008] 3 SA 232, 250 [30] (Constitutional Court).

[59] Ibid [37].

[60] For a discussion in relation to the doctrine of proportionality, see Richard Clayton and Hugh Tomlinson, *The Law of Human Rights* (Oxford University Press, 2000) 278–303.

[61] This formula represents a summary of the various steps required under *The Siracusa Principles on the Limitation and Derogation Provisions in the International Covenant on Civil and Political Rights*, UN ESCOR, 41st sess, Annex, [12], UN Doc E/CN.4/1985/4 (1984) [10].

[62] Ibid [11]–[12].

The judicial treatment of curfews within the USA provides a good illustration of the impact on a court's reasoning when it demands that a State provide objective evidence in support of its interference with children's rights to equality before the law and freedom of movement. Although curfews are common within many States in the USA they have generally been upheld when challenged in the courts. The exception to this trend was the decision of the US Court of Appeals for the Second Circuit in *Ramos v Town of Vernon* (2003).[63] Here the Court was not prepared to simply accept at face value the submissions of the authorities that the curfew was necessary to achieve aims such as a reduction in juvenile crime, the protection of the general public, and the protection of young people themselves. The court stressed 'the unreliability of assumptions and generalizations as justification for laws infringing on the constitutional rights of minors'[64] and sought to interrogate the authorities further and demand that evidence be provided in support of the claim that a curfew would achieve these aims. When no such evidence could be tendered—the court observed that there was 'a conspicuous lack of relationship between the contours of the problem identified by the Vernon Town Council and the curfew ordinance enacted in response'[65]—the curfew was held to be unconstitutional.

5.3 Courts' engagement with a rights based approach

5.3.1 An invisible rights approach

Not all courts adopt a substantive rights approach when dealing with matters that concern children. Indeed, the extent to which they do so can be located along a spectrum which ranges from the non-existent ('invisible rights approach') to the substantive rights approach with the following approaches in between—incidental, selective, rhetorical, and superficial. I have explained these approaches in detail elsewhere[66] and it is sufficient to note here that under an invisible rights approach, courts fail to identify the relevance of rights to any aspect of the proceedings and instead adopt an approach that conforms to the proprietary or welfare models.

5.3.2 An incidental rights approach

Under an incidental rights approach, children's rights are identified as being relevant but not essential to the conceptualization or resolution of the issues before a court. For example, the Canadian Case of *VM v British Columbia (Director of Child, Family and Community Service)*[67] involved a challenge to a blood transfusion for two infants whose parents were members of the Jehovah's Witness Church. The court identified the relevance of an infant's right to life but this concern was only incidental and the case was ultimately said to 'lie at the intersection of the rights and responsibility of parents to make sound health care decisions for their children and the duty . . . of the state to override that right in appropriate circumstances'.[68]

[63] 353 F 3d 171, 176–81 (Cardamone J for Cardamone and Sack JJ) (2nd Cir, 2003).

[64] Ibid 181 [30]. [65] Ibid 186 [7].

[66] See John Tobin, 'Judging the Judges: Are they Adopting the Rights Approach in Matters Involving Children?' (2009) 33 *Melbourne University Law Review* 579.

[67] 2008 BCSC 449 (13 June 2008). [68] Ibid [1].

5.3.3 A selective rights approach

A selective rights approach occurs when a court makes significant rather than incidental references to children's rights to inform or defend its resolution of the issues. However, it is selective in the sense that the analysis offered is not grounded in a comprehensive and internally coherent application of a rights based approach. A good illustration of this approach is the decision of the US Supreme Court in *Roper v Simmons*. The court held that the imposition of the death penalty on a person below the age of 18 was a form of cruel and unusual punishment and thus unconstitutional. In forming its decision the majority of the court drew on international law and the provisions of international instruments such as the CRC to confirm its position as to the illegality of the death penalty for children.[69] Remarkably, however, although the US Supreme Court thought it proper to embrace the first limb of article 37(a) of the CRC which prohibits the death penalty for juveniles, it overlooked the second limb of this provision which prohibits life imprisonment for children without the possibility of release. The adoption of such a selective approach to children's rights weakens the rigour of the court's decision and lends support to those who criticize recourse to international standards in domestic forums as a form of 'smorgasbording' whereby judges select only those standards that will confirm their position.[70]

5.3.4 A rhetorical rights approach

A rhetorical rights approach represents the dilemma that confronts courts as they seek to move from a welfare approach to a rights based approach. It is best illustrated in the context of matters which involve an attempt by a child to refuse medical treatment. The decision of the House of Lords in *Gillick* may have ushered in the idea of a rights based approach within common law jurisdictions. But it has been suggested that the application of this test, and similar versions which have been adopted in other jurisdictions, can be used to cloak paternalistic decisions regarding treatment of children in the rhetoric of their rights.[71] Potter, for example, has argued that courts have regularly held children to be competent in the context of access to contraceptive advice and abortions but repeatedly denied their competency when they seek to refuse life saving treatment despite evidence to suggest that the children in question are fully aware of the consequences of their decision.[72] Such an approach is termed the 'rhetorical rights approach' because it embraces the rhetoric of rights to the extent that children are told that their autonomy will be respected when in truth a welfarist approach model is adopted by a judge.

[69] *Roper v Simmons* 543 US 551, 578 [22]–[23].

[70] See, eg, Justice Antonin Scalia and Justice Stephen Breyer, 'The Relevance of Foreign Legal Materials in US Constitutional Cases: A Conversation between Justice Antonin Scalia and Justice Stephen Breyer' (2005) 3 *International Journal of Constitutional Law* 519, 521–2.

[71] Michael Freeman, 'Rethinking *Gillick*' (2005) 13 *International Journal of Children's Rights* 201, 206–8, 211–12; Melinda T. Derish and Kathleen Vanden Heuvel, 'Mature Minors Should Have the Right to Refuse Life-Sustaining Medical Treatment' (2000) 28 *Journal of Law, Medicine and Ethics* 109, 112–13.

[72] Jamie Potter, 'Rewriting the Competency Rules for Children: Full Recognition of the Young Person as Rights-Bearer' (2006) 14 *Journal of Law and Medicine* 64, 67.

5.3.5 The superficial approach

Finally, the superficial rights approach involves a court identifying the central relevance of children's rights to the issues to be decided but then fails to consider the actual scope and nature of the rights in question and/or fails to undertake a rigorous assessment as to the manner in which such rights must be balanced against any competing considerations. The decision of the International Court of Justice (ICJ) in the 2005 case *Armed Activities on the Territory of the Congo (Democratic Republic of Congo v Uganda)*[73] ('*Armed Activities Case*') provides an example of this approach. The ICJ had before it 'convincing evidence of the training in UPDF training camps of child soldiers and the UPDF's failure to prevent the recruitment of child soldiers in areas under its control'.[74] This in turn gave rise to a question as to whether Uganda had failed in its obligations with respect to the recruitment of child soldiers under international law. In addressing this concern the ICJ recited all the human rights and humanitarian law instruments to which the States were party.[75] It then listed the specific provisions of these instruments which Uganda was alleged to have violated and concluded that the UPDF 'did not take measures to ensure respect for human rights and humanitarian law in the occupied territories'.[76]

At no stage, however, did the ICJ engage in any substantive analysis as to the content and scope of the international obligations concerning child soldiers which Uganda had assumed.[77] It simply decided that the relevant instruments had been violated in light of evidence as to the training and recruitment of children. The facts may well have justified the ICJ's findings but its 'oracular'[78] tendencies create a void in its reasoning that undermines the legitimacy of its decision and provides an illustration of a superficial rights approach in judicial reasoning. This approach can be legitimately criticized for the quality of its reasoning. Moreover, in this case the ICJ did have jurisdiction to examine whether children's rights under international law had been violated but it failed to adopt a substantive rights approach. However, other courts may well be constrained by various factors in their ability to engage with this new way of thinking. The legitimacy of these constraints will be examined in the final part of this chapter.

[73] General List No 116 (Unreported, International Court of Justice, 19 December 2005).

[74] Ibid [210]. [75] Ibid [217]. [76] Ibid [211].

[77] More specifically its consideration of the evidence with respect to the training and recruitment of children was dissociated from the actual content of the provisions of Additional Protocols I and II to the Geneva Conventions, the Convention on the Rights of the Child, art 38 and the Optional Protocol on the Involvement of Children in Armed Conflict, none of which impose an absolute prohibition on the recruitment of children. See Protocol Additional to the Geneva Conventions of 12 August 1949, and Relating to the Protection of Victims of International Armed Conflicts (Protocol I), opened for signature 8 June 1977, 1125 UNTS 3, arts 77(2)–(3) (entered into force 7 December 1978) ('Additional Protocol I'); Protocol Additional to the Geneva Conventions of 12 August 1949, and Relating to the Protection of Victims of Non-International Armed Conflicts (Protocol II), opened for signature 8 June 1977, 1125 UNTS 611, arts 4(3)(c)–(d) (entered into force 7 December 1978) ('Additional Protocol II').

[78] See Antonio Cassese, 'The *Nicaragua* and *Tadić* Tests Revisited in Light of the ICJ Judgment on Genocide in Bosnia' (2007) 18 *European Journal of International Law* 649, 651, which argues with respect to *Application of the Convention on the Prevention and Punishment of the Crime of Genocide (Bosnia and Herzegovina v Serbia and Montenegro) (Merits)*, General List No 91 (Unreported, International Court of Justice, 26 February 2007) that 'the reader expecting a closely-argued decision will be left instead with the impression that the Court's holdings have a tinge of oracularity (oracles indeed are not required to give reasons)'.

5.4 The capacity of courts to engage with a substantive rights approach

A number of factors influence the level of engagement by courts with a rights based approach. These include the nature of the proceedings, procedural considerations,[79] and the capacity of lawyers to make submissions based on the rights of a child. Space does not permit a detailed discussion of these matters. Instead attention will be focused on two key factors that impact on the capacity of a court to adopt a rights approach—the existence of institutional constraints or opportunities to adopt this approach *and* the preparedness of a court to adopt an interpretative theory that embraces the notion of children as rights bearers.

5.4.1 The existence of institutional constraints and opportunities

Although nearly all States have ratified the CRC, in many jurisdictions the domestic legislative framework in relation to matters concerning children is still dominated by the welfare model. This represents a potentially serious institutional constraint on the extent to which courts can engage with a new way of thinking about children given that courts must interpret and apply the existing law. At the same time, the extent of this constraint should not be overestimated as an increasing number of States have adopted constitutions which actually recognize the rights of children and thus demand a consideration of these rights.[80] South Africa is an example of such a State. Indeed, it is for this reason that Justice Sachs in *M v State* declared that 'courts must function in a manner which at all times shows due respect for children's rights'.[81] As a consequence, far from operating as an institutional constraint, the domestic legal system in South Africa mandates that courts adopt a substantive rights approach in matters involving children.

But even in those jurisdictions where there is no constitutional or legislative protection of children's rights, there remains the potential for courts to adopt a construction of childhood that is consistent with a rights based approach. This is because the process of adjudication does not simply involve the identification and mechanistic application of the law to the facts in a case. Instead, as commentators such as Dworkin and Waldron have argued, an element of moral reasoning informs every aspect of the adjudicative process[82]—how a dispute is conceptualized, the procedures adopted, the content of each right, and where the balance is ultimately drawn between competing rights. When that moral reasoning is informed by the values that underpin a rights based approach, a court may be able to adopt decisions which conform to the *values* underlying this model despite the absence of express authority to do so.

There will of course be limits with respect to how far this model can be pursued by a judge. As Waldron has explained, the moral reasoning of judges is, in contrast to pure moral reasoning, constrained by legal precedents and/or legislative imperatives that cannot necessarily be swept aside. Judges are not free to 'drop inconvenient

[79] For example, whether the proceedings are initiated by adults or concern children directly and whether the system provides children with a right to representation.

[80] See generally John Tobin, above n 34, 110–15.

[81] *S v M* [2008] 3 SA 232, 244 [15] (Constitutional Court).

[82] Jeremy Waldron, 'Judges as Moral Reasoners' (2009) 7 *International Journal of Constitutional Law* 2, 12; Ronald Dworkin, *Law's Empire* (Belknap Press Cambridge Mass, 1986) 238–58.

lines of precedent or modify propositions embodied in authoritative texts'.[83] Or to borrow the words of Dworkin, the task of a judge is not 'to plant the flag of his [or her own moral] convictions over as large a domain of power or rules as possible'.[84] It is also true that in the absence of any form of express rights protection within a State, constitutional or otherwise, it is more difficult for a judge to justify the adoption of a substantive rights approach.

At the same time, courts are not completely precluded from the adoption of such an approach. As Dworkin has explained, 'the dynamics of interpretation *resist* as well as promote convergence' (emphasis added) and 'the centrifugal forces are particularly strong where the profession as well as the larger community is divided over justice'.[85] In other words, where there are competing visions of how to deliver just outcomes for children, there is more potential for judges to adopt a vision that represents a departure from the orthodox or established vision. With respect to the treatment of children, the historical insistence on the welfare model has been increasingly challenged by the rise of rights discourse as the most appropriate model to secure just outcomes for children. Indeed, it has been suggested by commentators that 'children's rights have…become perhaps the dominant programme within a social system which makes sense of the adult/child relationship'[86] and that advocacy for international children's rights is 'one of the most powerful social movements of the twentieth century'.[87] Although it remains debatable as to whether the status of children's rights has reached such a zenith, it is difficult to resist the argument that this concept has now taken a firm rooting in what Dworkin would describe as the 'general intellectual environment' in which judges think about the process of adjudication.[88]

Historically this environment, defined first through a prism of property rights and then welfarism, would have imposed a real and significant constraint on the capacity of judges to engage with a substantive rights approach when dealing with matters concerning children. The emergence of children's rights, however, provides an increasing opportunity for courts that engage with this model to occupy what Dworkin might describe as the 'cutting edge' of interpretation as opposed to offering idiosyncratic ramblings.[89] So while a court entertaining the idea of a child having rights may once have been considered heretical, shifting social values mean that this is no longer the case. A question remains, however, as to when and why a court would develop an interpretative theory in which the moral reasoning it adopts in the resolution of a dispute concerning a child will resist a traditional welfare model in favour of a rights based approach. It is to this final issue that I now turn.

5.4.2 Judicial receptivity to an interpretative theory that embraces the notion of children as rights bearers

Divergence amongst judges with respect to their engagement with the notion of children as rights bearers should not come as a surprise. It reflects Dworkin's observation that 'each judge's interpretative theories are grounded in his (sic) own convictions'[90] and the reality that 'Judges think about law…within society, not apart

[83] Waldron, above n 82, 13. [84] Dworkin, above n 82, 211. [85] Ibid 88.

[86] Michael King, 'The Child, Childhood and Children's Rights within Sociology' (2004) 15 *King's College Law Journal* 273, 275.

[87] Jude Fernando, 'Children's Rights: Beyond the Impasse' (2001) 575 *The Annals of the American Academy of Political and Social Science* 8, 10.

[88] Dworkin above n 82, 88. [89] Ibid. [90] Ibid 87.

from it'.[91] It therefore follows that in a general intellectual environment where the idea of children's rights is competing with alternative models of how best to deal with children, such pluralism will also be reflected in the construction of children by courts. Some judges will actively embrace the notion of children as rights bearers whereas others will be less familiar with or receptive to the model and lack the capacity or preparedness to apply it to the resolution of disputes involving children.

With respect to the treatment of children's rights by courts in the United Kingdom, for example, Fortin has identified 'a judicial ambivalence' over the extent to which courts are required to articulate matters concerning children in terms of their rights.[92] Even Justice Sachs himself admitted that his first inclination in the case of *M v State* was not to conceive of the issues in terms of the rights of the children. Thus, there is a degree of randomness in the extent to which courts engage with this new way of thinking. At the same time Sloth-Neilsen and Mezmur have observed that within the South African context, the trend towards 'the individual pre-disposition of some judges to raise children's rights *mero motu*' is linked to 'their prior history in the children's rights movement, some having participated in early conferences which shaped the drafting of the constitutional clause on children's rights'[93] under the South African Constitution.

The significance of this observation is that judicial engagement with elements of a substantive rights approach is assisted by prior exposure to the values that underpin this model. Although this is hardly a remarkable finding it tends to confirm the relevance of the recommendations which are repeatedly made by the CRC Committee that States provide training and education to judges in relation to children's rights.[94] Indeed, Sloth-Nielsen and Mezmur have noted in the context of South Africa that it was 'not unwarranted to mention that various training initiatives may already be showing an impact in the jurisprudence emanating from the courts'.[95] This tends to confirm the need for and benefit of training judges about children's rights as a way of shaping the framework of moral reasoning and interpretative theory they apply when resolving a case in a way that is consistent with the various dimensions of a substantive rights approach. It also affirms the important role of procedures which enable the rights of children to be brought to the attention of judges and the role of lawyers using those procedures to contribute to judges' awareness and understanding of children's rights.[96]

[91] Ibid 88. [92] Jane Fortin, above n 29, 305.

[93] Julia Sloth-Nielsen and Benyam D Mezmur, '2 + 2 = 5? Exploring the Domestication of the *CRC* in South African Jurisprudence (2002–2006)' (2008) 16 *International Journal of Children's Rights* 1, 3–4.

[94] See *General Comment No 5*, above n 27, [53]. Chief Justice Nicholson also confirmed the impact of education in exposing judges to new 'vistas' on various issues and allowing judges to recognize their own innate prejudices. He lamented, however, that judicial education about children's issues in the Australian context has been 'rudimentary': email from Chief Justice Alastair Nicholson to John Tobin, 16 February 2009.

[95] Sloth-Nielsen and Mezmur, above n 93, 27.

[96] See ibid (concluding, with respect to the increasing visibility of children's rights in the decisions of South African courts, that 'substantial credit must go to public interest litigators... for bringing children's interests to the fore in judicial proceedings'); Guggenheim, above n 20, 8 (observing that the most important legacy of the decision of the US Supreme Court in *Re Gault*, which was inspired by the submissions of lawyers, was 'the elevation of the prominence of lawyers in leading the modern children's rights movement').

5.5 Conclusion

In a recent case before the United Kingdom Supreme Court involving a challenge to a deportation of a child, Baroness Hale discussed the duty of courts to ensure the participation of children in such proceedings. She concluded with the observation that:

Children can sometimes surprise one.[97]

It may be a simple and short sentence but it is deeply embedded with a challenge to the traditional paradigms that have marked the construction of childhood by courts. No longer are adults to be the sole repository of wisdom and insight when it comes to the determination of a child's best interests. On the contrary children's voices must play an active role in this assessment. Indeed, Baroness Hale's commitment to hear and listen to children's voices provides the perfect bookend to Justice Sachs' commitment to see and consider the rights of children in matters where once they were invisible and ignored. Together, these sentiments underlie a new way of thinking for courts in which children, when conceived of as rights holders, are both seen and heard. This new way of thinking will prove challenging to some members of courts who are unable or unwilling to disenthrall themselves from a construction of childhood that is wedded to the proprietary or welfare model. But there is every indication that with the emergence and continued expansion of the idea of children's rights within social and political discourse,[98] this development will both inspire and be inspired by those courts which are prepared to *listen to and see* children in ways that have previously been overlooked.

[97] *Tanzania* [2011] 2 WLR 148, 163 [37].

[98] See generally Anna Holzscheiter, *Children's Rights in International Politics: The Transformative Power of Discourse* (Macmillan USA, 2010); John Wall, *Ethics in Light of Childhood* (Georgetown University Press, Washington DC, 2010).

6

Childhood, the United Nations Convention on the Rights of the Child, and Research: What Constitutes a 'Rights-Based' Approach?

Laura Lundy and Lesley McEvoy

6.1 Introduction

The United Nations Convention on the Rights of the Child[1] ('the CRC') makes no reference whatsoever to research or even to the need for information on the experiences of children within the signatory states. Nonetheless, 20 years after coming into force, the CRC has had a manifold impact on the focus and nature of childhood research. First, its main enforcement mechanism—periodic monitoring by the UN Committee on the Rights of the Child ('the Committee')—is heavily data-dependent. States are required to provide specified information at five-yearly intervals, as detailed in the Committee's guidelines for State Party reports.[2] While these data sets are often incomplete[3] and the Committee itself has recognized the lack of adequate national data,[4] it is inevitable that government-sponsored research throughout the signatory nations has been driven, at least in part, by their reporting obligations under the CRC.[5] The Committee has encouraged states to 'collaborate with appropriate research institutes and aim to build up a complete picture of progress towards implementation, with qualitative as well as quantitative data'.[6] Paralleling this, non-governmental organizations are increasingly undertaking research projects which 'challenge government assumptions'[7] and thus aid the alternative reporting

[1] United Nations (1989) United Nations Convention on the Rights of the Child Geneva: United Nations.

[2] United Nations Committee on the Rights of the Child (2010), *Treaty Specific Guidelines Regarding the Form and Content of Periodic Reports to be submitted by States parties under Article 44, paragraph 1(b) of the Convention on the Rights of the Child, CRC/C/58*, Geneva, United Nations.

[3] U. Kilkelly and L. Lundy, 'The Convention on the Rights of the Child: Its Use as an Auditing Tool' 2006 18(3) *Child and Family Law Quarterly* 331–50.

[4] United Nations Committee on the Rights of the Child, (2003) General Comment No. 5, General Measures of Implementation (CRC/C/GC/12). Geneva: United Nations, p. 19.

[5] P. Alderson (2008) 'Children as Researchers: Participation Rights and Research Methods' in P. Christensen and A. James (eds) *Research with Children: Perspectives and Practices* (2nd edition) London: Falmer Press, pp. 276–90.

[6] N. 4, above, 48.

[7] J. McKechnie and S. Hobbs (2004) 'Relevance, Evaluation and Dissemination: Childhood Studies' in S. Fraser et al (eds) *Doing Research with Children and Young People*, London: Sage, p. 273.

procedure which is a core component of the monitoring process for the CRC.[8] Moreover, not only has there been increasing recognition of the impact of CRC's monitoring mechanisms on research *agendas*, there is also a growing interest in the implications of the CRC's standards for research *processes*, for example in determining research questions and choosing methods.

The relationship between the CRC and research might be characterized therefore in a variety of ways, including: research that relates to children's rights (i.e. sheds light on an issue covered in the CRC); research about children's rights (that sets out directly to investigate the extent to which there is compliance with the CRC); research processes which are designed to be participatory (and are thus implementing, in particular, Articles 12 and 13 of the CRC); and research whose ethical frameworks are guided by CRC standards. The latter two have received most attention in academic discussions of childhood research, with several commentators having acknowledged the significance of CRC standards for participatory research with children[9] and ethical approaches to childhood research.[10] In particular, Ennew and Plateau[11] suggest that Article 12(1), Article 13(1), Article 33, and Article 36 have direct implications for research, in that: children's perspectives must be integral to the research; research methods employed must allow the child to express these perspectives freely; research must be conducted to the highest possible scientific standards; and children must not be exploited or harmed in any way during the entire research process. Combining these principles with the basic human rights principles of dignity and respect, they conclude that the child's 'right to be properly researched' is implicit in the CRC.[12]

In spite of the growing recognition of the implications of the principles of the CRC for research with children, nowhere in the existing academic literature has there been discussion of what it might mean for childhood research to be explicitly *rights-based*. The term 'rights-based' is often used broadly to describe activities which have a connection to international human rights standards, a defensible assertion since any activity which draws on these frameworks might legitimately be styled as rights-based. However, the concept carries a particular meaning and significance within established human rights discourse—one that has rarely been explored in the literature on childhood research.[13] The aim of this chapter, therefore, is to add to the discussion about the relationship between the CRC and childhood research through exploring what the application of a 'human rights-based approach', as commonly understood in the international human rights community, would mean if implemented systematically in the context of research with children. The implications of this are explored in relation to the three key chronological research stages:

[8] Children's Rights Alliance for England (2008) UK Implementation of the UN Convention on the Rights of the Child, England. Alternative Report to the UN Committee on the Rights of the Child, London, CRAE.

[9] P. Alderson (2008) n. 5, above; K. Winter (2010) 'The Perspectives of Young Children in Care and Implications for Social Work Practice', 15(2) *Child and Family Social Work*, 186–95.

[10] P. Alderson and V. Morrow (2011) *The Ethics of Research with Children and Young People: a practical handbook* London: Sage.

[11] J. Ennew and D. P. Plateau (2004) *How to Research the Physical and Emotional Punishment of Children* Bangkok: Keen Publishing (Thailand) Co., Ltd, International Save the Children Southeast, East Asia and Pacific Region Alliance.

[12] H. Beazley, S. Bessell, J. Ennew, and R. Waterson (2009) 'Editorial: the Right to be Properly Researched—Research with Children in a Messy, Real World' 7(4) *Children's Geographies* 365–78

[13] See L. Lundy and L. McEvoy (2009) 'Developing Outcomes for Educational Services: a Children's Rights-based Approach' 1(1) *Effective Education* 43–60 for an example of our initial attempt to engage the 'rights-based approach' as understood by the international human rights community.

framing, conducting, and disseminating children's rights-based research. However, before drawing out the features of such research, it is necessary to define first what it is we understand by the term 'rights-based'.

6.2 What does 'rights-based' research mean?

As noted above, the term 'rights-based' is used broadly to describe work influenced by the international human rights standards. However, these standards are in effect a legal articulation of a broader philosophical perspective. Therefore in order to understand more fully the meaning of the term 'rights-based' it is necessary to step behind the standards into the paradigm in which they are located: the concepts embedded within human rights discourse relating to the nature, source, and content of human rights and the processes through which these rights are realized. One such concept is what Dworkin has referred to as 'the vague but powerful idea of human dignity',[14] an idea recognized generally as central to contemporary conceptions of human rights[15] and an underpinning value of international human rights law.[16] The implication of this is that, from a human rights perspective, all human beings should be treated with a 'profound moral respect',[17] based on the inherent value of each individual. However, human rights are more than the values or aspirations that underpin them. What distinguishes human rights discourse from other moral discourses is that it 'draws our attention to the persons who have *rightful entitlements*'[18] and places concomitant obligations on the duty-bearer,[19] the state,[20] to respect the right-holders' enjoyment of their rights, to protect against deprivation, and to aid those whose rights have been violated.[21] Moreover, human rights, as codified in international human rights standards, provide the state, as duty-bearer, with both a moral standard and an international political benchmark of legitimacy against which to judge its actions.[22] Thus, within the human rights paradigm, the realization of a life of dignity is achieved through providing human rights standards to which the state is accountable and by empowering the individual to claim these rights. As Donnelly states:

> Human rights authorize and empower citizens to act to vindicate their rights; to insist that [human rights] standards be realized; to struggle to create a world in which they enjoy (the object of) their rights. Human rights claims express not merely aspirations, suggestions, requests, or laudable ideas, but rights-based demands for change.[23]

[14] R. Dworkin (1978) *Taking Rights Seriously* Cambridge MA: Harvard University Press, p. 198.

[15] F. Klug (2000) *Values for a Godless Age: The Story of the UKs New Bill of Rights* London: Penguin; J. Donnelly (2007) *International Human Rights* Colorado: Westview.

[16] P. Alston (1998) 'The Universal Declaration in a Era of Globalization' in B. van der Heijden and B. Tahzib-Lie (eds.), *Reflections on the Universal Declaration of Human Rights: A Fiftieth Anniversary Anthology* The Hague: Martinus Nijhoff.

[17] J. Mahoney (2007) *The Challenge of Human Rights: Origin, Development and Significance* Oxford: Blackwell, p. 146.

[18] M. Freeman (2002) *Human Rights* Cambridge: Polity, p. 61.

[19] C. Beitz (2009) *The Idea of Human Rights* Oxford: Oxford University Press.

[20] J. Donnelly (2007) *International Human Rights* (3rd edition) Cambridge MA: Westview Press, p. 28.

[21] H. Shue (1996) *Basic Rights: Subsistence and Affluence in U.S. Foreign Policy* Princeton: Princeton University Press.

[22] N. 20, above, p. 23.

[23] J. Donnelly (2003) *Universal Human Rights in Theory and Practice* New York: Cornell University Press, p. 12.

Unsurprisingly these concepts underpin the United Nations' definition of a 'human rights-based approach' as articulated in its Statement of Common Understanding[24] ('the Statement'). The Statement outlines three core principles which should guide a human rights-based approach (HRBA), summarized as follows: (i) activity should further the realization of human rights; (ii) human rights standards should guide all phases of activity; and (iii) activity should contribute to the development of the capacities of duty-bearers to meet their obligations and of rights-holders to claim their rights.[25] While this document set out to clarify what a HRBA meant in the context of development cooperation and development programming by UN agencies, its core principles have been deemed essential characteristics of human rights-based approaches more generally and have since been adopted as guiding principles for HRBAs by UN agencies and non-governmental organizations, for example in work with children[26] and in contexts such as education.[27] Moreover, in addition to the core principles, the Statement sets out a number of elements of good programming practices that are also essential under a HRBA,[28] including *inter alia* that: people are recognized as key actors in their own development; participation is both a means and a goal; strategies are empowering; and analysis includes all stakeholders. According to the Statement, these core principles and aspects of 'good practice' should apply to all aspects of developing programming, including the initial research carried out to inform planning, that is to assess the 'immediate, underlying, and structural causes of the non-realization of rights'.[29] The aspects of good practice evident in such an approach to research[30] are clearly transferrable into other contexts where a HRBA is sought, particularly in relation to the participation and empowerment of rights-holders.

We would suggest that the Statement, which is in essence a practical articulation of the concepts central to human rights discourse, offers a distinctive and potentially valuable framework for reflecting on the nature and conduct of *childhood research*. Central to the implementation of this are the dedicated children's rights standards contained in the CRC which not only provide a framework for research aims and questions, but also a blueprint for the treatment of children generally, and in particular their participation in all aspects of the research process. Thus, we would suggest that, applying the HRBA principles to research with children means that in a *children's rights-based approach to research*: the research aims should be informed by the CRC standards; the research process should comply with the CRC standards; and the research outcomes should build the capacity of children, as rights-holders, to claim their rights and build the capacity of duty-bearers to fulfil their obligations. Cutting across all of this is a requirement to ensure that the process furthers the realization of children's rights.

[24] United Nations (2003) *Statement of common understanding on a human rights-based approach to development co-operation* Geneva: United Nations. This is sometimes referred to as the 'Stamford' statement.

[25] N. 24, above.

[26] Save the Children (2007) *Getting it Right for Children: A Practitioners' Guide to Child Rights Programming* London: Save the Children UK.

[27] UNICEF/UNESCO (2007) *A Human Rights-based Approach to Education for All* New York: UNICEF/UNESCO.

[28] N. 24, above.

[29] N. 24, above.

[30] The approach is most commonly applied in the context of research or situational analyses which are integral to international development work. See N. 26, above. However, there is no discussion of it in the academic literature on childhood research methods.

The following sections of the chapter explore what a children's rights-based approach might mean in research relating to children. In doing so, it draws on the authors' work across a number of research studies which sought to apply the principles of the CRC to research processes.[31] That said, we would not claim that our own work to date has been fully 'rights-based', in the sense defined by the UN Statement. Whilst we have to date described some elements of our research as 'rights-based' particularly in relation to the participation rights of children involved in our studies, a more accurate description of our research would be 'rights-informed' or 'rights-compliant'. Likewise, in the discussion which follows reference is made to a range of other research projects conducted by childhood scholars which, although they do not usually claim to be rights-based, include approaches and techniques which would be useful and relevant to those attempting to adopt a rights-based approach to research with children. The overall aim of the chapter is to explore the implications of adopting a rights-based approach to childhood research, by reflecting in its application within three key chronological stages of research activity: framing, conducting, and disseminating research.

6.3 Framing children's rights-based research

A key stage in any piece of research will be the overall design of the study including defining the research aims and objectives, determining the research questions, and from this establishing the nature and the content of the research instruments.[32] A children's rights-based approach to this stage of research requires foregrounding the principles noted above as the study is being *designed* in order to ensure that the *conduct* of the research is also rights-based.

6.3.1 Using children's rights standards to inform research design

Research questions guiding a children's rights-based research project should be framed towards investigating breaches or otherwise, of rights, *in the language of rights*. There are many examples of research projects which have set out *explicitly* to investigate compliance with children's rights standards. Somewhat understandably, since their statutory remit requires it, this includes all research conducted by the various children's commissioners in the United Kingdom.[33] Other examples beyond this Ombudsman-generated research are less apparent; however specific rights have been identified in

[31] These projects include: L. Lundy and L. McEvoy (2008) *E-consultation with Pupils* Bangor: Department of Education Northern Ireland, a project researching children's and teachers' views on a range of e-consultation mechanisms; S. Miller, L. Lundy, L. Maguire, L. McEvoy, and P. Connolly (2008) *Ready to Learn* Belfast: Centre for Effective Education, a project funded by Barnardos Northern Ireland, investigating the relationship between educational achievement, social disadvantage, and children's self reported well-being; C. Murphy, K. Kerr, L. Lundy, and L. McEvoy (2010) *Attitudes of Children and Parents to Science Assessment* London: Wellcome Trust; L. Lundy, L. McEvoy, and B. Byrne (2010) *Ready to Learn: Involving Children in Service Design* Belfast: Centre for Effective Education.

[32] A. Bryman (2008) *Social Research Methods* Oxford: Oxford University Press.

[33] See, for example, U. Kilkelly, R. Kilpatrick, L. Lundy, P. Scraton, L. Moore, C. Davey, C. Dwyer, and S. McAlister (2005) *Children's Rights in Northern Ireland* Belfast: Northern Ireland Commissioner for Children and Young People, pp. 340; Scotland's Commissioner for Children and Young People (2008) *Handle with Care* SCCYP, Edinburgh.

some projects,[34] most commonly in the area of children's participation where Article 12 has achieved a significant degree of recognition.[35] Even in instances where the relevance of the research to children's rights is claimed, the research questions themselves are not usually framed explicitly in the language of entitlement and obligation. Moreover a large body of research conducted in the area of childhood, including much research in the fields of education, health, and social work, while pertaining directly to children rights is not framed within these standards, as will be evident from the wide range of research projects highlighted throughout this chapter.

Translating such research questions into the language of children's rights is not overly complex and indeed is facilitated by the CRC itself. While the CRC was recognized from the outset as limited[36] and its gaps have become even more apparent with age,[37] it still provides a comprehensive and accessible framework which covers most aspects of children's lives.[38] Moreover, when the CRC standards are read along with the Committee's General Comments, the standards are elastic enough to address, even in the broadest sense, most aspects of children's lives. In education, for example, commonly researched issues such as educational attainment, bullying, curriculum content, participation in school life, and discipline are all clearly rights-based issues linking directly to specific CRC obligations and associated jurisprudence. Translating non-rights-based research questions into rights-based questions not only situates the research from the offset within the CRC standards, but also draws attention to both the relationship of the rights-holders and duty-bearers to the issue in question, ultimately clarifying the goal of the research: the further realization of children's rights.

In addition to framing the research within CRC standards, a children's rights-based approach to research, as noted above, requires building the capacity of rights-holders to claim rights and the capacity of duty-bearers to fulfil their obligations. For the former, that entails not only meaningful involvement in the determination of the questions but also a requirement to develop the children's understanding of their rights, discussed below.

6.3.2 Building the capacity of rights-holders to claim their rights

In research projects carried out by the authors, the children we have worked with as co-researchers in Children's Research Advisory Groups (CRAGs)[39] were made

[34] See, for example, R.C. Mitchell (2000) 'Implementing Children's Rights in British Columbia using the Population Health Framework' *International Journal of Children's Rights* 8, 333–49.

[35] See, for example, A. Osler (2010) *Students' Perspectives on Schooling* Maidenhead: Open University Press.

[36] M. Freeman (2000) 'The Future of Children's Rights' *Children and Society* 14, 277–93.

[37] P.E. Veerman (2010) 'The Ageing of the United Nations Convention on the Rights of the Child' 18(4) *International Journal of Children's Rights* 585–618.

[38] N. 3, above.

[39] In each of our projects we have established Children's Research Advisory Groups (CRAGs) to work with the research team at all stages of the research process. The children in the CRAGs are not research subjects but rather are invited to participate on the basis of their contemporary experience as a child in a similar peer group as the research participants. As such the remit of CRAGs is to advise on the research process including how best to engage with other children on the issues, and assisting with the analysis and interpretation of the findings from interviews with other children; to provide insight on the main issues under investigation; and to identify potential solutions which might address the problems. See L. Lundy and L. McEvoy (2009) 'Developing Outcomes for Education Services: a Children's Rights-based Approach' 1(1) *Effective Education* 43–60; L. McEvoy and L. Lundy (2007) 'E-consultation with Pupils—a Rights-based Approach to the Integration of Citizenship Education and ICT' 16(3) *Technology, Pedagogy and Education*

aware from the outset that our approach was children's rights-informed and that in particular their involvement in the research was based on CRC principles. In some circumstances the children we worked with attended a 'Rights Respecting School' and as such were fairly well versed in key aspects of children's rights.[40] In other circumstances the children were not as aware of the CRC and its implications for their involvement in the research. In these cases time was taken in initial meetings with the CRAGs to explain the nature of children's rights and how these rights were informing the research processes in the project.[41] Efforts were also made in our projects to ensure that the children involved as research participants understood their position as 'rights-holders' in relation to the substantive issues under investigation, through explaining who was funding the research and how the research findings could be used by the funder to lobby government. For example, in a project exploring children's attitudes to science assessment, the children involved were aware from the outset that the funders, the Wellcome Trust, would use the findings to influence future government decisions.

Having established an understanding of the nature of rights and entitlement, children should be meaningfully engaged in the development of the research questions and the specific items employed in research instruments. In an ideal situation this would be child-led. There are many examples of innovative and empowering child-led research projects, from which principles of good practice in children's rights-based research could be drawn. For example Mary Kellett's work[42] positions children as active researchers, where they do not merely receive training in the research skills required for the specific project in which they are involved, but rather 'receive in depth training in generic research process so that they can apply, from the outset their knowledge and skills to the initial choice of research question, design and method'. This, she argues, allows children to set their own research agendas and generates knowledge with 'minimal adult filters'.[43]

The reality of many research projects, though, is that the research questions are established by research funders. Even so, there should still be scope for children's meaningful engagement. For example, in one of our projects[44] the research questions were clearly defined, focusing primarily on children's experience of and attitudes towards science assessment. However, within this set of research questions, the children involved in the CRAGs were able to develop specific questions for the research instrument that reflected the issues they had identified as salient to the research project: questions relating to the impact of assessment on family life and

305–20; L. Lundy, L. McEvoy, and B. Byrne (2011) 'Working with Young Children as Co-researchers: an Approach Informed by the United Nations Convention on the Rights of the Child' 22(5) *Early Education and Development* 714–36

[40] L. Lundy and L. McEvoy, N. 31, above, Miller et al, N. 31, above.

[41] See C. Murphy et al, N. 31, above. For another example of a research project where children's knowledge and the understanding of the CRC was explicitly developed see U. Kilkelly, R. Kilpatrick, L. Lundy, L. Moore, P. Scraton, C. Davey, C. Dwyer, and S. McAllister (2004) *Children's Rights in Northern Ireland* Northern Ireland Commissioner for Children and Young People.

[42] M. Kellett (2010) *Rethinking Children and Research: Attitudes in Contemporary Society* London: Continuum; M. Kellett (2005) *Children as Active Researchers: A New Research Paradigm for the 21st Century?* Methods Review Papers: ESRC National Centre for Research Methods; M. Kellett (2005) *How to Develop Children as Researchers: A Step by Step Guide to Teaching the Research Process* London: Paul Chapman Publishing.

[43] M. Kellett (2010) 'Small steps, Big steps! Empowering Children as Active Researchers' *American Journal of Community Psychology* 46, 195–203, 201

[44] See C. Murphy et al, N. 31, above.

friendship etc. While the children involved in this project were between 10 and 12 years old, age should not be a determining factor in relation to children's involvement in developing the focus of questions to be asked in a study. In our experience, even very young children can shape the research instrument. In a project funded by Barnardos Northern Ireland,[45] a leading children's charity, we were commissioned to engage in research with Primary 1 children (age 4–5) to explore the features of an out-of-school-hours service aimed at raising the educational attainment of children living in socially disadvantaged areas. The key research questions, set by the funder, were: What do Primary 1 children find hard about school? What would help them in an after-school club? The research team worked with a CRAG to develop research strategies to engage research participants meaningfully in the study. We developed a number of activities to help the CRAG think through what children their age might 'like about school', and also what they might 'find hard about school'. Following these activities, their most common suggestions were used to develop a picture survey which was used subsequently with the research participants, that is, other Primary 1 children. Since the images used for this activity were selected in light of discussion with the CRAG, the children had a direct influence on the questions and focus of the research, thus foregrounding the children's views and giving the CRAG a direct input into choosing main items in the research instrument.

6.3.3 Building the capacity of duty-bearers to fulfil their obligations

The determination of research questions offers an opportunity to frame the research in ways that can inform duty-bearers about the nature of the relevant rights and their obligations. For example, in the 'Ready to Learn' project,[46] the funders had commissioned a large scale baseline survey to ascertain the relationship between educational attainment, social disadvantage, and children's self-reported well-being. The research findings were to be used to design an educational intervention with specified outcomes for children: improved relationships with peers and school personnel; more pro-social behaviour; improved mental and physical health; and improved levels of engagement (such as attendance at school) as well as related outcomes for parents, schools, and communities. These outcomes were subjected to an audit against the children's rights standards in the CRC and the related commentary of the Committee. The audit not only assisted in articulating the potential outcomes of the intervention within a children's rights framework but also clearly identified the obligations of the duty-bearers to respect, protect, and fulfil these rights. Moreover, the audit assisted the funder in positioning itself in relation to the duty-bearers. As a non-governmental organization, the funder did not have direct obligations in relation to the rights identified in the audit. However the audit provided them with a language to convince government that the service they were developing not only met children's needs but if supported by government funding could assist in the state in fulfilling its international commitments to secure children's rights.[47]

In sum, in designing children's rights-based research, researchers need to ensure that the research aims to further the realization of the children's rights standards contained in the CRC; that an objective of the research should be to inform children involved about

[45] L. Lundy, L. McEvoy, B. Byrne, N. 39, above.
[46] L. Lundy and L. McEvoy (2009), N. 39, above and Miller et al, N. 31, above.
[47] L. Lundy and L. McEvoy (2009), N. 39, above.

their CRC rights and duty-bearers about their concomitant obligations; that research questions should be framed with CRC standards and associated jurisprudence; and that children's participation in the research design should be CRC-compliant. Whilst this may appear onerous, in reality it simply requires the research team to be committed to the realization of children's rights, cognizant of the standards in the CRC, and have competence in engaging children meaningfully in research processes.

6.4 Conducting children's rights-based research

The principles of a rights-based approach apply not only to the framing or design of the research, but also to the way in which the research is carried out, including the methods which are chosen for data collection as well as the treatment of child participants more generally. When these principles are applied a number of issues emerge as particularly significant for the conduct of the research: research ethics; children's participation in the research; and the relationship between the rights-holders and the duty-bearers. The issues are discussed in turn below.

6.4.1 Research ethics

For research to be children's rights-based it must be conducted in a way that respects and protects the rights of the children involved. As mentioned above, the link between the standards in the CRC and the *ethical treatment* of children in research has been the focus of some discussion in the academic literature. Alderson and Morrow, in particular, have consistently linked the ethical treatment of children to the principles of the CRC. They have drawn on the full plethora of CRC rights and argued that children are entitled to information about the research (Articles 13 and 17) in order to form their own views before giving consent (Article12).[48] Moreover, they suggest that giving due respect for consent and refusal prevents discrimination against disadvantaged groups (Article 2), the risk of abuse and exploitation (Articles 19, 32, 36, and 37), and unlawful interference with privacy and attacks on the child's honour and reputation (Article 17). Ennew has argued further that children have a right to be 'correctly described, researched and counted', an entitlement which entails a commitment on the part of the research community to ensure that *scientific* as well as ethical methods of data collection are used.[49] This, she asserts, means not using data collection instruments such as 'hasty, badly constructed questionnaires' but rather sound methods including careful observation, triangulation, control groups, and participatory data collection techniques. This focus on participatory data collection has a particular resonance with a children's rights-based approach and is discussed in more detail in the section below.

6.4.2 Children's participation in research

A considerable body of work has emerged on developing participatory research methods with children which, although not always identified as informed by the CRC, is

[48] N. 10, above, at p.86.

[49] J. Ennew (1995) 'Outside Childhood: Street Children's Rights' in B. Franklin (ed.) *The New Handbook of Children's Rights* London: Routledge, pp. 388–403.

undoubtedly respectful of children's participation rights. This sits within a general trend for children to be more actively engaged in research processes, with their position in the research less often characterized as the 'object' or 'subject' of research and more often as a research 'participant'.[50] This shift is often associated with the 'new sociology of childhood' which recognizes children as social actors, capable of making sense of and affecting the world around them.[51] Accordingly many childhood researchers are seeking to adopt research methods aimed at understanding the child's lived experience from the child's viewpoint and at exploring children's views and perspectives on matters affecting them.[52] This has resulted in the development of a wide range of participatory methods including the use of arts-based methods,[53] visual methods such as photographs,[54] stories and narratives,[55] role play and drama,[56] etc. all of which clearly foreground children's perspectives and provide them with opportunities to express their views freely. Furthermore, while some scepticism remains regarding children's ability to understand the research process,[57] children are being engaged routinely as researchers in many childhood research projects, as co-researchers,[58] peer-researchers,[59] and, more recently, in child-led research projects, noted above.[60]

[50] S. Greene and D. Hogan (eds) (2005) *Researching Children's Experiences: Approaches and Methods* London: Sage.

[51] J. Qvortrup, M. Bardy, G. Sgritta, and E. Wintersberg (1994) *Childhood Matters, Social Theory, Practice and Politics* Aldershot, UK: Averbury.

[52] E.K.M. Tisdall, J. Davis, and M. Gallagher (2009) *Researching with Children and Young People: Design, Methods and Analysis* London: Sage.

[53] See, for example, A. Veale (2005) 'Creative methodologies in participatory research with children' in S. Greene and D. Hogan (eds) *Researching Children's Experiences: Approaches and Methods* London: Sage, pp. 253–72; R. Leitch (2006) 'Researching Children's Narratives Creatively through Drawings' in P. Thompson (ed.), *Doing Visual Research with Children and Young People* New York & London: Routledge, pp. 37–59.

[54] See, for example, A. Clark (2010) 'Young Children as Protagonists and the Role of Participatory, Visual Methods in Engaging Multiple Perspectives', 46 *American Journal of Community Psychology*, 115–23; A. Clark (2004) 'The Mosaic Approach and Research with Young Children' in V. Lewis, M. Kellett, C. Robinson, S. Fraser, and S. Ding (eds) *The Reality of Research with Children and Young People* London: Sage, pp. 142–61; A. Clark and P. Moss (2001) *Listening to Young Children: The Mosaic Approach* London: The National Children's Bureau. The mosaic approach developed by Clark and Moss is a multi-method framework for gathering young children's views and experiences of their everyday lives. It uses observation, interviewing, and participatory visual and kinaesthetic approaches to build a picture or 'mosaic' of the child's life. See also T. Cook and E. Hess (2007) 'What the Camera Sees and from Whose Perspective? Fun Methodologies for Engaging Children in Enlightening Adults' 14(1) *Childhood*, 29–46.

[55] See, for example, E. Coates (2004) 'I forgot the sky: Children's stories contained within their drawings' in V. Lewis, M. Kellett, C. Robinson, S. Fraser, and S. Ding (eds) *The Reality of Research with Children and Young People* London: Sage, pp. 5–26.

[56] N. 53, above.

[57] See P. Christensen and A. Prout (2002) 'Working with ethical symmetry in social research with children' 8(4) *Childhood*, 165–76.

[58] See V. Lewis (2004) 'Doing research with children and young people' in S. Fraser, V. Lewis, S. Ding, M. Kellett, and C. Robinson (eds) *Doing Research with Children and Young People* London: Sage, pp. 15–26; S. Warren (2000) 'Let's do it Properly: Inviting Children to be Researchers' in A. Lewis and G. Lindsay (eds) *Researching Children's Perspectives* Buckingham, UK: Open University Press, pp. 122–34.

[59] N. Schafer and R. Yarwood (2008) 'Involving Young People as Researchers: Uncovering Multiple Power Relations Among Youths' 6(2) *Children's Geographies* 121–35; S. Cox and A. Robinson-Pant (2008) 'Power, Participation and Decision Making in the Primary Classroom: Children as Action Researchers' 16(4) *Educational Action Research*, 457–68; C. Murray (2006) 'Peer Led Focus Groups and Young People' 20 *Childhood and Society* 273–86.

[60] Nn. 42, 43, above; see also H. Shier (2010) 'Children as Public Actors: Navigating the Tensions' 24 *Children & Society* 24–37.

While such active involvement in research undoubtedly situates children at the centre of the research process, the emphasis has been on developing their capacity to undertake or participate in research rather than on the promotion of children's capacity to claim their rights in these contexts per se. We have sought to date, over a number of projects, to develop an explicit children's rights-compliant approach to participation in research which seeks to build the capacity of children to claim their rights.[61] As noted above, for us, this has involved the engagement of children as co-researchers, in CRAGs, and as research participants. In accordance with the HRBA principles this aspect of our research has been guided by the CRC and its associated jurisprudence. In particular we have contended that a children's rights-compliant approach to participation in research requires that children are assisted in both forming and expressing views (Article 12) through being provided with access to information (Article 17) and adult guidance (Article 5).[62] This approach brings with it a requirement to build the capacity of the children participating in the research on the substantive issues of the research. For children working as *co-researchers* in CRAGs this requires spending initial sessions developing their understanding of the body of knowledge associated with the research questions, rather than building their capacity to undertake research. For children who are the *research participants* this requires providing them with opportunities during data collection to form their views through access to information, before expressing their formed view.[63]

In addition to data collection, a significant stage in the conduct of any research project is the analysis and interpretation of findings; a crucial stage since this is the point at which meaning is given to the findings.[64] As noted above, an element of 'good practice' in a HRBA is the involvement of *all* stakeholders in this analysis.[65] Clearly, therefore, a children's rights-based approach to research necessitates that *children* are engaged in analysis and interpretation of findings. While this is not often the case in childhood research, Coad and Evans argue that involving children in data analysis can help to reduce the power imbalance between adult researchers and children and provide interesting case studies of children aged 10 and over being involved in the coding, analysis, and interpretation of interviews and questionnaires.[66] The involvement of children in the analysis and interpretation of qualitative data[67] and in the interpretation of findings from large scale quantitative surveys[68] has been a key feature of our own work. This interpretation was particularly significant in the 'Ready to Learn' project where the children's interpretation of the findings had a significant impact on the decisions made by the funders in relation to the educational intervention they were developing. We would contend that foregrounding children's rights in this project enhanced the children's authority as stakeholders and optimized

[61] This was based on a model of children's rights-based participation developed by one of the authors. See L. Lundy (2007) 'Voice is not Enough: Conceptualising Article 12 of the UNCRC' 33(6) *British Educational Research Journal* 927–42.

[62] See L. Lundy and L. McEvoy (forthcoming 2012) 'Children's Rights and Research Processes: Assisting Children to (In)formed Views' *Childhood* for a fuller exploration of this approach to research with children.

[63] N. 62, above. [64] N. 32, above. [65] N. 24, above.

[66] J. Coad and R. Evans (2008) 'Reflections on Practical Approaches to Involving Children and Young People in the Data Analysis Process' 22(1) *Children & Society* 41–52.

[67] L. Lundy and L. McEvoy, N. 39, above; C. Murphy et al, N. 31, above; L. Lundy and L. McEvoy (forthcoming) at N. 62, above.

[68] S. Miller at al, N. 31, above; L. Lundy and L. McEvoy (2009), N. 39, above.

their claims.[69] While children are not the only stakeholders who need to be involved in interpretation of findings, their 'take' on them is not just valuable but a requirement of a children's rights-based approach to research. As such, their perspective must be afforded due weight' in accordance with CRC standards, along with other stakeholder perspectives.

6.4.3 Relationship between rights-holders and duty-bearers during the conduct of research

The HRBA principles include a requirement to build the capacity of duty-bearers to fulfil their obligations across *all stages* of the activity. While the actual conduct of the research is a stage at which there is likely to be minimal input from the state agents who have the obligations in a particular area, even where they are the funders, there may, on occasion, be opportunities to involve them directly. We have attempted to engage duty-bearers with the children (as rights-holders) during the conduct of research through ensuring that the children involved in the research are made aware of a named person charged with responding to the research findings: a 'designated listener'.[70] For example, in the project exploring approaches to e-consultation with children[71] the participants were asked to complete a range of on-line consultation activities before engaging in a group discussion regarding their effectiveness. Before completing the activities participants were directed towards an embedded video where the 'duty-bearers' (in this case named civil servants responsible for taking the findings of the research forward) explained to the children why their views were important and why the government wanted to hear their views. When the children had completed the e-consultation activity they were informed, on-line, that their views would be sent to the named civil servant. It is notable that directly engaging the children with the 'duty-bearer' had an impact on how the children viewed their participation in the research and their position as 'rights-holders'.[72] Moreover, while this had undoubted benefits for the children, it was clear that the act of publicly stating their promise to the children in the video also underlined the officials' personal commitment to giving the respondents' views due weight.

In sum, in conducting children's rights-based research, we would suggest that researchers need to ensure that their engagement with children, either as child researchers or research participants, is guided at all stages by the CRC standards. In a children's rights-based approach this entails: ensuring that the conduct of the research respects the rights of the children involved; ensuring that research methods chosen are of a high quality and appropriate to address the issues being investigated; engaging children meaningfully in the choices that are made about methods as well as in how these methods are employed; taking deliberate steps to ensure that children are provided with opportunities to form and express their views freely across all stages of the research including the significance or meaning attributed to findings; making children aware of who has responsibility for acting upon the research findings; and, where possible, harnessing opportunities to engage with duty-bearers during the conduct of the research.

[69] N. 13, above.

[70] L. Lundy and L. McEvoy (2008), N. 31, above, p. 16.

[71] See L. Lundy and L. McEvoy (2008), N. 31, above; L. McEvoy and L. Lundy (2007), N. 39, above.

[72] L. McEvoy and L. Lundy (2007), N. 39, above.

6.5 Disseminating children's rights-based research

The dissemination of research is a further crucial stage in any research project which may be approached in different ways depending on the perspective of the researcher and their perceived relationship with their findings and responsibilities towards dissemination and impact. For some academic researchers, the ultimate goal is simply the general contribution to knowledge, in which case all that may be deemed necessary is the widespread dissemination of findings through professional and academic outputs. However, in line with the increasing emphasis in academia on the impact of research outputs, researchers are attempting to engage with those who can effect change, most notably policy makers and practitioners.[73] Given that the ultimate aim of rights-based research is to further the realization of rights, those seeking to adopt such an approach need to consider what role they can play in this, the ways in which they can engage children meaningfully in it, and the extent to which they are able or willing to influence the duty-bearers. We would suggest that, for research to be truly rights-based, there must be a deliberate and conscious effort to engage with children in meaningful ways to influence state actors whose policy and practices impact on their lives. In practice the approach adopted will depend on time and resources, the skills of the researcher, and, indeed, the nature of the research funding.

An essential element of a rights-based approach is that children contribute to the dissemination outputs. There are numerous examples of researchers working with children to develop meaningful ways of disseminating the findings to their peers and to the adults responsible for acting on them,[74] which may include the use of creative approaches such as drama.[75] In our own work we have, for example, incorporated children's interpretation of findings and their recommendations directly into research reports[76] and, in the context of a project with very young children, engaged a professional artist to work with the children in developing a visual representation of the findings for dissemination.[77] Such processes arguably develop the capacity of the children as rights-holders to claim their rights, in that they deepen their understanding of the nature of the issue and provide them with meaningful access to research evidence, which they may choose to use to lobby for change themselves.

Not only must children be engaged in shaping the dissemination outputs, a rights-based approach entails ensuring that these outputs build the capacity of the duty-bearers to fulfil their obligations to children. We would suggest that there is a variety of strategies which might be adopted in this respect. So for example, it may be sufficient for the researcher's relationship with the findings to end with its presentation to agencies that have a primary role in influencing government policy or informing practice. This might work best when the research has been commissioned by such a body. Provided this agency has a specific remit to engage with children and lobby government, and the capability to do so, the presentation of findings, framed explicitly within the language of rights and CRC principles in particular, may be all that is required to

[73] Within the UK, there is a government drive to encourage academic research which has social impact through, for example, the Research Excellence Framework (REF) and funding criteria used by bodies such as the Economic and Social Research Council.

[74] See for example, M. Kellett (2010), N. 42, above; P. Alderson and V. Morrow (2011), N. 10, above.

[75] A. Jones (2004) 'Children and Young People as Researchers' in S. Fraser, V. Lewis, S. Ding, M. Kellett, and C. Robinson (eds) *Doing Research with Children and Young People* London: Sage, pp. 113–30.

[76] See S. Miller et al; C. Murphy et al, N. 31, above.

[77] L. Lundy, L. McEvoy, B. Byrne, N. 39, above.

conclude the rights-based process. In fact, unless the researchers have specific expertise in working with children to effect change in their own lives, then this would be the most appropriate route to adopt in order for the research to continue to be rights-based. For example, research commissioned by the Northern Ireland Commissioner for Children and Young People (NICCY), sought the views of over 1000 children (and 350 adults) in order to identify the gaps, problems, and difficulties in the protection, promotion, and implementation of children's rights in Northern Ireland.[78] The research findings, a comprehensive audit of children's rights in the jurisdiction, provided NICCY with an evidence base on which to base its priorities for the office and to use in its interactions with government.[79] The final research reports, which included three different versions for children and young people, were disseminated widely, providing other children's organizations with a basis upon which to lobby government for rights-based change and the further realization of children's rights.

Alternatively the researchers might choose from the outset to work actively with children and young people to empower them to use the findings to lobby state and state actors. There are many excellent examples of young people using research evidence to lobby for change in their own communities, most usually in the context of community development work and programming.[80] Participatory Action Research (PAR) methods, in particular, which seek explicitly to empower participants to effect change in their lives, are being used increasingly with children.[81] The principles align well with rights-based approaches and their emphasis on empowering children to effect change in their own lives. However, while a number of researchers adopting PAR approaches link their work to the CRC, in particular Article 12's affirmation of the right 'to have a say in the decisions that shape their life',[82] this is often the extent of the engagement with rights discourse. Thus, in spite of the obvious consonance with the spirit of rights-based approaches, it is rare to find PAR research projects framed explicitly in terms of children's rights and the CRC.[83]

It might be queried whether it is possible for a genuinely rights-based process to conclude with the distribution of the findings without any engagement of the rights-holders in directly influencing the duty-bearers. While this is undoubtedly the ideal way to do it, it is at least arguable that, provided the findings shed light on a breach

[78] U. Kilkelly et al, N. 33, above. [79] U. Kilkelly and L. Lundy, N. 3, above.

[80] UNICEF, in particular, has led activity in this field, applying HRBA principles in its development work. See, for example, H. Eversole (2009) 'Asking Children: the Benefits from a Programming Perspective' 7(4) *Children's Geographies* 484–6. See also H. Shier (2010) 'Children as Public Actors: Navigating the Tensions' 24 *Children & Society*, 24–37 and A. Wheeler (2010) 'Children's Participation in Educational Projects and Sustainable Design—Comparing the UK and Nicaraguan Contexts: An Interview with Harry Shier, 17th January 2009 18(3) *International Journal of Children's Rights* 457–74 for an overview of Harry Shier's work with Nicaraguan coffee growers.

[81] For a recent review of these, see the Special Issue of *American Journal of Community Psychology* 46 (2010) on Participatory Action Research with Children.

[82] E. Newman Phillips, M.J. Berg, C. Rodriguez, and D. Morgan (2010) 'A Case Study of Participatory Action Research in a Public New England Middle School: Empowerment, Constraints and Challenges' 46 *American Journal of Community Psychology* 179–95, p. 181.

[83] An interesting exception is Mitchell's research which sought to investigate how the principles of the CRC were used by child health advocates in British Columbia. R.C. Mitchell (2000) 'Implementing Children's Rights in British Columbia using the Population Health Framework' 8 *International Journal of Children's Rights* 333–49. Not only was the research specifically framed by the CRC but there were considerable efforts made to ensure that children were subsequently able to use the research findings through, for example, the establishment of a Youth Advisory Council and a Children's Rights Symposium. However, the methods adopted do not appear to have involved children in the research design, conduct, or analysis.

of rights and children have been engaged throughout, including making a contribution to the dissemination outputs, then the presentation of the material to the duty-bearers may be a sufficient final step in a rights-based project, without any further engagement of children or the researchers. From a pragmatic perspective, there will not always be the capacity or resources to go further than this. Moreover, children might not be willing to be involved further in dissemination and active lobbying etc. While their engagement, either with or without the support of adults, would represent the ideal of ensuring that HRBA principles are applied throughout, it would seem unduly restrictive to describe research investigating compliance with children's rights, carried out in a children's rights-compliant manner and which presents findings to duty bearers in ways that enable them to meet their obligations under the CRC as not 'rights-based'.

6.6 Conclusions

There is increasing recognition of the implications of the CRC for childhood research. Within this, the term 'rights-based' has to date been used loosely (including by the authors) to describe research projects which are informed in some explicit way by the CRC. However, it has been seen that, within human rights discourse, this descriptor has been attributed a specific and particular meaning in the UN Statement of Common Understanding emanating from wider human rights discourse and principles. When the core principles of this are applied to the design and implementation of research processes, the implications for the conduct of childhood research are significant. In particular, there is a requirement that the goal of the research is to realize children's rights, that children's rights standards inform the process, and that children are engaged throughout in ways which build their capacities to assert their rights and the capacity of duty-bearers is increased to fulfil their obligations.

Existing childhood research provides manifest examples of strategies being adopted which would, if combined, constitute a 'rights-based' approach to research. However, it is rare to see this being followed through from start to finish. Research projects which are framed as investigations into rights often fail to use participatory methods or engage with children in dissemination. On the other hand, the projects which engage children actively throughout are framed rarely within the children's rights standards. Thus in spite of a growing awareness of the significance of the CRC, childhood researchers tend not to articulate their approaches to methods more fully within children's rights discourse. This is, perhaps, unsurprising given that the expertise is drawn mainly from sociology, psychology, and education, disciplines which generally do not focus on the substantive legal rights in the CRC, and wider human rights discourse. On the other hand, children's rights scholars, who have the requisite substantive knowledge of the CRC, tend not to conduct direct empirical research with children, the emphasis within the discipline of law being on doctrinal[84] and/or theoretical analyses.[85] Moreover, collaboration between legal scholars and those in

[84] G. Van Bueren (1995) *The International Law on the Rights of the Child* The Hague: Kluwer Law International; J. Fortin (2003) *Children's Rights and the Developing Law* (2nd edition) London: Butterworths.

[85] J. Eekelaar (1986) 'The Emergence of Children's Rights' 161 *Oxford Journal of Legal Studies* 170–1; M. Freeman (2007) 'Why it Remains Important to Take Children's Rights Seriously' 15(1) *International Journal of Children's Rights* 5–23.

other disciplines such as sociology has also been limited.[86] The net effect of this is that the international children's rights provisions contained within the CRC, while frequently attributed the status of a key driver in research with children, are integrated rarely into childhood research projects.[87] For this to change, all those conducting research with children should be informed and trained in the nature and scope of children's rights, which is in any event an obligation on the state under the CRC.[88] As the Committee has stated, the purpose of such training on the CRC should be 'to emphasize the status of the child as a holder of human rights, to increase knowledge and understanding of the Convention and to encourage active respect for all its provisions'.[89] The value of this for childhood researchers is that the CRC provides a comprehensive set of standards which embrace most aspects of children's lives, a language of rights and entitlement in which to frame the research and national and international mechanisms for implementation, thus providing leverage to those who wish to bring about change.

Practical leverage emanates from the existing monitoring mechanisms, national and international, which accompany children's rights standards, and thus provide a platform for those who want their research to have impact. The Committee itself has urged states to ensure that there is 'collection of sufficient and reliable data on children, disaggregated to enable identification of discrimination and/or disparities in the realization of rights'.[90] Moreover, the periodic (five-yearly) reporting process provides a focus for the research process: areas for investigation and avenues for dissemination. First, it highlights issues which are calling for further investigation and research. In particular, the Committee's Concluding Observations identify specific areas where states are not complying with the Convention and indicate issues which need to be investigated more fully. For example, in the most recent report on the United Kingdom the Committee points out, *inter alia*, a lack of data on the number of children seeking asylum, a need to assess why so many children with disabilities are in long term institutional care, and a need for an independent review of anti-social behaviour orders.[91] Secondly, the monitoring mechanisms provide a regular window of opportunity for those seeking for their research to have impact on policy. This can be achieved through conducting rights-based research either directly for the state or by working with non-governmental organizations to provide evidence for the alternative reporting process to the Committee. In either case, this provides a valuable opportunity for researchers to work alongside children not only to expose weaknesses in the implementation of the CRC and identify rights-based solutions but also to ensure that the research reaches an international audience which is capable of impacting on domestic law, policy, and practice.

Further leverage is grounded in human rights discourse itself. As Donnelly suggests, 'rights empower, not just benefit, those who hold them'.[92] Human rights place

[86] L. Alanen (2010) 'Editorial: Taking Children's Rights Seriously' 17(5) *Childhood* 5–8.

[87] See L. Lundy (2010) Review of J. Qvortrup, W, Cosaro, M-S. Honig (eds) (2010) *The Palgrave Handbook of Childhood Studies* Basingstoke: Palgrave, Macmillan in 18(2) *International Journal of Children's Rights* 655–8.

[88] Article 42 of the CRC requires the provisions of the Convention to be made widely known to children and adults alike.

[89] N. 4, above, para. 55.

[90] N. 4, above, para. 48.

[91] United Nations Committee on the Rights of the Child (2008) *Concluding Observations of the Committee on the Rights of the Child: United Kingdom of Great Britain and Northern Ireland* (UN/CRC/GBR/CO/4) (Geneva: United Nations).

[92] N. 23, above, p. 8.

an emphasis on entitlement rather than need and enable those who hold rights to demand a response from those who have both the duty and the power to effect change. Rights are thus a key resource for those who lack power, particularly children who are often powerless in their interactions with adults, being 'kept in an imposed and prolonged dependence which history and culture show to be neither inevitable nor essential'.[93] In the context of research, children have in the past been characterized in such a manner, with direct consequences for the methods adopted. However the last few decades have seen a shift in thinking about children's agency and competence with an associated emphasis on their participation in research.[94] Even so, it remains rare for children to be recognized as rights-holders, entitled not only to 'make their own lives rather than having their lives made for them'[95] but also to insist that those who bear them duties respect, protect, and fulfil their promises under the CRC.

Freeman has suggested that 'the Convention is international law's response to the paradigm shift in thinking about children'.[96] While this shift has undoubtedly brought about a change in the way in which childhood researchers view children and therefore conduct research, there is still much untapped potential for the application of the principles of children's rights in this context. The CRC may have been recognized as one of the initial drivers in the paradigm shift in childhood research, but its potential has not yet been fully harnessed. We would suggest that the children's rights-based approach, explored in this chapter, provides one way of taking this forward through a redefinition of both the purpose of childhood research and a reconsideration of the relationships between the researcher, children as rights-holders, and the adults who bear them duties under the CRC in these processes. Thus, research framed, conducted, and disseminated in accordance with international children's rights standards, and in the spirit of human rights discourse more generally, enhances the potential for childhood researchers to work with children to make a difference to their lives.

[93] M. Freeman (2010) 'The Human Rights of Children' in C. O'Cinneide (ed.) *Current Legal Problems Volume 63* Oxford: Oxford University Press, 1–44 at p. 16.

[94] P. Kirby (2002) 'Involving Young People in Research' in B. Franklin (ed.) *The New Handbook of Children's Rights: Comparative Policy and Practice* Abingdon: Routledge, pp. 268–84; A. Lange and J. Mieredorff (2010) 'Method and Methodology in Childhood Research' in J. Qvortrup, W. Cosaro, and M-S. Honig (eds) (2010) *The Palgrave Handbook of Childhood Studies* Basingstoke: Palgrave, Macmillan, pp. 78–95.

[95] N. 93, above, at p. 17.

[96] N. 93, above, at p. 19.

7

Child-Led Organizations and the Advocacy of Adults: Experiences from Bangladesh and Nicaragua

Manfred Liebel[1]

> *Time has wrapped itself around the adults—with its haste, its dread, its ambition, its bitterness and its long-term goals. They no longer see us properly and what they do see they have forgotten five minutes later.*
>
> *While we, we have no skin. And we remember them always.*
>
> From the novel by Peter Høeg, *Borderliners*, p. 144.

Sixteen years ago, I was invited to a Children's Rights Congress in Frankfurt am Main (van den Boogaart et al., 1996), to speak about my experience with 'new forms of interest articulation and participation of children in Latin America'. In particular, this covered initiatives and social movements that are run by children themselves and which seek to improve their precarious situation 'with their own force'. For seven years, I had the opportunity to witness such processes, and to accompany children on-site as an adult 'co-worker'. I would like here to once more return to what I learnt during that time, and to reflect on it in light of subsequent experiences, and in reference to experiences in other regions of the world. In doing so, I hope to better understand and to provide a better understanding of what the child-led organizations mean for the enjoyment of children's rights and in what ways they can contribute to attaining an understanding of participation suitable to the life situation of the children. In the process, it is indispensable to understand the pitfalls of and perspectives on 'advocacy' and organizations of adults, which children rely on, and which (want to) help and support children.

7.1 1995 flashback

At the Frankfurt Congress, in view of my experience with children's movements in Latin America, I presented the following (Liebel, 1996: 238; translation from German by the author):

[1] Institute of International Studies on Childhood and Youth, International Academy at the Free University Berlin, Germany.

As long as the child is understood only as a subject of rights, his/her claim to a dignified life remains abstract. According to the (children's rights) convention, all children have the same rights, yet how these rights are to be implemented and what difficulties must be overcome, only become more apparent when we comprehend children specifically as humans that have their own characteristics, worries, dreams, points of view, needs, experiences, etc. and which live under individual social conditions which can make it easier or harder for them to use their rights and self-actualise themselves as subjects.

Children's movements are a noteworthy example of this. They do not only refer to their rights as children, but also point to particular hostile characteristics of the societies they live in, and indicate alternatives. Foremost, they consider is to be a thorn in the side that children are systematically excluded from participating and taking on responsibilities in society, and that this is legitimised by their supposedly age-related 'immaturity' and 'imperfection'. They challenge, in what I see as a fundamental way, the paternalistic model of our existing society, by not only complaining that they are the subordinates (objects) of adults, but also insisting on that roles are newly distributed between age groups. It seems that children do not want to understand, why 'children's imagination' should be limited to children and 'responsibility' to adults. Therewith, they claim a new position in society for themselves, without having to stop being 'children'. And they make it clear, that a new understanding, we could also say: a new culture of childhood calls for a new culture of adulthood. Only in this way, can it be reasoned, that adults as well as children can become social subjects and remain social subjects for their whole lives.

In Latin America, this understanding of generational order and the personal support of children for it became known at the time as *Protagonismo Infantil,* which only translates badly into English, but is easily understood in this context (see Liebel, 2007). According to it, children do not necessarily just think about themselves and, where they organize themselves into social movements, are concerned not only about individual interests, but develop and get involved in ideas on a fairer society. Such a society can no longer fence children off and place them on the 'island of childhood', but rather has to offer them opportunities as early on as possible, to play a serious role, that is to be taken seriously, in society and accordingly in their surroundings. The understanding of participation expressed by this vision was at the time and is still today far from what children are granted usually as 'participation'. During my presentation at the Children's Rights Congress, I further explained (Liebel, 1996: 239; translation from German by the author):

In some Latin American countries, given the image that children's movements have, it is well-seen to speak in favour of the participation and protagonist's role of children. However, there is not always much behind this and the use of this vocabulary often only leads to veiling the continuation of a practice of little participation. Notably often, one can hear talk of, for example, engaging children in the process of their own change, which means nothing other than letting children search for the solutions to their problems themselves. Or the participation of children is understood simply as a method to keep children busy or to encourage them to take on activities whose aims and course of action have long been defined by adults. Or participation, under the condition that the child has to be 'sufficiently sensible', is perverted into a catch-phrase.

Also nowadays and in the minority world, when one speaks of child participation, one usually thinks of projects or initiatives that were created for children by adults. In contrast, children's own initiatives that arise out of their everyday life are not generally perceived and recognized as participation. They are, however, often taken up by organizations or institutions that lie in the hands of adults, to 'support' them, make them 'more effective' or otherwise 'accompany' them. The motives and aims of these organizations and institutions can be very varied. They can, for example, aim in instrumental ways, to use the initiatives of the children for their own image and to justify the existence of their own organization or profession. However, they can also be taken on with the only aim of standing by the side of children and bestowing their initiatives with more stability and efficacy. Ultimately, the children are themselves dependent on accompaniment and support and happily take up corresponding offers. The issue to be looked at here is in what ways the intervention of adults, regardless of their intentions, can affect active children. For this purpose, I will refer to a study from the South Asian country Bangladesh, and then take another look at my own experience in Latin America, which I will try to interpret anew from today's perspective. Finally, I shall delineate some conclusions aspiring to the advocacy of adults, which might be also relevant in a European context.

7.2 From self-organization to advocacy?

In a study of a group of children called *Amra* working on the streets in Bangladesh, Sarah White and Shyamol Choudhury (2010) explore how the aims and working methods of the group had changed under the influence of an NGO. The group that originated in the 1990s on the children's own initiative was made up, at the start of the investigation, of a core of eight to 10 boys who in turn worked together with around 70 children in various locations. About 30 adolescents, some of who had earlier belonged to the children's group, supported them. In the slum where they lived, the boys tried to teach other children to read and write and stood up for better health care in their neighbourhood. The group organized festivities with the children in the surrounding area, and planned a contact point and complaints office for children whose rights were violated.

In their activities, the group constantly faced problems and hindrances, which mainly resulted from the ubiquitous violence of the area and the complex informal and formal political structures that were usually also affected by violence. In Bangladesh, the slums are usually 'ruled' by so-called Mastaans, whose power is based on a mixture of offers of protection and the spreading of fear, and who control access to all-important resources. In order to achieve something in the neighbourhood, the children's groups consistently had to carry out a balancing act, of reaching arrangements with individual Mastaans without being identified with one or the other, and having to protect themselves from becoming tools of the local politicians for their purposes. The children were constantly having to interrupt and postpone their activities, to survive the conflicts between the various power groups of the neighbourhood. A lot of energy was also put into tackling the problems of the individual members and the protection of their group identity as the main basis of their solidarity, and in doing so, also securing their independence.

Some difficulties also arose in the attempts to establish relationships with the young persons in the direct surroundings. After having at first actively supported the group, some ultimately tried to use it as a drug trafficking spot and as a basis for illegal businesses. The earlier members of the group got caught up in the attempt to become a kind of Proto-Mastaans themselves. In addition came the fact that, because of evictions in the neighbourhood, most of the members of the group had to make use of the meeting room as a place to sleep. Some of the young persons of the neighbourhood saw an opportunity in this situation to make a kind of club where they could drink, smoke, consume drugs, and watch videos. The younger members of the group were afraid to defend themselves, and the older neighbours put enormous pressure on the 'club' to close. This crisis could only be overcome by lengthy talks and negotiations with all sides, where an adult who had been accompanying the group as a means of solidarity, played a key role.

The extent of their standing and influence is seen in the fact that despite all hindrances, the group finally managed to succeed, with the agreement of the local authorities and informal power groups, to gain the support of some NGOs for their fight for better living conditions in their neighbourhood. What is particularly impressive about this is the ability of the children to organize neighbourhood meetings and to activate many of the inhabitants of the neighbourhood. Their initial reluctance to be mobilized by children quickly faded to make way for wonderment and recognition for the aptitude of the group in getting off the ground a well co-ordinated network, which is capable of acting. Ironically, it was neither resistance towards the participation of children nor hostility of the residents of the neighbourhood that ultimately undermined the network, but rather the manner in which the NGOs intervened.

The NGOs saw a good opportunity to reach other children in the neighbourhood through the children's group Amra, and they invited the group to take part in vaccination campaigns, research programmes, and consultations of children. The backdrop for these kinds of activities, which took off around the year 2000, was the increased pressure on local NGOs to bring their work on children's rights into line, in particular to boost the participation of children and thereby demonstrating their legitimacy inwardly and outwardly. The interventions of NGOs had conflicting consequences for the children. On the one hand, they gave the children's groups the opportunity to convey their views and concerns to a broader public. On the other hand, the media attention attained by NGOs, the visible prominence, the experience of personal recognition, the availability of better food, and the investment of sums of money for the children that until then had been simply unimaginable, was a big temptation for them. The outcome was that participation in the activities of the NGOs gradually replaced the hard, uncomfortable grass-roots work on the streets, which brought little recognition. Over time, the orientation of the children changed: from direct action to advocacy, from groups to individuals, from the slum to the NGOs.

The daily experience of poverty, the organizational experience with the group, and the constantly active relationship with other children in the neighbourhood, allowed the members of the children's group to emerge as highly efficient advocates and were, in the eyes of the NGOs, an important complement to the programme's activities. The danger, however, that accompanied this model of child participation, was that the activists of the children's group distanced themselves more and more from the other children in the neighbourhood. The more opportunities they had in 'participation' and 'advocacy', the greater the distance became from the other children. The clearest example was offering Amra members the opportunity to travel to international meetings abroad. Wherever they showed up, they were celebrated as the 'true' representatives of the poor children of their country, and praised. Although, as delegated persons, they initially upheld their principles and, for example, insisted on always being re-elected 'by the base', after returning from the events they were seen in another way by the other children and unintentionally estranged themselves from them.

The new type of activities was reflected by changes in the group culture. In the interviews that Shyamol Choudhury and Sarah White had with the children and adolescents four years later, they observed a stronger interest at that time in more comfort and consumption. The children hardly spoke of their activities in the neighbourhood anymore, but rather emphasized their desire for grants, good food, travel and monetary allowances, and, above all, their connection to 'important' people, who later may be able to get them better jobs. For a select few the recognition as 'child-activists' had a stimulating effect, which was accompanied by increased self-confidence, but for most it resulted only in vague expectations of an easier life and an actual new dependence. The most marked effect was seen in a growing difference in power between the children. The core group hardly had any connections to the other children anymore. The younger and worse-off children from the neighbourhood hardly trusted themselves in the meeting place and only seldom spoke up at meetings. By trying, they risked being scorned. Amra—so they say—had become a 'borolok', that is to say a rich organization. White and Choudhury draw the conclusion that the dynamics of this model of participation are as concentric as they are exclusive: the few celebrated persons distanced themselves through this kind of participation bit by bit from those whose spokespersons they had become.

The self-directed actions of the children's group were in practice replaced by the input and initiatives of the NGO-workers. This does not mean that the children simply became passive objects. During the process, they enjoyed taking part in the new 'participatory' projects, doing street theatre, making videos, calendars, or statements for the media to produce, etc. Two or three of them could even fulfil a widespread childhood dream to find work 'in film'. Indeed, the notion that the children were 'autonomous' vanished into thin air. Ultimately, it depended on the available opportunities and forms of support.

White and Choudhury see here a new form of 'office-centred' models of participation, which they categorize as part of the 'theatre for development'. It was made up of an efficient use of time and minimum discomfort. The numerous meetings satisfied the bureaucratic need for activities that can be represented, and the creation of media products demonstrated tangible and quantifiable results. All of these demonstrative participatory practices could however also bring some individual benefits for the children, but served first to the benefit of the representatives and employees of the NGOs. They gained in repute, and in this way procured new opportunities to attain lucrative jobs or to place friends as advisors. 'The attraction of such approaches over the hard, low-capitalised, relatively invisible and highly uncertain work at street level, are very clear. (…) Despite the rhetoric of bottom-up development and the importance of local responsiveness, in the world of development the major financial and esteem rewards, both corporate and individual, derive not from the local but from the global "community"' (ibid.: 47).

The analysis of White and Choudhury draws attention to the fact that it is not enough to ask *whether* children participate, but *in what*, under *what framework*, for *which aim*, and in *whose interest* they do this. This leads to the question of what the implicit rules are that determine what counts as participation. In the case discussed above, a participations regime was established that was far away from the daily reality of the children and followed 'superimposed' rules that did not reflect this reality. This type of participation can lead to personal benefits for individual children, but it is not adapted to lead to changes in living conditions.

To make the latter possible, it is necessary first to give careful consideration to the complex, conflicting, and difficult life context of the children, and in particular their life experiences must be respected. This includes the fact that locally there are big differences in power and often violent conflicts—also among the children and adolescents themselves—and that the children move themselves in a field in which they cannot act as they wish, and absolutely not following pre-planned instructions. They have—like adults—the potential to get to grips with their daily problems and to organize themselves for this purpose and to overcome these problems. But for this they need their 'own space' and in the long run, not to be surrounded by (adult) persons that seek to understand, support, defend, and at any rate encourage them. This calls for, not a desire to 'teach them participation', but rather to recognize that they already practise this in their daily lives, usually of a kind and in a way that is not foreseen by 'participations models'. 'If we are serious about learning from child participation we need to "follow their feet" when marginalised children leave their air-conditioned office and design programmes that address the world they go and live within' (ibid.: 49).

7.3 From advocacy to self-organization?

I will take this opportunity, having discussed the study by Shyamol Choudhury and Sarah White, to once more reflect on my own experiences that I made in the 1990s in my work with children in Latin America, initially in particular in Nicaragua.

When I started working as a street worker in the early 1990s, working with children who mainly earned their living on the streets or at markets, a government had just taken power that aligned its policies with a neoliberal dictum. Within a few weeks, many children turned up on the streets looking for any opportunities to make money or to get to food. Some of these children begged, others robbed, others collected half-rotten fruit and vegetables at the markets or ravaged the waste bins for cans, bottles, scrap metal, and similar things, whilst others made an effort to get odd jobs or thought up some services in order to earn some money in a 'dignified' way, and many children also did many of these things simultaneously. Together with some colleagues, I quickly came to the conclusion that our street education work was too narrowly considered. For every child that we cared for in a project, within a short time came five, 10, or 20 further children that we should have included in our work. Our conclusion was that we should no longer advise the children that they could rely on our help, but rather that they should group together to jointly tackle their problems, and improve their awkward predicament. We would support them in this.

We based our thoughts on our observation that many children had already organized themselves into small groups in order to better face their situation. However, they often found themselves in competition or in conflict with one another. Many other children had or saw no other way than to get by on their own account. Our attempt to bring together the children with whom we had dealt in various projects or that we knew from the streets, was met with a positive response surprisingly quickly and unanimously. We invited children to workshops, which they could largely mould themselves. From these workshops sprung the initiative for a first larger meeting, in which around 100 boys and girls from numerous towns would take part. At the meeting, which lasted two-and-a-half days and was also largely organized by the children themselves, the decision was reached to form the 'Movement of Working Children of Nicaragua', and to allure other children into participating (on the formation of the movement see Liebel, 1994: 91–118).

At the meeting, it was demonstrated that the children were very efficient in producing their own ideas on how to organize themselves and what they wanted to achieve with their organization. As they, for example, voted an executive committee, they came to an agreement on the criteria that the members of the committee should fulfil. Amongst others, they had to be active, be able to speak, take initiatives, be honourable, responsible, serious, respectful, and not be a bragger; they should not be fearful and should not have any 'hair on their tongues', that is to say, they had to trust themselves to speak up even in situations to which they were unaccustomed; they should respect all children and defend their interests; they should fulfil the task at hand and be able to direct and instruct the children; and ultimately they should also see eye to eye with the adult co-workers of the movement (which at the time were still called 'educators'). In a heated debate, the attending girls managed to ensure that they were represented in equal numbers in the executive committee and that the younger children were also taken into consideration (the attending children were between the ages of 10 and 16 years old). In light of the everyday experiences of the children, which were wrought with degradation, discrimination, and violence, I was initially astonished at the self-confidence with which they took things into their own hands, and in the thoughtful way in which they dealt with each other. I put this down to the fact that at the meetings (as earlier at the workshops) they had the experience, which for them was probably very surprising, that (most) of the attending adults trusted them, dealt with them respectfully, and that they really could act in self-determined ways.

Of course it was not all sunshine and roses. There were arguments, heartaches, some at first tried to dominate others, girls had to defend themselves against flirting, and some boys beat each other up for futile reasons and much more. But the first really serious problems did not come about between the children, but rather between them and some adults. The reason for this lay in the fact that some of these adults, who were mainly acting as educators for projects of NGOs or church communities, despite best intentions, could not get used to the independence of the children and their way of managing the meetings, and therefore tried time and again to have unsolicited influence over the children. The adults had already been made to understand this at previous meetings, at which a section of them held the view that in the case of the formation of the children's movement, the adults should be integrated as quasi 'equal' members. Others, to which I belong, held the view that the children's movement should be an 'autonomous' endeavour of the children and that the adults should, in co-ordination with the children, find their role as 'outsiders' who support or advise the children.

Once the children had begun publicly to draw attention to their situation and to make accusations about the violation of their rights, they gained some friendly commentaries, but it must also be noted that they were not taken very seriously. Only once they started to pester journalists and politicians (by for example paying unannounced 'visits' to their offices), were they granted serious attention. Some media, for example, soon no longer spoke of 'street children', 'bummers', and 'no-good-ers', but rather of 'working children' whose parents stood by their side, or it was increasingly requested that the children be heard and their rights respected. But the difficulties and attacks quickly accumulated. Either it was alleged that the children had been manipulated by adults, or they were accused of behaving in an improper manner and there being a lack of respect towards adults. Some even saw 'order' or 'culture' as being under threat and called for a timely 'clamp down' and the restoration of 'authority'.

To my astonishment, the children were in no way intimidated by these attacks. They seemed familiar with them from their daily lives or saw them as a sign that they were finally being taken seriously. It also became clear, however, that the children felt that they were dependent on allies in the adult world. In particular they had very high expectations of us adults, who accompanied them as 'educators' and ensured our solidarity. These expectations sometimes went so far, that they idealized us as a kind of replacement father or mother, who would stand by their side unconditionally and whom they could trust almost without limits. Also from the NGOs that had since added children's rights to their banners, the children expected active support. A key issue turned out to be how the relationship between the autonomy that accompanied the children's movement, and which was claimed by the children, and the actual and perceived independence of the 'solidarity' adults and the 'co-operative' NGOs would develop.

With the growth of the children's movement, in which, in the meantime, up to 3,000 children were active, the self-awareness and the collective claim to autonomy of the children grew, but paradoxically the dependency on the adults also increased. The children's movement was increasingly dependent on space and money, to be able to plan and realize their activities. All of this could only be provided by adults, as only they had the necessary contacts and the right to conclude the contracts that the financial provider or lender usually insisted upon. The local UNICEF office, for example, offered financial support out of delight about the engagement of the children for their own rights; however it placed the condition that an NGO or contract partner act as an intermediary (which at the time the children rejected).[2] I, however, succeeded in convincing some child aid organizations or private persons to accept the children's movement as a direct partner even in granting money, but as a middleman I ended up in the role of the powerful benefactor, on whose benevolence the children depended. Despite the occasional unease, I had long underestimated the imbalance resulting from this and the one-sided labelling.

No less serious a matter, it turned out that some local NGOs and some of their appointed educators saw the children's movement as unfair competition, be it because they worried that the finances that they desperately needed for their own work would be snatched away from them, or because they did not want their monopoly over 'pedagogy' or the 'fight for children's rights' to be taken out of their hands. As a children's movement, then, it should subsist under their banner and the control of the NGO and 'their' educators, and make public appearances. Behind this hide both various institutional and personal interests and differing views on what is to be understood as children's rights and in particular the right to participation. I would like to use an example to clarify the challenges and expectations of the claim for autonomy of the children's movement and the way it was implemented.

With the increasing number of activities, the children faced the dilemma of no longer having enough time for all organizational affairs, all the more so as their time was highly in demand from their work, school, and sometimes family. To confront this dilemma, two 'experienced' and trustworthy adults were to be appointed for the children's movement centre[3] to continuously look after the 'bureaucratic things'.

[2] Here it was demonstrated that the right to participation accorded by the UNCRC, to form an association, is worth little if this association is not, legally speaking, able to act. This is precisely excluded, however, in all countries by legislation.

[3] It served not only as an office, but also as a kind of self-regulated child and youth centre, where the children met to talk and play, to celebrate festivities, to do homework, or to plan any activities.

The applicants—mostly educators and social-workers looking for jobs—found themselves in the unusual situation of coming before a selection committee that was mainly made up of children, to demonstrate their suitability and to submit to interrogation. This took some overcoming for most, but as they then waited over an hour for the decision of the committee, which meant subjecting themselves to the judgement of the children, almost all of them left in panic. This demonstrates how deeply-rooted the conviction was, even amongst adults who were allocated to the children and who wanted to advocate their rights, that children should not decide over adults but adults over children, and the adults should have the last word.

This tenor can be reinforced in organizations and institutions where adults are amongst other adults, however convinced they are about the significance of children's rights and the participation of children. Particularly where the application for children's rights is the organization's raison d'être and the basis for its economic existence, it stands to reason that they are careful to remain at the wheel. The children's movement learnt this the hard way, through countless attempts to secure NGOs' support. The support offered or accorded was either restricted to verbal demonstrations of sympathy or was subject to the condition that the children renounce their decision-making autonomy. The reason given for this was almost always that the children did not command the necessary competences to keep their organization alive and to deal with the corresponding duties. Every now and then, this came to a head with the allegation that the children were too impetuous or 'actionistic' and not sufficiently proficient in the 'strategic' intricacies of the 'political business'. In other words, it was suggested to them that they would do themselves and the 'children's right cause' more harm than good, if they did not entrust that cause to experienced specialists from the NGO.

This reflects more than just a generational problem. The interests of the NGOs in the legitimating of their own 'professional' actions also had a class-specific component. When it came to, for example, negotiations with the health ministry and police head office, in which the children called for more consideration for their particular situation as working children and better protection, some agents of the NGOs accused them of using 'vulgar speech' and lacking courtesy. Instead of respecting the forms of communication of the children and the strengths they have, they tried to press on them 'cultured' behaviour that fitted rather with their own social world than that of the children. In doing so, they contributed—possibly unintentionally—to devaluing the live experiences of the children and eroding their gradually increasing self-confidence, which was an essential base for the autonomy of action of their organization.

Their claim to autonomous action, which the children consistently voiced, was based on the experience of finding themselves in a situation of subordination from which they were seeking to free themselves. The subordination consisted, for one, in that as children they were refused recognition as equal partners, and also in that time and again they where disesteemed and discriminated against as *working children* or *children living on the streets*. Their own organization allowed them to abstract themselves from this double subordination, at least for a time, and to experience mutual respect and mutual recognition. These novel experiences for the children constantly made their self-confidence take wing, gave them back their sense of dignity, and allowed them to see their everyday life and work with new eyes. To the extent that they saw, for example, their way of working or living no longer as a defect in their childhood, but rather as being of positive value and a source of pride, their desire for respect and recognition, what they were, and how they saw themselves, grew. The refusal of the children to let themselves be put off by promises of a later life-phase or a better future, took the form of a phrase they often used: 'We are the present.'

A problem that was difficult to solve presented itself in the attempt to conciliate the autonomy demanded and practically achieved by the children's movement with the everyday local reality. As a social place, in a way the children's movement presented a kind of counter-reality to the daily indignity experienced in everyday life. At their meetings, the children were amongst themselves and could largely feel free there. However, this new awareness of life could also lead to the children hoping, through the children's movement, to escape their previous lives and to secure certain privileges, albeit modest ones. In order not to be removed from reality, they had constantly to remember that the reason for the movement lay not in the escape from problems, but that it should be the basis for an improvement of this everyday life.

The question that arose over and over was how to guarantee that the children, who as (usually elected) delegates of other children participated in meetings and assemblies of the children's movement, disseminate the conclusions reached communally and the communally developed ideas and demands, and engage in their local implementation. It was shown that the movement only had worth insofar as it could demonstrate its autonomy and ability to also act locally. On the contrary, it was also shown that the children acting locally were only taken seriously and could only gain influence to the extent to which the children's movement showed general public presence and 'made a name' for itself. For this, stable locally comprehensive structures and forms of actions in turn proved essential.

At the meetings of the children's movement these problems were contemplated again and again in a self-critical way and methods of self-correction sought. Some examples: Delegates who had not fulfilled their duties or who showed signs of arrogance were criticized or even discharged. When children (mostly girls) could not take part at meetings, because their parents feared for their welfare, a delegation would be sent to their home in order to convince the parents (which usually succeeded). When a 12-year-old girl, who belonged to the executive committee of the children's movement, no longer wanted to go to school (she did not feel she was taken seriously there), she was reminded that she was partially responsible for the credibility of the children's movement, which advocated the right to education for all children, and that she must be an example for other children. To reduce the dependency of the children's movement on financial aid, festivities with tombola and merchandising were organized in various city districts, to provide the local group with the necessary financial base.

In the search for solutions for problems that arose, advice and support from adults were also drawn upon. Their advice was usually taken up when it did not conflict with the 'frequency' of the children's movement and respected the decision-making autonomy of the children. However, in the case of children's movements, this autonomy always remained vulnerable, as it did not apply the power balance existing in the society between children and adults without force and also always—as shown above—involved dependencies. In the course of time, ideas were developed in different children's movements across Latin America on which exigencies are to be imposed on 'co-operative' adults or organizations. They boil down to the facts that adults should consider themselves 'co-protagonists', who not only respect the independent existence and form of organization and communication of the children's movement, but also act in their own field in the same way as they expect from children. The co-protagonism of adults is spoken of 'to designate the interdependence that makes us free and autonomous' (Cussiánovich, 2008: 71). In this sense, 'autonomous' networks of 'co-workers' of the children's movement, that is to say, not dependent on NGOs, parties, or institutions, have since appeared, which should promote both self-critical thinking and the social and legal recognition of children's movements.

7.4 Conclusion

The thoughts set out in this chapter may sound exotic, as for the most part it does not seem to be about putting an 'impetuous' children's movement on track, but rather prompting children actually to first create their own initiatives and increase their engagement with their own rights. But such an approach overlooks the fact that the alleged lack of engagement by children is also a consequence of a lack of opportunities and not least a concept of childhood that 'infantilizes' children and largely seals them off from the adult world.

I concluded my talk at the Frankfurt Children's Rights Congress with the words (Liebel, 1996: 243; translation from German by the author):

> A society, in which the participation of children becomes a reality, would not have much in common with the societies known up until today. Children alone cannot bring about such a fundamental change, however well organized they are. They are dependent on allies. But the children that are organising themselves contribute to making the adults more aware that a childhood that is not based on exclusion, but rather that shapes society, also offers them the chance to be a subject.

That was perhaps a naive thought. Participation is not a clear thing, on which there is agreement, and it does not only touch on the relationship of children and adults. But the quintessential is still topical: if participation is to be attractive for children and something to be taken seriously, it cannot only be conceded by adults. Children must be under the impression that their actions are not inconsequential, but can produce something. This is not only a question of arranged occasions and opportunities for participation, but regards the social position and the everyday life of children in general. Only where children are allocated vital duties and activities will they see sense in 'bending over backwards' for it. It would then also become apparent that the differences in power and competences between adults and children are not natural and absolute, but rather social products, relative and situational.

The manner in which the advocacy of children and their rights has been discussed until now does not sufficiently take this into consideration. They remain tightly trapped in the idea that children cannot represent their interests and rights by themselves. The practice of a child rights commissioner or a child rights observatory is usually conceptualized so that adults act *instead of* children, or the corresponding facilities are seen as a walk-in centre for children where they can go with their worries and requests. Here the unequal power dynamic between adults and children is untouched and not questioned, and sometimes even (unintentionally) reinforced.

There is no doubt that representative acting can be of use for children, in particular where they have little self-confidence or are severely limited in their opportunity to act (for example, very young or 'disabled' children who nowadays are referred to as children with 'special needs'). The same goes for situations in which children find themselves in a weak position and the decisions of adults are more or less provided (for example, in custody proceedings in family courts). But here it is also the case that the advocacy of children only makes sense where it is applied to work against the subordination of children and wherever possible, to strengthen the position of children. In this sense, forms of 'non-paternalistic' advocacy are favoured in international discussions nowadays, which are understood as being advice and encouragement of children and are directed at the extension of their possibilities to be of influence (see Oliver and Dalrymple, 2008). Thereby a difference is drawn between case-by-case, systemic, and cause-related advocacy in order to underline the fact that the individual support of children quickly reaches its limits, which in turn can only be overcome through structural changes in the balance of power. Adults who want to act as advocates for children in this way will not only insist on their independence (see Lansdown, 2001), but must also understand themselves—as in the case of the children's movements in Latin America—to be 'co-protagonists' of children.

References

Cussiánovich, A., *Treintaidos años de vida y acción de los NATs por la dignidad en el Peru* (Lima, Universidad Nacional Federico Villarreal & Ifejant, 2008).

Høeg, P., *Borderliners* (London, The Harvill Press, 1994).

Lansdown, G., *Independent Institutions Protecting Children's Rights* (Florence, UNICEF Innocenti Research Centre, 2001).

Liebel, M., *Protagonismo Infantil. Movimientos de niños trabajadores en América Latina* (Managua, Ed. Nueva Nicaragua, 1994).

Liebel, M., 'Neue Formen der Interessenartikulation und Partizipation von Kindern in Lateinamerika', in H. van den Boogaart, J. Fenske, G. Mankau, N. Struck, and W. Trede (eds), *Rechte von Kindern und Jugendlichen. Wege zu ihrer Verwirklichung. Beiträge zum Frankfurter Rechte-Kongress 1995* (Münster, Votum, 1996), 233–44.

Liebel, M., 'Paternalism, Participation and Children's Protagonism' (2007) 17(3) *Children, Youth and Environments* 56–73; online: <http://www.colorado.edu/journals/cye>.

Oliver, Ch. M. and J. Dalrymple (eds), *Developing Advocacy for Children and Young People. Current Issues in Research, Policy and Practice* (London and Philadelphia, Jessica Kingsley, 2008).

van den Boogaart, H., J. Fenske, G. Mankau, N. Struck, and W. Trede (eds), *Rechte von Kindern und Jugendlichen. Wege zu ihrer Verwirklichung. Beiträge zum Frankfurter Rechte-Kongress 1995* (Münster, Votum, 1996).

White, S. C. and S. A. Choudhury, 'Children's participation in Bangladesh: issues of agency and structures of violence', in B. Percy-Smith and N. Thomas (eds), *A Handbook of Children's and Young People's Participation. Perspectives from theory and practice* (London and New York, Routledge, 2010), 39–50.

8

Transforming Children's Human Rights—From Universal Claims to National Particularity

Ann Quennerstedt[1]

Interest in children's human rights is growing—globally as well as within nations. Often departing from the United Nations Convention on the Rights of the Child (UN 1989), in the political sphere, legal institutions, academia, and to some degree in practice, attention is increasingly focused on what children's rights include and mean and how they are realized (or not) in different parts of the world and in various areas of society. The establishment of a human rights convention especially for children, and the mounting interest in what the existence of such an international agreement means, reflects important changes in how children are viewed. Instead of seeing the child as the property of its parents (Quennerstedt 2009a), or as an object of development or socialization (James and James 2004), each child is now recognized as a human being in her/his own right with full human capacity and status. In other words, 'the child' is now included in the family of 'humans'.

In the Convention on the Rights of the Child the same rights are assigned to all children across the world, regardless of their contextual—social, economic, cultural, and religious—circumstances. Through the Convention, the rights of the child are accordingly made universal. This status of universality is an important prerequisite when justifying claims for and defending the rights of children worldwide. However, rights expressed in international treaties necessarily have to undergo a 'cultural journey' when they are put into practice in a certain society. Discourses that govern the perception and organization of, for example, law, family life, or education differ from one country to another. Given that political strategies that are designed to realize the rights expressed in the Convention are shaped within these discourses, national policy regarding the rights of the child will also differ between states, in spite of the universal status of the rights. Consequently, rights have to be transformed from the universal level to the particular policy and practice situation (Englund et al 2009), and in this process, the cultural, economic, and political situation in a state will influence the interpretation of children's rights in terms of content and how prioritizations between rights are made.

The Convention on the Rights of the Child often stands out as the ultimate definition of children's rights. Such a view of the Convention is visible in some research into children's rights, where the Convention itself often forms the point of departure

[1] Örebro University, Sweden

and main framework for the research. Instead, I would like to stress the importance of dealing with the Convention as a political document; an agreement between states made in a specific time and place. Likewise, Norberto Bobbio (1996) underlines that the meaning of human rights must not be regarded as carved in stone, and argues that the adoption of the UN Universal Declaration of Human Rights (UN 1948) marked the start of a process through which the concept of human rights is continuously enhanced, articulated, clarified, and updated. Bobbio considers the vast number of declarations and conventions connected to human rights that have emerged since the UN Universal Declaration of Human Rights, e.g. the Convention on the Rights of the Child, as the international community's way of allowing human rights to develop and move forward. Another essential feature of the constant revision of human rights is the critical examination of how universally expressed rights are received, interpreted, and acted upon in the various nations of the world. Such examinations can deepen our understanding of the transformation of supranational agreements into national discourses, law, and practice (Wahlström 2009), and thereafter be reflected back to the universal level.

The transformation of rights from the universal to the particular level is the very focus of this chapter. The specific interest is to explore how universally pronounced claims for children's human rights are brought from the international arena to the national, and how this transformation affects the perception of the rights. An approach to how the process of transformation and contextualization of rights can be theoretically understood will first be outlined. The elaborated approach will then be applied to a comparative policy study of how children's rights are interpreted in the area of education in the policies of two nations: Sweden and New Zealand.

8.1 Outlining a theoretical framework for understanding the transformation of rights from universality to particularity

A basic assumption, and a starting point for the analysis in this chapter, is that children's rights are part of a broader human rights framework (Alderson 1999, Bennet and Hart 2001). Grover (2007) emphasizes that children's rights are indistinguishable from human rights generally, and that the rights articulated in the Convention on the Rights of the Child are the same human rights entitlements that apply to all persons. Elsewhere, I have in the same vein argued that locating matters of children's rights within human rights may add a much needed theoretical framework to research into children's rights (Quennerstedt 2010b).

Bobbio (1996) describes children's rights as a step in the continuous expansion of human rights, and identifies two trends in the development of human rights that shed light on how rights for children have emerged and grown: universalization—a process in which rights have been increasingly perceived as universally valid for all humans—and the more contemporary process of proliferation—where universal rights are viewed as situated within contextual circumstances that have to be taken into account in the interpretation of rights. An important part of the proliferation trend is changing ideas about the basic entity of human rights, namely the replacement of an abstract man as the holder of rights with a specific human in a specific situation. The differences between individuals and groups of people, and the varying social status of human beings, are thereby recognized as aspects to consider with regard to human rights. In the proliferation of rights, children are identified as a group of humans that is embedded in specific social and status circumstances within which their human rights need to be specifically considered. The Convention on the Rights of the Child embodies this endeavour.

In the following, I will first reflect on the links between human rights, democracy, and citizenship. Inherent in this triad is a tension between the transcending supranational and national sovereignty. Seyla Benhabib's concept of *democratic iterations* (2004) is then suggested as a means to understand the mechanisms working in the reconciliation of claims from international commitments and the will of the sovereign people.

8.1.1 Human rights and democracy

The fundamental connection between human rights and democracy has been explored by a number of scholars. Both Bobbio (1996) and Benhabib (2004) tie human rights closely to democracy: they are the essential components of the same historic movement and the cornerstones of modern democratic states. They also precondition each other, i.e. without recognized and protected human rights we cannot talk about democracy and without democracy we lack the basic conditions for peaceful solutions of conflicts and the protection of human rights.

Bobbio (1996) and Benhabib (2004) discuss how human rights relate to rights given to citizens in democratic states. The first established rights (civil and political) were initially manifested as citizenship rights within states, and also the later established social rights took shape within states as citizenship rights (Marshall 1949/1964). Through the United Nations' adoption of the Universal Declaration of Human Rights in 1948, particular citizenship rights, earlier only pronounced for citizens in states, were transformed to a set of universally valid human rights recognized for all persons regardless of citizenship status. Bobbio (1996) and Benhabib (2007) agree that the universalization of rights has blurred the distinction between human and citizenship rights and has affected our understanding of what the base for having rights is—citizenship in a state or being a human.

In the indistinct relation between human and citizenship rights there is a tension between the universal and the particular. Benhabib (2004) identifies an irresolvable contradiction between the vision of the universal and the everyday reality of the particular; the universal human rights are expansive and inclusive, while citizenship rights limit and exclude those outside. The rights we are recognized as humans are not the same as those we uphold as citizens of a state. Benhabib points to a kind of uncertain space between the two sets of rights. Human and citizenship rights clearly overlap and affect each other, however. Citizenship rights gain their legitimacy from universal principles of human rights, and whether a person gets to enjoy the full range of human rights depends on her/his citizenship status in the place in which s/he resides.

Bobbio (1996) regards the universalization of rights as a step in the right direction towards global peace and democracy, although at the same time he points to problematic consequences for the protection of rights. Through the establishment of international agreements, the safeguarding of rights moves from strong legal systems within specific states to a weaker international system, where rights are often supported and upheld by the exertion of international social pressure rather than by the rule of law. Rights acknowledged for citizens in a state can be more specifically pronounced, and thereby more compelling, than what is possible in international human rights legislation, which often ends up as a set of vague compromises.

8.1.2 Harmonizing transnational agreements with the will of the democratic citizenry

In her work, Benhabib has examined how international law and the autonomy of a democratic citizenry can be understood as being linked. Benhabib (2004) argues that universal human rights and citizens' sovereign self-determination are both necessary foundations for the democratic state:

> 'We, the people' refers to a particular human community, circumscribed in space and time, sharing a particular culture, history and legacy; yet this people establishes itself as a democratic body by acting in the name of the 'universal'. (p. 44)

A democratic state's claim for sovereignty is first of all regarded as legitimate through the existence of a democratic constitution, and secondly by this constitution's conformity with universal principles of human rights. In this way, Benhabib emphasizes how the simultaneous presence of and tension between universal human rights and particular cultural and national circumstances are essential for democratic legitimacy.

Human rights and national sovereignty could be understood as contradictions, in that universal rights transcend the national context while the autonomy of a people is highly directed towards the situation within the boundaries of a nation. Benhabib (2004) argues that, in contemporary society, the importance of international agreements and international law has increased to the extent that it is now possible to talk about a 'human rights regime'. One consequence of such a regime is that state sovereignty is frayed: in some cases, national claims for the privilege of making decisions about citizens' conditions are internationally contested with reference to norms or principles deriving from human rights (Benhabib 2007). Consequently, states are no longer sovereign in the sense that they can decide whatever they like; not even if the decisions that are made adhere to democratic procedures. Instead, the actions of states are monitored and reviewed from the viewpoint of internationally acknowledged norms.

It may be seen as something of a paradox that in order to uphold democratic legitimacy, through which sovereign self-determination is justified, states have to bind their will and reduce their autonomy by committing to certain predetermined norms: the norms of human rights. However, in contrast to some strong liberal theorists who argue that human rights are substantively predefined and therefore not the object of national will formation, Benhabib claims that rights cannot be viewed as pre-political but must instead be understood as open to renegotiation and reinterpretation by the sovereign people (within limits). Through a constantly ongoing process of national reformulation, the commitments articulated in transnational agreements are brought into harmony with the particular political, cultural, and social situation of a specific state. There is accordingly 'a space of interpretation and intervention between transcendent norms and the will of democratic majorities' (Benhabib 2004, p. 181). Benhabib examines this space by developing the concept of *democratic iterations*:

> Democratic iterations are complex processes of public argument, deliberation, and learning through which universalist right claims are contested and contextualized, invoked and

revoked, throughout legal and political institutions as well as in the public sphere of liberal democracies. (2004, p. 19)

The term 'iteration' has been borrowed from the work of Jacques Derrida and refers to the act of repeating a term or a concept. In this repetition, a first or original usage of the term or its intended meaning is never replicated. Instead, every iteration is a variation that enriches and adds to the term and changes its meaning. Benhabib states that 'every act of iteration involves making sense of an authoritative original in a new and different context. The antecedent thereby is repositioned and resignified via subsequent usages and references' (2004, p. 180). To Benhabib, Derrida's concept of 'iteration' provides a tool that makes clear and understands the re-creation and re-interpretation of meaning that takes place in public conversations in various arenas, e.g. law, policy, and culture. In this way, there is an opening for democratic argument and deliberation in the space between universal norms and the will of democratic majorities. Democratic iterations constitute a link between the constitutional responsibility and local context of a specific state, and the state's allegiance to universal human rights (Benhabib 2007).

The global community is one arena in which democratic iterations are staged. Through taking part in iterations and negotiations in different international contexts, the commitment to human rights becomes an element in states' ongoing reflections of themselves as sovereign democracies. In the national arena, the people of a democracy need, through deliberation and formation of public opinion, to assume policies and legislation that correspond with international norms. At the same time, however, through democratic iterations the meaning of human rights will change in various directions, and the rights will be understood in new ways compared to authoritative originals and previous interpretations. Benhabib (2007) underlines that, while justification for sovereignty is needed in a democratic state, the outcomes of democratic iterations are not necessarily positive in the sense that discourses, public opinion, policies, and law will support the intentions in international human rights legislation. In other words, the democratic iterative process might also result in policies and decisions that other nations consider as contravening human rights.

8.2 An illustration of the argument—constructing children's rights in education in national policy

In the approach elaborated above as to how universal human rights are brought into agreement with the conditions and circumstances of particular states, national processes of democratic iterations are pointed out as central mechanisms. The democratic iterations will produce national versions of the universal rights, in which particular interpretations of the specific content of rights, and prioritizations between them, will be expressed. In this section, the aim is to demonstrate how the perception of rights can be affected through democratic iterations. In order to examine what national versions of children's human rights might look like and how they might differ from or resemble those of other nations, I have drawn on some of the results of a recent comparative policy study into how issues of children's rights in the field of education are constructed in the policies of two nations, namely Sweden and New Zealand.[2]

[2] The comparative policy study has been reported in Quennerstedt 2009b (New Zealand), 2010a (Sweden), and 2011 (comparison).

The will of the democratic citizenry becomes embodied in the policies that are pursued by governments and in the formulation of law. Analyses of the content of policies accordingly provide important insights into the process and outcomes of democratic iterations. The aim of the comparative policy study was to examine and compare the outcome of the process of interpretation in which universal claims of the child's rights to and in education are incorporated into the specific contexts of the two states. The more specific research focus was (i) to identify similarities and differences in the political constructions of children's rights in education, with regard to aspects of education that are proclaimed in policy as children's rights issues, and (ii) to explore how these similarities and differences can be understood as versions of universal children's rights transformed through democratic iterations.

The study was carried out in two steps. In the first step, text analyses of authoritative national political documents were done separately for each state. These analyses resulted in the identification of a range of issues in education that are constructed in the policies of the respective nations as relating specifically to children's rights. In the study's second step, the findings of the text analyses were compiled and compared. The comparison first of all focused on the outflow of the contextualization process of children's human rights in the two countries with the aim of identifying similarities and differences in the political constructions. Secondly, explanations for the similarities and differences were sought in the particular circumstances of the respective nation in terms of historical, cultural, political, and economic traditions and conditions. An overview of the major and minor rights issues that were identified in the study's first step is provided in Table 1.

In this chapter, the 'top issue' of each nation is discussed: student influence for Sweden and culturally responsive education for New Zealand. The educational matter proclaimed to be the most important children's rights issue in education accordingly differs between the nations. Moreover, the respective 'top issue' is only a minor issue in the other nation.

Table 1 Rights issues in education in Sweden and New Zealand as constructed in policy

Sweden	New Zealand
Major rights issues:	**Major rights issues:**
Student influence	Culturally responsive education
Participation in early childhood education	Participation in early childhood education
Teacher's knowledge about children's rights	Learning outcomes
Value formation	Value formation
Bullying	**Minor rights issues:**
Right to education	Bullying
Learning outcomes	Educational rights of students with disabilities
Minor rights issues:	Costs of education for families
Educational rights of students with disabilities	Disciplinary measures
Public funding	Student influence
Educational rights of students from minority groups	
Children's knowledge about their rights	

8.2.1 Student influence

In Swedish policy, student influence stands out as the most important of all children's rights issues in education. The political documents clearly and repeatedly state that in early childhood education and in school children have the right to participate in public will formation and decision-making and to influence the activities, learning content, and teaching methods. This claim is made with explicit reference to both national and international legislation:

> Children and youth shall be given influence and responsibility in school. The Education Act and curriculums regulate students' rights to influence the formation of their education. (Government Report Skr 2003/04:47, p. 38)

A closer examination of the motives given as to why influence is an important rights issue in education reveals three different lines of argument. The dominant motive is that influence is central to the fostering of tomorrow's citizens. Influence is closely connected to the explicit task assigned to Swedish early childhood education and school to educate for democracy. Children and students are to develop knowledge *about* democracy, but equally important is that they get to *practice* democracy and experience a democratic environment:

> The Government's aim is to strengthen the influence exerted by pupils and parents in school. Pupil influence is a prerequisite of the work which goes on in school. Pupils must be allowed influence, because the education of democratic citizens is one of the tasks of school. This in turn requires the pupils to have an opportunity to practise democracy in school. Pupil influence is also a precondition for participation and learning. (Sweden's second periodic report to the UN Committee on the Rights of the Child, p. 44)

A second justification for student influence is that it largely benefits the educational environment. Influence is first of all assumed to enhance learning, but is also expected to have a positive spillover into a number of other areas, e.g. the increase in a general sense of meaning, a reduction in bullying and the vandalizing of school buildings and property, and a reduction in stress levels:

> An interesting issue is how a well developed student democracy affects other matters in school, such as learning outcomes, stress, graffiti and the occurrence of bullying. (Government Report Skr. 2003/04:47, p. 41)

In these first two arguments for student influence the rights dimension is toned down—influence is perceived as a vehicle in the education of democratic citizens or as a quality factor. In the third motive for influence, the leading argument is that it is a question of rights; children and students are to be given influence because it is a human right as such, because as citizens they have the right to take part in the formation of public will—not because it is a means of achieving some other good:

> That students have influence in school is a *human right*. Students have a weak legal position in school...Against this background, it is particularly important to understand student influence in school as a right, and that schools develop this right through real content. (Official Report SOU 1997:116, p. 200, italics in the original)

In contrast to the Swedish perception, in New Zealand student influence is a rarely discussed rights issue in education. Although the need to strengthen children's influence and voice in society is pointed out in policy as an urgent concern in New Zealand, this need is hardly ever related to education. The matter of student influence does not receive much attention in policy, and reflection about children participating in informal decision-making in classrooms is more or less absent from the political discussion. When increased student influence is mentioned at all, it is mainly in terms of improving representation on the Board of Trustees, for example by having two student representatives instead of one, or allowing younger students to be represented:

> Several comments were made in submissions about children's participation at school. It was felt that schools should be more responsive to their students' views on how schools should be run. Some people believed that there needed to be two student representatives on school boards of trustees so that they can support each other and be more effective. Another suggestion was that children at primary and intermediate level also need a voice on the school board perhaps through an adult advocate. (Ministry of Youth Affairs 2000, p. 66)

The political rights of the child are specifically stated in Article 12 of the Convention on the Rights of the Child as the right to be heard and have your views taken into account. Influence is related to political human rights, i.e. the right to participate in the formation of public will and thereby take part in the exercise of power. A difference between New Zealand and Sweden concerns the interpretation of Article 12. Both nations maintain that efforts need to be made to strengthen the voice of the child in society, but take different stands on whether *education* is a central site for realizing children's political rights and for implementing Article 12. Sweden declares education to be a crucial place for this endeavour, whereas New Zealand looks to other societal arenas for the implementation of Article 12.

In Sweden's democratic iterations concerning the meaning and content of the rights of the child in the area of education, the nation's strong emphasis on the link between education and democracy—originating back to standpoints taken in educational policy after the Second World War—the matter of student influence as a human right of the child has been interpreted as connected to the responsibility of the education system to foster democratic citizens. The prioritization of student influence as an important children's rights issue in education can be understood in relation to this historical, political, and cultural background, and to the continuous will of Swedish society to assign education a fundamental role in upholding democracy. In New Zealand, the link between education and democracy is not as explicitly spelled out as in Sweden, and student influence is rarely proposed as a basis for maintaining democracy. When discussed at all, student influence is mainly linked to formal school governance in terms of boards of trustees or students' councils.

8.2.2 Culturally responsive education

In New Zealand policy, cultural responsiveness is proclaimed to be the most important rights-related matter in education. This claim is supported by references to international human rights instruments (e.g. Article 30 of the Convention on the Rights of the Child) and is also explicitly linked to obligations originating from the Treaty of Waitangi:[3]

> The whole child approach draws on UNCROC, which New Zealand ratified in 1993.... Specific rights include the right of indigenous children to preserve their own identity

[3] The Treaty of Waitangi was signed in 1840 by representatives of the British Crown and Māori chiefs. The Treaty established a British governor in New Zealand, recognized Māori ownership of their lands and other properties, and gave Māori the same rights as British subjects. Today it is generally considered to be the founding document of New Zealand as a nation, although disputes over what was agreed persist.

(Article 7) and the right of indigenous children to enjoy their own culture, religion and language (Article 30).... In addition, the Treaty of Waitangi requires the Crown to work in partnership with Māori to protect and respond to the collective and individual interests of Māori wellbeing and development. Together, the Treaty and UNCROC work to reinforce Māori children's rights. (Ministry of Social Development, 2002, p. 14)

Cultural responsiveness thus stands out as mainly connected to the rights of the minority Māori population in New Zealand; the right of the Māori child to be met by an education system that acknowledges and supports her or his cultural belonging, and that provides her or him with the possibility of developing a Māori identity, including language and culture, thinking, and world view:

In short, being able to live as Māori, imposes some responsibilities upon the education system to contribute towards the realisation of that broad goal. (Ministry of Education 2001, p. 4)

KaHikitia—Managing for Success acknowledges the Treaty of Waitangi as a document that protects Māori learners' rights to achieve true citizenship through gaining a range of vital skills and knowledge, as well as protecting te reo Māori as a taonga. (Ministry of Education 2008b, p. 2)

In New Zealand, the state's responsibility for arranging and funding a culturally responsive education system is perceived as very far-reaching and it permeates the organization of education. In order to meet all children's rights to a culturally responsive education, the New Zealand education system includes early childhood centres and schools with English language and Māori language instruction. The school system has two curriculums, one for English language schools and one for Māori language schools. Although the two curriculum documents are based on certain central and shared values, the Māori curriculum also promotes the cultural values and world views that are specific to the Māori community. Early childhood education has one joint curriculum for both English and Māori language centres, albeit with parallel texts:

This document recognises the distinctive role of an identifiable Māori curriculum that protects Māori language and tikanga, Māori pedagogy, and the transmitting of Māori knowledge, skills, and attitudes through using Māori language. (Ministry of Education 1996, p. 12)

Expectations that education should respond to cultural diversity are perceived in a significantly different way in Sweden, where claims for cultural responsiveness in education towards minority groups are rarely addressed as matters of rights. When the specific educational needs of students from minority groups are discussed in Swedish policy, it is mainly in terms of providing home language education for children belonging to a minority, and to some extent Swedish as a second language education.

However, the entitlement to home language education is not justified by references to the child's cultural human rights, or an idea that education should meet and promote cultural differences. It is instead promoted by arguments of beneficial effects for the child, such as a comprehensive home language being important for the development of the child's identity, or, since a successful learning of Swedish is closely connected to a developed home language, it will promote the integration of children from minority groups into Swedish society:

The purpose of home language instruction is to support the pupil's general linguistic development and in this way to promote progress towards active bilingualism. Entitlement to home language instruction is based on the individual pupil's need of linguistic support. (Sweden's second periodic report to the UN Committee on the Rights of the Child, p 136)

Different interpretations are evident in the two nations' policies about what education's responsibility for the child's cultural rights is. New Zealand holds as a fundamental rights issue that children from the nation's two official cultures are to be met by an education system that not only respects, but also advances their cultural belonging and develops appreciation for cultural diversity—an undertaking embodied in the design and funding of a parallel public school system with parallel curriculums for English and Māori schools. It can be noted, however, that the right to a culturally responsive education is not equally acknowledged for other cultural minorities in New Zealand. In Sweden, education is not perceived to have such an extensive responsibility for responding to the cultures of minorities, and the public education system is neither designed nor organized with the explicit aim of supporting minorities' cultural specificity.[4]

In bicultural New Zealand's understanding of human rights, the child's right to grow and develop within its culture is augmented. With a historical background of violent colonialism and relatively recent cruelty and injustices towards the Māori people, and the contemporary New Zealand vision of a nation that not only respects cultural diversity but also embraces it and is proud of it, the cultural rights of children belonging to one of the two official cultures of the nation are seen as vital to meet, protect, and promote. Education is viewed as a crucial site for this endeavour. In Sweden, the dominance of Swedish culture in education is rarely contested in policy. In the Swedish perception of human rights, children's cultural rights should be respected in everyday activities in educational settings, but cultural rights do not constitute a basis for organizing the public education system. Developing a cultural identity is more understood as a private matter than a responsibility of public education.

A decisive difference between the two nations is accordingly how cultural diversity is approached. In Sweden cultural particularity is to be respected—no discrimination on the basis of culture or ethnicity is accepted—but the fundamental societal line of thought is *integration*. The successful outcome of society's actions concerning cultural diversity is therefore well-integrated minorities that experience respect for their culture. In New Zealand, integration is not a way of thinking about the nation's biculturality, i.e. the Māori people are not to be culturally integrated, since integration is always a matter of a minority adapting to the majority and never the other way around. Against these different backgrounds, the democratic iterations in the respective nations have produced different interpretations of the content of children's cultural rights, how highly cultural rights are prioritized, and how the rights are connected to education.

8.3 Concluding remarks

This aim of this chapter has been to address the issue of how universally pronounced claims for children's rights are transferred from the international arena to the national, and how the understanding of rights for children is affected by this transformation process. A theoretical approach has been suggested, in which Benhabib's concept

[4] An exception is the Sami school, which is designed to support the indigenous Sami people's culture. However, the Sami school only offers education for Years 1–6, and has a very small number of students; in total about 170 students in five schools (which can be related to the size of the Sami population in Sweden: 20, 000). Further, the Sami school is not discussed in policy from either a children's rights or a cultural rights perspective.

of *democratic iterations* indicates national processes of public deliberation as central sites where transnational commitments meet and are negotiated with convictions held by that particular community. The perspective has been illustrated by showing how two nations have constructed issues of children's rights in education in policy. In this final section, I reflect on how the proposed perspective may offer tools for the examination of children's rights, or human rights generally, by filling a gap between universal rights documents and the everyday practices of a specific nation.

At the beginning of this chapter I argued that the Convention on the Rights of the Child should not be seen as the ultimate definition of children's rights. If studies of children's rights, e.g. concerning how rights are understood in a specific area of society or in a certain state, or the extent to which rights are met, only mirror their analyses and conclusions against the Convention itself, without giving attention to the space between the universal claim and the particular context, they might risk missing out on two important aspects. The first aspect is that the connection between children's human rights and democracy should be acknowledged. Human rights and democracy are interdependent and one cannot be placed above the other. Children's human rights, as expressed in the Convention on the Rights of the Child, can therefore not be regarded as situated outside the realm of the democratic people's political deliberations. That nations, through their democratic iterations, produce their own versions of children's human rights is a given and reasonable consequence of recognizing the right of a democratic people to form their own will. As indicated earlier, however, democratic iterations do not automatically result in actions that the global community would necessarily regard as being in line with human rights commitments. The national versions must therefore be critically examined. In such analyses, and together with theoretical perspectives, the Convention on the Rights of the Child is an important document.

The second aspect that could be neglected if the in-between space is not taken into account is that the content of human rights—what they are and what they mean—is the outflow of a continuous process; one that expands over time and space. The Convention constitutes the most authoritative agreement currently available in which children's human rights are considered with regard to the specific circumstances in which children, as a group of humans, are embedded. The Convention is an important milestone in the development of children's human rights, but it does not mark the end of the road. I would argue that the processes of democratic iterations across the world, within nations and between nations, are the terrain on which children's human rights are continuously articulated, contested, clarified, and enhanced. As these processes are the source of growth and change with regard to children's rights they should be closely studied.

Returning briefly to the example of Sweden's and New Zealand's understanding of children's rights issues in education, we can conclude that the nations' respective interpretations of student influence and cultural responsiveness of education reflect the public will that has been formed in democratic iterations in the nations. While both states recognize that the two issues are matters of children's rights in education, the specific historical background and political standpoints taken in each nation render one of them more important than the other. The analysis identifies two versions of how to view student influence and the cultural responsiveness of education as a matter of rights. Both versions are probably acceptable variations with understandable backgrounds. However, the analysis also gives grounds for posing critical questions to both nations, such as: Why are children's political rights so invisible in the area of education in New Zealand? And why is little attention given to children's cultural rights in Sweden?

The approach suggested in this chapter can contribute to a deeper understanding of the varying perceptions of children's human rights. By examining the space between universal human rights legislation and issues of children's rights in practice, justifiable variations can be understood as outflows of the will of democratic majorities. On the other hand, we might also be able to identify, and critically examine, differences that are not acceptable.

References

Alderson, Priscilla (1999) 'Human rights and democracy in schools do they mean more than "picking up litter and not killing whales"'? *The International Journal of Children's Rights*, 185–205.

Benhabib, Seyla (2004) *The Rights of Others* (Cambridge, Cambridge University Press).

Benhabib, Seyla (2007) 'Democratic Exclusions and Democratic Iterations: Dilemmas of "Just Membership" and Prospects of Cosmopolitan Federalism' *European Journal of Political Theory* 6(4), 445–62.

Bennet, John and Hart, Stuart N. (2001) 'Respectful Learning Communities: Laying the Foundations of Human Rights, Democracy and Peace in the New Millennium' in Stuart Hart et al (eds), *Children's Rights in Education* (London/Philadelphia, Jessica Kingsley Publishers, 2001), 191–216.

Bobbio, Norberto (1996) *The Age of Rights* (Cambridge/Malden, Polity Press).

Englund, Tomas, Quennerstedt, Ann, and Wahlström, Ninni (2009) 'Education as a Human and Citizenship Right—Parents' Rights, Children's Rights, or...? The Necessity of Historical Contextualization' *Journal of Human Rights* 8, 133–8.

Government Report Skr 2003/04: 47 *Utreckling av den nationella strategin för att förverkliga FN: s koventionomt barnets rättigheter [Development of the national strategy for the realisation of the UN Convention on the Rights of the Child]* Socialdepartementet [Ministry of Health and Social Affairs].

Grover, Sonja (2007) 'Children's right to be educated for tolerance: minority rights and inclusion' *Education and Law* 18(2–3), 149–60.

James, Allison and James, Adrian (2004) *Constructing Childhood. Theory, Policy and Social Practice* (Hampshire/New York, Palgrave Macmillan).

Marshall, Thomas H. (1949/1964), *Citizenship and Social Class* (Chicago, Chicago University Press).

New Zealand Ministry of Education (1996) *TeWhāriki.*

New Zealand Ministry of Education (2001) *A Framework for Considering Māori Educational Advancement.*

New Zealand Ministry of Education (2008) *KaHikita. Managing for Success. Māori Education Strategy.*

New Zealand Ministry of Social Development (2002) *New Zealand's Agenda for Children. Making life better for children.*

New Zealand Ministry of Youth Affairs (2000) *Second Periodic Report of New Zealand to the UN Committee on the Rights of the Child.*

Official Report SOU 1997:116 *Barnets bästa i främsta rummet. FN:s konvention om barnets rättigheter förverkligas i Sverige.* Barnkommitténs betänkande [*The best interest of the child in the first room. The UN Convention on the Rights of the Child made real in Sweden.* The Children's Committee's Final Report].

Quennerstedt, Ann (2009a) 'Balancing the Rights of the Child and the Rights of Parents in the Convention on the Rights of the Child' *Journal of Human Rights* 8, 162–76.

Quennerstedt, Ann (2009b) 'Children's Rights in Education—Transforming Universal Claims into New Zealand Policy' *New Zealand Journal of Educational Studies* 44(2), 63–78.
Quennerstedt, Ann (2010a) 'Den politiska konstruktionen av barnets rättigheter i utbildning' [The political construction of children's rights in education] *PedagogiskForskning i Sverige* [*Pedagogic Research in Sweden*] 15(3–4). In Swedish.
Quennerstedt, Ann (2010b) 'Children, But Not Really Humans? Critical Reflections on the Hampering Effect of the "3 p's"' *International Journal of Children's Rights* 18, 619–35.
Quennerstedt, Ann (2011) 'The Political Construction of Children's Rights in Education. A Comparative Analysis of Sweden and New Zealand' Submitted.
Sweden's second periodic report to the UN Committee on the Rights of the Child. UN Document CRC/C/65/Add.3.
United Nations (1948) *Universal Declaration of Human Rights*. General Assembly resolution 217 A (III), 10 Dec. 1948. U.N. Doc. A/RES/3/217/A.
United Nations (1989) *Convention on the Rights of the Child*. General Assembly resolution 44/25, 20 Nov. 1989. U.N. Doc. A/RES/44/25.
Wahlström, Ninni (2009) 'Understanding the Universal Right to Education as Jurisgenerative Politics and Democratic Iterations' *European Educational Research Journal* 8(4), 520–33.

9

Modern African Childhoods: Does Law Matter?

Julia Sloth-Nielsen[1]

9.1 Introduction

This chapter poses a question often aimed at lawyers, especially when they straddle a culturally diverse and contested terrain of human experience, such as the role of children and families in society: does law matter? The question is all the more pertinent in African contexts, due to the pervasive poverty, prevalence of practices harmful to children, and perceived inability of weak states to put legislative intentions into effect.

The backdrop is the sociology of childhood, more particularly, childhood in African contexts. The chapter commences in Part 9.2 with a discussion of pre-modern African childhood. Thereafter, Part 9.3 reviews the impact of colonial children's laws in constructions of childhood. It is argued that even the adoption of colonial children's legislation during the twentieth century failed to dislodge the primacy of culture in African childhood literature, and that by and large, formal law remained irrelevant to children's lives.[2] Nevertheless, some legacies of colonial laws can be detected, and these are explained. The article then examines, in Part 9.4, the implications of ratification of the UN Convention on the Rights of the Child (1989) (hereafter CRC) and the African Charter on the Rights and Welfare of the Child (1990) as far as the main question raised at the outset is concerned. In particular, the need for harmonization of domestic law with Convention and Charter principles is discussed, and the relevance of constitutionalism in modern Africa mentioned. The final part of this section examines the setting of an upper age of childhood, other age-related issues fundamental to modern African childhoods, marriage and gender equality, child participation, access to education, HIV/Aids as a driver of childhood constructs and socio-legal change, and harmful cultural practices. Part 9.5 contains a conclusion. It will be proposed that the introduction of a child rights discourse via the CRC and the African Charter on the Rights and Welfare of the Child, coupled with the implementation of large scale continental law reforms, has altered not only the legal landscape, but so too the present day understanding of childhood at a much more fundamental level. The conclusion

[1] Dean, Faculty of Law, University of the Western Cape, South Africa.

[2] Amanda Lloyd, 'Evolution of the African Charter on the Rights and Welfare of the Child and the African Committee of Experts: Raising the Gauntlet' (2002) 10 *The International Journal of Children's Rights* 183; Chuma Himonga, 'African Customary Law and Children's Rights: Intersections and Domains in a New Era' in Julia Sloth-Nielsen (ed), *Children's Rights in Africa: A Legal Perspective* (Ashgate, 2008) 73.

that this chapter puts forward is that law does matter: and that an irreversible journey has been set in place which redefines African childhood.

9.2 Pre-modern African childhood

Several propositions can be put forward to characterize childhood in African contexts (the word contexts is used here as no single or unified conception can purport to represent the universal experience of childhood in Africa).[3] But for some authors, there was in fact no concept of childhood, as commonly understood, in traditional African culture.[4] This view is contested: it belies the protections accorded children within the family by other means. For instance, it is well known that children's voices were heard through older relatives such as grandmothers whose role was to protect the children's interests thereby allowing for less formal and more interactive relationships between grandparents and their grandchildren.

The period during which a person was presumed in traditional African society to be a child was a diffuse one: on the one hand, children were expected to assume responsibilities towards the household from an early age. These could include adult-type responsibilities, such as child rearing in relation to younger siblings, tending crops and livestock, fetching water, and, in an overall sense, contributing in essential ways to the means of production and reproduction.[5] In this sense, 'childhood', as known in the western world today, was not a protected period of physical and psycho-social development in African societies. Rather it was a time-limited period of consummate dependency, followed by a gradual and inexorable progression into adult life: this progression commenced almost immediately a child could function independently.

Further, African childhood was generally marked by constant changes in status, roles, and responsibilities, rather than having a single exit point at a defined age.[6] The actual legal transition into a senior societal role was a functional outcome of various and different occurrences, procedures, or events. Establishing a hearth could be one, circumcision another, or taking a wife a third: the context and the cultural vehicle for transformation to adult status differed across cultures and tribes. This transition would have been neither automatic nor universal: in many instances, the perpetual minority status of women ensured that they never really migrated from childhood into adulthood; second or subsequent (male) siblings might have been similarly awarded lesser adult status, whatever their age, in view of the customary rules of primogeniture; and even widows, freed from the strictures of husband-rule,

[3] Julia Sloth-Nielsen and Benyam Mezmur, 'A Dutiful Child: The Implications of article 31 of the African Children's Charter' (2008) 52 *Journal of African Law* 159.

[4] Tom Bennett, 'Human Rights and the African Cultural tradition' (1993) 22 *Transformation* 30.

[5] K Mutua, 'The Banjul Charter and the African Cultural Fingerprint: An Evolution of the Language of Duties' (1995) 35 *Virginia Journal of international Law* 339. It is notable that African countries have expressed aversion to ratification of ILO Convention 132 relating to the Minimum Age of Admission to Employment, since child work is the norm and even an expected duty of maturation. See Jacqueline Gallinetti, 'An Assessment of the Significance of the Instrumental use of Children in the Commission of Offences as a Worst Form of Child Labour' (unpublished LLD thesis, University of the Western Cape, 2007) 207.

[6] Annika Hipple, 'Coming of Age Rituals in Africa: Tradition and Change' (2008) IV *Prudence International Magazine Journal*, available at <http://www.annikahipple.com/writing.samples> (accessed 28 June 2010); Manu Ampim, 'The Five Major African Initiation Rites' 2003, available at <http://www.manuampim.com/AfricanInitiationRites.htm> (accessed 28 June 2010).

would frequently be subject to ancillary customary laws and traditions which preserved minority status through leverite practices, widow cleansing, and such like.[7]

As in other cultures, the onset of puberty played an important role in child/adult transitions: a girl (especially) who had reached puberty was regarded as being of marriageable age. This link between puberty and adulthood affected not only the exit from childhood, but a range of other related themes, such as child marriage, child labour, and the rights of the child in and to education.[8]

Child protection, as a formal response to the abuse of the child within the family was an unknown societal phenomenon. This was likely because child rearing was a family concern, which did not involve the state or other institutions of governance. Instead the protection of children from excessively harsh treatment was a duty of other family members acting in a guardianship role towards children of the kinship circle or clan.

The harsh treatment of children was fairly commonplace, prevalent in practices which in places ranged from debt bondage of children to trafficking and sale of children. It is argued, though, that it is factually incorrect to depict the lack of attention to child protection as equivalent to the wholesale treatment of children as chattels or property in the family context: rather, children were cherished and valued, as semi-productive contributors of the future for the kinship unit.

There are many sayings, in cultures throughout Africa, which point to the value of children in family life, and it is crudely reductionist to equate this 'value' to monetary or fiscal terms.[9] Rather, 'value' in this sense bears a wide meaning: it entails that children are a form of emotional 'wealth' far beyond their present or potential economic contribution. Illustrative of the 'value' of children to the kinship group are the range of practices in customary law designed to enhance the child bearing and child rearing functionalism of the kinship group, such as leverite and sororite practices, women-to-women marriages, and so forth. From this, it can be deduced that children *qua* children were indeed beneficiaries of a customary conception of childhood, albeit that this differed from western versions.

Pre-colonial and to a significant extent even colonial Africa was a rural society, functioning with a pre-industrial subsistence economy, and with children as part and parcel of the means of production. Ariēs, Prout, and James and others have linked the emergence of childhood to the industrial revolution in western society, and law has been shown to be a critical adjunct to this process. Commencing with the emergence of laws restricting child labour,[10] the founding of the welfare system and the antecedents of the juvenile court,[11] the vision of childhood as an era of protective concern is a post-industrial period development. In Africa, however, the historical trajectory

[7] Lea Mwambene, 'The Impact of the Domestication of Rights in African Customary Family Laws: A Study of the Rights of Women in Malawi with some Reference to Developments in South Africa' (unpublished LLD thesis, University of the Western Cape, 2008).

[8] IRIN, 'Africa-Asia: Youth in Crisis: Coming of Age in the 21st Century' June 2010, available at <http://www.irinnews.org> (accessed 28 June 2010).

[9] See Bart Rwezaura, 'Competing "images" of childhood in the socio-legal systems of contemporary Sub Saharan Africa' (1998) 12 *International Journal of Law, Policy and the Family* 253 for a discussion of the notion of 'people-as-wealth' which emphasizes the communal value of intergenerational reproduction.

[10] See Jacqueline Gallinetti, 'An Assessment of the Significance of the Instrumental Use of Children in the Commission of Offences as a Worst Form of Child Labour' *op cit* note 5.

[11] See Julia Sloth-Nielsen, 'The influence of international law on South Africa's juvenile justice reform process' (unpublished LLD thesis, University of the Western Cape, 2001) 334 *et seq.*

of the development of child laws and a child rights discourse has been somewhat different to that in the north.

9.3 Colonization, children, and the law before 1990

It is somewhat unrealistic to assume that there might have been a leap from pre-colonial society to modern child rights-based legal systems without any intervening occurrences. In most African countries, as former colonies, legislation was adopted in the course of the twentieth century to create some kind of ad hoc legal framework relevant to juveniles or children. The review of legislation that preceded the adoption of the Kenyan Children's Act 2001 revealed the existence of more than 61 statutes affecting children, which the new law consolidated and modernized.[12] The Children's Act 38 of 2005 of South Africa repealed at least six discrete statutes dealing with children's status and welfare. The Law of the Child of Tanzania of 2009 repealed a number of previous enactments, and the Child Rights Act of Nigeria of 2003, in a similar vein, followed the Children and Young Persons Act of 1943, which was revised in 1958. This law related mostly to juvenile justice administration, and defined a child as a young person under the age of 14 years. The Namibia draft Child Care and Protection Act 2011 will repeal such enactments as 'The Children's Amendment Act (Rehoboth) 1981', and parts of a law called the 'Commonwealth Relations Act, 1962'. It will fundamentally replace the Children's Act of 1960, imported from South Africa before independence in 1990. The Lesotho (Child Welfare and Protection) Act finalized in 2010 has abrogated the colonial law which forbad the adoption of Basotho children by their own citizens of the country, privileging adoption for Europeans (sic) only.[13] Malawian colonial legislation has been very much in the public domain, thanks to the well publicized 'Madonna' series of cases.[14] The adoption law at stake in these cases dates to 1951.[15] Its enactment must be seen against the background that adoption as a customary law concept was for many peoples not only entirely unknown, but indeed contrary to basic tenets of ancestor and clan linkages, which are crucial to customary affiliation laws in many parts of the continent.[16] A number of countries appear to have enacted child protection laws in the 1970s, largely focused on juveniles in conflict with the law. Examples include Zanzibar, Mozambique, Botswana,

[12] See Godfrey Odongo, 'The Domestication of International Law Standards on the Rights of the Child with Specific Reference to Juvenile Justice in the African Context' (unpublished LLD thesis, University of the Western Cape, 2005).

[13] *Committee on the Rights of the Child: Concluding observations to the Lesotho Country Report*, CRC/C/15/Add.147 (26 January 2001). See also Itumeleng Kimane 2006, *The Lesotho Child Protection and Welfare Bill 2005: Why the delays in enacting the children's law?*, Unpublished paper presented at the University of the Western Cape/Miller Du Toit conference, 'The globalization of child and family law', 26–27 January (2005).

[14] Benyam Mezmur, 'From Angelina (to Madonna) to Zoe's Ark: What are the "A-Z" Lessons for Intercountry Adoptions in Africa?' (2009) *International Journal of Law, Policy and the Family* 1; Benyam Mezmur, '"As Painful as Giving Birth": A Reflection on the Madonna Adoption Saga' (2008) 41 *Comparative and International Journal of Southern Africa* 382; Julia Sloth-Nielsen, Belinda Van Heerden, and Benyam Mezmur, 'Intercountry Adoption from a Southern and Eastern African Perspective' (2010) *International Family Law* 86–97.

[15] In Botswana, adoption legislation was introduced a year later, in 1952: Act Proc. 63 of 1952 (Chapter 28:01, *Laws of Botswana*).

[16] For a historical trajectory of adoptions in traditional African societies, see Benyam Mezmur, 'Intercountry Adoption in an African Context: A Legal Perspective' (unpublished LLD thesis, University of the Western Cape, 2010) 30.

and Lesotho. These were at best partially implemented. By way of example, the 1971 Juvenile Code of Mozambique, enacted shortly before Portuguese exit from the country in 1975, was a model 'non-African' example: referring to non-existent structures and responsibilities, to be performed by non-existent functionaries.[17]

It can be concluded that African child law history demonstrates a pattern of the assimilation of law which mirrors some developments in the 'mother countries' and provides concrete evidence of colonial influence. Moreover, the institutions of the colonial era have found a place in many African countries, not just in law, but also in practice: borstals, approved schools, reformatories, schools of industry, and re-education facilities are (and were) part of the half-hearted attempts[18] to create separate institutions for children to underscore child welfare and juvenile justice systems.

Some colonial laws were racist in their content, others became so via their application. The *de jure* discrimination against nationals in the field of adoption in Lesotho has been noted. In South Africa, the child maintenance grant, a form of child support, was payable in practice only to white and mixed race persons until it was comprehensively overhauled in 1997 and replaced with a single child support grant payable to any primary caregiver of children who qualified on the means test. Zaal has written eloquently on the ways in which the apparently neutral children's court apparatus was used to promote apartheid ideology and further race classification for the purposes of racial segregation.[19]

Many colonial era child laws fell far short of a child rights orientation at even the most basic of levels: provisions for the reporting of child abuse did not feature at all, and the ideology of the delinquent, vagrant, promiscuous child (or child exposed to sexual exploitation) pervaded concepts of which children were in need of protection or care. State care systems, as such, were non-functional, and the 'duty' to provide child protection services rested mainly on civil society and religious organizations. Such juvenile justice statutory provisions as did exist were frequently encapsulated in isolated provisions of penal and criminal procedure codes. South Africa's position until 1 April 2010, when a dedicated Child Justice Act (75 of 2008) came into force, illustrates this point (Nigeria, Rwanda, and Ethiopia constitute three further examples). Fragmentation of statutes affecting children was evident in other areas as well, such as affiliation laws, inheritance laws, and laws relating to the maintenance of deserted wives and children.

Nevertheless, the existence of legislation relating to children before the CRC and African Charter did set in place the following legacies:

1) They created, in some places, the *expectations* of a discrete philosophy of childhood articulated through the creation of some separate institutions, through affiliation and family codes, through isolated provisions of criminal codes and procedural laws which contained some concession to youth or immaturity,[20]

[17] Julia Sloth-Nielsen and Jacqueline Gallinetti, *Report on the review of child law in Mozambique* (UNICEF and the Government of Mozambique, 2004).

[18] Half-hearted because many were set up with poor attention to infrastructural and maintenance costs. They remain sites for the abuse of children, rather than their rehabilitation or reintegration: see Julia Sloth-Nielsen and Benyam Mezmur, 'Surveying the Research Landscape to Promote Children's Legal Rights in an African Context' (2007) 7 *African Human Rights Law Journal* 330–53.

[19] Noel Zaal, 'Court Services for the Child in Need of Alternative Care: a Critical Evaluation of Selected Aspects of the South African System' (unpublished LLD thesis, University of the Witwatersrand, 2008) chapter 2.

[20] E.g. requiring children's identities to be protected in court procedures, or their cases to be separated from those of adults when alleged to be in conflict with the law.

and through the introduction of western law concepts such as contractual and other status-bearing events including the attainment of majority upon conclusion of a civil marriage. How deep this ran differed from place to place. South African and other Roman Dutch territories (Zimbabwe, Namibia, Botswana, Swaziland) as well as Uganda, Kenya, Tanzania, and Malawi, had an elaborate system of personal law by the time of the introduction of the CRC, based on a century of indigenous judicial precedent as well as the old statutes. Many texts on 'The Law of Persons', dating back to the 1900s, testify to this.

2) Second, some conception of *separation* of childhood from adult status did take root. There is no better testimony to this than the early declarations on children of the Organization for African Unity (OAU) (now the African Union (AU)), which predate the CRC and the international child rights movement to some extent.[21]

3) Third, a *welfarist* leaning was readily discernible, and a conflation of delinquency, danger, and disgrace were manifest. As recently as a decade ago, this was shown to prevail in studies analysing children's court proceedings in Kenya, where the majority of children appearing were street children, vagabonds, and urchins. This was possibly because of an underlying premise that welfare was the preserve of the African (extended) family. State intervention would occur only when public order was at stake, visibly so in the case of street children.

   South African trajectories were slightly different: the 'swart gevaar' (black danger) relegated children in any sort of trouble to the penal system, where they were disallowed the 'benefits' of the welfare system. It is no surprise that, at the dawn of democracy in 1996, children's welfare institutions were largely segregated by race, and mostly reserved for white and mixed race children—black children were rarely brought within the purview of the formal welfare system in South Africa for most of the previous century.[22]

4) Finally, the existence of the legislation for the welfare of children that prevailed did imply, in theory, a *state* system which could intervene to protect children where this was deemed necessary. But the idea of the 'least detrimental alternative' or 'minimum intervention' did not feature in law. Also, the indigenous systems of child protection, restorative justice, and community-based dispute resolution did not rise to the surface at all. It is only in the recent raft of child protection statutes that some attempt has been made to capture indigenous concepts and practices, a fuller discussion of which lies beyond the scope of this chapter.[23]

[21] Julia Sloth-Nielsen, 'Children's Rights in Africa' in M. Ssenyonjo (ed), *The African Regional Human Rights System 30 years after the ACHPR and Beyond* (Brill Publishing, The Netherlands, 2011).

[22] Julia Sloth-Nielsen, *op cit* note 11; Julia Sloth-Nielsen, 'A Short History of Time: Charting the Contribution of Social Development Service Delivery to Enhance Child Justice 1996–2006' (2007) 43(4) *Social Work/Maatskaplike Werk* 317–29.

[23] See, however, Julia Sloth-Nielsen and Benyam Mezmur, *op cit* note 18; Julia Sloth-Nielsen and Jacqueline Gallinetti, 'Just Say Sorry? *Ubuntu*, Africanisation and the Child Justice System in the Child Justice Act 75 of 2008' (paper presented at the conference on 'Ubuntu, Humanity and good faith/Equity as Flexible Principles in Law and Society in Southern Africa: Appropriate Principles in an Ever-changing world', Potchefstroom, 1–3 September 2010).

9.4 Implications of the CRC (1989) and the African Charter on the Rights and Welfare of the Child (1990)

African countries were amongst the first to ratify the CRC.[24] At the time of writing, 45 states (of the 53 member states of the African Union) are signatories to the regional treaty, the African Children's Charter.

The CRC requires a macro-level re-orientation of the relationship between state, family, and child, with a newly established role and set of responsibilities for the state in relation to the construction of childhood and its socio-political organization.[25] State parties undertake upon themselves a defined role in relation to the promotion, protection, and fulfillment of the rights of children, and thereby also irretrievably impact on and alter the rights of the family.[26] Thus, while articles 5 and 18 recognize the primacy of the role played by families in child rearing, a subsidiary role for states to support them in these endeavours is carved out. Article 19 crucially accords states a front line position in the protection of children within the family, and commits ratifying states parties to a range of actions and interventions to protect children, irrespective of in whose care they find themselves. This underlying orientation, which views childhood as a matter of public, and not merely private concern, is especially relevant for modern African childhoods.

Second, fulfillment of international obligations incurred by ratification is principally achieved through the reporting mechanism set up in the body of the treaty itself. Reporting carries with it the prospect of bringing the largely hidden-from-scrutiny-arena of child rearing into the public domain, at least on the international plane.[27] Hence, matters which relate to areas as varied as health, sexual exploitation, and cultural practices have increasingly been documented and placed under the spotlight of the international community through the reporting process, and cannot be shielded behind domestic particularity or local tradition. Female genital cutting is the most widely known example, but there are others: *ukuthwala* (seduction amongst the Xhosa), *trokosi* (sexual slavery in Ghana), targeting of children as witches (Burundi),[28] and killing of albino children (Tanzania). Largely since the adoption of the CRC, these and other issues have emerged from being merely anthropologically interesting to become *legally* significant.[29]

Third, and following on from the above, it is clear that ratification brings with it domestic responsibilities: the municipal dimension. Thus CRC's article 4 requires states parties to undertake 'all appropriate legislative, administrative and other measures for the implementation of the rights recognized in the Convention'. Harmonization of domestic law with international principles is therefore required, and it is thus that almost all countries in southern and eastern Africa, Northern Africa, and many in Central and West Africa have undertaken legislative reviews

[24] Ghana was the first country to ratify the CRC in 1990.

[25] Nigel Cantwell, 'The Origins, Development and Significance of the United Nations Convention on the Rights of the Child' in Sharon Detrick, *The United Nations Convention on the Rights of the Child: A guide to the travaux preparatoires* (Kluwer, The Netherlands, 1992) 26.

[26] Julia Sloth-Nielsen, 'Domestication of Children's Rights in National Legal Systems: Progress and Prospects' in Julia Sloth-Nielsen (ed), *Children's Rights in Africa: A Legal Perspective* (Ashgate, Dartmouth, 2008) 53.

[27] UNICEF, *Implementation handbook for the Convention on the Rights of the Child* (2007) ix.

[28] This has now been proscribed in the 2005 Constitution of Burundi.

[29] A host of laws proscribing female genital mutilation of fairly recent origin can be traced (Egypt, Ethiopia) as also recent anti-trafficking enactments (Benin, Mozambique, South Africa).

and have updated and remodelled their children's laws, this time with a principled and comprehensive treaty as guidance. In fact, two early starters, Uganda (1996) and Kenya (2001), are amidst the second wave of reform.[30]

The colonial enactments of the previous century are being replaced and expanded to produce a new set of principles and practices which define childhood, the state, and the family. Some of these are addressed in more detail shortly. A central question that arises for consideration is whether the project of domestication in turn impacts upon understandings of childhood at a micro level, or societally, generally; this is an issue to which I return in conclusion.

The development and formulation of the African Children's Charter in 1990 (in effect from 1999) is a relevant additional factor in answering the central question posed in this article. The Charter was advocated as a regional response to the development of a child rights discourse at the international level.[31] African countries, having played a rather marginal role in the overall framing of the CRC,[32] were persuaded that a regional children's rights treaty would be apposite not only to address the evident gaps and socio-political absence of African concerns from the dominant agenda, but also to reinforce the notion that an African conception of children's rights *did exist*. The concerns to which the African Children's Charter speaks include the use of child soldiers, children of imprisoned mothers, a culturally specific understanding of the concept and role of the extended family in matters of child care, the (then) plight of children living under apartheid, gender inequality in relation to female children and harmful practices, the position of refugee and displaced children, and the definition of the child. It has been asserted that adoption of the African Children's Charter was not simply evidence of an African rush to echo precepts already contained in the CRC, but rather substantiation of an abiding concern for children and protection of their rights within the OAU (now the AU).[33] The Charter followed a previous Declaration on the Rights of the Child as well as considerable activity at regional level on issues prevalent in children's rights discourse, especially on child health and child labour. The Charter also embodies an obligation to provide for its principles in domestic law.

Children's rights were thus not alien to Africa, or imposed, nor were they simply adopted and adapted from the north. Instead, they were alleged to have a strong local resonance, most aptly encapsulated in the preamble to the Charter and in article 31, setting out the duties of the African child.[34]

Treaties themselves are, of course, a form of law. Therefore, at a very simplistic level, the fact of ratification by states parties in Africa of both the international and the regional documents implies that there is strong support for the conclusion that 'law' does matter insofar as state obligations to a particular conception of childhood have been formally underwritten. This high level impact is bolstered by recognition of

[30] The author attended a workshop on proposed amendments to the Kenya Children's Act in Naivasha, May 2010, and a copy of the proposed draft Ugandan amendments are on file.

[31] Danwood Chirwa, 'The Merits and Demerits of the African Charter on the Rights and Welfare of the Child' (2002) 10 *International Journal on Children's Rights* 157; Dejo Olowu, 'Protecting children's rights in Africa: A critique of the African Charter on the Rights and Welfare of the Child' (2002) *International Journal on Children's Rights* 137; Frans Viljoen, 'The African Charter on the Rights and Welfare of the Child' in Trynie Boezart T (ed), *Child Law in South Africa* (Juta, Cape Town, 2010) 331; Benyam Mezmur, 'The African Charter v The UN Convention on the Rights of the Child: A Zero Sum Game?' (2008) 23 *SA Public Law* 1; Julia Sloth-Nielsen, *op cit* note 21.

[32] Only Egypt, Morocco, Algeria, and Senegal were actively involved in the drafting process of the CRC.

[33] Julia Sloth-Nielsen, *op cit* note 21.

[34] Julia Sloth-Nielsen and Benyam Mezmur, *op cit* note 3.

children as constitutional subjects: a majority of African constitutions refer explicitly to a variety of children's rights, ranging from education rights to protection rights.[35] South Africa takes a lead position internationally in constitutionalizing justiciable children's rights, which have, since the adoption of the 1996 constitution, resulted in a wealth of jurisprudence giving effect to a thoroughly modern conception of childhood rooted in human rights law and based on modern philosophies, such as child participation.

9.4.1 The upper age

The CRC, and the African Children's Charter unequivocally, set the age of childhood as extending to the age of 18 years. It has often been noted that the Charter affords higher protection than the CRC, since it does not permit of exceptions where national law provides for a lower age of majority, as does the CRC. Another obvious age-related issue concerns the minimum age of marriage, which the Charter establishes as a legal norm to be 18 years.

The *de facto* earlier entry into adulthood for African children which has prevailed has given way to a plethora of legal provisions which enshrine 18 as the age until which the protection of the status of childhood will endure. Colonial laws were uneven and insecure about defining childhood at all. In South Africa and some neighbouring states, the age of majority was set at 21, a position which changed in South Africa only in 2007, and which in Namibia will only change with the adoption of the Child Care and Protection Bill 2011. Previous legislation which set an age at below 18 has been revised upwards in some places (e.g. Mozambique).

It can be concluded that as regards the new provisions on age, law does matter: 18 has been established uncontroversially in many constitutions and domestic laws in accordance with the international treaty provisions, and customary conceptions have had to recede. The minimum age for extending protection against trafficking has been similarly set at 18 (e.g. in Law of Benin No 2006-04 of 10 April 2006; Chapter 17 of the Children's Act 28 of 2005 of South Africa).

9.4.2 Some other age-related concerns fundamental to the adult/child dichotomy in Africa

Culturally relevant events which raise flags in the discussion about whether law matters to African childhoods include marriage, especially child marriage, and the age of sexual consent. The fact of public outrage in Nigeria over the marriage of a 50-year-old senator to an Egyptian minor of 13 years in 2010 lends some credence to the contention that customary and religious conceptions of marriageability at puberty are receding. The 2003 Child Rights Act of Nigeria clearly provides for 18 years as the legal age for a valid marriage and the corresponding Egyptian law also prohibits child marriage. It is increasingly untenable to defend child marriages as excused by religious rights or the right to privacy, in the face of nationally and internationally binding agreements. The contention is that insofar as custom is being abrogated, law does matter.[36]

[35] Julia Sloth-Nielsen, *op cit* note 26.

[36] The National Agency for the Prohibition of Trafficking in Persons (NAPTIP) of Nigeria commenced investigations on the matter with a view to taking relevant action while the Supreme Council

The legal framework within which marriage of girls must be considered includes the Convention on the Elimination of Discrimination Against Women (CEDAW) and the African Women's Protocol (in force from 2007). Both take equality within marriage and freedom of choice (i.e. voluntary entry into marriage) as axiomatic, and enjoin states parties to ensure this through legislation.

But the colonial heritage of many states is legislation providing for different ages for the minimum age of consent to sexual intercourse for girls and boys. Frequently, the age for girls is lower, and is allegedly linked to their earlier physical maturation. Sexual consent laws are both contentious and confusing. South Africa's recent attempts to achieve a uniform minimum age for consent (at 16 years, below which sexual acts with a child constitute a statutory offence),[37] yet provide protection from exploitation, have led to the adoption of controversial provisions which criminalize consensual sexual acts between teenagers, which in turn raises the issue of children's autonomy and self-determination rights.[38] There is little unanimity regarding the ages of consent to sexual entrée in African legal systems, although where protective provisions relevant to HIV/Aids are concerned, the tendency is to permit voluntary testing for HIV at an age well below 18 years which indicates a certain degree of schizophrenia about when children should be recognized as sexual beings.[39]

Summarizing, the relevance of age to understandings of childhood in modern African systems, it is argued that there has been an inexorable movement towards agreeing that childhood up until 18 is a period of immaturity warranting differential treatment. This has occurred notwithstanding a cultural view that children still have responsibilities towards their families and duties to contribute to the maintenance of the family's means of production. Protection is also evident in the setting of a minimum age of marriage at 18 years in many new children's laws, and a more protective (legal) stance towards the age of sexual debut.

9.4.3 Non-discrimination

International law requires that legislative attention be paid to outlawing any form of discrimination against children on a variety of listed grounds, such as legitimacy, gender, and race. However, attempts to address equality in marriage laws that have been enacted in recent times in some African states have been controversial, the controversy extending to the position of extra-marital children.

Namibia adopted, after intense Parliamentary debates, legislation concerning child custody which provides for unmarried women and men equally to be appointed custodian of a child born out of wedlock, but only the one of them: the one *de facto* raising the child.[40] Payment of child support is also gender neutral (on paper), as the custodian parent is primarily responsible for the rearing of the child and the payment

for Sharia in Nigeria has challenged the Federal Government and the National Assembly of Nigeria in court.

[37] In *Geldenhuys v The State* 2008 ZASCA 47, the differential ages of consent to sexual intercourse for males and females (16 for girls and 18 for boys) was found to be unconstitutional, but with retrospective effect as the amended Criminal Law (Sexual Offences) Amendment Act 32 of 2007 had already equalized the minimum age via legislative reform.

[38] A constitutional challenge to the law is pending but at the time of writing had not been heard.

[39] The South African Children's Act 38 of 2005 (section 130) permits independent consent to HIV testing from the age of 12 or even below this age if the child is of an age and maturity to understand the implications of the test.

[40] Children's Status Act 6 of 2006, in force since 3 November 2008.

of all expenses. But apparent gender neutrality in attempts to give effect to the equality provisions of international and regional treaties can mask and even entrench traditional gender inequality, since it is most often mothers who raise children born out of wedlock.

Kenya's Children Act 2001 has become renowned for the lassitude granted errant fathers of children born out of wedlock to escape responsibility for their offspring. Numerous judgments have confirmed that the father must acknowledge paternity before acquiring rights, and that the duty to support a child does not arise before that event.[41] The 2010 Constitution of Kenya, which clarifies the responsibility of both parents to provide child support, will require a revision of the Children Act's scheme.

In South Africa, the Children's Act 37 of 2005 does not give full and completely equal recognition to biological fathers who were or are not married to the mother at or around the time of the child's birth. Section 21 of the Act provides a scheme whereby, provided the biological father satisfies certain predetermined criteria (some of which are objectively ascertainable, such as whether he was living with the mother at the time of the child's birth, and others of which are more amenable to interpretation—such as whether he has made a 'reasonable contribution' to the expenses and to the upbringing of the child'): he is vested with parental rights automatically.[42]

The abovementioned recent statutes addressing the position of unmarried fathers, and of gender equality outside of marriage, are bound up in the requirements of the CRC and African Children's Charter to ensure that children do not suffer discrimination on account of the marital status of their parents. The new children's laws giving effect to this on the continent alter customary affiliation rules and will ensure a greater obligation on unmarried fathers to provide material support to their offspring.

9.4.4 Child participation

Both the CRC and the African Children's Charter are unique in according children the right to participate in matters affecting them, and requiring their expressed views to be given due weight. This principle runs contrary to traditional conceptions of children in African contexts, grounded in children's respect for elders, which presupposes a hierarchical societal structure in which children are regarded as having insufficient societal status to express useful opinions or views.

In modern Africa, the concept of child participation is being given effect to in various forms. This development is undoubtedly inspired by the processes of domestication of the CRC and the Charter. Prominent examples include the establishment of children's parliaments,[43] the consultations with children held at the time of the UN Violence study, and in-country developments regarding legal representation of children charged with offences.[44]

[41] Julia Sloth-Nielsen, Nkatha Murungi, and Lorenzo Wakefield, 'Does the differential criterion for vesting parental rights and responsibilities of unmarried parents violate international law? A legislative and social study of three African countries' (2011) 55(2) *Journal of African Law* 203.

[42] When the Act came into force on 1 July 2007, qualifying fathers acquired parental responsibilities and rights in respect of their biological children retrospectively.

[43] Nigeria reported to the African Committee of Experts in November 2008 that the creation of 34 children's parliaments in 19 states was the vehicle for giving effect to hearing children's views, and that many children's clubs had been set up at state level. The ordinance of Burkina Faso establishing children's parliaments dates from 1998.

[44] Cheryl Frank and Louise Ehlers, 'Child Participation in Africa' in Julia Sloth-Nielsen (ed), *Children's Rights in African Context; A Legal Perspective* (Ashgate, 2008).

This new continental focus on hearing children's voices spreads far and wide. Concerning Niger, arguably amongst the most traditionalist (and Islamic) of African societies, it has been said that:

> The institutional organ, the youth parliament, is that it constitutes an environment of expression, concentration and permanent exchange which allows the children to call out to the public authorities and their parents on the matters of these times: violence in the family and school environment where they are the victims or authors. Based on this, they participate actively [in] the public and political life of the country and thus become full actors in the elaboration and reforms of the laws. Another advantage of this youth parliament is that it weakens the prevailing seniority principle which ensures that the young keeps quiet and obeys to the elders.[45]

Consultation about law reform with children is a fairly advanced endeavour, having commenced with consultations in the 1990s in South Africa at the time of drafting of the Child Justice Act and the Children's Act. The Mozambique legislation of 2008 was also preceded by a dedicated process of consultation with specific groups of vulnerable children (victims of child labour, or sexual exploitation and child prostitution, children in conflict with the law and so forth).[46] The recent development of the Namibian Child Care and Protection Bill of 2011 was furthered by innovative and multipronged methods of reaching children, including through classroom debates on certain key themes in the Bill, through newspaper inserts in several languages at periodic intervals, through a 'sms' campaign which saw children responding to questions such as 'what the minimum age of majority should be' and at what age the law should permit consent to medical treatment, followed with the establishment of a 'facebook' group for children and young people to discuss law reform questions.[47] This was supplemented by face-to-face consultations with groups in remote rural areas. The present process to develop a new children's law for the island territory of Zanzibar has been accompanied by probably one of the most extensive child participation exercises yet to take place, with village and district level child groups, formally constituted, debating child protection, child labour, responses to juvenile delinquency, and other intended aspects of the proposed new statute. Each and every district in the twin islands of Ungugaa and Pemba has been included in the consultation exercise.

Children's radio, hotlines for children, and access to justice initiatives flesh out the array of child participation strategies that have been identified. Celebrations of the Day of the African Child (an initiative launched by the African Committee of Experts on the Rights and Welfare of the Child, held annually on 16 June) typically involve children's participation in the exercise of their rights in a variety of media and via many models (drama, radio, debates, competitions, schools-based activities, and so on). In South Africa, March 2011 heralded the completion of the first national schools human rights moot competition, the final rounds of which saw children debating at the Constitutional Court.

NGOs, civil society organizations, and of course the international donor community are undoubtedly driving these developments. As a consequence, it may be contended that child participation is not organic, culturally approved, or a widespread

[45] African Child Policy Forum, 'Harmonization of Child Law in Central and West Africa' (forthcoming, copy on file with the author).

[46] Cheryl Frank and Louise Ehlers, *op cit* note 44.

[47] *Public Participation in Law Reform: Revision of Namibia's Draft Child Care and Protection Bill* (Final Report, 2010) Legal Assistance Centre and UNICEF, Windhoek, 2010.

and grassroots counter to the traditional invisibility of children in Africa. However, it may be suggested that even if child participation is occurring only to a fairly limited degree, the growing acceptance of hearing children's voices is worthy of note, insofar as traditional conceptions of the role of the child have had to shift to accommodate these new forms of child participation.

9.4.5 Access to education

Arlene Skolnick writes that '[t]he institution of schooling in Western societies has had profound effects on conceptions of childhood as well as on children themselves. It is school, along with the family, that defines the child's place in contemporary Western culture. For us school is the "natural habitat" of childhood, the school child is the child. The concept of childhood, the emergence of the private, emotionally intense family, and the idea of the school as part of the "normal" socialization of the child were different aspects of the historical process of modernization'.[48]

The CRC and the African Children's Charter enshrine the child's right to basic education without qualification. For Africa, the drive to spread access to education has assumed a new dynamic since the identification of universal primary education as one of the Millennium Development Goals. The effects have been dramatic, albeit that the goal of universal primary education for all will not be met by 2015. In many countries, enrolment rates have escalated sharply affecting both boys and girls. Comparing village life and town life in modern Uganda, Cheney explains the local effects of the drive towards education on childhood in Africa, and the way in which education severs the rural link and constructs a new African childhood.[49] This result is surely multiplied across the continent, where more and more children are now in school.[50] Implementation of the right to compulsory education brings with it a new experience of childhood for the African child of today.

9.4.6 HIV/Aids as a driver of understandings of childhood and concomitant legal changes

The impact of HIV upon children in Africa has been well documented and its impact felt upon policy and law reform initiatives since the mid-1990s. First, it has had a bearing on issues relating to consent to treatment and to HIV testing, where states have had to take account not just of children's evolving capacity to provide such consent *in abstracto*, as it were, but also on account of the potential lack of availability of parents and guardians able to furnish substitute consent due to the growing numbers of children orphaned by the disease. South Africa's Children's Act 38 of 2005 provides an example, as it provides for a new minimum age of consent to medical treatment (12 years, provided that child understands the nature and import of the treatment concerned: section 129), and a minimum age for consent to HIV testing (again 12 years, but without the proviso concerning sufficient understanding or maturity, and further providing that a child below the age of 12 years can furnish consent to a HIV

[48] Arlene Skolnick, 'The Limits of Childhood: Conceptions of Child Development and Social Context' 39(3) *Law and Contemporary Problems* Children and the Law (Summer, 1975).

[49] Kristen Cheney, '"Village Life Is Better Than Town Life": Identity, Migration, and Development in the Lives of Ugandan Child Citizens' (2004) 47(3) *African Studies Review* 1.

[50] See Benyam Mezmur and Julia Sloth-Nielsen, 'The Right to Education in Africa: Taking Stock' in C. J. Davel (ed), *Essays in Honour of Hans Visser* (Juta and Co, 2008).

test if such child is sufficiently mature to understand 'the benefits, risks and social implications of the test': section 130). Children will be considered mature if they can 'demonstrate that they understand the information on HIV Testing and can act in accordance with that appreciation' taking into account the child's age, knowledge of HIV and its implications, views, and personal circumstances.[51] A third highly contested provision[52] concerns access to contraceptives: section 134 of the Children's Act states that no person may refuse to sell condoms to a child over the age of 12 years or to provide these on request where they are available free of charge. Contraceptives other than condoms may be provided on request by a child, without parental consent or knowledge, if the child is aged 12 or older and the child is given proper medical advice and an examination to determine whether there are any medical contraindications to the provisions of a specific contraceptive. These provisions were prompted by concerns for children's reproductive health and policies that privilege the protection of children over cultural objections or opposition from parents. The HIV-related legislation illustrates the point that children's agency and evolving capacity is fundamentally altering the construction of childhood.[53]

The second arena where HIV/Aids has played a role in bringing modern African childhoods to the fore is in relation to alternative care. It has been noted that the pandemic has, in fact, spawned a new language in child rights policy circles:[54] of child headed households, OVCs (orphaned and vulnerable children), and kinship care, all slowly wending their way into policy and legal instruments. The impact of HIV/Aids on the breakdown of the extended family, burgeoning numbers in orphanages and children without parental care, has brought the issue of the traditional care of African children within family and clan structures to the surface, as numerous studies have shown the lack of coping ability of families devastated by HIV/Aids (even if the orphan estimates of the late 1990s and early 2000s have not played out to the extent that some predicted). Consequently, much current NGO and civil society work, not to mention policy initiatives and donor support, is geared towards shoring up community structures to enable the 'traditional family', often comprising only the older generation, with the middle generation having themselves been decimated by the ravages of the disease, to perform the care function that states are unable to do.

HIV/Aids has revealed, if nothing else, that the image of an idyllic rural childhood spent secure in a tight-knit family circle surrounded by a clan of diverse caregivers is, for many vulnerable children, a myth. Fieldwork over the last decade has pointed to children's extreme vulnerability to exploitation and deprivation of both basic and other (e.g. psycho-social) needs, and the inability of traditional family and kinship structures to step into the breach due to the HIV pandemic. Legal responses to the orphan crises are legion, ranging from formal recognition in civil law of kinship care arrangements (Namibia, South Africa, Tanzania), to new regulations governing the establishment and functioning of alternative care institutions (Kenya).

[51] Prinslean Mahery et al, *A Guide to the Children's Act for Health Professionals* (4th ed, 2010), Children's Institute, University of Cape Town, quoting the Department of Health *HIV Counselling and testing (HCT) Policy Guidelines* of March 2010 at 15.

[52] There was much adverse press coverage when this provision was put into operation on 1 July 2007.

[53] There is currently a national debate about a recent plan of the National Department of Health to conduct HIV testing in all secondary schools.

[54] Julia Sloth-Nielsen and Benyam Mezmur, 'Confronting Hydra Head On: Children's Rights in the Era of HIV/Aids' in Julia Sloth-Nielsen (ed), *Children's Rights in Africa: A Legal Perspective* (Ashgate, 2008).

9.4.7 Harmful cultural practices

Anecdotally, it is evident that the most objectionable harmful cultural practices which violate children's rights are in retreat. Thus, the full story of the extent to which female genital mutilation (FGM) is receding at grass roots level is one that needs to find expression: too many narratives focus on the practice as if the fact that it continues to occur indicates the impossibility of furthering children's rights in African context, and seem to point to the futility of legislative reform to prohibit and criminalize the practice.[55] Egypt's report to the African Committee of Experts on the Rights and Welfare of the Child is a benchmark in providing evidence of a steep decline in the practice, as the government has used village level approaches to combat and prevent FGM as an adjunct to formal law and policy.[56] Anecdotal reports suggest that in countries such as Ethiopia, programmes targeting village women are having similar effects.

9.5 Conclusion: laws do matter?

The conclusion postulated here is that law matters very fundamentally to childhood in modern African society, even if this might yet be in a way that differs from the modernized world. To an extent, the role of law remains aspirational; no one would argue that education has reached all qualifying children, or that early childhood marriage no longer occurs, or that children have been emancipated from their formerly subordinate position as non-actors in family or societal life.

But equally, the evidence is undeniable that there has been recognition of an evolving role for childhood in African society, a role that (as elsewhere) encompasses both a protectionist stance towards the very young, the marginalized, the orphaned, and the vulnerable, as well as a version which acknowledges children's evolving autonomy and agency. In this reconstruction of the African child, it is asserted that law has played a crucial role.

In pre-colonial times, children were the exclusive responsibility of families and clans. The constitutional project which has been underway across Africa since the 1990s has seen children specifically identified as beneficiaries of rights to be accorded them by states. South Africa's signal constitutional provision has rendered children's claims justiciable across an array of fronts, and can be regarded as trendsetting. Further to constitutional reform, the ratification of international and domestic treaties has spurred a continent-wide revision of the status of children as seen in new children's statutes across the continent. These, too, see the state as critical to children's lives and the fulfillment of their rights. Additionally, the ongoing drive towards legislating for gender equality, required by treaty law, has benefitted children in relation to affiliation, equal parenting rights in marriage, enhancement of access to child support, and inheritance.[57]

[55] See, e.g. Niger (Law No 2003–25 of the 13 June 2003 on FGM).

[56] Egypt enacted criminal sanctions for FGM which came into effect from June 2008. See Julia Sloth-Nielsen and Benyam Mezmur, 'Out of the Starting Blocks: the 12th and 13th meeting of the African Committee of Experts on the Rights and Welfare of the Child' (2009) 9 *African Human Rights Law Journal* 336.

[57] An example is the *Bhe* case (*Bhe and Others v Magistrate Khayeltisha and others (Commission for Gender Equality as Amicus Curiaie; Shibi and Sithole and Others; South African Human Rights Commission and Another v President of the Republic of South Africa and others)* 2005 (1) SA 580 (CC), in which the rule

The contents of the new children's laws are predominantly protectionist, yet contradictorily, to an extent more recognizing of autonomy (e.g. in HIV/Aids related/health matters) than are laws in the north. International and regional treaty law has changed the very definition of childhood itself, and there is widespread acceptance of childhood as the era that pertains until the attainment of the age of 18.

Law defines and constitutes childhood. In modern Africa, this is no less true. Whereas it may be contended that the law on paper can be but weakly associated with cultural changes, it is suggested rather that where law is accompanied by ever-increasing access to education, the rapid expansion of means of communication, intensifying urbanization, and the investment of states in dedicated structures (e.g. Ministries), for the delivery of services to children, law can and does have a powerful effect in redefining custom and tradition.

of male primogeniture was held to discriminate unfairly and unconstitutionally against girl children on the grounds of sex and birth, as it prevented them from inheriting from their deceased father.

10

The Age of Conflict: Rethinking Childhood, Law, and Age Through the Israeli-Palestinian Case[1]

Hedi Viterbo

10.1 Introduction: age, childhood, and law

'Are you a child?' To ascertain the answer to this question in relation to any given individual, contemporary society, and law in particular, readily resort to another question: 'How old are you?'[2] In both international child rights legislation[3] and national laws,[4] the term 'child' is defined solely as a matter of age. The prominence of age in relation to children is manifest in many other legal contexts, such as the ages of criminal responsibility, consent, driving, or drinking.[5]

This legal fetishism of age is, in itself, questionable for reasons beyond the scope of this chapter. Among other things, it ignores differences between same-age children, disregards disparities in the meaning of childhood in different societies and

[1] LSE. I wish to thank Emily Jackson, Jenny Kuper, and Nicola Lacey for their ongoing, dedicated, and supportive supervision of my doctoral research, of which the present chapter is part. I would also like to thank Mimi Ajzenstadt, Daniel Monk, and Adi Youcht for their helpful comments.

[2] Cf. Clayton A. Hartjen, *Youth, Crime, and Justice: A Global Inquiry* (Piscataway, New Jersey, 2008) 1–2. However, the understanding of childhood as primarily an age category seems most salient within contemporary Western societies: Allison James, Chris Jenks, and Alan Prout, *Theorizing Childhood* (Cambridge, 1998) 60–1. For an example of a competing conception of childhood in which age is not accorded as much prominence, see Thérèsa Blanchet, *Lost Innocence, Stolen Childhood* (Bangaladesh, 1996) 41–4.

[3] A 'child' is generally defined as any human being under the age of 18 years in, e.g., Convention on the Rights of the Child (adopted 1989; entered into force 1990), art. 1; African Charter on the Rights and Welfare of the Child (adopted 1990; entered into force 1999), art. 2. But see n. 127, below, and accompanying text. On the question of the applicability of the Convention on the Rights of the Child to the Occupied Palestinian Territories see Eyal Benvenisti, 'The Applicability of Human Rights Conventions to Israel and to the Occupied Territories' (1992) 26 *Israel Law Review* 24, 34–5; Philip Veerman and Barbara Gross, 'Implementation of the United Nations Convention on the Rights of the Child in Israel, the West Bank and Gaza' (1995) 3 *International Journal of Children's Rights* 296. A 'juvenile' is similarly defined as any person under 18 years of age in United Nations Rules for the Protection of Juveniles Deprived of Their Liberty (adopted 1990), art. 11(a).

[4] For a comparison of the age classification of young offenders in selected countries see Hartjen, n. 2, above, 5–6; John Winterdyk (ed), *Juvenile Justice Systems: International Perspectives*, 2nd ed (Toronto, 2002), XII–XIII.

[5] For further information, see, e.g., Hartjen, n. 2, above; Elizabeth S. Scott, 'The Legal Construction of Childhood' in Margaret K. Rosenheim (ed), *A Century of Juvenile Justice* (Chicago, 2002), 113, 113–14, 118–19, 121–2; Winterdyk, n. 4, above.

communities, and neglects the socio-economic circumstances of 'children'.[6] The aim of the present chapter, however, is neither to provide a thorough critique of age nor an alternative to it.[7] Instead, I endeavour to provide a contextualized investigation of some of the central factors which inform the intricate interplay between childhood, law, and age. To date, despite being a constitutive legal signifier of childhood, age has remained relatively unexplored and under-theorized—as opposed to the attention given to other social categories, such as gender, race, and class.[8]

The context chosen for this study is the Occupied Palestinian Territories (hereinafter: OPT), where children have played key roles, symbolically and practically.[9] An age perspective on the situation in the OPT may render children demographically salient. If we imagine, provisionally and doubtfully, a 'child' as anyone under the age of 18 years, most people residing in the OPT—53 per cent of Palestinians and a half of Israeli settlers—will appear to be children.[10] This population is significantly younger than populations in the West[11] and within Israel proper.[12] Furthermore, most Israeli soldiers serving in the OPT, while not 'children' according to the above definition, are confined to the relatively young age group of 18 to 21 years—another clue to the significance of age in this context.

[6] Erica Burman, 'Local, Global or Globalized?: Child Development and International Child Rights Legislation' (1996) 3 *Childhood* 45, 60–2; Allison James and Adrian James, *Key Concepts in Childhood Studies* (Los Angeles and London, 2008) 7–8, 15; David Jeffress, 'Neither Seen Nor Heard: The Idea of the "Child" as Impediment to the Rights of Children' (2006) 7 *Topias: Canadian Journal of Cultural Studies* 75, 75–6.

[7] Suffice it to note that alternatives of this kind, such as the 'evolving capacities' approach, might also be problematic. On some of the possible problems of the 'evolving capacities' approach see, e.g., Jeffress, n. 6, above, 80–2.

[8] On the relative disregard for age in the social sciences see, e.g., César Gonzáles, 'Age-Graded Sexualities: The Struggles of Our Ageing Body' (2007) 11 *Sex Cult* 31; Emma Halliwell and Helga Dittmar, 'Qualitative Investigation of Women's and Men's Body Image Concerns and Their Attitudes Toward Aging' (2003) 49 *Sex Roles: A Journal of Research* 675. More specifically, on the neglect of age in childhood studies and in criminology, see, respectively, Anja Müller, 'Introduction' in Anja Müller (ed), *Fashioning Childhood in the Eighteenth Century: Age and Identity* (Aldershot and Burlington, 2006) 1, 5; Rachel Pain, 'Theorising Age in Criminology: The Case of Home Abuse' in Mike Brogden (ed), *British Criminological Conferences: Selected Proceedings—Volume 2* (Belfast, 1997) 1.

[9] John Collins, *Occupied By Memory: The Intifada Generation and the Palestinian State of Emergency* (New York, 2004) 35–74; Daniel Dor, ' "Arafat Has Decided to Sacrifice Ishmael": The Intifada Children in the Israeli Press' in Naomi Bacon-Schnoor, Charles W. Greenbaum, and Philip E. Veerman (eds), *Protection of Children During Armed Political Conflict: A Multidisciplinary Perspective* (Oxford, 2006) 257; Jonathan Kuttab, 'The Children's Revolt' (1988) 17 *Journal of Palestine Studies* 26; New Profile—The Movement for the Civil-ization of Israeli Society, *Child Recruitment in Israel* (Ramat Hasharon, Israel, 2004); David Rosen, *Armies of the Young: Child Soldiers in War and Terrorism* (Piscataway, New Jersey, 2005) 91–131.

[10] Menachem Klein, 'The Intifada: The Young Generation in the Front', in Naomi Bacon-Schnoor, Charles W. Greenbaum, and Philip E. Veerman (eds), *Protection of Children During Armed Political Conflict: A Multidisciplinary Perspective* (Oxford, 2006) 45, 45–6. Forty-six per cent of Israeli settlers are aged 17 years or under: Israeli Central Bureau of Statistics, *Selected Data for International Child Day* (2008) (Hebrew), <http://www1.cbs.gov.il/reader/newhodaot/hodaa_template.html?hodaa=200811235>, 2.

[11] For example, in the US people under the age of 18 years comprise 23 per cent of the population: US Census Bureau, *Age and Sex* (2009), <http://factfinder.census.gov/servlet/STTable?_bm=y&-geo_id=01000US&-qr_name=ACS_2009_1YR_G00_S0101&-ds_name=ACS_2009_1YR_G00_&-_lang=en&-redoLog=false&-state=st&-CONTEXT=st>. In the UK people aged 19 years or under comprise 25 per cent of the population: Office for National Statistics, *Census 2001* (2001), <http://www.statistics.gov.uk/census2001/pop2001/united_kingdom.asp>.

[12] About 33 per cent of the Israeli population is under 18: The National Council for the Child, *A Collection of Data from the Annual 'Children in Israel—2009'* (2009) (Hebrew), <http://www.children.org.il/Files/File/Leket%20Shnaton2009.doc>, 1. This figure excludes non-citizen children, 74 per cent of whom reside in East Jerusalem: ibid., 2.

To a great extent, the Israeli occupation of the Palestinian Territories has been a legalistic one:[13] Israeli authorities have tended to rely on law as a basis to undertake and justify their actions.[14] Hence, the Israeli law in force in the OPT—which despite its importance has been largely understudied[15]— is an apt arena to examine age and childhood in this context. By focusing on the encounter between Israeli criminal law (domestic and military) and minors in the OPT, the present chapter rethinks the age-childhood-law triangle and explores its complexity.

The first part of the chapter explains how Israeli criminal legislation constructs two different childhoods along national lines in the OPT. Two central disparities concern the end of childhood and its uniformity: Israeli law defines 18 years as the age of majority for Israeli settlers in the OPT, and 16 years as the age of majority for Palestinians;[16] additionally, Israeli law constructs Israeli minority as mostly unitary, while dividing Palestinian minority into significant sub-categories, thereby constituting it as relatively fragmentary.

Despite this contingency of childhood and age upon nationality, the relationship between childhood, age, and law is not as simple as being merely determined along national lines. Contrasting demarcations of childhood, different dimensions of age, various meanings assigned to age, and conflicting age norms all bear on law's encounter with the child, and render age and childhood elusive. The second part of this chapter investigates the complex role these forces play in Israeli military law (which applies to Palestinians), especially with regard to four manifestations of the elusiveness of age and childhood. First, age categories in Israeli military law evince an ambiguous meaning. As will be explained, this terminological ambiguity is informed by competing demarcations of childhood and is linked to a broader incoherence which characterizes the military legal system. Secondly, several military court rulings have treated youth as an aggravating factor, thereby challenging prevalent age norms. Thirdly, Israeli military court judges have occasionally determined Palestinian minors' sentences in consideration of what they saw as those minors' physical age (rather than their chronological age). Through these cases I will explore how what I term the 'childhood body' functions as a 'body of evidence', and how, through this body, the judicial gaze establishes the child's 'true' age. Lastly, Palestinian minors are often simultaneously ascribed two different ages: their age at the time of the offences (which the court considers when determining their sentencing), and their age at the

[13] Characterizing the Israeli occupation as legalistic differs from determining its legality. Lisa Hajjar, *Courting Conflict: The Israeli Military Court System in the West Bank and Gaza* (London, 2005) 4, 27, 218–19, 248. Cf. Orna Ben-Naftali, Aeyal M. Gross, and Keren Michaeli, 'Illegal Occupation: Framing the Occupied Palestinian Territory' (2006) 23 *Berkeley Journal of International Law* 551.

[14] Hajjar, n. 13, above, 27–8, 49–61, 129, 235–6, 243–4, 247–8; Emma Playfair, 'Playing on Principle? Israel's Justification for its Administrative Acts in the Occupied West Bank' in Emma Playfair (ed), *International Law and the Administration of Occupied Territories* (Oxford and New York, 1992) 205; Idith Zertal and Akiva Eldar, *Lords of the Land: The War Over Israel's Settlements in the Occupied Territories, 1967–2007* (New York, 2007) 341, 343–4, 361–71. On the centrality of the Israeli military legal system see Hajjar, n. 13, above, 2–3, 16, 24, 26, 44, 187. On the centrality of the Israeli prisons see Esmail Nashif, *Palestinian Political Prisoners: Identity and Community* (London and New York, 2008) 70, 72, 94.

[15] Apart from the present chapter, there has been very little academic writing on Israeli military legislation, and virtually no writing on Israeli military court rulings.

[16] In 2011, the age of majority in the Israeli military legislation (applicable to Palestinians) was raised to 18 years. However, while this development might be of some symbolic significance, it is inconsequential in practice—among other reasons because even before the age of majority was formally raised, Palestinians aged under 18 years had already been tried separately in military youth courts. See n. 54, below, and accompanying text.

time of the sentencing (which determines their eligibility for maximum-sentence limitations). I will describe how, due to this coexistence of different ages in the same subject (the defendant), age and time both collapse and intensify.

The third part of the chapter focuses on two cases—one regarding a Palestinian defendant and the other concerning Israeli settler girls—in which law's subjects were seen as obscuring their age. The concerns and confusion evoked within the legal system are discussed in this section.

The chapter concludes by pointing, among other things, to the resonance of the issues discussed in this chapter with other contexts outside Israel-Palestine, including—but not limited to—international law, US law, and UK law. In light of the significant commonalities among these different contexts, the Israeli-Palestinian case is read as a 'super-experiment', through which to rethink how age functions and is utilized in the legal fabrication of childhood.

10.2 Age and nationality

Israel has concurrently operated two separate legal systems in the OPT (now excluding the Gaza Strip[17]), effectively dividing the population there along ethnic lines.[18] On the one hand, Palestinians have been subject to Israeli military law and tried in military courts[19] for all sorts of offences, including those considered unrelated to security.[20] Israeli settlers in the OPT, on the other hand, have been extra-territorially placed under domestic Israeli law,[21] which contains a considerably broader array of rights.

[17] Israel withdrew its military forces from the Gaza Strip and evacuated its settlements there in 2005. The courts now operating in the Gaza Strip are Palestinian military courts, run by the Hamas government. However, despite the formal pullout, Israel has occasionally arrested and interrogated Gazan Palestinians. See Defence for Children and Save the Children, *Child Rights—Situation Analysis: Right to Protection in the Occupied Palestinian Territory 2008* (Ramallah and Jerusalem, 2008) 63. If prosecuted, these Palestinians are tried in domestic Israeli courts. See Kathleen Cavanaugh, 'The Israeli Military Court System in the West Bank and Gaza' (2007) 12 *Journal of Conflict & Security Law* 197, 199; Defence for Children—Palestine, *Palestinian Child Prisoners* (Jerusalem, 2009) 8. The issue of whether the Israeli occupation of the Gaza Strip has terminated is in dispute. See, e.g., Susan Power, 'War, Invasion, Occupation—A Problem of Status on the Gaza Strip' (2009) 12 *Trinity College Law Review* 25; Yuval Shany, 'Binary Law Meets Complex Reality: The Occupation of Gaza Debate' (2008) 41 *Israel Law Review* 68, 76–7.

[18] See, e.g., Ben-Naftali, Gross, and Michaeli, n. 13, above, 584; Hajjar, n. 13, above, 58–61; Ardi Imseis, 'On the Fourth Geneva Convention and the Occupied Palestinian Territory' (2003) 44 *Harvard International Law Journal* 65, 106.

[19] However, there have been notable exceptions, when Palestinians from the OPT were tried in domestic Israeli courts. Cavanaugh, n. 17, above, 199–200; Hajjar, n. 13, above, 234. Furthermore, Palestinian residents of East Jerusalem are tried in either Israeli military courts or domestic Israeli courts, depending on where they are alleged to have offended. See, e.g., Defence for Children—Palestine, n. 17, above, 8. Additionally, the Palestinian Authority currently operates local courts in the West Bank (alongside the Israeli military courts), authorized to try Palestinians in civil and criminal matters which the Israeli military views as internal to Palestinian society. Asem Khalil, 'Formal and Informal Justice in Palestine: Dealing with the Legacy of Tribal Law' (2009) 184 *Etudes Rurales* 169; Shany, n. 17, above, 78. Palestinian citizens of Israel are tried in the domestic Israeli legal system.

[20] Hajjar, n. 13, above, 59, 255. See also Raja Shehadeh, *The Declaration of Principles and the Legal System in the West Bank* (Jerusalem, 1994) 23, 25; Sharon Weill, 'The Judicial Arm of the Occupation: The Israeli Military Courts in the Occupied Territories' (2007) 89 *International Review of the Red Cross* 395.

[21] Ben-Naftali, Gross, and Michaeli, n. 13, above, 584; Hajjar, n. 13, above, 58–9; Shehadeh, n. 20, above, 24–5. In principle, the military courts have jurisdiction over Israeli settlers living in the West

The national identity ascribed to suspects and defendants in the OPT thus determines how Israeli law classifies and treats them. One basic disparity in this regard is the age of majority. Whereas Israeli defendants are defined (by the domestic legislation) as minors up to the age of 18 years,[22] Palestinian defendants are defined as minors (by the military legislation[23]) up to the age of 16 years,[24] that is, two years younger.

Another nationally-based difference concerns the degree of fragmentation within childhood. The domestic law delineates Israeli minority as mostly unitary: for almost all purposes, 'minor' is the only age category in use.[25] Israeli military law, in comparison, constructs Palestinian minority as relatively fragmentary, by employing three sub-categories:[26] the first, 'child', denotes any person under the age of 12 years. Palestinians under the age of 12 years bear no criminal responsibility,[27] similarly to their Israeli peers.[28] The second sub-category is 'youth', referring to any person aged 12 or 13 years old. The maximum prison sentence which can be imposed on Palestinian 'youth' (12- and 13-year-olds) is six months,[29] whereas Israelis of the same ages cannot be sentenced to prison at all.[30] 'Tender adult', the third sub-category, denotes any person aged 14 or 15 years old. The maximum sentence for Palestinian 'tender adults' (14- and 15-year-olds) is one year, but only if the defendant is charged with offences for which the maximum sentence does not otherwise exceed five years.[31] This one-year limitation rarely applies, however, because Palestinian minors are usually charged with offences for which the maximum sentence does exceed five years.[32] For example, the maximum sentence for stone throwing—the most common charge against Palestinian minors—is 10 years, or, if the stones are thrown at a driving vehicle, 20 years.[33]

This classificatory system is not entirely unparalleled: similar fragmentary models have been in use in Germany, Switzerland, Finland, Hong Kong, and elsewhere.[34] Such fragmentary models of classification seem to echo psychological (mainly developmental-psychological) and sociological truth-claims about the

Bank but, almost invariably, settlers are tried by domestic Israeli courts: Hajjar, n. 13, above, 5, 58–9, 81, 255; Zertal and Eldar, n. 14, above, 372–3.

22 Youth Law (Adjudication, Punishment, and Modes of Treatment) (1971, 14th amendment 2008), art. 1.

23 Israeli authorities consider the military orders as constituting 'primary legislation corresponding to acts of Parliament or Laws'. David Yahav (ed), *Israel, The 'Intifada' and the Rule of Law* (Tel Aviv, 1993), 23. Cited in Shehadeh, n. 20, above, 31.

24 Order 1651 Concerning Security Provisions (Integrated Version) (Judea and Samaria) (2009) (Hebrew), <http://www.law.idf.il/SIP_STORAGE/files/5/685.pdf>, art. 136. Only for the purpose of release on bail, a 'minor' is defined as a person aged 12 to 17 years inclusive: ibid., art. 181(a).

25 Only in the particular context of obtaining evidence is the term 'child' used (denoting anyone under the age of 14 years). Law to Amend the Rules of Evidence (the Protection of Children) (1955), art. 1.

26 These three sub-categories are defined in Order 1651, n. 24, above, art. 1. I use literal translation of the Hebrew sub-categories which appear in the Israeli legislation.

27 Ibid., art. 191.

28 Penal Code (1977), art. 34(f).

29 Order 1651, n. 24, above, art. 168(b).

30 Youth law, n. 22, above, art. 25(d).

31 Order 1651, n. 24, above, art. 168(c).

32 According to my independent sample of military court cases. See also Defence for Children—Palestine, n. 17, above, 99–100.

33 Order 1651, n. 24, above, art. 212.

34 For example, German law uses the categories 'child' (up to the age of 13 years), 'juvenile' (ages 14–17), and 'young adult' (ages 18–20): Winterdyk, n. 4, above, 171–205. See also Donald J. Shoemaker (ed), *International Handbook on Juvenile Justice* (Westport, Connecticut, 1996) 127–8. On other fragmentary models of age classification used in Switzerland, Finland, Hong Kong, the Cayman Islands, the Philippines, and Nigeria see Paul C. Friday and Xin Ren (eds), *Delinquency and Juvenile Justice Systems in*

existence of standard stages of cognitive and emotional development and/or of socialization.[35] Through the fragmentation of childhood and the use of developmental-like terminology,[36] such models intensify age norms[37] and normalize age homogeneity.[38]

What is distinctive of the situation in the OPT is thus not the application of either model of age (the unitary or the fragmentary), but rather their simultaneous application, which contributes to constituting two different childhoods—Palestinian and Israeli—in the same territory.[39] For this reason, the Israeli-Palestinian case is a striking reminder of the need for childhood studies to acknowledge the intersectionality of 'child' and other social categories.[40]

10.3 The elusiveness of age

While childhood and age seem significantly contingent on nationality in Israel/Palestine, their legal construction is much more complex than merely an unequivocal echo of the dominant national imaginary. In fact, the boundaries of childhood—temporal (for instance, the ending of childhood, the time of transition between its supposed stages) and spatial (for example, the type of courts where defendants of a certain age are tried)—are considerably elusive. The present section identifies in Israeli military law four manifestations of this elusiveness—four different challenges to age demarcations and age norms, which exemplify that childhood and age are far from being stable, clear, or definite. Parenthetically but importantly, while the term 'elusiveness' describes here the equivocal demarcation of childhood, by no means am I implying that if only childhood could be tracked down and unmasked then it would be fixed and tangible; my understanding of childhood is as innately fluid (yet this issue exceeds the scope of this chapter).[41]

the Non-Western World (Monsey, New York, 2006) 56, 90; Hartjen, n. 2, above, 5–6; Winterdyk, n. 4, above, xii–xiii, 219.

35 On these psychological and sociological understandings of childhood see, e.g., James, Jenks, and Prout, n. 2, above, 20–4.

36 On developmentalist conception(s) of childhood see Lynn Fendler, 'Educating Flexible Souls: The Construction of Subectivity through Developmentality and Interaction' in Kenneth Heltqvist and Gunilla Dahlberg (eds), *Governing the Child in the New Millennium* (London and New York, 2001) 119; Nancy Lesko, *Act Your Age!: A Cultural Construction of Adolescence* (New York and London, 2001) 137; Nikolas Rose, *Governing the Soul: The Shaping of the Private Self*, 2nd ed (London and New York, 1999) 142–54.

37 The phrase 'intensification of age norms' is borrowed from Howard P. Chudacoff, *How Old Are You: Age Consciousness in American Culture* (Princeton, 1989) 65–91.

38 On the uniqueness attributed to different age groups, see Lesko, n. 36, above, 107.

39 Alongside the disparity between the legal treatment of Palestinians and Israelis in the OPT (children and adults), Hassin has pointed to the discrimination of Arab vis-à-vis Jewish juvenile delinquents in Israel proper. See Yael Hassin, 'Minority Juvenile Delinquents in the State of Israel and the Social Reaction to Their Delinquency' (1997) 17 *Hevra U-Revaha (Society and Welfare)* 283 (Hebrew).

40 On this need see, e.g., Peter Hopkins and Rachel Pain, 'Geographies of Age: Thinking Rationality' (2007) 39 *Area* 287, 289–90; Gill Valentine, 'Boundary Crossings: Transitions from Childhood to Adulthood' (2003) 1 *Children's Geographies* 37, 39.

41 For some work on the elusiveness and fluidity of childhood see David Buckingham, *After the Death of Childhood: Growing Up in the Age of Electronic Media* (Cambridge, 2000) 3–4, 10, 14, 21–40; Chris Jenks, *Childhood*, 2nd ed. (London and New York, 2001) 112, 117–18, 128, 130–1, 144–5, 147, 150; David Kennedy, *The Well of Being: Childhood, Subjectivity, and Education* (Albany, New York, 2006) xi-xii, 12, 15–17, 71–3, 95; Nick Lee, 'The Challenge of Childhood: Distributions of Childhood's Ambiguity in Adult Institutions' (1999) 6 *Childhood* 455; Helga Zeiher, Dympna Devine, Anne Trine

The Israeli-Palestinian case thus exemplifies the dialectical function of law in reproducing the very elusiveness that it seems to dread. On the one hand, law strives to forge and consolidate childhood through age demarcations (which, in turn, are informed by national demarcations). On the other hand, law not only makes but also unmakes age by reproducing and contributing to its elusiveness, as will now be demonstrated.

10.3.1 The ambiguity of age terminology

Israeli law's differential demarcation of childhood(s) along national lines in the OPT has been denounced repeatedly by various non-governmental and inter-governmental organizations . For instance, the UN Committee on the Rights of the Child recently expressed its concern that 'Israeli legislation continues to discriminate in the definition of the child between Israeli children (18 years) and Palestinian children in the occupied Palestinian territory (16 years)'.[42]

Notwithstanding their importance, such statements, by focusing on the Israeli legislation, ignore the question of how Israeli courts interpret and apply age categories in practice. Examining this overlooked issue may lead to the conclusion that, at least in relation to Palestinian minors, age demarcations have been considerably more elusive than both NGOs and Israeli legislation present them to be. As will be demonstrated, the meaning of age categories in Israeli military law is, in effect, indeterminate and ambiguous. This ambiguity is manifest in different ways which, as the following discussion will make clear, involve factors pertaining to broader complexities and elusiveness of both the military law and childhood.

As explained above, Israeli military legislation (applicable to Palestinians) currently defines a 'minor' as anyone under the age of 16 years.[43] But this definition is a very recent development. Until 2009, the military legislation did not include any definition of 'minor';[44] the age categories in use in this legislation were 'child' (under 12 years of age), 'youth' (12 or 13 years old), and 'tender adult' (14 or 15 years old).[45] Prior to 2009, it was only in the domestic legislation (applicable to Israelis) that 'minor' was defined, and there it has been defined as anyone under 18 years of age.[46]

Hence, unsurprisingly, until 2009 military courts offered two competing interpretations of the term 'minor'. On the one hand, some judges defined 'minor' as referring to Palestinians up to the age of 16 years.[47] This interpretive approach could

Kjørholt, and Harriet Strandell (eds), *Flexible Childhood? Exploring Children's Welfare in Time And Space* (Odense, Denmark, 2007) 11–12, 14, 49–51, 55–62.

[42] United Nations Committee on the Rights of the Child, *Consideration of reports submitted by States parties under article 8 of the Optional Protocol to the Convention on the Rights of the Child on the involvement of children in armed conflict—Concluding Observations: Israel* (2010), <http://www2.ohchr.org/english/bodies/crc/docs/CRC-C-OPAC-ISR-CO-1.pdf>, 2.

[43] N. 24, above, and accompanying text.

[44] More accurately, a definition of 'minor' appeared in the military legislation since 1975, but the legislation explicitly stated that this definition applied only for the purpose of release on bail: n. 24, above. This provision was originally anchored in Order 132 Concerning the Adjudication of Juvenile Delinquents (1967), art. 7a(e). Also, in 1988, an order—which has since then been annulled—defined a 'minor' as 'anyone who cannot be criminally prosecuted due to his [sic] age': Order 1235 Concerning the Supervision of Minors' Behaviour (1988), art. 1.

[45] Nn. 26–33, above, and accompanying text.

[46] N. 22, above, and accompanying text.

[47] See, e.g., Case 2651/09 *The Military Prosecution v. Hasnia* [2009] (Mil. Ct. App.) (stressing that a 16-year-old is not a 'minor' according to the military law). There are many similar rulings.

have derived mainly from the fact that the three age categories applicable to minor Palestinians—'child', 'youth', and 'tender adult'—extended up to the age of 16 years. On the other hand, in numerous military court rulings, judges classified and referred to Palestinians aged 16[48] and 17[49] years old as minors. This latter interpretation of minority may have been influenced by domestic Israeli law's definition of 'minor' as anyone under the age of 18.[50]

In July 2009, the military legislation was amended to add a definition of 'minor' (as anyone under 16 years of age), alongside the age categories 'child', 'youth', and 'tender adult', which remained in force. But while one might have expected this to resolve the interpretive incoherence among the judiciary, rulings given after this legislative revision indicate otherwise. For instance, a ruling by the Military Court of Appeals stated, in stark contradiction to the letter of the military legislation, that a defendant, who had been 'about *16 years old*'[51] when perpetrating the offences attributed to him, '*was a minor* when committing the offences'.[52]

Another amendment made to the military legislation in July 2009 was the stipulation that hearings concerning Palestinian 'minors' be held separately from those concerning adults. This separation between minors and adults could have been expected to be carried out along the age of 16 years, since this age was now defined in the military legislation as the age of majority. But here too, judicial practice rendered age much more ambiguous than the legislation (or the military's public statements[53]) alone would indicate: in practice, the military courts have voluntarily extended the separate adjudication of minors to Palestinians up to the age of 18 years.[54]

Thus, in the Israeli military courts, the meaning of 'minor' has remained highly ambiguous, even after a definition of the term was added to the military legislation in 2009. Furthermore, the ambiguity of age terminology in the military law concerns not only 'minor', but other age categories as well. For instance, whereas the military legislation unequivocally defines a 'tender adult' as anyone aged 14 or 15 years

[48] There are many examples. See, e.g., Case 66/03 *The Military Prosecutor v. Abu Safra* [2003] (Mil. Ct. App.); Case 2274/05 *The Military Prosecutor v. Abda* [2005] (Mil. Ct. App.); Case 3098/07 *The Military Prosecution v. Harfush* [2007] (Mil. Ct. App.); Case 1442/09 *Kuwasma v. The Military Prosecution* [2009] (Mil. Ct. App.).

[49] Here, too, the examples are numerous. See, e.g., Case 128/02 *Kudsi v. Military Prosecutor* [2002] (Mil. Ct. App.); Case 30/04 *Satita v. The Military Prosecutor* [2004] (Mil. Ct. App.); Case 4361/07 *Amarna v. The Military Prosecution* [2007] (Mil. Ct. App.); Case 2728/09 *Halil v. The Military Prosecution* [2009] (Mil. Ct. App.).

[50] N. 22, above.

[51] While the court's use of the word 'about' further illustrates the elusiveness of age, according to the information in the court ruling the defendant was indeed 16 years old at the time.

[52] Case 1528/09 *Massarwah v. The Military Prosecution* [2009] (Mil. Ct. App.) (emphases added). There are other military rulings which, even after the amendment to the military legislation, referred to defendants aged 16 and 17 years old as 'minors'. See, e.g., Case 2689/09 *The Military Prosecution v. Yamin* [2009] (Samaria Mil. Ct.); Case 3291/09 *The Military Prosecution v. John Doe* [2010] (Samaria Mil. Ct.); Case 4770/09 *The Military Prosecution v. Safadi* [2009] (Samaria Mil. Ct.).

[53] The Military Prosecution, *Annual Activity Report—2009*, at 91 (2010) (Hebrew), <http://www.law.idf.il/sip_storage//FILES/0/750.pdf> ('The [military] order was amended [...] so that a military youth court has been established, in which... cases of minors under the age of 16 would be heard.')

[54] Case 2919/09 *The Military Prosecutor v. Abu Rahma* [2009] (Mil. Ct. App.) ('the [military] courts have voluntarily adopted the age of minority in Israel [namely, 18 years], for the purpose of separating the proceedings of minors from those of adults.'). See also Hanan Greenberg, 'Military Ushers Juvenile Court Pilot Program' (9 June 2009) *Ynet News*, <http://www.ynetnews.com/articles/0,7340,L-3728449,00.html>.

old, Military Court of Appeals judge Daniel Friedman stipulated that a 17-year-old defendant 'is a tender adult, as he has not yet turned 18 years old'.[55]

The salient ambiguity of age terminology could be read against the backdrop of a wider incoherence, arguably characteristic of the Israeli military legal system. This institutional incoherence is manifest, among other things, in the substantial disparity which has been argued to exist between the sentences Israeli military courts issue for similar charges.[56] More specifically, military court rulings have been inconsistent in relation to the punishment and detention of Palestinian minors—as the Military Court of Appeals itself has admitted.[57]

Alongside the inconsistencies of the military legal system, what may also be at play in relation to the ambiguity of age categories is a collision between two competing demarcations of the child/adult divide. As explained, on the one hand, military law defines the age of 16 years as the threshold between childhood and adulthood. On the other hand, 18 years is probably the socially dominant (or at least a more dominant) drawing of the age of majority. The latter conception is manifest in myriad popular and professional representations of childhood, across various cultural, political, and legal sites.[58] These include domestic Israeli law, where 18 years marks majority not only with regard to offending, but also for many other purposes, such as voting, conscription, and various legal obligations and issues concerning the child-parent relationship. The different interpretations of 'minor' by military court judges may thus reflect different understandings of how to resolve the collision between these two competing demarcations of the end of childhood.

What links these two frontiers—the institutional incoherence of the military legal system and the collision between competing demarcations of childhood—is the indeterminate influence of domestic Israeli law on the military law: according to the military courts, while the domestic law is not operative in the OPT with regard to the adjudication of Palestinians, there are nevertheless some links between the domestic and military laws.[59] 'Some links' is the key phrase here, since the exact nature and strength of these links have been left to the discretion of each military court judge. Consequently, when determining the meaning of 'minor' and other age categories, some military court judges have ignored the domestic law, while others have advocated adherence to it (and to its marking of 18 years as the age of majority).[60] This has contributed to the aforesaid incoherence of the military law, and has sustained the collision between the competing demarcations of the age of majority.

One military court ruling advocating compliance with the domestic law stipulated, for instance, that '***a minor is a minor is a minor***, whether he [sic] lives where [domestic]

[55] Case 28/04 *Abu-AlShabab v. The Military Prosecutor* [2004] (Mil. Ct. App.).

[56] Hajjar, n. 13, above, 256.

[57] Case 355/03 *Abiyat v. The Military Prosecutor* [2004] (Mil. Ct. App.); Case 4497/08 *The Military Prosecution v. Hawajah* [2008] (Mil. Ct. App.). One military judge further described the military prosecution as inconsistent in relation to the sentences it requests to be imposed on minors: Case 1261/09 *The Military Prosecution v. Al-Farukh* [2009] (Judea Mil. Ct.).

[58] My use here of the terms 'legal', 'political', and 'cultural' is not aimed to mark them as disparate realms. On the indistinguishability of the 'legal' from the 'extra-legal' see, e.g., Nikolas Rose and Mariana Valverde, 'Governed by Law?' (1998) 7 *Social & Legal Studies* 541, 545–6; Pierre Schlag, 'The Dedifferentiation Problem' (2009) 42 *Continental Philosophy Review* 35.

[59] See, e.g., Case 2912/09 *The Military Prosecution v. Abu Rahma* [2009] (Mil. Ct. App.).

[60] Judges who have chosen to emphasize the influence of the domestic law on the military legal system, attributed this influence among other things to the fact that the legal education of military court judges, in Israeli higher education institutions, is based on the domestic law. See, e.g., Case 3975/04 *The Military Prosecution v. Nemer* [2006] (Judea Mil. Ct.).

Israeli law fully applies to him, or elsewhere [namely in the OPT], where [domestic] Israeli law indeed does not fully apply but there is a real influence of the [domestic] Israeli legal system'.[61] This ruling could be read as implying that, to some extent, the definition of 'minor' in the military legislation (as anyone under the age of 16 years) is only formal, and that the 'true' substance of 'minor' is different. This argument was expressed more explicitly in a ruling of the Military Court of Appeals from 2003. The two defendants in that case had been 16 years old at the time of the offence, and the judge declared that while they were '*[f]ormally*... adults according to the [military] law in the Area [that is, in the OPT],... their adulthood is *merely formal*'.[62] Another ruling of the Military Court of Appeals, from 2004, can be read as betraying a similar sentiment: in that case, the court rejected an appeal by a Palestinian defendant whose age, at the time of the offences, had been between 15 and 17 years. In its ruling, the court declared that 'the [defendant's] appeal is... grounded on... [his] age—or perhaps his "minority"'.[63] Why, one may wonder, did the court put the word 'minority' in quotation marks? A possible reading is that, in order to justify its decision, the court resorted—consciously or not—to portraying the defendant as not a minor in the full sense of the word, and hence the quotation marks. These rulings implicitly or explicitly depict the military legislation's demarcation of the age of majority as a formal demarcation, which supposedly coexists alongside a 'truer', more substantial demarcation of childhood. Sixteen- and 17-year-old Palestinian defendants are thereby labelled as both children (in what is seen as the socially dominant sense of the word) and non-children (in the formal, legal sense).

In interim conclusion, we have witnessed the ambiguous meaning of age categories in Israeli military law—ambiguity which has persisted even after a seemingly unequivocal definition of 'minor' was added to the military legislation. And as has been explained, this ambiguity—and the debate about the 'true' age of majority—are both linked to a broader incoherence of the military legal system, to an indeterminate relation between the military and the domestic laws, and to a collision between competing socio-legal demarcations of childhood.

10.3.2 Young and aggravating

The military legislation instructs courts, when determining a minor's sentence, to take into consideration his or her age at the time of committing the offence.[64] This instruction, adopted from the domestic legislation,[65] seems to be based on the prevalent association of childhood with innocence,[66] and the consequent conception—shared by many criminal legal systems worldwide—of young age as a mitigating factor. However, in practice, Israeli military court judges have held on several occasions that young age can, in fact, be an aggravating factor when determining the sentence. By so asserting, these judges departed from the prevalent understanding

[61] Case 2912/09, n. 59, above (emphasis in original). The judicial use of the term 'Israeli law' to denote only *domestic* Israeli law, which is typical of Israeli popular and legal discourses, reproduces the popular Israeli conception of the OPT as located outside Israeli space and time.

[62] Case 65/03 *The Military Prosecution v. Abu Hagier* [2003] (Mil. Ct. App.) (emphases added).

[63] Case 1553/07 *Karini v. The Military Prosecution* [2007] (Mil. Ct. App.).

[64] Order 1651, n. 24, above, art. 168(a). [65] Youth law, n. 22, above, art. 25(c).

[66] On this association see, e.g., David Archard, *Children: Rights and Childhood* (London and New York, 1993) 22, 37–41; James and James, n. 6, above, 50, 74–6, 140; Jenks, n. 41, above, 49, 58, 62–4, 75–6, 119, 124–5.

of childhood and young age, and in that sense undermined the child/adult differentiation.

An early case in which the court described young age as an aggravating circumstance dates back to July 1967—only a month after Israel completed its occupation of the Palestinian Territories, and more than a decade before the aforesaid consideration of age was introduced into the military legislation. In that case, military judge Avraham Fechter stated that under certain circumstances, youth could be an aggravating factor: 'As regards criminal terrorist activity which includes using weapons, *the defendants' young age works against them when determining the punishment*, inasmuch as for such roles and goals young people are the best suited, and when these people hold weapons to realize their intents, they should be punished severely in order to prevent other young people of their age from being tempted by adventures of this sort.'[67]

Young age was again depicted as a potentially aggravating factor in another military court ruling, more than three decades later. In 2003, military judge Ori Egoz conceded that young age is a mitigating factor in principle, but added that according to rulings by the Military Court of Appeals, 'the age consideration will be *an aggravating circumstance, when the minors are sent to carry out missions precisely because of their age* to prevent a stricter punishment from being imposed on the sender should he [sic] take action [instead of sending the minor to act for him]. . . . Implementing a lenient punitive approach might lead to the opposite of the desired result, and encourage the use of minors to interfere with public order and security. Young age cannot grant immunity to the imposition of deterring punishments (see: JSA A/291/91; JSA A/228/92[68]), and the court is obligated to make its contribution to eliminating this phenomenon'.[69]

The basis for judge Egoz's argument is a scenario in which Palestinian adults take advantage of the law's leniency towards children, by intentionally choosing young children to carry out terrorist attacks. To justify her stance, judge Egoz depicted this scenario as an epidemic, arguing that such use of 'young children and youth spread during the violent rampages in the beginning of the 90s when children were sent to throw stones and Molotov cocktails and to participate in violent disorderly conducts. Unfortunately, the circumstances of the case before us prove that a similar negative phenomenon might also spread nowadays, although through much graver crimes such as weapons smuggling and the execution of gunshot terrorist attacks'.[70]

This narrative, in which Palestinian children commonly serve as devices in the hands of adult terrorists, was designed to establish the necessity of judge Egoz's stance that young age could be an aggravating factor. 'I am not happy', stated Egoz, 'to [make] this harsh assertion from which derives the reduction of the relative weight which should be given to the fact that the offender is a young youth, but the state of affairs now in the region [that is, in the West Bank] and the worry of an increase in

[67] Abstract of the ruling in Case 331/68 *The Military Prosecutor v. Abd Al-Mussa and others* [possibly 1969] (Nablus Mil. Ct.) in Military Attorney General's Office, *Selected Rulings of the Military Courts in the Administered Territories—vol. 1* (1970), 252, 253. Some information on the case is unknown because the only two documents that have been published are a court decision (regarding one of the defendants, an adult) and a summary of the court's ruling.

[68] I currently do not have these two military court cases in my possession.

[69] Case 3900/03 *The Military Prosecutor v. Al-Nasirat* [2003] (Judea Mil. Ct.) (emphases changed).

[70] Ibid. (emphases changed).

such crimes, make this assertion inevitable.'[71] Eventually, judge Egoz translated her view of young age as aggravating into an exceptionally harsh sentence of 14 months (six months in prison and eight on probation). This ruling disregarded the fact that the defendant was 13 years old at the time of the sentencing, and that the military legislation therefore limits his sentence to six months.[72]

As we have seen, both judges Fechter (in 1967) and Egoz (in 2003) described youth as aggravating in order to accentuate the need for deterrence.[73] At the same time, the two judges hoped to deter different groups: Fechter aimed to deter 'other young people',[74] whereas Egoz endeavoured to discourage adults (from using minors for terrorist purposes).[75] This disparity is perhaps due to their different views of child-adult relationships: Egoz considered Palestinian minors to be passively and instrumentally used by Palestinian adults, whereas Fechter depicted them as calculated and potent.

In 2004, another military judge, Yoram Hani'el, voiced a stance similar to that of judges Fechter and Egoz: 'experience shows that the appellant's young age has a twofold consequence. On the one hand we take his age into consideration.... But on the other hand, *his age also has an aggravating consequence*, as it becomes clear time after time that there is a directing hand in the sending of minors by adults to actions endangering their lives as well as the lives of others. Their purpose is to receive a lenient sentence thanks to the [sic] young age.'[76]

Notwithstanding some differences in their reasoning, all three judges portray the Palestinian child as a challenge to age norms—and therefore as a challenge to childhood. The Palestinian child is said to be involved in executing terrorist attacks, and this depiction contests the common association between young age and innocence (which is the basis for seeing young age as a mitigating circumstance). Thus, the Palestinian child is portrayed as a Trojan horse: on the surface a child—an emblem of innocence—but in practice the ultimate challenge to childhood.[77]

10.3.3 Bodies of age

So far, we have seen how the elusiveness of the boundaries, meaning, and nature of childhood and age manifests itself through two different phenomena: the ambiguity of age terminology and the view of youth as aggravating. Disparate, sometimes conflicting, conceptions of age and childhood have appeared to be at play with regard to these two manifestations of elusiveness.

Also contributing to the elusiveness of age is the potentially competing 'evidence' according to which age can be determined. Several rulings of the Israeli military

[71] Ibid. (emphases changed).

[72] For this reason, the Military Court of Appeals reversed this ruling, and clarified that the six-month limit refers to the prison sentence together with the probation period. Case 358/03 *Al-Nasirat v. The Military Prosecutor* [2003] (Mil. Ct. App.).

[73] This raises the question, which in itself is beyond the scope of the present chapter, of how effective harsh sentences can be in deterring politically motivated perpetrators.

[74] N. 67, above.

[75] N. 69, above. However, the Military Court of Appeals eventually shortened the prison sentence imposed by judge Egoz from six to three months, and held that although 'the inclusion of minors in such [terrorist] offences should truly be discouraged,... this deterrence should be achieved through punishing those *adults* who exploit minors in their activity, as harshly as possible': Case 358/03, n. 72, above (emphasis in original).

[76] Case 30/04, n. 49, above.

[77] This portrayal is possibly shared also by the two rulings cited in judge Egoz's decision. See n. 68, above, and accompanying text.

courts, which will now be discussed, exemplify this 'competition of age'. In these rulings, judges examined and took into consideration the appearance of Palestinian minors' physical age, even when it was seen as discrepant from these minors' chronological age. As will now be demonstrated, the judges' willingness (and even desire) to observe children as 'bodies of evidence'[78] show age to be open for contention and negotiation.

Thus, in one case, a military judge justified a relatively short sentence (in Israeli military law terms), on the grounds, among others, that '[t]he defendant in this case is 13+ years old, *but physically he looks no older than 9 years*'.[79]

In another case, the court rejected the plea bargain reached by the parties, and instead imposed a significantly shorter sentence. The judge justified this decision by noting, *inter alia*: 'The defendant came across to me as honestly remorseful, an impression intensified by the fact that he was a young child who *according to his exterior appearance looks much younger than his age* [15 years old at the time of his arrest], *short, weak and undeveloped*'.[80] The military prosecution successfully appealed this decision, and the Military Court of Appeals doubled the length of the sentence, while nevertheless stipulating: 'I too have been able to *observe the appellant*, and I must concur with the assertions of the first instance court about *the level of his physical and mental development*.'[81]

In a later case, the court ordered a defendant's release from detention under certain restrictions, justifying this decision by describing the defendant as 'a 14 year old minor, *of a minor body size*, whom detention . . . will not benefit to say the least'.[82] A year later, in yet another case, the court justified the sentence it imposed, which was shorter than requested by the military prosecution, by contending, among other things: 'before me stands a defendant who has not yet turned 16 years old (and *it should be noted that his appearance is even younger*). . . . In such a case, prolonged incarceration . . . is likely to gravely harm his rehabilitation chances and consequently the public interest as well.'[83]

While young appearance was seen in these four cases as a mitigating factor, the lack of such appearance could correspondingly be seen, under certain circumstances, as an aggravating factor. This is illustrated by a ruling of the Military Court of Appeals, which stipulated: 'the appellant's young age [17 years at the time of the offences] cannot justify a substantial shortening of his punishment, since he is not a minor, but a

[78] This is a paraphrasing of Heather D'cruz, 'The Social Construction of Child Maltreatment: The Role of Medical Practitioners' (2004) 4 *Journal of Social Work* 99, 105. Of course, adulthood bodies have also been used as a source of evidence: for example, profiling and other techniques mark certain bodies as more or less threatening. See, e.g., Louise Amoore and Marieke de Goede, 'Transactions after 9/11: the banal face of the preemptive strike' (2008) 33 *Transactions of the Institute of British Geographers* 173.

[79] Case 1506/06 *The Military Prosecutor v. Sabih* [2006] (Judea Mil. Ct.) (emphasis added). This decision was reversed, less than a week later, by the Military Court of Appeals judge Nethanel Benisho, who sentenced the defendant to five months in prison, 10 months on probation, and a fine of 1000 New Israeli Shekels: Case 1413/06 *The Military Prosecutor v. Sabih* [2006] (Mil. Ct. App.). The Court of Appeals' ruling made mention of (but did not criticize) the first instance court's consideration of the defendant's young appearance ('the first court reached . . . [its] conclusion in reference to the . . . [defendant's] exterior looks').

[80] Case 4668/06 *The Military Prosecutor v. Halaf* [2006] (Judea Mil. Ct.) (emphases added).

[81] Case 1350/07 *The Military Prosecutor v. Halaf* [2007] (Mil. Ct. App.) (emphases added).

[82] Case 4380/08 *The Military Prosecution v. Hawajah* [2008] (Judea Mil. Ct.) (emphasis added).

[83] Case 1261/09, n. 57, above (emphasis added).

person who according to his age, and *also according to his looks*, should have understood well the severe consequences of his acts.'[84]

At the same time, in a legal system which has occasionally treated youth as an aggravating factor (as discussed earlier), young appearance was seen not only as a mitigating but also as an aggravating consideration. In 2003, in the Bet El Military Court, military judge Menashe Vahnish ruled that 18-year-old Muhamad Saleh Salim Sha'alan be held in detention until the end of the proceedings in his matter. In explanation of his decision, judge Vahnish contended that treating his young appearance as an aggravating factor could protect the defendant from unwanted adult influences: 'according to the evidence [in the case] and *a visual observation of the defendant's face*, he is a young youth in his adolescence who appears to be influenced by others.... [R]eleasing him [from detention] ... might bring him to be again under the influence of those people.'[85]

The six cases discussed thus far exemplify how the child's chronological age can be rivaled by the judge's gaze at the 'childhood body' (a phrase used here to convey the complexity of the body-child(hood) relationship[86]). The childhood body—a constitutive and inseparable part of the category 'child'[87]—serves as a means through which the court can produce claims about the 'true' age of the child. These claims, in turn, reflect and reproduce developmentalist conceptions of childhood (psychological and other),[88] and bodily stereotypes of 'the normal child'.[89]

To explore further the role of the childhood body in this context, the legal knowledge produced through the spectatorship of that body, and the implications for law's conceptualization of childhood, let us turn to two rulings of Military Court of Appeals judge Moshe Tirosh from 2003, which elucidate these issues. In these two cases, judge Tirosh rejected (fully or partly) appeals from the military prosecution, to increase the sentences of Palestinian minors convicted of illegally exiting the Gaza Strip, cutting the separation barrier, and entering Israel.

In the first of these two rulings of his, judge Tirosh held that the probation sentences imposed by the first instance court be prolonged, but the prison sentence and the fine imposed by that court remain unchanged. Tirosh noted: 'the court's eyes are in its head, and it can see before it three mere children, and despite the light moustache above their upper lip, their mother's milk has still not dried on their lips.' In the eyes of judge Tirosh—and it is indeed his eyes which largely determine the defendants' age—the defendants are the embodiment of competing signs of age: a hint of

[84] Case 149/02 *Harbawi v. The Military Prosecutor* [2002] (Mil. Ct. App.) (emphasis added).

[85] Case 1173/03 *The Military Prosecution v. Sha'alan* [2003] (Bet El Mil. Ct.) (emphasis added).

[86] Whereas phrases such as 'the child's body' reduce this relationship to a unidirectional ownership of the body by the child, the present chapter suggests that, to some extent, it is the body that appears to 'own' the child. Furthermore, the phrase 'childhood body' emphasizes the inextricability of childhood and embodiment. For another use of the term 'childhood body' see Alan Prout, 'Childhood Bodies: Social construction and translation' in Simon Johnson Williams, Jonathan Gabe, and Michael Calnan (eds), *Health, Medicine, and Society: Key Theories, Future Agendas* (London and New York, 2000) 109.

[87] Allison James, 'Embodied Being(s): Understanding the Self and the Body in Childhood' in Alan Prout (ed), *The Body, Childhood and Society* (London, 2000) 19, 27. See also Allison James, 'On Being a Child: The Self, the Group and the Category' in Anthony Paul Cohen and Nigel Rapport (eds), *Questions of Consciousness* (London, 1995) 60, 63–6.

[88] See nn. 35–8, above, and accompanying text.

[89] Allison James comments that such 'bodily stereotypes of "the normal child", historically derived and ultimately contingent, provide a measure of any individual child's conformity to that category of child': James, 'Embodied Being(s)', n. 87, above, 27. See also Berry Mayall, 'Children, emotions and daily life at home and school' in Gillian Bendelow and Simon Johnson Williams (eds), *Emotions in Social Life: Critical Themes and Contemporary Issues* (New York, 1998) 135, 144–5.

moustache implying that (masculine) maturity is nearing, and on the other hand babyish lips said to have recently been breastfed. The judge's self-proclaimed role, when facing these competing signs, is to 'uncover' the defendants' 'true' age.

For this purpose, judge Tirosh relies on developmental theory, as he perceives it, stating: 'We would not be introducing any innovation to developmental theory by saying that no 15- or 16-year-old is identical to any other 15- or 16-year-old. At this age, some are adults and some are still children. The appellants before us belong to the latter group.' Having inspected the defendants' appearance (an inspection legitimized by relying upon developmental concepts), judge Tirosh concludes: 'It could be said, jokingly, that they [the defendants] are not appellants, but rather mini-appellants.... [They are] not merely formally minors, but evidently immature.'[90]

The second military court case was heard later that day, and the defence attorney—who also represented the defendant in the above case—referred to judge Tirosh's decision in that case, and argued among other things: 'I have nothing to add to what His Honour noted in the verdict. These youths appear smaller than their real age. The court described this eloquently.... The prison sentence imposed [on the defendants... is appropriate] especially in light of... [their] age [and] body structure.'[91] Judge Tirosh concurred, and rejected the prosecution's appeal. In his ruling, judge Tirosh stipulated that '[f]ormally, the appellants are adults according to the [military] law in the area [that is, in the OPT]. Nevertheless, the court is under the impression that their adulthood is but formal.... We find no reason to change the decision [of the first instance court]..., given the necessary balance between the security of the area [that is, the OPT] and these appellants' age and physical and mental maturity, as they appeared to the [first instance] court'.[92]

The transformative judicial gaze at childhood bodies thus constitutes age as a site of competition between the corporeal and the chronological, between the unstable 'real' and the merely formal. The 'real' itself functions as neither a given nor a constant, as it can be located either in the chronological or in the physical, and perhaps in the mixture of both.[93]

10.3.4 Coevality—the coexistence of age(s)

After examining the interplay between different ages—physical age (as it appears to the court) and chronological age—let us turn to discuss another manifestation of the elusiveness of age, which involves the simultaneous application of two different ages to the same child defendant.

As noted earlier, the military legislation limits the maximum sentences which may be imposed upon Palestinian 'youth' (12- and 13-year-olds) and 'tender adults' (14- or 15-year-olds), to six months and a year respectively. However, these restrictions only apply to defendants who are 'youth' or 'tender adults' at the time of the sentencing. What matters is not the defendant's age at the time of the offence, but only how old the defendant is when the sentence is determined.[94] In comparison, no parallel provision exists in the domestic legislation (which applies to Israeli minors).

Indeed, in some cases, Palestinian defendants shift from one age category to another between their offending and sentencing. For example, in two cases, the

[90] Case 66/03, n. 48, above. [91] Case 65/03, n. 62, above. [92] Ibid.

[93] The 'real'/'formal' interplay also appeared in another form of elusiveness discussed earlier: the meaning of 'minority' (and the question of whether the defendant is 'really' or merely 'formally' a minor). Nn. 61–3, above, and accompanying text.

[94] Order 1651, n. 24, above, arts 168(b) and 168(c).

defendants were 15 years old ('tender adults') when they committed the offences, but reached the age of 16 years ('adults') by the time of their sentencing.[95] In another case, the defendant was 13 years old (a 'youth') at the time of his offending, and 14 years old (a 'tender adult') by the time his sentence was determined.[96]

In such cases, defendants are simultaneously ascribed two different ages, in a manner which deviates from the normalization of age groups and age homogeneity: their age at the time of the offending (which is a consideration in the sentencing[97]), as well as their age at the time of the sentencing (which determines their eligibility to the maximum-sentence limitations). Symbolically, a defendant thus can be, for example, simultaneously 13 and 14 years old (and therefore both a 'youth' and a 'tender adult'), or simultaneously 15 and 16 years old (both a 'tender adult' and an 'adult').

I shall term this coexistence of different ages and age groups, embodied concurrently in the same subject—the defendant—'coevality'. This is a state of different coeval regimes (two ages and/or two age groups) becoming coeval (in the sense of being applicable or realized at the same time). To a certain degree, the legal ambiguity of age categories such as 'minor', which we discussed earlier, renders coevality an integral component of Palestinian childhood: defendants of the same age can be classified, for example, as both 'minors' and 'adults'.[98]

The coevality of the sentencing in the military court makes it a moment when time both collapses and is intensified. It collapses because the distinction between past and present is challenged, by retrospectively narrating the defendant's past (the offending) through his or her present (the current age). It is intensified because not one but two ages—and hence two times—must be borne in mind.

This dual challenge—to the fixity of both age and time differentiations—is heightened with the passing of time between the moment of the offending and that of the sentencing. The longer it takes for the court to try defendants, the older these defendants become and the longer their sentence might be.[99] The NGO, Defence for Children—Palestine, succinctly described this situation, in 2007, as follows: '[a] child who is accused of committing an offence when s/he is 15, will be punished as an adult if s/he has a birthday whilst awaiting sentence. This places enormous pressure on a 15 year old child, the child's family and legal advisor to accept a plea bargain rather than risk court delays leading to the child being sentenced as an adult.'[100] Two years later, the NGO voiced a similar concern: 'a child who is accused of committing an offence when he or she is 15, is punished as an adult if he or she has a birthday whilst awaiting sentence.'[101]

These excerpts portray the defence's battle in such situations as a battle against time. In this battle, age norms are both idealized and dreaded: idealized—by criticizing the court's deviation from these norms (a deviation manifest in sentencing as an adult a defendant who offended at the age of 15); but age norms are also dreaded,

[95] Case 1091/02 *The Military Prosecutor v. Janam* [2003] (Hebron Mil. Ct.); Case 1001/04 *The Military Prosecutor v. Dib* [2004] (Judea Mil. Ct.).

[96] Case 4407/03 *The Military Prosecutor v. Harfush* [2004] (Judea Mil. Ct.).

[97] N. 64, above.

[98] See text accompanying n. 63, above.

[99] At the same time, courts may consider the passing of a long period of time between the crime and the sentencing as a mitigating factor. See, e.g., Case 3131/06 *The Military Prosecutor v. Arar* [2006] (Judea Mil. Ct.). However, the Military Court of Appeals described that case as unique and unrepresentative: Case 2481/06 *The Military Prosecutor v. Arar* [2006] (Mil. Ct. App.).

[100] Defence for Children—Palestine, *Palestinian Child Political Prisoners—2007 Report* (2007), <http://www.dci-pal.org/english/publ/research/2008/PCPReport.pdf>, 11.

[101] Defence for Children—Palestine, n. 17, above, 15.

which is illustrated when birthday—a quintessential social mechanism of age normalization[102]—is rendered a threat. Thus, the time with which the defence struggles is related not only to the moment of sentencing, but also to the day on which the defendant's age changes.

This turbulence of time and age may account for the anxiety which is not exclusive to the above excerpts from Defence for Children—Palestine, and has been expressed in other NGO documents as well.[103]

10.4 (Not) knowing age

As has been explained, the relationship between law and the child is informed by various, sometimes competing forces, which render age a matter of significant elusiveness. In this relationship, the legal system sees age and childhood as in need of being deciphered and known, and it considers itself to be the authorized producer of that knowledge. The following questions thus arise: how would the legal system react when its competence and ability to know the child's 'true' age are called into question? And, in particular, how would it react in circumstances in which it believes legal subjects to be able to hinder it from knowing their age?

A possible starting point to explore these questions is the following assertion, which an Israeli military prosecutor made when asked by ethnographer Lisa Hajjar about the young age of many Palestinian defendants. 'Don't let them fool you', said the prosecutor. 'They might look like children, but they are really adults. If they look fifteen, they are probably twenty-five. You can't trust Palestinians for anything, even their ages.'[104] This statement can be read in light of, and as complementary to, my discussion earlier of the legal knowledge produced around childhood bodies. That discussion highlighted how judges use childhood bodies as evidence of children's 'true', 'substantial' age. The military prosecutor's statement, brought here, illustrates again the significance of physical age, as well as law's desire to ascertain defendants' 'true' age. But what makes the prosecutor's assertion all the more intriguing is that it adds the figure of the legal subject to the legal interplay of 'truth' and age, and depicts that figure as subversive. The danger perceived from this figure (in this case—from the figure of the Palestinian defendant) lies in what is seen as its ability to use physical age as deception, as trickery, as a stratagem.

I wish not to question whether this statement is 'true' or 'false', accurate or paranoid. Instead, I would suggest using it as a preliminary example of how the legal

[102] On the significance of birthdays as cultural mechanisms of age normalization, see, e.g., Chudacoff, n. 37, above, 126–37; Lea Shamgar-Handelman and Don Handelman, 'Celebrations of Bureaucrocy: Birthday Parties in Kindergartens' in Esther Hertzog, Orit Abuhav, Harvey E. Goldberg, and Emanuel Marx (eds), *Perspectives in Israeli Anthropology* (Detroit, 2010) 111. On the celebration of birthdays as a Western ritual, which represents a different conception of age than conceptions dominant in other cultures, see, e.g., Blanchet, n. 2, above, 41–3.

[103] Defence for Children and Save the Children, n. 17, above, 67–8; Yesh Din—Volunteers for Human Rights, *Backyard Proceedings: The Implementation of Due Process Rights in the Military Courts in the Occupied Territories* (Tel Aviv, 2007) 155. In both these documents, it was argued that alongside the legal consideration of the defendant's age at the time of the sentencing, there is a common practice in Israeli military courts of prolonged proceedings. The combination of these two factors, contended the documents, inevitably makes many minor offenders likely to become adults by the date of their sentencing, which exerts pressure on their lawyers to bring trials quickly to an end. For more information on prolonged proceedings in the military courts, see Yesh Din, ibid., 18–19.

[104] Hajjar, n. 13, above, 117.

system may conceptualize the role of law's subjects in the production of knowledge about age—'their' age. For this purpose, two cases will now be examined—one regarding a Palestinian defendant, and the other concerning Israeli settler girls—in which the behaviour of legal subjects was seen as deviating from, or obscuring their 'true' chronological age.

10.4.1 Reverting to childhood

In 2001, the Israeli armed forces arrested 15-year-old Umar Abu Snima for illegally exiting the OPT. When deciding to sentence him to a month on probation, military judge Sigal Mishal noted that she was taking into consideration Abu Snima's young age.[105]

A year later, Abu Snima was once again arrested for illegally exiting the OPT. But this time, he presented himself to the interrogators as *Muhammad* Abu Snima—which the military court would later pronounce to be his real name.[106] When his fingerprints were taken, he was discovered to be 'about 20 years old', as the court would later put it.[107] Consequently, Abu Snima was charged not only with exiting the OPT but also with perjury. The Erez Military Court sentenced him to two-and-a-half months in prison, and 45 days on probation.[108]

Following an appeal by the military prosecution, the Military Court of Appeals increased Abu Snima's sentence to 10 months in prison and nine months on probation. Military Court of Appeals judge Sha'ul Gordon justified this decision by arguing that 'the offences of which the appellant has been convicted are very grave, and beyond the severity of exiting the Area [that is, the OPT] without permission are his false testimonies about his identity. The appellant hindered the interrogation and even managed to deceive the court and receive a short sentence by presenting himself as a minor'.[109]

In this case, Abu Snima's acts were conceptualized as bending, at least temporarily, the boundaries of childhood. Abu Snima's story, as told by the military court, is that of a legal subject turning back time, reverting to childhood, and by so doing, reversing one of the most basic assumptions for modern conceptions of childhood: that children become adults—not the other way around.[110]

As the eventual charges and sentence illustrate, this supposed 'manipulation' of the boundaries and foundations of childhood might not go unpunished. The court's actions further indicate its forcefully maintained self-image as the sole authorized determiner of the defendant's 'true' age. It is not that chronological age cannot be challenged, but rather that the court alone has the authority to challenge it. And as

[105] Case 164/01 *The Military Prosecutor v. Abu Snima* [2001] (Erez Mil. Ct.).

[106] Case 12/02 *The Military Prosecutor v. Abu Snima and others* [2002] (Mil. Ct. App.). The Military Court of Appeals speculated that Abu Snima's decision to use his 'real' first name when he was arrested for the second time was aimed to evade the enforcement of his probation sentence (from 2001). *Id.*

[107] Case 12/02, n. 106, above.

[108] Case 5/02 *The Military Prosecution v. Abu Snima* [2002] (Erez Mil. Ct.).

[109] Case 12/02, n. 106, above. My above description of Abu Snima as a 15-year-old was meant to reproduce, to some extent, the effect of his supposed impersonation.

[110] Although in practice, there are notable exceptions to this conception. For example, on the infantilization of the elderly and of 'Third World' peoples see, respectively, Sonia Miner Salari and Melinda Rich, 'Social and Environmental Infantilization of Aged Persons: Observations in Two Adult Day Care Centers' (2001) 52 *International Journal of Aging and Human Development* 115; Erica Burman, 'Innocents Abroad: Western Fantasies of Childhood and the Iconography of Emergencies' (1994) 18 *Disasters* 238.

we saw earlier, this authority has indeed been implemented, with courts occasionally giving precedence to defendants' physical age over their chronological age.

10.4.2 Withholding age

Whereas in Abu Snima's case, the behaviour denounced was his self-association with a supposedly 'wrong' age group, in the following case Israeli settler girls refused to disclose their ages altogether. This too was treated as an obstacle to law's resolve to know the age of the child-subject.

The background to this case is what Israel called its 'disengagement' from the Gaza Strip: the withdrawal of Israeli military from within the Strip and the evacuation of all Israeli settlements there, which took place in the summer of 2005.[111] This step encountered opposition from parts in the Israeli political right, which demonstrated, sometimes violently, and in some cases blocked transportation routes.

Minor settlers took an active part in those demonstrations, and a great number of them were detained as a result. Many refused to disclose their personal details to the police, including their ages. Consequently, some were held in detention for weeks, which instigated considerable public and legal debate in Israel. The Attorney General later explained these events from his perspective: 'Hundreds of minors refused to identify themselves. They said: we wouldn't identify ourselves, we don't care, even if we would have to sit in jail. The State then had the option to give in to that demand and release them without identification. This meant an inability to enforce the law on them, since it's clearly impossible to try an offender who hasn't identified himself. Therefore our policy, backed by the courts, was that a person who didn't identify himself . . . and which there was allegedly evidence that he committed an offence, would not be released until he identified himself. . . . Most of the minors who refused to identify themselves were identified within 24–48 hours. The big commotion revolved around a small group of girls who could not be identified.'[112]

While, in general, the settler girls' refusal to identify themselves baffled the legal system, it was the inability to 'know' conclusively their ages which was seen as particularly challenging. The legal system was thrown into confusion by what it saw as the virtually impossible task of placing these seemingly ageless girls in the legal array of age-based arrangements. Judge Galit Wigotsky-Mor, the president of the Youth Courts, pointed to this in a meeting of the Children's Rights Committee of the Israeli Parliament (the Knesset), which dealt with the prolonged detention of the settler girls. 'With regard to the detentions during the opposition to the disengagement', said judge Wigotsky-Mor, 'sometimes we [youth court judges] didn't even know whether the minor was over the age of criminal responsibility, 12 years, or under the age of criminal responsibility, in which case he [sic] couldn't even be arrested.'[113]

A similar dynamic interestingly took place two years later, in 2007. Two settler girls, 14 and 15 years old at the time (as would later be realized), were arrested for entering a sealed-off military area during a protest at an outpost in the West Bank.

[111] See also n. 17, above.

[112] Minutes number 11 of the meeting of the Children's Rights Committee of the 17th Knesset (17 October 2006) (Hebrew).

[113] Minutes number 32 of the meeting of the Children's Rights Committee of the 17th Knesset (12 June 2007) (Hebrew).

Like their predecessors, these girls also refused to state their age or any other identifying information to the police when they were arrested.[114]

The behaviour of both Abu Snima (the Palestinian defendant who 'posed' successfully as a child) and the settler girls who refused to disclose their age exemplifies the full potency of the utterance customarily directed at children: 'Act your age!' While expressing the dominance of age norms, this utterance also constitutes age as a matter of acting.[115] Through the eyes of Israeli law, both the Palestinian adult/child and the settler girls are seen to '*act* their age' (in an improper manner).

However, the case of the settler girls differs from Abu Snima's case in two respects which make it particularly notable. First, in the girls' case, not only is the determining of age attributed to legal subjects (rather than to legal professionals), but those legal subjects are defined as children[116]—which in itself is of great significance in such an adult-governed social field. An alarming capacity is thereby ascribed to the child: to confound, even temporarily, the seemingly stable regimes of age and law.

Also distinctive of the case of the settler girls is law's outright inability to know their age. Whereas in Palestinian defendant Abu Snima's case the law had his age 'wrong', with regard to the settler girls what was seen as so disturbing was law's failure to ascribe to them any age whatsoever. 'How old are you?'—the question which in this case was left unresolved—is generally of great social importance because it enables the enforcement of age norms, and more specifically because it allows society to place children along developmental-moral standards.[117] The legal urge to know a child's age can be read as a manifestation of a broader social urge to decipher the child.[118] Therefore, when a child is perceived to be evading or resisting law's desire to know her or his age, anxieties and confusion are almost bound to arise within the legal system.

Thus, when asked about their age, silence may (under certain circumstances) be perceived as a particularly challenging response children can give.[119] This deviates from the portrayal of silence as associated with impotence, an association traditionally drawn in many discourses about children and other groups defined as 'disempowered'.[120] But what rendered the settler girls' silence so effective, and in this

[114] Chaim Levinson, '5 Religious Girls Sue Police for Allegedly Strip-Searching Them' (31 December 2009) *Haaretz*, <http://www.haaretz.com/news/5-religious-girls-sue-police-for-allegedly-strip-searching-them-1.1012>.

[115] Gill Valentine argues that 'age is . . . , like gender, . . . a performative act that is naturalized through repetition and therefore is both fluid and contested': Gill Valentine, *Public Space and the Culture of Childhood* (Aldershot and Burlington, 2004) 55.

[116] The legal subjects' gender is also noteworthy, but I will not elaborate on this due to space limitations.

[117] The social centrality of the particular question 'how old are you?' is illustrated by Chudacoff's choice to use it as a title for his book: Chudacoff, n. 37, above.

[118] See, e.g., Jenny Hockey and Allison James, *Social Identities Across the Life Course* (Basingstoke and New York, 2003) 15, 18; Rose, n. 36, above, 135–54.

[119] Cf. Elaine Chase, 'Agency and Silence: Young People Seeking Asylum Alone in the UK' (2010) 40 *British Journal of Social Work* 2050, 2052, 2059–65; Ian Hutchby, 'Resisting the Incitement to Talk in Child Counselling: Aspects of the Utterance "I Don't Know"' (2002) 4 *Discourse Studies* 147, 149, 165.

[120] See, e.g., Jeffress, n. 6, above, 88–91; Alan Prout and Allison James, 'A New Paradigm for the Sociology of Childhood? Provenance, Promise and Problems' in Allison James and Alan Prout (eds), *Contemporary Issues in the Sociological Study of Childhood* (London and New York, 1997) 7, 7–8. For an example relating to the OPT, see Save the Children Sweden, *I Miss My House and My Pink Dress: Palestinian Children's Voices* (Stockholm, 2004). On the legislation and policies which have promoted 'child voice' in the UK since the 1990s, see Ann Lewis, 'Silence in the Context of "Child Voice"' (2010) 24 *Children & Society* 14, 14–15. For further critique of the association between silence and powerlessness (in the feminist context), see Susan Gal, 'Between Speech and Silence: The Problematics of Research

sense not silent at all, was the reaction of the Israeli police and courts to it: holding these girls in prolonged detention. It is due to this reaction that these girls' silence was heard loudly all the way to the Israeli Parliament, as was described earlier.

During the meeting of the parliamentary Children's Rights Committee, the representative of the Israeli Public Defense critically described as irrational and childish the state's insistence upon not releasing the girls from detention unless they sign an obligation concerning their probation conditions. The Public Defense lawyer further added: 'we would expect the [legal] system to take a deep breath. In the same way that we sometimes tell children to count to three and think how to get off the tree, here too a creative way to get off the tree was called for.... [As regards] those 13- or 14-year-old girls, minors who cannot even be legally sentenced to prison ...,[121] there should have been created conditions which do not depend on their active participation. Meaning, for instance, not forcing them to sign the obligation [regarding their probation conditions].'[122] Perhaps this comparison, by an Israeli public lawyer, of Israeli legal authorities to an impatient child who needs to be taught restraint and reason, implies that during Israel's 'disengagement' from the Gaza Strip childhood was not only an exterior force with which Israeli law had to reckon; the image of law as a child characterizes childhood as an interior characteristic of the legal system itself. To some extent, this might hint to another frontier of the question of elusiveness: not only is childhood elusive, but so is the basic distinction between 'childhood' and 'law'.

10.5 Conclusion: childhood, law, and age in Israel/Palestine and beyond

This chapter has explored the intricate relationship between childhood, age, and law through the Israel-Palestinian case, and particularly through Israeli (military and domestic) criminal law's conceptualization and construction of age and childhood in the OPT.[123] As we have seen, age is saliently contingent upon nationality in this context: the age-based demarcation of childhoods in the OPT varies significantly along national lines.

Also at the heart of the chapter is the elusiveness of age, four manifestations of which we have discussed: the ambiguity of legal age terminology; the legal conception of youth as aggravating; the punishment of minors according to what is seen as their physical age (rather than according to their chronological age); and the simultaneous application of different ages to the same minor. These four phenomena illustrate that both age and childhood are far from being stable, clear, or unequivocal.

Furthermore, we have examined how Israeli law conceptualizes and reacts to circumstances in which its subjects appear somehow to obscure their age. Such

on Language and Gender' in Micaela di Leonardo (ed), *Gender at the Crossroad of Knowledge: Feminist Anthropology in the Postmodern Era* (Berkeley, Los Angeles, and Oxford, 1991) 175.

121 See n. 30, above, and accompanying text.

122 Minutes number 11 of the meeting of the Children's Rights Committee, n. 112, above. Three other suggestions heard in the meeting of the committee were: to impose probation conditions on the girls even if they do not sign the conditions papers; to hold an immediate trial so that the girls are held in prolonged detention; and to release the girls and possibly even withdraw the charges altogether. Ibid., 39–40.

123 Due to space constraints, some of the complexities characterizing this context have been somewhat simplified, and some issues have remained unexplored.

circumstances seem to pose a formidable challenge to the legal system, which is largely governed by an urge to know the child's age.

While each of these different aspects of the legal construction of age and childhood is noteworthy in itself, it is only by jointly examining these aspects that a rich understanding of the relationship between childhood, age, and law can be gained. For example, the story of childhood and law would be partial if we were to describe it merely as dictated by the dominant national imaginary. While age and childhood are indeed constructed along national lines, their prominent elusiveness renders them irreducible to national demarcations. In a similar manner, the story of the elusiveness of childhood and age consists not only of the reproduction of elusiveness by the law, but also of circumstances in which children are the ones perceived (by the legal system) as bringing forth that elusiveness.

An amalgam of legal systems, of various—often competing—conceptions and constituents of childhood, the Israeli-Palestinian case could be read as a super-experiment for law and childhood. This experiment, while clearly involving unique interrelationships between childhood and law/politics, nonetheless resonates with other contexts.

For example, while the childhood-nationality linkage is salient in Israel/Palestine, the intersectionality of childhood and other social categories is prevalent elsewhere.[124] The definition of 16 years as the age of majority is also not unique to Israeli military law and can be found, for example, in US military law.[125] Additionally, the elusiveness of age and childhood is far from being exclusive to Israel/Palestine: for instance, the definition of 'child' in the UN Convention on the Rights of the Child as anyone under 18 'unless, under the law applicable to the child, majority is attained earlier',[126] renders the ending of childhood flexible and its beginning unresolved.[127] Similarly, youth has been regarded as aggravating outside Israel/Palestine—for example in several death penalty rulings of the Supreme Court of the US.[128] Issues pertaining to childhood bodies and law in Israel-Palestine also appear in many other contexts. Among these is the functioning of childhood bodies as evidence of the child's 'real' age, which is prominent, for example, in the British asylum system—where disputes often arise with regard to asylum seekers' age and the question of

[124] See, e.g., George S. Bridges and Sara Steen, 'Racial Disparities in Official Assessments of Juvenile Offenders: Attributional Stereotypes as Mediating Mechanisms' (1998) 63 *American Sociological Review* 554, 567; Nura Taefi, 'The Synthesis of Age and Gender: Intersectionality, International Human Rights Law and the Marginalisation of the Girl-Child' (2009) 17 *International Journal of Children's Rights* 345.

[125] Melissa A. Jamison, 'Detention of Juvenile Enemy Combatants at Guantanamo Bay: The Special Concerns of the Children' (2005) 9 *UC Davis Journal of Juvenile Law & Policy* 127, 136, 139, 151–3.

[126] Convention on the Rights of the Child, n. 3, above.

[127] Jenny Kuper, *International Law Concerning Child Civilians in Armed Conflict* (Oxford, 1997) 8–9.

[128] On the judicial and prosecutorial reference to youth as aggravating in *Roper v. Simmons* (where the Supreme Court held unconstitutional capital punishment for crimes committed by persons under 18 years of age), see Tamar R. Birckhead, 'The Age of the Child: Interrogating Juveniles After *Roper v. Simmons*' (2008) 65 *Washington & Lee Law Review* 385, 395–406; Elizabeth F. Emens, 'Aggravating Youth: Roper v. Simmons and Age Discrimination' (2005) *Supreme Court Review* 51, 51–2. The argument that youth is aggravating is not unique to *Simmons*, and such prosecutorial rhetoric appeared in at least seven other instances. Birckhead, ibid., 404–5; Emens, ibid., 75. See also Seung Oh Kang, 'The Efficacy of Youth as a Mitigating Circumstance: Preservation of the Capital Defendant's Constitutional Rights Pursuant to Traditional Eighth Amendment Jurisprudence' (1994) 28 *Suffolk University Law Review* 747, 774.

whether they 'truly' are children.[129] Similarly, the precedence of physical appearance over chronological age is clearly not exclusive to the context discussed in the present chapter, and characterizes, for example, the social recourse to plastic surgery and the use of cosmetic products.[130] Another commonality between Israel/Palestine and other contexts is the conception of the figure of the child as somewhat able to influence society's knowledge of her or his age.[131]

These and additional commonalities between the Israeli-Palestinian case and other contexts suggest the need further to explore the workings of age. The complex ways in which age functions and is utilized in the legal imagining and fabrication of childhood clearly require rethinking. Through its contextualized investigation of the childhood-age-law triangle, the present chapter offers a starting point for such an enterprise.[132]

[129] It has been argued that in this context, legal professionals, social workers, and other practitioners tend to rely on asylum seekers' physical appearance as an indicator of their age. Immigration Law Practitioners' Association and Heaven Crawly, *When is a child not a child? Asylum, age disputes and the process of age assessment* (London, 2007), <http://www.ilpa.org.uk/publications/ILPA%20Age%20Dispute%20Report.pdf>, 48–53. A more recent legal development with regard to the assessment of age of asylum seekers who claim to be children is the judgment of the UK Supreme Court in the case of *A v. London Borough of Croydon & Anor; M v. London Borough of Lambeth & Anor* [2009] UKSC 8, <http://www.supremecourt.gov.uk/decided-cases/docs/UKSC_2009_0106_Judgment.pdf>.

[130] Mike Featherstone and Mike Hepworth, 'The Mask of Ageing and the Postmodern Life Course' in Mike Featherstone, Mike Hepworth, and Bryan S. Turner (eds), *The Body: Social Process and Cultural Theory* (London, 1991) 371, 374 (describing how chronological age is discredited as an indicator of inevitable age norms, while different health regimens are prescribed to control biological age, which is argued to be the true index of how people should feel). See also Simon Biggs, 'Choosing Not to be Old? Masks, Bodies and Identity Management in Later Life' (1997) 17 *Ageing and Society* 553.

[131] For sociological writing on children's ability, under certain circumstances, to make their social age older or younger, see Lesko, n. 36, above, 144–5; Anne Solberg, 'Negotiated Childhood: Changing Constructions of Age for Norwegian Children' in Allison James and Adrian James (eds), *Constructing and Reconstructing Childhood: Contemporary Issues in the Sociological Study of Childhood*, 2nd ed (London, 1997) 126. See also Valentine, n. 40, above, 38.

[132] [Editor's Note: See further now Christina Alfreive in ed. J. Bhasha, *Children Without a State* (MIT Press, 2011), 67–88.]

11

Children's Participation in Court Proceedings when Parents Divorce or Separate: Legal Constructions and Lived Experiences

E. Kay M. Tisdall and F. Morrison[1]

Children's participation generally—and children's participation in court proceedings when their parents divorce or separate specifically—has gained considerable policy and practice prominence. This has been fuelled by the United Nations Convention on the Rights of the Child (UNCRC), with its requirements for children's views to be given due weight in all matters affecting the child (Article 12). Research developed immensely in the 1990s, gathering children's own views of their participation when their parents divorce or separate. This provided a grounded basis for changes in policy and practice[2] and numerous countries altered their law to facilitate children's views being considered in family law decisions.[3]

With all this activity have come new questions and new dilemmas. A very real concern is 'slippage', where leading legislation such as that of New Zealand is being negated by certain senior court decisions.[4] The pressure of fathers' rights groups—fathers who are unhappy with the contact they have with their children, following separation or divorce—has been successful in creating political attention. The policy and research gaze has narrowed to look intently at contested contact, including situations where domestic abuse has occurred or is alleged.[5] In a European context, the litigation of fathers has led to the European Court of Human Rights laying out how a parent's right to respect for his or her private and family life (Article 8) will need to

[1] Kay Tisdall is Professor of Childhood Policy and Co-Director of the Centre for Research on Families and Relationships, University of Edinburgh. She established the MSc in Childhood Studies in 2001, at the University, as one of the first interdisciplinary degrees underpinned by children's rights.

Fiona Morrison is a PhD student at the Centre for Research on Families and Relationships, University of Edinburgh.

[2] E.g. J. Cashmore and P. Parkinson, *The Voice of a Child in Family Law Disputes* (Oxford, 2008); G. Douglas, M. Murch, C. Miles, and L. Scanlan, *Research into the Operation of Rule 9.5 of the Family Proceedings Rules 1991* (2006, <http://www.dca.gov.uk/family/familyprocrules_research.pdf> (3.11.09)); C. Smart, B. Neale, and A. Wade, *The Changing Experience of Childhood: Families and Divorce* (Cambridge, 2001); A. Smith, N. Taylor, and M. Gollop (eds), *Children's Voices: Research, Policy and Practice* (Auckland, 2000).

[3] See Henaghan, chapter 4, this volume.

[4] E.g. see chapter 4 this volume.

[5] Scottish Government, *National Domestic Abuse Delivery Plan for Children and Young People* (Edinburgh, 2008); J. Hunt and A. Macleod, *Outcomes of applications to court for contact orders after parental separation or divorce* (2008, <http://www.justice.gov.uk/publications/docs/outcomes-contact-orders-briefing-note.pdf> (27.7.10)); Mruk Research Ltd, *2007 Child Contact Survey* (2008, <http://www.scotland.gov.uk/Resource/Doc/215624/0057695.pdf> (27.7.10)).

be balanced by the child's best interests and the child's own right under Article 8.[6] Debates continue about how best to facilitate children's participation in court proceedings: e.g. by legal representation of the child; by continuing the professional approach of expert reporting; and/or by the judge meeting with the child and speaking to the child personally.[7]

Scotland has followed these broad trends. In 1995, the Children (Scotland) Act was passed; it was the most radical, across UK children's legislation, in specifying the requirement for children's participation. The 1995 Act remains the foundation of current Scottish family law, with certain amendments in regards to contested contact. In 1999, the then Scottish Executive commissioned the first study on the relevant provisions.[8] The study analysed all related legislation and guidance, reported case law up until 2001, and undertook a feasibility study on investigating children's experiences of their participation. Key findings included:

- the individual focus of the family law proceedings, that caused problems for siblings and other horizontal relationships for children;
- the lack of information for children and their heavy reliance on parents' initiatives to become involved;
- adults' concern about children's welfare, and their young age, which could preclude children's involvement;
- problems with procedures, such as (lack of) intimation to children, children feeling that their views were not adequately taken into account by reporting professionals, and negative feelings about delayed proceedings;
- the appreciation of children who had been independently represented by a lawyer, even when the court decisions were not always what the children had wanted.

This chapter explores whether progress has been made, since the study was undertaken. After summarizing the relevant legal provisions, an updated review of reported case law is undertaken. The chapter then presents provisional findings from research with children about their participation in the contested area of child contact where there is a history of domestic abuse. The analysis concentrates particularly on the processes of participation and the 'weight' given to children's views, with accompanying consideration of how children and childhood are constructed within these. Children's participation in family law court proceedings is a particularly challenging requirement, for several reasons: courts are involving themselves in the private lives of families; parents have traditionally been seen as the parties involved, and not children; including children means involving them in adult disputes; and children

[6] E.g. *Glaser v United Kingdom* (2001) 33 EHRR 1.

[7] A. Parkes, 'The Right of the Child to be Heard in Family Law Proceedings' (2009) 4(Nov) *International Family Law Journal* 238; M. Potter, 'The Voice of the Child: Children's "Rights" in Family Proceedings' (2008) 3(Sept) *International Family Law Journal* 140; L. Trinder, C. Jenks, and A. Firth, 'Talking Children into being in Absentia?' (2010) 22(2) *Child and Family Law Quarterly* 234; N. Wilson, 'The Ears of the Child in Family Proceedings' (2007) 38(Sept) *Family Law* 808.

[8] Full reports are contained in K. Marshall, E.K.M. Tisdall, A. Cleland, with A. Plumtree, *Voice of the Child under the Children (Scotland) Act 1995*, Volume 1: mapping paper (Edinburgh, 2002); E.K.M. Tisdall, R. Baker, K. Marshall, A. Cleland, with A. Plumtree and J. Williams, *'Voice of the Child' under the Children (Scotland) Act 1995*, Volume 2: Feasibility Study (Edinburgh, 2002).

are frequently young. Children's participation is thus testing traditional attitudes towards childhood, children, and family law.

11.1 Children's participation in Scottish family law

Scotland is arguably still the most 'positive' in primary and secondary legislation about the possibility of children's participation, as compared to elsewhere in the UK.

First, the Children (Scotland) Act 1995 has a wide (if largely unknown) requirement on all those with parental responsibilities to consider a child's views when making 'any major decision' in exercising parental responsibilities or rights.[9] This is subject to the child's age and maturity. While the duty presumes that any child of age 12 and above will have sufficient age and maturity to have views considered, the duty nevertheless applies to all children. Similarly, a person who has 'care or control' of the child (but not parental responsibilities or rights) must consider a child's views when making 'any major decision' in relation to safeguarding the child's health, development, and welfare and/or surgical, medical or dental treatment or procedures.[10] These responsibilities are notable, as most parental separations, and subsequent decisions on residence, contact etc, do not reach court.

Second, should a case reach court, a child can participate in a number of ways. In family law proceedings, a court must consider a child's views when making an order in regard to parental responsibilities or rights.[11] To be more specific, the court, when considering whether or not to make an order:

> ... taking account of the child's age and maturity, shall so far as practicable –
> (i) give him an opportunity to indicate whether he wishes to express his views;
> (ii) if he does so wish, give him an opportunity to express them; and
> (iii) have regard to such views as he may express.[12]

Again, the presumption of age 12 is repeated: a child aged 12 or above will be presumed to have sufficient age and maturity to form a view.[13] A child can sue or defend proceedings in relation to any exercise of parental responsibilities and rights. A child under the age of 16 has the legal capacity to instruct a lawyer in any civil matter where the child has a general understanding of what it means to do so.[14]

Mechanisms have been established for children's involvement within court proceedings for s.11 orders on parental responsibilities and rights:

- If children were served with papers once the case enters the court process (called 'intimation'), they would receive a Form F9 requesting their views. The form goes back to the sheriff.[15]
- The court may appoint a court reporter or curator ad litem to report on the child's views.
- The sheriff may express the wish to hear directly from the child and ask for the child to be brought to the court.

[9] s.6. [10] s.6.

[11] s.11. Note the child's welfare remains the paramount consideration of the court.

[12] s.11(7)(b). [13] s.11(10). [14] Age of Legal Capacity (Scotland) Act 1991, s.2(4A).

[15] A sheriff is a professional judge in the second tier courts. A sheriff would hear most family law cases in the first instance—thus sheriff is typically used in this chapter—but some cases are heard in the Court of Session in the first instance or can be heard on appeal.

- A child may take independent legal advice. If this is done, the child's views may be expressed in several ways. First, the lawyer may help the child to fill in Form F9. Second, the lawyer may write to the court on the child's behalf or, third, the lawyer may seek to have the child involved as a party to the action.
- Alternatively, the lawyer may appear on the child's behalf at the Child Welfare Hearing to express the child's views. The Child Welfare Hearing was introduced following the 1995 Act to provide an early hearing to resolve any disputed issues in family actions, particularly in relation to children.

When a child has expressed a view, the sheriff or someone appointed by the sheriff must record the view. The sheriff may then decide whether it should be kept confidential.[16] As Raitt concludes, a Scottish sheriff has a wider set of participation modes and considerable discretion in selecting between or combining them, compared to English procedures.[17]

Family law proceedings under the 1995 Act remain substantially the same, with two amendments[18] of note: courts must consider whether it is appropriate to make an order when two or more relevant people would have to co-operate (to deal with contentious contact);[19] and courts must have regard to the need to protect the child from any abuse or risk of abuse, the effects of any such abuse, and the ability of a person to care for or meet the needs of the child.[20] These amendments are a reaction to the political furore and practical difficulties around contested contact.

11.2 Changing case law

An initial review up until March 2001 found that children's views were 'hidden' behind the reported case law.[21] Scottish case law rarely focused on the requirement to listen to children's views under the 1995 Act. Children's views may have been considered in many situations or, alternatively, their rights to be heard may have been breached. Either way, children's views were very seldom revealed in reported case law.

By 2010, this had substantially changed, clearly influenced by the Court of Session's pivotal decision in *Shields v Shields*.[22] In this case, a residence and specific issue order was requested, so that the child could relocate with his mother to Australia. The boy was seven-and-a-half years old at the time. The case was appealed and the Sheriff Principal commented negatively on the lack of attention to ensuring the child had an opportunity to state his views. The child had not been served with papers, and hence the Form F9, and no justification for this had been recorded beyond the boy's age. The Sheriff Principal still refused the appeal, on the basis that he would 'have to be satisfied that no Sheriff acting reasonably in the circumstances... could have refrained from seeking the views of an 8-year old child'.[23] The Court of Session disagreed.

[16] The Sheriff Ordinary Cause Rules 1993 (as amended) and the Child Care and Maintenance Rules 1997 (as amended) provide for children's views to be treated as confidential by the sheriff. The Court of Session has no similar rules (although does for adoption etc).

[17] F. Raitt, 'Hearing Children in Family Law Proceedings: Can Judges Make a Difference?' (2007) 19(2) *Child and Family Law Quarterly* 204.

[18] Made through the Family Law (Scotland) Act 2006. [19] s.11(7D).

[20] s.11(7A-C). [21] N. 8 above. [22] 2002 SC 246. [23] Para 4.

The child had an absolute right to discretion and reference could not be made to a hypothetical situation. Further, courts could not necessarily rest on an early decision but had to consider whether there was a material change in circumstances up until an order was made. The Court of Session agreed that the lapse of time (18 months) between intimation being dispensed with, and the decision being taken, was in this case such a material change.[24]

The Court of Session's subsequent observations have been vastly influential on the courts. Practicability is the 'only proper and relevant test' for giving the child an opportunity to make known his or her views, so the question becomes *how* rather than *whether* a child's views should be garnered: 'But, if, by one method or another, it is "practicable" to give a child the opportunity of expressing his views, then, in our view, the only safe course is to employ that method.'[25] Practicability is the first stage—and arguably sets a low threshold—and only then does the court weigh the child's views in the court's decision.[26]

Suitably taking account of children's views is now a recognized ground of appeal and, in some cases, has been the *sole* ground.[27] The processes of participation and how the reports say the views were weighed can now be commented upon.

11.2.1 Processes of participation

Observations in *Shields v Shields* cast doubt on the usefulness of Form F9 as a way for a child to express his or her views.[28] Reported case law shows a reliance on professional reports, written by court appointees and/or by psychological/psychiatric clinicians. These reports are pivotal in three ways: to establish the child's *capacity* to state views, the *content* of these views, and the *weight* these views should be given.[29] As Barnes writes, if a child's views might be called into question by reason of disability or learning difficulty, it would be wise to have a health professional's expert opinion that a child's views should be considered.[30] Reliance on such reports can fulfil the court's obligations for participation, if timely and well-prepared.

Most children's views are recorded and discussed when they are directly about the order requested: i.e. residence or contact. Case law suggests that a child's views will be considered more seriously when the topic is more 'focused' (e.g. *Shields v Shields*) than more generalized (on parental responsibilities, *C v McM*). The justification in the latter was that the child was less able to understand the generality of parental responsibilities. At least the case allowed for the wider considerations of a child to be discussed, such as school, friends, and physical activities. These considerations were also taken into account in certain other cases.[31] This shows some move to recognizing

[24] Although a gap of 16 months was not considered material in *C v McM* 2005 Fam LR 36.

[25] Para 11.

[26] This goes some way towards the UN Committee on the Rights of the Child's General Comment (2009): 'State parties should presume that a child has the capacity to form his or her own views and recognize that she or he has the right to express them; it is not up to the child to prove his or her capacity' (para 20).

[27] See also *C v McM*.

[28] Supported by early research by D. Christie, R. Mays, and L. Tyler, *The Child Welfare Hearings in Operation: Feasibility Study* (Edinburgh Scottish Executive Home Department, 2000).

[29] E.g. *Treasure v McGrath* 2006 Fam LR 100; *H v H* 2000 Fam LR 73.

[30] L. Barnes, 'A child is, after all, a child: ascertaining the ability of children to express views in family proceedings' (2008) 18 *Scots Law Times* 121.

[31] E.g. *Ellis v Ellis* Fam LR 77 mentions Jacob's wish 'to walk to the defender's house to play with his toys even if the defender is away' (para 15).

that the only issues at stake are not children 'choosing' between their parents but other aspects of children's lives affected by decisions on parental responsibilities and rights.[32]

In the earlier survey of reported cases, a slew of cases showed considerable concern about confidentiality.[33] On the one hand, courts recognized that children might be reluctant to state their views, if they were not kept confidential from one or both parents. To have their views revealed might jeopardize the children's welfare. The sheriff court could require children's views to be kept confidentially. On the other hand, if the views led to a certain decision, problems might arise about due process, especially in light of Human Rights Act 1998/European Convention on Human Rights' requirements. Notably, later reported case law has not continued with these debates, perhaps because sheriffs have managed to 'finesse the conflicts thrown up by confidentiality'.[34]

O'Malley v O'Malley[35] underlines judicial discretion on the mode of participation. In *X v Y*,[36] a party asserted that the children had lied to the clinical psychologist and the sheriff was asked subsequently to see the children himself. The sheriff refused, deeming himself 'not the appropriate person',[37] although he did see the children for a more generalized conversation as they had arrived at the court expecting to see him. Parties, then, cannot insist on the children's mode of participation; the sheriff decides.

The (possible) exception occurs when a child is separately represented. In early decisions, *Henderson v Henderson*[38] noted the reluctance of that sheriff to have children separately represented but the children remained parties to the case. More recently, in *D v H*[39] a 15-year-old sought a contact order for his sibling but a warrant for citation was refused as incompetent. Describing the *D v H* decision as 'premature', in *E v E*,[40] a 14-year-old took a plea of competency, arguing that she had a legitimate interest in contact with her siblings. The decision did not, however, make a clear statement that it would be competent for a contact order to be made in favour of a child.[41] But a possibility was opened for children's *own* horizontal relationships to be given a hearing, when they were affected by parental separation or divorce.

11.2.2 Due weight to children's views

The role of age was considered in the initial Scottish government feasibility study. There were concerns that the age of 12 would act as a threshold rather than a rebuttable presumption, particularly with less experienced legal professionals. Even the more experienced legal professionals expressed some concern with going below the age of eight for children's participation.

The citation of *Shields v Shields*, and its low threshold of practicability, has helped reduce this notional age threshold to under the age of three, but only this far: in *Stewart v Stewart*, including someone below this age was seen as 'wholly impractical'.[42] The court's view may well have been influenced by the overall disparaging of the appellant's 16 grounds of appeal as 'sterile and frivolous, and have

[32] See also Raitt for interviews with Scottish judges: n. 17, above.

[33] E.g. *Dosoo v Dosoo* 1999 SLT (ShCt) 86; *McGrath v McGrath* 1999 SLT (ShCt) 90.

[34] N. 17, above, 204. [35] 2004 Fam LR 44. [36] 2007 Fam LR 153. [37] 154.

[38] 1997 Fam LR 120. [39] 2004 SLT (ShCt) 73. [40] 2004 Fam LR 115.

[41] A. Cleland, 'Children's Voices in Legal Proceedings' in A. Cleland and E. Sutherland (eds), *Children's Rights in Scotland*, 3rd ed (Edinburgh, 2009) 9–58.

[42] 2007 CSIH 20, 13.

nothing to deal with the best interests of the child'.[43] This bundling is unfortunate because *Shields v Shields*' emphasis on method could allow in developing methods of working with very young children.[44] It follows Trinder and colleagues' concern that professionals use children's views as strategic resources, especially when they confirm their own perspectives and decisions, rather than as independent factors given due consideration.[45] Nonetheless, overall in reported case law, age is less likely to be used as a threshold and more likely as a factor to consider—it is regularly stated as part of the facts and often found in the justification—in deciding how to weigh a child's views. Age is highly influential when the child is near or over the age of 12,[46] due to the 1995 Act's presumption,[47] but courts now seem content to include the views of children who are much younger.[48]

Alongside age, other descriptors are used in decisions to justify the weight given to children's views. While the academic and legal literature discusses justifications around (rational) competency,[49] this was not a discourse used in reported cases. Instead, children's views were divided between those described as consistent, definite, and clear and views described as ambivalent or anxious. This contrast is illuminated by different descriptions of siblings, in a single case. For example, three siblings were described in *K v K*:[50]

- M expressed a strong view, and this has been consistent throughout...
- K is much more ambivalent and indeed from other information given to me it appears very likely that she may not be very happy in seeing her mother.
- X is really too young to have a definite view but he appears to be a happy child and one who should be resilient enough to deal with any problems that arise.

A similar contrast is made between two siblings in *H v H*:[51]

- LH was described as a mature and confident young woman, who knew her own mind... Her consistent view is that... It is articulated clearly in her letter...
- The position in respect of AH is much more difficult. Both psychologists were very concerned about him.... the distress and anxiety he has suffered... state of vulnerability...

[43] 31.

[44] P. Alderson, *Young Children's Rights: Exploring Beliefs, Principles and Practice*, 2nd ed (London, 2008); A. Clark and P. Moss, *The Mosaic Approach* (London, 2001).

[45] L. Trinder, C. Jenks, and A. Firth, 'Talking Children into being in Absentia?' (2010) 22(2) *Child and Family Law Quarterly* 234.

[46] And, according to Barnes (n. 30, above), age 12 remains a significant age for instructing a lawyer, as found in *Henderson v Henderson* (n. 38, above) and *C v McM* (n. 24, above).

[47] E.g. *G v G* 2002 Fam LR 120, 2-05.

[48] As an exception, the judge easily accepted the counsel's view that children aged seven and five were too young to be interviewed—with no justification of this (*McG v McG* 2007 Fam LR 62). This was an extremely contentious case, where the children were otherwise discussed as being 'coached' to make statements to their parents (64), which may offer an explanation for the judge's reluctance.

[49] J. Hemrica and F. Heyting, 'Tacit notions of childhood: an analysis of discourse about child participation in decision-making regarding arrangements in case of parental divorce' (2004) 11(4) *Childhood* 449.

[50] 2004 Fam LR 25, 27.

[51] 2010 SLT 395.

When views are described as consistent, clear, and definite, the court weighs them more heavily; if views were described as ambivalent or anxious, the views have substantially less weight.

A child's confidence or evident maturity might be commented upon, with no further linking justification to the weight given to the child's views.[52] Professional reports were frequent resources to support these evaluations of stability and clarity—or not—of children's views. Such descriptors underline that children can be moral agents, as autonomous rights-holders, capable of coming to rational views.

To be influential, however, on the court's decision about *weight*, reports must be 'balanced'. In *J v J*,[53] Professor Triseliotis' expertise was (at least on the surface) not questioned but his procedure was. He saw only the mother and the two children, and not the father. He saw the children in the mother's home only. In this way, he was described as not having sufficient comprehensive knowledge or ensuring that the children's views were sufficiently uninfluenced by context. This suggests that a child's views are more influential when they are contained within a report that assists the court with its *own* decision, which must be framed by welfare as the paramount consideration, the range of relevant evidence, and provide expert guidance on what weight should be given to the child's views.[54]

There is a particular emphasis on autonomy. Barnes writes of the undermining of children's views, when (legal) professionals think that the children have been manipulated (particularly by one of the parents).[55] The word 'manipulation'[56] is not found in the reported case law reviewed here but similar concerns can be seen in worries about being pressured by parental presence or material bribes[57] or the counter-assertions that a child's views were 'genuine'[58] and that the child 'knows her own mind'.[59] In *M v M*,[60] G's views were discounted, not because he was manipulated by a parent, but because he would want to please whoever asked him; thus how the questions were asked and in what context would heavily influence his decisions. A child's views could be deemed unascertainable because of loyalty to parents, or not wanting the child to feel responsible for a disloyal decision.[61] The possible manipulation of parents is not directly stated, although heavily implied by the decision in *Bailey v Bailey*.[62] But the court was more willing to state family influence directly when it involved the perceived influence of an older sibling's refusal of contact on her younger sibling.[63] Here, a contact order was made for the younger child despite her views against contact. In short, the weight of a child's views is fundamentally weakened if the views were (unduly?) influenced.

All the reported case law is adamant that the paramount consideration is a child's welfare, as required by the 1995 Act. The traditional weighing up is exemplified by *J v J*, where the children's current views are noted but are seen as contrary to their longer-term interests. These two children may not want to have contact with their father now, and seeing their father may cause upset and short-term distress. But having

52 E.g. *M v M* 2000 Fam LR 84.

53 2004 Fam LR 20.

54 See also child psychologist report in n. 31 above.

55 N. 30 above.

56 The term 'coached' is used within *McG v McG* (64) but notably for children's comments to parents and not specifically for reports etc to the court.

57 N. 31 above.

58 *S v S* 2004 Fam LR 127, 132; *G v G* 2002 Fam LR 120, 22-05.

59 E.g. *H v H* 2010 SLT 395, 31.

60 2008 Fam LR 90, 53.

61 *G v G* 2003 Fam LR 118; AH in *H v H* 2010 SLT 395, 37–8.

62 2001 Fam LR 133.

63 *White v White* 2001 SC 689.

contact is seen as in their long-term interest with the presumption that the upset and distress will dissipate.[64] These differences highlight particular views of childhood, well rehearsed in childhood studies literature:[65] the traditional focus on children as 'human becomings' as future adults and, more recently, as social investments for future society, in contrast to respecting children's childhoods now and their current state as 'human beings'. This is somewhat mitigated by the (now) common concerns for children's well-being should they move schools, friendships, need to travel between parents etc.[66] These raise more concurrent ideas of children's present well-being and not just their futures.

When the stated *views* of children are not considered sufficient for giving much weight, whatever a child's age, then recourse is made to *observed behaviour* of children. Of frequent note is whether the child seems loved, happy, and/or settled. Reactions at school are given high prominence. Such observations are not discussed as non-verbal expressions of children's views, but rather as indications of their welfare.

Moss and colleagues write about different perceptions of children and childhood, of the 'rich' child full of resources and capabilities in contrast to the 'poor' child, vulnerable and dependent.[67] When considering children's views, the 'rich' child is frequently presented in reported case law. Indeed, children are described as 'resilient' in *Ellis v Ellis*: 'I appreciate that children are resilient and can cope with change...' Note, however, that the statement then goes on to discount this, and to assert that children benefit from being settled: '...but I am not convinced that for the children to reside wholly with the pursuer would be so detrimental to their welfare that I should sacrifice the advantages they have gained from continuity and stability....'[68] Children, therefore, are not *that* resilient. In looking over the reported cases, the 'poor' child discourses are not associated with discussion of children's views, with one exception. The vulnerability of AH, in contrast to his sibling, is of 'great concern' to professionals and the court,[69] and leads to an occlusion of his views.

11.3 Lived experiences of family law proceedings

There has been much debate around the issue of child contact in the specific circumstances of domestic abuse. Research shows why contact in this context can be problematic. A wealth of studies has documented the negative impacts that domestic abuse has on children and that the presence of domestic abuse is a strong indicator for the direct abuse of children.[70] It is often assumed that abuse ends if women leave abusive partners. However abuse can continue and indeed intensify following

[64] The 2006 amendment in s.11(7)(D), on contentious contact, may diminish the precedence of *J v J*'s approach.

[65] A. James, C. Jenks, and A. Prout, *Theorizing Childhood* (Cambridge, 1998).

[66] E.g. *M v M* 2000 (n. 52 above), *M v M* 2008 (n. 60 above), *X v Y* (n. 36 above).

[67] P. Moss, J. Dillon, and K. Statham, 'The "Child in Need" and "the Rich Child": Discourses, Constructions and Practices' (2000) 20(2) *Critical Social Policy* 233.

[68] 95. See also *X v Y*: 'I accept that children can be quite resilient but unless there is a good reason for subjecting them to another major change in their lives then I believe that this should be avoided' (156).

[69] *H v H* 2010 (n. 61 above).

[70] See C. Humphreys, C. Houghton, and J. Ellis, *Literature Review Better Outcomes for Children and Young People Experiencing Domestic Abuse* (Edinburgh, 2006) for an overview of the effects of domestic abuse on children.

separation[71] and child contact is reported as a particular 'flash point' for such abuse to continue.[72] The research reported here[73] aims to explore children's own perspectives in these circumstances, an area that has been largely under-researched and missing from policy debates. As well as examining children's views of parental separation and the contact that does or does not take place, the research examines children's experiences of participating in family law proceedings.

The research involved separate in-depth interviews with children and their mothers (who were resident parents). Core to the research design were ethical considerations about informed consent, building respectful relationships with children and mothers, and their safety. A total of 15 mothers and 18 children participated in the study. The children's ages spanned from seven to 15 years. Participants were recruited to the study via domestic abuse support services like Women's Aid and local authority provided services. All of the families involved in the study had experienced domestic abuse (where fathers had been the perpetrator) and the parents had separated.

Drawing from the experience of an 11-year-old girl called Clare[74] who participated in the study, this part of the chapter examines Clare's views of her participation in family law proceedings. The purpose of this discussion is not to examine Clare or her mother's experience of domestic abuse. Nor does it intend to assess or make comment on whether contact with her father is in Clare's best interests. Rather this part of the chapter focuses on Clare's experience of participating in family law proceedings in a context of domestic abuse and contentious contact.

In many respects Clare's overall experiences were similar to those of other children who participated in the study. Contact had been a very fraught issue and disputes about it had been protracted. However in other respects Clare was not a typical case. She was very articulate and had been able to engage confidently with many of the family law processes that have been established to facilitate children's participation. She conveyed her feelings and wishes about contact on a number of occasions and through a variety of means. However, despite having a high degree of participation in the proceedings, Clare was extremely angry and frustrated about the decisions that were reached about contact with her father. Her anger emanated from a feeling that she had not been listened to or been able to influence the sheriff's decision about contact. Clare's experience has been selected for this chapter because of her feelings about participation. They led us to wonder: if children like Clare who are able to engage confidently with a ranges of mechanisms established for children's participation are left feeling unheard, what position may family law proceedings render children who are not able to participate so fully or confidently?

11.3.1 Clare's experience

Clare's parents first separated when she was four years old. Since then there have been disputes about the contact between Clare and her non-resident father. Thus, for

[71] R.E. Fleury, C.M. Sullivan, and D. Bybee, 'When Ending the Relationship Does Not End the Violence' (2000) 6 *Violence Against Women* 1363.

[72] C. Humphreys and R.K. Thiara, 'Neither Justice nor Protection: Women's Experiences of Post-separation Violence' (2003) 25(4) *Journal of Social Welfare and Family Law* 195.

[73] The research was undertaken as part of an Economic and Social Research Council PhD studentship at the Centre for Research on Families and Relationship at the University of Edinburgh and in collaboration with Scottish Women's Aid. Scottish Women's Aid is the membership organization for Women's Aid groups across Scotland.

[74] Not her real name.

almost three-quarters of Clare's life, there have been intermittent legal disputes about the contact that she has with her father. Several attempts to prevent contact have been made by Clare's resident mother. These stem from her concerns about Clare's father's ability to parent. When Clare was younger, her mother was concerned about Clare's physical safety when she was in the care of her father. Her mother described a series of occasions when, left alone with her father, Clare's physical safety had been compromised. On a few of these occasions she had sustained minor injuries: a cut to her hand that has left a scar and bruising to her head. Latterly concerns centered on Clare's strong feelings against contact. Both Clare and her mother in their separate interviews described how Clare became distressed before and after contact visits. This had at times manifested itself as physical symptoms, for example having an upset stomach or suffering from a headache.

11.3.2 Experiences of participation

During her interview, Clare recalled two main legal events where disputes about contact had been taken to court: once when she was around six years old and again more recently when she was ten years old. Clare exhausted many of the avenues open to her to convey her views and wishes about contact with her father to the court. During the first set of proceedings Clare had spoken directly to a court reporter who had been appointed by the court to investigate the circumstances of the contact dispute. In the most recent set of proceedings, Clare spoke again with a court reporter, completed a Form F9 with the support of an advocacy worker, and attempted to become legally represented. Whilst Clare's high level of participation shows that efforts were made by the court for Clare to have opportunities to express her views, her overall *experience* of participation was far from positive. Clare forcefully expressed through many ways that she does not want to have contact with her father. While the most recent contact order has significantly reduced the amount of contact taking place, Clare remains adamant that she does not want to see her father at all.

11.3.3 Due weight to children's views

For Clare, having the opportunity to express her view about contact has not been adequate, as she wanted to *influence* the court's decision so that it reflected her wishes. When explaining the ways in which court proceedings could be improved, Clare (and many of the other children in the study) placed great emphasis on the importance of listening to the child:

Clare: Listen to what the child says because after all it's the child's best interests and stuff.

As the quotation illustrates, Clare was familiar with the legal term 'best interests' and during the interviews she understood that this was the principle that underpinned the court's decision about contact. However for Clare her views were consistent with what was in her best interests.

Clare felt that the court's appreciation of her views was undermined because she could not give sufficient reason for her strong feelings about contact. Despite being articulate and confident, Clare struggled to provide reasons why she did not want to have contact with her father:

Clare: Cos that's the annoying part because apparently I don't have a good enough reason, because sometimes you don't need a reason sometimes you just have a feeling and you have to go by your instinct.

Clare's 'instincts' against contact were strong and she felt that these should be taken seriously. There appeared to be a disjuncture between what Clare and the court perceived to be valid reasons for contact to stop.

In Clare's case it was not clear to her what specific factors influenced the sheriff's decision about contact. Nor was it clear the weight accorded to Clare's views against contact, when conveyed in a Form F9 and when she met with the court reporter. Ultimately the sheriff ordered that she continue to have contact with her father (albeit a reduced amount of contact). Clare interpreted this decision as evidence that her views were not considered important, which left her feeling insignificant and powerless:

Clare: Unfair. Very unfair, cos in the court case that my mum went through I was nearly ignored. I mean it just makes you feel so small and yeah.

This focuses attention on a key challenge for children's participation in family law—the position that children are left in when the courts' decisions differ from the views expressed by the children. Courts are not legally required in Scotland to explain to children the reasons why courts have reached a particular decision. The sheriff's rationale for deciding to continue contact was not explained to Clare by the sheriff or anyone acting on the sheriff's behalf. Clare had no assurances that her views against contact had been heard and taken account of. Aside from raising questions about the respect that this affords children whose lives these decisions are concerned with (regardless of whether or not they have participated in proceedings), this lack of transparency can also create a vacuum where the child is left without any real understanding as to why a decision has been reached.

This vacuum can be filled by the child's own ideas and interpretations or by the perspectives of others. As well as interpreting the decision as evidence that her views were not considered important, Clare also believed courts placed more importance on issues that were not necessarily concerned with her individual circumstances or views. She described courts as having a strong commitment to ensuring that children and fathers have contact after parental separation. This meant that her views against contact were expressed in an environment that favoured contact, which made it difficult for her views to be heard and given weight:

Clare: ...nobody heard what I said, apart from my mum.... Because they didn't want to. Because in that court it is every children should see their fathers.... Um not actually listen to what the child thinks and stuff. Which I think should definitely change....

Clare believed that her views clashed with a dominant view that was held by the court about the relationships that children should have with their fathers, and as a consequence her views were overlooked.

As well as her perception that courts are pro-contact regardless of the child's views, Clare also identified her age as a barrier to influence the court's decision. She referred to this throughout the interview, highlighting that she looked forward to future birthdays because she believed that more weight would be given to her views or she would be sufficiently old to decide for herself whether she wanted to see her father:

Clare: ...I am really looking forward to my twelfth birthday cos that means I will be listened to much more, which will be very nice.

Clare: I am looking forward to when I am 12 cos that means they have to take me more seriously and I think I will definitely have stopped seeing my dad by the time I am sixteen.

It was not clear why Clare thought that reaching 12 would be the point where her views would be acted on by the court. The review of reported cases reveals that the child's age is not treated as a threshold; rather it is treated as one factor to take account of, amongst many others. However Clare's views highlight that children's age and the extent of their participation remain salient and connected issues for her. Clare perceived getting older as critical to her gaining influence within decision-making.

11.3.4 Participating in an adversarial process

There have been debates about whether participation in family law can over-burden children. It has been argued that it can leave children with an unenviable responsibility for choosing between parents.[75] This can be further complicated when considering the effects that domestic abuse can have on children's relationships with their mothers or fathers. For instance children may feel responsible for protecting their mother, fearful of their father, or not want to be disloyal to either.[76] Smart and colleagues' research with children on their participation in family law adds another dimension to these debates.[77] They report that in general children do not want to choose which parent they live with but do want to be involved in decisions about how they live. Particularly relevant to this chapter are the findings that children who had been abused want a greater say in decisions about residence and contact.

While children may want to be involved in decisions about issues like contact, it does not mean that children's participation is easy or without cost. The danger remains that, when participating in family law processes, children can become caught up in adversarial proceedings and indeed in conflict. During her interview Clare used words like 'battle', 'defence-weapon', and 'war' when referring to her experiences. These connotations of conflict are apparent throughout her discussion about the legal proceedings that have taken place.

When discussing the barriers that she experienced in expressing her views, Clare continued this theme of conflict with her description of the people who were involved in court proceedings. Clare described herself and her mother as being on one side and her father on another. Her idea of opposing sides extended beyond her and her parents. Clare perceived the court and all adults associated with it (even her mother's lawyer) to be allies of her father and therefore on his side. As a result Clare did not see the court as 'for' her or her mother; rather she saw the court as acting 'against' her and her mother:

> Clare: …Cos practically everybody in the court is against me and my mum and cos they are always saying right horrible things to her and praising my dad—it's strange. And stuff. So practically everybody in there is against us like even my mum's own lawyer so yeah. And stuff.

[75] R. Chisholm, 'Children's Participation in Family Court Litigation', in J. Dewar and S. Parker (eds), *Family Law: Processes, Practices, Pressures* (Oregon, 2003) 37.

[76] A. Mullender, G Hague, U. Imam, L. Kelly, E. Malos, and L. Regan, *Children's Perspectives on Domestic Violence* (London, 2002).

[77] C. Smart, B. Neale, and A. Wade, *The Changing Experience of Childhood: Families and Divorce* (Cambridge, 2001).

The notion that everyone associated with the court is against Clare and her mother angered and frustrated Clare. Her narrative reveals a sense of powerlessness:

Fiona: What or who are you most angry at? (referring to an emotion card selected by Clare)

Clare: Everything to do with him (court reporter). Everybody to do with the court case that wasn't on my side. Angry that it's as if I'm a tiny dot and they are humongous they are all this big circle.

Clare's construction of the court in this way highlights a very real challenge for family law and for parents: are there ways that children can participate in decisions about contact and be protected (as far as possible) from levels of conflict or antagonism that may exist?

11.3.5 Mechanisms for participation

During both sets of court proceedings Clare met with a court reporter on several occasions. He observed contact handovers, contact visits, and met with her at home and at school to gather her views about contact. The length of time the court reporter spent with Clare was considerable. However, her relationship with him has been fraught: as discussed earlier she constructed the court reporter as not being on her side but being on her father's side. Clare initially said that she felt able to give her views to the court reporter; however during her interview she highlighted a number of issues that had latterly made it difficult for her to express her views.

The first issue relates to how children's views are taken or more specifically the questions that are asked to elicit these views. The relationships children have with non-resident parents are complex. This can be magnified when there is a history of abuse. During the interview Clare described the court reporter as asking 'horrible' but 'normal' questions. She recalled him asking her questions about whether she loved her father or whether he loved her. The court reporter's questions appeared to stem from seeking a justification for why Clare did not want contact with her father:

Fiona: So what did he say when he (court reporter) came to meet you?

Clare: Um horrible stuff. Basically the normal questions—like why do you want to stop seeing your dad? Don't you love him? Doesn't he love you?

The implication of these questions is that children who love their fathers want contact and those who do not love their fathers do not want contact. As already discussed, children may have conflicted feelings about these relationships. Questions about love can be loaded and add to feelings of conflict that children may already have.

The second issue relates to the confidentiality of children's views. The implications of not treating children's views as confidential were evident in Clare's case. During one contact visit, the court reporter made an attempt to gather Clare's views about contact. Asked in front of her father and his new partner, Clare found it difficult to express her feelings about contact:

Clare: Um well he said are you happy? . . . And I couldn't really exactly say anything evil cos I mean come on my dad was sitting there. It was like one child against three adults. Guess who is going to win. . . .

Following the most recent contact decision, during a contact visit Clare's father recounted the views that she had given in her Form F9. This was an upsetting experience for Clare. She described feeling trapped and that her father had confronted her with these. It is not clear whether she had expected that her views on the F9 would be treated confidentially but the incident was upsetting, particularly as her father had misquoted her:

> Clare: ... um he said and when you wrote your court statement you wrote that I was mentally cruel to mum. And I said I don't remember writing 'cruel' and he said yes you did. And I actually put he 'also mentally hurt' my mother so I am so pissed off with him about that.

Clare's experiences bring to life some of the complexities around children's views and confidentiality. When asked her views about contact in front of her father, she was unable to express how she felt. Clare was however able to express her views in writing to the court, an activity she completed with the support of an advocacy worker. That these views were subsequently shared with her father during the court proceedings had negative consequences for Clare.

11.4 Concluding thoughts

On the surface of reported case law, there has been a substantial change in the overt recognition of children's views: most children will meet the low threshold of 'practicability' for their views to be considered; their views and the weight of those views are used more explicitly to justify court decisions. Not allowing children to have a chance to express views can be an appeal ground in itself. The case law demonstrates more sophisticated ideas about children's participation, at least on some issues, such as the need to consider change over time as children develop and to value children's present as well their future. All this can be seen as a considerable achievement, for those who normatively have argued for children's rights to participation in family law proceedings and elsewhere.

Children's views seem to have a clear influence in deciding certain cases. Family law proceedings can be seen, to a certain extent, as shifting paradigms:

> The welfare paradigm, which sees children as lacking the capacity and maturity to understand and assert their own needs, has been challenged by new paradigms, including children's rights, and children as social actors and young citizens. Within these new paradigms, children are not longer conceived as dependent, vulnerable, at-risk victims of divorce and passive objects of law, but are seen as subjects with agency.[78]

This progressive picture can be queried: practically, in reflecting on the empirical research; and conceptually, in questioning the reliance on autonomy, 'voice', and rationality.

Reported case law is but a small sample of cases and from the judges' perspectives. Children may not routinely have positive experiences of participation; even if procedures were followed as suggested in reported case law, children may still have different perspectives. Certainly, the empirical research reported here is less promising. Clare's account questions the *quality* of children's experiences: the procedures may be there, courts may even be ensuring they take place, but children may still not feel satisfied that their views are duly considered. Given the reliance on professional

[78] R. Hunter, 'Close Encounters of a Judicial Kind: "Hearing" Children's "Voices" in Family Law Proceedings' (2007) 19(3) *Child and Family Law Quarterly* 283, 283.

reports more generally, it is particularly important that practice is exemplary in gathering children's views.[79]

Here, the considerable discussion in England and Wales, engendered by the idea that judges should see children themselves, could be useful. One of the reasons articulated is a child's sense of inclusion:

> ... when considering the question of positive benefit to the child, the judge should not confine himself to the question of whether or not it will assist the judge to come to his decision, but should consider the potential benefit of affording to the child the chance to feel that he or she has participated in the process of deciding his or her own fate and has had his or her own 'shout' whatever the outcome.[80]

There is a risk that a focus on inclusion can fall back into listening to children's views as a kind of therapy, a panacea that has no real influence on decision-making. But Potter's wording is careful and instead identifies the potential benefit of inclusion as additional. Listening to children, according to Raitt, is 'a simple but potent mark of respect'.[81] This is an area worthy of further research, from child participants' perspectives. Potter also suggests that the judge should explain the decision to the child.[82] This would meet the gap for Clare, who was not told directly what the court decisions were, nor the reasons behind them.

There are also conceptual queries, which illuminate why certain tensions and dilemmas remain in children's participation in family law proceedings. With some irony, just as Scottish case law seems to be accepting the 'new' paradigm of children's citizenship and agency, academic childhood studies is just gaining its own maturity to question some of its underlying assumptions. While discursively powerful, the focus on children as social actors and as agents fails to incorporate post-modern ideas about identity and subjectivity. These can be seen as socially constructed, through relations of power and knowledge.[83] With such ideas, no one is truly an 'autonomous agent' and all views are contingent, interpreted, and contextually dependent. As Mantle and colleagues (2006) note:

> A naive positivism underlies any assumption that a child's wishes and feelings are simply 'out there waiting to be collected'. Interpretation is unavoidable and meanings are likely to be contested.[84]

Hunter argues that 'the quest for access to children's "true" or authentic wishes and feelings is misplaced'.[85] These arguments stand in sharp contrast to the reported case law's weight to (supposedly) consistent, firm, genuine, and uninfluenced views of children.

There has been an association, within childhood studies and/or child advocacy, of recognizing children as social actors and trying to put forward 'children's voices'.

[79] See criticisms of professional practice in England: A. James and S. McNamee, 'Turn Down the Volume? Not Hearing Children in Family Proceedings' (2004) 16(2) *Child Family Law Quarterly* 189.

[80] M. Potter, 'The Voice of the Child: Children's 'Rights' in Family Proceedings' (2008) 3(Sept) *International Family Law Journal* 140, 148.

[81] N. 17, above, 208. [82] N. 80, above, 150.

[83] M. Foucault, *Discipline and Punish* (London, 1997); G. Deleuze, *Difference and Repetition* (London, 1994, translated by P. Patton).

[84] G. Mantle, T. Moules, K. Johnson, with J. Leslie, S. Parsons, and R. Shaffer, 'Whose Wishes and Feelings? Children's Autonomy and Parental Influence in Family Court Enquiries' (2006) 37 *British Journal of Social Work* 785, 791–2.

[85] N. 78, above, 283.

This is typically done in research and participation activities, by direct verbal or written quotations from children and young people. But the selection of quotes, their framing and analysis are generally carried out by adults. Adults are determining what counts as a 'voice', representing that 'voice' textually, and interpreting what that 'voice' might be saying. The metaphor of 'voice' may unwittingly reproduce the very understandings of subjectivity that continue to marginalize children: the voice as the property of a rational, articulate, knowledgeable individual, capable of speaking for herself.[86] Focusing on voice privileges the comprehensible verbal utterances of individuals over other forms of communication, which risks excluding children and young people who communicate little or not at all through speech,[87] or who remain silent or laugh in response to questions.[88] All these trends can be seen in the reported case law. Behaviour is treated as evidence of best interests, in reported case law, but not as a communication form.[89] Further, most children are not directly 'voicing' their views in reported case law, because there are at least two layers of interpretation: first the reporting in the professional reports and second by the reported case. Thus, children's 'voices' are not unadulterated 'pure' representations of their views, but rather selected, framed, and presented for particular purposes and audiences.

Rather than agency and autonomy, the social sciences have gained an ever-increasing interest in relations and relationality.[90] A sharp distinction between emotions and rationality is not sustainable:

> Even to the present day, emotions are seen to be the very antithesis of the detached scientific mind and its quest for 'objectivity', 'truth' and 'wisdom'.... Such a view neglects the fact that rational methods of scientific inquiry, even at their most positivistic, involve the incorporation of values and emotions.[91]

Certain views have not been 'allowed in' by courts in family law proceedings because they are relational ('influenced') or emotional. Clare thinks, for example, that her feelings and 'instincts' were not taken seriously, as she could not articulate reasons for them. Views have been incorporated into family law under a rights approach that values autonomous, rational, articulate individuals. But these may be unhelpful standards, creating a mask that—should children deviate from it—will lead to their views being dismissed.

Scotland can be considered a success story, in its legislation and the evolution of its reported case law. But this must be qualified by certain trends that may undermine

[86] P. Alldred, 'Ethnography and Discourse Analysis: Dilemmas in Representing the Voices of Children' in J. Ribbens and R. Edwards (eds), *Feminist Dilemmas in Qualitative Research: Public Knowledge and Private Lives* (London, 1998).

These insights are attributed to Michael Gallagher.

[87] S. Komulainen, 'The Ambiguity of the Child's "Voice" in Social Research' (2007) 14(1) *Childhood* 11.

[88] K. Nairn, J. Munro, and A.B. Smith, 'A Counter Narrative of a Failed Interview' (2005) 5(2) *Qualitative Research* 221.

[89] N. Wilson, 'The ears of the child in family proceedings' (2007) 38(Sept) *Family Law* 808.

[90] A.R. Hochschild, 'Emotion Work, Feeling Rules and Social Structure' (1979) 85(3) *American Journal of Sociology* 551; L. McKie and S. Cunningham Burley (eds), *Families and Society: Boundaries and Relationships* (Bristol, 2005); C. Smart, 'Family Secrets: law and understandings of openness in everyday relationships' (2009) 38 *Journal of Social Policy* 551.

[91] S.J. Williams and G. Bendelow, 'Introduction: emotions in social life' in G. Bendelow and S.J. Williams (eds), *Emotions in social life* (London, 1998) xvi. This quotation, and more generally arguments about connecting emotion to reason, were brought to our attention by Louise Hill.

or sideline some or many children's views: a fixation on 'voice' and a façade of fixed, rational, autonomous views. Clare's case study certainly begs for more empirical research of children's own experiences, as well as other players within the court system, to check whether supposed progress is actually improving the experiences and outcomes for children. Children's participation is a marker of respect, a sign of inclusion, but it also should be part of ensuring the improved well-being of children.

12

Children's Consent and 'Assent' to Healthcare Research

Priscilla Alderson[1]

12.1 Introduction

The idea of children's 'assent' to medical research became part of English law in 2004. However, this overrides English legal traditions of children's consent. Although this chapter concentrates on English law and guidance, it has international relevance. English law integrates with European law and also has influence over more than a billion people in the 54 British Commonwealth countries. Ethics guidance in England on consent to research influences international projects, based in Britain and conducted in Europe and in every other continent. Discussions about children's consent and assent illuminate meeting points between law and childhood studies across the world.

This chapter will examine contrasting meanings of consent and 'assent', and will review the related law and ethics. I will discuss whether children's consent or their assent offers them best support and protection while they are considering whether to take part in research, and while they are research subjects. Examples of some present problems will be given, which indicate the need for broader understanding of children's consent.

12.2 Consent

Consent has a complex and tragic history, with deep roots in law, philosophy, and politics. Across the world, struggles for human rights against oppressive unjust rulers centred on campaigns for the democratic vote, which expresses the will or consent of the people. At the individual level, the law has long recognized that medical treatment and research conducted without the person's consent constitute assault. The first international definition of consent to research was enshrined in the *Nuremberg Code*[2] following the Nuremberg trials of Nazi atrocities in medical research including research on children. The *Code*'s authors were determined that such harms should never be repeated, and they began:

> 1. The voluntary consent of the human subject is absolutely essential. This means that the person involved should have legal capacity to give consent; should be so situated as to be

[1] Professor Emerita of Childhood Studies, Social Science Research Unit, Institute of Education, University of London.

[2] Nuremberg Code (1947) <http://ohsr.od.nih.gov/guidelines/nuremberg.htmlS>.

able to exercise free power of choice, without the intervention of any element of force, fraud, deceit, duress, over-reaching, or other ulterior form of constraint or coercion; and should have sufficient knowledge and comprehension of the elements of the subject matter involved as to enable him to make an understanding and enlightened decision.

This latter element requires that before the acceptance of an affirmative decision by the experimental subject there should be made known to him the nature, duration, and purpose of the experiment; the method and means by which it is to be conducted; all inconveniences and hazards reasonable to be expected; and the effects upon his health or person which may possibly come from his participation in the experiment.

Written by lawyers, the *Nuremberg Code* in its first clause gives clear standards and definitions, with the means of assessing the skill and knowledge of both medical researchers and of research subjects. The standards promote transparency and accountability. The *Code* is limited in covering only adults, and only 'non-therapeutic' research on 'healthy volunteers'; not research on patients. Children were excluded because they were deemed incapable of forming enlightened voluntary decisions. Ramsey[3] and McCormick[4] famously debated whether or not children should be forced to enter medical research programmes, but neither philosopher saw children as capable of altruism or consent.

The *Declaration of Helsinki*,[5] written by medical researchers and agreed by the World Medical Association, filled in gaps left by *Nuremberg. Helsinki* includes children, and patients who take part in clinical research. Whereas *Nuremberg* was concerned about unnecessary and unacceptable 'over-research', *Helsinki* was additionally concerned about 'under-research' in terms of the damage that medical treatment can do if it has been insufficiently tested. *Helsinki* was agreed a year after the Thalidomide tragedy, when inadequately tested medication given to pregnant women caused their babies to be born with tiny limbs. So again, protection of children played a key part in initiating advances in medical ethics. *Helsinki* begins by asserting that medical research aims 'to save suffering humanity'. Although it is very detailed and careful about information and consent, *Helsinki* does not mention consent until clause 16 (clause 9 in the initial 1964 version). Agency is invested in doctors, not in subjects.

16. The responsibility for the protection of research subjects must always rest with the physician or other health care professional and never the research subjects, even though they have given consent.

22. Participation by competent individuals as subjects in medical research must be voluntary. Although it may be appropriate to consult family members or community leaders, no competent individual may be enrolled in a research study unless he or she freely agrees.

24. . . . each potential subject must be adequately informed of the aims, methods, sources of funding, any possible conflicts of interest, institutional affiliations of the researcher, the anticipated benefits and potential risks of the study and the discomfort it may entail, and any other relevant aspects of the study. The potential subject must be informed of the right to refuse to participate in the study or to withdraw consent to participate at any time without reprisal. Special attention should be given to the specific information needs of individual potential subjects as well as to the methods used to deliver the information. After ensuring that the potential subject has understood the information, the physician or another appropriately qualified individual must then seek the potential subject's freely-given informed consent,

[3] Ramsey, P. (1970) *The Patient as Person*. New Haven, Conn: Yale University Press.

[4] McCormick, R. (1981) *How Brave a New World? Dilemmas in Bioethics*. Washington DC: Georgetown University Press.

[5] WMA—World Medical Association (1964/2008). Declaration of Helsinki. Fernay Voltaire <http://www.wma.org>.

preferably in writing. If the consent cannot be expressed in writing, the non-written consent must be formally documented and witnessed.

I have quoted clauses of *Helsinki* in detail because the essential criteria for informed consent are so well summarized. They act as a definition, a set of standards and a means of assessing whether potential participants' consent or refusal is adequately informed and respected. Many healthcare and other researchers today around the world are required by funders to sign a statement that they have read and will abide by the *Helsinki* standards.

In summary, law and medicine have combined in the aim to prevent recurrence of the research malpractice and negligence that shocked the world. Consent is seen as the essential and powerful means of ensuring adequate protection and adequate respect for individuals' voluntary informed decisions. The purpose of consent is to explain and transfer responsibility for risk from researchers to informed willing subjects, who decide for reasons of potential future self-interest or altruism to assist in the research.

English law's respect for minor patients' consent or refusal was illustrated in the three hearings of the *Gillick* case, by nine judges, about minors' legal right to consent to medical treatment. The Law Lords finally decided:

> As a matter of Law the parental right to determine whether or not their minor child below the age of sixteen will have medical treatment terminates if and when the child achieves sufficient understanding and intelligence to understand fully what is proposed [and has] sufficient discretion to enable him or her to make a wise choice in his or her own interests... Nor has our law ever treated the child as other than a person with capacities and rights recognised by law.[6]

Lord Scarman's very serious ruling, like *Nuremberg* and *Helsinki*, sets broadly applicable meanings and criteria for assessing standards. Years earlier, Lord Denning had stated that parents have a:

> dwindling right which the courts will hesitate to enforce against the wishes of the child. It starts with a right of control and ends with little more than advice.[7]

Scarman's ruling is, unfortunately, often overlooked in current UK guidance for children's services and replaced by Lord Fraser's limited ruling in the *Gillick* case:

1) the young person will understand the professional's advice;
2) the young person cannot be persuaded to inform their parents;
3) the young person is likely to begin, or to continue having, sexual intercourse with or without contraceptive treatment;
4) unless the young person receives contraceptive treatment, their physical their mental health, or both, are likely to suffer;
5) the young person's best interests require them to receive contraceptive advice or treatment with or without parental consent.

Fraser reduces the matter, in clauses 3–5, back into contraception, the substance of the *Gillick* case. Clause 1 assumes riskily uncritical faith in professionals' 'advice', information is not mentioned, whereas consent may be a necessary defence against professionals' negligence or abuse. Clause 2 ignores the majority of competent children

[6] *Gillick* [1985] 2 WLR 480.
[7] *Hewer v. Bryant* [1970] 1 QB 357, 369.

who do not either exclude or delegate to their parents, but who share decision-making with them. The replacement of Scarman's ruling by Fraser's invests power in professionals who can claim that young people refused to involve their parents. That could speed up young people's agreement with professionals' 'advice', whereas parents' experiences might lead them to be more cautious. The Fraser guidelines can belittle and erode the protection and autonomy that children's consent involves. In contrast, the Scarman ruling expresses real respect for minors and does not specify an age. In theory, therefore, the law supports doctors in the UK who, in their clinical judgement, deem a six- or eight-year-old competent to consent.[8]

For years, the UK government has advised that 'young people should be kept as fully informed as possible about their condition and treatment to enable them to exercise their rights', with respect for children's 'informed, free, express and specific consent' to healthcare treatment;[9] for their wishes and their right to refuse interventions.[10] Their views should be heard and given 'due weight'.[11]

In English law, those who can give valid consent to medical treatment for a child include the competent child and anyone who has parental responsibility for the child under the Children Act 1989. Following *Re R*,[12] the consent of only one of these people (child or parent) to treatment can overrule the refusal of all the others. Therefore treatment may be enforced on a resisting child if it is considered to be in the child's best interests. Lord Donaldson's rulings in 1991 and 1992, which narrowed the rights even of '*Gillick* competent' minors and even 16- and 17-year-olds to refuse medical treatment, have been much criticized.

There has been greater caution about minors' consent to research. Young children have had more power and protection as potential research participants than as patients. Adults were warned to take extremely seriously the refusal or resistance of even very young children to research, which is not associated with treatment,[13] and 'the investigator should reconsider whether it would be appropriate to proceed'[14] as well as working to enhance and encourage children's share in decision-making.[15]

> Either those included have given consent, or consent has been given on their behalf by a parent or guardian and those included do not object or appear to object in either words or action... When a child lacks sufficient understanding to consent, his willing cooperation should be sought.[16]

Children should be consulted and informed in terms they can understand.[17]

> When parental consent is obtained, the agreement of school age children to take part in research should also be requested by researchers... Research which could equally well be done on adults should never be done on children.[18]

[8] Age of Legal Capacity (Scotland) Act 1991, s 2(4).

[9] Department of Health (1991) *Welfare of children and young people in hospital* (London, HMSO).

[10] Children Act 1989, s 8. [11] UNCRC 1989, article 12. [12] *Re R* [1991] 4 All ER 177.

[13] RCPCH (2000/from BPA 1992) 'Guidelines on the Ethical Conduct of Medical Research Involving Children' *Archives of Disease in Childhood* 82: 177–182; BMA—British Medical Association (2001) *Consent, Rights and Choices in Healthcare for Children and Young People.* London: BMA, 234.

[14] RCP—Royal College of Physicians (1990a) *Research Involving Patients.* London: RCP.

[15] BMA—British Medical Association (2001) *Consent, Rights and Choices in Healthcare for Children and Young People.* London: BMA, 232.

[16] MRC—Medical Research Council (1991) *The Ethical Conduct of Research on Children* London, MRC; MRC (2004) *Medical Research Involving Children.* London: MRC.

[17] Freeman, M. (2006) 'Rethinking Gillick' in Freeman, M. (ed), *Children's Health and Children's Rights.* Leiden: Martinus Nijhoff Publishers.

[18] RCPCH, 2000/1992 op cit, n. 13.

The double standard of respect for children's consent to treatment, but for their refusal of research, raises difficulties when the research is about testing treatment, so-called 'therapeutic research'. Research cannot be therapeutic because it is about collecting, analysing, and reporting data. The findings might eventually benefit people in future, in the fairly rare event that they are reported and implemented to provide beneficial therapy. So it is important to unravel the different elements of consent to research, and to treatment, in clinical research.

In international law, the United Nations Convention on the Rights of the Child (UNCRC) relates to consent, and the assurance:

> To the child who is capable of forming his or her own views the right to express those views freely in all matters affecting the child: the views of the child being given due weight in accordance with the age and maturity of the child... The child shall in particular be provided the opportunity to be heard in any judicial or administrative proceedings affecting the child, either directly, or through a representative or appropriate body.[19]

Article 13 entails 'freedom of expression', so that children may express, discuss, and negotiate their concerns, reservations, and misunderstandings, and also have the 'freedom to seek, receive and impart information and ideas of all kinds... through any other media of the child's choice'. Leaflets, photographs, drawing, diagrams, dolls, and puppets can increase children's and parents' understanding of medical problems and treatments, such as 'battles' between blood cells and leukaemia treatment, or they can see contrasting images before and after orthopaedic surgery.

Yet the UNCRC does not go as far as English law in *Gillick*, and covers only levels 1–3 in the four levels of consent.[20] These levels are: 1) to be informed; 2) to express an informed view; 3) to have that view taken into account when decisions are made; 4) to be the main decision-maker about proposed interventions. It is often argued that children cannot and should not make major decisions, for reasons linked to these four levels: 1) They cannot understand the relevant information; 2) they cannot evaluate information in the light of lasting personal values; 3) they cannot know their own best interests, so that adults must act for them; 4) if things go wrong, children do not yet have the courage and resolve to stand by a decision, and will need to blame other people instead of enduring risk, guilt, and blame themselves. Doctors used all these arguments in the past to protect adult patients from complex and distressing information and decision-making about their treatment.

The versions of *Helsinki* in 1983 (clause 27) and 1996 (clause 28) referred to children:

> When a minor child is in fact able to consent, the minor's consent must be obtained in addition to the consent of the legally authorized representative.

However, 'assent' had crept into *Helsinki* by 2008:

> When a potential research subject who is deemed incompetent is able to give assent to decisions about participation in research, the physician must seek that assent in addition to the consent of the legally authorized representative. The potential subject's dissent should be respected.

[19] UN (1989) *Convention on the Rights of the Child* <http://www.ohchr.org>.

[20] Alderson, P. and Montgomery, J. (1996) *Health Care Choices: Making Decisions with Children*. London: Institute for Public Policy Research, 66.

12.3 Assent

Assent has not the power, clarity, or history of consent. It is vague in its definition, and therefore in its standard-setting and criteria for assessing ethical research practice. 'Assent' appeared in the US National Commission's report, stating that the consent of parents/guardians to research must be sought 'at all ages of the child; furthermore the child's assent should be sought from the age of 7 upwards'.[21] 'Assent' here is primarily non-refusal or simple agreement without the understanding, discretion, and legal validity associated with consent, and it continues to be promoted today.[22]

Consent involves a pause before the person makes and signifies the decision, usually by signing a consent form. When I researched parents' consent to children's heart surgery, some parents emphasized how vital that moment was to them, as the one time, they felt, when doctors had to defer to them, wait, listen, and reply to parents' questions and comments, before parents signed the consent form and the medical process once more hurried forward.[23] The consent form should record specific *Helsinki* conditions (see above) stating who informed the subject and replied to questions, and the freedom to withdraw at any time without prejudice and without having to give a reason. The informed decision to give or withhold consent is a choice not a duty.

Assent, however, need not involve that formal moment of choice and statement. Not only is 'non-refusal' a double negative instead of a positive concept, its nature is unclear. People may be too unaware, or uninformed, too afraid or shy to be able to refuse. So 'non-refusal' cannot be assumed to mean agreement. Assent does not involve information necessary for informed consent, but unless the child has enough basic information assent and consent would be meaningless. So to take seriously the 'assent' of an uninformed child could be a pretext or licence for researchers to proceed as if they have moral authority. The next section considers why this vague nonentity of assent has replaced consent in research on children.

12.4 Promotion of assent

One influence on European research is from North American doctors and lawyers who aim for one international standard for clinical research methods and ethics. The US not only adopts the lower standard of assent, its government is the only one in the world not to have ratified the UNCRC. Intense criticisms of children's rights emanate from the US.[24]

US state and federal laws respect decision-making from the age of majority of 18 or 19 years, with a few exceptions for 'mature minors'.[25] US experts frequently

[21] US National Commission for the Protection of Human Subjects of Biomedical and Behavioral Research (1977) *Research Involving Children*. DHEW, 77-0004 Washington DC: DHEW.

[22] NIH—National Institutes of Health (2007). <http://www.cancer.gov/clinicaltrials/understanding/childrensassent0101> (accessed 7 January 2011).

[23] Alderson, P. (1990) *Choosing for Children: Parents' Consent to Surgery*. Oxford: Oxford University Press.

[24] For example, Ross, L. (1998) *Families and Health Care Decision-making*. New York: Oxford University Press; Guggenheim, M. (2005) *What's Wrong with Children's Rights*. Cambridge MA: Harvard University Press.

[25] Gaylin, W. and Macklin, R. (1982) *Who Speaks for the Child*? New York: Plenum Press.

claim that 'Children cannot consent'[26] and 'Children cannot refuse'. Children can, of course, refuse by saying 'no'. The real questions are: Will adults hear and respect children's views? And can their consent or refusal be valid in law? In US law, children generally cannot consent. In UK law they can if they are deemed competent. The US preference for children's assent streamlines and strengthens the process, when it relies solely on parents' seldom-contested consent and avoids legal and cognitive ambiguities about competent children.

Another agency that promotes assent with the same motive of streamlining paediatric research is the pharmaceutical industry. There is concern about 'therapeutic orphans', diseases which have no known effective treatment. There is also worry about prescribing 'off-licence' medication for children, an estimated 85 per cent of all treatments, which have not been specifically tested for younger age groups during their years of rapid physiological change from birth onwards.[27] Evidence-based medicines have been tested in randomized controlled trials, usually conducted on men aged 16–60 years. Women tend to be excluded in case they might be pregnant. Children are seen as too vulnerable to be involved routinely: medically, children are especially vulnerable to adverse effects of trial drugs; ethically, they may be too easily pressured into entering and remaining in trials, and their protests and their own reports about adverse reactions may be ignored when adults' responses would be respected.

Besides developing new drugs, companies research for wider applications of their established drugs, including research into questionable new 'diseases' such as emotional and behavioural problems and obesity. There are also the 'me-too' drugs: research that validates small alterations to patented medications, and therefore supports a new name, new marketing, and a new, prolonged, profitable patent term. These can add to the burdens of research for children and young people without significantly adding to the benefits.[28] Big pharma faces financial difficulties. In July 2010, CMR International reported that just seven per cent of pharmaceutical sales came from medicines launched in the previous five years, and more new drugs are failing late-stage testing, incurring huge losses in companies' R&D investments. The industry has shared in promoting endorsement among practitioners and the public of the moral duty to develop medications to treat children and to test these more rigorously for each age group. So research has come to be seen as a positive imperative rather than a negative risk, and the *Nuremberg* traditions of consent may seem irrelevant.

Economic pressures can deter adults in several ways from 'wasting time' on ambiguous discussions with children. As researchers have to meet tighter deadlines and budgets, and as fears rise about the costly risks of complaint and litigation, consent itself is becoming more commercialized into a legal and business contract, when subjects agree to accept risks, and not to sue if these are realized. Attention shifts from the informed willing participant to the person who signs the contract, and who needs to have indubitable (adult) legal competence.

Underlying economic and legal considerations are two models of childhood. One is the traditional medico-psychological model of age-stage development, the mind growing as slowly as the body in a universal biologically unfolding pattern. The other

[26] NIH (2007) op. cit, n. 22.

[27] ABPI—Association of the British Pharmaceutical Industry (2004) *Current Issues in Paediatric Clinical Trials*. London: ABPI.

[28] Kolch, M., Ludolph, A., Plener, P., Fangerau, H., Vitiello, B., and Fegert, J. (2010) 'Safeguarding Children's Rights in Psychopharmacological Research: Ethical and Legal Issues' *Current Pharmacological Des.* June.

view is that young children's natural and inevitable immaturity is constructed, as discussed through this volume, and sometimes exaggerated, ascribed, and imposed by adults, partly to protect children but also to serve adult power and convenience. Children's competencies vary greatly in time and place and they relate more to opportunities, experiences, and expectations than to age, as seen, for example, in the courage and wisdom shown by the young patients in research interviews.[29]

In response to international pressures from research agencies, the UK Medicines for Human Use (Clinical Trials) Regulations 2004 (SI 2004/1031) transposed into law the European Clinical Trials Directive 2001/EC/20, to promote clinical trials with children. The Directive's Preamble states: 'Children represent a vulnerable population with developmental, physiological, and psychological differences from adults, which make age- and development-related research important for their benefit.' The European Regulation (EC) 1901/2006 on Medicinal Products for Paediatric Use amended previous Regulations and Directives, and came into binding force in all EC countries in January 2007.

The 2006 Regulation applies only to clinical medical trials, not to all other research. However, as the lawyer Hazel Biggs[30] points out, the National Research Ethics Service (NRES) requires these standards to be applied not only to trials, but to all research vetted by the healthcare research ethics committees, which the NRES oversees.[31] Biggs considers that this raises 'worrying discrepancies between the law and ethics', and that problems in the Regulation include:

1) ignoring both minors' consent and assent;
2) respecting parents' proxy consent which shall represent the minor's presumed will;
3) assuring 'the explicit wish of a minor who is capable of forming an opinion and assessing information to refuse participation in, or to be withdrawn from, the clinical trial at any time is considered by the investigator';
4) contradicting English common law and ethics standards;
5) having potential to confuse researchers and research ethics committees;
6) creating inconsistencies likely to have detrimental impact on autonomy of children in research;
7) posing worrying discrepancies between law and ethics;
8) being disrespectful and unrealistic.

Point 2 assumes, simplistically, that all parents know their child's views and feel willing and able to promote these unconditionally. So the researchers' and practitioners' own duty to discover and respond to children's views is unfairly, and not necessarily reliably, transferred on to parents. Point 3 is heavily age adapted, ignores younger children, and the verb 'considered' can be meaningless; researchers can still override children's protests with impunity. All eight points, as Biggs discusses, erode children's

[29] Alderson, P. *Children's Consent to Surgery. Buckingham*: Open University Press. 1993; (2008) *Young Children's Rights,* revised 2nd edition. London: Jessica Kingsley/Save the Children.

[30] Biggs, H. (2009) 'Competent Minors and Healthcare Research: Autonomy Does Not Rule, Okay?' 4(4) *Clinical Ethics*: 176–80, 177.

[31] NRES, National Research Ethics Service (2009) *Standard Operating Procedures for Research Ethics Committees: Version 4.0.* London: Department of Health: <http//www.nres.npsa.nhs.uk/news-and-publications/publications/>.

traditional English rights and consent in troubling ways that need to be challenged and changed.

Economic pressures are supported by a literature that assumes that children's rights inevitably oppose and erode parents' rights and therefore erode children's security and best interests. Efforts to 'protect' children from having to decide about healthcare research and treatment may then be intended to protect adult power rather than children's interests. The lawyer and professed 'child advocate', Martin Guggenheim,[32] insists that parents are the best deciders of children's interests. He regards children's rights simply as a screen for other adults (state officials) to interfere in family life.

The paediatrician Lainie Ross[33] argues that parents and not children should make healthcare decisions, because parents know how to balance everyone's interests in the 'intimate family'. While this is often a reasonable view, it is strange to favour setting the interests of the whole family before those of a child in need of healthcare, who may be very ill. Families usually willingly put the sick member first during such a crisis. An 'intimate family' also suggests intimate, trusting, respectful sharing of views and decisions between all the members, when parents know that children can have wise insights into their best interests. They expect that the rights (the basic needs and reasonable freedoms) of family members will converge rather than conflict. However, Ross's 'intimate family' sets potentially conflictual parental control first. This suggests that 'intimacy' is less an inner quality of the family, and more an outer protection from external interference into parents' rights.

Guggenheim, who has been thoroughly criticized,[34] and Ross appear to speak from the liberal tradition that separates public affairs and legitimate concerns of the state, from private intimate family and personal life. Yet feminist and child protection advocates point to the risks of lethal violence within such 'intimate families' and the crucial need for appropriate state intervention. Each week in Britain one or two women and one or two children still die from abuse at home.

Part of the dismissal of children's rights connects with mistrust of children. The transformation of women's status over the past century involved recognition that they are not 'like children', vulnerable emotional dependents on men, but that women can be as rational and capable as men. If children are to be accorded due respect, myths about their deficits have to be exchanged for due recognition of their intellectual, emotional, social, and moral capacities.

12.5 Are higher standards of respect for consent to research with children needed?

Over the past century, the benefits of clinical research have saved and enhanced the lives of countless children. However, research poses risks. The US paediatrician Lainie Ross explains the dangers of forcing into Europe the US commercial, bureaucratic standards. For example, many children with asthma use inhalers for daily prophylaxis (to prevent rather than treat asthma attacks). If they stop using inhalers,

[32] Guggenheim, M. (2005) *What's Wrong with Children's Rights*. Cambridge MA: Harvard University Press.

[33] Ross, op. cit. n. 24.

[34] Federle, K. (2009) 'Rights Not Wrongs' 17(2) *International Journal of Children's Rights* 321–9; Freeman, M. (2006) 'Review Essay: What's Right with Rights for Children' 14 *International Journal of Law in Context* 89–98.

they are likely to react for days or weeks by having more attacks. If the children take part in US randomized controlled trials, they may be 'patients' in a treatment arm, or they may be in the non-treatment arm, which has inhalers containing placebo (dummy treatment). In blind trials, for all that the families know, the children may be reacting to the new medication or to suddenly having none at all. Logic, ethics, and concern for children's safety, would suggest that the best trials compare a new treatment against the best known treatment, unless there is not yet an accepted treatment—but there are many established treatments for asthma.

It also seems obviously unscientific to compare the effectiveness of a new drug against non-treatment, and in a group of children who may be having severe withdrawal reactions after their usual asthma medication is suddenly withheld. Surely that would give an unfair and misleading advantage to the new drug. However, the Food and Drug Administration (FDA), the US agency responsible for medical research, prefers placebo trials[35] and is unduly influenced by commercial sectors.

As already mentioned, British guidance insists that children should be involved in medical research only if the research cannot equally well be done on adults, and if the findings are intended to benefit children. US guidance does not have this standard, so that children are recruited simply to increase numbers of subjects in trials with adult subjects, but with no guarantee that they will be studied as a separate group in order to benefit future child patients.[36] If US researchers had to observe *Helsinki* standards of respect for adequately informed consent of parents and children, these problems could be less common.

Pharmaceutical research can greatly benefit the vast majority of child patients who live in poorer countries. David Molyneux of the Liverpool Centre for Neglected Diseases reports that pharmaceutical companies have developed drugs, and donated billions of pounds worth of their products, for the treatment of diseases that blind, maim, and kill children. Most unfortunately, donors who are chiefly concerned with AIDS, tuberculosis, and malaria largely neglect these chronic conditions. However, despite the companies' benevolence, and increasing bioethics safeguards, harmful and fraudulent medical research and practices continue to be reported.[37] There is some evidence that certain researchers favour 'developing' countries with weaker ethical safeguards, to test dangerous experimental drugs on African children.[38] Researchers sometimes argue that consent is too individualistic and 'Western' a concept to be relevant to research with children in Africa. However, detailed, highly informed, and mutually respectful agreements are vital to protect children and their parents in risky research. African families may be concerned with communitarian and reciprocal trust and less with 'Western' concepts of autonomy and informed choices. Yet when things go wrong, without the support of welfare states and due compensation, impoverished African families can be even more severely affected, such as when they have to provide lifelong care for children damaged by research.

[35] Ross, L. (2006) *Children in Medical Research: Access Versus Protection*. New York: Oxford University Press.

[36] Ross (2006) op. cit., n. 24.

[37] Baughman, F. (2007) *The ADHD Fraud: How Psychiatrists make Patients of Normal Children*. Victoria B.C.: Trafford; Coppock, V. (2005) 'Meeting the Challenge? Voicing Children and Young People in Mental Health Research' in J. Goddard, et al. (eds), *The Politics of Childhood*. Basingstoke: Palgrave Macmillan; Sharav, V. (2003) 'Children in Clinical Research: a Conflict of Moral Values' 3(1) *American Journal of Bioethics* 1–99; Slesser, A. and Qureshi, Y. (2009) 'The Implications of Fraud in Medical and Scientific Research' 33(11) *World Journal of Surgery* 2355–9.

[38] Save the Children (2007) *Why Social Corporate Responsibility is Failing Children*. London: SCF.

For example, Pfizer held a two-week antibiotic trial in Kano, a slum city in Nigeria during 1996.[39] There was a meningitis epidemic, during which 11,000 people died. In the trial of 200 children, 100 were on the routine drug Rocephin, and 100 on the experimental drug Trovan. Eleven children died. Pfizer says only five of them were on Trovan. Many other children were disabled. Malam Musa Zango says his son Sumalia, then 12, is now deaf and mute.

Pfizer said that consent was given by the Nigerian state and the families, and produced a letter of permission from a Kano ethics committee. This was later found to be backdated, because the committee was not set up until 1997. Pfizer faced a US$8 billion fine, and the imprisonment of several staff. In April 2009, Pfizer was reported to have settled $75 million out of court. The case is immensely complicated in that the effects of the research drug and of the disease may be confused. However, the drug Trovan is no longer produced, and has been banned in Europe and withdrawn from sale in the US. Yet in 2010, Pfizer was accused of trying to unearth corruption in the Nigerian government in order to blackmail the attorney general into dropping the charges.[40] So 15 years later, compensation has still not been paid. The case shows how essential respect for informed and unpressured consent still is today.

12.6 Law and childhood studies

The law and childhood studies complement one another in grounding many areas of research, policy, and practice that affect children into the real 'adult' world of respect and justice, instead of banishing young people to some unreal 'world of childhood'. They can enrich understanding and implementation of formal legal standards, such as of consent and the UNCRC, through detailed research about children's real daily lives.[41] Central to psychological and social research is the legal concept of competence, and how adults and children perceive and perform competence. To assume children's incompetence sets them at a double disadvantage: it is hard for them to challenge powerful and dismissive adults, and it is also harder to demonstrate competence than incompetence, which can fairly easily seem to be proved by one or two mistakes or misunderstandings. The sociology of childhood demonstrates how childhood is partly a social construction in which adults and children constantly construct dyads of dependent child-providing adult, and victim child-rescuing adult. Traditions that children are incompetent and adults must decide for them reflect and reinforce these dyads. Yet they are not inevitable. Other dyads include respectful adult and capable child, in rising virtuous circles. These can be observed and researched once adults step outside restrictive developmental age-based concepts of childhood, which dominated the twentieth century in all aspects of the understanding and care and control of children, and are still powerfully influential.

[39] Independent (2009) <http://www.independent.co.uk/news/world/africa/pfizer-to-pay-16350m-after-deaths-of-nigerian-children-in-drug-trial-experiment-1663402.html> (accessed 24 February 2010).

[40] Boseley, S. (2010) 'Nigeria: drug trial tale of "'dirty tricks"' *Guardian Weekly*, 17/12/2010: 6–7, <http://www.independent.co.uk/news/world/africa/pfizer-to-pay-16350m-after-deaths-of-nigerian-children-in-drug-trial-experiment-1663402.html> (accessed 24 February 2010).

[41] Freeman, M. (2007) 'Why it Remains Important to Take Children's Rights Seriously' 15(1) *International Journal of Children's Rights* 5–23.

Psychological and social research finds early degrees and forms of competence. Children are meaning-makers from their early months,[42] and from their second year they begin to cooperate with medical treatment when it is carefully explained with support and reassurance. Young children can be 'maturely' responsible even when adults are not present. For example, four-year-old children share in managing their diabetes treatment, and can refuse sweets that their friends enjoy. They cope in sophisticated ways with being different yet sustaining friendships.[43]

As meaning-makers, unless they understand the reasons for painful or frustrating treatment and research interventions, children can be overwhelmed with fear or anger. When they are too young to understand consent, they still need to be informed as much as possible about the nature, purpose, and likely effects of interventions, to reduce fearful misunderstandings. These standards are emphasized in the ethics literature and guidance on children and consent, but tend to be missing in that on assent. Too often, consent is treated as all or nothing: children are either competent and fully involved, or else incompetent and excluded, whereas much decision-making is shared and it involves the four levels reviewed earlier. When the UNCRC Articles 12 and 13 endorse the first three levels of children's involvement, without any age barrier, they can recognize how children and adults can learn from children's own embodied feelings and experiences. It is only possible to care for babies through listening and learning from their expressed views about their constantly changing needs. Immensely detailed observations of premature babies find how subtly they express their views in a 'language' that can be 'read'.[44] Their need for quiet, for dim lighting and reassuring touching and talking, is used to transform some neonatal units towards 'baby-led' policies.[45]

The four levels of decision-making (1–3 in UNCRC, 4 in *Gillick*) provide questions for further detailed research about children's consent. One of my research studies involved interviewing 120 children having major surgery, their parents, and 70 hospital staff. They were asked about the age when the children were or would be able to understand the relevant information, and make an informed willing decision as well as their parents were able to. The replies[46] ranged from one surgeon saying 'never' to some adults and children stating ages from six years upwards. Much depended on the child, the family, and the condition and the beliefs of each interviewee. Most of the children wanted to share the decision-making with their doctors and parents; a few (not age-related) either wanted others to decide for them or else to be 'the main decider' about proposed surgery. Nurses said that after years of working with children they respected them at younger ages. The children's understanding appeared to depend far more on their experience than their age or ability.

In some respects, lawyers set a practical lead. For example, the Head of the Crown Prosecution Service London Homicide Team, lawyer Judith Reed, called a

[42] Siegal, M. (2008) *Marvelous Minds: The Discovery of What Children Know*. New York: Oxford University Press.

[43] Sutcliffe K., Sutcliffe R., and Alderson P. (2004) 'Can Very Young Children Share in their Diabetes Care? Ruby's Story' 16(10) *Paediatric Nursing* 24–6; Alderson P., Sutcliffe, K., and Curtis, K. (2006) 'Children's Consent to Medical Treatment' 36(6) *Hastings Center Report* 25–34.

[44] Als, H. (1999) 'Reading the Premature Infant' in Goldson E (ed.) *Developmental Interventions in the Neonatal Intensive Care Nursery*. New York: Oxford University Press, 18–85.

[45] Alderson P., Killen M., and Hawthorne J. (2005) 'The Participation Rights of Premature Babies' 13 *International Journal of Children's Rights* 31–50.

[46] Alderson, P. (1993) *Children's Consent to Surgery*. Buckingham: Open University Press, 143–74.

four-year-old victim of rape to give evidence at the central criminal court, the Old Bailey. Reed commented:

> Having viewed the video of her interview, I have to say she was really quite remarkable. I'd never seen a child so young give as clear and consistent an account… She was one of the best child witnesses of any age I've seen give evidence on video.[47]

During the trial, the child was cross-examined for 45 minutes by video-link. The rapist, who was convicted, had already been found guilty of the notorious murder of 'Baby P'. The example is relevant to healthcare decisions in showing young children's ability to understand, recall, and recount serious problems that affect their body. It refutes over-quoted papers such as 'There's a demon in your belly', demon being a mistake for oedema or swelling. The paper by Perrin and Gerrity[48] is often cited to 'prove' that even older children have fantasies, instead of questioning the efficiency of adults' information giving and their prejudices. Evidence from legal cases and childhood research can mutually enrich their knowledge and understanding of children's competencies.

12.7 Assessing competence

Outdated developmental age-stage views were quite prevalent in the hospitals in which I researched consent to surgery. Children were referred to one psychiatrist for competence assessment by surgeons in good faith. They did not realize that he was convinced that everyone aged under 18 was incompetent to decide about surgery. Such views are still promoted in ethics and medical journals that concentrate on vague assent and dismiss minors' consent because it is not legally validated in the US.

When assessing children's competence, it is therefore also important to take account of the assessors' values and knowledge, and to ask whether researchers and practitioners, who request assent or consent, are sufficiently able: to understand all the relevant information; to explain it clearly and resolve children's and parents' misunderstandings; to assist children and parents in their reasoned choice-making; and to respect children's and parents' decisions, putting no undue pressures on them? Much depends on the training and skills of practitioners and researchers, on their understanding of how childhood competencies are partly socially constructed dyads,[49] and also on the support or opposition they receive from colleagues when they risk advocating children's views and preferences against adults' assumptions.

Assessors of competence work with three models.[50] Status: is the person, for example, clearly a competent adult or else a non-competent baby? Outcome: does the assessor consider the person's decision is reasonable? Function: even if the assessor disagrees with the child's decision, does the child's reasoning, which explains and justifies the decision, seem to be valid? The first two views tend to favour the assessors' prior fixed assumptions, whereas the third approach is most likely to involve respectful,

[47] Reed, J. (2009) 'Why I let four-year-old rape victim give evidence in court', <http://www.cps.gov.uk/london/case_studies/why_i_let_rape_victim_age_> (accessed 15 July 2009).

[48] Perrin, E. and Gerrity, S. (1981) '"There's a Demon in your Belly": Children's Understanding of Illness' 76(6) *Pediatrics* 841–9.

[49] James, A. and Prout. A. (eds) (1997) *Constructing and Reconstructing Childhood.* London: RoutledgeFalmer.

[50] US (1977) op. cit, n. 21; Brazier, M. (1992) *Protecting the Vulnerable: Autonomy and Consent in Healthcare.* London: Routledge.

flexible consideration of the individual's competence and decisions through negotiation. Then the practitioner's/researcher's information can complement the patient's personal knowledge and values so that together they can make more informed decisions with mutual respect. In my study, some surgeons, for instance, described how they would operate on a slight spinal curve if a child were very distressed, but they would leave a more severe curve if it was safe to do so and the child did not appear to be concerned.

Clinical research involves many young people with long-term health problems. Although the following example involves consent to surgery and not to research, it is quoted to convey a little of the stoic, informed, practical reasoning of many children I interviewed. 'Niki' aged 11 had anterior horn cell damage, which wasted and twisted her body. She fought to be 'normal' and to attend mainstream school. Niki's mother explained the serious risks of spinal surgery for Niki's survival. I asked if she had told Niki before the operation.

Mother: Oh yes, oh yes, she was there, I wouldn't now, I don't think she could go through it if she didn't know.

PA: Is there anything you wouldn't talk about with Niki?

Mother: No. It's her body and her life. Kids can cope... I reckon kids understand what you tell them from whenever, there isn't an age. []

Niki: ... if your spine's twisted and your ribs go in, it would squash my lungs and all my inside, and then kill me after a while... My sister, she's 8 years old, she says that the hospital is practically saving my life.

Niki went on to say how she was supporting her anxious mother.[51]

Healthcare and research teams may have to test and stretch their own abilities to inform, and involve, and thereby increase the competence of their young patients. Along with respect for children's views and values, there needs to be realism about the limits of adults' clinical knowledge, skill, and 'factual' understanding, and of the daunting risks and uncertainties in some healthcare treatment and research.

12.8 Conclusions

This chapter has argued that healthcare research achieves great benefits but also poses serious and occasionally lethal risks. Legal rulings and guidance since *Nuremberg* give valuable, detailed definitions and standards of consent to research, which are as vital today as they were over 60 years ago. There is now greater understanding of children's rights, their views, and their competencies to become involved in different levels of decision-making. Childhood studies have assisted in showing how child-adult relations can reconstruct the same child as ignorant and incompetent or as informed, wise, and capable. So much depends on how children are informed and respected and encouraged. Competence is not a fixed fact to be measured but often a potential to be nurtured. It is formed from social experiences and relationships, and these do not correlate with fixed biological age-stages. Many healthcare practitioners, researchers, and parents skilfully inform and involve children, and useful guidelines

[51] Alderson (1993) op. cit., n. 46, 125.

promote these approaches, based on the law, and also the ethics of striving towards high standards.[52]

Progress in the UK has recently been undermined by new European-based law that requires parents' consent and mentions only children's 'assent'. This retrograde move has been influenced by commercial research companies and US doctors' promotion of uniform international standards for research on children. There is a risk that not only will children's views and decisions be ignored, but the crucial need to inform them adequately will also be neglected. This opens the way to the coercion of fearful, unwilling research subjects, who are treated as property and means used towards researchers' ends. Research ethics is founded on Kantian respect for persons as ends in themselves, who willing and altruistically agree to take part in research, hoping that the future knowledge might benefit them and/or their peers who have similar illnesses. There are now many research examples of children's altruism, once thought not to exist, in their work as carers and advocates, peace makers, and planners of better services.[53] Varma et al.[54] found that altruism was a motive for children to agree to take part in research. On the day this section was written, North Eastern Australia was suffering from unprecedented floods, and newspapers published photographs of Jordan Rice aged 13.[55] He died in the floods after telling rescuers, 'Save my brother first'. Altruism is not correlated with age.

Consent involves concepts of competence, respect, dignity, informed choice, and understanding. Freeman[56] adds making decisions that 'cohere with their system of values'. These concepts can be harder to define and assess in their positive forms than in their negative absence: in obvious incompetence, disrespect, violation, exploitation and abuse, misinformation, deceit, coercion, or misunderstanding. Professionals who aim to respect children therefore tend at first to have to risk taking children's competence partly on trust. Similarly, children initially have to trust that the adults will respect and not exploit or abuse them, until they can be reassured later by experiencing high standards of healthcare or research. Children with long-term conditions are frequently involved in treatment and research and are also likely to have experienced limits and failures of healthcare, so that their consent can be highly informed.

Respect for consent involves protecting the child's integrity of body, mind, personal identity, and reputation from unwanted invasion or intrusion when data are collected and later disseminated. Professionals who move beyond assumptions that their work is wholly benign and 'therapeutic' are able to appreciate children's own estimations of risks, costs, 'side-effects', or inconveniences.

Properly conducted, the consent process also protects professionals from subsequent criticisms, complaints, and litigation. However, all concerned increasingly need to realize and question the limitations of traditional consent in relation to work conducted by large teams, for future unknown purposes. Increasingly, data bases are sold on to other research teams for secondary analysis.

Consent is a paradox, combining Kantian notions of the autonomous wise agent who alone can make the correct personal decision, with the courage to make and stand by a best guess about uncertain futures. The protective courage shown by Niki

[52] RCPCH (2000) op. cit., n. 13; BMA (2001) op. cit., n. 13

[53] For example, Percy-Smith, B. and Thomas, N. (2010) *A Handbook of Children and Young People's Participation*. Abingdon: Routledge.

[54] Varma, S., Jenkins, T., and Wendler, D. (2008) 'How do Children and Parents Make Decisions about Pediatric Clinical Research?' 30(11) *Journal of Pediatric Hematology and Oncology* 823–8.

[55] *Guardian* London, 13 January 2011.

[56] Freeman (2006) op. cit., n. 17, 213.

towards her mother was repeatedly shown by children in the surgery study. Adults make mistakes and children may be able to make wise choices besides having unique and essential embodied knowledge, which adults need to understand if the decisions they make for and with children are to be informed.

A crucial part of consent is voluntariness. It is possible that the more professionals feel able to make informed, willing commitments to their work, the more they are able, willing, and confident enough to share information and risks, options and commitments with children, instead of trying to impose these on children. When research teams are democratic rather than hierarchical, the most junior researchers, usually those in closest touch with child subjects, can convey their views and influence the whole team more easily. It would be good to see researchers uniting to insist that higher standards of consent replace the muddle of assent in all law and guidance on research with children and young people.

Basic principles for consent to healthcare and research with children need to be more clearly agreed, and analysed into their many component practical questions for professionals to address. Ways of informing and consulting with children, respecting their autonomy and their vulnerability need to be refined further at every stage of research.[57] This will help to fulfil the long-standing guidance that 'research involving children is important for the benefit of all children and should be supported and encouraged, and conducted in an ethical manner'.[58] This involves acknowledging the interdependence and inalienable rights of 'every member of the human family' which are the foundations for solidarity, interdependence, equity, 'peace and justice in the world'.[59]

[57] Alderson, P. and Morrow, V. (2011) *Ethical Research with Children and Young People: A Practical Handbook*. Revised 3rd edition. London: Sage.

[58] RCPCH (2000) op. cit., n. 13, 117.

[59] UNCRC (1989), Preamble.

13

Children and Young People as Moral and Legal Actors: Findings from Studies Conducted in Northern Italy

Roberta Bosisio[1]

13.1 Children as moral actors

Children and childhood were studied for a long time in relation to other subjects and other conceptual fields, such as theories of education, sociology of family, and socialization.[2] This approach arose from the traditional concept of socialization, according to which children are social becomings and not social beings. For this reason children were not autonomous actors and they were not considered in the present tense as children, but as what they would become: adults.

Today, on the contrary, sociologists consider children to be individuals who participate in social life, starting with their specific perspective on the world, and according to models of action that may differ from those of adults.[3] They are no longer seen as passive recipients of the teachings of adults, but rather as actors who play an active role in their own development. Therefore, children, together with adults, participate in the construction of the social world that surrounds them, of childhood itself, and of the interpretative reproduction of their shared culture.[4]

[1] Roberta Bosisio is PhD in Sociology of Law; working as research fellow in Sociology of Law at the University of Milan (Italy) where she cooperates with the Department of Social and Political Studies. Her main fields of study and research are sociology of childhood and children's rights. She is interested in studying young people's lives from their point of views and voices.

Among her publications: 'Children's Right to Be Heard: What Children Think' (2011) 19 *International Journal of Children's Rights*, *Bambini e agire morale. Rappresentazioni delle norme e dei diritti nell'infanzia e nell'adolescenza* (Milano, 2010); '"Right" and "not right". Representations of Justice in Young People', (2008) 2 *Childhood*; *Non è giusto! Dilemmi morali e senso della giustizia nelle rappresentazioni degli adolescenti* (with Roberto Cammarata, Persio Tincani—edited by Paola Ronfani, Roma, 2007); 'La percezione dei diritti nell'infanzia e nell'adolescenza. Una ricerca empirica' (*Sociologia del diritto*, 1/2005); *Quello che ci spetta. I diritti fondamentali nelle rappresentazioni degli adolescenti* (with Luisa Leonini, Paola Ronfani, Roma, 2003).

[2] William Corsaro, *The Sociology of Childhood* (Thousand Oaks, 1997); Heinz Hengst, Helga Zehier (eds.), *Per una sociologia dell'infanzia* (Milano, 2004); Chris Jenks, 'Introduction: constituting the child', in Id. (ed.), *The Sociology of Childhood: Essential Readings* (London, 1982), 9.

[3] Allison James, Chris Jenks, Alan Prout, *Theorizing Childhood* (London, 1998).

[4] William Corsaro, *The Sociology of Childhood* (Thousand Oaks, 1997); Alan Prout, Allison James, 'Introduction', in Id. (eds.), *Constructing and Reconstructing Childhood* (London, 1990), 1; Jens Qvortrup, *Childhood as a Social Phenomenon. An Introduction to a Series of National Reports, Eurosocial Report* (Vienna, 1991), 36.

According to the new sociology of childhood, children also possess moral reasoning skills. As a matter of fact, it is noticeable that children, starting from their early years, are continuously faced with issues of justice and fairness in their everyday interactions, as well as with decision-making situations that carry moral implications.[5] For this reason, according to scholars, from a very early age they develop a good practical knowledge of moral concepts. However, adults usually do not recognize children as moral actors.[6]

The results of many studies show children's competence in terms of moral reasoning and action, and also their awareness of the discrepancy between their moral competence and the low moral status attributed to them by adults.[7] These findings confirm that teenagers internalize a developmental model of moral growth and that the low social position attributed by adults to them also influences children's self-image.[8]

13.2 Survey findings

We will present some examples drawn from the findings of three studies[9] on normative and legal socialization, which show that young people possess high moral and legal reasoning skills.

The first one was carried out in 2001–2002 among students attending the last year of lower secondary school in four schools in Milan and in two schools in two small towns in the north-west of Italy. One hundred and twenty interviews were conducted with the aim of ascertaining children's knowledge of the 1989 United Nations Convention on the Rights of the Child, collecting their opinions and perceptions on the rights granted, and gathering their normative social representations of the very concept of right. Many questions contained in the interview concerned rights pertaining to various spheres, where children's rights clash with those of adults: a) very personal rights, b) rights relating to everyday life situations, and c) rights

[5] William Damon, 'The Development of Justice and Self-interest during Childhood', in Melvin J. Lerner, Sally C. Lerner, *The Justice Motive in Social Behavior. Adapting to Times of Scarcity and Change* (New York, 1981), 57.

[6] Gary Matthews, *The Philosophy of Childhood* (Cambridge, 1994); Berry Mayall, *Towards a Sociology for Childhood. Thinking from Children's Lives* (Maidenhead, 2002); Berry Mayall, 'Lo status morale dell'infanzia: appunti dalla Gran Bretagna', in Heinz Hengst, Helga Zehier (eds.), *Per una sociologia dell'infanzia* (Milano, 2004), 124.

[7] Berry Mayall, 'Lo status morale dell'infanzia: appunti dalla Gran Bretagna', in Heinz Hengst, Helga Zehier (eds.), *Per una sociologia dell'infanzia* (Milano, 2004), 124.

[8] Leena Alanen, 'Women's Studies/Childhood Studies. Parallels, Links and Perspectives', in Jan Mason, Toby Fattore (eds.), *Children Taken Seriously. In Theory, Policy and Practice* (London, 2005), 31; Janet Holland, Rachel Thomson, Sheila Henderson, Sheena McGrellis, Sue Sharpe, 'Catching on, Wising up and Learning from your Mistakes: Young People's Accounts of Moral Development' (2000) 8 *The International Journal of Children's Rights* 271; Allison James, 'Life Times: Children's Perspectives on Age, Agency and Memory across the Life Course', in Jens Qvortrup (ed.), *Studies in Modern Childhood: Society, Agency, Culture* (New York, 2005), 248; Jens Qvortrup, 'Varieties of Childhood', in Id. (ed.), *Studies in Modern Childhood: Society, Agency, Culture* (New York, 2005), 1.

[9] The three studies mentioned in this work are part of the following national research programmes: *Citizenship Rights of children, Participation and Control* (reference n. 9914638391_004, year 1999); *Culture, Rights and Normative Socialization of Children and Adolescents* (reference n. 200314797_003, year 2003); *Mediation in Intercultural Practices, in Managing Conflicts, and in Social Promotion* (reference n. 2005145944_003, year 2005).

concerning more difficult decisions, such as children's right to be listened to if their parents decided to separate.

The second research was a study of perceptions of justice among teenagers, conducted in 2003–2004 in two towns in the north of Italy. It involved young people attending the first two classes of four different higher secondary schools with the aim of examining their representations of issues of justice. A total of 29 teenagers were interviewed individually, while 42 were involved in focus groups.

The interviews were conducted through the presentation of scenarios based on questions of justice. Girls and boys were presented with questions that ranged from simpler issues concerning respondents' everyday lives (decisions occurring in the family or among friends), to situations that were not part of their everyday experience and that interviewees were less familiar with (administrative and political decisions, issues concerning human rights violations). The focus groups were presented with a variety of moral dilemmas and the respondents were asked to have joint discussions on them.

Finally, the third study, conducted in 2007, analysed cultural mediation practices with separated children living in residential homes. This research, among other things, aimed at understanding whether the foreign children housed in those centres were aware of living within multiple normative and legal orders[10] and whether they had ever come across those conflicts that scholars dealing with mediation, namely cultural mediation, call 'normative conflicts', which occur when individuals have to live with different and often contradictory normative and legal systems. This study was carried out by means of in-depth interviews with 13 separated boys who had been living in reception centres in the north of Italy for at least one year. They came from different countries of strong migratory pressure and were aged between 12 and 18.[11] Their socialization and integration process had been underway for a relatively long time, under the guidance of social pedagogues and cultural mediators. Research findings focused on separated children's representations of their needs, interests, and fundamental rights, as well as the social and legal rules governing their relations with role model adults in their country of origin and in Italy.

13.2.1 Children's rights to be heard in proceedings concerning parental separation and divorce

With respect to the first study, children's analytical and moral reasoning skills are interestingly exemplified by the answers they gave about their right to be consulted if their parents decided to separate and their right to express their opinion about their custody.

The interviewees were asked if they should have the right to tell the judge which of their parents they would like to live with if they separate. The question was the following: *Chiara's parents are separating; do you think Chiara should have the right to tell the judge which of her parents she would like to live with?*

Almost all the respondents, except for five boys and three girls, claimed the right to be heard. Their arguments showed their awareness of the complexity of the situation. Most of them are fully aware that such choice would heavily affect their future life:

[10] Boaventura de Sousa Santos, *Estado, derecho y luchas sociales* (Bogotà, 1991).

[11] More precisely: six Moroccans, three Albanians, two Romanians, one Cameroonian, and one Pakistani.

She will be the one who'll have to live with her mother or with her father, so if she prefers one of them she should rightfully say so,

and, at the same time, of the fact that expressing a preference was often taken by the discarded parent as a demonstration of lesser affection:

Maybe she's afraid of losing . . . of disappointing the other parent,

with the risk that

the parent who is not chosen feels 'rejected' and might feel disappointed.

A girl, whose parents had been separated for five years, described her experience noting that it was still difficult for her to take a stand, since one of her parents 'reasons like a child' and took every choice she made to the advantage of the other parent as a lack of affection in his regard. She thus commented on this attitude:

Saying 'I want to stay with this one' is tantamount to saying that you don't love the other one. (. . .) I still notice that my father reasons like a child, so if I praise mum he'll start saying 'ah, you don't love me then', I mean, he doesn't actually say it but he shows it.

Several responses described the embarrassment or the worry involved when having to choose one parent over the other:

It is difficult to take a stand because you care for both in the same way and yet you have to decide between the two. I would find it embarrassing, because I would probably want to stay with my mother, but at the same time I would feel sorry for my father . . .

The account given by a now 13-year-old girl illustrates her awareness of the complexity of these questions very well:

Until you are fourteen, you are not allowed by law to tell who you wish to live with (. . .). As for me, on the contrary, I knew what I wanted very well, maybe not at seven, when my parents separated, but I surely did by the time I was ten. I went to talk to social workers, but I was accompanied by my father or my mother, so I could not speak my mind freely. I didn't say what I would have said if I had been alone. I don't like hurting people. The fact that I want to live with one parent does not mean that I don't love the other one (. . .). I think that children should be able to express their views, though not decide everything; they should just be able to voice their opinion because if, on the contrary, I should have to decide, I would feel guilty.

Other respondents, like this girl, recognized the difference between the right to express their opinions and the right to decide. They showed to be in favour of the right to express their opinion in a decision-making process affecting them—which the judge should take in due account—but, on the contrary, they were against making the child responsible for the decision. According to them, the decision should be up to the judge, also because he may be aware of some factors that might escape them:

Sure, she must have the right to have her say, but at the end of the day it is up to the judge to assess who she's better off with.

She has to endure difficult family circumstances; choosing the parent she prefers to live with would make it easier for her to go through this situation. However, one would need to check whether the parent she chooses is able to look after her, give her an education and keep her. One needs to assess whether that's feasible . . .

It is interesting to notice that half of the eight children who were against the recognition of the right to express a preference in order to determine their custody had experienced their parents' separation. They account for about one fourth of all the respondents with separated or divorced parents. It thus appeared that these children were less disposed to get the child involved in the proceedings concerning their custody. Three boys and one girl, in the light of their experience, reckoned that expressing their views in this regard would mean compromising their relationship with the non-custodial parent. They also did not feel they were ready to make such decision:

> I don't think it would be a good idea, because she would be put against her parents—I know this because my parents are divorced too. I will shortly have to see the judge and tell her that my father doesn't help us financially: it is already quite difficult to say that he never helps us, let alone if I was to say it in front of him...

> I think this is a difficult choice that would only complicate things (...). If the child has to choose one of the parents, whom she loves in the same way, the one who is left out...will feel disappointed.

The other four respondents argued that the child, as opposed to the judge, was not able to evaluate the most suitable solution correctly on the grounds of her age.

13.2.2 For justice's sake

With respect to the second research, which aimed to show adolescents' moral and legal reasoning, below are some findings from one of the focus groups organized in the framework of the study, focused on young people's sense of justice.

The scenario presented was taken from *Michael Kohlhaas*, a play written by German playwright Heinrich von Kleist in 1810. Von Kleist's work tells about Michael Kohlhaas, a horse dealer, who, in order to be allowed to cross the land of a local squire, was forced to leave two wonderfully bred horses as security. When he returned, he found his horses in a terrible state; he then refused to take them back and sued the squire for the damages he had suffered. Appalled at the judge's unfavourable ruling and even more at the loss of his own wife, who had been beaten to death by a Brandenburg's guard when she asked for the Governor's intervention in favour of her husband, Michael became the leader of a gang of rebels. In order to obtain justice, he made allies with the worst bandits, with whom he turned to looting and abuse. Since the judges did not behave as they should have done, he had a right, even a duty, to take justice into his own hands. The trial was re-opened, the court ruled in Kohlhaas's favour, but then he was arrested for his acts of banditry. He obtained justice for the damage he had suffered but, at the same time, he was sentenced to death for having threatened the order of the Empire. Finally, Kohlhaas died, but justice had been done.

The dilemma raised by this story is between the duty to disobey the law when it is not right and, on the other hand, the duty to obey it anyway because it is the law. This can be summed up in one key question: is it right to break a law you deem not right because it is contrary to your moral code? Or, on the contrary, should every law, even the most unjust, be obeyed because it is the law, in the name of a meta-law, a higher principle rooted in the need for political allegiance or social order?[12]

The question of obedience/disobedience to an unjust law has always been at the centre of philosophical debate, which is fuelled by opposing scholarly views on the conflict between moral and positive law from perspectives mostly related to moral and political philosophy and the philosophy of law. To put it very simply: on the one hand, there is the belief that every conflict between moral and positive law should be resolved in favour of the former. The opposing approach, on the contrary, maintains

[12] Vincenzo Ferrari, *Giustizia e diritti umani. Osservazioni sociologico-giuridiche* (Milano, 1995).

that legality and morality belong to separate spheres; thus, if the conflicts arising between them generate some moral dilemmas, these should not interfere with the general duty to obey the law. Consequently, all laws must be obeyed, even those that are wrong on moral grounds. Nevertheless, at the same time, people have the duty to make all lawful efforts to change these laws. According to this view, therefore, obedience to the law is a moral duty.

Kohlhaas's tragedy is in some ways similar to that of Antigone. Von Kleist's character, just like the main character of Sophocles's tragedy, experiences a profound conflict between two duties grounded in different normative frameworks: on the one hand, the legal system and, on the other hand, moral codes. Here too, we are faced with *non-dilemmas.*[13]

Just like Antigone, Michael Kohlhaas stimulated much thought among scholars, who have expressed conflicting views. As Thomas Mann remarked, Michael Kohlhaas's story could raise very mixed feelings among readers. On the one hand, it may stir admiration for the determination displayed by the main character, who becomes a hero and a defender of justice. On the other hand, however, the crimes he committed in his 'terror-bound frenzy to improve the world' and seek revenge could also cause horror and disgust.[14] In particular, Mann noted that Michael Kohlhaas received praise from Rudolf von Jhering who, in his 1872 work *The Struggle for Law,* mentioned von Kleist's play and wrote enthusiastically about the ideal feeling of justice held by the main character. For Jhering, standing up for one's rights is an individual's duty not only towards oneself but also towards society. Goethe, in contrast, as Mann remarked, had an opposite view. He defined Kohlhaas as an excessive character and his behaviour as an almost obsessive need to turn a personal matter into an issue of general interest.

Michael Kohlhaas's story also invites another important question. In fact, his fight for the recognition of the violation of his rights may not only serve to redress the injustice *he* had suffered, but eventually it could also secure justice for his fellow citizens. His struggle would then become of public interest. This is exactly the point Jhering made. He thought that the violation of a person's rights amounted to a violation of 'the Law'.[15] Within this framework, Kohlhaas is not a man 'obsessively confined in his narrow world of self-interest (...), but rather a staunch defender of the cause of law'[16] and justice, which is considered as a moral value that cannot be seen as separate from human dignity. Consequently, defending one's rights means preserving one's moral existence.

Finally, this story begs the question of whether it is fair to sacrifice innocent people in the name of a higher good, which, in this case, is justice.

Our focus group discussions were started with the question: 'How do you judge the behaviour of the main character of this story? Try to put yourselves in his shoes and say what you would have done in his place.'

[13] Persio Tincani, 'I dilemmi morali e le scelte tragiche', in Paola Ronfani (ed.), *Non è giusto! Dilemmi morali e senso della giustizia nelle rappresentazioni degli adolescenti* (Roma, 2007), 43.

[14] Thomas Mann, 'Heinrich von Kleist e i suoi racconti', in Id., *Nobiltà dello spirito e altri saggi* (Milano, 1997), 119.

[15] Rudolf von Jhering, 'La lotta per il diritto' [1872], in Roberto Racinaro (ed.), *La lotta per il diritto e altri saggi* (Milano, 1989), 71.

[16] François Chazel, 'Sentiment d'injustice, lutte pour le droit et rationalité axiologique: variations sur le "cas" de Michail Kohlhaas' (2003) 55 *Droit et Société* 774.

Almost all participants thought that Michael Kohlhaas's behaviour was wrong and called him 'stupid', 'naïve', 'crazy', 'fanatic', and 'selfish'. Their reasons drew on family and life values, which should not be sacrificed because of an injustice:

There are other values as well as justice, like the family.

It makes you wonder whether it was worth it. I don't think it was, I wouldn't sacrifice what he sacrificed: he lost everything in the name of a moral principle. Of course, everybody would do it in theory, but if you actually do it in practice you must be mad!

I think he did it all wrong, because, in order to obtain justice, he involved people who had nothing to do with it and then he died too. What use was justice to him in the end?

These opinions confirmed the importance of family in young people's scale of values. This is also shown in other studies,[17] where family ranks first.

Some participants, however, agreed with the ideal of justice supported by Kohlhaas, although they disapproved of his methods, thus showing their aversion to violence:

I don't agree with Kohlhaas's behaviour although maybe, if I put myself in his shoes, overwhelmed with rage, I would have taken justice into my own hands too. Still, I wouldn't have burned down houses and villages.

I don't agree because those who had their homes burned down suffered an injustice too and if they had behaved the way he did, it would have gone on forever.

The value of non-violence also underlay the criticism expressed by almost all participants when they were asked if it was legitimate to have a violent reaction when a public authority did not acknowledge a violation of legitimate rights and did not provide redress for the wrongs suffered. Placing oneself outside the law and taking justice into one's own hands after suffering an injustice was tolerated, but never through the use of violence:

I don't think it's right to use violence but I think it's right to rebel against injustice.

If we all reacted like that, following our instinct, we wouldn't be civilized people.

Others added that taking justice into one's hands should not involve the use of violence against innocent people:

There is a limit to everything. I mean, I accept the fact that he went and burned Von Tronka's castle to the ground but I do not accept his burning down villages and killing those who lived in them.

But some interviewees thought that

taking justice into one's hands is absolutely wrong because, even if a law is unjust, that's not the way to deal with it.

The general opinion was that the use of violence puts the victim at fault, leading to a spiralling sequence of abuses which it may become hard to get out of:

Then you'd become the bully because you're destroying villages. You'd get down to Von Tronka's level.

Some participants said that it was not worth fighting powerful people, even for a just cause, because in these cases defeat was on the cards. They thought that in the face of a court decision, albeit an unjust one, one should give in if up against very powerful people:

[17] Carlo Buzzi, Alessandro Cavalli, Antonio de Lillo (eds.), *Rapporto giovani. Sesta indagine dell'Istituto IARD sulla condizione giovanile in Italia* (Bologna, 2007).

Surrendering is wrong but unfortunately that's the way of the world. The just will always pay the price.

If I'd been in his shoes, after the court had ruled against me, I would have just given up.

Among the few who approved of Kohlhaas's behaviour, some of them called him 'heroic' and expressed their admiration for him. They pointed out that he had acted to defend a principle, the principle of justice, for which he had given up a life of comfort, his family and even his own life:

I think that Kohlhaas is to be admired because he had a sense of justice. His behaviour was extreme, that's true, but he pursued his ideal even at the cost of losing his wife and leaving his children. I don't think there would be people ready to do that nowadays.

Michael fought for justice. He lived in the 16th century, when people had to fight for justice. That's why we all have justice now, thanks to these people who fought for a principle.

Several focus group participants, even though they disapproved of Kohlhaas's behaviour, conceded that, if they had been in his shoes, they would have very likely behaved in the same way. In this case too, there was a discrepancy between what was considered as fair and unfair on an abstract level and, on the other hand, judgments expressed on the basis of experience:

I would have done exactly the same thing because suffering an injustice and not seeing it recognized would inevitably make me take justice into my own hands. I wouldn't accept the court's ruling which, in this case, appeared to be in favour of a powerful family.

Maybe, if I were to put myself in Kohlhaas's shoes, overwhelmed with rage, I would have taken justice into my own hands too. Still, I think that's absolutely wrong because, even if a law is unjust, that's not the way to deal with it.

The last question asked whether Michael Kohlhaas, by reclaiming his rights, only received redress for the wrong suffered or whether, on the contrary, he also secured justice for his fellow citizens. A high number of participants, both male and female, were convinced that Kohlhaas's actions would yield positive consequences:

People like Kohlhaas contributed to change the rules and the way we live as people and as a society. Nowadays, these things would be a lot worse if those people hadn't existed.

This story certainly made justice less dependent on power. Michael's rebellion toned down the arrogance of those squires.

On the opposite side, some focus group participants did not believe that actions of people like Kohlhaas helped fight injustice:

I don't think Kohlhaas's conduct secured justice for other citizens too, because he eventually only got justice for himself. The court probably couldn't take it anymore, von Tronka was fed up with the whole thing and so they gave him what he wanted. However, I don't think that those coming after him would get the same treatment, unless they used the same means as him and rebelled like him.

13.2.3 Separated children's representations of their rights and needs

The final examples of young people's moral reasoning skills are taken from research that sets itself apart from our previous studies. This is because, in the first place, the sample was not made up of Italian boys but it was composed of young people coming from countries of high migration pressure. Secondly, the sample belonged to a specific category of underage children: separated children, that is children, for the most part teenagers, who migrate to a foreign country by themselves.

This study admittedly has some limitations, due to the size and the particular nature of the sample, which was made up of separated children who started their settlement and integration process in residential homes. However, we believe this survey is particularly revealing since it focuses on the representations of needs and rights, which have been scarcely dealt with in previous research on separated children. For this reason, this work could provide an interesting contribution to the body of research that has developed in Italy and other European countries since the 1990s with the aim of identifying the social and age composition of separated children as well as the reasons behind their migration choice and their expectations for the future.[18] These studies are innovative with regard to the traditional research approach, which had focused almost exclusively on the so-called forced migration of children and which portrayed migrant children as 'passive, vulnerable and necessarily exploited' within the migration process,[19] with no possibilities or ability to make autonomous migration choices. These works, on the contrary, focus on the fact that separated children are usually *grands enfants*, not only in terms of age but also because almost all of them have reached a high degree of autonomy and sense of responsibility.[20]

In this regard, it should be pointed out that, while in 'rich countries' children's transition to adulthood has become increasingly extended, which entails a later assumption of adult responsibilities and the postponement of full independence, in 'poor countries', on the contrary, 'our' representation of childhood is hardly ever found; in fact, early access to adulthood implies a shorter childhood and no adolescence because poverty forces children to grow up fast and 'erases their rights'.[21] Moreover, in countries where everyday life is characterized by constant uncertainty due to economic and political instability, there is a different perception of risk compared to affluent countries: emigration is not considered as more difficult or hazardous than one's present life or future perspectives in the country of origin. Therefore, when reading and analysing respondents' narrations, we need to set aside our own representation of childhood, which, on the contrary, is more extended and clearly separated from adulthood; it is often idealized and, for this reason, it is equated exclusively with light-heartedness and carelessness.[22] Separated children should be approached in a more objective way, giving due consideration to their personal histories, their individual characteristics and their own specific needs.

[18] See Giovanna Campani, Zoran Lapov, Francesco Carchedi, *Le esperienze ignorate. Giovani migranti tra accoglienza, indifferenza, ostilità* (Milano, 2002); Monia Giovannetti, *Minori stranieri in movimento: percorsi e pratiche tra integrazione e devianza. Quaderni di Cittàsicure* 21 (vol. 2) (Bologna, 2000); Dario Melossi, Monia Giovannetti, *I nuovi sciuscià. Minori stranieri in Italia* (Roma, 2002); Clara Silva, Giovanna Campani, *Crescere errando. Minori immigrati non accompagnati* (Milano, 2004); Giovanna Campani, Olivia Salimbeni (eds.), *La fortezza e i ragazzini. La situazione dei minori stranieri in Europa* (Milano, 2006).

[19] Caitlin Farrow, 'A Review of European Research Findings on Children in Migration', in Save the Children, *Conference Report. Focus on Children in Migration* (2007) (<http://www.savethechildren.net/separated_children/publications/reports>), 6.

[20] See Irene Azzari, Olivia Salimbeni, 'Il minore straniero non accompagnato. Definizioni e legislazione internazionale', in Giovanna Campani, Olivia Salimbeni (eds.), *La fortezza e i ragazzini. La situazione dei minori stranieri in Europa* (Milano, 2006), 19.

[21] Giulia Di Bello, 'Prefazione', in Giovanna Campani, Olivia Salimbeni (eds.), *La fortezza e i ragazzini. La situazione dei minori stranieri in Europa* (Milano, 2006), 10; Vittoria Tola, 'Prefazione', in Giovanna Campani, Zoran Lapov, Francesco Carchedi (eds.), *Le esperienze ignorate. Giovani migranti tra accoglienza, indifferenza, ostilità* (Milano, 2002), 13.

[22] Alan Prout, Allison James (eds.), *Constructing and Reconstructing Childhood: Contemporary Issues in the Sociological Study of Childhood* (London, 1990).

Within the framework of this study, it is interesting to consider some examples of the reasoning developed by our young interviewees when they were asked to assess the rules regulating access to employment and compulsory education in their country of origin compared to Italy.

First of all, it should be noted that work was the most frequently cited reason for migrating. Our interviewees therefore seemed to consider work as their main need. Children migrating on their own, for the most part, aimed at integrating into Italian society through employment.[23] Almost all respondents declared they had decided to leave their country to find a way out of poverty and marginalization, a situation which, in their mind, could not be changed. They affirmed they left with a clear plan that had been agreed with their families, sometimes not without a struggle, with the aim of finding a job that could allow them to support themselves and their relatives as soon as possible.

Almost all these young boys, who had grown up before their time compared to 'Western' children, said they attended school irregularly and only for few years, while doing odd jobs or in some cases working every day, with or even without their parents' permission.

The interviewees' words reveal that, in their countries of origin, education is widely underrated: it is not regarded as a value in itself, a fundamental right, a means of emancipation but, on the contrary, it is often seen as preventing children from seizing the already scarce unskilled job opportunities that might arise, where no qualification is required anyway. In this regard, it is particularly revealing to notice that only a few interviewees declared they were aware of compulsory education laws in their country of origin while some of them ignored the very existence of compulsory education. Even those who were actually aware of those regulations declared they had often infringed them.

Once they got to Italy and learned that they could not access the labour market without having finished compulsory schooling, they assigned education an instrumental value.

> *When you were told that you would have gone to live in a residential care home, did you tell them what you would have liked to do?*
>
> Yes, I'd really like to find a job but then I understood that without a lower secondary school qualification I couldn't work… so I'd better finish lower secondary school, attend a course and look for a job (16 years old, Albanian).

It should be noted, however, that many respondents found it hard to accept the idea of postponing their access to the labour market—and, most importantly, postpone earning an income—to attend school, thus disappointing their families', as well as their own, expectations.

Some respondents claimed their need/right to work, affirming that education was a right they would forgo in favour of their need/duty to support their family. In those cases, the interviewees' current situation led to a rupture between what could be defined as an 'abstract right' (education) and, on the other hand, what was claimed as a 'concrete right' (work). In other words, there was a separation between what these young migrants thought the rights of people their age should be in theory and, on the contrary, what they reported as their concrete needs, on the basis of their social,

[23] Joseph Moyersoen, 'I minori stranieri non accompagnati', in Ermenegildo Ciccotti, Enrico Moretti, Roberto Ricciotti (eds.), *I numeri italiani. Infanzia e adolescenza in cifre—Edizione 2007* (Firenze, 2007), 89.

economic, and cultural background in their country of origin. This rupture could also be ascribed to the strong sense of responsibility these children felt towards their family: they did not want to disappoint them nor did they want to fail their expectations.

In Albania, is it normal for young people your age to work?

I think it would be better to go to school, but... in Albania, many children don't go to school, they'd rather work. When I was there, poor children started working even before the age of eleven. Now, though, I'm told that young children don't take to the streets to work anymore because nobody would hire them. I'm sorry to hear that, because their families need the money (16 years old, Albanian).

It is interesting to note that although some of them thought that it was right for Italian law to allow employment only to children over compulsory school age, at the same time, they were convinced that these provisions should not be introduced in their countries of origin because they would have negative repercussions on the already difficult financial situation of several families.

Under Italian law, children under 15 years of age are not allowed to work. Do you think that's right?

Yes, it is in Italy. In my country, on the contrary, it wouldn't be right because there you need to work at an earlier age and support your family (17 years old, Moroccan).

13.3 Some final comments

On the whole, the examples illustrated here show that young people possess the reasoning skills to face even complex questions with regard to situations affecting their everyday life, as well as more complex situations that are far from their experience. Boys and girls who participated in our interviews and focus groups showed high competencies and a good ability to use different justice and moral criteria as well as a strong and realistic sense of the complexity of different moral situations. Moreover, they displayed a considerable ability to draw on a vast array of rules and moral principles and also normative and legal systems, which they chose in a selective and complementary way according to each given situation.

Especially in focus group discussion, both boys and girls were able to reason and discuss the complex questions presented to them, displaying a good practical knowledge of moral concepts. Moreover, participants seemed to realize that they were confronted with dilemmatic situations and they appeared to be aware that it would have been difficult, if not impossible, to find a satisfactory and fair solution in all levels of judgment: every choice inevitably carries positive and negative consequences, which one needs to take responsibility for.

In particular, they were clearly aware of the existence of two different types of judgment: the legal and the moral. On several occasions, as mentioned above, they pointed out that what was 'legally right' could not always be considered as 'morally right'; it was also observed that, in a moral perspective—where specific values and criteria such as loyalty, trust, kinship, and friendship come into play—different situations would be considered in different ways, whereas, on the contrary, the law should deal with them all in the same way.

In the survey with separated children, respondents showed they were aware of the complexity of their situation; they also appeared to be able to form different judgements about laws, needs, and rights depending on the context and specific situation. In particular, it was noticed that they were aware of the gap between what the host society expected of them and viewed as a need for them and, on the other hand, what they expected of society and what they thought they needed. Finally, it was also possible to establish that there is often a separation between what respondents reckon the needs of people their age *should be* on an abstract level and, on the other hand, the *actual* needs they reported they had in their everyday life, on the basis of their past experience, their culture, and the context they lived in. Indeed, the variables relating to the interviewees' 'culture of origin' and the 'culture of their country of settlement' played a key role in shaping their opinions when they were asked to move away from abstract reasoning and express context-specific judgments.

14

Rights-Based Restorative Justice in Canada: From Silence to Citizenship

Shannon A. Moore[1] *and Richard C. Mitchell*[2]

14.1 Introduction

Numerous juvenile justice systems in democratic and non-democratic states alike are being re-shaped by the UN Convention on the Rights of the Child (hereafter CRC), but young people in conflict with the law remain 'the unwanted child' of the children's rights movement (Abramson, 2006; Moore & Mitchell, 2009). This notion is evidenced by the paucity of Canadian data investigating the implementation of the CRC within that country's juvenile justice settings, and this population of young people may now be identified—even more than other groups—as the nation's silenced citizens. Indeed, responding to myriad gaps in Canadian law and policy an exhaustive upper house legislative review by the Standing Committee on Human Rights entitled 'Children: The Silenced Citizens' (2007) repeats numerous recommendations raised by the Committee on the Rights of the Child in 1995 and 2003. As the current zeitgeist in the nation's capital returns to the old canard of 'getting tough on youth crime' (Canadian Coalition for the Rights of Children, 2011a; see also Simpson, 2011), it is now quite clear that CRC implementation within juvenile justice legislative, policy and practice settings is virtually non-existent across the country (see Moore & Mitchell, 2009 for one British Columbia exception).

Consider the following:

- youth custody rates are among the highest of industrialized nations,
- disproportionately higher rates of detention for ethnic minority and Aboriginal children,
- incarceration of youth within adult populations,
- shortage of effective alternative measures in securing custody,
- lack of training for child welfare authorities for early detection of at-risk children in conflict with the law,
- a shortage of preventative strategies (Senate of Canada, 2007: 86–98; see also Moore, 2007).

[1] Associate Assistant Professor, Director of Women's Studies Department and Department of Child and Youth Studies, Brock University, Canada.

[2] Associate Professor, Department of Child and Youth Studies, Brock University, Canada.

Criticisms abound due in no small measure to the far right-leaning ideological approach of the current federal Parliament despite the introduction of, and encouraging data from, juvenile justice legislation known as the Youth Criminal Justice Act (2003) designed by its predecessors (hereafter YCJA; Government of Canada, 2001; Senate of Canada, 2007: 90). Perhaps most notably for our purposes, the Act represents the first time that CRC principles and those pertaining to restorative justice practices have been statutorily articulated (Moore, 2007; Moore & Mitchell, 2009).

This chapter presents selected preliminary findings from an exploratory, qualitative study that began in 2008 utilizing grounded theory, analytical and methodological procedures (Glaser, 2005; Glaser & Strauss, 1967) to investigate Canada's compliance with alternative standards for juvenile justice found within numerous United Nations frameworks. The authors' research aim was twofold: first, to uncover barriers to compliance and secondly, to identify mechanisms to address these impediments. The analytical focus of the study relied on the concept of 'rights-based restorative justice' (Moore, 2008a; Moore & Mitchell, 2007a, 2007b, 2009), one that integrates the core principles of the CRC and those found within the Basic Principles on the Use of Restorative Justice Programmes in Criminal Matters (UN Economic and Social Council, 2002; hereafter UN Basic Principles; UN Office for Drugs and Crime, 2006). Data were organized by contextualizing current statutory and local practices of rights-based restorative justice programming across the country within international legal frameworks, by constant comparison of data to data and data to literature, and by presenting thematic findings elicited from eight key informant interviews through salient quotes.

14.2 Canadian context for justice

Astonishingly, as it turned 20 years of age across the globe the CRC remained misunderstood in Canada in both theory and practice, and effective responses within juvenile justice domains have yet adequately to interpret the human rights of young people (Senate of Canada, 2007: 90, preamble). It is also important to locate the broader historical context for the investigation in restorative justice practices found in both ancient and contemporary indigenous epistemologies as identified in more than 100 countries worldwide, including Canada (Van Ness, 2005; see also Braithwaite, 2002; Moore, 2007, 2008a, 2008b; Moore & Mitchell, 2009; White, 2002). Restorative justice practices respond to offending behaviours in an alternative manner to those adopted in the retributive systems commonly found in neo-colonial, industrialized states (Moore, 2007; Moore & Mitchell, 2007a, 2007b, 2009; Zehr, 1995). Moreover, restorative practice is built upon a communitarian worldview with a focus on full participation of all relevant members from the community as well as a profound respect for social and interpersonal relations. Similar to the human rights discourse, the voices of citizens who are more vulnerable due to age, ability, social circumstance, or victimization are emphasized. During restorative practice, the process of transforming harmful experience is paramount with oral and affective responses leading the way. The scope of these practices has a vast range and may include dyads, groups, or whole communities, with fact-sharing, acceptance of responsibility, mutual resolution, restitution, reduction in fear, and/or challenges to social inequity common features (Moore, 2007, 2008a; Moore & Mitchell, 2007a, 2007b, 2009; Nyp, 2004; UN Office of Drugs and Crime, 2006).

Notwithstanding the epistemological grounding of these practices within indigenous cultures over millennia (Moore, 2007, 2008a; Van Ness, 2005), it is true that restorative justice is still an emergent field within contemporary juvenile justice settings (Cormier, 2002). Only in the last decades of the twentieth century was the term applied to alternative approaches within adult or juvenile justice systems. This point is salient within the context of the lived experiences of Aboriginal Canadians (First Nations, Métis, and Inuit) represented so disproportionately in the criminal justice systems of the nation as both victims and offenders (Senate of Canada, 2007; Blackstock et al., 2004; Moore & Mitchell, 2009). Indeed, Aboriginal young people are described by researchers and policy-makers as the 'most vulnerable group of children and youth in Canada today, and in the future' (Finlay et al., 2005: 10). Aboriginal Canadians are more 'likely to be born into poverty, suffer health problems, be victims of maltreatment, be placed away from their families and communities in provincial and territorial child welfare systems or be incarcerated in youth correctional facilities'. The increased risk for young people in these communities to be involved in the youth justice system is evidenced by incarceration rates eight times higher than for non-Aboriginal youth. It is also evident that young people in contact with the welfare system often 'cross-over' into justice systems (Finlay et al., 2005: ibid). Such facts call attention to the need for more effective interventions and to the structural inequities in Canada rather than simply to a worldview of young offenders as 'law-breakers'. Restorative justice with its ancient indigenous roots could represent a significant new way forward in resolving some of the social problems in communities as diverse as those found among the various cultures of Aboriginal Canadians (Moore, Tulk & Mitchell, 2005).

In recent decades, Canada's higher comparative rates of incarceration of young people have been linked to previous legislation known as the Young Offenders Act. As noted above, for the first time the principles of two United Nations agreements—the CRC and UN Basic Principles—are embedded in the Youth Criminal Justice Act when it came into effect in 2003 (Denov, 2007; Moore, 2007; Moore & Mitchell, 2009). The socio-historical context has presented a unique research opportunity since the challenges of deploying fair, proportionate, and ethical responses by youth justice practitioners are of perennial international and national interest (Howe, 2008; Moore, 2007, 2008a; Senate of Canada, 2007; Moore & Mitchell, 2009). Notwithstanding, Canada's political system frequently obscures the clear understanding of compliance issues related to international legal standards because they are differently interpreted and implemented throughout the provinces and territories (Moore, 2007).

14.3 Rights-based restorative justice

Rights-based interventions in young peoples' lives are guided by core CRC principles which oblige practitioners to ensure that children are free from discrimination (Article 2); consider their best interests in all decisions (Article 3); support maximum healthy development and safety (Article 6); and allow participation in age-appropriate ways as full citizens in all issues that affect them (Article 12; see also Moore & Mitchell, 2007a, 2007b, 2009). CRC Articles 2, 3, 6, and 12 also provide a standard framework for reports submitted to the Committee on the Rights of the Child, and are integral to unlocking and understanding the interconnectedness of the remaining treaty provisions.

Ironically, Canadians contributed significantly in the drafting of both the CRC and the UN Basic Principles; both governmental and non-governmental delegates were promoters of these instruments in early days and demonstrated leadership during their early domestic implementation (Mitchell, 2000, 2005; Moore & Mitchell, 2009). The CRC serves as an 'umbrella treaty' for all 192 states who have ratified by further influencing new developments within international juvenile justice standards (Moore & Mitchell, 2009), and by offering basic guidance to greater coordination of implementation of both (Denov, 2007). As an instrument of international law, the treaty appears to have established itself as the 'industry standard' and offers a cross-cutting, interconnected framework for interpreting local youth justice programming throughout the world (Moore & Mitchell, 2009).

Specifically, justice provisions within CRC Articles 37 and 40 outline good practices for juvenile justice authorities and practitioners. Article 37 highlights how young people when deprived of liberty should be treated in a manner that acknowledges age-related needs for contact with family and friends, the right to play and to engage in leisure and cultural activities (see also CRC Articles 14, 30, 31), and the right to continue education (Articles 28 and 29). Canada has received targeted criticism from the Committee for the government's partial acceptance of CRC Article 37—while accepting in principle it has also reserved the right *not* to detain children separately from adults. In response, the Standing Senate Committee on Human Rights offered this imperative to legislators and policy-makers:

> In terms of alternative measures, the federal government needs to work proactively with the provinces and territories to ensure that alternative measures are effectively implemented for youth in conflict with the law. Restorative justice measures that focus on the offender's accountability to the victim, integration of the offender, and the restoration of harmony in the larger community, are important means of achieving this goal. As Article 37 insists, detention must be used only for the most serious crimes.
>
> The UN Study on Violence Against Children noted '[d]etention should be reserved for child offenders who are assessed as posing a real danger to others...' Otto Driedger of the University of Regina insisted that in order to come into compliance with the [CRC], restorative justice models were imperative—'not as an absolute alternative but as a parallel initiative, that will assist us to have a less polarized approach. But it will be a long process' (Senate of Canada, 2007: 94; also 87).

Likewise, Article 40 (1) discourages retributive responses by focusing on the need to avoid deprivation of liberty and emphasizing that young people are to be:

> ...treated in a manner consistent with the promotion of the child's dignity and worth, which reinforces the child's respect for human rights and freedoms of others and which takes into account the child's age and the desirability of promoting the child's reintegration and the child's assuming a constructive role in society.

Both CRC Articles 37 and 40 support the contextual analysis of youthful offences within a broader, systemic appreciation of the rights and needs of young people. To implement these principles, the Canadian government would benefit from the realization that there are often 'practical solutions to...pragmatic problems' (Senate of Canada, 2007: 97). Examples of such solutions are found within the *Rights-Based Restorative Practice: Evaluation ToolKit* (Moore, 2008a; Moore & Mitchell, 2009). The CRC offers the most widely accepted international human rights treaty in history while the UN Basic Principles is an instrument offering non-legally binding guidance for stakeholders. Accordingly, the integrated framework offered by the authors' argument for 'rights-based restorative justice' benefits from the CRC's status in international law and its ongoing reporting process under Article 44 with the notion of incremental growth towards new legislation, policy, and practice (Freeman, 2007; Mitchell, 2005, 2007).

Moreover, human rights education must be considered systemically from macro through to micro levels of implementation, a notion encapsulated in CRC Article 42. As one of us has noted (Mitchell 2005: 324–25), Article 42 and its 'principles and provisions' were conceived and included by negotiators as an 'international compliance indicator' for the entire treaty. At the same time, the Article represents the treaty's least ambiguous text—'States Parties undertake to make the principles and provision of the Convention widely known, by appropriate and active means, to adults and children alike'—and reinforces the notion that human rights relationships within and through education provide a cornerstone of such multi-systemic, rights-based approaches (Moore, 2008a; Mitchell, 2005; Moore & Mitchell, 2009; Tomaševski, 2007).

Finally, it must be emphasized that most of the previous pedagogical approaches in Canada have taken a top-down, developmental orientation towards civics citizenship curricula (see Howe and Covell, 2005: 123 as one example) with their implicit ideological assumptions of creating the type of 'docile citizen' noted in Raby's investigations (2005, 2008). This narrower analysis of the potential of the CRC for critical, active citizenship and pedagogy is also the antithesis to the kind of introduction to human, civil, social, and political rights argued for by Hyslop-Margison and Thayer (2009), Mitchell (2005, 2007), and others. It is perhaps a fundamental reason that 20 years on Canadian young people still describe themselves as 'silenced' from this important discourse. Hyslop-Margison and Thayer (2009: introduction) argue that in the current historical moment, the need to challenge corporate-driven, neo-liberal assumptions about 'vulgar capitalism' with alternative visions has never been greater, and 'a thick concept of democracy first constructed on a foundation of critical theory precepts and then properly implemented through public education can help us achieve this outcome'. The CRC offers adults and young people exactly this opportunity in 'extremely tenuous times' (Hyslop-Margison & Thayer, 2009: ibid.) with an alternative to retributive juvenile justice systems. As such, the core principles of the CRC articulated in Articles 2, 3, 6, and 12 are also emphasized here while reinforcing the potential of linking these with the basic principles of restorative justice. Again, as Hyslop-Margison and Thayer (2009) contend: 'Our role in education is not to prepare students for a new economic reality designed by others, but to prepare them to shape social reality in more progressive and socially just sorts of ways' (ibid.).

Restorative justice and young people's human rights similarly encourage the voices of victims, offenders, and young people to be heard through non-discriminatory, safe, authentic, and full participation (Moore, 2007; Moore & Mitchell, 2007a, 2007b, 2009). The integration of principles that ground rights-based restorative justice are summarized below:

Non-discrimination, Equality, and Mutuality: All young people have the same human rights regardless of social-cultural context or whether they are victims or perpetrators of harm; processes address the balance between equality and mutuality among stakeholders.

Best Interests, Well-Being, and Restoration: For all young participants involved there is a concern for their best interests, their well-being, and a restoration of equilibrium for all stakeholders. The aim is to heal harm done in the context of human relationships.

Survival, Development, and Safety: For young participants there is an appropriate consideration for the healthy development especially in the context of vulnerabilities and power relations typical in circumstances of victimization. Participants must feel a sense of safety.

Participation, Voice, and Volunteerism: All stakeholders must have an opportunity to fully participate and experience their views being meaningfully heard. All processes must be voluntarily engaged in by all stakeholders (Moore & Mitchell, 2009: 39).

Analyses of other UN instruments focused upon juvenile justice reveal complementary thinking to rights-based restorative justice paradigm including: the Riyadh Guidelines (UNOHCHR, 1990); the Beijing Rules (UNOHCHR, 1985); the Vienna Guidelines (UNECOSOC, 1997); Children's Rights in Juvenile Justice (UN Committee on the Rights of the Child, 2007). These judicial instruments also emphasize non-judicial interventions, and community, family, and school-based responses along with prevention strategies. Adapting such approaches to Canadian communities would reinforce movement from an over-reliance on retributive systems and the knee-jerk response perennially invoked to solve youth criminal justice issues towards holistic, and perhaps even preventative, measures (Moore & Mitchell, 2009).

14.4 Methodological and analytical framework

The main research aim in this study responds to the myriad gaps noted in legal, theoretical, and applied knowledge in Canada by exploring the nature and impact of compliance to CRC and UN Basic Principles within the juvenile justice system. Legal, policy, and practice impact were examined through the following question: 'How are juvenile justice stakeholders implementing the principles and provisions of international juvenile justice frameworks?' Methodologically, the investigation utilized a grounded theory approach with procedures and analysis first developed by Barney Glaser and Anselm Strauss (1967; see also Glaser, 2005; Mitchell, 2005; Mitchell & McCusker, 2008). The grounded theory approach offers a systematic set of inductive procedures that move outward from studying the lived experiences of individuals to a deeper conceptual understanding of these experiences. As such, the theory generated might also be expected to facilitate a greater understanding of how the implementation of the CRC and UN Basic Principles might be better facilitated within individual lives as well as within overarching systems of governance.

Eight key informants participated in this study through in-depth interviews in 2007–08, and salient excerpts from the larger data set have been integrated into the following sections for discussion. (Names of the participants were replaced by lettered acronyms: e.g. 'RBS', 'SCL', 'DDV', 'MVS', and 'KMY'). This cohort of participants were knowledgeable about both the human rights and restorative justice discourses in Canada and internationally, are currently stakeholders within both juvenile justice systems and community-based programmes, and have had central roles in shaping policy and practice in restorative justice at the federal and provincial ministerial levels in Canada, as well as during international negotiations. Selected preliminary findings were elicited first through open coding procedures utilizing research principles of constant comparison of data to data, and data to literature to guide analysis. In the following section, a preliminary selection of findings is presented.

14.5 Policy texts, power relations, and rights-based practice

To achieve a rights-based approach, all citizens living in democratic societies might be expected to benefit from accurate knowledge of accepted standards of human rights and justice—facilitated by statutory compliance and new policy development—congruent with international law. This is not the case in Canada, however, as numerous studies have indicated (Mitchell, 2000, 2005; Mitchell & McCusker, 2008; Senate of Canada, 2007). All participants in this study noted that accountability in juvenile justice decisions could be guided and better facilitated by clearer standards found within international frameworks offering larger political and legal contexts for practice. This process depends upon a common conceptual foundation (Abramson, 2006; Cormier, 2002; Mitchell, 2005, 2007; Moore & Mitchell, 2009) thus far woefully lacking in Canadian jurisprudence, policy, or practice settings, points emphasized below by key informant 'SCL':

> There is a lack of political will and legal reluctance on the part of the [Canadian] government, police, and crown attorneys to support and fund education of human rights and child rights specifically. Lack of knowledge and lack of understanding of human rights at the grass roots level are the greatest barriers to rights-based processes. We have a challenge in Canada in terms of our reception laws for human rights instruments that we ratify.
>
> Many contain a mandate for States to educate their citizens in the rights contained in the treaty, yet in Canada we assume that educating citizens about the Charter of Rights and Freedoms is adequate. Because of our dualist [federalist] system we don't have a straightforward mechanism for including them in our educational curricula at any level, much less reaching the public outside of formal educational institutions. Ignorance and denial are the biggest barriers to rights-based approaches in juvenile justice.

Practical dissemination of the core CRC principles is piecemeal and truncated throughout Canadian jurisdictions primarily because provincial and territorial Ministries of Education have not yet aligned themselves with international law or previous Committee on the Rights of the Child recommendations from 1995 and 2003 (Canadian Coalition for the Rights of Children, 2011b). Thus, the perpetual state of 'ignorance and denial' noted by 'SCL' continues. (See also Simpson, 2011 and his astute analysis for context).

Establishing rights-based approaches in educational curricula and within individual classrooms that are congruent with the CRC, congruent with the earlier notion of thick democracy and active citizenship, and congruent with treaty reporting and monitoring processes is a prerequisite to community-based justice initiatives since schools are also fundamental to the reintegration of young people in conflict with the law. Reciprocally, the CRC implementation process could be aided through the adoption of restorative justice principles in community settings, as another participant, 'RBS', explained:

> Fair process is central to human rights and essentially to what a restorative school is about. So if the young person feels they experienced a fair process they may not like the outcome, but that's okay because they have been part of a process where they had a voice, have been engaged, and understand why things have happened—there is explanation, expectation and clarity.

Moreover, effective implementation of right-based restorative justice within school systems would require active involvement by all stakeholders within that school community. Such an approach is challenging not only because it demands that educators emphasize equity in terms of rights and dignity, but because it undermines embedded power relations such as those observed by 'DDV' below:

It takes examining the systems we find ourselves working in as opposed to just thinking that the system is okay and we just need to get the young people to comply—to fit into the system. Many educators are willing to have students use restorative practices but they are afraid of using it in their own conflicts, and in their own inter-personal relationships with each other or with students. The heart of that fear is a sense of vulnerability.

There is a systemic structure in place in which educators are used to telling students what is right and wrong and how to behave. They have a hard time letting go and allowing students to contribute even to the development of school guidelines. It's about power and control. My experience of over 20 years of teaching is that students need to be invited into decision-making about their own education. This changes education—kids are happier and I was happier and learning was much more meaningful because the kids were doing things that were meaningful to them. It was about letting go of control. It was about the difference between authority and authoritarianism.

Restorative approaches are implicitly rights-based. There is a possibility for real change in the culture of communities and schools when restorative justice philosophy enters into the fray because it fundamentally alters the way adults in authority interact with young people, as confirmed by 'RBS':

In our schools when we use restorative questions to deal with issues, rather than asking the question 'why' and 'who's to blame'... we ask 'what happened?' and 'What were you thinking at the time?' 'Who has been affected by what you did and how?' and 'What can you do to make this right?' The conversation changes... It becomes critical that the young person is heard. It enhances their responsibility and accountability and is very respectful. If you can build and strengthen healthy relationships where people feel connected to one another conflicts will be worked out better. This takes a lot of respect and a lot of hearing and I think those are all related to rights.

Implementation of rights-based approaches is both implicit and explicit: it begins with adults in authority sustaining institutions and interpersonal relationships from the premise of mutual respect and dignity. By bringing together human rights and restorative justice principles, power relations may be re-addressed, but, as is so often the case, with policy-makers lagging behind, as 'SCL' observes: 'In our restorative justice circles, we work to uphold the dignity of all participants because it is one of the underlying principles of human rights. We do not see this in policy.' This analysis of the hidden citizenship potential of the CRC for facilitating the critical consciousness envisioned by Hyslop-Margison and Thayer (2009) is re-iterated by key informant 'SCL':

The responsibility rests at the feet of government—in terms of upholding its obligations to educate the public in human rights along with the treaties it signs. Part of the signing of conventions is to educate the public. And I think when we do human rights education in Canada we look at the Charter of Rights and Freedoms. Canadians are not given a good grounding in the commitments that we have made and the reasons behind those commitments—and I think that applies to the training of police, law enforcement offices and even lawyers particularly in the contexts of rights protected under international law. It is assumed in Canada that once we ratify a document that it is already in place domestically—somewhere, somehow.

But we do not have a system like, for example South Africa, which holds that if a convention is ratified it becomes part of domestic law, full stop. In Canada whose responsibility is it? The provinces are responsible for education. The Federal Department of Foreign Affairs is responsible for negotiating and ratifying these documents. The provinces report to the Federal Government about compliance and that is developed into a report to the Committee on the Rights of the Child. So if the government is not doing it we must attempt to bring education about children rights through restorative justice circles and practices.

Canada's denial of human rights education has an added, unintended consequence of sustaining juvenile justice as Abramson's 'unwanted child' within the children's rights movement, and confirms the status of young people involved in these processes as silenced citizens within a retributive system focused on punishment more than rehabilitation (Moore & Mitchell, 2009). As Abramson argues:

While the Convention on the Rights of the child is proving itself to be a highly successful human rights treaty, the potential of the CRC is not being realised with respect to the youngsters who are in trouble with the law. Of all of the major areas covered by the Convention, juvenile justice is the most neglected (2006: 15, 21).

Clearly, youth justice stakeholders require both theoretical and practical tools to allow this re-shaping of power relations through young people's rights and the concomitant transfer of knowledge negotiated through international consensus (Senate of Canada, 2007: preamble). Admittedly, academic literature linking the CRC with the UN Basic Principles is only a recent phenomenon (see Delens-Ravier, 2007; Moore, 2007, 2008a, 2009; Muncie, 2005), and as such, has rarely been linked to practice (Moore, Tulk & Mitchell, 2005; Moore & Mitchell, 2009). However, both sets of principles provide a rich alternative response to the diversity of local communities, and service delivery systems that risk being overly prescriptive, as Braithwaite cautions:

We must be careful how we regulate restorative justice... Unthinking enforcement of standards is a new threat to innovating with better ways of doing restorative justice... We can craft open textured restorative justice standards that allow a lot of space for cultural difference and innovation while giving us a language for uncontroversially denouncing bad practice (2002: 565).

For balance amongst and between universality, diversity, and a young person-centred approach, critical reflections on the source of authority in setting new standards for juvenile justice is also necessary, though frequent calls for a Child and Youth Commissioner have thus far been ignored in Canada. The integration of CRC and restorative justice principles in the 2003 YCJA provided some legitimacy to the development of rights-based restorative justice as a tool for community-based settings. Nevertheless, key informant 'RBS' discusses this legislative integration in the following:

The Act [YCJA] opens doors for the use of restorative justice and child rights because these principles and this philosophy are espoused in the preamble... I think it is critical that the act names things that we need to be concerned about: victims have a voice, young people are heard, young people should be involved in decisions that affect them; parent, families and communities have a chance to have their response; measures taken should be meaningful... So the act provides a foundation that opens the door and legitimises the use of RJ [restorative justice] for young people—at the same time it is a wide open door and not very directive... but that flexibility may also be its downfall.

There are two major challenges with the Act—reading the preamble [principles of restorative justice and child rights] without understanding the spirit of those principles or their effectiveness, and the lack of resources in the community.

In juvenile justice contexts, we find a double-edged sword where a general lack of knowledge about CRC fundamentals among legislators, policy-makers, and practitioners is coupled with juvenile justice's problematic relationship within the child rights movement in the first place:

> If the adults around children, their parents and other family members, teachers and carers do not understand the implications of the Convention, and above all its confirmation of the equal status of children as subjects of rights, it is most unlikely that the rights set out in the Convention will be realised for many children (Senate of Canada, 2007: 197).

The rhetoric of the rights-based preamble contained within the 2003 YCJA is another in the long list of missed Canadian opportunities to move in unity with other democratic states in supporting transmission of the CRC into effective legislation and new practices. This problem of active implementation is highlighted throughout this study, and throughout the Senate of Canada report (2007: 196–97) shows that key legal stakeholders are simply unaware the treaty exists, and whose authors admit that 'very little knowledge of the Convention exists outside of academic and advocacy circles'. Similarly, as Abramson (2006) argues, the CRC remains an untapped potential when young offenders continue to garner less sympathy than other young people in rights debates. A key concern is that social and theoretical constructions of young people as 'innocent and vulnerable' are wholly inconsistent with similar attributes characterizing young people in conflict with the law as 'deviant' (see also Moore & Mitchell, 2009; Roche, 1999). The Senate report suggests further that a primal fear of young people sustains the 'unwantedness' of those involved in juvenile justice proceedings within the children's rights movement. This analysis might help to explain some of the gap between Canada's international reputation as a rights-based nation and the empty rhetoric:

> The concept of 'rights' is often seen as dangerous or threatening to the rights of the more powerful. Margaret Somerville emphasized that in practice, children's rights often lose when they come into conflict with the rights of adults... Our societies are focused on intense individualism and on our rights; and since we are adults, children get left out... The Charter does apply to children; it is just that, in practice, they cannot claim their Charter rights. Everyone has rights under the Charter, and then there is the exercise of those rights. Children are not able to exercise their own rights. Furthermore, where they conflict with adults, the adults win (Senate of Canada, 2007: 35–6).

This critical notion that the Canadian Charter of Rights and Freedoms—its Constitution—can overshadow the CRC and thereby impede its implementation was echoed by study participant 'SCL':

> Public perception of youth, public perceptions of justice, and public ignorance about rights, and fear of the same—especially youth—are the greatest barriers to rights-based restorative justice. When child rights are linked with restorative justice I hear the retort, 'I don't believe in rights, I believe in responsibilities'. My experience is that parents, police and business persons do not want children and youth to know their rights because they fear the results.
>
> Parents seem to fear the interference of state in their home—and this is about the right to punish their children the way they want to—they did not know how to respond to a youth who is asserting his or her rights. I hear from community leaders and parents 'we don't want kids to know their rights'. I've observed that power relationships change during adolescence in a family and this can be frightening. Families need good communication and peace building toolkits.

The current inequitable status of 'thick democratic citizenship' (see also Hyslop-Margison & Thayer, 2009) between adults and young people in Canada is coupled with an ongoing, almost primal fear of educating young people about their Convention rights which propels individuals within adult-centred institutions towards a focus on control. Likewise, paramilitary philosophies informing systems of juvenile justice are particularly ill-equipped to engage restorative processes that focus on the voice and full participation of young people. Adultist goals of power and control can overshadow the search for deeper understanding regarding the meaning of behaviours in conflict with the law (Bazemore & Griffiths, 2003; Moore, 2007; Moore & Mitchell, 2009; Scraton, 1997). Study participant 'SCL' recalls similar observations from direct practice:

> Parents, police, business persons did not want children and youth to know their rights. They feared the results. It is also clear that many adults don't know their rights and fear that the exercise of the rights of others (children, minorities, indigenous peoples for example) will impact on them in a negative way. The most critical tool to change these power relations is human rights education at the grassroots level—we must reach families and business persons, police and legal counsel. Training in restorative justice must also include human rights.
>
> This would be facilitated through a participatory teaching and learning approach that is empowering for participants and results in attitudes (and hopefully practice) changes. In this type of methodology everyone teaches and everyone learns. This type of philosophy is parallel with restorative justice circles in which everybody is respected for their experience and wisdom—space is made for the voice of young, old, victims and perpetrators.

Fear of human rights education is sustained by a theoretical stance that suggests young people are adults-in-waiting, incompetent and problems to be solved, and the modernist notion that rights are interpreted and doled out by those in authority. This standpoint represents an ideology of adultism that denies even the notion of human rights as 'birthright'. As study participant 'MVS' suggests:

> Some people interpret rights language to be all about self-interest... as opposed to the need to protect each other, and protect vulnerable groups like children for instance... I think rights, restorative justice and conflict transformation belong to each other, and you really can't do any of them without the other. You can't do restorative justice without living a sense of rights. And I don't think you can do rights without living a sense of restoration.

Barriers to implementing a rights-based approach juvenile justice rest solidly in power networks within adultist-centred systems and related institutions (see also Scraton, 1997: 186 for trenchant analysis). This was confirmed by participant 'RBS':

> A shift in thinking is needed. The person in authority needs to understand that they don't lose their authority or their right to be listened to or respect when they work with young people. This idea challenges them. When we listen and respect the views of young people, when we engage a restorative philosophy we increase the rights of everybody, especially young people—it's not a case of losing rights or authority...
>
> So I think that if everybody operates under that mindset, that they are going to be concerned about rights of young people because they want to have kids be involved, have a voice, be more in charge of their discipline, be accountable for themselves and their actions. It begins to foster that type of individuals—self-learning begins to take place... so you create an environment where that begins to happen, and I think that's the fertile soil in which human rights are a bit more lived out.

This same participant added that a rights-based restorative justice approach appears to offer a nuanced challenge to traditional, hierarchically oriented retributive systems: 'The more punitive-based [the] system [is], the more challenging it is to move to a rights-based or restorative culture.' Practically speaking, restorative justice requires a transparent and accountable use of power that is best guided by clearly articulated standards; yet such benchmarks are most often set by 'top-down manergerialist' structures within the legal system which contradict attempts towards a more democratic ethos (Braithwaite, 2002: 563).

14.6 Preliminary conclusions

The authors' main argument supports the notion that a rights-based approach may be applied in juvenile justice decisions by integrating core principles and relevant provisions of the UN Convention on the Rights of the Child with the UN's Basic Principles of Restorative Justice. To support this notion, the chapter has reviewed relevant policy and legal texts drawn from international and Canadian law, and presented preliminary findings from an exploratory, grounded theory investigation. Beginning in 2008, eight key stakeholders experienced in shaping both international policy and domestic practice provided in-depth interviews, and our findings offer an analysis of underlying ideologies within Canadian legal and practice systems. Clearly, such antecedents and constraints are likely present in many juvenile justice settings across the world.

Four preliminary themes emerged in the study that the authors contend illuminate ideological, political, and legislative impediments to compliance with international standards noted from the literature. First, systemic gaps in human rights education have perpetuated an ongoing misinformation surrounding core treaty principles, and the subsequent lack of CRC compliance is perhaps the country's worst-kept secret. Along with most of Canada's young people, Canadian law-makers continue to be blissfully unaware of key CRC texts, or even that the treaty exists. This knowledge gap in human rights at the macro legal and policy levels filters down to micro levels of interaction between adults in charge of institutions and young people within direct-service, care, and education. The lack of knowledge is coupled with similar deficits concerning internationally negotiated standards found within the Riyadh Guidelines (UNOHCHR, 1990); the Beijing Rules (UNOHCHR, 1985); the Vienna Guidelines (UNECOSOC, 1997); and Children's Rights in Juvenile Justice (UN Committee on the Rights of the Child, 2007). Various levels of governance are culpable in sustaining this lack of knowledge in the country, yet the perennial lack of political will by elected officials to embed CRC Article 42 in relevant legislation—such as appointing a federal Child and Youth Commissioner—are perhaps the most important to note (Senate of Canada, 2007; Canadian Coalition for the Rights of Children, 2011b).

Second, the unique role of the CRC to protect the human rights of young people under the age of 18 years has been subsumed in dominant narratives of the Canadian Charter of Fundamental Rights and Freedom. Arguably, the Constitution protects the rights of everyone in Canada while implicitly avoiding the special status of young people as equal citizens in institutional and interpersonal relations with adults. For example, the Charter was used in a 2004 Supreme Court decision as an instrument to protect the primacy of families' and educators' rights to use corporal punishment as a means of social control and discipline. Central to that argument was the notion that what constitutes the 'best interests of the child' are adult rights under the Charter notwithstanding their incongruence with newer notions of social justice for and prevention of violence against young people (see Covell, 2005; Durrant, 2007 for incisive analyses).

Third, the dominant narrative of social control as opposed to a democratic, rights-based approach under the law currently finds a comfortable home within an ethical environment that constructs young people in conflict with the law as fearful. The underlying fear of young people held by many in Canadian society is reinforced in juvenile justice contexts in which the developmental notion of innocence is wholly incongruent. Adults in legal roles of authority are quite often reluctant or unable to inform young people about their rights, and this reluctance/fear is perpetuated by the lack of associating their CRC rights with those found under the Charter of Fundamental Rights and Freedoms, and by extreme examples of young offending behaviours publicized in the mass media (for impact of such accounts, see Denov, 2007). In reality, such extreme behaviours have been on the decline in Canada for a number of years, a statistical fact simply misrepresented in the current political climate and not well understood by those outside the academic discipline of criminology (see also Moore & Mitchell, 2009).

Finally, our analysis provides evidence that restorative justice practices have a clear potential to play a more active role in reshaping democratically oriented juvenile justice decisions and, concomitantly, to play a more active role in reshaping power relations implicit in CRC implementation and monitoring. The challenge is to deploy community-based alternatives to custody in transformative ways that translate top-down, human rights legal and policy texts to the lived experiences of young people. To implement such a rights-based approach, young people in conflict with the law need to find themselves at the centre of decision-making processes (as obliged in CRC Articles 2, 3, 6, and 12 at minimum) allowing the interconnected relationships among social justice, human rights, and well-being to be reinforced in local settings (see Mitchell, 2003a, 2003b; Moore & Mitchell, 2009; also Braithwaite, 2002; White, 2002). As key informant 'KMY' articulated:

> Change is from the inside out not from the outside in—we don't want to make it impossible for young people to offend we want young people to choose not to offend. That has to come from a mutual place of respect. I recognise that in society there is at times a need to restrain people from doing harm. But while recognising that... unless people can on their own volition choose to face up to their shortcomings, to the harm they have caused, and choose to make changes and be supported in that, it will always be a short term solution.

Opportunities for the sustained criticality necessary for 'thick democracy' to take hold, for young people to be heard authentically, for victim and offender needs for equity in power relations to be safeguarded, and for offenders to have opportunities for accountability and transformation are available by integrating both frameworks to reimagine juvenile justice practices. In so doing, a rights-based restorative justice system may be gradually implemented, and may yet emerge as the preferred mode of engaging young people in conflict with the law. While Canada often benefits abroad from its reputation as a bastion of human rights—one not entirely undeserved—this premise is increasingly being called into questioned since the nation has 'made [no] substantive progress in the actual implementation of the rights of the child' (Howe, 2008: 14). Although not alone amongst UN member states in the challenge to implement rights-based approaches fully within juvenile justice, Canada has received repeated criticism from the UN Committee on the Rights of the Child (1995, 2003) and from child advocates at home and abroad for its failure to move from rhetoric to reality (Canadian Coalition for the Rights of Children 2011a, 2011b; Howe, 2008; Moore & Mitchell, 2009; Senate of Canada, 2007). Indeed, as the current federal regime continues to avoid empirical evidence at all costs with its ideologically heavy-handed approach, the upcoming Concluding Observations offer only a negligible promise for any substantive change.

References

Abramson, B., 'Juvenile Justice: The "Unwanted Child"—Why the Potential of the Convention on the Rights of the Child Is Not Being Realized, and What We Can Do About It', in E. Jensen and J. Jepsen (eds.), *Juvenile Law Violators, Human Rights, and the Development of New Juvenile Justice Systems* (Oxford: Hart, 2006).

Bazemore, G. and Griffiths, C., 'Restorative Justice and Restorative Policing', *Police Practice and Research Police Reform* 2003 (4), 335–46.

Blackstock, C., Carke, S., Cullen, J., D'Hondt, J., and Formsma, J., *Keeping the Promise: The Convention on the Rights of the Child and the Lived Experiences of First Nations Children and Youth* (Ottawa: First Nations Child and Family Caring Society of Canada, 2004); retrieved 6 November 2011, from <http://www.fncfcs.com/sites/default/files/docs/KeepingThePromise.pdf>.

Braithwaite, J., 'Setting Standards for Restorative Justice', *British Journal of Criminology* 2002 (42), 563–77.

Canadian Coalition for the Rights of Children, *Bill C-10 and Young People* (Ottawa: Canada, 2011a); retrieved 4 November 2011, from <http://rightsofchildren.ca/young-people-and-bill-c-10>.

Canadian Coalition for the Rights of Children, *Alternative Report for Canada* (Ottawa: Canada, 2011b); retrieved 4 November 2011, from <http://rightsofchildren.ca/>.

Cormier, R.B., *Restorative Justice: Directions and Principles—Developments in Canada* (Ottawa: Office of the Solicitor General, 2002); retrieved 2 November 2011, from <http://dsp-psd.pwgsc.gc.ca/Collection/JS42-107-2002E.pdf>.

Covell, K., *Violence Against Children in North America: Report to the UN Global Study on Violence* (Toronto: UNICEF Canada, 2005).

Delens-Ravier, I., 'Restorative Justice in Belgium: From Dream to Reality', in A. Ang, I. Delens-Ravier , M. Delplace, C. Herman, D. Reynaert, V. Staelens, R. Steel, and M. Verheyde (eds.), *The UN Children's Rights Convention: Theory Meets Practice. Proceedings of the International Interdisciplinary Conference on Children's Rights, Ghent, Belgium* (Antwerp: Intersentia , 2007), 585–92.

Denov, M., 'Youth Justice and Children's Rights' in R.B. Howe and K. Covell (eds.), *A Question of Commitment: Children's Rights in Canada* (Waterloo, ON: Wilfrid Laurier University, 2007).

Durrant, J., 'Corporal Punishment: A Violation of the Rights of the Child', in R.B. Howe and K. Covell (eds.), *A Question of Commitment: Children's Rights in Canada* (Waterloo, ON: Wilfrid Laurier University, 2007).

Finlay, J., Parker-Loewen, D., and Mirwald, J., Submission to the Senate Standing Committee on Human Rights, 21 February 2005 (Ottawa, Canadian Council of Provincial Child and Youth Advocates, 2005).

Freeman, M., 'Why it Remains Important to Take Children's Rights Seriously', *International Journal of Children's Rights* 2007 (15(1)), 5–23.

Glaser, B., *The Grounded Theory Perspective III: Theoretical Coding* (Mill Valley, CA: Sociology Press, 2005).

Glaser, B. and Strauss, A., *The Discovery of Grounded Theory—Strategies for Qualitative Research* (Chicago: Aldine, 1967).

Government of Canada, *Canada's Youth Criminal Justice Act* (Ottawa: Department of Justice, 2001); retrieved 2 November 2011, from <http://www.justice.gc.ca/eng/pi/yj-jj/ycja-lsjpa/back-hist.html>.

Howe, R.B., 'Children's Rights as Crime Prevention', *International Journal of Children's Rights* 2008 (16(4)), 457–74.

Howe, R.B. and Covell, K., *Empowering Children: Children's Rights Education as a Pathway to Citizenship* (Toronto: University of Toronto Press, 2005).

Hyslop-Margison, E.J. and Thayer, J., *Teaching Democracy—Citizenship Education as Critical Pedagogy* (Rotterdam, Boston, and Taipei: Sense Publishers, 2009).

Mitchell, R.C., 'Implementing Children's Rights in British Columbia Using the Population Health Framework', *International Journal of Children's Rights* 2000 (8(4)), 333–49.

Mitchell, R.C., 'Ideological Reflections on the DSM–IV–R (or "Pay no attention to that man behind the curtain, Dorothy!")', *Child and Youth Care Forum* 2003a (32), 281–98.

Mitchell, R.C., 'Canadian Health Care and Child Rights—What are the Links?', *Canadian Journal of Public Health/Revue Canadienne de Santé Publique* 2003b (94), 414–16.

Mitchell, R.C., 'Postmodern Reflections on the UNCRC: Towards Utilising Article 42 as an International Compliance Indicator', *International Journal of Children's Rights* 2005 (13), 315–31.

Mitchell, R.C., 'Towards a Transdisciplinary Model within Child and Youth Rights Education', in A. Ang, I. Delens-Ravier, M. Delplace, C. Herman, D. Reynaert, V. Staelens, R. Steel, and M. Verheyde (eds.), *The UN Children's Rights Convention: Theory Meets Practice. Proceedings of the International Interdisciplinary Conference on Children's Rights, Ghent, Belgium* (Antwerp: Intersentia, 2007).

Mitchell, R.C. and McCusker, S., 'Theorizing the UN Convention on the Rights of the Child within Canadian Post-Secondary Education: A Grounded Theory Approach', *International Journal of Children's Rights* 2008 (16(2)), 159–76.

Moore, S.A., 'Making It Right: Inciting a Rights Based Restorative Justice Dialogue in Canada for Young People', in R.B. Howe and K. Covell (eds.), *The Rights of the Child in Canada* (Waterloo, Ontario: Wilfred Laurier University, 2007).

Moore, S.A., Rights Based Restorative Practice Evaluation ToolKit (Brussels: International Juvenile Justice Observatory, 2008a); retrieved 4 November 2011, from <http://www.oijj.org/documental_ficha.php?home=SI&cod=6231&pags=0&idioma=en>.

Moore, S.A., 'Social Justice and Education in a World Fit for Children?', in J.A. Kentel and A. Short (eds.), *Totems and Taboos Risk and Relevance in Research on Teachers and Teaching* (Rotterdam, Netherlands: Sense Publications, 2008b).

Moore, S.A. and Mitchell, R.C., 'Rights Based Restorative Justice: Towards Critical Praxis with Young People in Conflict with the Law' in A. Ang, I. Delens-Ravier, M. Delplace, C. Herman, D. Reynaert, V. Staelens, R. Steel, and M. Verheyde (eds.), *The UN Children's Rights Convention: Theory Meets Practice. Proceedings of the International Interdisciplinary Conference on Children's Rights, Ghent, Belgium* (Antwerp: Intersentia, 2007a).

Moore, S.A. and Mitchell, R.C., 'Herstelrecht volgens de mensenrechtenprincipes' (or 'Rights-based Restorative Justice'), *Het Tijdschrift voor Jeugdrecht en Kinderrechten* 2007b (5(4)), 251–9.

Moore, S.A. and Mitchell, R.C., 'Rights-Based Restorative Justice: Evaluating Compliance with International Standards', *Youth Justice* 2009 (9(1)), 27–43.

Moore, S.A., Tulk, W., and Mitchell, R.C., 'Qallunaat Crossing: The Southern-Northern Divide and Promising Practices for Canada's Inuit Young People', *First Peoples Child and Family Review* 2005 (2(1)), 117–29.

Muncie, J., 'The Globalization of Crime Control: The Case of Youth and Juvenile Justice: Neo-liberalism, Policy Convergence and International Conventions', *Theoretical Criminology* 2005 (9(1)), 35–64.

Nyp, G., *Pioneers of Peace: The History of Community Justice Initiatives in the Waterloo Region, 1974–2004* (Kitchener: Community Justice Initiatives, 2004).

Raby, R., 'Polite, Well-dressed and on Time: Secondary School Conduct Codes and the Production of Docile Citizens', *Canadian Review of Sociology and Anthropology* 2005 (42(1)), 71–92.

Raby, R, 'Frustrated, Resigned, Outspoken: Students' Engagement with School Rules and some Implications for Participatory Citizenship', *International Journal of Children's Rights* 2008 (16(1)), 77–98.

Roche, J., 'Children's Rights, Participation and Citizenship', *Childhood* 1999 (6(4)), 475–93.

Scraton, P. (ed.), *'Childhood' in "Crisis"?* (London: Routledge, 1997).

Senate of Canada, Standing Committee on Human Rights, *Children: The Silenced Citizens. Final Report on Implementation of Canada's International Obligations with Respect to the Rights of Children* (Ottawa: Senate of Canada, 2007); retrieved 2 November 2011, from <http://www.parl.gc.ca/Content/SEN/Committee/391/huma/rep/rep10apr07-e.pdf>.

Simpson, J. '"Tough on Crime" Agenda—There is no crime epidemic', *Globe & Mail*, 4 November 2011, p. A-19; retrieved 6 November 2011, from <http://m.theglobeandmail.com/news/opinions/jeffrey-simpson/there-is-no-crime-epidemic/article2224613/?service=mobile>.

Tomaševski, K., 'Are We Educating Children as People with Rights or Just Talking About It?' in A. Ang, I. Delens-Ravier, M. Delplace, C. Herman, D. Reynaert, V. Staelens, R. Steel, and M. Verheyde (eds.), *The UN Children's Rights Convention: Theory Meets Practice. Proceedings of the International Interdisciplinary Conference on Children's Rights, Ghent, Belgium* (Antwerp: Intersentia, 2007).

United Nations, *Convention on the Rights of the Child* (New York: United Nations, 1989).

United Nations Committee on the Rights of the Child, *Concluding Observations of the Committee on the Right of the Child: Canada* (Geneva: UNOHCHR, 1995); retrieved 2 November 2011, from <http://daccess-dds-ny.un.org/doc/UNDOC/GEN/G95/170/93/PDF/G9517093.pdf?OpenElement>.

United Nations Committee on the Rights of the Child, *Concluding Observations of the Committee on the Rights of the Child: Canada* (Geneva: UNOHCHR, 2003); retrieved 2 November 2011, from <http://daccess-dds-ny.un.org/doc/UNDOC/GEN/G03/446/48/PDF/G0344648.pdf?OpenElement>.

United Nations Committee on the Rights of the Child, *Convention on the Rights of the Child, General Comment no. 10 (2007): Children's Rights in Juvenile Justice* (Geneva: UNOHCHR, 2007).

United Nations Economic and Social Council, *UN Resolution 1197/30: Administration of Juvenile Justice: The Vienna Guidelines* (Geneva: ECOSOC, 1997).

United Nations Economic and Social Council, *UN Basic Principles on the Use of Restorative Justice Programmes in Criminal Matters* (Geneva: ECOSOC, 2002); retrieved 2 November 2011, from <http://www.un.org/en/ecosoc/docs/2002/resolution%202002-12.pdf>.

United Nations Office of Drugs and Crime, *Handbook on Restorative Justice Programmes: Criminal Justice Handbook Series* (Vienna: United Nations, 2006).

United Nations Office of the High Commissioner for Human Rights, *United Nations Standard Minimum Rules for the Administration of Juvenile Justice: The Beijing Rules* (UNOHCHR: United Nations, 1985).

United Nations Office of the High Commissioner for Human Rights, *United Nations Guidelines for the Prevention of Juvenile Delinquency: The Riyadh Guidelines* (Geneva: UNOHCHR, 1990).

United Nations Office of the High Commissioner for Human Rights, *United Nations Decade for Human Rights Education* (Geneva: UNOHCHR, 1998).

Van Ness, D., 'An Overview of Restorative Justice around the World', Paper presented at the United Nations 11th Congress on Crime Prevention and Criminal Justice, Bangkok,

Thailand (22 April 2005); retrieved 4 November 2011, from <http://www.icclr.law.ubc.ca/Publications/Reports/11_un/Dan%20van%20Ness%20final%20paper.pdf>.
White, S., 'Being Becoming and Relationship', *Journal of International Development* 2002 (14), 1095–104.
Zehr, H., *Changing Lenses: A Focus on Crime and Justice* (Scottsdale, PA: Herald Press, 1995).

15

New Zealand Children and Young People's Perspectives on Relocation Following Parental Separation

Megan Gollop and Nicola Taylor[1]

15.1 Introduction

Relocation disputes following parental separation are difficult to resolve by parents and the Family Court alike. Such disputes arise when the resident parent seeks to relocate with the children and that move will have a significant impact on the contact the children will have with their non-resident parent. In recent years these disputes have prompted greater domestic and international attention due to the higher rates of relationship breakdown, increased population mobility, and debate about whether the courts should allow or restrict relocations. We have recently completed a three-year study interviewing 100 New Zealand families where one parent sought to relocate. This chapter reports on interviews we conducted with children and young people from these families about their experiences. Ascertaining their unique perspectives is consistent with Childhood Studies that places children's own views at the heart of research enquiry. The research literature on the impact of parental separation and relocation is first reviewed, with particular emphasis on studies that focus on children and young people's perspectives on these issues. We then outline and discuss the themes that emerged from the interviews with the children and young people who took part in our study.

[1] *University of Otago, Dunedin, New Zealand.* The authors would like to express their appreciation to the parents and children who participated in this study and to the New Zealand Law Foundation for generously funding the project.

15.2 The effects of parental separation on children

There is now a substantial body of research examining the impact of parental separation on children. Several early reviews of the research evidence have concluded that parental separation does pose a risk to children's well-being.[2] However, while short-term distress at the time of the separation is common, long-term negative outcomes are only experienced by a minority of children whose parents separate. These children, however, are at approximately twice the risk of having adverse outcomes than those children from intact families.[3] Essentially, the majority of children from separated families do not experience long-term negative outcomes, but as a group, children whose parents have separated or divorced are more likely than those from intact families to have poorer outcomes.

The contemporary approach is more concerned with evaluating which factors contribute to poorer outcomes for children and which ones act as buffers or protective mechanisms—a risk and resilience perspective[4] that views parental separation as a stressor for children. It is now also widely recognized that separation and divorce is not a discrete event but rather an ongoing process of family transition and adjustment which children and young people negotiate.[5] As such, the impact of separation on children and their adjustment to it is also an ongoing process with 'multiple changes and potential challenges for children'.[6] It is the presence of unalleviated or multiple stressors that can increase the risk of adverse outcomes for children[7] with the number of stressors that children experience predicting their post-separation well-being and adjustment.[8]

Many such stressors have been identified including: inter-parental conflict, loss of important relationships, economic hardship, poor parental adjustment and parenting competence, remarriage or repartnering, and stressful or negative life experiences, such as the initial separation, moving, or changing schools.[9] Protective factors that can moderate these risk factors include: support from family and friends, the child's coping skills and resilience, therapeutic support, competent parenting, contact with non-resident parents, diminished inter-parental conflict, the quality of the parent-child relationship, and parents' ability to co-parent authoritatively.[10] It is therefore the particular combination of risk and protective factors in each child's individual situation that will determine how their parents'

[2] B. Rodgers and J. Pryor, *Divorce and Separation: The Outcomes for Children* (York, Joseph Rowntree Foundation, 1998); P. R. Amato and B. Keith, 'Parental Divorce and the Well-being of Children: A Meta-analysis' (1991) 110 *Psychological Bulletin* 26.

[3] Rodgers and Pryor, N. 2, above.

[4] J. B. Kelly and R. E. Emery, 'Children's Adjustment Following Divorce: Risk and Resilience Perspective' (2003) 52 *Family Relations* 352.

[5] Rodgers and Pryor, N. 2, above.

[6] N. 4, above, 352.

[7] N. 4, above.

[8] P. R. Amato, 'The Consequences of Divorce for Adults and Children' (2000) 62 *Journal of Marriage and Family* 1269.

[9] N. 4, above; N. 8, above.

[10] N. 4, above; P. R. Amato, 'Parenting Through Family Transitions' (2004) 23 *Social Policy Journal of New Zealand* 31.

separation will initially impact on them and will then affect their adjustment and well-being over time.

15.3 Relocation following parental separation

One particularly significant risk factor for children following their parents' separation is relocation. Residential mobility is often an inevitable consequence of relationship breakdown, with divorced parents being far more likely to shift and to change residences more often than those who remain married.[11] However, children tend to act as anchors in their separated parents' movement decisions. So while moving is common, the distance is usually restricted to enable each parent to continue playing a role in their child's life.[12] Legal disputes over relocation therefore arise when the distance is much greater and will affect the child's ability to retain contact easily with their non-moving parent.

When a child relocates to another location they leave behind their school, neighbourhood, friends, and their non-moving parent, which can be a disruptive and stressful life event, increasing instability in the child's life. Moving may impact on the continuity a child can have in their relationship with their non-resident parent and may erode other important relationships in their lives, which can remove some of the protective factors identified above, such as peer support.[13]

The risk of negative outcomes due to parental separation may also be increased by the reduction in social capital available to children—the social capital of the family is disrupted when one parent leaves the household, and also the community-based social capital is withdrawn.[14]

However, there may be beneficial outcomes for children who relocate. If children are relocating to a location in close proximity to extended family this will increase the family's social capital. Children may benefit from the challenges and opportunities presented by a new neighbourhood and school and a relocation may also serve as a means of reducing harmful exposure to parental conflict if the move puts distance between conflicted parents. In addition, if a resident parent's well-being is enhanced by the move, then this may impact positively on their parenting competence and relationship with their child, thereby having a positive impact on the child's adjustment and well-being.[15]

While there is substantial research literature on the effects of residential mobility on children in intact families and following parental separation, the findings are

[11] A. Booth and P. Amato, 'Divorce, Residential Change, and Stress' (1992) 18 *Journal of Divorce & Remarriage* 205; W. G. Austin, 'Relocation, Research, and Forensic Evaluation, Part 1: Effects of Residential Mobility on Children of Divorce' (2008) 46 *Family Court Review* 137.

[12] Bruce Smyth, Jeromey Temple, Juliet Behrens, Rae Kaspiew, and Nick Richardson, 'Post-separation Geographic Mobility in Australia: Some Preliminary Data on Behaviour, Disputes and Attitudes' in (eds.) Juliet Behrens, Bruce Smyth, and Rae Kaspiew, *Symposium Proceedings: Relocation Disputes in Australia: What Do We Know, What are the Implications for Family Law and Policy*? (Canberra, The Australian National University, 2008), 13.

[13] N. 10, above.

[14] S. J. South, K. D. Crowder and K. Trent, 'Children's Residential Mobility and Neighborhood Environment following Parental Divorce and Remarriage' (1998) 77 *Social Forces* 667.

[15] W. G. Austin, 'Relocation, Research, and Forensic Evaluation, Part II: Research in Support of the Relocation Risk Assessment Model' (2008) 46 *Family Court Review* 347; J. B. Kelly and M. E. Lamb, 'Developmental Issues in Relocation Cases Involving Young Children: When, Whether, and How?' (2003) 17 *Journal of Family Psychology* 193.

somewhat mixed.[16] Some studies reveal beneficial effects of relocating while others report negative outcomes for children.[17] The research in this field is highly diverse and negative outcomes associated with relocation may be explained by other factors that lead to frequent residential mobility.[18]

Overall, research findings indicate 'heightened risk' for a child who relocates, particularly when there have been multiple moves and changes to family structure,[19] which can increase or exacerbate the instability and disruption created by parental separation.[20] The risk of negative outcomes can be heightened by such factors as moving due to family disruption, a negative parental attitude towards the move, the number of moves and their frequency, the distance moved, and the existence of multiple stressors.[21]

Children from separated families are regarded as being at greater risk of adjustment problems after a residential move. Similar to the research findings outlined above in relation to the impact of separation on children, whether a relocation will have a positive or negative impact on children depends on many variables,[22] and will be determined by the combination of risk and protective factors present in each individual case.[23] The principles and factors to be taken into account are generally identified in various statutes, case law, professional commentaries, and custody evaluation protocols.[24] However, no research has yet been conducted to specifically identify the key risk and protective factors which can account for individual differences in outcomes for children who relocate after their parents' separation or who are the subject of a relocation dispute.

Relocation disputes are widely regarded as one of the most difficult and controversial issues in family law internationally.[25] New Zealand relocation law applies to proposed moves within and between provinces of New Zealand, as well as internationally. The child's welfare and best interests are the paramount consideration and there is no presumption for or against relocation in statute or in the case law. New Zealand guardians must agree on a change of the child's residence that may affect the child's relationship with their parents or guardians.[26] If they cannot agree,

[16] For a review see B. Horsfall and R. Kaspiew, 'Relocation in Separated and Non-Separated Families: Equivocal Research Evidence From Social Science Literature' (2010) 24 *Australian Journal of Family Law* 34.

[17] N. Taylor and M. Freeman, 'International Research Evidence on Relocation: Past, Present and Future' (2010) 44 *Family Law Quarterly* 317.

[18] N. 16, above.

[19] J. Kelly, 'Relocation of Children Following Separation and Divorce: Challenges for Children and Considerations for Judicial Decision-Making' (2009), Paper presented at the 5th World Congress on Family Law and Children's Rights, 23–6 August, Halifax, Canada.

[20] K. Waldron, 'A Review of Social Science Research on Post Divorce Relocation' (2005) 19 *Journal of the American Academy of Matrimonial Lawyers* 337; Austin, N. 11, above, 142.

[21] C. Humke and C. Schaefer, 'Relocation: A Review of the Effects of Residential Mobility on Children and Adolescents' (1995) 32 *Psychology, A Journal of Human Behaviour* 16.

[22] M. Gindes, 'The Psychological Effects of Relocation for Children of Divorce' (1998) 15 *Journal of the American Academy of Matrimonial Lawyers* 119.

[23] Austin, N. 11, above.

[24] See, for example, W. D. Duggan, 'Rock-paper-scissors: Playing the Odds with the Law of Child Relocation' (2007) 45 *Family Court Review* 193, who identifies 36 factors distilled from American Court decisions on relocation.

[25] M. Thorpe, 'Relocation—The Search for Common Principles' (2010) 1 *Journal of Family Law and Practice* 36.

[26] Section 16(2)(b) Care of Children Act 2004.

permission for the proposed relocation must be obtained from the Family Court.[27] This approach contrasts with the situation in England/Wales where permission is required only for international relocations or where a court has made a prohibited steps order. Moves within the United Kingdom are usually regarded as the prerogative of the parent who is primarily caring for the child. Clear policy differences are thus evident between these jurisdictions. In England/Wales, applicants are routinely granted permission to relocate based on the likely effect of a 'refusal of the application on the mother's future psychological and emotional stability'.[28] Conversely, in New Zealand the courts tend to refuse more applications as they work through a broader range of statutory principles to take account of the child's relationship with others and their current environment.[29]

15.4 Childhood Studies and children's perspectives

Much of the research on the impact of separation and relocation is focused on outcomes for children, with children constructed as the passive victims of their parents' separation and regarded as objects of the research rather than as subjects.

The interdisciplinary field of Childhood Studies challenges views of children as incompetent, passive recipients in need of protection and instead constructs them as social actors who have their own purposes and meanings, and are capable of expressing their own views. This conceptual framework has given rise to research that emphasizes children's own accounts and perspectives, the aim of which has been to 'do research *with* children rather than *on* or *about* them and in the process, to give their views legitimacy'.[30] In order to more fully understand the impact of separation and divorce, children should therefore be the subjects of research rather than the objects.[31]

A small body of qualitative, child-centred research now exists which investigates and explores children's lived experiences and accounts of their parents' separation and subsequent family transitions. This research shows that children and young people are highly capable of reflecting on their experiences and articulately expressing their views on family transitions following parental separation. While children do report the distressing nature of experiencing the separation of their parents, they also demonstrate resilience and adjustment over time.[32]

[27] By an application under section 47(1)(a) Care of Children Act 2004 for a parenting order with a condition that the child may move, or by an application under section 44 of the Act for the Court to resolve a dispute between guardians.

[28] 'In most relocation cases the most crucial assessment and finding for the judge is likely to be the effect of the refusal of the application on the mother's future psychological and emotional stability' *Payne v Payne* [2001] EWCA 166, [2001] 1 WLR 1826, para 32 per Thorpe LJ.

[29] Nicola Taylor, Megan Gollop, and Mark Henaghan, *Relocation Following Parental Separation: The Welfare and Best Interests of Children* (Dunedin, University of Otago, 2010). The importance of the six principles set out in section 5 Care of Children Act 2004 as relevant to a child's welfare and best interests has also been affirmed by the NZ Supreme Court in its recent decision of *Kacem v Bashir* [2010] NZSC 112.

[30] Carol Smart, Bren Neale, and Amanda Wade, *The Changing Experience of Childhood: Families and Divorce* (Cambridge, Polity Press, 2001), 14.

[31] Kari Moxnes, 'Children Coping With Parental Divorce: What Helps, What Hurts?' in (eds.) An-Margritt Jensen and Laura McKee, *Children and the Changing Family: Between Transformation and Negotiation* (London, Routledge/Falmer, 2003), 90.

[32] Ann Marie Halpenny, Shelia Greene, and Diane Hogan, *Children's Perspectives on Coping and Support Following Parental Separation* (Dublin, School of Social Sciences and Law, Dublin Institute

Two common themes arising from this line of research focus on children's knowledge and understanding of their parents' separation and the degree to which children were consulted on and participated in any family decisions that affected them. Having information in order to help understand and cope with their family transition is important to children.[33] Children who are denied information express anger and resentment[34] or feel confused and distressed.[35] Children also emphasize the importance of being consulted on and participating in decisions which impact on their lives.[36] The degree to which children are consulted, listened to, or able to influence contact or residence arrangements impacts on their satisfaction with such arrangements.[37] Children can feel disempowered if they lack information about family transitions in which they are embroiled and need this information and understanding to be able to form their views and contribute to family and legal decision-making processes.

Another theme emerging from the research ascertaining children's perspectives is the support children and young people have in helping them to deal with their parents' separation. Friends are commonly reported as an important source of support,[38] and as key confidants[39] for children, especially at a time when parents may be too consumed by their own pain and distress to provide their children with the support they need. In addition to being a listening ear for children, friends can also help by acting as a source of distraction by involving children in activities that take their minds off their upsetting family situation.[40] Friends can be 'accessed independently, without adult knowledge and at the child's initiative' and can offer 'non-judgemental, egalitarian support, along with the opportunity for a reciprocal exchange of experiences' in a confidential, safe space with no consequences.[41]

of Technology, 2008); I. Butler, L. Scanlan, M. Robinson, G. Douglas, and M. Murch, 'Children's Involvement in their Parents' Divorce: Implications for Practice' (2002) 16 *Children & Society* 89; Margaret Robinson, Ian Butler, Lesley Scanlan, Gillian Douglas, and Mervyn Murch, 'Children's Experience of their Parents' Divorce' in (eds.) An-Margritt Jensen and Laura McKee, *Children and the Changing Family: Between Transformation and Negotiation* (London, Routledge/Falmer, 2003), 76.

[33] Robinson et al., N. 32 above; A. B. Smith and M. M. Gollop, 'What Children Think Separating Parents Should Know' (2001) 30 *New Zealand Journal of Psychology* 23.

[34] Halpenny et al., N. 32, above.

[35] Judy Dunn and Kirby Deater-Deckard, *Children's Views of their Changing Families* (Layerthorpe, York, Joseph Rowntree Foundation, 2001).

[36] M. M. Gollop, A. B. Smith, and N. J. Taylor, 'Children's Involvement in Custody and Access Arrangements After Parental Separation' (2000) 12 *Child and Family Law Quarterly* 383; C. Smart and B. Neale, '"It's my life too"—Children's Perspectives on Post-Divorce Parenting' (2000) March *Family Law* 163; Smith and Gollop, N. 33, above; Butler et al., N. 32, above; J. Cashmore and P. Parkinson, 'Children's and Parents' Perceptions on Children's Participation in Decision Making After Parental Separation and Divorce' (2008) 46 *Family Court Review* 91.

[37] Butler et al., N. 32, above; Gollop et al., N. 36, above; Robinson et al., N. 32, above; P. Parkinson, J. Cashmore, and J. Single, 'Adolescents' Views on the Fairness of Parenting and Financial Arrangements After Separation' (2005) 43 *Family Court Review* 429.

[38] Butler et al., N. 32, above; Ian Butler, Lesley Scanlan, Margaret Robinson, Gillian Douglas, and Mervyn Murch, *Divorcing Children: Children's Experiences of their Parents' Divorce* (London, Jessica Kingsley, 2003); Robinson et al., N. 32, above; Diane Hogan, Ann Marie Halpenny, and Shelia Greene, *Children's Experiences of Parental Separation* (Dublin, Children's Research Centre, Trinity College Dublin, 2002); Dunn and Deater-Deckard, N. 35, above.

[39] Dunn and Deater-Deckard, N. 35, above; J. Dunn, L. C. Davies, T. G. O'Connor, and W. Sturgess, 'Family Lives, and Friendships: The Perspectives of Children in Step-, Single Parent, and Nonstep Families' (2001) 15 *Journal of Family Psychology* 272; Butler et al., N. 32, above.

[40] Hogan et al., N. 38, above.

[41] B. Neale, 'Dialogues with Children: Children, Divorce and Citizenship' (2002) 9 *Childhood* 455, at 464.

Grandparents too are regarded by children and young people as an important source of support.[42] The close physical proximity of extended family (particularly grandparents) living nearby[43] and emotional closeness to maternal grandparents is reported to contribute to better child adjustment.[44]

Until recently, children's perspectives have been largely absent from the published literature on residential mobility, yet they provide a unique insight into the impact of relocation following parental separation by those most directly affected.

A few studies reporting on children's perspectives of parental separation touch on children's feelings and experiences of moving. Moxnes[45] found that children described changing residences as difficult, particularly if they moved to a new location and had to make new friends and settle into a new community. This difficulty was heightened if the distance moved negated frequent contact with their friends and if their parents were unable or unwilling to assist their children with this transition and help them maintain their old friendships. However, those children who were well informed and prepared for the move and had been able to maintain contact with friends fared better.

Hogan, Halpenny, and Greene[46] also reported that moving house was an important change for children, which some children said they had difficulty adjusting to. Moving to another location impacted on their friendships, contact with non-resident parents and grandparents. Those children who had to regularly travel in order to have contact with their non-resident parent found the travel a strain but saw it as necessary in order to maintain their relationship.

Continuity and normality at the time of their parents' separation was valued by children in a study by Butler, Scanlan, Robinson, Douglas, and Murch.[47] Remaining at the same school and keeping in contact with friends was therefore very important to the children. Some children feared having to change schools and losing their friends. Norford and Medway found that adolescents cited leaving existing friends and having to make new ones as the worst aspect of relocating.[48]

However, none of these studies specifically focus on the issue of children and young people's perspectives on relocation following parental separation. Until very recently no such research existed. However, in the last few years, two socio-legal qualitative research projects have been undertaken in New Zealand[49] and Australia[50] that directly seek the perspectives of children (and parents) about a relocation dispute and/or moving subsequent to parental separation.

This chapter reports on data from one of these projects conducted in New Zealand during 2007–2009. This research was the first undertaken in New Zealand on relocation, and amongst the first worldwide to explore family members' perspectives on this issue. The purpose of our study was to explore families' experiences of a post-separation relocation dispute and we now turn to outline the methodology and report on the findings from our interviews with 44 children and young people.

[42] Robinson et al., N. 32, above; Butler et al., N. 38, above; Butler, et al., N. 32, above; Hogan et al., N. 38, above; Dunn and Deater-Deckard, N. 35, above.

[43] Butler et al., N. 38, above.

[44] Dunn and Deater-Deckard, N. 35, above.

[45] Moxnes, N. 31, above, 90.

[46] Hogan et al., N. 38, above.

[47] Butler, et al., N. 32, above; Butler et al., N. 38, above.

[48] B. Norford and F. Medway, 'Adolescents' Mobility Histories and Present Social Adjustment' (2002) 39 *Psychology in the Schools* 51.

[49] Funded by the New Zealand Law Foundation. See Taylor et al., N. 29, above.

[50] The Australian Research Council is funding a prospective, longitudinal study of relocation being undertaken by Patrick Parkinson, Judy Cashmore, and Judi Single at the University of Sydney.

15.5 Method

15.5.1 Participants

One hundred New Zealand families took part in our study on relocation following parental separation. Families were recruited where a parent had relocated (or sought to relocate) with the children, and that move would have a significant impact on contact arrangements with the other parent. This recruitment was achieved through family lawyers, newspaper articles and advertisements, and word of mouth.

The participants included 114 parents (73 mothers and 41 fathers; in 14 families both parents took part), and 44 children (23 girls and 21 boys) from 30 of the 100 families. The children and young people ranged in age from 7.6 to 18.1 years (mean age = 12.1 years). The parents of the majority (77 per cent) of the children and young people described their children's ethnicity as European; 16 per cent of children were identified as Māori and European; two per cent as Māori, and five per cent were described as Asian.

Three-quarters of the children and young people had experienced a residential move as a result of a relocation 'issue'; while the remaining 25 per cent had not. For seven of the 33 children who had moved, the move was not permanent. For those children and young people who had moved, seven could recall an international move. Several children had had multiple relocations (some which did not impact on their contact with their other parent) and seven had had several multiple international relocations—either moving to or from New Zealand more than once.

At the time of the interview, the majority (91 per cent) of the children and young people had a parent who lived in a different country, city, or town from themselves, with nine per cent living in the same location as both of their parents.[51] Ten children (from seven families) had parents who lived in a different country.

15.5.2 Data collection

While the parents were interviewed twice, separated by 12–18 months, the majority of the children and young people were interviewed at the time of their parents' first interview.

Most of the children and young people were interviewed at one of their parents' homes—64 per cent were interviewed at their resident parent's home; 14 per cent at their contact parent's home; 11 per cent of the children had a shared care arrangement and were interviewed at one of their homes, with the remaining 11 per cent of the children and young people coming into our University research centre for their interview.

Most often the children and young people spoke with the interviewer by themselves; however, 16 children from six families chose to be interviewed with their siblings, and six spoke to the interviewer with one of their parents present. The children's interviews were around 20–30 minutes in duration.

The interviews with the children and young people covered their:

- family and living arrangements;
- knowledge and understanding about their parents' separation;

[51] Either the proposed relocation had not proceeded or in some cases the non-resident parent followed their children or the resident parent and/or children had returned.

- current and past contact and residence arrangements and how they felt about these;
- knowledge of and involvement in the relocation decision;
- experience and understanding of any professionals involved;
- experiences of moving if applicable;
- advice they would give other children and parents in similar circumstances.

The interviews with the children and young people were transcribed and a content analysis of the transcripts undertaken to identify common themes. The themes emerging from these interviews are outlined below and focus on: children's understanding of the (proposed) relocation; their initial reaction to hearing about the relocation; their adjustment to the relocation; positive experiences; negative aspects; changing schools; what helps children adjust; children's contact and relationships with their non-resident parents; consultation and amount of say the children had; their experience and understanding of legal processes and professionals; and advice for children.

15.6 Findings

15.6.1 Understanding about the relocation

Generally, the children and young people[52] demonstrated a good understanding of why the relocation occurred and their parent's motivation for wishing to move. These reasons usually matched the parent's actual motivation for the move. They could see that their resident parent wished to move to make a fresh start, to get away from their other parent, or to be with a new partner, for employment/career opportunities, or to obtain family support. Some of the children showed an understanding of the emotional needs of their parents, describing how their parents were stressed or in need of support:

I think Mum wanted to get away from it all.... I just remember it being hard and Mum was stressed all the time.... I think Mum needed to get back into life and so she came here and got a good job and life was fine for her. (Will, aged 17)

Mum was scared of Dad. She was being real scared. (Charlie, aged 8)

I think it was just because probably Mum was struggling a bit and so she probably needed her parents' support, with me. (Laura, aged 14)

As well as generally understanding why their resident parent wished to relocate, the children could also see their other parent's perspective, particularly how hard it was for the left-behind parent:

I remember getting up at like three o'clock in the morning to leave for the plane. It was the first time I saw my Dad cry.... I was just like, 'Whoa, he's crying'.... He wasn't very happy. (Louise, aged 13)

Dad came home [after Court decision]. He wasn't happy when he got home.... Sitting on the couch hugging and listening to him talk to us telling us, and he was crying. (Chloe, aged 11)

52 The children's names and any identifying details have been changed to preserve their, and their family's, anonymity.

15.6.2 Initial reaction to hearing about the relocation

Generally, the prospect of moving was regarded positively. The children and young people spoke of being excited and happy to be moving, seeing it as an adventure, with new experiences and opportunities. Other children reported that they were sad or nervous, while some reported mixed emotions, feeling both excited but also sad about leaving friends and family behind:

I was kind of excited... but also a bit sad just to leave everything here.... It was going to be cool but it wasn't that great leaving everything. (Jacob, aged 16)

Some of the children reported a negative reaction to the news they were moving, but said they were happier about it by the time of the actual move and had begun to look forward to it:

Oh, when Mum told me I burst out crying. I remember that.... Cos I had all my friends, but when I was going I think I'd got a bit used to it so it was fine. (Laura, aged 14)

15.6.3 Children's adjustment to the relocation

One of the most common themes that emerged from the interviews with the children and young people was an acceptance of and satisfaction with their current situations. However, it should be noted that the parents of children who had had a particularly difficult and/or traumatic experience did not tend to give consent for their children's participation in our study.

Several children described a relatively easy relocation. For example, Jenny (aged 16) had had a very smooth adjustment to living in a different country:

It was good. They were all really nice friendly people over there and they made it really easy to get settled in and going to a new school wasn't too bad. Everything went quite nicely for me. (Jenny, aged 16)

For her the good things about relocating included:

Just meeting the people, sort of going to a new school, getting along with everyone really well and playing new sports and just having a real good time I think. We just settled in really fast and everything went really nicely.... I don't know if I would change anything actually because it was pretty awesome everything that we did, and getting to go around the world. It was really cool. (Jenny, aged 16)

Only two of the children and young people reported a predominantly negative experience. The Family Court refused to allow Nina (aged 13) to relocate with her mother when she was younger and she was placed in her father's care despite a strong desire to move with her mother. Nina was very unhappy living with her father and felt unwanted, unloved, and that she was 'a burden on people' and described her experience as 'being through hell'. Rachel (aged 14) was struggling with her recent move and thought that moving:

Stuffs you up big time. It sucks so much.... and it hurts your family so bad. (Rachel, aged 14)

However, the majority of the children seemed relatively happy and liked where they lived. While some children acknowledged that things had been difficult for them initially, they reported growing accustomed to their new lives and being relatively satisfied with their current situations. Much of the advice that the children said they would give other children and young people facing a similar situation focused on a reassurance that moving was not so bad and that things would turn out fine:

I'd probably say you just get used to it. It might be hard in the beginning but you'll get used to it. You'll be able to see your parents hopefully. (Laura, aged 14)

I'd probably say to them it's actually not as bad as you think.... I just think it's actually not that bad.... Like it's not that hard as long as they stay close. (Chloe, aged 11)

If you're like scared that everything's going to change, it doesn't actually change. Your parents still love you. But it's not actually a big deal when you get the hang of it. It's actually just a small little thing like breaking a pencil, or breaking a pencil tip. (Adam, aged 11)

I think it's like just trust in [the place you move to]. Like you've got to know that you're still going to have contact with your parents and stuff but it's going to be hard for the first few years. But you've just got to trust [the place], make friends and just try and settle in as easy as you can. (Will, aged 17)

Some of the children did report difficulties at the time of the relocation but could see in hindsight that things had worked out well for them. In some instances the children reported that while it was hard initially, they were now in a better situation and the move was ultimately beneficial. Many could also see both good and bad things about the relocation:

It's pretty hard moving away.... It would have made it easier if Mum didn't have to move so far away, but then again that's one of the things I liked so much about it. It was kind of sad leaving, but it was a pretty good experience in the end for us.... Highs and lows, ups and downs, but I think the positives would almost outweigh the negatives. (Jacob, aged 16)

As illustrated above, the children and young people could generally identify both beneficial and detrimental aspects about relocating and/or living in a different location to one of their parents. Since the children were generally happy about the moves they had experienced there were relatively more positive than negative issues reported in the interviews.

15.6.4 Positive aspects of relocating

Many positive factors about moving that the children described related to where they had moved to, with some preferring their new location to the place they had left. For some it was about the actual location, such as it having better weather or a slower, more relaxed pace of life, or there being more to do. For other children, feeling safer and more secure, or no longer being bullied or socially isolated was the reason they preferred their new location.

Several children liked the contrast between the two different locations their parents lived in. This meant they got to experience and enjoy two different lifestyles in each parent's location and to also have experiences they might not otherwise have had, particularly those whose parents lived overseas:

It was real good cos I was travelling across the world. One time we stopped off in Los Angeles for two weeks and did the whole Disneyland thing which was awesome. And you can go the other way through Singapore and you get to see all the different countries. (Fraser, aged 16)

I went to Euro Disney and Lego Land. When I go to London, I go there every year. Usually once a year we go to Spain with my grandparents cos they have a holiday house down there. (Daniel, aged 7)

You get to experience two different lives kind of. And you meet new people. (Kylie, aged 14)

I kind of get a city life and a country life. Bit of both. (Sophie, aged 11)

Many of the positive aspects about relocating that the children identified emphasized the importance of family, particularly moving to a location where lots of extended family members lived:

I loved it there. Cos we've got heaps of family and... we had heaps of cousins. It was great fun. (Ross, aged 15)

When we moved down there it was kind of like a big impact cos we never see our family very much and we were living with them all of a sudden. It was a good thing. It was really cool. (Paige, aged 10)

Making new friends was regarded as a positive feature about moving, particularly for those children who may have been bullied or did not have many friends at their old schools. For these children, relocating had meant a fresh start.

15.6.5 Negative aspects of relocating

As noted earlier, the children did not report many things that they did not like about relocating. However, a couple of children disliked the place they had moved to, either not liking their new school or being bullied and feeling threatened in their new location. Others found that only having one parent in close proximity was difficult, as it meant that that parent had all the say about decisions involving them.

Large distances between their parents' homes was hard for some children as it meant long travelling times and hindered their ability to visit family. Leaving family behind was frequently mentioned as a difficult consequence of relocating:

Just leaving Dad I think and friends. Just leaving everything behind, everything you'd sort of known. [Saying goodbye to] all the family, pretty tough. (Jacob, aged 16)

I was a bit sad because I was going to leave my Dad and lots of my friends down there.... I had my grandparents, my Dad, my cousins and my aunties there. (Sean, aged 11)

By far the most commonly cited negative aspect of relocating (or reason for not wishing to move) was having to move away from friends:

I had this one girl, we'd known each other since we were like three and we absolutely adored each other and then we moved away. But we're still in contact. (Paige, aged 10)

My friends in [town] were probably the best friends I've ever had, and it was hard moving away from them. (Will, aged 17)

I wanted to stay in [city] cos that's where all my friends are. They did [ask me what I wanted] and I wanted to stay down here cos that's where my friends are. (Sam, aged 11)

I was kind of sad, cos my best friend was there, and I don't get to see her until the holidays. (Chloe, aged 11)

An inevitable consequence of moving for many of the children and young people was starting a new school. Some found this daunting at the beginning, but most came to enjoy their new schools. However, a few of the children had found it difficult changing schools. The first day at a new school could be particularly hard:

Then going to a new school... you always dread the first day of school. (Jacob, aged 16)

It was really hard for me moving schools. I didn't actually know what was going on. Didn't know much people. Here, I know lots of people and it's like a totally different world. (Sally, aged 9)

*Cos it was like really f***ing horrible on the first day.... It's like totally different.... I hate school. It's horrible... Like in my old school it was so easy going. Like down here, it's so uptight.* (Chris, aged 14)

Well, it was pretty rough there... I felt good at first but then about a year later I got bullied lots, so yeah, in four years there I learnt to put up with people who are just really mean. Cos like everyone there was like that, except for some people. (Sean, aged 11)

Just settling into a new school again [was hard]. We got moved around quite a lot as kids. I think [brother] had it a bit harder but I settled in again quite easily but, yeah, the first few weeks were a bit [hard]. (Will, aged 17)

15.6.6 What helps children adjust to relocating?

The children and young people were asked what had helped them adjust to either the move or to living in a different place to one of their parents, or what had made the process easier for them.

Moving to a place where extended family lived was seen as an important factor, as they were a source of support and also a way of meeting new friends:

Having family there was good too, like cousins our age made it easy to make friends.... If we didn't have family, it would be a lot harder. It would be pretty rough. (Jenny, aged 16)

It was definitely good I think knowing that we did have family here that would help us if we got into trouble. (Will, aged 17)

Making new friends was seen by many children as something that helped them adjust to the move and was a key part of settling into a new school. Getting involved in sports and extra-curricular activities was regarded as one way of making friends at a new school and in the community:

We went and joined the local tennis club.... But just coming back to school, I think what made it easy to settle in was being quite good at sport. So everyone was sort of like, 'Whoa. Where did you come from?' and made heaps of friends from there. (Jacob, aged 16)

When I went to school... it was alright cos on the first day I made a few friends, and then that just carried on, and I got known better and I got to know people better. And I did well at that school.... I liked that school better than the other one. (Louise, aged 13)

I made friends pretty quickly actually. I got into all extra-curricular activities and stuff and just started making friends again... so it was quite easy actually. (Will, aged 17)

Several children commented on the age when children relocated. They regarded moving as preferable when children were younger as it was easier for them to make friends then, whereas it was considered harder for teenagers:

We were pretty young when we moved so I think that made it a lot easier. So I'd say that there's quite a bit to do with the age and stuff. [If I moved now] I'd say it would be a different game. If we were going somewhere new again it would just be weird. Cos everybody's, they're all settled in there and stuff. (Andrew, aged 15)

I was a lot younger so it didn't really bother me that much cos it's not hard to make friends at that age. You just kind of play with someone. (Will, aged 17)

Like if you're young, it's okay to move. If you're really young, like quite young, they're not going to remember it. But it's really hard, especially for teenage people, like to be completely moved.... It's easier to move away when you're younger than when you're older.... Young kids it's okay because they can make more new friends. (Claire, aged 17)

Given that so many of the children found it difficult to leave their friends behind when they relocated it was of interest to learn what helped them to maintain these relationships. The children and young people reported considerable variety in whether they did maintain these friendships. Some children had lost touch with their old friends while others, particularly those who regularly returned to their original location for contact with their left-behind parent, still kept in touch with their old friends. Contact visits thereby also allowed contact with old friends, and some children reported spending a lot of time with them during holidays while staying with their non-resident parent.

15.6.7 Contact with their non-resident parent

Maintaining their relationships with their contact parent was also important for the children and young people. Generally, they were positive about the face-to-face contact they had with the parent they did not live with. Having to travel to another location to see their contact parent meant that for some children their time with that parent had a holiday feel, particularly when contact occurred during school holidays. Some children experienced visits to the place where their contact parent lived, but also liked it when their contact parent came to visit them in their new locations, so their parent could meet their friends and watch them take part in school, cultural, or sporting activities. Contact often involved not just contact with the non-resident parent, but also with extended family such as grandparents, aunts, uncles, and cousins and also friends. This was very much valued by the children.

Relocation, and the resulting distance between parents' homes, meant that travel was inevitable in order for children to have contact with their left-behind parent (unless it was the parent who did the travelling). Nearly all of the children and young people had experienced a variety of modes of travel in order to see their contact parent. They had mixed responses about how they felt about this travel. Travel by airplane or train was popular whereas long car trips were not, particularly if children suffered from motion sickness. None were extremely negative about the travel and many just accepted it:

I don't mind the travel. You get used to it after a while. (Emily, aged 11)

Those that travelled by airplane generally liked the experience, although long, international flights could be taxing and 'boring'. Most of the children, however, enjoyed flying, and found airports exciting. Flying unaccompanied could be a challenging experience for some of the children, but most coped well:

It was a bit daunting at first and I was sort of worried, but it turned out quite nicely cos of course business class and they are quite friendly people and the air hostesses always looked after you. (Jacob, aged 16)

It was pretty scary but I think I got some of the airplane people to help me and take me to this kids' room or something. [What did you find scary about it?] Probably thinking about, 'Oh, I'll fall asleep and then they'll fly off with me.' (Sean, aged 11)

The first time it was [scary]... not having Mum or Dad.... The hostesses are really nice to you. They give you more attention. They give you extra lollies.... I was scared. And the thought of going all by myself... I feel for the kids that are only children, and their parents split up, and they fly like from one end of the country, and they fly all by themselves. I don't think I could do that, like I would be so scared.... Not having anyone with you, just the two of us, is kind of weird. (Chloe, aged 11)

A few children travelled by train by themselves and this seemed more manageable:

I do it by myself.... Oh, pretty cool. I have my wallet and money so I can just buy Coke and chocolate on the train.... I go up and then after the weekend or the holidays I just hop back on the train and go back down again. [Was it scary?] Sort of, sort of. I'm used to it.... The first time I just texted my Mum and Dad every time I got to a station. I had a book or a Gameboy. Eventually I got a Nintendo DS and played that.... It's actually a long time. I'm not sure how long, but it's long. (Sam, aged 11)

You kind of get used to the travel after a while and it's quite fun to go on a train.... I'm coming to the age when I can go on the train by myself so I'll be going on the train by myself. I think it's going to be pretty cool. (Madison, aged 11)

Several children wished for more frequent contact and others said they would prefer their parents to live in the same town/city or country or would just like their parents to live closer to each other. The cost of travel was a related issue for some of the children we spoke with that sometimes limited more frequent contact, particularly when this involved air travel:

. . . if there was plays that I'm performing in I kind of want him to see them and stuff, but he's down in [city]. I'd want them to be closer . . . I'd be able to see him more. He would be able to come up for plays every now and then. (Andrea, aged 14)

If I could have a wish, I would probably just wish that practically [the two towns] were all around that same place so they could be a bit closer cos sometimes the travel does get a bit annoying but as I said before you get used to it. (Emily, aged 11)

If you could push New Zealand, and it was like closer to Europe. I like the flight but just hate that it's so expensive. (Claire, aged 17)

Six children from three families wanted to reduce the amount of time they spent with their contact parent—reasons included wanting weekend time with their resident parent and not wanting to spend their entire holidays with their contact parent. When planned contact interfered with the children and young people's lives this could be problematic for them.

The children reported a variety of ways to keep in touch with their contact parent between face-to-face visits. These included phone calls, emails, texting, Skype, MSN, and, infrequently, letters. Such modes of communication were sometimes seen as superficial and not as good as face-to-face contact:

It's not the same as talking to him in person. (Olivia, aged 15)

It's more light and fluffy. We don't really talk about anything, any actual problem. . . . If you really talk to him, face-to-face it's better. (Claire, aged 17)

I can text him on Mummy's phone, so at least I can talk to him sometimes, but sometimes I'm a bit sad because I can't actually talk to him and hear his voice. (Stephanie, aged 9)

Phone or email contact could be sporadic, difficult, or inconsistent for some of the children. They found it difficult when their contact parent did not adhere to agreed-upon arrangements to call and did not like the lack of immediacy with email as a form of communication. Children's independent contact with the parent they didn't live with was sometimes thwarted when their mobile phones were broken or lost and the use of mobile phones was expensive when ringing or sending texts to an overseas number:

We can email, but he probably wouldn't reply to it for another few days. (Aaron, aged 15)

We made an arrangement a while back that every second Sunday we'd ring him and every Sunday that we didn't ring him that he'd ring us. He hasn't kept up that arrangement. (Louise, aged 13)

It costs money on our cell phones or to check our voicemails. (Olivia, aged 15)

I was a bit gutted cos we didn't have a phone so I couldn't keep in contact with him, and the only communication we had was a cell phone. (Louise, aged 13)

He can text us messages but we can't text back. . . . If it wasn't to an overseas country we could try texts more often. (Claire, aged 17)

Only a few children (particularly those whose fathers lived overseas) mentioned successfully using Skype or MSN:

Mum's computer has a special camera and we go on Skype usually. . . . Maybe about two times in three weeks. If the Skype thing is a bit damaged or if one of our computers isn't working, we just call. It's just as good. (Daniel, aged 10)

I talk on Gmail a lot. Gmail's a Google mail. You can talk on-line. . . . It depends, like if he's at work. He does some work, like on the computer at home at night. (Olivia, aged 15)

However, many of the children did not have access to such technology to keep in touch with their contact parent or it was unreliable or problematic. It was difficult to use Skype and the like when one of the parents did not have broadband, internet access, or a webcam. The children found Skype frustrating when the internet connection was slow or patchy:

Mum she said she would get the internet. [Mum's boyfriend's] has a computer but I don't want to ask him for it. (Bernadette, aged 14)

We have used Skype before, but it didn't really work.... the connection's like really off and we were talking to him and we'd start the conversation and stop cos he was talking at the same time. (Olivia, aged 15)

We don't have a computer, but at my grandparents' we do, but they don't have a camera, but my Dad's friend's laptop does, but I can't talk to him because I don't have one. (Stephanie, aged 9)

15.6.8 Children's relationships with their contact parents

Many of the children said they missed the parent they did not live with. However, there was a sense that they grew accustomed to not seeing their contact parent as often as they had when they lived in the same location. Some of the children thought the relocation had changed their relationship with their contact parent while others did not. A few commented on the diminished role their contact parent had in their life following the relocation:

[Dad is] almost a part-time parent. (Jed, aged 12)

Kind of not like a parent-child relationship because he doesn't really see us much.... He doesn't really have any control over us any more. So he's kind of a bit taken aback when he finds out the changes [in us].... Not like a parental relationship anymore because they're not there. Like you know how parents are there 24/7, watching, kind of control you. There's nothing like that anymore, like it's completely different. (Olivia, aged 15)

Mum can tell us not to do stuff and ground us, and tell us what we can and can't do, like wear clothes and that, and he can't.... He hasn't got any power really. He just comes over and we go shopping and stuff. (Claire, aged 17)

The distance and amount of contact between children and their contact parents could impact on how well parents knew their child:

I'm a different person now from when I last talked to my Dad in person.... Like if he lived [here], he probably would know who I am and stuff like that. But because he lives away, I talk to him by technology which is not representing myself, in person, like the way I talk and my body language. And you can kind of tell that he doesn't really know me that well because of birthday and Christmas presents. (Olivia, aged 15)

For some, not living in the same location as their contact parent had actually improved their relationship:

I think maybe it's a bit better because you know how you get grumpy with your parents? I don't usually do that, like when I get grumpy with him, he'll be like 'Ah, well we've only got this little time. Let's make the most of it.' It's stronger and you don't really do that any more. (Chloe, aged 11)

I get on with him better [since the relocation]. Because I don't see him often enough and before that he was sort of like always telling me off. (Louise, aged 13)

I probably miss him more and enjoy staying with him. So it's probably made it more better probably. But then it's broken it away that we're not seeing each other as much, so it's like half and half. (Sean, aged 11)

Several children reported difficult, strained, or distant relationships with their contact parent. In most cases this did not appear to be due to the relocation or the geographical distance but rather was a feature of their relationship *prior* to the relocation. For some, it was their contact parents' lack of affection and/or commitment to maintaining contact after the separation, but prior to them moving, that made the relationship difficult:

I just don't think he cares. I don't feel cared for. I mean before it was so different. Before I was the star on top of the Christmas tree but now I'm just the little pot. I'm nothing and I don't really care, cos I just get on with life.... At the start my dad was expressing such love for me but then his love died away and then it became clear to me that I wasn't much to him. (Nina, aged 13)

Then we got a bit distant... we kind of drifted apart.... The time spans between contact are getting long, and so maybe in the near future if he wants contact maybe I'll have to start the flame.... My Dad kind of doesn't have that much of a commitment thing going on and he forgets a lot. I felt kind of disappointed because I was used to seeing my Dad quite a lot and then it's not so much, but then I got used to that and now it's like nothing. It felt really, really odd. (Tara, aged 10)

While some children described a distant kind of relationship with their contact parent, others expressed stronger negative feelings towards them and some were angry with their contact parent about the separation and that parent's subsequent behaviour:

I hated him. I didn't talk to him for six months. [Brother] was a bit more placid about it. He stayed and talked to him, but I left.... I wasn't really interested in seeing him at all. Like for the first six months he would ring me up. He'd talk to [brother] and then he'd ask if I'd talk to him, and I said no.... I just got over it. (Claire, aged 17)

When he first left I had quite a bit of hate for him and I was a really angry kid. Like I used to get into a lot of trouble and stuff, but now he contacts us more, we have a fine relationship and stuff.... We were definitely closer as kids I think if I remember correctly, but it's just kind of distant now. I still talk to him and everything, we still get along. (Michael, aged 17)

While such anger was resolved by the time of the relocation for some children, for others it had an ongoing effect, resulting in children no longer wishing to have contact with their parent after the relocation:

I don't really want to have contact with him cos it seems like every time he calls it seems something happens.... it's like you go a step backwards. It's so much better when we don't have any contact with him cos we can just get on with our lives.... There's like too many complications like, 'Oh, come and visit' and all this stuff, and we don't really want to.... Mum's like, 'If you want to see him you can', but I don't want to see him. (Johanna, aged 12)

We just don't want to [see Dad] and don't particularly like him and his decisions he's made.... He's never made an effort to come and see us. It's kind of for the better that my Dad left because we never got along. Like before he left he kind of always got really angry at me.... So life is definitely a lot more happier and pleasant. So it's kind of worked out for the better, in this situation anyway. (Kara, aged 18)

Other children found their contact parent's continued animosity towards their other parent difficult and this impacted on their relationship with their contact parent:

Well, I kind of missed him, but I thought it was kind of like good to get away from him as well.... He went through a... well he still is... a hatred stage with Mum. And he always seems to like take it out on me. He just calls her all these horrible names behind her back to me and I just hang up. I hate it. (Louise, aged 13)

15.6.9 Consultation and amount of say

There was quite a lot of variety in the children's reports of how much say they were given in the decision to relocate and/or the subsequent contact arrangements. Some children were consulted and had a lot of input into the decision about whether or not they moved and who they lived with. For example:

I know that Mum always said that I had a choice... and she always told me I had a choice and she didn't mind if I chose either way, but I like spending time with both my parents.... I did have quite a lot of say cos I talked to my lawyer and I said [what I wanted] so they worked it out so [parents] had about the same time.... I get quite a lot of say. (Emily, aged 11)

Other children reported they had very little say and were just informed they were moving. Some children, however, did not want to be asked for their views, or did not wish to make a choice between their parents.

Those children who were not consulted or who did not get a say about the relocation and/or the contact they had with their other parent thought it was important that children had a voice. Their advice to parents or professionals making decisions about relocation included:

The kids should be deciding and their parent because then they know what the kid wants. (Charlie, aged 8)

I think that they [children] deserve to have a voice, but I think that they should negotiate sort of thing because like when we moved I didn't get to have a say in anything except for who I wanted to live with and it was either Mum or Dad. (Louise, aged 13)

Listen to your kids.... They should let you do whatever you want instead of having to go through all the Courts and spend all their money on lawyers. (Connor, aged 11)

Talk to them and see if they actually want to move. (Charlotte, aged 10)

Nina acknowledged that while it was hard for young children to speak up, she thought it was important that they did:

I just want to let the judges and the lawyers and all the people they're having to deal with, I just want them to know that they should get involved, like talk to the child about what's really going on.... they won't, at the start... if they're all as young as I was they probably won't understand what was going on, they won't tell you what's really going on inside their mind.... I believe that children need to know that they have to stand up, cos if they don't act now, it will really close off a lot of things in the future. Cos I was timid at the start and then I slowly came to understand, to realize or comprehend what was going on around me and what could happen if I didn't do something and make sure that everyone knew what I believe was best for me. (Nina, aged 13)

15.6.10 Experience and understanding of legal processes and professionals

Children from 30 families took part in this study. Sixteen of these 30 families had some form of Family Court involvement in their family's relocation issue. Twenty-five (57 per cent) of the children (from these 16 families) had had experience with or knowledge of the Family Court and/or legal professionals in relation to the relocation issue. Those children and young people who knew something about the court varied in their understanding, but most children who were asked knew it was the judge who made the decision about the move. Their experience of legal processes and professionals was described by some children as 'a bit of pain', 'awkward' or 'weird'.

Fourteen children spoke about having a lawyer appointed to represent them, and they varied in how positive this experience was. Some children really liked their lawyer:

It feels like he understands you, like when he's talking to you, and he asks you all the questions, like he doesn't hurry you into answering them. (Chloe, aged 11)

She's really nice. We wouldn't just talk about the things we needed to do. We'd also just talk about daily life. (Emily, aged 11)

While other children clearly did not feel the same way about their lawyer:

He was a stinker! Just because I didn't like him. Cos I just don't trust him. Just don't trust him. (Charlie, aged 8)

In addition to lawyers, the children spoke of other professionals who had met with them and several were not happy about having to talk with strangers about their family situation. For example, Connor (aged 11) found it 'sad... you have to speak to a stranger. I don't like talking about Mum and Dad breaking up to a stranger'.

Children who felt reluctant to speak with lawyers or other court-appointed professionals sometimes felt pressured to make a choice between their parents and refused to engage in the process:

They were pretty tough questions, like what parent do you like best, what parent do you want to spend the night with? I didn't answer any of them. I said, 'Dunno'.... I got pretty annoyed sometimes... I think they were just lining up who can crack the code, who can make him say 'I want to live at that house.' (Adam, aged 11)

Half the time I just wanted to get out of [lawyer's] office, so I would say whatever would come to my mind so she would let me go.... I just wanted to escape from that. I wanted to live a normal life instead of continually going to see a lawyer and a psychiatrist and a psychologist and a social worker.... All I wanted was a normal life. (Nina, aged 13)

Well, a lady asked me questions. I always said like, 'I don't know. I don't know. I dunno, I dunno. I'm not sure. I'm not sure'. And I kept on playing games with her.... I just didn't want to talk to her. I wasn't sure about anything really.... And I didn't know anything. I didn't say yes or no to anything. (Lucy, aged 8)

Those children who had a negative view of legal and court professionals all related how they felt that they were not listened to by these professionals. For example, Nina (aged 13) had repeatedly told her lawyer she was unhappy living with her father and wanted to move to live with her mother who had relocated. She was very unhappy with her lawyer, whom she felt did not listen to her or understand her situation:

I think I was a burden on [lawyer]. I used to ask to see her a lot cos I really wanted to live with my Mum. I don't feel she was doing her job.... I don't think she understood that my future was resting on her shoulders, and I don't think she took the time to understand just what she was doing.... How important her role is and I don't think she took it seriously.... Maybe she took it seriously, but I don't think she worked hard enough.... It's her job to help people.... I told her what I wanted but she obviously wasn't doing as much as she could.... This is [lawyer's] job. She's getting paid to do what she's doing and she wasn't taking responsibility for it, cos she had a lot of power over what would happen to me and then you say that with power comes great responsibility and I don't think she was being responsible enough with what she was doing... It's like she was hearing but she wasn't actually listening. (Nina, aged 13)

She thought that her views were not given as much weight because of her young age:

I don't believe they understood that a child as young as I could make decisions for her future, but my decision hasn't changed over time. (Nina, aged 13)

Several other children were angry that while their views had been listened to, they were reported to the court incorrectly:

She [lawyer for the child] decided for us.... She said like the total opposite thing I wanted to do. I said I didn't want to go see my Dad and she said to the Court he does want to see his Dad. (Brandon, aged 10)

Adam was clear that 'I decided I don't want to decide' and knew that he had not indicated a preference for either parent and was angry it was reported that he had:

I don't know what I said but I'm sure I didn't say I don't want to stay with Dad. I didn't.... Listen to the kids, not make their own decisions. They have to listen. I made it clear, but they didn't listen. (Adam, aged 11)

Adam was also angry with the judge:

I got really pissed off with the Judge—all of the decisions he made. I didn't want to choose, and he said that I wanted to live with Mum and I never said that. I never said that. (Adam, aged 11)

15.6.11 Advice for children

The children and young people were asked what advice they would give another child facing a relocation issue. Generally, their responses fell into the four categories: staying in contact with your parent(s); having a voice; a reassurance that things will work out; and just 'going with the flow'. For example:

Just try ringing them and stuff. And if you can get your Mum or Dad or whoever you're living with, get them to get airplane tickets or bus tickets or anything just to see them. Or just write letters and send photos and stuff. (Sean, aged 11)

I'd ask them what they want and then say for them to tell their Mum their opinion and then she might take that into consideration. (Lucy, aged 8)

Maybe like keep your hopes up, don't bring yourself down cos everything's changing. Cos sometimes change can be good and sometimes it can be really bad, but you can work your way through it. (Paige, aged 10)

I suppose it's never really a good experience having your parents break up and all that fighting and stuff that comes with it and then breaking up and going in two different ways and not being able to see one parent or the other. But I suppose if it happens you've just got to get on with it and try to keep everything like normal and just be yourself and just do what you normally do and try just and carry on as if everything's fine. (Jacob, aged 16)

15.7 Discussion

The children and young people in our study spoke articulately about their experiences of their family situation, family relationships, relocating (or not being able to move), their contact arrangements, and the legal processes and professionals they encountered. This provides yet more evidence of children and young people's ability to reflect on and express their experiences, and reinforces the value of researching children's perspectives on the challenges they sometimes face within their families and the Family Court. Asking children to reflect back on their experiences provides an insight into post-separation family transition issues that cannot be captured by more outcome-based research.

The children and young people demonstrated maturity in their understanding of the issues surrounding their family's relocation experience. They evidenced an ability to see the issues from a balanced viewpoint—understanding and appreciating why their resident parent wished to relocate but also empathizing with the parent who was left behind. In addition to being able to see their parents' perspectives on the relocation issue, the children and young people could also outline both the advantages and disadvantages of moving. While initially traumatic and/or difficult, looking back, they could also see that the move had ultimately been a good thing to happen to them.

Generally, the prospect of moving was regarded positively. The children and young people spoke of being excited and happy to be moving, seeing it as an adventure, with new experiences and opportunities. However, they did acknowledge the negative aspects—moving away from friends and family, the nervousness of starting a new school, and having to make new friends.

What came through very strongly in these interviews was that for the most part, the children and young people were relatively happy, well-adjusted, and satisfied with how things had worked out for them and their families. This is not to say that the relocation experience was not difficult or traumatic for some, but rather there was the sense that they had adjusted and become accustomed to their new situations. This was particularly true of those children and young people for whom the relocation issue had occurred some years previously. This is consistent with the large body of research on the effects of parental separation that demonstrates that while short-term distress is common, children do adjust over time and the majority come through the experience relatively unscathed. Like parental separation, relocation is a risk to children's well-being, but fortunately the majority of the children and young people in our study did adjust well. However, as mentioned earlier, the parents of children who had had a particularly difficult and/or traumatic experience did not tend to give consent for their children's participation in our study and so the 44 children and young people we did interview may have been a particularly well-adjusted group. Some of the 114 parents who were interviewed as part of the larger study gave anguished accounts of the traumatic and distressing events their children had experienced. We will capture these parental perspectives on their children's adjustment to a relocation dispute in future publications arising out of our data and thereby provide a fuller account of the likely range of outcomes for children.

From a risk and resilience perspective what emerged from the interviews with the children and young people was the importance of relationships. The loss of relationships could make the process harder (or more risky) for some children, while having supportive relationships was a protective factor. Two overarching themes that emerged from the many topics discussed by the children and young people was the importance of family and the importance of friends. Moving to be with extended family was regarded as a positive aspect of moving, while shifting away from family and a parent and missing them was considered one of the hard things about moving. Family support was important in helping children and young people adjust to a relocation.

Similarly, saying goodbye to friends was the most common difficulty the children and young people reported when moving to a new location. Being able to maintain these friendships was valued, while making new friends was a significant factor in helping the children and young people settle in after a move. The importance of friends was repeatedly mentioned within and across the interviews with the children and young people. Butler et al.'s[53] conclusion that the 'importance of a child's friends

[53] Butler et al., N. 38, above, at 81.

during the crisis of parental separation should not be underestimated', also holds true in the relocation context.

This is important information for parents who are proposing to relocate. Children will need support and encouragement to make new friends after a move. These new friends are particularly important in helping children adjust to a new school and community, at a time when their resident parent may themselves be stressed and distracted with the process of moving house and starting a new job. The children and young people told us that getting involved in sports and extra-curricula activities was a good way of making new friends and parents can help with this by encouraging their children to join such activities and facilitating the process.

It is also important for both resident and contact parents to be aware of the importance of their children being able to maintain relationships and links with their old friends after moving away. Non-resident parents should allow their children to spend time with these friends (and other family members) while they are back on contact visits. Resident parents should encourage their children to keep in touch (via phone, internet etc) with their old friends and to ensure that their children have access to such modes of communication so as to facilitate the maintenance of these important peer relationships.

The loss of important relationships is a mediating factor that can lead to poor outcomes for children after parental separation. Moving away from one parent usually means a decrease in the frequency and amount of time children can spend with their contact parent. Most of the children in this study were satisfied with the contact they had with the parent they did not live with—a few would have liked more contact or for their parents to live closer together, but the distance and in some cases infrequent face-to-face contact was something the children appeared to grow accustomed to. Some children travelled extensive distances in order to have contact but they did not really complain about this, and did get used to it.

The use of technology such as texting, email, Skype, MSN, and the like was used by quite a few of the children and young people, but many described problems with it. Face-to-face contact was generally preferred. Clearly it was important to the children to be able to maintain contact with their non-resident parent between visits but this could be a source of frustration and in some instances result in superficial communication. If parents and judges make agreements and orders which include the use of modern technology such as mobile phones, emails, webcams, and the internet—so called 'virtual visitation'[54]—this should be regarded as supplementary to, not a replacement for, face-to-face visits.[55] While these modes of communication

[54] E. Bach-Van Horn, 'Virtual Visitation: Are Webcams Being Used as an Excuse to Allow Relocation?' (2008) 21 *Journal of the American Academy of Matrimonial Lawyers* 171; C. R. Flango, 'Virtual Visitation—Is this a New Option for Divorcing Parents?' (2003) *2003 report on trends in the State Courts* 20, retrieved from <http://www.ncsconline.org/WC/Publications/Trends/TrendsSum/CustodTrSum.html>; S. L. Gottfried, 'Virtual Visitation: The Wave of the Future in Communication Between Children and Non-custodial Parents in Relocation Cases' (2002) 36 *Family Law Quarterly* 475; S. L. Gottfried, 'Virtual Visitation: The New Wave of Communication Between Children and Non-custodial Parents in Relocation Cases' (2003) 9 *Cardozo Women's Law Journal* 567; A. Levasseur, 'Virtual Visitation: How Will Courts Respond to a New and Emerging Issue?' (2004) 17 *The Quinnipiac Probate Law Journal* 362; A. Schepard, 'Virtual Visitation: Computer Technology Meets Child Custody Law' (2002) *New York Law Journal* 228; K. R. Shefts, 'Virtual Visitation: The Next Generation of Options for Parent-Child Communication' (2002–2003) 36 *Family Law Quarterly* 303; D. Welsh, 'Virtual Parents: How Virtual Visitation Legislation is Shaping the Future of Custody Law' (2008) 11 *Journal of Law and Family Studies* 215.

[55] Bach-Van Horn, N. 54, above.

might, in theory, seem a clever solution, they can be unreliable or inaccessible. The availability of such technology (whether each parent has the necessary equipment and the financial ability to fund it) should be ascertained or reality tested[56] to determine whether such virtual contact is feasible.

The children gave mixed accounts about how the relocation impacted on their relationships with their contact parent. Some thought it had made no difference, while a few thought the relationship had become more distant and less parental. Several children had distant, difficult, or strained relationships with their contact parent but this appeared to be due to factors independent of the relocation, such as the contact parent's behaviour or failure to maintain regular contact. However, for the most part, the relocation did not appear to change the existing nature of the parent-child relationship in a detrimental way and in some instances, for children who had more fraught relationships with their contact parent, the relationship had actually improved due to the move.

The children and young people's experiences of the legal processes and professionals were also mixed. Some children liked their lawyers, while others did not feel their lawyer had listened to them or accurately reported their views. Those who spoke about the Family Court had a reasonably correct understanding of its role in the decision-making process.

In accord with previous research,[57] being consulted and listened to was important to the children and young people we spoke with. Those children who were given a say and contributed to the relocation decision valued this opportunity. Those who had not, or who had felt they were not listened to, were unhappy about this. The children who had been able to decide which parent they lived with appeared very happy about this and with their current living and contact arrangements, but other children did not wish to make this choice. It is important to remember that consulting children does not equate to giving children the responsibility of being the decision-maker, and that children will vary in terms of their desire to contribute to such a decision.

Furthermore, if children and young people are to be consulted this needs to be more than just a token gesture. If children are consulted they need to be listened to and heard. There were several accounts of children being consulted and given the opportunity to express their views but then not being heard or listened to—either the child continually expressed an opinion that was ignored or misreported, or they specifically chose *not* to express their views or contribute to the relocation decision and yet were reported as doing so. Such situations resulted in anger and distress for these children, which could have been avoided had the professionals involved really listened to what the children were saying.

The children and young people were predominantly happy, well-adjusted, and satisfied with their lives—many were thankful that they had had such a good experience and knew that there were other children who were not so fortunate. Features of their experiences that could account for their successful adaptation included their relatively good knowledge and understanding about the relocation, the reasons for it, and the associated legal processes and the maintenance of important relationships in their lives. Most of the children had a good relationship with their contact parent. Those that did not tended to have a poor relationship prior to the relocation and so

[56] P. Parkinson, J. Cashmore, and J. Single, 'The Need for Reality Testing in Relocation Cases' (2010) 44 *Family Law Quarterly* 1.

[57] N. 36, above.

the relocation did not impact on the relationship, or if it did, it did so in a positive way. Only a small number of children were having no contact at all with their non-resident parent and this was also the case prior to the relocation.

Many of the children moved to, rather than away from, the support of extended family (or experienced no change), and none of the children reported any difficulties in making new friends, while also maintaining old friends. Therefore, the identified protective factors of peer and family support were present in many of these children's lives. Few experienced the risk factor of the loss of important relationships.

The time delay between the relocation and the interview also varied in this sample of children. For some it had been several years between the two events. While this was helpful in allowing the children to reflect on the ongoing process of their post-relocation family life, the passage of time may have also been a factor in the positive nature of their adjustment. There was certainly the sense that these children had just grown accustomed to their new lives over time and saw the distance from their contact parent and the travel involved in maintaining contact as something that they had grown 'used to'. The age of the children may also have been a factor. Most of the children who had moved did so prior to their teenage years, when perhaps their peer relationships were not as important to them as they would have been had they moved as adolescents.

Analysis of the interviews with the parents of these children and young people is ongoing and future publications will shed further light on the features of these children's situations that contributed to their positive adjustment. Comparisons between the accounts of these parents with those of parents whose children did not fare so well will also be possible, allowing a more comprehensive analysis of the risk and protective factors present in the lives of these children.

15.8 Conclusion

Most existing research on the impact of parental separation and relocation on children does not directly engage with those most directly affected—the children themselves. The other qualitative studies examining family members' experiences of relocation disputes in the context of the Australian[58] family justice system have successfully recruited parents but have had much greater difficulty in including children and young people. Our study is therefore important in contributing this significant perspective to help provide families, legal professionals, the courts, and policy-makers with valuable new information about relocation. The three themes dominating the children's accounts—the importance of family and friends; the importance of being consulted and listened to; and children's resilience and ability to adjust to family transition—build on the findings of earlier research on parental separation and family mobility. They illustrate the importance of evaluating the known risk and protective factors in each individual case so as to arrive at an outcome that will best promote the child's welfare and best interests.

[58] Parkinson et al., N. 56, above; J. Behrens, B. Smyth, and R. Kaspiew, 'Australian Family Law Court Decisions on Relocation: Dynamics in Parents' Relationships Across Time' (2009) 23 *Australian Journal of Family Law* 222. An English study focused exclusively on adult perspectives and did not seek to recruit children: Marilyn Freeman, *Relocation: The reunite Research*. Research report (London, Research Unit of the Reunite International Child Abduction Centre, 2009).

16

Vulnerability, Children, and the Law

Jonathan Herring[1]

16.1 Introduction

Latey J, a wise and experienced family law judge, once said:

children are especially vulnerable. They have not formed the defences inside themselves which older people have, and, therefore, need especial protection. They are also a country's most valuable asset.[2]

Such a perspective plays a powerful role in the law's response to childhood. Vulnerability is commonly cited as a reason why children should not receive rights, or at least not the same rights as adults. We are told that if the law were to give children the same rights as adults we would see more exploitation of children, not less.[3] David Archard argues 'granting fundamental liberties to a child before he possesses the capacities to be the guardian of his own life is cruel'.[4] Children's vulnerability is seen as justifying the extensive child protection law that we have and the vast array of criminal offences that are designed to protect children from the many dangers they face.[5] Indeed the welfare principle[6] itself, which is at the heart of the Children Act 1989, is often supported in the name of protecting children.[7]

The vulnerability rhetoric not only explains the law's response to childhood, it is also a theme prevalent in the portrayal of children in media.[8] We hear much of 'the crisis in childhood'.[9] Stevi Jackson and Sue Scott write that '[c]hildhood is increasingly being constructed as a precious realm under siege from those who would rob children of their childhoods, and as being subverted from within by children who refuse to remain childlike'.[10] The Archbishop of Canterbury attracted considerable

[1] Fellow in Law, Exeter College, University of Oxford. I am particularly grateful to Jo Bridgeman, Kirsten Johnson, and Helen Reece for comments on a draft of this chapter.

[2] *Re X (A Minor) (Wardship: Jurisdiction)* [1975] Fam 47.

[3] Jane Fortin, *Children's Rights and the Developing Law* (Cambridge, 3rd edn, 2009), 5.

[4] David Archard, 'Philosophical Perspectives on Childhood' in (ed.) Julia Fionda, *Legal Concepts of Childhood* (Oxford, 2001), 52.

[5] Laura Hoyano and Catherine Keenan, *Child Abuse* (Oxford, 2010).

[6] Children Act 1989, s. 1.

[7] Jonathan Herring, 'Farewell Welfare' (2005) 27 *Journal of Social Welfare and Family Law* 159.

[8] Phil Scraton (ed.), *Childhood in Crisis* (London, 1997).

[9] Mary Kehily, 'Childhood in crisis? Tracing the Contours of "Crisis" and its Impact upon Contemporary Parenting Practices' (2010) 32 *Media Culture Society* 171; The Children's Society, *Children: Good Childhood Inquiry Report Debate* (London, 2008).

[10] Stevi Jackson and Sue Scott, 'Risk Anxiety and the Social Construction of Childhood' in (ed.) Deborah Lupton, *Risk and Sociocultural Theory: New Directions and Perspectives* (Cambridge, 1999), 86.

attention when he declared that childhood was under threat, being damaged by commercial pressures, family breakdown, and parents who refuse to grow up.[11]

There are plenty of authors who have criticized the way that the law and media have presented children as being vulnerable. It undermines children's agency and justifies inappropriately paternalistic interventions in the lives of children. It involves exaggerating the risks children face and downplays their abilities. Children, it is loudly asserted, are a great deal more competent and able than we give them credit for. I agree with much that has been written making such points. This chapter will, however, take a rather different line. It will be argued that the law is right to regard children as vulnerable, where it is at fault is in failing to recognize the vulnerability of adults. Children are vulnerable as is everyone. In children we adults see our own vulnerability and flee from it. I, therefore, do not reject claims that children are vulnerable: I think they are, even if the claims are often exaggerated and distorted to achieve adult purposes. The failure is to recognize that children's vulnerability is, in essence, no different from that faced by adults.

16.2 Defining vulnerability

16.2.1 The meaning of vulnerability

My argument will be that everyone is vulnerable. It is an inevitable part of the human condition. But before exploring this, more needs to be said about the notoriously vague concept of vulnerability.[12] It is used in many disciplines and without a consistent meaning.[13] According to the *New Oxford Dictionary of English*, to be vulnerable means 'to be exposed to the possibility of being attacked or harmed, either physically or emotionally'.[14] That seems a very broad definition: you would need to be wrapped up in substantial quantities of cotton wool not to face any risk of harm! It need hardly be said that on this definition we are all vulnerable: we brush with emotional harm or physical attack daily. But there are other aspects of the notion of vulnerability that merit further discussion.

16.2.2 The source of vulnerability

To some vulnerability refers to a failure to be able to protect oneself, rather than an external state of affairs. So, a person who has suffered in an earthquake is not automatically vulnerable, unless they lack the ability to protect themselves. Vulnerability therefore rests in a physical, mental, or emotional weakness of the individual in the face of a threat. This may be that the person lacks the physical ability to save him or herself from dangers or their mental capacity is such that they cannot perceive or

[11] BBC News Online 'Childhood "in crisis"' 18 September 2006.

[12] Barbara Fawcett, 'Vulnerability. Questioning the Certainties in Social Work and Health' (2009) 52 *International Social Work* 473; Samia Hurst, 'Vulnerability in Research and Health Care; Describing the Elephant in the Room?' (2004) 7 *Medicine, Health Care and Philosophy* 281; Michael Kottow, 'Vulnerability: What Kind of Principle is it?' (2004) 7 *Medicine, Healthcare and Philosophy* 281.

[13] Michael Dunn, Isabel Clare, and Anthony Holland, 'To Empower or to Protect? Constructing the "Vulnerable Adult" in English Law and Public Policy' (2008) 28 *Legal Studies* 234.

[14] *Oxford English Dictionary* (Oxford, 2010).

avoid danger.[15] Such an understanding is captured by the Council for International Organizations of Medical Science (writing about vulnerability in the context of medical research) as follows:

> 'Vulnerability' refers to a substantial incapacity to protect one's own interests owing to such impediments as lack of capability to give informed consent, lack of alternative means of obtaining medical care, ... or being a junior or subordinate member of a hierarchical group.

Doris Schroeder and Eugenijus Gefenas[16] take a rather different, and preferable, approach. For them vulnerability is to be exposed to the possibility of harm (what they describe as the external element of vulnerability) *and* to be substantially unable to protect oneself from that possibility (what they describe as the internal element). They therefore define vulnerability in this way: 'To be vulnerable means to face a significant probability of incurring an identifiable harm while substantially lacking ability and/or means to protect oneself.' In adopting such an approach one might accept that everyone suffers the external elements of vulnerability to some extent, but that it is the internal elements where the differences arises. However, the distinction between external and internal risks is probably artificial. An individual characteristic can only be a source of vulnerability in the context of particular social circumstances. Being unable to walk might, or might not, render one at greater risk of being mugged depending on a wide range of social circumstances. It is better, therefore, not to rely on a distinction between inherent characteristics and external circumstances, but rather simply to focus on the risk of harm being faced.[17] One might say that vulnerability is situational.

16.2.3 Subjective/objective understanding of vulnerability

Another distinction which is relied upon by some is the perspective of the vulnerability. Michael Dunn, Isobel Clare, and Anthony Holland distinguish 'etic' and 'emic' understandings of vulnerability:

> 'Etic' approaches equate vulnerability with risk, and assess an individual's vulnerability in terms of the risk facing that person, justifying intervention as a means of managing that risk with regard to objectively determined standards.[18] 'Emic' approaches, in contrast, are based on the experiential perception of 'exposure to harm through challenges to one's integrity... [It] places vulnerability in a psycho-social cultural context'[19], and focus on the subjective reality of a person's everyday life.... [V]ulnerability exists as lived experience. The individual's perception of self and challenges to self, and of resources to withstand such challenges, define vulnerability.[20]

[15] Samia Hurst, 'Vulnerability in Research and Health Care; Describing the Elephant in the Room?' (2004) 7 *Medicine, Health Care and Philosophy* 281.

[16] Doris Schroeder and Eugenijus Gefenas, 'Vulnerability Too Vague and Too Broad' (2009) 18 *Cambridge Quarterly of Healthcare Ethics* 113.

[17] Samia Hurst, 'Vulnerability in Research and Health Care; Describing the Elephant in the Room?' (2004) 7 *Medicine, Health Care and Philosophy* 281.

[18] See, for example, Lu Aday, *At Risk in America: The Health and Health Care Needs of Vulnerable Populations in the United States* (San Francisco, 2001).

[19] Judith Spiers, 'New Perspectives on Vulnerability using Emic and Etic Approaches' (2000) 31 *Journal of Advanced Nursing* 715, 718.

[20] Michael Dunn, Isabel Clare, and Anthony Holland, 'To Empower or to Protect? Constructing the "Vulnerable Adult" in English Law and Public Policy' (2008) 28 *Legal Studies* 234.

This distinction is helpful because it opens up the possibility of recognizing that what might be regarded as vulnerability from the outside might not be so regarded by the individual. The benefit is that it involves listening to the voice of the person that is said to be disadvantaged to ascertain what it means to be vulnerable. This is an important point and is one we will return to later.

16.3 Vulnerability and children

Vulnerability has played an important role in the construction of childhood.[21] Anneke Meyer usefully separates out the alleged forms of childhood vulnerability into three categories: physical, social, and structural. References to physical vulnerability highlight that children's bodies tend to be smaller and they tend to be physically weaker than adults. Social vulnerability relates to the fact that children lack certain social skills which means they cannot use social tools to protect themselves from harms. Structural vulnerability refers to the power relations between children and adults which can be manipulated to harm children.

The emphasis on vulnerability sits alongside a range of other discourses about childhood: as evil; innocent; dangerous; and sources of potential.[22] Many commentators have noted the contradictory descriptions of children. For example, their innocence is emphasized when children are seen as the victims of crime[23] and their evil when viewed as perpetrators. We have seen in recent times these combine so that children who commit crime or anti-social behaviour are subject to increasingly stringent control, whereas at the same time their innocence is deemed to require ever increasing regulation and protection. Both lead to restrictions on the freedom of children. I would support Anneke Meyer's argument that the notion of innocence and vulnerability combine to provide childhood with a form of 'moral rhetoric' meaning that 'children and childhood function to explain and legitimize any practice or opinion as right while removing the necessity to provide reasons: children are the reason'.[24]

16.3.1 The consequences of the construction of vulnerability

The current construction of vulnerability has three particular consequences for the law's interaction with childhood that I wish to emphasize:

16.3.1.1 Paternalism

As children are regarded as vulnerable to a range of harms from which they cannot protect themselves, the law is authorized to protect children. Adults are permitted to use force to ensure their protection.[25] Children are regarded as at significantly greater risk of serious harms than adults and as lacking the ability to protect themselves. Nikolas Rose has explained how this presentation of the child as vulnerable renders her an object for adults to work on:

[21] Anneke Myer, 'The Moral Rhetoric of Childhood' (2007) 14 *Childhood* 85.

[22] Christine Piper, *Investing in Children* (Cullompton, 2008).

[23] Gill Valentine, 'Angels and Devils: Moral Landscapes of Childhood' (1996) 14 *Environment and Planning* 581.

[24] Anneke Myer, 'The Moral Rhetoric of Childhood' (2007) 14 *Childhood* 85, 93.

[25] Children Act 2004, s. 58 authorizes parents to use force which causes less than actual bodily harm by way of punishment.

The modern child has become the focus of innumerable projects that purport to safeguard it from physical, sexual and moral danger, to ensure its 'normal' development, to actively promote certain capacities of attributes such as intelligence, education and emotional stability.[26]

The most practical way the law protects children is by granting parents legal authority to control, discipline, and organize their children.[27] These are seen as necessary for parents to carry out their primary function of nurturing and protecting children,[28] so that in due course the child can become a rational and full citizen.[29] Education, and the requirement that children receive education, plays a central role in this too.[30] But it is not just parents or schools who have this function. As Allison James, Penny Curtis, and Joanna Birch put it:

[T]he Law operates as one of the main regulatory devices that shape the space of childhood. It does this through developing social policies . . . that seek to control the kinds of activities that children can do; the social and material environments they inhabit and the resources they have access to.[31]

The role, then, for children under this model is one that emphasizes obedience, so that the risks they face are minimized. Children must accept the wisdom of adults. One nine-year-old boy is quoted as saying:

Adults like children when they behave and help with cleaning or tidying up and do what they are told, but not if they cry and shout and hit the adults—but sometimes also if they [children] say something funny.[32]

The mature child will appreciate how little they know and will respect their elders and betters. So obedience is seen as a sign of maturity and disobedience a sign of immaturity. A child seeking to disagree with an adult cannot win.

This can be particularly apparent in cases where, especially in the context of contact disputes, the courts seem deeply suspicious of children who say they do not want to see their fathers. Such children are commonly seen as suffering from so-called 'alienation syndrome' or as not appreciating the long-term gains of knowing one's parents.

16.3.1.2 The quietening of children

One of the aspects of vulnerability of children emphasized by lawyers is that children lack the capacity to be able to make decisions for themselves. They lack the ability to comprehend the significance of facts; to project into the future; and suffer from an inability to focus on long-term goals, preferring short-term pleasures. In any event their decisions may reflect the views of adults rather than their own as children are liable to be mouthpieces for the views of adults or peer pressure.[33] Guggenheim

[26] Nikolas Rose, *Governing the Soul* (London, 1989), 121.

[27] Of course, the irony is that many children suffer harm at the hands of their parents.

[28] Ron Taffel and Melinda Blau, *Nurturing Good Children Now* (New York, 1999).

[29] Felicity Kaganas and Alison Diduck, 'Incomplete Citizens: Changing Images of Post-Separation Children' (2004) 67 *Modern Law Review* 959.

[30] Education Act 1996, s. 7.

[31] Allison James, Penny Curtis, and Joanna Birch, 'Care and Control in the Construction of Children's Citizenship' in (eds.) Antonella Invernizzi and Jane Williams, *Children and Citizenship* (London, 2008).

[32] Anneke Myer, 'The Moral Rhetoric of Childhood' (2007) 14 *Childhood* 85.

[33] Martin Guggenheim, *What's Wrong with Children's Rights* (Cambridge, Massachusetts, 2005).

writes that '"children's rights" has become a mantra invoked by adults to help them in their own fights with other adults'.[34]

Further, we see the reluctance of the courts to take seriously the job of listening to children in court proceedings. Despite some positive pronouncements in the Court of Appeal about the importance of involving children in litigation,[35] the lack of finance to back this up reflects a failure to take children's involvement seriously.[36] More significantly, children are silenced through the pressure to encourage parents to resolve disputes themselves. Jane Fortin writes:

> the pressure imposed on separating parents to settle their disputes out of court often reinforces their children's isolation, ensuring that outsiders are kept totally unaware of their unhappiness and helplessness, with plans for their upbringing made over their heads.[37]

It is most revealing, as Michael Freeman notes, that the concerns over the involvement of children in litigation regarding their future family lives contrasts markedly with the willingness to prosecute children in the criminal courts.[38]

16.3.1.3 The confinement of children

Vulnerability can be seen as rendering children private and justifying restrictions on their movement. Given the many risks children face it is safest to keep children in their homes and away from public spaces. The parents of children are entrusted to protect children from the harms of the outside world.[39] Typically children are seen to 'embody a state of innocence, purity and natural goodness that is only contaminated on contact with the corrupt outside world'.[40] Restricting where children can go and their interactions with adults naturally follows from such a perception.[41]

Jenny Kitzinger has argued how 'Childhood is presented as a time of play, an asexual and peaceful existence within the protective bosom of the family'.[42] Promoting privacy of family restricts the access of adults to children and thereby reduces risk. Of course, the language of vulnerability can also be used to justify state intervention in family life, in order to protect children. But even there, the aim is usually to find a safer private place for the child.

16.4 Dangers of the current construction of vulnerability

It is not difficult to be suspicious about the claims made above on the vulnerability of children. The needs of children and children's agency are defined by adults and on adult terms. Streets and public places may be seen as dangerous for children, but in fact children are more street-wise than adults.[43] Computers are seen as a source of

[34] Martin Guggenheim, *What's Wrong with Children's Rights* (Cambridge, Massachusetts, 2005), xii.

[35] *Mabon v Mabon* [2005] EWCA Civ 634.

[36] Jane Fortin, *Children's Rights and the Developing Law* (Cambridge, 2009), chapter 6.

[37] Jane Fortin, *Children's Rights and the Developing Law* (Cambridge, 2009), 284.

[38] Michael Freeman, 'The Child in Family Law' in (ed.) Julia Fionda, *Legal Concepts of Childhood* (Oxford, 2001).

[39] Annette Appell, 'The Pre-Political Child Of Child-Centered Jurisprudence' (2009) 46 *Houston Law Review* 703; Pia Haudrup Christensen, 'Childhood and the Cultural Constitution of Vulnerable Bodies' in (ed.) Alan Prout, *The Body, Childhood and Society* (Harlow, 2000).

[40] Mary Kehily, *An Introduction to Childhood Studies* (Buckingham, 2004), 5.

[41] Gill Valentine, *Children's Geographies* (London, 2000).

[42] Jenny Kitzinger, 'Defending Innocence: Ideologies of Childhood' (1988) 28 *Feminist Review* 77.

[43] Elizabeth Scott, 'Legal Construction of Adolescence' (2000) 29 *Hofstra Law Review* 547.

sexual danger yet children are often more adept with the technology than adults. I can think of a whole host of areas about which my children are more knowledgeable than I am. Much more could be said about the down-playing of the abilities of children, but others have done so extensively elsewhere.[44] I want to highlight some other reasons for being sceptical about the emphasis on vulnerability.

16.4.1 Selective

The first is that the discourse of vulnerability is typically selective of the dangers children face. These are commonly seen in terms of sexual abuse or physical harm. There is good reason to be sceptical about this. Where are the dangers posed to children by the environmental, social, or economic harms? The 'vulnerability' used in the media presents the government as posing no risk to children: the risk is from individuals. The government is the protector of children. Further, the risk is seen in terms that reinforce the protection offered by the traditional private family unit.

More importantly, the vulnerability of children emphasizes children's lack of ability or personal resources, rather than the dangers adults pose to children. So much has been written on the 'dangers' of the internet for children, and so little on what adults do with computers that poses risks. More on that later.

16.4.2 Homogenization

A second point to emphasize at this stage is that the language of vulnerability essentializes children. Children are classified as bound together in their weakness, innocence, and vulnerability. That fails to recognize the diversity of children and their range of childhood experiences.

Annette Ruth Appell writes of the construction of childhood as vulnerability:

> ...this construction of childhood formulates the child as raceless (i.e., white) and middle-class, much like the raceless (i.e., white) middle-class man who is the liberal subject that feminist and critical theorists have exposed and contested. No matter who this child is or from whence she or he comes, this same child is expected to become the white, male, middle-class, adult liberal subject upon reaching adulthood. Childhood's defining characteristics as natural, dependent, and private mask the differences among children while reinforcing the normative middle-class child as the measure of childhood; moreover, these characteristics further obfuscate the inequalities among the adult liberal subjects children are expected to become.[45]

As must be obvious, the fears of the Western parent that their children are at risk of obesity, overly-materialistic, or suffering low self-esteem have little resonance for those in the developing world.[46] The Western concern for children's vulnerability says little about the actual children, but much about the kind of society they live in and the worries of the adults. Treating childhood as a special form of vulnerability fails to appreciate the particular skills and talents (and particular vulnerabilities) that individual children have.

[44] E.g. Priscilla Alderson, *Young Children's Rights* (London, 2008).

[45] Annette Appell, 'The Pre-Political Child Of Child-Centered Jurisprudence' (2009) 46 *Houston Law Review* 703, 750–1.

[46] Virginia Morrow, 'Editorial: At the Crossroads' (2007) 14 *Childhood* 5.

16.4.3 Endangerment

A third reason to be sceptical about the use of vulnerability is that the vulnerability rhetoric can itself create dangers for the child. For example, to emphasize the horrors of child abuse, much is made of the sullying of the innocence of childhood. It is, however, a dangerous approach. As Kitzinger argues, it is this very kind of language of innocence and purity which plays a role in fuelling the paedophilic imagination.[47] Further, she explains:

> Innocence, then, is a problematic concept because it is itself a sexual commodity and because a child who is anything less than 'an angel' may be seen as 'fair game', both by the courts and by other men who will avail themselves of a child they know has previously been abused.[48]

If the defiling of innocence is the mark of child abuse then where the child is not innocent, the abuse seems less. This should not be.

Referring back to a point made earlier, the vulnerability discourse encourages children to accept obedience and respect their parents and adults.[49] Childhood compliance with adult demands and rules is deeply imbedded into our society's construction of childhood. Ironically, it is this which renders children so vulnerable in the arena of sexual contact.[50]

So far I have sought to explain the dangers in the vulnerability rhetoric in relation to children. However, to abandon it entirely and emphasize children's capabilities and resilience carries dangers too. I want to take a different tack. The law in its treatment of children based on vulnerability exaggerates the vulnerability of children and exaggerates the capacity of adults. I would make the following points in suggesting an alternative approach.

16.5 Challenges to vulnerability discourse

16.5.1 Adults vulnerable too

I argue that we should accept vulnerability as an inherent human characteristic.[51] As Levinas states: 'The I, from head to foot and to the bone-marrow, is vulnerability.'[52] As adults we like to emphasize our independence, capacity for rational thought, and autonomy. However, we puff ourselves up with such talk. In fact, we are all too aware of our own limitations. Very few people consenting to medical treatment or people making financial decisions are able to make a fully informed decision or to act on the basis of a rational decision-making processes.[53] Unsurprisingly, we often delegate such decisions to others.[54]

[47] Jenny Kitzinger, *Framing Abuse: Media Influence and Public Understandings of Sexual Violence against Children* (London, 2004).

[48] Jenny Kitzinger, 'Defending Innocence: Ideologies of Childhood' (1988) 28 *Feminist Review* 77.

[49] Jenny Kitzinger, *Framing Abuse: Media Influence and Public Understandings of Sexual Violence against Children* (London, 2004).

[50] James Kincaid, *Erotic Innocence: The Culture of Child Molesting* (London, 1998).

[51] Margrit Shildrick, *Embodying the Monster: Encounters with the Vulnerable Self* (London, 2002); Angharad Beckett, *Citizenship and Vulnerability* (Basingstoke, 2006).

[52] Emmanuel Levinas, *Humanismo Del Otro Hombre* (Madrid, 1993), 123.

[53] For a discussion of the non-rational dimension to much decision making see D. Redelmeier, P. Rozin, and D. Kahneman, 'Understanding Patients' Decisions: Cognitive and Emotional Perspectives' (1993) 270 *Journal of the American Medical Association* 72.

[54] Susan Adler Channick, 'The Myth of Autonomy at the End-of-life: Questioning the Paradigm of Rights' (1999) 44 *Villanova Law Review* 577.

Martha Fineman has argued that looking at a typical life span there will be times of different capacity and strengths. The typical 'adult liberal subject' focuses on just one part of that life span and essentializes this as the norm of people. We could take other sections of the typical life span and have a very different ideal around which to base a legal system. As Martha Fineman argues:

> The vulnerability approach recognizes that individuals are anchored at each end of their lives by dependency and the absence of capacity. Of course, between these ends, loss of capacity and dependence may also occur, temporarily for many and permanently for some as a result of disability or illness. Constant and variable throughout life, individual vulnerability encompasses not only damage that has been done in the past and speculative harms of the distant future, but also the possibility of immediate harm. We are beings who live with the ever-present possibility that our needs and circumstances will change. On an individual level, the concept of vulnerability (unlike that of liberal autonomy) captures this present potential for each of us to become dependent based upon our persistent susceptibility to misfortune and catastrophe.

I would go further and question whether even in our 'prime' we do have the kind of autonomy and capacity traditional liberalism claims for adults.

Consider, for example, the work of Samia Hurst. In examining international guidelines of research ethics and setting out who might be regarded as vulnerable, she produces a list of vulnerable groups which include the following:

- Racial minorities
- The economically disadvantaged
- The very sick
- The institutionalized
- Children
- Prisoners
- Pregnant women and foetuses
- Incompetent persons
- Persons susceptible to coercion
- Persons who will not derive direct benefits from participation
- Persons for whom research is mixed with clinical care
- Junior or subordinate members of a hierarchical group ... [such as] medical and nursing students, subordinate hospital and laboratory personnel, employees of pharmaceutical companies, and members of the armed forces or police
- Elderly persons
- Residents of nursing homes
- Patients in emergency rooms
- Homeless persons
- Refugees or displaced persons
- Patients with incurable disease
- Individuals who are politically powerless
- Members of communities unfamiliar with modern medical concepts

No doubt more could be added to this list.[55] But notice how enormously lengthy the list is. There must be few people who do not fall into one category or another. And her list is not unusual. The Declaration of Helsinki states that vulnerable groups include 'the economically and medically disadvantaged'; 'those who cannot give or refuse consent for themselves'; 'those who may be subject to giving consent under duress'; 'those who will not benefit personally from the research' and 'those for whom the research is combined with care'.[56] Again the majority of the population could fit in with this description of vulnerability.

The extent of departure from the autonomous ideal within the adult population is easily underestimated. While not suggesting that the following groups are necessarily vulnerable, the next list indicates the widespread issues faced by adults which manifest a departure from the autonomous hyper-competent man which is the heart of liberal approaches to the law:

- 75 per cent of the population have an IQ of less than 110.[57]
- 1 in 4 people will experience some kind of mental health problem in the course of a year.[58]
- 2.04 million contacts from new clients were made to Councils with Adult Social Services Responsibilities (CASSRs) in England in 2007–08.[59]
- In England in 2008, 38 per cent of men drank over four units on at least one day in the week prior to interview and 29 per cent of women drank more than three units on at least one day in the week prior to interview. Twenty-two per cent of men reported drinking over eight units and 15 per cent of women reported drinking over six units on at least one day in the week prior to interview.[60]
- In 2008, almost a quarter of adults (24 per cent of men and 25 per cent of women aged 16 or over) in England were classified as obese (BMI 30kg/m2 or over).[61]
- In 2008–09, 10.1 per cent of adults had used one or more illicit drug within the last year, compared with 9.6 per cent in 2007–08. However, over the longer term this shows an overall decrease from 11.1 per cent in 1996.[62]
- In 2008–09, there were around 18.7 million first outpatient attendances. Of these, 10.1 million resulted from GP referral, 3.4 million from other consultants, 1.1 million from referral by an Accident & Emergency department, and the remainder from other sources.[63]
- Total unemployment stood at 2.47 million for the three months to July 2010.[64]

[55] C. Coleman, 'Vulnerability as a Regulatory Category in Human Subject Research' (2009) *Journal of Law, Medicine and Ethics* 12.

[56] World Medical Association, *Declaration of Helsinki* (Ferney-Voltaire, 2008), at A(9).

[57] George Boeree, *Intellegence and IQ* (Shippenberg, 2009).

[58] Mental Health Foundation, *Statistics on Mental Health* (London, 2010).

[59] NHS, *Community Care Statistics 2008–09: Social Services Activity Report, England* (London, 2010).

[60] NHS, *Statistics on Alcohol, England* (London, 2010).

[61] NHS, *Statistics on Obesity, Physical Activity and Diet, England* (London, 2010).

[62] NHS, *Statistics on Drug Misuse: England* (London, 2009).

[63] NHS, *Hospital Outpatient Activity, 2008–09* (London, 2010).

[64] Office of National Statistics, *Employment* (London, 2010).

- The population of the UK is ageing. Over the last 25 years the percentage of the population aged 65 and over increased from 15 per cent in 1983 to 16 per cent in 2008, an increase of 1.5 million people in this age group.[65]
- There are over 6.9 million disabled people of working age, which represents 19 per cent of the working population.[66]
- In 2007–08, 13.5 million people in the UK were living in households below the low-income threshold. This is around a fifth (22 per cent) of the population.

My point is more than identifying the number of people who could typically be labelled as vulnerable.[67] Rather, my point is that we are *all* vulnerable. We are all profoundly dependent on others for our physical and psychological well-being. Our society has built up a wide range of structures and forms of assistance which disguise our vulnerability. Indeed, we are forced by a wide range of societal pressures to disguise or mitigate our vulnerability so that we can behave in an acceptable way in the public realm.[68] In a powerful article Kate Lindemann contrasts the emphasis that is paid to the accommodations for disabled people so as to minimize the impact of their disability, with the lack of appreciation of the accommodations for the able bodied:

> Colleagues, professional staff members, and other adults are unconscious of the numerous accommodations that society provides to make their work and life style possible. ATM's, extended hours in banks, shopping centres and medical offices, EZpass, newspaper kiosks, and elevators are all accommodations that make contemporary working life possible. There are entire industries devoted to accommodating the needs of adult working people. Fast food, office lunch delivery, day time child care, respite care, car washing, personal care attendants, interpreters, house cleaning, and yard and lawn services are all occupations that provide services that make it possible for adults to hold full time jobs.[69]

We thus highlight the facilities used to deal with the vulnerabilities of others, while overlooking the accommodations 'we' need to deal with our vulnerabilities.

A similar point can be made about children. There are a mass of social structures which push children towards a passive, non-autonomous role, and a mass of social structures which enable adults to live apparently independent and autonomous lives. These often go unnoticed and assumed as normal.[70] We readily class those who need care from others as vulnerable, without seeing the vulnerability that caring creates for the carer.[71] This is particularly so in the case of children, as will be discussed next.

16.6 Children's vulnerability is adults' vulnerability

In fact, children's vulnerability is a source of adults' vulnerability. For parents there is ever constant fear that the child out of eyesight or earshot is in danger. Every parent

[65] Office of National Statistics, *Ageing* (London, 2010).

[66] Disability Rights Commission, *Statistics* (London, 2009).

[67] Barbara Fawcett, 'Vulnerability: Questioning the Certainties in Social Work and Health' (2009) 52 *International Social Work* 473.

[68] I am grateful to Jo Bridgeman for this point.

[69] Kate Lindemann, 'The Ethics Of Receiving' (2003) 24 *Theoretical Medicine and Bioethics* 501.

[70] Alan Peterson and Iain Wilkinson, *Health, Risk and Vulnerability* (London, 2007).

[71] Bill Hughes, Linda McKie, Debra Hopkins, and Nick Watson, 'Love's Labours Lost? Feminism, the Disabled People's Movement and an Ethic of Care' (2005) 39 *Sociology* 259.

knows the sinking stomach when the child is not in the place you expected her to be.[72] The nagging questions: is it safe to let them walk to the shop? visit the friend? be photographed by someone at the sports day? etc. Parenthood is in danger of becoming a time of near constant fear. While a somewhat polemical book, Frank Furedi's *Paranoid Parenting*[73] captures well the fear that many parents feel not only at the many 'risks' children face, but their inability to protect their children from those risks.

Part of this fear is that what one does as an adult can have a profound impact on the child. As Beck-Gersheim puts it:

> A child can no longer be accepted as it is, with physical idiosyncrasies, perhaps even flaws. Rather, it becomes the target of a diversity of efforts. All possible flaws must be corrected... all possible talents must be stimulated... Countless guides to education and upbringing appear on the book and magazine market. As different as each one is, at bottom they all have a similar message: the success of the child is defined as the private duty and responsibility of the parents/the mother. And the duty reads the same everywhere: the parents must do everything to give the child 'the best start in life'.[74]

As this quotation indicates, the greater the perceived vulnerability of the child, the greater the levels of care required, and that in turn creates its own form of vulnerability for the carer.[75] Ironically, while the impact of parenting on children is much discussed, the impact of children on parents goes barely noticed. I remember well a lecture in which I set out the ways my children had 'parented' me that morning: it took some time to go through it all!

There is a further argument here and that is that many of our concerns about children's vulnerability are in fact a projection of adult's own vulnerabilities. Chris Jenks once perceptively stated:

> The child cannot be imagined without considering the idea of 'adult' just as it is impossible to picture the adult and society without positing 'the child.'[76]

Our construction of childhood is therefore part of defining what it is to be an adult. Adults seek to deny their own vulnerability by projecting it onto children. Shelley Day Sclater and Christine Piper[77] have discussed this projection. They explain:

> 'Projection' refers to an unconscious process whereby painful feelings are expelled from inside the self and located in another person. The subject can then deal with those feelings, as it were, at one step removed, as though they were characteristics of another. At its simplest, projection is happening when a part of the self is perceived in someone else, and we are therefore assisted, by a psychological defence mechanism, to avoid deeply painful emotions. It must be emphasized, however, that psychological mechanisms like projection are ordinary processes and are not indicative of pathology; projection is actually commonplace and ordinary.[78]

[72] Mary Jane Kehily, 'Childhood in Crisis? Tracing the Contours of "Crisis" and its Impact upon Contemporary Parenting Practices' (2010) 32(2) *Media, Culture & Society* 171–85.

[73] Frank Furedi, *Paranoid Parenting* (London, 2001).

[74] Elizabeth Beck-Gersheim, 'Individualization and "Precarious Freedoms": Perspectives and Controversies of a Subject-orientated Sociology' in (eds.) Paul Heelas, Scott Lash, and Paul Morris, *Detraditionalization* (Oxford, 1996), 23, at 48.

[75] Charlotte Chorn Dunham and Julie Harms Cannon, '"They're Still in Control Enough to be in Control": Paradox of Power in Dementia Caregiving' (2008) 22 *Journal of Aging Studies* 45.

[76] Chris Jenks, *Childhood Projection* (London, 2005), 87.

[77] Shelley Day Sclater and Christine Piper, 'Social Exclusion and the Welfare of the Child' (2001) 28 *Journal of Law and Society* 409.

[78] Shelley Day Sclater and Christine Piper, 'Social Exclusion and the Welfare of the Child' (2001) 28 *Journal of Law and Society* 409, 411.

They argue that, 'If adults can legitimately position children as vulnerable with reference to the welfare discourse, they may then have little incentive to confront the vulnerable feelings inside themselves'. They go on to argue:

In a divorce situation, the welfare discourse both permits individuals to fight for the perceived needs of vulnerable children and allows children to become repositories for the overwhelming feelings of parents. It is difficult to avoid the conclusion that we, as adults, have an emotional investment in seeing things in the way that we do and in acting in the way that we do. Our analysis of the operation of the welfare principle in relation to divorce and separation would suggest that we are comfortable when regarding our children as vulnerable because this serves an emotional purpose for us. This, perhaps, is why achieving participation and autonomy rights for children is proving to be such a difficult thing to do.[79]

16.7 Vulnerability is good

David Archard has written:

There may be features of childhood but not of adulthood which are valuable, such as innocence, wonder and trust. There may, correspondingly be features of adulthood but not childhood which are valuable, such as experience and independence. It is also evident that there may be features of childhood but not of adulthood which are not valuable, such as dependence and vulnerability.[80]

This dislike of dependence and vulnerability is not restricted to philosophers. John Moore, then the Secretary of State for Social Security commented:

A climate of dependence can in time corrupt the human spirit. Everyone knows the sullen apathy of dependence and can compare it with the sheer delight of personal achievement.[81]

I think both of these are profoundly mistaken. Vulnerability and dependence are not only inevitable parts of humanity, as argued above, they are greatly to be welcomed. They are often virtues, not vices.

Comments such as that from John Moore are common. Self-reliance has become a dominant theme in social policy.[82] Be it lone parents or care in the community, autonomy and independence has become a key policy goal. But this ignores the fact that as humans we are interdependent.[83] Any personal achievements of the kind referred to by Moore are in reality the product of many people's efforts.[84] Any academic will readily acknowledge their debt to the writings of earlier academics and discussions with others in the production of research.

[79] Shelley Day Sclater and Christine Piper, 'Social Exclusion and the Welfare of the Child' (2001) 28 *Journal of Law and Society* 409, 412.

[80] David Archard, 'Philosophical Perspectives on Childhood' in (ed.) Julia Fionda, *Legal Concepts of Childhood* (Oxford, 2001), 52.

[81] John Moore, UK Secretary of State for Social Security, 1987, quoted in Michael Fine and Caroline Glendinning, 'Dependence, Independence or Interdependence? Revisiting the concepts of "Care" and "Dependency"' (2005) *Ageing and Society* 601, 601.

[82] Knut Halvorsen, 'Symbolic Purposes and Factual Consequences of the Concepts "Self-Reliance" and "Dependency" in Contemporary Discourses on Welfare' (1998) 7 *Scandanavian Journal of Social Welfare* 56.

[83] Susan Dodds, 'Gender, Ageing, and Injustice: Social and Political Contexts of Bioethics' (2005) 31 *Journal of Medical Ethics* 295.

[84] Michael Fine and Caroline Glendinning, 'Dependence, Independence or Interdependence? Revisiting the Concepts of "Care" and "Dependency"' (2005) *Ageing and Society* 601, 601.

The vulnerability narrative tends to promote disablist approaches to the issue. As many writers from disabilities studies have written, there is great pressure to be perceived to be independent and lacking vulnerability. Success for a person with a disability is measured by the extent to which they may be able to be (or present themselves as being) independent and autonomous. In short, to be 'normal'.[85]

Being vulnerable is an aspect of many of the great values. Relationships; intimacy; care; all of these things in their nature render us vulnerable.[86] It is only by properly appreciating our vulnerable nature that the importance of human rights is appreciated.[87] Similarly, dependency should not be something to be afraid of or ashamed of. Something has gone very wrong with our care of vulnerable older people when 'not being a burden' is reported as the main goal of their lives by patients living in nursing homes.[88] Dependency on others is an aspect of our humanity. From our earliest beginnings we are in relationships of dependency and we continue so for much, if not all, of our lives. Sometimes receiving, sometimes giving, care; often doing both. Relationships of dependency are central to our lives.

16.7.1 Elevation of the rational

Part of what is behind the distinction drawn between children and adults is an elevation of rational thought as being the key marker of personhood. We can see this in its most extreme with those who question whether people with severe mental disability should or should not be regarded as moral people.[89] Children are seen as *potential* citizens, and as regarded as having 'the right to a free future'.[90] Children are not there yet, but are on their way.

Eva Feder Kittay[91] has written movingly of the attitudes displayed towards her severely disabled daughter, Sesha:

> Sesha's life is a human life, but a tragic one because her situation is such that she can never achieve functioning of all the capabilities to some satisfactory degree. I believe that were Sesha capable of replying, she would remind us that people with disabilities have worked hard to insist that life with impairments, even serious impairments need not be 'tragic'. What is tragic is the failure of the larger society to include people with variant bodies and modes of functioning. Yes, when Sesha was born I had envisioned a different future for her. Yes, when I learned of her very significant impairments I saw a human tragedy. But I have since learned—from her, from the disability community and from my own observations—that she is capable of having a very good life, one full of joy, of love, of laughter: a life that includes the appreciation of some of the best of human culture, great music and fine food, and the delights of nature, water, the scent of flowers, the singing of birds. No, she cannot participate in political life, she cannot marry and have children, she cannot read a book or engage in moral reasoning, but her life is richly human and full of dignity. We need to work hard to see that her life is not tragic...

[85] Tom Shakespeare, *Help* (London, 2000).
[86] George W. Harris, *Dignity and Vulnerability* (Berkeley, California, 1997).
[87] Bryan Turner, *Vulnerability and Human Rights* (University Park, Pennsylvania, 2006), chapter 2.
[88] S. Pleschberge, 'Dignity and the Challenge of Dying in Nursing Homes: the Residents' View' (2007) 36 *Age and Ageing* 197.
[89] E.g. Peter Singer, 'Speciesism and Moral Status' (2009) 40 *Metaphilosophy* 56.
[90] Claudia Mills, 'The Child's Right to an Open Future?' (2003) 34 *Journal of Social Philosophy* 499.
[91] Eva Kittay, 'Equality, Dignity and Disability' in (eds.) Mary Ann Lyons and Fionnuala Waldron, *Perspectives on Equality* (Dublin 2005), 95.

Eva Kittay in this passage shows how the disabled can be branded and defined by their lack of abilities in accordance with the norm. Yet, her emphasis is on Sesha's capabilities. We could make similar points about children. If we value in humanity not, or not only, a certain kind of rational thought, but the capacity for wonder, for unconditional loving, intense feeling, then many children have these to a greater extent than many adults.

Kittay concludes her discussion of dignity with a central point:

> I urge that we not look for the basis of dignity in attributions we have as individuals, but in the relationships we bear to one another. Relationships of caring serve as conduits of worth—the worth of the caregiver is conferred on the one to whom she devotes herself.

Although I would want to add that in relationships of care it is hard to separate out who is the cared for and who is carer.[92] There is often an interdependency and interchange which means the obvious categories of care and cared for break down. How easily we overlook the care children provide adults. Not only in the small things: the overlooking of child carers of adults in much of the literature on care is significant. If our source of value, dignity, and humanity is not our intellect but our feelings, relationships, care, love, then separation between children as the vulnerable and adults the non-vulnerable collapses.

16.8 Power, not vulnerability

A more profitable way of considering the issues of children's vulnerability is to look at the use of power over children, rather than vulnerability. And not only the power of adults over children but the power that children can exercise over children. Jenny Kitzinger suggests if we replace the words vulnerability with oppression then we begin to get a more accurate picture.[93] Some of children's vulnerability does not rest in the nature of childhood, but the use of power by adults. The use of power not only creates the vulnerability, it thereby creates the justification for its own use.

The lack of legal power for children is itself a source of vulnerability, but can be explained by it. We can see too the law's acceptance of corporal punishment which is justified in the name of enabling parents to exercise control over children in order to protect children from risk. Yet the practice and acceptance of corporal punishment reveals a diminished acceptance of children's rights and personhood. It creates its own range of vulnerabilities. Social structures can legitimize dependency and vulnerability.[94] Susan Dodds writes:

> Any limitations on such individuals are to be construed as either chosen (and hence the cost should be borne by the individual) or as problems peculiar to the individual, rather than as a predictable effect of dominant social norms, given the kinds of things human people are.[95]

[92] Jonathan Herring, 'Caregivers in Medical Law and Ethics' (2008) 25 *Journal of Contemporary Health Law and Policy* 1.

[93] Jenny Kitzinger, 'Who are You Kidding? Children, Power and the Struggle Against Sexual Abuse' in (eds.) A. James and A. Prout, *Constructing and Reconstructing Childhood* (London, 1997).

[94] Michael Fine and Caroline Glendinning, 'Dependence, Independence or Interdependence? Revisiting the concepts of "Care" and "Dependency"' (2005) *Ageing and Society* 601, 601.

[95] Susan Dodds, 'Gender, Ageing, and Injustice: Social and Political Contexts of Bioethics' (2005) 31 *Journal of Medical Ethics* 295.

The perception of vulnerability of children can distract from an appreciation of the power exercised by adults. The power is seen as a natural response to the vulnerability. It also disguises the power that children can exercise over adults. An appreciation of the common and interlocking vulnerabilities of adults and children can reveal what can otherwise be an unrecognized use of power.

16.9 Developing a legal response

At the heart of a legal response which seeks to recognize the vulnerability of all people, both adults and children, should be two elements: first a centralizing of vulnerability; and second an emphasis on caring relationships.

16.9.1 Centralizing vulnerability

The law tends to assume that adults have capacity, are autonomous, and able to make decisions for their life which are worthy of respect. The general law's rules apply to such people. There are then special areas of the law which are marked off for those lacking capacity. For example, there are special exceptions to the rules of contract which apply to minors, those under undue influence, or those lacking mental capacity. Children are seen as falling within one of these exceptional cases deserving of special rules. We can see this in the very structure of the law syllabuses at most UK law schools where the subjects of contract, land, and tort dominate, and the subjects of child law, mental health law, welfare law, and elder law are very much to the side, if visible at all. They are seen as exceptional cases. Indeed an undergraduate could work through their law degree reading only a tiny number of cases in which a child or a person lacking capacity is involved. It may be the world of a select group of law firms, but it is not the real world, as any high street solicitor or social worker will be aware.

We could, and should, present a rather different legal system, which starts with an acknowledgement of everone's vulnerability.[96] Law degrees would have the law on mental health, child law, carer law, elder law, and undue influence at their hearts. This would produce a different way of looking at the world. Gone would be the special 'concessions' involved in protecting especially disadvantaged groups such as the disabled or children. Instead, they would be regarded as the norm and the focus would be on the special privileges that are given to the able bodied or some adults.

Martha Fineman summarizes that approach in this way:

> I argue that the 'vulnerable subject' must replace the autonomous and independent subject asserted in the liberal tradition. Far more representative of actual lived experience and the human condition, the vulnerable subject should be at the centre of our political and theoretical endeavours. The vision of the state that would emerge in such an engagement would be both more responsive to and responsible for the vulnerable subject...[97]

The significance of this shift in perspective is significant. Vulnerability, rather than being regarded as a form of deprivation or pathology, would be regarded as the normal state for people to be in. Our focus would be on the privileges the lucky few have,

[96] Piers Blaikie, Terry Cannon, Ian Davis, and Ben Wisner, *At Risk: Natural Hazards, People's Vulnerability, and Disasters* (London, 2003).

[97] Martha Fineman, 'The Vulnerable Subject: Anchoring Equality in the Human Condition' (2008) 20 *Yale Journal of Law and Feminism* 1.

rather than the vulnerability of the most. Fineman argues that vulnerability is a 'universal, inevitable, enduring aspect of the human condition that must be at the heart of our concept of social and state responsibility'. She explains that our embodiment carries with it the ever present risk of harm, injury, and misfortune. Life has the risk of accidents or tragedies. These are beyond human control. All manner of natural disaster, illness, are a risk of harm. This leads her to argue that 'society can and does mediate, compensate, and lessen our vulnerability through programs, institutions, and structures. Therefore, because both our personal and our social lives are marked and shaped by vulnerability, a vulnerability analysis must have both individual and institutional components'.

As Fineman argues, current liberal thought around the liberal subject as a social actor is based on autonomy, self sufficiency, and self determinacy.

The significance of this approach is spelt out by Fineman:

> When we only study the poor, the rich remain hidden and their advantages remain relatively unexamined, nestled in secure and private spaces, where there is no need for them or the state to justify or explain why they deserve the privilege of state protection. We need to excavate these privileged lives. While sometimes this will be a difficult and complex undertaking, there are certainly abundant records and instruments of privilege all around us that can be accessed relatively easily. These archives are located in corporate boardrooms and in the rules setting up or limiting state and national regulatory regimes. They can be gleaned from tax and probate codes, history books, literature, political theories, and of course, from the language and logic of the law.[98]

It is not just the 'subjects' that make up the law degree that is the problem, it is the norm of independence, autonomy, and non-vulnerability that is perpetuated. So even where child law is studied, the discussion tends to centre on the way children depart from that norm.

Susan Dodds also argues that we need a legal and social system which is not premised on individualistic conceptions of autonomy but an acceptance of our vulnerability:

> A vulnerability-centered view of the self and of persons is better able to capture many of our moral motivations and intuitions than can be captured by an autonomy-focused approach. We are all vulnerable to the exigencies of our embodied, social and relational existence and, in recognizing this inherent human vulnerability, we can see the ways in which a range of social institutions and structures protect us against some vulnerabilities, while others expose us to risk. We do not have to view our obligations towards those who lack the capacity to develop or retain autonomy as having a different source from our obligations towards those whose autonomy is made vulnerable due to a degree of dependency. It may be easier to recognize the social value of provision of care if it is viewed as something on which we all have been dependent and on which we are all likely to be dependent at different points in our lives, rather than altruistic behaviour extended to those who lack 'full personhood'.[99]

The law focuses on adults and independent adults as the norm, and children and other 'vulnerable adults' as departures from that norm requiring special protections or privileges. The power exercised by adults over children is lost with these assumptions and the emphasis placed on vulnerability. The role of the law could shift to

[98] Martha Fineman, 'Equality: Still Illusive After All These Years' in (eds.) Joanna Grossman and Linda McClain, *Social Citizenship and Gender* (Cambridge, 2010).

[99] Susan Dodds, 'Depending On Care: Recognition of Vulnerability and the Social Contribution of Care Provision' (2007) 21 *Bioethics* 500, 507.

restricting and reducing the power of the powerful, rather than seeking to protect the vulnerable from an exercise of power.[100]

An interesting example, perhaps, of this is the creation of a jurisdiction in the courts for vulnerable adults, even though they have capacity.[101] This definition of a 'vulnerable adult' reflects closely the definition offered by the Lord Chancellor's Department in the consultation document, *Who Decides? Making decisions on behalf of mentally incapacitated adults*:

> A vulnerable adult is defined as someone over the age of 18 who is or may be in need of community care services by reason of mental or other disability, age or illness and who is or may be unable to take care of him/herself or unable to protect him/herself against significant harm or exploitation.[102]

The case law on vulnerable adults is still developing. In *Re SK (An Adult) (Forced Marriage: Appropriate Relief)*, Munby J stated that:

> [i]n the context of the inherent jurisdiction I would treat as a vulnerable adult someone who, whether or not mentally incapacitated, and whether or not suffering from any mental illness, or mental disorder, is or may be unable to take care of him or herself, or unable to protect him or herself against significant harm or exploitation, or who is deaf, blind, or dumb, or who is substantially handicapped by illness, injury or congenital deformity. This, I emphasize, is not and is not intended to be a definition. It is descriptive, not definitive; indicative rather than prescriptive.[103]

It is interesting that in *Re A*[104] Munby J heard two cases together which he explained raised 'essentially the same important issue',[105] namely the circumstances in which it was permissible to remove someone from the care of their families. What, however, is striking is that one case involved a child and the other a vulnerable adult. To Munby J, despite the fact the statutory and case law might differ the essential question was the same for each. The cases raise some interesting issues, and this is not the place to go into those, but there is an acknowledgment here that even if it is accepted that vulnerability is an appropriate criterion to use, it does not automatically lead to children being treated differently from adults.

The approach taken to vulnerable adults indicates perhaps a chipping away at the assumption that the autonomous adult is the ideal, with the exceptions for children and those lacking mental capacity. It indicates an acceptance that adults can be vulnerable. Using Munby J's test, how many people are able to look after themselves or protect themselves from significant harm or exploitation, at least on their own? No doubt Munby J was imagining that the jurisdiction would apply to a limited number of people, but the logic of his approach can be applied much more widely.

[100] Samuel Bray, 'Power Rules' (2010) 110 *Columbia Law Review* 1172.

[101] *Re SA (Vulnerable Adult with Capacity: Marriage)* [2006] 1 FLR 867, discussed by Mary Welstead, 'Vulnerable adults: The inherent jurisdiction and the right to marry' (2007) 19 *The Denning Law Journal* 258.

[102] Lord Chancellor's Department, *Who Decides? Making Decisions on Behalf of 'Mentally Incapacitated' Adults* (London, 1997).

[103] [2004] EWHC 3302 (Fam), at [82] per Munby J.

[104] [2010] EWHC 978 (Fam).

[105] At [3].

16.9.2 Centralizing care

Alongside a recognition of our shared vulnerability should be an acknowledgement of the importance of care.[106] Mutual care is essential for the functioning society. As Joan Tronto writes:

> Care is not a parochial concern of women, a type of secondary moral question, or the work of the least well off in society. Care is a central concern of human life. It is time we began to change our political and social institutions to reflect this truth.[107]

Care work therefore needs to be recognized and valued within the legal system.[108] The legal and social response to caring provides a challenge to the way legal rights and responsibilities are understood.[109] Much of the law is based on the assumption that we are competent, detached, independent people who are entitled to have our rights of self-determination and autonomy fiercely protected.[110] However, the reality is that we are ignorant, vulnerable, interdependent individuals, whose strength and reality is not in our autonomy, but our relationships with others.[111]

Much of the writing on ethics of care offers alternatives to individualistic approaches.[112] There is an extensive literature on this and only a very brief summary will be offered here. These regard the role of law to promote caring relationships, rather than the pursuit of individual rights. Rights have been misused as tools to keep other people out of my life. They need not be so understood. They can be used in progressive ways of protecting and promoting values of community and mutuality. In failing properly to acknowledge care work, the law misses an important and inevitable aspect of life. Eva Feder Kittay wrote of our interdependence:

> My point is that this interdependence begins with dependence. It begins with the dependency of an infant, and often ends with the dependency of a very ill or frail person close to dying. The infant may develop into a person who can reciprocate, an individual upon whom another can be dependent and whose continuing needs make her interdependent with others. The frail elderly person . . . may herself have been involved in a series of interdependent relations. But at some point there is a dependency that is not yet or no longer an interdependency. By excluding *this* dependency from social and political concerns, we have been able to fashion the pretense that we are *independent*—that the cooperation between persons that some insist is *inter*dependence is simply the mutual (often voluntary) cooperation between essentially independent persons.[113]

[106] Martha Fineman, *The Autonomy Myth* (New York, 2004), xvii; Steven Levy, 'The Relational Self and the Right to Give Care' (2006) 28 *New Political Science* 547, 548.

[107] Joan Tronto, *Moral Boundaries: A Political Argument for an Ethic of Care* (London, 1993), 180.

[108] Fiona Williams, 'The Presence of Feminism in the Future of Welfare' (2002) 31 *Economy and Society* 502, 509.

[109] Rosemarie Tong, 'The Ethics of Care: A Feminist Virtue Ethics of Care for Healthcare Practitioners' (1998) 23 *Journal of Medicine and Philosophy* 131.

[110] Liz Lloyd, 'Mortality and Morality: Ageing and the Ethics of Care' (2004) 24 *Ageing and Society* 235.

[111] Christopher Meyers, 'Cruel Choices: Autonomy and Critical Care Decision-Making' (2004) 18 *Bioethics* 104; Joan Tronto, *Moral Boundaries* (London, 1993), 167–70.

[112] E.g., Carol Gilligan, 'Moral Orientation and Moral Development' in (eds.) Eva Kittay and Diana Meyers, *Women and Moral Theory* (Savage, Maryland, 1987); Marilyn Friedman, 'Liberating Care' in (ed.) Marilyn Friedman, *What Are Friends For?* (Ithica, New York, 1993); Selma Sevenhuijsen, *Citizenship and The Ethics of Care* (London, 1998); Ruth Groenhout, *Connected Lives: Human Nature and an Ethics of Care* (Savage, Maryland, 2004); Virginia Held, *The Ethics of Care* (New York, 2006); Daniel Engster, *The Heart of Justice. Care Ethics and Political Theory* (Oxford, 2007).

[113] Eva Feder Kittay, *Love's Labor: Essays on Women, Equality and Dependency* (New York, 1999), xii (emphasis in original).

In relationships of caring and dependency our interests become intermingled.[114] We do not break down into 'me' and 'you'. To harm a caregiver is to harm the person cared for; to harm the person cared for is to harm the caregiver. There should be no talk of balancing the interests of the caregiver and the person cared for: the question rather should be emphasizing the responsibilities they owe to each other in the context of a mutually supporting relationship.[115]

Indeed, it is simplistic to imagine we can identify in a caring relationship who is the caregiver and who is the cared for; their relationship is marked by interdependency. The 'cared for' provides the 'caregiver' with gratitude, love, acknowledgement, and emotional support, which will be of great emotional value to him. Indeed, often a 'caregiver' will be the 'cared for' in another relationship. As Diane Gibson noted, our society is made up of overlapping networks of dependency.[116]

Caring relations often involve a complex interplay of dependencies and vulnerabilities.[117] As Michael Fine and Caroline Glendinning argued:

> Recent studies of care suggest that qualities of reciprocal dependence underlie much of what is termed 'care'. Rather than being a unidirectional activity in which an active care-giver does something to a passive and dependent recipient, these accounts suggest that care is best understood as the product or outcome of the relationship between two or more people.[118]

When assessing the rights of any individual or the medical needs of an individual, such a person should be considered in a situational context. Never should it be a matter of assessing a person in isolation. Rather, each person's needs and rights must be considered in the context of their relationships.

An approach based on an ethic of care is one that recognizes that care is part of the human condition and that it involves a recognition of our mutual vulnerabilities that makes care a necessary, and rewarding, part of life. Without a recognition of our common vulnerability there is a danger, as some critics have complained, that 'care ethics' can be seen to valourize the carer, and devalue the 'cared for'.[119] Once our common vulnerability and the mutuality of care is recognized this criticism to a large extent is dissipated.

My digression on to care is a central part of understanding vulnerability. Once we accept that we all are, to some extent, in relationships of care, then we see that we are all, to some extent, vulnerable. Children are only one aspect of that vulnerability, and it is wrong to regard them as especially vulnerable.

16.10 Conclusion

This chapter has considered the claims made about the vulnerability of children and explored the impact that the perceived vulnerability of children has had on the legal

[114] Tom Shakespeare, *Help* (London, 2000) and Tom Shakespeare, 'The Social Relations of Care' in (eds.) Gail Lewis, Sharon Gewirtz, and John Clarke, *Rethinking Social Policy* (Bristol, 2001), 53.

[115] Grace Clement, *Care, Autonomy and Justice: Feminism and the Ethic of Care* (Boulder, Colerado, 1996), 11; Virginia Held, *The Ethics of Care* (New York, 2006), chapter 1.

[116] Diane Gibson, *Aged Care: Old Policies, New Solutions* (Cambridge, 2005), 185.

[117] Charlotte Chorn Dunham and Julie Harms Cannon, '"They're Still in Control Enough to be in Control": Paradox of Power in Dementia Caregiving' (2008) 22 *Journal of Aging Studies* 45.

[118] Michael Fine and Caroline Glendinning, 'Dependence, Independence or Inter-Dependence? Revisiting the Concepts of Care and Dependency' (2005) 25 *Ageing and Society* 601, 616.

[119] See e.g. Tom Shakespeare, *Help* (London, 2000).

responses to children. While sympathetic to the writings which have sought to deny the vulnerability of children, this chapter has sought rather to emphasize the vulnerability of adults. It has argued that vulnerability is the common lot of humanity. The portrayal by adults of children as especially vulnerable is part of an attempt to hide from the vulnerability of adults. It helps bolster the image of the autonomous independent man on which so much legal analysis and thought is based. He is the figure who so dominates the law books and law courses. The more realistic picture of the vulnerable interdependent relationship is sidelined and overlooked. Yet that is our reality. We need to rejoice in our vulnerability, for it is that which is central to our humanity. Our law needs to centralize common human vulnerability and the resulting need for networks of care as the cornerstone of a legal system.

17

'When the Kissing has to Stop': Children, Sexual Behaviour, and the Criminal Law

Heather Keating[1]

17.1 Introduction

There are, perhaps, few areas where our confused and conflicting constructions of childhood are brought into such profound tension as that concerning the law relating to consensual sexual behaviour between children or young people.[2] This chapter highlights these tensions and considers the way in which the current law, contained within the Sexual Offences Act 2003, attempts to resolve them. It does so, by reflecting briefly on constructions of childhood, children's sexuality, and what is known about their sexual behaviour, before exploring the legal framework. That legal framework includes not only the Sexual Offences Act 2003 but also the age of criminal responsibility. The chapter considers whether prohibiting sexual activity, including even kissing, cuddling, and petting, below the age of 16 (the age of consent) is the most appropriate legal response in achieving the difficult 'balance between protection from abuse... on one hand and permitting sexual expression of young people as they proceed through to adulthood on the other'.[3] It focuses particularly on the current protective strategy to resolving that dilemma by which such behaviour, which we know children engage in, is criminal but prosecutorial discretion is relied upon to prevent 'normal', mutually agreed early teenage sexual behaviour being prosecuted. The chapter argues that this, taken together with an age of criminal responsibility which is fixed at 10, renders the law inconsistent, illogical, and strikingly confused: children are held to be incapable of giving valid consent on the one hand and responsible for their behaviour on the other.

The essay concludes with a consideration of alternative approaches, chiefly from recent reforms in Scotland, and argues that if justice is to be done to children, reform is needed to both the age of criminal responsibility and the law relating to sexual offences involving older children.

[1] Senior Lecturer in Law, University of Sussex. With thanks to Michael Freeman for the suggested title (adapted from the novel, *When the Kissing had to Stop* by Constantine Fitzgibbon (1960, Cassell and Co, London)). I am also grateful for the helpful comments made by the reviewer.

[2] The term 'children' will be used throughout this essay to avoid repetition of children and young people.

[3] Arfan Khan, 'Sexual Offences Act' (2004) 68 *Journal of Criminal Law* 220 at 220.

A key concern of this chapter is, thus, to analyse the law's response to consensual behaviour (although not recognized as such) between children aged between 13 and 15 years old. However, given that the chapter explores the juxtaposition of an age of consent which is fixed at 16 and an age of criminal responsibility set at 10 years old, it begins with an account of the recent and much publicized conviction of two boys aged 10 and 11 for attempted rape in May 2010 of an eight-year-old girl. The boys, who were tried at the Old Bailey, were said to have 'dragged' or 'lured their victim to secluded spots near their homes', to have forced her to remove her underwear and tried to have sex with her.[4] The defence claimed that what had happened was simply childish sexual experimentation—'that age-old game, doctors and nurses'[5] and that there was real doubt as to whether both boys knew what 'sex' entailed. By contrast, in her closing argument, counsel for the prosecution told the jury: 'It would be so much easier and so much nicer to believe that this was all a case of innocent sexual experimentation: a game of "If you show me yours I'll show you mine." Just because it would be easier, just because we do not want to really have to consider these things really did happen is not the way to decide this. One has to look at the evidence, not the way we would like things to perhaps be.'[6] The jury found the boys guilty of attempted rape by a majority of ten to two.[7] A subsequent appeal failed to overturn the convictions but led Hughes LJ to state that 'like the [trial] judge, we have found this a painful case to consider and a difficult one in which to apply the rules which we are obliged to apply'.[8]

Clearly, the law must protect any victim who does not consent to sexual activity. Further, this chapter does not in any way argue that children as young as the victim in this case should be deemed to have the capacity to consent. The reason this case is included is that it forces us to think about childhood, sexuality, and the role of law, both in terms of sexual offences and the age at which children are held to account for their behaviour.

17.2 Childhood and children's sexuality

In what has proved to be a highly influential study, James and Prout assert that: 'the immaturity of children is a biological fact but the ways in which that immaturity is understood and made meaningful is a fact of culture.'[9] That there is, at the very least, a 'schizophrenic dualism'[10] about how we construct childhood has become

[4] One of the many troubling aspects of this trial was the capacity of this little girl to give evidence, albeit by video link. Her evidence changed during the course of the cross-examination from one of coercion to one of participation in a game, which was covered up when telling her mother because she was afraid of being denied sweets. Rather than withdrawing the case from the jury on the basis of no case to answer, the trial judge decided to leave it to the jury to determine the truth (*The Times*, 24 May 2010).

[5] *The Independent*, 25 May 2010. [6] Ibid.

[7] The boys were acquitted of rape. Subsequently, the boys were each sentenced to three-year supervision orders. Their names were placed on the sex offenders' register for two-and-a-half years (although their mothers were permitted to sign it on their behalf). Both boys' mothers were given one-year parenting orders: *Guardian*, 18 August 2010.

[8] *R v W and M* [2010] EWCA Crim 1926 at [37].

[9] Allison James and Alan Prout, 'A New Paradigm for the Sociology of Childhood? Provenance, Promise and Problems' in (eds.) Allison James and Alan Prout, *Constructing and Reconstructing Childhood: Contemporary Issues in the Sociological Study of Childhood* (1997, Falmer Press, Basingstoke), 7.

[10] Sheila Brown, *Understanding Youth and Crime* (2005, Open University Press, Maidenhead), 8.

abundantly clear. Childhood may be constructed as a time of innocence, to be nurtured and not 'lost' by too early 'corruption' by adult concerns. Children may be seen as vulnerable and in need of protection so as to have the opportunity to develop into reasoning, autonomous adults. But childhood may also be constructed as a period in which children's ignorance (rather than innocence) and even evil has to be brought under control. Childhood may thus be something to be treasured or feared: however, radically different although these constructions are, both construct the child as 'other'. While we may think that we can consign this dualism to history—most notably to the Victorian age[11]—the impact of such different constructions upon the way in which (real) children are still treated by society, by law, and by policy makers is profound. In so far as the law is concerned, very broadly speaking, family law has adopted a paternalistic approach based upon a construction of childhood as a period of vulnerability and development during which children's best interests should be protected by the adults who care for them with the support of the law if necessary. In recognition of their growing maturity, and in line with some acknowledgment at least of what studies have revealed about the psychological development of children, older children may be given some rope—but not enough with which they could hang themselves.[12] Again very broadly speaking, the criminal law, on the other hand, regards children (other than the very youngest) as responsible actors, who are accountable for their actions and, if found guilty, are liable to be punished.[13] Some of the discourse surrounding children and crime (and certainly that which pervades much of the tabloid press) would appear to be shaped by (and fuel) a fear of childhood as innately uncontrolled. However, Fionda offers a different interpretation: 'the youth justice process increasingly denies young offenders their childhood, since as devils, they are assigned *adult-like* attributes of evil and the competence of free will.'[14] The 'normal' innocence of childhood and the protection that children thus ordinarily merit is lost or forfeited by children behaving in a way that falls outside the construction. As Fionda also comments, the falsely dichotomous labels of 'angel' or 'devil' are 'defined from an adult perspective and framed upon a false memory of our own childhood and unrealistic expectations of what young people can be or indeed, are, in their own social world'.[15]

But, as well as seeking to identify and punish the blameworthy, criminal law also seeks to protect members of society, particularly vulnerable members of society from harm—even harm to which, ostensibly, they have consented. Ost has commented that 'the protectionist discourse surrounding children and sexual abuse has become so compelling that it is difficult to respond objectively when we perceive children to

[11] See, for example, Hendrick, who describes six different constructions which developed during this period in history: Harry Hendrick, 'Constructions and Reconstructions of British Childhood: An Interpretive Survey 1800 to the Present' in (eds.) Allison James and Alan Prout, *Constructing and Reconstructing Childhood: Contemporary Issues in the Sociological Study of Childhood* (1997, The Falmer Press, Basingstoke).

[12] *Re W (a minor) (medical treatment: court's jurisdiction)* [1993] 1 FLR 1 adapting Lord Donaldson's dicta at 12. See further, Jane Fortin, *Children's Rights and the Developing Law* (2008, Cambridge University Press, Cambridge), 81–103; Michael Freeman, 'The Limits of Children's Rights' in (eds.) Michael Freeman and Philip E. Veerman, *The Ideologies of Children's Rights* (1992, Martinus Nijhoff Publishers, Dordrecht).

[13] These ideas are developed further in, Heather Keating, 'The "Responsibility" of Children in the Criminal Law' (2007) 19 *Child and Family Law Quarterly* 183.

[14] Julia Fionda, *Devils and Angels: Youth Policy and Crime* (2005, Hart Publishing, Oxford), 6 (my emphasis).

[15] Ibid, 4.

be at threat'.[16] Although written in the context of an extension to the legal protection afforded to children in relation to fabricated pornographic images[17] we need to ensure that objectivity is not also lost in wider discussions of children's sexual behaviour.

It is certainly the case that such discussions are controversial. The construction of childhood as a period of innocence, coupled with the idea that sexuality is a 'special area of life' reserved for adults has resulted in an increasingly powerful social taboo.[18] Jackson has commented, 'Our feelings about children and sex are not a normal response to people of a particular age but result from the way in which childhood is defined within our society'.[19] Thus, just as constructions of childhood have changed over time (and, as commentators have shown, differ across cultures[20]) so too have views about children's sexuality. Foucault has analysed this change in terms of adult power over children's sexuality.[21] In his view, gaining control was 'a key feature in the development of educational provision and social policy in western Europe' which has led to the constant monitoring of children's sexuality over the last two centuries.[22] The efforts made during, in particular, the Victorian age to repress sexuality (including, for example, telling children that masturbation would lead to blindness) and the influence of the social purity movement have been well documented.[23] Children's sexuality is no longer seen in such negative and damaging terms. But many would still prefer to pretend that it does not exist. Furthermore, measures taken to protect childhood and children's innocence from sexual matters are not without risk. Kitzinger, writing about the prevention of the sexual abuse and exploitation of children, has argued, for example, that the sometimes extreme rhetoric surrounding the innocence of childhood can serve to reinforce children's desirability to potential abusers as sexual objects. More fundamentally, she argues:

> [T]he reason why it is counterproductive to use 'innocence' in the fight against child sexual abuse is that it is an ideology used to deny children access to knowledge and power and hence actually increases their vulnerability to abuse.... Those adults who champion 'childhood' use innocence as an excuse to exclude children from the 'adult world' and indeed, to isolate them from other children's experiences.[24]

In so far as early sexual experimentation between older children is concerned (rather than adult/child abuse), there is growing acceptance that this is 'normal'. However, that acceptance does not extend to its decriminalization.

[16] Suzanne Ost, 'Criminalising Fabricated Images of Child Pornography: a Matter of Harm or Morality?' (2010) 30 *Legal Studies* 230 at 232.

[17] See the Coroners and Justice Act 2009, sections 62–8.

[18] Mary Jane Kehily and Heather Montgomery, 'Innocence and Experience' in (eds.) Martin Woodhead and Heather Montgomery, *Understanding Childhood* (2003, The Open University Press, Milton Keynes), 236.

[19] Stevi Jackson, *Childhood and Sexuality* (1982, Oxford, Basil Blackwell), 22, cited in Kehily and Montgomery, n. 18, above, 236.

[20] See, for example, William Crocker and Jean Crocker, *The Canela: Bonding Through Kinship, Ritual and Sex* (1994, Fort Worth, Texas, Harcourt Brace College Publishers).

[21] Michel Foucault, *The History of Sexuality* (1976, Penguin, Harmondsworth).

[22] Kehily and Montgomery, n. 18, above, 241.

[23] See Matthew Waites, *The Age of Consent, Young People, Sexuality and Citizenship* (2005, Palgrave Macmillan, Basingstoke) and references cited therein.

[24] Jenny Kitzinger, 'Who are you kidding? Children, Power and the Struggle Against Sexual Abuse' in (eds.) Allison James and Alan Prout, *Constructing and Reconstructing Childhood: Contemporary Issues in the Sociological Study of Childhood* (1997, The Falmer Press, Basingstoke), 167.

Finally, it would be wrong to ignore the importance of gender when considering changes in attitudes towards children's sexuality. The increase in the age of consent from 12 to 13 and then 16 for girls in the late nineteenth century[25] was fought for in order to protect vulnerable young girls from older and more powerful male adults; the battle to save such children from prostitution and sexual abuse needed to be won,[26] but these changes in the law also took place against a gendered construction of sexuality: it was 'founded on a polarised view of male and female sexuality whereby the "beast" of male lust required containment to preserve the virtue of passive, innocent female sexuality'.[27] As Waites comments, 'the question of an age of consent for men did not arise, due to the overwhelming assumption that women did not initiate sexual activity'.[28] The law has since moved towards gender neutrality and, as will be seen, has achieved it in the context of the age of consent, but it would still be wrong, as the next section illustrates, to ignore the issue of gender.

17.3 Children's sexual behaviour

Despite these long-term attempts to control and regulate children's sexual behaviour, research reveals that many children are sexually active below the age of 16. In a national survey of attitudes and lifestyles conducted in 2000, Wellings and colleagues found that the average age of first sexual experience was 14 for girls and 13 for boys. The median age for first heterosexual intercourse was 16 for both boys and girls. 30 per cent of boys aged between 16 and 19 first had sexual intercourse before the age of 16; the corresponding figure for girls was 26 per cent.[29] In *Setting the Boundaries* (the report which reviewed adult and child sexual offences and made recommendations for far-reaching reform)[30] earlier studies are cited in which it had been found that 28 per cent of under-age boys and 19 per cent of under-age girls were sexually active in 1991,[31] while the average age at which teenagers had their first sexual experience was 15.3 years old.[32] However, a significant proportion of those who have sexual intercourse at an early age later express regret that they 'had not waited'; this is particularly true of girls.[33] Further, first sexual intercourse is more likely to be unprotected among the youngest age groups: when first sex occurred between the ages of 13 and 14, 31 per cent of men and 33.6 per cent of women did not use a condom; and 18 per cent of men and 22 per cent of women used no contraception at all. However, these figures are much lower than those obtained in the 1990 survey where the equivalent figures were 60 per cent of men and over half of women.[34]

[25] By the Sexual Offences Act 1875, section 4 and the Criminal Law Amendment Act 1885, section 5 respectively.

[26] See Jennifer Temkin, *Rape and the Legal Process* (2002, Oxford University Press, Oxford), 136–40.

[27] N. 23, above, 70.

[28] Ibid.

[29] Kaye Wellings et al, 'Sexual Behaviour in Britain; Early Heterosexual Experience' (2001) 351 *The Lancet* 1835. See also the earlier survey: *Sexual Behaviour in Britain: the National Survey of Attitudes and Lifestyles* (1994, Penguin, Harmondsworth).

[30] Home Office, *Setting the Boundaries: Reforming the Law on Sexual Offences* (2000, HMSO, London).

[31] Social Exclusion Unit, *Teenage Pregnancy Report*, Cmnd 4342 (1999, TSO, London).

[32] The Durex Global Sex Survey 1999, cited in *Setting the Boundaries*, n. 30, above, para 3.2.10.

[33] Wellings et al, n 29, above.

[34] Ibid.

We do not know whether more children are engaging in under-age sexual intercourse or whether there is now a greater openness about such behaviour. Certainly, the last figures would appear to be indicative of a greater willingness to seek contraceptive advice and treatment. In its report, the Teenage Pregnancy Unit suggested that the law itself had little influence on children's behaviour: indeed, *Setting the Boundaries* cited the 'graphic quote' that 'If someone wants to have sex, they won't go –ah I can't because I'm breaking the law'.[35] By contrast, one study at least has found that one-fifth of girls aged between 13 and 14 would like to see the age of consent raised to 18.[36] This ties in perhaps with the finding of the Teenage Exclusion Report that girls often feel that they are pressurized into early sexual activity.[37] As will be seen, this finding helped to shape the protective stance adopted by *Setting the Boundaries* and subsequent legislation.

17.4 Responsible criminal children

In stark contrast to such protection, the age of criminal responsibility in England and Wales is set at 10, having been raised from seven at common law to eight in 1993 and then to 10 in 1963.[38] Legislation which would have raised it to 14 has never been implemented[39] and was finally removed from the statute books in 1991.[40] From the age of 10 children are, thus, 'generally mature enough to be accountable for their actions'.[41] While the criminal law does indeed rest upon the principle that individuals can be called to account for their behaviour, viewing children as young as 10 as possessing such capacity responsibility has become increasingly controversial.[42]

Further, the presumption of *doli incapax*, which applied up to the child's fourteenth birthday, was abolished in 1998[43] on the basis that it was 'archaic, illogical and unfair in practice'.[44] This presumption required courts to consider whether the child defendant before them understood his or her behaviour to be 'gravely wrong, seriously wrong' rather than merely 'naughty'.[45] If not, the child could not be tried for the offence with which he or she had been charged. The presumption may not, especially towards the end of its existence, have protected many child defendants in practice (when it seemed to be taken as axiomatic, for example, by some judges

[35] N. 30, above, para 3.5.6 (at n. 46), citing n. 31, above, 47.

[36] *The Times*, 8 September 2000.

[37] N. 31, above, 42–3.

[38] The Children and Young Persons Act 1933, section 50 as amended by the Children and Young Persons Act 1963, section 16.

[39] Children and Young Persons Act 1969, section 4.

[40] Criminal Justice Act 1991, section 72.

[41] *No More Excuses: A New Approach to Tackling Youth Crime in England and Wales*, Cm. 3809, (1997, HMSO, London), 1–2.

[42] See further, Keating, n. 13, above. A further illustration of the governmental view that children aged 10 and above are generally responsible is provided by its rejection of the Law Commission's proposal that the developmental immaturity of a defendant aged under 18 should be included in the partial defence of diminished responsibility (available to a charge of murder only): Law Commission, *Murder, Manslaughter and Infanticide*, Law Com No. 206 (2006, TSO, London), para 5.125 and Ministry of Justice, *Murder, Manslaughter and Infanticide: Summary of Responses and Government Position* (2009, TSO, London), paras 97–103.

[43] Crime and Disorder Act 1998, section 34. An argument that this section abolished the presumption but not the defence of *doli incapax* itself was rejected by the House of Lords in *R v JTB* [2009] UKHL 20.

[44] Home Office, *Consultation: Tackling Youth Justice* (1997, HMSO, London), para 7.

[45] *Gorrie* (1919) 83 JP 136.

and commentators that children 'grow up more quickly' and that education would have taught the child right from wrong[46]) but one has to wonder whether it might just have come to the aid of the two boys convicted of attempted rape last year: in sentencing them, the trial judge, Saunders J, told the boys, 'I do not accept that what happened was a game but I do accept that you did not realise how serious what you were doing was.'[47] It is perhaps worth reminding ourselves that these boys are among the very youngest children ever to be convicted of attempted rape.[48] Indeed, it seems that there has been a general increase in the number of children being prosecuted;, for example, IPPR research reveals an increase of 35 per cent in children aged below 15 being prosecuted between the years 2002–2006.[49] It seems likely, however, that this increase results not only from the abolition of the presumption but also from other punitive developments since 1998.[50]

Some concessions are made in relation to proceedings against young defendants. Many will be diverted from formal criminal justice proceedings by means of the system of reprimands and warnings. Of those prosecuted, most child defendants will be tried in the youth courts, where proceedings are not open to the public and efforts are made to reduce the formality of the occasion.[51] But children, even young children just over the age of criminal responsibility, who are charged with serious offences, are still tried in the Crown Court. This is exactly what happened, of course, with the infamous trial of Venables and Thompson (who were aged 11 and 10 at the time of the trial) for the murder of James Bulger, as a result of which the United Kingdom was found to be in breach of the boys' right to a fair trial under Article 6 of the European Convention on Human Rights and new guidelines had to be introduced.[52] However, concern remains about the appropriateness of the Crown Court for very young defendants. That disquiet is fully justified is demonstrated by the recent trial of the two boys for attempted rape. While dismissing the appeal of the two boys against conviction, Hughes LJ commented that the court was 'dismayed' that the case had been heard in the Crown Court and not in the youth court.[53] Hughes LJ was particularly concerned with the impact the trial on a public stage would have had upon the little girl but his dismay extended to the defendants as well.

The age of criminal responsibility, the process by which young defendants are treated by the criminal justice system, and the increasingly punitive policies adopted by successive governments, have all been subject to deserved and intense criticism both domestically and internationally.[54] But for the purposes of this chapter the

[46] See, for instance, n. 41, para 8. It is noteworthy, however, that in the House of Lords decision of *C v Director of Public Prosecutions* [1996] AC 1, which acted as a catalyst for the abolition of the presumption by the government, Lord Lowry did not associate himself with this view (at 33).

[47] *Guardian*, 8 August 2010.

[48] The legal presumption that boys under the age of 14 were incapable of sexual intercourse was abolished by the Sexual Offences Act 1993, section 1.

[49] Joe Farringdon-Smith and Lucia Durante, *Towards and Popular, Preventative Youth Justice System* (2009, IPRR, London), 14.

[50] See further, John Graham, 'Responding to Youth Crime' in (ed.) David J. Smith, *A New Response to Youth Crime* (2010, Willan Publishing, Cullompton) and *R v G* [2010] EWCA Crim 2134 at [25] on developments which may have made prosecutions for sex offences by young defendants more likely.

[51] See Magistrates' Courts (Children and Young Persons) Rules 1992.

[52] *T and V v The United Kingdom* (1990) 30 EHRR 121; *Practice Note (trial of children and young persons: procedure)* [2000] 2 All ER 285.

[53] *R v W and M* [2010] EWCA Crim 1926 at [38]–[40].

[54] See, further, Heather Keating, 'Being Responsible, Becoming Responsible and Having Responsibility Thrust Upon them: Constructing the "Responsibility" of Children and Parents' in (eds.)

chief point of criticism is that 'this presumption of capacity responsibility [from the age of 10] by the criminal justice system stands in marked contrast with what appears almost as a presumption of incapacity... in other legal arenas'.[55] It is against this backdrop of disparity that the chapter now considers the law relating to sexual behaviour between children.

17.5 The Sexual Offences Act 2003: children and consent

It is undeniable that the law relating to sexual offences prior to the passage of the Sexual Offences Act 2003 was in need of substantial reform. The law had developed in a piecemeal way over many years and was rightly condemned as 'archaic, incoherent and discriminatory'.[56] Modernization was needed to reflect 'changes in society and social attitudes',[57] core concepts needed to be clarified, anomalies removed, and there was overwhelming agreement that increased protection of children from sexual abuse was necessary,[58] not least from new ways in which children could be exposed to danger.[59] The legislation which resulted from the reform process is in many ways a significant improvement upon the previous law but the Sexual Offences Act 2003 is also complex and there is a worrying and potentially confusing degree of overlap between offences.[60]

Central to the reform was the creation of a new range of child-specific offences,[61] the primary focus of which would be 'to protect children from abusive (coerced and unwanted) sexual behaviour from older people and other children'.[62] There can be no argument with such an objective. But in drawing up its recommendations for a coherent range of offences *Setting the Boundaries* had to consider the age of consent and allied to this, the role of the law in dealing with under-age sex. Its deliberations on the age of consent are prefaced by an indication of the range of comments received during consultation and they are worth repeating here:

> The age of consent 'is one of the most contentious areas of sexual offences legislation. The law holds that a person below the age of consent is incapable of consent. I believe this is condescending and often offensive and distressing to couples caught up in age of consent offences.'...
>
> We would protest against the policy of police and prosecutors to recognise the sexual autonomy of children, which is resulting in an increasing number of cautions rather than

Jo Bridgeman, Heather Keating, and Craig Lind, *Responsibility, Law and the Family* (2008, Ashgate, Aldershot).

[55] Barry Lyons, 'Dying to be Responsible: Adolescence, Autonomy and Responsibility' (2010) 30 *Legal Studies* 257 at 274.

[56] Home Office, *Protecting the Public, Strengthening Protection against Sexual Offenders and Reforming the Law on Sexual Offences*, Cm. 5668 (2002, TSO, London), para 8.

[57] Ibid, para 4.

[58] N. 30, above, para 3.1.3.

[59] For example, the offence of meeting following grooming was created: see the Sexual Offences Act 2003, section 15.

[60] Containing 52 offences in total (some of which are new and some of which are substantial revisions of existing offences).

[61] Although such offences do not preclude other offences such as rape under the Sexual Offences Act 2003, section 1 being charged where appropriate.

[62] N. 30, above, para 3.9.2.

prosecutions, where unlawful sexual intercourse... is involved, probably due to the notion that a child can give his 'informed consent'.[63]

Against the backdrop of divided opinion, the need to introduce gender neutrality and the desire to increase protection against abuse, the report states:

It is clear that children now mature physically at a much younger age, and are exposed to sexual images and pressure to engage in sexual activity by media when they are very young. However, society has to protect children from inappropriate sexual activity at too early an age when it has the potential to cause physical, emotional and psychological harm. The risks of early pregnancy are well documented and there is evidence linking early sexual activity with increased risk of development of sexually transmitted diseases and cervical cancer.[64]

Have early arguments about protection of childhood innocence and prevention of corruption now been translated into medicalized arguments? The report also noted the evidence that some teenage girls can be put under pressure and 'consent grudgingly, if at all, to early sexual activity'.[65] The different ages of consent elsewhere in the world (for example, that it is 15 in France, Sweden, and Denmark)[66] are acknowledged but the report concludes that it did not see:

any argument for reducing the age of consent—the variation in the rates at which children mature physically and emotionally varies greatly, making any age an arbitrary one. The present age is well established, well understood and well supported. We think there is a real need to maintain an age of consent to ensure that children are protected, and as a matter of public policy, the age of consent should remain at sixteen.[67]

These are valid concerns, which the government later accepted, although one would have wanted much more detailed consideration of such an important issue.[68] However, the principal problem which arises from the perspective of this chapter is the impact this recommendation has upon mutually consensual sexual behaviour between under-age children. It is, of course, accepted that behaviour between under-age children can be as exploitative and non-consensual as between an adult and a child but it cannot, or should not, all be swept away as such. *Setting the Boundaries* comments that 'the role of the law in dealing with under age sex is much more difficult' and that some members of the review had questioned the need for an offence of sex between minors.[69] In trying to resolve the dilemma the report may stand accused of erring on the side of protecting children and, thus, reinforcing the construction of childhood as innocent, at the expense of recognizing children's agency. However, at least it cannot be accused of wishing to keep children in ignorance about sexual advice and knowledge. It makes clear that in seeking such guidance neither children nor their advisors are breaking the law.[70] Quite what children are meant to do with this advice, say, about safe sex, is problematic. There are further difficulties with the arguments: despite acknowledging the finding of the Teenage Pregnancy Report (cited earlier) that the law has little impact upon the behaviour of children who wish

63 Ibid, para 3.3.2.

64 Ibid, para 3.5.5.

65 Ibid, para 3.3.7.

66 Ibid, para 3.5.4.

67 Ibid, para 3.5.7.

68 For a detailed and scholarly analysis of the age of consent, see further, Waites, n. 23, above.

69 N. 30, above, paras 3.9.2–3.9.4.

70 Ibid, paras 3.3.7, 3.8, 3.9.4. The report acknowledges the 'overwhelming message' obtained from discussion groups with children that what was wanted 'was more and better sex education, particularly for boys' (para 3.3.9). The Sexual Offences Act 2003, section 73, provides a defence against aiding, abetting, or counselling certain sexual offences involving children (sections 5, 6, 7, 9, and 13) where the person's purpose is, for example, to protect the child from pregnancy or sexually transmitted disease.

to have sex, the view taken in *Setting the Boundaries* is that the law 'plays a significant social role in setting parameters for behaviour, and we want to discourage under-age sex'.[71] Little wonder then, that in commenting on the review, Lacey states that this is 'an ambitious view of the potential social functions of criminal law'.[72]

The conclusion reached and the one reflected subsequently in sections 5 to 8 of the Sexual Offences Act 2003[73] is that there should be a distinction between children aged below thirteen and those aged between 13 and below 16. For children aged under 13 consent is irrelevant on the basis that it is 'absolutely wrong to engage in sex' below this age.[74] There is a good deal of wisdom of such protective provisions although one cannot help wishing, perhaps unfairly, that the report had at least acknowledged that its view that children aged 12 or under do not have 'the knowledge or understanding of consequences' to have capacity stands in complete contrast to the view taken of children as defendants.[75]

These offences impose strict liability: there is no need to prove *mens rea* on the part of the defendant in relation to the child's age. While these provisions were intended to and do criminalize adults who engage in sexual activity with children under 13, they also catch a much younger person who engages in sexual activity with the (irrelevant) consent of a child under 13. The wording of the offences means that it is possible that a boy of 13, who has kissed and fondled a girl of 12 with her consent, could be convicted of causing a child to engage in sexual activity[76]—even if he believed she was aged 13 or over.

Between the ages of 13 and up to 16, children 'ought not to have sex'.[77] However, the report recognizes 'that children have sex with each other and will continue to do so'.[78] The solution adopted, about which the review members clearly thought very carefully, is complex and given the decision to leave the age of consent at 16 can only provide very limited recognition of children's sexual behaviour. In addition to the range of adult offences against children which are created,[79] where the defendant must be over 18, the recommendations which became law (after substantial reworking by the government and debate during the Bill's passage) provide for a specific offence where the defendant is aged below 18 and the other party is below 16. Section 13 of the Sexual Offences Act 2003, in attempting to provide for more lenient treatment of consensual under-age sex, makes punishable

[71] Ibid, para 3.9.5.

[72] Nicola Lacey, 'Beset by Boundaries: The Home Office Review of Sex Offences' [2001] *Criminal Law Review* 3 at 9.

[73] These offences are rape of a child under 13, punishable by life imprisonment (section 5); assault of a child under 13 by penetration, punishable by a maximum of life imprisonment (section 6); sexual assault of a child under 13 punishable by a maximum of 14 years' imprisonment (section 7); causing or inciting a child under 13 to engage in a sexual activity, carrying a maximum of 14 years' imprisonment (section 8).

[74] N. 30, above, para 3.3.6.

[75] In fact, the only consideration the age of criminal responsibility receives is when the report rejects the age of 10 as the benchmark for consent being irrelevant as 'too low to offer proper protection' (para 3.5.10).

[76] By virtue of the Sexual Offences Act 2003, section 8.

[77] N. 30, above, para 3.3.6.

[78] Ibid, para 3.9.2.

[79] These offences are sexual activity with a child, carrying a maximum of 14 years' imprisonment (section 9); causing or inciting a child to engage in sexual activity, with a maximum of 14 years' imprisonment (section 10); engaging in sexual activity in the presence of a child, with a maximum of 10 years' imprisonment (section 11); causing a child to watch a sexual activity, carrying a maximum of 10 years' imprisonment (section 12). There are additional offences, for example the abuse of trust and familial abuse provisions, not considered here.

by a maximum of five years' imprisonment anything done by a person under 18 which would have been an offence under sections 9 to 12 had that person been 18 or over.

Many commentators have been deeply critical of this solution. Lacey asserts, 'for a Review committed to reflecting contemporary views of "right and wrong", and which sets out from the recognition that criminal law is not the best way to intervene in the area of teenage sex, this is little short of extraordinary'[80] and during the House of Lords' debates on the Bill, Baroness Jay argued that the law would 'reinforce youthful opinions that the adult world is totally alien to their experience. We may regard early sexual experience as immoral, misguided or simply precocious but there is nothing to suggest that by making it automatically criminal, we do anything except, perhaps, make it excitingly illicit'.[81] Finally, Spencer has commented that the offences 'cover... all forms of sexual behaviour between consenting children. The result is to render criminal a range of sexual acts, some of which are usually thought to be normal and proper, and at least not seriously harmful.'[82]

Setting the Boundaries recognized, of course, the potential problems of the approach taken and considered that just as prosecutions for under-age sex between willing teenagers had already become rare in practice, so too under the new law it would 'normally not be acceptable to put them through the mechanism of the criminal justice system'.[83] The government agreed that just as there were no oppressive prosecutions under the old law, this would be the case under the new law because the Crown Prosecution Service would have written guidelines.[84] Prosecutorial discretion thus becomes critical.

17.6 Prosecutorial discretion

The CPS Code for Crown Prosecutors for the Sexual Offences Act 2003 (where the defendant is under 18)[85] opens by quoting Lord Falconer during the passage of the Bill:

> Our overriding concern is to protect children, not to punish them unnecessarily. Where sexual relationships between minors are not abusive, prosecuting either or both children is highly unlikely to be in the public interest. Nor would it be in the best interests of the child.[86]

There are two related issues here. One is a question of principle: 'if the distinction between the cases where we do and do not want to prosecute can be set out in written guidelines, it can, and should, be stated in the Act'.[87] To do otherwise can be said to run contrary to the notion of the rule of law.[88] The second issue is whether, in fact,

[80] Lacey, n. 72, above, 9. Bennion goes considerably further in his criticism: 'One might plausibly call this pathetic effort the Sex Hate Bill' (Francis Bennion, *Sexual Ethics and the Criminal Law* (2003, Lester Publishing, Oxford), 6).

[81] *Hansard* HL Deb, vol 644, col 861 (February 13 2003); similar concerns were expressed, for example, by Baroness Noakes (col 777) and Baroness Gould of Potternewton (col 785).

[82] John Spencer, 'The Sexual Offences Act 2003: (2) Child and Family Offences' [2004] *Criminal Law Review* 347 at 354.

[83] N. 30, above, para 3.19.9.

[84] N. 82, above, 354.

[85] CPS, *Sexual Offences Act 2003, Code for Crown Prosecutors (child defendants (under 18))* (2009).

[86] *Hansard* HL Deb, vol 646, col 1174 (1 April 2003).

[87] Spencer, n. 82, above, 354.

[88] Ibid.

it has been safe, in the years since the implementation of the Act, to rely upon police and prosecutorial discretion.

One can reflect again on the story that emerged in the attempted rape case last year. Given that the age of criminal responsibility does stand at 10 and given the original story told by the eight-year-old girl, the decision to prosecute can be understood: as a spokesperson for the CPS stated, 'the allegations made by the girl were very serious. She has the same right to the protection of the law as an adult and that is why, after very careful consideration of all the evidence, the case was put before a jury'.[89] But as the trial proceeded, the difficulties with establishing what had really happened became clear, with very different stories emerging. While the little girl in question lacked the capacity to give consent, if she had willingly participated in a game with the boys, was the public interest served by the trial continuing? In other words, even when an initial decision to prosecute is justifiable, in instances such as this counsel and judges should be alert to the need to reconsider their decisions, if the oppressive use of the law is to be avoided. Trials cannot become unstoppable juggernauts.

The second case to consider, which is deeply worrying for similar reasons, is that of *R v G*.[90] The defendant, a boy of 15, pleaded guilty to rape of a child under 13 (she was 12 years old). She stated that she had not consented to sexual intercourse and it was on this basis that the most serious charge of rape with a child under 13 under section 5 of the Sexual Offences Act 2003 was proceeded with. The boy argued that the girl had consented and told him she was 15, but pleaded guilty when told that neither her consent nor his reasonable belief as to her age was relevant.[91] His plea was accepted by the prosecution on the basis of his version of facts and that the girl had agreed that she had said she was 15. She did not retract her statement in relation to lack of consent but did not want to give evidence in court because she was too frightened to do so. She and her mother, therefore, agreed to the boy's version of the facts.

The case went to the House of Lords where the defence argued that, given the basis upon which the plea of guilty was accepted, the prosecution should have exercised discretion to reduce the charge to the lesser offence under section 13. The claim was made that proceeding with section 5 (the rape offence) breached the boy's Article 8 rights as a disproportionate interference with his right to respect for his private life. By a majority, the House of Lords rejected the defence arguments. It was held that although Article 8 might be infringed if a child is prosecuted for an offence under section 5 that is not justified under Article 8.2, in this instance, the initial section 5 charge was correct and there was no duty to substitute a section 13 charge. Thus, 'any infringement will turn on the individual facts of each case'.[92] The Court of Appeal had also stated (and a majority of their Lordships did not reject this view) that if it transpires that the facts are less serious than originally alleged, the judge can pass an appropriate sentence to reflect this.[93] This hardly seems to be fair labelling: the

[89] Alison Saunders, Chief Crown Prosecutor for London, *Independent*, 25 May 2010.

[90] [2009] 1 AC 92 (House of Lords).

[91] The House of Lords confirmed that offence was one of strict liability as to the age of the child: Lord Hoffmann at [3].

[92] CPS, n. 85, above. See also *R v G* [2006] 2 Cr App R 17 at [45].

[93] N. 90, above, at [46]. The fact that the boy was given a conditional discharge for an offence carrying a maximum of life imprisonment is, as Ashworth comments, illustrative of the disproportionality of the charge: Andrew Ashworth, *Principles of Criminal Law* (2009, Oxford University Press, Oxford), 345.

defendant may have been an opportunist[94] but the designation as 'rapist' is inaccurate on the basis of the agreed facts.

In her speech, Baroness Hale (in the majority) stressed the positive obligation of the state under Article 8 which might:

> require the criminal law to provide effective protection for those who cannot protect themselves from the sexual attentions of others ... whether they like it or not. ... [A]nyone who has practiced in the family courts is only too well aware of the long term and serious harm both physical and psychological, which premature sexual activity can do. And the harm which may be done by premature sexual penetration is not necessarily lessened by the age of the person penetrating.[95]

Ashworth rightly comments that, this is 'a strong argument, but it is questionable whether it is strong enough to justify convicting of this serious offence a young person of 15 on facts such as those that formed the basis of plea in this case. Important as it is to assert the Art.8 rights of the girl of 12, the question in the case also concerns the Art.8 rights of the 15-year-old'.[96]

It seems clear that a 'heavy responsibility has been placed on the prosecuting authorities, where both parties are of a similar young age, to discriminate between cases where the proscribed activity was truly mutual on the one hand and those where the Complainant was subjected to an element of exploitation or undue pressure on the other'.[97] If the offences are not prosecuted, as one would very much hope would be the case with consensual teenage sexual exploration, children may come to perceive the law as making empty threats. If offences are prosecuted, not only may individual injustices result, but also as Spencer has commented, 'so far are these provisions out of line with the sexual behaviour of the young that ... they will eventually make indictable offenders of the whole population'.[98] Some children may be deterred from seeking medical advice in relation to both contraception and treatment for STDs.

Prosecutorial discretion is, therefore, problematic and it is not surprising that in the light of *R v G* the detailed list of factors to be considered by Crown Prosecutors has been revised. It now includes: the age and understanding of the offender (this may include whether the offender has been subjected to any exploitation, coercion, threat, deception, grooming, or manipulation by another which has led him or her to commit the offence); the relative ages of the parties (that is that they are the same age or there is no significant disparity in age); whether the complainant entered into sexual activity willingly (that is, did the complainant understand the nature of his or her actions and that (s)he was able to communicate his or her willingness freely?); parity between the parties in regard to sexual, physical, emotional, and educational development; the relationship between the parties, its nature, and duration and whether this represents a genuine transitory phase of adolescent development; whether there is any element of exploitation, coercion, threat, deception, grooming, or manipulation in the relationship; the nature of the activity (for example, whether it is penetrative or non-penetrative activity); what is in the best interests and welfare of the complainant; and what is in the best interests and welfare of the defendant.[99] It is perhaps too

[94] See Lord Hope at [33].

[95] [41], [49].

[96] Andrew Ashworth, 'Sexual Offences: Sexual Offences Act 2003, s.5—Rape of a Child under 13—Defendant under 18' [2008] *Criminal Law Review* 818 at 820.

[97] Lord Hope at [14].

[98] Spencer, n. 82, above, 354.

[99] N. 85, above.

early to tell if these revised guidelines will appropriately identify those cases where prosecutions should be brought. The decision to prosecute the 10- and 11-year-old boys for rape and attempted rape would have been made by reference to them but, as already stated, that decision can be understood on the basis of the initial version of events at least. However, the point of principle remains.

17.7 Should we be considering other ways of dealing with under-age sexual behaviour?

The age of consent has not been fully reviewed for 30 years.[100] Lord Millett has argued that, 'the age of consent has long ceased to reflect ordinary life, and in this respect Parliament has signally failed to discharge its responsibility for keeping the criminal law in touch with the needs of society'.[101] After an extensive review of the debates, Waites has argued that the age of consent ought to be set 'not with reference to young people's own competence in assessing risks' but 'through consideration of young people collectively, at an age which can contribute to reducing risks and potential negative consequences to an acceptable level'.[102] He advocates a reduction to 14 but only with a two-year 'age span provision'; thus, a 14-year-old child could legally have sex with those aged 14 to 16.[103] The age of 16 would remain the age of consent in relation to adults over 18.[104] The age of 15 is common within the EU, although there are European countries with both similar (for example, Belgium) and lower ages of consent (for example, Germany) than England and Wales.[105] What is striking about other European countries is how much less divergence there is between the age of consent and the age of criminal responsibility. If coherence is sought then it would seem that other European countries have much to offer us by way of example: in Germany, for instance, the age of criminal responsibility is 14—a gap of one year compared to the six-year gap in this country.[106]

However, given the protective rationale of the current law it seems very unlikely that a proposal to lower the age of consent would obtain the support of government. It is against this backdrop that the recent reforms made in Scotland may represent a way forward. The Sexual Offences (Scotland) Act 2009 distinguishes between, on the one hand, young children (those under 13)[107] where a belief that the child is over 13 is no defence and, on the other hand, older children (those between 13 and below 16),[108] just as the law in England and Wales does. These latter offences, such as the offence of having sexual intercourse with an older child,[109] apply if the defendant is aged 16 or over and the child is aged between 13 and up to 16 years old. There is a specific offence of older children engaging in sexual conduct with each other (including penetration) which carries a maximum penalty of 10 years'

[100] The Policy Advisory Committee on Sexual Offences, *Report on the Age of Consent in Relation to Sexual Offences*, Cmnd. 8216 (1981, HMSO, London).

[101] *R v K* [2002] 1 AC 462 at [44].

[102] Waites, n. 23, above, 234.

[103] Such provisions have been adopted in many of the states in the United States: see further Waites, n. 23, above, ibid, 239.

[104] Ibid, 234, 238.

[105] See further, ibid, 44–53.

[106] See also Lyons, n. 55, above, who discusses this issue in the context of the discrepancy between the age of criminal responsibility and the age of majority (at 276).

[107] Sections 18–27.

[108] Sections 28–37.

[109] Section 28.

imprisonment.[110] Where the other child gives consent he or she also commits an offence punishable by a fine. However, there is a defence to charges in respect of 13- to 15-year-old complainants of reasonable belief that the child was aged 16 or over (and the defendant had not been previously charged with a relevant sexual offence).[111] Most significantly, it is a defence to certain sexual conduct (not amounting, for example, to penetration)[112] to a charge of engaging in sexual activity with an older child[113] that there is no more than a two-year age difference between the children engaged in the activity. These provisions are complex and do not go as far as the Scottish Law Commission had wished[114] (and, of course, have gone too far for others[115]) but they are provisions that would take England and Wales a little way towards greater coherency. A review of our law is needed to assess whether this is a model which would provide sufficient recognition of children's agency without undermining the protection the law needs to afford.

What of younger children, under 13? Clearly, a law which regards the sexual offence as taking place irrespective of the child's 'consent' is one which commands very considerable support. But here too we might have another, albeit different, lesson to learn from Scotland. The Criminal Justice and Licensing Act 2010 amends the law so that no child under the age of 12 may be prosecuted for an offence.[116] It does not raise the age of criminal responsibility, which is still eight in Scotland; indeed an amendment to change the age of criminal responsibility to 12 was lost. But it does ensure that no child will face a criminal prosecution until he or she is at least 12 years old, younger children being dealt with by means of the system of children's hearings.[117] England and Wales cannot simply adopt this reform because we do not have a system of children's hearings. But we should take on board the message that underpins the reform: children should not be accountable to the criminal law below the age of 12. An even bolder reform would be to put the age of criminal responsibility at 13.[118] Not only would this be more in line with our understanding of childhood development but it would then also mirror the provisions designed to protect younger children who are victims of sexual crimes. While the current prospects for reform are bleak, indeed, in the wake of the concern which accompanied the trial of the boys of 10 and 11 for attempted rape, the Ministry of Justice announced that 'the government has no plan to raise the age of criminal responsibility as we believe children aged 10 are able to weigh up right and wrong in the same way that older children

[110] Section 37. [111] Section 39.

[112] By virtue of section 39(3). Under section 39(4) there is no defence if there is penetration of B's vagina, anus, or mouth with A's penis or penetration of B's vagina, anus, or mouth with A's mouth, tongue, or teeth. There is also no defence if the sexual touching involves B's vagina, anus, or penis being touched sexually by A's mouth, tongue, or teeth.

[113] Section 30.

[114] It wished to exclude all consensual activity between children in this age group, although referral to a children's hearing would have been possible: Scottish Law Commission, *Report on Rape and Other Sexual Offences*, Scottish Law Com. No. 209 (2007, TSO, Edinburgh), paras 4.52–4.57.

[115] For a strongly argued critique of the (then) proposed reforms in Scotland, see The Christian Institute, *Undermining the Age of Consent* (2008, The Christian Institute, Edinburgh).

[116] Section 38.

[117] See further, Claire McDiamid, *Childhood and Crime* (2007, Dundee University Press, Dundee).

[118] I have argued elsewhere (n. 13, above), that the most principled reform would be to introduce a test along the lines of the *Gillick* test of competence. However, pragmatic objections to such a change are likely to be insurmountable and, thus, a blanket raising of the age of criminal responsibility is strategically the best way to secure reform.

or adults can',[119] this should not lead commentators to abandon the argument for reform. The age of criminal responsibility should be raised.

17.8 Conclusion

This chapter has sought to demonstrate the 'strikingly muddled'[120] thinking that pervades the criminal law in these contexts. This is seen both in the approach taken to older children's normal sexual experimentation and in the relationship between those provisions and the age of criminal responsibility. The law is currently inconsistent in its treatment and incoherent in its underlying rationale, perhaps influenced by different constructions of childhood. The reality, of course, is (adopting Fionda's terminology) that children are neither 'devils' nor 'angels'[121] and the law has to find a way to respond to real children's needs, claims, and behaviour which is based upon evidence, not only of the risks associated with too early sexual experiences but also children's psychological development. What we know is that there is a world of difference between the capacities of the average 10-year-old child and the average 13- to 14-year-old child.

It is, of course, the case that inconsistencies in law are virtually inevitable. As Fortin comments, the law has a 'collection of bizarrely arbitrary age limits'[122] some of which are of little practical significance and even may be 'a source of amusement',[123] but the inconsistencies explored here are of grave and practical significance. The official commentary to the Beijing Rules states that 'the modern approach is... that there is a close relationship'[124] between the age of criminal responsibility and other social rights and responsibilities (such as, for example, the age at which one can vote or marry). Judged by this yardstick we fail children: not only do we have a six-year disparity between the age of criminal responsibility and the age of consent but we are also completely out of line with most other European countries.

A protective approach to younger children is entirely justified. Young children should be protected from sexual abuse and exploitation *and* from the consequences of what would otherwise be criminal behaviour. The current law adheres to this in so far as children under the age of 10 are concerned. But thereafter the approaches fundamentally diverge. From this point on the criminal law protects children from abuse but punishes children who offend. While 10- and 11-year-old children can be tried in the Crown court as responsible for their behaviour, 14-year-old children lack the capacity lawfully to engage in kissing or other forms of sexual intimacy. Do we really want older children growing up with the message that these are 'furtive activities punishable by a gaol term'?[125] Although there is a strong presumption against prosecution, we need to ask ourselves if relying on prosecutorial discretion is the best we can do and in this context the Scottish Law Commission has given a clear lead:

[119] *Guardian*, 18 August 2010. A review of how children are treated in court, was, however, announced.

[120] Spencer n. 82, above, 354, writing in the context of the child sex provisions of the Sexual Offences Act 2003.

[121] Fionda, n. 14, above. [122] Fortin, n. 12, above, 108. [123] Ibid, 109.

[124] Official Commentary to Rule 4 of the Beijing Rules (the United Nations Standard Minimum Rules for the Administration of Juvenile Justice 1985).

[125] *Hansard* HL Deb, vol 644, col 869 (13 February 2003) (*per* Baroness Walmsley).

In making [our] recommendation we are particularly struck by anomalies which would follow in criminalising consenting sexual activity between teenagers, which would extend to activities such as kissing each other. We are not impressed by the argument that such criminal activity would be theoretical only and in the vast majority of cases there would be no criminal prosecutions. Such an approach fails to take account of the possibility that older children might still be subject to investigation by the police, even if prosecution in the courts is unlikely. More fundamentally, there is an important point of principle involved. If consenting sexual activity between young people is not to attract criminal liability, then the activity should not be criminal.[126]

When the Sexual Offences Bill was before Parliament, Baroness Walmsley urged that amendments be made so as to bring 'common sense, humanity and justice'[127] to the law. With this vital objective in mind, the first stage to reform should be a review of both our sexual offences law and the age of criminal responsibility.

[126] N. 115, above, para 4.55.

[127] *Hansard* HL Deb, vol 646, col 1174 (1 April 2003).

18

Tackling Cyber-Bullying from a Children's Rights Perspective

Anne S.Y. Cheung[1]

It is said that words can craft peace and declare war, encourage and forbid, forgive and intimidate. Words can also both heal and hurt and sometimes, as we will discover, they can kill. In the high technology landscape, the power of words and their destructive force are manifested in the growing problem of cyber-bullying carried out by children against their peers.

Despite the lack of a universal definition of cyber-bullying, it usually refers to situations where a child is threatened, humiliated, embarrassed, or otherwise targeted by another child or children through electronic means, which includes interactive and digital technologies, the internet, and mobile phones.[2] It often takes the form of mockery, insult, gossip, harassment, or exposing someone else's personal information on the internet. Unlike traditional bullying, cyber-bullies are less inhibited about restraining their behaviour because bullying of this kind can be done in an anonymous, impersonal way.[3] Technological advances have also provided the bullies with the ability to infiltrate the private spaces of victims beyond the schoolyard, making them unable to seek refuge at home. Besides, bullying can also easily take place whether or not the perpetrators have a strong physical build. In other words, in the context of this information age, bullying is no longer confined to face-to-face confrontation but is rather a combination of online and offline harassment, 24 hours a day, seven days a week, involving multiple aggressors, up to hundreds or even millions, against a single victim. These victims, therefore, often feel helpless, unable to trace the initial perpetrator nor to secure the co-operation of telecommunications companies or internet service providers (ISPs) in filtering, blocking, or removing the offending messages or photos. As a result, studies in the US have shown that victims of cyber-bullying often suffer from depression notwithstanding a definite link between cyber-bullying and teenage suicide.[4] Unfortunately, technological advancement now has the capacity to bring out a greater cruelty and violence in human nature than that

[1] Department of Law, The University of Hong Kong. This project was funded by the Outstanding Young Researcher Award of the University of Hong Kong.

[2] WiredSafety, 'What is Cyberbullying, exactly?' at <http://www.stopcyberbullying.org/what_is_cyberbullying_exactly.html>. WiredSafety is an international charity organization working to fight cyber-bullying and is based in North America.

[3] Sameer Hinduja and Justin W. Patchin, *Bullying Beyond the Schoolyard: Preventing and Responding to Cyberbullying* (Thousand Oaks, California, 2009), 21–2.

[4] Sameer Hinduja and Justin W. Patchin, 'Bullying, Cyberbullying, and Suicide' (2010) 12(3) *Archives of Suicide Research* 206, also available at <http://www.cyberbullying.us/cyberbullying_and_suicide_research_fact_sheet.pdf>.

demonstrated in William Golding's classic novel *Lord of the Flies*, and in an unprecedented altered and amplified form.[5]

The urgency of the matter has prompted various attempts at the national and regional levels to regulate the 'high tech playgrounds for intimidation'.[6] However, legal actions are lengthy and costly, and common law causes of action such as defamation and harassment, for example, have often proved to be inadequate. Attempts to hold ISPs liable for failing to mitigate the damage caused by harmful messages or postings have also proved to be an uphill battle as weighty constitutional issues of freedom of expression and privacy have yet to be evenly balanced.[7] In the education sector, while noble efforts have been made to tackle the problem of cyber-bullying and to hold schools to be responsible, this approach often fails to reach those who carry it off-campus.[8]

In order to tackle the problem of cyber-bullying in an integrated and coherent manner which can combine legal intervention, education, and regulation from the telecommunications industry, this chapter advocates an alternative approach of co-regulation based on children's rights. According to the United Nations Convention on the Rights of the Child (UNCRC), which has been ratified by 140 states since 1989, states have a duty to prevent violence and harm inflicted on children.[9] This implies that states should take actions for the protection of children from cyber-bullying through law and policies which co-ordinate efforts between the stakeholders including parents, schools, industries, and children themselves. This approach will enable a responsive and adaptive model, requiring stakeholders to develop their code of practice, and enabling policy makers to overcome the hurdle of legislation that is lagging behind technological advancement. Perhaps the closest model that has reflected a children's rights based approach is the European Commission Safer Internet Programme launched in 1999.[10] It has involved 30 state governments and 20 social networking companies in the efforts to combat cyber-bullying in Europe. While this model has provided a significant reference for governance, the present European Commission's framework is not a co-regulatory model for it is wholly dependent on the voluntary participation of the industry, without any monitoring mechanism and sanctioning power.

In order to explore the necessity and advantage of a children's rights based approach to co-regulation, this chapter begins in Part 18.1 by discussing the nature, manifestation, prevalence, and harm of cyber-bullying, with an illustration of notorious examples of cyber-bullying in different countries. The harm and violence inflicted by children against their peers should not be underestimated. Furthermore, the

[5] The reference to William Golding's Nobel prize winning novel, *Lord of the Flies*, is drawn by Shaheen Shariff, *Confronting Cyber-Bullying* (New York, 2009), 3.

[6] Stacy Chaffin, 'The New Playground Bullies of Cyberspace: Online Peer Sexual Harassment' (2008) 51 *Howard Law Journal* 773.

[7] Cara J. Ottenweller, 'Cyberbullying: The Interactive Playground Cries for a Clarification of the Communications Decency Act' (2007) 41 *Valparaiso University Law Review* 1285.

[8] Shira Auerbach, 'Screening Out Cyberbullies: Remedies for Victims on the Internet Playground' (2009) 30 *Cardozo Law Review* 1642.

[9] Article 19 of the UNCRC stipulates that States Parties shall take all appropriate legislative, administrative, social, and educational measures to protect the child from all forms of violence. By October 2010, 140 out of 193 states had ratified the treaty, United Nations Treaty Collection at <http://treaties.un.org/Pages/ViewDetails.aspx?src=TREATY&mtdsg_no=IV-11&chapter=4&lang=en>.

[10] European Commission Information Society, 'Safer Internet Programme: the Main Framework for European Policy' at <http://ec.europa.eu/information_society/activities/sip/policy/programme/index_en.htm>.

discussion will map out the statistics from different countries to show how widespread and serious the problem of cyber-bullying is across the globe (in the United States, Canada, United Kingdom, Continental Europe, and Asia). Although the major concern of our subject matter is peer-to-peer bullying among minors, references will also be made to cyber-bullying among university students. Part 18.2 will then examine the current legal attempts in the United Kingdom and the United States to tackle the problem and the inadequacies of the positivist legal approach. The reason for focusing on the United Kingdom is because it has laid down the ground rules and doctrines of civil causes of action for many other common law countries, indirectly setting the contours of available remedies for cyber-bullying victims. In addition, it is noteworthy that because of the UK's membership in the European Union (EU), it has joined the EU's project of developing other and various approaches to tackle the problem of cyber-bullying. On the other hand, the United States has also been chosen as the subject of study due to its strong stance in favour of protecting freedom of speech and because it is the home of leading internet companies including Yahoo, Facebook, and Google. In the final section of Part 18.3, I argue that a co-regulatory model based on children's rights will provide a viable and more effective solution to the problem of cyber-bullying, in which schools and ISPs play an essential role. In particular, the ISP should develop its code of practice within a model of compliance, of having a mechanism for reporting, follow-up, and notice and take-down of harmful materials.

18.1 Cyber-bullying: its nature, manifestation, and prevalence

18.1.1 The nature and manifestation of cyber-bullying

Shariff and Hoff assert that cyber-bullying is a 'psychologically devastating form of social cruelty among adolescents'.[11] This is an extension of traditional bullying which has been customarily manifested in overt physical aggression such as beating and shoving, but covert bullying which aims to exclude the victims by gossips, verbal threats, or harassment,[12] exists side by side with overt bullying. The case of cyber-bullying is often a variation of covert bullying through electronic media, not only crossing various electronic media (mobile phone and internet) but also blurring the boundaries between the online and offline worlds. In their report to the Anti-Bullying Alliance in the United Kingdom, Peter Smith and his colleagues have identified seven types of cyber-bullying, which include sending abusive text messages, emails, or phone calls to the victims and their social circle; taking pictures or video clips of the victim without consent and posting them online; bullying in online chatrooms and social networking sites.[13]

The content of cyber-bullying includes harassment or threats to the victims of physical and sexual violence and the sending of damaging statements about the victims to other students. Also, it can be a form of technological attack by shutting down

[11] Shaheen Shariff and Dianne L. Hoff, 'Cyber Bullying: Clarifying Legal Boundaries for School Supervision in Cyberspace' (2007) 1 *International Journal of Cyber Criminology* 76.

[12] Shariff and Hoff, N. 11 above, 80.

[13] Peter Smith, Jess Mahdavi, Manuel Carvalho, and Neil Tippett, 'An Investigation into Cyberbullying, Its Forms, Awareness and Impact, and the Relationship between Age and Gender in Cyberbullying: A Report to the Anti-Bullying Alliance' (July 2006) at <http://www.education.gov.uk/research/data/uploadfiles/RBX03-06.pdf>.

the victims' blogs, or hacking into their accounts and sending offensive messages in their names to others.[14] Another strategy involves setting up internet polling or rating sites targeting the victims.[15] The discussion below highlights some examples of cyber-bullying during which lives of victims were being torn apart.

Defamation can be a grotesque form of cyber-bullying as experienced by David Knight, a Canadian high school student who had been bullied by his classmates for most of his school years.[16] The final blow came in 2001 when the classmates set up a website accusing him of committing paedophilic criminal activities. From then on, he received horrible email messages. With the threat of litigation, it took almost six months before Yahoo decided to remove the site. Meanwhile, Knight could not take the pressure any longer and had to withdraw from school. In his own words, he felt 'even more trapped' by cyber-bullying, with six billion people watching, rather than just being taunted by 30 people in the cafeteria.[17]

Equally devastating to the victims is the dissemination of their personal information without consent which would create a deep sense of violation in individuals. Notorious cases involved two other students in North America: a 15-year-old Canadian student called Ghyslain Raza and an American university student named Tyler Clementi. In 2003, Raza's home video, showing him pretending to wield a Star Wars light saber, was posted onto YouTube without his consent. Since then, he has been dubbed the Star Wars Kid, with his video clip reaching an internet hit rate of 900 million by 2006. As a consequence of the ridicule, Raza suffered from depression and, similarly, had to withdraw from school. He eventually ended up in a child psychiatric facility for a year. His parents sued the classmates and the case was eventually settled.[18] But to this day, one can still view the video clip of the Star Wars Kid on YouTube and it has become part of the archive, memorialized on the internet for everyone to search.

As indicated earlier, cyber-bullying is not confined to high school students. In 2010, a student named Clementi was in his first year studying at Rutgers University in the US. He was secretly filmed by two of his fellow students having sex with another man. The video clip was broadcast on the internet through webcam. Shortly after Clementi was made aware of the incident, he committed suicide.[19] Not only did this tragedy involve gross violation of privacy, it also illustrates the catastrophic side of the results of cyber-bullying.

Another deeply disturbing practice of cyber-bullying is ironically known as 'happy slapping', which involves recording (often through mobile phone) a physical attack and posting it online. In 2010, a 16-year-old Canadian girl was allegedly drugged and raped by a group of five to seven young men at a party. Another teenage boy who was present took photos of the incident and then uploaded them onto the social-networking site Facebook.[20] In 2006, in Italy, an autistic boy was beaten

[14] Hinduja and Patchin, N. 3, above, 38

[15] Hinduja and Patchin, N. 3, above, 28. Rating sites include 'Pick the Hottie' or 'Hot or Not'.

[16] Joan Leishman, 'Cyber-bullying' CBC News, March 2005 at <http://www.cbc.ca/news/background/bullying/cyber_bullying.html>.

[17] Leishman, N. 16, above.

[18] BBC, 'Star Wars Kid is Top Viral Video' BBC News, 27 November 2006 at <http://news.bbc.co.uk/2/hi/entertainment/6187554.stm>.

[19] Laura Trevelyan, 'Shock at Student's Suicide over Sex Video' BBC News, 4 October 2010 at <http://www.bbc.co.uk/news/world-us-canada-11464617>.

[20] Glenda Luymes, 'Gang-rape Photos Posted on Net' *The Province*, 17 September 2010 at <http://www2.canada.com/theprovince/news/story.html?id=96b674f9-83ea-45db-a3c6-47b5618eab8b>.

and insulted by four high school students. The attack was recorded by mobile phone and then uploaded onto YouTube. The clip was available on YouTube for more than two months before Google took it down after receiving a formal police complaint. In 2010, Google was convicted and received a suspended sentence for violating the Italian Privacy Code.[21] In these two horrific accounts of violence and abuse, the victims are victimized twice over, both in the online world and after going through traumatic physical abuse.

Despite the multiple forms of cyber-bullying, it has become a serious global and cross-cultural problem.

18.1.2 The prevalence of cyber-bullying

In the United Kingdom, according to a survey done in 2009, it was revealed that 22 per cent of secondary school students were victims of cyber-bullying.[22] What is more worrying in the study is the spread of cyber-bullying to primary schools revealing that one in five (20 per cent) of Year 6 primary school students aged 10 or 11 had been cyber-bullied in the previous 12 months and 22 per cent of the same age group of students did not know how to protect themselves against it.

A similar pattern is detectable in other parts of Europe. A study on internet safety and children's interests sponsored by the European Union and carried out between 2006 and 2009 covered 21 member states. This reported that 20 per cent of teenagers had been cyber-bullied,[23] and 10 per cent of teenagers in Germany, Ireland, and Portugal had received unwanted sexual comments online, while 25 per cent to 30 per cent of teenagers in Iceland, Norway, the United Kingdom, and Sweden had a similar experience. The most serious problem was in Poland where 50 per cent of teenagers have had this unpleasant experience.

Again, in the United States, a study in 2010 revealed that 20 per cent of students between 10 and 18 years old had experienced cyber-bullying,[24] the most common form being carried out through mobile phone (83 per cent) while the most popular means on the internet was through Facebook (50 per cent). However, the first set of figures actually represents a significant drop in cyber-bullying by 50 per cent compared with 2004.

In Canada, a survey conducted in the Greater Toronto Area in 2008 showed that 20 per cent of grades 6 and 7 students had been cyber-bullied by others while 29 per cent reported that they had been perpetrators.[25] Contrary to the common perception that cyber-bullying was often done anonymously, in reality 68 per cent of the victims

[21] Rachel Donadio, 'Larger Threat Is Seen in Google Case' *New York Times*, 24 February 2010 at <http://www.nytimes.com/2010/02/25/technology/companies/25google.html>.

[22] Anti-Bullying Alliance, 'New Research on Cyberbullying Highlights the Role of Parents in Prevention' 16 November 2009 at <http://www.anti-bullyingalliance.org.uk/press_centre/news_archive/new_research_on_cyberbullying.aspx>.

[23] Sonia Livingston and Leslie Haddon, *EU Kids Online: Final Report* (2009), 20 at <http://eprints.lse.ac.uk/24372/1/D6.5_EU-Kids-Online-Final-Report.pdf>

[24] Sameer Hinduja and Justin W. Patchin, 'Cyberbullying: Identification, Prevention and Response' at <http://www.cyberbullying.us/Cyberbullying_Identification_Prevention_Response_Fact_Sheet.pdf>. The survey covered 4441 students between 10 and 18 years old.

[25] Faye Mishna, Charlene Cook, Tahany Gadalla, Joanne Daciuk, and Steven Solomon, 'Cyber Bullying Behaviors Among Middle and High School Students' (2010) 80(3) *American Journal of Orthopsychiatry* 362. The study surveyed more than 2000 elementary and high school children in 30 schools in the Greater Toronto Area.

reported that they had been bullied by a friend or a student at their own school or at another school.[26]

The situation is equally worrying in Asia. In Hong Kong, a survey conducted between November 2009 and February 2010 on primary five- and six-year students revealed that 50 per cent of them had been victims of cyber-bullying while 30 per cent had been perpetrators.[27] Another study conducted in the same period on secondary school students showed that 30 per cent had been victims.[28] Different anecdotes of cyber-bullying in China, Japan, South Korea, and India have been documented by Shariff in her work.[29]

18.1.3 Harm to the victims and perpetrators

Regardless of where cyber-bullying takes place, the harm suffered by the victims ranges from physical to psychological. They often feel terrorized, and ostracized, losing their sense of personal security, self-esteem, and identity.[30] Their ability to participate in online and offline societies is severely impaired, resulting in a profound sense of isolation, which many described as a form of 'social death',[31] or as previously stated in the earlier section, driven to commit suicide.

In an increasingly sophisticated high tech landscape, there are no obvious rules or boundaries, and no supervision or monitoring, so that users let loose their worst instincts for so-called omnipotence. In such circumstances, both overt and covert bullying create a power imbalance between the perpetrators and the victims. Current literature confirms the obvious view that minorities in general are first to be victims in the social hierarchy and are likely to face various forms of cyber-attack, such as women, homosexuals, the black community, and members of other traditionally disadvantaged groups.[32] For example, a study in Finland found that 16 per cent of female teenage respondents were cyber-bullied by boys, while only five per cent of male respondents were harassed by girls.[33] Clearly, cyber-bullying has mirrored the power abuse and its related problems in the offline world whilst allowing anonymous aggressive behaviour and contributing to a hostile learning environment and to future social problems.

While cyber-bullying is a relatively current phenomenon, research on bullying is rich and can provide useful references. Psychiatric studies have established that many bullies have been victims of bullying themselves by their parents or other

[26] Ibid.

[27] SingTao News, '30 per cent of Senior Primary School Students had CyberBullied Others' 24 August 2010 at <http://hk.news.yahoo.com/article/100823/3/jumh.html> (in Chinese). The survey was conducted by The Chinese University between November 2009 and February 2010, interviewing 626 primary school students.

[28] SingTao News, 'Survey Revealed 30 per cent of Secondary School Students had been Cyberbullied' 3 July 2010, <http://hk.news.yahoo.com/article/100703/3/iz26.html> (in Chinese). The study was conducted by the Hong Kong Family Welfare Society and The Chinese University interviewing 1800 secondary school students.

[29] Shariff, N. 5, above, 67–74.

[30] Danielle Keats Citron, 'Cyber Civil Rights' (2009) 61 *Boston University Law Review* 62, 64, 89.

[31] Robin M. Kowalski, Susan P. Limer, and Patricia W. Agatson, *Cyberbullying* (Oxford, 2008), 49.

[32] Citron, N. 30, above. Citron was writing about cyber-harassment in general.

[33] Andre Sourander et al, 'Childhood Bullying Behavior and Later Psychiatric Hospital and Psychopharmacologic Treatment' (2009) 66(9) *Archives of General Psychiatry* 1005–1012. The survey covered 5038 Finnish children born in 1981.

students.[34] And both victims and bullies are likely to be social delinquents when they grow up.[35] Other research on bullying focused on onlookers and bystanders, reveals that 30 per cent tend to support perpetrators rather than defending the victims, and the longer the bullying persists, the more bystanders will join in the abuse.[36] Directly on cyber-bullying, scholars in Taiwan found that the dominant attitude of cyber-bullies and bystanders was indifference, with a low level of empathy for others.[37] Devastating and tragic cases involve victims in retaliation, resorting to extreme forms of aggressive and violent behaviour as their final protest. What is more, it is now understood that all the aggressors of campus shootings who have recently shocked the world had been victims of bullying: these included the Columbine High School shooting in Colorado in 1999 where two senior students killed 12 of their fellow students and one teacher; the Virginia Polytechnic shooting in 2007 where one student killed 32 other students; and the Ecole Polytechnique Montreal shooting where a student killed 28 others.[38] In these cases and others, the victims-turned-aggressors committed suicide after the shootings but they had resorted to violence only after the school administration had repeatedly failed to intervene as in the case of Columbine and Virginia.[39] The lessons from these tragic events are that the victims, the bullies, and the bystanders are all victims of a discourse that has endorsed the use of violence.

Other than the harm caused to the social and psychological development of both the immediate child victims, perpetrators, and bystanders, we shall return in more detail to the problem caused by excessive exposure to social networking sites and the likely harm to children's brain development in Part 18.3.

18.2 Legal attempts and hiatus

The bullying that flares up in the high tech landscape has posed unprecedented legal challenges to the authorities. Apparently, both civil remedies under tort law and sanctions under criminal law are readily available. Attempts have also been made to hold ISPs responsible. Yet, the above endeavours have not yielded the results that had been hoped for. As we will see in the discussion below, the inherent limitations of the existing legal approach is highly dependent on actions being brought individually or directly against the perpetrator, but in cyber-bullying, the identity of the initial perpetrator may not be known since there are often infinite audience numbers or participants involved, which makes the gathering of evidence and the bringing of civil action or the instigation of prosecution an almost insurmountable problem.

[34] Denise L. Haynie, Tonja Nansel, Patricia Eitel, Aria Davis Crump, Keith Saylor, Kai Yu, and Bruce Simons-Morton, 'Bullies, Victims, and Bully/Victims: Distinct Groups of At-Risk Youth' (2001) 21 *The Journal of Early Adolescence* 29, 44; Xin Ma, 'Bullying and Being Bullied: To What Extent are Bullies also Victims?' (2001) 38 *American Educational Research Journal* 351. Both studies found that bullies are likely to come from authoritarian, hostile, and rejecting parents. The second study also showed that victims of bullying at school had a tendency to bully other students.

[35] Clayton R. Cook, Kirk R. Williams, Nancy G. Guerra, Tia E. Kim, and Shelly Sadek, 'Predictors of Bullying and Victimization in Childhood and Adolescence: A Meta-analytic Investigation' (2010) 25(2) *School Psychology Quarterly* 65, 66. Ma, N. 34, above, 352.

[36] Shariff and Hoff, N. 11, above, 85.

[37] Yun-yin Huang and Chien Chou, 'An Analysis of Multiple Factors of Cyberbullying Among Junior High School Students in Taiwan' (2010) 26 *Computers in Human Behavior* 1581.

[38] Shariff, N.5, above, 23.

[39] Shariff, N.5, above, 23.

18.2.1 Common law action of defamation

In the common form of cyber-bullying which involves spreading rumour, gossip, or slander, one can rely on the common law remedy of defamation. Accordingly, a plaintiff has to prove there has been a publication of a defamatory statement about him,[40] the meaning of which is described as an action calculated to injure the reputation of another by exposing him to hatred, contempt, or ridicule, or a tendency to lower the plaintiff in the estimation of right-thinking members of society generally.[41] The alleged statement is presumed to be false by the court so it is for the defendant to raise the defence of truth.

In recalling the plight of David Knight, the Canadian student that we have discussed in Part 18.1 of this chapter, it would seem the case would easily conform to the above definition on what constitutes defamation. Knight was falsely described as a homosexual, a paedophile, and a rapist in a website titled 'Welcome to the Page that Makes Fun of Dave Knight'.[42] Not only did the site attack Knight, but it also attacked all his family members. But all that Knight knew was that the website was set up in Thailand. In order to start a legal battle, he had to discover the identity of the defamers and needed to overcome the jurisdictional problem. Eventually, as we know, it took the Knight family six months to get the ISP company to remove the site. Arguably, on closer inspection, Knight could have lost a defamation lawsuit because the title of the website suggested that it was meant to be a joke. In that event, the court is likely to hold that, given the context, it would not satisfy the legal test of being a defamatory statement which lowered the reputation of Knight and his family members in the mind of right-thinking members of the community despite the fact that it was a cruel and crude joke.

Along the same line of legal logic, defamation action may not be able to help victims who have been targeted in polling or rating sites such as—'who is the ugliest', 'who is the most promiscuous', or 'who should be the next to die'.[43] This is because the above examples are about the invitation and mere expression of opinions, which may not be considered to satisfy the legal test of defamation.[44] Furthermore, offensive or insulting words sent directly to the victim's mobile phone or email account would not constitute defamation because there has been no publication to a third party. Likewise, disclosure of personal information or photos without consent will not be protected under defamation action, and common law has been traditionally weak in

[40] Helen Fenwick and Gavin Phillipson, *Media Freedom under the Human Rights Act* (Oxford, 2006), 1043.

[41] Fenwick and Phillipson, N. 40, above.

[42] Ottenweller, N. 7, above, 1285.

[43] The US case of *Emmett v Kent School District No. 415*, 92 F. Supp. 2d 1088 (WD Wash. 2000) was concerned about a senior student who set up a website on mock obituaries allowing visitors to vote who the next to die in the school should be. The student was suspended and successfully brought an action under the free speech clause of the First Amendment. The court found that the school had failed to demonstrate there was any threat or violence intended by the plaintiff.

[44] The position that value-judgment is a protected form of speech has been accepted by the US Court and the European Court of Human Rights. The English position is not entirely clear at this stage. For the position in the US, see American Law Institute, Restatement of the Law—Torts (1977, current through August 2010) § 566. For discussion of the European Court and the English position, see Alison L. Young, 'Fact, Opinion, and the Human Rights Act 1998: Does English Law Need to Modify its Definition of "Statements of Opinion" to Ensure Compliance with Article 10 of the European Convention on Human Rights?' (2000) 20(1) *Oxford Journal of Legal Studies* 89.

the protection of privacy rights.[45] Victims like Raza (the Star Wars Kid discussed in Part 18.1 of this chapter), whose private or embarrassing moment was captured by a recording device for distribution, might not be able to avail themselves of a common law remedy of defamation nor protection of privacy because the image distributed is true and may not satisfy the test of being personal information in itself. Often in those cases, the more truth, the more the violations.

18.2.2 Harassment

In the light of these limitations under the defamation law, is it not possible for the victim to seek recourse under harassment law and legislation?

In English common law, the tortious action of intentional harassment where physical or psychological harm arises is well recognized.[46] Under the classic rule laid down by *Wilkinson v Downton* back in 1897, any word said or act done, whether directly or indirectly, with the intention of inflicting harm, incurs tortious liability as long as harm is actually caused,[47] and this harm refers both to bodily or recognized psychiatric illness, meaning that a victim suffering from mere distress is highly unlikely to make a successful claim.

This high threshold set by common law has presented difficulties for victims of stalking and harassment in the workplace which has eventually led to the enactment of the Protection from Harassment Act in 1997.[48] Under s. 2 of the Act, it is an offence to pursue a course of conduct which amounts to the harassment of another where the accused knew or ought to have known that the course of conduct amounts to harassment. The Act has left open the definition of harassment,[49] so that the term is not clearly defined other than the inclusion of alarm and distress under s. 7(2). In addition, a person would have committed an offence if he pursues a course of conduct which causes another to fear that violence will be conducted against them (s. 4). Speech is specifically covered (s. 7(4)), and 'a course of conduct' refers to conduct on at least two occasions (s. 7(3)). Therefore, the Act provides civil and criminal measures to the victims under s. 3 and s. 5 of the Act, whereby a restraining order is available (s. 5). But what is unclear is whether being bullied once could still be considered as harassment? And what about being cyber-bullied by different people in an uncoordinated way but each of the perpetrators has only bullied the victim once? Would that constitute a course of conduct?

Perhaps, in those situations, we have to rely on another 'rag bag of statutes' dealing with harassment in the United Kingdom.[50] Under s. 5(1) of the Public Order Act, it is a criminal offence for anyone to use threatening, abusive, insulting words or behaviour in a public or a private place that is likely to cause harassment, alarm, or distress.[51]

[45] Nicole Moreham, 'The Protection of Privacy in English Common Law: a Doctrinal and Theoretical Analysis' (2005) 121 *Law Quarterly Review* 628–56.

[46] Anthony M. Dugdale, Michael A. Jones, Daniel Alexander, and John Federic Clerk, *Clerk and Lindsell on Torts* (London, 2006), 1–24.

[47] *Wilkinson v Downton* (1897) 2 QB 67.

[48] Protection from Harassment Act 1997, Ch. 40.

[49] David Ormerod, 'R. v Curtis (James Daniel): Harassment—Protection from Harassment Act 1997 s.4(1)' (2010) 8 *Criminal Law Review* 638–40. Ormerod explains that it is a deliberate attempt to accommodate a flexible approach for the court to deal with the numerous varieties of harassment and stalking.

[50] Subhajit Basu and Richard Jones, 'Regulating Cyberstalking' (2007) 2 *Journal of Information, Law and Technology* 2, at 12.

[51] Public Order Act of 1986, Ch. 64.

The likely legal hurdle that a victim has to overcome is whether the cyber space or telecommunications will be considered as a 'place'. Directly governing telecommunications is s. 127(1)(a) of the Communications Act, under which a person can be guilty of 'improper use of a public electronic communications network' for sending a message that is grossly offensive, indecent, obscene, or menacing.[52] Under s. 127(2) of the Communications Act, a person can be guilty of sending a message known to be false through the public electronic communications network for the purpose of causing annoyance, inconvenience, or needless anxiety to another. In addition, other than the sanctions above, s. 1 of the Malicious Communications Act punishes the sending of the said electronic communication which conveys a threat and causes distress.[53] However, the Communications Act will not apply if data is sent through a local area network, rather than a public one.

Other forms of harassment and cyber-bullying, like sending obscene photos of the victims (or the recording of the happy slapping case of the rape victim, which was later disseminated on the internet), will also be covered by s. 2 of the Obscene Publications Act,[54] and the act of 'hacking' could easily satisfy the definition of authorized access into another computer's material account under s. 1 of the Computer Misuse Act.[55] However, in the United Kingdom, though there has been no reported judgment on cyber-bullying and harassment, and the term cyber-bulling is not mentioned in any of the statutory provisions, arguably it is covered by other pieces of legislation.[56] But even so, how is the victim going to bring legal actions against unknown and multiple aggressors?

Equally unsatisfactory is the US legal position. The United States has a federal law banning harassment but not cyber-bullying.[57] By July 2010, while 45 states have legislation criminalizing the acts of bullying, and 30 states have laws on electronic harassment, only five states have legislation specifically on cyber-bullying.[58] Of the above, only seven states have imposed criminal sanctions while the remaining 37 rely on the method of school sanctions.[59] This reflects an old assumption that bullying mainly takes place in the schoolyard, which is not true for cyber-bullying. Despite the armoury of law available to victims, it is far from effective for their protection.

Take the case of Jake Baker, a student at the University of Michigan who was involved in posting a story on an internet newsgroup and sending email messages to a previously unknown man called Gondola in Ontario, Canada.[60] The story and messages that Baker had sent graphically described the torture, rape, and murder of a woman who was named as Baker's classmate. The story was posted on an electronic bulletin board as well as the newsgroup so it was publicly available, while the email exchanges between Baker and Gondola were private. Baker was charged under the Federal Penal Code for transmitting in interstate or foreign commerce any

52 Communications Act of 2003, Ch. 21.

53 Malicious Communications Act of 1988, Ch. 27.

54 Obscene Publications Act of 1959, Ch. 66.

55 Computer Misuse Act of 1990, Ch. 18.

56 Louise Ellison and Yaman Akdeniz, 'Cyberstalking: The Regulation of Harassment on the Internet' (1998) *Criminal Law Review* 29.

57 Federal legislation outlaws wilful injury, intimidation, interference, or attempted intimidation towards an individual by force or threat of force because of one's race, colour, religion, or national origins. 18 U.S.C. s245(b0(2)(2000)). For further discussion, see Auerbach, N.8, above, 1663.

58 Sameer Hinduja and Justin Patchin, 'State Cyberbullying Law: A Brief Review of State Cyberbullying Laws and Policies' Cyberbullying Research Centre 1 at <http://www.cyberbullying.us/Bullying_and_Cyberbullying_Laws_20100701.pdf>.

59 Hinduja and Patchin, N. 58, above, 1.

60 *US v Baker*, 890 F. Supp. 1375 (1995).

communication containing any threat to kidnap any person or any threat to injure the person of another.[61] Baker successfully relied on his constitutional right of free speech under the First Amendment as a defence. The US District Court ruled that pure speech could not be considered as a 'true threat' despite the fact that it may be unsettling or alarming in nature. Neither was the fear of serious injury alone enough to justify suppression of free speech,[62] because a threat that warrants legal intervention must satisfy the requirement of being unconditional, unequivocal, immediate, and specific.[63] The potential target or targets must be sufficiently specific and the recipient be foreseeable.[64] In other words, the US approach is dominated by the notion of imminent physical harm. Short of this, free speech almost trumps in most cases; for the court, it was better to leave it to the university to discipline Baker than for the prosecutor to bring the case to court.

The story of Megan Meier in 2006 is another illustration. In 2006, Meier was a 13-year-old girl from Missouri and suffering from depression and attention deficit disorder.[65] She enjoyed communicating on MySpace where she met Josh on the social network site. This was a romantic, amicable, online relationship with him which lasted about a month. The relationship suddenly changed when Josh started sending hostile messages to her, with the last one ending 'the world would be a better place without you' and Meier committed suicide on that same night. It turned out that Josh had never existed. This was a disturbing story of a virtual identity created by Meier's 47-year-old neighbour, Lori Drew, whose daughter did not get along with Meier, and who, as an adult, deliberately got close to a child, gained her confidence, and exploited her vulnerabilities after knowing her medical background and intimate thoughts. Drew's identity was revealed six weeks later by a classmate who knew about the hoax. At that time, Missouri did not have an anti cyber-bullying law. The state prosecutor decided not to press charges against Drew under harassment law knowing that it was difficult to prove an intent to harm, stalk, endanger, or harass.[66] Instead, she was indicted in California for conspiracy and three counts of computer fraud under the Computer Fraud and Abuse Act. However, eventually, she was acquitted of all charges by the California Supreme Court, who found that any attempt to secure a criminal conviction based on intentional violation of a website's terms of service by setting up a false account would be too vague and broad under First Amendment principles.[67] Perhaps the only consolation in this tragedy is that, in 2008, it prompted Missouri to enact its own law on cyber-bullying.[68]

Although there is legal protection from defamation and online harassment in both the United Kingdom and the United States, the use of these laws will be confined inevitably to relatively straightforward cases in which there are identifiable offenders

[61] 18 USC § 875(c).

[62] *US v Baker*, 890 F. Supp. 1375, 1387 (1995).

[63] N. 62, above, 1382–3. [64] N. 62, above, 1386.

[65] ABC News, 'Parents: Cyber Bullying Led to Teen's Suicide' ABC News, 19 November 2007 at <http://abcnews.go.com/GMA/story?id=3882520&page=1>.

[66] Auerbach, N. 8, above, 1662, footnote 129.

[67] *US v Drew*, 259 F.R.D. 449 C.D.Cal., 2009.

[68] Under Missouri Revised Statute § 565.090 (Supp. 2008), harassment is a misdemeanor unless it is '[c]ommitted by a person twenty-one years of age or older against a person seventeen years of age or younger', in which case it is a felony. When a distinction is needed, the cyber-bullying of a child by an adult will be called 'felony cyber-bullying'. Further discussion, see Andrew M. Henderson, 'High-Tech Words Do Hurt: A Modern Makeover Expands Missouri's Harassment Law to Include Electronic Communications' (2009) 74 *Missouri Law Review* 379.

within the specific country.[69] This is far from adequate given the multi-faceted nature of cyber-bullying, the anonymity of most perpetrators, the huge numbers of people involved, and the borderless nature of cyberspace.

18.2.3 The role of ISPs as responsible

Attempts have, thus, been made to hold ISPs accountable for they are usually more resourceful than the individual perpetrator and more effective at removing, blocking, and filtering materials. Lichtman and Posner have also argued convincingly that ISPs should be held responsible for the malicious acts of their users based on a common law doctrine of indirect liability for those who are in a position to control the 'bad actors' or mitigate the harm generated by them.[70] Also, the ISPs are deriving benefits indirectly from their users by attracting advertisers' sponsorship on their sites. Understandably, the industries concerned would not support the above stance because the debate necessarily involves a delicate balance between the right to free speech and other countervailing interests such as reputation or privacy.

In 1999, UK ISPs were held liable in *Godfrey v Demon Internet*[71] unless they could invoke the defence of innocent disseminator, meaning that they did not have knowledge. In *Godfrey*, a plaintiff brought an action against an American service provider for a defamatory posting by an unknown person. He notified the managing director of Demon and asked for the message to be removed, with which Demon failed to comply. The court relied on the UK Defamation Act of 1996, which provides that a person has a defence to defamation proceedings if he shows that he was not the author, editor, or publisher of the statement and that he has taken reasonable care in respect of its publication.[72] Although the court held that the defendant was not a publisher under the statute, it could not claim immunity after it had received notice. The case was widely criticized as being too stringent on ISPs.[73]

Since then, developments have forged a new direction. To limit the liability of ISPs in certain areas including defamation on the internet, the UK Government and the English courts must follow the EU standard under the Electronic Commerce (EC Directive) Regulations in 2002.[74] The EC Directive defines the circumstances in which internet intermediaries should be held accountable for material which is hosted,[75] cached,[76] or carried by them but which they did not create. In effect, it provides a 'safe haven' for the exemption of ISPs' liability when they are mere conduits,[77]

[69] Ellison and Akdeniz, N. 56, above, 35.

[70] Doug Lictman and Eric Posner, 'Holding Internet Service Providers Accountable' (2006) 14 *Supreme Court Economic Review* 221. Lichtman and Posner's discussion was on ISPs' role and liability in the creation and propagation of computer virus and malware, but the same legal argument applies to the regulation of cyber-bullying.

[71] [1999] 4 All ER 342.

[72] Section 1(1) of the UK Defamation Act 1996, Ch. 31.

[73] See discussion in Diane Rowland, 'Free Expression and Defamation' in *Human Rights in the Digital Age*, 66 (Mathias Klang and Andrew Murray eds., 2005).

[74] SI 2002/2013, implementing the Directive on Electronic Commerce, Directive 2000/31/EC of June 2000 [2000] OJ L178/1 at <http://www.opsi.gov.uk/si/si2002/20022013.htm>.

[75] Directive on Electronic Commerce, N. 75, above, article 14, <available at http://eur-lex.europa.eu>.

[76] Directive on Electronic Commerce, N. 75, above, article 13.

[77] Directive on Electronic Commerce, N. 75, above, article 12.

unless they have actual knowledge of unlawful activity or information,[78] and have failed to act expeditiously to remove the materials.[79] Article 15 of the Directive clearly stipulates that there is no general duty on ISPs to monitor information which passes through or is hosted on their system.

In 2006, the English court had an opportunity to clarify the position of ISPs in defamation litigation in *Bunt v Tilley*.[80] The claimant brought a defamation action against six defendants, including three ISPs. Having benefitted from consideration of both *Godfrey* and the Electronic Commerce (EC Directive) Regulations 2002, the court held that for an ISP to be held responsible for defamatory publication, there must be 'knowing participation'[81] to incur liability: a passive role in facilitating postings is not sufficient to incur liability.[82] In distinguishing *Godfrey* from the case at bar, the court ruled against the claimant for failing to serve actual and effective notice to the defendant ISPs. In effect, the UK decision has provided the model of a notice and take-down system.

Unlike the European standard, the US is often seen as taking a liberal stance to protect free speech. ISPs enjoy almost complete immunity from civil liability under s. 230(1)(c) of the Communications Decency Act 1996 which states that 'no provider or user of an interactive computer service shall be treated as the publisher or speaker as of any information provided by another content provider'.[83] In the controversial case of *Zeran v America Online, Inc. (AOL)*,[84] the plaintiff was a victim of defamatory postings on AOL message boards, from which he received death threats and abusive phone calls. AOL refused to post a retraction of the original message and failed for several days to remove it in spite of complaints by the plaintiff. Yet the Court of Appeals ruled that AOL was an interactive computer service and should not be held liable.

It has been argued that the US courts have misinterpreted the Communications Decency Act and have mixed up the legal liabilities under common law principles of defamation between publishers and distributors.[85] While the former bears a higher duty based on their capacity to supervise and monitor, the latter are being held to a much lower standard based on failure to remove contentious materials upon notice. The US position has been content to leave victims of cyber-bullying without legal recourse and remedies if they could not identify the initial perpetrator, or when the ISPs refuse to remove the objectionable materials. In evaluating the efforts of both the English courts (in reality, the European Union approach) and the American courts in order to find a satisfactory solution between the balance of a claimant's rights solely on the issue of reputation and the interests of ISPs, Eric Barendt compellingly argues that the English and European Union approaches are preferable because they have provided a more effective remedy than the American one, especially when victims are facing blatantly unfounded and malicious allegations.[86]

So far, our analysis on ISPs' liability has concentrated on internet defamation disputes, yet the adoption of a notice and take-down regime is equally apposite for

[78] Directive on Electronic Commerce, N. 75, above, article 13.

[79] Directive on Electronic Commerce, N. 75, above, article 14.

[80] [2006] EWHC 407 (QB) at <http://www.bailii.org/ew/cases/EWHC/QB/2006/407.html>.

[81] *Bunt v Tilley*, N. 80, above, at para. 23.

[82] *Bunt v Tilley*, N. 80, above, at para. 36.

[83] 47 USC s.230 (1996).

[84] 129 F 3d 327 (4th Cir., 1997).

[85] Ottenweller, N. 7, above, 1301–11.

[86] Eric Barendt, *Freedom of Speech* (Oxford, 2006), 466.

reputation damage, harassment, privacy violations, and other forms of bullying on the internet.

18.3 Children's rights and the model of co-regulation

When looking at the problem of cyber-bullying and in our anxious search for a direct legal answer, it is easy to think that there is only one group of direct victims who have been taunted and mocked by the bullies. In fact, the bullies and the bystanders who joined in are also victims themselves in a broader sense. As discussed earlier, existing research in psychology has shown that the social and psychological developments of the bullies, bystanders, and victims are all adversely affected in this hostile, abusive, and violent form of interaction.[87] Contemporary neuroscience research has also revealed that excessive and sustained exposure to social networking sites is likely to affect brain development of young children, which may partly explain their behaviour associated with cyber-bullying. Baroness Susan Greenfield, who is an eminent neuroscientist at the University of Oxford and a member of the House of Lords in the UK, explained the above point to the Parliament,[88] where she elaborated her theory of 'plasticity of the human brain', referring to the changing nature of human brains by prolonged exposure to a new and unprecedented type of ongoing environment, including the screen.[89] As children's experiences on social networking sites are 'devoid of cohesive narrative and long term significance', their brain systems might easily be 'infantilized', characterized by short attention spans, sensationalism, inability to empathize, and a shaky sense of identity.[90] Thus, she urged that it is necessary for the Government to build safeguard measures for children in the use of social networking sites. Unsurprisingly, Baroness Greenfield's view has proved to be controversial.[91] While conclusive evidence has yet to be gathered, her warning on the systematic desensitization caused by technology and excessive use of social networking sites should not be brushed aside lightly.

Considering that bullying and cyber-bullying is a form of violence inflicted on children by children themselves, and the health factors related to social, psychological, and biological development of the younger generation, a purely legal approach to the holding of the children as defendants either liable in civil action or culpable in criminal prosecution may not be the best solution.

18.3.1 International legal regime on children's rights

The United Nations Convention on the Rights of the Child (UNCRC), in setting out the international and legal standard and guidelines for the protection of children,

[87] Tord Ivarsson, Anders G. Broberg, Tomas Arvidsson, and Christopher Gillberg, 'Bullying in Adolescence: Psychiatric Problems in Victims and Bullies as Measured by the Youth Self Report (YSR) and the Depression Self-Rating Scale (DSRS)' (2005) 59 *Nordic Journal of Psychiatry* 365–73; Petra Gradinger, Dagmar Strohmeier, and Christiane Spiel, 'Traditional Bullying and Cyberbullying: Identification of Risk Groups for Adjustment Problems' (2009) 217(4) *Journal of Psychology* 205–13.

[88] Baroness Susan Greenfield's speech, House of Lords: *Hansard* (UK), 12 February 2009 at <http://www.publications.parliament.uk/pa/ld200809/ldhansrd/text/90212-0010.htm>.

[89] Greenfield, N. 88 , above, column 1291.

[90] Greenfield, N. 88, above, column 1293.

[91] 'Four Authors Respond to the Social Networking Controversy' *Neuronarrative*, 12 March 2009 at <http://neuronarrative.wordpress.com/2009/03/12/four-authors-respond-to-the-social-networking-controversy/>.

has emphasized that 'the best interests of the child' should be the primary consideration for the states (article 3). Under article 19 of the Convention, States parties have the obligations to protect children from all forms of physical or mental violence.[92] It also obliges the state to enact preventive measures to ensure that all child victims of violence receive the support and assistance they require.

The notion of violence is broad enough to encompass bullying as supported by the Rapporteur's Report to the United Nations General Assembly in 2007 which condemned all forms of violence including bullying.[93] The Report urged all states to strengthen efforts to prevent and protect children from all such violence through a 'comprehensive approach and to develop a multifaceted and systematic framework', to foster international co-operation and mutual assistance, and to implement preventive and anti-bullying policies.[94] In 2009, in the Stockholm Call for Action to the European Member States at l'Europe de l'Enfance, cyber-bullying was listed to be a form of violence that warrants the development of state intervention and national strategies.[95] Indeed, in Annex II of the same document, it was stated that violence against children, including bullying, was one of the primary concerns listed by children themselves

Above all, this international human rights approach based on a children's rights perspective is no longer grounded on a traditional vertical relationship between state and individuals, largely with negative obligations incumbent on states to refrain from human rights violation like torture or degrading treatment.[96] Rather, it is based on a horizontal relationship with obligations on states to enforce rights between individuals and to offer adequate protection to them. This would have required the state to implement protective and preventive measures against cyber-bullying for children's welfare and their best interest regardless of who the perpetrators are and how many. As we have discussed in the earlier section on defamation and harassment actions which are responsive, the children's rights based approach differs from the traditional form of legal intervention and calls for a pro-active response from the states: namely, as advocated by the Stockholm Call for Action, national strategies should include a reporting system accessible to children themselves, and a mandatory action plan

[92] The full text of article 19 reads: '1. States Parties shall take all appropriate legislative, administrative, social and educational measures to protect the child from all forms of physical or mental violence, injury or abuse, neglect or negligent treatment, maltreatment or exploitation, including sexual abuse, while in the care of parent(s), legal guardian(s) or any other person who has the care of the child.

2. Such protective measures should, as appropriate, include effective procedures for the establishment of social programmes to provide necessary support for the child and for those who have the care of the child, as well as for other forms of prevention and for identification, reporting, referral, investigation, treatment and follow-up of instances of child maltreatment described heretofore, and, as appropriate, for judicial involvement.'

[93] Tebatso Future Baleseng, 'Promotion and Protection of the Rights of Children' Report of the Third Committee to the United nations General Assembly, 66 Session, 3 December 2007 (A/62/435) at <http://www.ohchr.org/documents/press/a.62.435.pdf>.

[94] Baleseng, N. 93, above, paras. 54, 57(c) and (k)

[95] It was an NGO statement signed by 46 groups across Europe addressing l'Europe de l'Enfance, a ministerial group among European Union Member States set up to protect children's rights in Europe (the inter-governmental group was set up in 2000. Information available at <http://www.childoneurope.org/ee/history.htm>). The Stockholm Call for Action, NGO Statement to the EU Member States at the Meeting of the Permanent Intergovernmental Group l'Europe de l'Enfance, 20 November 2009 at <http://www.tfal.org.mt/MediaCenter/PDFs/1_The%20Stockholm%20Call%20for%20Action.pdf>.

[96] Wouter Vandenhole, 'Cyber Bullying from a Children's Rights Perspective' *The Legal Aspects of Cyberbullying: Cost Action ISO0801 Workshop Abstract* 37, 26 May 2010 at <http://sites.google.com/site/costis0801/>.

in each school to prevent and handle bullying and cyber-bullying.[97] Here, I would further advocate a similar mandatory action plan of reporting, handling, and preventing of cyber-bullying on ISPs under a co-regulatory governance regime.

18.3.2 The alternative approach of co-regulation

The existence of a children's rights based approach indeed necessarily entails a co-regulatory model of governance simply because it is a shared responsibility among various parties for the care of our future generation. In writing on child protection in the digital era, Eva Lievens reminds us that parents and educators should play a primary role, with the state and industry coming next. In her work, Lievens defines co-regulation as a regulatory strategy which consists of elements of both direct state regulation and elements of self-regulation.[98] While the state should remain as the primary architect of the regulatory regime and the primary guarantor of human rights, Lievens urges us to think outside the traditional legislation box of a centred command-and-control model when dealing with children's issues in the digital age.[99] One reason is that the law struggles to keep pace with technological advances, and the problem of cyber-bullying is no exception. In addition, as mentioned earlier, there are multi-stakeholders involved, and it is in the nature of cyber-bullying to be often anonymous with multiple aggressors involved. Therefore, a model of co-regulation will offer a workable solution with key building blocks, such as parental control tools, awareness action, reporting system, code of conduct by the industry, and co-operation across borders.[100] The stakeholders involved should include children, parents, NGOs, the government, and the industry. The closest model that we have so far is the European Commission's Safer Internet Programme launched in 1999, with 30 countries participating, and with three major aims: promoting the safer use of the internet and other communication technologies, particularly for children and young people; educating users, particularly children, parents, carers, teachers, and educators in this regard; and fighting against illegal content and harmful conduct online.[101] The Programme includes an education campaign to raise awareness, to involve parents, to conduct studies on the issue of cyber-bullying, and to involve ISPs as one of the major key actors.[102] During 2010, 20 major social networks companies have joined, including Bebo, Facebook, MySpace, and Google/YouTube.[103]

18.3.2.1 Role of schools

It is not difficult to understand the role of schools in the co-regulatory model. In fact, it is indispensable in tackling the problem of cyber-bullying as most bullying takes

[97] Stockholm Call for Action, N. 95, above, paras. 32 and 33.

[98] Eva Lievens, *Protecting Children in the Digital Era: The Use of Alternative Regulatory Instruments* (Leiden, 2010), 208.

[99] Lievens, N. 98, above, 87.

[100] Lievens, N. 98, above, 105.

[101] Europe's Information Society, 'Policy: Making the Internet Safer for Europe's Children' at <http://ec.europa.eu/information_society/activities/sip/policy/index_en.htm#programme>.

[102] Europe's Information Society, 'Safer Internet Day 2009: Commission Starts Campaign against Cyber-Bullying' 10 February 2009 at <http://europa.eu/rapid/pressReleasesAction.do?reference=MEMO/09/58>.

[103] Europe's Information Society, 'Social Networking: Commission brokers agreement among major web companies' 10 February 2009 at <http://ec.europa.eu/information_society/newsroom/cf/itemlongdetail.cfm?item_id=4672>.

place in schools so that cyber-bullying and bullying often go hand-in-hand. Many of their victims in schools find it a form of unbearable pressure and are forced to withdraw from study, as we have already seen in the plight facing Knight and Raza discussed in Part 18.1. As a result, a child's right to education guaranteed under articles 28 and 29 of the UNCRC would be indirectly compromised.

While it is important to have anti-bullying policies in schools, it may not be an adequate remedy if the scope of the policies is based on a strict division between on-campus and off-campus activities being contingent on whether school resources (e.g. school computer, web-based system) have been employed. This deficiency is illustrated in the US. Critics have pointed out that victims of cyber-bullying have to face the huge obstacles in proving that online bullying has caused substantial and material interference or disruption to learning at school.[104] Short of satisfying this legal standard, First Amendment free speech rights will trump in most situations. Yet it is not clear whether the learning of the whole class has to be adversely affected in order to satisfy the test of 'substantial and material interference' to learning, or whether it is adequate to prove that the learning of one or two children has been substantially and materially disrupted. On top of this, although 42 states in the US require schools to have an anti-bullying policy, many have not defined the meaning of bullying or even alluded to cyber-bullying.[105]

In comparison, the United Kingdom has provided an alternative, although its effectiveness is hard to predict and judge since it is still in its experimental stage. As far as we can tell, consistent with the approach of children's rights, in 2004 the UK Government formulated the *Every Child Matters* policy, the aim of which is for every child and young person from 0–19 years to achieve the following: be healthy; stay safe; enjoy and achieve; make a positive contribution; achieve economic well-being.[106] Schools have a statutory responsibility to ensure that they have in place an anti-bullying policy and behaviour management practices that satisfy current UK legislation on children's rights. For instance, s. 89(1) of the Education and Inspections Act of 2006 requires all schools to have anti-bullying measures and empowers schools to have their jurisdiction extended to related off-campus activities under s. 89(1) and s. 89(5).[107] Likewise, the School Standards and Framework Act requires head teachers to have measures in place to prevent all forms of bullying among pupils under s. 61(4).[108] In addition to statutory duties, the Government's guidance of 2007 requires schools to adopt a comprehensive anti-bullying policy that includes staff training as well as disciplinary sanctions against students who bully.[109] Moreover, the school curriculum would cover issues of internet safety and the handling of cyber-bullying. The new primary curriculum will come into force in September 2011, while the secondary curriculum in England has, in fact, included this aspect since 2008.[110]

[104] Auerbach, N. 8, above; Renee L. Servance, 'Cyberbullying, Cyber-Harassment, and the Conflict between Schools and the First Amendment' (2003) *Wisconsin Law Review* 1213.

[105] Hinduja and Patchin, N. 58, above 2, 7. For instance, Arizona, Michigan, and Mississippi only mention the concept of bullying but not cyber-bullying.

[106] The Department for Children, Schools and Families, 'Every Child Matters Outcome Framework' at <http://www.dcsf.gov.uk/childrensplan/downloads/ECM%20outcomes%20framework.pdf>.

[107] Education and Inspections Act of 2006, Ch. 40.

[108] School Standards and Framework Act of 1998, Ch. 31.

[109] The Department for Children, Schools and Families, 'No Hiding Place for Bullies—Ed Balls' *DFES News*, 21 September 2007 at <http://www.dcsf.gov.uk/pns/DisplayPN.cgi?pn_id=2007_0168>.

[110] Tanya Byron, *Do We Have Safer Children in a Digital World? A Review of Progress Since the 2008 Byron Review* (2010) 17 at <http://www.dcsf.gov.uk/byronreview/pdfs/do%20we%20have%20safer%20children%20in%20a%20digital%20world-WEB.pdf>.

In other words, the United Kingdom has adopted a combined approach of empowerment (awareness-raising, protection, and prevention) and punishment as part of education for all children.

18.3.2.2 The role of ISPs

While legal duties have been imposed directly on schools with teachers and school principals willingly embracing the above measures, the telecommunications industry is so far exempted from direct legal intervention on their role in combating cyber-bullying. One may also question the basis and justification of imposing such a responsibility on ISPs because, after all, they are not educators nor are they child carers. But as discussed in the earlier section on 'Harassment', the imposition of liabilities on third parties who are in a position to control and mitigate the harm is actually consistent with the underlying principles of tort law.

Besides, private telecommunications companies have created a public space, which plays a key role in contemporary youth culture. In 2009, MySpace and Google alone had 42 million monthly European users of social networking sites.[111] By July 2010, Facebook, the most popular social networking site, has reached 500 million registered members, that is eight per cent of the world's population.[112] According to the International Telecommunications Union Report in 2010, 11 per cent of Facebook users in the US were aged 13 to 17, while 28 per cent were aged 18 to 25. It was estimated that globally, 55 per cent of Facebook users were between 13 and 17 years old.[113] According to another study in 2009 on internet usage among teenagers in the US, it was found that 73 per cent use social networking sites.[114] Posting comments, either to a picture, page, or wall remains the most popular among teens who use these sites, with 86 per cent posting comments to a friend's page or wall, and 83 per cent adding comments to a friend's picture. This reiterates our concerns that social networking sites are a common breeding ground for cyber-bullying.

Although Facebook is one of the members of the Europe's Safe Internet Programme, the mechanism under the Programme is based on a voluntary and self-regulatory model. According to the evaluation report released in early 2010, it was commented that the principles to which the ISPs have signed up have remained aspirational instead of legal. Despite the fact that major social networking sites have to make a self-declaration on their intentions to conform with the principles of self-regulation,[115] and 20 companies have pledged to introduce a report misuse button for their users, and to alert local authorities to inappropriate contact from or conduct by another user, on close inspection, this is far from ideal. For example, on Facebook, there is no report mechanism for wall posts and comments: it is only available for

[111] Jemima Kiss, 'Social Networking Sites Sign EU Pact to Fix Cyber-Bullying' 19 February 2009 at <http://www.guardian.co.uk/media/pda/2009/feb/19/socialnetworking-myspace>.

[112] Facebook, 'Timeline' at <http://www.facebook.com/press/info.php?timeline>.

[113] International Telecommunications Union, 'Child Online Protection Statistics Framework and Indicators, (Draft)' 7 June 2010, para. 202–3 at <http://www.itu.int/council/groups/wg-cop/second-meeting-june-2010/COP_Stat_Framework_7%20June_2010.pdf>.

[114] Amanda Lenhart, Kristen Purcell, Aaron Smith, and Kathryn Zickuhr, 'Social Media and Young Adults', Pew Research Center, 3 February 2010 at <http://www.pewinternet.org/Reports/2010/Social-Media-and-Young-Adults/Part-3/1-Teens-and-online-social-networks.aspx>. The survey interviewed 800 adolescents between 12 and 17, in the period from June to September 2009.

[115] Europe's Information Society, 'Implementation of the Safer Social Networking Principles for the EU', 9 February 2010 at <http://ec.europa.eu/information_society/activities/social_networking/eu_action/implementation_princip/index_en.htm>.

photos, videos, and notes. After a user has reported an abuse, an administrator will look at the complaint, but the user will not be notified of any action taken.[116] This illustrates the shortcomings of a voluntary self-regulatory model; thus, if a co-regulatory model is to be effective, mandatory reporting and handling systems must be implemented by the ISPs and enforced by the regulators. Although legal regulations would not be able to spell out every detail for regulation due to the ever-changing and flexible technological infrastructure, they cannot give an entirely free hand to the industry as it is, of course, unlikely to solve cyber-bullying.

Whether or not the ISPs are able to implement a fully filtered mechanism after complaints have been made, their role in the control of cyber-bullying is crucial. For instance in China, in 2007, when Zhang Shufan, a 13-year-old high school girl gave a television interview condemning the corrupting trend of the internet as too violent and too pornographic, she was immediately attacked by angry netizens who mobilized public opinion, and used the internet to track her down.[117] Within five days, there were 1200 postings giving her personal information (including her primary school record), and running for 12 full web pages on the bulletin discussion board, commonly known in China as BBS, of Baidu. Her picture was also posted and more information about her was called for and flooded the internet, including stories that she was not as pure and good as she had presented. Eventually, it was Baidu who intervened after eight days of internet frenzy created by netizens.[118] The web company decided to freeze posting for eight days though viewing was still allowed. Baidu explained that this was done to protect the interest of minors in society and 'to maintain healthy discussion' on its site.[119]

At this point, one might question whether the duty imposed on the ISP would be too onerous. Are we not asking them to be both censors and arbitrators? Bearing in mind the European model of E-Commerce Directive, ISPs are exempted from liability when acting as mere conduits, or just hosting or caching information from third parties unless they have actual knowledge of the unlawful information. A children's rights based model only requires a minimum standard of compliance with a reporting mechanism, effective action plan, support mechanism to victims, and a notice and take-down system upon complaints. Lievens has proposed a benchmark system with indicators on when ISPs' action is needed to remove the materials.[120] Obvious illegal materials or information would include child pornography (including doctored photos of a victim, or estranged boyfriends sending intimate photos of their girlfriends after the relationship has turned sour), and dissemination of sensitive personal information without consent and video-clips of happy slapping. In the light of the above, a framework with a number of clear indicators may also be designed for

[116] Bojana Lobe and Elisabeth Starksrud, 'Evaluation of the Implementation of the Safer Social Networking Principles for the EU Part II: Testing of 20 Providers of Social Networking Services in Europe', European Commission Safer Internet Programme (January 2010) 22 at <http://ec.europa.eu/information_society/activities/social_networking/docs/final_report/sec_part.pdf>.

[117] The account was from *Pupil: Web pages are very pornographic and very violent* at <http://epaper.xkb.com.cn/view.php?id=184695> (in Chinese), posted on 7 January 2008.

[118] Zhang expressed her view on 12 December 2007 on CCTV. The first posting to attack her was immediately posted on that evening. Other attacks followed which lasted until 8 January 2008 when Baidu intervened and stopped further discussion. It was only on 16 January 2008 that posting was allowed. See Yang Xuan, 'What Does this Egao Incident Show?' *People's Daily*, 11 January 2008 at 11 at <http://paper.people.com.cn/rmrb/html/2008-01/11/content_38069275.htm> (in Chinese).

[119] Baidu, *Gong Gao: Guan Yu Zhang Shu Fan Ba De Wei Hu Shuo Ming [Notice: Declaration on the Protection of Zhang Shufan]*, 8 January 2008 at <http://tieba.baidu.com/f?kz=308107848>.

[120] Lievens, N. 98, above, 360.

less clear cases (e.g. defamation or harassment). In this way, the role for ISPs can be easily clarified.

18.4 Conclusion

Cyber-bullying is more than simply an old problem in a new disguise. It is unique. Unlike traditional schoolyard bullying, cyber-bullying does not need to have direct encounters with the victims. While the perpetrators can hide behind the cloak of anonymity, the victims are at the mercy of numerous aggressors synchroniously and instantaneously, regardless of time and space. To the victims, it seems there is unending suffering, and no 'home' where they can run to for safety. Every time they go online, victims suffer repeated humiliation. Once words enter cyberspace, they do not 'disappear into the air',[121] but become part of the permanent memory of an internet system that will haunt the victims for the rest of their lives. The dark side of the dot.com revolution is that modern information technology has not only become an easy tool for bullying, but has also made it much more powerful and pernicious.

While no one can honestly deny the seriousness of the problem, we are at a loss as to how to overcome the difficulties associated with individual perpetrators who are often unknown or impossible to track down. Adding to this, there is the viral nature of the internet message which spreads like wild fire and is ingrained into the memory of cyberspace. But conventional legal causes of action, such as defamation and harassment, are ill-equipped to deal with the cyber-bullies who are often anonymous individuals or an anonymous crowd, amounting to hundreds or even millions, who act in an uncoordinated, spontaneous manner. Commentators have remarked that cyberspace has stretched the applicability of legal regulation beyond breaking point.[122] Adding to the legal problem, psychologists and neuroscientists have warned that excessive exposure to digital activities at an early age can impede the social, emotional, and even brain development of children, with implications for risking a loss of empathy, on the one hand, and, on the other, an increase in aggressive behaviour.

In facing this problem of cyber-bullying, a children's rights based approach offers an alternative strategy. Rather than relying on a reactive legal mechanism, largely dependent on a victim's decision to take action, the state will design a co-regulatory model based on doctrines of international children's rights intended to serve the best interests of children. To this end, it will be necessary to adopt pro-active measures of prevention and empowerment involving children, parents, schools, and the industry. Unfortunately, although the European Commission has designed a model aiming to implement the above principles, this well-intentioned effort has yet to bear any fruit. This is largely due to the lack of a mandatory compliance and regulatory regime imposed on ISPs. Given the increasing role that the telecommunications industry has been playing in the life of the younger generation and the profits that they have generated from online activities and mobile phone services, it is vital that the industry should develop a minimum code of practice and safety for their users. Reliable safety mechanisms of reporting, follow-up, notice, and take-down of harmful materials for victims of cyber-bullying must be implemented and monitored by the authorities.

[121] Luc Beirens, 'Police Experiences with Cyberbullying—the Belgian Case' *The Legal Aspects of Cyberbullying: Cost Action ISO0801 Workshop Abstract* 9, 26 May 2010 at <http://sites.google.com/site/costis0801/>. Luc Beirens is the Head of the Federal Computer Crime Unit in Belgium.

[122] Basu and Jones, N. 50, above, 21.

Just like the real world, digital space is not a bed of roses. Technology has filled us with fascination, excitement, and fear. But in order to help the younger generation navigate safely the complexities of life, online and offline, the law needs to bring in both industry and educators to develop a multi-dimensional road map of best practice for victims and bullies, users, and business.

19

Exploring the Contested Role of Mandatory Reporting Laws in the Identification of Severe Child Abuse and Neglect

Ben Mathews

Significant numbers of children are severely abused and neglected by parents and caregivers. Infants and very young children are the most vulnerable and are unable to seek help. Many of these children experience both initial harm and enduring effects, at substantial cost to the individual and society. These situations present complex normative and practical questions. Should measures be taken to identify these situations? If so, what measures should be adopted? Once cases are identified, what responses should be implemented? This chapter is primarily concerned with aspects of the second question, of what measures should be adopted to detect cases of severe child maltreatment. It proceeds from a position that any liberal democracy, to be consistent with its values and organizing principles, should take some kind of socio-legal measures to identify cases of severe child maltreatment.[1]

Many liberal democratic jurisdictions have enacted legislation requiring designated professionals such as doctors, nurses, police, and teachers to report suspected cases of severe child abuse and neglect. These 'mandatory reporting laws' have been created on the basis that such cases would otherwise remain hidden because of the nature of both the situation and the conduct, which generally means the parent will not seek help, and because the child victim usually cannot or will not seek help.[2] In contrast, other jurisdictions including the United Kingdom have not adopted this legislative approach. This seems to be at least partly motivated by a concern that, as reflected in some academic criticism, the laws produce dramatic increases in unwarranted reports, which, it is argued, lead to investigations which infringe on people's privacy, cause trauma to innocent parents and families, and divert scarce government

[1] Apart from making some general observations about the third issue of what appear to be the most appropriate overall strategies for dealing with different manifestations of maltreatment, this chapter does not explore the diverse and complex issues regarding this question. As well, for reasons of space, this chapter is limited to an exploration of the issue on a whole population level without addressing any specific issues regarding subgroups of the population, such as indigenous peoples, where there may be additional issues.

[2] Discussed further below. Arguably, this premise is very strong for some types of child maltreatment such as sexual abuse and physical abuse, but is weaker for many cases of other types such as neglect. Accordingly, the differences between different types of maltreatment are the basis for differential response systems, discussed later.

resources from deserving cases.[3] However, such jurisdictions often do impose industry-based policy requirements on similar classes of designated persons to report suspected cases of maltreatment, and these professionals are often bound by a common law duty to report known and suspected severe maltreatment.[4] Hence, even where legislative reporting duties have not been preferred, other types of reporting duties exist. This suggests that, while criticism has been levelled at perceived adverse consequences of legislative reporting duties, their motivating principle is a compelling feature of a society seeking to protect vulnerable children. This principle is that where a person in a professional relationship with a child knows or suspects the child is a victim of severe maltreatment, the child's situation should be brought to the attention of helping agencies.

The primary purpose of this chapter is to explore in some further detail the extent to which opposition to mandatory reporting laws is valid based on the claim that the laws produce 'overreporting'. This is an important exercise because evidence supporting this claim has significant implications for child protection systems. Exploring this claim requires legal and historical analysis, and use of empirical data about child victimization and reporting patterns. Accordingly, the first part of this chapter revisits the original mandatory reporting laws, discusses their development into various current forms, explains their relationship with policy and common law reporting obligations, and situates them in the context of their place in modern child protection systems. This part of the chapter will show that in general, contemporary reporting laws have expanded far beyond their original conceptualization, but that there is also now a deeper understanding of the nature, incidence, timing, and effects of different types of severe maltreatment, an awareness that the real incidence of maltreatment is far higher than that officially recorded, and that there is strong evidence showing that the majority of identified cases of severe maltreatment are the result of reports by mandated reporters. The second part of this chapter discusses the apparent effect of mandatory reporting laws on 'overreporting' by referring to Australian government data about reporting patterns and outcomes, with a particular focus on New South

[3] G. Melton, 'Mandated Reporting: A Policy Without Reason' (2005) 29 *Child Abuse & Neglect* 9; F. Ainsworth, 'Mandatory Reporting of Child Abuse and Neglect: Does it Really Make a Difference?' (2002) 7 *Child and Family Social Work* 57; see also R. Lonne, N. Parton, J. Thomson, and M. Harries, *Reforming Child Protection* (Routledge, London, 2009). Melton went so far as to urge repeal of the laws, and to recommend that jurisdictions which had not yet adopted them should not do so. Two articles responded to this: B. Drake and M. Jonson-Reid, 'A Response to Melton Based on the Best Available Data' (2007) 31 *Child Abuse & Neglect* 343; B. Mathews and D. Bross, 'Mandated Reporting is Still a Policy with Reason: Empirical Evidence and Philosophical Grounds' (2008) 32(5) *Child Abuse & Neglect* 511. On the issue of traumatic investigations, it seems reasonable to conclude that some investigations of child protection referrals, especially but not only those involving suspected sexual abuse, may be traumatic for some families, and there are some accounts of such trauma: see for example P. Davies, 'The Impact of a Child Protection Investigation: a Personal Reflective Account' (2010) *Child and Family Social Work* 1, <http://doi:10.1111/j.1365–2206.2010.00732.x>; G. Dumbrill, 'Parental Experience of Child Protection Intervention: a Qualitative Study' (2006) 30 *Child Abuse & Neglect* 27; and see *Sullivan v Moody* (2001) 207 CLR 562. However, other studies have found little trauma and high levels of familial satisfaction with investigation processes, suggesting that much depends on jurisdictional and practitioner practice and expertise: see G. Fryer, D. Bross, R. Krugman, D. Denson, and D. Baird, 'Good News for CPS Workers' (1990) 48(1) *Public Welfare* 38; D. English, S. Brummel, J. Graham, T. Clark, and L.Coghlan, *Factors that Influence the Decision not to Substantiate a CPS Referral III: Client Perceptions of Investigation* (Department of Health and Social Service, Office of Children's Administration Research, Olympia, Washington, 2002); R. Huebner, M. Jennings, and S. Schaaf, *Customer Satisfaction: Feedback Results in User-Provider Partnerships* (State Government News, Kentucky, 2002); D. Finkelhor, 'Is Child Abuse Overreported?' (1990) 48(1) *Public Welfare* 22.

[4] *JD v East Berkshire Community Health NHS Trust* [2005] UKHL 23.

Wales. It will be seen that raw descriptive data about report numbers and outcomes appear to show that reporting laws produce both desirable consequences (identification of severe cases) and problematic consequences (increased numbers of unsubstantiated reports). Yet, to explore the extent to which the data supports the overreporting claim, and because (as will be seen) numbers of unsubstantiated reports alone cannot demonstrate overreporting, this part of the chapter asks further questions of the data. Who makes reports, about which maltreatment types, and what are the outcomes of those reports? What is the nature of these reports; for example, to what extent are multiple numbers of reports made about the same child? What meaning can be attached to an 'unsubstantiated' report, and can such reports be used to show flaws in reporting effectiveness and problems in reporting laws?

Before proceeding further, some preliminary comments are warranted. This chapter does not seek to provide final answers to complex issues concerning overreporting, but it does seek to shed further light on the overreporting claim. Any exploration of the claim that mandatory reporting laws produce 'overreporting' is difficult because this is a complex claim, the numerous facets of which have not been articulated and explored with precision by either critics of the laws or their defenders. As well, analysing this claim must draw on empirical evidence about the consequences of enacting reporting laws, but often such evidence is nonexistent, partial, or ambiguous. In addition, a 'substantiated' report is commonly used as standard to measure whether a report was 'warranted' and an 'unsubstantiated' report is seen as one which was unwarranted, but the use of this standard is questionable. This exploration is also complex because 'child maltreatment' is not a uniform phenomenon; classes of maltreatment are qualitatively different. Child sexual abuse is clearly different in numerous ways from child neglect. Discussion of issues concerning 'child abuse and neglect', including those regarding reporting laws and overreporting, often proceed without distinguishing between different forms of abuse, instead conflating them. This is problematic because the aetiological and legal differences between types and extents of abuse can clearly have significance when evaluating the justifiability of legal and social responses to them. A case of the worst type of sexual abuse is far different from a case of mild neglect produced by poverty. Additionally, the severity of cases differs within each type of abuse, and this affects what types of responses may be required. Finally, the questions of whether reporting laws should exist and in what form, and of whether they produce 'overreporting' are best explored in the context of the aims of a society's whole child protection system, and with reference to the economic and human resources the jurisdiction is willing to devote to that system. A system with wider goals than can be met with the resources devoted to it is set up to fail.

It will be suggested that available evidence from Australia is not sufficiently detailed or strong to demonstrate the overreporting claim. However, from this exploration it is also apparent that, whether adopting an approach based on public health and or other principles, much better evidence about reporting needs to be collected and analysed by government systems. As well, more nuanced research needs to be conducted to identify what can reasonably be said to constitute 'overreports', and efforts must be made to minimize unsatisfactory reporting practice, informed by the relevant jurisdiction's context and aims. It is also concluded that, depending on the jurisdiction, the available data may provide useful indicators of positive, negative, and unanticipated effects of specific components of the laws, and of the strengths, weaknesses, and needs of the child protection system. At the same time, in light of the aetiology of severe child maltreatment and the contribution made by mandated reporters to case identification, and despite the presence of practical (and in some cases, theoretical) problems with elements of reporting laws, a broad claim that the laws should be repealed in their entirety because they cause unjustifiable overreporting is, at least for now, neither sound nor evidence-based. Given the still relatively early stage of child protection efforts, and the complexity of the context, it is to be expected that problems and challenges will arise with reporting laws. However, unless and until there exists a proven system of case identification which is superior to the contribution made by mandated reporters, these challenges should be identified and faced, rather than prematurely abandoning the whole strategy.

19.1 Legal and social contexts of reporting laws

19.1.1 Kempe, the 'battered-child syndrome', and the first mandatory reporting law

The impetus for the first mandatory reporting law was the work of the Colorado paediatrician C. Henry Kempe and his colleagues in identifying cases of severe child physical abuse, and conceptualizing this as the 'battered-child syndrome'.[5] It is important to note that Kempe's work was not about any manifestation of physical abuse no matter how slight; the battered-child syndrome was defined as:[6]

> A term used by us to characterize a clinical condition in young children who have received serious physical abuse, generally from a parent or foster parent... It is a significant cause of childhood disability and death. Unfortunately, it is frequently not recognized or, if diagnosed, is inadequately handled by the physician because of hesitation to bring the case to the attention of the proper authorities... The battered-child syndrome may occur at any age, but, in general, the affected children are younger than 3 years.

Kempe and his colleagues proceeded to discuss the type and number of cases they were seeing in their hospitals; an example was given of one day's intake including four infants suffering parent-inflicted battering, two of whom died, another of whom died four weeks later, with the fourth recovering. Kempe acknowledged that battering occurred on a spectrum, with less severe cases through to extremely severe cases. However, the emphasis was on severe injury, especially cases involving bone fractures (whether of the skull, arms, or legs) and or subdural hematoma.[7] Kempe asserted that appropriate management by doctors involved making:[8]

> the correct diagnosis so that he can institute proper therapy and make certain that a similar event will not occur again. He should report possible wilful trauma to the police department or any special children's protective services that operate in his community. The report that he makes should be restricted to the objective findings which can be verified and, where possible, should be supported by photographs and roentgenograms.

It is important to note that the authors tried to ascertain the national incidence of severe battering through a national survey of hospitals (only 71 responded) and a survey of 77 district attorneys. As a result, nationwide they found 749 known cases

[5] C. H. Kempe, F. Silverman, B. Steele, W. Droegemueller, and H. Silver, 'The Battered-Child Syndrome' (1962) 181 *Journal of the American Medical Association* 17.
[6] Kempe, N. 5, above, 17.
[7] Kempe, N. 5, above, 19–24.
[8] Kempe, N. 5, above, 23.

reported by these sources in a one-year period (302 reported by the hospitals and 447 by the attorneys).

Kempe's work was accompanied by intensive, successful lobbying efforts for legislative reform. As a result, the first mandatory reporting laws were enacted in every State of the USA (except Hawaii) between 1963 and 1967, and in accordance with the limited scope of Kempe's work at this time, these laws were initially limited to requiring medical professionals to report suspected serious physical abuse inflicted by a child's parent or caregiver.[9] It is important during any exploration of issues concerning mandatory reporting laws that the intent and expression of the laws was and would remain[10] focused on the requirement not to report any or all abuse, but only to report cases of suspected significant, serious harm. This point, which is far more than academic, is often missed by commentators.[11]

19.1.2 Expansion of the law, and adoption by other countries

Profound changes then occurred which dramatically broadened the scope of the reporting laws. In all States of the USA, the scope of the initial laws expanded in three ways, motivated in part by federal legislation—the 1974 Child Abuse Prevention and Treatment Act (CAPTA) which allocated funds to States based on the parameters of their laws. First, members of additional professional groups were required to report suspicions of abuse. Second, the types of reportable abuse were expanded beyond physical abuse, to also include sexual abuse, emotional or psychological abuse, and neglect. Third, a broader spectrum of cases were required to be reported, by a lifting of prior limits which restricted reportable cases to those involving serious harm.[12] Importantly, this final expansion would later be reversed, reinstating the 'serious harm' qualification.[13]

Since the initial developments in the USA, many jurisdictions including the States and provinces of Canada and Australia have engaged with the challenge of detecting cases of maltreatment at an early stage, to protect children and facilitate provision of services to families.[14] Many legislatures have adopted the principle animating the first reporting law, and have extended it to different professional groups, and to different types of child maltreatment. In Canada, and particularly in Australia, with each jurisdiction possessing constitutional power to legislate for matters relating to child protection, this has meant that States and Territories have adopted different measures at different times. The laws in these jurisdictions have continued to evolve in response

[9] B. Nelson, *Making an Issue of Child Abuse* (University of Chicago Press, Chicago, 1984).

[10] An exception, suggesting legislative and or policy error, arguably occurred in New South Wales, as will be seen.

[11] This omission is seen in even some of the best work: D. Scott, 'Child Protection: Paradoxes of Publicity, Policy and Practice' (1995) 30(1) *Australian Journal of Social Issues* 71, 77; R. Lonne, N. Parton, J. Thomson, and M. Harries, N. 3, above, 3.

[12] S. Kalichman, *Mandated Reporting of Suspected Child Abuse: Ethics, Law and Policy* (American Psychological Association, Washington: DC, 1999), 15–16.

[13] The Child Abuse Prevention and Treatment Act s 5106g(2) now defines 'child abuse and neglect' as 'at a minimum, any recent act or failure to act on the part of a parent or caretaker, which results in death, serious physical or emotional harm, sexual abuse or exploitation, or an act or failure to act which presents an imminent risk of serious harm'.

[14] Many other countries have also enacted reporting laws in various forms, such as Brazil, Denmark, Finland, France, Hungary, Israel, Malaysia, Mexico, Norway, South Africa, and Sweden: B. Mathews and M. Kenny, 'Mandatory Reporting Legislation in the USA, Canada and Australia: a Cross-jurisdictional Review of Key Features, Differences and Issues' (2008) 13 *Child Maltreatment* 50.

to new phenomena (such as domestic violence), evidence of successes and defects in child protection systems, and, arguably, perceived political imperatives. In Australia, legislation was first enacted in South Australia in 1972, and ever since, the eight States and Territories have incrementally expanded mandatory reporting requirements. Even now, the legislation continues to develop. In Queensland the then Education (General Provisions) Act 1989 (Qld) was amended in 2004 to require teachers to report suspected child sexual abuse by school staff, and in 2005 the Public Health Act 2005 (Qld) was amended to require nurses to report all four classical types of abuse and neglect. In Western Australia, which had been the only Australian State not to have reporting laws in any form, provisions in the Children and Community Services Act 2004 (WA) commenced in 2009 requiring doctors, nurses, midwives, police, and teachers to report child sexual abuse. In Tasmania, changes were made in 2009 to the Children, Young Persons and Their Families Act 1997 (Tas) to accommodate a heightened emphasis on differential response systems. In New South Wales, amendments to the Children and Young Persons (Care and Protection) Act 1998 commencing in 2010 have the effect of requiring reports only of 'significant' harm, and of heightening the use of differential response; these changes will be returned to later.[15]

19.1.3 Common elements and significant differences in the laws

It is important to recognize that while they have similar guiding principles and common elements, mandatory reporting laws contain significant differences between jurisdictions. Law and policy created to assist the detection and reporting of, and the responses to, abuse and neglect are complex, and exist alongside political, economic, social, and cultural forces in each society. This point is important because it means that simplistic dichotomous arguments about whether or not 'mandatory reporting laws' are justifiable are at the very least misguided because they do not distinguish between the different forms, purposes, and contexts of the laws.

A number of elements are common to the laws. The legislation will usually define: which persons are required to make reports; what state of mind a reporter must have before the reporting duty is activated (usually described as where the person 'suspects on reasonable grounds', or a synonymous expression); the types of abuse and neglect that must be reported; the degree of abuse or neglect which requires a report (hence also defining extents of abuse and neglect that do not require reports). Further definitions of types of abuse and neglect may be detailed, and these may include not only exposure to harm, but exposure to risk of future harm. Penalties for failure to report will be set out although the intention is to encourage compliance, not to threaten prosecution.[16] A guarantee of confidentiality is provided concerning the reporter's identity, and the reporter is endowed with immunity from any legal liability arising from a report made in good faith. Mechanisms will be described regarding when and how the report is to be made, and to whom. A separate related provision usually enables any person to make a report in good faith even if not required to do so, and provides confidentiality and legal immunity for these persons.

[15] Pursuant to the Children Legislation Amendment (Wood Inquiry Recommendations) Act 2009 Sch 1.1 [1]–[4].

[16] It has been argued, but not proved, that penalty provisions produce 'defensive' reporting of 'even the most marginal events', a manifestation of overreporting: F. Ainsworth and P. Hansen, 'Five Tumultuous Years in Australian Child Protection: Little Progress' (2006) *Child and Family Social Work* 33, 39.

Differences between jurisdictions' reporting laws illustrate differences in normative preferences, child protection systems and social realities, all within the context of desired effective yet feasible government agency intake and response. Four areas of difference are of particular significance: who is made a mandated reporter; what types of maltreatment must they report; what extent of suspected harm activates the reporting duty; and are reports required only of past maltreatment, or also of suspected risk of maltreatment. Each of these parameters will broaden or narrow the scope of the reporting laws; hence it is clear that the scopes of different reporting laws occur on a spectrum ranging from very limited to extremely wide.

19.1.3.1 Which persons are mandated reporters?

Two approaches to this parameter are discernible. In most cases, the legislation appoints as mandated reporters members of designated professions who are likely to come into contact with children in their work, and who are seen as well placed by virtue of their occupation, training, and knowledge to detect abuse and neglect. This occupation-specific model often includes those involved in education, law enforcement, welfare, and health systems, but it can extend to others. These designated reporters are usually required to report suspicions developed in the course of their work, but some jurisdictions compel reports regardless of the context in which such a reporter's suspicion arises. The second approach, more common in Canadian provinces, and present in 18 States in the USA, is to impose reporting duties on all citizens. However, some jurisdictions have limited the scope of the legislation in this regard: legislation in Queensland, for example, expressly requires only doctors and nurses to make reports.

19.1.3.2 What types of maltreatment must be reported?

Legislative developments have often commenced with reporting duties limited only to severe physical abuse, with medical practitioners the only group of professionals required to report. Incremental developments have then been made to embrace newly recognized types of child maltreatment—sexual abuse, neglect, and psychological abuse—and to require additional professional groups to report suspected cases. This has resulted in the current situation where most commonly, legislation requires reports concerning the four classical types of maltreatment: physical abuse, sexual abuse, psychological abuse (sometimes called emotional abuse), and neglect. However, some jurisdictions have limited the scope of the laws in this regard. In Australia, for example, Victoria and the Australian Capital Territory do not require reports of psychological abuse or of neglect, and Western Australia requires only reports of sexual abuse.

More recently, influenced by changing social circumstances and new knowledge about the effects on children of certain phenomena, some jurisdictions have extended mandatory reporting requirements beyond the four classical types to new specific types of abuse and neglect. One of these, most notable in the USA, is the duty (typically imposed on medical practitioners) to report prenatal substance abuse when substance-exposed newborns are encountered.[17] Another is the duty to report

[17] In the USA, this new duty is largely a result of a provision inserted in CAPTA by the Keeping Children and Families Safe Act of 2003; CAPTA s 5106(b)(2)(A)(ii) now includes as a condition of States' eligibility for federal funding the presence of policies and procedures to address the needs of

exposure of a child to illegal drug activity.[18] However, the most significant new type of conduct which some jurisdictions are requiring to be reported is the exposure of a child to domestic violence. In Australia, New South Wales expressly requires reports of the risk of serious psychological or physical harm to a child as a consequence of exposure to domestic violence.[19] Tasmania requires a report where a child's safety, psychological wellbeing, or interests are 'affected or likely to be affected' by family violence.[20] In Canada, seven jurisdictions include exposure to domestic violence as a circumstance where a child is in need of protection.[21] In contrast, only a few states in the USA clearly require such reports (Montana, West Virginia, and the District of Columbia); however, other States' definitions of psychological abuse may have the indirect effect of requiring the exposure of a child to domestic violence.[22]

19.1.3.3 What extent of suspected harm is required to activate the reporting duty?

At least for physical abuse, psychological abuse, and neglect, the laws are not intended to require reports of any and all 'abusive' or 'neglectful' acts or omissions. Reporting laws are not directed at isolated, long-past, or trivial incidents of less than ideal parenting. Consistent with the original reporting laws, modern mandatory reporting legislation is concerned with acts and omissions that cause significant harm to the child's health, safety, wellbeing, or development, or which are likely to so cause. Accordingly, save for sexual abuse (which is less controversial in this respect), legislation defines the extent of harm thought to have been caused or likely to eventuate, which limits the scope of cases to be reported. An exception to this, which has recently been rectified by legislative amendment, was New South Wales, where the reporting legislation did not clearly limit the reporting duty to cases of significant harm; this will be returned to later.

These definitions (and their implementation in training) of the extent of harm thought to have been caused to the child or to be likely to befall the child which triggers the reporting duty are one of the most problematic features of the entire context. On a policy level, this generates the question of which types of cases of actual maltreatment and risk of future maltreatment a jurisdiction wants to capture: how wide is the child protection net to be cast? On a definitional and implementation level, there are then the dual challenges of accurately describing in the legislation which types of cases need to be reported (and, by logical extension, which do not), and then the practical challenge of conveying this in training to reporters. Inevitably, different jurisdictions have adopted different approaches to these challenges, for each category of abuse and neglect.[23]

infants born and identified as being affected by illegal substance abuse or withdrawal symptoms from prenatal drug exposure.

[18] Mathews and Kenny, N. 14, above, 57.

[19] Children and Young Persons (Care and Protection) Act 1998 (NSW) s 23(1)(d).

[20] By the operation of the Children, Young Persons and Their Families Act 1997 (Tas) s 14(2)(a) and the Family Violence Act 2004 (Tas) s 4. The concept of 'family violence' is defined broadly: Family Violence Act 2004 (Tas) s 7.

[21] One (Newfoundland and Labrador) requires a report of exposure to domestic violence even if there is no harm or risk of harm to the child; the other six (Alberta, Manitoba, the Northwest Territories, Nova Scotia, Prince Edward Island, and Saskatchewan) require reports only where the child has been harmed, is 'likely to suffer harm', or is at 'substantial risk' of harm as a result of the domestic violence: Mathews and Kenny, N. 14, above, 57–8.

[22] Mathews and Kenny, N. 14, above, 57–8.

[23] Mathews and Kenny, N. 14, above, 54.

19.1.3.3.1 Physical abuse

For physical abuse, four different approaches are evident.[24] First, a majority of 29 States in the USA refers in broad terms to 'harm or threatened harm' through physical abuse or physical injury, without defining what constitutes sufficient injury, and nearly all Canadian provinces also simply refer to physical harm or injury without further definition. Second, a substantial group of jurisdictions require a higher degree of harm than that of the first approach, but does so in conceptual terms rather than specifying types of injury; for example, requiring 'serious' injury or 'substantial' impairment of health. This conceptual approach is also used in seven Australian States, which require 'significant' harm or a synonymous variation of this. Third, some jurisdictions detail an exhaustive list of the injuries constituting physical abuse which must be reported, termed as 'any case in which a child exhibits evidence of skin bruising, bleeding, malnutrition, failure to thrive, burns, fracture of any bone, subdural hematoma, soft tissue swelling, or death'. Uniquely, combining the second and third approaches, Alberta requires 'substantial and observable injury' evidenced by any of an enumerated list of injuries. Fourth, some States in the USA give a nonexhaustive list of the injuries which can constitute physical injury sufficient to require a report.

19.1.3.3.2 Psychological or emotional abuse

Many jurisdictions require a certain extent of harm caused by psychological, emotional, or mental injury to qualify it as reportable.[25] In Australia, the qualification is usually in terms such as 'significant' or 'serious' harm, or significant detriment to development. In the USA, jurisdictions generally require an observable and/or substantial impairment in ability to function.

19.1.3.3.3 Neglect

Many jurisdictions define neglect ambiguously in terms of failure to provide 'basic', 'adequate', 'proper', or 'necessary' care, without specifying a degree of harm required to activate the reporting duty.[26] Some jurisdictions in the USA and Australia require a higher degree of consequence of the neglect to require a report, but the terms used remain ambiguous and easily susceptible to misinterpretation; they include 'serious impairment' (Indiana), 'substantial impairment' (Louisiana, New Hampshire), 'endangerment of child's life or development or impairment of the child's functioning' (Pennsylvania), 'serious physical impairment evidenced by severe bodily malfunctioning' (Northern Territory), 'significant detrimental effect' (Queensland), and 'physical or psychological injury detrimental to the child's wellbeing or jeopardizing the child's physical or psychological development' (South Australia and Tasmania). Provisions regarding neglect are usually directed at parents' intentional acts or grievous omissions. Accordingly, most jurisdictions in the USA expressly exclude poverty-based neglect from the definition of reportable 'neglect'.[27]

[24] Mathews and Kenny, N. 14, above, 58.

[25] Mathews and Kenny, N. 14, above, 59.

[26] Mathews and Kenny, N. 14, above, 59–60.

[27] While beyond the scope of this chapter, this raises an important question. If a primary function of the child protection system is to assist children and their families, does the exclusion of poverty-based 'neglect' inappropriately exclude many children and families? It may be that legislatures are cautious to avoid the potential for the child protection system to remove children from families on the basis of poverty alone. Yet, it would appear to defeat a major purpose of the child protection system if children who suffer poverty-related neglect are excluded from, or are less likely to receive, services because their cases

19.1.3.4 Major dimensions of variation

Clearly, then, mandatory reporting laws in different jurisdictions have significant differences, and these reflect the normative preferences in a given jurisdiction and the relationship between the reporting law and the child protection system. The key differences concern who is designated as the reporters, which types of abuse and neglect they must report, what state of mind is required to activate the reporting duty, and what suspected extent of harm is required to trigger the duty.[28] Recognition of significant differences between the laws, and of the multi-dimensional choices that a jurisdiction is faced with when creating such a law, shows these laws are not and need not be uniform. Because of this, it becomes problematic to make an absolute claim that 'mandatory reporting laws' as a whole lead to or are associated with specific consequences. In the same jurisdiction, one feature of the reporting law may lead to largely positive results while another may lead to negative results. What researchers must do is to target which aspects of a law causes or is associated with which types of outcome, and to try and isolate the factors influencing these outcomes. Arguably, this must be done in each jurisdiction, because other variables (such as reporters' training and the characteristics of the child protection system) will affect reporting practices and outcomes. In this way, positive outcomes can be reinforced and further strengthened, and negative outcomes can be identified and decisions made on what to do about them.

19.1.4 Policy-based duties and common law obligations

Other jurisdictions including the United Kingdom have not enacted reporting laws.[29] Yet, there may be other sources of a reporting duty where legislation is absent. Industry-based policies often require members of relevant professions (such as medical and educational professionals) to report suspected child maltreatment. In the United Kingdom, for example, the General Medical Council declares that a doctor's first concern must be the safety of the child, a report must be made of any reasonable concern that a child is at risk of abuse, and a doctor will justifiably raise such a concern even if eventually shown to be groundless, if done honestly and based on reasonable belief.[30] In 2007, the Department for Children, Schools and Families and the Department of Health released a statement of advice to paediatricians in England and Wales, which declared that a paediatrician's first duty is to the child, whose well-being is paramount.[31] The advice cited *JD v East Berkshire Community Health NHS*

have less chance of being brought to the attention of helping agencies. Arguably, such cases are perfect candidates for differential response.

[28] Another issue, which would require extended treatment and is beyond the scope of this chapter, concerns whether reports are required only of suspected past or present abuse, or are also required of suspected risk of future abuse that has not occurred yet: see further D. Besharov, '"Doing Something" About Child Abuse: The Need to Narrow the Grounds for State Intervention' (1985) 8(3) *Harvard Journal of Law and Public Policy* 539.

[29] But see E. Munro and N. Parton, 'How Far is England in the Process of Introducing a Mandatory Reporting System?' (2007) 16 *Child Abuse Review* 5; and see Criminal Law (Northern Ireland) Act 1967 s 5, as discussed in L. Bunting, A. Lazenbatt, and I. Wallace, 'Information Sharing and Reporting Systems in the UK and Ireland: Professional Barriers to Reporting Child Maltreatment Concerns' (2010) 19 *Child Abuse Review* 187.

[30] General Medical Council, *0–18 Years: Guidance For All Doctors*, Rules 60–61, <http://www.gmc-uk.org/guidance/ethical_guidance/children_guidance/56_63_child_protection.asp>.

[31] Department for Children, Schools and Families, Department of Health, *Joint statement on the duties of doctors and other health professionals in investigations of child abuse*, 2007. After the 2010

Trust[32] to confirm that where a paediatrician suspects child abuse, the paediatrician owes a legal duty of care to the child, no competing duty is owed to the parents (so if a report of suspected abuse is not proved the parents cannot sue for negligence), and the proper protection for a parent is that the paediatrician's investigations be conducted in good faith. An accompanying letter recognized practitioners' concerns about parents' complaints but urged that this 'should not deter anyone from reporting suspected cases of child abuse provided they have acted in good faith'.[33] Teachers in the UK also have strong policy-based duties to report child abuse and neglect.[34] As well, even in the absence of a legislative duty, the law of negligence may create a common law duty for a professional dealing with a child to report known and suspected severe maltreatment, so that failure to report suspected abuse may expose medical and educational professionals and their employers to liability in negligence.[35] Despite these reporting duties in policies and at common law, which often impose substantially identical reporting obligations as their legislative counterparts (but without the protections afforded to reports by the legislation[36]), there is a relative lack of opposition to these reporting duties when compared with the opposition to legislative reporting duties.

19.1.5 Legal extensions and changed social contexts

In most jurisdictions having mandatory reporting legislation, the scope of the reporting duties has been extended far beyond the ambit of the original law influenced by Kempe's work. Inclusion of neglect, particularly where resulting from poverty rather than parental malfeasance, is perhaps the clearest example of how far the laws have departed from the original principle. The addition in some jurisdictions of exposure of a child to domestic violence is also a manifestation of this. Psychological abuse, while clearly more closely related to the original concept, and while known to be potentially extremely damaging, is at the same time clearly a much different type of context than physical or sexual abuse. In many cases, neglect is also qualitatively different from intentional harm. The constructs of 'domestic violence' and of a child's 'exposure' to it are also conceptually far different from situations of direct physical assault of a child. The extension of reporting duties to professionals who are unable to conduct physical examinations of a child and to ask questions of the child's parent,

general election, the Department for Children, Schools and Families was replaced by the Department of Education. The General Medical Council now has several documents confirming doctors' duties in this context, including *0–18 Years: Guidance For All Doctors*, <http://www.gmc-uk.org/guidance/ethical_guidance/children_guidance_contents.asp>.

[32] [2005] UKHL 23.

[33] K. Brennan and A. Keen, *To Health Professionals and Safeguarding Children Stakeholders*, 20 July 2007, <http://www.chimat.org.uk/resource/item.aspx?RID=56263>

[34] For teachers, see Department for Children, Schools and Families, *Working Together to Safeguard Children* (London, 2010), <http://publications.education.gov.uk/>; read with Department for Education and Skills, *What to do if you're worried a child is being abused*, 2006, 9–14, <http://www.dcsf.gov.uk/everychildmatters/>.

[35] See for example *JD v East Berkshire Community Health NHS Trust* [2005] UKHL 23; *AB v Victoria* (Unreported, Supreme Court of Victoria, Gillard J, 15 June 2000); *B v Attorney General (New Zealand)* [2003] UKPC 61; see also *Brown v University of Alberta Hospital* (1997) 145 DLR 4th 63, and *Landeros v Flood* (1976) 551 P 2d 389. However, not every jurisdiction may recognize such a duty: see L. Hoyano and C.Keenan, *Child Abuse: Law and Policy Across Boundaries* (Oxford University Press, Oxford, 2007), 369.

[36] B Mathews, H Payne, C Bonnet, and D Chadwick, 'A Way To Restore British Paediatricians' Engagement With Child Protection' (2009) 94(5) *Archives of Disease in Childhood* 329.

also represents a departure from the context of the original laws. As well, concepts within the original law that were always inherently problematic, such as the vague concepts of 'reasonable suspicion' and 'significant harm' used to avoid unduly limiting reports, have not generally been improved upon. Empirical studies and critical evaluations have shown that the vagueness and ambiguity of concepts like 'reasonable' cause and 'significant' harm cause problems for reporters,[37] and there is widespread agreement that these concepts need to be clarified.[38] This means that, in an already difficult operational context for reporters, the task of understanding and complying with reporting duties has been further complicated. This may have consequences for reporting practice, leading to either or both failing to report some cases that should be reported, and reporting other cases that clearly should not be reported.

However, it must be borne in mind that while the laws have expanded in the sense of requiring reports of different types of maltreatment, they have also developed in the sense of the methods of response made to reports. It is far from true that every report made is subject to formal investigation. Especially in recent times, there is an emphasis on enabling wherever possible a speedy, sensitive, and nonintrusive response to identify the child's and family's needs and attempts to provide services which fulfil those needs.[39] Such 'differential response' assesses the family's needs and is particularly appropriate for low-risk and moderate-risk cases, especially for cases involving possible neglect. It is becoming more popular in the USA, with over 20 States now implementing these systems.[40] Australian jurisdictions including New South Wales, Victoria, and Tasmania are also making renewed efforts to implement these systems. The irony is that child protection systems appeared to become more investigative the more reports they received, whereas greater efforts should have been made to respond efficiently with a non-intrusive, service-based approach to cases of neglect. These dextrous, adaptable response systems, equally able to deal with the multiplicity of cases from sexual abuse reports requiring urgent investigation, to poverty-induced neglect requiring no investigation but provision of services, were in fact always the intended partner of the laws, as expressed in the NSW legislation enacted in 1998. This demonstrates that a major challenge, and possibly the dominant challenge, in this context is sound public administration.

19.1.5.1 Social differences: current knowledge about the nature, incidence, timing, and effects of severe maltreatment

There are significant social differences in the modern context when compared with Kempe's era. Since the time of Kempe's concern with severe physical abuse, different maltreatment types have been recognized: sexual abuse, neglect, and psychological abuse. Nonexistent in Kempe's era, bodies of evidence of the often severe and

[37] See Bunting, Lazenbatt, and Wallace, N. 29, above.

[38] See for example David Finkelhor, 'The Main Problem is Underreporting Child Abuse and Neglect' in (eds) Donileen Loseke, Richard Gelles, and Mary Cavanaugh, *Current Controversies on Family Violence* (Thousand Oaks, California, 2005), 299; Douglas Besharov, 'Overreporting and Underreporting Child Abuse and Neglect Are Twin Problems' in (eds) Donileen Loseke, Richard Gelles, and Mary Cavanaugh, *Current Controversies on Family Violence* (Thousand Oaks, California, 2005), 285; C. Johnson, 'Child Maltreatment 2002: Recognition, Reporting and Risk' (2002) 44 *Pediatrics International* 554.

[39] Child Welfare Information Gateway, *Differential Response to Reports of Child Abuse and Neglect* (United States Department of Health and Human Services Administration for Children and Families, Washington DC, 2008), <http://www.childwelfare.gov/pubs/issue_briefs/differential_response>.

[40] A. Conley and J. Berrick, 'Community-Based Child Abuse Prevention: Outcomes Associated With a Differential Response Program in California' (2010) 15 *Child Maltreatment* 282.

long-lasting effects of these different maltreatment types, and of their incidence, have since developed.[41] Further, there is growing evidence about even 'newer' forms of maltreatment such as exposure to domestic violence.[42]

There is also now a different understanding of the incidence of severe maltreatment. The survey Kempe conducted was nowhere near exhaustive, so it is wrong to claim that he thought there were only hundreds of cases annually of severe physical abuse in the USA at that time. However, the now known numerical scale of severe child maltreatment is far beyond what may reasonably have been contemplated by legislators enacting the first reporting laws and those enacted soon after which embraced other maltreatment types. In the USA in 2008/09, for example, there were 121,137 substantiated cases of physical abuse.[43] These are only the identified cases: national incidence studies indicate the real incidence is substantially higher,[44] and it is accepted by leading scholars worldwide that the real incidence is substantially higher than that shown in government data.[45] Incidence and prevalence studies have found substantially greater frequencies of maltreatment in all categories than are recorded

[41] For a systematic review regarding all types of maltreatment, see R. Gilbert, C. Widom, K. Browne, D. Fergusson, E. Webb, and S. Janson, 'Burden and Consequences of Child Maltreatment in High-income Countries' (2009) 373(9657) *Lancet* 68; on physical abuse, see E. Gershoff, 'Corporal Punishment by Parents and Associated Child Behaviors and Experiences: A Meta-analytic and Theoretical Review' (2002) 128 *Psychological Bulletin* 539; J. Landsford, K. Dodge, G. Pettit, J. Bates, J. Crozier, and J. Kaplow, 'A 12 year Prospective Study of the Long-term Effects of Early Child Physical Maltreatment on Psychological, Behavioural, and Academic Problems in Adolescence' (2002) 156 *Archives of Pediatric and Adolescent Medicine* 824; K. Springer, J. Sheridan, D. Kuo, and M. Carnes, 'Long-term Physical and Mental Health Consequences of Childhood Physical Abuse: Results from a Large Population-based Sample of Men and Women' (2007) 31 *Child Abuse & Neglect* 517; on sexual abuse, see L. Chen, H. Murad, M. Paras, K. Colbenson, A. Sattler, E. Goranson, M. Elamin, R. Seime, G. Shinozaki, L. Prokop, and A. Zirakzadeh, 'Sexual Abuse and Lifetime Diagnosis of Psychiatric Disorders: Systematic Review and Meta-Analysis' (2010) 85 *Mayo Clinic Proceedings* 618; E. Paolucci, M.Genuis, and C. Violato, 'A Meta-analysis of the Published Research on the Effects of Child Sexual Abuse' (2001) 135 *The Journal of Psychology* 17; on psychological abuse see B. Egeland, 'Taking Stock: Childhood Emotional Maltreatment and Developmental Psychopathology' (2009) 33 *Child Abuse & Neglect* 22; and on neglect, see K. Hildyard and D. Wolfe, 'Child Neglect: Developmental Issues and Outcomes' (2002) 26 *Child Abuse & Neglect* 679.

[42] S. Holt, H. Buckley, and S. Whelan, 'The Impact of Exposure to Domestic Violence on Children and Young People: A Review of the Literature' (2008) 32 *Child Abuse & Neglect* 797; D. English, J. Graham, R. Newton, T. Lewis, R. Thompson, J. Kotch, and C. Weisbart, 'At-Risk and Maltreated Children Exposed to Intimate Partner Aggression/Violence' (2009) 14 *Child Maltreatment* 157; S. Hamby, D. Finkelhor, H. Turner, and R. Ormrod, 'The Overlap of Witnessing Partner Violence with Child Maltreatment and Other Victimizations in a Nationally Representative Survey of Youth' (2010) 34 *Child Abuse & Neglect* 734; M. Bair-Merritt, M. Blackstone, and C. Feudtner, 'Physical Health Outcomes of Childhood Exposure to Intimate Partner Violence: a Systematic Review' (2006) 117 *Pediatrics* 278; D. Wolfe, C. Crooks, V. Lee, A. McIntyre-Smith, and P. Jaffe, 'The Effects of Children's Exposure to Domestic Violence: A Meta-analysis and Critique' (2003) 6(3) *Clinical Child and Family Psychology Review* 171.

[43] US Department of Health and Human Services, *Child maltreatment 2008* (US Government Printing Office, Washington: DC, 2010), 47 (Table 3-12).

[44] In the UK, for example, see S. May-Chahal and P. Cawson, 'Measuring Child Maltreatment in the United Kingdom: A Study of the Prevalence of Child Abuse and Neglect' (2005) 29 *Child Abuse & Neglect* 969; in Canada, see B. Fallon, N. Trocme, J. Fluke, B. MacLaurin, L. Tonmyr, and Y. Yuan, 'Methodological Challenges in Measuring Child Maltreatment' (2010) 34 *Child Abuse & Neglect* 70; and in the USA, see A. Sedlak and D. Broadhurst, *Third National Incidence Study of Child Abuse and Neglect* (Westat, Rockville, MD, 1996); D. Finkelhor, R. Ormrod, H. Turner, and S. Hamby, 'The Victimisation of Children and Youth: a Comprehensive, National Survey' (2005) 10 *Child Maltreatment* 5.

[45] See for example R. Gilbert, A. Kemp, J. Thoburn, P. Sidebotham, L. Radford, D. Glaser, and H. MacMillan, 'Recognising and Responding to Child Maltreatment' (2009) 373(9658) *Lancet* 167; P. Kohl, M. Jonson-Reid, and B. Drake, 'Time to Leave Substantiation Behind: Findings From A National Probability Study' (2009) 14(1) *Child Maltreatment* 17; May-Chahal and Cawson, N. 44, above;

Table 1 Officially recorded incidence of four main maltreatment types: USA, Canada, and Australia, 2008

	USA 2008	Canada 2008	Australia 2008–09
Physical abuse	121,137	17,212	7801
Sexual abuse	68,002	2607	3735
Psychological abuse	54,258	7423	12,397
Neglect	534,066	28,939	8708

by government statistics presenting the results of substantiated investigations,[46] and it has been argued that failure to detect and report cases of maltreatment is a more serious concern than overreporting.[47] However, even the government data, representing the minimum known incidence for the four classical types of maltreatment, present numbers of substantiated cases which are of great concern.[48]

19.1.5.1.1 Ages of victimization

The ages at which children are most frequently victimized are also a significant factor in considering issues concerning reporting. The most detailed statistics, maintained and published in the USA,[49] show beyond doubt that younger children are generally more vulnerable to maltreatment. There are some variations by type of abuse: for example, children aged under four are relatively less likely to be sexually abused than older children, and there are similar numbers of physically abused children from age one. However, younger children are much more likely to suffer neglect, medical neglect, and psychological abuse. Further, except for sexual abuse, there is a clear developmental vulnerability: infants under one are the most vulnerable to every type of maltreatment (including physical abuse), followed by infants aged one, aged two, and so on. Three-quarters of victims (75.0 per cent) had no history of prior victimization.[50] Three-quarters of all victims were aged under 12 years old: nearly one-third (32.6 per cent) were younger than four years old, another quarter (23.6 per cent) were aged four to seven, and almost another one-fifth (18.9 per cent) were aged eight to 11.[51]

K. Ronan, D. Canoy, and K. Burke, 'Child Maltreatment: Prevalence, Risk, Solutions, Obstacles' (2009) 44(3) *Australian Psychologist* 195.

[46] See for example Finkelhor, Ormrod, Turner, and Hamby, N. 44, above; May-Chahal and Cawson, N. 44, above; Sedlak and Broadhurst, N. 44, above.

[47] D. Finkelhor, N. 3, above; N. 38, above.

[48] These data about the primary recorded category of substantiated maltreatment are extracted from: US Department of Health and Human Services, N. 43, above, 47 (Table 3-12); Public Health Agency of Canada, *Canadian Incidence Study of Reported Child Abuse and Neglect—2008: Major Findings* (Ottawa, 2010), 31 (Table 4-1); Australian Institute of Health and Welfare, *Child protection Australia 2008–09* (Canberra, Australian Capital Territory, 2010), 57 (Table A1.4)—hereafter referred to as Australian Institute of Health and Welfare (2010). The three countries also detail numbers of victimizations in other recorded categories not detailed here, such as 'medical neglect' and 'other abuse' (USA) and 'exposure to intimate partner violence' (Canada). The official recorded rate of victimization per 1000 children differs across these countries, being 10.3 in the USA, 14.19 in Canada, and 6.9 in Australia: US Department of Health and Human Services, N. 43, above, 23; Public Health Agency of Canada (2010), 31; Australian Institute of Health and Welfare (2010), 16.

[49] US Department of Health and Human Services, N. 43, above, 47 (Table 3-12). Data from previous years also show these patterns: US Department of Health and Human Services, *Child maltreatment 2007* (US Government Printing Office, Washington: DC, 2009), 47 (Table 3-11).

[50] US Department of Health and Human Services, N. 43, above, 40 (Table 3-7).

[51] US Department of Health and Human Services, N. 43, above, 25 (Figure 3-3).

Table 2 USA 2008/09, numbers of children victimized, by age and maltreatment type

	Physical abuse	Sexual abuse	Psychological abuse	Neglect
Less than 1 year old	15,658	470	4171	71,968
1 year old	5917	558	3634	44,166
2 years old	5780	968	3327	41,431
3 years old	5678	2394	3221	37,011
4–7 years old	27,510	15,232	13,373	126,918
8–11 years old	23,480	16,122	12,233	96,755
12–15 years old	26,644	23,959	10,584	84,627
16–17 years old	9819	7946	3419	29,270

19.1.6 Sources of substantiated reports: the successful side of reporting

How are substantiated cases of victimization identified? The best available data show that the majority of cases, for each type of maltreatment, are identified as a result of a report made by a mandated reporter. Non-mandated reporters make a significant but far smaller contribution to case identification. Perpetrators are rarely the source of substantiated reports, and victimized children hardly ever report their own situation.[52] The most complete data are from the USA for the year 2007, and Canada has also published useful information for the year 2003.[53] Australia does not publish equivalent data, but does detail the sources of reports of investigated cases, showing similar patterns of the infrequency of perpetrator and child reports, and the predominance of reports by mandated reporter groups, especially police and health and educational personnel.[54]

Table 3 Percentage of substantiated reports by maltreatment type and report source

	USA 2007				Canada 2003		
	Mandated reporters	Nonmandated reporters (including child victim)	Child	Perpetrator	Mandated reporters	Nonmandated reporters (including child victim)	Child
Physical abuse	78.1	21.9	0.6	0.1	79%	19%	5%
Sexual abuse	74.0	25.9	0.8	0.1	62%	39%	3%
Psychological abuse	68.7	31.3	0.8	0.1	71%	26%	2%
Neglect	63.6	36.4	0.3	0.1	63%	26%	2%

[52] Although especially for older children, some reports made by mandated reporters probably result from a disclosure by the child to the reporter, who then makes the report.

[53] Data are extracted from US Department of Health and Human Services, *Child maltreatment 2007*, N. 49, above, 45 (Table 3-9); and N. Trocme, B. Fallon, B. MacLaurin, J. Daciuk, C. Felstiner, T. Black, L. Tonmyr, C. Blackstock, K. Barter, D. Turcotte, and R. Cloutier, *Canadian Incidence Study of Reported Child Abuse and Neglect—2003: Major findings* (Minister of Public Works and Government Services, Canada, 2005), 86 (Table 8-1)—hereafter referred to as the *Canadian Incidence Study of Reported Child Abuse and Neglect*.

[54] Australian Institute of Health and Welfare (2010), N. 48, above, 58 (Table A1.5).

These statistics suggest mandatory reporting does work to identify the majority of cases of severe child maltreatment that are detected. The nature of the acts constituting severe maltreatment, the incidence of severe maltreatment, the ages at which children are particularly vulnerable, the effects of severe cases, and the limits of differential response, all point to a continuing justification of reporting laws in some form. There simply is not sufficient evidence to suggest that most parents and caregivers who severely maltreat their children, in many cases committing violent criminal acts, and accompanied by situations of drug use, will be prepared to voluntarily seek assistance both to help their child and to help themselves. It is important to again emphasize that the reporting laws were (and in general, remain) directed only at cases of severe maltreatment, not at any and all maltreatment. Nevertheless, it is undeniable that when compared with the first law and its context, the differences in modern reporting laws and the societies in which they exist raise questions about the justifiability of broader reporting laws. Essentially, the question presented is whether, even if accepting the soundness of the principle animating the original law—that a child who is known or thought to have been severely physically harmed by their parent or caregiver should have their maltreatment stopped by bringing it to the attention of helping authorities—extensions to the original law are, on balance, desirable developments. The claim that these broader reporting laws have produced massive numbers of unsubstantiated reports offers an ostensibly powerful critique of the laws and reporting practices.

19.2 Evidence about reporting

Is there evidence to support the claim that mandatory reporting laws cause intolerable levels of overreporting? If so, what is that evidence, how powerful is it, and what implications does it have? This part of the chapter adduces evidence regarding these questions by detailing data about reporting patterns and reporting outcomes. In particular, Australian data will be referred to, with a focus on evidence of reporting in New South Wales, the most populous jurisdiction in Australia. In an area where it is often difficult to obtain evidence, New South Wales is a useful study for three reasons. A recently completed inquiry into the New South Wales child protection system referred to relatively detailed evidence of reporting practice which would otherwise not be readily available; there have been substantial changes in the parameters of the reporting law which enable some conclusions to be drawn regarding their effects; and a published study of the effects of introducing a specific reporting duty also provides data from which some conclusions can be drawn.

As will be seen, there are strong indications that the introduction of reporting laws does appear to result in the identification of cases of severe maltreatment. However, the laws also appear to produce increased numbers of reports, many of which are not 'substantiated' by government child protection agencies. Criticism of mandatory reporting laws has been based on the global claim that the laws produce large increases in unsubstantiated reports, which are equated with the concept of 'overreporting', without exploring or explaining the precise evidence-based details of this claim.[55] This is unfortunate, because while a global claim can readily be opposed on the basis that mandated reporters make the majority of substantiated reports and

[55] See for example Melton, N. 3, above, and Ainsworth, N. 3, above.

hence clearly make a substantial contribution to child protection, more precise claims about overreporting may have credence. If there is evidence of demonstrated, specific overreporting practices, then there are important lessons to be learnt by child protection systems which have the potential to improve systems and outcomes for children, families, and communities, and which may suggest that an element of a reporting law is entirely unwarranted. To develop a more accurate picture of reporting practice and outcomes, a more nuanced examination[56] of the data is needed, which may indicate evidence about key questions including:

- Do numbers of reports appear to increase after the introduction of a legislative reporting duty?
- If so, which reporter groups make how many reports, regarding which types of maltreatment, and what trends are apparent in whether these reports are substantiated or unsubstantiated?
- What is the nature of 'overreports': for example, are a large proportion of them made about the same small group of children, and if so, why?
- To the extent that there are 'unacceptable' numbers of 'unsubstantiated' reports, to what extent are these made by mandated reporters, as opposed to non-mandated reporters?

This exploration will therefore attempt to shed some light on these questions. Yet, this endeavour is further complicated by the fact that a number of researchers have powerfully argued that it is not appropriate to equate unsubstantiated reports with overreporting. Drake has concluded that:[57]

> Even some of the very best researchers in the field have a tendency to view the appropriateness of a report and substantiation as similar or identical concepts. The evident conceptualization of substantiation assumes that unsubstantiated reports represent invalid reports, instances of overreporting…The critical factor in understanding substantiation data is to question the common tendency to assume that unsubstantiated reports represent situations in which maltreatment did not occur and in which the family does not need services…this conclusion does not logically follow from the inability of a CPS worker to substantiate a case; a report may be unsubstantiated for many reasons.

Accordingly, this discussion will also make some remarks about the nature of an 'unsubstantiated' report, and when it may be appropriate and inappropriate to use this outcome as evidence of undesirable reporting practice.

19.2.1 The problem of incomplete and incomparable data

Before continuing, an important observation should be made about the inability to compare data across jurisdictions within the same country because of different systems of recording, nomenclature, and systemic responses, the lack of data within jurisdictions about the questions germane to this endeavour, and even the inability to chart trends within a jurisdiction because of changes to recording and disposition practices. In undertaking this exercise, both accessing publicly available documents

[56] The best evidence would emerge from detailed quantitative and qualitative research in each jurisdiction, regarding each reporter group (whether or not mandated), for each type of maltreatment.

[57] B. Drake, 'Unraveling' 'Unsubstantiated' (1996) 1(3) *Child Maltreatment* 261, 262–3.

and by communicating with staff at government departments,[58] it became clear that even within jurisdictions there is a lack of both available and published data which presents serious problems not only for researchers, but for policymakers and the public. Whether framed wholly or partly as a social issue, a criminal issue, or, increasingly, as a public health issue,[59] the child maltreatment field is impeded from identifying and solving problems regarding reporting and identification of maltreatment (and of subsequent responses including service provision) because there is a lack of detailed quantitative and qualitative data about reporting. This problem is particularly evident in Australia and the United Kingdom. The Australian Institute of Health and Welfare only collects and publishes data submitted to it by State and Territory government departments, and this is limited to data regarding numbers of notifications, numbers of substantiations, numbers of children in substantiated notifications by type of abuse, and reports made by reporter group which led to an investigation. Data published by State and Territory government departments is variable but does not provide details about reports by abuse type, reporter group, and outcome of report. In the United Kingdom, the relevant Department does not collect data regarding the numbers of referrals of suspected abuse and neglect, or the source of those referrals, or data about the outcomes of those referrals by type and reporter group.[60]

Despite the limits of the available data, the ensuing discussion will detail descriptive evidence which seeks to provide richer information than is usually presented about several of these issues. In this way, a more comprehensive understanding of reporting practices and outcomes, and the law's influence on them, may be developed.

[58] And drawing on the author's experience of the time and difficulty involved in accessing detailed data from three Australian States regarding the reporting of one type of abuse only, by one class of reporters: B Mathews, K Walsh, D Butler, and A Farrell, *Teachers Reporting Suspected Child Sexual Abuse: Towards evidence-based reform of law, policy and practice* (Queensland University of Technology, Brisbane, 2010).

[59] M. O'Donnell, D. Scott, and F. Stanley, 'Child Abuse and Neglect—is it Time for a Public Health Approach?' (2008) 32(4) *Australian and New Zealand Journal of Public Health* 325; R. Krugman, 'Time to Medicalise Child Maltreatment' (2009) 373 *Lancet* 19; D. Scott, 'Towards a Public Health Model of Child Protection in Australia' (2006) 1(1) *Communities, Families and Children Australia* 9. While beyond the scope of this chapter, based on the history of public health see B. Turnock, *Public Health: What It Is and How It Works* (4th ed, Jones and Bartlett, Sudbury, MA, 2009); L. Gostin, *Public Health Law: Power, Duty, Restraint* (2nd ed, University of California Press, Berkeley, CA, 2008), the issue of whether criminal acts of sexual assault inflicted by an adult on a child are properly characterized as a public health issue is debatable, although some have claimed this: J. Mercy, 'Having New Eyes: Viewing Child Sexual Abuse as a Public Health Problem' (1999) 11(4) *Sexual Abuse: A Journal of Research and Treatment* 317.

[60] Personal communication, Graham Knox, 14 October 2010. This is the Department for Children, Schools and Families, which publishes data about child protection referrals, assessments, and child protection plans: see Department for Children, Schools and Families, *Referrals, assessment and children and young people who are the subject of a child protection plan, England—Year ending 31 March 2009*, <http://www.education.gov.uk/rsgateway/DB/SFR/s000873/index.shtml>. In Canada, the published data is slightly more informative: see for example the *Canadian Incidence Study of Reported Child Abuse and Neglect*, N. 53, above. The USA publishes the most detailed data, including using data from 48 States, a breakdown of substantiated maltreatment victims by type of maltreatment and by report source (US Department of Health and Human Services, N. 49, above, Table 3-9); although the latest report for 2008 did not include this. A request was made for this data but at the time of writing it had not been provided.

19.2.2 What appears to happen after enactment of a legislative reporting duty: a rare study from New South Wales

Child welfare legislation had existed in New South Wales for many decades,[61] but it was not until 1 July 1977 that new provisions required any member of a professional group to report a named type of abuse. The Child Welfare (Amendment) Act 1977 (NSW) required medical practitioners to report 'reasonable grounds to suspect that a child has been assaulted, ill-treated or exposed'.[62] A decade later, this mandatory reporting provision was expanded when medical practitioners were required to report suspected child sexual abuse.[63] At this time, two more future expansions to the law were enabled: first, s 22(2)(b) enabled other professions to be added to the category of mandated reporters, by Regulation; and second, s 22(3) enabled other professions to be required to report sexual abuse, by Regulation. This second expansion was then realized on 19 July 1987 when teachers were required to report suspected sexual abuse.[64] While more dramatic changes would occur in 2000, as detailed shortly, the change to teachers' reporting duties informed a rare study by Lamond of the effect on reporting practice of a new legislative reporting duty.[65]

Lamond accessed government data about reports of each type of maltreatment, from different reporter groups, for two three-month periods before and after the legislative change. Lamond concluded that the new legislative duty to report, accompanied by training about how to comply with that duty, increased substantiated reports of child sexual abuse. Reports by this group of reporters of suspected sexual abuse almost tripled after the duty was introduced, increasing from 98 to 286. The substantiation rate of these reports remained stable at around 70 per cent, with the result that the number of substantiated cases increased from 69 to 189; this also meant that the number of unsubstantiated cases increased from 29 to 85. Lamond concluded that the intensive training effort associated with the extension of the reporting duty assisted in the positive outcomes, and minimized the potential for larger increases in unsubstantiated reports which had been reported in other jurisdictions

[61] As long ago as 1939, New South Wales legislation created offences specifically regarding child abuse and neglect. The Child Welfare Act 1939 (NSW) s 148(1) provided that 'any person, whether or not the parent of the child or young person, who without reasonable excuse neglects to provide adequate and proper food, nursing, clothing, medical aid, or lodging for any child or young person in his care' would commit an offence. Section 149(1) made it an offence for any person to assault, ill-treat, or expose any child or young person, if it resulted or appeared likely to result in bodily suffering or permanent or serious injury to the child's health.

[62] Schedule 5 added s 148B to the Child Welfare Act 1939 (NSW).

[63] Children (Care and Protection) Act 1987 (NSW) s 22(2), s 22(4).

[64] There is a complex legislative history but in essence the change was made by a Regulation amending the Child Welfare Regulation 1940, inserting r 74, which contained the duty. After enactment of the Children (Care and Protection) Act 1987, the Children (Care and Protection—General) Regulation 1988 (NSW) r 10 embodied the duty (this commenced on 18 January 1988: r 2). Regulation 10(1) named teachers, counsellors, social workers, and early childhood teachers at schools as reporters, and r 10(3) defined a 'school' as a State school or a registered school within the meaning of the Education and Public Instruction Act 1987, which effectively included nongovernment schools within the remit of the reporting duty. On 1 September 1996, the Children (Care and Protection) Regulation 1996 (NSW) repealed the Children (Care and Protection—General) Regulation 1988 and replaced it with a substantially identical provision in r 16, which provided that for the purposes of s 22(3), the same four groups were prescribed as reporters; curiously r 16(3) defined a 'school' as a government school within the meaning of the Education Reform Act 1990. Subsequently, the Children (Care and Protection) Amendment (Notification of Child Abuse) Regulation 1997 (NSW), No 101 of 1997 extended the duty to teachers at registered nongovernment schools, with r 2 adding 'or a registered non-government school' to r 16 of the 1996 Regulation.

[65] D. Lamond, 'The Impact of Mandatory Reporting Legislation on Reporting Behaviour' (1989) 13 *Child Abuse & Neglect* 471.

after introduction of mandatory reporting obligations. These findings are important because they suggest that a reporting duty, with appropriate training, results in the identification of substantially more cases of serious abuse. These are also contextually significant results: in a single three-month period, school personnel alone identified an additional 120 cases of child sexual abuse. However, the findings also indicate that a higher number of unsubstantiated reports will be produced.

Yet, there are further indications about reporting patterns from the data cited by Lamond, which were not discussed in his analysis. Re-examination of the data yields information about reporting practices of different reporter groups, for different types of abuse and neglect, in situations of both presence and absence of a legislative reporting duty. In particular, there are indications about the number of reports made, and their outcomes. These statistics provide information over two time periods about who made reports (whether or not legislation required them to), and the numbers of reports, about each type of abuse. It is clear that:

- in each period, neglect was the maltreatment type most commonly reported;
- over both periods, reports of neglect accounted for over one-third of all reports;
- in each period, as a group, members of the public made the most total reports, making over 50 per cent of all reports in the first period and almost 50 per cent of reports in the second period;
- in each period, as a group, members of the public made the most reports for each maltreatment type, except for sexual abuse in the second period;
- in the first period, teachers, who were not legislatively mandated to report, still did report 460 cases, most commonly physical abuse and neglect;
- in the second period, when teachers were legislatively required to report only sexual abuse, teachers' reports of sexual abuse almost tripled, their reports of physical abuse increased slightly, and their reports of neglect and emotional abuse decreased;

Table 4 Number of reports made by all reporter groups, for all types of abuse and neglect, before and after legislative mandatory reporting by school personnel of sexual abuse[66]

	Number of reports in 3-month period before mandatory reporting of sexual abuse, by reporter group, by type			Totals	Number of reports in 3-month period after mandatory reporting of sexual abuse, by reporter group, with numerical increase/decrease by type			Totals, with increase/decrease
	Teachers	Other human services	Members of the public		Teachers	Other human services	Members of the public	
Emotional abuse	60	280	331	671	46 (-14)	248 (-32)	262 (-69)	556 (-115)
Neglect	140	527	887	1554	109 (-31)	412 (-115)	775 (-112)	1296 (-258)
Physical abuse	162	356	537	1055	193 (31)	324 (-32)	455 (-82)	972 (-83)
Sexual abuse	98	362	400	860	286 (188)	515 (153)	393 (-7)	1194 (334)
Total	460	1525	2155	4140	634 (174)	1499 (26)	1885 (-270)	4018 (-122)

66 Data from Lamond, N. 65, above, 473–4 (Tables 1 and 2).

- between the two periods, total numbers of reports declined substantially for neglect, emotional abuse, and physical abuse, while the number of reports of sexual abuse increased (with the increase produced by reports of teachers and other human services staff).

Therefore, members of the public, who were not mandated to report and did not work professionally with children, made the majority of all reports and were far more frequent reporters than the professionals, although their reports declined in the second period. Neglect was the most frequently reported issue. For school personnel, substantial numbers of reports were made for each type of maltreatment even when legislation did not require reports. However, school personnel's reports of sexual abuse almost tripled after their training and commencement of the legislative reporting duty. Reporting of sexual abuse by other professionals also increased substantially in the second period, suggesting that the introduction of teachers' reporting duty (and possibly media exposure, or training of other professionals) may have also sensitized other professionals to reporting of sexual abuse. Reporting of other abuse types by school personnel and other professionals declined in the second period, except for sexual abuse, and for physical abuse reported by teachers. This may suggest that increased attention to the importance and/or reporting of one abuse type may result in less sensitivity to other types.

As well as these associations with numerical changes in various types of reports, questions arise about the effects on reporting 'effectiveness' of the reporting duty and training about it. Did the duty produce more substantiated reports, more unsubstantiated reports, or both? In addition, even if substantiation rates are used as a measure for reporting effectiveness,[67] how accurate are teachers at reporting all types of child abuse and neglect, and did this change over the two time periods?

These statistics provide information over two time periods about the substantiations of teachers' reports for each type of abuse and neglect, in a context where teachers were required to report only sexual abuse, and only in the second time period, and had received training to prepare them for the reporting duty. It is apparent that:

- over each period, before and after the legislative duty and training, the substantiation rate of teachers' reports of sexual abuse was almost identical;
- for sexual abuse, this produced almost three times the number of substantiated reports, and three times the number of unsubstantiated reports, in a three-month period;
- in the first period, teachers' reports were substantiated at approximately 70 per cent for sexual, physical, and emotional abuse, while the rate for neglect reports was lowest at 59 per cent;
- in the second period, teachers' reports of physical abuse had slightly higher substantiation rates, while substantiation rates of reports of emotional abuse were significantly lower (see Table 5).

Therefore, the legislative duty and training about it coincided with a significant increase in the number of reports, with an almost identical substantiation rate. This suggests a heightened awareness of possible cases of sexual abuse, and also perhaps reaffirms the fact that detecting sexual abuse is inherently difficult and that an unrealistically high substantiation rate should not be expected, even with the delivery of

[67] See the discussion below about why this is unsound.

Table 5 Outcome of reports made before and after legislative mandatory reporting by school personnel of sexual abuse[68]

	Teachers' reports in 3-month period before mandatory reporting, by type and outcome				Teachers' reports in 3-month period after mandatory reporting, by type and outcome			
	Reports	Substantiated (same; or different, type as suspected: subtotal)	Not substantiated	Substantiation rate	Reports	Substantiated (same; or different, type as suspected: subtotal)	Not substantiated	Substantiation rate
Emotional abuse	60	(36;4): 40	16	71.5%	46	(18;7): 25	17	59.5%
Neglect	140	(59;21): 80	55	59.2%	109	(37;23): 60	38	61.2%
Physical abuse	162	(89;22): 111	48	69.8%	193	(110;26): 136	50	73.1%
Sexual abuse	98	(62;7): 69	29	70.4%	286	(165;23): 189	85	68.8%
Total[69]	460	(246;54): 300	148	67.0%	634	(330;79): 409	190	68.3%

[68] Data from Lamond, N. 65, above, 475 (Table 3).

[69] Totals do not add up to the total numbers of reports because in the first three-month period, 12 children were unlocatable, and in the second period, 35 were unlocatable.

training programmes to professional reporters. If substantiation is used as a measure of effectiveness, it also indicates that teachers' reports of suspected sexual abuse prior to the legislative and training initiatives were remarkably successful.

19.2.3 Data about reporting in Australian States and Territories 2004/05–2008/09

By 2004, all Australian States and Territories except Western Australia had enacted reporting laws. These were of various breadth, with those in New South Wales being the broadest by virtue both of requiring reports of domestic violence and not clearly limiting the reporting duty to cases of significant harm.[70] It is not possible to provide a nationwide historical trend over time charting the impact of the introduction of reporting laws, partly because each State and Territory has enacted laws at different times, with different breadths. The exploration later in this chapter of the New South Wales experience will seek to trace how reporting changes over time within a jurisdiction, influenced by legal developments. However, because commentators often refer to 'nationwide trends', it may be useful to detail the numbers of notifications, and substantiations, in each jurisdiction, over the last five years.

In the last five years, higher numbers of notifications were made in most jurisdictions.[71] However, the great majority of the increase occurred in New South Wales, the most populous State.[72]

[70] The NSW provisions are discussed below. For a recent national comparison, see Mathews and Kenny, N 14, above. Western Australia now has a reporting provision regarding sexual abuse only, which commenced on 1 January 2009.

[71] Data are taken from Australian Institute of Health and Welfare (2010), N. 48, above, 13 (Table 2.3). The annotations show not only that comparisons cannot be made across States, but that even within States, trends over time cannot readily be discerned because of changes to recording practices. The notes explain that Tasmania experienced an increase in reports from police about family violence because of changes to legislative reporting requirements in 2004; that Victoria's data from 2006/07 onwards is not comparable with earlier years due to changed reporting practice; that Queensland changed recording practice in 2006/07 so that additional 'concerns' received about an open case were no longer treated as an additional notification but were added to the file; that in Western Australia, notifications increased after 2005/06 because all 'concern for child' reports were counted as notifications, where previously only those that were investigated were so counted; and from February 2008, selected subsequent contacts about open cases in Tasmania were not included as notifications but as 'case notes'. It should also be noted that in the Northern Territory, the Care and Protection of Children Act 2007 (NT) s 15(2), supported by the Domestic and Family Violence Act 2007 (NT), introduced exposure to physical violence into the definition of harm, with an example provided of exposure to domestic violence. This amendment commenced on 7 May 2008. Previously, the Community Welfare Act (repealed by the Care and Protection of Children Act 2007) did not include exposure to physical violence as one of the forms of maltreatment to be reported. Partly as a result of these changes, and partly due to the federal government's intervention, reports of suspected child maltreatment tripled in the three years from 2006/07 to date: M. Bamblett, H. Bath, and R. Roseby, *Growing them Strong, Together: Promoting the Safety and Wellbeing of the Northern Territory's children, Summary Report of the Board of Inquiry into the Child Protection System in the Northern Territory 2010* (Northern Territory Government, Darwin, 2010), 21.

[72] At June 2009, the populations of Australia's eight States and Territories were: New South Wales: 7.1 million; Victoria: 5.4 million; Queensland: 4.4 million; Western Australia: 2.2 million; South Australia: 1.6 million; Tasmania: 0.5 million; Australian Capital Territory: 0.35 million; Northern Territory: 0.2 million: Australian Bureau of Statistics, *3101.0—Estimated Resident Population, States and Territories*, <http://www.abs.gov.au/AUSSTATS/abs@.nsf/DetailsPage/3101.0Mar%202010?OpenDocument>.

At 30 June 2009, the national population of children aged 0–17 inclusive was 5,062,034; and the population in each State and Territory of children aged 0–17 inclusive was: New South Wales: 1,625,316; Victoria: 1,220,487; Queensland: 1,071,091; Western Australia: 530,041; South Australia: 354,846;

Table 6 Total notifications, 2004/05 to 2008/09, Australian States and Territories

Year	NSW	Vic	Qld	WA	SA	Tas	ACT	NT
2004/05	133,636	37,523	40,829	3206	17,473	10,788	7275	2101
2005/06	152,806	37,987	33,612	3315	15,069	13,029	8064	2863
2006/07	189,928	38,675	28,511	7700	18,434	14,498	8710	2992
2007/08	195,599	41,607	25,003	8977	20,847	12,863	8970	3660
2008/09	213,686	42,851	23,408	10,159	23,221	10,345	9595	6189

Table 7 Total substantiations, 2004/05 to 2008/09, Australian States and Territories

Year	NSW	Vic	Qld	WA	SA	Tas	ACT	NT
2004/05	15,493	7,398	17,307	1,104	2,384	782	1,213	473
2005/06	29,809	7,563	13,184	960	1,855	793	1,277	480
2006/07	37,094	6,828	10,108	1,233	2,242	1,252	852	621
2007/08	34,135	6,365	8,028	1,464	2,331	1,214	827	756
2008/09	34,078	6,344	7,315	1,523	2,419	1188	896	858

In some jurisdictions, the numbers of substantiations actually decreased over the same period, or only increased moderately, despite increased numbers of notifications.[73]

19.2.3.1 Notifications and substantiations relative to children involved

For the purpose of this discussion, it is relevant to note that relatively low proportions of notifications were substantiated. Also, it is evident there can be more than one notification and substantiation per child. Data for 2008/09 demonstrates this.[74]

Due to the difficulties already noted in charting trends within States across time, and in comparing jurisdictions, it is not possible to draw definitive conclusions about the data detailed above. However, a conservative reading of the data appears to suggest the following:

- the largest numerical increase in notifications occurred in NSW;
- the largest proportional increase in notifications occurred in Western Australia and the Northern Territory;
- several jurisdictions had no increase or only a small increase in notifications;

Tasmania: 118,397; Australian Capital Territory: 78,490; Northern Territory: 62,738: Australian Bureau of Statistics, *3201.0—Population by Age and Sex, Australian States and Territories, June 2009*, <http://www.abs.gov.au/AUSSTATS/abs@.nsf/DetailsPage/3201.0Jun%202009?OpenDocument>.

[73] Data are taken from Australian Institute of Health and Welfare (2010), N. 48, above, 13 (Table 2.4).

[74] Data are taken from Australian Institute of Health and Welfare (2010), N. 48, above, 18 (Table 2.7). While it is beyond the scope of this chapter to further discuss this theme, use of the population data and the numbers of children in substantiations in each jurisdiction, the rate of officially recorded child maltreatment per 1000 children can be calculated in each State and Territory for 2008/09, as follows: NSW: 8.6; Vic: 5; Qld: 6.2; WA: 2.7; SA: 5.4; Tas: 9; ACT: 7.8; NT: 12.2.

Table 8 Numbers of notifications and substantiations, with numbers of children involved, 2008/09

	NSW	Vic	Qld	WA	SA	Tas	ACT	NT
Notifications	213,686	42,851	23,408	10,159	23,221	10,345	9595	6189
Children in notifications	112,035	33,640	20,959	8892	15,227	7240	5157	4312
Substantiations	34,078	6344	7315	1523	2419	1188	896	858
Children in substantiations	14,052	6129	6628	1463	1916	1075	613	765

- three jurisdictions (WA, SA, ACT) had no greater numbers of substantiations despite substantially increased notifications;
- in NSW, which experienced the highest numerical increase in notifications, there was in fact a higher proportionate increase in substantiations than notifications, with substantiation numbers more than doubling while notifications increased by less than that amount;
- some jurisdictions receive multiple notifications for every child involved in a notification.

For the purpose of this chapter, it is clear that in New South Wales and other States which have experienced an increase in reports, little close examination of reporting practices has occurred. There is scant government data about the details of reporting practices and outcomes, which must be rectified if problems in reporting are to be identified, and if laws, policies, and practices are to be improved. This is especially important if child welfare and child protection are to be seen as public health concerns, since a central tenet of public health is that to facilitate the diagnosis and resolution of problems, phenomena must be measured and systems must be monitored and evaluated. As well, apart from Lamond's study there is very little published academic research analysing detailed empirical effects of reporting laws on overreporting. The absence of studies may be due to the fact that to conduct sophisticated, rigorous studies with both quantitative and qualitative elements requires substantial time, money, and skilled personnel. However, considering that many jurisdictions have enacted reporting laws as an important part of the whole child protection effort, the evidentiary vacuum is surprising. To offer some new insights, the next part of this chapter explores the New South Wales experience after major legislative change.

19.2.4 The New South Wales experience after major legislative change in 2000

The most significant legislative change occurred on 18 December 2000, when the Children and Young Persons (Care and Protection) Act 1998 (NSW) ss 23 and 27 extended the reporting duties of all reporter groups to additional types of abuse and neglect (including exposure to domestic violence where the child was at risk of serious physical or psychological harm). In some cases there was a requirement to report not only maltreatment thought to have already occurred but also to suspected risk of future maltreatment. As well, in some situations (such as psychological abuse), there was also a duty to report a case where the abuse had occurred with the harm not yet apparent but with a perceived risk of future harm. Section 27 imposed the reporting duty, and s 23 defined when a child was 'at risk of harm', setting out the types of case to be reported. Subsections (a) and (b) related to situations of neglect, (c) covered physical and sexual abuse, (d) related to harm caused or risked from exposure to domestic violence, and (e) included situations of psychological abuse:

(a) the child's or young person's basic physical or psychological needs are not being met or are at risk of not being met,

(b) the parents or other caregivers have not arranged and are unable or unwilling to arrange for the child or young person to receive necessary medical care,

(c) the child or young person has been, or is at risk of being, physically or sexually abused or ill-treated,

(d) the child or young person is living in a household where there have been incidents of domestic violence and, as a consequence, the child or young person is at risk of serious physical or psychological harm,

(e) a parent or other caregiver has behaved in such a way towards the child or young person that the child or young person has suffered or is at risk of suffering serious psychological harm.

It is critical to note that the principles to be applied in administering the Act included that the child's safety, welfare, and well-being were the paramount consideration (s 9(a)), and that in deciding what legal or administrative action was necessary to protect a child, the least intrusive course consistent with the child's welfare had to be followed (s 9(d)). Chapter 3 (Requests for assistance and reports) set up a system aimed at enabling the provision of assistance through various means, and of enabling multiple methods of response including not only investigation, but referral to helping services. Clearly then, the explicit and entirely sound intention at the outset was to establish a system which included and emphasized principles of 'differential response', rather than focusing exclusively on investigation.[75] Chapter 3 established a system where assistance could be sought by a child (s 20) or by a child's parent (s 21); a person who was not mandated to report suspected harm to a child was enabled to report it (s 24); and a person who was mandated to report suspected harm to a child was required to report it (s 27). The system was conceptualized so that either a request for assistance or a report of suspected harm could both be dealt with by means *other than* assessment and investigation. The Act made it clear that a determination of the appropriate response could result in any of the following:[76] no response; referral to another agency; provision of information or services (including financial assistance, counselling, parenting education, drug and alcohol counselling; health services; counselling for sexual assault or domestic violence; respite care; family support; accommodation). However, unlike most reporting laws, the legislation did not clearly state that only cases of significant harm were to be reported.

[75] As systems including mandatory reporting have been criticized for: see for example Melton, N. 3, above.

[76] In the Act as made, see the note to s 22, and the diagrams at beginning of Chapter 3 of the Act.

Table 9 Number of 'notifications' detailed in Australian Institute of Health and Welfare (AIHW) Reports, NSW, 2002/03–2008/09

Year	Number of notifications as detailed in AIHW reports
2002/03	109,498
2003/04	115,541
2004/05	133,636
2005/06	152,806
2006/07	189,928
2007/08	195,599
2008/09	213,686

19.2.4.1 Increased numbers of notifications and reports, and substantiation rates

The expanded mandatory reporting provisions coincided with a consistent increase in the number of notifications, as shown in the data from the AIHW (see Table 9).[77]

However, the data reported by the AIHW does not represent the complete picture of reporting and actually *underrepresents* the number of reports made to the Department.[78] In New South Wales, a 'report' is the name given to the initial contact made to the Department, and it only *becomes* a 'notification' as labelled by the AIHW if it is both screened in and not diverted to another agency, or given information or advice, or simply had the information forwarded for recording only. So, in NSW, 'notifications' are the *subset* of 'reports' which have not been dealt with by differential response. Therefore, numbers of 'reports' and 'notifications' are distinct, and 'substantiation rates' need to distinguish between whether it is a substantiation rate of 'reports' or only of 'notifications'.

To give an example, in 2006/07, the AIHW report stated there were 189,928 notifications, 37,094 of which were substantiated,[79] an overall substantiation rate of 19.5 per cent. In contrast, Departmental statistics[80] stated there were 286,033 reports, of which 40,472 were substantiated. Of all reports, 84,825 were closed at intake (by either simply forwarding the information to the Department, providing advice or referral to another agency, or finding that no further assessment was required). The other 201,208 were referred for assessment: these are the reports that became 'notifications'.[81] According to the Department's figures, therefore, there were 286,033 reports, and overall a substantiation rate of 14.2 per cent. Therefore, Departmental statistics show an apparently worse situation

[77] Australian Institute of Health and Welfare, *Child protection 2005–06* (Canberra, Australian Capital Territory, 2007), 21; Australian Institute of Health and Welfare, N. 48, above. The numbers of notifications were even smaller before 2002/03. However, the annotations stipulate that data for 2002/03 onwards cannot be compared with previous years because of changes to the data system during 2002/03.

[78] To be fair, the AIHW report cannot offer a comparative national picture because States and Territories differ in their reporting systems, nomenclature, and methods of dealing with reports. However, the AIHW report would be improved by giving a complete picture of each State and Territory's system, and more detail about the number of initial 'reports' and their outcomes. It may be that this data is not readily available in State and Territory departments.

[79] Australian Institute of Health and Welfare, *Child protection 2006–07* (Canberra, Australian Capital Territory, 2008).

[80] As detailed in J. Wood, *Report of the Special Committee of Inquiry into Child Protection Services in New South Wales*, 2008, Volume 1, 150–1, copy on file with author.

[81] Wood, N. 80, above, 156.

Table 10 Number of 'reports' and 'notifications' as detailed in NSW Departmental statistics, and substantiation rates, 2004/05–2007/08

Year	Number of substantiations	Number of 'reports'	*Substantiation rate of all 'reports'*	Number of 'notifications'	*Substantiation rate of all 'notifications'*
2004/5	15,493	216,386	7%	140,184	11%
2005/6	29,809	241,003	12%	160,842	18%
2006/7	40,472	286,033	14%	201,208	20%
2007/8	36,129	303,121	12%	205,283	17%

of 'overreporting' than the AIHW data.[82] It can also be noted that Departmental data show the number of reports increasing from 216,386 in 2004/05 to 303,121 in 2007/08 (see Table 10).[83]

If one assumes that most reports are made by mandated reporters, these data appear to indicate that mandatory reporting produces both an increase in reports, and an increase in unsubstantiated reports. However, a closer examination of these broad categories of data is necessary.

19.2.4.2 Reporting practices by maltreatment type and reporter type: who reports what, and how often? An analysis of data from 2006/07

Records of reports for the year 2006/07 provide insights into reporting practices characteristic of recent years before systemic changes in New South Wales in 2010. These data were included in the report published after a recent inquiry into the child protection system in New South Wales (the Wood Inquiry), and as they are similar to the following year's data, they can be relied on to represent a reasonably representative picture of reporting practices in this State at this time (see Table 11).[84]

Several significant findings emerge from these data about how many reports are made, about which types of maltreatment, and by which reporter groups. Domestic violence was by far the most commonly reported issue,[85] followed by neglect and physical abuse. Of all reports, suspected physical abuse constituted only 14.2 per cent and sexual abuse 7.1 per cent. As well as domestic violence reports, a substantial proportion of 17.4 per cent of all reports related to carer-related issues (mental health, drugs, alcohol). Of all reports, mandated reporters made 74.1 per cent and nonmandated reporters made 25.9 per cent.[86] These proportions were similar for reporting

[82] Wood, N. 80, above, 156; Australian Institute of Health and Welfare, N. 48, above. Complicating matters further is the complex structure New South Wales has of dealing with those reports that are referred for further assessment (that is, those that become 'notifications'). Each notification can result in either one or two stages of 'secondary assessment'. A notification can be closed, or referred to a service, after a Stage 1 assessment only, and such a notification will not be labelled as a 'substantiated' case. Other notifications will receive both Stage 1 and Stage 2 assessments, and it is these that result in findings of 'substantiated' or 'unsubstantiated': A. Zhou and M. Chilvers, *Child Protection Reporting in NSW and Australia: an Analysis of Comparability Issues* (Sydney, New South Wales), 6.

[83] Wood, N. 80, above, 119, 137.

[84] These data are extracted from Wood, N. 80, above, 150–1. The data include categories beyond main maltreatment types: carer drug/alcohol; carer mental health; child risk taking (drug/alcohol use, suicide risk, and runaway).

[85] At least by primary reported issue; although over one-third of reports related to one issue only.

[86] This reflects an enduring trend since 2001/02: Wood, N. 80, above, 172. Of reports made by mandatory reporters, police make about one-third, health personnel 15 per cent, and school/child care reporters about 13 per cent.

Table 11 Number of child protection reports, by reporter type and primary reported maltreatment type, NSW 2006/07

	Domestic violence	Neglect	Physical abuse	Carer drug and alcohol	Psychological abuse	Carer mental health	Sexual abuse	Child risk taking	Total reports by reporter type*
Police	54,376	7327	6590	6340	5318	2954	3709	3632	**93,069**
Health	6342	4765	6022	6172	3394	9677	3414	2046	**43,870**
Education	2518	5091	10,141	1937	4661	1374	4430	2859	**35,741**
Other mandated reporter	5534	8154	5944	2901	3647	2882	3467	3906	**39,336**
Total mandated reporters	68,770	25,337	28,697	17,350	17,020	16,887	15,020	12,443	**212,016**
Nonmandated reporters	5513	16,610	11,862	10,945	8569	4531	5184	3156	74,017
Total reports by maltreatment type	**74,283** (26.0%)	**41,947** (14.7%)	**40,559** (14.2%)	**28,295** (9.9%)	**25,589** (8.9%)	**21,418** (7.5%)	**20,204** (7.1%)	**15,599** (5.5%)	286,033

* Including 18,139 'Other' reports. Total reports by reporter type include data from this category and so differ from the sum of the subtotals listed

of physical and sexual abuse, but domestic violence was overwhelmingly reported by mandated reporters. Nonmandated reporters made approximately two in every five reports of neglect, and one in three reports of psychological abuse. Of all mandated reporter groups, police contributed by far the most reports, making almost one half of all mandated reports and almost one-third of all reports. Reports by police, health, and education personnel constituted 76 per cent of all reports made by mandated reporters. Police reports of domestic violence were easily the single largest group of reports, constituting over two-thirds of all reports of domestic violence, and almost one-fifth of all reports. Approximately 70 per cent of all reports concerned children under 12.

19.2.4.3 Outcomes of reports

An assessment path of these reports for the year 2006/07 indicates how they were dealt with, and combined with the information above may indicate problematic and successful aspects of reporting practice, and can illuminate systemic issues. Breakdowns by type of abuse and, where possible, reporter group, indicate areas of interest (see Table 12).

These raw numbers about the disposition of reports show that almost 30 per cent of all reports were not referred for further assessment. Numerically, reports of domestic violence were the largest contributor to this group, and reports by police were most often not referred. One in four reports by the three main mandated reporter groups (police, health, education) were not referred for any further assessment. Because these data are only quantitative, it is not possible to make firm claims about the quality of these reports unless the substantiation status of the report is used as a measure of reporting quality. Recalling that the legislation was enacted to implement principles of differential response as well as investigative responses where appropriate, the data raise questions about systemic responses. In particular, there was a large number of 77,567 cases which were referred for further assessment but were then nearly all closed before secondary assessment for the listed reason of 'competing priorities'. As well, a further 76,884 cases received only Stage 1 secondary assessment, with the reasons for most of these case closures given simply, and enigmatically, as 'Close' or 'Case Closure Policy' and only 10.5 per cent were stated as 'Eligible Early Intervention'. It is unfortunate that there is not further information in this respect, or a complete breakdown of outcomes by reporter type and maltreatment type. In addition, the richest data, showing reports by type of maltreatment *and* by reporter type *and* by report outcome (including whether services were provided *or* were thought necessary), are not available. This data would arguably shed the most light on the reporting effectiveness of different reporter groups for each maltreatment type.

Some further findings can be gleaned from these data concerning the number and nature of substantiated cases, and the source of their reports. In New South Wales, a notification can result in either one or two stages of 'secondary assessment'. A notification can be closed, or referred to a service, after only a Stage 1 assessment, and such a notification will not be labelled as a 'substantiated' case. Other notifications will receive both Stage 1 and Stage 2 assessments, and it is these that result in findings of 'substantiated' or 'unsubstantiated'.[87] Nearly all reports reaching SAS 2 were substantiated. Of all reports having a completed SAS 2, the most common primary issues were neglect, physical abuse, domestic violence, carer drug or alcohol,

[87] Zhou and Chilvers, N. 82, above.

Table 12 Assessment path of all child protection reports by primary reported issue, NSW, 2006/07

Total number of reports	Total not referred for any further assessment	Total referred for further assessment	Closed before secondary assessment	Secondary Assessment Stage 1 only completed	Secondary Assessment Stage 2 completed	SAS 2 substantiations	Substantiation rates: SAS 2/all reports
286,033 (involving **123,690** children)	**84,825*** (29.7%)	**201,208** (70.3%) (involving 102,098 children)	77,567 (in 99.8% of cases because of 'competing priorities')	76,884	43,295	**40,472#** Involved 14,010 children.	93.5%/14.2%
Subtotals by primary reported issue							
Domestic violence: **74,283**	23,302	50,981	25,441	18,404	6451	**6274**	97.2%/8.4%
Neglect: **41,947**	9838	32,109	9587	13,266	8498	**8004**	94.2%/19.1%
Psychological abuse: **25,589**	9586	16,003	7207	5691	2894	**2699**	93.3%/10.5%
Physical abuse: **40,559**	9296	31,263	11,657	11,688	7299	**6618**	90.7%/16.3%
Risk taking: **15,599**	6542	9057	3447	3229	2280	**2136**	93.7%/13.7%
Carer D/A: **28,295**	6257	22,038	7979	7880	5766	**5483**	95.1%/19.4%
Sexual abuse: **20,204**	5620	14,584	4235	5721	4407	**3874**	87.9%/19.2%
Carer mental health: **21,418**	5055	16,363	5172	7178	3708	**3533**	95.3%/16.5%
Subtotals by reporter type							
Police: **93,069**	29,932	63,137	29,417	21,977	10,850	n/a	n/a
Health: **43,870**	10,266	33,604	11,187	13,949	7842	n/a	n/a
Education: **35,741**	8859	26,882	11,805	9454	5162	n/a	n/a
Other: **113,353**	35,768	77,585	25,158	31,504	19,441	n/a	n/a

* Of these, 51,546 forwarded information to the Department, 23,299 were provided with information, advice, or a referral, 9827 were judged as requiring no further assessment, and 153 had an unspecified outcome: Wood, N. 80, above, 137.

\# Of these substantiations, 28,335 were of actual harm and 12,137 were of risk of harm.

and sexual abuse. The raw numbers indicate that substantiation rates of *all reports* by the three main mandated reporter groups are approximately one in six (health), one in seven (education), and one in eight (police).[88] However, if the more appropriate unit of analysis is the *number of children* involved in those reports, and arguably it is, then the substantiation rate of reports by these three reporter groups are approximately one in three (health), two in seven (education), and one in four (police). These face-value substantiation rates, which are substantially lower than those detailed in Lamond's study, may be seen by some to be an outstanding contribution to child protection, but others may interpret them as an unacceptably low rate of accuracy. Before making any further observations about these outcomes, it is necessary to explore the limits of substantiation rates as an evaluative measure.

19.2.4.4 Limits of substantiation rates: multiple reports and the nature of substantiation

Only tentative conclusions can be drawn from this data, for reasons including the fact that there are not breakdowns of final outcomes by reporter type and maltreatment type. Perhaps more importantly, due to systemic and other factors, it is impossible to conclude that a report was unwarranted if it was unsubstantiated or did not reach investigation, or did not have an investigation concluded. Some tentative conclusions informed by the data will be drawn shortly, but it is necessary to explain why the bare quantitative data need to be treated with circumspection. In particular, two important concepts emerge. First, because of multiple reporting and re-reporting, the number of reports far exceeds the number of children who are the subject of those reports. Second, due to a number of factors, whether a report is substantiated is not a reliable indicator of the justifiability or merit of the report, and consequently, overall rates of 'substantiation' are not reliable indicators of the efficacy of reporting behaviour.

19.2.4.4.1 Multiple reports and re-reporting

In general, reporting systems do not function on the basis that one report is made for each child involved; rather, multiple reports can be made about the same child. Because of this, soaring numbers of reports alone can be misleading and overall substantiation rates underestimate the reality. In the New South Wales context, this phenomenon appears to have been prominent. The Wood Inquiry found that a substantial proportion of all reports were made about a relatively small concentration of the same children. In 2006/07, the top 20 per cent of frequently reported children accounted for more than half the total number of reports, and the top one per cent of frequently reported children accounting for 8.9 per cent of reports.[89] A related finding was that as a proportion of total children, the number of children who were the subject of a report for the first time had fallen every year since 2001/02.[90] These findings hence indicate that, rather than the child protection net capturing ever greater numbers of children, greater numbers of reports about the same children are being made, possibly influenced by systemic difficulties such as failure to respond. Multiple reports can be made by the same person about the child, or by a number of different

[88] Using the total numbers of reports by police, health, and education reporter groups, the numbers of these reports undergoing SAS 2, and applying the 93.5 per cent substantiation rate of all SAS 2 assessments.

[89] Wood, N. 80, above, 170. [90] Wood, N. 80, above, 170.

persons. There can be many reasons for this multiple reporting behaviour, including the same reporter making multiple reports out of a perception that nothing has happened, failure to provide feedback to the reporter about what is happening, or continuation of the abuse after intervention[91] or when no intervention has occurred. The Wood Inquiry observed that multiple reporting has increased over time,[92] and this is borne out by an independent analysis of the data which shows that the ratio of reports to children involved in reports has grown from an average of 1.878 reports per child in 2001/02, to 2.316 reports per child in 2007/08.[93] Related to this, the Wood Inquiry identified a substantial increase over time in the occurrence of subsequent reports within seven days of the initial report about the same child regarding the same issue: these are 're-reports'. Between 2004/05 and 2007/08, re-reporting by *any* type of reporter accounted for 15–18 per cent of the total reports made.[94] By 2007/08 there had been 51,933 re-reports by any reporter about the same issue the subject of the initial report, accounting for 17.1 per cent of all reports made.[95] The increase in re-reporting over time indicated the presence, and possibly growing influence, of systemic problems.

19.2.4.4.2 Substantiation rates

Several authors have argued at length that it is inappropriate to use rates of unsubstantiated reports as a measure of 'overreporting', and that it is incorrect to think that maltreatment occurred in only those cases that are officially 'substantiated'.[96] There are two broad arguments. First, many 'unsubstantiated' cases do involve maltreatment but are either not assessed at all, or, if assessed, do not end with a conclusion of substantiation. Failure to assess the case can occur through lack of agency resources. However, even if assessed, there can be numerous reasons for a finding of 'unsubstantiated'. Differential response methods may have been used, which usually entail not making a finding of whether the maltreatment has occurred. There may have been an absence of sufficient evidence of maltreatment despite evidence of harm, particularly in cases involving preverbal children. Alternatively, there may be insufficient evidence of harm despite evidence of maltreatment, particularly in cases involving psychological abuse, or neglect. Factors influencing an 'unsubstantiated' finding can relate to characteristics of the child (such as the child's age), the type of abuse, and the family (such as admission of maltreatment and compliance). Finally, the availability of services can influence the finding.

Second, many 'unsubstantiated' cases involve maltreatment which is at levels beneath the threshold required for a 'substantiation', but these cases are in fact ideal candidates for service provision to prevent a continuance or escalation of maltreatment. Hence, it is inappropriate to conclude that reports regarding such cases were inappropriate. Data from the USA confirms this, as numerically, more unsubstantiated cases receive services than do substantiated cases. Proportionally, in 2008, 63.3 per cent of substantiated cases and 28.5 per cent of unsubstantiated cases received

[91] Wood, N. 80, above, 171.

[92] Wood, N. 80, above, 120.

[93] Wood, N. 80, above, 120.

[94] Wood, N. 80, above, 170. Short term re-reports by the same reporter type accounted for six to seven per cent of all reports.

[95] Wood, N. 80, above, 170, 130–1 (Table 5.14).

[96] Drake, N. 57, above; Kohl, Jonson-Reid, and Drake, N. 45, above; T. Cross and C. Casanueva, 'Caseworker Judgments and Substantiation' (2009) 14(1) *Child Maltreatment* 38; Drake and Jonson-Reid, N. 3, above.

post-investigation services.[97] On this argument, in the New South Wales context the reported cases that received services and were not subject to SAS 2 are not 'overreports', and nor are those that should have but did not receive services where the assessment was discontinued before SAS 2.

If these claims are correct, then together with the phenomenon of multiple reporting there are flaws in any argument that numbers and proportions of unsubstantiated cases alone demonstrate overreporting and a consequent related claim that reporting laws should be abandoned. This is certainly not to say that the numbers of reports, and the proportion of these that are not substantiated, are not a major cause of concern for child welfare and child protection systems. In fact, there appears to be compelling evidence of system burden. It is understandable that there may be an impulse to attribute all or some of the blame for this on increased numbers of reports, and that if this is in turn a result of reporting laws, the prospect of their repeal seems a ready panacea. Anyone genuinely interested in child welfare and the health of child protection systems must feel profound sympathy for those working in overburdened systems, and frustration about the lack of adequate support conveyed to administer these systems. Nevertheless, it is not a principled conclusion that simply repealing the laws will solve current problems of child protection, family assistance, and public administration.[98]

Without seeking to be definitive, some observations might be made about the difficult question of what might be said to constitute an 'overreport'. Certainly, intentionally false reports are 'overreports'. Reports made in good faith that have no basis whatsoever and are made from a lack of awareness of the nature of maltreatment can also fairly be said to be overreports. There may also be reports that have some basis but which contain so little useful information that agency intake cannot use them to inform a decision about how to proceed, and some of these may be said to be overreports. Poorly judged reports of clearly innocent or trivial incidents beyond the intention of the law may also be viewed as overreports. There is possibly another, contextual sense in which a report could be termed an overreport, relative to a particular jurisdiction's approach to child welfare, and the scope of its child protection system. That is, if it appears that reports about a particular kind of act or omission are being received as a result of poorly-drafted legal provisions, or of policy that has been poorly-conceived or inadequately implemented, then these could be deemed to be overreports in the sense that the jurisdiction was not intending to receive these types of reports. However, in any given jurisdiction, what is required to contextually and thoroughly assess overreporting, both by mandated and nonmandated reporters, for each type of maltreatment, is a qualitative examination of reports that have been made, and quantitative and qualitative study of reporters' knowledge, attitudes, beliefs, and reporting practice.

19.2.4.5 Conclusions of the Wood Inquiry and reforms in 2010

The Wood Inquiry noted there 'was limited, and primarily academic support expressed to the Inquiry for abolition of the mandatory reporting provisions' with the main reason given being that the system was 'flooded with reports, the response to which used up scarce resources and diverted attention from those families whose

[97] US Department of Health and Human Services, N. 43, above, xiv.

[98] Mathews and Bross, N. 3, above.

children were in need of the State's intervention'.[99] The Inquiry concluded that 'the requirement to report should remain',[100] for several reasons including that child protection system workers generally supported mandatory reporting while endorsing amendments to how it operated; there was no 'evidence of a flood of reports with a reduction in outcomes, at least by reference to investigations and substantiations'; that reporting was increasing elsewhere, that substantiation rates had almost doubled in three years, that reports receiving SAS 2 had more than doubled since 2004/05; and that abolishing the laws may leave people obliged to report under industry policy without the protections in the legislation.[101]

It was concluded that rather than abolishing the reporting laws, the system needed greater effectiveness in reporting and more appropriate treatment of cases, including by differential response:[102]

> The preferable approach to deal with the large numbers of reports, and one which is reflected in this report, is for the system of reporting and assessment to be modified to ensure that children at risk of significant harm receive the attention of [the Department] and its NGO partners while families in need of assistance are directed to services, be they universal or more targeted in orientation. Further, that those outside [the Department] working in child protection, be encouraged to improve the quality of their reports, more frequently exercise their professional judgement and work collaboratively and cooperatively with [the Department] to better use their resources in the best interests of children. Education of mandatory reporters and enhancing the availability of differential responses should reduce multiple reporting rates.

Informed by these conclusions, the legislation was amended in 2010 to limit matters to be reported to cases of suspected risk of significant harm, rather than any harm.[103] This remedied the initial error in the 2000 legislation and realigned the legislation with that existing elsewhere and the principle motivating Kempe's original law. As well, associated changes sought to restore the originally-sought, and entirely sound, emphasis in New South Wales on differential response.

Preliminary data indicate this has had a decisive impact on reporting practice, especially regarding reports by police.[104] In the June quarter there were 47,766 calls, compared with the previous year's quarterly total of 71,879. Calls by police to the Department in that quarter had fallen by 64 per cent compared with the previous year's quarter (21,891 to 7863), with the major reason being that the bulk of police reports were made to the police child well-being unit (the differential response destination), with only suspected cases of significant harm being reported to the Department.[105] The Department was anticipating an annual reduction in reports of over one-third. Yet, in a sense, this may have simply shifted the destination of

[99] Wood, N. 80, above, 179. [100] Wood, N. 80, above, 181.

[101] This point has been made in the UK context: Mathews, Payne, Bonnet, and Chadwick, N. 36, above.

[102] Wood, N. 80, above, 181–2.

[103] Children and Young Persons (Care and Protection) Act 1998 (NSW) ss 23, 27, as amended by the Children Legislation Amendment (Wood Inquiry Recommendations) Act 2009 (NSW) Sch 1.1.

[104] A. Horin, 'Rule change brings drop in child helpline calls' *Sydney Morning Herald*, 15 November 2010, <http://www.smh.com.au/action/printArticle?id=2043433>.

[105] The New South Wales *Keep Them Safe: Annual Report 2009–10* details the new system of referring only cases of suspected significant harm to the Department, while cases of concern which do not reach this threshold are referred to other departments' child well-being units run by professional groups eg doctors, teachers, police, which are then able to refer children and families to services: Department of Premier and Cabinet, *Keep Them Safe* (Sydney, 2010), <http://www.dpc.nsw.gov.au/__data/assets/pdf_file/0004/107761/KTS_Annual_Report_2009-10.pdf>.

different types of reports so that while some system burden has been reduced, an overall reduction in reporting may not have occurred, and nor may the need for services. Indicating some enduring challenges, a Departmental executive stated:[106]

> Child protection teams are as busy as they always were; we're not feeling any relief... families we never got to in the old system are not being referred to us any more. We're still getting the same number of serious child protection referrals and we have not had any additional case workers.

19.3 Conclusion

Despite its limitations, the data about reporting may suggest areas where reporting and response systems contain strengths and weaknesses, and indicate where legislative and policy provisions may have been misconceived or have had unintended effects, or where an emphasis on differential response approaches is required instead of an investigative approach. It may be that, while the data alone cannot show the precise nature or extent of 'overreporting' by reporters, it can indicate patterns of overall reporting pursuant to the enactment of legislative reporting duties, patterns in reporting by different reporter groups and by different maltreatment types, and some of the methods of disposition most common to each type. This may enable legislators, policymakers, and researchers to reflect on the benefits and disadvantages of having enacted certain provisions, such as the domestic violence requirement. This may also inform considerations regarding appropriate systemic response methods for reports about different types of maltreatment. It can also inform understandings of systemic resourcing, service provision, and prevention needs.

The data do suggest that most substantiated cases of child abuse are identified as a result of a report by a mandated reporter, that some types of maltreatment are far more frequently reported by a specified class of reporter (especially, in the case of New South Wales, police reports of exposure to domestic violence, but also neglect and physical abuse), and that the introduction of a legislative reporting duty tends to produce both more substantiated and more unsubstantiated reports. The data also indicate that, depending on the jurisdiction and its system burden, there can be a substantial amount of multiple reports made about the same relatively small group of children. It may also be observed that in New South Wales in the relevant year studied, one-quarter of all reports were made by nonmandated reporters, and that using the numbers of children involved in reports, the overall substantiation rate of reports made by the three major mandated reporter groups relative to the children involved in those reports was approximately one in four. As well, data from New South Wales raises the question of the magnitude of systems burden and the effect this has on both the provision of services to children and families through differential response, and the capacity to investigate appropriate cases.

Ultimately, questions about specific features of overreporting are unanswerable without richer evidence than is provided by descriptive reporting numbers. In addition, the overarching question of whether there is 'too much' overreporting depends largely on the characteristics of the particular jurisdiction's laws, reporting practices,

[106] Horin, N. 104, above. Indicating the fragmentation that had been produced, the executive stated that the Department would not know if these diverted families were receiving assistance because 'we're not the agency that runs the whole system any more'.

systemic responses, systemic burdens, and on what number and proportion of 'over-reports' (however defined) the jurisdiction is willing to bear relative to its aims. It is certainly true that since the creation of the original reporting laws, most modern reporting laws have expanded in many ways, and that this has led to a higher number of reports. As well, it is strongly arguable that on occasion, as in the case of New South Wales, a jurisdiction has drafted provisions in such a way that they appear to have produced unintended and or unanticipated effects regarding the number of reports received.

Scott has observed correctly that 'child protection services are merely one component in a complex web of child and family services at the primary, secondary and tertiary levels of prevention'.[107] Arguably, the most justifiable approach must embrace all three methods of responding to severe child maltreatment. Given the characteristics of much severe child maltreatment and the apparently low likelihood that such cases will come to the attention of helping agencies without being reported by someone beyond the child's family, the validity of the principle motivating the original reporting law still appears intact. Where used, these laws must be framed so that their content fits the realistic ambition of the jurisdiction's overall child protection and family welfare plan. Whatever the scope of such a plan, it should be considered, coherent, and adequately resourced. The relationship of reporting laws with differential response and investigative responses must be soundly designed, both these response methods should be implemented appropriately, and reporting behaviour[108] should be monitored quantitatively and qualitatively so that problems can be identified and resolved.

[107] Scott, N. 11, above, 85.

[108] For mandated reporters, training must enable reporters to know the indicators of abuse and neglect, know when a report is and is not required, and know how to make a report that both satisfies the reporting requirements and provides useful assistance to child protective services intake.

20

Domestic Violence, Contact, and the ECHR

Shazia Choudhry[1]

The effect of domestic violence upon children has become an issue of serious concern. Research has demonstrated that children can experience domestic violence not only as direct victims but also as witnesses. At least 750,000 children a year witness domestic violence[1A] and in London 30 per cent of domestic violence murders are witnessed by children.[2] The effects are serious; children who live with domestic violence are at increased risk of behavioural problems, emotional trauma, and mental health difficulties in adult life.[3] Nearly three-quarters of children deemed to be 'at risk' live in households where domestic violence occurs and 52 per cent of child protection cases involve domestic violence.[4]

The impact of the research on the effects of witnessing or experiencing violence on children has not been confined to so-called 'intact' families. It has also led to an increased awareness of the continued risks posed to child victims during post separation contact with the abusive parent. The concern is such that it has led to a number of calls for a legal presumption against contact in such cases, such as that adopted in New Zealand.[5] However, although the domestic family law courts have shown an increasing awareness of the potential effects of domestic violence on children it is fair to say that there has been a reluctance to implement such a presumption largely due to an interpretation of the paramountcy principle[6] which has, as the next section will demonstrate, made it difficult for courts to refuse contact. Thus, even where domestic violence is a factor, it must, like all other factors, if necessary, be overridden by what is in the best interests of the child. Facilitating post separation contact between a child and a parent has generally been viewed as being in the best interests

[1] Law, Queen Mary, University of London.

[1A] Department of Health, 'Secure Futures for Women: making a difference' (London, Department of Health, 2002).

[2] Metropolitan Police, 'Findings from the Multi-Agency Domestic Violence Murder Reviews in London' (London, 2003), 10.

[3] J. Kolbo, E.H. Blakely, and D. Engleman, 'Children who Witness Domestic Violence: a Review of Empirical Literature' (1996) 11 *Journal of Interpersonal Violence* 281–93; R. Morley and A. Mullender, 'Domestic Violence and Children: What we Know from Research' in (eds.) A. Mullender and R. Morley, *Children Living with Domestic Violence: Putting Men's Abuse of Women on the Childcare Agenda* (London, Whiting and Birch, 1994); M. Hester, C. Pearson, and N. Harwin, *Making an Impact: Children and Domestic Violence: A Reader* 2nd edition (London, Jessica Kingsley, 2007).

[4] N. 1, above; E. Farmer and M. Owen, *Child Protection Practice: Private Risks and Public Remedies* (London, HMSO, 1995).

[5] See M. Kaye, 'Domestic Violence, Residence and Contact' (1996) 8 *Child and Family Law Quarterly* 285; M. Hester and C. Pearson, 'Domestic Violence and Children—the Practice of Family Court Welfare Officers' (1997) 9 *Child and Family Law Quarterly* 281; A. Perry, 'Safety First? Contact and Family Violence in New Zealand' (2006) 18 *Child and Family Law Quarterly* 1.

[6] See *Re H (Minors) (Access)* [1992] 1 FLR 148 as an example of the application of the test to contact cases and *Re H (Contact: Domestic Violence)* [1998] 2 FLR 42 at 56A–D.

of the child and as a result is very rarely entirely refused. This chapter will assess the current legal response to the issue within the context of the relevant provisions of the Human Rights Act 1998 (HRA) and the European Convention on Human Rights (ECHR) and whether the implementation of a legal presumption against contact in cases involving domestic violence would represent a breach of those provisions.

20.1 Current legal responses to children, domestic violence, and contact disputes

The leading authority in this area is the conjoined appeals of *Re L; Re V; Re M; Re H (Contact: DV)*,[7] in which the Court of Appeal stressed that there was no presumption against contact in cases involving domestic violence and that it was one important factor in the overall balancing exercise of section 1(3) of the Children Act 1989. The decision was particularly significant for the fact that the court commissioned and took into account expert evidence on the effects of domestic violence from academic psychologists, which concluded that domestic violence in itself was not a reason to refuse contact. As a result, the court set out a two-stage approach that should be taken in cases involving allegations of domestic violence. First, the court should decide whether or not the allegations concerning domestic violence are made out. Second, if they are made out the court should weigh up the risks involved and the impact of contact on the child against the positive benefits (if any) of contact. Any risk of harm to the resident parent should also be considered. A number of other, more detailed guidelines were referred to, the aim being that, although there was no presumption against contact in such cases, they would at least ensure that the courts would take the matter seriously and allow the courts to refuse contact if necessary. In addition to this decision there was a general consensus by judges that fears concerning the commitment of the father and the security of the mother where contact was granted, could be alleviated by allowing either indirect[8] or supervised contact only either at a relative's home or at a contact centre as a prerequisite to unsupervised contact in the future.[9]

Nonetheless, problems remained with this position. First, it quickly became apparent that the decision had little effect on the refusal of contact in such cases. According to Smart et al, despite the fact that violence is raised as a reason for restricting contact in 22 per cent of disputes reaching the courts[10] and according to NAPO is established/admitted in over a third of cases requiring welfare reports,[11] contact is refused in comparatively few cases. A report by the Judicial Statistics Department in 2005 revealed that of the 28,641 applications for contact made in 2005 only 58 resulted in a non-contact order, and more recent figures show a further decrease.[12] Second, there were a number of examples of court decisions in favour of contact that could

[7] [2000] 2 FLR 334.

[8] See *Re H (Contact: Domestic Violence)* [1998] Fam Law 392 (CA).

[9] *Re O (Contact: Imposition of Conditions)* [1995] 2 FLR 124 at 128.

[10] C. Smart, V. May, A. Wade, and C. Furniss, *Residence and Contact Disputes in Court, Volume 1* (London, Department for Constitutional Affairs, 2003).

[11] NAPO, 'Contact, Separation and the Work of Family Court Staff' a briefing from NAPO and the Trade Union and Professional Association for Family Court and Probation Staff (2002).

[12] From a 2005 report by the Judicial Statistics Department quoted in evidence from the Men's Advice Line at paragraph 288 of the Home Affairs Sixth Report (Home Affairs Committee Publications, 2008).

be doubted on the grounds of child welfare.[13] In 2001, a survey involving 127 refuge organizations found that contact orders are even being granted to parents convicted of offences against children and to parents whose behaviour caused children to be placed on the Child Protection Register. In some of these cases unsupervised contact was granted or visits were ordered to take place at contact centres which had no facilities for supervision.[14] Finally, the often used tactic of ordering supervised contact in order to minimize risk can only be successful if that supervision is available and effective. Unfortunately, there is an acute shortage of facilities for supervised contact. Only 12 per cent of contact centres in England provide individual supervision for high risk cases.[15]

The results of the courts getting the decisions wrong are serious. One piece of research which surveyed a number of cases where contact had been ordered despite the presence of domestic violence as a factor, suggested that 25 per cent of children were abused as a result of the contact.[16] Subsequent to this, a study by Women's Aid in 2004 found that 29 children in 13 families were killed between 1994 and 2004 as a result of contact arrangements in England and Wales.[17] The findings were so disturbing that it prompted a report into the cases by Nicholas Wall J[18] to the President of the Family Division.[19] There was also concern that allowing contact would enable the violent former partner to continue to dominate and exercise power over the resident parent and, more worryingly, use such arrangements to discover her whereabouts.[20] A further report by the Family Justice Council was subsequently commissioned to consider, and make recommendations about, what approach should be adopted by the court when asked to make a contact order by consent, in cases where domestic violence was present.[21] As a result, in recent evidence to the Home Affairs Select Committee, the Council stated 'a cultural change is required, with a move away from "contact is always the appropriate way forward" to "contact that is safe and positive for the

[13] See for example *Re J-S (A Child) (Contact: Parental Responsibility)* [2002] 3 FCR 433 and *Re E (children) (domestic violence: direct contact)* [2005] All ER (D) 86 (Apr).

[14] H. Saunders, *Making Contact Worse?* (Bristol, Women's Aid Federation of England, 2001).

[15] C. Furniss, 'Family Contact Centres: The Position in England, Wales & Scotland' (Leeds University: Centre for Research on Family, Kinship and Childhood, 1998).

[16] M. Hester, 'One step forward and three steps back? Children, Abuse and Parental Contact in Denmark' (2002) 14 *Child and Family Law Quarterly* 267.

[17] H. Saunders, *Twenty-nine Child Homicides: Lessons Still to be Learnt on Domestic Violence and Child Protection* (Bristol, Women's Aid Federation of England, 2004).

[18] Nicholas Wall, a Lord Justice of Appeal, 'A Report to the President of the Family Division on the Publication by the Women's Aid Federation of England Entitled *Twenty Nine Child Homicides: Lessons Still to be Learnt on Domestic Violence and Child Protection* With Particular Reference to the Five Cases in which there was Judicial Involvement' (March 2006).

[19] However, his report concluded that eight of the 11 children who had died in these cases did so as a result of parental actions, which could not reasonably have been foreseen or anticipated by the court on the material available before it. The remaining three children were the subjects of two cases, in both of which the judge was presented with consent orders agreed between the representatives of the parties. It was not clear, however, whether the court should have been more proactive in investigating the circumstances and refusing contact despite such agreement.

[20] See M. Kaye, J. Stubbs, and J. Tolmie, 'Domestic Violence and Child Contact Arrangements' (2003) 17 *Australian Journal of Family Law* 93; J. Masson and C. Humphreys, 'Facilitating and Enforcing Contact: the Bill and the Ten Per Cent' (2005) 35 *Family Law* 548; and J. Hardesty and G. Chung, 'Intimate Partner Violence, Parental Divorce and Child Custody: Directions for Intervention and Future Research' (2006) 55 *Family Relations* 200.

[21] J. Craig, '"Everybody's Business"—How applications for contact orders by consent should be approached by the court in cases involving domestic violence. The Family Justice Council's Report and Recommendations to the President of the Family Division' (February 2007). Can be found at: <http://www.family-justice-council.org.uk/docs/contactsummary.pdf>.

child is always the appropriate way forward" '.[22] In pursuance of this aim the Council has recently issued a new practice direction for the courts along these lines, which is accompanied by very strict guidelines.[23] Of particular note is the requirement for the court to consider whether, subject to the seriousness of the allegations made and the difficulty of the case, it is appropriate for the child who is the subject of the application to be made a party to the proceedings and be separately represented.[24] It also makes the point that where abuse is disputed, and where (if established) it is likely to affect the order that is going to be made, the court must hold a fact finding hearing in order to establish whether or not the abuse has occurred.[25] There is some evidence that the various campaigns and reports on the issue have had some effect upon the attitude of some members of the judiciary towards contact in cases involving domestic violence. Sir Nicholas Wall has recently admitted that the judiciary was late in realizing the impact of domestic violence upon children, which coupled with a rather naïvely optimistic interpretation of the ethos of the Children Act may have led to some incorrect decisions on contact in the past.[26] However, criticism of the current system remains, with many arguing that the implementation of a presumption against contact in such cases would be a far simpler, safer, and effective method of protecting vulnerable adults and children rather than relying on individual judicial interpretation of regularly issued guidance. Concern also remains about the continued use of supervised contact in circumstances that pose too great a risk to the child and adult involved.

20.2 The impact of the HRA 1998

Re L was also significant for one further reason which has since failed to be picked up on by subsequent guidance and judicial comment; its discussion, albeit brief, of the applicability of the HRA 1998.[27] In response to a fairly detailed submission by counsel on behalf of one of the appellant fathers, Dame Elizabeth Butler Sloss conducted a brief examination of some of the relevant European Court of Human Rights (ECtHR) authority and concluded that there had been no failure in refusing to order contact, by the judge, under Article 8(1), to have proper respect for family life on the basis that there was a real risk of emotional harm to the child which was protected by the provisions of Article 8(2). There was, however, no discussion of any other relevant articles or a detailed examination of *all* the parties' rights in this regard. This is not

[22] House of Commons, Home Affairs Committee, 'Domestic Violence, Forced Marriage and "Honour" Based Violence' Sixth Report of Session 2007–8, Vol. 1, HC 263-I (2008) at para. 287.

[23] 'Practice Direction: Residence and Contact Orders: Domestic Violence and Harm'. The Practice Direction can be accessed on the Family Justice Council's website at: <http://www.family-justice-council.org.uk/docs/Domestic_Violence_PD.pdf>.

[24] Ibid., para. 17.

[25] However, guidance on the practice direction has since been issued by Sir Nicholas Wall (*Guidance*, [2010] 2 FCR 271) due to the fact that 'judges had been holding unnecessary fact finding hearings, sometimes lasting several days, as a result of which they find facts which are not relevant to the ultimate issue'. Paragraph 5 of speech to the National Resolution Domestic Abuse Conference (15 October 2010).

[26] See his speech to the National Resolution Domestic Abuse Conference on 15 October 2010: 'The ethos of the Children Act 1989 was perceived by many, myself included, as non-blameworthy, un-recriminatory. Look forward, not back. The relationship is over: don't spend time raking over its embers: look to the future. I suspect that this attitude prevented a number of us from investigating allegations of domestic abuse, and also stopped us permitting victims to advance abuse as a reason—to take just one example—for denying contact.'

[27] N. 7, above. See Butler Sloss LJ at para. 277.

that surprising given that the case was decided before the HRA was implemented but the failure to follow up the analysis in subsequent case law demonstrates the general lack of attention given to the Act by the family law bench. This is regrettable, not only because this failure demonstrates a breach of the judiciary's obligations under the HRA but also because it demonstrates a failure to utilize, as the author has argued previously,[28] an alternative model which does not presuppose the outcome of an application by elevating what is currently assumed to be in the best interests of children as the only consideration. It is thus, rather ironically, the very existence and operation of the paramountcy principle which may have exacerbated some of the problematic decision-making mentioned above. The ECHR model, in contrast, allows for a detailed, case-by-case, consideration of what is the best outcome for all the parties concerned. Although the welfare of the child is a highly relevant factor which is given priority by the ECtHR, this priority will only be accorded after a detailed consideration of all the rights of the parties involved. Crucially, the ECtHR does not elevate its consideration to that of paramountcy.[29] The next section of this chapter will examine how, and to what extent, if at all, the domestic response to the issue fits in with the requirements of the ECHR and will outline how legal decision-making in such cases would be affected by using the ECHR model. Before doing so, a brief discussion of the applicability of the most relevant articles, Article 3 and Article 8, is necessitated and will now be undertaken.

20.3 Article 3

Article 3 of the ECHR states: 'No one shall be subject to torture or to inhuman or degrading treatment or punishment.'

The phrase 'ill treatment' in Article 3 includes actual bodily harm or intense physical or mental suffering.[30] 'Degrading treatment' includes conduct which humiliates or debases an individual; shows a lack of respect for, or diminishes human dignity. It also includes conduct which arouses feelings of fear, anguish or inferiority capable of breaking an individual's moral and physical resistance.[31] In considering whether treatment is 'degrading' the Court will have regard to whether its object was to humiliate and debase the victim and the effect on the victim.

Article 3 not only prohibits the State from inflicting torture or inhuman or degrading treatment on its citizens, it also requires the State to protect one citizen from torture or inhuman or degrading treatment at the hands of another.[32] A State will infringe an individual's right under Article 3 if it is aware that she or he is suffering the necessary degree of abuse at the hands of another and fails to take reasonable,[33] adequate,[34] or effective[35] steps to protect that individual.[36] There is a particular

[28] See S. Choudhry and J. Herring, *European Human Rights and Family Law* (London, Hart, 2010).

[29] See S. Choudhry, 'The Adoption and Children Act 2002, the Welfare Principle and the Human Rights Act 1998—A Missed Opportunity' (2003) 15 *Child and Family Law Quarterly* 119 and S. Choudhry and H. Fenwick, 'Clashing rights, the Welfare of the Child and the Human Rights Act 1998' (2005) 25 *Oxford Journal of Legal Studies* 453 for a detailed analysis of the difference in reasoning.

[30] See *Ireland v. UK* [1978] 2 EHRR 25.

[31] See amongst recent authorities, *Price v. UK*, Application no. 33394/96, ECHR 2001-VII, paras 24–30, and *Valašinas v. Lithuania*, Application no. 44558/98, ECHR 2001-VIII, para. 117.

[32] *A v. UK* [1998] 3 FCR 597; *E v. UK* [2002] 3 FCR 700.

[33] *Z v. UK* [2001] 2 FCR 246.

[34] *A v. UK*, N. 32, above, para. 24.

[35] N. 33, above, para. 73.

[36] *E v. UK*, N. 32, above.

obligation on the State to protect the Article 3 rights of vulnerable people, such as children. The obligations imposed on the State include ensuring that there is an effective legal deterrent to protect victims from abuse; to ensure that there is proper legal investigation and prosecution of any infringement of the individual rights; and where necessary to intervene and remove a victim from a position where she or he is suffering conduct which is prohibited by Article 3. Hence States have been found to infringe Article 3 when they have been aware that children are being abused but have not taken steps to protect children;[37] where the law on sexual assault required proof that the victim had physically resisted the sexual assault;[38] and where the police failed properly to investigate or take steps to prosecute men alleged to have committed sexual assaults.[39]

The right under Article 3 is an absolute one. Unlike many of the other rights mentioned in the ECHR there are no circumstances in which it is permissible for the State to infringe this right. This makes it clear that the rights of another party cannot justify an infringement of someone's Article 3 rights. So, for example, it cannot be successfully argued that a family's right of privacy justifies non-intervention by the State if that non-intervention infringes one family member's Article 3 rights. Indeed, and perhaps this is more controversial, it is suggested that other rights of the victim cannot justify an infringement of Article 3. In other words, the State cannot justify its failure to protect a victim's Article 3 rights in a contact case by referring to that person's right to respect for private life.

20.3.1 The positive duty of the State under Article 3

Article 3 imposes primarily a negative obligation on States: to refrain from inflicting serious harm on persons within their jurisdiction. Most cases involving Article 3 have involved State agents or public authorities inflicting treatment on individuals.[40] However, the ECtHR has been developing a certain level of flexibility in addressing the application of Article 3 within the 'private context'.[41] The Court has, for example, recognized that the State can be under positive obligations to protect one individual from having her or his rights under Article 3 infringed by another individual.[42]

A positive obligation on the State to provide protection against inhuman or degrading treatment from another individual has thus been found to arise in a number of cases. In *A v. United Kingdom*,[43] a child applicant successfully complained that the Government had failed to protect him from degrading treatment (caning) carried out towards him by his stepfather. The Court reasoned that Article 3 required States not only to protect individuals from treatment which breached Article 3 administered by private individuals, but also that: 'Children and other vulnerable individuals, in particular, are entitled to State protection, in the form of effective deterrence, against such serious breaches of personal integrity.'[44] A violation of Article 3 had therefore occurred.

[37] Ibid. [38] *MC v. Bulgaria* (2005) 40 EHRR 20. [39] Ibid.

[40] Cases have ranged from prison and detention: (see *Ireland v. UK*, N. 30, above) to corporal punishment (see *Tyrer v. UK* (1978) 2 EHRR 1, para. 31).

[41] See *D. v. UK*, judgment of 2 May 1997, *Reports* 1997-III, p. 792, para. 49.

[42] See *E and Others v. UK* Application no. 33218/96 (2003) 36 EHRR 31.

[43] (1999) 27 EHRR 611.

[44] Ibid., para. 22. Reference was also made to the United Nations Convention on the Rights of the Child, Articles 19 and 37.

However, it was not until the decisions in *Z and Others v. United Kingdom*[45] and *E v. United Kingdom*[46] that the nature and extent of positive obligations under Article 3 arising within English civil law came before the Court. Both cases concerned allegations that the respective local authorities had failed to take adequate protective measures in respect of the severe neglect and abuse which the applicants, as children, had suffered at the hands of their carers, contrary to Articles 3 and 8. These alleged breaches, it was argued, were due to the House of Lords having held that,[47] as a matter of principle, local authorities could not be sued for negligence or for breach of statutory duty in respect of the discharge of their functions concerning the welfare of children. Their action for damages for negligence and/or breach of statutory duty had, therefore, been struck out as revealing no cause of action.[48] In respect of Article 3 the Court found that there had been a violation, as it was clear that the neglect and abuse suffered by the children reached the threshold of inhuman and degrading treatment.

In its judgments the Court reiterated the principle that States should provide effective protection in relation to children and vulnerable adults, particularly where the authorities had or ought to have had knowledge of abuse.[49] Of particular note is the Court's response to the Government's argument that, notwithstanding any acknowledged shortcomings, it had not been shown that matters would have turned out any differently:

> The test under Art.3 however does not require it to be shown that 'but for' the failing or omission of the public authority ill-treatment would not have happened. A failure to take reasonably available measures which could have had a real prospect of altering the outcome or mitigating the harm is sufficient to engage the responsibility of the State.[50]

As a result, the Court was satisfied that the pattern of lack of investigation, communication, and co-operation by the relevant authorities amounted to a breach of Article 3.

20.3.2 Is domestic violence suffered/witnessed by a child inhuman and degrading treatment for the purposes of Article 3?

As the research outlined at the beginning of this chapter demonstrates, the effects of witnessing or experiencing domestic violence upon children will often be sufficiently intense to engage Article 3. Physical abuse is likely to fall within Article 3, unless it is physical injuries of a minor kind. Emotional abuse, intimidation, or debasement can

[45] N. 33, above. [46] N. 32, above.

[47] Reported as *X and Others v. Bedfordshire County Council* [1995] 3 All ER 352.

[48] This decision became the leading authority in the UK in this area. However, it was distinguished by the House of Lords in two significant judgments concerning the extent of liability of local authorities in child care matters. In *W and Others v. Essex County Council* [1998] 3 All ER 111, foster parents who brought a claim for damages for negligence against a local authority who placed a known suspected sexual abuser within their home had their appeal against the striking out of their action upheld by the House of Lords in relation to the sexual abuse and psychiatric illness suffered by their three children and inflicted by the foster child. In *Barrett v. London Borough of Enfield* [1999] 3 WLR 79, the plaintiff, who had been in care most of his life, claimed that the local authority had negligently failed to safeguard his welfare causing deep-seated psychiatric problems. Here, the House of Lords held that the judgment in *X and Others v. Bedfordshire* did not, in this case, prevent a claim of negligence being brought against a local authority by a child formerly in its care.

[49] See para. 88. *Z v. UK* applied. See also *Stubbings v. UK*, 1996-IV, para. 64.

[50] At para. 99.

also fall within Article 3 as 'degrading treatment', particularly when these aspects of the practice are intended to humiliate and demean the victim.[51] In addition, young victims in particular may find themselves in an abusive and dangerous situation against their will with no power to seek help. It can thus constitute a form of child abuse leading to criminal sanctions against the carer perpetrator or the carer who fails to protect.

Although the question of whether a child victim of domestic violence can fall within the definition of Article 3 treatment has not specifically been addressed by the ECtHR,[52] the more general question of whether domestic violence can fall within the definition of Article 3 treatment has now been settled. The question was directly addressed by the ECtHR for the first time in its highly significant decision in *Opuz v. Turkey*,[53] in which the applicant, a victim of domestic violence, alleged that the injuries and anguish she had suffered as a result of the violence inflicted upon her by her husband had amounted to torture within the meaning of Article 3 of the Convention. Furthermore, by consistently failing to take any action to protect her from his violence in response to her repeated requests for help, the State had made her feel debased, hopeless, and vulnerable. The ECtHR agreed, coming to this conclusion by a straightforward application of the principles that it had developed in relation to Article 3 discussed above. Of particular relevance was the principle that children and other vulnerable individuals, in particular, are entitled to State protection, in the form of effective deterrence, against serious breaches of personal integrity. The Court thus considered, as the author had earlier predicted,[54] that the applicant and therefore other victims of domestic violence could fall within the group of 'vulnerable individuals' entitled to State protection that was referred to in *A v. United Kingdom*.[55] Relevant factors in coming to this conclusion that were cited by the Court were the violence suffered by the applicant in the past, the threats issued by her husband following his release from prison, and her fear of further violence. Importantly, the Court also acknowledged that domestic abuse which is non-physical can also come within Article 3:

> The Court observes also that the violence suffered by the applicant, in the form of physical injuries *and psychological pressure*, were sufficiently serious to amount to ill-treatment within the meaning of Article 3 of the Convention.[56] (emphasis added)

The Court then turned to the question of whether the national authorities had taken all reasonable measures to prevent the recurrence of violent attacks against the applicant's physical integrity. After reviewing the response of the authorities in some detail, the Court considered that it had not. Although the authorities had responded each time a complaint had been made, the reliance upon the applicant's continued involvement for further action and the general inadequacy of the measures taken against her

[51] A harrowing account of the forms of domestic abuse can be found in S. Edwards, *Sex, Gender and the Legal Process* (London, Blackstone, 1996).

[52] This question did come up in the later case of *Bevacqua and S. v. Bulgaria*, Application no. 71127/01, 12 June 2008, but the Court declined to consider Article 3 opting instead to consider it under Article 8 alone. This case will be discussed in the next section on Article 8.

[53] Application no. 33401/02, 9 June 2009.

[54] See S. Choudhry and J. Herring, 'Domestic Violence and the Human Rights Act 1998: A New Means of Legal Intervention' (Winter 2006) *Public Law* 752 and S. Choudhry and J. Herring, 'Righting Domestic Violence' (2006) 2 *International Journal of Law, Policy and the Family* 1.

[55] N. 32, above.

[56] N. 53, above, para. 161.

husband meant that the local authorities had failed to demonstrate the required diligence to prevent the recurrence of violent attacks against the applicant.[57]

The potential significance of this decision for *all* victims of domestic violence cannot be underestimated. First, it demonstrates the acceptance and application by the ECtHR of a number of international instruments and decisions in relation to domestic violence. Second, it demonstrates that a State's obligation under Article 3 cannot simply be satisfied by the passing of appropriate legislation alone. What is also required to be demonstrated is that the legislation is reasonably *effective*. The decision thus underlines the need to fully implement and carefully monitor the effectiveness of domestic violence policy and legislation. Finally, although uncontested in *Opuz*, it is nevertheless clear that the Court's willingness to refer to the reports provided by NGOs and advocacy groups means that such evidence will be of considerable importance when it comes to any future assessment by the Court of a State's obligation in this regard.

20.3.3 Conclusions on Article 3 within the context of contact and domestic violence

In summary therefore, the Court has established that particular regard will be given to children and vulnerable adults when considering the extent of the positive obligations that are to be imposed on member States towards them, notwithstanding that the 'treatment' at issue is being meted out by private individuals. Liability under Article 3 will thus be incurred if the following criteria are met:

- the treatment concerned comes within the definition established under Article 3;
- the State ought to have or had knowledge that such treatment was occurring;
- the State failed to take reasonably available measures that could have mitigated the resulting harm.[58]

Thus, although Article 3 is drafted in absolute terms, the *duties* imposed by it on States are not. The police, local authorities, and courts are only under a duty to intervene in *so far as is reasonable* to protect a victim of domestic violence, including children affected by domestic violence, where the violence amounts to torture, inhuman, or degrading treatment. The British Government has certainly demonstrated some effort towards complying with this duty, in terms of both prevention and response. In relation to adult victims there has been a significant amount of policy and resource commitment. Crown Prosecution Services, Association of Chief Police Officer, local authority, and judicial guidance are regularly updated and take into account the substantial amount of research in the area. Further, in compliance with Recommendation 5 of the Council of Europe (2002),[59]

[57] Ibid., paras 166–75.

[58] J. Rogers, 'Applying The Doctrine Of Positive Obligations In The European Convention On Human Rights To Domestic Substantive Criminal Law In Domestic Proceedings' (2003) *Criminal Law Review* 690 emphasizes that it will need to be shown that the criminal law provides an effective deterrent.

[59] Recommendation Rec(2002)5 on the protection of women against violence, adopted by the Committee of Ministers of the Council of Europe on 30 April 2002. The Recommendation specifically asks that Member States 'consider establishing a national plan of action for combating violence against women', as a means towards 'ensuring that all measures are co-ordinated nation-wide and focused on

the Government has published and updated its National Domestic Violence Delivery Plan[60] on how it intends to achieve the goal of the protection of women against violence. In addition, the definition of harm was amended by the Adoption and Children Act 2002[61] to make clear that when a court is considering whether a child has suffered, or is likely to suffer harm, it must consider harm that a child may suffer, not just from domestic violence, but also from witnessing it. Section 7 of the Children and Adoption Act 2006[62] also extends the duty to private law Children Act proceedings in requiring officers from the Children and Family Court Advisory and Support Service (CAFCASS), to carry out risk assessments in such proceedings where they consider that there is cause to suspect that a child is at risk of harm. The officers are then required to inform the court of their findings in respect of the risk of the child who is suffering harm, so that the court can consider what action should be taken. Notwithstanding such efforts, it must be remembered that when an assessment is undertaken of the conduct of the State in relation to Article 3 cases the real issue is whether the State was properly to be regarded as responsible for the conduct that was prohibited by Article 3 rather than whether this was as a result of legitimate government policy. Thus, the actual implementation of such policies must be closely monitored in order to ensure that State obligations are really being fulfilled. In practical terms, this could mean that in civil cases a failure by the courts to provide protection to a vulnerable child and/or adult against direct contact with a violent parent where Article 3-type treatment or the risk of it can be evidenced may also lead to a breach of their obligations under section 6 of the HRA towards that child and/or adult. At present, such cases are often dealt with in conjunction with the public law elements of the Children Act 1989 and, if relevant, criminal law proceedings. Although one would hope that this would mean it is highly unlikely that direct contact would be awarded in cases where the Article 3 threshold has been met, the research discussed at the beginning of the chapter unfortunately demonstrates that direct contact has in fact sometimes been erroneously awarded. It is precisely these kinds of cases that have the potential to be most affected by an application of this analysis. It is also precisely these kinds of cases that demonstrate the most serious failure to harness the potential of the HRA where direct contact is nonetheless allowed. This is due to the fact that the denial of direct contact should be a relatively straightforward exercise in judicial reasoning for, according to the terms of the article itself, the balancing of the rights and interests of others is not required. If Article 3-type treatment or the risk of it is proved then that is the end of the matter. The refusal to award direct contact to the applicant who has meted out, or is judged to be at risk of meting out, such treatment to a child can easily be legally justified. Any competing claims under Article 8 as a qualifying article should not, as the next section makes clear, override a finding that Article 3 as an absolute article has been breached. The effects of the failure to harness this provision cannot be underestimated. A judiciary which

the needs of the victims and that relevant state institutions as well as non-governmental organisations (NGOs) be associated with the elaboration and the implementation of the necessary measures'.

[60] The plan and the updated progress reports can be found on the Home Office Website at: <http://www.crimereduction.homeoffice.gov.uk/dv/dv017.htm>.

[61] Implemented in January 2005.

[62] Section 7 of the Act came into force on 1 October 2007. However, revised forms (commonly known as 'Gateway' forms), for applications for child contact and residence were introduced on 31 January 2005. Courts are now required to consider whether incidents of domestic violence—not just from direct violence but also from witnessing violence towards another—has had an adverse impact on the child, or might affect the child in the future.

fails to do so is failing in its duties towards protecting vulnerable children from further harm.

Not all cases will, however, meet the threshold for Article 3-type treatment, perhaps where the child has not directly experienced the violence but there is some basis for believing that a risk remains to the child. In these cases, the applicability of Article 8 and the competing claims that will arise under it must be considered.

20.4 Article 8

Article 8 provides:

1. Everyone has the right to respect for his private and family life, his home, and his correspondence.
2. There shall be no interference by a public authority with the exercise of this right except such as in accordance with the law and is necessary in a democratic society in the interests of national security, public safety or the economic well being of the country, for the prevention of disorder or crime, for the protection of heath or morals, or for the protection of the rights and freedoms of others.

The ECtHR has held that although Article 8 is primarily concerned with protecting individuals and families from unwanted State intrusion, it also imposes positive obligations upon the State. It is necessary to consider this issue in relation to all aspects of Article 8.

20.4.1 The right to respect for 'private and family life'

The right to private life is a wide-ranging right. Of particular relevance to the domestic violence context are two points. First, 'the concept of private life covers the physical and moral integrity of the person'.[63] In *X and Y v. The Netherlands*,[64] the lack of effective protection under the criminal law against sexual assault for a mentally ill woman was said to amount to an infringement of her right to private life. The State, it was said, is required under Article 8 to protect one person's right to private life against unwanted contact or infringements to moral integrity. The State may thus be required to protect a citizen from serious violence under Article 3, and less serious incidents under Article 8.[65] Mental health and stability is said to be part of a person's moral integrity.[66] Second, the ECtHR has stated that Article 8 is concerned with protecting a person's physical and psychological integrity[67] and her/his right to identity and personal development.[68] Once this is identified as at the heart of Article 8, domestic violence can readily be seen as involving an interference with the parties' right to develop their personality. Clear links have been established between being a victim of domestic violence and a variety of emotional and psychological problems.[69]

Article 8 imposes positive obligations on the State. Most of the case law has concerned the positive obligations imposed on a State to protect the family life between

63 *X and Y v. The Netherlands* (1986) 8 EHRR 235.

64 Ibid.

65 *Costello-Roberts v. UK* (1995) 19 EHRR 112.

66 *Bensaid v. UK* (2001) 33 EHRR 10.

67 *Pretty v. UK* (2002) 35 EHRR 1, para. 61.

68 *Bensaid v. UK* (1995) 19 EHRR 112, para. 45.

69 Parliamentary Assembly, Council of Europe, Committee on Equal Opportunities for Women and Men, *Domestic Violence* (2002), para. 12.

a parent and child. It is well established in the Court's case law that the mutual enjoyment by parent and child of each other's company constitutes a fundamental element of family life, and domestic measures hindering such enjoyment can amount to an interference with the right protected by Article 8 of the Convention.[70] There may be, in addition, positive obligations inherent in effective 'respect' for private or family life.[71] Thus, where the existence of a family tie has been established, the State must, in principle, act in a manner calculated to enable that tie to be developed and take measures that will enable a parent and child to be reunited.[72] This applies not only to cases dealing with the compulsory taking of children into public care and the implementation of care measures, but also to cases where contact and residence disputes concerning children arise between parents and/or other members of the children's family.[73]

However, the Court has also made it clear that the State's positive obligations concerning the reunification of a parent and a child on the breakdown of the parental relationship are not absolute. In *Kosmopoulou v. Greece*,[74] it was held that whilst national authorities must do their utmost to facilitate such a reunion, any obligation to apply coercion in this area must be limited. This is due to the need to take into account the interests as well as the rights and freedoms of all concerned and, more particularly, the best interests of the child and his or her rights under Article 8 of the Convention. Where contact with the parent might appear to threaten those interests or interfere with those rights, it is for the national authorities to strike a fair balance between them.[75] The key consideration is, therefore, whether the State has taken all such steps to facilitate contact as can reasonably be demanded in the particular circumstances of each case.[76] Regard must also be had to the fair balance that must be struck between the competing interests of the individual and the community as a whole, including other concerned third parties. In both cases, the State enjoys a certain margin of appreciation.[77]

Thus, it can be seen that within the context of domestic violence the State may be required to intervene in order to protect the family lives of the abused parent and any children under its Article 8 obligations.[78] If the relationship between the child and parents is being severely disrupted by violence (even if it is not being directed at the child), there is a strong case for claiming that both the child's and the abused parent's right to family life are being interfered with. This may then, in turn, create a positive obligation upon the State to intervene to protect their rights of family life.

[70] See, amongst others, *Johansen v. Norway* (1997) 23 EHRR 33, para. 52.

[71] See N. 63, above.

[72] See, amongst others, *Eriksson v. Sweden* (1990) 12 EHRR 183, para. 71; *Gnahoré v. France*, Application no. 40031/98, ECHR 2000-IX, para. 51; *Zawadka v. Poland*, Application no. 48542/99 23 June 2005; *Bajrami v. Albania*, Application no. 35853/04, 12 December 2006; and *Sobota-Gajic v. Bosnia and Herzegovina*, Application no. 27966/06, 6 November 2007.

[73] *Hokkanen v. Finland* (1995) 19 EHRR 159, para 55.

[74] [2004] 1 FLR 800, para 45.

[75] *Ignacollo-Zenide v. Romania*, Application no. 31679/96, ECHR 2000–I, para. 94.

[76] *Hokkanen v. Finland* (1995) 19 EHRR 159, para. 58. See also *Chepelev v. Russia*, Application no. 58077/00, 27 July 2007.

[77] See *Z and others v. UK* (2002) 34 EHRR 3, para. 41.

[78] Where a child is being affected by the violence her or himself, the case is likely to fall within Article 3. It may even be argued that if the family life is characterized by abuse, the family life ceases to be entitled to respect and so is no longer protected by Article 8: J. Herring, 'Respecting Family Life' (2008) 75 *Amicus Curiae* 21.

The ECtHR has recently considered this very issue in *Bevacqua and S v. Bulgaria*[79] in which, following the parents' separation and during extended custody proceedings in Bulgaria, the applicant mother agreed to the father having contact with the three-year-old child. However, the father subsequently refused to return the child to the mother's care, and thereafter refused the applicant contact. After recovering the child from kindergarten, the applicant was threatened by the father who eventually entered her home to recover the child and used violence against her. The applicant then moved to a hostel for victims of domestic violence in another town, but the authorities threatened to prosecute her for abduction of the child. To make matters worse, the Bulgarian courts then failed to make an interim order concerning the custody of the child in response to the applicant's request. In order to avoid prosecution the applicant then agreed that she and the father would care for the child in alternate months. However, while the child was living with the father there was further violence by the father against the applicant and after a series of further proceedings, the applicant was eventually granted custody of the child, the domestic courts having accepted that witnessing such behaviour from the father was a bad example for the child. Crucially, however, the father was not prosecuted for any of the violence used against the applicant both before and subsequent to this decision. As a result the applicants (mother and child) complained that the authorities had failed to take the necessary measures to secure respect for their family life and failed to protect the first applicant against the violent behaviour of her former husband relying on Articles 3, 8, 13, and 14 of the Convention. However, the ECtHR considered that, in this case, the complaints fell to be considered under Article 8 alone although it was also emphasized that a State's positive obligations in this context could arise in some cases under Article 2 or 3 and in other instances under Article 8 taken alone or in combination with Article 3 of the Convention.[80] After a detailed examination of the facts the Court went on to hold that the authorities' duty under Article 8 towards both applicants (parent and child) had required the examination of the interim measures application with due diligence and without delay and to secure the enjoyment of both applicants' right to normal contacts between them; however, this had not occurred:

> The cumulative effects of the District Court's failure to adopt interim custody measures without delay in a situation which affected adversely the applicants and, above all, the well-being of the second applicant and the lack of sufficient measures by the authorities during the same period in reaction to Mr N.'s behaviour amounted to a failure to assist the applicants contrary to the State positive obligations under Article 8 of the Convention to secure respect for their private and family life.[81]

There are a number of significant aspects to this decision. First, the judgment reiterates the development of a positive obligation to include, in certain circumstances, a duty to maintain and apply in practice an adequate legal framework affording protection against acts of violence by private individuals.[82] Second, there is the reliance by the Court on a number of international instruments to emphasize the particular vulnerability of the victims of domestic violence and the need for active State involvement in their protection. The terms of the Recommendation Rec(2002)5 of the Committee of Ministers of the Council of Europe on the protection of women

[79] N. 52, above. [80] Ibid., para. 65. [81] Ibid., para. 84. [82] Ibid., para. 65.

against violence[83] and the United Nations General Assembly Declaration on the Elimination of Violence against Women Article 4(c)[84] were quoted in detail as were comments by the Special Rapporteur on violence against women and the case law of a number of international bodies concerning the issue of domestic violence.[85] Thus, although the Court reiterated that the sphere of the relations of individuals between themselves was in principle a matter that fell within the domestic authorities' margin of appreciation it was also able to rely on the absence of compliance with the aforementioned provisions as a means of emphasizing the failure to respect the Article 8 rights of the victims in this case notwithstanding the application of this margin.[86] Finally, and of most significance, was the articulation by the Court of the second applicant's (the child's) right to respect to family life and the ability to effectively exercise his right to regular contact with his mother. Of particular note was the clear recognition by the Court of the adverse affects upon him of having to witness the violence between his parents.[87]

Although not discussed in *Bevacqua*, the fact remains that the father in such cases is also entitled to claim his right to exercise family life with his child under Article 8. Moreover, a domestic court, unlike the ECtHR, will be required to consider *all* the Article 8 claims of those involved even though this will inevitably result in a clash of rights between those family members. The issue is not just one of ensuring that family members are protected from violence under Article 8, but also that doing so does not disproportionately interfere with the right to mutual enjoyment of family life in terms of contact between the non-resident parent and the child and the effect this may have on the family life of the resident parent who has experienced violence from the other. It is at this juncture, however, that the debate concerning the appropriate balancing of the individual Article 8 rights of all the parties involved intersects with the domestic debate concerning the appropriateness of allowing contact between a child and a formerly violent parent.

20.4.2 Balancing Article 8 rights in civil cases and the process of qualification

When considering an application to restrict an abusive partner's contact with his/her child/children, the court will have to undertake a balancing exercise between the competing individual Article 8 rights of the parties. The respondent can, for example, make a claim concerning his own rights to respect for private and family life and the right to respect for the home. As Article 8 is a 'qualified' right, once the Court has decided that Article 8(1) is 'engaged' by an alleged interference with the right it will then turn to a detailed consideration of whether the qualifications contained in Article 8(2) have been established. As is well known, this will require an assessment of whether the interference was prescribed by the law, whether the interference was necessary in the interests of one of the listed, legitimate, aims, and finally, whether

[83] See N. 59, above. It states that Member States should introduce, develop, and/or improve where necessary national policies against violence based on maximum safety and protection of victims, support and assistance, adjustment of the criminal and civil law, raising of public awareness, and training for professionals confronted with violence against women and prevention.

[84] Which urges States to 'exercise due diligence to prevent, investigate and, in accordance with national legislation, punish acts of violence against women, whether those acts are perpetrated by the State or private persons'.

[85] N. 52, above, para. 53.

[86] Ibid., paras 82 and 83.

[87] Ibid., para. 79.

the interference was necessary in a democratic society in pursuance of the legitimate aim.

Thus, any interference with a right must be shown to have been in response to a pressing social need to act for that purpose and to be a proportionate response to that purpose.[88] Proportionality thus becomes a 'vehicle for conducting a balancing exercise' by requiring a balance between the nature and extent of the interference against the reasons for interfering.[89] Generally, when determining the issue of proportionality and whether the measures taken are 'necessary in a democratic society', the Court will consider whether, in the light of the case as a whole, the reasons adduced to justify them were relevant and sufficient for the purpose of Article 8(2).[90] In making this assessment, the Court will afford the national authorities a margin of appreciation, in recognition of the fact that they are better placed to the primary judgment as to the needs of the parties involved and the appropriate balance to be struck between them. The extent of the margin of appreciation to be accorded to States in such circumstances will, however, vary in the light of the nature and seriousness of the interests at stake.[91] The margin also varies according to the context of the individual facts of a case.[92]

20.4.3 Balancing cases involving children

When approaching any question concerning Article 8, the ECtHR starts from the stance that wherever family life is found to be in existence, each of the family members will be entitled independently to respect for their family life. It does not regard the child's interests in this respect as paramount, that is, as displacing considerations of other members' rights.[93] Each family member's right to respect for family life (private life is not usually considered separately, although in some circumstances this might be a significant possibility) is accorded equal weight before a decision is made as to what extent, if at all, the rights of family members are in conflict. The Court will then consider whether any interference with the rights of family members is justified as 'necessary' under Article 8(2); it is only at this point that the welfare of the child becomes relevant[94] and will not inevitably result in the child's interests prevailing.[95]

[88] See *Silver v. UK* (1983) 5 EHRR 344, para. 97.

[89] See Feldman, *Civil Liberties and Human Rights in England and Wales* 2nd edition (Oxford, 2002), 57.

[90] See *Olsson v. Sweden (No. 2)* (A/250) (1992) 17 EHRR 134, para. 68.

[91] *K and T v. Finland* (2001) 31 EHRR 18, para. 166 and *Kitzner v. Germany* (2002) 35 EHRR 25, para. 67.

[92] See *Johansen v. Norway* (1996) 23 EHRR 33, para. 64 and *K v. Finland* (2003) 36 EHRR 18, para. 168.

[93] For a recent example where paramountcy was not applied see *Hansen v. Turkey* [2004] 1 FLR 142, para. 98. The Court has, however, recently used the word 'paramount' in relation to children's interests in *Zawadka v. Poland* (2007) 44 EHRR 9, para. 67, but diluted this term by referring, in the same paragraph, to the need to take into account 'more particularly' the best interests of the child. It does not seem, therefore, that the Court used 'paramount' in the same sense as the Children Act 1989.

[94] Although the welfare of the child will, to some extent, be relevant when the Court considers its right to family life at the first stage under Article 8(1) it will not be considered in relation to the Article 8(1) rights of the other parties.

[95] This is contrary to the current domestic judicial interpretation of Article 8. See: S. Choudhry and H. Fenwick, 'Taking the Rights of Parents and Children Seriously: Confronting the Welfare Principle under the Human Rights Act' (2005) 25 *Oxford Journal of Legal Studies* 453; H. Fenwick, 'Clashing Rights, the Welfare of the Child and the Human Rights Act' (2004) 67 *Modern Law Review* 889, which attacks the effect of the principle in the case of clashes between media freedom and the privacy of the child; S. Choudhry, 'The Adoption and Children Act 2002, the Welfare Principle and the HRA 1998—a

It is also clear that although the Court is prepared to concede a margin of appreciation to the national authorities in private family law cases where clashes between the Article 8 rights of the child and the parent occur, it is not as wide as in certain 'clash of rights' instances in other contexts:[96] the Court is prepared to be fairly interventionist where the right of one party to family life would be almost entirely abrogated by the restriction in question.[97] However, Strasbourg clearly accords special importance to the best interests of the child: where a significant conflict between the claims of another party and those interests arises, it will tend to allow the child's interests to determine the outcome.

The Court has also demonstrated a greater willingness to give special consideration to children's rights,[98] which in turn has been attributed to the growing influence upon the Strasbourg jurisprudence[99] of the United Nations Convention on the Rights of the Child (the CRC).[100] Both the Commission and the Court have referred to the provisions of the CRC in children's cases since it came into force in 1990, and this development in approach is evidenced by a number of recent cases.[101]

More significantly, in succeeding judgments, the Court has reaffirmed the established position whereby the varying Convention rights of the parties concerned are considered by starting from a basis of presumptive equality.[102] In other words, within the margin of appreciation of the Member State, a fair balance must be struck between the Article 8 rights of the child and those of the parent, albeit attaching particular importance to the former, thereby ruling out the use of a presumption that precludes that balancing exercise.

20.4.4 The 'parallel analysis' approach

It is thus apparent from the Strasbourg jurisprudence that an individual right cannot figure merely as an exception to another individual right and, in addition, that it cannot be entirely abrogated without an application of the paragraph 2 tests. Instead, the

Missed Opportunity', N. 29, above; H. Fenwick, D. Bonner, and S. Harris-Short, 'Judicial Approaches to the HRA' (2003) 52 *International and Comparative Law Quarterly* 549 at 572–84, especially at 582–4.

[96] See *Otto-Preminger Institut v. Austria* (1994) 19 EHRR 34; *Tammer v. Estonia* (2003) 37 EHRR 43.

[97] *Johansen v. Norway* (1997) 23 EHRR 134.

[98] The ECHR itself contains few explicit references to children and their rights, which is generally believed to be due to the era of its inception.

[99] See U. Kilkelly, 'The Best of Both Worlds for Children's Rights? Interpreting the European Convention on Human Rights in Light of the UN Convention on the Rights of the Child' (2001) 23 *Human Rights Quarterly* 308 and M. Woolf, 'Coming of Age? The Principle of the Best Interests of the Child' (2003) 2 *European Human Rights Law Review* 205 for an overview of how the principle has been interpreted by the European Court of Human Rights and the UK courts within the context of the UN Convention on the Rights of the Child 1989.

[100] Article 3 of the CRC states: 'in all actions concerning children, whether undertaken by public or private courts of law, administrative authorities or legislative bodies, the best interests of the child shall be a *primary* consideration.' The UK has ratified the CRC and is therefore bound under international law to comply with its requirements. It is still, however, not part of UK law.

[101] See *L v. Finland* (2001) 31 EHRR 30, para. 118; *Elsholz v. Germany* [2000] 2 FLR 486.

[102] Thus, in *Hansen v. Turkey* [2004] 1 FLR 142 the Court found, 'the rights and freedoms of all concerned must be taken into account, and more particularly the best interests of the child and his or her rights under Article 8 of the Convention. Where contacts with the parent might appear to threaten those interests or interfere with those rights, it is for the national authorities to strike a *fair balance* between them' (emphasis added). See also *Gorgulu v. Germany* Application no. 74969/01, para. 43 and *Hoppe v. Germany* (2004) 38 EHRR 15, para. 44 for evidence of this approach.

'parallel analysis' approach must be utilized: both rights must be considered as exceptions to the other, by applying all the tests within paragraph 2 of Article 8.[103] Unlike Strasbourg, the domestic court will have all the family members as parties before it and all will claim that their rights are equally at issue. As a result the domestic courts will need to deal explicitly with the question of clashing rights. Of significant note is the requirement to attach particular importance to the best interests of the child when carrying out the balancing exercise concerning Article 8. This should provide a powerful justification to reinterpret any existing domestic requirements to hold such interests as paramount[104] but will also, if necessary, introduce a relatively higher consideration towards the interests of children where no such requirement currently exists.

20.4.5 Conclusions on contact, domestic violence, and Article 8

It is clear therefore that the ECHR does allow for a proportionate interference with violent parents' Article 8 right to family life as long as the interference satisfies the process of qualification within Article 8(2). Further, due to the number of Article 8 claims at play in a contact dispute that involves domestic violence, the parallel analysis will also need to be employed. This means that all three Article 8 rights must be considered as exceptions to the other, by applying all the tests within paragraph 2 of Article 8. The court should also acknowledge that, although not paramount, the interests of any children involved should be of particular importance. The key consideration in such a case will therefore be whether the State has taken all the necessary steps to facilitate contact between the violent parent and the children as can reasonably be demanded in the special circumstances of the case. It may be that in striking a fair balance between the competing rights of the family members involved, the nature and extent of the violence is considered too great to grant a request for any form of contact where such contact could threaten the interests or interfere with other family members' rights. However, it may also be the case that allowing supervised or unsupervised contact may, according to the individual facts of a case, be the more proportionate response bearing in mind the positive obligations that are owed to parents, under Article 8 to facilitate contact between a parent and child, if possible. What is also important to bear in mind is the recent acknowledgement by the ECtHR of the detrimental effects that witnessing domestic violence may have on a child and therefore *his/her* right to family life. It may follow that a cautious approach such as the implementation of a presumption against contact where domestic violence has been proved, perhaps where an order has already been made under the Family Law Act 1996,[105] would not be regarded as disproportionate under Article 8.

[103] See S. Choudhry and H. Fenwick, N. 29, above, and G. Phillipson, 'Transforming Breach of Confidence? Towards a common law right to privacy under the HRA' (2003) 66 *Modern Law Review* 726. For recent examples of judicial application of the parallel analysis see *Campbell v. MGM* [2004] 2 AC 457 and *Re S* [2005] 1 AC 593.

[104] In proceedings brought under the Children Act 1989 by virtue of section 1 and the so-called 'paramountcy principle'. See S. Choudhry and H. Fenwick, N. 29, above, for a detailed consideration of how the parallel analysis should be applied in such cases and why compliance with the HRA necessitates a reinterpretation of the paramountcy principle.

[105] In addition, separate legislation in New Zealand dealing with contact features a rebuttable presumption that there should not be contact unless the court can be sure that the mother and child will be safe. The Guardianship Act contains a risk assessment checklist that must be considered by the court before contact is awarded. All children are represented in family proceedings. There is no power to imprison a mother who refuses to comply with a contact order or similar agreement. Children have a right to oppose access—the older and more mature a child is the more weight will be given to his/her wishes.

This would mirror the provisions of New Zealand's Domestic Violence Act of 1995 which provides that when there is a protection order in place, the respondent may not contact any child of the applicant's family, unless contact is permitted under any order or written agreement.

Despite the fact that there is no explicit reference to it either in the case law or relevant reports, the current state of domestic law on contact in such cases would appear, in the main, to comply with the requirements of Article 8. The practice direction in particular allows for a detailed consideration of exactly the kind of issues that would be relevant to the proportionality exercise and a separate consideration of the child's interests. Separate representation or at the very least, separate consideration of the child's interests must, however, be ensured.

20.5 Conclusion

It is clear from the analysis conducted above that some elements of the current legal response to this issue comply with the requirements of the HRA. However, the question remains whether this is a result of accident rather than design; the most problematic feature identified is the general failure to employ *any* human rights analysis as a matter of course in such cases. Should this occur, it is clear that an application of the principles established by the ECtHR under Article 3 would easily enable the refusal of direct contact in the large majority of cases where the children involved have been sufficiently adversely affected by the violence they have experienced. Where Article 3 is not of relevance, the balancing exercise required under Article 8 may, as Dame Elizabeth Butler Sloss argued in *Re L*, be employed to justify the refusal of contact on the basis that the risks to the child's welfare, being of crucial importance, outweigh any competing rights of the abusive parent. Importantly, the process under Article 8 also allows for the consideration of the risks to the welfare of the carer of the child who is also a victim of the violence. The key point to emerge from the analysis conducted in this chapter, however, is that neither Article 3 nor 8 precludes the employment of a rebuttable presumption against contact in cases involving domestic violence. The crucial difference that employing a human rights analysis under Article 8 makes from the domestic method is that it allows for a reframing of the concept of child welfare in a way which permits the equal consideration of the rights and interests of all involved. More crucially, it enables a much more effective challenge to the view that contact is always in the best interest of the child and rarely to be denied. Employing a human rights analysis is thus, certainly in this context, preferable to the operation of a principle that, in essence, renders redundant any consideration of the competing interests involved and prevents the introduction of legal presumptions that may serve the very aim for which it professes to strive.

21

Reframing the Practice of 'Son Preference' Through the Millennium Development Goals

Michelle Ratpan[1]

'Girl's rights are inferior to human rights in general and to children's rights in particular.'

Ladan Askari[2]

21.1 Introduction

UNICEF has estimated that in India, more than one million female babies die each year from malnutrition and abuse who would have lived had they been boys.[3] These deaths are largely due to the widespread belief that there is a greater social, cultural, and economic utility to having sons over daughters. In academic literature, the view that sons are more valuable than daughters has been referred to as the social phenomenon of 'son preference'.[4]

This chapter describes the preference of sons over daughters in northern India. This preference results in the deliberate neglect of girls causing their eventual death from disease and/or malnutrition. The justifications for this practice are largely based on community and religious values that support discriminatory attitudes and behaviour. To date, various local, national, and international remedies have been suggested to combat this problem. Despite the implementation of local programmes, passing of national laws, and ratification of international treaties, empirically, the ratio of girl children to boys in northern India continues to decline. The biologically normal sex ratio in a population is approximately 105 boys per 100 girls at birth, which declines to achieve gender balance at around age 20.[5] The most

[1] BCL/LLB (McGill University, 2005), LLM (Georgetown University Law Center/Graduate Institute Geneva, 2010). The author wrote this chapter during her graduate studies in Global Health Law and is currently counsel for the Department of Justice (Canada). The views expressed herein are solely the author's and do not, in any way, represent the views of the Attorney General of Canada, Department of Justice, or of any of their officials.

[2] Ladan Askari, *Girl's Rights Under International Law: An Argument for Establishing Gender Equality as a Jus Cogens*, California Review of Law and Women's Studies 3 1998–1999, at 12 [Askari].

[3] Lara M. Gardner, *A Dubious Designation: how one simple label legitimizes human rights abuse*, International Legal Perspectives 16 2004, at 19 [Gardner].

[4] Shelley Clark, *Son Preference and Sex Composition of Children: Evidence from India*, Demography, Volume 37-Number 1, February 2000: 95–108 at 95.

[5] Douglas Almond et al., *Son Preference and the Role of Culture: Evidence from Asian Immigrants to Canada*, <http://www.econ.ubc.ca/kevinmil/almond-edlund-milligan-SIChildren.pdf>, at 3 [Almond].

recent census taken in India in 2001 revealed that there were 933 females for every 1000 males.[6] As such, the social and legal remedies in place are necessary but not sufficient to bring about change.

This chapter suggests that it is time for a reframing of the issue of 'son preference'. The focus in both national and international legal discourse needs to move towards an agreement on what constitutes the universal children's right to equal treatment and equal access to available health services. This chapter examines how India may reduce the practice of 'son preference' through a commitment to achieving the Millennium Development Goals, particularly goals one to four. In doing so, the Indian Government may successfully take the focus away from attempting to change a negative social practice, towards achieving a positive social outcome.

21.2 The practice of 'son preference' in India

While the practice of 'son preference' exists throughout India, the problem appears to be more serious in the wealthier northern region. For instance, in the northern state of Haryana there are 820 girls per 1000 boys[7] and in Punjab, there are 793 females for every 1000 males.[8] On the whole, 80 per cent of districts in India recorded a rise in child sex ratios between 1991 and 2001.[9] In the overall Indian population, there are 36 million fewer women than men, making it among the countries with the worst male to female ratios in the world.[10] According to the Government of India's first periodic report to the UN Committee on the rights of the Child, 2001:

> Every year, 12 million girls are born—three million of whom do not survive to see their 15th birthday. About one third of these deaths occur in the first year of life and it is estimated that every sixth female death is directly due to gender discrimination.[11]

The Global Gender Gap Report 2007, which is an international survey published by the World Economic Forum, ranks India 126 out of 128 countries on its 'health and survival' index. In part, the 'health and survival' index aims to capture the practice of 'missing women', prevalent in many countries with strong son preference. The Report states that India's sex ratio at birth fell to 0.89 girls for every boy, causing its score to decrease.[12]

The preference of sons over daughters in India is a serious phenomenon that requires both national and international attention. The first documentation of

[6] India, <www.searo.who.int/LinkFiles/Improving_maternal_newborn_and_child_health_india.pdf>, at 2.

[7] Nisha Sinha and Joanne Yoong, *Long-Term Financial Incentives and Investment in Daughters, Evidence from Conditional Cash Transfers in North India*, The World Bank, Poverty Reduction and Economic Management Network Gender and Development Group, March 2009, <http://www-wds.worldbank.org/external/default/WDSContentServer/IW3P/IB/2009/03/09/000158349_20090309091453/Rendered/PDF/WPS4860.pdf>, at 4 [Sinha and Yoong].

[8] Niraja Gopal Jayal, *Left Behind? Women, Politics and Development in India*, 14 Brown Journal of World Affairs 91, 2008 at 95 [Jayal].

[9] Almond, *supra* note 5, at 3.

[10] Kristi Lemoine and John Tanagho, *Gender Discrimination Fuels Sex Selective Abortion: The Impact of the Indian Supreme Court on the Implementation of and Enforcement of the PNDT Act* 15 University of Miami International and Comparative Law Review 203 2007–2008, at 217 [Lemoine and Tanagho].

[11] Infochange Agenda, Status of children on India: <http://infochangeindia.org/agenda/child-rights-in-india/status-of-children-in-india.html>.

[12] Jayal, *supra* note 8, at 3 and 5.

son preference was by British officials in the form of female infanticide in the late eighteenth century.[13] Since then there have been a number of attempts to outlaw the practice of female infanticide and more recently, female feticide. 'Female infanticide' is the killing of a young child because of the child's gender. This killing can take on a variety of forms including strangulation, poisoning, starvation, and drowning.[14] In many cases girls are not killed after their birth. Instead, they die during the first few years of life.[15] Some authors have used the term 'female infanticide' to include both the outright killing of a child and the purposeful neglect of a child that causes the child's death.[16] Others use the term 'extended infanticide'[17] to refer to a more passive process intended to deprive girls of fair access to nutrition and health services leading to reduced chances of survival.[18] In this chapter the term 'extended female infanticide' will be used in reference to the process whereby a family member or community neglects the health needs of a daughter, ultimately leading to her death. The term 'son preference' will be used in reference to the social and cultural factors that cause 'extended female infanticide'.

The neglect of girls in India manifests itself in a number of ways; girls may be breast fed for shorter periods of time than boys,[19] they often suffer from discriminatory food distribution[20] and are thus the last family member to eat,[21] they may not receive vaccinations necessary to combat preventable diseases,[22] and they may not be taken to the hospital when they are ill thereby lacking adequate or equitable access to health care services.[23] Girls may also suffer discrimination in terms of opportunities for education.

While the practice of extended female infanticide exists throughout northern India, it is unlikely to be reported due to the fact that neglect through malnutrition and lack of access to health care services is far more difficult to detect than the outright murder of a child.[24]

[13] Lemoine and Tanagho, *supra* note 10, at 207.

[14] Kirsten M. Backstrom, *The International Human Rights of the Child: Do they Protect the Female Child?* George Washington Journal of Internationa Law and Economics 541 1996–1997, at 544 [Backstrom].

[15] Ibid., at 544.

[16] Lemoine and Tanagho, *supra* note 10, at 207, cite other authors who refer to 'female infanticide'.

[17] Ibid., at 208. Note that the authors refer to the practice of deliberately neglecting a child as 'extended infanticide'. I have adopted this term but added the word 'female' to highlight that this practice predominantly affects girl children.

[18] Christophe Z Guilmoto, *Sex Ratio Imbalance in Asia: Trends, consequences and policy responses* <http://www.unfpa.org/gender/docs/studies/summaries/regional_analysis.pdf>.

Jonathan Todres, *Women's Rights and Children's Rights: A Partnership with Benefits for Both*, 10 Cardozo Women's Law Journal 603, 2003–2004, at 607 [Todres].

[19] Ibid.

[20] Askari, *supra* note 2, at 15.

[21] Todres, *supra* note 18, at 607.

[22] Fred Arnold et al, *Son Preference, the Family Building Process and Child Mortality in India*, Population Studies 52 1998, at 301–15. Authors found that in 'India as a whole, boys have a slight, but consistent, advantage over girls in immunization coverage for each of six major vaccine-preventable childhood diseases' at 307 [Arnold].

[23] Todres, *supra* note 18, at 607. See also, Cynthia Price Cohen, *The United Nations Convention on the Rights of the Child: A feminist Landmark*, 3 William and Mary Journal of Women and the Law 29 1997, at 41.

[24] Lemoine and Tanagho, *supra* note 10, at 208.

21.3 Causes for extended female infanticide

There are numerous causes for extended female infanticide in northern India. Many authors cite the predominant cause as traditional or cultural practices within northern Indian society.[25] It is important to recognize that since these traditional practices are based on a patriarchal social structure, they are generally used against the most vulnerable segment of society: girls and women. In general, the prevalence of the practice of extended female infanticide is supported by the fact that much of northern Indian society places little to no value on girls.[26]

In India, approximately 83 per cent of the population is Hindu.[27] In the Hindu religion there is a strong preference for sons. According to the Hindu religion, sons are required to cremate the deceased parents because only sons, or in their absence grandsons or other men in the family, can light the funeral pyre. It is said that sons help in the salvation of the souls of the dead parents by performing *pinddaan*, offering food and clothing to Brahmins, during certain times of the year.[28] In contrast, daughters are neither permitted by religion nor considered competent under Hindu tradition to perform this service.

In India, sons have greater economic utility in the family. Men have higher wage earning capacity, particularly in agrarian communities,[29] and are able to provide security in the case of illness of family members.[30] Sons also carry on the family name, receive the family inheritance, and are responsible for supporting their parents.[31] In addition, families with a greater number of sons receive the financial benefit from dowry payments. In contrast, there is little economic utility in daughters who are considered unable to perform laborious tasks and, after marriage, join their husband's family and often have little contact with their birth parents.[32]

Perhaps the greatest and most oft-cited reason for son preference in India is the existence of the dowry system. In India it is said that raising a daughter is like watering someone else's field.[33] When a daughter is of marrying age, her family is generally required to provide her husband's family with a dowry. The dowry is a payment from the bride's family to the groom's family in money or property. Although dowries were outlawed in India in 1961,[34] this social custom still remains.[35] The average cost of dowry payments is US $35,000. The average citizen in India earns US $3,500 a year.[36] When a bride's family is unable to pay the dowry demanded by the groom's family, the new wife will often be verbally or physically abused and even murdered. It is estimated that over 13,000 brides are killed every year in India over dowry disputes.[37] As such, families who are unable to afford dowry payments or do not wish to provide a dowry, may neglect or mistreat their daughters causing extended female infanticide.[38]

[25] Gardner, *supra* note 3, at 16. [26] Ibid., at 18.

[27] Indian Child, <http://www.indianchild.com/population_of_india.htm>.

[28] Arnold, *supra* note 22, at 301. [29] Lemoine and Tanagho, *supra* note 10, at 218.

[30] Arnold, *supra* note 22, at 301. [31] Lemoine and Tanagho, *supra* note 10, at 218.

[32] Arnold, *supra* note 22, at 301.

[33] Alison Wood Manhoff, *Banned and Enforced, The Immediate Answer to a Problem Without an Immediate Solution—How India Can Prevent Another Generation of Missing Girls*, 38 Vanderbilt Journal of Transnational Law 889 2005, at 899 [Manhoff].

[34] Manhoff, *supra* note 33, at 901. The author notes that dowries were outlawed by the Dowry Prohibition Act of 1961. The ineffectiveness of the Act is shown by the fact that during the first 24 years of its existence less than one per cent of dowry related deaths were prosecuted under the law in Delhi.

[35] Ibid., at 891. [36] Gardner, *supra* note 3, at 19. [37] Manhoff, *supra* note 33, at 901.

[38] Ibid., at 900.

Discrimination against girls is so ingrained in the religious and social construct of much of northern India that it may be necessary to examine external mechanisms to combat this practice. The following section explores the various local, national, and international methods suggested to eradicate the practice of extended female infanticide.

21.4 Scholarly perspectives on eradication of extended female infanticide

Scholars rely on a combination of micro and macro level changes. On a micro level, it is posited that greater education, media attention concerning the social and cultural value of girls, and state subsidies are required to foster equality. At the macro level it is believed that national laws enacted to protect girls will assist in the provision of equitable access to nutrition, education, and health services. Moreover, India's continued commitment to international treaties that protect the equality rights of girls will support the decline in the sex ratio between children.

21.4.1 Micro level changes

It has been suggested that empowering the Hindu-Indian woman through education regarding her human rights and the rights of her child is critical to foster change in the traditional devaluation of girls.[39] This empowerment can be achieved through local education programmes or through media coverage of census results that show sex discrimination as a serious and combatable phenomenon in India.[40] While the individual empowerment model is an important step towards the equalization of treatment between genders, it is not sufficient to combat the religious and social constructs inherent in northern Indian society that perceive girls as economic liabilities and boys as economic assets.

To address the need for financial stability in the northern Indian family, several states have supported governmental and non-governmental programmes that provide preferential policies towards families upon the birth of a daughter. An example of such a programme, the *ApniBetiAPnaDhan* (Our Daughter, Our Wealth), was set up in the northern Indian state of Haryana in 1994. To be eligible, a family must be below the poverty line or from a disadvantaged caste background and their daughter must be the first, second, or third child in the family.[41] Eligible parents who give birth to daughters are given an immediate financial grant, coupled with a long-term savings bond redeemable by an unmarried daughter at the age of 18.[42]A study examining the 10-year period after the implementation of this programme shows positive effects on the sex ratio of the total living children in Haryana. The study shows that

[39] V.G. Julie Rajan, An Assessment of Human Rights Violations Against Women in Modern-Day India as a Result of Son Preference, <http://www.sawnet.org/articles/Son_preference.html>, at 9 [Rajan].

[40] United Nations Population Fund, 4th Asia Pacific Conference on Reproductive and Sexual Health and Rights October 29–31, 2007, Hyderabad India, *Sex-Ratio Imbalance in Asia: Trends, consequences and policy response, Executive Summary, Regional Analysis*, <http://www.unfpa.org/gender/docs/studies/summaries/reg_exe_summary.pdf>, at 11 [UNPF].

[41] Sinha and Yoong, *supra* note 7, at 4. [42] Ibid., at 2.

families made greater post-natal health investments in girls after the programme was implemented than before.

While the success of this programme is a promising step in the right direction, there are some serious drawbacks with providing financial incentives to families to encourage adequate health care and nutrition for their daughters. At its base, the notion of endowing financial utility to girls in order to counteract their perceived lack of social utility is morally reprehensible. Such government programmes simply reinforce the notion that girls are not valuable and that a small remittance will be sufficient to change socially ingrained discrimination against girls. Furthermore, while studies have shown that these programmes may garner some success, statistically, discrimination towards girls in northern India is more likely to occur among urban, educated, and well-to-do families, rather than their rural, more impoverished counterparts.[43] Therefore, the families who are eligible for remittances through these state supported programmes are not the families most likely to engage in extended female infanticide.

21.4.2 Macro level changes

Many authors have noted that state regulation through legislation banning infanticide and feticide (through sex selective abortion) may be effective in slowing the rate of death of the girl child. It is true that since the Infanticide Act of 1870, the Government of India has taken a number of steps to combat the existence of son preference and female infanticide in India. The use of ultrasounds and other sex selection technologies were banned throughout India in 1994 through the Prenatal Diagnostic Techniques (Regulation and Prevention of Misuse) Act ('PDTA'). The PDTA banned the use of prenatal technology to determine a fetus' sex, prohibited the communication of sex information to the patient, and allowed the devices to be used only in registered genetic testing clinics.[44] While the PDTA is laudable in theory, in practice, between the enactment of the PDTA in 1994 and 2000 there were no convictions of individuals who violated the ban.[45] It appears that the ban has only served to push the practice of sex selection underground as well as allow wealthy people to pay private clinics to inform them of the sex of their unborn child.[46] It is true that legislation against infanticide and banning sex determination ultrasounds is an important step in ensuring gender parity, but it is doubtful that any such ban will have a deterrent effect on the practice of extended female infanticide,[47] a practice that is both difficult to detect and unlikely to be reported.

At the international level, there are various instruments that support the equal treatment of children and their equal access to available health care services. The Universal Declaration of Human Rights (1948), the subsequent International Covenant on Civil and Political Rights (ICCPR), and the International Covenant on Social, Economic and Cultural Rights (ICSEC) each set out and reiterate the principle of non-discrimination and equal treatment of the sexes as a fundamental right. The Universal Declaration of Human Rights states that everyone is entitled to all the rights and freedoms of the Declaration without distinction based on sex.[48]

[43] UNPF, *supra* note 40, at 4.

[44] Manhoff, *supra* note 33, at 894. [45] Ibid., at 895. [46] Ibid., at 905.

[47] Ibid., at 891.

[48] Universal Declaration of Human Rights, <http://www.un.org/en/documents/udhr/.> Article 2. See also, Cohen, *supra* note 23, at 30.

The ICSEC declares that the parties to the covenant undertake to guarantee that the rights enunciated in it will be exercised without discrimination based on sex.[49] The ICCPR goes further in Article 24 by speaking to the responsibility of the family, society, and the state to foster the equal treatment of children:

> Every child shall have, without any discrimination as to race, colour, sex, language, national or social origin, property or birth, the right to such measures of protection as are required by his status as a minor, on the part of his family, society and the State.

With regard to the right to health, Article 12 of the ICESC recognizes the 'right of everyone to the enjoyment of the highest attainable standard of physical and mental health'. With regard to the child's right to health, Article 12.2(a) goes on to state that the steps taken by State Parties to achieve the realization of this right shall include those necessary for:

> The provision for the reduction of the stillbirth-rate and of infant mortality and for the healthy development of the child.[50]

While none of the preceding Conventions devotes itself entirely to the rights of the child or, more specifically, the particular needs of the girl child, they set the foundation for the importance of non-discrimination based on sex and the right to health under international law. The landscape of children's rights changed dramatically in 1989 with the completion of the United Nations Convention on the Rights of the Child (UNCRC). The UNCRC came into force on 2 September 1990 and reached near universal ratification by 1996.[51] It is the most widely ratified human rights convention in the world and is the first international human rights convention to use gender-neutral language.[52] The UNCRC recognizes the child as having individual rights, separate and distinct from his or her parents' rights. The child is no longer considered to be the property of the family[53] and in situations of mistreatment, abuse, or neglect the state is required to intervene on behalf of the child.[54] Pursuant to Article 2(1), the UNCRC recognizes the child's right to freedom from 'discrimination "of any kind" irrespective of the child's race, color, sex, language . . . birth or other status'. The UNCRC also recognizes the right of the child against discrimination in the family environment. Article 2(2) of the UNCRC states:

> States Parties shall take all appropriate measures to ensure that the child is protected against all forms of discrimination or punishment on the basis of the status, activities, expressed opinions or beliefs of the child's parents, legal guardians or family members.

The UNCRC provides a wide variety of protections with regard to the health of the child. In particular, Article 24(1) states that:

> States Parties recognize the right of the child to the enjoyment of the highest attainable standard of health and to facilities for the treatment of illness and rehabilitation of health. States Parties shall strive to ensure that no child is deprived of his or her right of access to such health care services.

[49] International Covenant on Economic, Social and Cultural Rights, <http://www2.ohchr.org/english/law/cescr.htm> Article 2(2).

[50] Ibid.,at Article 2(2)(a).

[51] Cohen, *supra* note 23, at 29.

[52] Todres, *supra* note 18, at 613.

[53] Backstrom, *supra* note 14, at 565.

[54] Ibid., at 565. See also, United Nations Convention on the Rights of the Child, <http://www2.ohchr.org/english/law/crc.htm>, at Article 19 [UNCRC].

The UNCRC supports the child's right to the 'enjoyment of the highest attainable standard of health' and provides that 'States Parties shall take all effective and appropriate measures with a view to abolishing traditional practices prejudicial to the health of children'.[55] While this provision was intended to refer primarily to the practice of female genital mutilation,[56] it is clear that it may apply equally to the practice of extended female infanticide. Read together, Articles 2(1), 2(2), and 24(1) of the UNCRC establish an obligation on States Parties to take appropriate measures to ensure that a child is protected against discriminatory practices based on sex, engaged in by family members, which result in the inadequate provision of health care services to the child. In effect, the UNCRC can be read to provide a full protection against the practice of extended female infanticide.

Despite the breadth of the UNCRC and the aforementioned conventions, India's ratification and accession to many international treaties and conventions has not eliminated the practice of extended female infanticide. While treaty ratification is an important step towards the protection of the equality rights of girls and their access to adequate nutrition and health services, the ratification of treaties is not sufficient to guarantee such rights.[57] In order to combat the problem of non-implementation, it has been thoughtfully suggested that a bold change in the framing of gender equality in international law is required. Ladan Askari suggests that in order to protect the girl child's human rights, gender equality must rise to the level of a *jus cogens* norm,[58] that 'by elevating gender equality to the level of a peremptory norm, the flaw of treaty law which prevents girls' human rights from being fully protected, will be alleviated'.[59] Treaty ratification will no longer be required as a pre-requisite to prohibit gender discrimination. Under this rationale, the harmful practice of son preference and discriminatory food distribution will constitute violations of the peremptory norm against gender discrimination and will be punishable as such.[60]

In line with this enlightened notion of reframing the issue of gender equality to the level of a *jus cogens* norm, I suggest that it is time to look at the practice of son preference through the lens of achieving the targets set out in the Millennium Development Goals. Several of the goals will not be met without the eradication of the practice of extended female infanticide in India. While it remains important to engage in local, national, and international interventions in support of the rights of girls, the Millennium Development Goals may provide the Indian Government with an opportunity to successfully reframe the international focus away from attempting to change a negative social practice, towards achieving a positive social outcome.

21.5 The Millennium Development Goals and the health of the girl child

In September 2000, the world leaders of 189 countries gathered together at the Millennium Summit to discuss the world's most pressing international development needs. As a result of the Millennium Summit, the nations in attendance unanimously

[55] UNCRC, *supra* note 54, at Article 24(3).
[56] Cohen, *supra* note 23, at 52.
[57] Askari, *supra* note 2, at 29.
[58] Ibid., at 3.
[59] Ibid., at 4.
[60] Ibid., at 15.

adopted the United Nations Millennium Declaration (UNMD).[61] This Declaration was translated into a roadmap setting out eight specific goals, referred to as the Millennium Development Goals (MDGs), to be reached by 2015. The UNMD and the subsequent goals are non-binding on States Parties. While some have criticized non-binding declarations or 'soft law' as 'not law at all', a preferable view is to see such declarations as the crystallization of certain commitments which have already been established in treaty law or which may develop into binding law at a later date.[62] In fact, the MDGs build on agreements made at United Nations conferences in the 1990s and represent a compact between countries of the developing world and those of the developed world to work together to reduce poverty and hunger, decrease ill-health, gender inequality, lack of education, access to clean water, and environmental degradation.[63] As such, the MDGs incorporate many of the goals regarding non-discrimination and the right to equal access to health services for children outlined in the ICCPR, CEDAW, ICESC, and UNCRC respectively. The optimism with regard to the UNMD as opposed to other non-binding and even binding international instruments is that, for the first time, there is a near unanimous nation-state commitment to meeting goals whose foundation is to further a universal children's right to health.

While achievement of all of the MDGs is important to the well-being of children, there are several goals that cannot be achieved unless there is a decline and eventual eradication of the neglect and mistreatment of girls in India. These goals and relevant targets are examined in the next four sections. By reframing the issue of son preference through the lens of the MDGs the right of the girl child to equal treatment and equal access to available health services becomes paramount, and debates over culture, religious beliefs, and economic utility become secondary.

21.5.1 Eradicate extreme poverty and hunger

The first goal of the MDGs is to eradicate extreme poverty and hunger with a target of decreasing by one half, between 1990 and 2015, the proportion of people who suffer from hunger around the world. Two indicators for monitoring progress towards this goal include an assessment of the prevalence of underweight children under the age of five years and the proportion of the population living below the minimum level of dietary energy consumption.

The most recent statistical information shows that in the developing world, one out of every four children under the age of five years is underweight.[64] Indian children make up one-third of the world's malnourished children.[65] The prevalence of child undernutrition in India is among the highest in the world, nearly double that

[61] To date 192 UN member states and 23 international organizations have agreed to achieve the MDGs by 2015, <http://en.wikipedia.org/wiki/Millennium_Development_Goals>.

[62] Patricia Birnie and Alan Boyle, *International Law and the Environment*, Oxford University Press, 2002, at 25.

[63] MDG Monitor, Tracking the Millennium Development Goals, <http://www.mdgmonitor.org/aboutMDG.cfm>.

[64] The World Bank—An Online Atlas of the Millennium Development Goals, <http://devdata.worldbank.org/atlas-mdg> [WB Devdata].

[65] UNICEF, India, Overview—Millennium Development Goals, <http://www.unicef.org/india/overview_3696.htm>.

of Sub-Saharan Africa.[66] As of 2009, in India, the percentage of children under the age of five who were malnourished was 46 per cent of the total population.[67] Child malnutrition is estimated to play a role in about 50 per cent of all child deaths. Malnutrition plays a role in 57 per cent of child deaths from malaria, 61 per cent of deaths from diarrhoea, 52 per cent of deaths from pneumonia, and 45 per cent of deaths from measles.[68] As of a 2005 statistic, underweight prevalence was found to be higher among girls (48.9 per cent) than boys (45.5 per cent) in India.[69] With regard to poverty, as of 2005, nearly half of the Indian population was living on less than $1.25 a day.[70]

At the national level India has implemented a programme in response to child malnutrition called the Integrated Child Development Services Programme (ICDS). The programme was established in 1975 as part of the National Policy for Children. The programme offers a wide range of health, nutrition and education services to children, adolescent girls, and women. However, it has been suggested that a key problem with this programme is the fact that it is focused on food supplementation to the detriment of not providing enough attention to improving childcare behaviour.[71]

In a recent academic paper, Manisha Chakrabarty shows the importance of childcare behaviour and how a lack of adequate nutrition and health services negatively affects the gender distribution in a community. Chakrabarty examined the existence of gender bias by using the World Bank's Living Standard Measurement Study (LSMS) survey data designed to monitor poverty in rural areas of two states of northern India; Bihar and Uttar Pradesh (UP) for 1997–1998.[72] UP has the largest population of all of the Indian states and the highest number of people living below the poverty line. Bihar has the lowest per-capita income in India, with an estimated 55 per cent of people living below the poverty line.[73] Chakrabarty found that of the total number of households with one child, the proportion of girl children to boy children was 86 to 331. Of the total number of households with two or more children, the ratio of first surviving girl child to boy child was 428 to 1174. Chakrabarty concludes that 'If every birth has more or less an equal probability of being a boy then this pattern can indirectly express a hard fact of less concern and care for the girl child, leading to few families left with [a first] survived child as a girl'.[74] Based on Chakrabarty's study we can conclude that while government programmes that supply food and clean water for children are important in decreasing levels of malnutrition, the distribution of these services between girls and boys is also extremely important in eliminating overall levels of malnutrition and disease.

While malnutrition affects both girls and boys in India, the statistics show that girls are more likely to die from malnourishment. It appears that many families may be using the limited available food and health resources preferentially for their sons.

66 Michele Gragnolati et al, *India's Undernourished Children A Call for Reform and Action*, August 2005, <http://siteresources.worldbank.org/SOUTHASIAEXT/Resources/223546-1147272668285/IndiaUndernourishedChildrenFinal.pdf> [Gragnolati].

67 WB Devdata, *supra* note 64. See also, <http://www.humanrights.asia/news/ahrc-news/AHRC-STM-216-2009>.

68 Gragnolati, *supra* note 66, at xvi.

69 Ibid., at xvi.

70 WB Devdata, *supra* note 64.

71 The Integrated Child Development Services Program (ICDS)—Are Results Meeting Expectations? <http://siteresources.worldbank.org/SOUTHASIAEXT/Resources/223546-1147272668285/undernourished_chapter_2.pdf>, at 30.

72 Manisha Chakrabarty, *Son Preference And Its Determinants In Rural India—An Analysis Based on A Composite Measure of Gender Bias*, <http://www.keele.ac.uk/depts/ec/web/wpapers/kerp0502.pdf>, February 2005, at 2 [Chakrabarty].

73 Ibid., at 2.

74 Ibid., at 3–4.

This supports the theory that extended female infanticide remains a hindrance to achieving the first goal of the MDGs. Absent the elimination of this practice in India as a whole, achieving the targets set out under the first goal will be impossible. In order to meet this goal, local and state level interventions, which provide health services and nutrition counselling, must be directed towards girls. Similarly, education programmes at the local level must be oriented towards changing child caretaking behaviour within households.[75]

21.5.2 Universal primary education

The second goal seeks the achievement of universal primary education by 2015 for all children. The relevant targets for this goal are enrolment in primary education, completion of primary education, and literacy of 15–24 year olds, female and male.

Today, more than 100 million children of primary school age remain out of school, most of them in South Asia and Sub-Saharan Africa and the majority of them are girls.[76] In India, as of 2007, the ratio of female to male children who were enrolled in primary school was 95.7 girls for every 100 boys. The completion rate for female children of primary school was 83.1 per cent.[77] While these national disparities do not appear alarming, the statistics are misleading. The national averages mask larger disparities at the state level. For instance, gender disparity in enrolment in primary schools is the greatest in the northern states of Bihar, Uttar Pradesh, and Rajasthan, where the gross primary enrolment rate for girls is about two-thirds or less than that for boys. In some other northern Indian states, such as Punjab, Haryana, Sikkim, and Kerala, data sources suggest that there is near parity enrolment rates between girls and boys in primary school. However, this perceived equality masks the fact that with the growing private sector education, parents tend to enrol their sons in private schools while enrolling their daughters in government schools. The theory that fewer girls are completing primary and secondary school than boys is borne out by the literacy rates in India. As of 2007, the literacy rate for children over the age of 15 was 54.5 per cent of females and 76.9 per cent of males.[78]

The lower enrolment rates for girls in primary school education and the lack of encouragement to continue with their education or to learn to read are symptoms of the larger social devaluation of girls and women in India. India will not meet the goals and targets related to primary education if the practice of extended female infanticide continues. In fact, the continuation of this practice will mean that in the future, there will be even fewer girls enrolling in primary school education because the ratio of girls to boys in the general population will decline. This will lead to an even greater disparity in primary school completion and literacy rates for young girls. If young girls are not enrolling in and completing primary school education they will not have the tools to empower themselves and make use of available programmes and information to put an end to the cycle of discrimination against future generations of girls in India.

[75] Gragnolati, *supra* note 66, at xvii. [76] WB Devdata, *supra* note 64.

[77] Millennium Development Goals—India, <http://ddp-ext.worldbank.org/ext/ddpreports/ViewSharedReport?&CF=&REPORT_ID=1336&REQUEST_TYPE=VIEWADVANCED> [MDG WB Report].

[78] Ibid.

21.5.3 Promoting gender equality in women

The third MDG seeks to eliminate gender disparity in primary and secondary education by 2005 and at all levels by 2015. As a target to achieve this goal, assessment of the ratios of girls to boys in primary, secondary, and tertiary education is necessary.

The ratio of female to male children in India enrolled in secondary school in 2007 was 83.3 of female children per 100 male children.[79] The importance of enrolment of girls in primary and secondary education for their health and for the achievement of all of the MDGs cannot be overstated. According to statistics from the National Family Household Survey in 2007,[80] girls who did not receive any education had their first child at the average age of 18.7 years old. Their child had an under-five mortality rate of 94.7 out of 1000 and the percentage of their children that were malnourished was 52 per cent. This can be contrasted with girls that received education past the age of 12 years old. The average age of motherhood for this group was 24.8 years old, the under-five mortality rate for their children was 29.7 out of 1000 and the percentage of their children that were malnourished was 17.9 per cent.

The statistics show a large disparity between the enrolment rates for girls and boys in secondary education. This gender disparity has far-reaching effects on other health-related goals. It is evident that the goals of eradication of poverty and hunger and child mortality will not be achieved if the practice of extended female infanticide persists. While there are already several local and national programmes in place to encourage primary and secondary school education for girls,[81] there is an urgent need for an increased awareness of the long-term health consequences for all children if girls are not encouraged to complete their education.

21.5.4 Reduce child mortality

The fourth goal of the MDGs is to reduce by two-thirds between 1990 and 2015 the under-five mortality rate.[82] Three indicators for monitoring progress are the under-five mortality rate, the under-one infant mortality rate, and the proportion of one-year-old children immunized against measles.

Every year over 10 million children in developing countries die before the age of five years.[83] With regard to the first indicator for monitoring progress, in Asia as a whole, more young girls die than young boys. In every other region, the rates are approximately equal and at times, boys die at a higher rate. In 2009, the under-five mortality rate in India was 57 children per 1000.[84] In the northern Indian states of Haryana, girls are two times more likely than boys to die between the ages of one and four.[85] On the whole, girls from India aged one to five are 50 per cent more likely to die than boys who are the same age.[86]

[79] Ibid. [80] Wilson Center on Demand, <http://www.wilsoncenter.org/ondemand>.

[81] For instance the Sarva Shiksha Abhiyan programme, <http://en.wikipedia.org/wiki/Sarva_Shiksha_Abhiyan>.

[82] MDG Monitor—Tracking the Millennium Development Goals, <http://www.mdgmonitor.org/browse_goal.cfm>.

[83] Global Monitoring Report 2007, <http://www.who.int/whr/2003/chapter1/en/index2.html>.

[84] WB Devdata, *supra* note 64. [85] Sinha and Yoong, *supra* note 7.

[86] Nicholas D. Kristof and Sheryl Wudunn, *Half the Sky: Turning Oppression Into Opportunty for Women Worldwide,* Alfred A. Knopf, New York, 2009 [Kristof and Wudunn].

The second indicator shows that as of 2008, the under-one mortality rate was 54 children per 1000.[87] While both girls and boy children are affected by these mortality rates, malnutrition, lack of adequate health care, and substandard provision of hygiene are more common among young girls than boys. A study in West Bengal finds that it is three times more likely that malnourished girls (between the ages of seven to eight months) will be kept at home rather than given proper medical care in comparison to boys of the same age.[88]

With regard to levels of immunization, the percentage of children aged 12 to 23 months who were immunized in India against measles as of 2008 was 67 per cent, one of the lowest rates of all countries.[89] In areas where son preference is common, the lower level of resources devoted to female children means that they are less likely to be vaccinated.[90] A study of two states of northern India, Bihar and Uttar Pradesh (UP), for 1997–1998[91] substantiates this finding showing a gender bias in the average proportion of immunized children between the ages of zero to five years old was 0.174 girls in proportion to 0.207 boys.[92]

In order to meet the fourth goal and the target of reducing the under-five and under-one mortality rates, all Indian girls and babies must be guaranteed equal access to nutrition and life-sustaining resources.[93] It is evident that the practice of extended female infanticide seriously hinders the potential for progress under this goal. Progress could be made with a focus on encouraging equitable access to the distribution of food, vaccinations, and other health-related resources between children. There is also a need for local and national education programmes to improve domestic childcare and feeding practices and micronutrient supplementation for girls.[94]

21.6 Conclusion

The social phenomenon of 'son preference' is prevalent in much of northern India and often results in extended female infanticide. As a solution to this practice, this chapter has suggested the possibility of reframing 'son preference' through the lens of the Millennium Development Goals, thereby removing the focus from religious or cultural justifications and focusing on the international goal of protecting and promoting the health of all children. This reframing process is in no way intended to exclude local, national, and international measures whose purpose is to combat sex-based discrimination and to uphold the rights of the girl child. On the contrary, it is intended to be complementary by bringing the issue of the right to health into the forefront of the discussion of extended female infanticide.

The importance of discussing the practice of extended female infanticide at this moment in our global history cannot be overemphasized. This practice affects young girls exclusively and is but one instance of a larger phenomenon of the disappearance of young girls and women throughout the world. In their poignant book entitled *Half the Sky*, Nicholas D. Kristof and Sheryl Wudunn write:

[87] MDG WB Report, *supra* note 77.

[88] Rajan, *supra* note 39.

[89] WB Devdata, *supra* note 64.

[90] Department of Gender and Women's Health, World Health Organization, En-gendering the Millennium Development Goals, <http://www.who.int/gender/mainstreaming/en/MDG.pdf>, at 4.

[91] Chakrabarty, *supra* note 72, at 2.

[92] Ibid., at 5–6.

[93] Rajan, *supra* note 39.

[94] The World Bank, <http://web.worldbank.org>.

> The global statistics on the abuse of girls are numbing. It appears that more girls have been killed in the last fifty years, precisely because they were girls, than men were killed in all the battles of the twentieth century. More girls are killed in this routine 'gendercide' in any one decade than people were slaughtered in all the genocides of the twentieth century.[95]

The global statistics are astounding. While the practice of extended female infanticide is not new, there has never been a better time for change. Globalization has created a serendipitous interconnection that we can no longer escape. As members of the global community we are equipped with the statistics, the information, and the painful details of the neglect and mistreatment of young girls that occurs every day in other parts of the world. The only step that remains is to search for practical mechanisms and solutions to help the victims of this neglect and abuse avoid experiencing unnecessary suffering.

[95] Kristof and Wudunn, *supra* note 86, at xvii.

22

Time to Grow Up: The UN Committee on the Rights of the Child's Jurisprudence of the Right to Development

Noam Peleg[1]

Introduction

Since 1924, the year the League of Nations adopted the Declaration on the Rights of the Child,[1A] the conceptions of 'the child' as a developing human being and the time of 'childhood' as a journey toward adulthood have dominated international children's rights law. The 1989 UN Convention on the Rights of the Child[2] is based upon, and promotes, the very same conceptions. The protection of the child's rights to life, survival, and development in Article 6 probably best reflects these conceptions. It states:

1. States Parties recognize that every child has the inherent right to life.
2. States Parties shall ensure to the maximum extent possible the survival and development of the child.

The right to development is mentioned in five other Articles: Article 18 (parental responsibilities), Article 23 (children with disabilities), Article 27 (adequate standard of living), Article 29 (aims of education), and Article 32 (economic exploitation). These Articles refer to eight dimensions of an individual child's development—physical, mental, moral, social, talents, cultural, spiritual, and personal.

In this chapter I ask how the UN Committee on the Rights of the Child ('the Committee') understands the meaning of the right to development of children.

I begin by briefly presenting two conceptions of childhood—children as 'becoming' and children as 'being'. I argue that, although an apparent paradigm shift in conceptualizing 'childhood' took place during the 1970s and 1980s, moving from the former to the latter concept, there is a doubt whether the Convention and the Committee reflect this shift. Using this presumption, I analyse the Committee's jurisprudence of the right to development of children. I argue that the Committee's interpretation results in the Committee being entrenched within a conception of

[1] University College London, Faculty of Laws. I would like to thank Arif Jamal, Marika Samson, and Zvika Triger for their helpful comments on earlier drafts. Many thanks to my PhD supervisors, Michael Freeman and Colm O'Cinneide, for their support and encouragement. Special thanks to Lana Tatour.

[1A] League of Nations O.J. Spec. Supp. 21, at 43 (1924).

[2] UN Convention on the Rights of the Child 1989.

children as 'becoming' human beings and therefore it is mostly vague, lacks meaningful content, and undermines children's agency.

22.1 Two concepts of childhood

'The child' and the stage of 'childhood' are socially constructed phenomena.[3] As such, they are neither neutral nor natural concepts but rather products of time, place, class, race, gender, and generation.[4] Science, religion, psychology, and law are the dominant social instruments that construct the meaning of this period of human live. According to Ariès' classic study *Centuries of Childhood*,[5] the concept of childhood emerged in Western Europe only in the 17th century, together with the rise of the modern state.[6] This is not to imply that children did not exist prior to that time, but rather that there existed no conception of 'childhood', in the sense of identifying a distinct social group composed of non-adults and injecting distinct meaning to it. In fact, the phrase 'age of maturity' is in itself a socially constructed concept.

Despite many critiques of Ariès's work,[7] it should not be easily dismissed. *Centuries of Childhood* is an important research work for many reasons, and two of them need to be addressed here. Ariès not only saw childhood as a social conception (and, as such, its meaning changes over time), but more importantly he illuminated the difficulties in speaking about one universal, paradigmatic, and timeless 'child'. However, despite these difficulties, many persist in trying.

From the Enlightenment, when Ariès argues that 'childhood' was born, up to and until the late 20th century, the dominant view of childhood characterized children as human 'becomings'.[8] Different theoretical approaches offered different descriptions or explanations to the process of transition from childhood to adulthood. Most, if not all, of these approaches, shared the view that children are incompetent, irrational, dependent, and lacking in agency.[9] Children were primarily described as 'not yet adults',[10] or as human beings on 'a journey toward a destination'.[11] According to

[3] Alan Prout and Allison James, 'A New Paradigm for the Sociology of Childhood? Provenance, Promise and Problems' in (eds.) Allison James and Alan Prout, *Constructing and Reconstructing Childhood* (Routledge, London, 2nd edition, 1997), 10–29; Allison James and Adrian L. James, *Constructing Childhood—Theory, policy and social practice* (Palgrave, London, 2004).

[4] Michael Freeman, 'The Human Rights of Children' in (eds.) George Letsas and Colm O'Cinneide, *Current Legal Problems 2010*, 1, 9–15; Leena Alanen, 'Exploration in Generational Analysis' in (eds.) Alanen et al., *Conceptualizing Child-Adults Relations*, (Routledge, London, 2001), 11–22.

[5] Philippe Ariès, *Centuries of Childhood—A Social History of Family Life* (translated by Robert Baldick, Jonathan Cape, London, 1962).

[6] Nick Lee, *Childhood and Society* (Open University Press, London, 2001), 37.

[7] See, for example, David Archard, *Children Rights and Childhood* (Routledge, London, 2nd edition, 2004), 20–3; Rex and Wendy Stainton Rogers, *Stories of Childhood* (University of Toronto Press, Toronto, 1992); Philip E. Veerman, *The Rights of the Child and the Changing Image of Childhood* (Martinus Nijhoff Publishers, Dordrecht, 1992), 4–10; Richard T. Vann, 'The Youth of Centuries of Childhood' (1982) 21 *History and Theory* 279.

[8] Lee, N. 6 above, 37.

[9] Allison James, 'Agency' in (eds.) Jens Qvortrup et al., *The Palgrave Handbook of Childhood Studies* (Palgrave, London, 2009), 34–45.

[10] Archard, N. 7 above, 39.

[11] Lee, N. 6 above, 8.

this view, the child's destination is the eventual transformation into a 'full' human being, i.e. into an adult.[12]

Writing in 1919, Emile Durkheim set the tone for generations to come:

The essential function of this age, the role and purpose assigned to it be nature, may be summed up in a single world: it is the period of *growth*. That is to say, the period in which the individual, in both the physical and moral sense, does not yet exist, the period in which he is made, develops and is formed... in everything the child is characterized by the very instability of his nature, which is the law of growth.[13]

Since then, '*the law of growth*' has been the predominant conception of childhood studies in general and of childhood sociology in particular. Consequently, developmental psychology and developmental biology became the two main frameworks to understand the time of childhood 'scientifically'. As James, Jenks, and Prout argue, it is 'the principle of certainty by which people within Western culture "know" that children... simply "grow up" '.[14]

Different streams of developmental psychology aspire to identify the various stages of personal development and to explain the meaning of the 'period of growth'. These theories, as any other scientific or semi-scientific theories, presume to offer a universal truth concerning human lives and contribute to inculcate the 'becoming' approach. All the dominant developmental psychology theories of Freud, Erikson, and Piaget espouse the 'becoming' model, and tell a very powerful story about childhood, which makes it 'difficult for us to view childhood any differently'.[15] However, these theories should be viewed as products of their time, their contexts, and their proponents, who are often, as in this case, white, upper-middle class, Western European men. As such, none of these theories should be seen as representing a universal truth about children and childhood.

Developmental biology emerged concurrently with developmental psychology. This approach highlights the 'neutral' biological fact that the child is smaller in size and weight than an adult, and adds a socially constructed meaning to this reality.[16] It takes the chronological age of the person as the primary indicator of the child's stage of development,[17] considering it to be 'an inevitable and invariant process driven by a biologically rooted structure which the child inherits'.[18] Developmental biology surrenders to the temptation to see childhood as a neutral and universal phenomenon,[19] taking children's competences and skills to be 'facts of their ongoing physiological and psychological development despite the cultural context in which this takes place'.[20] Like developmental psychology, developmental biology supports a presumption about the objective neutrality of childhood, ignoring any subjective factors that might influence the time of childhood or the experience of numerous children.

[12] Harry Hendrick, *Children, Childhood and English Society 1880–1990* (Cambridge University Press, Cambridge, 1997), 3–4.

[13] Emile Durkheim, 'Characteristics of Childhood' in (ed.) W.S.F. Pickering, *Essays on Morals and Education* (1919, translated by H.L. Sutcliffe, Routledge, London, 1979), 150 (emphasis in original).

[14] Allison James, Chris Jenks, and Alan Prout, *Theorizing Childhood* (Polity, Cambridge, 1998), 196.

[15] Michall Wyness, *Childhood and Society* (Palgrave, London, 2006), 18.

[16] Archard, N. 7 above, 25–6. [17] Wyness, N. 15 above, 132.

[18] Archard, N. 7 above, 44.

[19] Jo Boyden, 'Childhood and the Policy Makers: A Comparative Perspective on the Globalization of Childhood' in *Constructing and Reconstructing Childhood*, N. 3, above, 190–229, 218.

[20] *Constructing and Reconstructing Childhood*, N. 3 above, 18.

The failure to create a unified understanding of childhood,[21] together with the increasing global awareness of the inadequacy of many children's living conditions,[22] resulted in a paradigm shift in childhood studies during the 1970s and 1980s. Under the new paradigm, childhood is conceptualized as a time with its own importance, rather than only as a path toward adulthood. According to this new view, childhood was no longer conceived as merely a time of 'becoming' and began to be seen as a time of 'being'.

The underlying assumption of this concept is that children are active persons who construct their own lives, the lives of those around them, and of the societies in which they live. As James and Prout claim: 'what is vital is to focus on children not only as protoadults, future beings, but also on children as beings-in-the-present'.[23] The concept of 'being' is 'not based on stability, completion and independence but on its own rights'.[24] It relates to children as they are, and not mainly by comparing them to adults. This approach confers importance to children's experiences as children and to children's point of view on the world, their wishes, opinions, and fears. As Smart, Neale, and Wade argue: 'children no longer had to be seen as empty vessels being passively socialized for adulthood, but could be conceptualized as active and interactive practitioners of social life'.[25]

However, it is arguable whether current studies of childhood have actually followed the assumed shift, or if they are not, in practice, perpetuating the view of children as creatures in a mode of transition.[26] According to Lee, this might be explained because childhood is often still considered to be a journey toward adulthood,[27] and children to be 'unfinished adults'.[28] It seems that the conception of 'becoming' is still embedded in contemporary culture and practice,[29] probably as a result of 'our strange obsession with the physical and developmental stage through which... "childhood" itself is most often conceptualized'.[30] Engaging in these kinds of arguments does not usually result in acknowledging children's agency or children's 'being'.

The confusion between the two concepts is not only an issue for sociologists, psychologists, or anthropologists, but for lawyers also. The law is one of the most powerful social instruments and has an important role in constructing childhood in the domestic and the international arenas. Subsequently, international children's rights law was not created and neither is implemented in a vacuum. It is linked to social attitude, or attitudes, toward children and childhood. International children's rights law has helped to create and shape the conception of childhood during the 20th century and 21st century. The Convention has created a specific image of childhood to be adopted and followed by each of the 193 States Parties.

[21] John R. Morss, *Growing Critical* (Routledge, London, 1996); Erica Burman, *Deconstructing Developmental Psychology* (Routledge, London, 2nd edition, 2008); *Stories of Childhood*, N. 7 above.

[22] Alan Prout, *The Future of Childhood* (Routledge Falmer, Abingdon, 2005).

[23] Allison James and Alan Prout, 'Re-presenting Childhood: Time and Transition in the Study of Childhood' in *Constructing and Reconstructing Childhood*, N. 3 above, 230, 245.

[24] Lee, N. 6 above, 54.

[25] Carol Smart, Bren Neale, and Amanda Wade, *The Changing Experience of Childhood* (Polity, Cambridge, 2001), 12–13.

[26] Adrian L. James, 'Competition or Integration? The Next Step in Childhood Studies?' (2010) 17 *Childhood* 485, 487–9; Michael-Sebastian Honig, 'How is the Child Constituted in Childhood Studies?' in (eds.) Jens Qvortrup et al., N. 9 above, 62–77.

[27] Lee, N. 6 above, 8.

[28] Archard, N. 7 above, 42.

[29] Archard, N. 7 above, 39.

[30] *Constructing Childhood*, N. 3 above, 15.

The Convention holds a mixed conception of childhood. It is not clear whether the Convention imagines children as human beings, human becomings,[31] as both, or whether it holds a coherent conception of childhood at all. Nevertheless, as far as the right to development is concerned, the paramount conception of the Convention is the view of children as 'human becomings'.[32] This right was incorporated into the Convention under the perception of a universal-biological child, as Adam Lopatka, the Chairperson of the Working Group that drafted the Convention, concedes:

> [T]he physical and mental nature of the child is identical everywhere . . . the process of growth and adolescence takes a similar course in all children. Their physical and mental needs are also similar.[33]

Accordingly, it is not surprising that the Convention's ultimate goal is to promote the child's 'harmonious development'.[34] The Convention is a forward-looking document, aspiring to enable the perfect conditions for the child to grow up to his or her fullest potential. The Convention's right to development focus is on the child's future, while the child's life at present is regarded as less significant.

22.2 The UN Committee on the Rights of the Child's jurisprudence of the right to development

The UN Committee on the Rights of the Child was established by the Convention.[35] It serves as its monitoring mechanism and has a significant role in interpreting the Convention.[36] As the body that receives information concerning the status of children's rights in all 193 States Parties (from official governmental reports, UN agencies, and NGO's shadow reports), the Committee has the most comprehensive and up-to-date information about the situation of children worldwide. It is expected to use this knowledge and its important institutional position to promote recognition and protection of *all* rights of *all* children. This includes the right to development.

Soon after it was established, the Committee defined the right to development as one of the Convention's general principles,[37] and in 2003 it stated it to be one of the Convention's four guiding principles,[38] declaring that its meaning should be understood 'as a holistic concept, embracing the child's physical, mental, spiritual, moral, psychological and social development'.[39]

[31] Lee, N. 6 above, 95; Freeman, N. 4 above, 20.

[32] Noam Peleg, 'What Do We Mean When We Speak about the Right to Development?' in (ed.) Kerstin Nordlöf, *Sovereignty of Children in Law* (Scholarly Press, Cambridge, 2012).

[33] Adam Lopatka, 'The Rights of the Child are Universal: The Perspective of the UN Convention on the Rights of the Child' in (eds.) Michael Freeman and Philip Veerman, *The Ideologies of Children's Rights* (Martinus Nijhoff, Leiden, 1992), 47, 49.

[34] Preamble to the Convention.

[35] Article 43.

[36] See John Tobin, 'Seeking to Persuade: A Constructive Approach to Human Rights Treaty Interpretation' (2010) 23 *Harvard Human Rights Journal* 201.

[37] UNCRC, 'General Guidelines Regarding the Form and Content of Initial Reports To Be Submitted By States Parties Under Article 44, Paragraph 1(a), of the Convention' (30 October 1991) UN Doc CRC/C/5.

[38] UNCRC, 'General Comment No. 5 (2003)—General Measure of Implementation of the Convention on the Rights of the Child (arts. 4, 42 and 44, para. 6), (27 November 2003) UN Doc CRC/GC/2003/5.

[39] Ibid.

The Committee began reviewing States Parties' implementation reports in 1993. In the first 17 Concluding Observations it published in 1993 and 1994, little attention was given to the right to development. During those days, the Committee focused on the practical steps that States Parties should take in order to incorporate the Convention into their domestic legislation and policies. In the following years, the Committee gradually began referring to specific rights, including the right to development, focusing on particular components such as nutrition,[40] early childhood development,[41] and the minimum age for marriage.[42] Later, it broadened its scope to include more aspects of the child's life.

In order to analyse the Committee's interpretation to the right to development of children, I used discourse analysis methodology[43] and reviewed all 341 Concluding Observations and 12 General Comments published by the Committee between 1993 and 2009.[44] By referencing the Committee's own views on the subject, I endeavour to encompass the child's life broadly, taking the child's course of life as the underlying narrative for analysis. I start with the time of the birth of the child, which allows me to consider the influence of characteristics such as gender and disabilities on the child's ability to enjoy the right to development. Next, I discuss the period of early childhood and the connection between the right to development and the right to education and the right to health. I finish my analysis by discussing the connection between the right to development and child labour.

A review of the Committee's work could have taken other forms, such as contrasting how children's rights are understood in northern or southern states, or in developed as opposed to developing countries. However, such categorizations do not place the child at the centre of attention, but rather the society or state in which she or he is living. My position affirms that, in interpreting children's rights, children themselves should be the prime focus and other aspects should be accorded only a secondary importance.

My approach has its own problems, and two of them are particularly worth raising. The first is that the focus on the child assumes a somewhat universal meaning of childhood and of children's rights, an assumption contradicted by my earlier analysis. The second, closely related to the first, is that this position ignores, at least to some extent, differences among individual children, but also differences between societies and societal contexts. However, since I am following the Committee's own course of analysis, these apparent difficulties should be seen as part of my critique of the Committee's work, as the Committee itself does not rigorously attend to the persistent problem of universalism (despite some States Parties raising the issue).[45]

[40] UNCRC, 'Concluding Observations of the Committee on the Rights of the Child: Honduras' (24 October 1994) UN Doc CRC/C/15/Add. 24.

[41] UNCRC, 'Concluding Observations of the Committee on the Rights of the Child: Jamaica' (15 February 1995) UN Doc CRC/C/15/Add. 32.

[42] UNCRC, 'Concluding Observations of the Committee on the Rights of the Child: Nicaragua' (20 June 1995) UN Doc CRC/C/15/Add. 36.

[43] Rosalind Gill, 'Discourse Analysis' in (eds.) Martin Bauer and George Gaskell, *Qualitative Research with Text, Image and Sound* (Sage Publishing, London, 2000), 179.

[44] After the paper had been submitted, the Committee published 'General Comment No. 13—'Article 19: The Right of the Child to Freedom from all Forms of Violence'. Due to its importance, I have accommodated some comments about it, mainly in relation to the connection between the right to development and violence against children. UNCRC, 'General Comment No. 13 (2001)—Article 19: The Right of the Child to Freedom from all Forms of Violence' (17 February 2011) UN Doc CRC/C/GC/13.

[45] Sonia Harris-Short, 'International Human Rights Law: Imperialist, Inept and Ineffective? Cultural Relativism and the UN Convention on the Rights of the Child' (2003) 25 *Human Rights Quarterly* 130, 146–63.

22.2.1 Discrimination

The child's ability to enjoy fully his or her right to development is influenced by social and legal attitudes toward the child's personal and family characteristics, such as race, gender, disability, and class. Therefore, the Committee concludes that a child's right to non-discrimination, guaranteed in Article 2 of the Convention, should be protected not only for its own merit, but also in order to prevent a 'negative effect' on the child's development.[46]

The Committee specifically refers to two practices of discrimination as a violation of the right to development. The first is the usually lower marriage age for girls, which has an inevitably impact on both girls' and boys' 'health, education and social development'.[47] The second is the gap between the time when compulsory education ends and paid work is permissible. This gap can expose children to economic exploitation and therefore jeopardize their development.[48]

Children with disabilities are seen by the Committee as a particular vulnerable group, as they are often excluded from society by adults and children alike. Therefore, protecting their right to non-discrimination is a means to guarantee their future development. Discriminating against children with disabilities 'threatens their survival and development if it goes as far as physical or mental violence'.[49]

The Committee makes an important link between the right to non-discrimination and children's future development, which indicates the significance of the child's future, to the Committee's interpretation of the right to development. It is clearly evident that it is not the discriminated child's life at present with which the Committee is concerned, but rather the effects on the child's future. However, the Committee does not shed much light on what children's future should look like and, more importantly, what their right to development means in the future, let alone in present time as children.

22.2.2 The child's family

Beside the child's own personal characteristics, the child's family has a major influence on the child's development, according to the Convention's preamble:

> Recognizing that the child, for the full and harmonious development of his or her personality, should grow up in a family environment, in an atmosphere of happiness, love and understanding...

[46] 'General Comment No. 5', N. 38 above. UNCRC, 'Concluding Observations: Canada' (20 June 1995) UN Doc CRC/C/15/Add. 37; UNCRC, 'Concluding Observations: United Kingdom of Great Britain and Northern Ireland' (15 February 1995) UN Doc CRC/C/15/Add. 34; UNCRC, 'Concluding Observations: Germany' (26 February 2004) UN Doc CRC/C/15/Add. 226; UNCRC, 'Concluding Observations: Burundi' (16 October 2000) UN Doc CRC/C/15/Add. 133; UNCRC, 'Concluding Observations: Cameroon (6 November 2001) UN Doc CRC/C/15/Add. 164; UNCRC, 'General Comment No. 4 (2003)—Adolescent Health and Development in the Context of the Convention on the Rights of the Child' (1 July 2003) UN Doc CRC/GC/2003/4.

[47] UNCRC, 'Concluding Observations: India' (26 February 2004) UN Doc CRC/C/15/Add. 228; 'Concluding Observations: Nicaragua' 1995 N. 42 above.

[48] 'Concluding Observations: Nicaragua' 1995 N. 42 above; UNCRC, 'Concluding Observations: Sri Lanka' (21 June 1995) UN Doc CRC/C/15/Add. 40; UNCRC, 'Concluding Observations: Kuwait' (26 October 1998) UN Doc CRC/C/15/Add. 96.

[49] UNCRC, 'General Comment No. 9 (2006): The Right of Children with Disabilities' (27 February 2007) UN Doc CRC/C/GC/9.

The Convention goes on to define the parents and members of the extended family as responsible for the upbringing and development of the child (Articles 18 and 4, respectively).

In interpreting these Articles, the Committee promotes a traditional, patriarchal, and gender bias division of responsibilities for the upbringing of the child. The Committee concludes that a traditional family unit, composed of monogamist-heterosexual parents, will best fulfil the child's right to development.[50] The Committee's jurisprudence then provides a prescription for a family composition, overlooking parenting and child-rearing practices and their impact on children's right to development.

The Committee argues that parents should not be 'too young', although it gives no indications for what is deemed to be 'too young'. Furthermore, should parents fall into that category, then 'continuing attention [should] be given to the risks of early parenthood'.[51] Moreover, the Committee assumes that a single-parent family is headed by a mother and therefore argues for the promotion of a higher level of involvement of fathers in the 'upbringing and development of the child'.[52] The Committee does not refer to parents who are 'too old' to rear their children or to the impact that such parents might have on their children's development. The Committee also ignores other types of single-parent families, such as those in which the father is the caregiver rather than the mother. Nor does the Committee discuss 'less traditional' family units, which are increasing in numbers in recent years, such as families headed by same-sex parents, or those raising children born from sperm or egg donors. It also ignores families of adopted children, and the potential impact that such family structures might have on children's development.

The Committee gives no explanation for any of its positions or assumptions, either the explicit or the non-explicit ones. Its perceptions of the preferred family unit represent traditional concepts of the 'good parent' or the 'good family', which are neither common among all States Parties, nor necessarily the only models for 'good' parenting, nor the one which best supports the child's development.[53] Even if by adopting the Committee's point of view concerning parental roles and children's future, one could have expected that it would have discussed the connection between the child's identity and development in light of Articles 7 and 8 of the Convention.[54] But the Committee has not done so, save the issue of birth certificates which is discussed below.

Two exceptions to the general terms in which the Committee discusses child-rearing are mothers' roles and traditional practices. With respect to the role of mothers, the Committee's comments follow its conservative approach, designating special roles for mothers in promoting the right to development of their children. It claims

[50] For example: UNCRC, 'Concluding Observations: Denmark' (15 February 1995) UN Doc CRC/C/15/Add. 33.

[51] UNCRC, 'Concluding Observations: Barbados' (24 August 1999) UN Doc CRC/C/15/Add. 103; UNCRC, 'Concluding Observations: Zambia' (2 July 2003) UN Doc CRC/C/15/Add. 206.

[52] UNCRC, 'Concluding Observations: Barbados' (24 August 1999) UN Doc CRC/C/15/Add. 103; UNCRC, 'Concluding Observations: Zambia' (2 July 2003) UN Doc CRC/C/15/Add. 206.

[53] See, for example, a recent study indicating that adolescents reared in lesbian-mother families since birth demonstrate healthy psychological adjustment. Nanetta Gartrell and Henny Bos, 'US National Longitudinal Lesbian Family Study: Psychological Adjustment of 17 Years Old Adolescents' (2010) 126 *Pediatrics* 28.

[54] Ya'ir Ronen, 'Redefining the Child's Right to Identity' (2004) 18 *International Journal of Law, Policy and the Family* 147, 149–50.

that if a mother decides to work outside the family home and to put her children into nursery care, then States Parties should ensure sufficient resources to 'enable full physical, mental and intellectual development of [those] children'.[55] As far as fathers are concerned, the Committee encourages greater involvement by fathers in the upbringing of the child, in order to support their child's development.[56]

With regard to traditional practices, the Committee focuses on female genital mutilation, forced marriage, and infanticide, which are usually performed by family members in order to fulfil their beliefs and customs, and result in violating human rights of children. From the early days of its work, and despite some States Parties arguing that cultural relativism justifies these acts,[57] the Committee considered these practices as violations of children's rights, mainly the right to health.[58] In 2001 the right to development, of girls and boys alike, was added to the list.[59] However, the Committee clarifies neither the relationship between these practices and the right to development, nor why they constitute a violation of the right to development. Furthermore, although the Committee declares that traditional practices violate the rights of both boys and girls, it mainly focuses on female genital mutilation.

Focusing on female genital mutilation omits another common traditional practice, male circumcision. Arguably, and by applying the Committee's own approach to the subject, there should be no difference between male circumcision and female genital mutilation, as both are acts of violence conducted by adults against children in the name of cultural or religious belief. There may be different explanations to this omission. One can argue that a cultural bias of the Committee dictates this omission; the different degrees of force employed in these two practices is another possible explanation; boy's right to cultural heritage can be a third option.[60] These explanations justify male circumcision as less aggressive than female genital mutilation and as an act that causes less long-term damage, and therefore does not constitute a violation of the boy-child's rights.[61] However, generating hypothetical explanations misses the point that the Committee does not even discuss male circumcision, let alone decide whether it constitutes a violation of any right, not least the right to development, or not. Boy-children can at least expect that the Committee will address this act and ask if it violates their rights.

[55] UNCRC, 'Concluding Observations: Nigeria' (13 April 2005) UN Doc CRC/C/15/Add. 257.

[56] 'Concluding Observations: Barbados' 1999, N. 52 above; 'Concluding Observations: Zambia' 2003, N. 51 above.

[57] Sonia Harris-Short, N. 45 above, 146–63.

[58] See, for example, UNCRC, 'Concluding Observation: Ethiopia' (24 January 1997) UN Doc CRC/C/15/Add. 67.

[59] UNCRC, 'Concluding Observations: United Republic of Tanzania' (9 July 2001) UN Doc CRC/C/15/Add 156; UNCRC, 'Concluding Observations: Nepal' (21 September 2005) UN Doc CRC/C/15/Add. 261; UNCRC, 'Concluding Observations: Kenya' (7 November 2001) UN Doc CRC/C/15/Add. 160; 'Concluding Observations: India' 2004, N. 47 above; UNCRC, 'Concluding Observations: Benin' (20 October 2006) UN Doc CRC/C/BEN/CO/2.

[60] Michael Freeman, 'A Child's Right to Circumcision' (1999) 83S(1) *British Journal of Urology International* 74.

[61] Marie Fox and Michael Thomson, 'Short Changed? The Law and Ethics of Male Circumcision' in (ed.) Michael Freeman, *Children's Health and Children's Rights* (Martinus Nijhoff, Dordrecht, 2006), 161–81. A different point of view is reflected by UK courts, which focus on the question of parents' consent to the procedure. Gilbert criticized this approach, arguing that it fails to scrutinize the need of the state to defend one's physical integrity from being violated. Howard Gilbert, 'Time to Reconsider the Lawfulness of Ritual Male Circumcision' (2007) *European Human Rights Law Review* 279.

22.2.3 Children deprived of family environment

Driven by its ideal model of child-rearing and taking the position that growing up without a family environment poses a 'serious risk' to the child's development,[62] the Committee intensively addresses the issue of children who are deprived of a family environment. The Committee identified four categories of children who face such risk: children of separated parents; children who live in institutions; children who have imprisoned parents; and refugee, stateless, and unaccompanied children. Except for children of separated parents, all of these children have one or both parents in state facilities, usually prisons or hospitals, and some of them often live in these institutions as well.

The Committee expresses its concerns for well-being and development of children who live in institutions, and it urges States Parties to consider whether a decision to place a child in an institution, to which his or her caregiver was committed, would serve the child's best interests and the child's 'healthy development'.[63] States Parties are also asked to 'ensure the adequate development'[64] of these children and to create an 'environment that would allow for fuller development of the child' inside the state's institution.[65] With regard to imprisoned children, the Committee asks States Parties, in accordance with Article 37 of the Convention, to 'take all necessary measures to ensure that children are not ill-treated in detention, that conditions in detention facilities are not contrary to the child's development'.[66] While the child is living in an institution, she or he should be able to keep contact with the outside world, and the state ought to ensure that 'living conditions in prisons are adequate for the child's development'[67] and suitable for the 'harmonious development' of the child.[68] In the case of young children, those living standards should be adequate for their 'early development'.[69]

Upon release from the institution, children should be provided with 'educational opportunities, including vocational and life-skills training, and recovery and social reintegration services, in order to support their full development'.[70] Following Article 25 of the Convention, the Committee further asks States Parties to develop alternatives to institutional care 'with the best interests of the child as a primary

[62] UNCRC, 'General Comment No. 7 (2005)—Implementing Child Rights in Early Childhood' (20 September 2006) UN Doc CRC/C/GC/7/Rev. 1.

[63] UNCRC, 'Concluding Observations: The Plurinational State of Bolivia' (2 October 2009) UN Doc CRC/C/BOL/CO/4.

[64] UNCRC, 'Concluding Observations: Nicaragua' (24 August 1999) CRC/C/15/Add. 108.

[65] UNCRC, 'Concluding Observations: Russian Federation' (23 November 2005) UN Doc CRC/C/RUS/CO/3.

[66] UNCRC, 'Concluding Observations: Venezuela' (5 October 2007) UN Doc CRC/C/VEN/CO/2; UNCRC, 'Concluding Observations: Sierra Leona' (20 June 2008) UN Doc CRC/C/SLE/CO/2; UNCRC, 'Concluding Observations: Chad' (12 February 2009) UN Doc CRC/C/TCD/CO/2.

[67] UNCRC, 'Concluding Observations: Bolivia' (11 February 2005) UN Doc CRC/C/15/Add 256, 640; UNCRC, 'Concluding Observations: The Islamic Republic of Iran' (31 March 2005) UN Doc CRC/C/15/Add 254; UNCRC, 'Concluding Observations: Mexico' (2 June 2006) UN Doc CRC/C/MEX/CO/3.

[68] UNCRC, 'Concluding Observations: Nepal' (21 September 2005) UN Docs CRC/C/15/Add. 261.

[69] UNCRC, 'Concluding Observations: Philippines' (21 September 2005) UN Doc CRC/C/15/Add.259.

[70] UNCRC, 'Concluding Observations: China (Including Hong Kong and Macau Special Administration Regions)' (24 November 2005) UN Doc CRC/C/CHN/CO/2; UNCRC, 'Concluding Observations: Jordan' (29 September 2006) UN Doc CRC/C/JOR/CO/3; UNCRC, 'Concluding Observations: Kenya' (19 June 2007) UN Doc CRC/C/KEN/CO/2.

consideration, as well as the promotion of his or her harmonious development and preparation for responsible participation in society'.[71]

Refugee, stateless, and unaccompanied children receive special attention from the Committee. It determines that the common practice of detaining them can lead to 'harmful consequences on children's mental and physical health and overall development',[72] and therefore States Parties should 'provide for adequate accommodation, taking into account the state of development of all unaccompanied and separated asylum-seeking children'.[73] Stateless children should also enjoy a 'minimum standard of living, including housing, clean water and sanitation, and have access to play, cultural activities, educational and health care institutions and services in their neighbourhood needed for their development'.[74] The Committee also expresses its concern for unaccompanied children and children outside their country of origin, since they are especially exposed to various risks to their rights to life, survival, and development.[75]

Consistent with its stand on the issue of family composition, the Committee concludes that children who grow up with separate parents can have their development distorted (although having separated parents does not necessarily mean lacking in a parental role or a family composed of a biological and non-biological parent) and therefore it encourages courts who deal with family disputes to ensure that both parents share the responsibilities for the 'upbringing and development of the child'.[76]

It seems that the Committee has a strong position about children who are deprived of their family environment and the impact of this situation on children's right to development. It views this situation as having negative consequences for children's future development and therefore places obligations on States Parties, with the aim of taking care of the child's future well-being.

22.2.4 The right to be registered after birth

The child's right to be registered immediately after birth (Article 7) does not seem to have, at least at first glance, any connection to the right to development. Nevertheless, as part of its effort to connect every aspect of the child's life to the child's right to development, the Committee makes such a link.

The Committee takes the position that having a birth registration mechanism and ensuring that each child is issued with a birth certificate are two pre-conditions for fulfilling the right to development. Lack of such mechanism, it determines, 'can impact negatively on a child's sense of personal identity and children may be denied entitlements to basic health, education and social welfare'.[77] Once again it is the child's future that is protected by issuing a birth certificate, not only as a future adult, but as a child as well.

[71] UNCRC, 'Concluding Observations: Bulgaria' (24 January 1997) UN Doc CRC/C/15/Add. 66.

[72] UNCRC, 'Concluding Observations: Australia' (20 October 2005) UN Doc CRC/C/15/Add. 268.

[73] UNCRC, 'Concluding Observations: Austria' (31 March 2005) UN Doc CRC/C/15/Add. 251.

[74] UNCRC, 'Concluding Observations: Dominican Republic' (11 February 2008) UN Doc CRC/C/DOM/CO/2.

[75] UNCRC, 'General Comment No. 6 (2005)—Treatment on Unaccompanied and Separated Children Outside Their Country of Origin' (1 September 2005) CRC/C/GC/2005/6.

[76] UNCRC, 'Concluding Observations: Equatorial Guinea' (3 November 2004) UN Doc CRC/C/15/Add 245.

[77] 'General Comment No. 7', N. 62 above.

22.2.5 The socio-economic conditions of the child's life

Like the personal characteristics of the child, the socio-economic conditions into which the child is born or in which he or she lives have an immense impact on the right to development. These conditions are external to the child's personality or the choices he or she makes, but nevertheless should not be ignored even when the child is placed at the centre of attention.

In light of Articles 3, 4, 6, 26, and 27 of the Convention, the Committee focuses on the socio-economic status of the child's family and holds States Parties responsible for supporting 'families in a difficult economic and/or social situation in order to ensure, to the maximum extent possible, the survival and development of all children'.[78] Although the Committee does not specify which kind of support and what measures will meet this standard, it does say that a social safety net and social security policy, sufficient to enable families living in poverty to provide their children with an adequate standard of living, will meet this requirement.[79]

22.2.6 Poverty and adequate standard of living

The Committee's discussion on children's poverty and standard of living echoes the public-policy theory of development. According to this theory, which emerged in the late 1940s in the USA, economic growth will trickle down to all parts of society and result in reducing poverty and a better life for everyone.[80] Similarly, the Committee argues that eliminating poverty will improve children's ability to enjoy their rights to survival, development, and well-being,[81] and recommends a three-step plan to reduce poverty and improve children's material living conditions. According to this plan, every State Party should first define a poverty line.[82] Then, based on this local definition, each state should formulate poverty alleviation policies. Thirdly, every State Party should support families living in economic hardship.[83]

Poverty is indeed a challenge to the promotion of human rights, but the Committee's somewhat simplistic three-step plan does not account for children's unique position within economic hardship and overlooks the impact of poverty on children, which is different from the impact on adults, either male or female.[84]

The right to an adequate standard of living, protected in Article 27 of the Convention, is closely related to poverty. Article 27 guarantees a right to a living standard that protects five different elements of an individual child's development: physical, mental, spiritual, moral, and social development. Based on this article, the

[78] UNCRC, 'Concluding Observations: Latvia' (21 February 2001) UN Doc CRC/C/15/Add. 142; UNCRC, 'Concluding Observations: Georgia' (27 October 2003) UN Doc CRC/C/15/Add. 222.

[79] UNCRC, 'Concluding Observations: Jamaica' (4 July 2003) UN Doc CRC/C/15/Add. 210; UNCRC, 'Concluding Observations: France' (30 June 2004) UN Doc CRC/C/15/Add. 240.

[80] Gustavo Esteva, 'Development' in (ed.) Wolfgang Sachs, *The Development Dictionary* (Zed Books, London and New York, 1992), 6, 6–23; Arthur Lewis, *The Theory of Economic Growth* (Allen and Unwin, 1955); Paul A. Baran, *The Political Economy of Growth* (Harmondsworth, Penguin Books, 1957); Peleg, N. 32 above.

[81] UNCRC, 'Concluding Observations: Honduras' (24 October 1994) UN Doc CRC/C/15/Add. 24; UNCRC, 'Concluding Observations: Venezuela' (5 October 2007) UN Doc CRC/C/VEN/CO/2.

[82] 'Concluding Observations: Australia' 2005, N. 72 above.

[83] UNCRC, 'Concluding Observations: Ethiopia' (21 February 2001) UN Doc CRC/C/15/Add. 144; UNCRC, 'Concluding Observations: Ireland' (29 September 2006) UN Doc CRC/C/IRL/CO/2; UNCRC, 'Concluding Observations: Lithuania' (17 March 2006) UN Doc CRC/C/LTU/CO/2.

[84] See Amartya Sen, *Development as Freedom* (Oxford University Press, Oxford, 1999), 193.

Committee has determined that an inadequate standard of living negatively impacts children's 'quality of life',[85] but does not elaborate on the meaning of this.[86]

Other than stating that the right to an adequate standard of living is fundamental to a child's ability to enjoy the right to development, the Committee does not elaborate further, and leaves the meaning of these two rights vague.

One group of children who obviously do not enjoy adequate standard of living is singled out for special attention: children who live on the street. The Committee determines that States Parties have the responsibility to take all measures necessary, in order to support the 'full development'[87] of these children. But after establishing this vague obligation, the Committee does not say more about it.

22.2.7 Early childhood development

Over the years, the Committee has extensively discussed the connection between the time of 'early childhood' and child's development. Fixed with the psychological and biological development models, the Committee has characterized the time of 'early childhood' as a period in which the child experiences the most rapid growth of the nervous system, communication skills, abilities, and interests. It also describes it as the time when the child forms relationships with other children and adults, creates a perspective on the world, and establishes the foundations for his or her mental and physical health, emotional security, and cultural and personal identity.[88]

Therefore, 'early childhood development' programmes should be available to children as soon as they are born.[89] These programmes should target infants with low birth weight and ensure universal immunization programmes.[90] Baby-friendly hospitals ought to be available, newborn infants should not be separated from their mothers after birth,[91] and early childhood diseases such as acute respiratory infections, diarrhoea,[92] chronic malnutrition,[93] bacterial infection, measles, and pneumonia[94] need to be treated by medical staff trained to work with children. Other factors influencing the child's development at this age, such as inadequate sanitation, hygiene and diet,[95] access to safe drinking water,[96] and household food insecurity,[97] should also be targeted by States Parties.

The way that the Committee describes the period of early childhood demonstrates the thin line distinguishing between the right to life, the right to survival, and the

[85] UNCRC, 'Concluding Observations: United Kingdom of Great Britain and Northern Ireland' (20 October 2008) UN Doc CRC/C/GBR/CO/4.

[86] The term 'Quality of life' has a great significant in development theory. See Martha Nussbaum and Amartya Sen (eds.) *Quality of Life* (Oxford University Press, Oxford, 1993).

[87] UNCRC, 'Concluding Observations: Turkey' (9 July 2001) UN Doc CRC/C/15/Add. 152; UNCRC, 'Concluding Observations: The Republic of Moldova' (31 October 2002) UN Docs CRC/C/15/Add. 192; 'Concluding Observations: Zambia' 2003, N. 52 above.

[88] 'General Comment No. 7', N. 62 above.

[89] 'Concluding Observations: Jamaica' 1995, N. 79 above.

[90] UNCRC, 'Concluding Observations: Hungary' (24 June 1998) UN Doc CRC/C/15/Add. 87.

[91] UNCRC, 'Concluding Observations: Republic of Serbia' (20 June 2008) UN Doc CRC/C/SRB/CO/1.

[92] UNCRC, 'Concluding Observations: Ivory Coast' (9 July 2001) UN Doc CRC/C/15/Add. 155.

[93] 'Concluding Observations: Cameroon' 2001, N. 46 above.

[94] 'Concluding Observations: Nepal' 2005, N. 59 above.

[95] UNCRC, 'Concluding Observations: Marshall Islands' (19 November 2007) UN Doc CRC/C/MHL/CO/2.

[96] 'Concluding Observations: Ivory Coast' 2001, N. 92 above.

[97] UNCRC, 'Concluding Observations: Djibouti' (7 October 2008) UN Doc CRC/C/DJI/CO/2.

right to development in this stage of the child's life. High mortality rates of children at these ages also indicate a low potential to survive, thereby impacting the ability of these children to grow up and develop. Nevertheless, the life-survival-development continuum is not without significance.

22.2.8 Violence against children

There are many reasons why children should grow up in an environment free from violence, and one of them is that violence threatens their right to life, survival, and development.[98] Violence can occur inside or outside the family home, at school, on the playground, or in any other state or private facility. It can be used as a punitive measure, as a matter of discipline, or as an abusive act. Regardless of the form or forum of its perpetration, children should be protected from it.[99]

In general, violence has a 'devastating impact' and negatively impacts children's survival and their 'physical, mental, spiritual, moral and social development'.[100] In General Comment No. 13 the Committee emphasized over and over that violence threatens the child's development and well-being, both 'in childhood and when becoming adults' and therefore States Parties are asked to form a rights-based approach plan to eliminate violence against children. This kind of plan, the Committee determined, should take development in 'its broadest sense as a holistic concept, embracing the child's physical, mental, spiritual, moral, psychological and social development. Implementation measures should be aimed at achieving the optimal development for all children'.[101] This last comment introduces another undefined standard of development—'optimal' development.

Corporal punishment is probably the most common form of violence against children, and as such gains rapid attention. 'Corporal punishment and other degrading forms of punishment', the Committee has declared, 'may inflict serious damage to the physical, psychological and social development of children.'[102] The Committee goes on to designate corporal punishment not only as a violation of the right to development, but also of Articles 3, 19, 27, 28, 37, and 39 of the Convention,[103] and recommends that States Parties ban corporal punishment in legislation, educate the public about the negative impact it has on the development of the child, and promote positive, violence-free, disciplinary methods.[104]

Another situation of violence propagated against children addressed by the Committee is armed conflict. Unlike corporal punishment, an armed conflict is institutionalized, often state-initiated violence (or in a case of civil war, initiated by adults detached from their capacity as parents or educators), which does not take place in the 'private' sphere. While it does not target only children, it too often

[98] UNCRC, 'Concluding Observations: Peru' (22 February 2000) UN Doc CRC/C/15/Add. 120; 'General Comments No. 13', N. 44 above.

[99] Article 19. 'General Comment No. 13', N. 44 above.

[100] 'General Comment No. 13', N. 44 above. [101] Ibid.

[102] UNCRC, 'General Comment No. 8 (2006)—The Right of The Child To Be Protected From Corporal Punishment and Other Cruel and Degrading Forms of Punishment' (2 March 2007) UN Doc CRC/C/GC/8.

[103] General Comment No. 8, N. 102 above; UNCRC, 'Concluding Observations: Australia' (21 October 1997) UN Doc CRC/C/15/Add. 79; UNCRC, 'Concluding Observations: Fiji' (24 June 1998) UN Docs CRC/C/15/Add. 89.

[104] 'Concluding Observations: Barbados' 1999, N. 51 above; UNCRC, 'Concluding Observations: New Zealand' (27 October 2003) UN Doc CRC/C/15/Add. 216.

victimizes them. Children do not initiate armed conflicts, but nonetheless they find themselves being forcibly recruited into armed forces, losing parents and relatives, suffering from the economic hardship created by war, dealing with lasting emotional traumas, and in some cases being exposed to torture and killing. It is clear, then, why the Committee considers armed conflicts to have negative effect on children's rights to life, survival, and development.[105]

The impact that the course of wars has on the right to development is not addressed by the Committee, which only links it to the child's right to life. One exception is the issue of land mines.

In many war zones, land mines are left in the ground for years after the hostilities end, often in places open to the public, and these 'pose a continuing threat' to children's development.[106] In addressing the aftermath of war and following Articles 38 and 39 of the Convention, the Committee emphasizes the need to carry out rehabilitation measures, which should include psychosocial, psychological, and physical rehabilitation. These measures should also be available to children who were directly and indirectly involved in the hostilities.[107] The physical and emotional traumas caused by armed conflicts are well-known, so one can wonder why only the child's right to life is discussed in connection with the immediate effect of armed conflicts on children, and not on the right to survival or development also.

22.2.9 Education

The Convention dedicates Articles 28 and 29 to the right to education. Article 28 recognizes the right to education for itself and Article 29 lays down the aims of education. The Convention declares that the first aim of education is to develop the child's 'personality, talents and mental and physical abilities to their fullest potential'.[108] In this context, the Committee articulates the view that personality, talent, and mental and physical development constitute part of the child's 'holistic development'.[109]

Although the Convention does not explicitly acknowledge the duty of the state to facilitate access to the right to education prior to the primary level,[110] declaring that only the latter should be 'compulsory and available to all',[111] the Committee recognizes the importance of education to the child's development and the need to have pre-school age formal education. Therefore, it goes beyond the obligations set out in the Convention, arguing in favour of a much earlier start for compulsory

[105] UNCRC, 'Concluding Observations: India' (23 February 2000) UN Doc CRC/C/15/Add. 115; UNCRC, 'Concluding Observations: Columbia' (16 October 2000) UN Doc CRC/C/15/Add. 137.

[106] 'Concluding Observations: Kuwait' 1998, N. 48 above; UNCRC, 'Concluding Observations: Iraq' (26 October 1998) UN Docs CRC/C/15/Add. 94; UNCRC, 'Concluding Observations: Angola' (3 November 2004) UN Doc CRC/C/15/Add. 246;

[107] 'Concluding Observations: Angola' 2004, ibid; UNCRC, 'Concluding Observations: Algeria' (12 October 2005) UN Doc CRC/C/15/Add. 269; 'Concluding Observations: Philippines' 2005, N. 69 above; UNCRC, 'Concluding Observations: Thailand' (17 March 2006) UN Doc CRC/C/THA/CO/2; UNCRC, 'Concluding Observations: Pakistan' (15 October 2009) UN Doc CRC/C/PAK/CO/3-4.

[108] Article 29(1)(a).

[109] UNCRC, 'General Comment No.1 (2001): The Aims of Education' (17 April 2001) UN Doc CRC/GC/2001/1.

[110] Mieke Verheyde, *Article 28: The Right to Education* (Martinus Nijhoff Publishers, Leiden, 2006), 15–23.

[111] Article 28(1)(a).

education and asking States Parties to make it available to children after birth.[112] Furthermore, in order to support the early development of children aged five to six, the Committee encourages States Parties to create compulsory pre-primary school education programmes,[113] stating that these kinds of programmes are particularly important for children from ethnic minorities, for children with disabilities, and for children growing up in economic hardship.[114] Once again, like the right to development itself, these programmes should also be addressed holistically.[115]

In light of the overall aims of education set out in Article 29, the Committee notes that the education process should be child-friendly and inspire and motivate the child.[116] To this end, curricula should focus on the 'personal development and vocational training of students',[117] and schools ought to seek 'innovative means for promoting the cognitive, social and emotional development of children'.[118] One example of such a programme is the Chinese 'all-round development' policy, which contains a 'curriculum promoting children's active learning capacities and which also focus on a child's right to play and leisure'.[119]

Having said that, the Committee also argues that putting too much emphasis on success in school can also damage the child's right to development. This is the case when schools are too competitive, that they can 'place additional burdens on children and may hamper the development of the child to his or her fullest potential',[120] leaving the child with a 'consequent lack of time for leisure, physical activities and rest'.[121]

In unusually long and detailed discussions, the Committee has established a relatively clear connection between the right to education and the right to development. It specifies that the aim of education is to promote the child's right to development, and that the education system should be designed to achieve this goal. This discussion also reflects the unified model of childhood that the Committee holds. When it encourages States Parties to make formal education available to toddlers, it ignores cultures and customs where toddlers are educated outside a formal education system or other skills or competence are considered more important to the child's development, than those that are encouraged in Western societies.[122] Similarly, criticizing cultures where schools are designed to be too-competitive institutions reflects the Western 'free-from-responsibilities' conception of childhood, which is closely related to the 'becoming' model, and rejects other cultures, where the schools system in

[112] 'General Comment No. 7', N. 62 above.

[113] UNCRC, 'Concluding Observations: Malaysia' (25 June 2007) UN Doc CRC/C/MYS/CO/1.

[114] UNCRC, 'Concluding Observations: Bulgaria' (23 June 2008) UN Doc CRC/C/BGR/CO/2; UNCRC, 'Concluding Observations: Georgia' (23 June 2008) UN Doc CRC/C/GEO/CO/3.

[115] UNCRC, 'Concluding Observations: Bangladesh' (25 June 2009) UN Doc CRC/C/BGD/CO/4.

[116] Ibid.

[117] UNCRC, 'Concluding Observations: Macedonia' (23 February 2000) UN Doc CRC/C/15/Add. 118; UNCRC, 'Concluding Observations: Brazil' (3 November 2004) UN Doc CRC/C/15/Add. 241.

[118] UNCRC, 'Concluding Observations: Poland' (30 October 2000) UN Doc CRC/C/15/Add. 194.

[119] 'Concluding Observations: China' 2005, N. 70 above.

[120] 'Concluding Observations: Thailand' 2006, N. 107 above.

[121] UNCRC, 'Concluding Observations: Japan' (24 June 1998) UN Doc CRC/C/15/Add. 90; UNCRC, 'Concluding Observations: Republic of Korea' (18 March 2003) UN Doc CRC/C/15/Add. 197; UNCRC, 'Concluding Observations: Japan' (26 February 2004) UN Doc CRC/C/15/Add. 231.

[122] See, for example, Catherine Snow et al., 'Talking and Playing with Babies: Ideologies of Child-Rearing' in (eds.) Robert A. LeVine and Rebecca S. New, *Anthropology and Child Development* (Blackwell, Oxford, 2008) 115–26; Charles Stafford, *The Road of Chinese Children: Learning and Identification in Angang* (Cambridge University Press, Cambridge, 1995).

particular, and education in general, may serve different social purposes but nevertheless also aim to promote the child's development.[123] Furthermore, designing minimum and maximum requirements for education systems confines a narrow margin in which educational processes can take place, which leads to a specific interpretation of the right to development, that fits the 'human becoming' model.

22.2.10 The right to rest and leisure and access to information

The right to rest and leisure is protected in Article 31 and is one of the unique human rights of children. In its first years of operation, the Committee tended to ignore this right, and only later began addressing it and linking it to the right to development.

According to the Committee, play and leisure activities should be complementary to children's physical and psychological development,[124] encouraged by States Parties and available to all children, especially members of vulnerable groups.[125] The Committee dictates that children need to play not only with other children, but also with their mothers, taking the view that mother-child activities 'have a crucial bearing on the development of the child's cognitive abilities and their social and emotional development'.[126] Later, the Committee refers to the need to play with 'parents',[127] not only with mothers.

However, it is not always clear whether the Committee sees the importance of play only through the prism of the child's future development, as part of the child's socialization and cognitive development, for example, or whether play and leisure also have meaning in present time for the child. As play is often characterized as one of the archetypes of childhood, linking it to the child's future development is unsurprising, but it can also be expected that a much clearer link be made to the child's life as a child.

As an increasing number of children spend their leisure time watching television or playing on a computer, the Committee dedicates attention to these activities—thereby ignoring those who do not have access to these luxuries—arguing that media performs an important function by providing information and influencing the child's social, spiritual, and moral well-being and mental and physical health.[128] Accordingly, it asks States Parties to ensure that children have access to 'appropriate information',[129] aimed at promoting 'the child's development and physical and mental health'[130] and the child's 'cultural development'.[131] The questions about what 'cultural development' stands for and what sort of information will meet this standard remain open.

[123] See Heather Montgomery, *An Introduction to Childhood* (Wiley-Blackwell, Oxford, 2009), 49–50.

[124] UNCRC, 'Concluding Observations: Lithuania' (1 February 2001) UN Doc CRC/C/15/Add. 146; 'Concluding Observations: Lithuania' 2006, N. 83 above.

[125] 'Concluding Observations: Benin' 2006, N. 59 above.

[126] UNCRC, 'Concluding Observations: Belize' (10 May 1999), UN Doc CRC/C/15/Add. 99.

[127] UNCRC, 'Concluding Observations: Mauritania' (6 November 2001) UN Doc CRC/C/15/Add. 159.

[128] Article 17. But see the claim that the Convention is not capable of dealing with the new digital media age: Philip E. Veerman, 'The Ageing of the UN Convention on the Rights of the Child' (2010) 18(4) *International Journal of Children Rights* 585, 589–93.

[129] UNCRC, 'Concluding Observations: Cambodia' (28 June 2000) UN Doc CRC/C/15/Add. 128.

[130] UNCRC, 'Concluding Observations: Marshall Islands' (26 October 2000) UN Doc CRC/C/15/Add. 139.

[131] UNCRC, 'Concluding Observations: Lebanon' (7 June 1996) UN Doc CRC/C/15/Add. 54.

22.2.11 The child's health

Article 24 protects the child's right to the 'highest attainable standard of health', and although it does not explicitly address any developmental aspects of the child, the Committee has connected some aspects of it to the right to development. Inadequate access to safe drinking water, as well as air and water pollution,[132] were identified as having 'negative consequences for children's health and development'.[133] As four million children under the age of five die each year from diarrhoea, malaria, or pneumonia,[134] epidemic diseases are defined as a violation of the right to life and as a barrier to full enjoyment of the right to development.[135]

Similarly, HIV/AIDS is described as an epidemic that poses an increasing risk to children's lives, survival, and development,[136] and 'affects all of the child's rights', determined that children should 'benefit from economic and social policies that will allow them to survive into adulthood and develop in the broadest sense of the word'.[137] The latter recommendation indicates that it is not the quality of these children's lives as children that necessarily counts. It is not their current physical, mental, spiritual, moral, economic, and social well-being as children that matters. But rather, the Committee once again asks children to obey the 'law of growth' by asking States Parties to provide children who have HIV/AIDS with 'a standard of living adequate for their physical, mental, spiritual, moral, economic and social development, including access to psychosocial care, as needed'.[138]

22.2.12 Adolescent health

As the child grows up, he or she presumably moves from one development stage to another, and therefore the way that the right to development is manifested should change accordingly. However, the Committee only attends to this shift in matters of health and the right to health, dedicating General Comment No. 4 to 'adolescent health'.[139]

The Committee states that adolescence 'poses new challenges to health and development',[140] and emphasizes the need of States Parties to give more attention to adolescent 'healthy development', but does not elaborate on its meaning. However, it does identify sexuality, pregnancy, and eating disorders as the central foci for adolescent health. More specifically, early marriage and pregnancy, traffic accidents, mental disorders, and psychosocial illnesses including depression, eating disorders and self-destructive behaviour, lack of access to health services, and insufficient information on health issues are highlighted as having a negative impact on the adolescent's development.[141] Adolescent psychological development is also

[132] Article 24(2)(c).

[133] UNCRC, 'Concluding Observations: Vanuato' (10 November 1999) UN Doc CRC/C/15/Add. 111; UNCRC, 'Concluding Observations: Haiti' (18 March 2003) UN Doc CRC/C/15/Add. 202; UNCRC, 'Concluding Observations: Uzbekistan' (2 June 2006) UN Doc CRC/C/UZB/CO/2; UNCRC, 'Concluding Observations: Bangladesh' (27 October 2003) UN Doc CRC/C/15/Add. 221; 'Concluding Observations: Thailand' 2006, N. 107 above.

[134] UNICEF, *The State of the World's Children 2009* (UNICEF, New York), 2–4.

[135] UNCRC, 'Concluding Observations: Mali' (2 November 1999) UN Doc CRC/C/15/Add. 113.

[136] UNCRC, 'General Comment No. 3 (2003)—HIV/AIDS and the Rights of the Child' (17 March 2003) UN Doc CRC/GC/2003/3.

[137] Ibid.

[138] Ibid.

[139] 'General Comment No. 4', N. 46 above.

[140] Ibid.

[141] Ibid.

mentioned as an issue requiring special attention, in order to ensure protection of the adolescent's healthy development.[142] This is the case notably in relation to the consumption of alcohol and drugs, which are considered as having a negative effect on the physical, emotional, and psychological development and well-being of the (adolescent) child.[143]

The Committee recognizes the need to modify the way in which the child is being perceived as she or he grows up, and alters the meaning of the right to development as a consequence. But rather than providing satisfactory explanations for the changes in its understanding of development, the Committee settles for highlighting new areas of consideration.

22.2.13 Children and labour

Article 32 of the Convention does not prohibit any form of child labour, and only protects the child from 'economic exploitation and from performing any work that is likely to be hazardous or to interfere with the child's education, or to be harmful to the child's health or physical, mental, spiritual, moral or social development'. Based on this Article, the Committee demands States Parties protect the right to development of working children.[144] It emphasizes that long working hours, especially for young children who are still subject to compulsory education, have a negative effect on school attendance and hence on these children's 'full and holistic development'.[145] This is consistent with yet another vague desire to defend children's full and holistic development.

22.3 The need to deconstruct the Committee's conception of childhood

The origins of the Committee's approach to the right to development lie in the Convention and the emphasis it puts on protecting children's development and the process of growing up.

Between 1993 and 2009, the Committee put a lot of effort into interpreting and ascribing meaning to the right to development of children. This has resulted in a detailed directory of what can constitute a violation of, or interference with, children's right to development. The Committee gathered almost every aspect of children's lives and almost every human right of the child into this directory, as well as rights that are not mentioned in the Convention, such as the right to freedom of movement.[146] However, as broad and detailed as the Committee's interpretation is, it

[142] UNCRC, 'Concluding Observations: Romania (12 June 2009) UN Doc CRC/C/ROM/CO/4.

[143] UNCRC, 'Concluding Observations: Democratic People's Republic of Korea (27 March 2009) UN Doc CRC/C/PRK/CO/4.

[144] UNCRC, 'Concluding Observations: Lao People's Democratic Republic' (21 October 1997) UN Doc CRC/C/15/Add. 78.

[145] UNCRC, 'Concluding Observations: Central African Republic' (18 October 2000), UN Docs CRC/C/5/Add. 138; 'Concluding Observations: Cameroon' 2001, N. 46 above; UNCRC, 'Concluding Observations: Madagascar' (27 October 2003) UN Doc CRC/C/15/Add. 218; 'Concluding Observations: Jamaica' 2003, N. 79 above; UNCRC, 'Concluding Observations: Czech Republic' (18 March 2003) UN Doc CRC/C/15/Add. 201; 'Concluding Observations: Malaysia' 2007, N. 113 above.

[146] UNCRC, 'Concluding Observations: United Kingdom of Great Britain and Northern Ireland' (20 October 2008) UN Doc CRC/C/GBR/CO/4.

amounts to a failure to meet the interpretative standard it set itself, when requesting that State Parties interpret 'development' in its broadest sense as a 'holistic concept, embracing the child's physical, mental, spiritual, moral, psychological and social development'.[147] Its interpretation does not amount to any holistic concept but rather remains a fragmented structure of distinct components of development.

The Committee's interpretation of the right to development shifts between two poles. It either defines a violation of one human right of the child as a simultaneous violation of the right to development (for example, violation of the right to non-discrimination), or it defines development to be the aim of protecting other human rights (like the right to education). Nonetheless, the Committee's rhetoric has resulted neither in a meaningful nor holistic understanding of the right to development. Neither of these two approaches provides a distinct and substantial meaning to the right to development itself, nor does it clarify whether the right to development should be understood to protect the process of development, its outcome or both. This ambiguity is a result of the traditional, conservative, and binary conception of childhood as time of 'becoming' that the Committee holds, unable or unwilling to divert from what Diduck calls a 'romantic developmentalism' approach towards children.[148]

It is no surprise then that the right to freedom of expression[149] or the right to participation[150] are two of the very few rights that the Committee has not expressly linked to the right to development. Unlike the rest of the Convention's rights, these two rights are not solely forward-looking rights, but rather they attribute meaning to children's lives in the present and acknowledge children's agency. A child who expresses his or her opinions or executes his or her right to participation in a decision concerning his or her future, deconstructs the binary distinction between the 'becoming' and 'being' models. These kinds of children are 'being' and 'becoming' simultaneously and do not fit the image of 'the child' that the Committee holds. These children are not only growing up, but also live their meaningful lives as children.

22.4 Conclusion

The UN Committee on the Rights of the Child is not a homogenous body. Its members come from different geographical, personal, and professional backgrounds and during the 17 years of work reviewed in this research, the Committee's composition has changed little. However, notwithstanding its diversity and though different aspects of children's lives were in focus during the years, the overall approach to the right to development has remained the same.

When the Committee urges States Parties to respect and promote children's right to development, it pays only lip service to children and their rights. Its perceptions of what qualifies as adequate child-rearing or how children should be educated are the direct result of the Committee's anachronistic 'human becoming' approach, which sees children only through the prism of their future selves. It seems that the Committee understands the right to development of children to be nothing more than the right to become an adult.

[147] 'General Comment No. 5', N. 38 above.

[148] Alison Diduck, *Law's Families* (Lexis-Nexis, London, 2003), 79.

[149] Article 13.

[150] Article 12.

While the right to development does have significant forward-looking elements, it has other potential meanings as well. As Janusz Korczak wrote:

> Children are not people of tomorrow, but are people of today. They have a right to be taken seriously, and to be treated with tenderness and respect. They should be allowed to grow into whoever they were meant to be—the unknown person inside each of them is our hope for the future.[151]

These words were written in 1919, five years before the League of Nations adopted the Declaration on the Rights of the Child. Almost 100 years later, these words should be a reminder that the meaning of the right to development for children surpasses the one so far ascribed to it by the UN Committee on the Rights of the Child.

[151] Janusz Korczak, *Loving Every Child* (originally published in 1919; translated by Sandra Joseph, Algonquin Books, New York, 2007), 19.

23

CRC's Performance of the Child as Developing

Ashleigh Barnes[1]

> The account of children's rights should be both realistic and unsentimental about the facts of childhood and adulthood... Indeed, there are so many similarities and continuities between childhood and adulthood that it is hard, without lapsing into sentimental romanticism, to say what is so different about the two phases other than the way social structures treat them... Yet there are *important natural differences* between childhood and adulthood... central to them is the notion of maturity.[1A]

Law is enslaved to child welfare and child development experts.[2] The agitation of a particular identity, or a categorization based upon alleged 'natural' characteristics, has been done in the context of gender, race, sexual orientation, etc., to expose the unnaturalness and difference within that category. In an attempt to explore a similar critique of the child, a Foucauldian critique of power and truth/knowledge will be recruited to make the argument that the category 'child' is not based upon a set of natural and fundamental characteristics shared by those aged 0–18, the operating presumption of the child in the UN Convention on the Rights of the Child (CRC). If there is no universal 'child', on what ground do the politics behind and the power relations dependent upon the fictitious universal child in the CRC stand? 'Realistically' and 'unsentimentally', we must ask whose 'facts' are being employed in the CRC, on what basis, and to what end?

Yet, what does it mean to be a child? What characteristics make a person a 'child'? It is a grouping deemed by the international community to be collectively unique enough to justify the creation of a singular category in the context of international law, irrespective of gender, class, ethnicity, nationality, and so on. While other fields of study have agitated the 'naturalness' of the 'developing child', legal international discourse on the child and rights of the child remains stuck on the 'developing child'. For example, sociologists agitated the 'naturalness' and essential nature of childhood some 40 years ago.[3] Nonetheless, several 'truths' are presented in the CRC about the

[1] Ph.D. Candidate Australian National University; Assistant Professor Jindal Global Law School.

[1A] Coady, C. (1992) 'Theory, Rights, and Children: A Comment on O'Neill and Campell' 6 *Int. J. L. and Fam.* 44, emphasis added.

[2] King, Michael and Piper, Christine (1995) *How the Law Thinks about Children*, 79.

[3] See for example: Ariès, P. (1962) *Centuries of Childhood: A social history of family life;* Archard, D. (2004) *Children: rights and childhood*, 2nd Edition; Archard, D. (2003) *Children, Family, and the State*; Freeman, M. (1998) 'The Sociology of Childhood and Children's Rights' 6 *International Journal of Children's Rights* 433; Erikson, E. (1977) *Childhood and Society*; Holloway, S.L. and Valentine, G. (2000) 'Spatiality and the New Social Studies of Childhood' 34(4) *Sociology* 763–83; Holloway, S.L. and Valentine, G. (eds.) *Children's Geographies: Living, playing, learning*; Holt, J. (1974) *Escape from Childhood*; James, A. (1979) 'Confections, Concoctions and Conceptions' 10(2) *Journal of the*

child: passive, innocent, dependent, subversive, developing, vulnerable, incapable, and so on. The focus of this chapter will be development because the term 'development', as this chapter will argue, is one of the most influential and believable 'truths' about childhood.[4] Additionally, the term 'development' has an interesting relationship with all the other discourses/'truths' of childhood. The term 'development' encapsulates, explains, and even 'cures' (i.e. is the means to surmount) the child as passive, incapable, dependent, vulnerable, subversive, in need of discipline. The term 'development' accounts for the 'need' for adult intervention in the lives of both the Apollonian and Dionysian child.[5]

While the terms 'vulnerability', 'incapacity', 'dependence' and 'passivity' lack a certain concreteness (and result in a never-ending discussion), development (and the child's need for it) is virtually unquestionable.[6] Notably, the discussion surrounding and reflected in the CRC is not about whether a child is developing, but rather about who is in the best position to guide the child through this 'golden' but dangerous time.[7] The discussion surrounding and reflected in the CRC is not whether the child's

Anthropology Society of Oxford 83; James, A. and Prout, A. (eds.) (1997) *Constructing and Reconstructing Childhood*; James, A., Jenks, C., and Prout, A. (1998) *Theorizing Childhood*; James, A. and Jenks, C. (2004) 'Constructing childhood sociologically', in Kehily, M. (ed.) *An Introduction to Childhood Studies* Maidenhead; James, A. and James, A. (2004) *Constructing Childhood: theory, policy, and social practice*; James, A. and Prout, A. (1990) *Constructing and Reconstructing Childhood: Contemporary issues in the sociological study of childhood*; Jenks, C. (1982) 'Constituting the Child' in Jenks, C. (ed.) *The Sociology of Childhood—Essential Readings*; Jenks, C. (1994) 'Child Abuse in the Postmodern Context: an Issue of Social Identity' 2(3) *Childhood* 111; Jenks, C. (1996) 'The Post-modern Child' in Brannen, J. and O'Brien, M. (1994) *Children in Families: Research and policy*; Mayall, B. (ed) *Children's Childhoods: Observed and Experienced*; Mayall, B. (2002) *Towards a Sociology for Childhood: Thinking from Children's Lives*; Prout, A. (2000) 'Children's Participation: Control and Self-realisation in British Late Modernity' 14(4) *Children and Society* 30; Prout, A. (2004) *The Future of Childhood. Towards the Interdisciplinary Study of Children*; Prout, A. (2005) *The Future of Childhood*; Prout, A. and Hallett, Ch. (eds.) (2003) *Hearing the Voices of Children: Social Policy for a New Century*; Qvortrup J. et al. (eds.) (1994) *Childhood Matters: Social Theory, Practice and Politics;* Qvortrup, J. (2005) 'Varieties of Childhood' in Qvortrup, J. (ed.) *Studies in Modern Childhood: Society, Agency and Culture,* Basingstoke: Palgrave; Qvortrup, J. (1993) *Childhood as a Social Phenomenon: Introduction to a Series of National Reports*; Stainton Rogers R. and Stainton-Rogers, W. (1992) *Stories of Childhood: Shifting Agendas of Child Concern*; Veerman, P. (1992) *The Rights of the Child and the Changing Image of Childhood*; Valentine, G. (1996) 'Angels and Devils: Moral Landscapes of Childhood' 14 *Environment and Planning D: Society and Space* 581–99; Valentine, G. (2003) 'Boundary Crossings: Transitions from Childhood to Adulthood' 1(1) *Children's Geographies* 37; Zelizer, V. (1985) *Pricing the Priceless Child. The Changing Social Value of Children.*

[4] Woodhead, M. (1990) 'Psychology and the Cultural Construction of "Children's Needs"' in Woodhead, M., Light, P., and Carr, R. (eds.) *Growing up in a Changing Society.*

[5] Jenks, C. (2005) *Childhood,* 72. The Apollonian child is angelic, naturally good, innocent, asexual, the best of human nature, and untainted by the world, natural goodness; such children play and chuckle, smile and laugh. The Apollonian child is pre-Eve and her apple. Under this children are not curbed or beaten into submission, they are encouraged, enabled, facilitated. The Dionysian child or the 'inherently bad' child, who is like this prince of wine, revelry, and nature, comprises of the idea that children possess an initial evil or corruption, which for example has as its major buttress in the doctrine of Adamic original sin. The child harbours a potential evil and if adults allow them to stray away (from adults) this force will mobilize. Jenks argues that: 'These images are informative of the shifting strategies that Western society has exercised in its increasing need to control, socialize and constrain people in the transition towards modernity.'

[6] See for example: Stainton Rogers, R. and Stainton Rogers, W. (1992) *Stories of Childhood: Shifting Agendas of Child Concern*; Jenks, C. (2005) *Childhood*; Archard, D. (2001) 'Philosophical Perspectives on Childhood' in Fionda, J. *Legal Concepts of Childhood*; Mayall, B. (2000) 'The Sociology of Childhood in Relation to Children's Rights' 8 *International Journal of Children's Rights* 245.

[7] Lansdown, G. (2005) *The Evolving Capacities of the Child*, Innocenti Insight, x: Assumptions about child development and evolving capacities of the child. Conventional child development theory influences current thinking based on five key assumptions: 1) child development is a universal process, 2) adulthood has normative status, 3) development goals are universal, 4) deviation from the norm indicates risk for

alleged state of development should affect the child's bundle of rights, but rather the extent to which the child's development should affect the child's bundle of rights.[8]

To justify the bundle of rights given to children and thus to cast the category 'child' as less than human, a strong case must be made; a particularly believable 'truth' must be put forward to accomplish such discrimination. The derogation of 'fundamental' rights, which are allegedly available to all humans on the basis of their humanness, requires a sturdier ground on which to stand. While justifying the child's 'lesser' bundle of rights on the basis of the other truths in the Convention would (arguably) be more difficult, this chapter argues that justifying the child's bundle of rights on the basis of the more persuasive (and scientific!) term 'development' has greater political purchase. Ultimately the CRC's construction of the child as developing, through its allocation of 'rights' to children, sustains and supports a hierarchy of power of the state (as a back-up parent) and the parent over the child. This hierarchy of power is made 'ok'/condonable/even 'necessary' through the deployment of knowledge regarding 'the child's development'. This hierarchy of power makes possible the regulation and control of childhood.

To examine the CRC's child, one must start by exploring the shape of rights given to the child. When these rights diverge from the rights given (or emphasized[9]) to all other humans, one must look at the justification that is offered. The identification of that justification illuminates the CRC's true child, as though we are seeking to

the child, 5) childhood is an extended period of dependence in which children are passive recipients of adult protection, training, wisdom, and guidance rather than contributors to their social environments.

[8] See for example: Brems, E. (2002) 'Children's Rights and Universality' in Willems, J. *Developmental and Autonomy Rights of Children: Empowering Children, Care-givers, and Communities*, reproduced in Dillon, S. (2010) *International Children's Rights*; Olsen, F. (1992) 'Children's Rights: Some Feminist Approaches to the CRC' 6 *International Journal of Law and the Family* 192; Miljeteig-Olssen, P. (1990) 'Advocacy of Children's Rights—The Convention as More than a Legal Document' 12 *Human Rights Quarterly* 148.

[9] It was noted during the drafting of the Convention that 'there are still those who believe that a convention on the rights of the child was not necessary—that children's rights were, if not totally, at least adequately covered by existing human rights instruments applicable to all, and that it is dangerous or unwarranted to pinpoint children as a special and separate category of human beings. We can recall that it was not because of the Convention that children were singled out as a special group, but because of the realization, seventy years ago, that children's specific needs and vulnerability demanded particular responses from the international community. We can note in that regard that global human rights instruments were not drawn up with children in mind, that they have been developed over a period of a decade, and that as a whole they therefore contain a number of inconsistencies and certainly do not reflect current knowledge and experience with regard to children's issues. But in addition . . . is the usefulness for promoting knowledge and understanding of children's issues'. See Detrick, S. (1992) *The United Nations Convention on the Rights of the Child, A guide to the 'Travaux Preparations'*, 29. Germany suggested that 'All states shall ensure a) that all human rights recognized by them also apply to children, b) that general human rights as enshrined in the ICCPR even apply to children, if a state party to the present convention is not a party to the Covenant'. Germany argued that many of the rights in the International Covenants already apply to children, were included again specifically in the draft Convention, but on the other hand not all the rights guaranteed by the Covenants appeared in the draft Convention, for example the right of self-determination, the equal rights of men and women, the ban on slavery, the right of a person arrested or detained to be brought promptly before a judge, even though they should also apply to children. The delegate said that this selective double-regulation of rights would create problems and even contradictions with the Covenants and a general clause ensuring the application of general human rights to children should be substituted for the present Article 1. Australia said that to do so was totally new, bringing into question the whole approach of the Convention to existing rights. It may well have been a better way to proceed had it been introduced years before, but that had not happened and now its acceptance would only serve to delay adoption of the Convention. Ultimately Germany withdrew its proposal. See Detrick, S. (1992) *The United Nations Convention on the Rights of the Child, A guide to the 'Travaux Préparatiores'*, 131.

understand Pinocchio's goal: what it means to be a 'real' [child], in this case a 'real' child according to the CRC. This chapter argues that to be a 'true' or 'real' child, a person nominated a child must be 'developing'. This chapter then argues and seeks to explicate how the hierarchy of power surrounding the child is made possible.[10] Section 23.1 discusses the 'disciplines' and 'knowledges' that underline and support childhood as being defined as a state of development. Section 23.2 will examine specific articles in the Convention that reference the child's development and will examine how development operates (i.e. what the term 'development' makes possible) in each of those articles.

23.1 Childhood as a state of development and its implications

The CRC uses the word 'development' 18 times; 14 of which refer to the child's development.[11] Childhood as the site of development was accepted in the Convention without any discussion during the drafting of the Convention.[12] The acceptance of childhood as a state of development is not explained in the Convention or by the drafters, outside perhaps of the Preamble by 'bearing in mind that, as indicated in the Declaration on the Rights of the Child, the child, by reason of his physical and mental immaturity, needs special safeguards and care'.[13] Children are assumed immature and thus in need of development. Childhood characterized as a unique state of development is presented as a 'truth' in the CRC, apparently too obvious to require discussion.[14] This section will discuss the various knowledges that support development as a 'truth' of childhood, and then discuss the implication of the CRC's adoption of childhood as a state of development.

23.1.1 The basis of childhood development

The CRC assumes that there is a model of childhood development that is universally descriptive of all children.[15] However, the Convention's version of childhood as a period of development is far from unique. The performance of the child as developing

[10] Hammarberg, T. (1990) 'The UN Convention on the Rights of the Child and How to Make it Work' 12 *Human Rights Quarterly* 101: the triangular relationship between the child, the guardians, and the state was of course a sensitive issue during the drafting.

[11] Other references to 'development' relate to the state's obligation for development of programmes, institutions, etc. For example Article 18(2) states, '[f]or the purpose of guaranteeing and promoting the rights set forth in the present Convention, States Parties shall render appropriate assistance to parents and legal guardians in the performance of their child-rearing responsibilities and shall ensure the development of institutions, facilities and services for the care of children'.

[12] See generally Detrick, S. (1992) *The United Nations Convention on the Rights of the Child, A guide to the 'Travaux Préparatiores'*.

[13] 1989 Convention on the Rights of the Child, UN Doc. A/RES/44/25 (1989), entered into force September 1990, Preamble. Detrick, S. (1992) *The United Nations Convention on the Rights of the Child, A guide to the 'Travaux Préparatiores'*.

[14] Detrick, S. (1992) *The United Nations Convention on the Rights of the Child, A guide to the 'Travaux Préparatiores'*.

[15] In support of this view see: Brems, E. (2002) 'Children's Rights and Universality' in Willems, J. *Developmental and Autonomy Rights of Children: Empowering Children, Care-givers, and Communities*, reproduced in Dillon, S. (2010) *International Children's Rights*, 69. For a critique see: Pupavac, V. (2001) 'Misanthropy without Borders: The International Children's Rights Regime' 25(2) *Disasters* 101; Boyden, J. (1994) 'Children's Experience of Conflict Related Emergencies: Some Implications for Relief Policy and Practice' 18 *Disasters* 256.

matches dominant knowledges about childhood: psychological and even 'common sense' understandings of childhood.[16] The dominant developmental approach to childhood, provided by psychology, is based on the idea of natural growth.[17] It is essentially an evolutionary model: the child developing into an adult represents a progression from simplicity to complexity of thought, from irrational to rational behaviour.[18] The persuasiveness of psychological reasoning is attributed to developmental psychology's heavy reliance on ways of thinking already found particularly influential in natural sciences.[19] Socialization is portrayed as a process analogous to the creation of a compound out of base elements. *Sodium + Chloride = Salt; Heredity + Environment = socialized individual.*[20] However, unlike the chemist, but like the alchemist, some academics contend that psychologists have never had any clear idea of how their metaphorical process (melding together of nature and nurture) actually operates.[21] Psychologists can only speculate in extremely vague terms about the way socialization may operate, let alone how it may fail, be reversed, break down, etc.[22] The interplay between nature and nurture requires theoretical and moral resolutions and extrapolations, rather than some objective description.[23] Development does not signify a 'natural' process, but makes reference to a socially constructed sense of change during childhood, which is encoded within a series of benchmarks made relevant by predominate discourses/knowledges placed on the child.[24]

Though the process of development is argued to be no more than a story or 'truth-claim', some maintain that it has become a story with such compelling plausibility it has overwhelmingly acquired the seeming status of incontrovertible truth: development during the course of childhood is the way children *really are.*[25] 'Natural children' are then tracked and plotted as they 'develop' through the 'socialization process' into adulthood, which is itself taken for granted in the prevailing social order.[26] Stainton Rogers and Stainton Rogers, in their book, *Stories of Childhood: Shifting Agendas of Child Concern*, label the phenomenon of childhood development as 'developmentalist hegemony' because of its potency.[27] Jenks argues that while

[16] Stainton Rogers, R. and Stainton Rogers, W. (1992) *Stories of Childhood: Shifting Agendas of Child Concern*, 51.

[17] Prout, A. and James, A. (1997) 'A New Paradigm for the Sociology of Childhood? Provenance, Promise and Problems' in James, A. and Prout, A. *Constructing and Reconstructing Childhood: Contemporary Issues in the Sociological Study of Childhood*, 10–11.

[18] Prout, A. and James, A. (1997) 'A New Paradigm for the Sociology of Childhood? Provenance, Promise and Problems' in James, A. and Prout, A. *Constructing and Reconstructing Childhood: Contemporary Issues in the Sociological Study of Childhood*, 10–11.

[19] Stainton Rogers, R. and Stainton Rogers, W. (1992) *Stories of Childhood: Shifting Agendas of Child Concern*, 38; Mayall, B. (2000) 'The Sociology of Childhood in Relation to Children's Rights' 8 *International Journal on Children's Rights* 244.

[20] Stainton Rogers, R. and Stainton Rogers, W. (1992) *Stories of Childhood: Shifting Agendas of Child Concern*, 38.

[21] Stainton Rogers, R. and Stainton Rogers, W. (1992) *Stories of Childhood: Shifting Agendas of Child Concern*, 38.

[22] Stainton Rogers, R. and Stainton Rogers, W. (1992) *Stories of Childhood: Shifting Agendas of Child Concern*, 38.

[23] Stainton Rogers, R. and Stainton Rogers, W. (1992) *Stories of Childhood: Shifting Agendas of Child Concern*, 39.

[24] Jenks, C. (2005) *Childhood*, 39.

[25] Stainton Rogers, R. and Stainton Rogers, W. (1992) *Stories of Childhood: Shifting Agendas of Child Concern*, 39–40.

[26] Stainton Rogers, R. and Stainton Rogers, W. (1992) *Stories of Childhood: Shifting Agendas of Child Concern*, 51.

[27] Stainton Rogers, R. and Stainton Rogers, W. (1992) *Stories of Childhood: Shifting Agendas of Child Concern*, 41.

social sciences have critically addressed and debunked dominant ideologies of, for example, capitalism in relation to social class, colonialism in relation to race, and patriarchy in relation to gender, the ideology of development in relation to childhood has remained relatively intact.[28]

Moving beyond psychology, our everyday understandings of children and childhood have been more broadly monopolized by a knowledge industry manufactured by the practitioner and academic entrepreneurs working in the fields of education, anthropology, sociology, social work, and so on.[29] These industries' manufactured knowledge legitimates a particular set of discourses upon the child, representing their knowledge as fundamental, invariable truths about the nature of all children, past and present.[30] This chapter argues that the CRC is a highly persuasive knowledge manufacturer, legitimating a particular set of discourses on the child. The CRC produces and legitimates its performance of childhood as fundamental, invariable truth about the category child. The CRC's claim to 'truth' (child = developing) masquerades as a description of 'how things are', rather than a production/prescription of 'how things must be'.

23.1.2 The implications of development

One author writes that the undeveloped child is incomplete, lacking full maturity, and unfinished.[31] In this way the child is defined negatively, in the sense of what the child lacks.[32] Archard, in his essay, 'Philosophical Perspectives on Childhood', argues that the defining feature of childhood is that the child is unfinished relative to a human *telos*:

> In the biology, the child is viewed as unfinished in his or her growth as a human animal; in the ethics, unfinished in the training of virtue; in the politics, unfinished in the education for adult life as a responsible citizen.[33]

Children are viewed as 'becoming' rather than being.[34] The focus of adults then is not on childhood in and of itself, but on how the desired characteristics of adulthood are acquired.[35] Put another way, the fixation on childhood is on the process of

[28] Jenks, C. (2005) *Childhood*, 4. See also Aitken, S.C. and Herman, T. (1997) 'Gender, Power and Crib Geography: Transitional Spaces and Potential Places' 4(1) *Gender, Place and Culture* 63.

[29] Stainton Rogers, R. and Stainton Rogers, W. (1992) *Stories of Childhood: Shifting Agendas of Child Concern*, 51.

[30] Stainton Rogers, R. and Stainton Rogers, W. (1992) *Stories of Childhood: Shifting Agendas of Child Concern*, 51.

[31] Fionda, J. (2001) 'Legal Concepts of Childhood: An Introduction' in Fionda, J. *Legal Concepts of Childhood*, 12.

[32] Archard, D. (2001) 'Philosophical Perspectives on Childhood' in Fionda, J. *Legal Concepts of Childhood*, 43, referring to Hendrick, H. (1997) *Children, Childhood, and English Society, 1880–1990.*

[33] Archard, D. (2001) 'Philosophical Perspectives on Childhood' in Fionda, J. *Legal Concepts of Childhood*, 43, quoting Matthews, G. (1998) 'Socrates' Children' in Turner, S. and Matthews, G. (eds.) *The Philosophers's Child: Critical Essays in the Western Tradition*, 21. See also Erny, P. (1973) *Childhood and Cosmos, The Social Psychology of the Black African Child*, 11: The child is distinguished from the adult by the fact that he[/she] has not yet reach maturity. He/she is still in a stage of development, on the way to completion. From this reasons he/she cannot be described in his/her full and stable state, since he/she is essentially a dynamism, a tension, progress toward a more perfect state. Neither the child nor his/her personality can be considered under any aspect but that of becoming.

[34] Archard, D. (2001) 'Philosophical Perspectives on Childhood' in Fionda, J. *Legal Concepts of Childhood*, 43.

[35] Archard, D. (2001) 'Philosophical Perspectives on Childhood' in Fionda, J. *Legal Concepts of Childhood*, 43–4.

development. Development teleology condemns children to being viewed exclusively as developmentally adaptive, hence correct or developmentally defective, hence incorrect.[36] The focus then is on what children 'need'. As will be argued in Section 23.2, the CRC's performance of the child as developing enables the 'need' for adults who have responsibility for/power over children. The child's 'need' for a 'responsible' adult significantly alters the child's rights, even rights that are considered to be fundamental for all humans. In the context of the CRC this chapter argues that the CRC's performance of the 'child' as a unique state of development is the basis for deviating from the 'equal and inalienable rights of all humans'.[37] Notably, whether rights are the 'solution' has been widely discussed and criticized; however a full discussion will not take place here. Regardless of whether one agrees with the efficacy of rights, how these rights are constructed contribute to the production of an identity for the category child. Some argue that the Convention reinforces and reifies the systematic oppression of young people.[38] It is argued that the child becomes a site for progress, a reflection of the community's progress and therefore an object of regulation.[39]

If the basis on which we (read 'adults') 'know' children is an unessential, unnatural social construction, how can we (read 'adults') validate how children are talked about and therefore treated, in the Convention and otherwise? By portraying the child as incomplete/developing and therefore in need of his/her wiser counterparts, the Convention not only justifies the restriction of some very basic rights, but entrenches a vastly inequitable relationship between the child and his/her family and his/her community. Quite simply, casting the child-as-developing allows the Convention (adults, states, institutions, discourses) to side-step what would be considered unthinkable for any other category of persons within the human family.

23.2 Development in the CRC

This section now turns to how the term 'development' is deployed in the Convention. To unpack the operation of 'development' in the Convention, this section will utilize Woodhead's 'needs equation' from her article, 'Psychology and the Cultural Construction of "Children's Needs"'. Woodhead argues that childhood is predominately conceptualized in terms of needs; a term that she argues conceals a complex practice of latent assumptions and judgments about children.[40] Her equation, 'X

[36] Campbell, T. (1993) 'The Rights of the Minor: As Person, As Child, As Juvenile, and Future Adult' in Archard, D. et al. (eds.) *Children, Rights, and the Law*, 17.

[37] Preamble.

[38] Stainton Rogers, R. and Stainton Rogers, W. (1992) *Stories of Childhood: Shifting Agendas of Child Concern*.

[39] Jenks, C. (2005) *Childhood*, 3; Grahn-Farley, M. (2003) 'Beyond Right and Reason: PieerSchlag, The Critique of Normativity, and the Enchantment of Reason: A Theory of Child Rights' 57 *University of Miami Law Review* 867, for the discussion relating to children: 'The rights of a person tell us more about that person's place in society than about the rights themselves. Rights are signs of what the human has been made to not be. Rights are the void. Rights are emptiness. Rights are the emptiness that remains when a person is made to be less than human. The language of rights takes the place of the unspeakable pain and suffering that is inflicted on people, by people. Rights are the bandages on already-inflicted injuries. Bandages do not heal; they cover and hide wounds. Instead of seeing the harms inflicted, one sees the bandages. Instead of seeing the pain and suffering, one sees the right.'

[40] See Woodhead, M. (1990) 'Psychology and the Cultural Construction of "Children's Needs"' in Woodhead, M., Light, P., and Carr, R. (eds.) *Growing up in a Changing Society*, 37, 40: Woodhead maintains that children might be better served if 'children's needs' were outlawed from all professional

needs Y for Z', is a method for analysing and breaking down who needs what and why, questions often difficult to ascertain. The simplicity of this method to deconstruct the components of the language behind the words is precisely why this equation is being used, as though we are again in English class doing sentence diagrams. As applied to the CRC, X [the child] needs Y [a particular thing that is secured in the form of a right] for Z [to accomplish some measure].[41] This analysis will be used even when the 'need' is implied. As a reminder, this chapter does not endeavour to engage in black letter law analysis. Obviously, if so, an easy counter-argument would be that rights given under other international conventions, such as the International Covenant on Economic, Social and Cultural Rights (ICESR) and the International Covenant on Civil and Political Rights (ICCPR), would be applicable to children. Rather, this chapter seeks to examine the story told by the CRC. As such, the rights that are included and excluded, as well as rights that are modified in this Convention, are all of interest. The specific bundle of rights found in the CRC and, therefore, the bundle of identified issues/needs of childhood tell a very specific tale of childhood, as compared to the story told of adult right holders in other conventions.[42]

23.2.1 Preamble[43]

The Preamble to the CRC reads:

the child, for the full and harmonious **development** of his or her personality, should grow up in a family environment, in an atmosphere of happiness, love and understanding... taking due account of the importance of traditions and cultural values of each people for the protection and harmonious **development** of the child. (emphasis added)

Applying Woodhead's 'needs equation' X Y Z model to these two sentences:[44]

X	needs	Y	for	Z
The child		A family environment (defined as an atmosphere of happiness, love, and understanding) that takes into account traditions and cultural values		Full and harmonious development

discourse, policy recommendations, and popular psychology. Woodhead argues that 'needs' often serve as a very credible veil for uncertainty and even disagreement about what is 'in the best interest of the child'.

[41] Woodhead, M. (1990) 'Psychology and the Cultural Construction of "Children's Needs"' in Woodhead, M., Light, P., and Carr, R. (eds.) *Growing up in a Changing Society*, 37.

[42] Detrick, S. (1992) *The United Nations Convention on the Rights of the Child, A Guide to the 'Travaux Préparatiores'*, 130–1: Indeed the German delegate expressed concern that certain rights from other human rights conventions were included in the CRC while others were not (citing the right to self-determination, the ban on slavery, the equal rights of men and women, the right of a person arrested or detained to be brought promptly before a judge). The delegate pointed out that this selective double-regulation of rights would create problems and even contradictions with the other human rights conventions. Ultimately the German delegate argued that there should be a general clause noting the applicability of general human rights to children. The Australian delegate argued that if the German delegate's suggestion was followed, this would be a whole new approach to the Convention, and would derail the entire process, particularly at such a late stage in the drafting process. Ultimately the German delegate withdrew its proposal. Given this discussion, one could argue that even under a black letter law analysis it is uncertain what the effect of the CRC's selective 'double-regulation' is.

[43] The legal significance of the Preamble as compared to the articles themselves will not be discussed here, the reason being that this chapter investigates the performance of the child in the Convention in its entirety, rather than its black letter law importance.

[44] Woodhead, M. (1990) 'Psychology and the Cultural Construction of "Children's Needs"' in Woodhead, M., Light, P., and Carr, R. (eds.) *Growing up in a Changing Society.*

According to this statement, the result needed for the child is 'full and harmonious development'. During the drafting of the Convention, no discussion took place as to what was meant by any of these three terms: 'full', 'harmonious', or 'development'.[45] The non-discussion of the usage of the term 'development' in relation to the child is consistent throughout the drafting of the Convention. Apparently, the term was too obvious to require discussion. The terms 'full' and 'harmonious' are interesting adjectives used to describe the child's development. What do 'full' and 'harmonious', much less 'development', mean? Harmonious could mean 'appropriate' or 'agreeable'. Yet, what is 'appropriate' for the child's development? Is there agreement/could there be agreement regarding what is or is not suitable for the child's development?[46] How one defines 'harmonious' would depend on one's vision of what childhood should be. Given that the Preamble notes that the aim of childhood is where 'the child should be fully prepared to live an individual life in society', 'full' implies the time at which the child graduates from childhood into adulthood. Outside of the legally delineated time defined in Article 1 of when the child graduates, what does a fully developed child look like? 'Full' seems to imply the point at which the child fully reaches his/her binary opposition: adulthood/a state of responsibility. If the answer is an adult, what does an adult look like? Regardless, the picture drawn of the child in this article is that the child is inherently incomplete, lacking, and insufficient, and thus requiring development. By attaching 'full' and 'harmonious', the CRC not only makes adulthood the normative aim of childhood, but indicates that the process itself has to meet certain norms of what is or is not appropriate for childhood. In this way, the process of development becomes an object of regulation (it must be full and harmonious); the child becomes a site of regulation. Indeed Mayall in her article, 'The Sociology of Childhood in Relation to Children's Rights', argues that the perceived 'need' to monitor children's development has led to unprecedented surveillance of childhood, whether at school or at home.[47]

Here the child seems to need two things: 1) to develop and 2) a family environment. More specifically, the child needs the family *for* his/her development. 'Needs' statements (here the child needs full and harmonious development) carry authority not just because of their straightforward descriptive quality.[48] Woodhead contends that 'needs' statements convey considerable emotive force, inducing a sense of responsibility, and even feelings of guilt if those statements are not followed. This power, she argues, comes partly from the connotation of helplessness and passivity of any individual who is 'in need' and partly from the implication of the dire consequence that will follow if the need is not met through appropriate intervention.[49] Here if the child does not have a family environment in line with traditions and cultural values, the child will not develop, fully or harmoniously. If the child does not have a family,

[45] Detrick, S. (1992) *The United Nations Convention on the Rights of the Child, A guide to the 'Travaux Préparatiores'*, 102–10.

[46] Lansdown, G. (2005) *The Evolving Capacities of the Child*, Innocenti Insight, Foreword: 'The understanding of childhood varies significantly around the world. No universal consensus can be found as to what children need for their optimum development, what environments best provide for those needs, and what form and level of protection is appropriate for children at a specific age.'

[47] Mayall, B. (2000) 'The Sociology of Childhood in Relation to Children's Rights' 8 *International Journal of Children's Rights* 243.

[48] Woodhead, M. (1990) 'Psychology and the Cultural Construction of "Children's Needs"' in Woodhead, M., Light, P., and Carr, R. (eds.) *Growing up in a Changing Society*, 40.

[49] Woodhead, M. (1990) 'Psychology and the Cultural Construction of "Children's Needs"' in Woodhead, M., Light, P., and Carr, R. (eds.) *Growing up in a Changing Society*, 40.

the child's development will be incomplete and tumultuous. Given that the Preamble notes that the aim of childhood is where 'the child should be fully prepared to live an individual life in society', the undeveloped child would be a 'dire consequence'. The entire aim of childhood (development into a normal adult) would not be reached.

The family becomes the 'proper' place for childhood. The portrayal of the child as developing makes possible and even necessary the family. In the Convention, the family and the community are made up of hierarchical relationships of adults over children. For example, traditions, cultural values, and parents'[50] judgment trump the child's right to information, thought, and religion,[51] and even the right to be free from abusive traditional practices or as the Convention more lightly puts it 'traditional practices that are prejudicial to the health of children'.[52] By making the family a requirement of childhood, the CRC solidifies and rationalizes the hierarchical relationship of adults,[53] in particular parents and the state as a back-up parent,[54] over children.[55] The child and her/his development are in need of regulation and thus it is the parents that must first exercise such control.

23.2.2 Article 6: right to life

The first article that includes the word 'development' is the right to life in Article 6, which states,

1. State Parties recognize that every child has the inherent right to life.
2. State Parties shall ensure to the maximum extent possible the survival and development of the child.

[50] The words 'parents' and 'care-givers' are used interchangeable. The terms 'adult' and 'parents' are used interchangeably in this chapter, and mean those who have responsibility for the child. The issue of the Convention giving preference to biological parents will not be pursued here.

[51] See Articles 14(2) and 17(e).

[52] See Article 24(3), particularly when read with Article 18: 'States Parties shall take all effective and appropriate measures with a view to abolishing traditional practices prejudicial to the health of children.' Interestingly, given that the Convention presents children as vulnerable, in need of protection, etc., the state is not required to ensure the abolishment of traditional practices. Further, given that assault against children (otherwise known as 'smacking') is widely practised, one wonders whether, if children were allowed to participate, both measures regarding traditional practices and 'smacking' might be different. But then again, 'smacking' probably could be justified under the need for development, in particularly as outlined in Article 29, to develop respect for one's parents.

[53] For example, 'Responsibility for', in Articles 5 and 18, becomes a grant of power to the parent over the child, where parents are empowered to impose their beliefs and opinions on the child. For further discussion see Barnes, A. 'The CRC's Natural Family: the Parent, the State and the Child' (forthcoming).

[54] Article 20(2).

[55] Interestingly, in the discussions that took place during the drafting of the Convention, the terms 'family'/'care' and 'parent' became almost synonymous. It is not that the terms 'family' and 'parent' are synonymous, but rather that 'family' and 'parental control' were used synonymously. For example regarding Article 5, the Canadian delegate noted the concern that 'in protecting the family from the state, *the family must not be given arbitrary control over the child*. Any protection from the state given to the family must be equally balanced with the protection of the child within the family.' Canada argued that the Convention was a 'delicate balance between the rights of the child and the correlative rights of the parents'. In the first two sentences the delegate refers to the family and the child, and in the third refers to the parents and the child. Further, the Canadian delegate expressed the fear that 'the family' must not be given arbitrary control over the child. As the family is only made up of parents and children, the Canadian delegate must have meant that the *parents* must not be given arbitrary control. 'Parental power' becomes interchangeable with the term 'family'. See: Detrick, S. (1992) *The United Nations Convention on the Rights of the Child, A guide to the 'Travaux Préparatiores'*, 160. Emphasis added.

Under Woodhead's model:

X	needs	Y	for	Z
The child		The state		The child to be able to survive and develop and thus to be able to enjoy the right to life

Here, the right to life refers to 'survival and development'. The required result is the 'survival and development' of the child. Yet what does development, but also survival mean? Further, how do 'survival' and 'development' relate to the right to life? During the drafting of this article there were some concerns expressed that the concept of survival was not legally defined and could be 'harmful' to the concept of the right to development.[56] The Italian representative noted that 'the two words "survival" and "development" had come to acquire the special meaning of ensuring the child's survival in order to realize the full development of his or her personality, both from the material and spiritual points of view'.[57] This special meaning was not articulated by the Italian representative and arguably is not obvious from the Convention or the discussions that took place during the drafting of the Convention.

In the commentary on Article 6, Nowak takes a positive view of the coupling of the right to life/survival with development in Article 6 arguing that such coupling illustrates that the right to life was interpreted in a comprehensive manner.[58] Though Nowak does not expound on what he means by 'comprehensive', he goes on to argue that concept of development in the CRC would be understood better through Article 1 of the United Nations Declaration on the Right to Development (UNDRD). Article 1 of the UNDRD defines the right to development as 'an inalienable human right by virtue of which every human person and all peoples are entitled to participate in, contribute to, and enjoy economic, social cultural and political development, in which all human rights and fundamental freedoms can be fully realized'.[59] Nowak argues that the right to development has been characterized as a participatory process which ultimately leads to the full realization of all human rights and fundamental freedoms.[60] While similar vocabularies are being used in the CRC and the UNDRD, a vastly different paradigm of rights is being articulated. Though this point will be further developed in this chapter, far from full participation in economic, social, cultural, and political development, the child's development relates little to full participation in anything, including the matters that directly relate to the child.

While the right to life under the CRC refers to 'survival and development', the ICCPR only requires freedom from arbitrary deprival of life.[61] This article seems to

[56] Detrick, S. (1992) *The United Nations Convention on the Rights of the Child, A guide to the 'Travaux Préparatiores'*, 120.

[57] Detrick, S. (1992) *The United Nations Convention on the Rights of the Child, A guide to the 'Travaux Préparatiores'*, 123.

[58] Nowak, M. (2005) 'Article 6: The Right to Life, Survival and Development' in Alen, A. et al. (eds.) *A Commentary on the United Nations Convention on the Rights of the Child*, 2.

[59] Nowak, M. (2005) 'Article 6: The Right to Life, Survival and Development' in Alen, A. et al. (eds.) *A Commentary on the United Nations Convention on the Rights of the Child*, 47.

[60] Nowak, M. (2005) 'Article 6: The Right to Life, Survival and Development' in Alen, A. et al. (eds.) *A Commentary on the United Nations Convention on the Rights of the Child*, 47.

[61] 1966 International Covenant on Civil and Political Rights, UN Doc. A/RES/2200A (XXI), entered into force 23 March 1976, Article 6.

suggest that unlike adults, children, by mere the fact of being a child, must apparently struggle to survive. The Preamble states that children around the world are living in exceptionally difficult circumstances. Further, given that the Convention does not recognize that children suffer from social discrimination and at the same time does recognize that children are fundamentally immature, the child's struggle to survive would be a result of the child's inherent immaturity, at least as understood in the Convention.[62] The child needs the state to ensure her/his survival and development, as if the latter is an obvious necessary attachment for the child to enjoy the right to life. This brings up images of the Apollonian child, who of course does not have to worry about life being arbitrarily deprived by the state.[63] This child is too innocent, too passive. This child needs to be encouraged (towards development) and protected (to survive).

While the ICCPR refers to purely negative obligations (not to deprive life), the CRC mandates positive obligations (the state shall ensure survival and development).[64] What the state is required to do in the name of 'survival and development' is unclear. The inclusion of a positive obligation, while potentially viewed as 'progressive', also permits more control. In this way, by requiring the state to ensure the child's

[62] Although the Preamble mentions that everyone is entitled to the rights of the CRC without distinction of any kind and that all 'members of the human family' enjoy 'equal and inalienable rights', the CRC does not explicitly mention that the child enjoys equal or full rights, nor does it mention that children suffer from exceptional discrimination based on their status as a 'child'. The aim of the CRC, one could argue, is not towards protection of the children's claim to equal rights and freedom from discrimination, as least equal rights to adults and freedom from discrimination based on their status as 'children'. The CRC does not mention any social barriers that children experience that inhibit their full participation. Rather, the CRC only mentions the child's (physical and mental) immaturity. Meaning that while a state cannot discriminate based on race or gender for example, it may do so on the basis of age. In this way, the state may discriminate against all children, but may not discriminate among children. Many international children's right scholars agree that the law should treat the child differently, based on the idea that children are fundamentally different and thus require different protections and rights altogether. See for example: Van Bueren, G. (2006) 'Article 40: Child Criminal Justice' in Alen, A. et al. (eds.) *A Commentary on the United Nations Rights of the Child*, 19; Abramson, B. (2008) 'Article: 2. The Right of Non-Discrimination', in Alen, A. et al. (eds.) *A Commentary on the United Nations Convention on the Rights of the Child*, ix: the author does not recognize the differential treatment of children as a form of discrimination. The author states 'generally speaking, people understand that human rights include children. In addition, because of their *particular position*, children have been given special provision, the CRC can be considered *lex specialis* with regard to the Universal Declaration of Human Rights'. Emphasis added. Thorgeirsdottir, H. (2006) 'Article 13: The Right to Freedom of Expression' in Alen, A. et al. (eds.) *A Commentary on the United Nations Convention on the Rights of the Child*, 4: 'Affording children this right [to expression] in a special instrument in addition to the other instruments that do not distinguish between children and adults in being holders of this right, is a recognition of the significance of children acquiring cognitive, emotional, social, and moral competencies absorbing influence from the environment and expressing their reaction, opinions, and sentiments.' If not equal rights and full participation, what does the CRC guarantee children, now that the CRC has identified children as biologically and essentially immature? As will be argued throughout this chapter, the CRC guarantees dependency and vulnerability as markers of childhood.

[63] See Jenks, C. (2005) *Childhood*, 69–73: Jenks argues that the Apollonian and Dionysian images of the child are informative of the shifting strategies that Western society has exercised in its increasing need to control, socialize, and constrain people in the transition towards modernity.

[64] Detrick, S. (1992) *The United Nations Convention on the Rights of the Child, A guide to the 'Travaux Préparatiores'*, 121. It was noted that right to survival carried with it more positive obligations than the right to life such as prolonging the child's life. The right to life was argued to be so important that its inclusion should be necessary and should be extended to positive obligations on the state. The representative of Venezuela felt that the inclusion of paragraph 2 would diminish the concept of the right to life conferred on all human beings in existing international instruments and requested that thought be given to that.

development and survival, the child becomes an object of regulation by the state. As states are charged with this task of ensuring survival and development, the state is at once given the power to define what both 'survival' and 'development' mean, as well as to define what measures need to be taken to ensure the state's definitions of 'survival' and 'development' are realized. One can imagine what could be done in the name of this very persuasive banner, 'rights of the child'. How can one argue against ensuring the survival and development of this precious child, whose protection is even mandated in an international convention? Would the method of protection even matter? In this way, Article 6's use of development portrays the child as a virtually helpless and innocent object requiring state intervention. While the Preamble's usage of development authorizes the control of children by the family (i.e. parents), in Article 6 the child's state of development enables the state to exercise greater control and regulation of childhood; an argument that will be made throughout this chapter and the next.

23.2.3 Article 18: Parents are responsible for their child(ren)

Article 18 provides that:

1. States Parties shall use their best efforts to ensure recognition of the principle that both parents have common responsibilities for the upbringing and development of the child. Parents or, as the case may be, legal guardians, have the primary responsibility for the upbringing and development of the child. The best interests of the child will be their basic concern.
2. For the purpose of guaranteeing and promoting the rights set forth in the present Convention, States Parties shall render appropriate assistance to parents and legal guardians in the performance of their child-rearing responsibilities and shall ensure the development of institutions, facilities and services for the care of children.
3. States Parties shall take all appropriate measures to ensure that children of working parents have the right to benefit from child-care services and facilities for which they are eligible.

X	needs	Y	for	Z
The child		Responsible adults that are assisted by the state		The child's development and upbringing

The required result of Article 18 is the child's development and upbringing. Again these words portray the child as incomplete. Thus, a responsible adult is required to oversee such development and upbringing of the child. During the drafting of this article the focus of the discussion was on ensuring that parents had the primary role in the development and upbringing of the child, and thus minimizing state intervention in the relationship between the parent and child.[65] Also, the discussions revolved around not only protecting the position of the parent in relation to the child, but also

[65] Detrick, S. (1992) *The United Nations Convention on the Rights of the Child, A guide to the 'Travaux Préparatiores'*, 265–7.

minimizing the state's obligation in relation to providing for the child.[66] In this way, this article secures the hierarchical matrix of the parent over the child, with the state as a backup over the parent. Article 18 talks in terms of responsibility; but 'responsibility for' another person is an enactment of power, and as such is a right held by an adult to exercise power over the child. Responsibility here arguably is about the parent's right to control the child. This responsibility enables the adult to determine and dictate what is or is not in the best interests of the child. Parents' 'responsibility' over the child trumps the child's right to information, thought, and religion,[67] and even the right to be free from abusive traditional practices or, as the Convention more lightly puts it, 'traditional practices that are prejudicial to the health of children'.

One can imagine if the CEDAW included, for example, the 'responsibility' of a woman's husband to provide for the woman (the subject of the Convention) and therefore had responsibility for all of her financial matters.[68] 'Responsibility for' in the context of man and woman becomes more easily seen as 'power over'. In a Convention that addresses the rights of the child, I find it (not so) odd that it contains rights of those who are given control over children. Indeed, during the drafting of this article, the American delegate noted that it was 'strange' for an international human rights convention to place responsibilities on private individuals (i.e. parents) when a convention can only create binding obligations for ratifying governments.[69] If 'responsibility for' is read as the right to have power over another human, this article is indeed strange. However, when viewed in line with the traditional right to family privacy for adults, which includes the right to raise one's children, this article is less about obligating parents, and more about recognizing the parents' right to privacy.[70]

The child's state of development here again makes necessary the hierarchical relationship between the parent and the child. If development is but one version of the state of childhood, then why is this type of relationship necessary? Further suspect is that the rights of those who are on the upper side of this power equation (i.e. adults) are included in a Convention that is supposed to address those who require their own convention, those who had no voice in this Convention's creation. Yet, care-givers appear in almost every article as a right holder: 'responsibility for' as actually a right to exercise power over.[71]

23.2.4 Article 27: Adequate standard of living

Article 27 enumerates that:

1. States Parties recognize the right of every child to a standard of living adequate for the child's physical, mental, spiritual, moral and social development.

[66] Detrick, S. (1992) *The United Nations Convention on the Rights of the Child, A guide to the 'Travaux Préparatiores'*, 265–7.

[67] See Articles 14(2) and 17(e).

[68] If one views the child as fundamentally different from adults, and thus inherently immature, one would argue that analogy to the category 'woman' would be irrelevant. This chapter rejects the idea that there exists some fundamental, universal, inherent 'child'. Thus, as there is no essential woman, there too is no essential child.

[69] Detrick, S. (1992) *The United Nations Convention on the Rights of the Child, A guide to the 'Travaux Préparatiores'*, 270.

[70] See generally Hafen, B. and Hafen, J. (1996) 'Abandoning Children to Their Autonomy: The United Nations Convention on the Rights of the Child' 37 *Harvard International Law Journal* 460.

[71] Parents are rights holders 16 times whereas children are rights holders 22 times (most of which include rights to protection).

2. The parent(s) or others responsible for the child have the primary responsibility to secure, within their abilities and financial capacities, the conditions of living necessary for the child's development.

3. States Parties, in accordance with national conditions and within their means, shall take appropriate measures to assist parents and others responsible for the child to implement this right and shall in case of need provide material assistance and support programmes, particularly with regard to nutrition, clothing and housing.

4. States Parties shall take all appropriate measures to secure the recovery of maintenance for the child from the parents or other persons having financial responsibility for the child, both within the State Party and from abroad. In particular, where the person having financial responsibility for the child lives in a State different from that of the child, States Parties shall promote the accession to international agreements or the conclusion of such agreements, as well as the making of other appropriate arrangements.

X	needs	Y	for	Z
The child		Parents, supported by the state, to ensure an adequate standard of living		The child's physical, mental, spiritual, moral, and social development

Similar to Article 6's right to life, the right to adequate standard of living is heavily attached to the child's development. Further, development in Article 27 includes a laundry list of the specific areas in which the child needs to develop: physically, mentally, spiritually, morally, and socially. 'Adequate' attaches to the living conditions necessary for the child's physical, mental, spiritual, moral, and social development.[72] Why is this laundry list necessary for the child's right to an adequate standard of living? Reference to development not only casts the child as incomplete/immature, development is portrayed yet again as an essential 'truth' of the child. The focus on development seems to underline the assumed precarious nature of being a child. The child as immature/incapable could be seen in turn to underscore the child as in need of development, and thus to underscore children's difference from adults. Yet, is the standard of living that is adequate for a six-year-old different from a 50-year-old? The assumption is always: yes, the needs of the six-year-old, who is immature and must develop maturity, will be quite different from a 50-year-old, who is mature and does not require any relevant sort of development. However, are the basic needs of all children, those which would make possible an 'adequate' standard of living, really that different from all adults? Many would answer affirmatively. Yet others argue that childhood is a set of experiences neither more nor less internally coherent that those of adults.[73] A comparison of Article 27 with the ICESCR's Article 11 gives insight into how the CRC answers this question in the affirmative. While Article 11 of the ICESCR has been interpreted to focus on housing and food, Article 27 of the CRC

[72] Eide, A. (2006) 'Article 27: The Right to an Adequate Standard of Living' in Alen, A. et al. (eds.) *A Commentary on the United Nations Convention on the Rights of the Child*, 17.

[73] See generally Campbell, T. (1993) 'The Rights of the Minor: As Person, As Child, As Juvenile, and Future Adult' in Archard, D. et al. (eds.) *Children, Rights, and the Law*, 1.

has been interpreted to focus on development. One author writes that Article 27 means that the 'child shall enjoy conditions which facilitate its development into a fully capable and well functioning adult person'.[74]

Article 27, like Article 11 in the ICESCR, mandates the right to an adequate standard of living.[75] However, unlike the ICESCR, the reason for having such a right is included in the CRC: the child's development. The ICESCR only states the right to an adequate standard of living and the measures that the state is required to take are mentioned.[76] Additionally, the means for realization of the right to an adequate standard of living are different under the two Conventions: in the CRC, the focus is on providing parents with assistance to provide for the child[77] and in the ICESCR the focus is on how generally to make food and shelter more readily available.[78] As children are incomplete/immature and thus require development, and indeed according to Article 27 require development in all sorts of areas of their personality and physicality, the child needs parents to secure their right to an adequate standard of living. Again development justifies making adults responsible for the child.[79] As such, perhaps the inclusion of multiple areas of the child's 'development' (i.e. inclusion of the multiple areas of the child's deficiencies) in this article was to justify the child's 'need' for an intermediary. Indeed most of the discussion during the drafting of this article focused on the extent of the obligation placed on the state to provide assistance, and not whether the child should also be provided direct assistance by the state.[80] This article states that the caregiver has the primary responsibility for ensuring this standard of living, and that the state 'shall take appropriate measures' to help those responsible for the child. Under the ICESCR Article 11, the right holder does not have this intermediary. As was argued regarding Article 18, 'responsibility for' is a grant of power over, as it requires the child to be dependent on the adult who is responsible. Giving parents 'primary responsibility' has been interpreted to 'protect parents . . . against

[74] Eide, A. (2006) 'Article 27: The Right to an Adequate Standard of Living' in Alen, A. et al. (eds.) *A Commentary on the United Nations Convention on the Rights of the Child*, 17. The usage of the term 'it' in relation to a person is an usual and possibly insightful reference, which may indicate some sort of subhuman status.

[75] 1966 International Covenant on Economic, Social and Cultural Rights, UN Doc. A/RES/2200A (XXI), entered into force 3 January 1976, Article 11: '1. The States Parties to the present Covenant recognize the right of everyone to an adequate standard of living for himself and his family, including adequate food, clothing and housing, and to the continuous improvement of living conditions. The States Parties will take appropriate steps to ensure the realization of this right, recognizing to this effect the essential importance of international co-operation based on free consent. 2. The States Parties to the present Covenant, recognizing the fundamental right of everyone to be free from hunger, shall take, individually and through international co-operation, the measures, including specific programmes, which are needed: (a) To improve methods of production, conservation and distribution of food by making full use of technical and scientific knowledge, by disseminating knowledge of the principles of nutrition and by developing or reforming agrarian systems in such a way as to achieve the most efficient development and utilization of natural resources; (b) Taking into account the problems of both food-importing and food-exporting countries, to ensure an equitable distribution of world food supplies in relation to need.'

[76] ICESCR, Article 11. [77] Article 27(2)(4). [78] ICESCR, Article 11(2).

[79] Cowan, D. and Dearden, N. (2001) 'The Minor as (a) Subject: the Case of Housing Law' in Fionda, J. (ed.) *Legal Concepts of Childhood*: These authors note that the political agenda in the welfare system which seeks to reinforce the dependence of the child is 1) to restrict access to declining resources, or 2) to discipline/punish those who cannot or will not fit within the norms of childhood.

[80] Detrick, S. (1992) *The United Nations Convention on the Rights of the Child, A guide to the 'Travaux Préparatiores'*, 371–7.

excessive state intervention ... [and] indicate that parents ... could not expect the State always to intervene, because the provision of the conditions of living necessary for the child's development is primarily [the parents'] responsibly'.[81] In his commentary on this article, Eide argues that under Article 27 the child is the right holder and the parent is the duty holder.[82] Yet he does not conceptualize the state's obligation not to intervene in the parents' exercise of primary responsibility as a 'right' the parents hold.[83] As argued in relation to Article 18, this Article also includes the parent's right to privacy. The child is made dependent on the parent, rather than being provided direct assistance to secure adequate housing for her or himself.

23.2.5 Article 29: Education

Article 29 states that:

1. States Parties agree that the education of the child shall be directed to:

(a) The **development** of the child's personality, talents and mental and physical abilities to their fullest potential;

(b) The **development** of respect for human rights and fundamental freedoms, and for the principles enshrined in the Charter of the United Nations;

(c) The **development** of respect for the child's parents, his or her own cultural identity, language and values, for the national values of the country in which the child is living, the country from which he or she may originate, and for civilizations different from his or her own;

(d) The preparation of the child for responsible life in a free society, in the spirit of understanding, peace, tolerance, equality of sexes, and friendship among all peoples, ethnic, national and religious groups and persons of indigenous origin;

(e) The **development** of respect for the natural environment.

2. No part of the present article or article 28 shall be construed so as to interfere with the liberty of individuals and bodies to establish and direct educational institutions, subject always to the observance of the principle set forth in paragraph 1 of the present article and to the requirements that the education given in such institutions shall conform to such minimum standards as may be laid down by the State.

[81] Eide, A. (2006) 'Article 27: The Right to an Adequate Standard of Living' in Alen, A. et al. (eds.) *A Commentary on the United Nations Convention on the Rights of the Child*, 19, citing Detrick, S. (1992) *The United Nations Convention on the Rights of the Child, A guide to the 'Travaux Préparatiores'*, 459.

[82] Eide, A. (2006) 'Article 27: The Right to an Adequate Standard of Living' in Alen, A. et al. (eds.) *A Commentary on the United Nations Convention on the Rights of the Child*, 19.

[83] Eide, A. (2006) 'Article 27: The Right to an Adequate Standard of Living' in Alen, A. et al. (eds.) *A Commentary on the United Nations Convention on the Rights of the Child*, 19.

X	needs	Y	for	Z
The child		→ to be directed to the development of: 1. The child's self 2. respect for human rights 3. respect for the child's parents 4. respect for her/his own cultural identity, language, and values 5. respect for national values 6. respect for her/his country 7. respect for other civilizations 8. respect for the environment → to be directed to prepare for responsible life		????—does not say

Article 29 is one of two articles that address the child's education.[84] The curriculum posited by the Convention in this article seems strange when compared to other human rights conventions. Yet, this article seems to embrace the most influential and contemporary accounts of that education: a developmental view which represents that progress of the child towards the acquisition of full adult rationality as segmented into distinct incremental stages, each appropriate to a certain age band, each defined in terms of a particular set of abilities and skills, and each representing a clear advance upon the preceding stage.[85] Four of the five paragraphs in Article 29(1) focus on education that ensures development. The other is aimed at 'preparation', which also indicates that the child is incomplete and therefore not ready for 'free society'. The first aim of education is to ensure the development of the 'child's personality, talents, and mental and physical abilities to their fullest potential'. This designates that the child is obviously in a state of incompleteness, which education is supposed to aim to remedy.

Outside of the critique describing children as merely 'incomplete', this article's educational aims are not just focused upon 'developing' the child 'potential'. The next developmental aims are about developing the child's respect 1) for human rights, 2) for the child's parents, culture, country, national values, and other civilizations, and 3) for the 'natural environment'. These educational aims are thinly veiled code words that aim to discipline the subject. Fostering respect for this list has nothing to do with developing the child's 'potential' but rather places limits on the child under the name of 'respect'. Requiring the child to learn unilateral respect for this list contributes to the child's submissive positioning in the CRC. These educational aims demonstrate the arbitrariness of what is justified in the name of 'development'.[86]

[84] See also Article 28.

[85] Archard, D. (2001) 'Philosophical Perspectives on Childhood' in Fionda, J. *Legal Concepts of Childhood*, 46.

[86] Minow argues in Minow, M. (1996) 'Rights for the Next Generation: A Feminist Approach to Children's Rights' in Ladd, R. (ed.) *Children's Rights Re-Visioned*, 44: 'However appealing [the justification that care and custody is provided when a child is incompetent and rights and autonomy when they are competent] may be as a normative theory, it fails to describe the current legal universe. It seems bizarre to justify the variable treatment of young people currently manifested in the patchwork of legal regulations as though it expressed careful judgments about their competencies for various tasks and responsibilities. Why would an eighteen-year-old be competent to consent to her abortion but not entitled to miss school from her doctor's appointment w/o parental permissions? Why would the seventeen-year-old be competent to be treated as an adult in criminal court but not competent to sign a contract?'

First, the child needs to *learn* respect for her/his parents (the child's more powerful binary opposite). During the drafting of the Convention, the Yugoslavian and Canadian delegates proposed the addition of respect for parents, which was adopted without comment.[87] Respect for parents was not in the original draft.[88] Again thinking of the CEDAW, how would an article about a need to respect men (women's more powerful binary opposite) be perceived? I would imagine that such a unilateral requirement would be an impossibility. Not once in the Convention are parents or any adults required to 'respect' children.[89]

Second, that children's education is to be directed towards fostering (again this word) 'respect' for the 'natural environment' in a treaty about children's rights seems misplaced, in the sense that it is not required explicitly of any other category of persons.[90] Whether respect for the natural environment should be required of everyone will not be discussed here, regardless of merit. What is of interest here is that this respect is required uniquely of children. Nowhere in the ICCPR or the ICESCR is respect for the natural environment found. Rather, states are required to respect the right of peoples to dispose of natural resources as part of the right to self-determination.[91] This notably does not include teaching those peoples to respect their environment. It seems that the inclusion of this was to encourage educators to ensure that our Apollonian child is exposed to his/her 'natural' environment (i.e. nature), or to ensure that the Dionysian child is taught not to harm his/her 'natural' environment. Regardless, the inclusion of this educational aim from the beginning of the drafting of the CRC is curious, particularly as it arguably preceded environmentalism becoming of more concern to the international community.[92]

Third, the focus on developing the child's respect for human rights is also interesting here in the sense that human rights focus on protecting the individual from the state. The ICCPR, for example, is about obliging the state to respect human rights and thus possessing certain protection from the state. In this case, the article is about *teaching* the *rights holder* (i.e. children) to respect *human rights*, their culture, and other cultures. The CRC presents a very different conception of the child rights holder, as compared to the adult rights holder. The CRC's requirement that

[87] Detrick, S. (1992) *The United Nations Convention on the Rights of the Child, A guide to the 'Travaux Préparatiores'*, 406.

[88] Detrick, S. (1992) *The United Nations Convention on the Rights of the Child, A guide to the 'Travaux Préparatiores'*, 406.

[89] Article 5 of the CRC only states that '*States Parties shall respect the responsibilities, rights and duties of parents* or, where applicable, the members of the extended family or community as provided for by local custom, legal guardians or other persons legally responsible for the child, to provide, *in a manner consistent with the evolving capacities of the child,* appropriate direction and guidance in the exercise by the child of the rights recognized in the present Convention'.

[90] The original text read 'in harmony with nature'. See Detrick, S. (1992) *The United Nations Convention on the Rights of the Child, A guide to the 'Travaux Préparatiores'*, 400.

[91] Article 1(2) and (3) of the ICCPR states: '(2) All peoples may, for their own ends, freely dispose of their natural wealth and resources without prejudice to any obligations arising out of international economic co-operation, based upon the principle of mutual benefit, and international law. In no case may a people be deprived of its own means of subsistence. (3) The States Parties to the present Covenant, including those having responsibility for the administration of Non-Self-Governing and Trust Territories, shall promote the realization of the right of self-determination, and shall respect that right, in conformity with the provisions of the Charter of the United Nations.'

[92] The initial draft stated that the child should be educated 'in harmony with nature'. The *final* draft stated that the child should be educated to develop 'respect for the natural environment'. See: Detrick, S. (1992) *The United Nations Convention on the Rights of the Child, A guide to the 'Travaux Préparatiores'*, 400.

the *child* should *learn respect for* what the CRC is supposed to be *providing the child*, again makes sense only if the child is performed as lacking, as developing. Fourth, interestingly this article requires the inculcation of respect for one's state, or 'national values'. As in the previous paragraph, rights generally focus on the protection of individuals from the state, in a sense, the obligation of the state to respect the individual. However, in the CRC, it is the child who must learn respect for his/her state. By mandating that the child learn respect for her/his state, the state becomes included and entrenched in the CRC's hierarchy of power. Where human rights typically restrict the state's power over the individual, the CRC requires the *teaching* of the *right holder* respect for *the state.*

Finally, this article does not include the *child's right to anything.* This article does not require states and/or parents to finance a child's education or for the state to make available education, as is done in Article 28.[93] The child has no right to an education or curriculum of her/his own choice. The article does not include the right of the child to be respected at school, by the state, or by parents. This article is about helping this poor, ignorant child who needs to learn respect for her/his parents, the natural environment, human rights, and the state. The term 'development' in Article 29 justifies the curriculum and focus of the child's education. While Article 29(1)(a) relates to the child's development, Article 29(1)(b)–(e) regarding developing respect hardly seems to relate to the child's development, much less any right the child might posses. This article seems to be about underlining the hierarchy that surrounds the child of the parents and state over the child—all because of the child's development. Put another way, the child is put under the 'care' (i.e. control) of adults all because that person is nominated a child and because all persons nominated a child are envisioned in the CRC as developing/lacking/incomplete, making the superior positioning of the adult over the child 'necessary'.

23.2.6 Article 32: Freedom from work

Article 32 asserts that,

1. States Parties recognize the right of the child to be protected from economic exploitation and from performing any work that is likely to be hazardous or to interfere with the child's education, or to be harmful to the child's health or physical, mental, spiritual, moral or social development.
2. States Parties shall take legislative, administrative, social and educational measures to ensure the implementation of the present article. To this end, and having regard

[93] Article 28: '1. States Parties recognize the right of the child to education, and with a view to achieving this right progressively and on the basis of equal opportunity, they shall, in particular: (a) Make primary education compulsory and available free to all; (b) Encourage the development of different forms of secondary education, including general and vocational education, make them available and accessible to every child, and take appropriate measures such as the introduction of free education and offering financial assistance in case of need; (c) Make higher education accessible to all on the basis of capacity by every appropriate means; (d) Make educational and vocational information and guidance available and accessible to all children; (e) Take measures to encourage regular attendance at schools and the reduction of drop-out rates. 2. States Parties shall take all appropriate measures to ensure that school discipline is administered in a manner consistent with the child's human dignity and in conformity with the present Convention. 3. States Parties shall promote and encourage international cooperation in matters relating to education, in particular with a view to contributing to the elimination of ignorance and illiteracy throughout the world and facilitating access to scientific and technical knowledge and modern teaching methods. In this regard, particular account shall be taken of the needs of developing countries.'

to the relevant provisions of other international instruments, States Parties shall in particular:

(a) Provide for a minimum age or minimum wages for admission to employment;

(b) Provide for appropriate regulation of the hours and conditions of employment;

(c) Provide for appropriate penalties or other sanctions to ensure the effective enforcement of the present article.

X	needs	Y	for	Z
The child		Protection from economic exploitation and performing work that is hazardous		Development and education

Article 32 is peculiar especially when read against the ICCPR and the ICESCR, as the CRC can be seen as a hybrid of the two, yet modified to accommodate the CRC's portrayal of the child as developing. The focus of the CRC's rights relating to work, how they are constructed and even organized, tell a very different tale for the 'needs' of the child as opposed to the 'needs' of the working adult. Although already stated, this chapter does not engage in a black letter law analysis. Rather, it focuses on the story told about the child in the CRC by the CRC's allocation of rights. It is interesting that this article, unlike most other articles, asserts explicitly that State Parties must take into consideration the 'relevant provisions of other international instruments'.[94] Why were other international instruments explicitly mentioned and which ones would be considered relevant? Further, why must states 'in particular' focus on that which is listed in Article 32(2)(a–c)? Does that mean that states may ignore that which is not listed in Article 32(2)? Four points can be made. First, this article does not include the right to work, as found in the ICESCR's Article 6. The child does not have the right in the CRC to 'the opportunity to gain his [or her] living by work which [she/] he freely chooses or accepts'.[95] The denial of such a right could have serious implications for children as they are again forced to be dependent on parents or the state. Further, the focus on protecting the child's development underlines the immaturity, incapacity, and 'special status' of the child, who is as a result made in 'need' of both the parents and the state for support. Would the inclusion of the right to work be viewed as encouraging children to work, and thus be incongruent with the prevailing identity of the child as dependent and at the same time incongruent with the prevailing identity of the adult as responsible?

Second, the article refers to two types of prohibited work: 1) economic exploitation, and 2) work that is 'likely to be' hazardous and/or interferes with the child's development. This article speaks nothing about what would qualify as economic exploitation.

[94] This was included on the suggestion of the representative of the International Labour Organisation. See Detrick, S. (1992) *The United Nations Convention on the Rights of the Child, A guide to the 'Travaux Préparatiores'*, 422.

[95] Article 6 of the ICESCR: '1. The States Parties to the present Covenant recognize the right to work, which includes the right of everyone to the opportunity to gain his living by work which he freely chooses or accepts, and will take appropriate steps to safeguard this right. 2. The steps to be taken by a State Party to the present Covenant to achieve the full realization of this right shall include technical and vocational guidance and training programmes, policies and techniques to achieve steady economic, social and cultural development and full and productive employment under conditions safeguarding fundamental political and economic freedoms to the individual.'

At what point does doing chores around the house or babysitting for younger siblings become exploitative? At what point does working for the family business become exploitative? Indeed one speaker noted during the drafting of this article that the establishment of a minimum age of employment should not prevent the 'participation of children, under the direction of their parents and so as not to interfere with their education, in culturally related family hunting, fishing, or agricultural activities not regularly employing unrelated workers'.[96] This speaker also noted that this article was not intended to prohibit family subsistence activities.[97] Additionally, as discussed above, most curious is that Article 38 of the Convention does not prohibit children between the ages of 15 and 17 from being directly involved in 'hostilities'. Military service for the state, including direct combat, is not considered by the CRC to be at odds with the child's 'development', nor is it considered 'hazardous'. It seems that if the child is working for the family, working for the state's military, or engaged in some 'cultural' activity, there is less concern about the conditions of the child's labour.

Third, although the ICCPR does not refer to the right to work, it does include the right to be free from slavery and/or servitude (related to economic exploitation).[98] Interestingly however, the powerful words, 'slavery' or 'servitude', are left out of the CRC.[99] The implications of this omission abound. For example, although there is a prohibition on trafficking,[100] the absence of a specific prohibition on slavery could have analogy for a child whilst in care, quite separate from the issue of being illegally abducted. Additionally, though the CRC includes a prohibition on all forms of exploitation,[101] the prohibition against slavery has been recognized as *jus cogens*[102]

[96] Detrick, S. (1992) *The United Nations Convention on the Rights of the Child, A guide to the 'Travaux Préparatiores'*, 422.

[97] Detrick, S. (1992) *The United Nations Convention on the Rights of the Child, A guide to the 'Travaux Préparatiores'*, 422.

[98] Article 8 of the ICCPR, a non-derrogable right: '1. No one shall be held in slavery; slavery and the slave-trade in all their forms shall be prohibited. 2. No one shall be held in servitude. 3. (a) No one shall be required to perform forced or compulsory labour; (b) Paragraph 3(a) shall not be held to preclude, in countries where imprisonment with hard labour may be imposed as a punishment for a crime, the performance of hard labour in pursuance of a sentence to such punishment by a competent court; (c) For the purpose of this paragraph the term 'forced or compulsory labour' shall not include: (i) Any work or service, not referred to in subparagraph (b), normally required of a person who is under detention in consequence of a lawful order of a court, or of a person during conditional release from such detention; (ii) Any service of a military character and, in countries where conscientious objection is recognized, any national service required by law of conscientious objectors; (iii) Any service exacted in cases of emergency or calamity threatening the life or well-being of the community; (iv) Any work or service which forms part of normal civil obligations.'

[99] Notably, the CRC does not include *any* non-derogable rights.

[100] Article 35: 'States Parties shall take all appropriate national, bilateral and multilateral measures to prevent the abduction of, the sale of or traffic in children for any purpose or in any form.'

[101] Article 32: '1. States Parties recognize the right of the child to be protected from economic exploitation and from performing any work that is likely to be hazardous or to interfere with the child's education, or to be harmful to the child's health or physical, mental, spiritual, moral or social development. 2. States Parties shall take legislative, administrative, social and educational measures to ensure the implementation of the present article. To this end, and having regard to the relevant provisions of other international instruments, States Parties shall in particular: (a) Provide for a minimum age or minimum ages for admission to employment; (b) Provide for appropriate regulation of the hours and conditions of employment; (c) Provide for appropriate penalties or other sanctions to ensure the effective enforcement of the present article.' Article 34: 'States Parties undertake to protect the child from all forms of sexual exploitation and sexual abuse. For these purposes, States Parties shall in particular take all appropriate national, bilateral and multilateral measures to prevent: (a) The inducement or coercion of a child to engage in any unlawful sexual activity; (b) The exploitative use of children in prostitution or other unlawful sexual practices; (c) The exploitative use of children in pornographic performances and materials. Article 36: 'States Parties shall protect the child against all other forms of exploitation prejudicial to any aspects of the child's welfare.'

[102] Arrest Warrants Case was the first time the ICJ mentioned the term. See *Case Concerning the Arrest Warrant of 11 April 2000* (*Democratic Republic of the Congo v. Belgium*), Judgment of 14 February 2002,

or at least is universally condemned, and therefore could be a more effective tool in combating some of the situations in which children find themselves whilst 'in care' of someone. Was this prohibition so clear that it was not deemed necessary to include? Is slavery not a particular problem for children and their development? Or would the inclusion of this prohibition challenge some of the extreme contexts in which children are required to live, considering 1) the few rights given to children to challenge the dependency in which they are required to live, and 2) the few restrictions on the parents' dominance over the child? Could making such a linkage be an extremely effective tool against such exploitation and deprivation of rights, as slavery has such political purchase?[103] Would it not be an effective tool to challenge the presumption that the parents *will have* the best interest of the child as their basic concern? Or is that precisely the problem?

Fourth, even in the event that the child does work, the child, under the CRC, is not given fundamental safeguards associated with the right to work such as the right to 'fair wages', equal pay for equal work, or 'equal opportunity of promotion'.[104] Would providing such rights in the Convention be viewed as a feared encouragement to work, a contradiction to the prevailing image of childhood in the CRC? Finally, Article 7 of the ICESCR secures not only fair wages and equal opportunity for promotion, but also '[r]est, leisure and reasonable limitation of working hours and periodic holidays with pay, as well as remuneration for public holidays'. The child's right to 'rest, leisure, and play' is an entirely separate article that provides for no other safeguards regarding their work.[105] Why do children need a separate article to ensure their right to 'rest, leisure, and play', when they did not get (at least in this Convention) the right to equal pay for equal work, much less freedom from slavery?

Again the idea may be that the authors of the CRC did not want in any way to encourage child labour, so play was emphasized, where competitive pay, for example, was not. Article 32 together with Article 31 bring up the old idea that childhood is a 'golden age' where children should have little responsibility in order to

[2002] 41 ILM 536. The Vienna Convention on the Law of Treaties also mentions the term where if a treaty conflicts with *jus cogens* then the treaty is void: 1969 Vienna Convention on the Law of Treaties 8 ILM 679 (1969). Neither the case nor the Vienna Convention offer examples of norms of *jus cogens*. The ILC Draft Articles on State Responsibility, 1980 YILC, Vol. 34 II, Article 40 does give the prohibition of slavery as an example of *jus cogens*.

[103] Is the exclusion of 'slavery' from the CRC a blacklash of sorts to Hafen, B. and Hafen, J. (1996) 'Abandoning Children to their Autonomy: The CRC' (1996) 37 *Harvard International Law Journal* 449? Thus, the CRC is not abandoning children to their rights, as Hafen and Hafen argue in their article, 'Abandoning Children to their Autonomy: The CRC', but arguably, in some cases, not providing protection for children against their parents even in extreme circumstances.

[104] Article 7 of the ICESCR: 'The States Parties to the present Covenant recognize the right of everyone to the enjoyment of just and favourable conditions of work which ensure, in particular: (a) Remuneration which provides all workers, as a minimum, with: (i) Fair wages and equal remuneration for work of equal value without distinction of any kind, in particular women being guaranteed conditions of work not inferior to those enjoyed by men, with equal pay for equal work; (ii) A decent living for themselves and their families in accordance with the provisions of the present Covenant; (b) Safe and healthy working conditions; (c) Equal opportunity for everyone to be promoted in his employment to an appropriate higher level, subject to no considerations other than those of seniority and competence; (d) Rest, leisure and reasonable limitation of working hours and periodic holidays with pay, as well as remuneration for public holidays.'

[105] Article 31: '1. States Parties recognize the right of the child to rest and leisure, to engage in play and recreational activities appropriate to the age of the child and to participate freely in cultural life and the arts. 2. States Parties shall respect and promote the right of the child to participate fully in cultural and artistic life and shall encourage the provision of appropriate and equal opportunities for cultural, artistic, recreational and leisure activity.'

enjoy themselves, particularly when read with other articles that deny (or deemphasize) children('s) responsibility (e.g. right to work) and capacity (e.g. certain criminal procedural rights).[106] Surely these articles denote the Apollonian child, frolicking with no cares or worries. Not only are children then incapable of responsibility, they are encouraged not to 'worry' about responsibility. The CRC's combination of deletions and additions in Articles 32 and 31, as compared to the ICCPR and the ICESCR, has strong implications about the 'nature' of the childhood as in a safe, warm environment where children 1) have no cares but to rest and play, 2) should not have to work, and 3) have responsible adults to provide for them. By envisioning the child in this way, the CRC is at the same time justifying the 'need' for a responsible adult.

23.2.7 Article 23: Rights of the disabled child

The only other article that deals with the child achieving 'the fullest possible social integration and individual development, including his or her cultural and spiritual development' is Article 23 which focuses on the rights of the child with disability. This article asserts that:

1. States Parties recognize that a mentally or physically disabled child should enjoy a full and decent life, in conditions which ensure dignity, promote self-reliance and facilitate the child's active participation in the community.
2. States Parties recognize the right of the disabled child to special care and shall encourage and ensure the extension, subject to available resources, to the eligible child and those responsible for his or her care, of assistance for which application is made and which is appropriate to the child's condition and to the circumstances of the parents or others caring for the child.
3. Recognizing the special needs of a disabled child, assistance extended in accordance with paragraph 2 of the present article shall be provided free of charge, whenever possible, taking into account the financial resources of the parents or others caring for the child, and shall be designed to ensure that the disabled child has effective access to and receives education, training, health care services, rehabilitation services, preparation for employment and recreation opportunities in a manner conducive to the child's achieving the fullest possible social integration and individual development, including his or her cultural and spiritual development
4. States Parties shall promote, in the spirit of international cooperation, the exchange of appropriate information in the field of preventive health care and of medical, psychological and functional treatment of disabled children, including dissemination of and access to information concerning methods of rehabilitation, education and vocational services, with the aim of enabling States Parties to improve their capabilities and skills and to widen their experience in these areas. In this regard, particular account shall be taken of the needs of developing countries.

[106] See Freeman, explaining how this conception of children is utilized to deny children rights: Freeman, M.D.A. (ed.) (2004) *Children's Rights*, Volumes I and II; Freeman, M.D.A. (1983) *The Rights and Wrongs of Children*; Freeman, M.D.A. (2007) 'Why It Remains Important to Take Children's Rights Seriously' 15(1) *The International Journal of Children's Rights* 5–23.

X	needs	Y	for	Z
The disabled child		The state to provide assistance to the disabled child and to the child's parent		The promotion of self-reliance, facilitation of the child's active participation in the community, and the achievement of the fullest possible social integration and individual development

Article 23(2) is unlike all other articles in the Convention. Uniquely it states that disabled children's assistance should be given to 'the eligible child and those responsible for his or her care.' Notably, this is the only article that explicitly provides for assistance from the state to be given to the child *and* the parent, as opposed to just the parent, as in Article 27 (standard of living) or Article 18 (parent's responsibility for the child). Notably, the original text of this article made no mention of providing assistance to the child's family.[107] Most of the discussions during the drafting of this article focused on providing support to the child. Not until 1982 (three years into the drafting process) was the child's family included upon the suggestion of Argentina and the United Kingdom.[108] One must wonder why assistance is envisioned differently in the case of a child with a disability from that for children more generally.

Furthermore, while this article refers to the child's development, it also states that the child should live in conditions that 'promote self-reliance and facilitate the child's active participation in the community' and the 'fullest possible social integration'. The Polish delegate pushed for the inclusion of self-reliance, active participation, and dignity in conjunction with the Australian, Canadian, British, and American delegates.[109] This language was accepted without discussion.[110] Certainly, no other article exclusively focuses on the unqualified promotion of self-reliance and full social integration for the child. This article seems to reflect the Convention on the Rights of Persons with Disabilities (CRPD) more so than other articles within the CRC: promoting participation and self-reliance in the instance of dependency.

One must ask: why was the child with a disability given more autonomy as compared to other children and more equality as compared to the adults responsible for the child with a disability? It would seem that because of the greater likelihood of dependence of the child with a disability, the aim is to ensure respect for this child's autonomy. Yet, why is this approach not more globally applicable for the normative conception of the child? If the CRC desires to couple the child with the parent, why not put the two members of the family on a more equal footing as envisioned to a greater degree in the case of children with disabilities? Quite possibly the 'disabled' child is less threatening to the status quo matrix of power by mere virtue of his/her

[107] Detrick, S. (1992) *The United Nations Convention on the Rights of the Child, A guide to the 'Travaux Préparatiores'*, 332–3. The original article did take into consideration the circumstances of the child's parents.

[108] Detrick, S. (1992) *The United Nations Convention on the Rights of the Child, A guide to the 'Travaux Préparatiores'*, 332.

[109] Detrick, S. (1992) *The United Nations Convention on the Rights of the Child, A guide to the 'Travaux Préparatiores'*, 332–3.

[110] Detrick, S. (1992) *The United Nations Convention on the Rights of the Child, A guide to the 'Travaux Préparatiores'*, 332–3.

disability. As if somehow children with disability have less capacity to buck the hierarchical relationships that surround the child in the CRC's version of childhood.

23.3 Conclusion

The CRC tells its story of the child. The 'nature' of the child as portrayed in the CRC rests on a foundational 'truth-claim': children are in a state of development. The CRC performs the child as passive, dependent, an object of care and love, requiring the child to be developed towards adulthood. Thus, adults must have responsibility for/control over the child for the duration of childhood. As discussed in Section 23.1, the perception that children are in state of development is consistent with not only scientific understandings of childhood, but also everyday understandings: consider the words of America's 44th President in his inaugural speech, '[w]e remain a young nation, but in the words of Scripture, the time has come to set aside childish things'.[111] But who determines what qualifies as 'childish things', much less who gets to determine that those things are 'lesser'? These are all important questions as the performance of the child as developing enables the hierarchical relationship of adults over children. Section 23.2 argued that the CRC presents a rationality that children are in a state of development and that this state of development justifies a hierarchical relationship with the adults charged with the task of 'caring' for those who are deemed a child. Children must, under the Convention, rely on adults for financial support, yet defer to them about the child's right to freedom of religion, thought, expression, education, in sum the assessment of what is in their best interest. The CRC dictates the abdication of a wide spectrum of possibility for autonomy and choice, all in the name of the child's development. The story told by the CRC is that the CRC is about 'protecting' children from themselves because children are incomplete and therefore in need of adults' help, and providing children with rights when adults determine children are worthy of those rights. Yet, how does this story about what children are 'really' made of relate to the flesh and blood of those who are nominated a child? What about those who are responsible, but are not adults? What about adults who are not responsible, but are not children?

Further, adults are assumed to have at heart the child's best interest. As with the notion of development—the alleged altruism that adults feel towards a child is equally a social construct, where the appearance of care disguises the reality of control.[112] Dependency that results from the child's state of development when viewed through the lens of power, relates not to the spontaneous loving bonds, but mechanisms that serve to sustain particular versions of the status quo.[113] The CRC becomes not about 'protecting' children or providing children with rights, but rather portraying a particular 'truth' about children to enable the sustainment of status quo, propping up the adult-child binary opposition where children are the Other. The CRC is then about fortifying and rationalizing the adult's and the state's ability to intervene in the lives of children on the basis of a 'truth' that does not exist, and in ways that have nothing to do with 'protecting children' but rather about entrenching the position of adults over children, moulding children into what adults and society think

[111] Delivered on 20/01/2009. See: <http://www.msnbc.msn.com/id/28751183/>.

[112] Jenks, C. (2005) *Childhood*, 42.

[113] Jenks, C. (2005) *Childhood*, 42.

this category of persons should be. Development becomes an instrument of social and cultural reproduction.[114] As one author wrote:

> We are compelled to care about the well-being and prospects of other peoples' children as a condition of preserving our nationhood... [A] call to recast the ground of public discourse on the collective status of children... to recover... traditions of common intent essential to sustain our nationhood into the next century.[115]

Children become a conduit through which nationhood is preserved and sustained. Without the control of children—how else would proper gender, class, and sexuality be performed? How else would 'good' citizens be made?

The child's 'need' for development justifies almost anything and evades virtually all critical inquiry. The notion of development enables the avoidance of critical, yet fundamental, questions such as 1) what is meant by development, 2) why is it necessary, and 3) what is made possible by development. At best development creates a credible veil for uncertainty and even disagreement about what is in the 'best interest' of the child—all without critical inquiry into the idea of speaking 'for' children.[116] At worst, it enables the oppression and exploitation of the humans who are nominated a child, through the legitimatization of power hierarchies. This chapter does not argue that children should be treated as adults. Rather it argues that the foundation upon which the differential treatment of children rests requires thorough and critical inquiry, to gauge whether the differential treatment is justified. If all humans are born free, then how do we explain that some (here children) are less free than others? As Freeman has argued 'a true rethinking of children would also address citizenship rights... the [CRC], unsurprisingly, did not do so'.[117] As such, children remain 'aliens',[118] 'serfs',[119] 'passive spectators',[120] and 'savages'.[121]

[114] Jenks, C. (2005) *Childhood*, 48.

[115] O'Neill, John (1994) *The Missing Child in Liberal Theory*, vii-x.

[116] Woodhead, M. (1990) 'Psychology and the Cultural Construction of "Children's Needs"' in Woodhead, M., Light, P., and Carr, R. (eds.) *Growing up in a Changing Society*, 40.

[117] Freeman, M. (2000) 'The Future of Children's Rights' 14 *Children & Society* 287.

[118] Van Bueren, G. (1995) *The International Law on the Rights of Children*, 141.

[119] Beck (1997) 'Democratisation of the Family' 4 *Childhood* 161.

[120] Freeman, M. (2000) 'The Future of Children's Rights' 14 *Children & Society* 287.

[121] Jenks, C. (2005) *Childhood*, 3.

24

Minding the Gap? Children with Disabilities and the United Nations Convention on the Rights of Persons with Disabilities

Bronagh Byrne[1]

The United Nations Convention on the Rights of Persons with Disabilities (CRPD) was adopted by the UN General Assembly on 13 December 2006 and came into force on 3 May 2008.[2] The first human rights treaty of the 21st century, the CRPD has placed the spotlight firmly upon the breadth and depth of exclusionary and oppressive practices experienced by people with disabilities and which had hitherto been rendered invisible by an 'able-bodied' human rights discourse. The awakening of a disability movement throughout the latter part of the 20th century and its subsequent prominent role in shaping the CRPD during the treaty negotiation process has shaken the corporeal foundations on which society is based; that of a so-called 'normal' homogenous population and whose complete and functioning corporeality is the barometer against which all born into our society are measured. It is against this barometer that children with disabilities have traditionally been measured and found wanting. The development of a thematic convention is indicative of the increasing recognition accorded to the complexity of disability issues and the conclusion reached by the international community that the difference of disability is such that it has not been, and cannot be, effectively addressed by so-called 'mainstream' human rights treaties.

The marrying of disability and human rights discourse, and the challenges these have posed to the discourses of each other, has prompted valuable scholarship on a range of issues pertaining to the CRPD.[3] Conspicuous by its absence in this 'new' scholarship is a detailed exploration of the positioning of and rights accorded to children with disabilities within the CRPD, such has been the assumed and

[1] Queen's University Belfast.

[2] As of 1 November 2011, 106 States have ratified the Convention and there have been 153 signatories; 64 States have ratified the Optional Protocol and there have been 90 signatories. The Convention came into force on 3 May 2008, 30 days after ratification by Ecuador, the 20th State. Both the UK and Ireland signed the Convention at the first opportunity on 30 March 2007. The UK ratified on 8 June 2009, albeit with reservations relating to employment in the armed forces (Article 27), liberty of movement (Article 19), education (Article 24), and equal recognition before the law (Article 12). Ireland has yet to ratify. The Optional Protocol also came into force on 3 May 2008 and the UK ratified the Protocol on 7 August 2009.

[3] See for example Frédéric Mégret, 'The Disabilities Convention: Human Rights of Persons with Disabilities or Disability Rights' (2008) 30 *Human Rights Quarterly* 494; Rosemary Kayness and Phillip French, 'Out of the Darkness, Into the Light? Introducing the CRPD' (2008) 8 *Human Rights Law Review* 1; OddnýMjöll Arnardottir and Gerard Quinn (eds.), *The UN Convention on the Rights of Persons with Disabilities* (Martinus Nijhoff Publishers, Leiden, 2008).

unquestioned emphasis on the notion of a homogenous, and adult, disabled subject. Like adults with disabilities and children generally, children with disabilities have not traditionally been viewed as 'rights holders'. Children with disabilities can experience 'double jeopardy',[4] falling short of non-disabled norms on the one hand, and adult-based norms on the other. In addition, they have often been perceived as lacking the competence and capacity to be 'reliable witnesses' of their own lives and denied the opportunity to participate in decisions affecting them. These norms have also been a feature of international human rights law both respectively and cumulatively and children with disabilities have either not been acknowledged at all within the core treaties, or where they have been acknowledged, most notably within the Convention on the Rights of the Child, the resultant approach has been one of undue welfarism and/or medicalization of disabled children's lived experiences. The implications of such an approach is significant given the role of international human rights law in the production and maintenance of particular 'truths'; in offering a 'discourse of both freedom and domination'; and as a key agent of socialization and acculturation more generally.[5] The way in which international law conceptualizes and legitimizes the intersection between childhood and disability, and the disabling practices that result, has significant implications for influencing States to 'right' or 'wrong' behaviour in their treatment of children with disabilities, in determining what constitutes 'right' or 'wrong' behaviour, and in legitimizing the nature and content of the rights that children with disabilities can claim. The normative power of rights is thus of particular significance for a population group whose restoration to as complete a state of corporeal normality as possible has long been the primary concern for welfare professionals with little or no regard for either experiential childhood factors or the social dimensions of disability therein.

This chapter provides a critical assessment of the approach adopted by the CRPD towards children with disabilities and its implications for socializing States Parties to both 'right' and 'rights' behaviour. It discusses the ways in which 'rights talk' for children with disabilities, itself a relatively recent development in this context, has been predominantly needs based in its substantive content and explores whether the exacerbated disadvantage experienced by children with disabilities as a result of the particular interaction between disability and childhood is effectively addressed and given due weight by the new Convention. The CRPD's provisions are discussed in the context of children with disabilities and their potential to provide effective redress assessed. The chapter concludes with some critical reflections on the extent to which the CRPD can really be understood as minding the gap for children with disabilities. It suggests that whilst the combined mainstreaming approach adopted in the CRPD has the potential to make rights 'real' for children with disabilities, the double jeopardy hitherto experienced by this population group will continue unabated unless children with disabilities are accorded explicit attention throughout the full range of implementation and monitoring procedures mandated by the Convention. It is also crucial that future 'rights talk' with respect to children with disabilities does not again become undermined by welfarist discourse. The CRPD provides a key opportunity to revisit the medically oriented and individualized 'rights' base to which

[4] Gerison Lansdown, *The Evolving Capacities of the Child* (UNICEF/Save the Children, Florence, 2005).

[5] Tony Evans, 'International Human Rights Law as Power/Knowledge' (2005) 27 *Human Rights Quarterly* 1049. See also Ryan Goodman and Derek Jinks, 'How to Influence States: Socialization and International Human Rights Law' (2004) 54 *Duke Law Journal* 621.

children with disabilities have been subject. For the purpose of this chapter, 'disability' is understood as a socially constructed concept; specifically as resulting from the complex interaction between: impairment; the imposition of restrictions and barriers by cultures, structures, and institutions; and the legitimation of ablist ways of 'being' and 'doing' as exerted by educational, medical, and social discourses.

24.1 From welfare talk to (empty) rights talk?

The ways in which respective debates on understandings of disability and of childhood have persisted in compartmentalizing 'children' and 'disabled people' has not been helpful in highlighting the complexity of the lived experiences of children with disabilities. The categorical nature of identity ascription that assumes a single, fixed identity has prioritized either the corporeal 'normality' of childhood or the adult experience of disability. There are a number of common themes to be found across the fields of childhood and disability. Traditional developmental understandings have conceptualized childhood as 'natural, passive, incompetent'[6] and as 'lacking the capacities, skills and powers of adulthood',[7] while traditional medicalized understandings of disability have reduced disabled people to positions of powerlessness, unable to fully participate unless they can be restored to some form of specified 'normality'. Disability and childhood have been commonly presented in their respective spheres as dependent and incomplete states, constitutive of diminished capability and seemingly bereft of any meaningful capacity and agency until they are either 'cured' or 'grow up'. Children with disabilities have found it difficult to escape these traditional conceptualizations since:

> Judged against . . . normative yardsticks, the imperfectable bodies . . . of disabled children were inevitably constructed as inferior—as 'backward' or 'developmentally delayed'. Moreover, as children were exposed to ever more scrutiny, so children with impairments became disproportionately subject to new forms of surveillance, discipline and control (through institutional 'care', 'special' schooling, medical treatment, 'corrective' surgery, 'remedial therapy', eugenic abortions and genetic 'screening').[8]

Social policy relating to both childhood and disability has been underpinned by an ethic of care and dependency. The terms 'disability' and 'childhood' are commonly used in their respective fields as administrative and distributive constructs; a means of legitimating access and entitlement to resources, services, and opportunities through, for example, diagnosis and labelling, and acceptance or rejection of expressed need against set criteria. Mayall's observation that 'whole armies of health and social workers work to modify childhood' is amplified in the context of children with disabilities.[9] In this way, social policy has facilitated the policing of children

[6] Allison James and Alan Prout, *Constructing and Reconstructing Childhood* (Falmer Press, Basingstoke, 1990), x.

[7] David Archard, *Children, Rights and Childhood* (Routledge, London, 2004), 39.

[8] Mark Priestley, 'Childhood Disability and Disabled Childhoods—Agendas for Research' (1998) 5 *Childhood* 243.

[9] Berry Mayall, 'The Sociology of Childhood in Relation to Children's Rights' (2000) 8 *International Journal of Children's Rights* 243.

with disabilities through its establishment of 'boundaries of normalcy in an idealised version of the normal life course'.[10]

As such, children with disabilities are particularly vulnerable to forms of additive discrimination; that is, discrimination on the grounds of age like other children, because they too are children; and discrimination on the grounds of disability like other people with disabilities, and which increases the 'quantitative nature of the experience of discrimination'.[11] Significantly, children with disabilities can also experience *intersectional discrimination* since they may experience discrimination in a way that is distinct both from other children and from other people with disabilities. As Crenshaw illustrates with reference to black women: 'often they experience double discrimination—the combined effects of practices which discriminate on the basis of race, and on the basis of sex. And sometimes they experience discrimination as Black women—not the sum of race and sex, but as Black women.'[12] Similarly, children with disabilities can experience discrimination not simply as the sum of childhood and disability, but distinctively as *children with disabilities*. For example, children with disabilities: are more likely than children without disabilities to live away from home for substantial periods of time;[13] are more likely to experience neglect, and emotional, physical, and sexual abuse than children without disabilities;[14] and are far less likely to be involved in decision making processes[15] with a tendency for their interests to be inextricably linked with that of the family.

International human rights law has mirrored these categorical and welfarist understandings of both disability and childhood, with a social model of disability particularly slow to penetrate the human rights arena. 'Rights talk' has been regarded as irrelevant and inappropriate for a group of children whose restoration to as close a state of 'normality' as possible remains the immediate concern—and priority—for professionals and families. Engagement with particular aspects of these discourses by the international human rights framework is crucial; not only in socializing States to 'right' behaviour, but in determining what constitutes 'right' behaviour, and the implications of such norm setting for the rights children with disabilities can claim. The international human rights framework has, however, perpetuated and legitimated a form of rights behaviour that has been fundamentally disabling of children with disabilities.

With limited exceptions, the core UN human rights treaties have not expressly addressed the human rights of children with disabilities. Indeed, the international human rights domain has itself been guilty of perpetuating negative and disempowering views of disability. Understandings of disability as constitutive of individual deficit and relative 'inability' has manifested itself in the ablist norms which underpin

[10] Mark Priestley, 'Adults Only: Disability, Social Policy and the Life Course' (2000) 29 *Journal of Social Policy* 427.

[11] Nicholas Bamforth, Maleiha Malik, and Colm O'Cinneide (eds.), *Discrimination Law: Theory and Context* (Sweet and Maxwell, London, 2008), 528.

[12] Crenshaw (1989) cited in Bamforth et al. (2008) N. 11 above, 532.

[13] Luke Clements and Janet Read, *Disabled People and the European Convention on Human Rights* (Policy Press, Bristol, 2003); Janet Read and Luke Clements, *Disabled Children and the Law* (Jessica Kingsley Publishers, London, 2001).

[14] Jenny Morris, *Still Missing? Disabled Children and the Children Act, Vol.2* (The Who Cares? Trust, London, 1998). Ruth Marchant and Marcus Page, *Bridging the Gap: Investigating the Abuse of Children with Disabilities* (NSPCC, London, 1992); Helen Westcott, *Abuse of Adults and Children with Disabilities* (NSPCC, London, 1993).

[15] Anita Franklin and Patricia Sloper, 'Supporting the Participation of Disabled Children and Young People in Decision-Making' (2009) 23 *Children and Society* 3.

rights discourse and to which children with disabilities have been subject. Prior to the adoption of the CRPD, the Convention on the Rights of the Child was the only core human rights treaty to make explicit reference to disability. Other human rights treaties have subsumed disability under 'other status', as demonstrated in Article 2(1) of the International Covenant on Civil and Political Rights (ICCPR) (1966) and Article 2(2) of the International Covenant on Economic, Social and Cultural Rights (ICESCR) (1966). In 1994, the Committee on Economic, Social and Cultural Rights developed a General Comment on disability, recognizing that children with disabilities were especially vulnerable to exploitation, abuse, and neglect and thus entitled to special protection.[16] However, the ICESCR, like the ICCPR, was clearly not designed with children or people with disabilities in mind and subsequently has had little impact in addressing issues particular to either children or people with disabilities, lest *children with disabilities* specifically. The textual absence of children with disabilities in the core treaties prior to the CRC has served only to embed the invisibility of this particular group within the mainstream human rights paradigm; itself based on 'able-bodied', adult norms. One could argue that the UN human rights machinery has itself been as disabling and discriminatory as the practices it has sought to challenge by seemingly situating children with disabilities outside of human rights norms. While the universality of human rights is oft proclaimed with vigour, such universality has been ill-applied to children with disabilities in practice.

The United Nations Convention on the Rights of the Child (CRC) is the most comprehensive human rights instrument dedicated solely to the promotion and protection of children's rights. As the 'touchstone' for children's rights across the world,[17] the Convention contains extensive standards covering almost all areas of children's lives, including, *inter alia*, health, education, play, and standard of living. It also contains provisions specific to particular groups of children such as refugee children; children with disabilities; children in conflict with the law; and children who have been subject to abuse and exploitation. As such, it is a key source of rights for children with disabilities. Article 2 of the CRC, for the first time in binding international law, prohibits discrimination in the enjoyment of the Convention rights on the grounds of disability. In its General Comment on disability, the Committee on the Rights of the Child expressly stated that children with disabilities should enjoy all the Convention rights *without discrimination of any kind*.[18] Recognition of the need for substantive equality measures and of the multiple forms of discrimination experienced by children with disabilities is also evident:

> [The] explicit mention of disability as a prohibited ground for discrimination in article 2 is unique and can be explained by the fact that children with disabilities belong to one of the most vulnerable groups of children. In many cases forms of multiple discrimination—based on a combination of factors... increase the vulnerability of certain groups.... Discrimination takes place—often de facto—in various aspects of the life and development of children with disabilities.[19]

Article 23 of the CRC specifically addresses the rights of children with disabilities to, *inter alia*, enjoy a 'full and decent life'[20] and to 'special care' and 'assistance'.[21]

[16] Committee on Economic, Social and Cultural Rights, General Comment 5: Persons with Disabilities (1994) 32.

[17] Jane Fortin, *Children and the Developing Law* (Cambridge University Press, Cambridge, 2005), 49.

[18] Committee on the Rights of the Child, General Comment 9: The Rights of Children with Disabilities (CRC/C/GC/9, 2006) 8.

[19] N. 18 above, 11.

[20] Article 23(1) CRC.

[21] Article 23(2) CRC.

The Committee has made clear that the applicability of the CRC to children with disabilities is not limited to this right.[22] In its General Comment on children with disabilities, the Committee has stated that the underlying principle of this provision is that children with disabilities should be included in society. The effectiveness of Article 23 in addressing the rights of children with disabilities has been called into question. Kilkelly for example has observed that, in contrast to other provisions such as Article 22 on refugee children which requires States Parties to take 'all appropriate measures' to ensure they receive the care and protection they need, Article 23(2) stops short of specifying how the right of children with disabilities to 'special care' is to be achieved.[23] While Article 23(1) recognizes that children with disabilities 'should' enjoy a full and decent life, it does not place any obligation on States Parties to take measures to this end.[24] Similarly, Article 23(3), whilst requiring the provision of assistance, makes this subject to available resources, 'wherever possible', and 'taking into account the financial resources of parents or others caring for the child'. The language of the disability specific provision in the CRC and of the general comment on disability is heavily grounded in a welfarist and medicalized approach to disability with emphasis on 'special care', 'treatment', and 'rehabilitation', suggesting that there remains a tendency to regard all children with disabilities as necessitating predominantly protective measures rather than as active holders of rights more generally. The emphasis has thus been one of 'normalization', that is, upon the 'therapeutic' process of bringing an individual as closely as possible towards the 'normal'. Thus the purpose of rights talk and action for children with disabilities in the context of the CRC has been to focus on ways of overcoming the gap between the 'impaired being' and a 'normal becoming'. Children with disabilities are accepted not for who they are, but for what they fail to be and what they might become. The perceived work and input needed on the part of States Parties for children with disabilities to achieve the normal status that is held in such high esteem, not only devalues disabled children for who they are but fails to recognize the role of States Parties in the disabling process. Significantly, the overall goal that children with disabilities should be *included in society,* and the measures to be taken to this end, fails to problematize the ablist and adult-based foundations on which society is based, preferring instead to place responsibility for change and adaptation upon a seemingly delinquent subject. Conceptualizing children with disabilities in this way exemplifies the crucial role of the international human rights community in socializing States Parties to particular behaviours and actions, not least in inducing States Parties to medically oriented and deficit-based 'rights' behaviour and legitimizing particular understandings of children with disabilities in the process. Ultimately, the CRC has sought only to positively address one aspect of disabled children's lives; that of their inherent '*childhood*', with the experience of '*disability*' remaining 'locked' into an individual, medical approach.

It is acknowledged that the Committee on the Rights of the Child has begun to offer a more positive appraisal of disabled children's lives in its General Comments, and which have been bolstered by the drafting of the CRPD at that time. Yet the General Comment on children with disabilities, whilst purporting to draw upon

[22] N. 18 above, 5.

[23] Ursula Kilkelly, 'Disability and Children: the Convention on the Rights of the Child' in (eds.) Gerard Quinn and Theresia Degener, *Human Rights and Disability: The Current and Future Potential of United Nations Human Rights Instruments in the Context of Disability* (OHCHR HR/PUB/02/1, Geneva, 2002), 194.

[24] N. 23 above.

the social model-based definition of disability set out in the CRPD,[25] continues to confuse disability with impairment and emphasizes the need for measures which will 'enable [children] to adjust and live better with *their* disabilities'[26] and 'psychological support that is sensitive to the *stress and difficulties* imposed on families of children with disabilities';[27] the stress and difficulties imposed perceived as an inevitable and inherent result of caring for a disabled child. There remains a danger that the experiences of children with disabilities is construed as a 'burden' upon their adult caretakers and 'subsumed into the collective notion of the disabled family'.[28] By placing undue attention on the functional limitations of impairment, the CRC has contributed to the socially constructed and negative existential status of disability. In so doing, the child with the impairment is subsequently positioned as the key barrier to their own rights discourse.

Another major shortcoming of the CRC lies in the 'inevitable arbitrariness' with which disability issues are considered by the Committee on the Rights of the Child.[29] An analysis of the Committee's 2002 Concluding Observations to the UK's second periodic report uncovers only passing reference to children with disabilities[30] with the Committee's most recent 2008 report on the UK's combined third and fourth periodic reports (post adoption of the CRPD and following adoption of the General Comment on the rights of children with disabilities) paying increased attention to this group of children.[31] It will be interesting to observe: whether the Committee on the Rights of the Child accords increased attention to children with disabilities in the long term given the co-existence of the CRPD; whether the CRPD will be perceived by the latter Committee as the natural home for detailed commentary on children with disabilities; or indeed whether arbitrariness will endure. Finally, the lack of an individual complaints mechanism under the CRC, combined with the under-resourcing and heavy workload of the Committee on the Rights of the Child, has further limited the CRC's potential to provide effective redress to children with disabilities.[32] Nevertheless, the positioning of children with disabilities as rights holders within the CRC is a major achievement, in particular given that *adults* with disabilities remained implicitly protected in the other core human rights treaties and not expressly so. As shall be seen, given the relatively adult-centric manner in which the CRPD was drafted, it is highly unlikely that the CRPD provisions which are directly applicable to children with disabilities would have been so extensive had the CRC not already been in place.

[25] N. 18 above, 7. [26] N. 18 above, 27, emphasis added. [27] N. 18 above, 41.

[28] Vanessa Singh and Anita Ghai, 'Notions of Self: Lived Realities of Children with Disabilities' (2009) 24 *Disability and Society* 131.

[29] N. 23 above, 194.

[30] Committee on the Rights of the Child, Concluding Observations: United Kingdom of Great Britain and Northern Ireland (2002), Thirty-first session. CRC/C/15/Add.188 at paras 15, 22 and 47.

[31] Committee on the Rights of the Child, Concluding Observations: United Kingdom of Great Britain and Northern Ireland (2008), Forty-ninth session. CRC/C/GBR/CO/4, at paras 32, 45, 52, 53, 66, 69, 81.

[32] The UN Human Rights Council adopted the final draft Optional Protocol on a communications procedure for children's rights violations in June 2011. The new protocol will enable the Committee on the Rights of the Child to examine communications from children and their representatives alleging violations of their rights.

24.2 Unpacking the CRPD

The CRPD is structured in a typical fashion. It comprises 50 articles and its Optional Protocol comprises 18 articles. The treaty begins with a series of introductory (Preamble) and interpretive articles (Articles 1 and 2); continues with general obligations (Articles 3 to 9) and substantive rights (Articles 10 to 30), and establishes implementation and monitoring processes (Articles 31 to 40). It also sets out the rules which govern the operation of the Convention such as how States become party and when it will come into force (Articles 41 to 50). Through the Optional Protocol, an individual complaints procedure is established, allowing individuals and groups of individuals to raise complaints with the treaty body where they have exhausted domestic and regional remedies. It also establishes an inquiry procedure in relation to gross or systematic violations of the rights contained in the Convention. The Convention adopts a holistic approach and contains a full range of civil, political, economic, social, and cultural rights. While many of the rights specified in the CRPD are also specified in other human rights instruments, the Convention focuses on the actions that States Parties must take to ensure that people with disabilities enjoy these rights on an equal basis with others.

Somewhat significantly, the CRPD departs from the definition of disability adopted by previous treaty monitoring bodies. Its Preamble recognizes that disability is an 'evolving concept' which results from 'the interaction between persons with impairments and attitudinal and environmental barriers', while Article 1 of the CRPD makes clear that:

> Persons with disabilities *include* those who have long-term physical, mental, intellectual or sensory impairments which in interaction with various barriers may hinder their full and effective participation in society on an equal basis with others.[33]

Whilst proponents of a social model of disability in its purest form would no doubt critique the seemingly overlapping boundaries between impairment and disability in this statement, it is nonetheless the first expression of a social constructionist view of disability in a human rights treaty, and for this reason should be built upon rather than undermined. In the context of education, for example, the focus should be on those socially constructed educational barriers, which, *in interaction with* impairment, hinders the full and effective participation of children with disabilities on an equal basis with their peers. Whilst undoubtedly imperfect, it does represent progress in international law since, prior to the adoption of the CRPD, approaches to disability were characterized wholly by their medicalization. It is also testament to the difficulties inherent in the process of treaty negotiation and wherein attempts to reach consensus on a definition of disability was the subject of much debate between proponents of individual and social models of disability. In the CRPD, and in contrast to Article 23 of the CRC, no reference is made to 'special needs' or 'care'. This is interesting in itself and is indicative of a more positive approach to, and nuanced understanding of, the lived experiences of both children and adults with disabilities. It is also perhaps reflective of the extent of participation by people with disabilities themselves in the negotiation process. However, the failure explicitly to distinguish between and separate 'disability' and 'impairment' from the outset, and the

[33] Emphasis added.

subsequent vagueness that is implied, may fail adequately to challenge the entrenchment of disablist norms within States Parties by providing something of a legitimate escape route to 'safer' individualized climes. It remains to be seen if, and how, the Committee on the Rights of Persons with Disabilities approaches disability as a concept in its Concluding Observations and whether it will issue a General Comment on the issue. Intuition suggests that given the potential controversy this may elicit, it may be some time before the Committee is ready to take this step.

The CRPD adopts a combined mainstreaming approach to the rights of children with disabilities per se with numerous references to the specificity of children's lives throughout and obligating States Parties to provide age-appropriate assistance alongside a specific article addressing issues specific to children with disabilities not addressed elsewhere. The key overarching provisions relating to children with disabilities are contained within Article 3 (General Principles) and Article 7 (Children with disabilities). In contrast to the underlying principles of the CRC, which were identified *later* by its Committee, the CRPD itself explicitly sets out eight 'general principles'. All provisions of the Convention must therefore be read in light of these principles. Significantly, in addition to principles relating to, inter alia, full participation, equality, accessibility, and non-discrimination, Article 3(h) establishes as a general principle:

> (h) Respect for the evolving capacities of children with disabilities and respect for the right of children with disabilities to preserve their identities.

Article 7 (Children with Disabilities) reads:

1. States Parties shall take all necessary measures to ensure the full enjoyment by children with disabilities of all human rights and fundamental freedoms on an equal basis with other children.
2. In all actions concerning children with disabilities, the best interests of the child shall be a primary consideration.
3. States Parties shall ensure that children with disabilities have the right to express their views freely on all matters affecting them, their views being given due weight in accordance with their age and maturity, on an equal basis with other children, and to be provided with disability and age-appropriate assistance to realise that right.

These provisions clearly draw upon rights contained in the CRC with Article 3(h) CRPD drawing upon Article 5 CRC, and Article 7 CRPD drawing upon two of the cross-cutting principles contained in the CRC; that of best interests (Article 3 CRC) and of the right to be heard (Article 12 CRC). It is important to note in the context of the CRPD that the principle of respect for evolving capacities is not restricted to the confines of parental autonomy but must guide the interpretation of *all* CRPD rights.[34] The explicit inclusion of this concept and its prime location therein, is of great significance for a group of children who have often been perceived as incapable of demonstrating any meaningful capacity or competence. There is a presumption that, not only do children with disabilities have capacity, but that, like children more

[34] The concept of evolving capacities is stated in Article 5 CRC with respect to parental direction and guidance in the exercise by the child of the Convention rights. It is repeated in Article 14 CRC with respect to parental direction and guidance on the child's right to freedom of thought, conscience, and religion. 'Evolving capacities' is linked to the requirement of Article 12 CRC that the views of children should be given due weight in accordance with the age and maturity of the child.

generally, their capacity for autonomous decision making will develop over time. The Committee on the Rights of the Child has referred to evolving capacities as constitutive of a 'positive enabling process' and encompassing 'processes of maturation and learning whereby children progressively acquire knowledge, competencies and understanding'.[35] In their periodic reports to the Committee on the Rights of Persons with Disabilities, States Parties are required to report on the manner in which the general principles have been implemented, and to provide examples.[36] There remains, however, as Lansdown asserts more generally in the context of the CRC, a potential for conflict when children's assessment of their capacities do not concur with those of parents, educationalists, and health professionals, among others.[37] This concept may therefore be perceived as particularly challenging in the context of children with disabilities given the lower baseline capacity they may be viewed as possessing and the extrinsic barriers to the meaningful exercise of capacity that children with disabilities may experience in contrast to children without disabilities, such as higher levels of overprotection and low expectations; a legacy of the intersection between disability and childhood. While children's capacities evolve to differing degrees and at different rates, the extent to which the capacities of children with disabilities are *de facto* enabled may diverge from that which is possible, becoming contingent upon adult views and understandings of what is considered acceptable and 'safe' for a disabled child to achieve, and/or the type of support that may either be available or perceived as appropriate in particular instances. It is imperative that if the principle of evolving capacities is to effectively inform the realization of all other CRPD rights, the extrinsic barriers to processes of maturation and learning experienced by children with disabilities are recognized and challenged by the Committee on the Rights of Persons with Disabilities in its commentary to States Parties.

The language of Article 7 CRPD is in stark contrast with the medicalized discourse evidenced in Article 23 CRC. It is also in opposition to the first draft of the child-specific article proposed during the CRPD negotiations which took the latter as its starting point, and which made reference to the need for children with disabilities and their adult caretakers to be provided with 'counselling' and for the provision of 'assistance' and 'care' appropriate to the 'child's condition and the circumstances of their parents'.[38] This marrying of the needs of children with that of their parents was removed in the final provision. The final article is much more positive in language. Article 7(1) obligates States Parties to take all *necessary* measures to 'ensure the full enjoyment by children with disabilities of all human rights and fundamental freedoms on an equal basis with other children'. Nonetheless, what is considered 'necessary' will vary between States Parties.

Article 7(2) clearly sets out the best interests principle. The best interests of the child are to be a primary consideration in *all actions concerning children with disabilities*. The wording of this principle indicates that its scope is very wide, potentially extending to public and private bodies and to private family settings. It remains to be seen just how extensively the Committee will interpret this provision. As in the CRC, the best interests principle is not determinative but is only one primary

[35] Committee on the Rights of the Child, General Comment No.7 'Implementing child rights in early childhood' (CRC/C/GC/7Rev.1, 2005), 17.

[36] Committee on the Rights of Persons with Disabilities, Reporting Guidelines (CRPD/C/2/3, 2009), 7.

[37] Lansdown N. 4 above, 344.

[38] <http://www.un.org/esa/socdev/enable/rights/ahcstata24bkgrnd.htm> accessed 10 January 2011.

consideration. This raises the question of which other values should prevail or outweigh the best interests consideration. The reduction of best interests to 'a primary' consideration is a considerable weakening of the original draft proposal that best interests should in fact be the *paramount* consideration in all actions concerning children with disabilities.[39] The inclusion of Article 7(2) is problematic and theoretically deficient. There was no attempt by the Ad Hoc Committee or Working Group to define the concept of best interests; a fundamental flaw in ensuring its effective applicability since 'for some best interests can be reduced to a satisfaction of material needs... Others will emphasize emotional security, psychological well-being, attention to developmental interest. Some... will stress moral and religious welfare'.[40] The welfarist discourse with which the concept is associated with respect to children with disabilities in particular, risks reaffirming and entrenching rather than challenging the paternalist practices to which children with disabilities continue to be subject. Moreover, as Archard and Skivenes have observed in the context of children generally: 'By whom and according to what procedures are judgements of best interests made? Clinicians... may be accomplished diagnosticians, but they need not be the best placed to judge whether or not a life is worth living.'[41] Similarly, what happens when the interests of parents, professionals, and children collide? How should best interests be measured? Is it in the 'best interests' of a child with a disability to be brought as closely as possible to the culturally, socially, and biologically 'normal'? What is the relationship between the general principle of 'respect for difference and acceptance of persons with disabilities as part of human diversity and humanity' as established in Article 3 of the CRPD and the best interests principle here? Take, for example, a deaf child in whose medical interests it has been established would be to receive a cochlear implant, but which would potentially lead to the exclusion of that child from the signing Deaf Community of which the child is part, and thus may not be in that child's cultural interests? Which set of interests or considerations should prevail? Consideration of the child's best interests is vital; however it is the unproblematized vagueness of the concept within the CRPD combined with the deeply entrenched welfarist underpinnings of 'best interests' as used in the context of both disability and childhood which could prove to be the undoing of the glossy allusions presented in Article 7. As it currently stands, continuation of such usage with respect to children with disabilities would be quite legitimate.

Some reassurance may be found in Article 7(3): the right of children with disabilities to express their views freely on all matters affecting them and for their views to be given due weight in accordance with their age and maturity.[42] The explication of disability *and* age-appropriate assistance in realizing this right is cognizance of the realities of multiple discrimination experienced by children with disabilities on the grounds of both childhood and disability. In its recent response to the UK's third and fourth periodic reports, the Committee on the Rights of the Child expressed concern that 'insufficient action has been taken to ensure that the rights enshrined

[39] Paramountcy of the child's best interests is established in Article 23(2) of the CRPD; respect for home and family in relation to the guardianship, wardship, trusteeship, or adoption of children, reflecting a similar provision in Article 21.

[40] Michael Freeman, *A Commentary on the Convention on the Rights of the Child: Article 3: The Best Interests of the Child* (Martinus Nijhoff Publishers, Leiden, 2007), 27.

[41] David Archard and Marit Skivenes, 'Balancing a Child's Best Interests and a Child's Views' (2009) 17 *International Journal of Children's Rights* 8.

[42] Thus drawing upon Article 12 CRC.

in Article 12 are applied to children with disabilities'.[43] Children with disabilities are often perceived as a justifiable exception to participative processes for three reasons: a belief that they have no views to express; an assumption that the interests and lived experiences of children with disabilities will always be best articulated by adult caretakers; and concern that any attempts to facilitate children's views will be too expensive or too difficult. It is hoped that the further elaboration of this right in the CRPD will encourage States Parties to take their obligations more seriously in this respect. Lundy writing on Article 12 CRC, has identified four key factors underpinning successful implementation of this right: first, 'space'—children must be given the opportunity to express a view in a space that is safe and inclusive. For children with disabilities such spaces must also be physically accessible. Second, 'voice'—children must be facilitated to express their views. The proliferation of 'voice' for children with disabilities will necessitate particular forms of support or adjustment where appropriate, alongside recognition of the range of verbal and non-verbal ways in which views can be expressed. Third, 'audience'—the view must be listened to; and finally, 'influence'—the view must be acted upon as appropriate.[44] It is interesting to note that whilst Article 12 CRC is assured only 'to the child who is capable of forming his or her own views',[45] no such restriction is placed upon its CRPD equivalent. The inclusion of 'evolving capacities' as a key principle strengthens the potential of Article 7 in bringing the voices of children with disabilities to the fore. However, as Lundy rightly observes in the context of the CRC, 'At some point, attention needs to focus on the extent of influence; what constitutes the "due" in the "due weight"' as well as the danger that 'the adults who act as gatekeepers to Article 12 rights may decide that children are not sufficiently mature to express a view'.[46] The latter concern is exacerbated when the intersection between disability and childhood is brought to the fore. Attention needs to be paid to *which* children with disabilities are approached to participate in decision-making processes. There remains a danger that only older children who have impairments which are perceived to be relatively inexpensive to accommodate or who require only minimal or readily available forms of support are given the opportunity to express their views, or that some forms of verbal or written means of expression are prioritized at the expense of other specialized or less well known modes and which may thus be deemed as secondary in importance for this purpose.

Article 4(3) (General Obligations) stipulates that:

> In the development and implementation of legislation and policies to implement the present Convention, and in other decision-making processes concerning issues relating to persons with disabilities, States Parties shall closely consult with and actively involve persons with disabilities, including children with disabilities, through their representative organizations.

Article 4(3) is reflective of the unprecedented level of engagement by civil society in the negotiation process. Civil society in this context largely encompassed organizations OF people with disabilities as opposed to organizations FOR people with disabilities. At first glance Article 4(3) appears to be a fairly strong obligation advocating direct engagement. During the negotiation process, it was proposed that the latter

[43] Committee on the Rights of the Child, Concluding Observations: United Kingdom of Great Britain and Northern Ireland (CRC/C/GBR/CO/4, 2008), 32.

[44] Laura Lundy, '"Voice" is not Enough: Conceptualising Article 12 of the UNCRC' (2007) 33 *British Educational Research Journal* 927.

[45] Article 12(1) CRC.

[46] N. 44 above, 937.

part of this provision should read '…involve persons with disabilities, including children with disabilities, *and* their representative organizations'. The replacement of the word 'and' with 'through' weakens this obligation. Nonetheless, Article 4(3) requires States Parties to actively *involve* children with disabilities through organizations that are *representative*, recognizing that children, and not just adults, have an important role to play. It requires such involvement both in processes relating to the implementation of the Convention and *in other decision-making processes* concerning issues relating to people with disabilities. Article 4(3) is clearly complemented by Article 7(3) of the CRPD with respect to children.

The Convention rights apply equally to all people with disabilities, including children. The Ad Hoc Committee responsible for drafting the Convention text recognized, however, the need to articulate rights in ways that would effectively address the combined effects of practices on the basis of disability and other grounds such as gender and age. The CRPD in its mainstreaming approach makes explicit references to children and/or age in articles outside of those already discussed. In Article 8(1)(b), States Parties are required to 'undertake to adopt immediate, effective and appropriate measures' to combat stereotypes, prejudices, and harmful practices relating to people with disabilities, including on the basis of sex and age, in all areas of life.[47] Interestingly, the CRPD also requires States Parties to take measures to foster 'an attitude of respect' for the rights of disabled people at all levels of the education system, 'including in all children from an early age'.[48] Reference to 'age-appropriate accommodations' is made in the context of ensuring effective access to justice for people with disabilities,[49] while the right of children with disabilities to registration of birth, to a name, to acquire a nationality, and, as far as possible, to know and be cared for by their parents is set out in Article 18(2).[50]

The right to be free from all forms of exploitation, violence, and abuse is established in Article 16. This right is crucial in recognizing the greater likelihood of people of disabilities to experiences of abuse and exploitation, both inside and outside the home through placement in care and educational, social, or medical institutions. The Committee on the Rights of Persons with Disabilities has, in its reporting guidelines, stipulated that States Parties should pay particular attention to women and children with disabilities in this context.[51] States Parties are obliged to take protective and preventive measures, including ensuring that protection services and support are 'age, gender and disability sensitive'.[52] States Parties are also required to take account of 'age specific needs' in supporting the recovery, rehabilitation, and social reintegration of persons with disabilities who become victims of any form of exploitation, violence, or abuse.[53] Paragraph 5 of Article 16 requires States Parties to implement legislation and policies, *including child-focused legislation and policies* to ensure that instances of exploitation, violence, and abuse are identified, investigated, and, where appropriate, prosecuted. The pattern of, and for many children with disabilities, negative consequences of long-term institutionalization, is illuminated in Article 23—respect for home and family. This article presents a detailed set of provisions for children with disabilities. It should be recalled at this point that in implementing Article 23,

[47] Article 8 CRPD, Awareness-raising. [48] Article 8(2)(b) CRPD.

[49] Article 13(1) CRPD, Access to justice.

[50] Article 18 CRPD, Liberty of movement and nationality.

[51] Committee on the Rights of Persons with Disabilities, Reporting Guidelines (CRPD/C/2/3, 2009), 11.

[52] Article 16(2) CRPD, Freedom from exploitation, violence and abuse. [53] Article 16(4).

as with all other rights, States Parties are required to take account of the CRPD's general principles and to ensure that the views of children with disabilities are given due weight in accordance with their age and maturity, adding additional weight to its provisions. Under Article 23(3), States Parties are to ensure that children with disabilities have equal rights with respect to family life. In addition:

3. [...] With a view to realizing these rights, and to prevent concealment, abandonment, neglect and segregation of children with disabilities, States parties shall undertake to provide early and comprehensive information, services and support to children with disabilities and their families.

4. States parties shall ensure that a child shall not be separated from his or her parents against their will, except when competent authorities subject to judicial review determine..., that such separation is necessary for the best interests of the child. In no case shall a child be separated from parents on the basis of disability of either the child or one or both of the parents.

5. States parties shall, where the immediate family is unable to care for a child with disabilities, undertake every effort to provide alternative care within the wider family, and failing that, within the community in a family setting.

Article 23(4) reflects the potential conflict that could arise between a child's views and that which is perceived by the relevant authorities as being in their best interests, while Article 23(5) clearly challenges States Parties to avoid institutionalization of children with disabilities as far as possible. In addition, Article 23(1)(c) obliges States Parties to ensure that people with disabilities, *including children*, retain their fertility on an equal basis with others.

The right to an effective education is crucial for children with disabilities. For the parents of children with disabilities, the key debate centres on whether they should access mainstream educational provision or be educated within a segregated, 'special' school environment. Whilst educational achievement and progression is clearly important for all, educational provision for children with disabilities has been negatively skewed towards the lower end of the non-academic spectrum in a way that has been pejorative to the moral worth and social inclusion of people with disabilities more generally. Article 24 CRPD accords the right of people with disabilities to education without discrimination and on the basis of equal opportunity. It requires States Parties to ensure an inclusive education system at all levels, and draws on Article 29 CRC in establishing the aims to which such a system should be directed.[54] However, no attempt is made to explicitly define what is meant by 'inclusion' other than to state that children with disabilities should not be excluded from the general education system on the basis of disability,[55] and that they should receive the support required *within the general education system*, to facilitate their *effective education*.[56] This would appear to signify a positive approach to inclusion; one wherein the presumption is in favour of education in mainstream settings, with the provision of support to ensure that education really is inclusive and not reduced to mere integration. No attempt was made during the negotiation process to define 'inclusion' or to include any such definition in Article 2 of the CRPD which defines the terms 'communication', 'language', 'discrimination on the basis

[54] Set out in Article 24(1), that is, to 'the full development of human potential and sense of dignity and self-worth, and the strengthening of respect for human rights, fundamental freedoms and human diversity', and 'the development by persons with disabilities of their personality, talents and creativity, as well as their mental and physical abilities, to their fullest potential'.

[55] Article 24(2)(a).

[56] Article 24(2)(d).

of disability', 'reasonable accommodation', and 'universal design' for the purposes of the Convention. The remainder of Article 24 does elaborate further on what would appear to be the prerequisites for an inclusive education system. In addition to measures to 'enable persons with disabilities to learn life and social development skills to facilitate their full and equal participation in education',[57] States Parties are required to provide reasonable accommodation and individualized support measures in 'environments that maximize academic and social development' and which are 'consistent with the goal of full inclusion'.[58] The concept of 'reasonable accommodation' permeates the Convention. This is the first time reasonable accommodation has been both included and defined in a core human rights treaty. Article 2 defines reasonable accommodation as:

> Necessary and appropriate modification and adjustments not imposing a disproportionate or undue burden, where needed in a particular case, to ensure to persons with disabilities the enjoyment or exercise on an equal basis with others of all human rights and fundamental freedoms.

The explicit inclusion and definition of the concept is, on the one hand, a crucial component of the CRPD, recognizing the ways in which people with disabilities, including children, have been disadvantaged by the immanent rules of a 'game' designed by and for a non-disabled and adult majority which has already begun, not least in education and social settings, and of the remedies needed to ensure a more level 'playing field'.[59] However, the concept of reasonable accommodation contained in the CRPD remains inherently problematic, and fails to depart significantly from welfarist assertions of assistance contained in other human rights treaties. Whilst the grounding of the CRPD in a social model of disability is to be clearly welcomed, the CRPD fails to recognize the way in which 'reasonable accommodation' can itself become a barrier which may 'hinder full and equal participation' of children with disabilities 'in society on an equal basis with others'. It does not challenge the legitimacy of prevailing ways of being and doing, focusing only on the need to instigate change where absolutely necessary. The complexity of reasonable accommodation and the justifiable discrimination it implies has been highlighted by Riddell et al, in the context of national disability discrimination legislation, rightly arguing that '[t]he notion of "reasonableness" is evidently a somewhat slippery concept which may be interpreted differently in a variety of contexts'.[60] What is understood as 'reasonable' by one State Party may be wholly different from another. Consideration also needs to be paid to what constitutes an 'undue burden'. Implicit within understandings of justifiable discrimination and reasonable adjustment is the idea that children with disabilities and their needs are both burdensome and expensive and wherein the notion of reasonableness and its subjective parameters risks becoming something of a safety net and/or an institutional conservation strategy against structural change. That children, and adults, with disabilities can still be subject to justifiable discrimination is something that would be deemed intolerable and inappropriate for those whose differences are grounded in gender, ethnicity, religion, or class. In this regard

[57] Article 24(3). These measures include, inter alia, facilitating learning of Braille, sign language, and alternative means of communication and mobility skills.

[58] Article 24(2).

[59] Iris Marion Young, 'Equality of Whom? Social Groups and Judgements of Injustice' (2001) 9 *The Journal of Political Philosophy* 1.

[60] Shelia Riddell, Teresa Tinklin, and Alastair Wilson, *Disabled Students in Higher Education: Perspectives on widening access and changing policy* (Routledge, London, 2005), 79.

reasonable accommodation becomes something of a double-edged sword: a precursor to a form of *conditional rather than absolute inclusion*, and ultimately to a *conditional rights discourse.* Such conditionality emanates from the implicit designation of some children with disabilities and those children with more complex needs in particular, as having needs that are 'unreasonable', 'too costly', and 'burdensome'. Whilst viewed as a key avenue through which disabling barriers can be eradicated and of achieving substantive equality, the continuing justification for practices that are clearly discriminatory, but 'unreasonable' to remove, locates the 'problem' of disability with the disabled child who, but for their costly requirements perceived as resulting from individual need, would be 'able' to participate fully and/or avail of a particular right. This subtle practice of blame transfer is clearly reminiscent of processes of 'othering', not least because '*The Different Ones are seen as less competent, less skilled, less knowing...*'[61]

Finally, Article 25(b) accords children with disabilities the right to health services needed specifically because of disability, including early identification, intervention, and prevention,[62] while Article 30(3)(d) requires States Parties to ensure that children with disabilities have equal access to participation in play, recreation, and leisure and sporting activities, including those activities in the school system.[63]

24.3 Monitoring the CRPD's monitoring provisions

As with all human rights treaties, the Convention contains a number of monitoring provisions. Particular aspects of these provisions are innovative, largely unprecedented in other human rights treaties. The overarching objective of monitoring is to ensure effective implementation of the provisions of a treaty, and that those intended to benefit from these provisions are able to do so. Monitoring processes are of critical importance to ensuring the rights of children with disabilities. Aside from reporting procedures which are common to all treaties, the relative diversity of monitoring provisions across the core UN treaties with respect to individual complaints mechanisms highlights the lack of consensus about how implementation can be best achieved. There is, however, general consensus that the work of treaty bodies should be heavily weighted towards encouraging and facilitating the development of national systems and processes which support and defend the articulated rights.[64] The inclusion in the CRPD of Article 33 on national implementation and monitoring is recognition of the need for strong systems of monitoring so as to ensure the transmission of and engagement with the Convention's standards at national level. Such processes are crucial in socializing States Parties to 'right' and 'rights' behaviour. Effective implementation of the CRPD is ultimately premised on establishing a 'domestic architecture for change' as envisaged by Article 33 of the CRPD.[65] This requires States Parties to designate one or more focal points within government for

[61] William Ryan, *Blaming the Victim* (Random House, New York, 1976), 10.

[62] Article 25 CRPD, Health.

[63] Article 30 CRPD, Participation in cultural life, recreation, leisure and sport.

[64] Anne Gallagher, 'Making Human Rights Treaty Obligations a Reality: Working with New Actors and Partners' in Phillip Alston and James Crawford (eds.), *The Future of UN Human Rights Treaty Monitoring* (Cambridge University Press, Cambridge, 2000), 201.

[65] Gerard Quinn, 'Resisting the "Temptation of Elegance": Can the Convention on the Rights of Persons with Disabilities Socialise States to Right Behaviour?' in O.M. Arnardottir and G. Quinn (eds.), *The UN Convention on the Rights of Persons with Disabilities* (Martinus Nijhoff Publishers, Leiden, 2008), 219.

matters relating to the Convention;[66] maintain, strengthen, designate, or establish a framework to promote, protect, and monitor implementation;[67] and ensure that civil society, in particular, people with disabilities, and their representative organizations are involved and participate fully in the monitoring process.[68] It is not yet clear how well this will work in practice and, with no comparator in the human rights treaty system, it is likely to be some time before effective national level systems of monitoring are developed. There has already been debate among and within States Parties that the 'framework' referred to in Article 33(2) necessitates only the designation of a national human rights institution as opposed to the collaborative effort and partnership of a number of bodies, including civil society, that close reading of the article would suggest. Nonetheless, the deliberate inclusion of these provisions is something of a natural progression given the wider debate on enhancing the effectiveness of treaty monitoring by the international community. As such the CRPD is illustrative of a shift towards more participative forms of monitoring in which people with disabilities play a central role. In taking a more considered approach to processes of implementation and monitoring, Article 33 has the potential to promote greater and more meaningful compliance with human rights norms at domestic level and to act as a powerful disincentive to violating behaviour. The role of Article 33 in enhancing the domestic internalization of norms is, on one level, exciting and to be highly welcomed. Ironically, however, it also has the potential to become a double-edged sword where the norms it seeks to inculcate are grounded in conceptions of individual deficit, and wherein added legitimacy is granted to concepts such as reasonable accommodation in its present form.

The role of children with disabilities within the monitoring process remains under question given that they are not explicitly mentioned anywhere in Article 33. It would be somewhat misleading to assume that the phrase 'persons with disabilities' is here all encompassing in the eyes of States Parties. Whilst theoretically so, the default use of 'persons' in international law to date has, in practice, been exclusive of people with disabilities and children generally unless otherwise stipulated, much less children with disabilities. The lack of reference to children here is particularly disappointing given the numerous references to children throughout the CRPD's substantive provisions as well as the requirement for children with disabilities to be involved in the development of legislation and policies relating to the implementation of the Convention under Article 4(3). In contrast to Article 4(3), however, Article 33(3) requires people with disabilities to be involved in the monitoring process *alongside*, that is, in addition to, their representative organizations rather than merely *through* these organizations. There is a risk that the potential of the CRPD with respect to ensuring the rights of children with disabilities and in developing truly participative forms of monitoring will be undermined by the absence of express reference to children in relation to national monitoring specifically as experience in relation to international human rights law more generally demonstrates.

In contrast to the current status of the CRC, the Optional Protocol to the CRPD establishes an individual complaints procedure, allowing individuals and groups of individuals to raise complaints with the treaty body where they have exhausted domestic and regional remedies. This would appear to offer much hope in enabling children with disabilities to bring forth individual complaints. As Freeman has observed: '[T]he sight of children hauling their own state before an international

[66] Article 33(1) CRPD. [67] Article 33(2) CRPD. [68] Article 33(3) CRPD.

court would be particularly gratifying.'[69] Examination of the CRPD's Optional Protocol suggests that this has not been designed with children in mind and it remains to be seen how effective this will be in practice for children with disabilities, or indeed people with disabilities more generally. Unlike the text of the CRPD itself, the Optional Protocol is disappointingly standard. There is no reference to disability or age-specific assistance or support in the complaints process. There is no reference to submission of complaints or exchange of information in alternative formats or cognizance of any barriers within the complaints process that may arise. Whilst the individual complaints procedure would appear to be ill-conceived for adults with disabilities, the intersection between disability and age and failure to take this into account would appear to exclude children with disabilities even further from effective redress of rights violations.

24.4 Conclusion

The United Nations Convention on the Rights of Persons with Disabilities has generated expectations of urgent redress for the long-overdue advancement of human rights for people with disabilities throughout the world. In determining what constitutes 'right' or 'wrong' behaviour, international human rights law undoubtedly plays a key role in the enunciation and development of norms at both international and national levels. It would be misleading, however, to assume that such explication will inevitably be positive. In determining the content and nature of the rights that designated rights holders can claim and the parameters of the duties to be exercised on the part of States Parties, the legitimating role of international human rights law can cause the human rights framework itself to become a part of the disabling processes it purports to challenge. This has been particularly evident in the case of children with disabilities wherein the human rights system prior to the CRPD has itself been guilty of perpetuating the 'otherness' of children with disabilities by placing undue attention on overcoming the functional limitations of impairment through highly individualized and welfarist-based solutions rather than on eradicating the disabling effects of society. Nor has the human rights system addressed the intersectionality of disability and childhood with any great success.

The development of a thematic convention in the form of the CRPD is therefore crucial; not only in challenging persistent human rights violations on the ground, but in providing the human rights system with a much needed opportunity to revisit and reassess the less than satisfactory nature of the rights discourse to which both adults and children with disabilities have been subject. As such the CRPD's success is highly anticipated and its coming into force heralded as a major achievement in itself. While not altogether unwarranted, such celebration must be kept in perspective and close attention paid to the implications of that which is presented in the CRPD lest children with disabilities become subject to little more than an illusionary vessel. The CRPD clearly enhances the textual visibility of children with disabilities within international human rights law. Such textual visibility is a legacy of the mainstreaming approach that was adopted by the treaty's drafters towards children with disabilities and of the high involvement of civil society in that process. Of especial importance is the explicit applicability of the CRPD rights across disabled children's lives and

[69] Michael Freeman, 'The Future of Children's Rights' (2000) 14 *Children and Society* 290.

cognizance not just of the intersection between disability and childhood per se but of the intersection between childhood, impairment, and the imposition of restrictions and barriers by structures and institutions. The success of such an approach remains untold, however, and it is vital that these intersections are given not only textual voice, but are given practical voice in the ever developing processes of implementation and monitoring that seek to give effect to these rights. Children with disabilities must be accorded equal status to adults with disabilities both by the Committee on the Rights of Persons with Disabilities and by States Parties and not positioned as a mere addendum or afterthought. Indeed, while it is much too early to assess the CRPD's progress to date, one wonders whether the CRPD's long-term success in effectively minding the gap for children with disabilities might have been enhanced by naming the treaty the 'Convention on the Rights of Children and Adults with Disabilities' given the extent to which disability has been perceived as located outside of human rights norms by virtue of its textual absence in human rights discourse and the extent to which childhood has fallen victim to a homogenous and inevitably adult-based disability discourse. Indeed, human rights discourse has too often concealed positions of power under the guise of universality. The traditional use of 'persons' as an all-encompassing term has served only to conform to, and reaffirm, an ablist and adult-oriented status quo by rendering silent that which is taken for granted. In this way a thematic convention and the textual visibility of children with disabilities therein must be understood as positive. What is not yet certain is how well this will be translated into practice.

Some aspects of the CRPD are of concern and, to some extent, continue to locate children with disabilities within a welfarist discourse albeit in reconstituted forms. This is most evident through attempts by the international community to address issues relating to 'reasonable accommodation'. Undoubtedly a complex and challenging issue for the Committee, not least in obtaining consensus among States Parties, the way in which this has been conceptualized has created space for the legitimation of exclusionary practices within State Parties. Whilst the reality of resources will always be an issue, of particular concern here is the way in which the problem of resources becomes understood as the problem of 'disability' in its medicalized form, and wherein the child with the impairment subsequently becomes the key barrier to their own rights discourse.

In conclusion, the combined mainstreaming approach to childhood adopted by the Ad Hoc Committee in developing the Convention alongside elaboration of key CRC rights in the context of disability denotes a substantial window of opportunity in providing effective redress to the human rights violations experienced by children with disabilities across the world. The coming into force of the Convention and its ratification by States Parties across the developing and developed world is but one step in realizing the rights therein for children. Whilst States Parties' obligations in promoting, protecting, and respecting the fundamental rights and freedoms of children with disabilities have been made substantively clearer than has hitherto been the case, the realization of these obligations will remain elusive on the ground unless effective implementation and monitoring systems are in place. It will be up to the Committee on the Rights of Persons with Disabilities to set the standard by elaborating upon the nature and content of these rights, and in so doing inducing States to 'rights' and 'right' behaviour in a positive and meaningful manner. One hopes that this is a challenge that the Committee will take on with vigour and understanding so that the CRPD really does mind the gap in realizing the rights of children with disabilities.

25

'Special' Treatment, 'Special' Rights: Children Who Hear Voices as Doubly Diminished Identities

China Mills[1]

Introduction

I think I'd have liked them to believe me about everything... The abuse and the voices because it's real to me.[2]

Her mental disorder... was such that on other days she was not only Gillick incompetent, but actually sectionable. No child in that situation can be regarded as Gillick competent.[3]

While the recognition of children as subjects of rights is mandated in legislation, this chapter begins to query the medico-legal frameworks for such recognition; what do they take for granted and what do they foreclose? In doing this I want to attend to how rights discourse, psychiatry, and developmental models of the 'normal' child can converge to embody disciplinary effects that regulate children's lives and discursively frame certain children as 'problems'. Appearing before the law as subjects of rights, and within psychiatry as 'mentally ill', the 'child with mental health problems' enters into specific realms of appearance and frameworks of recognition that delimit and foreclose what sort of subject that child can be and how that child can come to understand their experiences. This chapter explores how it is that the strategies that young people develop to survive inequality and distress often become pathologized as 'symptoms' within psychiatric frameworks of understanding.

In this way, the medical model through its conceptualizations of children's behaviour as pathological, works to divest children's behaviour of any political significance, rendering their lives, in Agamben's terms, as 'bare', as 'life unworthy of being lived'.

[1] China Mills is currently studying for a PhD at the Education and Social Research Institute, at Manchester Metropolitan University. She is exploring the intersections between post-colonial and political theory for conceptualizing the medicalization of people's resistance to psychiatric and pharmacological frameworks of recognition within the arena of global mental health and disability, in the UK and India. China has previously carried out research for the Hearing Voices Network, with young people who hear voices, and has previously worked with young people who have physical and learning disabilities, in the UK and India.

[2] All quotes, unless otherwise stated, are taken from research undertaken by the author into 'Young People's Stories about Hearing Voices' (funded by the Research Institute of Health and Social Change, at Manchester Metropolitan University, in 2008). (All names have been changed throughout to ensure anonymity.)

[3] Lord Donaldson, cited in P. Fennell, V. Harpwood, and C. Ngwena, 'Medical Law' (1991) *All ER Annual Review*.

Through attending to the survival strategies and resistance of such children, we might begin to recognize and trouble how children are subjected to 'treatment' often in the form of medication justified within a normative matrix that sets the parameters of what counts as a 'normal' child, and childhood.

Drawing upon my previous research around young people's lived experiences of hearing voices, and survivor literature on self-injury, this chapter aims to bring into question the medico-legal frameworks of intelligibility that regulate what can be constituted as normal/rational and what can be publicly recognizable as reality. I want to explore what conditions the distinction between what we recognize as a 'normal' child and that which we construct as 'abnormal'. How does this construction of the 'normal' child condition our responses to children who have unusual experiences or who are distressed? How do terms such as 'normal' and 'child' work, what do they foreclose, and what are they used to justify? As more and more children are framed as 'mentally ill', with increasing amounts of medication prescribed to children, such questions are pertinent.

This chapter will explore the processes by which children framed as being 'mentally ill', and particularly here children who self-injure or hear voices, present us with a limit figure to current child rights discourse. In engaging with this limit figure, this chapter aims to examine the parochial frameworks drawn upon within legal decisions around children's rights to refuse 'treatment'. In fact it aims to interrogate how psychiatric frameworks foreclose what can be understood to be 'treatment' in the first place. In contesting the frameworks by which the 'child with mental health problems' comes to be constituted, it will engage with young people's own stories to enable dissonant and plural frames of recognition to come into view.

Reading the stories that people who heard voices as children have told me, alongside the work of Giorgio Agamben and Judith Butler, particularly their theses around 'bare' and 'precarious' lives, enables further understanding of how dominant schemes of intelligibility may work to medicalize childhood experience; normalizing the absence of children with mental illness and pathologizing their presence within rights discourse.[4] Thus we might conceptualize child rights as being a 'violating enablement' for children.[5]

25.1 Competence, consent, and coercion

Within the law, children under the age of 16 have the right to consent to or to refuse medical treatment without parental consent, as a result of the landmark *Gillick* ruling.[6] However reinterpretations of *Gillick* within Court of Appeal rulings have meant that this potentially progressive legislation carries 'veto clauses'.[7] Significantly, such vetoes are particularly visible in cases that have involved young people (under 18 years) who are understood to have mental health problems. This chapter will highlight certain themes that have emerged in casework as lenses through which to

4 Ann Phoenix, 'Theories of Gender and Black Families', in (eds.) G. Weiner and M. Arnot, *Gender Under Scrutiny* (Hutchinson, London, 1987) 50.

5 Gayatri Chakravorty Spivak, *Outside in the Teaching Machine* (Routledge, London, 1993) 44.

6 *Gillick v West Norfolk and Wisbech Area Health Authority and Another* [1986] AC 112.

7 B.A. LeFrancois, '"It's Like Mental Torture": Participation and Mental Health Services' (2008) 16 *International Journal of Children's Rights* 233.

explore constructions of the child with mental health problems as such a limit figure to understandings around child rights and competence.

Two rulings by the Court of Appeal have been significant in reinterpreting *Gillick*, setting the precedent for current legislation.[8] According to Mike Shaw these rulings have been responsible for largely curtailing young people's ability to refuse treatment.[9] In both these cases the Court of Appeal decided that any person with parental responsibility, or the High Court, could in certain situations override a child's right to refuse medical treatment. It is relevant for this chapter that these cases involved young people with mental health problems and in both cases the child's right to refuse treatment was overridden; both young people were given compulsory medical treatment against their wishes.

One of these cases (*Re R*[10]) involved a young woman (aged 15 years) who experienced 'auditory and visual hallucinations', and who refused medical advice to take anti-psychotics. Despite the *Gillick* decision, Lord Donaldson, in the Court of Appeal, stated that 'no minor of whatever age has the power by refusing consent to treatment to override a consent to treatment by someone who has parental responsibility for the minor' or by the court.[11] He went on to to say that: 'parental power to consent to medical treatment on behalf of a child was not lost when the child acquired competence to give consent.'[12] Such parental power could be used to authorize treatment when a child refused. Thus, despite the *Gillick* decision, Lord Donaldson's guidance assumes that 'children under 16 are never competent, even if they are *Gillick* competent, to refuse treatment as long as someone else with a concurrent power of consent agrees to it'.[13]

Lord Donaldson went on to justify his stance in saying that he felt that R (the young woman) could not possibly have understood the implications of medical treatment because even if she understood on 'a good day', her 'mental disorder' 'was such that on other days she was not only *Gillick* incompetent, but actually sectionable. No child in that situation can be regarded as *Gillick* competent'.[14] Similarly Lord Justice Farquharson (another of the three Lord Justices that reviewed the case in the Court of Appeal) argued that the *Gillick* test was 'not apt to a situation where the understanding of the child varies from day to day according to the effect of her illness'; he went on to say that he would reject the use of the *Gillick* test in such a situation.[15]

However the recognition that children are subjects of rights is mandated in legislation, embodying a normative conviction that children have particular rights, and should be treated as such. Dickenson points out that 'If people have rights, it is not because they pass a rationality test'.[16] Competent adults can refuse medical

[8] *Re R (A Minor) (Wardship: Medical Treatment)* [1992] 1 FLR 190, and *Re W (A Minor) (Consent to Medical Treatment)* [1993] 1 FLR 1.

[9] Mike Shaw, 'When Young People Refuse Treatment: Balancing Autonomy and Protection', in (eds.) Rt. Hon Lord Justice Thorpe and Catherine Cowton, *Delight and Dole: The Children Act 10 Years on* (Family Law, Jordan Publishing, Bristol, 2002).

[10] *Re R (A Minor) (Wardship: Medical Treatment)* [1992] 1 FLR 190.

[11] Lord Donaldson cited in M. Roberts, 'R v M Refusal of Medical Treatment' (1999) 159 *Childright* 14

[12] J. Masson, 'Adolescent Crisis and Parental Power' (1991) 21 *Family Law* 528.

[13] P. Fennell, 'Informal Compulsion: the Psychiatric Treatment of Juveniles under Common Law' (1992) 4 *Journal of Social Welfare and Family Law* 311.

[14] Lord Donaldson cited in *Re R (A Minor) (Wardship: Medical Treatment)* [1992] 1 FLR 603.

[15] Lord Farquharson cited in P. Fennell, V. Harpwood, and C. Ngwena, 'Medical Law' (1991) *All ER Annual Review*.

[16] D. Dickenson, 'Children's Informed Consent to Treatment: is the Law an Ass?' (1994) 20 *Journal of Medical Ethics* 206.

intervention for reasons that are 'rational or irrational or for no reason',[17] and case law shows that adults with mental health problems, including schizophrenia, are not always assumed to be incompetent.[18] Thus, while adults are presumed to be competent unless there is evidence to the contrary, children are not.

25.2 Children who cannot refuse

In this way children's refusal comes to be framed as 'irrational', as 'part of their illness' and can thus be overridden, meaning that a 'competent child under 16 has the right to say "yes" but not to say "no" to medical treatment'.[19] While statute law appears to constitute children as subjects of increasing numbers of rights, case law, on which much clinical practice is based, gives children fewer and fewer choices regarding their own treatment, meaning that young people under 18 'now have no right to refuse treatment'.[20]

This provides a lens through which to see the implicit psychiatric underpinnings of the concept of competency, where, to be viewed as competent, children seem to have to demonstrate illness acceptance or treatment compliance. This tacit acceptance of psychiatry defines the parameters of consent and competence, and means that within current case law a child can never be conceptualized as competent if they are simultaneously framed as mentally ill. Devereux notes the 'catch 22 by which patients whose competence is in doubt will be found rational if they accept the doctor's proposal but incompetent if they reject professional advice'.[21]

However Fennell questions 'the automatic assumption that refusal is irrational and can be overridden whether or not the patient is competent'.[22] Similarly, Dickenson argues that any power to give consent must also mean the right to withhold consent, otherwise 'the right to consent would seem to be no more than the right to agree with the medical practitioner'.[23] Indeed, if 'meaningful consent implies the possibility of saying "no" and having this refusal respected',[24] then the denial of children's ability to say 'no' would seem to stand in direct contrast to rights discourse, where children have a right to express and have their views given due weight 'according to age and maturity'.[25] But who decides what age is 'old enough', or who is and is not mature? Such conceptualizations of rights to refuse and consent to treatment do not currently take into account the asymmetrical power relations weaved into the fabric of children's everyday lives.

This needs to be taken particularly seriously in relation to dilemmas around medical treatment when they involve children, where power relations between

[17] T. Ford and A. Kessel, 'Feeling the Way: Childhood Mental Illness and Consent to Admission and Treatment' (2001) 179 *The British Journal of Psychiatry* 384.

[18] *Re C (Refusal of Medical Treatment)* [1994] 1 FLR 31.

[19] See P. Fennell, V. Harpwood, and C. Ngwena, 'Medical Law' (1991) *All ER Annual Review*.

[20] D. Dickenson, 'Children's Informed Consent to Treatment: is the Law an Ass?' (1994) 20 *Journal of Medical Ethics* 205.

[21] J.A. Devereux, D.P.H. Jones, and D.L. Dickenson, 'Can Children Withhold Consent to Treatment?' (1993) 306 *British Medical Journal* 1459.

[22] P. Fennell, 'Informal Compulsion: the Psychiatric Treatment of Juveniles under Common Law' (1992) 4 *Journal of Social Welfare and Family Law* 311

[23] D. Dickenson, 'Children's Informed Consent to Treatment: is the Law an Ass?' (1994) 20 *Journal of Medical Ethics* 205.

[24] M. Roberts, 'R v M Refusal of Medical Treatment' (1999) 159 *Childright* 15.

[25] United Nations Convention on the Rights of the Child (Article 12).

adult professionals and children labelled as 'mentally ill' are particularly unequal. LeFrancois notes that 'nowhere is the acceptance of children's irrationality more prevalent, in terms of legislation, policy and practice, than in the area of child and adolescent mental health'.[26] In this arena not only does the position of 'child' delegitimate the young person's views, but the deeming of that young person as 'mentally ill' (by an adult professional) constructs their beliefs and demands as irrational; positioning them as doubly incompetent, doubly diminished identities.

'In this context, adults hold sole discretionary power in defining children as irrational, based both on their age and their psychiatric diagnosis, thereby stripping them of any rights they might otherwise have to make decisions that could influence their treatment.'[27]

Current case law then puts adults in the sole position to determine children's 'rationality' and to veto children's wishes. This is made explicit by Lord Donaldson, who in discussing the *Gillick* ruling, stated that '[I]n a case in which the "*Gillick* competent" child refuses treatment, but the parents consent, that consent enables treatment to be undertaken lawfully'.[28] It is thus 'virtually impossible to envisage a situation where a child or young person with a negative mental health label could ever refuse treatment'.[29]

This makes visible the paternalism of child rights discourse, where bio-medical definitions of welfare are privileged over children's autonomy and self-determination. Here appeals to the principle of working in children's 'best interests' may serve as 'an additional adult veto to children's decision making in the name of protection', diverting attention from the maintenance of adult interests and inequality.[30]

Building on this analysis, I propose that the discourse of child rights and best interests also neutralizes and depoliticizes children's experiences, leaving bio-medical and psychiatric assumptions unproblematized within the law.

Shaw argues that a young person should not be treated against their will unless they are more than likely to 'suffer significant harm without treatment'.[31] However, I suggest that there is a need to attend to medical and psychiatric frameworks of recognition and their impact on what can be constituted as a 'crisis' or an 'emergency', what can be understood as 'harm' and what can be conceptualized as 'treatment'. While decisions around competency claim neutrality, Roth argues that judgements of competency are not straightforward applications, but rather 'reflect social considerations and societal biases as much as they reflect matters of law and medicine'.[32] It seems that one key bias here is the implicit dominance and hegemony of bio-medical psychiatry and the pharmaceutical industry.

[26] B.A. LeFrancois, '"It's Like Mental Torture": Participation and Mental Health Services' (2008) 16 *International Journal of Children's Rights* 212.

[27] Ibid. 213.

[28] Lord Donaldson, cited in Mike Shaw, 'When Young People Refuse Treatment: Balancing Autonomy and Protection', in (eds.) Rt. Hon Lord Justice Thorpe and Catherine Cowton, *Delight and Dole: The Children Act 10 Years on* (Family Law, Jordan Publishing, Bristol, 2002) 48.

[29] Vicky Coppock, '"Mad", "Bad" or "Misunderstood"?', in (ed.) P. Scranton, *Childhood in 'Crisis'?* (London, 1997) 157.

[30] B.A. LeFrancois, '"It's Like Mental Torture": Participation and Mental Health Services' (2008) 16 *International Journal of Children's Rights* 213.

[31] Mike Shaw, 'When Young People Refuse Treatment: Balancing Autonomy and Protection', in (eds.) Rt. Hon Lord Justice Thorpe and Catherine Cowton, *Delight and Dole: The Children Act 10 Years on* (Family Law, Jordan Publishing, Bristol, 2002) 50.

[32] L.H. Roth, A. Meisel, and C.W. Lidz, 'Tests of Competence to Consent to Treatment' (1977) 134 *American Journal of Psychiatry* 279.

25.3 Psychiatry, children, and 'bare life'

The bio-psychiatric framing of hearing voices, mandated and funded by pharmaceutical companies, monopolizes media representations and public understandings, regulating what can be seen and heard, deciding 'what will and will not be publicly recognizable as reality' and as normal.[33] Within this framework anything outside of this limited boundary (based on assumptions of a unitary rational masculine subject) comes to be framed as irrational and mentally ill. Thus medico-legal judgments of competency are invested with cultural assumptions of what constitutes a 'good' childhood and a 'life worth living'.

While children with mental health problems do not feature in the work of Italian philosopher Giorgio Agamben, drawing upon his work we might begin to explore how these children's lives and behaviour are discursively framed within a medico-legal matrix as lives 'unworthy of being lived'.[34] Agamben points to how every society determines the threshold beyond which life is devoid of meaning, cast outside the polis and constructed as apolitical. Such life then ceases to have any juridical value and is thus portrayed as 'incurably lost'; as 'bare life'.[35] Although Agamben makes scant reference to children's lives, I would like to explore how Agamben's work may enable us to theorize how psychiatry constructs children as 'bare life', depoliticizing their experiences and their refusals by framing them as 'symptoms' of illness. Similarly, what do such children, framed as mentally ill, do to Agamben's thesis? I want to engage with these conceptual resources to examine how they may help us to make sense of and to understand psychiatric and legal constructions of children, and particularly the overriding of children's refusals and psychiatry's legitimization of force.

To do this we need to examine the mechanisms and techniques within psychiatry by which particular behaviour comes to be discursively framed as problematic and pathological. One key framing device within developmental psychology, psychiatry, and legal discourse is the medicalization of children's behaviour, 'where individual actions come to be read as "signs" of a more enduring problem' and thus of a pathology.[36] Such pathologization and subsequent medicalization of children's behaviour and experiences were very apparent in the stories that people told me during my research with people who heard voices as children.

In asking people to focus their narrative around their experiences of disclosing that they heard voices, and of other people's responses and reactions to this, it was possible partially to explore how hearing voices was discursively framed by those people to whom the children had disclosed their experiences of voice hearing. Often the framing device took the form of pathologization of children's experiences of hearing voices, and the construction of these voices as a 'problem'.

The voices are not always the problem, it's other people's reactions

They meant more to them [professionals] than what it did to me

[33] Judith Butler, *Precarious Life: The Power of Mourning and Violence* (Verso, London and New York, 2004) 147.

[34] Giorgio Agamben, *Homo Sacer: Sovereign Power and Bare Life* (Stanford University Press, 1998) 137–8.

[35] Ibid. 138

[36] M MacLure et al, 'Becoming a Problem: How Children Develop a Reputation as "Naughty" in the earliest years at School: Full Research Report' (2008) 3.

The frequent reports by children of having their experiences framed in this way may be partly explained by the dominance of psychiatry and the pharmaceutical industry to mediate particular experiences within a specific medical framework of intelligibility. Such frameworks, given medical legitimacy in the Diagnostic and Statistical Manual (DSM IV-TR), construct the experience of hearing voices as 'auditory hallucinations', seen to constitute the 'psychotic dimension' of 'positive symptoms' of schizophrenia.[37] In this way children's experiences come to be framed within a psychiatric lens. One young woman described how '*these very ordinary feelings of adolescent insecurity were immediately interpreted as symptoms of a diseased mind*'.[38] This then affected how children went on to frame their own experience of hearing voices, as one young woman noted:

But now something is happening to me that I think people think is abnormal and which I am also seeing as being more abnormal too.[39]

The Mental Health Act frames children's experiences and refusal of treatment as irrational, as part of an illness. This delegitimates and depoliticizes such refusal through decontextualizing it, where the 'the reasonableness (or unreasonableness) of the objection is irrelevant'.[40] Using Agamben we could say that children's refusals are cast outside the polis and deemed apolitical. Not only does this push us to question who has the power to make such decisions, but to attend to the public frame of what constitutes 'reasonableness' and to what can be understood as being 'treatment'.

25.4 Violent 'treatment'

A new approach recently developed in the USA for 'correcting' the 'behaviour problems' associated with autism provides a glimpse into how such constructions and justifications of 'treatment' take place.[41] Here an eight-year-old boy who performed self-injurious behaviour constructed as 'not responsive to treatment' was given a course of Electro-Convulsive Therapy (ECT) as a last resort. The fact that this course of 'treatment', involving 15 sessions of ECT, reduced his self-injury is thus seen as a justification to develop this 'therapy' for use on more children with autism. Here the irony of conceptualizing ECT as a 'treatment' to stop self-harm is lost as its justification operates within a normative rational/ableist matrix that claims that the 'life of a disabled person is not worth living unless an intervention or accommodation raises their existence to an acceptable "quality of life" ', even if this intervention itself causes injury.[42]

While the use of ECT on children is currently rare, medicating children has become much more common. In 1993, 3500 prescriptions were given in the UK for Ritalin for Attention Deficit Hyperactivity Disorder (ADHD); by 2006 the NHS

[37] Diagnostic and Statistical Manual IV-TR (American Psychiatric Association, Arlington, 2000) 299.

[38] C. Campbell, 'The terrifying ordeal of a brilliant student who started hearing voices and then fell into the abyss of insanity' (2008) *The Daily Mail* (7 February 2008).

[39] Quote from a girl at the Children's Hearing Voices Conference, in Amsterdam, 1993, reported by Terence McLaughlin.

[40] Department of Health, 'Code of Practice: Mental Health Act 1983' (2008) 23.17, 183.

[41] D. Chieco, 'Case Study Suggests New Therapy for Autism' (2009) *The John Hopkins News-Letter*.

[42] J. Overboe, 'Disability and Genetics: Affirming the Bare Life (the State of Exception)' (2007) 44 *Canadian Review of Sociology and Anthropology CRSA/RCSA* 224.

gave out approx 250,000 prescriptions; and in the USA doctors write 2 million prescriptions a month.[43] If we bear in mind that the National Institute for Health and Clinical Excellence (NICE) estimates that using the DSM-IV criteria, ADHD is thought to affect three to nine per cent of school-age children,[44] then we can glimpse the wide impact this medicalization of childhood could potentially have.

On a recent television documentary about ADHD in the UK, one mother reported that her son was first medicated at age five with little effect so the doctor upped the dose by six times the normal dose. When he was 14 he was put on Risperdal, an antipsychotic drug, used for schizophrenia. The mother said it was like her son had been replaced by a zombie.[45] By 2008, around 8000 children and young people in the UK were being treated with Ripserdal or Zyprexa, despite side effects (including brain tumours).[46] There are further reports that GPs prescribe antipsychotics inappropriately, which is worrying for drugs with such severe side effects.[47]

It would thus seem that once constructed within medico-legal understandings as 'bare life', or what Judith Butler understands as precarious lives that are 'already lost',[48] children can be subjected to often aggressive medical and surgical interventions justified in the name of 'treatment' to restore that person to a 'normal' life. This is also significant for children framed as being disabled.[49] It thus seems that psychiatry depoliticizes self-injury and hearing voices, through placing 'mental illness' (or 'psychosis') as explicitly *outside* the realm of human experience and thus outside the parameters of human rights.[50] This helps us to understand how violence against children in the name of 'treatment' can coexist alongside the strong push for children's rights, through a process of framing hearing voices as 'psychotic', as outside the realm of 'normal' childhood experiences, and thus outside the parameters of child rights. Schrag and Divoky note that consequentially:

> millions of children are no longer regarded as part of the ordinary spectrum... but as people who are qualitatively different from the 'normal' population.[51]

Here we can see some of the implications of a creeping medicalization and bio-politicization of childhood and of children's rights. This establishes specific parameters of human intelligibility, framing certain experiences (particularly psychosis and self-harm) as 'outside' of 'normal' childhood experience, and thus as in need of 'treatment', usually through medication. This is despite much research and service user testimony that suggests that children are more likely to recover when they do not

[43] G. Fowler, 'Turning Children into Mental Patients: ADHD in the UK' (2010) 17(2) *Asylum* 20.

[44] National Institute for Health and Clinical Excellence, 'Attention Deficit Hyperactivity Disorder: Diagnosis and management of ADHD in children, young people and adults' (2008) *Clinical Guidance* 72.

[45] Panorama, 'What Next for Craig'? BBC One (12 November 2007).

[46] G. Fowler, 'Turning Children into Mental Patients: ADHD in the UK' (2010) 17(2) *Asylum* 20.

[47] Kendall (2007) cited in G. Fowler, 'Turning Children into Mental Patients: ADHD in the UK' (2010) 17(2) *Asylum* 21.

[48] Judith Butler, *Precarious Life: The Power of Mourning and Violence* (Verso, London and New York, 2004).

[49] Human Rights Joint Committee, Memorandum submitted by Scope (<http://www.Parliament.co.uk>, 2009) (accessed 5 June 2009).

[50] H. Spandler and T. Calton, 'Psychosis and Human Rights: Conflicts in Mental Health Policy and Practise' (2009) 8 *Social Policy and Society* 248.

[51] Peter Schrag and Diane Divoky, *The Myth of the Hyperactive Child: and Other Means of Child Control* (Penguin, Harmonsworth, 1981) 36.

accept the illness model.[52] It interests me that while the diagnosis of ADHD has gained much critical recognition as the medicalization of oppositional behaviour and thus as a mechanism of social control, behaviours and experiences labelled as 'psychosis' or self-injury continue, even within critical writing, to be viewed from a psychiatric gaze as 'outside' of normality, as 'real' disorders, thus justifying 'treatment' through medication. For example, after a thoughtful discussion of how the label ADHD operates as a mechanism of social control, Vicki Coppock goes on to say that admission to adolescent psychiatric units appeared appropriate (in her review of the literature), though not unproblematic, in cases of 'deliberate self-harm and severe psychosis'.[53] While not necessarily seeking to refute this, I am interested in why self-harm and 'psychosis' are viewed as justifying medical treatment or detention, when the 'treatment' of ADHD is seen as regulatory. It seems that hearing voices and self-injury act as tropes in which children undergo a suspension of their ontological status as children, where the absence of such children in legal discourse is normalized, while their presence is seen as pathological.[54]

Such children are then subjected to 'treatment' that outside of this psychiatric 'state of exception' would be constituted as legal battery and child abuse.[55]

Healy points out that 'the drugs used to treat ADHD are the same [chemically] as speed and cocaine. We react with horror to the idea that our kids would use such drugs, but don't react about drugs such as Ritalin being given to them', by doctors.[56] This raises important ethical questions around what governs our affective responses to different forms of violence against children and what regulates when we will and when we will not feel horror. According to Judith Butler, '"[h]orror" and "outrage" are differentially distributed' and we thus need to examine the occasions on which we feel horror as our dominant affective response and those where feelings of horror are absent.[57] Although Butler is discussing these issues in relation to acts constructed as terrorism, such dilemmas have particular relevance for what is constructed as 'treatment' for children who are distressed, and when and how this can be understood to be violent. This raises questions of how we can conceptualize contemporary forms of 'treatment', how they alter our normative distinctions, how we can compare such forms of 'treatment' and name new normative judgements, and in what vocabulary we will make these judgements.[58]

If we assume that some violence is justified, by the law, the state, and psychiatry, then normative judgements about what can be understood as violence and as 'treatment', and who counts as human, are built into our very definition of 'treatment'. Some of the terms in which violence, normality, and the child can be conceptualized then may 'dispose us in advance towards certain kinds of moral responses and normative conclusions'.[59] This is particularly important in debates about what constitutes

[52] S. Escher, M. Morris, A. Buiks, P. Delespaul, J. Van Os, and M. Romme, 'Determinants of Outcome in the Pathways through Care for Children Hearing Voices' (2004) 13 *The International Journal of Social Welfare* 208.

[53] Vicki Coppock, 'Medicalising Children's Behaviour', in (ed.) Bob Franklin, *The New Handbook of Children's Rights: Comparative Policy and Practice* (Routledge, London, 2003) 142.

[54] Ann Phoenix, 'Theories of Gender and Black Families', in (eds.) G. Weiner and M. Arnot, *Gender Under Scrutiny* (Hutchinson, London, 1987) 50.

[55] H. Spandler and T. Calton, 'Psychosis and Human Rights: Conflicts in Mental Health Policy and Practise' (2009) 8 *Social Policy and Society* 245.

[56] David Healy, cited in G. Fowler, 'Turning Children into Mental Patients: ADHD in the UK' (2010) 17(2) *Asylum* 21.

[57] Judith Butler, *Frames of War: When is Life Grievable?* (Verso, London and New York, 2009) 159.

[58] Ibid. 159. [59] Ibid. 156.

'treatment', what counts as an emergency, and thus how to respond to a child who hears voices or who performs self-injury.

25.5 Troubling the 'normal' child

It seems such frames of pathologization and medicalization are given coherence through assumptions of a normal developmental trajectory for children, in pursuit of the 'normal' child. Thus those children who do not 'fit', who do not meet the developmental milestones described (and prescribed) within developmental psychology are constructed in deficit, and often pathologized. However, such milestones and norms are developed from statistical analysis, from means, medians, and modes that strip children from all that tied them to their context and render their lives into abstraction. Diken and Laustsen point to how in this way statistics reduce life 'to one aspect of its being'.[60] It is thus possible to see how we might usefully expand the conception of bare life to conceptualize how legal and medical understandings of children as statistics, abstracted and atomized from their everyday lived realities, can render children's lives as 'bare'.

Such statistical measurement is fundamental to the biopolitical paradigm,[61] and to the governance of subjects, including children. Thus 'children are regulated and measured … in relation to fictitious norms elaborated by dominant models'.[62] The requirement of a certain kind of subject within child rights legislation and discourse institutes a slip from description of that subject to prescription, and diagnosis of who and what that subject, and thus that child, should be. In this process certain lived experiences and subjectivities are dismissed, or rendered solely as pathological.

The construction of children with mental health problems as 'bare life' could thus be seen as a tactic by which to 'manage' and regulate those children who do not 'fit' developmental psychology's fictitious norms. Here the medicating of such 'problem' children works as a techno-political technique to render certain children's bodies as docile, and thus as governable. In this way, psychiatric frameworks work differentially to 'manage' specific populations through derealizing the humanity of particular subjects, such as children with mental health problems. One such technique for managing a population then is to construct them as less than human, or as in the case of hearing voices and self-injury, as outside of what is publicly recognized as 'normal' human experience. Thus 'managing' children with mental health problems (or any population) is not just a process whereby subjects are constituted as a subject (i.e. as psychotic), it is also a process of de-subjectivation and regulation.[63]

Here we might fleetingly glimpse how 'the law is never impartial but always caught up with strategies of power and with a discursive violence that seeks to grasp and domesticate the troublesome other'.[64] In this way, the law, shot through with psychiatric assumptions, works to domesticate those 'troublesome' children who do not

[60] B. Diken and C.B. Laustsen, 'Zones of Indistinction: Security, Terror and Bare Life' (2002) Department of Sociology, Lancaster University, 3.

[61] Ibid. 3.

[62] Erica Burman, *Developments: Child, Image, Nation* (Routledge, London and New York, 2008) 176.

[63] Judith Butler, *Precarious Life: The Power of Mourning and Violence* (Verso, London and New York, 2004) 68.

[64] M. Shildrick, 'Transgressing the Law with Foucault and Derrida: some Reflections on Anomalous Embodiment' (2005) 47(3) *Critical Quarterly* 31.

easily 'fit', often through psychiatric 'treatment' to construct a reformed Other, who is 'almost the same, but not quite',[65] who is almost 'normal', but not quite.[66] Here attempts to make children 'normal' raise important ethical questions around what we claim to 'treat' children for.

In attending to young people's stories of their experiences within the psychiatric system it would seem there is a mismatch between children's lived realities and the 'normal' child conjured by developmental discourse. This 'normal' child bears no relation to most children's lived experience and yet it serves to construct and delimit children's realities in many ways. It is on the body and in the minds of those children, framed as mentally ill, where developmental psychology, abjection, and biopower converge and interweave, becoming a technology of normalization that is translated into material violence. This prevents those categories of children who are framed as being of 'unsound mind' or as 'incompetent' from being conceptualized as having rights, meaning that everything such children do and say is deemed illegitimate by definition and thus politically insignificant (including their refusals). The implications of this framing for children's lives are made explicit in the following story of Marie's experiences.

Marie had heard voices for a long time; they helped her and comforted her while her parents sexually abused her. However sometimes they caused her distress, usually a sign for her that she was getting stressed or a reminder that she should tell someone about the abuse she experienced as a child and kept secret for a long time afterwards. After a particularly distressing experience she found herself sectioned, face to face with a psychiatrist. She found the courage and told him for the first time she had never told anyone that she was abused as a child. He told her 'you're saying that because you're ill'.[67]

Unfortunately, this response is not uncommon, highlighting how psychiatric frameworks for understanding children work to depoliticize and delegitimate young people's experiences. This process, alongside the legal overriding of young people's refusals to take medication or undergo 'treatment', can greatly exacerbate feelings of loss of control, potentially replaying the traumatic circumstances a young person may have experienced in the first place. The emphasis on medical intervention, and in the case of 'schizophrenia' particularly drug treatments, can also be traumatic for young people. The following quote from a young person in an adolescent mental health in-patient unit highlights this:

I'm against any form of medication 'cos... I don't like to think of it as brain chemicals all in the wrong. That makes me feel that it's out of my control and medication put forward to solve those problems, again is out of my control. I don't like, you know, how these things can alter the way I think and the way I am... It's an anti-psychotic.... I don't like the idea that it changes who I am. They say they are fine but I don't want to lose something that is me... I think it's, I mean, I don't think that medication is the answer and I think people should be given a choice whether

[65] Homi Bhabha, *The Location of Culture* (Routledge, London and New York, 1994) 85.

[66] My current research explores how the colonial relation is mobilized within 'treatment' of children labelled as mentally ill, and how postcolonial theory may enable an informative (re)reading of children's strategies of resistance and survival. See C. Mills, 'The Tyranny of the "Normal" Child: Hearing Voices, Sly Normality and Resistance', Paper presented at Lancaster Disability Studies Conference, September 2010.

[67] Story told to me during research with people who heard voices when they were children (Research Institute of Health and Social Change, MMU, 2008). (Names have been changed to ensure anonymity.)

we want medication or not. I mean, it's your body and they shouldn't threaten you and things like that.[68]

In order to make a valid treatment decision the British Medical Association states that a child should 'be capable of choosing and understand why a choice is needed', 'have information about risks, benefits and alternatives' and 'make a free choice (i.e. free from undue pressure)'.[69] However the young person's story above highlights a number of problems here. First, such guidelines assume that there is an actual choice between at least two viable alternatives. However, in practice, within child and adolescent mental health services, 'choice' often means choosing if you want to take your medication in the form of pills or injection; it rarely seems to materialize into choosing whether or not you actually want to take medication. If we expect young people to take an interest in being well-informed about 'treatment' then their choices will have to actually count,[70] and there will have to be actual choices to choose from.

Secondly, due to the dominance of pharmaceutical frameworks for understanding children's behaviour, non-medical alternatives rarely figure as a choice for young people. In fact the medical profession constitutes the key target of pharmaceutical company marketing strategies, and research consistently shows that marketing strategies and interaction with drug company representatives largely influences doctors' prescribing practices.[71] Joanna Moncrieff points to how the influence of the pharmaceutical industry on psychiatry reinforces narrow biological conceptions of experience, drives expansion of bio-medical frameworks of understanding into wider areas of everyday life, and forecloses public debate about the adverse effects of psychiatric drugs.[72] Such pharmaceutical colonization and medicalization of children's everyday lives is particularly worrying because the huge commercial incentive to construct particular experiences as 'mental illness' changes our view of what it means to be a child, and ultimately to be human.

25.6 Hearing voices and survival

Dominant medical frameworks for understanding the experience of hearing voices and self-injury tend to conceptualize these experiences as 'symptoms' of an 'illness'. However many young people who hear voices and/or self-injure do not understand their experiences in this way. Sometimes young people had always heard voices and to them the experience was 'normal':

At first I thought everyone shared this experience, but when I talked to a friend about it she said she had not had this experience and she thought I was strange because she had not heard about anyone who heard voices. At the same time, I thought she was strange because to me hearing a voice was normal.[73]

[68] B.A. LeFrancois, '"It's Like Mental Torture": Participation and Mental Health Services' (2008) 16 *International Journal of Children's Rights* 221.

[69] British Medical Association, 'Advance decisions and proxy decision-making in medical treatment and research: Guidance from the BMA's Medical Ethics Department' (2007) 2.

[70] D. Dickenson, 'Children's Informed Consent to Treatment: is the Law an Ass?' (1994) 20 *Journal of Medical Ethics* 206.

[71] A. Wazana, 'Physicians and the Pharmaceutical Industry. Is a Gift Ever Just a Gift'? (2000) 283 *Journal of the American Medical Association* 373.

[72] J. Moncrieff, 'Is Psychiatry For Sale? An Examination of the Influence of the Pharmaceutical Industry on Academic and Practical Psychiatry' (2003) Institute of Psychiatry, London.

[73] Comment from a young girl, at the Children's Hearing Voices Conference (Amsterdam, 1993).

Similarly, Ellie was not threatened by the voice that she heard when she first started university; she found that, '*it was a useful indicator to me of how I was really feeling*', '*far from being some sinister psychiatric symptom, the phenomenon was probably no more than my own externalised thoughts*'.[74]

It also became apparent, in my research, that many young people understood hearing voices as a coping strategy, an aid to survival in an unequal and often abusive adult world. For example, Jenny has heard voices for as long as she can remember and at first they helped her and reassured her when her mother neglected her. Pete's voices reminded him he should tell someone about the abuse he had experienced. Ellie's voices serve as a reminder to her when she's stressed.

However the DSM states:

> Diagnostic criteria for Schizophrenia: A. Characteristic Symptoms: Two (or more) of the following, each present for a significant portion of time during a 1-month period (or less if successfully treated):
>
> (1) delusions
> (2) hallucinations…
> Note: Only one Criterion A symptom is required if delusions are bizarre or hallucinations consist of a voice keeping up a running commentary on the person's behavior or thoughts, or two or more voices conversing with each other.[75]

What happens to this framework when we juxtapose it with the writing of Donna Williams, who self-identifies as autistic?:

> The more I became aware of the world around me, the more I became afraid… I was frightened… My world was full of imaginary friends. They were far more magical, reliable, predictable and real than other children… Other people did not understand the symbols I used.[76]

Children and young people's own understandings of hearing voices highlight a major paradox within psychiatry. Here voices which may actually be a coping strategy (even though sometimes unpleasant) and which have enabled the voice hearer to survive, are framed by psychiatry as in need of eradication, often through medication. Thus children's coping strategies are pathologized, diverting attention from exploring the often difficult and traumatic lived realities of children, and the very reasons why they may hear voices in the first place. The young people and adults with whom I spoke during my research highlighted how the responses of adults, professionals, and services often contributed to their distress through denying them a voice, framing the voices they heard as problematic or pathological and not believing them. In fact many psychiatrists refuse to engage in conversation about the voices people hear in fear of 'colluding with people's delusions':

> *The doctors told the other staff not to pay attention to me when I spoke about the voices; they said it would be playing into my delusions.*[77]

For a number of people, the voices they heard actually only became distressing after telling others about them, as Pete pointed out, '*quite often people have no issues with*

[74] C. Campbell, 'The terrifying ordeal of a brilliant student who started hearing voices and then fell into the abyss of insanity' (2008) *The Daily Mail* (7 February 2008).

[75] Diagnostic and Statistical Manual IV-TR (American Psychiatric Association, Arlington, 2000) 312.

[76] Donna Williams, *Nobody Nowhere* (Jessica Kingsley Publishers, London, 1992).

[77] Chloe Hadjimatheou, 'Embracing the Dark Voices Within' (2009) BBC World Service. Date Accessed: 17 September 2010 <http://news.bbc.co.uk/1/hi/health/8232555.stm>.

the voices until they disclose'. This was, as one young man said, because his voices '*were worried the doctors were gonna medicate them away*'. He felt that before taking any medication he first needed to understand what the voices were trying to tell him and why they were there in the first place.

Smith describes how hegemony does not operate solely, or sometimes at all, through brute force but entails 'the delimitations of the intelligible... To fail to achieve an adequate fit within an officially recognised position is to be de-authorised—to be denied recognition as an author of the text and to have one's text dismissed from the start as incoherent, illegitimate or unbelievable'.[78] Smith could easily be referring here to the hegemony of bio-psychiatry, where diagnosis works to dismiss children's own texts; the voices they hear, the pain they feel, labelling them as irrational and unbelievable from the start. This urges us to contest the limits that are placed on who is able to speak with authority about children's lives and what they can say, attending to the 'rarefaction of the speaking subject'.[79] For many adults whom I interviewed, being believed would have made all the difference when they disclosed to people that they heard voices as children:

> *They did'nae believe things I was saying, they said it was all in my head but I tried to tell them it was real to me, that was what was happening.*
>
> *I tried to tell people but I was never believed about the abuse. And I sort of shut up and I stopped talking about them. Because nobody was believing me, I stopped talking about the voices.*
>
> *I think I'd have liked them to believe me about everything... The abuse and the voices because it's real to me. I mean I'm not saying they have to say 'Oh aye we hear them as well' but if they said well you know 'Well I can understand that must be frightening'.*

The above quotes make clear that belief does not mean saying you can hear the voices too; it means accepting that the voices are 'real' to that child; that they may be distressing, that they may be personally and politically meaningful, and thus engaging with that meaningfulness. It means acknowledging that children's survival strategies and ways of understanding the world are not represented by the language of pathology which underpins many children's services and legal assumptions.[80]

This begs the question: at 'what point does such mental activity become pathological, however, as opposed to necessary, creative, imaginative or even pleasurable' and who decides?[81] We must attend to children's diverse strategies for communicating their experiences and take these seriously, working 'to develop approaches which help to preserve rather than deny the real' of children's experiences, and to search vigorously for ways we can 'access' the views of children labelled as mentally ill.[82] This also 'means accepting a child's knowledge of terrible experiences'.[83] While children may indeed speak or communicate to us, it may be in a language that professionals deem socially unacceptable, such as communicating distress through self-injury or hearing voices. This means professionals need to attend to narratives of experience that are not restricted by psychiatric vocabulary of deficits and pathologies; but to a multi-voicedness or heteroglossia of ways of understanding children's lives and distress.

[78] Anna Marie Smith, 'The Regulation of Lesbian Sexuality through Erasure: The Case of Jennifer Saunders', in (ed.) Karla Jay, *Lesbian Erotics* (New York University Press, New York, 199) 169.

[79] Michel Foucault, *The Archaeology of Knowledge* (Tavistock Publications, London, 1972).

[80] T. Billington, 'Working with Autistic Children and Young People: sense, experience and the challenges for services, policies and practices' (2006) 21(1) *Disability and Society* 1.

[81] Ibid. 8. [82] Ibid. 11.

[83] V. Sinason, *Mental Handicap and the Human Condition* (Free Associations, London, 1992) 209.

While legal definitions of capacity emphasize rationality, this does not solely determine children's and adult's decision making; emotion, social context, and experience also all play a part.[84] We thus need to acknowledge that, '[w]e make a mistake . . . if we take a single definition of the human, or a single model of rationality, to be the defining feature of the human'.[85] Attending to children's other worlds, voices and self-injury may enable dissonant and disruptive frames of what it means to be a normal or rational child to come into view, pushing current frameworks of recognition to the point of rupture.

25.7 The limit figure of the child

The lives of children who are mentally distressed thus work to belie the assumption that adults are best situated to protect children and act upon them in their 'best interests'. As Spandler and Calton note in relation to human rights,[86] we might infer that children with mental health problems operate as a limit case to universalist claims of child rights discourse. Thus children with mental health problems act as zones of indistinction between adult and child, and human and non-human, exposing the limitations of rights based conceptions that employ 'modalities of exception'.[87]

When professionals begin to question the normality of a child or of a particular experience, such as hearing voices, they are calling on a parochial frame for understanding normality, drawing on a restricted framework for understanding what it means to be 'normal' and to be a child. If this single parochial model (applied with little problematization from developmental psychology) is employed within legislation and child rights then we will be led to wonder if those children who do not 'fit' with dominant understandings of rationality (arguably Western and patriarchal), or those children who do not fit within our normative boundaries and definitions of childhood, are still children (or still human), or if they are 'exceptional' or 'special', thus presenting us with a limit case of the child.[88] This points to how rights claims are deployed within a normative context; thus when a subject is not seen to meet specific normative requirements or not to 'fit' particular parameters of legal intelligibility then they are accorded 'special' rights. According to Shildrick, such 'special' rights denote a person's failure to achieve particular normative standards, positioning their 'difference as an inadequacy', and constantly re-interpellating them within the law as a devalued identity marked out for regulation.[89] Such issues lead us to grapple with how those children who serve as limit cases of the 'normal' child, challenge us to rethink our notions of child rights and what it means to be a child. Instead

[84] D. Dickenson, 'Children's Informed Consent to Treatment: is the Law an Ass?' (1994) 20 *Journal of Medical Ethics* 205.

[85] Judith Butler, *Precarious Life: The Power of Mourning and Violence* (Verso, London and New York, 2004) 90.

[86] H. Spandler and T. Calton, 'Psychosis and Human Rights: Conflicts in Mental Health Policy and Practise' (2009) 8 *Social Policy and Society* 245.

[87] Hester Parr, *Mental Health and Social Space: Towards Inclusionary Geographies* (Blackwell, Oxford, 2008) 175.

[88] See Judith Butler, *Frames of War: When is Life Grievable?* (Verso, London and New York, 2009) for further discussion of limit cases in constructions of 'terrorism'.

[89] M. Shildrick, 'Transgressing the Law with Foucault and Derrida: Some Reflections on Anomalous Embodiment' (2005) 47(3) *Critical Quarterly* 36.

of framing children in terms of deficit within a pathogenic model, we might explore what new conceptualizations of life might mean.

In pioneering research conducted by Helen Spandler, one young person who self-injured said that services should provide, 'recognition that it's your way of coping even though they might not agree with it'.[90] Another urged professionals to, 'let people hang onto the control that they've already took by whatever means (self-harm if they want)'.[91] Lucy Johnstone summarizes the philosophy of the psychiatric approach as removing power and control from a person, denying their feelings, and ignoring the meaning behind that person's actions. She points out that these are the very circumstances that are likely to have led a person to self-injure, or indeed to hear voices, in the first place.[92] The medicalization and pathologization of children's lives prevents children's resistance and survival from being read politically. It can repeat the initial trauma that children may have experienced through forcibly 'treating' them (arguably infringing on their right to their bodily integrity) or through denying the legitimacy of their experiences. Children's very resistance and distress becomes pathologized and sanitized through medical and legal understandings and diagnoses. This explicit denial of personal and political meaning to children's experiences and distress could indeed more helpfully be seen as a process of constituting 'bare life', excluding such children further through domains of intelligibility and empathy.

However while exploring how psychiatry may construct these lives as 'bare', it seems important from the point of view of young people's stories to resist such a conceptualization. Although Agamben may say that resorting to acts of resistance through the body epitomizes 'bare life',[93] for example through self-injury, it seems key for young people to conceptualize their experiences and strategies as politically significant. Thus we must recognize children's experiential right to develop their own understanding of their experiences. In this way, 'bare life' is not just a description of certain children's experiences, it is a critique of psychiatry's frameworks of intelligibility, and a call to action. This will involve engaging with children's experiences and behaviour, survival strategies, and acts of resistance, as meaningful, and often coherent, responses to material and discursive violence. In this way, experiences such as hearing voices and self-injury can be read as not only personally meaningful but politically meaningful, in that they may constitute 'rational and resistant reactions to maladaptive environments'.[94]

Judith Butler raises concerns about the application of Agamben's seemingly exclusionary logic to political debate around 'life worth living', because his distinction between life and politics seemingly serves to depoliticize life and lived experience once again. While I have similar reservations about the political implications of 'bare life', I have found Agamben's thesis to be a useful conceptual tool in rethinking how bio-psychiatry constructs and represents certain children's lives. If we bear in mind that decisions over what constitutes a 'life worth living' are explicitly political questions of biopower, then we can glimpse how bio-psychiatry's construction

[90] Young person cited in Helen Spandler, *Who's Hurting Who?* (Handsell Publications, Gloucester, 1996) 99.

[91] Ibid. 95.

[92] L. Johnstone, 'Self-Injury and the Psychiatric Response' (1997) 7(3) *Feminism and Psychology* 421.

[93] B. Diken and C.B. Laustsen, 'Zones of Indistinction: Security, Terror and Bare Life' (2002) Department of Sociology, Lancaster University, 1–14.

[94] D. Goodley, '"Learning Difficulties", The Social Model of Disability and Impairment: Challenging Epistemologies' (2001) 16(2) *Disability and Society* 215.

of some children's lived experience as 'bare life' may prevent us from engaging with how we might otherwise recognize and represent children's lived experiences of distress, hearing voices, or self-injury. As Butler remarks in relation to the experiences of Palestinians living under Israeli occupation, and in which here we might see in relation to children's realities, these 'are not undifferentiated instances of "bare life" but highly juridified states of dispossession'.[95] Lives constructed by psychiatry as lost are then 'both expelled and contained... saturated with power'.[96] This calls for the need to develop new conceptual understandings of how children's lives that are constituted as 'lost' may be cast outside the polis while remaining explicitly politicized.

25.8 Rupturing dominant frames

It is paradoxical and dangerous that professional and medical claims to take children's best interests seriously, an assertion key to the UN Convention on the Rights of the Child, often conflict with children's actual interests and can work to deny children's lived experiences. Difficult issues need to be addressed here. What are the ethical implications of 'treating' or 'fixing' children if we conceptualize their experience not as a pathology or mental illness but as an emotional protest to social inequality, or as survival strategies and resistance to traumatic conditions?

This raises the 'question of how power forms the field in which subjects become possible at all or, rather, how they become impossible'.[97] Rather than asking what tools we need to bring such children's lives into the public domain, based on recognition and identity struggles, we need to begin by 'calling into question the framework that silences the question of who counts as a "who"—in other words, the forcible action of the norm on circumscribing a grievable life'[98] and a livable life. Who confers recognition and what is *it* that is being recognized? Attending to young people's stories of their experiences within the psychiatric system it would seem there is a mismatch between children's lived realities and the 'normal' child conjured by developmental discourse. Here we can see how issues affecting children may be 'cloaked in a discourse on rights that, in effect, both diagnoses and prescribes' the limits of publicly recognizable childhoods in the name of the normal child, eclipsing alternative constructions and frameworks that may be more practical or desirable for children.[99]

We need to engage with this limit case of the child, the child who is uncontainable within current mental health and child rights legislation, because when people's human status, or their status as a child, is called into question it is a sign that we have 'made use of a parochial frame for understanding the human, and failed to expand our conception of human rights to include those whose values may well test the limits of our own'.[100] To come up against this limit case of the child challenges us to rethink how terms such as 'child' and 'mental illness' work. What do they occlude and foreclose? Who counts as a child? And whose childhoods count as 'real' childhoods?

This rethinking is central to a democratic project of challenging and reimagining child and human rights jurisprudence. Such a project points to the need for the

[95] Judith Butler, *Frames of War: When is Life Grievable?* (Verso, London and New York, 2009) 42.

[96] Ibid. 40. [97] Ibid. 163. [98] Ibid. 163.

[99] P. Reynolds, O. Nieuwenhuys, and K. Hanson, 'Refractions of Children's Rights in Development Practice: A View from Anthropology' (2006) 13 *Childhood* 292.

[100] Judith Butler, *Precarious Life: The Power of Mourning and Violence* (Verso, London and New York, 2004) 89.

development of non-medicalized support for young people who are distressed and urges us to search alongside children for more ethical frames by which to recognize and 'treat' children with mental health problems.

An ongoing task of child rights, then, is to reconceive the 'child' and to (re)imagine, rework, and reconfigure childhood through engaging with and enabling overlapping and dissonant frames for understandings children's lives. This needs to come not from a normative perspective of pathology but from an affirmative stance that embraces a pluralism of what it can mean to be a child, what it can mean to be distressed, and of more equitable ways for children and adults to exist together in the world.

Acknowledgements

I would like to dedicate this chapter to all the young people and adults who helped me with my research; and particularly to Kate Crawford, Peter Bullimore, Julie Downs, and Becky Harper who made the Manchester Hearing Voices Network a home from home, and whose dedication and courage is humbling. Thanks to Michael Freeman for making the 'Law and Childhood' colloquium such a wonderful space for discussion and exchange. I would also like to acknowledge the continuous support and inspiration from my doctoral supervisor Erica Burman; and those at the Discourse Unit, and the Education and Social Research Institute at Manchester Metropolitan University. Lastly, a million thanks to Liam O'Hanrahan.

26

The Child's Right to Privacy and Article 8 European Convention on Human Rights

Kirsty Hughes

This chapter looks at the child's right to privacy. It argues that whilst in theory children have a right to privacy under Article 8 European Convention on Human Rights (ECHR), in practice there is an absence of rights-based reasoning in the privacy jurisprudence concerned with children. This chapter looks at a number of areas in which the courts have been faced with cases relating to the Article 8 ECHR privacy rights of the child. By analysing the manner in which the courts have addressed the right in these cases, it becomes apparent that the only situations in which the courts have given serious consideration to the child's right to privacy are situations in which either a high degree of protection is afforded to that privacy-related interest in the adult context or where the child is vulnerable to a clearly identifiable harm. This is problematic because the right to privacy is not usually, and should not be, contingent upon the individual suffering harm. Moreover, children may require greater and different privacy protection than adults. It is therefore argued that the child's right to privacy is not being adequately analysed or protected.

The structure of this chapter is as follows: first, it looks at why the child's right to privacy should be considered separately from the adult's right to privacy and the special issues which are raised by children's privacy; second, it examines how the courts have dealt with cases raising issues related to children's privacy; it concludes by considering the problems that need to addressed.

26.1 Why does the child's right to privacy need to be considered separately from an adult's right to privacy?

The child's right to privacy is not wholly distinct from the adult's right to privacy. Both will raise questions, for example, about the extent to which the individual can be subjected to surveillance, what information can be regarded as private, and which relationships should be regarded as confidential. Thus many of the issues and questions that are relevant to the adult's right to privacy will also apply to the child's right to privacy. However, this chapter argues that the child's right to privacy raises a number of special issues that justify examining it separately from that of the adult. First, that children have different privacy needs to adults; and second, that due to the complexity of claims involving the child's right to privacy, there is a danger that the child's right to privacy will be neglected in the process, thus to guard against this the child's right to privacy needs to be clearly identified and analysed.

26.1.1 Children have different privacy needs

One reason for considering the child's right to privacy as distinct from an adult's right to privacy is that *age* is a factor that affects experiences of, needs for, and one's capacity to obtain, privacy. There are two relevant factors here. First, social norms will evolve over time, and will affect generational perceptions and understandings of privacy. Second, individuals may have different privacy needs at different points in their life. Thus, a teenager's need for privacy may not be the same as an elderly person's need for privacy—because both their socially created perceptions of privacy, and their physical and psychological reasons for needing privacy, may be different. Some research has been conducted into this aspect of privacy in the behavioural sciences.[1] It is suggested that children find it harder to obtain privacy than adults, that privacy is important to children, that children have different needs at different stages of their development, and that the availability of privacy affects their development. It has been suggested that:

> Privacy matters more to older children and is more central to their development and integrity than it is to younger children; consequently the intrusion both *is* and is *experienced* as more violative of the older child than by the younger child. This is not just because older children have greater expectations of privacy than do younger children. It is because privacy plays a bigger role in their development than it does in younger children's lives, and intrusions would have much greater impact on parent-child relationships in the case of older children... privacy is a major managing instrument in this close context.[2]

Thus children have different privacy needs at different stages of their development, they have different privacy needs from adults, and they may be more vulnerable to the impact of an invasion of privacy. This means that children may need different interests protected by Article 8 ECHR, and they may also require a greater degree of protection, as they may be less able to set boundaries for themselves.

26.1.2 The child's right to privacy tends to clash with more rights and interests than an adult's right to privacy

The second reason for considering the child's right to privacy separately, is that the right to privacy often runs up against other competing rights or interests. In most

[1] Maxine Wolfe 'Childhood and Privacy' in I. Altman and J. F. Wohlwil (eds.) *Human Behavior and Environment, Volume 3: Children and the Environment* (Plenum, New York, 1978); Maxine Wolfe and Robert S. Laufer 'The Concept of Privacy in Childhood and Adolescence' in D. H. Carson and S. T. Margulis (eds.) *Man-Environment Interactions: Evaluations and Applications, Part II, Volume 6: Privacy* (Dowden, Stroudsburg, 1975); Ross Parke and Douglas Sawin 'Children's Privacy in the Home: Developmental, Ecological and, Child-rearing Determinants' (1979) 11 *Environment and Behavior* 87; Karyn McKinney 'Space, Body and Mind: Parental Perceptions of Children's Privacy Needs' (1998) 19 *Journal of Family Issues* 75; Cindy Weigel-Garrey, Christine Cook, and Mary Jane Brotherson 'Children and Privacy: Choice, Control and Access in Home Environments' (1998) 19 *Journal of Family Issues* 43; Gary Melton 'Minors and Privacy: Are Legal and Psychological Concepts Compatible?' (1983) 62 *Nebraska Law Review* 455; Sandra Petronio *Boundaries of Privacy: Dialectics of Disclosure* (State University of NY Press, Albany, 2002), 6–9, 73–5, 93–4, 153–5 and 164–5.

[2] Ferdinand Schoeman 'Adolesecent Confidentiality and Family Privacy' (1986–1987) 20 *The John Marshall Law Review* 641, 653.

adult privacy cases there are two parties pulling in opposite directions. The paradigm case is one in which a celebrity wants to rely upon the right to privacy to prevent publication, and a newspaper wants to rely upon the right to freedom of expression to justify publication.[3] Striking the balance between these interests is problematic in the adult context. However, where children are concerned there is often a more complex mix of competing interests and rights. As with other types of cases involving children, there are often a number of actors in child privacy cases, typically the child, the child's parents, and the state. There may also be third parties involved. Each of these parties may be seeking to argue in favour of different interests. Given the complexity of these claims, there is a danger that the child's right to privacy may be neglected in the process.

In addition to the number of parties involved, further complexity stems from the fact that the child's *own* Article 8 ECHR right may pull in different directions. As one commentator has acknowledged, 'the child's Convention rights may not only clash with those of adults but may be internally inconsistent, in that they may clash with each other'.[4] For example, the child's right to autonomy may conflict with the child's right to physical and psychological well-being; or the child's right to family life may conflict with the child's right to respect for private life. Thus striking the balance between these rights and interests is highly complex. It is crucial in striking that balance that the child's *right* to privacy is not neglected and, therefore, the child's right to privacy demands separate analysis.[5]

26.1.3 Background problems to the child's right to privacy

Before we examine the jurisprudence it is worth noting some further background problems to the child's right to privacy. This chapter does not seek to argue the case for the child's right to privacy. Children already have a right to privacy under the UN Convention on the Rights of the Child (CRC) and children are entitled to a right to privacy under Article 8 ECHR. There is also empirical evidence that children need privacy and that the availability of privacy affects their development. Ultimately, whether one believes that this 'need' justifies or is best met by a legal right to privacy is a matter of debate. However, given that children have this right, a more interesting question is whether the child's current right to privacy is effective. Nevertheless, in answering that question, it is worth giving some brief consideration to some of the potential challenges to a child's right to privacy to highlight some of the difficulties that arise in this area.

At a basic level there are those scholars that object to, or question, the concept of human rights,[6] the notion of children's rights,[7] and the idea that 'children' are a

[3] See the House of Lords decision in *Campbell v Mirror Group Newspapers* [2004] UKHL 22, [2004] AC 457; and the European Court of Human Rights decision in *Von Hannover v Germany* (App. no. 59320/00) (2005) 40 EHRR 1.

[4] Andrew Bainham 'Can we Protect Children and Protect their Rights?' (2002) *Family Law* 279.

[5] Andrew Bainham, ibid, has made the more general point comparing children's rights to the welfare principle that 'the express recognition and separation out of specific individual rights lay bare the different values in a way that is not so obvious on an application of the welfare principle'.

[6] For discussion of the critiques applied to human rights see Marie-Bénédicte Dembour *Who Believes in Human Rights: Reflections on the European Convention* (Cambridge University Press, Cambridge, 2006).

[7] For general discussion of judicial approaches to children's rights post Human Rights Act 1998, see Jane Fortin 'Accommodating Children's Rights in a Post Human Rights Act Era' (2006) 69(3) *Modern Law Review* 299.

distinct group.[8] These issues raise complex philosophical questions that are beyond the scope of this chapter. This chapter operates on the presumption that human rights are an effective tool, that children are entitled to and need a right to privacy, that we need to ensure that children are able effectively to enjoy this right, and that whilst children are not a homogenous group, they are best served in this context by being considered as a separate group from adults. The need to consider the child's right to privacy can also be grounded in a broader feminist and child law critique, namely that in the same way:

> ...the societal disadvantages faced by women are not overcome by treating women as if they were men. Likewise, the appropriate response to the social conditions of children is not to treat them as if they were adults. Children should not have to fit into adult categories when their values, priorities, interests and desires may be different.[9]

In addition to these general criticisms, there are three specific issues that we need to consider: first, the argument that there are other rights or interests which are being neglected by focusing upon the right to privacy; second, the question of whether the courts should focus upon rights or welfare; and third, the argument that children are adversely affected by some forms of privacy protection. All of these arguments may affect judicial analyses of the child's right to privacy, and thus they need to be considered here.

26.1.3.1 Privacy is not a priority for children

Some scholars would argue that other rights and interests are more important than a right to privacy, or other autonomy-based rights. The issue here is not whether children need privacy, but whether a right to privacy is a priority for children, or whether children need other interests or rights, which are being neglected by focusing on rights such as privacy.

Fortin has identified a number of the criticisms which have been levelled at the notion of 'rights talk' for children, in particular that the focus on illusory 'moral rights' undermines real rights, that many of the rights are aspirational rather than real, that it encourages individualistic concerns rather than notions of care, and that it undermines relationships, particularly familial ones.[10] At a fundamental level,

[8] A problem with focusing upon the child's right to privacy is that children are not a homogenous group. Their needs and abilities will be affected by a number of factors, such as their race, sex, social-economic status, personality, and family life. This relates to a broader critique advanced in third-wave feminism, which criticizes the notion of 'women' as a group with uniform needs and interests. The same argument can be advanced with respect to the notion of the 'child'. For discussion see, Hilary Charlesworth and Christine Chinkin *The Boundaries of International Law—A Feminist Analysis* (Manchester University Press, Manchester, 2000), 46–8. Frances Olsen has made this point in relation to the Convention on the Rights of the Child: 'The concerns of post-modern feminism that bear most closely on the Convention of the Rights of the Child include the whole notion of a universal document to deal with all children, throughout the world; the concern that such an effort will almost inevitably result in a western-oriented document that merely purports to be universal; and more positively, the question of the category "child" and the status of that category.' Frances Olsen 'Children's Rights: Some Feminist Approaches to the United Nations Convention on the Rights of the Child' (1992) 6 *International Journal of Law and the Family* 192, 215.

[9] Jo Bridgeman and Daniel Monk 'Introduction: Reflections on the Relationship Between Feminism and Child Law' in Jo Bridgman and Daniel Monk (eds.) *Feminist Perspectives on Child Law* (Routledge-Cavendish, London, 2000), 11.

[10] Jane Fortin *Children's Rights and the Developing Law* (CUP, Cambridge, 2009, 3rd ed.), 9–11.

some scholars object to children having 'autonomy-based' rights on the basis that they are simply not able to make such decisions.[11] Fortin has cautioned that we:

> ... must be careful not to claim rights for children that are difficult to substantiate and which devalue the currency of rights talk. Above all, we should avoid using the language of spin to embroider our commitment to children's rights, while at the same time failing to deliver what children really require.[12]

This is imperative, for the adequate protection of children's interests, and for human rights discourse. Thus this chapter will look at whether the child's right to privacy is empty rhetoric or whether it actually provides protection for children's interests.

26.1.3.2 Rights or welfare

We must also acknowledge a broader debate which is at the heart of child law scholarship, namely whether we should be concerned with children's welfare, rather than children's rights; and whether welfare and rights are compatible. This chapter does not seek to address the welfare-versus-rights question. It also does not deal with how the courts have addressed rights claims in cases where s.1(1) Children Act 1989 and the paramountcy principle apply.[13] There is an extensive body of literature on this issue.[14] Instead, this chapter focuses upon how the courts have addressed the Article 8 ECHR rights of children in general. Nevertheless, it is worth being aware of the tension between welfare and rights because the fact that in other contexts the welfare of the child is the paramount consideration may indirectly affect the court's reasoning in rights cases.

26.1.3.3 Children are victims of privacy

The third issue that we need to consider is the idea that children are victims of privacy (particularly privacy within the family home). This idea relates to the well-developed body of feminist literature on the problems with the concept of 'private'.[15] It is

[11] See discussion in Jane Fortin *Children's Rights and the Developing Law* (CUP, Cambridge, 2009, 3rd ed.), 19–21.

[12] Jane Fortin 'Children's Rights—Substance or Spin' (2006) 36 *Family Law* 757.

[13] Children Act 1989 s.1(1): 'when a court determines any question with respect to-
(a) the upbringing of a child, or
(b) the administration of a child's property, or the application of any income arising from it, the child's welfare shall be the court's paramount consideration'.

[14] For discussion of the welfare principle in the HRA era see: John Eekelaar 'Beyond the Welfare Principle' (2002) *Child and Family Law Quarterly* 237; Jonathan Herring 'The Human Rights Act and the Welfare Principle in Family Law—Conflicting or Complementary' (1999) *Child and Family Law Quarterly* 223; Shazia Choudhry and Helen Fenwick 'Taking the Rights of Parents and Children Seriously: Confronting the Welfare Principle Under the HRA' (2005) *Oxford Journal of Legal Studies* 453.

[15] Some feminists have cautioned that excluding the state from the home means that issues that particularly concern women and children, such as domestic violence, are ignored: see Anita Allen *Uneasy Access: Privacy for Women in a Free Society* (Rowman and Littlefield, Totowa, NJ, 1988); Tracy E. Higgins 'Reviving the Public/Private Distinction in Feminist Theorizing' (1999–2000) 75 *Chicago-Kent Law Review* 847; Catherine A. MacKinnon 'Privacy v Equality: Beyond Roe v Wade' in Catherine A. MacKinnon *Feminism Unmodified: Discourses on Life and Law* (Harvard University Press, Cambridge, MA, 1987); Catherine A. MacKinnon *Towards a Feminist Theory of the State* (Harvard University Press, Cambridge, MA, 1989); Linda C. McClain 'Inviolability and Privacy: the Castle, the Sanctuary and the Body' (1995) 7 *Yale Journal Law and Humanities* 195; Frances Olsen 'Feminist Critiques of the Public/Private Distinction' (1993) 10 *Constitutional Commentary* 327; Carole Pateman 'Feminist Critiques of the Public/Private Dichotomy' in C. Pateman *The Disorder of Women, Democracy, Feminism and Political Theory* (Stanford University Press, Stanford, CA, 1989), Ch.6; Laura W. Stein

important to note that feminists do not have 'one voice', and conflicting views on any given issue often emerge in feminist scholarship. However, despite these differences, it is probably fair to say that most feminists criticize the public/private divide.[16] The same unease that feminists have expressed about the impact of privacy (and in particular family privacy) applies where there are child members of a family.[17] Broadly speaking, some feminists are concerned that privacy (and in particular family privacy) may shield harmful behaviour from public scrutiny. This is a very important issue for family privacy. However, this chapter focuses upon the child's right to privacy, and therefore it is not concerned with many of the family privacy cases that would concern feminists, for example the claims of parents that corporal punishment falls within the right to respect for family life.[18] Thus many of their concerns about the concept of private are not applicable here, and at a fundamental level, one would argue that trepidation about family privacy does not tell against and therefore should not impede the independent development of the child's own right to privacy. Nevertheless, one must be cautious, as the child's right to privacy is rarely litigated by the child: many of the cases are brought by parents, either in their own capacity or on behalf of the child. Thus we need to consider whether it is really the child's right that is being protected here.

With these issues in mind, we now turn to examine the jurisprudence.

'Living with the Risk of Backfire: A Response to the Feminist Critiques of Privacy and Equality' (1993) 77 *Minnesota Law Review* 1153; Donna Sullivan 'The Public/Private Distinction in International Human Rights Law' in J. Peters and A. Wolper (eds.) *Women's Rights Human Rights: International Feminist Perspectives* (Routledge, London, 1995); and Nadine Taub and Elizabeth M. Schneider 'Women's Subordination and the Role of the Law' in D. Kairys (ed.) *The Politics of Law: A Progressive Critique* (Pantheon Books, New York, NY, 1990, 1st ed.).

[16] See Ruth Gavison's analysis of feminist opposition to the public/private divide: Ruth Gavison 'Feminism and the Public/Private Distinction' (1992) 45 *Stanford Law Review* 1.

[17] Anita Allen provides a clear example of the concerns raised by family or group privacy. The example is based upon the arrest in 2001 of a Reverend and a number of parents who were members of the House of Prayer. The arrests followed the discovery that a child had been beaten with a rod which had left welts upon his body. It was standard practice of the House of Prayer to discipline children in this way and those that were arrested had encouraged or participated in the beatings. The members of the House of Prayer complained about this interference with their way of life and their decisions regarding their own children. As Allen explains, situations like this demonstrate why we may at times need to 'rip down the doors of "private" citizens in "private" homes and "private" institutions... to protect the vital interests of vulnerable people': Anita L. Allen *Why Privacy isn't Everything: Feminist Reflections on Personal Accountability* (Rowman & Littlefield Publishers, Lanham, Maryland, 2003), 195–6.

[18] Physical punishment of children can raise issues under Articles 3 and 8 ECHR. Some groups have argued that banning parents from physically punishing their children breaches parents' rights to respect for family life and to freedom of religion. However, the Commission has declared these arguments inadmissible: *Seven Individuals v Sweden* (App. no. 8811/79) Commission Decision 13 May 1982, D.R. 29, 104. If the conduct is severe enough to trigger Article 3 ECHR, then the punishment cannot be justified as Article 3 ECHR is an absolute right. In *A v United Kingdom*, the Court held that beating a step-child with a cane constituted a violation of Article 3 ECHR and that the state had an obligation to ensure that measures were in place which constituted 'an effective deterrence against such serious breaches of personal integrity': (App. no. 25599/94) (1999) 27 EHRR 611 at [22]. In *Costello-Roberts v United Kingdom* (App. no.13134/87) (1995) 19 EHRR 112, the Court suggested that some acts which fall short of Article 3 ECHR will engage Article 8 ECHR. However, the Court took the view that the punishment in question (the child had been smacked by his headmaster three times with a gym shoe) did not fall within the scope of Article 8 ECHR because it did not entail sufficient adverse effects for the child's physical and moral integrity. Setting a minimum threshold of physical violence and harm before Article 8 ECHR is engaged restricts the protection afforded to children; the Court's focus upon adverse effects is wrong and should not be a pre-requisite for the Convention right to be engaged.

26.2 Article 8 ECHR jurisprudence: case studies of the child's right to privacy

Under some international treaties, children have an express right to privacy.[19] However, there are no specific children's rights under the ECHR.[20] Article 1 ECHR provides that the rights in the Convention are to be secured to 'everyone' and Article 14 ECHR provides that enjoyment of the rights under the Convention shall be secured without discrimination, which includes discrimination based upon 'age'.[21] Thus children have the same rights as adults, and they should not be discriminated against in their enjoyment of Convention rights. Some scholars have questioned whether this is sufficient in the context of children's rights generally.[22] This chapter focuses on whether the fact that the right to privacy applies equally to children is sufficient.

The analysis offered focuses upon a series of case studies, which have raised issues relating to the child's right to privacy. The first case study considers the privacy rights of children involved in, or indirectly affected by, legal proceedings. The second case study looks at children and publicity. The third case study looks at cases involving the taking or publishing of photographs of children. The fourth case study examines cases where information relating to a child is disclosed on the internet. The fifth case study looks at cases concerning medical confidentiality. It should be noted that it is rare for applications to be made directly by children; cases are usually brought either by the child's parents on behalf of the child, or by the child's parents in their

[19] Convention on the Rights of the Child, UNGA Res 44/25, Articles 16 and 40(2)(vii); and the African Charter on the Rights and Welfare of the Child, Article 10. The effect of the CRC has been described as 'to question the public/private dichotomy . . . and . . . to disaggregate the rights of children from the rights of "families", to constitute children as independent actors with rights vis-à-vis their parents and vis-à-vis the state': see Bettina Cass 'The Limits of the Public/Private Dichotomy: A comment of Coady and Coady' in P. Alston, S. Palmer, and J. Seymour (eds.) *Children, Rights and the Law* (Clarendon Press, Oxford, 1992), 140–7, 142.

[20] Council of Europe Deputy Secretary General Maud de Boer-Buquicchio at the launching ceremony of the Council of Europe's *Initiative against Corporal Punishment of Children*, 15 June 2008, Zagreb, Croatia asserted that: 'the European Convention on Human Rights is for everyone and there is no footnote in it which says that the human rights are for adults only'. See Council of Europe Press Release 'Council of Europe launches pan-European campaign against corporal punishment of children' Press Release 439 (2008) <https://wcd.coe.int/ViewDoc.jsp?id=1308361&Site=DC&BackColorInternet=F5CA75&BackColorIntranet=F5CA75&BackColorLogged=A9BACE> (accessed 31 August 2009).

[21] Article 14 ECHR does not expressly refer to age; however the list provided in Article 14 ECHR is non-exhaustive and it is clear from the Explanatory Report to Protocol 12 that Article 14 ECHR does prohibit discrimination on the basis of age: see Explanatory Report to Protocol No. 12 to the Convention for the Protection of Human Rights and Fundamental Freedoms, at [20].

[22] Philip Alston and John Tobin *Laying the Foundations for Children's Rights: An Independent Study of some Key Legal and Institutional Aspects of the Impact of the Convention on the Rights of the Child*, UNICEF, <http://www.unicef-irc.org/publications/pdf/ii_layingthefoundations.pdf>. Alston and Tobin have identified and considered three arguments, which are advanced to justify the non-inclusion of children's rights in the ECHR, namely: (i) the civil and political rights protected by the Convention apply to children; (ii) children's rights are adequately dealt with in the European Social Charter; and (iii) the Council of Europe has adopted a range of specialist treaties some of which focus on the rights of children. They conclude that these justifications are not sufficient and that a comprehensive children's rights convention is necessary.

own capacity. This may have impacted upon the way that the Court has analysed the rights in particular contexts.[23] These issues will be highlighted below.

26.2.1 Children involved in legal proceedings

The first category of cases are those where the child is involved in legal proceedings. The scope and impact of the child's right to privacy in this context depends upon the nature of the proceedings being brought and the role that the child has in the proceedings.

26.2.1.1 Children as suspected offenders

The strongest degree of protection is afforded in cases where the child is a suspect. The child's privacy interests may be affected at a number of different stages in the process of investigation and prosecution. The European Court of Human Rights has examined some of the measures used by states as part of their criminal investigations, and has noted that special caution must be taken when the suspected offender is a child. The leading case is *S and Marper v United Kingdom* (the case in which the Court held that the UK's DNA database violated Article 8 ECHR).[24]

The first applicant, S, was only 11 years old when he was charged with attempted robbery and his fingerprints and DNA samples were taken. He was subsequently acquitted, and he asked for his fingerprints and DNA samples to be destroyed. The police refused to do so and proceedings were brought; these proceedings were unsuccessful in the Administrative Court, the Court of Appeal, and the House of Lords.[25] A claim was eventually brought to the European Court of Human Rights.

Before the European Court of Human Rights, the applicants argued that the DNA database violated Article 8 ECHR, and they 'stressed in particular the social stigma and psychological implications' of the database for children.[26] The Court held that the 'blanket and indiscriminate nature of the powers of retention' constituted a disproportionate interference with Article 8 ECHR.[27] Significantly, the Court also emphasized the harmful and detrimental impact that the measure could have upon a child's development and a child's integration into society. It stated:

> The retention of the unconvicted persons' data may be especially harmful in the case of minors... given their special situation and the importance of their development and integration in society... the Court considers that particular attention should be paid to the protection of juveniles from any detriment that may result from the retention by the authorities of their private data following acquittals of a criminal offence...[28]

This was a significant statement of the vulnerability of the child, and the relevance of this for Article 8 ECHR. However, one must be cautious, as the impact of the database on the child was not determinative of the outcome in *S and Marper*. Nevertheless,

[23] Most troubling is the suggestion that there is a 'stark contrast' between the way that the European Court of Human Rights has dealt with cases which are based upon parents rights, compared to those genuinely brought on behalf of the child; indeed Fortin has argued that 'the ECtHR often plays a poor part in championing children's rights, as opposed to those of their parents': *Children's Rights and the Developing Law* (Cambridge University Press, Cambridge, 2009, 3rd ed.), 64.

[24] (App. nos. 30562/04 and 30566/04) (2009) 48 EHRR 50.

[25] *R (on the application of S) v CC of South Yorkshire & Another*, [2002] EWHC 478 (Admin), [2002] Po. LR 273; Court of Appeal [2003] EWCA Civ 1275, [2002] 1 WLR 322; House of Lords [2004] UKHL 39, [2004] 1 WLR 2196.

[26] N. 24, above, at [60]. [27] N. 24, above, at [125]. [28] N. 24, above, at [124].

the Court's suggestion that greater protection is necessary where a child is concerned is notable, because as we will see below, the courts have not approached other cases in this manner.

A further reason for caution is the UK's response to *S and Marper*. Whilst one would hope that *S and Marper* would lead to a careful consideration of the impact of such measures on children, the responses following the ruling are mixed. An initial notable improvement for young children was the removal in 2009 of all DNA profiles from children aged under 10.[29] However, the legislation proposed by the last Government left significant cause for concern about the degree of protection afforded to older children. The Crime and Security Act 2010 recommended the indefinite retention of a DNA profile of an individual under the age of 18 who was convicted of a serious offence, or more than one minor offence; retention for five years of the DNA profile of an under-18-year-old convicted of a single minor offence; retention for six years of the DNA profile of 16- and 17-year-olds arrested but *not convicted* of a serious offence; and retention for three years of all other under-18-year-olds *arrested but not convicted*. It is submitted that these proposals would not give sufficient protection to children. The provisions are not yet in force, and they require a commencement order to be brought into force, see s.59(1) Crime and Security Act 2010. In the meantime, the coalition Government is proposing to make some amendments to the DNA database to bring it further in line with the more restrictive Scottish model that was favourably highlighted by the European Court of Human Rights in *S and Marper*.[30] Under the Scottish model, DNA samples must be destroyed if the individual is not convicted, although there is an exception if the person is suspected of certain sexual or violent offences, in which case the data may be retained for three years.[31] This would be an improvement although it still would not provide sufficient protection for children. A better response would be that which Liberty has campaigned for, namely a presumption in favour of removing DNA profiles and fingerprints once a child reaches 18.[32] This presumption could be rebutted by factors such as the seriousness of the offence for which the child has been convicted, and the number of offences for which they have been convicted.[33] It is submitted that this proposal needs serious consideration.[34]

[29] National DNA Database *Annual Report 2007–2009* <http://www.npia.police.uk/en/docs/NDNAD07-09-LR.pdf, 21>.

[30] HM Government *The Coalition: Our Programme for Government* <http://www.cabinetoffice.gov.uk/media/409088/pfg_coalition.pdf>, 11. See *S and Marper*, at [109].

[31] Criminal Procedure Act 1995.

[32] Liberty has campaigned for the removal of all unconvicted children's data from the DNA database, although it has contemplated a possible exception where a 16- or 17-year-old is arrested for a more serious sexual or violent offence but is ultimately acquitted or has charges dropped. In this situation they suggest that DNA removal could take place a year after acquittal or the dropping of the charges: Liberty *Liberty's Response to Home Office's 'Your Freedom' Consultation* <http://www.liberty-human-rights.org.uk/pdfs/policy10/liberty-s-response-to-the-your-freedom-consultation-october-2010.pdf> at [21].

[33] N. 32, above, at [22].

[34] It should also be noted that the UN Committee on the Rights of the Child has also expressed concern about the impact of the DNA database on children: see Committee on the Rights of the Child, 49th session, *Concluding Observations on UK*, 20 October 2008 <http://www2.ohchr.org/english/bodies/crc/docs/AdvanceVersions/CRC.C.GBR.CO.4.pdf>, at [36].

26.2.1.2 Children on trial

If legal proceedings are brought against a child, then the child may be able to claim that the proceedings should be held in private.[35] This is based upon Article 6 ECHR, rather than Article 8 ECHR. Article 6 ECHR, the right to a fair trial, provides that proceedings should be held in public, but that the press and public may be excluded from all, or part, of a trial in the interests of juveniles. Thus Article 6 ECHR does not provide children with a right to privacy during trials; it merely provides an exception to the general right to a public trial.[36] This exception is designed to recognize the vulnerability of children, but ultimately whether the trial will be held in private will depend upon the balance to be struck in each case between the child's interests and the interests in a public trial.

Obviously where the child is the defendant, he or she is the primary holder of the Article 6 ECHR right to a fair trial, and it is therefore easier to argue that proceedings should be held in private. This was the case in *T v United Kingdom*[37]/*V v United Kingdom*.[38] The children (aged 10 at the time of the crime and 11 at the time of trial) were convicted of murdering a two-year-old toddler (Jamie Bulger). Although a number of special measures were used, the trial was a public one and the children's names were published following conviction. The children claimed that the public nature of the trial, and the release of their names post-conviction, violated Articles 3 and 6 ECHR (no arguments were made on the basis of Article 8 ECHR). The Court rejected the Article 3 ECHR argument. However, it held that Article 6 ECHR had been violated. In deciding that Article 6 ECHR was violated, the Court was strongly influenced by the special protection afforded to children's privacy under international

[35] Under English law if proceedings take place in the youth court, on appeal from a youth court, or in certain circumstances in a magistrates' court, then s.49 Children and Young Persons Act 1933 prohibits the reporting of the name, address, school, picture, or any particulars likely to lead to the identification of any child or young person concerned in the proceedings. However, for serious crimes, proceedings may be transferred to the Crown Court. A judge is entitled to restrict reporting which might lead to the identification of a child or young person in a Crown Court trial under s.39 Children and Young Persons Act 1933 (s.107(1) Children and Young Persons Act 1933 defines a 'child' as a person under the age of 14 years, and a 'young person' as one who has attained the age of 14 years and is under the age of 18). However, if the judge refuses to restrict reporting, then currently there is no opportunity to challenge that refusal. In 2010, the Law Commission reported that the protection of children's Article 8 ECHR rights required there to be a right of appeal in cases where their names are to be made public in relations to crimes they have committed. It asserted: '. . . our view is that the protection of the Article 8 rights of children and young people is sufficiently important for there to be a right of appeal against a ruling which allows a child or young person in a trial on indictment to be identified. The rationale for restricting reporting of criminal proceedings in relation to child defendants is, we believe, their immaturity and the expectation that they will change. If their names are made public for crimes committed when children, their chances of rehabilitation may well be damaged. The European Court of Human Rights has commented on what it called, "the special position of minors in the criminal-justice sphere" and has noted "in particular the need for the protection of their privacy at criminal trials". Law Commission (Law Com No.324) *The High Court's Jurisdiction in Relation to Criminal Proceedings* (London, The Stationery Office, 2010) at [10.4]': It should be noted that this analysis was conducted under the auspices of Article 8 ECHR as opposed to Article 6 ECHR. This suggests that at least some public bodies regard Article 8 ECHR as relevant to the child's right to privacy in this context. Thus Article 8 ECHR may yet come into play to protect the rights of children on trial.

[36] For an argument that all proceedings should be held in public and that there should be no exception based upon the privacy of the child, see James Michael 'A Child's Right to Privacy or Open Justice' in G. Douglas and L. Sebba (eds.) *Children's Rights and Traditional Values* (Ashgate, London, 1998).

[37] Application no. 24724/94 [1999] ECHR 170.

[38] Application no. 24888/94 [1999] ECHR 171.

law, and the strong trend towards protecting the privacy of juveniles, in particular.[39] Thus, where the child is a defendant, Article 6 ECHR offers significant, albeit indirect, protection to the child's privacy. The protection afforded to child suspects and defendants needs to be compared with the protection afforded to the children of suspected offenders and children involved in other types of legal proceedings.

26.2.1.3 Children indirectly involved in criminal proceedings

The European Court of Human Rights has yet to consider the Article 8 ECHR rights of children indirectly affected by criminal proceedings. However, this issue has arisen on a number of occasions in English law. Under s.39 Children and Young Persons Act 1933, a judge is entitled to restrict reporting which might lead to the identification of a child or young person in a Crown Court trial.[40] However, if the child is not a defendant or a witness to criminal proceedings then s.39 Children and Young Persons Act 1933 does not apply.

The leading case is the House of Lords decision in *Re S (FC) (a child)*.[41] In *Re S* the child's mother was accused of murdering S's brother. The mother was on trial and an injunction was sought to prevent publication of the mother's identity, on the ground that revealing her identity would lead to the identification of S (an eight-year-old child). Evidence was presented to the effect that the child would suffer psychological harm as a result of the publicity. The Lords proceeded on the basis that the Article 8 ECHR right of the child favoured restricting publication of the child's mother's identity, whereas the Article 10 ECHR rights of the press favoured disclosure.[42]

The Lords accepted that Article 8 ECHR was engaged. However, they drew a distinction between juveniles who are directly involved in criminal trials (like in *T and V*), and children (like S) who are indirectly affected. They noted that whilst publication would be distressing for S, it was 'not of the same order when compared with cases of juveniles, who are directly involved in criminal trials'.[43] Lord Steyn looked at the special protection given to juveniles by the Convention on the Rights of the Child (CRC), and concluded that the CRC 'does not protect the privacy of children if they are only indirectly affected by criminal trials.[44] It is worth noting that in determining that the CRC offers no protection to children indirectly affected by a trial, Lord Steyn cited Articles 17 and 40.2(vii) CRC, but made no reference to Article 16 CRC. Article 17 CRC provides children with a right of access to information and material from a diversity of national and international sources, especially those aimed at the promotion of social, spiritual, and moral well-being and physical and mental health. It does not seem relevant to the issues raised by *Re S*. Article 40.2(vii) CRC is concerned with the right of juveniles to privacy during proceedings. This obviously was relevant to *Re S*. However, the fact that child defendants have a right to privacy does not mean that the CRC offers no protection to the privacy of children indirectly affected by legal proceedings. Moreover, as noted above, Lord Steyn made no reference to Article 16 CRC. On first glance, it seems plausible that his reference to Article 17 CRC may have been intended to be a reference to Article 16 CRC, but one must reject that possibility as Lord Steyn also cited some academic commentary which related to Article 17 CRC.[45] The lack of Article 16 analysis is peculiar. Article 16

[39] N. 37, above, at [85]; and N. 38, above, at [87].
[40] See N. 35, above.
[41] [2004] UKHL 47, [2005] 1 AC 593.
[42] N. 41, above, at [15].
[43] N. 41, above, at [27].
[44] N. 41, above, at [26].
[45] See Lord Steyn's reference in *Re S*, N. 41, above, to Geraldine Van Bueren *The International Law on the Rights of the Child* (Martinus Nijhoff, Dordrecht, 1994), 141 and 182.

CRC states that no child shall be subjected to arbitrary or unlawful interference with his or her privacy, and that the child has the right to the protection of the law against such interference or attacks. Thus it would appear to be at least arguable that this provision could provide some protection to children indirectly affected by criminal trials, particularly given that the Lords accepted that the similarly worded, albeit not child-specific, Article 8 ECHR would apply on these facts. The omission appears to be anomalous.

Returning to the court's analysis of Article 8 ECHR, the court accepted that Article 8 ECHR was engaged; however it drew a distinction between the Article 8 ECHR rights of children on trial and the Article 8 ECHR rights of those indirectly affected by criminal proceedings. As noted above, this distinction was partly based on the Lords' analysis of the CRC. In addition to the CRC, the Lords also grounded their argument that greater protection was afforded to child juveniles in the European Court of Human Rights' decision in *T and V v United Kingdom.*[46]

Certainly, *T and V* advocates strong protection for child defendants, but *T and V* was based on Article 6 ECHR, not Article 8 ECHR, and therefore it does not really offer any guidance as to the relevant weight of the Article 8 ECHR rights of child defendants or those indirectly affected by legal proceedings. Thus it is submitted that Lord Steyn was wrong to conclude that the CRC and *T and V* state that less weight should be afforded to children indirectly affected by proceedings. Nevertheless, it is probably correct that in principle less weight should be afforded to the rights of those indirectly affected. However, the problem in *Re S* was not that *less weight* was given to children indirectly affected, but in fact that *no real weight* was given to their Article 8 ECHR rights. As Rachel Taylor has noted, the difficulty with Lord Steyn's approach is that:

> By deciding that indirect involvement is *necessarily* less weighty than direct involvement, the House of Lords avoided the need for detailed consideration of the specific impact on [S]. No further analysis of his Article 8 right was given.[47]

Certainly the court did not accept that the fact that a child was affected was relevant to Article 8 ECHR. In fact, Lord Steyn noted that if the claim were allowed then adults could also seek injuctions and this 'would confront newspapers with an ever wider spectrum of potentially costly proceedings and would seriously inhibit the freedom of the press to report criminal trials'.[48] There was no consideration of whether the fact that the individual affected was a child should alter the weight afforded to Article 8 ECHR in striking the balance between Articles 8 and 10 ECHR and ultimately, the House of Lords came down in favour of freedom of expression.[49]

Shortly after *Re S,* in *A Local Authority v W* (*Re W*), an injunction was sought by the local authority to protect the identity of two children whose mother had pleaded guilty to knowingly infecting the father of one of the children with HIV.[50] The injunction sought would prohibit the publication or broadcasting of names, addresses, or

[46] N. 37, above.

[47] Rachel Taylor 'Re S (A Child) (Identification: Restrictions on Publication) and A Local Authority v W: Children's Privacy and Press Freedom in Criminal Cases (2006) *Child and Family Law Quarterly* 269.

[48] N. 41, above, at [32].

[49] For a critique of the decision see Helen Fenwick 'Clashing Rights, the Welfare of the Child and the Human Rights Act' (2004) 67(6) *Modern Law Review* 889–927.

[50] This is an offence under s.20 Offences Against the Person Act 1861: *A Local Authority v W* [2005] EWHC 1564 (Fam), [2006] 1 FLR 1.

photographs of the parents, and any details that were likely to lead to the identification of the children, including details of their nursery placements, carers, and any photographs. Sir Mark Potter, President of the Family Division drew upon the House of Lords decision in *Re S*, a decision by which he was bound, and noted:

Although the decision is contained in the single judgment of Lord Steyn, with whom the remainder of their Lordships agreed, it is on analysis by no means easy to apply. That is because it makes clear on the one hand that, in performing the balancing exercise between the competing rights of freedom of the press under Article 10 and the rights of a child under Article 8, there is no presumption of priority as between those rights, while on the other hand it is stated that in European jurisprudence and domestic practice the ordinary rule that the press may report everything which takes place in a criminal court can only be displaced by 'unusual or exceptional circumstances' (per Lord Steyn at paragraph [18]); see also the reference to a requirement for 'most compelling circumstances' (at paragraph [20]).[51]

However, having reviewed the various authorities, including *Douglas v Hello!*, the House of Lords decision in *Campbell v MGN*, and *Re S* itself, the judge concluded that parallel analysis was required.[52] He then distinguished *Re S* and *Re W*, emphasizing in particular, that in *Re W* there was a good possibility that the children could be protected from publicity; that any publicity could jeopardize the prospects of the children being placed in care; and that the problems derived not from the mother's criminal conviction, but from the fact that the children would be adversely treated by their community if it were suspected that they had HIV.[53] Crucially, the judge also cast doubt on the distinction drawn in *Re S* between children directly and indirectly involved in proceedings:

At paragraph 27 of his judgment, Lord Steyn stated that interference with the Article 8 rights of a child not a party to or involved in criminal proceedings, however distressing to the child, was not of the same order when compared with the cases of those directly involved in criminal trials. That is of course correct (a) in the general sense that, ex hypothesi, the interference is in one case a direct effect of the court proceedings, whereas in the other it is an indirect effect; (b) in the particular sense that a child directly involved in a trial is likely to undergo trauma from that very fact, whereas the damage to a child who is not involved is limited to stress arising from knowledge of the trial and the criminality of the child's parent if found guilty. If, however, it is clear from the evidence that real and substantial damage to the child's Article 8 rights is likely to result if the injunction is not granted which would not otherwise occur, it does not seem to me that the distinction adverted to by Lord Steyn goes to the core of the balancing exercise as articulated by Latham LJ in *Re: S* at paragraph 76, (as quoted at para 37 above).[54]

It is submitted that further consideration of the impact upon the child is crucial if the child's Article 8 ECHR right is to mean anything in this context, particularly with regard to the protection afforded by that right to 'physical and psychological integrity'.[55] Moreover, as Rachel Taylor has noted, the judge's 'statement must be correct if it is accepted that the balancing exercise ... requires close consideration of the specific rights claimed'.[56] In *Re W* the judge granted the injunction, having particular regard to the vulnerability of the children and the prospect of a 'widespread and far longer-lasting inroad into the privacy and family life to which these children

[51] N. 50, above, at [24]. [52] N. 50, above, at [52]–[53]. *Douglas v Hello!* [2001] QB 967.
[53] N. 50, above, at [55]–[58].
[54] N. 50, above, at [60]. [55] See *Von Hannover*, N. 3, above, at [50].
[56] Rachel Taylor 'Re S (A Child) (Identification: Restrictions on Publication) and A Local Authority v W: children's privacy and press freedom in criminal cases (2006) *Child and Family Law Quarterly* 269.

are entitled and of which they are in such need'.[57] This was a significant statement of the Article 8 ECHR rights of the child, albeit as we will see below, the judge's reference to 'real and substantial damage' has bitten in the subsequent cases.[58]

Re W was the high watermark for children's privacy in this context, and in two subsequent cases the balance has fallen back in favour of freedom of expression. In *A Local Authority v PD* (*Re PD*) the High Court refused to grant an injunction prohibiting publication of the identity of a father (PD) who was on trial for murdering his wife.[59] The facts were particularly gruesome: the father had chopped up his wife and placed her body parts in a freezer.[60] This case was also heard by Sir Mark Potter (President of the Family Division); however, in this case he refused to grant an injunction on the ground that there was nothing of such an exceptional or compelling nature that would justify granting anonymity. Having advocated the use of the balancing exercise the judge went on to assert:

> The burden of proving the case for grant of an injunction always lies upon the applicant. In the special case of an injunction *contra mundum*, and in particular one which restrains the press from exercising its right unrestrainedly to report criminal proceedings, the burden is a heavy one. The necessity is to show unusual and exceptional circumstances. The entire tenor of the judgment in *Re S* demonstrates the difficulties facing the applicant in a case of this kind.[61]

It is submitted that the need for 'unusual and exceptional circumstances' undermines the judge's assertion in both *Re W* and *Re PD* that a balancing exercise must be conducted which operates on the basis that neither right takes priority. Indeed this is implicit in his acknowledgment of the difficulties that applicants face in these cases. The lack of real protection afforded to Article 8 ECHR is also apparent in the judge's conclusion in *Re PD*:

> Thus, unusual and sensational as the *facts* of this case may be, the proposed identification of the defendant in connection with the criminal proceedings cannot be shown either to cause or create serious, let alone irremediable, damage to G in the enjoyment of her private of family life. It is certainly far from sufficient to outweigh the plain and substantial interference with the right of the press to identify the father and otherwise to report the criminal proceedings in which she [sic] is being tried.[62]

If 'irremediable damage' is required, then this is a very high threshold, and one that would exclude many cases. However, even if only 'serious damage' is required, it is submitted that this also undermines Article 8 ECHR. Put simply, Article 8 ECHR is a poor relation to Article 10 ECHR, if the child needs to prove serious damage to rebut the presumption that the press are entitled to publish. Moreover, this problem is compounded by the fact that the courts do not appear to be giving sufficient consideration to the vulnerability of children, and the impact of publicity in determining whether there is serious damage.[63]

[57] N. 50, above, at [78].
[58] See text to n. 54 above.
[59] [2005] EWHC 1832 (Fam), [2005] EMLR 840.
[60] N. 59, above.
[61] N. 59, above, at [30].
[62] N. 59, above, at [38].
[63] In *Re S* the court received the following evidence from a psychiatrist; however even this was not sufficient to rebut Article 10 ECHR: 'CS attends school and once the news of the charges against his mother becomes public, he will have to cope with the curiosity of his peers, and possible bullying and teasing. If the reporting was confined to the time of the trial and [S's] name and the name of the family was not mentioned, and photos not published, it would be possible to plan for the minimum of adverse effects by removing [S] from the country for a holiday during the trial itself and for sensitive work to be done with his peers by the school in his absence. However if there is a long period of adverse named publicity, the effect on this vulnerable boy, who has already lost a brother by death and has been deprived of his

Most recently, in *Crawford v CPS* the High Court again refused to grant an injunction on the basis that there was no evidence that the children would suffer any harm, other than the embarrassment that may stem from other people knowing that their father had been convicted of a criminal offence.[64] It should be noted that *Crawford* was a far less-convincing case: the offences were less serious, Mr Crawford had been convicted of harassment of his former wife and her partner, not murder, and the father had a high profile (he was himself a judge); there was therefore a legitimate concern that if an injunction were granted that it would appear that Mr Crawford was being permitted to use the law to protect his own reputation. It was therefore perhaps understandable that the injunction was refused. Nevertheless, this trend for requiring serious harm to tip the balance in favour of Article 8 ECHR is troubling, particularly when coupled with the lack of consideration given to the question of whether the child will suffer harm.[65]

26.2.1.4 Children involved in civil proceedings

Whilst the European Court of Human Rights has not considered the privacy rights of children indirectly involved in criminal proceedings, it has had the opportunity to consider the privacy rights of children involved in other types of legal proceedings, for example, custody proceedings. Custody proceedings are usually held in private to protect the privacy of the child. However, in a number of cases parents have argued that holding custody proceedings in private is a violation of their (the parents') Article 6 ECHR right to a fair trial. On the face of it, this would appear to pit the parents' Article 6 ECHR right against the child's Article 8 ECHR right. This would raise interesting questions about the balance to be struck between these interests and the degree of protection afforded to the child. However, in practice, whilst the Court has alluded to these issues, it has not directly addressed the child's Article 8 ECHR right.

In *B and P v United Kingdom* the Court had to consider whether holding residence proceedings in private violated the applicants' Article 6 ECHR right to a fair trial. English law stated that such proceedings should normally be held in private, and the European Court of Human Rights held that this rule did not violate Article 6 ECHR because private proceedings were necessary to protect the privacy of the child.[66] The Court asserted that 'such proceedings are prime examples of cases where the exclusion of the press and public may be justified in order to protect the child'.[67] Yet, despite this reference to the child's needs, no consideration was given to any rights that the child may have under Article 8 ECHR. This is an example of how the fact that cases are brought by parents may affect the Court's reasoning. This may be particularly

mother's care (and it has to be said that there is no evidence that she was anything other than a good and caring parent to [S]) would, in my opinion be significantly harmful. It would not be possible to protect him in the way I mention above. The effect of bereavement on a child of this age is to enhance the risk of developing a depressive disorder five-fold. [S] therefore, whilst at present well-functioning carries this enhanced risk which may not manifest itself immediately. The risk continues into adult life. The addition of the stress of coping with the curiosity and possible teasing and bullying of his peers would be to significantly increase the possibility of his developing a psychiatric disorder.' N. 41, above, at [10].

[64] [2008] EWHC 854, at [31]–[32] and [42].

[65] See Jacob Cook's critique of the presumption of open justice and its application in *Crawford v CPS*: Jacob Cook 'Press Freedom and the Privacy of Non-Victim Children: Resolving Conflict Between Open Justice and Human Rights' (2010) *Communications Law* 108.

[66] (App. nos. 36337/97 and 35974/97) (2002) 34 EHRR 19.

[67] N. 66, above, at [38].

problematic where parents have a strong argument under Article 6 ECHR, as there is a danger that appropriate weight will not be afforded to the child's interests if the reasoning is not carried out under the auspices of Article 8 ECHR.

A case where the parent had a strong claim under Article 6 ECHR was *Moser v Austria*.[68] In *Moser*, the applicant's son had been taken into care, and the applicant argued that the state's refusal to hold a public hearing violated Article 6 ECHR. The Court agreed. It distinguished *Moser* from *B and P* on the basis that *B and P* involved a dispute between the mother and the father, whereas in *Moser* the proceedings were between the mother and the state. This was a valid distinction. However, the child potentially had a number of rights that needed to be considered. On the one hand, this was a case where the child may also have had a strong interest in the proceedings being held in public: if the child were taken into care this would impact on the child's Article 8 ECHR right to respect for family life. Indeed, the case was brought on the basis that taking the child into care interfered with both the mother's and the child's right to respect for family life.[69] It was accepted by the Court that the mother had a right to bring the claim on behalf of herself and her son.[70] On the other hand, the child's Article 8 ECHR right to respect for private life may have pointed in the direction of private proceedings. Yet, despite these complexities, the Court gave no consideration to the child's interests under Article 8 ECHR, and how those interests should weigh in favour, or against, the claim of the mother that the proceedings should have been held in public, and that the decision should have been publically declared. The Court held that the private nature of the proceedings violated Article 6 ECHR.[71]

In both *B and P* and *Moser*, the Court noted that the protection of children was a valid reason for holding proceedings in private.[72] However, in both cases the Court focused upon the parents' right to a fair trial under Article 6 ECHR and the limits of that right. Thus at best, the child's privacy was construed as an exception or limit to that right. In neither case did the Court link this privacy interest to Article 8 ECHR, to analyse how this right sat with the parents' right under Article 6 ECHR. One needs to be cautious here and to acknowledge that this is not unusual. In fact, this is the Court's standard approach, as others have acknowledged:

> ...when Strasbourg hears cases brought by individuals alleging a violation of a Convention right, competing rights figure only as possible means of justification for the respondent State and thus as an exception to the primary right whose infringement is alleged.[73]

However, whilst it is evident that the Strasbourg Court has a different role from the domestic courts, one of the Court's roles is to interpret the Convention and to provide guidance to the state parties faced with the task of enforcing the rights. Thus, at the very least it should acknowledge that other rights are engaged. Otherwise, there is a danger that these rights will be neglected at the domestic level.

[68] (App. no. 12643/02) [2007] Fam Law 20.

[69] It was accepted by the Austrian Government that this would interfere with the right to respect for family life, although it was argued that the interference was justified. N. 68, above, at [62].

[70] N. 68, above, at [60].

[71] N. 68, above, at [98] and [104].

[72] N. 66 above, and N.68, above, at [95].

[73] Helen Fenwick and Gavin Phillipson 'The Doctrine of Confidence as a Privacy Remedy in the Human Rights Act Era' (2000) 63(5) *Modern Law Review* 660.

26.2.2 Children and publicity

The courts have also had to consider cases where the child has been, or is about to be, the subject of publicity, outside the context of legal proceedings. The European Commission of Human Rights considered such a case when it decided *A, Byrne and Twenty-Twenty Television v United Kingdom*.[74] The case was brought by the child's mother who wanted the child to participate in a documentary. The domestic courts had refused to vary or discharge injunctions to allow the making and broadcasting of the documentary. The mother argued that this refusal constituted a violation of her right to respect for private and family life. The Commission considered the case under the right to respect for family life and held that whilst the right was interfered with, this was justified. In determining that the interference was justified the Commission noted that the domestic courts were concerned to protect the privacy of the child and the child's welfare. However, at no point in the Commission's analysis did the Commission state that this was a case where the domestic courts were required to balance competing rights, the rights of the mother and the rights of the child. The focus was entirely upon the question of whether the interference with the mother's right was justified. The mother, the producer of the documentary, and the production company, also sought to argue that the injunction constituted an interference with their Article 10 ECHR rights. The Commission proceeded on the basis that Article 10 ECHR was engaged but again found this interference to be justified. The analysis was similar to the Article 8 ECHR analysis, in that there was no discussion of the child's rights under Article 8 ECHR. Thus this is another example of the absence of Article 8 ECHR reasoning in cases where children's rights are affected.

In the more recent domestic cases the courts have confronted Article 8 ECHR head on and they have applied the balancing exercise that was advocated in *Re S*.[75] This is apparent from the earlier case, *Campbell v MGN* (which advocated the balancing exercise in misuse of private information cases) and in the later child privacy case *Murray v Big Pictures Ltd*.[76] The weight afforded to Article 8 ECHR will depend upon the facts of the case. As we will see below, there seems to be more scope in this context (than in the cases concerned with children indirectly affected by legal proceedings) for arguing that greater weight should be given to the Article 8 ECHR rights of children. What is also interesting in these cases is that (in addition to the rights of the press) there may be an Article 10 ECHR right of a third party, perhaps a parent, or another child. Moreover, the child concerned may also have Article 8 and Article 10 ECHR rights pulling in different directions.

Re Roddy (A Child) (Identification: Restriction on Publicity) illustrates some of these complexities.[77] In *Re Roddy*, reporting restrictions had been put in place in 1999 and 2000 to protect a 13-year-old mother—Angela Roddy, her baby 'Y', and the father of the child 'X', who was also about 13 years old. Angela had been placed in foster care and Y had been adopted.[78] In 2003, a newspaper and Angela sought a variation of the order. In her witness statement, Angela stated that she wanted to let others know what the care system was like, and to inform them of the consequences of having unprotected sex.[79] She also stated that she was 'happy to be named and photographed for the purposes of the newspaper article and [that she had] considered the

[74] (1998) 25 EHRR CD 159. [75] N. 41, above.
[76] [2008] EWCA Civ 446, [2008] 3 WLR 1360.
[77] [2003] EWHC 2927 (Fam), [2004] 1 FCR 481. [78] N. 77, above, at [2].
[79] N. 77, above, at [6].

consequences of this'.[80] The local authority agreed that the order could be varied in respect of Angela; however the authority was concerned to protect X and Y. Thus the matter came before the High Court.

Munby J noted that whilst *Re Roddy* raised further complexities to *Re S*, the same balancing exercise applied:

In *Re S* the balancing exercise was not particularly complicated. Although Article 6 was also implicated the essential contest was between the rights of the child under Article 8 and the rights of the media under Article 10. In the present case, as we shall see, the exercise is more complicated. On one side there are ranged ANL's [Associated Newspaper Limited's] rights under Article 10 and, as she would have it, Angela's rights under both Article 10 and Article 8. On the other side there are ranged Article 8 rights asserted on behalf of both X and Y and also, on one view, Angela's rights under Article 8. But although the exercise may be more complicated (though no more complicated than the somewhat similar exercise I had to undertake in *Clibbery v Allan* [2001] 2 FLR 819, affirmed on appeal, *Clibbery v Allan* [2002] EWCA Civ 45, [2002] Fam 261) the essential task remains that identified by Hale LJ in *Re S*.[81]

Thus, the judge had to balance the rights of the various interested parties. The task was made easier by the fact that neither the newspaper, nor Angela, wished to reveal information that would lead to the identification of either X or Y. Thus, whilst the publication would impact on the private lives of X and Y, X and Y would remain anonymous, and therefore the impact was thought to be minimal.[82] However, consideration needed to be given to the question of whether Angela's own rights pointed in favour of, or against, varying the order. In making that assessment the judge addressed a number of crucial questions concerning the child's right to privacy, and children's rights generally. First, he acknowledged that a child has autonomy rights under the Convention, but those rights may be challenged:

A child is, of course, as much entitled to the protection of the Convention—and specifically of Articles 8 and 10—as anyone else. But, as Mr Arnot correctly pointed out, the personal autonomy guaranteed by Article 8 (and, I would add, by Article 10) is necessarily somewhat qualified in the case of a child. For, depending on the circumstances, decision-making power may rest not with the child but with the child's parents or even with the court. I must return to this topic in due course. For the moment I observe only that there may well be cases where a child wishes to go to the media—wishes, in other words, to avail himself of what he asserts are his Article 10 and Article 8 rights to make public that which would otherwise be private—whilst his parents, or the court, may think that his interests are better served by asserting his right under Article 8 to keep such matters private.[83]

The judge then considered the crucial question of whether children should be allowed to exercise these rights. It is worth setting out this aspect of the judgment in full because it is a significant statement of the importance of children's rights:

There is in fact a very important point of principle lurking behind all this. Are children of Angela's age to be allowed to exercise for themselves the rights they have under the Convention—here the vitally important rights under Articles 8 and 10? Are we to recognise that Angela should in relation to her Convention rights enjoy the same autonomy, the same decision-making power, as she will undoubtedly have when she reaches the age of 18 in just one year's time? Are we to trust Angela to decide for herself whether that which is private (and

[80] N. 77, above, at [6].

[81] N. 77, above, at [21]. It should be noted that the *Re S* decision that Munby J was referring to was the Court of Appeal decision; however, the balancing exercise discussed by the Court of Appeal is the same as the later House of Lords decision

[82] N. 77, above, at [43] and [80].

[83] N. 77, above, at [37].

not merely private—what we are talking about here is something extremely personal and intimate) should remain private or whether it should be shared with the whole world? Are we, in other words, to take children's rights seriously and as our children see them? Or are we to treat children as little more than the largely passive objects of more or less paternalistic parental or judicial decision-making?

I repeat, because the point is so important, that Angela is seeking to enforce what she says are her *rights* under the Convention. What underlies ANL's claim to be entitled to publish Angela's story is not only its own rights under Article 10, nor merely the fact (important though it is) that, by giving her consent, Angela may be said to have waived her privacy. What underlies the whole case is Angela's right, as she would have it, to tell her story to the world—a right, and it is nothing less, securely founded in Articles 8 and 10.

What we are actually talking about here is the extent to which we are prepared to recognise the autonomy of the 16-year-old; in particular, the extent to which we are prepared to recognise that 16-year-olds have rights to freedom of expression secured to them by Articles 8 and 10. Some academic commentators complain that these are matters to which the courts have not hitherto given serious consideration. That may or may not be so. But I entirely agree that these are very important issues.[84]

Having clearly identified the question of competence Munby J then reviewed the cases where the courts have had to deal with questions of competence, and he concluded that *Gillick* competence should apply in this context:

The courts must face reality. We must, as Lord Scarman said, be sensitive to human development and social change. Angela may not yet be quite 17 years old but she is a young woman with a mind of her own and, as her solicitor B has said, a mature and articulate young person. We no longer treat our 17-year-old daughters as our Victorian ancestors did, and if we try to do so it is at our—and their—peril. Angela, in my judgment, is of an age, and has sufficient understanding and maturity, to decide for herself whether that which is private, personal and intimate should remain private or whether it should be shared with the whole world. She is what Ward LJ described in *In re Z (A Minor) (Identification: Restrictions on Publication)* [1997] Fam 1 at p 30 as a 'competent teenager taking [her] story to the press'. She is, to use the language of Woolf J (as he then was) in *Gillick v West Norfolk and Wisbech Area Health Authority* [1984] QB 581 at p 596, 'capable of making a reasonable assessment of the advantages and disadvantages' of what is proposed.

In my judgment (and I wish to emphasise this) it is the responsibility—it is the duty—of the court not merely to recognise but, as Nolan LJ said, to *defend* what, if I may respectfully say so, he correctly described as the *right* of the child who has sufficient understanding to make an informed decision, to make his or her own choice. This is not mere pragmatism, although as Nolan LJ pointed out, any other approach is likely to be both futile and counter-productive. It is also, as he said, a matter of principle. For, as Balcombe LJ recognised, the court must recognise the child's integrity as a human being. And we do not recognise Angela's dignity and integrity as a human being—we do not respect her rights under Articles 8 and 10—unless we acknowledge that it is for her to make her own choice, and not for her parents or a judge or any other public authority to seek to make the choice on her behalf.[84a]

This was a crucial statement for children's rights. Where children seek to express their views, and to engage in the public sphere, we sometimes fear that children do not understand the need for privacy, and we sometimes respond to this by providing children with 'privacy' for their benefit, or in other words, silencing

[84] N. 77, above, at [46]–[48].
[84a] N. 77, above, at [56]–[57].

them.[85] However, it is submitted that whilst we need to be aware of children's vulnerability, and their difficulties in obtaining privacy in some contexts, we also need to be careful that we do not assume that children are ignorant of the need for privacy. We need to ensure that children have both a right to privacy and a right to freedom of expression.[86] As one commentator has noted, 'if the child's right to privacy is going to enhance rather than diminish his need for autonomy, then serious consideration must be given to the child's desire to have his voice heard'.[87] It should also be noted that Munby J thought that Angela's right to decide to tell her story, engaged her *Article 8 ECHR right* as well as her Article 10 ECHR right. A core element of Article 8 ECHR is autonomy, and it crucial that children are also able to benefit from that aspect of the right.

Finally, it is worth noting that whilst *Re Roddy* was a rather easy case because the order was not opposed by the local authority, Munby J held that he would have come to the same decision even if the application had been opposed by Angela's parents or the local authority:

> In fact Angela's decision is supported by her parents and not opposed by the local authority. But neither of those facts can be determinative. I wish to make it clear that, giving proper weight to Angela's evidence and the evidence of her solicitor, B, I should unhesitatingly have come to precisely the same conclusion even if Angela's wish to tell her story to the world had been opposed both by the local authority and by her parents. The decision, I repeat, is for Angela: it is not for her parents, the local authority or the court.[88]

Thus, *Re Roddy,* whilst actually allowing disclosure of private information, provided perhaps the strongest statement of children's rights to autonomy—a crucial aspect of Article 8 ECHR.

Another publicity case concerning teenage pregnancy is *Re Stedman and Patten.*[89] Chantelle (aged 15) gave birth to a child, Maisie, and it was alleged that Alfie (aged 13) was the father. A phenomenal degree of publicity in the national and international press followed. Indeed the High Court noted that even the phrase 'media circus' could not 'adequately describe what went on in the first week or so after

[85] Research into children's use of the internet suggests that children have some awareness of the need for privacy online and of some of the threats that they may encounter when using the internet. The research also suggests that younger children tend to use the internet as a space in which to experience privacy and to engage in private discussion that would not be possible face-to-face because of the constant presence of others: LSE UK *Children go Online: Emerging Opportunities and Dangers,* First Project Report *'UK Children Go Online: Listening to Young People's Experiences'* <http://www.lse.ac.uk/collections/children-go-online/UKChildrenGoOnlineReport1.pdf>. The Final Report of the LSE project suggests that whilst children are sometimes naïve about external threats to their privacy they are very protective of their privacy in relation to their parents: LSE UK *Children go Online: Emerging Opportunities and Dangers,* Final Project Report *'UK Children Go Online: Final Report of Key Project Findings'* <http://www.lse.ac.uk/collections/children-go-online/UKCGO_Final_report.pdf> 25.

[86] The child's right to freedom of expression is equally contested. In particular what forms of expression and forums in which a child can express views and the right to receive expression. This issue is beyond the scope of this chapter but there is a vast body of fascinating literature on this topic. In particular, highlighting the differences between liberal and communitarian approaches to this issue see Amitai Etzioni 'On Protecting Children From Speech' (2004) 79 *Chicago-Kent Law Review* 3; Colin M. Macleod 'A Liberal Theory of Freedom of Expression for Children' (2004) 79 *Chicago-Kent Law Review* 55; Marjorie Heins 'On Protecting Children—From Censorship: A Reply to Amitai Etzioni' (2004) 79 *Chicago-Kent law Review* 229; William Galston 'When Well-being Trumps Liberty: Political Theory, Jurisprudence, and Children's Rights' (2004) 79 *Chicago-Kent Law Review* 279.

[87] Jaclyn Moriarty 'Children, privacy and the Press' (1997) *Child and Family Law Quarterly* 217.

[88] N. 77, above, at [59].

[89] [2009] EWHC 935 (Fam), [2009] 2 FLR 852.

Maisie's birth'.[90] What was perhaps most troubling was that Alfie's and Chantelle's mothers had subjected these children to this media attention.[91] The local authority intervened and obtained an order making Maisie, Chantelle, and Alfie wards of court.[92] A number of reporting restrictions were then put in place, including one which prevented the parents of Alfie and Chantelle from having any further contact with the media.[93] However, it subsequently transpired that Alfie was not the father of the child, and due to a loophole in the original order, the *Daily Mirror* was able to publish an article disclosing this fact, together with a photograph of Alfie and Maisie. Further reporting restrictions were sought namely: (i) to prevent the publication of any photographs of Alfie, Maisie, and Chantelle, regardless of whether they were already in the public domain; and (ii) to prohibit any reports of Alfie's DNA test, again, regardless of whether this information was already in the public domain.[94] The judge held that Alfie's, Chantelle's, and Maisie's Article 8 ECHR rights would be engaged if these details were published.[95] However, he refused the injunction, on the basis that it would constitute a disproportionate interference with the Article 10 rights of the press, and Alfie, and that it would be futile, given that extensive material was already in the public domain.[96]

Of course this was a case where Alfie had a strong claim under Article 10 ECHR; indeed he may also have had a strong claim under Article 8 ECHR (the right to reputation) to 'set the record straight'; thus the outcome in *Re Stedman* may be a just one. However, it is submitted that greater consideration needs to be given to two issues. The first is the fact that it was the children's parents who had originally brought the children to the attention of the media. There is a troubling and unresolved issue in the judgment, namely the newspaper's argument that the children could not have a reasonable expectation of privacy because their parents had courted publicity.[97] This issue was not resolved because the defendant conceded that the children's Article 8 ECHR rights were engaged.[98] However, this argument has also arisen in other cases and thus it is addressed in more detail, below.

The second (and related) problem is what the judge referred to as the 'public domain qualification or 'Canute principle', namely that if the information is already in the public domain, there is no point in imposing restrictions on future publication.[99] In *Re Stedman* the judge decided that as the information had been seen and read by millions of people, an injunction would be 'futile'.[100] This is problematic, because as noted above, the information had come into the public domain as result of the actions taken by the children's parents. Moreover, as the local authority argued, whilst it may be true in confidentiality cases that courts should not restrict the publication of information already lawfully published, 'that may not be so in privacy cases involving vulnerable children who are wards of the court'.[101] This was rejected by the judge, who held that:

> ... the requirement under s 124(a)(i) of the Human Rights Act to consider the extent to which the material has become available to the public applies equally whether the material is confidential or private and whether it relates to adults or children.[102]

[90] N. 89, above, at [7]. [91] N. 89, above, at [2]–[3]. [92] N. 89, above, at [8].
[93] N. 89, above, at [10]. [94] N. 89, above, at [21]. [95] N. 89, above, at [49].
[96] N. 89, above, at [96]–[97]. [97] N. 89, above, at [46]. [98] N. 89, above, at [48].
[99] N. 89, above, at [74]–[99].
[100] N. 89, above, at [97]. The court heard evidence that the story had been reported all over the world and had been the subject of comment in Parliament, that a Google search of the name Alfie Patten produced about 359,000 results and 25,100 images. The story in the *Daily Mirror* has also been viewed online 84,000 times, at [75].
[101] N. 89, above, at [81]. [102] N. 89, above, at [81].

It is submitted that whilst s.124(a) emphasizes Article 10 ECHR, and directs the courts to have regard to the extent to which the information is already in the public domain, it has been clear since *Douglas v Hello!* that this does not provide a definitive answer and that the courts also need to look to Article 8 ECHR.[103] Moreover, as the local authority argued, 'a distinction needs to be made between confidentiality and privacy; once confidentiality is lost it is lost for all time, a photograph on the other hand is capable of being a fresh intrusion on the subject's privacy with every fresh publication'.[104] Indeed as the judge acknowledged:

> It is right that the photographs are not of themselves offensive but that does not mean they are not capable of causing distress and being an invasion of privacy each and every time they are published showing, as many of them do, Alfie as 'father' with Chantelle and his 'daughter' Maisie.[105]

Yet despite this, the judge concluded that 'she had to deal with the reality of the situation regardless of whether or not the *Daily Mirror* article was published lawfully'.[106] In other words, the 'public domain qualification' was not restricted to cases where the information had already been lawfully published, but applied even if the information had been unlawfully published. This is illogical because it creates a system in which once privacy is breached, it is acceptable repeatedly to publish the information. It is submitted that this pragmatic approach to the 'reality of the situation' does not afford sufficient protection to privacy rights in general, or the privacy rights of children in particular.

26.2.3 Photographing children

The extent to which individuals are free to take, retain, and disseminate photographs of others, particularly where the images are taken in public places, is a difficult legal issue which has arisen in a number of privacy cases.[107] One of the issues that needs to be considered is whether greater protection should be afforded to children captured in photographs.

The European Court of Human Rights has held in a number of cases that taking or disseminating photographs of an individual can engage Article 8 ECHR.[108] In *Reklos and Davourlis v Greece* the Court was required to consider whether Greece had failed to protect the rights of a child by rejecting legal proceedings brought against a photographer who took the child's photograph without the child's consent, and without the consent of the child's parents.[109] The applicants in *Reklos* were the parents of a new-born baby. A professional photographer working in a hospital took photographs of the baby in a sterile unit and offered to sell them to the applicants. The applicants objected to the photographs having been taken without their consent, and demanded that the photographer hand over the negatives. The photographer refused to do so, and the parents subsequently brought legal proceedings on the basis that the photographer had infringed the personality rights of their child. This claim was dismissed

[103] *Douglas v Hello!* [2000] EWCA Civ 353, [2001] 2 WLR 992, at [133].

[104] N. 89, above, at [83].

[105] N. 89, above, at [85].

[106] N. 89, above, at [91].

[107] Including: *Campbell v MGN*, N. 3, above; *Von Hannover v Germany*, N. 3, above; *Murray v Big Pictures Ltd*, N. 76, above. See also the New Zealand case *Hosking v Runting* [2004] NZCA 35, [2005] 1 NZLR; and the Canadian case *Aubry v Éditions Vice-Versa inc.* [1998] 1 SCR 591.

[108] See *Von Hannover*, N. 3, above; *Sciacca v Italy* (App. no. 50774/99) (2006) 43 EHRR 20; and *Egeland and Hanseid v Norway* (App. no. 34438/04) (2010) 50 EHRR 2.

[109] (App. no.1234/05) [2009] EMLR 16.

as 'too vague' by the Supreme Court of Greece and the parents lodged an application with the European Court of Human Rights.

The applicants alleged that there had been an unlawful interference with the child's right to respect for his private life.[110] The Greek Government argued that there had been no interference with Article 8 ECHR on the basis that: the photographs had not been published; there had been no commercial exploitation of the baby's image; and the mental maturity of the baby was not sufficiently developed for the baby to sense any infringement of his personality rights.[111] The Court refused to deal with the general question of whether the right to one's image depends on the individual being aware of an interference.[112] It should be noted that if this were necessary, then this would clearly curtail the rights of young children. However, the Court limited its task to the question of:

> whether the taking of the photographs in question without the parents' prior consent, together with the retention of the negatives, was capable of interfering with the baby's right to respect for its private life as guaranteed by Article 8 of the Convention... [and therefore] whether the domestic courts afforded sufficient protection to the private life of the applicants' son.[113]

The Court accepted that it had to consider whether there had been an interference with the son's right to respect for private life, even though the images had not been published.[114] The Court stated that Article 8 ECHR 'encompasses the right to identity... and the right to personal development, whether in terms of personality or of personal autonomy'.[115] Having accepted that these principles underpin Article 8 ECHR, the Court noted that one's image is one of the most fundamental elements of one's personal development, that it is therefore essential that an individual can control their image, and that to control one's image, one must not only have the opportunity to refuse to consent to one's image being published, but also to oppose the taking, conservation, or reproduction of one's image by another.[116] Significantly the Court held that the effective protection of the right:

> ...presupposes in principle and in the circumstances such as those of the present case obtaining the consent of the person concerned at the time the picture is taken and not simply if and when it is published. Otherwise an essential attribute of personality would be retained in the hands of a third party and the person concerned would have no control over any subsequent use of the image.[117]

After applying these principles to the facts, the Court held that the act of taking the photographs and the retention of those photographs had violated the child's Article 8 ECHR right.[118] The Court asserted that the right to one's image requires photographers to obtain the consent of the person concerned at the time that the picture is taken, and not simply when it is published, but that where the person photographed was a minor, the child's parents should oversee the exercise of the child's right:

> ...the person concerned was a minor and the exercise of the right to protection of his image was overseen by his parents. Accordingly, the applicants' prior consent to the taking of their son's picture was indispensable in order to establish the context of its use.[119]

[110] N. 109, above, at [29].
[111] N. 109, above, at [30]–[31].
[112] N. 109, above, at [34].
[113] N. 109, above, at [34].
[114] N. 109, above, at [38].
[115] N. 109, above, at [39].
[116] N. 109, above, at [40].
[117] N. 109, above, at [40].
[118] N. 109, above, at [41]–[43].
[119] N. 109, above, at [41].

Thus the Court rendered consent essential, and as the applicant was a 'minor' it was parental consent which was necessary. It should be noted that the fact that the 'victim' was a child did not alter the *degree of protection* afforded by the Court in *Reklos*. In fact, the Court gave no consideration to the question of whether children needed greater protection than adults in this context. Of course, by stating that consent is necessary before taking someone's photograph, the Court had already found that Article 8 ECHR offers a high degree of protection and thus it was not necessary to go further and to add greater protection to children. However, whilst it was perhaps not a problem in this particular case because the Court afforded no weight to Article 10 ECHR (a fact that is also contentious), it is submitted that the weight to be afforded to Article 8 ECHR will be essential in cases where the Court finds that the right conflicts with another competing right, such as freedom of expression.[120] It is submitted that the fact that a child is affected should be relevant to the question of what weight is to be afforded to Article 8 ECHR, and the extent of the state's positive obligations.

A further problem stems from the manner in which the Court shifted the role of consent from the child to the child's parents in *Reklos*. This was essential in *Reklos* because the applicant was a new-born baby, and thus lacked the capacity to consent. However, the decision suggests that parental consent is necessary in *all* cases involving minors. As noted above, the Court held that the consent of the child's parents was 'indispensable'.[121] It also held that:

> ... *the key issue* in the present case is not the nature, harmless or otherwise, of the applicants' son's representation on the offending photographs, but the fact that the photographer kept them without the *applicants' consent*. The baby's image was thus retained in the hands of the photographer in an identifiable form with the possibility of subsequent use *against the wishes of the person concerned and/or his parents*. [emphasis added][122]

Of course, the Court was focusing upon the specific facts of *Reklos*, and as that case concerned a new-born baby shifting consent to the parents was sensible. Nevertheless, the Court's reasoning raises a number of questions, namely: at what point are children able to consent for themselves; and what is the relationship between parental consent and the child's consent. These questions need exploring as the Court's blanket assertion that consent lies with the parents has the potential to undercut the very status of the child's Article 8 ECHR right as a 'right' held by the child.

Some of the domestic cases also give cause for concern about the role of parental consent. In *Murray v Big Pictures Ltd*, a freelance photographer surreptitiously took photographs of the infant son of the famous author, J.K. Rowling, and sold them to a newspaper.[123] The *Sunday Express* published a photograph depicting Mr and Mrs Murray walking down a public street with the child in a push chair. The photograph had been taken covertly, using a long-lens camera, and neither the claimant, nor his parents, had consented to the taking, or the subsequent publication, of the photograph.

Proceedings were brought on behalf of the infant based on the tort of misuse of private information. At first instance the claim was struck out on summary judgment.[124] However, the claimant successfully appealed.[125] The Court of Appeal held

[120] For discussion see Kirsty Hughes 'Photographs in Public Places and Privacy' (2009) 1(2) *Journal of Media Law* 159.

[121] See text to n. 119, above.

[122] N. 109, above, at [42].

[123] N. 76, above.

[124] *Murray v Express Newspapers and Anor* [2007] EWHC 1908, [2007] EMLR 583.

[125] N. 76, above.

that 'the fact that [the applicant] is a child is in our view of greater significance then the judge thought' and that the 'position of an adult may be very different from that of a child'.[126] Crucially, the court expressed the view that:

> The law should indeed protect children from intrusive media attention, at any rate to the extent of holding that a child has a reasonable expectation that he or she will not be targeted in order to obtain photographs in a public place for publication which the person who took or procured the taking of the photographs knew would be objected to on behalf of the child.[127]

Thus *Murray* is significant and a welcome decision because the court expressly stated that the claimant's status as a 'child' was significant. However, the case is also disappointing because the court left open the possibility that a child's right to privacy may be waived by his or her parents. It asserted that:

> If the parents of a child courted publicity by procuring the publication of photographs of the child in order to promote their own interest, the position would or might be quite different from a case like this, where the parents have taken care to keep their children out of the public gaze.[128]

It is submitted that under no circumstances should a child's Article 8 ECHR rights be waived as a result of the behaviour of his or her parents. As noted above, the uncertainty created by this statement was also apparent in *Re Stedman*.[129]

To conclude, whilst Article 8 ECHR is engaged in these photograph cases, the European Court of Human Rights in *Reklos* did not give sufficient consideration to the question of whether children require a greater degree of protection, whereas the Court of Appeal in *Murray* held that greater protection may be necessary when the case concerns a child. However, worryingly, both the European Court of Human Rights, and the English courts, have left the rights of the child in the hands of the child's parents. In both *Reklos* and *Murray*, this was not problematic as the parents wanted to protect the privacy of the child, and given the age of the children involved this was probably desirable. However, problems could arise with older children if the child has different wishes to his or her parents. Thus, this reasoning does not sit well with Munby J's analysis in *Re Roddy*.[130] Moreover, it is submitted that in no circumstances should a child be denied a right to privacy on the ground that on previous occasions his or her parents have courted publicity. Given these ambiguities, further guidance from the European Court of Human Rights is desirable, as to the scope of, and weight to be afforded to, a child's right to privacy under Article 8 ECHR.

26.2.4 Publishing children's details on the internet

This is an area in which the European Court of Human Rights has offered strong protection to children's privacy. This is apparent in the case of *KU v Finland*.[131] KU was 12 years old when someone placed an advertisement on an internet dating site claiming that the boy was looking for an intimate relationship with a boy of his own age or older. The boy's father asked the police to identify the person who had placed the advertisement on the internet so that proceedings could be brought against him or her. The police asked the service provider to identify the person who had placed the advertisement, but the service provider refused to divulge that information, because

[126] N. 76, above, at [45] and [56].
[127] N. 76, above, at [57].
[128] N. 76, above, at [38].
[129] N. 89, above, at [46].
[130] N. 77, above.
[131] (App. no. 2872/02) (2009) 48 EHRR 52.

doing so would mean breaching confidentiality laws. The Finnish Court refused to order disclosure as there was no explicit legal provision authorizing such an order, and KU subsequently brought proceedings to the European Court of Human Rights.

The Court held that there was no question that Article 8 ECHR was engaged, and it emphasized the potential threat to the applicant's physical and mental welfare and in particular the vulnerability of children.[132] Moreover, the Court held that Article 8 ECHR had been violated. In considering the scope of Finland's positive obligations, and the margin of appreciation, the Court stressed the fact that the applicant was a minor and that the advertisement made him a target for paedophiles.[133] The Court also asserted that the state had a positive obligation to protect the child's physical and moral welfare by prohibiting such disclosures, and by having an effective criminal justice process.[134] Thus, the disclosure of children's details on the internet is one context in which the Court has offered greater protection to children than it would have done to adults.

26.2.5 Children and medical confidentiality

A crucial area in which the child's right to privacy has come up in litigation is in the context of medical confidentiality. A fundamental issue, which the courts have had to consider, is whether the child has a right to keep details of medical advice and treatment from his or her parents. The European Court of Human Rights has held that medical confidentiality is protected under Article 8 ECHR.[135] Similarly, the House of Lords in *Campbell v MGN* held that details of treatment for drug addiction were private.[136] Thus, there is a general rule that details of medical treatment and conditions will be protected by Article 8 ECHR. The question is whether children can rely upon this right.

The European Court of Human Rights has not considered this issue but it has been considered in domestic cases. In a pre-Human Rights Act 1998 case, *Gillick v West Norfolk and Wisbech Area Health Authority and the Department of Health and Social Security*, the House of Lords held that a doctor could lawfully prescribe contraception to a girl under 16 years of age, without the consent of her parents, if the girl was sufficiently mature to understand the nature and implications of the treatment.[137] This became known as *Gillick* competence. More recently, in *R (on the application of Axon) v Secretary of State for Health*, the claimant (a parent) sought judicial review of a Department of Health document advising health professionals on giving advice and treatment on sexual matters to people under the age of 16.[138] The claimant argued that a health professional should not be obliged to keep confidential details of medical advice and treatment, and that he or she should not provide such advice or treatment without the knowledge of the child's parents, unless the child's physical or mental health would be prejudiced. Alternatively, the claimant argued that, at the very least, advice relating to an abortion and the performance of an abortion should not occur without the knowledge of the child's parents, unless the child's physical or mental health would be prejudiced. The claimant also sought to

[132] N. 131, above, at [41].
[133] N. 131, above, at [45].
[134] N. 131, above, at [46].
[135] (App. no. 22009/93) [1997] ECHR 10, at [95].
[136] N. 3, above.
[137] [1986] AC 112.
[138] [2006] EWHC 37 (Admin), [2006] QB 539.

argue that this would violate parents' Article 8 ECHR rights to respect for family life. Silber J rejected the claimant's arguments. In doing so he asserted:

> The ECHR and the [CRC] show why the duty of confidence owed by a medical professional to a competent person is a high one and which therefore should not be overridden except for a powerful reason. In my view, although family factors are significant and cogent, they should not override the duty of confidentiality owed to the child. It must not be forgotten that this duty was described in *Z v Finland* (supra) as '*a vital principle in the legal system of all Contracting Parties to the Convention*'.
>
> Mr Havers [counsel for the claimant] points out that the claimant in that case was not a child but that is not a distinction of decisive or any great importance especially where the child is sufficiently mature to be able to understand the consequences of his or her decision. I am fortified in reaching that conclusion by the fact that in *Yousef v Netherlands* (2003) 36 EHRR 20, the European Court of Human Rights explained with emphasis added that in '*judicial decisions where the right under article 8 of parents and of a child are at stake, the child's rights* must *be the paramount consideration*' [73]. By parity of reasoning, I consider that the child's claim to confidentiality should not be overridden in the way which Mr Havers advocates.[139]

On the face of it this looks very promising for children; it is a strong assertion of the child's rights to medical confidentiality, and the fact that the child's parents' rights cannot override this. However as one scholar has noted, whilst the judge rejected the mother's claim, rights-based analysis was not fully applied when the court came to assessing the clash between the claimant's right and the rights of her children:

> But these comments were embedded in his analysis of the general principles of law applying to Sue Axon's application and were not developed when dealing with her Art 8 claims, In this later part of his judgment, he gave a variety of reasons for his view that the State could justify infringing her right to family life but made no real attempt to analyze the rights that her daughters themselves had under the European Convention. In many ways, Silber J's reasoning was very similar to that adopted in a host of family law cases involving a potential clash between the rights of parents and children. As pointed out elsewhere, in these cases, the judiciary only clearly analyze the rights that adults have and fail to articulate those of the children... The consequence of such an approach in the *Axon* case was that the learned judge reached a very important decision affecting the lives of teenage girls generally without clearly setting out and discussing the specific Convention rights they themselves had which might clash with their mother's rights.[140]

Thus, yet again we encounter an absence of rights-based reasoning, even in a case where the court was attuned to interests of children. Moreover, it is apparent that the lack of analysis of children's rights is not restricted to the Strasbourg jurisprudence.

26.3 Conclusion

Having considered a number of case studies we now need to draw the threads together. It should be apparent that judicial approaches to the child's right to privacy vary significantly depending upon the type of case. The strongest statements of the child's right are located in cases concerning criminal investigative

[139] N. 138, above, at [64]–[65]. See also [127].
[140] N. 12, above, 764.

measures, photographs, medical confidentiality, and the internet. A high degree of protection is afforded to photographs and medical confidentiality because these are interests which attract a high degree of protection in the adult context. There are only two cases in which the European Court of Human Rights has afforded greater protection to children than it has to adults. They are *S and Marper v UK* (the UK DNA database case), and *KU v Finland* (the case concerning the publication of a child's details on an internet dating website). In both of these cases the Court emphasized the vulnerability of children. In *S and Marper*, the Court suggested that whilst both adults and children's rights were affected by the DNA database, greater care needed to be taken when children were affected. In *KU v Finland*, the Court emphasized the danger that the internet posed as a means by which paedophiles could contact children. Thus in *KU* the Court afforded protection to a child, which it probably would not have protected in the adult context, and it is the only case in which the Strasbourg Court has protected what appears to be a child-specific privacy interest. The Court's analysis of children's needs in *S and Marper* and *KU* is significant; however, it is notable that both of these cases were cases where there was a well-recognized threat, and where children are readily perceived as vulnerable. Protection against those threats is crucial, but there is also a need for further consideration of the child's right to privacy in contexts where the harm is not so readily visible.

Yet in the majority of cases there has been little engagement with the question of whether children need further protection. In privacy cases relating to legal proceedings, a number of approaches have emerged: cases concerning the privacy of juveniles are dealt with under Article 6 ECHR; cases concerning the privacy rights of children indirectly affected by legal proceedings are considered under Article 8 ECHR; and cases concerning the privacy rights of children directly affected by custody proceedings have not been addressed under the remit of either right, but have simply been considered as a limit to the child's parent's/s' rights under Article 6 ECHR. There are some explanations for these differences in approach. Clearly, Article 6 ECHR is only relevant to cases directly concerned with legal proceedings, and thus it would not apply to children who are not participating in legal proceedings, but are indirectly affected by publicity given to those proceedings. In the cases where children are on trial they are afforded significant protection, albeit that this occurs under Article 6 ECHR, not Article 8 ECHR. In the other cases there has been no real consideration of children's needs. However, the problem is not the absence of Article 6 ECHR reasoning in these cases, but the absence of Article 8 ECHR reasoning in the child custody proceedings, and the lack of weight afforded to Article 8 ECHR in the cases where children are indirectly affected by publicity.

In the child custody proceedings cases, the Strasbourg Court has emphasized the importance of children's privacy in examining whether custody proceedings should be held in private, but the Court has not drawn upon the child's rights under Article 8 ECHR in this analysis. Instead, it has regarded the child's privacy interest, as an exception to, or somehow related to, Article 6 ECHR. As noted above, one explanation for the Court's failure to address Article 8 ECHR directly in these cases is that the Strasbourg Court focuses upon the rights of the applicant. This approach was critiqued on the ground that the Court has an obligation to interpret the Convention and to provide guidance to state parties faced with the task of reconciling competing rights. Moreover, there is a further critique, which is that even if it were acceptable to focus exclusively on the rights of the applicant, in one of these cases the child was an applicant and the Court still did not address this issue.[141]

It is important to acknowledge here that most cases are either going to be brought by parents acting in their own capacity, or by parents on behalf of their children. It is therefore imperative that the Court fully addresses the child's rights in cases where the child is not the applicant. The Court has done this in cases where the parent argues that taking the child into care breaches the parent's right to respect for family life. There are some inconsistencies in the jurisprudence, but it is nevertheless clear that the Court acknowledges and examines the child's right under Article 8 ECHR and that the parent's right cannot trump the child's right.[142] This alleviates one of the concerns of feminists that family privacy can be used as a shield. However, the child's right also needs to be considered when questions are raised about whether the proceedings should be held in private.

Turning to the other case studies, it is clear that Article 8 ECHR has a role in cases where children are indirectly affected by news stories about legal proceedings, and cases where children are the focus of news stories. However, the weight afforded to Article 8 ECHR varies significantly in these cases. In the cases where children are indirectly affected by publicity given to legal proceedings, the domestic courts have set a very high threshold before Article 8 ECHR will outweigh Article 10 ECHR: it must be established that the child will suffer 'irremediable or serious damage'. This threshold is set too high and it completely undermines Article 8 ECHR, contradicting the repeated assertions of the Strasbourg Court and the domestic courts that Article 8 and Article 10 ECHR are of equal status.[143]

Logically, greater weight has been afforded to Article 8 ECHR in cases where children are the subject of news stories. However, even in these cases we have yet to see

[141] In *Moser*, the mother brought the application on behalf of herself *and* her child, yet the child's interest in private proceedings was not addressed under Article 8 ECHR. To deal adequately with the question of whether the mother's rights and the child's rights were compatible, this issue needed to be expressly addressed.

[142] In *Johansen v Norway*, a case in which a child had been taken into care, the Court noted: 'a fair balance has to be struck between the interests of the child in remaining in public care and those of the parent in being reunited with the child. In carrying out this balancing exercise, the Court will attach particular importance to the best interests of the child, which, depending on their nature and seriousness, may override those of the parent. In particular, as suggested by the Government, the parent cannot be entitled under Article 8 of the Convention to have such measures taken as would harm the child's health and development.' (App. no. 17383/90) (1997) 23 EHRR 33, at [78]. Thus *Johansen* suggests that the child's welfare may trump the rights of the parents but that a fair balance must be struck between the competing interests, with the caveat that a parent cannot rely upon his or her rights where this would harm the child's health and development. A different approach emerged from the Court in *Yousef v Netherlands*, another child custody case: '[t]he court reiterates that in judicial decisions where the rights under art.8 of parents and those of a child are at stake, the child's rights must be the paramount consideration. If any balancing of interests is necessary, the interests of the child must prevail' (App. no. 33711/96) [2002] 3 FCR 577, at [73]. Thus, the Court afforded much more weight to the child's rights in *Yousef* compared to the balancing exercise that was envisaged in *Johansen*. However, some scholars have suggested that the *Johansen* case is the most consistent with the rest of the Convention jurisprudence: Sonia Harris-Short 'Family Law and the Human Rights Act 1998—Restraint or Revolution?' (2005) 17 *Child and Family Law Quarterly* 32, 35 and 37–8. For discussion see Sonia Harris-Short and Joanna Miles *Family Law: Text, Case and Materials* (Oxford University Press, Oxford, 2007), 621–5. For our purposes, it is worth noting that even under *Johansen* the rights of the parent are restricted by the child's health and development needs, and that a balancing exercise is envisaged. Thus the right to respect for family life does not act as a shield in the sense that is envisaged by some feminist critiques of family privacy.

[143] See *Campbell v MGN*, N. 3, above, at [111]. Council of Europe Parliamentary Assembly Resolution 'Resolution on the Right to Privacy' Resolution 1165 (1998) affirmed that Articles 8 and 10 ECHR 'are neither absolute nor in any hierarchical order, since they are of equal value'.

a strong statement of the child's right to privacy. In the Commission decision *A, Byrne and Twenty-Twenty Television* there was no discussion of the child's Article 8 ECHR right.[144] The domestic courts have addressed the child's rights under Article 8 ECHR, although it should be noted that in both *Re Roddy* and *Re Stedman and Patten*, the interference was justified.[145] This was probably appropriate because both cases also concerned the Article 10 ECHR rights of children: Angela (in *Re Roddy*) and Alfie (in *Re Stedman and Patten*). The right to freedom of expression is an important autonomy right too. Nevertheless, it will be interesting to see whether the courts will take a more robust approach to the child's Article 8 ECHR right in a case where the only Article 10 ECHR right engaged is the right of the press. There were some suggestions that this may be the case in *Murray v Big Pictures*, but that was a case concerning photographs, and as noted above photographs receive strong protection under Article 8 ECHR. A further problem which needs to be addressed is the troubling suggestion in *Re Stedman*, that a child may no longer be able to enforce his or her Article 8 ECHR right if the information is already in the public domain. This is not an appropriate approach to the right to privacy in general (the right to privacy is violated by repeated attention) and it is particularly problematic when children are involved where repeated publication could impact on their development.

What emerges from these case studies is that there is a lack of coherence in the analysis of the child's right to privacy. The first step in developing the child's right to privacy is to ensure that there is a clearer understanding of the applicability of Article 8 ECHR. Only once we have firmly established that Article 8 ECHR is engaged, will we be able to give proper consideration to the question of whether children require greater protection. As noted above, at present this question is only being addressed where there is a clearly identifiable harm (*S and Marper*, youth justice system and *KU v Finland*, threat posed by paedophiles on the internet). This is not sufficient: all invasions of privacy are inherently harmful, and further steps need to be taken to ensure that the child's right to privacy is fully developed.

Whilst perhaps only a few children's privacy cases are reaching the courts, there are a vast array of policies and measures which impact on the child's right to privacy, including the policy of fingerprinting children in schools, nursery and school webcams and CCTV technology, and the large number of databases that hold information on children.[146] The type of 'harm' that results from extensive surveillance and the collection of data is not nearly as visible as the forms of harm identified above; therefore a robust approach needs to be taken to Article 8 ECHR to ensure that children's rights are not neglected.

Finally, we have to consider whether there are child-specific, privacy-related interests which need protecting. One of the problems with children's rights is that children are rarely involved in the dialogue surrounding these rights. Unlike the feminist movement, the child law movement is rarely progressed by children themselves; it is adults' voices that dominate this movement, and adult's perceptions of children's interests:

> ... to challenge the adult view and allow different understandings to emerge, it is necessary, first to enable children to express their views and detail their experiences of, for example, the

[144] N. 74, above. [145] N. 77 and N. 89, above.

[146] For discussion of the comprehensive range of measures applied to children see: Information Commissioners Office *Protecting Children's Personal Information: ICO Issues Paper*; and Action on Rights for Children *Privacy Guide for Parents*.

law; and secondly, to ensure that analysis of what they have to say is not framed by understandings and expectations of children held by others.[147]

One way of overcoming this is to include children in policy-making, and in fact a number of law reform bodies have included studies of children's perceptions of, and desires for, privacy in their projects.[148] Further research of this nature is vital if the child's right to privacy is to be meaningful.

[147] N. 9, above, at 12.

[148] The Australian Law Reform Commission interviewed children and completed privacy workshops in schools as part of their privacy reform project. Australian Law Reform Commission 'For Your Information: Australian Privacy Law and Practice' (ALRC 108, Sydney, 2008). The University of Ottawa included a panel of children in its conference on privacy to discuss their uses and understanding of social networking sites on the internet: *Revealed I—a conference on privacy and identity*, University of Ottawa, Canada, 25–27 October 2007.

27

Foster Care Partnerships in Finland 1990–2010: From Social Task to Ensuring Better Market Share?

Petra Kouvonen[1]

27.1 Introduction

A common issue in the field of child welfare, as in other social services, is how to tailor services so that clients receive the most suitable form of care. All current legal regulations in use in the field of child welfare emphasize that measures for children deprived of care in their original families should be free of discrimination, which might be seen as a presumption of the right of each child to receive equal care.[2] Equality in care might be interpreted in two senses: as care being equally available to all children and as care being individually suitable. Equal care for all children in both these senses is however not always self-evident, especially if a service field has gone through structural changes as will be discussed in this chapter, using the Finnish foster care field as a case. In the chapter foster care will be the concept used to discuss all non-institutional substitute care for children placed outside their homes. Thus the definition includes foster care provided by private households or private companies.

Basically two problems regarding the right of all children to receive suitable care stand out in the current field of child welfare in Finland. The first obstacle in the service chain is the overall rapid increase in the number of child welfare cases, which has doubled since the economic recession in the early 1990s. A total of 16,608 children are currently placed outside their homes (2008), compared to some 8000 cases then. The percentage of children placed outside their homes is over one per cent of the Finnish population under the age of 18. In the capital area the percentage is 2.3.[3] An outstanding trend throughout the country has been the strong increase in young people aged 12–15 placed outside their homes. This group of teenagers today represents 55 per cent of all out-of-home placements,[4] which is some 20 per cent more than 20 years ago. This cohort can be seen as one of the most fundamental challenges for the Finnish child welfare system in recent years. The group has introduced new

[1] Nordic Centre for Welfare and Social Issues.

[2] UN Convention on the Rights of the Child § 2; Finnish Act on Child Welfare § 8.

[3] <http://www.stakes.fi/EN/tilastot> [accessed 26 October 2010].

[4] Tarja Heino, 'Lastensuojelun tilastot, asiakkaat ja palvelut' in (ed.) Marjatta Bardy, *Lastensuojelun ytimessä* (Helsinki, 2009), 59.

types of problems into the field, which the system has often failed to respond to.[5] The second set of problems in current Finnish child welfare that are related to equality in care are the large regional differences in type and organization of services across the country.[6] This is probably most visible in the role institutional care takes in relation to other forms of substitute care. The number of institutional places has increased fast. Today 84 per cent of all places are institutional. Most of these places are produced by non-public service providers.[7]

All of the above-mentioned problems are signs of a dysfunctional service chain, where demand and supply often fail to meet. A new feature introduced aiming more effectively to meet current needs in social services in Finland and elsewhere has been to strengthen the role of non-governmental service providers, civil society, and its citizens. This process has led to the appearance of new *partnerships* including a mixture of public, private, and third-sector-driven service providers.[8] By decentralizing of power and compensation from rigid hierarchical structures partnerships are on such occasions seen as providing a solution for a number of problems, such as changes in client constellations or arbitrary service provision.[9] Rod Rhodes[10] speaks of self-organizing, interorganizational networks, where State power is being exerted through plural institutions in a dispersed system of power. The process has been highly visible in the field of Finnish foster care. An upsurge of new partnership constellations, including outsourced service providers have been put in action since the early 1990s to tackle obstacles in the service chain.[11] The promise to meet current needs, however, does not seem to have been fulfilled in light of the obstacles still present, as explained above.

At the national level partnerships were first introduced through the 'valtionosuusuudistus' reform in early 1990s. The municipalities, responsible for organizing services such as child welfare, played a key role in the implementation of the reform, commonly known as New Public Management.[12] Municipalities were at the same time given more freedom to involve other actors in the provision of child welfare and other similar social services while their responsibility for organization and supervision also increased. Secondly, the base for State funding became more closely connected to the municipalities' own abilities to raise funds, and public saving was encouraged.[13] Simultaneously, at the international level, procuration was introduced as a means to promote free competition and equal opportunities through the adoption of the European Trade Agreement (ETA) and the Act on Public Procurement (1505/1992). These national and international reforms replaced the welfare-based financing policy where funds for welfare services were earmarked for certain purposes by State

[5] Tarja Heino and Marjanne Johnson, 'Huostassa olleet lapset nuorina aikuisina' in (eds.) Ulla Hämäläinen and Olli Kangas, *Perhepiirissä* (Helsinki, 2010), 285.

[6] Ministry of Social Affairs and Health/Memorandum, 2006: 25.

[7] <http://www.stakes.fi/EN/tilastot> [accessed 26 October 2010].

[8] Janet Newman and John Clarke, *Publics, Politics & Power. Remaking the Public in Public Services* (London, 2009), 2–3.

[9] M. Daly, 'Governance and Social Policy' (2003) 32:1 *Journal of Social Policy* 116.

[10] R.A.W Rhodes, 'The New Governance: Governance without Government' (1996) 44(4) *Political Studies* 660.

[11] Ministry of Social Affairs and Health/Working Group Memorandum, 2003:11

[12] Michael Power, *The Audit Society* (Oxford, 1997).

[13] Raija Julkunen, *Suunnanmuutos. 1990-luvun Sosiaalipoliittinen reformi Suomessa* (Helsinki, 2001), 117–19.

authorities[14] and introduced a market environment in which 'independent' and presumably 'equal' service providers could operate. The role of municipalities changed from service providers to mainly service purchasers.[15] At the same time those providing services increasingly became competing actors, looking for ways to convince municipalities of their competencies, with the aim of entering successful partnerships with them. These new duties involved entirely new tasks for the service providers. The process in which these tasks were added to the field of child welfare has not yet been studied in a Finnish context. This chapter endeavours to fill that gap.

The dissatisfaction with the abilities of partnerships to meet social demands is not an isolated phenomenon. In other countries where reforms have been carried out, great dissatisfaction with the ability of the new partnerships to provide better and more targeted services has been revealed.[16] In light of this criticism it seems that the promises of the new partnerships in the field of child welfare are highly contentious, but identifying this controversy has contributed only a little to the understanding of *why* a gap between the rhetoric of inclusiveness and practices of exclusion seems to be present.[17] In order to tackle this question the present chapter looks into the changed positions of stakeholders in the field of foster care in the forming of partnerships. The more precise question addressed is to what extent representatives of foster care are able to work in partnerships from a 'social' perspective, e.g. by responding to obstacles in care, when new needs produced by the market seem to have become increasingly important for their survival. The approach adopted here follows Ian Mc Donald's[18] suggestion to look at partnerships as forms of social actions offering different possibilities for freedom and constraint by those who implement them. He claims that such an approach contributes to a better understanding of values, meanings, and power relations attached to partnership activity.

The assumption that guides the writing in this chapter is that the emergence of partnerships, when approached from the point of view of the partners themselves, in fact might be explained by reasons other than any formal goal, such as providing access to more equal and suitable care, for example.[19] Previous studies in the field of public choice have argued that bureaucrats often act more in order to maintain their positions than according to the demands placed upon them, when new initiatives are introduced.[20] Competition between different forms of services in a certain field might then often lead to the adaption of strategies and organizational design of other partners without necessarily making them more efficient.[21] Whether such an

[14] Markku Salo and Mari Kallinen, *Yhteisasumisesta yhteiskuntaan. Mielenterveyskuntoutujien asumispalveluiden tila ja tulevaisuus* (Pori, 2007).

[15] Briitta Koskiaho, *Hyvinvointipalvelujen tavaratalossa* (Tampere, 2008), 26–8.

[16] I. McDonald, 'Theorising Partnerships: Governance, Communicative Action and Sport Policy' (2005) 34 *Journal of Social Policy* 581; J. Newman, M. Barnes, H. Sullivan, and A. Knops, 'Public Participation and Collaborative Governance' (2004) 33 *Journal of Social Policy* 213–17; K. Rummary, 'Towards a Theory of Welfare Partnerships' in (eds.) Caroline Glendinning, Michael Powell, and Kirstein Rummery, *Partnerships, New Labour and the Governance of Welfare* (Bristol, 2002), 229–45.

[17] McDonald, N. 16, above, 581–2.

[18] McDonald, N. 16, above, 596

[19] Julia Elyachar, *Markets of disposessions. NGO's, Economic Development and the State in Cairo* (Durham, NC, 2005); Pernille Hohnen, *A Market Out of Place? Remaking Economic, Social and Symbolic Boundaries in Lithuania* (Oxford, 2003).

[20] Patrick Dunleavy, *Democracy, Bureaucracy and Public Choice. Economic Explanations in Political Science* (Exeter, 1991), 211–13.

[21] Paul J. Di Maggio and Walter W. Powell, *The New Institutionalism in Organizational Analysis* (Chicago, 1991), 63–4.

assumption holds true in the field of Finnish foster care will be approached in what follows.

Theoretically, partnerships are in this chapter regarded as a form of governance where partners, on the one hand, are made willing to act in accordance with new requirements introduced by policy requiring flexibility, networking, and self regulation,[22] but on the other, are active subjects in interpreting and making use of the demands placed at them. The empirical cases presented here look into the argumentation of two interest groups active in this field: the Professional Foster Care Association (PFA) and Finnish Federation of Foster Care Associations (FFC). The first is closely connected to public service distribution by representing service providers who work on commission for the local municipalities, while the other represents private service providers, who sell services to the municipalities. The research material from the associations consists of policy documents, chronicles, professional magazines, and interviews with stakeholders in the field. I use the concept of *translation*, introduced by Bruno Latour,[23] in interpreting the process of action, where the partners make use of previous knowledge and habits in acting and also simultaneously absorb new expectations held of them.[24] The form that action takes in partnerships is the result of a translation, in which the actors attempt to transform themselves in relation to both new and old sets of requirements.

27.2 Governing by partnerships

The Finnish foster care field today represents what is usually called a quasi market. This means that it involves elements of rigid hierarchical public service provision combined with the involvement of an expanding market of private service providers.[25] In Foucauldian terms[26] the mix can be visualized as a process in the manner of a shepherd who knows what is in the best interest of his flock, i.e. a pastoral form of governance has been partly replaced by collective forms of governance, such as partnerships, contracts, and mechanisms of empowerment.[27] The pastoral form of governing, that to a great extent was present in the welfare state, has in many cases today lost its legitimacy and has opened up ways for negotiated forms of power, where steering through partnerships replaces ordering and intervention by command.[28] At the same time, duties have become a shared issue. Governing practices that work in

[22] Mitchell Dean, *Governmentality. Power and Rule in Modern Society* (London, 1999); Nikolas Rose, *Powers of Freedom. Reframing Political Thought* (Cambridge, 1999); Ilpo Helén, 'Hyvinvointi, vapaus ja elämän politiikka. Foucault'lainen hallinnan analytiikka' in (eds.) Jani Kaisto and Miikka Pyykkönen Hallintavalta, *Sosiaalisen, politiikan ja talouden kysymyksiä* (Helsinki, 2010), 27–48.

[23] Bruno Latour, *The Pasteurisation of France* (Cambridge, 1988); Bruno Latour, 'Ethnography of Hightec: About the Aramis Case' in (ed.) Pierre Lemonnier, *Technological Choices: Transformation in Material Cultures since the Neolithic* (New York, 1993); Bruno Latour, *Reassembling the Social. An introduction to Action-Network-Theory* (Oxford, 2005).

[24] Jani Kaisto, 'Kääntämisen sosiologia hallinnan analytiikan työkaluna' in (eds.) Jani Kaisto and Miikka Pyykkönen Hallintavalta, *Sosiaalisen, politiikan ja talouden kysymyksiä* (Helsinki, 2010), 49–71.

[25] Tom Christensen and Per Laegrid, *New Public Management—The Transformation of Ideas and Practice* (Aldershot, Ashgate, 2001).

[26] Mitchell Dean, *Governmentality. Power and Rule in Modern Society* (London, 1999), 83.

[27] Kati Rantala and Pekka Sulkunen, *Projektiyhteiskunnan kääntöpuolia* (Helsinki, 2003), 480.

[28] Pekka Sulkunen, *The Saturated Society: Regulating Lifestyles in Consumer Capitalism* (Helsinki, 2010).

ways where the subject is made willing to act through negotiation is what Foucault[29] calls 'conduct of conduct'. In this chapter we can even talk of *conduct of conduct of conducts*, since the demands placed upon those who represent services in the field are the target of current governing practices.

Adopting governing practices where partnerships and collaboration are introduced as means to provide suitable care does not mean that other governing practices are abandoned.[30] Several forms of governing practices, including pastoral power, present in more hierarchical service provision within the welfare state, often overlap each other in the new order.[31] Tension that might be caused by such overlapping is visible in the current Finnish child welfare market, where the actors involved in partnerships must manage old sets of rules as well as be flexible in adapting to new requirements when they appear, in addition to carrying out their primary duty of ensuring quality in care. These 'new' requirements are seen here as being caused by an extensive decentralization of duties that seems to push partners into competition for market share. Such competition brings in new demands. On top of the old sets of social requirements, such as providing suitable care, the actors might have to refashion their positions in order to survive. Partnerships might then be used to maintain or shape market positions. Stakeholders, such as the interest organizations focused on here, play a key role together with municipalities in the making of these partnerships, as will be outlined in what follows.

27.3 Partnerships in Finnish foster care

In the case of legally regulated partnerships, municipalities still have the main responsibility for organizing foster care and other child welfare services in Finland, as before. Thus the State through its connection with the municipalities is involved in all measures taken when children are placed outside their homes.[32] This relationship has, however, changed recently as municipalities increasingly have had to manage the planning and procuration of services while the service providers have had to prove that they are trustworthy partners. The most visible recent change in the relationship between municipalities and service producers in the field of foster care has occurred due to a gradual transition towards *purchase agreements* between private entrepreneurs, such as Professional Foster Homes, and the municipalities, since the early 1990s. The transition towards foster care provided on the basis of purchase agreements has occurred partly at the expense of traditional forms of foster care partnerships where the care is not bought, but instead private households work *on commission* for the municipalities. Partnerships based on commission can be seen as part of the provision of public services.

Generally, the costs of care varies widely in child welfare. Costs for the kind of care offered by the FFC, namely foster care based on commission, has remained at some €400 per month for one child,[33] while the transactional costs for the municipalities

[29] Michel Foucault, *Seksualisuuden historia: tiedontahto, nautintojen käyttö, huoli itsestäsi*. Original texts: 1976, 1984. Transl. Kaisa Sivenius (Helsinki, 1998).

[30] J. Newman, M. Barnes, H. Sullivan, and A. Knops, 'Public Participation and Collaborative Governance' (2004) 33 *Journal of Social Policy* 213–17.

[31] N. 25, above, 20–1.

[32] Virge Mikkola, *Lastensuojelu Euroopassa ja Venäjällä* (Helsinki, 2008).

[33] According to the most recent changes in the Family Care Act (948/2006) the fee for private households is, after index adjustments in 2009 at a minimum 336, €41 per month per child for foster parents

for work performed according to purchase agreements, as in the case of the PFA, are approximately €150 per child per day, which means approximately €4500 per month. Paradoxically, a continuous increase in partnerships between municipalities and private service producers has occurred despite the high transactional costs for municipalities. This has resulted in an upsurge of new private companies and an increasing number of children placed in these units. The number of children placed in Professional Foster Homes was 3159 in 2008,[34] four times higher than in the mid-1990s. The number of children placed in private households as part of the public distribution within the municipality was 5486 in 2008. Although this number still exceeds that for children placed by private companies, the amount did however increase only slightly in the 1990s and has thereafter remained the same with even a decline since 2002.[35]

This declining trend in the use of publicly provided foster care represented by the FFC that has taken place despite the low costs, points at obstacles to committing to partnerships for such service provision, especially when private service providers have increasingly managed to commit to such partnerships with municipalities at the same time. Several reasons may explain why municipalities might prefer partnerships with expensive service providers, such as Professional Foster Homes, rather than continue networking with local foster homes, which are part of the public service provision. A common explanation is the lack of private households among service providers. Another explanation, particularly focused on in this chapter, but seldom touched upon, is the changed market situation in which the service provider, representing private households, remains in an uneven market position compared to private companies. Households working for the municipalities are, for instance, only able to sell services to their local municipality, which limits their market.[36] Private companies, on the other hand, might offer their services all over the country. In practice this means that private companies such as Professional Foster Homes might have children from different regions living in their units, while publicly provided foster care in households might only provide care to children from a local municipality.

The concern for diminishing foster care provided by private families has been addressed nationally in the government programme of Prime Minister Matti Vanhanen in 2007, but without any significant effect on activating municipalities to produce new partnerships with local households. The rapid outsourcing of services has only slowly affected national policy making, although the Concluding Observations of the Committee on the Rights of the Child sent to Finland in 1996 and 2000[37] have remarked on the question as well. According to the Committee, the problem in the Finnish foster care market does not concern only the increased use of private companies, but rather the whole chain of decentralization, where duties of the State have been devolved to the municipalities, which then further have been obliged

who work outside their homes. For full-time foster parents the fee might be higher. The minimum fee for expenses is €375.08 per month and child according to the index adjustments in 2009.

[34] <http://www.stakes.fi/tilastot/tilastotiedotteet/2010/Tr29_10.pdf> [accessed 26 October 2010].

[35] Tarja Heino, 'Lastensuojelun tilastot, asiakkaat ja palvelut' in (ed.) Marjatta Bardy, *Lastensuojelun ytimessä* (Helsinki, 2009), 55–6.

[36] Jari Ketola,'Perhehoito ennen ja nyt' in (ed.) Jari Ketola, *Perhehoito. Tekemisen ja tukemisen arvoista työtä* (Juva, 2008), 32.

[37] Concluding Observations of the Committee on the Rights of the Child, Finland (CRC/C/15/Add. 53/1996 and CRC/C/15/Add. 132/2000): <http://formin.finland.fi/public/default.aspx?contentId=68142andnodeId=31460> [accessed 1 March 2010].

to outsource services. The process of outsourcing occurred in Finland hand in hand with the economic recession that took place in the early 1990s, when the number of child welfare cases also grew.[38] The resources of many municipalities for child welfare thus remained scarce when problems increased and outsourcing gave local actors greater responsibility for services. These actors not only acquired new duties, but increasingly new and more severe problems to manage as well.

Elsewhere I have argued that new fundamental governing practices in such a demanding area as child welfare might ultimately lead to demands for stricter control, when practices underlining the autonomy of its subjects fail in their aims. Often this failure occurs in situations where the problems turn out to be too severe to be solved by practices that emphasize the agency of its subjects.[39] In the service field such risks might be present since the gap between service planning and provision has become wider at the same time as child welfare cases seem to have become not only more numerous, but also representative of more severe problems. Added to these demands are the new duties, for instance handling the 'market', that seem to have been introduced in addition to 'social' demands such as providing services tailored to the current clientele in foster care. This analysis will therefore look at the adjustments that have taken place among two representatives of foster care, in attempting to respond to these multiple requirements.

27.4 Materials and method

The material used here consists of data on two associations: the above-mentioned PFA and the FFC. The associations act for two different service providers. As outlined the PFA represents private companies which sell their services to municipalities while the FFC is the interest group for traditional foster care provided on commission by private households.

The documentation used as data are: policy documents, chronicles, professional magazines (26 issues),[40] and seven expert interviews. A total of 716 pages (371 for FPA and 345 for FFC) were included in the analysis. The chapters picked out from the FFC chronicle include detailed descriptions of the association from its founding in 1983 to today, while the PFA, established in its present form in the first half of the 1990s, has summarized its history in the 1/2002 issue of its professional magazine named '*Amppeli*'. The limited historical description of the latter has for this chapter been complemented by including other issues of *Amppeli* in the analysis, that go back to the introduction of the magazine in 1999. Expert interviews and policy documents were used as background and were not analysed in detail. The expert interviews often provide new information and also an opportunity to dig deeper into relevant sources.[41] I therefore used written sources mentioned in the interviews to validate the relevance of the information that I gained from the interviews. The first

[38] Hannele Sauli, 'Lasten ja lapsiperheiden toimeentulo' in (eds.) Leena Kartovaara and Hannele Sauli, *Suomalainen lapsi* (Helsinki, 2007), 269–86.

[39] Petra Kouvonen, 'Vulnerable, Guilty or on their Own? Institutional Identities of Substance Abusing Children and Families within Finnish Child Welfare' (2009) 26(6) *Nordic Studies on Alcohol and Drugs* 483–503.

[40] 12 issues of the magazine *Perheboito* (2008–2010) and 22 issues of the magazine *Amppeli* (1999–2009).

[41] Alexander Bogner, Beate Littig, and Wolfgang Menz, *Interviewing Experts* (London, 2009).

expert interview took place in May 2008, the last in April 2010. The two years spent on the study made it possible to make use of information from the first interview and follow it up in the succeeding years.

The analysis was done in two stages. First, all articles or material in which *descriptions of networking or other collaboration* between the interest groups and other actors, were selected. The first stage resulted in 256 pages of such data (151 for the PFA and 105 for the FFC). The texts were read two to three times before moving on to the next stage, where excerpts in which partnerships were discussed explicitly *as a means to overcome difficulties in the field, i.e. provide suitable services or improve the market position* were also selected. This stage resulted in 493 excerpts (210 from the PFA and 283 from the FFC).

In the second stage the excerpts were analysed according to the meanings that the partnerships were given by the authors. Attention was thus paid to the argumentation and positions taken by those in the field rather than to investigating how things actually were. To explore the perspective taken I have examined the selected excerpts picked out in a narrative way by using social semiotics.[42] The enunciative modalities are a dimension in the social semiotics, where a description of reality is described from a certain perspective, in which the 'speaker' wants to approach an imaginary audience, called the 'reader'. The speaker, in this chapter being mostly the writers in the professional magazines, often tells a story about current challenges in the field of foster care for the audience, which in this case is primarily the readers of these magazines. Such stories of 'how things are' are a form of enunciative modalities named veridictory modality. After the challenge has been presented, the speaker might switch over to telling how the challenge 'should be' interpreted. The presentation of the solution or right answer in such cases is called the epistemic modality.[43] I found the semiotic approach fruitful since the situation where partnerships are established is based on the position interest groups take with respect to each other. In the process, convincing and negotiating are often used as a means of gaining access to or sometimes avoiding new partnership constellations.

Finally, I use the concept of translation to interpret the views expressed in the texts. The concept was originally introduced by Bruno Latour in connection with his Action-Network-Theory (ANT).[44] According to Latour translation is a way to explore innovators' attempts to create a network in which all the actors agree that the network is worth building and defending. In this chapter the interest lies in the making of partnerships as a sort of network. Here attention is paid to whether the network or partnership is used in order to respond to obstacles in the service chain or whether the remaking of partnerships is instead guided by other aims, such as defending market share. The process of meaning-making is a dynamic one, which makes the ANT well suited for exploring different kinds of negotiated power.[45] In what follows the results of such meaning-making will be explored, first by looking into the main approaches towards partnerships present here in the data and, secondly, by looking more closely at the two interest groups studied in the chapter.

[42] Pekka Sulkunen and Jukka Törrönen, *Semioottisen sosiologian näkökulmia. Sosiaalisen todellisuuden rakentuminen ja ymmärrettävyys* (Helsinki, 1997), 99.

[43] N. 42, above, 113–18.

[44] Latour, *Resembling the Social*, N. 23, above.

[45] N. 24, above, 50–3.

27.5 Three approaches to partnerships

Three main responses to the new governing practices were found in the data when analysed in the first stage. The two first approaches were related to what could be interpreted as ways of preserving or gaining new positions in the field of foster care, for example by defending market share. The last approach to partnerships was more explicitly used in terms of defending social rights, such as provision of equal access to suitable care.

External cooperation. Partnerships were first discussed from a perspective that I call *external cooperation*. In this approach the need for networking with public authorities, such as the municipalities, Ministry of Social Affairs and Health and State Provincial Office, responsible for the supervision of foster care services, was touched upon by the speakers in the texts. Often partnerships in the sense of external cooperation seemed to be a means by which misunderstandings or gaps in the communication with authorities was avoided. The situations were connected to the establishment of a formal position for the service providers and their interest organizations.

Internal cooperation. The second perspective on partnerships, also closely linked to the formal positions in the foster care market, was to view partnerships as channels for shaping and promoting a group's image in and between member associations. I call this approach *internal cooperation*. Such cooperation meant for instance that an association would have introduced mutual quality standards. Both associations studied in this chapter work as interest organizations for service providers and networking in and between actors can therefore be seen as one of their core activities. Internal cooperation, when explicitly emphasized, can however become essential for many reasons due to the changing environment and the contradicting demands placed on the service providers and their representatives. Often internal and external networking also went hand in hand. An internal consensus regarding issues such as introduction of quality standards was thus often a way to establish sustainable external partnerships with representatives from the public authorities. The quality standards internally agreed upon then also served as a channel to be accepted as an official partner by the authorities.

Cooperation with social aims. Thirdly and finally, partnerships were approached as a way to provide equal care for children in relation to access and suitability, which might be regarded as meanings that came closest to the original purpose or promise of introducing a differentiated policy in order to meet social needs more effectively. For this reason I call this approach *cooperation with social aims*. Since the challenge in the case of better service matching in the Finnish child welfare context increasingly has been to find suitable out-of-home placement for young people aged 15–17,[46] partnerships in such statements in the data were primarily seen as a means of closing the current gaps in the distribution of service for this group. Cooperation with social aims was also visible in the material depicting discussions about regional inequalities in the provision of services. Both these questions regarding common obstacles in the Finnish foster care service chain were however underrepresented in the data compared to approaches more concerned with defending the formal positions of the member units through external or internal cooperation.

[46] N 34, above, 57.

The overall activity surrounding the issue of partnerships as part of the organization or production of services was highly visible. The number of excerpts in which partnerships were discussed as part of foster care totalled 493. However, the meanings attached to partnerships varied widely. In only 99 excerpts were partnerships explicitly approached with social aims, while 394 excerpts dealt with the stance the service providers took regarding the new order, as well as their market position. Although social aims, such as better service matches, were probably part of the reason why the external and internal cooperation was emphasized, such aims were most often displaced by aims more concerned with problems related to the role of the service provider in relation to others. In relation to each other the organizations also differed regarding how partnerships were interpreted. However, the differences were not very clear in terms of numbers and pointed to similar adjustments with most meanings attached to maintaining or establishing *external cooperation* (PFA/103, FFC/130). Partnerships in the sense of *internal cooperation* were the second most prevalent meaning visible (PFA/83, FFC/78). In the 99 excerpts where *cooperation with social aims* such as equal access to suitable care was touched upon, the FFC data included 75 such discussions while only 24 were found in the PFA data. The main approaches presented above consequently reveal that most argumentations seemed to be attached to work aimed at strengthening the formal and informal positions of the interest groups. Social questions such as obstacles in access or suitability of care were clearly in a minority.

In what follows the question of how the underrepresentation of excerpts dealing explicitly with social aims should be interpreted will be examined in more detail. Both associations are presented separately from the perspective of their adjustments in the field. The approaches presented above are often overlapping in the data and are dynamic in the sense that the meanings might change over time and in relation to the context. The following presentation proceeds in a narrative way, starting with a look at the perception of current challenges caused by a policy that stresses collaboration between partners and then moves on to a presentation of possible new positions in partnerships that seem to have emerged in line with new demands. The enunciative modalities of social semiotics are used to highlight such changes in the positions taken by the interest groups.

27.6 The Finnish Federation of Foster Care Associations (FFC): translating demands into new structures

The FFC works to secure a high standard of home-based care for children, the disabled, the elderly, and the chronic ill. The FFC receives most of its funding from Finland's Slot Machine Association (RAY), which raises funds through gambling operations to support Finnish health and welfare organizations. The FFC was established in 1983 and works as an umbrella for 25 membership organizations, with a total of 3700 members. The adoption of the Family Care Act in 1992 was the first step in recognizing foster care in private homes as an official service provision.[47] In relation to foster care for children and young people placed outside their home, the FFC has since its establishment worked for the right of all children to grow up in a family-like environment. According to the FFC the family setting is the most natural

[47] Leea Markkanen, *Perhehoidon tukena 20 vuotta. Perhehoitoliiton historiikki* (Jyväskylä, 2003).

environment for children to grow up in, since it makes the establishment of stable relationships possible. The federation underlines that foster care in private households is basically non-commercial in character. The task of fostering is therefore seen as more of a mission than as a matter of working duty.[48]

In the data analysed from the FFC external cooperation is the most prevalent meaning attached to partnerships. Internal support systems probably function well within the organization, which might explain why partnerships are less mentioned as a means to internal cooperation. The internal strategies within the association seems however to have had to react to such external factors as the social challenge of changes in clientele, where small children often have been replaced by teenagers. The following quote where the current head of the association interprets the aims of the association and its member organizations in the following way illuminates the issue:

The smaller the child is, the more important it is that it is a usual family. One of our slogans is 'Ordinary families and special tasks'. The slogan could today be the other way around as well, being then 'special families and ordinary tasks'... in a way that describes that the work is specific and special (Chair of the FFC, Interview/February 2010).

The quote above underlines some of the ambivalences and challenges currently faced by the FFC in achieving mutual understanding within internal partnerships. The emphasis on specific groups in child welfare has so far been on small children. For the most part, the families have committed themselves to taking in foster children, which underlines that the task is not comparable to professional work and also why the families can be seen as 'ordinary'. Today the fostering of children does, however, according to the speaker increasingly call for certain requirements. This means full-time work and specialization, which is not how it was.[49] This kind of argumentation of contesting views, is a typical example of enunctiative modality structures that appear in situations where new interpretations of a phenomenon, such as changes in clientele, appear.[50] The speaker compares different kinds of interpretations and possible solutions in the new situation. Here it is the care of demanding teenagers that has forced the association to think that the supply of services might need to include a more varied set of families, including those families with specialized competences. The double meaning of the slogan above refers to revised views. From the perspective of governance, it seems then that the association stands open to self evaluation and possible internal changes in response to the new clientele.

Reactions toward reforms that have taken place in the remaking of the public sector were also strongly visible in the data. The lack of support from authorities was for instance a continuously discussed matter in the FFC when the decline in foster care provided by its member units was touched upon. The most common explanation for the situation in the debate has been that an increase in family-based care is not possible since: 'not enough families are available and the children are too traumatized to be cared for in families'. The FFC has refused to accept this argument, as can be seen in the following quote:

I or the association have never been convinced by that argument. If no family care providers are recruited, educated and supported systematically, there cannot be new ones coming in at once. And if children in need of foster placement are not taken into custody in time, reparating their damage requires so many multi-professional skills that ordinary families are unable to provide such help. (Chair of the FFC, Perhehoito 01/2008, 5)

[48] N 35, above, 41–2. [49] N 35, above, 41. [50] N 42, above, 43–4.

The speaker above, being the FFC chair, explains by the use of veridictory modality how things currently are in relation to the cooperation between local foster families and municipalities. The speaker does not recognize the argument that the producers of family-based foster care should just accept the current situation, in which children come late into care, by continuing as partners with the municipalities without getting anything in exchange. Partnerships in the form of multi-professional work are not seen as an attractive alternative, which might reflect that the quote is from 2008. Those working in the field were at the time well aware of the problems caused by the reform of the public sector. The establishment of multi-professional teams had since the early 1990s been viewed as a solution to all types of obstacles in social services. The speaker in the quote wants to point out that local partnerships within the municipality, if including proper education and support from municipalities, in fact could serve as an alternative to multi professional teams needed when problems are very serious. At the time the statement was made such support seems to be absent however, according to the speaker. This has caused a decline in families willing to commit to partnerships with municipalities. Another problem in the partnership between municipalities and family-based foster care touched upon in the data was that the actors were seen as having unequal opportunities to influence decision making within social services. Hierarchical power mechanisms were seen as highly present in the partnerships, as the following quote describes:

For maintaining its (social work) duty it has to fulfill its control function AND provide family-based foster care as part of social work… one might wonder then how far teamwork might be improved under such circumstances. Active involvement in a team would mean that all members would have the same degree of formal power. (Article in Perhehoito: tekemisen ja tukemisen arvoista työtä, 2008, 161–162)

Municipal social work as the organizer of foster care is in this quote seen as 'sitting on two chairs'. Municipalities control the procuration and select services, but they also have the duty to provide qualitatively good foster care. The example points to obstacles that may arise in external partnerships where two different systems working according to different power mechanisms are present.[51] Partnerships are then introduced as a means to avoid rigid hierarchical structures and provide social services more smoothly. On the other hand, the system also seems to work according to a hierarchical structure that seems to prevent the realization of social tasks. The service providers might feel powerless and frustrated over the work performed in such partnerships. This is also evident in the quote below, where the lack of equal opportunities to influence the work is made explicit:

At its best those in social work are aware of the contradictions in the field that are caused by the different courses of action required in bureaucratic and multi professional work and try to minimize the disadvantages that appear. The family-based foster care provider should have a special position in the team, which should be based on detailed knowledge of the one she/he provides care to. (Perhehoito, 2/2008, 6–7)

In this quote the speaker explains that work in partnerships might be accepted if those providing family-based foster care are treated as equal partners. Networks might in such cases be useful, but only if equal opportunities means something in practice. Thus, the speaker is not translating the requirements of cooperation as such, but rather the meaning of partnerships by remaking the circumstances under which

[51] N 26, above, 20–1.

such cooperation might work. The speaker is emphasizing a clearer division of labour in multi professional networks. As well, previous research has shown that an unclear division of labour causes a great deal of frustration in social work performed by multi professional teams.[52] An explanation of such frustration is that the expectations to provide better care might be buried under a 'searching' for right solutions instead of actually doing anything concrete to tackle the problems.[53] The partnerships' inability to solve the problems they encounter was also visible in the data. This might explain why partnerships mostly were discussed in connection with other than social aims, such as access to suitable care. Finding qualitatively good care for all children was simply often considered impossible under the current circumstances. Partnerships were considered a possible solution to good care, but apart from structural changes, changes in attitudes were also considered necessary if a better match in care was to be achieved.

Overall governing through partnerships in its current form seemed to present a dilemma to representatives of family-based foster care. These representatives appear dissatisfied with the situation in which their member families are expected to take care of children who are offered societal support at a late stage and therefore often suffer from severe problems. At the same time, support from the public authorities is meagre. Partnerships as such are not turned down as a solution, but the external partnerships with authorities would require a mutual commitment, that today is often lacking. Partnerships, when discussed in the FFC, therefore mean adapting only up to a certain stage. Reform is considered necessary for future qualitative work and, for example, opportunities to provide equal access to suitable care. These developments have in practice led the FFC to consider partnerships with new non-public actors who could take over the work of the social sector, as can be seen from a quote taken from an article in the FFC chronicle:

. . . it is also an honest question to ask if it is possible to overcome the structural problems in relation to the power relations, expertise, monopolies on knowledge, support and control of social work. Would we need other compensating structures, besides family care organized by social work, that could take over the duties of family-based foster care organized by social work? (Article in Perhehoito, tekemisen ja tukemisen arvoista työtä, 162)

The speaker here, being an FFC expert, is not only explaining how things are but is providing a solution to the situation. The speaker's expertise becomes visible by the use of epistemic modality.[54] Similar views expressed by the interest organization have recently also influenced policy making in practice. A new regime, including the relevant actors, that would take over duties from the municipalities, has recently been suggested in the working group recommendation on reform needs concerning legislation on family care from the Ministry of Social Affairs and Health.[55] Some non-public actors, such as *Perhehoitokumppanit*, a private company working under the multinational company British Foster Care Associates, have already established themselves in the field. Today however, the legislation only considers municipalities as legal partners for family-based foster care, which makes the establishment of new

[52] K. Rantala and P. Sulkunen, 'The Communatarian Preventive Paradox: Preventing Substance Misuse without the Substance' (2003) 23(4) *Critical Social Policy* 491–3.

[53] M. Määttä, 'Moniammatilliset ryhmät ehkäisevän päihdetyön toteuttajina Helsingissä' (2004) 4 *City of Helsinki Urban Facts* 24.

[54] N. 41, above, 113–14.

[55] Lainsäädännön muutostarpeet perhehoidossa, Ministry of Social Affairs and Health, 2010: 15.

actors difficult. A change in the legislation is needed and the FFC has taken an active role in advocating that change as can be seen in the quote above.

The actions of the FFC in recent years reveal that actors representing family-based foster care not only accept changes that have occurred in the field, but instead of simply accepting current partnership constellations, they are creating new alternatives. By doing so they *translate* the demand of partnerships into new partnership constellations and structures that they find acceptable. These efforts in strengthening the position of the interest group seem to be made in order to create acceptable conditions for work, which are seen as necessary to enable partnership cooperation with social aims.

27.7 The Professional Foster Care Association (PFA): translating demands to fit its own agenda

The PFA is an association of private service providers in the field of foster care in Finland. The predecessor of the organization was established first as a non-profit-based association in 1987. Shortly after, the association was refused public financing. Its members saw no option other than turning the member units into private companies in 1991. The current working association was finally established in 1992. The PFA has approximately 100 member units. The title Professional Foster Home was first widely used for a variety of units that began to appear more and more frequently in the 1990s. In 1997 permission from the State Provincial Office was required for the establishment of a Professional Foster Home in order to prevent inappropriate service providers from entering the field. However, the supply of professional foster care continued to expand rapidly and the companies were successful in entering into partnerships with the municipalities. This quick expansion did not necessarily mean easy entry into the field. As can be seen in the following quote, private companies often felt unwanted during their establishment in a field dominated by publicly organized services. As a former PFA chair reflects upon the obstacles met during her presidency in the mid-1990s:

'it was IN to talk about quality and we discussed different approaches to that in our meetings. We knew that we were a 'problem' and a 'challenge' for the State Provincial Offices. We believed in finding a mutual vision and feeling at the national level. (Chair of PFA 1996, Amppeli, 1/2002,12)

Together with internal cooperation, external cooperation was the most prevalent meaning attached to partnerships in the PFA. As can be seen in the above quote a way of establishing trust in service purchasers and supervising authorities was to invest in mutual internal quality standards between the member units. By approaching the need for both internal and external changes the speaker makes the demand for adjustment clear. Contesting views are evident, but they are not impossible to reconcile. The epistemic judgment made by the speaker is that it is worth approaching the views expressed by the official policy to try to find a mutual commitment in order to make mutual partnerships possible.[56] Instead of looking for change, conforming is seen as a necessity in the process of being accepted.

In reality, this adjustment has meant that the association works in two directions, internally and externally, in order to build up sustainable relations with other

[56] N. 41, above, 114.

partners in the field. For instance the PFA also introduced the requirement of permission from the State Provincial Office before such permission became obligatory in 1997. Internal 'quality work' seems to have been closely linked with the new requirements while partnerships have in this light meant investments into creating a balance between external demands and internal strategies, rather than exerting pressure on the authorities. Specific social aims, such as partnerships guided by such demands as equal care, were included in the quality work but were seldom seen as arguments in the data. This does not mean that the aim of equal care would have been off the agenda. Rather, it reflects that the primary aims attached to partnerships in the PFA during the last two decades have been elsewhere, namely in becoming a 'trustworthy partner' as is clear in the above quote. In contrast to the FFC, whose challenge has been the changing environment, the PFA seems to have flexibly adjusted to external changes, but has had instead to overcome prejudices and concerns in connection with being a new kind of service provider on the stage. These concerns seem not to have been entirely groundless as is evident in the following quote by a representative of the municipality Vantaa, here in the role of a purchaser of foster care services:

Private service providers began to establish and market themselves in the field of foster care, and their number grew all of a sudden. The procuration and need of supervision in our city was obvious. At the same time we needed to learn how to manage partnerships with new private companies who were offering their services, plan the steering of clients into foster care placement, and overall organize a rapidly changing activity into a manageable totality where all partners are served in the best possible way. (Head Social Worker, Vantaa, in the foreword of the unpublished guide 'Procurament in Foster Care, Inspection and Supervision, 2009', 3)

The speaker presenting her views on the new partnering situation that was introduced is here a purchaser, not a service provider. The quote expresses that the changing relationships in the domain of foster care also affected the work of other actors in the field, such as the municipalities responsible for organizing out-of-home placements. The speaker first explains how things have changed and how it was thus expedient to enter into partnerships with new providers. Partnerships can thus be seen as an alternative option to avoid unwanted consequences, for both those who offer and those who purchase the services. In reality suspicion and demands for stronger quality control increased, especially after an incident in a private foster home community named Kuttula. The case received wide public attention when the original parents of children placed in the Kuttula units accused the service providers of abuse, violence, insufficient staff education, arbitrary use of restrictions, etc. As a result of the investigation that followed, the State Provincial Office of Eastern Finland was charged with insufficient supervision by the Decision of the Parliamentary Ombudsman Riitta-Leena Paunio in 2000. The case can be seen as an example of a system based on independent and presumably equal partners evolving into a situation where governing through partnership was no longer considered sufficient. More restrictive regulations followed thereafter in the recommendations by the Working Group on the Supervision of Private Child Welfare Services set up shortly after the incident.[57] The result was a system in which both negotiated and pastoral forms of power were eventually combined.

[57] Lastensuojelun yksityisten palvelujen valvontatyöryhmän muistio. Ministry of Social Affairs and Health, 2001: 29.

As a consequence of the Kuttula case, suspicion was cast upon all private service providers. This affected the association in a way that pushed its work even more strongly in a direction where internal quality standards were met in relation to demands posed from the outside. Partnerships with the aim of stabilizing the association and adjusting the balance were formed extensively for example by organizing mutual meetings with the State Provincial Office, establishing a membership journal and introducing quality standard handbooks. The internal cooperation was at this point focused more on quality than increasing the quantity of units, as can be seen from the following quote:

In 1999 the number of new memberships increased by 10 units. After applying our membership criteria, that had been formulated over a long period of time, many units were excluded. The 'bad feeling' arising from the case of Kuttula, began to vanish and we got along with matters that concerned the association. (Chair of the PFA, 1999–2000, Amppeli 1/2002, 14)

According to the speaker, the association had in the end won the battle. Municipalities continued to purchase their services and a system to control the service providers had been set up internally. The internal efforts were continuously conducted in line with the external ones, such as the establishment of the Working Group on the Supervision of Private Child Welfare Services that followed the decision in the Kuttula case. The challenges were, as mentioned above, somewhat different from those experienced by the already established service provider FFC. One could say that the PFA stands out as a child of its time. This means for instance that the interest group's critique or the expectations of the public sector have been minor compared to those of the FFC. The PFA does not seem to have expected the public sector to provide support in the same way as the local service providers represented by the FFC. What the PFA did expect was, however, to be taken seriously and be considered as an equal partner to be approached by negotiation, not by command. This position is evident in a comment from a partnership meeting where representatives from the State Provincial Office, private service providers, as well as municipal social workers met in order to discuss Professional Foster Homes at the time of the Kuttula scandal:

One of the representatives from the western social services suggested a care agreement to be followed by all service providers. We tried as amicably and clearly as possible to explain to the representative of this social work unit that it was no longer possible to issue any unilateral commands towards service units of an association of this size. Care agreements are issues to be mutually negotiated in contracts between two equal contractors. (Commentary from the meeting in Amppeli, 2/1999, 7)

The last quote points to the different position the PFA has taken in relation to the authorities. Here the speaker wants to express that the relationship between the partners has changed. With the use of epistemic modality the speaker assumes the position of an actor having equal expertise when he or she explains the episode that took place at a meeting.[58] By using that example, the speaker underlines the views he or she has on the changing field. The critique is not concerned with specific expectations regarding the tasks carried out by social services. Instead the PFA is clearly more concerned with being regarded as a serious and equal actor. While the FFC until recently recognized positive aspects of the public authorities' capabilities, the PFA seems on the contrary to distance itself from the 'old' forms of governing by command. By entering into partnerships with the PFA, the expectations placed on support services are not an issue: as long as the PFA is regarded as an equal partner in the relationship

[58] N. 41, above, 115.

it can adjust to external requirements. Translation of external demands in the case of the PFA has thus first and foremost meant changes within its own organization, while the PFA translation has created new alternative structures to the public sector. The success of the PFA in entering into partnerships, as well as the new private companies currently introduced between municipalities and local foster families, together increase the amount of private contribution in the field of Finnish foster care. This creates new private-public partnership constellations. For the time being 'the making' of these partnerships seems to be using up most of the energy. To what extent the work will create structures that are more responsive to the service users' needs in the future remains to be seen.

27.8 Preliminary discussion

The aim of this chapter has been to interpret the meanings attached to partnerships by two different representatives of service providers in the field of Finnish foster care, the PFA and FFC, by asking whether social demands, such as equal access to suitable care, or possible other aims such as defending market share, seem to be guiding the action. As discussed in the introduction, partnerships and other empowered forms of decision making are currently not seen as successful in meeting social needs, such as providing equal access to suitable care. The question of why new ways of collaboration do not seem to have contributed to more suitable care has thus been approached by looking into the reasoning of these two interest groups in the foster care field.

The analysis of the two actors is situated in the changing power relations that have occurred as a consequence of a more general reorganization of the public sector in the early 1990s, which took place in tandem with an economic recession in Finland.[59] The field of Finnish foster care stands out as a sector where the simultaneous effects of the recession and the public sector reform are highly visible in increased dissatisfaction with the system. Salient problems include unequal service distribution throughout the country and increasing numbers of children and teenagers taken into care late.[60] From the perspective of power relations, two kinds of power are seen as being present in a situation where a mixture of private and public service organizations are currently working in parallel[61] as a result of the recent reform. On one side are negotiated forms of power introduced by partnerships, and on the other are remaining hierarchical power mechanisms that are often reframed in the new constellation. An example of such reframing in the field of Finnish foster care has been the new demands concerning supervision which have been produced by the new policy, as in the Kuttula case presented earlier.

The claim that actors in organizational structures often operate more in line with preserving or maintaining their positions when new initiatives are introduced rather than working towards official goals[62] seems to hold true in the data analysed here. Both associations seemed to place more emphasis on creating or defending their positions in the field rather than using social aims as an argument when considering working in partnerships. This finding contributes to the understanding of *why* obstacles are still present in the service chain regardless of the new initiatives introduced by the public sector reform. However, the way the two interest groups have worked

[59] N. 13, above, 69–71.
[60] N. 3, above, 55–8.
[61] N. 25, above, 20–1.
[62] N. 20, above, 211–13.

in order to maintain their positions seems to differ. The representative of traditional foster care (the FFC) has during the last 20 years endeavoured to more systematically coordinate the work of public services. The association has loudly criticized the current policy, which is also blamed for the increased numbers of children and youngsters coming into care late.[63] Current partnerships are not, according to the analysis, providing the units that the FFC represent with as satisfactory results in a supportive partnership as it seems. This has led the association to build new structures. Ultimately, the new structures even make it possible to avoid dysfunctional partnerships with local municipalities. If the reforms suggested by the working group established by the Ministry of Social Affairs and Health[64] pass, it will mean that a new kind of private-private partnership will appear side by side with the already existing purchase agreements between companies such as Professional Foster Homes and the municipalities. By taking an active role in policy making and implementation and in the formation of new service providers the FFC then stands out as an actor not only committed to partnerships but one that also forms new partnerships in order to establish new structures.

In the case of the PFA a changed position towards requirements posed to the service was witnessed a decade earlier during and shortly after the Kuttula incident. When the incident occurred the association had been functioning only for a few years. Even the case of Kuttula, however, did not impede continuing success of partnerships that had been established between the member organizations and municipalities. The success of the member units represented by the PFA can in the light of this chapter be explained by the quick adjustment to current requirements under the lead of the PFA. The formation of the association took place alongside the reforms carried out in the public sector. The member associations of the PFA were further able to benefit from increasing numbers of children taken into custody. The adjustment made member units of the PFA attractive partners in the eyes of municipalities. The PFA accordingly created no visibly new structures but the increasing partnerships with municipalities did strengthen their own position. This also strengthened the role of private service provision in foster care partnerships more generally.

From the perspective of children's social rights, such as equal access to suitable care, the result of partnership formation in the field of foster care does not reveal a success story. The result of the present analysis shows that equal care is only seldom explicitly discussed in the meaning of making of partnerships. Working in partnerships has, as this chapter has illustrated, rather for the moment led to efforts to maintain market positions in a changing service field. Such a result gives reason to argue that a displacement of social tasks seems to have taken place. The self-organizing and interorganizational networks,[65] including a variety of actors, redirected actions aimed at children's social rights towards a status quo where social aims come second. Taking precedence are partnerships, tools used on a battlefield where actors' market shares are the main concern. Nikolas Rose[66] defines the displacement of the 'social' as a logic where the social is produced by the entrepreneurial activity of each and everyone instead of being produced equally for all. In the first meaning the activity lies in the subject, while in the second the activity is produced by the State or some other actor. The description fits well with how children's rights to equal access to suitable

[63] N. 36, above, 32–5.
[64] N. 55, above.
[65] N. 10, above, 660.
[66] Nikolas Rose, 'The Crisis of "social". Beyond the Social Question' in (ed.) Sakari Hänninen, *Displacement of Social Policies* (Jyväskylä, 1998), 69–70.

care are being framed in current Finnish policy, where a lack of central coordination exists. In this situation the activity falls upon local networks of service providers and municipalities as the responsible organizers. Although many of the partnerships seem to be established to provide suitable care for new groups of clients, the lack of central coordination is forcing the associations to use partnerships more, in order to create structures, either by themselves or by facilitating new initiatives. Under such conditions the 'social' is being changed into separate and diverse activities in the field, which inevitably creates separate markets and regional differences in service distribution. Demands concerning supervision, as witnessed following the Kuttula case, are features arising with the field becoming more diverse and the coordination of activities failing. The situation where the service provider might choose its clients is probably also creating a state of affairs in which client selection might take place, where the right to individually appropriate care becomes a right only for those who are considered suitable. Further research into both these consequences and possible alternatives to them would be needed to determine how the absent social question could be made more visible in current public-private partnerships.

The present chapter clearly shows that despite great concern and awareness in Finland with regards to the unequal provision of services, acknowledged by the Committee of the Rights of Children and by the associations studied here, the task of providing more suitable services is considered secondary when partnerships are introduced as a governing practice simultaneously with a rapid reorganization of the public service sector. The new system has not, at least initially, produced greater equality, when collaboration in partnerships is perceived as various activities for ensuring better market share of actors instead of being a centrally coordinated activity for the benefit of children placed outside their homes.

28

Parental Discipline, Criminal Laws, and Responsive Regulation

Bronwyn Naylor[1] *and Bernadette J. Saunders*[2]

28.1 Introduction

In the debate around physical discipline of children, neither children's need to be disciplined nor parents' obligation to discipline their children constructively is particularly contentious. Contention arises in relation to whether physical punishment is a necessary component of parental discipline and whether it can be legally or morally justified. In this chapter, we first outline the clear international human rights-based support for criminalizing physical punishment of children, and summarize the current law permitting physical punishment in Australia and the UK. We consider the reform process in a number of countries that have prohibited physical punishment, identifying the political and legal factors leading to the reforms, the impact upon attitudes and incidence of physical violence, and the ways in which the criminalizing of physical punishment has been implemented in practice. Finally, we look critically at the use of criminal laws in this area and propose a framework for an acceptable regime which both makes a clear statement of the unacceptability of physical punishment and engages with parents to achieve social change without inappropriate stigmatization.

The effectiveness or otherwise of physical discipline is irrelevant to law reform that promotes alternatives and, above all, emphasizes recognition of children's human rights. Effectiveness is nonetheless often highlighted by proponents of physical punishment, and those who rationalize it.[3] In many countries that have not banned physical punishment, the motivation given for its use is pedagogical, ostensibly in the child's best interests. Meta-analyses of research on the effectiveness of corporal punishment show that it is of limited effect. It may produce immediate compliance, but it fails to self-motivate morally appropriate behaviour, and increases the risk of aggression and psychological harm.[4] Further, research suggests that parents'

[1] Law Faculty, Monash University.

[2] Social Work, Faculty of Medicine, Nursing and Health Sciences, Monash University. The authors thank Katie Barnett for her helpful comments on a draft of this chapter, and acknowledge with gratitude the support of the Legal Services Board (Victoria) for their ongoing research on parental discipline.

[3] See, for example, Robert E Larzelere (2000) 'Child Outcomes of Non-abusive and Customary Physical Punishment' *Clinical Child and Family Psychology Review* 3(4) 199–221.

[4] Elizabeth T Gershoff (2002) 'Corporal Punishment by Parents and Associated Child Behaviors and Experience: A Meta-Analytic and Theoretical Review' *Psychological Bulletin* 128(4) 539–79.

intentions when physically 'disciplining' children may bear little resemblance to the outcomes. Children have been injured and have even died when physical 'discipline' has escalated beyond 'reasonable' limits.[5] Parents also express remorse and regret.[6]

Physical punishment is in many countries no longer acceptable as a social practice. This is an indication of changes in understandings of both the individual autonomy of a child, and family power relations. The family was once sacrosanct in law. Men, in previous times, were entitled to physically discipline their servants and wives as well as their children. Such physical violence may well have 'worked', that is caused compliance and subservience, but it is in current times unacceptable for the separate reason that such people have their own human rights to being treated without violence. With regard to children's rights, Durrant observes that:

> It should not be necessary, on an issue of fundamental human rights, to demonstrate conclusively that violation of those rights leads invariably to harm before ensuring that those rights are protected. Nor should the 'putative' benefits of a rights violation be used to justify the violation.[7]

All people have the right to be treated with respect and to be protected from harm and humiliation. Children, as small people, have the right to dignity and integrity and therefore ought not to be subjected to any degree of unnecessary pain or violence. Indeed children's vulnerability, given their size and stage of human development, ought to entitle them to special respect, constructive guidance, well informed care, and thus enhanced protection from physical and emotional harm.

28.2 The human rights background

International and domestic charters of rights have for decades recognized the rights of children, in both the general prohibition on torture and on 'cruel, inhuman or degrading' punishment[8] and the specific provision that 'Every child shall have, without any discrimination... the right to such measures of protection as are required by his [sic] status as a minor, on the part of his family, society and the State'.[9] International and domestic instruments also provide specifically for the equal application and protection of the law:

> Every person is equal before the law and is entitled to the equal protection of the law without discrimination.[10]

[5] See for, example, Olav Nielssen et al. (2009) 'Child Homicide in New South Wales from 1991 to 2005' 190/1 *MJA* 7–11, Lord Laming (Victoria Climbié inquiry) House of Commons (2003) Health Committee Minutes, 27/3/03, Question 71. Available at <http://www.publications.parliament.uk/>.

[6] See for, example, Bernadette J Saunders and Chris Goddard (2010) *Physical Punishment in Childhood: the Rights of the Child* Wiley-Blackwell, UK, 146–9.

[7] Joan Durrant (2011) 'The empirical rationale for eliminating physical punishment', in Joan Durrant and Anne Smith (eds) *Global Pathways to Abolishing Physical Punishment: Realizing Children's Rights* Routledge, NY, 42.

[8] International Covenant on Civil and Political Rights (ICCPR) art. 7; Charter of Human Rights and Responsibilities Act 2006 (Vic) s.10; Human Rights Act 2004 (ACT) s.10.

[9] ICCPR art. 24(1); also the Australian human rights charters, Victorian Charter s.17(2); ACT Human Rights Act s.11(2).

[10] Charter (Vic) s.8(3); Human Rights Act (ACT) s.8(3); ICCPR art. 26.

Children's human rights are more specifically addressed in the United Nations Convention on the Rights of the Child (CROC) (1989) which requires that signatories take all 'legislative, administrative, social and educational measures' to protect children from:

> all forms of physical or mental violence, injury or abuse, neglect or negligent treatment, maltreatment or exploitation, including sexual abuse, while in the care of parent(s), legal guardian(s) or any other person who has the care of the child.[11]

Despite these clear statements, however, children are not provided with equal protection. In fact the only situation where physical force is now allowed as discipline is for people who are young, and where the perpetrator is the child's parent or carer. Similar behaviour would be a criminal offence in any other situation.

The words 'all forms of physical... violence, injury or abuse' in Article 19 and 'the prohibition on torture or other cruel, inhuman or degrading treatment or punishment' in Article 37 of the CROC (1989) clearly include corporal punishment, and the UN Committee on the Rights of the Child has confirmed this interpretation.[12] The Committee on the Rights of the Child characterizes corporal punishment as 'a form of violence, defined as any punishment in which physical force is used and intended to cause some degree of pain or discomfort, however light, to the child'.[13]

However, arguments persist that gentle educative 'corporal punishment' is not 'violence, injury or abuse' and is therefore not proscribed by the Convention. This appears to be the reading adopted by the 166 countries that are signatories to the Convention but have not prohibited corporal punishment in the home, including Australia, the UK, and Canada.[14] Such arguments frequently emphasize the protection given to 'appropriate direction and guidance' in Article 5 of the Convention, which endorses the rights of parents to make decisions about their child's upbringing.[15]

Balancing the privacy of the home against State intervention in parenting practices can be challenging, as highlighted by the perceived tensions between Article 5 and Articles 19 and 37 combined. All countries that have ratified the CROC must consider the implications of intervening in the privacy of home, and the political and philosophical implications of criminalizing parental behaviours. As a guide, the Committee on the Rights of the Child made the following remarks in its 2006 General Comment No. 8 related to the prosecution of parents:

[11] UN Convention on the Rights of the Child, G.A. Res.44/25, U.N. GAOR, 44th Sess., Supp. No. 49, U.N. Doc.A/44/49 (20 November 1989): Article 19. CROC Article 37 also states that no child shall be subjected to 'cruel, inhuman or degrading treatment or punishment'.

[12] For the most recent confirmation of this position see Committee on the Rights of the Child 56th Session 17 February 2011 General Comment No. 13 'Article 19: The right of the child to freedom from all forms of violence' (2011).

[13] Council of Europe, Council of Europe Policy guidelines on integrated national strategies for the protection of children from violence, 2009, p.32.

[14] <http://www.endcorporalpunishment.org/>.

[15] Article 5 provides, 'States Parties shall respect the responsibilities, rights and duties of parents or, where applicable, the members of the extended family or community as provided for by local custom,... to provide, in a manner consistent with the evolving capacities of the child, appropriate direction and guidance in the exercise by the child of the rights recognized in the present Convention'. Benjamin Shmueli (2008) 'The Influence of the United Nations Convention on the Rights of the Child on Corporal Punishment—A Comparative Study' *Oregon Review of International Law* 10, 189, reviews the claim that 'corporal punishment administered for the purpose of education' does not fall within Article 19; compare for example Michael D A Freeman (2010) 'Upholding the Dignity and Best Interest of Children: International Law and the Corporal Punishment of Children' *Law and Contemporary* Problems 73, 213.

The de minimis principle—that the law does not concern itself with trivial matters—ensures that minor assaults between adults only come to court in very exceptional circumstances; the same will be true of minor assaults on children.... the aim should be to stop parents from using violent or other cruel or degrading punishments through supportive and educational, not punitive, interventions.... Prosecuting parents is in most cases unlikely to be in their children's best interests.[16]

Physical discipline law reform aims to accord children the full protection from assault that adults take for granted. This is the focus of this chapter.

We begin by outlining the current criminal laws relating to corporal punishment, and the minor reforms to these laws, in Australia and the UK (with brief reference also to Canada), noting the entrenched resistance to banning physical punishment. Our focus then moves to Sweden, Germany, and New Zealand to examine motivations for banning physical punishment in those countries, and the impact of the legislative changes. An approach to reform in Australia and the UK, using the framework of 'responsive regulation', is then proposed.

28.3 The current law in Australia and the United Kingdom

In Australia it is not unlawful for parents to discipline their children using physical force, despite Australia's ratification of the CROC in 1990. The Australian Government has shown little response to the UN Committee's 1996 and 2005 critical feedback in relation to Australia's tolerance of parental physical discipline and lack of progress toward law reform that affords children the same protection from assault as adults.[17] Nor has it responded to the criticism of the UN Committee against Torture in 2008:

The Committee notes that corporal punishment of children is not explicitly prohibited in all States and Territories and may still be applied as 'reasonable chastisement'.

The State party should adopt and implement legislation banning corporal punishment at home and in public and private schools, detention centres, and all alternative care settings in all States and Territories.[18]

The criminal law of assault penalizes the application of physical force to anyone unless the perpetrator has a lawful excuse. Australian criminal law is based on common law in the United Kingdom, which provides an excuse for 'reasonable chastisement'. This was articulated in the 1860 case of *Hopley* as follows:

...a parent or a schoolmaster...may for the purpose of correcting what is evil in the child inflict moderate and reasonable corporal punishment, always, however, with this condition, that it is moderate and reasonable. If it be administrated for the gratification of passion or of rage, or if it be immoderate and excessive in its nature or degree, or if it be protracted beyond

[16] General Comment No. 8 (2006) on 'The right of the child to protection from corporal punishment and other cruel or degrading forms of punishment (arts. 19; 28, para. 2; and 37, inter alia)', para. 26. Available at <http://www.unhchr.ch/tbs/doc.nsf/(Symbol)/CRC.C.GC.8.En?OpenDocument>. Comment No. 8, paras. 40 and 41.

[17] Committee on the Rights of the Child (2005). Concluding Observations: Australia. 20/10/2005. CRC/C/15/Add.268. Retrieved 28 August 2009, from <http://www.unhchr.ch/tbs/doc.nsf/%28Symbol%29/CRC.C.15.Add.268.En?Opendocument>.

[18] 22 May 2008, CAT/C/AUS/CO/1, Concluding observations on third report, para. 31 (cited in <http://www.unhcr.org/refworld/country,,CAT,,AUS,,4885cf7f0,0.html>).

the child's powers of endurance, or with an instrument unfitted for the purpose and calculated to produce danger to the life or limb; in all such cases the punishment is excessive, the violence is unlawful, and if evil consequences to life and limb ensue, then the person inflicting it is answerable to the law...[19]

Australian law similarly recognizes a 'lawful excuse' where a parent (or guardian) assaults their child for the purpose of 'discipline'. It must be moderate and reasonable, and must be for the purpose of correction. The defence of 'reasonable chastisement' or 'lawful correction' exists in various forms in all Australian states and territories.[20] The 1955 judgment in *Terry* framing the defence in Victoria and the Australian Capital Territory defines it as follows:

...there are strict limits to the right of a parent to inflict reasonable and moderate corporal punishment on his or her child for the purpose of correcting the child in wrong behaviour. In the first place, the punishment must be moderate and reasonable. In the second place, it must have a proper relation to the age, physique and mentality of the child, and in the third place, it must be carried out with a reasonable means or instrument.[21]

It is important to note that the defence is only available for physical violence 'for the purpose of correct[ion]', or 'to discipline, manage or control'.[22] As made explicit in *Hopley*, and implicit in *Terry*, there is no defence for actions carried out in anger or frustration or vengeance. This is a significant distinction which is discussed further below.[23]

28.3.1 Jurisdictions that have modified the defence of lawful correction

The only Australian state to have restricted the defence is New South Wales (NSW), which in 2002 adopted legislation to limit the defence of 'lawful correction' to 'reasonable' force. In NSW, force will be unreasonable if it is applied to the head or neck of the child, or if it could harm the child 'for more than a short period'.[24]

The UK, also a signatory to the CROC, has similarly restricted but not abolished the defence, after regular criticism from the UN Committee on Children,[25] and after a number of judicial decisions considering the effect of the European Convention and the UK Human Rights Act.[26] The Children Act 2004 s.58 now restricts the

[19] *R v Hopley* 175 ER 1204 (1860). UK law has been amended, as discussed further below.

[20] See *R v Terry* [1955] VLR 114, 116 for the common law formulation; the defence is also explicit in the Code states. Corporal punishment in the home is regulated at state level, under the common law in the Australian Capital Territory and Victoria, and by statute in the Northern Territory Criminal Code Act s.27; Queensland Criminal Code Act 1899 s.280; South Australia Criminal Law Consolidation Act 1935 s.20; Tasmania Criminal Code Act 1924 s.50; and Western Australia Criminal Code 1913 s.257. See for example, the defence of reasonable force for 'correction' (Criminal Code WA s.257) or for 'correction, discipline, management or control' (Criminal Code Qld s.280).

[21] *R v Terry* [1955] VLR 114, 116.

[22] Queensland Criminal Code Act 1899 s.280: 'by way of correction, discipline, management or control'; Northern Territory Criminal Code Act s.27(p): 'to discipline, manage or control'.

[23] See discussion in Heather Keating (2006) 'Protecting or Punishing Children: Physical Punishment, Human Rights and English Law Reform' 26 *Legal Studies* 394, 397–8, 400.

[24] Crimes Act 1900 (NSW) s.61AA(2)(b).

[25] Discussed in Michael D A Freeman (2010) 'Upholding the Dignity and Best Interests of Children: International Law and the Corporal Punishment of Children' (2010) *Law and Contemporary Problems* 73, 211–51.

[26] See *A v United Kingdom* (1999) 27 EHRR 611: acceptance of the defence of reasonable chastisement where stepfather beat boy with cane held to be in violation of Art 3 of European Convention for the Protection of Human Rights and Fundamental Freedoms 1950 (which prohibits torture, and inhuman or degrading treatment or punishment). Subsequent UK decisions have tended to see the UK law as

availability of the defence of 'reasonable punishment' to minor assaults.[27] The defence can be raised to the offence of common assault (where no mark is left[28]) but not to the more serious charge of assault occasioning actual bodily harm.

In a review of English-speaking jurisdictions, it should be noted that the defence has also been modified, but not banned, in Canada. The Canadian Criminal Code provides for the reasonable correction defence in s.43, which states that a parent is justified in using force for correction provided it 'does not exceed what is reasonable under the circumstances'. Canada is also a signatory to the CROC. In 2004 the Canadian Supreme Court rejected a constitutional challenge to s.43. It concluded that neither the Canadian Charter equality guarantee nor the CROC prohibited reasonable physical punishment, and that punishment was 'reasonable' if it was 'minor corrective force of a transitory and trifling nature'. This was held to exclude corporal punishment of children under two or over 12, or punishment using objects or involving blows or slaps to the head, any 'degrading, inhuman or harmful conduct', and acts of anger.[29]

Both English and Canadian critics have pointed out that, far from producing a shift in parental attitude away from use of physical punishment, these modified excuses place a greater focus on the *right* to use force. Indeed, Freeman observes, 'the message it gives to parents is that they may hit their children'.[30] As Keating observed with disappointment in the context of the UK reforms, these amendments were a missed opportunity to establish the clearest possible statement of principle that violence is as unacceptable towards a child as it is towards an adult.[31]

28.3.2 The politics of change

Physical punishment has been described as the 'primordial violence' from which much other violence in society stems.[32] Condoning any degree of physical discipline arguably sets the foundation for exceeding often ill-defined limits, whether through escalation or in anger and frustration. Language is important here. Reframing corporal punishment, or 'smacking', as 'violence' and 'assault' can be powerful, as these words usually refer to 'unlawful, irresponsible acts that are unacceptable in humane, civilised societies'.[33] Yet child homicides have resulted from excessive physical punishment used to control or discipline children, frequently in response to normal

being compatible with Art 3: see *R v H (Assault of Child: Reasonable Chastisement)* [2002] 1 Cr App R 7. See discussion in Keating (2006), n. 23 above, and Freeman (2010), n. 25 above.

[27] It is no longer available in relation to any more serious injuries imposed as punishment, for example those causing 'grazes, scratches, abrasions, minor bruising, swelling, superficial cuts or a black eye': Crown Prosecution Service, *Reasonable Chastisement Research Report* July 2007. <http://www.cps.gov.uk/Publications/research/chastisement.html> at 27 January 2009.

[28] Freeman (2010), n. 25 above, 218

[29] *Canadian Foundation for Children, Youth and the Law v Canada* [2004] 1 SCR 76, 2004 SCC 4; discussed in Anne McGillivray and Cheryl Milne (2011) 'Canada: The rocky road of repeal' in Joan Durrant and Anne Smith (eds) *Global Pathways to Abolishing Physical Punishment: Realizing Children's Rights* Routledge, NY, 98–112.

[30] Freeman (2010), n. 25 above, 218; see also Joan Durrant et al. (2009) 'Protection of children from physical maltreatment in Canada: An evaluation of the Supreme Court's definition of reasonable force', *Journal of Aggression, Maltreatment and Trauma* 18, 1–24.

[31] Keating (2006), n. 23 above, 296.

[32] Murray Straus (2009) The Special Issue on Prevention of Violence Ignores the Primordial Violence *Journal of Interpersonal Violence* 23, 1314–20, 1314.

[33] Saunders and Goddard (2010), n. 6 above, 120

childhood behaviours such as crying and toileting accidents.[34] Indeed Duncanson in her report, 'Child Deaths and Serious Injury as a Result of Assault in Sweden and New Zealand', concludes that:

...ensuring that the law contains no acceptance of violence towards children is one factor in achieving a shift to lower child injury and death rates from assault, and to more positive community and parental attitudes towards children.[35]

The deeply entrenched acceptance of physical punishment can make it difficult to challenge but the language chosen to describe actions directed at children can motivate desirable attitudinal and behavioural changes, and therefore impact on law reform processes.[36] Clarity and avoidance of confusion in language is paramount. Sadly, however, it may take a particularly horrific case of severe or fatal abuse to alter perceptions of what is and what is not acceptable parental behaviour. When these cases occur, some people are motivated to see the connections between lawful correction and severe or fatal injuries yet others resist seeing the connections, choosing instead to emphasize the disparity between what they perceive to be *lawful* correction and the unacceptable extremes of abusive physical punishment.

Concern about serious injuries and deaths in which physical discipline appears to be an element is a significant impetus for consideration of legislative reform. Prominent examples in Australia, the United Kingdom, and New Zealand include Daniel Valerio in Australia in 1992, Victoria Climbié in 2000 in the UK, and James Whakaruru in New Zealand in 1999. All of these children were subjected to frequent, harsh physical punishment at the hands of their 'carers', and in each child's life beatings started with small 'smacks'.[37] Before the repeal of section 59 in New Zealand, and eight years after James Whakaruru's death at the hands of his mother's partner Ben Haerewa, Coddington reported in the *New Zealand Herald* that, for four-year-old James:

...smacks were every-day—nay, every-hour—'discipline'...Mum's busy; smack over the head. Dad's hungover; smack around the ear. Stop grizzling; smack around the bum. Smack, smack, smack. That's often the only touching many New Zealand children receive from those they look to for love and affection.[38]

Lord Laming, Chairman of the UK Climbié Inquiry, remarked that 'a major context' for the Victoria's abuse was 'discipline and punishment...Victoria's abuse began with little smacks' and her 'great aunt told the inquiry that there was nothing wrong with smacking'. Lord Laming recalled acting in cases of child abuse and 'losing cases on a defence of reasonable chastisement'. 'I would have thought', he reflected, 'that violence towards children should be taken as seriously—or more seriously—than

[34] See Nielssen et al. (2009), n. 5 above; Murray Straus (2000) 'Corporal Punishment and Primary Prevention of Physical Abuse' *Child Abuse & Neglect* 24(9), 1109–14, Anne Smith et al. (2005) 'The Discipline and Guidance of Children: Messages from Research', Children's Issues Centre and the Office of the Children's Commissioner, University of Otago, Wellington, US Advisory Board on Child Abuse and Neglect (1995), 'A Nation's Shame: Fatal Child Abuse and Neglect in the United States', Washington.

[35] Mavis Duncanson (2006) 'Child Deaths and Serious Injury as a Result of Assault in Sweden and New Zealand' Office of the Commissioner for Children, Wellington.

[36] Kai-D Bussmann (2004) 'Evaluating the Subtle Impact of a Ban on Corporal Punishment of Children in Germany' *Child Abuse Review* 13, 292–311.

[37] As noted earlier, 'smack' is a colloquial, euphemistic term that effectively minimizes the act of hitting a child to modify, control, or admonish the child's behaviour.

[38] Deborah Coddington (2007) 'The Smacking Debate Story: Bradford's Law Will Save our Children' *The New Zealand Herald*, 18 March 2007.

violence towards adults.'[39] As noted earlier, the United Kingdom has since modified the availability of the chastisement defence but the government is not considering total abolition. Roger Singleton's recent independent report on physical punishment explicitly avoided discussion of parental punishment, focussing on punishment in various care settings. The Terms of Reference excluded parental punishment, whilst noting:

> The Government does not condone smacking children and we want to progress to the point where smacking is seen as unacceptable by the vast majority of parents and is only used as a last resort, if at all . . . [40]

However Singleton noted that the Secretary of State had made it clear that the Government did not believe a full ban on smacking was needed, and 'does not intend to criminalize parents who administer a mild smack'.[41] On the other hand the Singleton Report noted that the Crown Prosecution Service (CPS) reports very little use of the reasonable punishment defence—two cases since 2007, and 12 cases where the defence may have been a factor and where the case resulted in acquittal or discontinuance in the period 2005–2007.[42]

In Australia in 1992, two-year-old Daniel Valerio was murdered at the hands of his step-father Paul Aiten. Aiten was recently released from prison reportedly expressing no remorse.[43] Significantly, tolerance of physical discipline and confusion about lawful correction were factors in Daniel's tragic and extremely brutal demise.[44] Many community professionals were aware of Daniel's vulnerability but did not act to protect him. Media reporting and community concern subsequently led to the introduction of mandatory reporting of abuse. Yet, many more children have since died in not dissimilar circumstances, sometimes described as physical 'discipline' gone awfully wrong.[45] In 2007 Stuart McMaster was tried in Victoria, Australia over the death in 2005 of five-year-old Cody Hutchings. Cody suffered from Williams syndrome, a genetic condition that the judge said linked with developmental delays, associated challenging behaviours, poor sleep patterns, and irritability. The court heard that McMaster, Cody's mother's partner, would 'discipline' Cody severely using a belt that McMaster had modified to become a heavy strap. McMaster frequently and mercilessly assaulted Cody. Cody would plead: 'Don't call the strap man dad', but to no

[39] Lord Laming (Victoria Climbié inquiry) House of Commons (2003). Health Committee Minutes, 27/3/03, Question 71. Available at <http://www.publications.parliament.uk/>.

[40] Roger Singleton (2010) *Physical Punishment: Improving Consistency and Protection* March 2010 [35].

[41] Singleton (2010), n. 40 above [10]. In 2003 an internet forum was discussing the topic 'Should parents be banned from smacking their children?' (<http://my.opera.com/community/forums/topic.dml?id=22655&t=1297746097&page=2#comment191804>). One contributor posted 'Tony Blair has rejected calls from MPs who want the smacking of children banned. The Prime Minister's official spokesman said: "We continue to believe this is a matter of individual choice for parents." So there we are then. Blair has to smack his kids and so can we'. A response from 'A Norwegian member' then appeared, 'Hmmmm. . . . then I must say my children are lucky that they grow up in Norway . . . where we are civilised enough to have laws against this cruelty. . . . ' Both 24 June 2003.

[42] Roger Singleton (2010), n. 40 above [31]. This may mean that few parents raise the defence; but it may also mean that 'clear' cases of reasonable discipline are simply not prosecuted, at the discretion of the police or prosecutors.

[43] Anthony Dowsley and Wayne Flower (2011) 'Daniel Valerio's killer walks free but locals furious' *Herald Sun* 14 January 2011.

[44] Chris Goddard (1996) *Child Abuse and Child Protection: A Guide for Health, Education and Welfare Workers* South Melbourne, Churchill Livingstone.

[45] This expression is commonly used in mitigation of serious abuse in the press: it reveals recognition that excessive physical punishment can begin with benevolent intent but, in the guise of 'discipline', can nevertheless result in serious and even fatal consequences for the child.

avail. Over 160 bruises on Cody's head, neck, chest, abdomen, arms, legs, penis, and buttocks were revealed at his post-mortem examination. He had also suffered a gash to the forehead, a tear in the mouth, two skull fractures, a torn liver, and a tear to the mesentery holding his internal organs in place.

In Victoria calls for a 'ban' on corporal punishment have followed some horrendous cases but such calls have not so far been acted upon. In 2008, retired Chief Justice of the Family Court, Alistair Nicholson, called on state governments to abolish the defence of reasonable chastisement,[46] and his arguments attracted broadly supportive media attention with discussion of positive parenting options in the popular press.[47] However, readers' responses were less enthusiastic.

Similarly, in January 2009, the *Medical Journal of Australia* published a study of child homicides in New South Wales which concluded that 'lives could be saved by measures that reduce the incidence of child abuse, including the prohibition of corporal punishment of children'.[48] This research was reported in supportive terms in the main Australian newspapers.[49] However, the popular press in Victoria characteristically invited readers to vote online on the question 'should smacking be banned?'. The concerning result, though not unexpected, was that 93.8 per cent of readers who took the time to respond to a phone-in poll voted against a ban.[50]

In NSW the recent decision by police to charge with assault a mother who hit her 16-year-old daughter across the face—in a police station—was heavily criticized in the popular press. Under the headline, 'Mum jailed for slapping drunken daughter', it was reported that the magistrate hearing the charge dismissed the case and recorded no conviction, thereby defining hitting the face of a 16-year-old young person as acceptable parenting.[51] The magistrate reportedly said, 'This is just a parent exercising their right to be a parent—this [charge] is absolutely ludicrous'. (It will be recalled that that 2002 reforms to the NSW criminal law limited the defence of 'lawful correction' to 'reasonable' force and provided that force will be unreasonable if it is applied to the head or neck of the child, or if it could harm the child 'for more than a short period' (Crimes Act 1900 (NSW) s.61AA(2)(b)). The case clearly fell within this definition of 'unreasonable', yet the magistrate dismissed the incident as 'trivial' under the Crimes (Sentencing Procedure) Act 1999 s.10.

In New Zealand, prior to law reform in 2007, too many cases of parental violence toward children in the context of discipline or control of children had attracted media attention, and many people now acknowledge the connection.[52] The successful proponents for the removal of the reasonable chastisement defence under section 59 asserted that in addition to amending a breach of children's rights to live without fear of violence or the threat of violence, removal of the defence 'would have a longer

[46] Alistair Nicholson (2008) 'Choose To Hug, Not Hit' *Family Court Review* 46, 11.

[47] Faye Burstin (2008) 'Judge wants ban on smacking kids' *Herald Sun* (Melbourne), 21 February 2008.

[48] Olav Nielssen et al., (2009) 'Child Homicide in New South Wales from 1991 to 2005' *Medical Journal of Australia* 190, 1, 7.

[49] 'Call for ban on hitting children' *Herald Sun* (Melbourne), 5 January 2009; 'Child Homicide rate twice UK's' *The Australian* (New South Wales), 5 January 2009.

[50] *Herald Sun* (Melbourne), 6 January 2009; 2064 responses were received.

[51] Lisa Mayoh (2010) 'Mum jailed for slapping drunken daughter' *The Sunday Telegraph* 9 May 2010.

[52] Beth Wood, Ian Hassal, and George Hook (2008) *Unreasonable Force: New Zealand's Journey Towards Banning the Physical Punishment of Children* Wellington, Save the Children.

term effect in reducing the amount of physical force used on children, and with that the risk of serious physical injury or death'.[53]

The New Zealand reforms required considerable negotiation and compromise but the amended bill was ultimately supported by 113 out of 121 members of Parliament.[54] Nevertheless, when the legislation passed there were media claims that parents were now unable to correct or discipline their children, and that children were even threatening to report parents to the police. The Director of Family First New Zealand reportedly claimed, 'We are creating a "paranoid parenting" environment'.[55]

In 2009, the legislation's critics initiated a citizen's referendum. The referendum question was phrased in highly loaded terms: 'Should a smack as part of good parental correction be a criminal offence in New Zealand?'[56] The results were overwhelmingly against the 'anti-smacking' reforms, with 87.4 per cent voting 'no' in a voter turnout of 57 per cent of eligible voters.[57] Nonetheless the Government made it clear that it would not be influenced by the outcome and there have been no amendments. A private members bill to legalize smacking was defeated 115–5 on its first reading in Parliament in September 2010.[58]

The UN Committee on the Rights of the Child welcomed the New Zealand legislation in its February 2011 state review and re-emphasized the importance of continuing to promote non-violent forms of child discipline.[59]

28.4 The experience of law reform in Sweden, Germany, and New Zealand

A broad suite of reforms has been effected across the world, in Scandinavia, Europe, and South America, and more recently in Africa and the Middle East.[60] We review evaluations of the reforms in Sweden, Germany, and New Zealand. We then outline an approach to reform based on John Braithwaite's principles of 'responsive regulation', diagrammatically represented in the form of a pyramid of actions. This model emphasizes that the criminal law has a place, but only as the end point in a stepped series of interventions.

[53] Wood et al. (2008), n. 52 above, 25

[54] Wood et al. (2008), n. 52 above, 186.

[55] 'Smacking case shows law works—Bradford' *New Zealand Herald* (Auckland), 22 November 2007.

[56] Under the Citizens Initiated Referenda Act 1993, NZ citizens can initiate a referendum if they can show the support of 10 per cent of registered voters.

[57] <http://www.electionresults.govt.nz/2009_citizens_referendum/2009_referendum_results.html>.

[58] 'New smacking bill defeated' 8 September 2010 <http://www.3news.co.nz/New-smacking-bill-defeated-/tabid/419/articleID/175074/Default.aspx>.

[59] 'The Committee welcomes new section 59(1) of the Crimes Act (1961), which abolishes the legal use of parental force for the purposes of correction. The Committee recommends that the State party heighten public awareness about the law and continue to promote positive and non-violent forms of discipline in childrearing': <http://www.occ.org.nz/__data/assets/pdf_file/0013/8014/UN_recs_periodic_report_07.01.2011.pdf>.

[60] See summary of reforms in Adam J Zolotor and Megan E Puzia (2010) 'Bans against Corporal Punishment: a Systematic Review of the Laws, Changes in Attitudes and Behaviours' *Child Abuse Review* 19, 229–4, 232–4.

28.4.1 A summary of approaches in countries which have 'banned' corporal punishment[61]

Approaches in countries which have banned corporal punishment have included the removal of the 'reasonable chastisement' defence, making an assault prosecution available, but also the legislative inclusion of positive statements of children's rights, and programmes of education and welfare support. Some include explicit legislative statements of a child's right to be brought up without physical violence,[62] though interpretations of 'physical violence' may be narrow. Such positive rights are not generally seen as specifically enforceable by the child, but are given force by the existence of criminal sanctions (with removal of the defence) and through child welfare and family law measures.

Reforms have aimed:

- to remove the express defence of 'lawful correction',
- in some cases, to explicitly restate parents' right to use force to protect their children from harm (the 'necessity' defence),
- to leave the criminal law of assault by default, as a 'backstop',
- to encourage/mandate police and prosecutorial discretion, and even non-prosecution,
- to make explicit statements about children's positive rights (for example to a non-violent upbringing),
- to produce cultural and attitudinal change through
  - education
  - public information
  - resourcing welfare agencies and support sources
  - explicitly preferring a 'therapeutic' disposition to a criminal one (for example, in Germany).

Sweden's reform is the longest-standing and, along with Germany's, has been widely evaluated. Both countries have legal systems based on Civil Codes. Thus, after a review of reforms and their impact in Sweden and Germany, we examine the 2007 New Zealand reforms to better understand their provenance and impact in a common law country that is most comparable, historically and politically, to Australia and the UK. First, we will outline the reforms. We then evaluate the impact on attitudes to, and incidence of, corporal punishment and on the decision whether, and when, to prosecute.

28.4.2 Sweden

Sweden abolished the defence of reasonable chastisement in the penal code in 1957. However, media attention to two cases of child maltreatment, and ongoing media debate about parental rights following this reform, led to a parliamentary inquiry

[61] See for a review of international reforms, Freeman (2010), n. 25 above.
[62] See summary in Zolotor and Puzia (2010), n. 60 above, 232–4

into children's rights. The Swedish Parliament then expressly prohibited the physical punishment of children in 1979.

The Swedish reform did not criminalize corporal punishment as such. Recognizing that the law of assault already applied to any substantial act of violence to a child, the legislature added a provision specifying that children were entitled to be treated with respect, and that they were not to be subjected to corporal punishment.[63] The provision appears in the civil Children and Parents Code and does not carry a separate sanction. Behaviour falling within the definition of assault is punished under the general criminal law in the Penal Code. The Ministry of Justice confirmed in its public information materials that the criminal law already allowed punishment, under the crime of assault, for physical chastisement that caused 'bodily injury or pain . . . more than of very temporary duration', and that the new law made no change to this. At the same time, it continues to be the case that 'trivial offences will remain unpunished, either because they cannot be classified as assault, or because an action is not brought'.[64] The rights of children were recognized and protected, without removing any right of parents to discipline their children within accepted limits.[65]

28.4.3 Germany

In Germany an amendment to the Civil Code in 2000 (entitled an 'Act Outlawing Violence in Education') created a 'right to a non-violent upbringing'.[66] This does not create a right of private action in the victim, but has implications for both criminal and family/child protection laws. A parent charged with a criminal offence for use of physical punishment can no longer argue any 'right' to discipline. The behaviour will only be criminal if it exceeds 'a certain degree of intensity', but 'this level of intensity is now reached when a child is slapped'. The parent is then liable to be punished for 'causing bodily injury pursuant to Art 223 of the Criminal Code' as they would be for an assault on anyone else. At the same time, there is no duty under the Code on social services or counselling agencies, or any citizen, to report violations, and 'the public prosecutor's office will still only press criminal charges in serious cases'. Further, the prosecutor can 'waive these [charges] when the family accepts social education, family-oriented therapy or other supporting measures'.[67]

In the context of family law the new provision is also to be taken into account 'in assessing whether there is a danger to the best interests of the child' per Article 1666p, 1666a German Civil Code. 'If the welfare of the child is endangered, the Family Law Court (Familiengericht) shall be obliged to take the measures necessary to eliminate

[63] See Foraldrabalken (Swedish Children and Parents Code) ch. 6; Joan Durrant (1999) *A Generation without Smacking: The Status of Swedish Children and Youth Since the Passage of the 1979 Corporal Punishment Ban* London, UK, Save the Children, 7.

[64] Durrant (1999), n. 63 above, 7.

[65] Staffan Janson, Bodil Langberg, and Birgitta Svensson (2011) 'A 30-year ban on physical punishment' in Joan Durrant and Anne Smith (eds) *Global pathways to abolishing physical punishment: Realizing children's rights* Routledge, NY.

[66] Art 1631 German Civil Code para. 2 sentence 1: 'Children have a right to a non-violent upbringing'. 'Violence' defined: 'Corporal punishment, psychological injuries and other degrading measures are impermissible' (para. 2 sentence 2). Parents can intervene to protect children, but 'every form of violence, which is intended as a punishment', is now absolutely prohibited: 'Violence in Upbringing. An assessment after the introduction of the right to a non-violent upbringing' 2003 Federal Ministry for Family Affairs, Senior Citizens, Women and Youth, and Federal Ministry of Justice ['Violence in Upbringing'].

[67] Violence in Upbringing, n. 66 above, 5.

the danger (instructions, orders or prohibitions or, if necessary, withdrawal of the parent's right to custody of the child).'[68]

28.4.4 New Zealand

New Zealand was the first English-speaking country to prohibit corporal punishment, in 2007. The New Zealand Crimes (Substituted Section 59) Amendment Act 2007 abrogates the former defence permitting the use of reasonable force for the purpose of correction, but restates the right of parents to protect or control their child. Indeed the legislation first articulates the positive rights of parents to use force to protect or control their children, and then states that this does not include any right to use force for 'the purpose of correction'. Section 59 headed 'Parental control' provides now as follows:

(1) Every parent of a child . . . is justified in using force if the force used is reasonable in the circumstances and is for the purpose of—

(a) preventing or minimising harm to the child . . . ; or

(b) preventing the child from engaging . . . in conduct that amounts to a criminal offence; or

(c) preventing the child from engaging . . . in offensive or disruptive behaviour; or

(d) performing the normal daily tasks that are incidental to good care and parenting.

(2) Nothing in subsection (1) or in any rule of common law justifies the use of force for the purpose of correction.

(3) Subsection (2) prevails over subsection (1).

(4) To avoid doubt, it is affirmed that the Police have the discretion not to prosecute complaints against a parent of a child or person in the place of a parent of a child in relation to an offence involving the use of force against a child, where the offence is considered to be so inconsequential that there is no public interest in proceeding with a prosecution.

The legislation did not create a new offence. The legislation removed the existing defence for force 'for the purpose of correction', whilst reaffirming the general defence of necessity, that is, the recognition that parents may need to use force to prevent harm to the child.

28.5 How have these approaches worked? Do they appear to have changed behaviour?

Our review of law reform in Sweden, Germany, and New Zealand leads to two key questions: first, have the reforms worked—have they changed attitudes and behaviour?; and secondly, have they led to legal interventions? Or, for people critical of greater regulation in this area, have the reforms tipped the state/privacy balance too far, with inappropriate prosecutions? We will look at each of these questions in turn.

[68] Violence in Upbringing, n. 66 above, 4–5.

28.5.1 Changes in attitudes and incidence[69]

28.5.1.1 Sweden

The impact of Sweden's 1979 legislation is the subject of much discussion and some contention in the literature.[70] The emphasis of the reform was on cultural change, with the reasoning that '[i]nformation and education to alter the attitudes of parents... is preferable to relying on penal sanctions'.[71] Information campaigns were initiated in the media; this extended to distribution of information brochures with advice about alternative disciplinary strategies (in all major community languages) and information printed on milk cartons. By 1981, 99 per cent of Swedes were aware of the law.[72]

Despite this awareness of the law, Sorbring et al. observed that a small number of Swedish parents continue to use physical punishment because they are stressed, their children continuously misbehave, or for religious reasons, but generally children do not now expect physical discipline. Verbal control or a 'firm command' is the normal disciplinary approach.[73] However, some children, especially boys, may still expect to be hit for transgressions such as hitting a sibling or pursuing a dangerous activity such as touching a stove.[74]

More recently, Janson, Langberg, and Svensson have reported research conducted by the Swedish Government's Committee on Child Abuse initiated in the mid-1990s following concerns over increased family violence.[75] Of significance to this chapter, Janson et al. reported that while in the 1960s most parents had hit their preschool children from occasionally to regularly, by 2006 only 13–14 per cent of middle-school children reported ever being smacked:

> ... children in the 2000s are smacked considerably less often and with less force than children in the 1980s [and] almost an entire generation who experienced physical punishment themselves as children refrained from inflicting it when they became parents... In the 1960s, corporal punishment was seen as a justified and useful tool in bringing up children; today most parents look upon such behaviour as deviant.[76]

[69] See for an overview of research to date, Zolotor and Puzia (2010), n. 60 above, 235–9 (attitudes) and 240–1 (prevalence).

[70] See, for example, Chris Beckett (2005) 'The Swedish Myth: The Corporal Punishment Ban and Child Death Statistics' *British Journal of Social Work* 35, 125–38; J Roberts (2000) 'Changing Public Attitudes towards Corporal Punishment: The Effects of Statutory Reform in Sweden' *Child Abuse & Neglect* 24(8), 1027–35.

[71] See Barbro Hindberg (2001) *Ending Corporal Punishment* Ministry of Health and Social Affairs 13 <http://www.endcorporalpunishment.org/pages/pdfs/ending.pdf> at 23 March 2009.

[72] Durrant (1999), n. 63 above, 8.

[73] E. Sorbring, M. Rodholm-Funnemark, et al. (2003) 'Boys' and Girls' Perceptions of Parental Discipline in Transgression Situations' *Infant and Child Development* 12, 64

[74] ibid.

[75] Staffan Janson, Bodil Langberg, and Birgitta Svensson (2011) 'A 30-year Ban on Physical Punishment' in Joan Durrant and Anne Smith (eds) *Global Pathways to Abolishing Physical Punishment: Realizing Children's Rights* Routledge, NY, 241–55. The research included a representative sample of 2500 parents, in 1980, 2000 and 2006, contributing information about upbringing, conflicts, and punishment of a particular child during the previous year; representative samples of 11-, 14- and 16-year-old children surveyed in 1994, 2000, and 2006–2007 about their attitudes toward and experiences of physical punishment; 20-year-old young people providing information about their experiences of physical punishment and other bullying and abuse; and tracking of adults' attitudes towards physical punishment from 1965, drawing on various research studies.

[76] Janson, Langberg, and Svensson (2011), n. 75 above, 250–1.

Nevertheless, evaluations find that some parents' motivation for using physical punishment remains strong despite the ban. Therefore, education about child development and alternatives to physical punishment will continue to be important, along with the child and family supports well established in Sweden.

28.5.1.2 Germany

In Germany, the physical punishment ban in 2000 was promoted using three strategies: nationwide media campaigning; local family welfare organizational campaigning; and the integration of simultaneous research into publicity campaigns.[77] A reduction in the incidence of physical punishment in Germany was reported following a comparison of self-reported incidents before and after the 2000 reforms. Parents' self-reports of having 'beaten their children's bottoms' reduced from 33.2 per cent in 1996 to 26.4 per cent in 2002. Children's self-reports of having been 'thrashed' reduced from 30 per cent in 1992 to an impressively low three per cent in 2002.[78] Bussmann's research indicates significant shifts in parents' awareness of their own motivations, with 57 per cent of parents now justifying their use of corporal punishment in terms of 'the excessive demands and stress in daily family life and their feeling of helplessness' rather than using 'educational reasons'.[79]

Bussmann also found high levels of agreement that the new laws were useful; that it was good to have clear statutory statements about such issues. Only 12.6 per cent agreed that 'the law should not become involved in the life of the family; parents must be allowed to set their own limits' and 15.8 per cent agreed that 'the rearing of their child is the natural right of parents; no one has a right to tell parents what to do, not even the lawmakers'.[80] He concluded that banning physical discipline impacted on the following three dimensions thus demonstrating 'its symbolic meaning':

- Increase of legal sensibility and consciousness
- Sensitized perception and definition of physical punishment as violence
- Stimulation of family discussions on sanctioning styles and on the legal limits of physical punishment.[81]

In 2005, Bussmann was commissioned to conduct a representative survey involving 1000 parents of children between 12 and 18 years old; 1000 adolescents aged between 12–18, and 350 staff from counselling and welfare agencies.[82] He found that parents' knowledge of the law increased to almost 40 per cent between 2001 and 2005. However, adolescents' knowledge remained fairly steady at 28 per cent with a slight decrease to 25 per cent among adolescents who had experienced violence in childhood. An intensive school education campaign was consequently recommended. Results of incidence studies in 2001, 2005, and 2007 indicated a decrease in childrearing violence, with the exception of parents who resort to extreme violence; approximately 13–17 per cent of parents continue to fall into this category. However, Bussmann asserts that:

[77] Kai-D Bussmann (2011) 'Background and Legal Consequences of the Right to be Raised Without Violence' , in Joan Durrant and Anne Smith (eds) *Global Pathways to Abolishing Physical Punishment: Realizing Children's Rights* Routledge, NY, 134–45, 138.

[78] Violence in Upbringing, n. 66 above, 9 [79] Ibid, 13. [80] Ibid, 14.

[81] K D Bussmann (2004) 'Evaluating the Subtle Impact of a Ban on Corporal Punishment of Children in Germany' *Child Abuse Review* 13, 292–311.

[82] Discussed in Bussman (2011), n. 77 above.

> ...the new right to be reared without violence has begun to fulfil its function as a model and orientation aid on various levels—both in families and in the counselling practices of many centers. Nowadays, one can clearly see a general condemnation of the use of violence in childrearing...the law has attained its goal...In 2005, 76% of...parents wanted to...avoid using corporal punishments like slaps on the face...compared to 67% in 2001...91% of adolescents considered that 'Parents should try to talk to their children more, and not be too ready to hit them'.[83]

The experience of Sweden and Germany demonstrates that there can be shifts in attitude away from the use of physical punishment in parenting, and that the law can be a part of such cultural change. The European and Scandinavian political and historical contexts may allow greater acceptance of government regulation than occurs in common law countries.[84] Further, there is a history of Codes being used to spell out rights, which often provide a starting point for community debate. Common law countries present a different context, and New Zealand is the only common law country to ban physical punishment. It therefore provides a valuable illustration of the reform process.

28.5.1.3 New Zealand

After one year's operation, an independent survey of 750 adults over 18 years of age found that whilst many respondents were aware of the law reform (91 per cent), fewer understood its implications (18 per cent knew 'a lot' about the law, 54 per cent 'a fair amount'). Forty-three per cent of respondents supported the law, 28 per cent opposed it, and 26 per cent were neutral (three per cent were unsure). There was a high level of support for the idea that children deserved equal protection from assault as adults (89 per cent). Just over one-third of respondents were firmly opposed to the use of physical discipline, and support for the practice appeared to be in decline, although 58 per cent thought physical punishment of children was acceptable in some situations.[85] Whilst at odds with the finding of support for the legislation, this figure was a significant reduction on the 87 per cent response to this question in 1993.[86]

In New Zealand, the educational goal of the reform could therefore tentatively be said to be achieving some success, in raising the profile of children's rights, without evidence that the reform has significantly increased state intervention in appropriate parental practices. As discussed earlier, a 'citizen-initiated referendum' challenging the 'anti-smacking' legislation was held in 2009 and the right to smack supported by almost 90 per cent of voters; on the other hand, a subsequent attempt to re-legalize smacking was resoundingly unsuccessful in the Parliament.

A factor in the New Zealand reforms was that New Zealand has adopted human rights legislation which includes the widely-recognized protections against 'cruel, inhuman and degrading treatment or punishment' and articulates rights to equal treatment and dignity. The New Zealand reforms were driven by recognition of human rights obligations both domestically and internationally, in a specific political and historical context.[87]

[83] Ibid, 139

[84] This is the view of Janson et al in relation to Sweden: Janson et al., (2011), n .65 above, 253.

[85] Omnibus Survey Report *One Year On: Public Attitudes and New Zealand's Child Discipline Law, Report from the Office of the Children's Commissioner*, 2008 November.

[86] Ibid.

[87] See discussion of the combination of factors leading to the passing of the legislative amendment in Taylor, Wood, and Smith (2011), 'The Achievements and Challenges of Prohibition' in Joan Durrant and Anne Smith (eds) *Global Pathways to Abolishing Physical Punishment: Realizing Children's Rights* Routledge, NY, 184–9.

Such legislation has recently been rejected in Australia, although two jurisdictions, Victoria and the ACT, have state-based human rights legislation.

This is in contrast to the approach in the UK, noted above. The UK has also adopted human rights legislation, and its human rights obligations have been raised in many of the cases on physical punishment of children but have not ultimately been regarded as requiring total abolition. The UN Children's Committee remonstrances have to date been ignored. As also noted earlier, Canada's modified defence has similarly been accepted as consistent with its Charter of Rights despite the expressed qualms of some judges.

Law reforms to protect the rights of children have therefore taken different forms in Scandinavia, in Europe, and in New Zealand. A common feature however has been abolition of the defence of reasonable chastisement, re-engaging the criminal law. Criminal prosecutions, appear to occur rarely and inconsistently, and are perceived to be problematic.

28.5.2 Implementing the criminal laws—prosecution and balancing the interests of 'state' and 'privacy'

28.5.2.1 Sweden

The 1979 reform did not pass without challenge, and there was some public concern that it would lead to many citizens being branded as criminals.[88] Initially prosecutions for corporal punishment in the family home could only be commenced if one of the parents made a complaint or admitted the abuse, a limitation that was removed in 1982.[89] While the 1979 law was framed within the civil Children and Parents Code, and designed to be educative rather than punitive,[90] injured children can sue for damages, parents' use of physical punishment may influence custody cases, and the Penal Code provides for prosecution of parents for actions amounting to assault.[91] As Janson et al. note, referral to welfare services is however prioritized, whether or not the police decide to prosecute.

Family members' reporting of child abuse quadrupled in Sweden from early 1980 to the late 1990s.[92] This was thought to be a result of greater sensitivity to adults' responses to children, and knowledge that abusive parents may have significant family or other problems that affect the law's impact.[93] Annerback et al.'s analysis of all suspected child abuse reports to police in one district of Sweden between 1986 and 1996 revealed that reports mainly related to suspected abuse by socially disadvantaged biological parents. This, they contend, may have been because these parents were more closely monitored. They note that families in which severe abuse has occurred are often already known to social services in relation to previous reports of less serious abuse. Janson et al. observe that:

[88] Janson et al. (2011), n. 65 above, 247.

[89] Ibid, 249.

[90] C. Flynn (1996) 'Normative Support for Corporal Punishment: Attitudes, Correlates and Implications' *Aggression and Violent Behavior* 1, 47–55

[91] Michael Freeman (1999) 'Children are Unbeatable' *Children and Society* 13, 130–41.

[92] Eva-Maria Annerback et al. (2007) 'Severe Child Abuse: a Study of Cases Reported to the Police' *Acta Paediatrica* 96, 1760–4.

[93] Peter Newell (1989) *Children are People Too: The Case against Physical Punishment* London, Bedford Square, 85.

Violence which used to be a family secret, is more likely to be reported today because Swedes are less likely to excuse or minimise the physical abuse of children.[94]

A 2001 study by the Swedish National Council for Crime Prevention found that minor child assault reports to police increased but not reports of moderate to severe child assault.[95] In Sweden prosecutions have not increased; Janson et al. propose that this is largely because the law primarily aimed to be educative, and because welfare measures are favoured above criminal prosecution. At the same time prosecution also presents obstacles, such as the difficulties of prosecuting crimes taking place inside the home, with few if any witnesses and a high burden of proof. Rather than prosecution, all alleged maltreatment is investigated, and a range of supportive and preventative services are available to children in need of protection and families in need of education and support.[96]

28.5.2.2 Germany

In Germany, as noted above, criminal prosecution of parents for hitting their children remains highly unlikely.[97] Bussmann observes, however, that fines have occasionally been imposed in some recent cases:

...the threshold to a punishable bodily integrity is certainly lower than it was under the previous law. In 1987, for example, the Federal Supreme Court still failed to view hitting a child with a 1.4-cm thick length of sturdy hosepipe as a clear transgression of the parental right of chastisement. Through the impact of the new law...local penal courts [in some cases]...no longer exempt violent parents so broadly from their penal responsibilities.[98]

A criminal prosecution must be found to be in the public interest, and Bussman points out that there are at least two inherent obstacles to criminal prosecution: first, the victim (the child or the child's representative) must lodge the complaint, and secondly the child's parent must grant the child consent to lodge the complaint. Needless to say the intervention threshold is very high, except in cases of serious bodily injury or severe cases:

...public prosecutors continue to have reservations about prosecuting parents...The guidelines for criminal prosecution emphasize the particular importance of supporting the family through socio-educational measures, family therapy, or other interventions...public interest in a criminal prosecution can also be dropped in cases of child abuse when such measures are implemented or seem to promise success. Hence, this domain is guided by the principle of providing assistance rather than punishment...The legislature can rightly claim that criminalization of parents is not intended and will also not occur in practice, even though every slap technically constitutes a punishable criminal assault...this legal reform is truly a case of symbolic law.[99]

28.5.2.3 New Zealand

Following legislative reform in New Zealand, there was no rush to prosecute, as had been feared, nor evidence of a significant increase in notifications to welfare agencies. It was reported that '[t]he main feedback...is that people are more willing to report violence against children in public places'.[100] The New Zealand Police conduct

[94] Janson et al. (2011), n. 65 above, 251.
[95] Reported in Janson et al. (2011), n. 65 above. [96] Ibid, 248.
[97] Bussmann (2011), n. 77 above. [98] Ibid, 142.
[99] Ibid, 143–4. [100] *New Zealand Herald* (Auckland), 22 November 2007.

ongoing reviews of the legislation. Initial findings were that there had been little impact on police activity. In the first three months after enactment of the legislation, police attended 111 child assault events. Three involved 'smacking' and 12 involved minor acts of 'physical discipline'; all were considered 'inconsequential and not in the public interest to prosecute'.[101]

The most recent six-monthly review, covering the period December 2009 to June 2010, was the seventh review since the passing of the amendment.[102] It was reported that police attended 416 'child assault events' during the period, of which 25 were identified as involving 'smacking' and 38 involved 'minor acts of physical discipline'.[103] One of the 'smacking' events and two of the 'minor acts of physical discipline' resulted in prosecution.[104] Some of the other cases resulted in warnings, and about half of all the cases also led to referrals to support agencies. The police noted that in none of the three cases did the parent argue that their use of force had been 'reasonable'. The review notes that the third prosecution for a 'smacking event' since the passing of the amendment in June 2007 occurred during this seventh review period. A review of the operation of the amendment carried out for the Ministry of Social Development in 2009 concluded that there was:

> ...no evidence to show that parents are being subject to unnecessary state intervention for occasionally lightly smacking their children or any other unintended consequences of the Act.[105]

On the basis of this outline, we are arguing that the law plays an important role in stating that physical discipline is unacceptable, whether through the removal of any defence, or through positive affirmation of children's rights. It can change attitudes and incidence of the behaviour. At this stage, however, there is little evidence for concern that such legal changes lead to intervention in family life through inappropriate criminal prosecution or other procedures.

28.6 'Responsive regulation' as a new conceptual framework: 'speaking softly but carrying a big stick'

The role of the criminal law is to censure and punish actions that cause harm to individuals and society. On any interpretation, physical discipline of children causes pain, and it can be argued that it therefore falls into this category. As censure, the criminal law is vital in articulating unambiguously the values of the society.

The extent to which criminal laws should *reflect* current values, and to which they can themselves *change* values in a society, is always contentious, particularly

[101] See *Third Review of Police Activity following the Enactment of the Crimes (Substituted Section 59) Amendment Act 2007*, 18 December 2008, 1 <http://www.police.govt.nz/resources/2008/section-59-activity-review/section59_crime_ammendment_act_2007.pdf> at 23 March 2009.

[102] <http://www.police.govt.nz/seventh-review-police-activity-enactment-crimes-substituted-section-59-amendment-act-2007>.

[103] This may be compared with (e.g.) 258 'child assault events' in the third review period. The report notes: 'There is an increase in the number of events attended by police during this review period which is consistent with reduced tolerance and increased reporting of child assault events.'

[104] Two of the cases were prosecuted as 'assault child' and one as 'common assault'. The outcomes were one discharge without conviction, one withdrawn by leave, and one convicted and sentencing adjourned subject to good behaviour.

[105] *Report to the Minister for Social Development and Employment pursuant to section 7(2) of the Crimes (Substituted 59) Amendment Act* 2009, 3.

where the aim of legislating is to claim a normative social value. The examples of Sweden, Germany, and New Zealand support the capacity for law reform to effect real changes in attitudes. Keating optimistically observes that 'in the light of experiences elsewhere in Europe, [law reform in the UK] could be expected to effect real changes in attitudes and practice among parents'.[106]

It must be kept in mind that an angry or frustrated 'smack' is already an assault under Australian and UK law, because the case law has determined that there is no defence for actions carried out in anger, frustration, or vengeance. Ironically, this is the type of behaviour for which there seems to be some sympathy, judging by the commonly-stated concern that loving parents will be inappropriately punished. A 'smack' or 'slap' may, however, be excused as 'trivial' by either the police or the courts. What is protected under the defence is a premeditated assault imposed with the intention of correcting a child's behaviour. Indeed, this intentional correctional behaviour is much more amenable to being changed in response to legal penalty than any emotional and stressed behaviour.

The intervention of the state into the private sphere of family life through the criminal justice process is always controversial. As noted earlier, engagement with intimate partner violence was historically resisted, but has in more recent times become acceptable and indeed expected. This can be explained by reference to developing understandings of women's autonomy and rights, and the shifting balance between privacy and rights. Nonetheless, the use of criminal law does not have to be solely punitive, and can operate as a lever for attitudinal change and social reform. This has been shown in jurisdictions where corporal punishment has been banned. Where there is resistance to law reform of parental physical chastisement, in English-speaking countries other than New Zealand, we endorse a more nuanced approach to criminal law. It can be viewed as one of a range of responses to corporal punishment by parents, which we expect will ultimately be regarded as at least equally abhorrent as domestic violence directed at women. John Braithwaite has evocatively characterized this regulatory approach as 'walking softly and carrying a big stick'.[107]

We propose a principled framework based on the model of 'responsive regulation', outlined by Braithwaite and Ayres. Underlying this model is the idea that behaviour should be regulated 'responsively', allowing the regulated group to show their good intentions (or not) before considering any further intervention.[108] Following from this assumption, it is proposed that initially the least intrusive level of intervention needed to achieve the desired outcome should be employed. More intrusive options are held in reserve for use where the regulated individual is unresponsive or recalcitrant. The regulator (the state, police, prosecutor) requires a sequence of sanctions which can be progressively employed as needed or withdrawn on evidence of compliance and remorse.[109]

The concept of responsive regulation is often represented in the form of a pyramid of actions. The base represents the least interventionist regulations, which should be the most widely employed, and the apex signifies the least-used and most onerous

[106] Keating (2006), n. 23 above, 396

[107] John Braithwaite (1997) 'On Speaking Softly and Carrying Big Sticks: Neglected Dimensions of a Republican Separation of Powers' *University of Toronto Law Journal* 47, 305–61.

[108] Ian Ayres and John Braithwaite (2002) *Responsive Regulation: Transcending the Deregulation Debate* New York, Oxford University Press.

[109] Very serious harm would of course immediately be addressed with more serious responses or sanctions.

regulations, in this case criminal penalties. In the area of parental behaviour we can identify two specific goals, each of which can be elaborated using an Ayres and Braithwaite pyramid model (see Figure 1 below). The first is the establishment of broad social values that demonstrate respect for children, and the second is the establishment, encouragement, and enforcement of parental behaviours that demonstrate respect for children.

To establish the first goal, of desired broad social values, a pyramid of state *actions* aimed at changing social attitudes to parenting in general might have at its base community education campaigns and the provision of child development and parental skills training. More interventionist forms of actions might include sanctions for actions and policies that communicate disrespect for or intolerance of children.

For the second goal, a pyramid of individual *sanctions* aimed at unacceptable parental behaviour can be developed:

Figure 28.1 A pyramid of enforcement responses[110]

The wide base of the pyramid could represent positive approaches such as awareness raising, the provision of information, or a requirement of attendance at an educational programme. It might move on to the offer of parenting support, or the requirement to accept parenting support. Child protection mechanisms may be next, with a hearing or group conference to consider whether removal of the child ought to be posed as an option if behaviours toward the child are not modified. At the apex of the pyramid would be criminal prosecution with the ultimate threat of imprisonment. Criminal procedures would themselves be differentiated into a diversion programme and community based/treatment options, with punitive/custodial options reserved for the worst cases. Depending on the seriousness of the harm or risk, the process might of course immediately begin at the criminal justice level.

It should be recognized that the regulation of behaviours can be achieved through both unorchestrated and intentional/managed mechanisms. Probably the most effective forms of regulation are those that are not directed by the state at all; they are positive cultural values and social attitudes. It is anticipated that people will voluntarily moderate their behaviour to fit in with dominant attitudes and values in the particular society. Cultural and attitudinal change are forms of 'regulation' which are highly

[110] Ayres and Braithwaite (2002), n. 108 above, 35.

desirable, but not always readily achieved. State measures are then put in place to both explicitly promote and hasten such change.

When applying this model to 'common' forms of parental corporal punishment such as pushing or 'smacking', the first avenue would be the encouragement to learn other disciplinary approaches, followed by warnings, and only then would criminal sanctions be considered. As Bussmann observes:

> ... like the Swedish law on which it is modelled, the German legislation is primarily intended as an appeal, since it is not used to extend criminal prosecution to parents. In particular it is seen to satisfy the expectations of the majority of the parents and their children that the law should protect children against violence to the same extent as it does adults.[111]

A similar approach is achieved in New Zealand with the explicit statement in the New Zealand legislation that police should not prosecute 'inconsequential' parental violence.

In the UK, a total ban was seen as risking unacceptable state intervention in the home, making parents fearful of engaging with welfare agencies, and overstretching already-limited child protection resources.[112] However an opinion survey of UK parents also found that over half (58 per cent) supported law reform provided they could be sure that parents 'would not be prosecuted for trivial smacks'.[113] Further, it would be fully anticipated that positive parenting strategies would reduce the need for any more interventionist approaches, as highlighted by the responsive regulation model. For example, Keating notes that:

> ... the development and success of [parenting] programmes suggests that if parents do receive support, the need for child protection agencies to intervene may be much more limited than is feared.[114]

The shift 'upscale' or 'up pyramid' involves decision making at various points, including police and prosecution exercises of discretion whether to proceed. The New Zealand reforms embody criteria for the exercise of police discretion 'where the offence is considered to be so inconsequential that there is no public interest in proceeding'.[115] Guidelines or standing orders would need to be established in each jurisdiction.

Many areas of law affecting private behaviour adopt the approach of positive engagement to encourage compliance, and limited use of available criminal sanctions. Zolotor and Puzia conclude their recent meta-review of the research:

> Anti-corporal punishment legislation should support families and children, not criminalise parents. Herein lies the challenge to governments, to send a clear and strong message to parents without the undue burden of punishment.[116]

This is a widely accepted approach in other areas of law. As one example, the legal requirement across Australia that adults use seat belts in cars was controversial in the 1970s but now entirely accepted, and implemented with community education as well as police checks when carrying out traffic duties. The legal requirement that a child be held securely in a car seat has been implemented with community education,

[111] Violence in Upbringing, n. 66 above, 21.

[112] Keating (2006), n. 23 above, 408–9.

[113] Ibid, 403. [114] Ibid, 409.

[115] s.59(4). See Jeremy Johnson (2009) '"Anti-smacking" Law and Judicial Review' *New Zealand Law Journal* 11–13 for discussion of possible grounds for challenging prosecutorial decisions on the basis of this section.

[116] Zolotor and Puzia (2010), n. 60 above, 244.

availability of low-priced car seats, and hire of seats from child welfare agencies, with the aim of protecting children and minimizing the need for criminal prosecution. A breach is nonetheless a criminal offence.

28.7 Conclusion

We have argued that the notion of a child's right to respect and to equal treatment makes it impossible to endorse the continued lawfulness of physical violence to children, under any guise. As Freeman recently affirmed, emphasizing dignity is 'to engage with our conception of what it is to be human... it is definitive and universal. It is not a value that tolerates either derogation or dissent'.[117]

Removal of the lawful correction defence to assault would not only prevent a parent who assaults his or her child causing injury from defending the assault on the grounds of acceptable discipline. It would encourage all parents to seriously consider the reasonableness of hitting children and promote the use of non-violent, constructive disciplinary methods. It would provide a clear statement of the respect with which all children are held in this society.

If physical punishment was unlawful in Australia parents who unthinkingly use very mild physical responses to children as discipline would not need to fear prosecution, nor do they deserve punishment. In present times, both the legal principle of 'de minimus' and police discretion guard against this. As noted above, many parents indeed admonish themselves for not choosing better disciplinary alternatives.

'Walking softly' therefore appears to be the most palatable approach, with ongoing attention to changing the culture of parenting to enhance parents' skills in non-violent discipline. This model must nonetheless be backed up by a genuine 'threat' or 'big stick' to more confidently ensure desirable behavioural and attitudinal change, and to advance progress toward a society that does not tolerate or condone any violence directed at children in any context. This approach is already being employed, with the valuable changes in behaviour and attitudes summarized earlier, and should be embraced in Australia and the UK.

We nevertheless look for the arrival of the time when the assault of children does not seem to require different legal or procedural rules to any other assaults. Murray Straus observes that there continues to be a 'cultural myth' that mild physical discipline by well-intentioned parents is occasionally necessary; this is however:

> just as contradictory as being against slapping a spouse for misbehavior, while also believing that a slap may sometimes be necessary, and is harmless if done in moderation by a loving partner. We do not insist on providing training in conflict resolution skills as a precondition for a no-wife-slapping educational effort, and we should not require it for a no-corporal punishment educational effort.[118]

As a number of members of the House of Lords wrote to the *Guardian* newspaper in 2004, children:

> are people, albeit smaller and more vulnerable, and they have human rights like the rest of us. However, children are the only members of society who can be legally assaulted

[117] Freeman (2010), n. 25 above, 251.

[118] Straus (2000), n. 34 above, 111.

and, as a matter of conscience, we are determined to put right that longstanding wrong.[119]

Violent responses to children in any guise are neither an acceptable nor a private matter. Even in relationships between parents and children, laws can encourage people to behave morally. Children's human rights and equality must at last be recognized in 21st century society.

[119] Keating (2006), n. 23 above, 410–11, quoting 'Letter by 17 peers', *Guardian*, 5 July 2004.

29

Litigating the Child's Right to a Life Free from Violence: Seeking the Prohibition of Parental Physical Punishment of Children Through the Courts

Aoife Nolan[1]

29.1 Introduction: the move towards the abolition of parental physical punishment

The right of parents to punish their children physically (or to carry out corporal punishment in the home) seems to be under threat.[1A] While the first explicit legal prohibition of parental corporal punishment was enacted by Sweden in 1979, the last three decades have seen such treatment being proscribed in a wide range of countries with different social, cultural, and legal traditions, including Israel, Croatia, Kenya, Iceland, Nepal, and New Zealand.[2] Thirty-one countries,[3] including 22 members of the Council of Europe, have explicitly abolished all corporal punishment.[4] As of December 2010, a further 23 states have made an explicit commitment to prohibition

[1] Law, Durham University.

[1A] Corporal or physical punishment has been defined by the Committee on the Rights of the Child as 'any punishment in which physical force is used and intended to cause some degree of pain or discomfort, however light' (ComRC, *General Comment No.8 on the right of the child to protection from corporal punishment and other cruel or degrading forms of punishment (arts. 19; 28, para.2, and 37, inter alia), para 11)* (2006), UN Doc. CRC/C/GC/8. This will be the definition employed in this chapter.

[2] Information taken from Global Initiative to End All Corporal Punishment of Children, *Ending legalised violence against children: Global Report 2007*, 6–7.

[3] Global Initiative to End All Corporal Punishment of Children/Save the Children Sweden, *Ending legalised violence against children: Global Report 2010* (Nottingham, Russell Press Limited, 2010) 23. According to this report, the following 29 states have prohibited corporal punishment in all settings, including the home: Austria (1989); Bulgaria (2000); Costa Rica (2008); Croatia (1998); Cyprus (1994); Denmark (1997); Finland (1983); Germany (2000); Greece (2006); Hungary (2004); Iceland (2003); Israel (2000); Kenya (2010); Latvia (1998); Liechtenstein (2008); Luxembourg (2008); Netherlands (2007); New Zealand (2007); Norway (1987); Poland (2010); Portugal (2007); Republic of Moldova (2008); Romania (2004); Spain (2007); Sweden (1979); Tunisia (2010); Ukraine (2003); Uruguay (2007); Venezuela (2007). Togo (2011) and South Sudan (2011) have since abolished parental physical punishment. For accounts of a range of different national experiences in relation to the legal prohibition of PPP, see J. Durrant and A. Smith (eds), *Global Pathways to Abolishing Physical Punishment* (Abingdon, Routledge, 2011).

[4] Other Council of Europe members states have committed themselves to explicit law reform (Source: Council of Europe, 'Eliminating Corporal Punishment: A Human Rights Imperative for Europe's Children').

in all settings and/or are actively considering prohibiting legislation.[5] In December of 2007 alone, Spain, Venezuela, and Chile passed measures resulting in the prohibition of the corporal punishment of children. Uruguay had done so the previous month.

The abolition of parental physical punishment (PPP) has generally occurred through the amendment of national codes and legislation to either repeal legal defences, laws, or regulations authorizing corporal punishment, and/or by enshrining explicit prohibitions of corporal punishment in legislation applying to the home and family.[6] Some prohibitions are explicitly child rights-based,[7] while others are not.[8] Many of these national changes are reflective of the ever-more assertive opposition towards parental and other forms of corporal punishment being articulated by international and regional human rights bodies.[9] Such opposition has been most notably expressed by the UN Committee on the Rights of the Child in its 2006 *General Comment No.8 on the right of the child to protection from corporal punishment and other cruel or degrading forms of punishment*.[10] The Committee has made it clear that a failure to prohibit the PPP of children amounts to a violation of multiple provisions of the Convention on the Rights of the Child (CRC); it has stated that 'the Convention requires the removal of any provisions (in statute or common-case law) that allow some degree of violence against children (e.g., "reasonable" or "moderate" chastisement or correction), in their homes/families or in any other setting'.[11] According to the Committee:

> simply repealing authorisation of corporal punishment and any existing defences is not enough. In addition, explicit prohibition of corporal punishment and other cruel or degrading forms of punishment in their civil or criminal legislation, is required in order to make it absolutely clear that it is as unlawful to hit or 'smack' or 'spank' a child as to do so an adult,

[5] Global Initiative to End All Corporal Punishment of Children/Save the Children Sweden, *Ending legalised violence against children: Global Report 2010* (Nottingham, Russell Press Limited, 2010) 7.

[6] Such legislative measures have been identified by the Global Initiative to End All Corporal Punishment of Children as 'key elements of law reform' required for the effective prohibition of corporal punishment (Global Initiative to End All Corporal Punishment of Children, *Prohibiting corporal punishment of children: A guide to legal reform and other measures*, 8).

[7] See, e.g., Article 32a of the Venezuelan Ley Orgánica para la Protección de Niños, Niñas y Adolscentes, which provides that: 'All children and young people have a right to be treated well. This right includes a non-violent education and upbringing, based on love, affection, mutual understanding and respect, and solidarity.' (English translation from the Spanish at: <http://www.crin.org/resources/infoDetail.asp?ID=15885&flag=news>).

[8] See, e.g., Uruguay, where an article incorporated into an older law (Law No. 17.823 of 7 September 2004 (Código de la Niñez y la Adolescencia)) to give effect to the abolition made no reference to the rights of the child (Source: <http://www.crin.org/docs/FileManager/uruguay_castigo_senado_ag_07.doc>). There was, however, a reference to the rights of the child elsewhere in the law being amended.

[9] See, e.g., the campaign for the abolition of all corporal punishment of children being carried out by the Council of Europe discussed below. For a discussion of the approach of different international regional human rights bodies to PPP, see M. Freeman, 'Upholding the Dignity and Best Interests of Children: International Law and the Corporal Punishment of Children' (2010) 73 *Law and Contemporary Problems* 213.

[10] This concern about all forms of violence against children amongst UN member states was been demonstrated by the adoption of *UN GA Resolution A/RES/62/141 on the Rights of the Child*, 18 December 2007 by the UN General Assembly, creating the new position of Special Representative of the Secretary-General on violence against children. Bearing in mind that this resolution was voted for by a number of governments that have expressed opposition to the prohibition of parental physical punishment (only the US voted against the resolution), the author is certainly not making the case that the adoption of this resolution constitutes definitive evidence of a common belief on the part of states voting in favour that there should be a complete abolition of corporal punishment in the home.

[11] See ComRC, General Comment No. 8, para 10.

and that the criminal law on assault does apply equally to such violence, regardless of whether it is termed 'discipline' or 'reasonable correction'.[12]

However, while much has been achieved in terms of the battle for the legal proscription of the physical punishment of children, a large number of countries remain resistant to the concept of the total abolition of corporal punishment by parents. One example of this is the October 2007 decision of the South African National Assembly's Portfolio Committee on Social Development to remove draft Section 139 banning all corporal punishment of children by their parents from the Children's Amendment Bill[13] due to 'the need for further investigation of the matter'.[14] This excision—which resulted from the resistance of a range of politicians to an abolition of parental physical punishment—occurred despite the objections of numerous national children's rights organizations.[15] It is notable that this instance of a failure by law-makers to take a decisive step to prohibit PPP occurred in a country which has one of the most emphatic and detailed range of child rights protections at both the constitutional and statutory levels in the world. In a similar vein, 2010 saw the UK Government's Chief Adviser on the Safety of Children publish a report that recommended smacking should be banned in all places outside the home.[16] According to the Adviser, 'any attempt to define those family categories or circumstances to which the availability of the defence ought or ought not to apply would be cumbersome, bureaucratic, largely impractical and very difficult to communicate'.[17] In terms of UK politicians' views, 2004 saw an effort to add a new clause to the Children Bill removing the common law defence of 'reasonable chastisement' being defeated overwhelmingly by MPs from a range of different political parties.[18]

These and other domestic examples of law-makers refusing to legally enshrine a prohibition of PPP demonstrate that there can be no general presumption that elected representatives will inevitably favour, or be convinced by, arguments that PPP should be prohibited. This is true even in jurisdictions where there are relatively high levels of awareness of children's rights. The difference in the attitudes of elected representatives on the issue seems likely to be reflective of (and is certainly consistent with)

[12] ComRC, General Comment No. 8, para 34.

[13] B19F of 2006. Now the Children's Amendment Act 41 of 2007.

[14] Portfolio Committee on Social Development Report. Parliament Of The Republic Of South Africa, Announcements, Tabling And Committee Reports, Wednesday, 24 October 2007 [No 126–2007], Fourth Session, Third Parliament cited in Children's Rights Institute, *Children's Bill Progress Update: Changes to the Children's Amendment Bill by the National Assembly* (November 2007): <http://www.ci.org.za/depts/ci/plr/pdf/progress/5%20Nov%20Progress%20Update.pdf>, 11.

[15] See, e.g., the submissions of the Working Group on Positive Discipline, a coalition of children's rights organizations and others in relation to the Child Amendment Act at: <http://www.rapcan.org.za/wgpd/default.asp>. The Committee did state, however, that it anticipated this matter being finalized in a proposed amendment bill to be introduced in 2008. (Portfolio Committee on Social Development Report, above n. 14, 11.) This has not yet occurred, however. The Committee also made amendments to Section 144 on *Purposes of prevention and early intervention programmes*, stating that 'Prevention and early intervention programmes must focus on—*(b)* developing appropriate parenting skills and the capacity of parents and care-givers to safeguard the well-being and best interests of their children, including the promotion of positive, non-violent forms of discipline'.

[16] Chief Adviser on the Safety of Children, *Physical punishment: Improving Consistency and Protection: An Independent Report by Sir Roger Singleton, Chief Adviser on the Safety of Children* (March 2010): <http://publications.dcsf.gov.uk/default.aspx?PageFunction=productdetails&PageMode=publications&ProductId=DCSF-00282–2010>.

[17] Ibid, 2.

[18] 'MPs oppose moves to ban smacking', *BBC News*, 3 November 2004: <http://news.bbc.co.uk/1/hi/uk_politics/3972453.stm>.

evidence that views on the desirability or effectiveness of PPP vary between both different societies[19] and members of the same ones.

In addition to lobbying and conducting campaigns aimed at the political branches of government, children's rights advocates have also sought to bring about the prohibition of PPP through challenging state measures permitting such treatment of children before domestic and international judicial and quasi-judicial decision-making bodies. Some of these cases have involved an individual challenge arising out of a particular factual situation. For instance, the European Court of Human Rights (ECtHR) decision in *A v UK* involved an application made by a nine-year-old boy who had been subjected to repeated beatings by his stepfather with a garden cane applied with considerable force.[20] His stepfather was charged with assault occasioning actual bodily harm but was found not guilty on the basis that it was a defence to a charge of assault on a child under English law that the treatment in question amounted to 'reasonable chastisement'. The ECtHR considered that the treatment in question reached the minimum level of severity necessary to fall within the scope of Article 3 (prohibition on torture and inhuman or degrading treatment or punishment) and concluded that English law did not provide adequate protection to the applicant in terms of that provision.[21]

Other litigation has been taken as part of broader campaigns centred on child protection and/or the abolition of parental physical punishment. Examples include the collective complaints brought before the European Committee of Social Rights (European Committee) by the World Organization against Torture/Organisation Mondiale Contre la Torture (OMCT) against a range of European states, as well as the litigation brought before the Northern Irish courts by the Northern Ireland Commissioner on Children and Young People (NICCY), respectively. These are discussed below.

In addition to seeking the establishment of a prohibition through the resolution of a specific legal case, children's rights advocates have sought the abolition of PPP by appealing to the advisory (or non-contentious) jurisdiction of domestic courts or international quasi-judicial bodies. In one celebrated instance, Save the Children Sweden and the Andean Commission of Jurists requested the Inter-American Commission on Human Rights to declare all corporal punishment of children a breach of their human rights.[22] They requested further that the Commission would seek an advisory opinion on the issue from the Inter-American Human Rights Court.[23] The Court ultimately refused to hand down an advisory opinion on the

[19] See, e.g., the research findings quoted in the Independent Expert for the United Nations Secretary-General's Study on Violence against Children, *World Report on Violence against Children* (Geneva, United Nations, 2006) 53, which demonstrate the sharply divergent attitudes towards parental corporal punishment held by adults in a range of different jurisdictions.

[20] *A v UK* (1999) 27 EHRR 61.

[21] The applicant also complained before the Commission that the state had failed to protect him from ill-treatment by his stepfather, in violation of Articles 3 and/or 8 of the Convention; that he had been denied a remedy for these complaints in violation of Article 13; and that the domestic law on assault discriminated against children, in violation of Article 14 in conjunction with Articles 3 and 8. The applicant ultimately did not pursue his claim in relation to these latter two points before the Court. Given its finding in relation to Article 3, the Court did not regard it as necessary to examine whether the inadequacy of the legal protection provided to A against the ill-treatment that he suffered also breached his right to respect for private life under Article 8.

[22] 'Inter-American Commission on Human Rights: Call to End All Corporal Punishment of Children', 5 October 2005: <http://www.crin.org/../violence/search/closeup.asp?infoID=6367>.

[23] Ibid.

basis that 'answers to the questions asked . . . can be drawn from a full analysis and interpretation of the body of jurisprudence of the Tribunal regarding the rights of the child and relating to other criteria established for the child, as well as from the obligations issued by other international instruments ratified by the States in the region'.[24] Having referred extensively to provisions of the CRC, as well as General Comment No. 8, the Court stated that its jurisprudence constituted a positive answer to the questions asked by the Commission in its Request; namely, whether states should regulate paternal authority and protection in such a way as to protect children against all forms of corporal punishment, and whether states are under the obligation to adopt legislative and other measures in order to ensure that children are not subjected to corporal punishment as a method of discipline in the family, at school, or in institutions.[25]

Litigation efforts seeking the prohibition of PPP have met with mixed success. While some judicial and quasi-judicial bodies have been prepared to hold that such activity is a violation of a variety of children's rights, others have refused to do so. This chapter focuses on a number of recent rulings by courts and international quasi-judicial bodies involving challenges to state permission of physical punishment of children by their parents.[26] I have selected these cases on the basis that they involve the courts and quasi-judicial bodies under consideration specifically addressing the issue of the absolute prohibition of PPP in the context of exercising contentious jurisdiction. The cases addressed are amongst the most celebrated examples of judicial engagements with PPP.[27]

The chapter analyses these decisions with the primary aim of identifying common or contrasting elements in terms of the reasoning employed by judges and other decision-makers in either upholding or striking down the legality of PPP. It argues that approaches adopted by the decision-makers under consideration to the issue of PPP vary widely in terms of, amongst other things, judicial or quasi-judicial understandings and weighting of children's rights, the balance struck between such rights and parental autonomy, and the role played by international child rights standards and comparative experiences in relation to the prohibition of PPP. The chapter considers how these variations operate in relation to determining whether or not a court will be prepared to find in favour of a prohibition of PPP.

The chapter opens with a discussion of the 'value' of a legal prohibition of PPP. The following section outlines the key facts of the decisions under consideration. Next, I outline common elements and divergences in the legal reasoning adopted by different bodies addressing the question of the permissibility of PPP. This includes a discussion of the particular understandings of 'children' as right-holders (or not) demonstrated by those decision-makers, as well as a consideration of the connection between such and judicial/quasi-judicial willingness to proscribe PPP. I conclude by considering

[24] Inter-American Court of Human Rights, Decision on Request for Advisory Opinion Presented by the Inter-American Commission on Human Rights, 30 March 2009, para 15: <http://www.endcorporalpunishment.org/pages/pdfs/ResolutionIACHR.pdf>.

[25] Ibid, paras 9–11

[26] For the sake of convenience, both judicial and quasi-judicial decision-making bodies that are discussed in this chapter will be referred to as courts, albeit that the author is fully aware of the difference between, amongst other things, the binding nature of the decisions made by such bodies.

[27] While I would also have liked to address Decision No. 4909 of 16 May 1996 of the Italian Court of Cassation which is discussed briefly below at n. 42, I was unable to do so due to an inability to locate a full translation of that decision.

the implications that the chapter's findings will have in terms of indicating when and where litigation seeking the abolition of PPP will be successful.

29.2 The value of the legal prohibition of PPP: a question of symbolism rather than impact?

Before launching into a consideration of the relevant case law, it is important to consider what is at the heart of children's rights activists' quest to have the courts prohibit parental corporal punishment.[28]

According to the UN Study on Violence, 'studies from many countries in all regions of the world suggest that up to 80 to 98 per cent of children suffer physical punishment in their homes, with a third or more experiencing severe physical punishment resulting from the use of implements'.[29] The legal abolition of parental corporal punishment is considered by many children's rights activists to be a key element in the quest to bring an end to violence against children in the home.[30] Indeed, the presumption underlining the work of those seeking the abolition of PPP by the courts is that such a prohibition will lead to a reduction in parental violence against children and an increased enjoyment of children of the right to protection from all forms of violence, set out most notably in Articles 19 and 37 of the CRC.[31] Certainly,

[28] This chapter does not involve an in-depth consideration of whether parental physical punishment of children is unjustifiable. For a general discussion of different theorists on the question of whether corporal punishment of children including PPP can be morally or legally justified, see S. Turner, 'Justifying Corporal Punishment of Children Loses Its Appeal' (2003) 11 *International Journal of Children's Rights* 219. Archard has pointed out that for corporal punishment to be 'seriously wrongful' or 'subabusive', it would need to be established that such punishment does the child more harm than good, has serious harmful effects on a child's development, or that the feasible alternative forms of disciplining children are just as effective (D. Archard, *Children, Rights and Childhood*, 2nd Edn (London, Routledge, 2004), 197–8). Certainly, there appears to be evidence that this is the case. Durrant argues in her review of empirical findings on the impact of PPP that there now exists an 'overwhelming amount of evidence that has accumulated over past decades to demonstrate that physical punishment predicts negative developmental outcomes with remarkable consistency' (J. Durrant, 'The Empirical Rationale for Eliminating Physical Punishment' in J. Durrant and A. Smith (eds), *Global Pathways to Abolishing Physical Punishment* (Abingdon, Routledge, 2011) 42, 42). For an overview of the literature addressing the impact of PPP on children, see E. Gershoff and S. Bitensky, 'The Case against Corporal Punishment of Children: Converging Evidence from Social Science Research and International Human Rights Law and Implications for US Public Policy' (2008) 13(4) *Psychology, Public Policy and Law* 231, 233–40. See also R. Larzelere, 'Child Outcomes of Nonabusive and Customary Physical Punishment by Parents: An Updated Literature Review' (2000) 3 *Clinical Child and Family Psychology Review* 199. For an argument that the leading theories of children and childhood predict that physical punishment, including PPP, will be detrimental to children's development, see A. Smith, 'The Theoretical Rationale for Eliminating Physical Punishment' in J. Durrant and A. Smith (eds), *Global Pathways to Abolishing Physical Punishment* (Abingdon, Routledge, 2011), 27.

[29] *Report of the Independent Expert for the United Nations Study on Violence against Children*, UN Doc. A/61/299, para 28.

[30] For instance, the prohibition by the state of all forms of violence against children, in all settings, was a key recommendation of the independent expert for the United Nations study on violence against children in his report (*Report of the Independent Expert for the United Nations Study on Violence against Children*, UN Doc. A/61/299, para 98). It should be noted, however, that neither the independent expert nor children's rights organizations that are in favour of the abolition of PPP regard legal proscription as capable of bringing about the elimination of PPP in the absence of other accompanying measures.

[31] See, e.g., the statement of the Global Initiative to End All Corporal Punishment of Children that '[w]ithin the family, corporal punishment is in most countries explicitly condoned in the law, giving parents active encouragement and legitimacy in using it in bringing up their children. In some countries, the law is silent on the issue, failing to challenge traditional assumptions that hitting children

that is the view of the Committee on the Rights of the Child which has stated that '[t]he first purpose of law reform to prohibit corporal punishment of children within the family is prevention: to prevent violence against children by changing attitudes and practice, underlining children's right to equal protection and providing an unambiguous foundation for child protection and for the promotion of positive, non-violent and participatory forms of child-rearing'.[32]

As with all laws criminalizing particular behaviour, one might query whether a ban on PPP does or will, in fact, serve as a deterrent. This chapter does not argue that the prohibition of physical punishment will necessarily deter adults from employing violence in chastising their children in all—or even many—cases. Bearing in mind that the prohibition of PPP is reactive in nature, it seems highly unlikely to ameliorate (or indeed, address to any significant degree) underlying causes of violence against children such as poverty, or societal or cultural factors such as gender discrimination, adultism, and patriarchy.[33] There is certainly some evidence that would suggest that the prohibition of PPP does reduce the incidence of such parental activity. For instance, follow-up studies on the effects of the Swedish prohibition of PPP, seem to indicate that the use of physical punishment among Swedish parents has decreased significantly.[34] Indeed, it would seem surprising that an explicit recognition that PPP was illegal and (very importantly) the establishment of a system concerned with the effective enforcement of that ban would have no impact whatsoever on levels of PPP—especially if accompanied by awareness-raising, parental education programmes, and policies and programmes aimed at supporting families.[35]

At the most basic level, the reduced incidence of PPP in countries with prohibitions on such activity is almost certainly reflective of a society that is more child rights-conscious.[36] However, the introduction of such a ban seems likely to have an educative effect in itself, resulting in greater societal awareness of children's rights.[37] Thus, to some extent, we are faced with a 'chicken and egg' scenario.

is acceptable. Only where the law expressly bans its use is there a clear message to parents and others that hitting children is wrong' (Global Initiative to End All Corporal Punishment of Children/Save the Children Sweden, *Ending legalised violence against children: Global Report 2010* (Nottingham, Russell Press Limited, 2010), 30).

[32] ComRC, General Comment No. 8, para 38.

[33] For a discussion of causes of or factors contributing to violence in the home and family, see Report of the Independent Expert for the United Nations Study on Violence against Children, UN Doc. A/61/299, 68–72; 398; D. Ghate, 'Family Violence and Violence Against Children' (2000) 14 *Law & Society* 395, 398.

[34] See, G. Jutengren and K. Palmérus, 'A Comparison of Swedish and US Fathers' Self-reported Use of Parental Discipline' (2002) 16 *Children & Society* 246, 248; S. Janson, 'Response to Beckett, C. (2005) "The Swedish Myth: The Corporal Punishment Ban and Child Death Statistics", *British Journal of Social Work*, 35(1), 125–38' (2005) 35(8) *British Journal of Social Work* 1411.

[35] The key role of educational and information campaigns in contributing to a reduction in PPP following a legal ban is demonstrated by a comparison of the difference in the levels of reduction of PPP in jurisdictions where a prohibition of such activity was accompanied by ongoing nation-wide awareness campaigns and those jurisdictions where it was not. See, e.g., K. Bussmann, C. Erthal, and A. Schroth, 'Effects of Banning Corporal Punishment in Europe: A Five-Nation Comparison' in J. Durrant and A. Smith (eds), *Global Pathways to Abolishing Physical Punishment* (Abingdon, Routledge, 2011), 299.

[36] This is reflected in the fact that campaigns directed towards the prohibition of PPP are frequently heavily couched in the language of children's rights or that legal prohibitions of PPP often take place in the context of child rights-based legislation.

[37] See, e.g., the experience in Sweden where Durrant notes that, 'What is clearly the case is that as each reform was made, public attitudes changed—and as attitudes changed, support for further reform increased. All of these changes—attitudinal and legislative—took place within the context of increasing knowledge of child development and parenting, as well as growing recognition of children as holders of

However, the justification for the legal abolition of parental corporal punishment is not simply based on the effect that such a ban would have on the incidence of parental corporal punishment. The prohibition of PPP of children has strong symbolic value as it involves the acknowledgement of children as autonomous individuals who are entitled to state protection from being the victims of violations of the right to freedom from all forms of violence. It is a statement that this right adheres to them regardless of who perpetrates such violence and what aim the perpetrators are seeking to achieve. It thereby ensures that children's dignity and bodily integrity are to be respected and recognizes children's equality with other members of society whose right to live free from violence is already guaranteed under the law. As Freeman has noted: 'nothing is a clearer statement of the position that children occupy in society, a clearer badge of childhood and what we associate with it, than the fact that children alone of all people in society can be hit with impunity. There is probably no more significant step that could be taken to advance both the status and protection of children than to outlaw the practice of physical punishment.'[38]

The imposition of a legal obligation on a particular state to prevent PPP empowers children to claim protection from that state. In doing so, it challenges the subordination of the individual autonomy of the child to that of the parents/family. It also explicitly limits the rights of parents in relation to the education and disciplining of the child. Thus, while the actual 'impact' of a prohibition of PPP may be open to question, its symbolic value is undeniable.

29.3 Introducing the cases

My analysis in this chapter focuses on two sets of decisions. The first involves instances in which courts or international quasi-judicial decision-making bodies have held that PPP is impermissible. This includes a group of decisions made by the European Committee of Social Rights in relation to a number of collective complaints brought by the OMCT against Belgium, Portugal, Italy, Ireland, and Greece,[39] all of which are states parties to the European Social Charter and/or Revised Charter. In these complaints, the OMCT alleged that, by failing explicitly and effectively to prohibit parents and 'other persons' from inflicting corporal punishment on children, and by offering children no effective protection against corporal punishment in the family or various other contexts,[40] the states parties in question had failed to comply with Article 17 of the European Charter or the Revised Charter.

human rights' (J Durrant, 'Legal Reform and Attitudes Toward Physical Punishment in Sweden' (2003) 11 *International Journal of Children's Rights* 143, 152). For a claim that legislative reform did not reduce the level of public support for parental use of corporal punishment as a means of disciplining children in Sweden but rather that changes in public opinion may have generated the legal reform, see J. Roberts, 'Changing Public Attitudes Towards Corporal Punishment: The Effects of Statutory Reform in Sweden' (2000) 24(8) *Child Abuse and Neglect* 1027.

[38] M. Freeman, 'The Future of Children's Rights' (2000) 14 *Children & Society* 277, 287.

[39] 21/2003, *World Organization against Torture (OMCT) v Belgium*, 26 January 2005; 20/2003, *OMCT v Portugal*, 26 January 2005; 19/2003, *OMCT v Italy*, 26 January 2005; 18/2005, *OMCT v Ireland*, 26 January 2005; 17/2003, *OMCT v Greece*, 26 January 2005; 34/2006, *OMCT v Portugal*, 5 December 2006.

[40] For example, in *OMCT v Greece*, ibid, the complainant alleged that Greece did not explicitly and effectively prohibit corporal punishment against children in secondary schools and other institutions and forms of care for children, as well as in the family. In *OMCT v Ireland*, ibid, the complainant

In all of the OMCT decisions, the European Committee stated that its case law was to the effect that the prohibition of all the forms of violence must have a legislative basis and that 'the prohibition must cover all forms of violence regardless of where it occurs or of the identity of the alleged perpetrator. Furthermore, the sanctions available must be adequate, dissuasive and proportionate'.[41] In doing so, the European Committee emphasized that the Charter is a living instrument that must be interpreted in light of developments in the national law of member states of the Council of Europe as well as relevant international instruments. In its interpretation of Article 17 of both instruments, the European Committee referred in particular to Article 19 CRC as interpreted by the Committee on the Rights of the Child, Article 3 ECHR as interpreted by the European Court of Human Rights, Recommendations adopted by the Council of Europe Committee of Ministers on the medico-social aspects of child abuse and on violence within the family, as well as Parliamentary Assembly Recommendation 1666 (2004) on a 'Europe-wide ban on corporal punishment of children'.

The European Committee found all of the respondent states, bar Italy and Portugal, to be in violation of Article 17. According to the European Committee, domestic judicial interpretations by the Italian and Portuguese courts of particular legislative provisions essentially amounted to the prohibition of all forms of violence in those jurisdictions having a legislative basis.[42] In the later decision of *OMCT v Portugal*, the Committee stated further that Article 17 required that 'The relevant provisions must be sufficiently clear, binding and precise, so as to preclude the courts from refusing to apply them to violence against children'.[43] Moreover, de jure legal reform was not enough—states are obliged to act with due diligence to ensure that such violence is eliminated in practice.[44]

Two domestic cases, both of which involved the application of criminal law to PPP, also resulted in a finding that PPP must be prohibited by the state. The first, *Plonit v Israel*,[45] involved an appeal taken by a mother against her conviction and sentence for the crimes of abuse and assault of a minor resulting from her violence

highlighted the state's failure to prohibit the corporal punishment of children in the home, foster care, residential homes, and in the care of certain child minders.

[41] See, e.g., *OMCT v Belgium*, above n. 39, para 39.

[42] In Decision No. 4909 of 16 May 1996, the Italian Court of Cassation held that violence against children, no matter how slight, is never a 'lawful' correctional measure, any abuse of which would be punishable under Article 571 of the Italian Criminal Code on 'Abuse of correctional measures or discipline'. Rather such violence comes under the ill-treatment provided for in Article 572 on 'Ill-treatment in the family or of children', which makes provision for more serious penalties. The Committee's finding in relation to this is arguably problematic in light of the fact that, due to Italy's civil legal system, this decision is, in theory at least, not binding on other courts in terms of precedent in the way that it would be under a common law system. (For more on this decision, including the question of the enforceability of the court's rulings on other courts, see S. Bitensky, 'Spare the Rod, Embrace our Humanity: Toward a New Legal Regime Prohibiting Corporal Punishment of Children' (1998) 31 *University of Michigan Journal of Law* 353. In the case of Portugal, the Supreme Court made a ruling subsequent to the Committee's original finding of compliance finding that moderate punishments administered to the minor by the person entitled to do it and whose purpose is exclusively educational and adequate to the situation, are not unlawful (5 April 2006 (06P 468)). OMCT subsequently brought a second complaint and the Committee found Portugal to be in violation of Article 17 of the Revised Charter (34/2006, *World Organization Against Torture (OMCT) v Portugal*, 5 December 2006).

[43] *Portugal v OMCT*, para 20. [44] *Portugal v OMCT*, para 21.

[45] CrimA 4596/98 *Plonit v Israel* [2000] IsrSC 54(1) P.D. 145. The references below are taken from an unofficial translation: <http://www.endcorporalpunishment.org/pages/pdfs/Israel_Judgment.pdf>. For useful analyses and critiques of this decision, the legal, societal and political responses thereto and its impact, see Y. Kaplan, 'Corporal Punishment of Children in Israel: A New Trend in Secular and Religious Law' (2006) 14 *International Journal of Children's Rights* 363; R. Schuz, 'Three Years On:

towards her two children. Here, the Israeli Supreme Court concluded that reasonable parental corporal punishment no longer constituted a defence to criminal assault and that regular use of hitting/beating as a method of discipline came within the crime of child abuse, and, as a behavioural rather than a causative crime, did not require proof of intent to cause an injurious result. In doing so, the court considered the evolution of the notion of 'reasonable' parental corporal punishment in UK, US, and Canadian law,[46] as well as the position of the child as a right-holder under both the CRC and the Israeli legal framework.[47] It concluded that 'corporal punishment of children, or humiliation and derogation from their dignity as a method of education by their parents, is entirely impermissible, and is a remnant of a societal educational outlook that has lost its validity'.[48] The court emphasized that 'we cannot leave "open" the definition of "reasonable" and thus compromise at the risk of danger to the health and welfare of children',[49] choosing instead to adopt a 'professional-educational approach which rejects corporal punishment as an educational tool'[50] and 'that stresses the right of the child to dignity, bodily integrity and health of mind'.[51]

In *Writ Number 57 of the year 2061 (2005)*,[52] the Nepal Supreme Court considered a proviso to Section 7 of the Children's Act 2048 (1992), which prohibited children being subjected to torture or cruel treatment. This provision stated that 'any act by the mother, father of family member, guardian or teacher to scold the child or give him/her minor beating for the sake of his or her interest shall not be deemed to violate this Section'. The decision resulted from a petition brought by advocates of persons working against torture, including that of children.[53] The court ultimately held that the section was contrary to the spirit of Articles 14(4) and 25(8) of the Nepalese Constitution. Article 14(4) provides that no person shall be subjected to physical or mental torture nor shall be given any cruel, inhuman, or degrading treatment. Article 25(8) sets out the obligation of the state to make necessary arrangements for the safeguard of the rights and interest of children. The court issued a directive order, requiring the executive to 'pursue appropriate and effective measures to prevent physical punishment as well as other cruel, inhuman or degrading treatment of punishment being imposed or inflicted on and likely to be imposed or inflicted on children'.[54]

This chapter also addresses two national cases in which courts were not prepared to hold PPP to be impermissible. The first, *Canadian Foundation for Children, Youth and the Law v Canada*,[55] centred on a challenge to Section 43 of the Canadian Criminal Code, which provides a defence to assault for parents, guardians, and teachers who use reasonable force in disciplining children.[56] The complainants argued that the

An Analysis of the Delegalization of Physical Punishment of Children by the Israeli Courts' (2003) 11 *International Journal of Children's Rights* 235.

[46] In doing so, it explicitly criticized the legislative approach adopted in Section 43 of the Canadian Criminal Code which is discussed below in the context of *Canadian Foundation for Children, Youth and the Law v Canada (Attorney General)* 2004 SCC 4.

[47] For more, see below at 29.4.4.

[48] *Plonit v Israel*, 11. [49] Ibid, 6. [50] Ibid. [51] Ibid.

[52] 6 January 2005. References are taken from the translation of the decision provided at: <http://www.endcorporalpunishment.org/pages/hrlaw/judgment-nepal.html>.

[53] While the court also addressed the issue of physical punishment in an educational context, this chapter will focus on its findings with regard to PPP.

[54] *Writ Number 57*.

[55] *Canadian Foundation for Children, Youth and the Law v Canada (Attorney General)* 2004 SCC 4.

[56] Section 43 provides that '[e]very schoolteacher, parent or person standing in the place of a parent is justified in using force by way of correction toward a pupil or child, as the case may be, who is under his care, if the force does not exceed what is reasonable under the circumstances'.

provision violated Section 7 (right to life, liberty, and security of person and the right not to be deprived thereof except in accordance with the principles of fundamental justice) and Section 12 (right not to be subjected to any cruel and unusual treatment or punishment) of the Canadian Charter of Rights and Freedoms. Finally, it was claimed that the provision impugned Section 15(1) (right to equality before and under law and the right to equal protection and equal benefit of the law without discrimination) because it denied children the legal protection against assaults that is accorded to adults. A majority of the court found against the claimants on all three points.

While the court (and the defendant state) conceded that Section 43 adversely affected children's security of the person, it disagreed that the provision offended a principle of fundamental justice. The applicants claimed that no less than three principles were offended. First, that the child must be afforded independent procedural rights; second, that legislation affecting children must be in their best interest; and third, that criminal legislation must not be vague or overbroad. With regard to the first point, the court concluded that thus far its jurisprudence has not recognized procedural rights for the alleged victims of an offence but—even on the assumption that it had—Section 43 provided adequate procedural safeguards to protect this interest as the child's interests were represented at trial by the Crown.[57] The court also stated that while the best interests of the child was a 'recognized legal principle' and 'a factor for consideration in many contexts',[58] it did not constitute a principle of fundamental justice as it did not satisfy the condition of being 'vital or fundamental to our societal notion of justice' and was not 'capable of being identified with some precision'.[59]

The court also ruled that 'properly construed' Section 43 was not unduly vague.[60] First, the force must be for the purposes of education or corrective purposes.[61] The court conceded that the words 'reasonable under the circumstances' were broad but stated that 'implicit limitations' add precision.[62] In establishing the meaning of that phrase, the court stated that Section 43 was 'limited to only the mildest forms of assault' and referred to Canada's international treaty obligations, including various provisions of the CRC and the International Covenant on Civil and Political Rights (ICCPR). It held that 'determining what is "reasonable under the circumstances" in the case of child discipline is also assisted by social consensus and expert evidence on what constitutes reasonable corrective discipline'.[63] In doing so, the court effectively construed PPP as a socio-cultural norm. The court found that:

> When these considerations are taken together, a solid core of meaning emerges for 'reasonable under the circumstances', sufficient to establish a zone in which discipline risks criminal sanction. Generally, s. 43 exempts from criminal sanction only minor corrective force of a transitory and trifling nature. On the basis of current expert consensus, it does not apply to corporal punishment of children under two or teenagers. Degrading, inhuman or harmful conduct is not protected. Discipline by the use of objects or blows or slaps to the head is unreasonable. Teachers may reasonably apply force to remove a child from a classroom or secure compliance with instructions, but not merely as corporal punishment. Coupled with the requirement that

[57] *Canadian Foundation for Children*, para 6.

[58] Ibid, para 10.

[59] Ibid, paras 10, 11. For a criticism of the court's focus on 'social consensus' in this context, see S. Anand, 'Reasonable Chastisement: A Critique of the Supreme Court's Decision in the "Spanking" Case" (2004) 41 *Alberta Law Review* 871, 874–5.

[60] *Canadian Foundation for Children*, para 14.

[61] Ibid, para 24.

[62] Ibid, para 29.

[63] Ibid, para 36.

the conduct be corrective, which rules out conduct stemming from the caregiver's frustration, loss of temper or abusive personality, a consistent picture emerges of the area covered by s. 43. It is wrong for law enforcement officers or judges to apply their own subjective views of what is 'reasonable under the circumstances'; the test is objective. The question must be considered in context and in light of all the circumstances of the case. The gravity of the precipitating event is not relevant.

Nor did the court find Section 43 to be overbroad, given Parliament's decision to confine the exemption to 'reasonable correction'.[64]

With regard to Section 12, the court found that Section 43 did not permit conduct that amounted to being 'cruel and unusual'. It also found no violation of Section 15(1) of the Charter. In considering whether discrimination had taken place in this context, the court's analysis centred on the 'correspondence between the distinction and the claimant's characteristics or circumstances'.[65] While it found that Section 43 made a distinction on the basis of age (which is one of the proscribed grounds of discrimination under Section 15).[66] Chief Justice McLachlin concluded that 'a reasonable person acting on behalf of a child, apprised of the harms of criminalization that s. 43 avoids, the presence of other governmental initiatives to reduce the use of corporal punishment, and the fact that abusive and harmful conduct is still prohibited by the criminal law, would not conclude that the child's dignity has been offended in the manner contemplated by s. 15(1)'.[67] According to the court, the force permitted by Section 43 was limited and had to be set against the reality of a child's mother or father being charged and pulled into the criminal justice system, 'with its attendant rupture of the family setting, or a teacher being detained pending bail, with the inevitable harm to the child's crucial educative setting'.[68] Thus, Section 43 was 'not arbitrarily demeaning' and did not discriminate; '[r]ather, it is firmly grounded in the actual needs and circumstances of children'.[69] In effect, the non-criminalization of parents was deemed to be rendered necessary by children's needs/circumstances.

Three judges dissented wholly or in part with the majority ruling. Justice Binnie found that Section 43 denied children the protection of the criminal law against the infliction of physical 'force' that would be a criminal assault if used against an adult, thereby violating Section 15. He held, however, that this infringement of children's equality rights was saved by Section 1 of the Charter in relation to parents as it constituted 'a reasonable limit prescribed by law as can be demonstrably justified in a free and democratic society'.[70] Justice Arbour dissented as a whole, finding that Section 43 infringed the rights of children under Section 7 of the Charter. She concluded that as Section 43 was 'unconstitutionally vague', it did not satisfy the requirement under Section 1 that any limitation on rights must be 'prescribed by law'. Justice Deschamps, also dissenting, agreed with Justice Arbour's arguments on Section 7 but preferred to address the question in terms of Section 15. She concluded

[64] Ibid, paras 45–7.

[65] These factors are addressed below in my discussion of the court's conceptualization of the child as a rights-bearer.

[66] *Canadian Foundation for Children*, para 54 [67] Ibid, para 68. [68] Ibid.

[69] Ibid. Binnie J took express issue with this finding of the majority in his decision, arguing that use of force cannot be said to 'correspond' to a child's 'needs, capacities and circumstances' from the vantage point of 'a reasonable person acting on behalf of a child who seriously considers the child's views and developmental needs'. (para 102).

[70] Section 1 of the Charter provides that, 'The *Canadian Charter of Rights and Freedoms* guarantees the rights and freedoms set out in it subject only to such reasonable limits prescribed by law as can be demonstrably justified in a free and democratic society'.

that the inferior protection that Section 43 afforded to children resulted in a violation of their constitutional equality rights, which was not saved by Section 1.

In the final case considered here, *In the Matter of An application for Judicial Review by the Northern Ireland Commissioner for Children and Young People of Decisions Made by Peter Hain The Secretary of State and David Hanson the Minister of State*,[71] NICCY sought judicial review of the decision of the defendants to introduce a provision which provides for a defence of reasonable chastisement of a child to a charge of assault.[72] This provision was enacted into English law, and subsequently Northern Irish law, in order to meet concerns raised in the ECtHR's decision in *A v UK* discussed above. NICCY based its action on, amongst other things, the fact that such an order was ultra vires because it breached Articles 3 (right to freedom from torture and inhuman or degrading treatment or punishment), 8 (right to respect for private life), and 14 (non-discrimination) ECHR, as well as various provisions of the CRC.[73] The first matter determined by the court was whether the applicant had the 'victim' status necessary to bring a challenge to the impugned legislation under the Convention. Having considered jurisprudence of the UK courts and the ECtHR, Justice Gillen in the High Court held that she did not. However, in case he was incorrect on this issue, the judge was prepared to proceed to consider the position as if the applicant had established victim status. Upon appeal, the High Court's decision on the point of the lack of 'victim' status of the Commissioner was upheld by the Court of Appeal.[74] However, this chapter focuses on the decision of the High Court as, unlike the Court of Appeal, Justice Gillen engaged with the issue of the permissibility of the PPP.[75]

[71] [2007] NIQB 115. All references are taken from a copy of the judgment found at <http://www.bailii.org>.

[72] Article 2, Law Reform (Miscellaneous Provisions) (Northern Ireland) Order 2006. The Order came into law in September 2006 and provides:

'(1) In relation to any offence specified in paragraph (2), battery of a child cannot be justified on the ground that it constituted reasonable punishment.
(2) The offences referred to in paragraph (1) are –
  (a) an offence under section 18 of the Offences against the Person Act 1861 (c.100) (wounding, or causing grievous bodily harm, with intent)
  (b) an offence under section 20 of that Act (malicious wounding or grievous bodily harm)
  (c) an offence under section 43 of that Act (aggravated assault)
  (d) an offence under section 47 of that Act (assault occasioning actual bodily harm and common assault)
  (e) an offence under section 20(1) of the Children and Young Persons Act (Northern Ireland) 1968 (c.34) (cruelty to persons under 16)
(3) Battery of a child causing actual bodily harm to the child cannot be justified in any civil proceedings on the ground that it constituted reasonable punishment.
(4) For the purposes of paragraph (3) 'actual bodily harm' has the same meaning as it has for the purposes of section 47 of the Offences Against the Person Act 1861.
(5) In section 20 of the Children and Young Persons Act (Northern Ireland) 1968 subsection (6) is hereby repealed.'

[73] NICCY claimed that this was contrary to Section 6 of the HRA 1998 or Sections 24 and 26 of the Northern Ireland Act 1998. Section 6 makes it unlawful for a public authority to act in a way which is incompatible with an ECHR right. Under Sections 24 and 26, no Minister or Northern Ireland department has the power to make, confirm, or approve any subordinate legislation, or to do any act, so far as the legislation is incompatible with any ECHR rights, while, where the Secretary of State for Northern Ireland considers that any action proposed to be taken by a Minister or Northern Ireland department would be incompatible with any international obligations, he may order that the proposed action shall not be taken.

[74] *Northern Ireland Commissioner for Children and Young Peoples' Application* [2009] NICA 10.

[75] Upon appeal, the Court of Appeal stated that 'If the Court were to rule that the common law defence contravenes the application of the Convention rights pursuant to the 1988 Order and that it cannot be called in aid by a parent prosecuted for an assault on a child when he alleges that he is exercising

While the judge held that the provision engaged Article 8, he concluded that this interference with 'a child's right not to be assaulted' was justified in terms of Article 8(2).[76] This was because, first, it was 'prescribed by law'. The judge found 'nothing vague, imprecise or unlawful about the use of the phrase "reasonable chastisement"',[77] referring positively to the comments of the Canadian Supreme Court on this point in *Canadian Foundation for Children*.[78] Second, he held that the interference for which the law provided was directed towards the 'protection of children from any physical violence outside reasonable chastisement and even then this is confined to the offence of assault' and hence fell within the ambit of the second paragraph of Article 8. The court also held that the interference was proportionate:

> Confining the matter to assault effectively ensured that only a modest and measured degree of physical chastisement could ever be deployed to come within the defence of reasonable chastisement. Not only has the chastisement to be reasonable, but it has to be actual chastisement and not merely loss of temper, acts of frustration or irrational outbursts by a parent unconnected with reasonable punishment within the confines of the offence of assault... I am satisfied that such an approach does strike a fair balance between the rights of the individual children and interests of the community.[79]

With regard to Article 3, having reviewed ECtHR jurisprudence, the influence of the CRC on the ECtHR, and the interrelationship between the two instruments, the court concluded that Article 3 does not require the total abolition of corporal punishment—even in the case of children as not every case of corporal punishment would achieve the minimum level of severity to engage Article 3.[80] Justice Gillen also refused to accept that the impugned legislation brought about discriminatory treatment of children and young people amounting to a breach of Article 3 in the way that, for instance, race would, stating that 'children are justifiably treated differently from adults in a number of legal areas for their welfare and protection. Such justification can never arise in the case of racial discrimination'.[81] Turning to Article 14, the court rejected the claim that the failure to extend to children and young people the full protection of the criminal law against assault in the same way as it is extended to adults unlawfully discriminated against them in the enjoyment of their rights and freedoms under Articles 3, 6, and 8, thus breaching Article 14. In his view:

> [there are] objective and reasonable justifications in many instances for treating children differently from adults... Children and young people are treated differently under the law inter alia to protect them and to ensure their education and welfare. I do not believe therefore that Article 14 forbids such discrimination. The Convention does not require that there be strict equality of treatment between children and adults.[82]

a parental right to punish, this would appear to have the effect of turning an act which is presently unlawful into an offence. To accede to the applicant's application would very arguably run counter to the provisions of Section 7(8) [HRA] which provides that nothing in the HRA creates a criminal offence' (*Northern Ireland Commissioner for Children and Young Peoples' Application* [2009] NICA 10, para 21).

[76] Article 8(2) ECHR provides that: 'There shall be no interference by a public authority with the exercise of this right except such as is in accordance with the law and is necessary in a democratic society in the interests of national security, public safety or the economic well-being of the country, for the prevention of disorder or crime, for the protection of health or morals, or for the protection of the rights and freedoms of others.'

[77] *Northern Ireland Commissioner for Children and Young People*, para 40.

[78] Ibid. [79] Ibid, para 47. [80] Ibid, para 67.

[81] Ibid, para 69. [82] Ibid, para 76.

In Justice Gillen's view, even if he was wrong on this point, the interference was justifiable in terms of the Convention.[83]

Having outlined the cases under consideration, I now turn to consider what these decisions suggest about the different approaches adopted by courts to the issues surrounding parent-administered corporal punishment.

29.4 A tale of common themes and divergences: child protection, parental rights, international standards, comparative experiences, and the child as right-holder

This section investigates four common and contrasting elements in terms of the legal reasoning employed in the decisions addressed in this chapter. First, I consider the various approaches adopted to the issues of child protection, the child's family rights, and parental rights in the context of PPP. I then address the role played by international child rights standards in the decisions in question, as well as the weight accorded to comparative experiences in relation to the prohibition of PPP. The final topic discussed is the understanding of 'children' as right-holders and members of a vulnerable social group (or not) demonstrated by the decision-makers under scrutiny.[84]

29.4.1 Of child protection, family rights, and parental rights

All of the decisions addressed the key issue of child protection (expressed variously as a 'need' and 'a right'). The interpretation and weight accorded to child protection varied considerably, however, between decision-making bodies. This was particularly so when it came to striking a balance between the child's right to protection and the child's right to family. Where the courts address the position of the child target of PPP in terms of children's rights, this entails a recognition of the dignity and agency of children. In contrast, where the courts centre on parental powers, rights, and duties, it suggests a perception of the child as a passive object whose rights are secondary to those of others. Thus, where the courts primarily focus upon parental rights, one might assume that this will lead to a predisposition towards 'shoring up' those rights, thus resulting in a reduced likelihood that they will find PPP to be impermissible. But is this the case in practice?

In its decision, the Canadian court acknowledged that, as vulnerable members of Canadian society, 'children need to be protected from abusive treatment... and Parliament and the Executive act admirably when they shield children from

[83] NICCY had also made arguments under traditional grounds of judicial review, making its claims on the bases that: (i) the provision constituted a denial of the reasonable expectation that NICCY would be consulted with before a policy decision was taken by the respondents on the question of the physical punishment of children; (ii) the provision constituted a denial of the reasonable expectation that the respondents would not depart from the Office of Law Reform consultation document on 'Physical Punishment in the Home: Thinking About the Issues, Looking at the Evidence', and the Children's Strategy in the absence of any cogent explanation for doing so. The applicant argued that these documents effectively amounted to a governmental policy commitment to implement the CRC; (iii) there had been breaches of the principles of fairness and unreasonableness in failing to take account of various relevant and important matters; and (iv) there was irrationality on the grounds of perversity and of mistaken understanding of the facts. The court also found against NICCY on these grounds.

[84] For more on the conceptualization of social groups, see Iris Marion Young, *Inclusion and Democracy* (Oxford, Oxford University Press, 2000), Chapter 3.

psychological and physical harm'.[85] However, while the court acknowledged that in doing so, the government was responding to 'the critical need of all children for a safe environment',[86] it proceeded to state that children also depend on parents and teachers for guidance and discipline, to protect them from harm and to promote their healthy development within society'.[87] The court thus appeared to prioritize the child's need for a 'stable and secure family and school setting' above their need to protection from PPP.[88] This contrasts with the approach of the Nepal Supreme Court which, in holding PPP to be impermissible, emphasized that 'the environment conducive for development and the opportunity to develop their personality while spending a respectful life free from torture are the most essential elements for the overall development of children'.[89]

Furthermore, it is clear that the child's family rights are not the only 'balancing rights' that courts will take into account in addressing the child's need for protection when holding PPP to be permissible. Notably, while the Northern Ireland High Court explicitly acknowledged what it termed 'the child's right not to be assaulted in the context of Article 8',[90] it also highlighted 'the right of *parents* to bring up their children, guiding and disciplining them appropriately within a safe and loving family setting without invoking the criminal law' as forming part of legislative objective for the impugned provision.[91] Indeed, a concern with 'parental rights'—particularly parents' right to raise children without undue state interference—is an underlying theme of both of the decisions considered that involved a judicial refusal to hold PPP to be impermissible.

In contrast, the bodies in favour of proscribing PPP that are discussed in this chapter demonstrated a reluctance to engage in any depth with the issue of parental rights. For instance, the European Committee of Social Rights did not explicitly address the issue of parents' rights in its decision-making. This was despite the reference to such rights in a range of the domestic legal frameworks under consideration (albeit that none of the defendant countries suggested that PPP was permissible under Article 17 due to the existence of such rights).[92] The lack of discussion of parental rights was particularly notable in the context of the European Committee's complaints against Ireland, Portugal, and Italy which involved allegations of violations of Article 17 of the Revised Charter. That Article requires states to take measures 'to ensure that children and young persons, *taking account of the rights and duties of their parents*, have the care, the assistance, the education and the training they need, in particular by providing for the establishment or maintenance of institutions and services sufficient and adequate for this purpose'.[93] This wording would appear to have offered the Committee an opportunity to 'factor in' or to get involved in a balancing act between the rights of parents and children had it chosen to do so.

Judicial trepidation about the impact of a prohibition of PPP upon parental rights or interests is thrown into sharp relief in discussions of the potential 'criminalization' of parents resulting from such a prohibition. Such concern was clear in *In the Matter of An application for Judicial Review by the Northern Ireland Commissioner*

[85] *Canadian Foundation for Children*, para 58. [86] Ibid. [87] Ibid. [88] Ibid.

[89] *Writ Number 57.* [90] *Northern Ireland Commissioner for Children and Young People*, para 37.

[91] Para 47. Italics added by author.

[92] In contrast, in his dissenting opinions on *OMCT v Greece*, *OMCT v Ireland*, and *OMCT v Belgium*, Lucien Francois stated that he found it 'shocking to lump together categories of people as different as child abusers and parents who take care to use moderate correction towards their children'.

[93] Article 17(1)(a). Italics added by author.

for Children and Young People when the court referred to evidence submitted by the Secretary of State that 'such a ban could result in the criminalization of parents. This would not be conducive to the parent/child relationship or in the best interests of either party'.[94] In doing so, the court quoted the statements of the majority decision in *Canadian Foundation for Children* approvingly.[95] In that decision, the Canadian Supreme Court was explicit in its concern about the potential of a ban on all forms of PPP in terms of the criminalization of parents, stating that Section 43 'is sensitive to children's need for a safe environment. But s. 43 also ensures the criminal law will not be used where the force is part of a genuine effort to educate the child, poses no reasonable risk of harm that is more than transitory and trifling, and is reasonable under the circumstances'.[96] Notably, the court stated that 'introducing the criminal law into children's families and educational environments in such circumstances would harm children more than help them'.[97] The court claimed that the decision not to criminalize PPP was not grounded in 'devaluation of the child, but in a concern that to do so risks ruining lives and breaking up families—a burden that in large part would be borne by children and outweigh any benefit derived from applying the criminal process'.[98] In effect, the non-criminalization of parents was deemed to be rendered necessary by children's needs/interests.

Such an approach directly conflicts with the views of the Committee on the Rights of the Child which recently stressed that 'the interpretation of a child's best interests must be consistent with the whole Convention, 'including the obligation to protect children from all forms of violence'.[99] According to the Committee a child's best interest cannot be used to justify practices, including PPP, which conflict with the child's human dignity and right to physical integrity.[100] In the same statement, the Committee highlighted that parental rights and duties with regard to child-rearing cannot be used to override the child's right to freedom from PPP, iterating that 'an adult's judgment of a child's best interests cannot override the obligation to respect all the child's rights under the Convention'.[101]

A similarly child-centric approach is evidenced in the Israeli Supreme Court's decision in *Plonit*. The court in that case stated that 'parents are first and foremost responsible for their children, and the rights and duties granted to them by law give them discretion in the rearing and education of their children'.[102] However, while acknowledging the general understanding that, under normal circumstances, parental discretion is the best means to ensure appropriate decision-making vis-à-vis child-rearing, the court emphasized that this discretion did not mean that parents are 'completely autonomous' with regard to decisions affecting their children.[103] Crucially, '[p]arental discretion is limited and always subject to the needs of the child, his or her welfare and rights'.[104] When addressing the question of the criminalization

[94] *In the Matter of An application for Judicial Review by the Northern Ireland Commissioner for Children and Young People*, para 48.

[95] *Canadian Foundation for Children*, para 58 cited at para 49.

[96] Ibid, para 59. The central legislative purpose of Section 43 was one of parental rights not of child protection: 'The heading in the *Code* under which s. 43 is placed—"Protection of Persons in Authority"—confirms that this justification was aimed at protecting parents and teachers from prosecution and not to protect children from the intrusion of the criminal law' (para 235).

[97] Ibid. [98] Ibid, para 62.

[99] ComRC, *General Comment No.13 on Article 19: The right of the child to freedom from all forms of violence* (2011) UN Doc.CRC/C/GC/13, para 54.

[100] Ibid. [101] Ibid.

[102] *Plonit v Israel*, 9. [103] Ibid. [104] Ibid.

of parents, the court emphasized that parents could still make use of all the defences already codified in the criminal law and that the criminal law possessed enough filters, such as prosecutorial discretion, that 'unimportant cases' would not be included in its sweep.[105] In contrast, the Canadian Supreme Court rejected the notion of prosecutorial discretion playing a role in the prevention of the criminalization of parents should Section 43 be found unconstitutional, stating that 'our goal should be the rule of law, not the rule of individual discretion ... Moreover, if it is contrary to s. 15(1) for legislation to deny children the benefit of the criminal law on the basis of their age and consequent circumstances, it is equally discriminatory for a state agent ... to choose not to charge or prosecute on the same basis'.[106]

The cases considered in this chapter thus support the view that, where a court chooses to focus primarily upon parental rights, this appears likely to lead to a predisposition towards 'shoring up' those rights, thereby reducing the probability that they will find PPP to be impermissible.

29.4.2 The role of the CRC

Another shared element of all of the decisions considered was reference to international law, and to the CRC in particular. However, the interpretation and employment of those international human rights law standards thereof varied considerably. One might assume that where courts refer to, or rely on international children's rights standards, this will be indicative of a willingness to construe those standards in such a way as to give effect to international law statements that argue in favour of the prohibition of the PPP. The question is whether this is, in fact, borne out by the case law.

Unsurprisingly, all of the bodies that found PPP to be impermissible quoted the CRC approvingly, using it as either a basis or a support for their conclusions. As stated above, the European Committee emphasized that in its interpretation of Article 17 of the Charter/Revised Charter it referred, in particular, to Article 19 of the United Nations CRC as interpreted by the Committee on the Rights of the Child.[107] This involved an implicit incorporation of the Committee's interpretation of Article 19 as entailing a prohibition of PPP into the interpretation of Article 17.[108]

In *Plonit*, the Israeli Supreme Court made it clear that 'the current judicial attitude to the position of the child and his or her rights' must be given effect to in

[105] Ibid, 12. For an argument that existing criminal defences could serve to prevent the criminalization of parents in the Canadian context, see *per* Arbour J in *Canadian Foundation for Children*, paras 196–209.

[106] Para 63. For a useful discussion of how prosecutorial discretion might operate in the context of the abolition of Section 43, see M. Carter, 'Corporal Punishment and Prosecutorial Discretion in Canada' (2004) 12 *International Journal of Children's Rights* 41.

[107] *OMCT v Belgium*, para 38(a); *OMCT v Portugal*, para 34(a); *OMCT v Italy*, para 41(a); *OMCT v Ireland*, para 63(a); and *OMCT v Greece*, para 31(a).

[108] While the Committee only released its General Comment No. 8 in 2006, it had previously repeatedly recommended the prohibition of PPP in its concluding observations on states parties' reports. For more, see the database on 'Committee on the Rights of the Child comments and recommendations regarding corporal punishment made following examination of states' reports, January 1993 to February 2011': <http://www.endcorporalpunishment.org/pages/frame.html>. Furthermore, in its recommendations following its two General Discussion Days on 'State violence against children' and 'Violence against children within the family and in school', respectively, the Committee urged states parties to ensure that all forms of violence against children, however light, were prohibited. (See, UN Doc CRC/C/97, para 8, and UN Doc. CRC/C/111, para 715).

Israel.[109] This was incumbent in the period after the enactment of the 1992 legislation on Israeli Basic Law: Human Dignity and Liberty. Notably, however, the court highlighted that 'no less significant in this respect is Israel's status as a signatory to the Convention on Children's Rights'.[110] Later in its decision, the court stated that 'the outlook which recognises the child's rights to protect his or her physical and mental integrity received clear expression in the Convention on Children's Rights', emphasizing that the Convention 'explicitly forbids the use of physical or mental violence against children, and obligates the state to take measures to prevent violence against children'.[111] Thus, the position of the CRC vis-à-vis PPP strongly influenced the court's decision.[112]

In *Writ Number 57*, the petitioners argued that Nepal was legally bound to observe a range of treaties prohibiting torture, inhuman, or degrading treatment or punishment and violence against children in terms of the Nepal Treaties Act 2047.[113] The Nepal Supreme Court agreed, making reference to a wide range of international human rights instruments in its ruling, including the CRC, the ICCPR, the Universal Declaration of Human Rights, and the Convention against Torture and Other Cruel Inhuman or Degrading Treatment or Punishment. The court concluded that, given Nepal's ratification of those instruments, it was not proper or lawful to make laws contrary to their provisions.

The CRC and other international human rights standards were also cited in the decisions of the Canadian Supreme Court and the Northern Ireland Human Rights Commission. Perhaps unsurprisingly, those bodies did not accord the same weight to those provisions as the decision-makers that found PPP to be impermissible. More worryingly, both courts proceeded to engage in an activity that can—most generously—be described as a 'selective' application of the CRC.

In its majority decision, the Canadian Supreme Court directly engaged with the CRC, citing Articles 5, 19(1), and 37(a) of that instrument. According to the court, it followed from these provisions and Article 7 ICCPR that 'what is "reasonable under the circumstances" [in terms of Section 43] will seek to avoid harm to the child and will never include cruel, inhuman or degrading treatment'.[114] The court then proceeded to state that neither the CRC nor the ICCPR 'explicitly require state parties to ban all corporal punishment of children',[115] highlighting that while the Human Rights Committee has expressed the view that corporal punishment of children in schools engages Article 7's prohibition of degrading treatment or punishment, it had not done the same vis-à-vis 'parental use of mild corporal punishment'.[116] In doing so, it ignored multiple statements of the Committee on the Rights of the Child on the issue. This is particularly striking given the point made by Justice Arbour in her dissenting judgment that the Committee's Concluding Observations on Canada's first state report submitted in terms of the CRC included a recommendation that physical punishment of children in families should be prohibited.[117] Indeed, as Justice Arbour noted in arguing that the protection accorded to children by Section 7 of the Charter should be informed by Canada's international obligations, the Committee's

[109] *Plonit.* [110] Ibid. [111] Ibid.

[112] Similarly, Kaplan notes that, 'The principles of the Convention on the Rights of the Child are one of the major sources of inspiration in the decision of the Israeli Supreme Court' (Kaplan, above n. 45, 364).

[113] See Article 9(1).

[114] *Canadian Foundation for Children*, para 32. [115] Ibid., para 33.

[116] Ibid. [117] Para 87.

Concluding Observations on Canada's subsequent state report specifically targeted Section 43. Here the Committee bemoaned the fact that Canada had taken no action to remove it, while recommending that the state adopt 'legislation to remove the existing authorization of the use of "reasonable force" in disciplining children and explicitly prohibit all forms of violence against children, however light, within the family, in schools and in other institutions where children may be placed'.[118] The fact that the majority decision in *Canadian Foundation for Children* did not address these statements—even if only to dismiss them—resulted in the court providing only a partial picture of the obligations imposed by the CRC.

In its decision, the Northern Ireland High Court appeared to adopt a more positive approach to international human rights law—at least initially. Here, the judge made reference to evidence on a wide range of international standards, including the CRC and General Comment No. 8, as well as information on bans in other jurisdictions.[119] When discussing the CRC, the court stated that 'even if an international treaty such as this has not been incorporated into domestic law, our domestic legislation should be construed so far as possible so as to comply with the international obligations which we have undertaken when two interpretations are possible'.[120] Justice Gillen stated further that, '[w]here children are involved I consider the interpretation chosen should be that which better complies with the commitment to the welfare of children which this country has made by ratifying the United Nations Conventions on the Rights of the Child'.[121] The court proceeded, however, to argue that, '[c]areful perusal of the UNCRC itself has to be made to ensure that the instrument itself amounts to the prohibition against corporal punishment'.[122] In doing so, Justice Gillen proceeded effectively to express agreement with Chief Justice McLachlin's statement in *Canadian Foundation for Children* quoted above. Justice Gillen did concede that, since that decision, the UN Committee on the Rights of the Child 'has criticised the continued existence of the parental right of chastisement and recommended its abolition'.[123] In his view, however, the fact that Article 19(1) of the UNCRC required states parties to 'take all *appropriate* legislative measures to protect the child from all forms of physical or mental violence' justified Chief Justice McLachlin's interpretation. In Justice Gillen's words:

> It is the Committee on the Rights of the Child which has arguably taken the matter a stage further in recent times by recommending the abolition of all corporal punishment for children. Even had the Government committed itself to fully implementing the UNCRC, which I do not believe it has done, it has not committed itself to accepting the interpretation of Article 19(1) placed on it by that Committee.[124]

One cannot quibble with the fact that the statements of the Committee on the Rights of the Child are merely 'soft' law, as opposed to the binding obligations imposed by the treaty provisions.[125] However, Justice Gillen's rejection of the authoritative

[118] Para 88. Citing ComRC, 'Concluding Observations: Canada', UN Doc. CRC/C/15/Add. 215 (2003), at paras 32–3

[119] Para 30. [120] Para 109. [121] Ibid.

[122] *In the Matter of An application for Judicial Review by the Northern Ireland Commissioner for Children and Young People*, para 112

[123] Ibid, para 113. [124] Para 113.

[125] For more on the status of General Comments in international human rights law, see Conway Blake, 'Normative Instruments in International Human Rights Law: Locating the General Comment' NYU Center for Human Rights and Global Justice Working Paper Series No. 17 of 2008: <http://www.chrgj.org/publications/wp.html>.

interpretative statement of the CRC provided in General Comment No. 8 belies his stated preference for an interpretation 'which better complies with the commitment to the welfare of children which this country has made by ratifying the United Nations Conventions on the Rights of the Child'. Furthermore, his statement that the Government had not committed itself fully to implementing the CRC (as opposed to domestically incorporating that instrument, which may have been what he meant)[126] reflects an apparent misunderstanding on Justice Gillen's part of the nature of the obligations that the UK assumed upon ratifying the CRC.

Above, I suggested that where courts or other decision-makers refer to or rely extensively on international children's rights standards, this is likely to suggest a willingness to construe those standards in such a way as to give effect to international law statements that argue in favour of the prohibition of PPP. The decisions considered make it clear that this is not necessarily the case. On the one hand, the fact that the CRC was considered by decision-making bodies finding both for and against the prohibition of PPP demonstrates the stature and ever-increasing influence of that instrument. On the other, the refusal of the Northern Irish and Canadian courts to adopt a progressive (or, rather, an accurate) interpretation of the CRC in their decision-making illustrates how the protections contemplated in that instrument can be undermined and even perverted by being subject to selective interpretation. Thus a body's engagement with international standards will not necessarily signify, or result in, a greater readiness to find PPP impermissible.

29.4.3 The impact of comparative experiences

In addition to varying in terms of their approach towards international human rights law standards pertaining to PPP, there was a clear divergence between the bodies that found PPP to be prohibited and those that did not in terms of their treatment of comparative developments in relation to the prohibition of PPP.

In its decision, the Israeli Supreme Court highlighted the fact that the 'professional-educational approach' which it embraced in its decision had manifested in the legislation of a range of different states that had prohibited or severely limited parents' authority to carry out such punishment. It cited in particular the examples of Sweden, Finland, Denmark, Norway, and Austria.[127] The Nepal Supreme Court referred to information presented to it on comparative developments in relation to the prohibition of PPP, concluding that 'universally laws have been made fully restricting physical punishment to be imposed on children in the course of discipline or in the name of child welfare',[128] and listing a range of different countries in which physical punishment had been 'restricted' as result of legislation, judicial decisions, and governmental directives. The court therefore concluded that '[t]here seems no reason for Nepal not to take an initiative in the universal campaign against physical punishment or torture'.[129] In contrast, the European Committee of Social Rights did not refer to specific domestic examples, albeit that, as stated earlier, it made it clear that its interpretation took place in light of Parliamentary Assembly Recommendation 1666 (2004) on a 'Europe-wide ban on corporal punishment of children'. That Recommendation saw the Council of Europe Parliamentary Assembly welcome 'the

[126] See *Northern Ireland Commissioner for Children and Young People*, para 10.
[127] *Plonit v Israel*, 6. [128] *Writ Number 57*. [129] Ibid.

current global initiative to end all corporal punishment of children'.[130] The same measure invited the Council of Europe's Committee of Ministers 'to launch a co-ordinated and concerted campaign in all the member states for the total abolition of corporal punishment of children'[131] and 'to recommend that the member states enact appropriate legislation prohibiting the corporal punishment of children, particularly within the family'.[132]

In contrast, the Northern Ireland High Court highlighted that 'a common stance has not been adopted or implemented in Europe outlawing all corporal punishment of children'.[133] This was despite the fact that Justice Gillen expressly made reference to the Council of Europe Parliamentary Assembly Recommendation 1666 (2004) discussed above. As discussed above, he did, however, make approving reference to the majority decision in *Canadian Foundation for Children* in his judgment. Notably, the court in the latter case made no reference to other jurisdictions in which PPP was banned. Indeed, the sole reference to any such experience was Justice Binnie's response to evidence that other jurisdictions including Sweden did without a parental defence: 'Sweden, at least, has a very different criminal law regime applicable to physical assaults.'[134]

Therefore, the approach adopted to comparative experience in relation to the prohibition of PPP constituted a clear point of divergence between the courts drawing opposing conclusions in relation to the permissibility of PPP.

29.4.4 Conceptualization of the child as 'rights-bearer' and the prohibition of PPP

The final element addressed in this section relates to the conceptualization of the child as a rights-bearer and a member of a vulnerable social group in the decisions under examination.

All of the decisions addressed in this chapter referred to the child as a rights-bearer. However, the most detailed examination of the position of the child as rights-bearer took place in the *Plonit* judgment. Here, the Israeli Supreme Court stated that, '[t]oday it is possible to rule that in a society such as ours the child is an autonomous human being, possessed of independent interests and rights of his or her own, and that society has the obligation to defend the minor and his or her rights'.[135] It quoted a range of different Israeli judges' statements emphasizing the 'personhood' of children and that the concept 'children's rights' affords constitutional protection to the child while constituting 'a recognition of children's rights and the totality of rights acts a guarantee of the security of the child's welfare'.[136]

The European Committee of Social Rights did not engage in any extensive analysis of the role of child as right-holder or as a social group but made it clear through the sources it employed in its interpretation of Article 17 (a child right-specific protection) that it regarded the child as a rights-bearer in terms of the international human rights law understanding of that status. The Nepal Supreme Court adopted a

[130] Council of Europe Parliamentary Assembly, Recommendation 1666 (2004) 'Europe-wide ban on corporal punishment of children' (23 June 2004), para 4.

[131] Ibid, para 7.

[132] Ibid, para 9(i).

[133] *In the Matter of An application for Judicial Review by the Northern Ireland Commissioner for Children and Young People*, para 120.

[134] *Canadian Foundation for Children*, para 118.

[135] *Plonit v Israel*, 10.

[136] Ibid.

somewhat more expansive approach in its decision, making it clear that children were right-holders in terms of both domestic and international law and ruling that the state was obliged to create an environment that is conducive to their overall development. Notably, it directly affirmed the personhood of children, by highlighting that the Constitution guarantees that no one can subject 'any person' to torture or inhuman or degrading treatment and holding that the impugned provision was therefore unconstitutional on that basis.

But what of those bodies that upheld the permissibility of PPP? The majority of the court in *Canadian Foundation for Children* noted the nature of the interest affected by Section 43—'physical integrity'—was profound,[137] that '[c]hildren often feel a sense of disempowerment and vulnerability' and that 'this reality must be considered when assessing the impact of s. 43 on a child's sense of dignity'.[138] However, it did not focus to any degree on the question of the status of the child as a right-holder per se. This was despite its reference to the CRC. For instance, instead of adopting a child rights-centric analysis of Section 15, its consideration centred on the language of children's 'needs'. The court also failed to engage in any in-depth analysis of the position of the child as a social group.[139] While it acknowledged that the children were a 'highly vulnerable group' for the purposes of its investigation into whether discrimination had occurred,[140] it failed to address the question of their 'pre-existing disadvantage'.

In contrast, Justice Deschamps in her minority judgment focussed on both the status of the child as a rights-bearer and as a member of a historically marginalized social group. Having highlighted that 'children as a group face pre-existing disadvantage in our society',[141] and that their vulnerability was entrenched by the traditional legal treatment of children as the property of their parents or guardians,[142] she asserted that:

> Fortunately, this attitude has changed in modern times with a recognition that children, as individuals, have rights, including the right to have their security and safety protected by their parents, families and society at large.[143]

She critiqued Section 43 as a throwback to old notions of children as property, arguing that it reinforced and compounded children's vulnerability and disadvantage by denying them the protection of the criminal law.[144] In her view, the fact that the accused was most likely to be the person charged with their control and trusteeship exacerbated the already vulnerable position of children.[145] Unlike the majority she emphasized that 'the status of children as persons deserves equal recognition'.[146]

The emphasis on the personhood and status of the child as rights-bearer would thus seem to serve as a dividing line between decisions in which PPP is found to be permissible or impermissible. The water is muddied, however, by the decision of *In the Matter of An application for Judicial Review by the Northern Ireland Commissioner for Children and Young People*. In his judgment, Justice Gillen employed strong rhetoric on the child as a rights-bearing member of a 'vulnerable group'.[147] Indeed, paragraph 32 of his judgment contains a trenchant recognition of the child as a rights-bearing member of a vulnerable group:

[137] *Canadian Foundation for Children*, para 56.
[138] Ibid, para 68.
[139] See *Canadian Foundation for Children*, paras 55–6, 58–60 and 68.
[140] Ibid, para 55.
[141] Ibid, para 225.
[142] Ibid.
[143] Ibid.
[144] Ibid, para 226.
[145] Ibid.
[146] Ibid.
[147] See, e.g., *Northern Ireland Commissioner for Children and Young People*, para 63.

Children are a vulnerable group in our society. Smacking children to whatever degree is likely to involve their human dignity, their personal development and their own sense of self and autonomy. Children are real persons not abstractions...children are not just passive recipients of other people's concern for their best interest, but they are moral actors in their own right with points of view of their own which are entitled to respect.

As we have seen, however, this did not result in a finding that PPP was an unjustifiable violation of what the court termed 'the child's right not to be assaulted in the context of Article 8'.[148] Thus, while an assertive construal of the child as rights-bearer would seem to bode in favour of the judicial or quasi-judicial prohibition of PPP, this will not inevitably be the case.

29.5 Conclusion

This chapter has focused on a range of decisions by courts and international quasi-judicial bodies in relation to challenges to state permission of PPP. In doing so, it has highlighted a number of elements in terms of the reasoning employed by decision-makers in either upholding or striking down the legality of PPP.

Admittedly, extrapolating from a limited number of individual decisions does not constitute adequate support for making broad-ranging, unqualified arguments in the way that reliance upon a range of comprehensive empirical studies would, for instance. Furthermore, the decisions presented are unavoidably embedded in particular cultures and contexts that may not 'translate' to other jurisdictions. The features identified and discussed do enable some preliminary conclusions to be drawn, however.

Perhaps unsurprisingly, my analysis of the decisions under consideration demonstrated that where a court chooses to focus primarily upon parental rights, this will reduce the likelihood of a finding that PPP is impermissible. As might also have been predicted, where a court or quasi-judicial decision-making body is dismissive of, or has only limited regard to, comparative experiences of the prohibition of PPP, this results in a greater probability that PPP will be found permissible. Of greater interest, however, is the finding that a body's engagement with international children's rights standards will not necessarily signify, or result in, a greater readiness to prohibit PPP—albeit that this will depend on how such standards are interpreted. Finally, while an assertive construal of the child as a rights-bearer and as a member of a vulnerable social group would seem to bode in favour of the judicial or quasi-judicial prohibition of PPP, this will not always be the case.

The number of cases being brought by advocates seeking the proscription of PPP through the courts is on the rise. This chapter therefore constitutes an important first step towards identifying factors that affect the likelihood that litigation seeking the abolition of PPP will be successful.

[148] Ibid, para 37.

30

Discipline and the Ethics of Care—Constructing Caregiver Discourses from an Urban Poor Area in Tanzania

Sofia Johnson Frankenberg

Most caregivers[1] regard it as their responsibility to teach children to behave appropriately. What is appropriate behaviour and how to make children behave as they should varies according to the local context. The term 'discipline' can be defined as actions taken by caregivers in order to make sure that children behave according to what is accepted; however it is also commonly used to define the use of stronger directives such as threats, strong words, raised voice, as well as harsh punishment such as corporal punishment. Corporal punishment as a discipline strategy is commonly used in many parts of the world (Pinheiro, 2006).[2] The United Nations Committee on the Rights of the Child considers corporal punishment a violation of article 19 of the Convention on the Rights of the Child (CRC), which states that children should be protected against physical as well as psychological violence. In Tanzania, although a signatory to the CRC, corporal punishment is lawful in schools,[3] in the penal system, in families,[4] and in alternative care institutions (End All Corporal Punishment Now, 2011). This is clearly in contravention of the CRC (United Nations, 2006, 2007). The use of corporal punishment in Tanzanian schools is widespread (MKUKUTA Monitoring System, 2007). A study from Iringa region (Feinstein and Mwahombela, 2010) with students and teachers in secondary schools showed that corporal punishment was the most common disciplinary measure used for both major and minor offences and that teachers

[1] The term 'caregivers' signifies any person having caregiving responsibilities for a child, including parents, grandparents, relatives, siblings, neighbours, house girls, and professional caregivers.

[2] Corporal punishment as discipline is just one form of violence against children. The first national survey on violence against children (13–18 years) in Tanzania shows that violence in general is a serious problem. The study identifies that nearly three-quarters of both females and males have experienced physical violence, nearly three in 10 females and approximately one in seven males have experienced sexual violence, and one-quarter have experienced emotional violence prior to the age of 18 by an adult or intimate partner (United Republic of Tanzania, 2011).

[3] The use of corporal punishment in schools is restricted to four strokes and it is exclusively to be administered by the head master (Ministry of Education, 2008).

[4] 'Corporal punishment is lawful in the home in mainland Tanzania and in Zanzibar. Provisions against violence and abuse in the Penal Codes and other laws are not interpreted as prohibiting corporal punishment in childrearing. In mainland Tanzania, the Law of the Child Act (2009) states that parents should protect children from all forms of violence (article 9), includes beatings which cause harm in the definition of child abuse (article 3) and prohibits "torture, or other cruel, inhuman punishment or degrading treatment" (article 13). However, it allows for "justifiable" correction (article 13) and does not exclude all forms of corporal punishment from such correction.' (End All Corporal Punishment Now, 2011, p. 2)'.

were in favour of its use. In the neighbouring country, Kenya, corporal punishment in schools is also widespread despite its prohibition in 2001 (Meru, 2010). There is currently a debate in Tanzania regarding the abolition of corporal punishment in schools. It has been a global trend that a ban on physical punishment in school precedes the abolition of smacking by parents. Globally more than 40 per cent of children are protected against physical punishment in school while only two to three per cent have legal protection from violence in the family (Modig, 2009).

The extent of corporal punishment being used in the rearing of children below eight years has not been systematically investigated in Tanzania but there are indications that it is also frequently used in the home (Makame, 2001). Young children have the same right to be protected against abuse as older children and more knowledge about the use of corporal punishment in the home is urgently needed.

The uses of corporal punishment as well as the negative effects of corporal punishment are well researched in the Euro-American context (Gershoff and Bitensky, 2007). Some research in other parts of the world has also been undertaken. A cross-cultural study from China, India, Italy, Kenya, the Philippines, and Thailand found that physical discipline was related to both aggression and anxiety in the children (Landsford et al., 2005). Ember and Ember (2005), using a worldwide sample of largely pre-industrialized societies, related the use of corporal punishment to the closeness of the relationship between the child and the caregiver, and state that corporal punishment is less common in societies with exclusively parental caregivers than in societies with more non-kin caregivers. Payet and Franchi (2008) stress the complexity of corporal punishment and state that a universal ethical perspective such as article 19 'cannot capture the intrinsic dynamic of a perspective that is at once individual and collective, psychological and social and whose reasons are dictated by experience and shaped by its contradictions' (Payet and Franchi, 2008: 167). Studying corporal punishment in schools in South Africa, these authors argue that there is a relationship between corporal punishment and an environment of *care* as they are both based on a relationship of closeness, and in practice may be inseparable from other forms of care such as compliments, listening, and other ways of showing affection. In environments where corporal punishment is widely accepted, corporal punishment may be regarded as necessary for the desired development of the individual. Brownlie and Anderson (2006: 479), studying parental views on corporal punishment in Scotland, argue that campaigns against corporal punishment need to be 'informed by an understanding of the parent-child relationship as well as the meaning(s) disciplining has for parents'. These findings suggest that further exploration of the complexities of the caregiving relationship and corporal punishment in the home is required in order to find alternative discipline strategies for young children.

In a previous article (Frankenberg, Holmqvist, and Rubensson, 2010) caregivers' conceptions of corporal punishment have been explored. This chapter takes point of departure in these findings and takes them a step further by investigating how they can be understood in the light of the caregiving relationship using the concepts *zone of intimacy* and *ethics of care* (Hundeide, Pramling Samuelsson, and Hundeide, 2010; Cockburn 2005; Tronto 1993).

30.1 The study

The study on which this discussion is based has been described in more detail (Frankenberg, Holmqvist, and Rubenson, 2010) and will briefly be described here.

Data were collected in focus group discussions with mothers, fathers, grandmothers, and grandfathers. In total 80 participants divided into 13 focus groups were selected in collaboration with the local government in Temeke in Dar es Salaam. Participants were selected by purposive sampling. The main selection criterion was that all participants should have at least one child or grandchild under the age of eight years in their household. Participation was voluntary and after being informed about the project by the first author and research assistant, an oral informed consent was given by the participants before the start of the discussions. Discussions focused on the situation of young children in the area as well as views on discipline and corporal punishment focusing on questions such as: What unwanted behaviour is common among young children? What different discipline strategies are used and how do different caregivers believe they affect the child? How much corporal punishment is accepted and where are the limits regarding when it is seen as child abuse? During the discussions, participants were encouraged to give examples and to give their opinions on different examples brought forward by the group. The analysis was inspired by a social constructivist version of grounded theory (Charmaz, 2006), emphasizing process and actions and attempting to create a theoretical, abstract, and interpretive understanding of the data.

30.1.1 Living conditions of the participants

The residents of Temeke 'live in informal settlements, typically experiencing overcrowding and a lack of adequate shelter and resources, such as land. One in three people in Temeke lives below the poverty line. The vast majority of residents earn income through informal employment such as petty trade and small scale fishing. There are also high incidences of crime, domestic violence, pollution, poor environmental sanitation, and flooding during the rainy seasons' (UNICEF, 2009). Data for the current study were collected in five streets (*mitaa*) in one ward in an urban district of Dar es Salaam. Two streets are squatter areas, where the houses are built without city planning; they are small and lie closely together with only narrow paths separating them. The other three areas consist mainly of government houses, formerly built for government employees but now inhabited by a mixture of people. The ground is covered with a sandy soil creating a very dusty environment. Most people in the area collect water in buckets from communal taps. Childcare is the responsibility of the family including siblings and extended family. Some parents also describe collaboration with neighbours. There are both government run and private pre-schools in the area but these are limited to a couple of hours per day and there are no day care services for children with working parents. Participants state that few families can afford a house girl[5] to take care of the children in order to assist working parents and many are concerned that it is difficult to protect children from harm in the area. The main source of income for the participants was petty business, casual labour, and employment as guards or mechanics. Participants describe how they struggle to afford the basic needs for their children such as medicine, nutritious food, and school uniforms. The inhabitants of Temeke originate from all over Tanzania. Among the participants, 25 per cent were from the coastal

[5] House girls are frequently mentioned in Tanzania. International research has shown how difficult it is for poor families in many countries to afford domestic workers. A study referred to by Hein (2005) in three sugar cane plantations in Tanzania reported that a large number of women had to either bring their children to work or leave them in the care of young child minders.

region, 19 per cent were from Dar es Salaam, 41 per cent were from other parts of the country, and 15 per cent were of unknown origin. Religion plays an important role in Tanzania, but national statistics regarding religious affiliation are not available. Religious leaders and sociologists generally estimate that the Christian and Muslim populations are approximately equal, each accounting for 30 to 40 per cent of the population, with the remainder consisting of atheists and practitioners of other faiths and indigenous religions (US Department of State, 2009). A government official in Temeke estimates that the inhabitants in Temeke correspond to the estimated national figures.

30.1.2 Findings

According to the caregivers in the study, young children do bad things because they do not understand or because they are mischievous. Discipline strategies are used for different reasons, such as preventing the child from getting hurt, to make the child understand, to make the child change bad behaviour, to prevent the child from repeating mistakes, and to make the child behave according to the norms of society. Both long-term and short-term strategies for changing child behaviour are described, with short-term strategies aiming at protecting the child from danger and making the child behave in the present, and long-term strategies aiming at internalizing what is right and wrong in order for the child to act appropriately later on without the involvement of the caregiver.

Different caregivers have different discipline responsibilities and may use different strategies. The different strategies also require different capacities from the caregiver. The strategies used are based on the role of the caregiver as well as the caregivers' understanding of how child development can be influenced. The analysis of the data discovered the following discipline strategies: *to beat with care*, representing a commonly used 'legitimate' form of corporal punishment; *to treat like an egg*, representing a powerless and soft attitude common for grandparents; *as if beating a snake*, representing caregivers' conceptions of overly harsh corporal punishment which seriously hurts the child; and *the non-care of non-beating*, representative of caregivers who neglect their children.

30.1.2.1 To beat with care

Beating with care takes place within a loving and caring relationship based on emotional involvement from the caregiver and the corporal punishment is intended to be controlled and moderate. Parents and grandparents stress the importance of combining discipline with love. If the parent or grandparent does not act lovingly the child will not develop appropriately and the punishments will be ineffective:

> Also you need to use care and patience. At other times you show him you love him and if he makes a mistake you beat him a little bit.

Caregivers argue that corporal punishment is necessary because in the neighbourhood where they live, it is difficult to control the children and prevent them from playing with other children who may have 'bad' habits:

> Because our children, without the stick you will not be able to raise them well. Many times they are mischievous coming in from outside. They meet with many people when they are playing. If you don't use the stick it is difficult for the child to listen. Therefore you punish him in order for him to be able to have good habits.

Beating with care is performed in the best interests of the child, in order to teach what is right and wrong and prevent the child from getting injured or causing accidents. As caregivers are occupied with other chores, it is important that the children learn to avoid accidents as early as possible and corporal punishment is regarded as an effective strategy:

The child who you can show something and he will understand is from 3 years old. He is able to take a knife and start to play with it or play with the fire. You beat him and tell him 'this fire is hot, if I see you again playing with the fire, I will beat you'. Another day he will be afraid, he will remember: I touched here; mama was beating me I should not play with that again.

Within the logic of *beating with care*, it is important, particularly regarding young children, that the punishment is given shortly after the misdemeanour in order for the child to understand the relationship between the mistake and the punishment:

Or he is hitting his friend and you beat him right away. Don't wait until the time has passed he will not remember what he has done; right away you beat him.... His brain will be developing well. But if you leave him for 10 minutes and then you beat him he will not remember what he did.

Caregivers are often busy with household chores or absent from the house working in other places, and disciplining shortly after the misdemeanour is not always possible. The participants describe how small children from an early age are left alone at home or in the neighbourhood when the mother goes to work. When she comes back a neighbour might inform her about something wrong the child has done during the day. The caregiver then must choose either not to discipline at all or to corporally punish even if it is difficult for the child to understand the connection between the misdemeanour and the punishment. Trying hard to fulfil their caregiving responsibilities, caregivers in that situation may choose to punish, not because they believe punishment will make the child understand but because they feel there is no alternative.

To beat with care also means that corporal punishment is used as a strategy in combination with other discipline strategies such as instructing, bribing, and threatening:

Maybe I should tell you an example myself, I said, I have a grandchild of my own.... He is mischievous, he doesn't listen. We were beating him and telling him [what is right] many times.

We use a lot of words of God [religious threats]: if you do like this it is a sin, if you do this it is wrong and you go to hell, also it [the threats] helps to bring [the child] back to a good condition [behave properly].

A child that has stolen something can be threatened by the parent that a hand will be cut off. To threaten the child that the police will come to take the child away is also used to scare the child and make him or her understand the proper way to behave.

Some participants describe using corporal punishment very frequently while others are more restrictive. There are a few parents among the participants who do not beat their children at all. These caregivers, nevertheless, state that they would beat the child if necessary. One technique of corporal punishment used for young children under five is to cane them a couple of times on the leg. Another method is to burn the child with a lit match or stick. Some parents stress the importance of relating the punishment to what the child has done. If the child has run away the child will be caned on the legs, if the child plays with fire he or she will be burnt, if the child has stolen something he or she will be caned on the hands. For less serious misdemeanours, the parent might pinch the child.

It can be concluded that the discipline strategy *to beat with care* is based on a relationship of *love* and *control. Love* is transmitted to the child through caregiving involvement, while *control* is acted out through instilling fear in the child through the use of corporal punishment.

30.1.2.2 To treat like an egg

Some of the grandparents interviewed have primary caregiving responsibilities for their grandchildren. Reasons mentioned for grandparents' taking care of grandchildren are parental divorce and parental death. Grandparents usually speak affectionately about their grandchildren, indicating close and loving relationships. However, there is concern among the respondents that grandparents, as primary caregivers, cannot raise their grandchildren properly. There is a popular expression commonly used in Tanzania mentioned in the interviews by both grandparents and parents:

> We grandparents we treat our grandchildren like eggs.

Treating the child like an egg means being too gentle when setting limits, begging the child to do as they say, and not daring to be strict with the child. Grandparents compare themselves with parents and agree that parents are generally much stricter with their children, meaning that they beat them more and harder and that they do not bother to get an explanation from the child about the reason for the wrongdoing. Grandparents describe how they used to be much stricter but now, in line with the African tradition, they have softened as they have got older. The discourse of *treating the child like an egg* appears ambiguous. On the one hand, grandparents seem proud of how they make an effort to understand the perspective of the child instead of immediately punishing the child. Grandparents describe that it is good to be closer to the children:

> We are buddies me and my grandchild.

Participants describe how grandparents spend more time at home and that they have more time to spend with their grandchildren, facilitating a closer relationship. On the other hand, both grandparents and parents are seriously concerned about the consequences of children *being treated like eggs*. Both grandparents and parents describe the grandparenting style of being too soft as a problem. There are a number of explanations provided by grandparents and parents as to why they are less strict. Grandparents describe having too much love and sympathy for the child to be able to be strict. Also grandparents comment on how unclear authority relationships between parents and grandparents have an effect on the grandparents' authority:

> We have a lot of sympathy and that [child] which we raise is not ours. For example, if his father beats him it is different from how I, the grandfather, would beat him. If the child cries his mother will see that we, the grandfather or grandmother, beat him a lot. So then we get the blame. That is why we, the old, say it is not possible to beat the grandchildren much.

In this case, the grandparent cannot corporally punish the child as he or she thinks best because the mother will accuse him or her of being too harsh. Thus grandparents cannot discipline the grandchild efficiently unless the parent has handed over the responsibility for disciplining the child to the grandparent and supports the discipline strategy used. Among the participants, most of the grandparents have the main responsibility for the grandchildren. In situations where the parents are present in the household, the grandparent's softer attitude can be considered to be functional and in the best interests of the child. However, if the parents are absent, both parents and grandparents are concerned that the grandparents are unable to take good care of the grandchildren. Children growing up with their grandparents are described as developing weak morally:

> We the grandfathers we have a lot of love for our grandchildren. We raise them badly; different from if he is raised by his father or mother. It happens sometimes that the child is ruined because we raise him in a grandfather's way, when he is big he will not be obedient. . . . We the old, we raise the children like eggs. . . . The childrearing of grandfathers and grandmothers is destroying our grandchildren. Yes we say the government should help us and we should contribute so that we can give children the good upbringing they need.

It can be concluded that the strategy *to treat like an egg* is based on a relationship where the caregiver provides a combination of *love* and *freedom* to the child. *Love* is transmitted to the child through caregiving involvement while *freedom* is the result of caregivers not setting limits for the child.

30.1.2.3 The non-care of non-beating

When asked if there were parents who never beat their children, the participants primarily referred to cases where the parents were disinterested, detached, or indifferent to their children and where the children grew up without boundaries. These cases were described as horror scenarios where the lack of discipline at a young age results in the children developing into villains, thieves, or drug addicts with no sense of right and wrong:

> For those who don't beat the children, the child will end up doing bad things; even the parent will not be able to stop him [then] because he left the child without admonishing him since he was a child. Therefore even if the parent [then] tries to admonish the child, that child will not agree [and] the parent will leave him to do what he wants.

As mentioned earlier, there are caregivers who state that they do not corporally punish their children, because the children are so well behaved that they do not need to. However if it were necessary they would not hesitate to use corporal punishment. These cases are included in the *beating with care* strategy and are not characteristic of the *non-care of non-beating* strategy.

The non-care of non-beating as a discipline strategy is based on a relationship where the caregiver *ignores* the child while also *giving* the child freedom. By ignoring the child the caregiver neglects the child, which also results in the child getting too much freedom without the necessary limits to what is age-appropriate guidance and control of the child.

30.1.2.4 As if beating a snake

There are other types of beatings which do not represent the good caregiving described in *beating with care*. The category *as if beating a snake* represents child abuse, as defined by parents and grandparents. These beatings are also delivered to correct the child's misbehaviour and are given so the child understands that he or she has made a mistake. However, in *as if beating a snake* the punishment is too harsh and may be directly harmful to the child's physical well-being. In one of the groups, a mother described how she excessively beat her seven-year-old daughter and the rest of the group agreed that this happened frequently:

Interviewer: And can it happen that you beat a child too much, or are there some people that beat the children so much that it is not good for them?

Mama: Usually it happens, some beat a lot until they hurt the children, I have already beat [my daughter] until I have hurt her. My child is very naughty, she doesn't like to go to school instead she likes to play. I found, her, she was playing with dirty water in the drain, I stopped her, she didn't listen, I decided to get the belt and to thrash her. She was injured on her head.

Beating *without* care is described as having a negative influence on the child. And there are limits to what should be regarded as legitimate beatings of children. There is consensus among the groups that many children are beaten far too much and there are descriptions of children being beaten nearly to death, or where they faint or are seriously injured:

The way we take care of them is not good. Last week in the house where I live there was a child that was beaten close to death—he was a thief who had been cared for badly.

For my side, I witnessed my neighbour—it is not good to mention their name—but he beat the child until he fainted. After that they had to splash water on him, it took two hours then the child stood up; that is what I saw, two hours, he could have died.

Respondents described how *as if beating a snake* can result in severe child abuse. An additional consequence of *as if beating a snake* is that the child may lose his or her positive feelings for the caregiver:

But if you beat him a lot it will be [like] an illness. Also love will get less for the father and mother, he sees you as poison.

As if beating a snake can also lead to children running away from home to live on the streets; something regarded as a negative consequence by the participants.

The strategy *to beat like a snake* is based on a relationship where the caregiver *controls* the child by instilling fear into the child while *ignoring* the child as well by simply not caring.

30.1.2.5 The caregiving discipline model

The four variables, to love, to control, to ignore, and to give freedom, describe relational qualities resulting from the caregiving discipline strategies used by the caregivers. The participants describe involvement and fear as two major factors influencing child behaviour and related to the quality of the caregiving relationship. There are also descriptions of caregiving where the child gets too much freedom or where the child is ignored by the caregiver. The strategy for obtaining a relationship based on controlling the child is fear, on loving the child is involvement, on giving freedom to the child is to be too gentle or not to set limits for the child, and on ignoring the child is neglect. Combining the four discipline strategies *to beat with care, to treat like an egg, the non-care of non-beating,* and *as if beating a snake* with the relational variables of loving, controlling, ignoring, and giving freedom in an axial diagram gives the model shown in Figure 30.1.

The diagonal *to beat with care* and *the non-care of non-beating* represents a continuum of care provided by the caregiver to the child. *To beat with care* has the highest

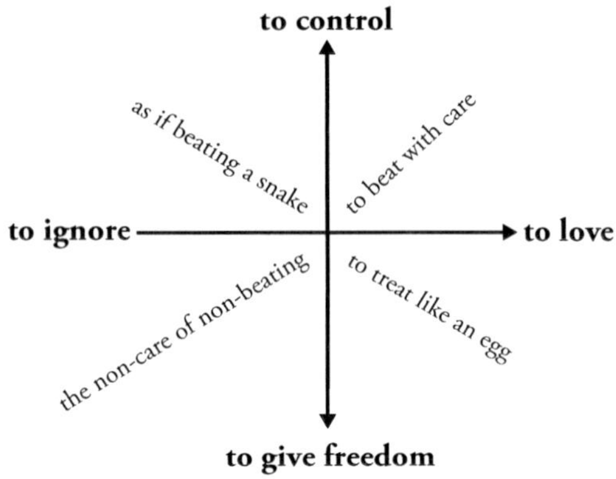

Figure 30.1 The Caregiving Power Discipline Model

level of care and *the non-care of non-beating* has the lowest level of care. The diagonal *as if beating a snake* and *to treat like an egg* represents a continuum of force used within the relationship between the child and the caregiver. *As if beating a snake* represents an excessive use of force whereas *to treat like an egg* represents a form of caregiving lacking in force. The model shows that the quality of the caregiving relationship and the force being used within a relationship are interdependent in the context studied.[6]

According to the views of the caregivers, the strategies of *treating the child like an egg* and *the non-care of non-beating* risk creating irresponsible and disrespectful citizens. It is *beating with care* that achieves the long-term goal of well-adapted citizens according to the participants. The preferred discipline strategy *to beat with care* is based on a combination of control and love and it is commonly stated that instilling fear in the child will make the child understand the difference between right and wrong.

30.1.3 Discussion

The participants regard it as responsible caregiving to punish the child corporally and without its use there is fear that the goals of caregiving may not be met. *Beating with care* has the effect of emotional arousal in the child, described by Quinn (2005) as being an essential feature for effective childrearing aiming at the child developing into a culturally accepted adult. However, not all interaction with children is driven by the goal of effective childrearing and the analysis of the data indicates that there is a dividing line between what is regarded as rational and appropriate corporal punishment and what is regarded as abuse. Participants say that corporal punishment in some cases crosses the line of acceptable punishment, or *beating with care*, and turns into *as if beating a snake*, resulting in child abuse in the home. International research confirms a connection between the use of corporal punishment and child

[6] It is noted that the model presented shows similarities with the structural analysis of social behaviour model developed by Benjamin (1974) as well as the parental disciplinary patterns described by Baumrind (1978). Analysis of similarities and differences, however, is not within the scope of this chapter.

abuse (Gershoff and Bitensky, 2007) and there is evidence of parental loss of control contributing to excessive violence against children.

30.1.3.1 Zone of intimacy

The line between acceptable punishment and abuse may be understood in the light of the concept *zone of intimacy*, introduced by Hundeide, Pramilng Samulesson, and Sommer (2010), describing variations in human intimacy, defined as 'the zone in which a child can be included and cared for through empathetic identification and sensitive availability of the caregiver to the child's needs.' (p. 83) From this perspective the discipline strategies represented by *beating with care* and *to treat as an egg* can be categorized as taking place within the 'zone of intimacy'. The parent and grandparent discourses categorized within these strategies include references indicating empathetic connectivity with the child as opposed to the strategies *as if beating a snake* and *the non-care of non-beating*. The caregiver who manages to include the child in her or his zone of intimacy makes it possible to elicit empathetic identification with the child and in that way provides a more genuine and sustainable basis of care. Empathetic identification means identifying with the point of view of the child. This facilitates seeing the child as a person, which is the first step towards humanization and inclusion (ibid.). In particular the discourse presented under the category *as if treating like an egg* expresses the capacity of identification with the child and seeing the child as a person with whom it is desirable to have a relation.

Hundeide et al. (2010) stress that 'a child may also be expelled from the zone of intimacy with subsequent blockage of empathetic identification, affective withdrawal leading to neglect, and possible abuse' (p. 83). From this perspective children who are subjected to treatment characterized as the *non-care of non-beating* and *as if beating a snake* can be characterized as having been excluded from the 'zone of intimacy' and are subjected to neglect and abuse.

The participants in this study state that there are many threats to the children outside the home, making it difficult to protect the children from harm. This inability of the participants to make their neighbourhood more child-friendly may result in a conviction that control of the child through corporal punishment is necessary. The perspective of 'zone of intimacy' further explains the psychological mechanism that may determine whether or not the caregiver will have the conditions of treating the child with dignity. Hundeide et al. (2010) stress the necessity of being close to the child in order to arrive at the emotional sensitivity which characterizes the 'zone of intimacy'. This may explain why it is the grandparents' discourses that most clearly express a relationship based on the respect of treating the child as person. Grandparents in the areas where the data was collected often have more time to spend with the children than parents who are occupied with work and household shores.

The transferability of the findings in this study to other settings requires further national and international investigations as well as contributions from a historical point of view. The tendency to regard corporal punishment not as violence but as an act of love and a necessary form of discipline, as in *beating with care*, is far from unique and is a common argument used among defenders of corporal punishment as a discipline strategy (Lansdown, 2000). The common use of corporal punishment in other countries in Africa (Stavropoulos, 2006) as well as other parts of the world indicates that ideals such as *to beat with care* may be common elsewhere. The question of what local childrearing circumstances contribute to *beating with care* as an ideal disciplining strategy should be further explored. There was a common saying in

Sweden around the beginning of the 20th century, 'the one you love you beat'.[7] Since then the discourse on child discipline in Sweden has changed along with the overall stance towards children.

The universalist claims of the CRC have been criticized (Twum-Danso, 2009) and the resistance in many countries to a complete ban on corporal punishment highlights the gap between universal rules and regulations and the everyday practice of caregiver-child relationships. Inspired by feminist theory Cockburn (2005) has suggested that the implementation of the CRC should be undertaken within a framework of 'ethics of care' (Tronto, 1993). Morality is formed through social practice and customs and the enactment of ethical judgement in situations of care can therefore only be realized if related to caregivers' feelings and opinions. An 'ethics of care' can 'be described as a moral activity, the "activity of caring", rather than a set of principles which can be followed' (Cockburn, 2005: 73). An ethics of rights emphasizing rules and rights may be regarded as abstract and formal while an 'ethics of care', on the other hand, emphasizes responsibilities and relationships and may therefore more easily be related to concrete situations of care. The Caregiving Discipline Model primarily describes the relationship between caregivers and children grounded in concrete situations of guidance and control in a local Tanzanian context and can as such be interpreted as moral discourses illustrating the 'ethics of care' in this local context.

Finally, it may be argued that the Caregiving Discipline Model also illustrates the interdependence between childhood relationships and law in the sense that the horizontal axis describes the relational qualities of involvement between child and caregiver during childhood whereas the vertical axis describes the caregiver-child relationship in relation to the law or in a wider sense; what is regarded as right and wrong. The model thus highlights a fundamental interdependence between the relationship between the child and the caregiver and the implementation of the law. The law in this sense addresses both the child, in terms of what is accepted and not accepted behaviour in society, and the caregiver in terms of laws protecting the dignity and wellbeing of the child. These findings indicate that an ethics of rights represented by the CRC must go hand in hand with an 'ethics of care'.

Funding

The empirical findings presented in this chapter were produced with the support of The Nordic Africa Institute, Uppsala, Sweden.

Acknowledgements

A previous version of this chapter, entitled 'The Care of Corporal Punishment: Conceptions of Early Childhood Discipline Strategies Among Parents and Grandparents in a Poor and Urban Area in Tanzania' by J.S. Frankenberg, R. Holmqvist, and B. Rubenson, has been published in the journal *Childhood: A Journal of Global Child Research* vol. 17(4) 2010. Copyright © 2010 by SAGE publications. Reprinted by Permission of SAGE.

[7] 'Den man älskar agar man'.

References

Baumrind, D. (1978) 'Parental Disciplinary Patterns and Social Competence in Children' *Youth and Society* 9(2): 236–67.

Benjamin, L.S. (1974) 'Structural Analysis of Social Behavior' *Psychological Review* 81(5): 392–425.

Brownlie, J. and S. Anderson (2006) 'Beyond Anti-Smacking: Rethinking Parent-Child Relations' *Childhood* 13(4): 479–98.

Charmaz, C. (2006) *Constructing Grounded Theory: A Practical Guide through Qualitative Analysis.* London: Sage.

Cockburn, T. (2005) 'Children and the Feminist Ethic of Care' *Childhood* 12(1): 71–89.

Ember C.R. and R. Ember (2005) 'Explaining Corporal Punishment of Children' *American Anthropologist* 107(4): 609–19.

End All Corporal Punishment Now (2011) *United Republic of Tanzania, Country report, Summary of necessary legal reform to achieve full prohibition.* Accessed 5 November 2011, from <http://www.endcorporalpunishment.org/pages/frame.html>.

Feinstein, S. and L. Mwahombela (2010) 'Corporal Punishment in Tanzania's schools' *International Review of Education* 56: 399–410.

Frankenberg, S., R. Holmqvist, and B. Rubenson (2010) 'The Care of Corporal Punishment: Conceptions of early childhood discipline strategies among parents and grandparents in an urban and poor area in Tanzania' *Childhood* 17(4): 455–69.

Gershoff, E.T. and S.H. Bitensky (2007) 'The Case against Corporal Punishment of Children: Converging Evidence from Social Science Research and International Human Rights Law and Implications for US Public Policy Psychology' *Public Policy and Law* 13(4): 231–72.

Hein, C. (2005) *Reconciling Work and Family Responsibilities: Practical Ideas from Global Experience.* Geneva: International Labour Organization.

Hundeide, K., I. Pramilng Samuelsson, and D. Sommer (2010) *Child Perspectives and Children's Perspectives in Theory and Practice.* Dordrecht: Springer.

Landsford, J., L. Chang, K. Dodge et al. (2005) 'Physical Discipline and Children's Adjustment: Cultural Normativeness as a Moderator' *Child Development* 76(6): 1234–46.

Lansdown, G. (2000) 'Children's Rights and Domestic Violence' *Child Abuse Review* 9(6): 416–26.

Makame, V. (2001) *A Rapid Assessment of Child Rearing Practices Likely to Affect Child's Emotional, Psychological and Psychomotor Development: A Case Study of Kibaha District, Costal Region—Tanzania.* Dar es Salaam: UNICEF Tanzania.

Meru, M. (2010) 'Why Are Kenyan Teachers Still Using Corporal Punishment Eight Years After a Ban on Corporal Punishment?' *Child Abuse Review* 19: 248–58.

Ministry of Education and Vocational Training, National Website of the United Republic of Tanzania. (2008). Accessed 15 February 2008, from <http://www.moe.go.tz>.

MKUKUTA Monitoring System: Research and Analysis Working Group and Communications Technical Working Group, Ministry of Planning Economy and Empowerment (2007) *Tanzanian Children's Perceptions of Education and Their Role in Society Views of the Children 2007.* Dar es Salaam.

Modig, C. (2009) *Never Violence—Thirty Years on from Sweden's Abolition of Corporal Punishment.* Government offices of Sweden and Save the Children.

Payet, J.P. and V. Franchi (2008) 'The Rights of the Child and "the Good of the Learners": A Comparative Ethnographical Survey on the Abolition of Corporal Punishment in South African Schools' *Childhood* 15(2): 157–76.

Pinheiro, P.S. (2006) *World Report on Violence against Children*, Independent Expert for the United Nations. New York: UN.

Quinn, N. (2005) 'Universals of Childrearing' *Anthropological Theory* 5(4): 477–516.

Stavropoulos, J. (2006) *Violence against Girls in Africa: A Retrospective Survey in Ethiopia, Kenya and Uganda.* Addis Ababa: The African Child Policy Forum.

Tronto, J. (1993) *Moral Boundaries: A Political Argument for an Ethic of Care.* London Routledge.

Twum-Danso, A. (2009) 'Reciprocity, Respect and Responsibility: The 3Rs Underlying Parent-Child Relationships in Ghana and the Implications for Children's Rights' *International Journal of Children's Rights* 17: 415–32.

UNICEF Tanzania (2009) 'Fact Sheet Temeke District'.

United Nations (2006) 'CRC/C/TZA/CO/2 Consideration of Reports Submitted by State Parties under Article 44 of the Convention, Concluding Observations: United Republic of Tanzania', 21 June, Committee on the Rights of the Child, Geneva.

United Nations (2007) 'CRC/C/GC/8 General Comment No. 8: The Right of the Child to Protection from Corporal Punishment and Other Cruel or Degrading Forms of Punishment', Committee on the Rights of the Child, Geneva.

United Republic of Tanzania (2011) *Violence Against Children in Tanzania: Findings from a National Survey 2009*, Multi Sector Task Force on Violence Against Children Secretariat: UNICEF Dar es Salaam, Tanzania.

US Department of State (2009) Accessed 13 August 2009 from <http://www.state.gov/g/drl/rls/irf/2006/71328.htm>.

31

Caring for Children: Risks and Responsibilities in the Law of Tort

Jo Bridgeman[1]

31.1 Responsibilities to children

In this chapter, I explore responsibilities to children through consideration of civil liability claims for compensation brought on behalf of children. Whilst academic analysis has offered a critique of the increased use of the criminal law, in recent years within the UK, to make parents *take* responsibility for their children,[2] the expectations of parents, other adults, and children as revealed through civil law jurisprudence has not received the same scrutiny.[3] Not surprisingly, these cases are consistent with constructions of children in many areas of law as dependent, incompetent (less able than adults to 'foresee risk and exercise self-restraint and skill'),[4] unruly (both 'hazardous and irresponsible'),[5] and as 'becoming' (that is, children need to take risks in order to learn how to manage risks). Consequently, children require supervision and adult failure to supervise may result in children causing harm to themselves or to others. The risks children pose take on particular significance in a world which is preoccupied with the management and avoidance of risk and in which anxiety about risk is a 'constant and pervasive feature of everyday consciousness, managed through everyday practices; it might be fuelled by public discussions of risk, but individuals are left to find their own ways of coping with the uncertainty it engenders'.[6] The risks children take, or are to be allowed to take, feature prominently in discussions of our health and safety culture. And civil claims brought on behalf of children for

[1] Sussex Law School, University of Sussex.

[2] For example, Heather Keating, 'Being Responsible, Becoming Responsible and Having Responsibility Thrust upon Them: Constructing the "Responsibility" of Children and Parents' in (eds.) Jo Bridgeman, Heather Keating, and Craig Lind, *Responsibility, Law and the Family* (Ashgate, 2008), 125–43; Jo Bridgeman, 'Accountability, Support or Relationship? Conceptions of Parental Responsibility' (2007) 58 *Northern Ireland Legal Quarterly* 307–24; Helen Reece, 'From Parental Responsibility to Parenting Responsibly' in (ed.) Michael Freeman, *Law and Sociology: Current Legal Issues* (Oxford University Press, 2006).

[3] One exception being Roderick Bagshaw, 'Children Through Tort' in (ed.) Julia Fionda, *Legal Concepts of Childhood* (Hart, 2001), 127–50. Paula Giliker considers 'Parental Liability for Harm Caused by Children: A Comparative Analysis' in (eds.) Rebecca Probert, Stephen Gilmore, and Jonathan Herring, *Responsible Parents and Parental Responsibility* (Hart, 2009), 333–51.

[4] Julia Fionda, 'Legal Concepts of Childhood: An Introduction' in (ed.) Julia Fionda, *Legal Concepts of Childhood* (Hart, 2001), 3–17, at 11.

[5] N. 4, above, 15.

[6] Sue Scott, Stevi Jackson, and Kathryn Backett-Milburn, 'Swings and Roundabouts: Risk Anxiety and the Everyday Worlds of Children' (1998) 32 *Sociology* 689–705, at 690.

harm sustained when engaging in risky activities are often reported, in the media and political debate, in terms of a compensation culture. Together they contribute to 'contemporary meanings of childhood... shaped by the past and the present, located in residual notions of childhood in the popular imagination and in contemporary accounts of risk and crisis'.[7]

Recent judicial consideration of children's risk-taking and of responsibilities to 'other people's children' is offered by the bouncy castle case, *Perry v Harris*.[8] Of this case, David Cameron, then leader of the opposition, in a speech announcing a review for the Conservative Party by Lord Young of the 'health and safety and compensation culture',[9] said in December 2009:

> In one case, parents who put up a bouncy castle for a children's party were successfully sued when a boy was injured after colliding with another child. Eventually it was overturned by the Court of Appeal, but what message does this send parents about allowing their children to play with others? This has all helped to create a legal hypersensitivity to risk, accident and injury. And this has had a direct knock-on effect on the health and safety culture.[10]

It has been suggested that this 'hypersensitivity' extends so far that 'childhood is becoming undermined by risk aversion'.[11]

In this chapter, I take up the question posed above by David Cameron and explore civil law responsibilities to children. First, I examine the nature, scope, and extent of the civil responsibilities of parents to children, then the professional responsibilities of teachers, before turning to responsibilities to 'other people's children'. My analysis of the cases considers the nature of responsibility to children, expectations of children and of parents, teachers, and other adults caring for children and what they reveal of the nature of relationships between adults and children.[12]

31.2 Parents

The legal principles established in tort cases, for damages for harm sustained whilst a child, brought against foster carers (considered below), which demonstrate a reluctance to identify the standard of care owed within the domestic sphere, are thought by many textbook writers to apply to parents.[13] This is based upon the obiter opinion of Browne-Wilkinson VC in *Surtees* that the duty owed by the foster parents in the case before him was 'exactly the same as that owed by the ordinary parent to his or

[7] Mary Jane Kehily, 'Childhood in Crisis? Tracing the Contours of "Crisis" and its Impact upon Contemporary Parenting Practices' (2010) 32 *Media, Culture & Society* 171–85, at 171–2.

[8] *Harris v Perry* [2008] EWHC 990, QB; *Perry and Another v Harris (A Minor)* [2008] EWCA Civ 907.

[9] Lord Young, *Common Sense Common Safety, A report by Lord Young of Graffham to the Prime Minister* (Cabinet Office, Crown Copyright, September 2010).

[10] David Cameron, 'Reducing the burden and impact of health and safety', <http://www.conservatives.com/News/Speeches/2009/12/David_Cameron_Reducing_the_burden_and_impact_of_health_and_safety.aspx1>, December 2009.

[11] Tim Gill, *No Fear: Growing Up in a Risk Averse Society* (Calouste Gulbenkian Foundation, London, 2007), 10.

[12] Shauna Van Praagh, '"Sois Sage"—Responsibility for Childishness in the Law of Civil Wrongs' in (eds.) Jason W. Neyers, Erika Chamberlain, and Stephen G.A. Pitel, *Emerging Issues in Tort Law* (Hart, Oregon, 2007), 63–84, at 64.

[13] For example, Nicholas J. McBride and Roderick Bagshaw, *Tort Law* (Longman, 3rd ed, 2008), 184; John Murphy, *Street on Torts* (Reed Elsevier (UK) Ltd, 11th ed, 2003), 651; WVH Rogers, *Winfield & Jolowicz on Tort* (Sweet & Maxwell, 17th ed, 2006), 174.

her own children'.[14] Actions against parents have been dominated by claims founded upon allegations of a failure to prevent abuse; and thus a failure to fulfil the parental responsibility to *protect from harm*. The inability of claimants to bring claims against the perpetrators of abuse, due to the interpretation of statutes of limitation, forced claimants to reconstruct actions as breach of duty arising from a failure to prevent or stop the abuse. In *Stubbings and Webb*,[15] the House of Lords held that the abuse, as a battery, came within s.2 of the Limitation Act 1980 with a six-year limitation period (after reaching the age of majority) and not within s.11 with a three-year limitation period commencing at the date of the breach or upon knowledge of the person injured (s.14) and with judicial discretion to allow claims out of time (s.33). This remained the position for 15 years until the House of Lords, revisiting the issue in *A v Hoare and other appeals*,[16] considered that *Stubbings* had been wrongly decided and had resulted in the lower courts distinguishing cases on artificial and unsatisfactory grounds. Lord Hoffmann noted the case of *S v W and Another (Child Abuse: Damages)*,[17] as 'perhaps the most remarkable example of the anomaly' created by the application of the statute. In *S v W*, the claim against the father as the perpetrator of the abuse, actionable in trespass, was statute barred whereas the claim against the mother, who was aware of the father's actions, based upon breach of her duty to protect her child came within ss. 11, 14, and 33 of the Limitation Act 1980. Both Millett LJ and Sir Ralph Gibson expressed the view that the effect of the application of legal principles by which they were bound was both illogical and surprising.

Lord Woolf in *Barrett v Enfield LBC*, a case concerning whether the council owed a duty with respect to decisions affecting the welfare of a child in its care, considered that *decisions* made by parents should not be subject to civil claims. Obiter, his Lordship said:

> If a parent when driving a car injures his child who is a passenger, then of course as is the case with any other driver there is no reason why he should not be liable for damages. However parents are daily making decisions with regard to their children's future and it seems to me that it would be wholly inappropriate that those decisions, even if they could be shown to be wrong, should be ones which give rise to a liability for damages.[18]

On appeal to the House of Lords,[19] Lord Hutton agreed that children should not seek damages against their parents with respect to decisions related to their upbringing

[14] *Surtees v Kingston-upon-Thames Borough Council; Surtees v Hughes and Another* [1991] 2 FLR 559, 583.

[15] In *Stubbings and Webb* [1993] AC 498 the claimant sought to bring an action against her stepfather and stepbrother for sexual and physical abuse and against her stepmother for physical abuse. Lord Griffiths in the House of Lords did not consider that 'breach of duty [included] a deliberate assault. The phrase lying in juxtaposition with negligence and nuisance carries with it the implication of a breach of duty of care not to cause personal injury, rather than an obligation not to infringe any legal rights of another person'. The ECtHR rejected the claim that this amounted to a breach of Articles 6(1), 8, and 14 of the ECHR in *Stubbings and Others v The United Kingdom* [1997] 1 FLR 105, criticised by Alastair Mullis, 'Case Commentary: The Abuse Continues?' (1997) 9 *Child and Family Law Quarterly* 291.

[16] *A v Hoare and other appeals* [2008] UKHL 6. Coulson J exercised discretion under s.33 enabling the claim in *Hoare* to proceed to trial, *A v H* [2008] EWHC 1573. None of the cases concerned an action against a parent; rather they alleged vicarious liability of an employer, systemic failures, and in *Hoare* itself the perpetrator of attempted rape subsequently won £7million on the lottery whilst on day release, rendering him claimworthy.

[17] *S v W and Another (Child Abuse: Damages)* [1995] 1 FLR 862. Although the argument in this case was confined to whether ss. 2 or 11 applied, not whether the action could proceed beyond three years under ss. 14 or 33.

[18] *Barrett v Enfield LBC* [1998] QB 367, 377.

[19] *Barrett v Enfield LBC* [2001] AC 550.

which subsequently turned out to be wrong. However, his Lordship considered that it did not then follow that the local authority should not be held to account in respect of decisions, such as taking a child into care or placing for adoption, which would not fall within the remit of parents. Reflecting upon *Barrett* and *X v Bedfordshire*,[20] it has been suggested that:

> A common law duty of care on parents would be an additional positive weapon in the hands of the state (through its judicial system) to enforce the statutory 'parental responsibility' which the law imposes upon parents.[21]

We should note that the courts have not denied that parents owe duties of care to their children—indeed, the parent-child relationship is one commonly cited as involving a positive duty to act in addition to the duty to act carefully—rather they have been reluctant to identify the standard of care owed by parents to their children. Secondly, albeit in principle rather more than in practice, these duties hold parents to account *to their child* for harm resulting from their actions or inactions rather than to the state.

In an essay, the focus of which is parental responsibility *for* the harms caused *by* their children rather than *to* them, Shauna Van Praagh argues that the parental role includes 'develop[ing] the separate responsibility of the child'[22] but that of greater significance is 'the mutual responsibility—to teach and to learn, to guide and to grow'.[23] The primary responsibility to protect, care for, secure the wellbeing of, nurture, and guide, children rests with parents, a responsibility which attracts duties to act and to act carefully. Fulfilling parental responsibilities to children involves assessing risks and making decisions, largely discharged in the private domain; a chaotic place where risks are taken and, consequently, minor injuries may be inevitable.[24] The law imposes duties but is reluctant to articulate standards except in cases of gross derelictions of care involving a 'violation of a relationship of trust'.[25]

The application of general principles operates to determine standards according to common practice, assessment of the likelihood and severity of risk, and the cost and practicality of precautions. The majority of parents take care of their children, try to maximize their wellbeing, do the best for them that they can, and assess as best they can the risks which their children should take in the interests of developing their skills and abilities. Most parents will meet and surpass any legal standards set by ordinary tortious principles, not because the law requires it of them, but because as parents they are most profoundly concerned with the needs and interests of their child. If the law can establish standards of care towards strangers in chance encounters, it must surely be able to identify those arising in the most intimate, caring relationship. Failure to extend the protective reach of the civil law to children, in the

[20] *X and Others (minors) v Bedfordshire County Council; M (a minor) and Another v Newham London Borough Council and Others; E (a minor) v Dorset County Council; and other appeals* [1995] 2 AC 633.

[21] Dr Susan Maidment, 'Children and Psychiatric Damages—Parents' Duty of Care to their Children' (2001) 31 *Family Law* 440–4, at 444.

[22] N. 12, above, 77. [23] N. 12, above, 80.

[24] Although both adults and children see the home as a place of safety with risks associated with places beyond the home: Jeni Harden, Kathryn Backett-Milburn, Sue Scott, and Stevi Jackson, 'Scary Faces, Scary Places: Children's Perceptions of Risk and Safety' (2000) 59 *Health Education Journal* 12–22; P. Kelley, S. Hood, and B. Mayall, 'Children, Parents and Risk' (1998) 6 *Health and Social Care in the Community* 16–24.

[25] Joanne Conaghan, 'Tort-Litigation in the Context of Intra-familial Abuse' (1998) 61 *Modern Law Review* 132–161, at 161.

belief that it would be an 'intrusion' which could 'disturb family harmony',[26] is to fail to recognize harm to children and reinforces a construction of children as becoming not being. Where a child is injured, it will be the child's parents who assume the burden of caring for the child. As such not only the cause but also the consequences of injury are privatized; confined to the home. Responsibility for children is thus individualized and privatized. The responsibility for children rests with their parents, the responsibility to care for children rests with their parents. Parents are responsible for, rather than to, their children.

31.3 Teachers

Children leave the private sphere of the home and enter the quasi-public realm of school. During school hours, the physical and emotional care of children is delegated to teachers. At school, children are not only taught their lessons but develop practical, emotional, and social skills; teachers, like parents, guide and direct children and contribute in significant ways to securing children's wellbeing. However, unlike parents, teachers feature heavily amongst those with respect to whom concerns about the legal consequences of their responsibilities to children have been expressed.

One area in which the responsibilities of teachers and the wellbeing of children has received attention, within the context of concern surrounding a 'compensation' or 'blame' culture, is that of school trips and civil actions against teachers when children have come to harm under their supervision outside school. As the House of Commons Education and Skills Select Committee noted, the media report these 'tragic but isolated incidents' giving them extensive publicity which deters future school trips:[27]

> High profile reporting of isolated incidents and some tabloid journalism misrepresents the incidents of serious accidents on school trips, which is actually very low indeed. There have been 57 fatal accidents on school visits since 1985 (this figure includes adults accompanying visits and road traffic accidents en route to and from off-site visits). In England in 2003, there were between seven and ten million 'pupil visits' involving educational or recreational activity, but only one fatality. Whilst every fatality is clearly tragic for those involved, these statistics compare extremely favourably with other routine activities such as driving or being driven in a car, or simply the likelihood of an accident at home or in school.[28]

David Cameron welcomed as a 'start' s.1 of the Compensation Act 2006, aimed at reducing the fear of litigation and risk averse behaviour by providing reassurance that the standard which must be met is one of reasonableness and that the court will consider whether a finding of liability would prevent or discourage a desirable activity.[29] But he argued that:

[26] *Surtees v Kingston-upon-Thames Borough Council; Surtees v Hughes and Another* [1991] 2 FLR 559, per Beldam LJ.

[27] House of Commons Education and Skills Select Committee, *Education Outside the Classroom*: Second Report of Session 2004–5 (HMSO, 2005) 6.

[28] N. 27, above, para. 19.

[29] House of Commons Constitutional Affairs Committee, Third Report of Session 2005–06, *Compensation Culture* (Stationery Office, HC 754–1, 2006) Baroness Ashton of Upholland, Parliamentary Under Secretary of State, Dept for Constitutional Affairs, quoted at para. 54. The HCCAC observes that the House of Lords in *Tomlinson v Congleton BC and Others* [2003] UKHL 47 referred to the social value of activity, not 'desirable activity' as in s.1.

we should consider whether further protection should be provided in cases involving adventure training and other outdoor activity by schools.

Those activities allow children to develop character, show leadership and work as a team—and it's a tragedy that they are being denied these possibilities because teachers and organisers fear the consequences if something goes wrong. . . . By providing [teachers] with greater assurance, I believe we can provide our children with greater opportunity.[30]

This begs the question whether the case law supports the view that these fears are well-founded or that further reassurance is required about the responsibilities of teachers to children in their care when they engage in risk-taking, character-building, team-working activities.

In *Outdoor Activities, Negligence and the Law*,[31] Julian Fulbrook offers a comprehensive analysis of the incidents of harm to children on school trips.[32] In exceptional cases, these incidents have resulted in prosecutions of the local authority for breach of the Health and Safety at Work etc Act 1974, punishable by a fine,[33] and, in the worst cases teachers have been prosecuted.[34] In the event of the death of a child, claims for damages, confined to bereavement damages, are likely to be settled. In 2001, following a number of fatal incidents, teachers' union NASUWT adopted the policy of advising members against taking pupils on school trips.[35] Reducing the opportunities for children to go on school trips reduces their range of experiences, opportunities to take risks in a controlled environment, and to develop skills and experiential knowledge. Children benefit from risk-taking: through taking risks children learn how to deal with those risks; children crave risks and if not provided with situations in which they can experience risks will create them for themselves, in potentially

[30] David Cameron, 'Reducing the burden and impact of health and safety', <http://www.conservatives.com/News/Speeches/2009/12/David_Cameron_Reducing_the_burden_and_impact_of_health_and_safety.aspx1>, December 2009.

[31] Julian Fulbrook, *Outdoor Activities, Negligence and the Law* (Ashgate, Hampshire, 2005).

[32] The deaths of four teenagers Dean Sayer (17), Simon Dunne (16), Claire Langley (16), and Rachel Walker (16) from Southway School, Plymouth (Fulbrook, N. 31, above, 17) in Lyme Bay in 1993 resulted in the successful prosecution for manslaughter of the company OLL Ltd, which was fined £60,000, and its managing director, Peter Kite, who received a three-year custodial sentence (Fulbrook, N. 31, above, 27; *R v Kite* [1996] 2 Cr. App. R. (S.) 295). Civil claims, for bereavement damages, were settled (Fulbrook, N. 31, above, 27). A private member's bill led to the Activity Centres (Young Persons Safety) Act 1995, establishing the Adventure Activities Licensing Authority (AALA). There was, in Fulbrook's words, 'unedifying further action' on the part of the company (Fulbrook, N. 31, above, 27). In *OLL Ltd v Secretary of State for Transport* [1997] 3 All ER 897, the activity centre claimed under the Civil Liability (Contribution) Act 1978 against the Secretary of State for an indemnity or contribution to negligence damages on the basis that the coastguard had acted negligently in the conduct of the search. The action was struck out. Lord Young has recently recommended the abolition of the AALA: Lord Young, *Common Sense Common Safety, A report by Lord Young of Graffham to the Prime Minister* (Cabinet Office, Crown Copyright, September 2010) 36.

[33] For example, Leeds City Council was fined at Leeds Crown Court following the deaths of Hannah Black (13) and Rochelle Couvet (14) in October 2000 whilst riverwalking during a residential outdoor course in Stainforth Beck, Yorkshire, despite the river being swollen following heavy rain: Roger Barker, 'Hard lessons on school trips' (2003) *Tolley's Health and Safety at Work* 22.

[34] For example geography teacher, Paul Ellis, pleaded guilty to gross negligence manslaughter after the death of 10-year-old Max Palmer who drowned whilst pool plunging in Glenridding Beck, Cumbria. He was imprisoned for 12 months in 2003. Julian Fulbrook concludes that the trial and HSE report 'reveal a hopelessly reckless disregard for safety judged against any guidelines or indeed against even plain common sense' (Fulbrook, N. 31, above, 3).

[35] Fulbrook, N. 31, above, 5.

more dangerous environments; and risk-taking enables children to develop 'adventurousness and entrepreneurialism', 'resilience and self-reliance'.[36]

The case law establishes that teachers have a dual duty towards pupils in their care; an educational duty and a health and safety duty 'in loco parentis' which may include a duty to act:[37]

> [T]he school undertakes to educate [the pupil] in as wide a sense as it reasonably can. This involves the school having pupils in its care and it involves the pupils in various activities in the classroom, in the chapel, in the gymnasium, on the sports field and so on. There are risks of injury inherent in many human activities, even of serious injury in some. Because of this, the school, having the pupils in its care, is under a duty to exercise reasonable care for their health and safety.[38]

The one reported case arising from a school trip[39] concerned the behaviour of a sixth-form boy injured whilst skiing rather than a 'cavalier or reckless' disregard on the part of his teachers. The allegation of negligence was in failing to provide supervision of the nature or type appropriate for a school trip organized for younger pupils which the claimant, along with two other sixth-form pupils, had been allowed to join, and failure to monitor the claimant's skiing and to provide adequate instruction. Whilst being under the general control of the teachers, the trip involved unsupervised skiing upon condition that the boys were mature and responsible. Leveson J considered that it was understood by the claimant, his parents, and teachers that:

> [T]he teachers taken together represented responsible adults who would broadly supervise what the boys were doing in exactly the same way that parents supervise their own children allowing greater freedom to those in their later teens providing, of course, that such greater freedom is not abused.[40]

This became the crux of the case as Leveson J found the breach of duty in the failure 'to impose substantial sanctions for deliberately skiing off-piste', telling the boys off but not removing their skiing passes was not the reasonable response of a teacher acting in the place of a parent[41] which was the (legal) cause of the accident which followed when the claimant was skiing too fast and paying insufficient attention to the risks. The teachers should have determined that the boys had not demonstrated the required level of maturity or skied responsibly and so were not to be trusted to ski alone; the boys had behaved irresponsibly, continued to do so, and this caused the accident in which the claimant was rendered paraplegic[42] and for which he was held 50 per cent contributorily negligent. The Court of Appeal disagreed with the conclusion that the reprimand given was not within the 'range of reasonable responses for a teacher in his position,[43] acting as a reasonably careful parent'[44] and allowed the appeal. It is of note that here the central issue was the role of the teacher responsible for a pupil on a school trip exercising judgement about discipline and punishment balanced against respect for the age, experience, and greater independence to be extended to an older pupil.

[36] Gill, N. 11, above, 15–16.

[37] *Hippolyte v Bexley London Borough*, CA, 23 November 1994.

[38] *Van Oppen v Clerk to the Bedford Charity Trustees* [1989] 3 All ER 389, CA per Balcombe LJ quoting from Boreham J at trial [1989] 1 All ER 273, 291–2.

[39] *Chittock v Woodbridge School* [2001] All ER (D) 342, QBD.

[40] N. 39, above, at [12].

[41] N. 39, above, at [43].

[42] N. 39, above, at [51].

[43] Where there are a number of options available the teacher is not negligent if he acts 'within a reasonable range of options for a reasonable teacher exercising that duty of care in the circumstances' applying *Bolam*, *Woodbridge School v Chittock* [2002] ELR 735, at [18].

[44] N. 43, above, at [27].

The health and safety duty has also been applied to injuries sustained during PE lessons when the failure is in the level of direction or assistance with the prescribed activity or use made of equipment.[45] It has been applied to claims following from injuries caused by the condition of school buildings (where the action was also, and technically correctly so, under the Occupiers' Liability Act 1957): swing doors, flint walls in the playground, and a Wendy house being the alleged cause of harm.[46] The health and safety duty has been breached where children have been injured on the road after making their escape from school premises or where young children have been allowed to leave school premises before the end of the school day.[47] To protect children from injuries caused by other children adequate supervision is required during lessons[48] and at playtimes[49] but not before or after school.[50] And during playtimes, the level of supervision must be sufficient to exercise control over what children play with.[51] The professional educational standard of 'reasonable members of the teaching profession'[52] has been applied to the response of the school to reports of bullying[53] and failure to diagnose dyslexia.[54] Whether to communicate directly to a child's parents information concerning the child's experience at school is a matter of professional judgement. Whilst the parents of the boys involved in an incident of harassment of a 13-year-old girl on school premises had been informed, the decision to inform the girl's parents or to tell her to inform them was a matter of professional judgement.[55]

The *extent* of these duties was considered in a case concerning psychiatric harm alleged to have been caused by bullying by other pupils:

The school does not have the charge of its pupils all the time and so cannot directly protect them from harm all the time. At a day school that charge will usually end at the school gates, although the school will have a duty to take reasonable steps to ensure that young children who are not old enough to look after themselves do not leave the school premises unattended: [see *Carmarthenshire CC v Lewis* [1955]]. One can think of circumstances where it might go

[45] *Cotton v Kent County Council*, 15 July 1983; *Cassidy v The Council of the City of Manchester*, 12 July 1995, CA.

[46] *Meehan v Lancashire County Council*, 24 November 1988; *Ward v Hertfordshire County Council* [1969] 2 All ER 807, QBD; *Ward v Hertfordshire County Council* [1970] 1 All ER 535; *Smart v Gwent County Council*, 25 April 1991, CA, <http://www.lexisnexis.com/uk/legal/>.

[47] *Jenney v North Lincolnshire County Council* [1999] All ER (D) 1463; *Barnes (an infant) v Hampshire County Council* [1969] 3 All ER 746, HL; *Nwabudike v The Mayor and Burgesses of the London Borough of Southwark*, *The Times*, 28 June 1996. In the better known case of *Carmarthenshire County Council v Lewis* [1955] 1 All ER 565, HL, the injury was to a lorry driver who was killed when he swerved to avoid the child who had left the classroom, gone through the playground and through the gate onto the road. The House of Lords avoided the conclusion that the nursery teacher, who had been delayed by tending to a cut on the knee of another child, had been negligent but held the local authority liable for failure to ensure that the playground was secure in that it should not have been possible for a young child to open the gate.

[48] *Mullin v Richards*, 6 November 1997, CA although the claim against the local authority based upon lack of supervision in the classroom failed.

[49] *Palmer v Cornwall CC* [2009] EWCA Civ 456, CA.

[50] *Wilson v Governors of the Sacred Heart Roman Catholic School*, 5 November 1997, CA.

[51] *Beaumont v Surrey County Council* (1968) 66 LGR 580 (strong elastic which had been left in the bin by a teacher); *Kearn-Price v Kent County Council* [2002] All ER (D) 440 (ban on playing with full size leather football not enforced); *Palmer v Cornwall County Council* [2009] EWCA Civ 456 (rock thrown at a seagull).

[52] *Gower v London Borough of Bromley* [1999] ELR 356, per Auld LJ at 359.

[53] *Bradford-Smart v West Sussex County Council* [2002] EWCA Civ 07; *Shaw v Redbridge LBC* [2005] EWHC 150, QB.

[54] *Phelps v Hillingdon LBC* [2001] 2 AC 619.

[55] *Shaw v Redbridge LBC* [2005] EWHC 150.

beyond that, for example if it were reasonable for a teacher to intervene when he saw one pupil attacking another immediately outside the school gates. It will clearly extend further afield if the pupils are on a school trip, educational, recreational or sporting. But the school cannot owe a general duty to its pupils, or anyone else, to police their activities once they have left its charge. That is principally the duty of parents and, where criminal offences are involved, the police.[56]

Responding to events outside school is a 'matter of discretion rather than duty'. Thus, the Court of Appeal overturned the first instance decision finding liability in *Wilson v Governors of the Sacred Heart Roman Catholic School*, in which a child was injured by the deliberate act of another child whirling an anorak around their head as the children left school at the end of the day. Supervision was required at lunchtimes, not as children left school.[57]

The legal duties owed by teachers are thus limited in extent according to their professional role; likewise the standard of care set is appropriate to the nature of the teacher/pupil relationship. Lord Slynn in the House of Lords in *Phelps v Hillingdon LBC* approved of the standard of care as it had been articulated by Auld LJ in *Gower v London Borough of Bromley*:

(i) teachers have a duty to take such care of pupils in their charge as a careful parent would have in like circumstances and (ii) teachers have a duty to exercise the reasonable skills of their calling in teaching and otherwise responding to the educational needs of their pupils.... The duty is to exercise the skills and care of a reasonable teacher on the basis of what would have been acceptable to reasonable members of the teaching profession.[58]

In other words, the health and safety duty standard is that of the reasonable parent, although the courts have shown realism in the willingness to adapt that standard to the circumstances; as in, 'a prudent parent of a large family';[59] the care 'a reasonable father would take of the children of his family having regard to the number of children involved, the conditions of school life and the sort of behaviour of which children are capable on being let loose at the end of the school day';[60] or to take proper and reasonable steps 'bearing in mind the known propensities of boys and girls between the ages of 11 and 18'.[61] The educational duty is the standard of the reasonable teacher to which *Bolam* applies.[62]

Recently, in another case which has been cited in discussions of our 'compensation culture', the High Court overturned the decision of the county court and, without appearing to criticize directly, implied that it was the expectations and behaviour of the child's mother, rather than his teachers, which were to be called into question.[63] A five-year-old boy, attending a school sports day on a village playing field, pretending to be Superman, jumped off a swing—which he should not have been on—and broke his arm. The claim was based upon failure of his teachers to supervise and to warn him of the dangers presented by the swing and to warn his mother that he was unsupervised whilst playing on the swing. Those arguments failed but the claim initially succeeded on the unpleaded case that the local authority was in breach on the

[56] *Bradford-Smart v West Sussex County Council* [2002] EWCA Civ 7.
[57] *Wilson v Governors of the Sacred Heart Roman Catholic School*, 5 November 1997, CA.
[58] *Phelps v Hillingdon LBC* [2001] 2 AC 619, 659.
[59] *Ward v Hertfordshire County Council* [1969] 2 All ER 807, QBD.
[60] *Wilson v Governors of the Sacred Heart Roman Catholic School*, 5 November 1997, CA.
[61] *Beaumont v Surrey County Council* (1968) 66 LGR 580.
[62] *Shaw v Redbridge LBC* [2005] EWHC 150.
[63] *Simonds v Isle of Wight Council* [2003] EWHC 2003.

grounds that it did not do enough to remove or restrict the hazard such as immobilizing the swings, taking them down, or putting tape around them.[64] The High Court observed that it is easy to identify, after the event, things that might have been done to have prevented the accident but the question was whether the defendant was under a duty to do those things, and concluded that the duty had been fulfilled by adequate supervision.[65] Gross J observed that the claimant's mother had been at the event and that the incident occurred just after they had finished their picnic and as the afternoon's activities commenced. At this point the claimant's mother had left but rather than take her child to his teachers she had told him to go to them. He did not do as he was told but went on the swing where the accident occurred.

The specific duty which teachers owe children arises from their professional responsibility to educate them. More generally, the care of children is delegated to teachers during school hours and, outside these times, when engaging in school activities or trips. There are, of course, practical reasons why the local authority may find itself defending an action in respect of harm sustained by a child whilst under the supervision of its teachers, when, had the child been in the care of his or her parent, no claim would have been initiated.[66] Whilst claims are brought against the local authority, it is the individual teacher whose conduct is subject to scrutiny. However, the case law does not support the view that teachers should fear the law or that they should need to be given further reassurance about the scope of their legal duties to take care of children in their charge. The courts have shown themselves able to identify the scope of the health and safety and educational duties and the standard appropriate to the professional relationship of care, notably with reference to a modified version of the standard of care owed by parents.

As is apparent from the cases, children brought together in the quasi-public space of school require supervision. If the home is a chaotic place where many things are happening at once, so much more so are schools where children present the risk of causing harm not only to themselves but also to others.[67] In this context, the expectations of teachers, in terms of the legal duties owed and the standards set by law, are tailored appropriately. It has been suggested that the privatization and individualization of responsibility for children encourages a sense amongst parents that the care of children is *solely* their responsibility[68]—that parents, alone, are responsible for their children. Gillian Thomas and Gina Hocking argue that the effect of increased individualism has been to 'push responsibility for children back towards the immediate family and household, and to reduce community responsibility'. Having children is seen as parental choice and the welfare of children is considered to be the parents' responsibility alone.[69] Thomas and Hocking suggest that the result is greater parental desire for control, supervision, and management of children's time, lives, and activities. This, in turn, fuels parental uncertainty about those things which are outside their control such as the risks to which their child may be exposed in the park or on school trips;[70] and, furthermore, this encourages the willingness of parents to criticize or challenge the decisions of others when harm befalls children whilst in the care

64 N. 63, above, at [16]. 65 N. 63, above, at [26].

66 As noted by Beldam LJ in *Surtees v Kingston-upon-Thames Borough Council; Surtees v Hughes and Another* [1991] 2 FLR 559.

67 Sue Scott, Stevi Jackson, and Kathryn Backett-Milburn, 'Swings and Roundabouts: Risk Anxiety and the Everyday Worlds of Children' (1998) 32 *Sociology* 689–705, at 691.

68 Gillian Thomas and Gina Hocking, *Other People's Children* (Demos, London, 2003), 17, 40.

69 N. 68, above, 17. 70 N. 68, above, 23, 52.

of others. Where their child is seriously injured whilst in another's care, parents who face the responsibility of meeting their child's needs and maximizing their quality of life will inevitably act protectively in relation to their child seeking accountability and a compensation claim as the means by which to secure the resources that would better enable them to meet the needs of the child.

31.4 Others

Tort lawyers will be familiar with the case of *Surtees*, commonly cited as authority for the proposition that courts are reluctant to find a duty owed by parents to their children where the harm was alleged to have been caused to the claimant whilst in foster care many years earlier. Sir Nicholas Browne-Wilkinson VC adopted the stance that it was not possible to assess the standard of care of activities within the home, by 'ordinary loving and careful mothers... to individual children, given the rough-and-tumble of home life'.[71] The standard of care owed to other people's children was at issue in the recent case of *Perry*. The defendant hired a bouncy castle and bungee run for her triplets' tenth birthday party, erecting them on the playing field behind their house. The claimant, who had been attending a football training session at the field, went on the bouncy castle and was seriously injured by another child who hit him on the head with his foot whilst doing a somersault. He suffered a skull fracture which resulted in 'severe, permanent cognitive, behavioural, emotional and social consequences'.[72] The court at first instance found that the defendant had given the claimant permission to go on the bouncy castle and that she breached the duty owed to him. The breach of duty comprised inadequate supervision,[73] failure to forbid the children from doing flips or somersaults, and failure to ensure that the children on the castle were all of a similar size and weight.[74] The breach caused the harm because, although the accident happened very soon after claimant went on the bouncy castle, the evidence of the child who hit the claimant was that he would not have done the somersault had he been told not to.[75] Notably, the claimant's father, who was with the claimant at the playing field, tidying up after a football training session, was joined in the proceedings on the basis that he had failed to prevent the claimant from going on the bouncy castle or to provide sufficient supervision; that he was in breach of a 'continuing duty of a parent for a child'.[76] The claim against the father failed at first instance on the evidence that he had told his son that he could not go on the bouncy castle as it was obviously a private party but that he was content for the claimant to seek permission, that the claimant had, and that the father had assumed that the castle was supervised.

[71] *Surtees v Kingston-upon-Thames Borough Council; Surtees v Hughes and Another* [1991] 2 FLR 559, 583, Sir Nicholas Browne-Wilkinson VC. Although in *S v Walsall MBC and Others* [1986] 1 FLR 397 damages were awarded against a foster mother in respect of severe burns to the soles of the feet of the claimant when she was two-and-a-half. The judge refuted any suggestion that the injuries were deliberately inflicted and invoked the doctrine of *res ipsa loquitur* in the absence of any explanation to hold the foster mother liable in negligence for the injuries.

[72] *Perry and Another v Harris (A Minor)* [2008] EWCA Civ 907, at [4].

[73] *Harris v Perry* [2008] EWHC 990, QB, at [19].

[74] The child who injured the claimant was a 'gentle giant' who should not have been permitted to be on castle at same time as smaller children, N. 73, above, at [24].

[75] N. 73, above, at [22].

[76] N. 73, above, at [35].

The Court of Appeal overturned the decision of the lower court, noting that there was very little precedent addressing the duty a parent owes to their own, or to other, children whilst playing together.[77] It would be impractical, and not in the public interest, for the law to impose a duty upon parents of constant supervision.[78] Further, it is not possible to exclude all risk that children will injure themselves whilst playing and minor injury is common. Whilst some circumstances, or activities, impose greater risks, the duty is then to provide adequate supervision to reduce risk to an acceptable level.[79]

The defendant submitted that the standard of care owed was that of a reasonably prudent parent to her own children, the claimant that it was 'to act as would any reasonable provider and supervisor of these kind of inflatables for use by young children'. The Court of Appeal considered that these amounted to the same thing, requiring it to ask, 'what positive steps would a reasonable parent take for the safety of a child of the claimant's age playing on a bouncy castle?'[80] The Court of Appeal held that the judge at first instance had applied too high a standard of care. Constant supervision was not required; it was reasonable to supervise both inflatables at the same time. Neither was it a breach of duty to allow children of different sizes on to the bouncy castle at the same time.[81] Whilst it was reasonably foreseeable that, if there was boisterous behaviour, there may be a collision and injury, injury of the severity sustained was not foreseeable.[82] This was 'a freak and tragic accident [which] occurred without fault'.[83]

So, what message does this case send about responsibilities to other people's children? Despite there being no pre-existing relationship, by giving the child permission to go on the bouncy castle the defendant accepted a duty to take care to supervise him on the equipment, a duty which, in the circumstances, she fulfilled. A duty existed but, on the facts, there was no liability to this child, who sustained severe, permanent brain damage whilst under the supervision, however reluctant, of someone else's parent. This case is thus not authority for the proposition that adults owe duties of care to other people's children; those duties only arise where they have, however reluctantly, been accepted. And then the standard owed is that of a reasonable parent to a child of this age engaging in this particular activity: thus, it was not a breach of the standards of a reasonably prudent parent to permit two 'entirely sensible, responsible' 14-year-old boys to practise shot put together.[84] The primary responsibility for children rests with their parents; teachers have responsibilities to children during school hours; and responsibilities to children may be imposed upon other adults who accept the duty to care for them. Responsibilities to children are individually assumed, not collectively assigned.

31.5 Supervising, and caring for, children

Children require supervision because they behave in childish ways, taking risks adults would not, engaging in conduct adults would not—sword-fighting with

[77] N. 72, above, at [34].
[78] N. 72, above, at [34].
[79] N. 72, above, at [34].
[80] N. 72, above, at [37].
[81] N. 72, above, at [42]–[46].
[82] N. 72, above, at [38].
[83] N. 72, above, at [47].
[84] *Porter v London Borough of Barking and Dagenham*, *The Times*, 9 April 1990.

plastic rulers, for example.[85] They are seen not to possess the skills of the 'reasonable man' in the judgement of risks and precautions. The Court of Appeal judges in *Mullin v Richards*, following the Australian case of *McHale v Watson*, modified the standard of care owed by children. Butler-Sloss LJ quoted Kitto J:

> In regard to the things which pertain to foresight and prudence experience, understanding of causes and effects, balance of judgement, thoughtfulness it is absurd, indeed it is a misuse of language, to speak of normality in relation to persons of all ages taken together. In those things normality is, for children, something different from what normality is for adults; the very concept of normality is a concept of rising levels until 'years of discretion' are attained. The law does not arbitrarily fix upon any particular age for this purpose, and tribunals of fact may well give effect to different views as to the age at which normal adult foresight and prudence are reasonably to be expected in relation to particular sets of circumstances.[86]

For the same reasons, children require the supervision of adults. In *Paranoid Parenting*, Frank Furedi argues that parenting has been redefined from 'nurturing, stimulating and socializing children' to 'monitoring their activities'[87] and that risks are avoided rather than managed, children's activities controlled, and freedom limited.[88] The primary responsibility for children rests with their parents and '[t]he fusion of risk anxiety with protectiveness engenders a need for constant vigilance in order to anticipate and guard against potential threats to children's well-being'.[89] This in turn fuels a desire to control children's activities, to be critical of the standard of care taken by others when the care of children is delegated to them, and to respond both to existing risks and to those which are imagined.[90]

There are a range of reasons why claimants pursue a civil claim for damages including to: hold another to account; secure an explanation, acknowledgement that harm has been caused or an apology; prevent the same harm befalling another; or obtain financial compensation to support the provision of care that is now required. Some of the cases considered above could rightly be dismissed as opportunistic attempts to gain compensation for minor injuries, although they can equally be understood in terms of an increased willingness on the part of parents to criticize the standards of others caring for their children. The successful claims in *Lewis*, *Jenney*, and *Barnes* involved a nursery school-aged child, an eight-year-old with developmental problems, and five-year-old child respectively either finding their own way out of the school premises or being let out of school early with serious consequences for other road users or the child themselves in a situation where parents had entrusted their child to the care of others. In these cases the claim for compensation combines with a desire to hold to account those in whose care the child was, to secure an explanation and apology for what happened, and to highlight failings in an effort to prevent a similar

[85] Although the age of majority does not protect from reckless conduct which has devastating consequences for the individual: *Tomlinson v Congleton BC and Others* [2003] UKHL 47; *Donoghue v Folkstone Properties Ltd and Another* [2003] QB 1008; *Rhind v Astbury Water Park Ltd and Another* [2004] EWCA Civ 756.

[86] *Mullin v Richards*, 6 November 1997 (<http://www.lexisnexis.com/uk/legal/>), per Butler-Sloss LJ quoting Kitto J in *McHale v Watson* [1966] 115 CLR 199, at 213.

[87] Frank Furedi, *Paranoid Parenting: Why Ignoring the Experts May be Best for Your Child* (Chicago Review Press, Chicago, 2002), 5.

[88] N. 87, above, 31.

[89] Sue Scott, Stevi Jackson, and Kathryn Backett-Milburn, 'Swings and Roundabouts: Risk Anxiety and the Everyday Worlds of Children' (1998) 32 *Sociology* 689–705, at 691.

[90] N. 89, above, 700.

incident occurring in the future. In other cases, such as *Chittock* and *Perry v Harris*,[91] the child was seriously and permanently injured and, as a consequence, required life-long care. Both the school and the hirers of the bouncy castle were insured and thus, in both cases, compensation claims represented a means of securing the resources to buy the goods and services necessary to maximize the future quality of life of the child. Both ultimately unsuccessful, the families were left to fall back upon their own individual, private resources to care for their children.

It has been suggested that civil claims brought seeking damages in redress for harm to children demonstrate a search to find someone else to blame. Analysis of the cases, to the contrary, reveals the privatization and individualization of the care of children. Children are the primary responsibility of their parents although their care is delegated to teachers during school hours or activities and may be temporarily accepted by others. Children will take risks and in doing so risk harming themselves and others.[92] The individualizing and privatizing imperative which places the responsibility for children with their parents and leaves them alone to care in the event of injury makes the imposition of tortious responsibility for harm caused by parents to their children appear superfluous, renders inevitable parental concern for greater control over their children, and makes parents critical of the standards of others when caring for their children.

[91] For example, severe brain damage after asthma episode in *Hippolyte v Bexley London Borough*, 23 November 1994, CA; severe spinal injury in a school rugby match in *Van Oppen v Clerk to the Bedford Charity Trustees* [1989] 3 All ER 389, CA; paraplegia in a skiing accident in *Woodbridge School v Chittock* [2002] ELR 735; fractured skull when hit head on flint boundary wall of playground, successful at first instance, overturned on appeal, *Ward v Hertfordshire County Council* [1969] 2 All ER 807, QBD, *Ward v Hertfordshire County Council* [1970] 1 All ER 535.

[92] The majority of accidents occur to children within the home, in the form of falls, scalds and burns, and poisoning, <http://www.rospa.com/HomeSafety/Info/child-accidents-2008.pdf#dup20> (accessed 30/11/10).

Index of Names

Index of Subjects